D1289361

The Wiley-Blackwell Handbook of Childhood Cognitive Development

Wiley-Blackwell Handbooks of Developmental Psychology

This outstanding series of handbooks provides a cutting-edge overview of classic research, current research, and future trends in developmental psychology.

- Each handbook draws together 25–30 newly commissioned chapters to provide a comprehensive overview of a sub-discipline of developmental psychology.
- The international team of contributors to each handbook has been specially chosen for its expertise and knowledge of each field.
- Each handbook is introduced and contextualized by leading figures in the field, lending coherence and authority to each volume.

The *Wiley-Blackwell Handbooks of Developmental Psychology* will provide an invaluable overview for advanced students of developmental psychology and for researchers as an authoritative definition of their chosen field.

Published

Blackwell Handbook of Infant Development
Edited by Gavin Bremner and Alan Fogel

Blackwell Handbook of Childhood Social Development
Edited by Peter K. Smith and Craig H. Hart

Blackwell Handbook of Childhood Cognitive Development
Edited by Usha Goswami

Blackwell Handbook of Adolescence
Edited by Gerald R. Adams and Michael D. Berzonsky

The Science of Reading: A Handbook
Edited by Margaret J. Snowling and Charles Hulme

Blackwell Handbook of Early Childhood Development
Edited by Kathleen McCartney and Deborah A. Phillips

Blackwell Handbook of Language Development
Edited by Erika Hoff and Marilyn Shatz

Wiley-Blackwell Handbook of Childhood Cognitive Development, 2nd edition
Edited by Usha Goswami

Not yet published

Wiley-Blackwell Handbook of Infant Development, 2nd edition
Edited by Gavin Bremner and Theodore D. Wachs

Wiley-Blackwell Handbook of Developmental Psychology in Action
Edited by Rudolph Schaffer and Kevin Durkin

Wiley-Blackwell Handbook of Adulthood and Aging
Edited by Susan Krauss Whitbourne and Martin Sliwinski

Wiley-Blackwell Handbook of Childhood Social Development, 2nd edition
Edited by Peter K. Smith and Craig H. Hart

The Wiley-Blackwell Handbook of Childhood Cognitive Development

Second edition

Edited by

Usha Goswami

WILEY-BLACKWELL

A John Wiley & Sons, Ltd., Publication

This second edition first published 2011

Edition history: Blackwell Publishers Ltd (1e, 2002)

Blackwell Publishing was acquired by John Wiley & Sons in February 2007. Blackwell's publishing program has been merged with Wiley's global Scientific, Technical, and Medical business to form Wiley-Blackwell.

Registered Office
John Wiley & Sons Ltd, The Atrium, Southern Gate, Chichester, West Sussex, PO19 8SQ, United Kingdom

Editorial Offices
350 Main Street, Malden, MA 02148-5020, USA
9600 Garsington Road, Oxford, OX4 2DQ, UK
The Atrium, Southern Gate, Chichester, West Sussex, PO19 8SQ, UK

For details of our global editorial offices, for customer services, and for information about how to apply for permission to reuse the copyright material in this book please see our website at www.wiley.com/wiley-blackwell.

Library of Congress Cataloging-in-Publication Data

The Wiley-Blackwell handbook of childhood cognitive development / edited by Usha Goswami. – 2nd ed.
p. cm. – (Wiley-Blackwell handbooks of developmental psychology)
Rev. ed. of: Blackwell handbook of childhood cognitive development. 2003.
Includes bibliographical references and index.
ISBN 978-1-4051-9116-6 (hardcover : alk. paper)
1. Cognition in children. I. Goswami, Usha C. II. Goswami, Usha C. Wiley-Blackwell handbook of childhood cognitive development. III. Title: Wiley-Blackwell Handbook of childhood cognitive development.
BF723.C5B5 2010
155.4'13–dc22

2010003122

A catalogue record for this book is available from the British Library.

Set in 10.5 on 12.5 pt Adobe Garamond by Toppan Best-set Premedia Limited
Printed and bound in Singapore by Fabulous Printers Pte Ltd

01 2011

To Ella Elisabeth Thomson
who asked when I would dedicate another book to her,
so here it is.

Contents

Acknowledgements

Once again, I would like to thank my contributors for making my editorial duties in preparing this volume both interesting and enjoyable. As previously, the quality of their contributions has been outstanding, and I have learned a lot from reading their views. Our field has developed tremendously since the last edition of this handbook, and its vibrancy and excitement is conveyed in all of the chapters. New developments in brain science look set to increase activity in the field even further, and to show the critical importance of developmental studies to the understanding of cognition in adulthood. I would like to thank St John's College, Cambridge, for providing the perfect environment for working on this book. I would also like to thank Nichola Daily for her secretarial support.

List of Contributors

Glenda Andrews, Griffith University

Renée Baillargeon, University of Illinois

Simon Baron-Cohen, Autism Research Centre, Department of Psychiatry, Cambridge University

Patricia J. Bauer, Department of Psychology, Emory University

Peter Bryant, Department of Education, University of Oxford

Trix Cacchione, Universität Zürich

Malinda Carpenter, Department of Developmental and Comparative Psychology, Max Planck Institute for Evolutionary Anthropology, Leipzig, Germany

Adam E. Christensen, Pennsylvania State University

Sharon Crosbie, Clinical Centre for Research, University of Queensland, Australia

Harry Daniels, Centre for Sociocultural and Activity Theory Research, Department of Education, University of Bath

Judy S. DeLoache, University of Virginia

Joanne Deocampo, Department of Psychology, Emory University

Barbara Dodd, Clinical Centre for Research, University of Queensland, Australia

Susan A. Gelman, University of Michigan – Ann Arbor

György Gergely, Cognitive Development Center, Central European University, Budapest

Yael Gertner, University of Illinois

Matthew Gingo, University of California, Berkeley

Silke M. Göbel, University of York

Usha Goswami, University of Cambridge

Graeme S. Halford, Griffith University and University of Queensland

Annette Karmiloff-Smith, Developmental Neurocognition Laboratory, School of Psychology, Birkbeck, University of London

Barbara Koslowski, Cornell University

Deanna Kuhn, Teachers College Columbia University

Marina Larkina, Department of Psychology, Emory University

Erin M. Leddon, Northwestern University

Jie Li, University of Illinois

Lynn S. Liben, Pennsylvania State University

Angeline Lillard, University of Virginia

Amy Masnick, Hofstra University

Andrew N. Meltzoff, Institute for Learning and Brain Sciences, University of Washington

Patricia H. Miller, University of Georgia

Ulrich Müller, University of Victoria

Larry P. Nucci, University of California, Berkeley

Terezinha Nuñes, Department of Education, University of Oxford

John E. Opfer, The Ohio State University

Ashley M. Pinkham, University of Virginia

Paul C. Quinn, University of Delaware

Wolfgang Schneider, University of Würzburg, Germany

Eric Smith, University of Virginia

Margaret J. Snowling, University of York

Robert J. Sternberg, Tufts University

Michael S. C. Thomas, Developmental Neurocognition Laboratory, School of Psychology, Birkbeck, University of London

Michael Tomasello, Department of Developmental and Comparative Psychology, Max Planck Institute for Evolutionary Anthropology, Leipzig, Germany

Sandra R. Waxman, Northwestern University

Henry M. Wellman, University of Michigan

Gert Westermann, Department of Psychology, Oxford Brookes University

Friedrich Wilkening, Universität Zürich

Di Wu, University of Illinois

Philip David Zelazo, University of Minnesota

Introduction

Usha Goswami

Since the first edition of this Handbook, the field of developmental cognitive neuroscience has begun in earnest. In my view, this will have a lasting impact on our understanding of childhood cognitive development. Neuroscience has the potential to have a transformative effect on our theories and our explanatory frameworks. This is because understanding the neural codes that the brain uses to organize and transmit information will provide insights into developmental causal mechanisms. These insights may transform our views about cognitive development.

For example, the formats that are provided by neural coding mechanisms will inevitably affect how the brain develops a cognitive system from sensory inputs. One powerful metaphor is the idea of neural ensembles, groups of active cells that represent a particular percept or concept via the spatial or temporal patterning of their firing. Different cells in the same ensemble (neural network) that represent a percept or concept will be linked to each other, so that when there is noise in the input, or partial information, the ensemble can still activate – the cells that do fire will perform a pattern-completion process and trigger the other cells that represent the percept or concept. This pattern-completion process is in principle equivalent to what is traditionally termed generalization, as it enables abstraction and categorization – argued by Quinn (chapter 5, this volume) to be the primitive in all behavior and mental functioning.

Indeed, neuroimaging reveals that even the brains of young infants show sustained activity based on abstracted dependencies in the absence of sensory input, for example, when a hidden object disappears unexpectedly (Kaufman, Mareschal, & Johnson, 2003). The sensory processing of spatio-temporal structure can in principle yield the abstracted dependencies traditionally discussed as "prototypes" of concepts, as "causal knowledge" about physical systems, and as "naïve psychology" (e.g., Rosch, 1978; Shultz, 1982; Wellman & Gelman, 1998; see Goswami, 2008, for a fuller discussion). Sensory learning is rapid, and so the brain is frequently responding not to a particular sensory event itself, but to the abstract dependencies that are typical of that class of events, or to the dependencies that occur between patterns of sensory events, that may in essence comprise concepts or causal systems. In principle, these neural learning mechanisms are analogous to the "generalization across instances" that traditionally has been assumed to underpin conceptual development.

How can such neural mechanisms give rise to causal knowledge? For example, while the specific perceptual features of two objects in a launching event may vary, the spatio-temporal dynamics (and therefore the causal structure, e.g., the fact that A causes B to move) will vary less. The ensemble of cells that responds to the spatio-temporal motion of one particular launching event will therefore also trigger some of the other cells that were responsive in previous, but perceptually slightly different, launching events. As more such launching events are experienced, the neural network will in effect abstract and represent the "knowledge" that A causes B to move. The perceptual illusion of causality during launching and other visual events noted by Michotte (1963) is one example of how sensory perceptual dynamics enable the development of conceptual representations (see also Scholl & Tremoulet, 2000).

The highly distributed nature of neural representations means that cognitive behavior will reflect properties of these distributed representations (Szűcs & Goswami, 2007). An example is infants' behavior when apparently reasoning about physical events (Baillargeon, Li, Gertner, & Wu, chapter 1, this volume). For example, rather than postulating completely distinct neural networks for, say, occlusion events versus containment events, it could be that a weaker neural network representation of a hidden object suffices for occlusion events than for containment events. As discussed by Munakata (2001), a neural representation can be graded in terms of (for example) the number of relevant neurons firing, their firing rates, the coherence of the firing patterns, and how "clean" they are for signaling the appropriate information. Graded representations offer an alternative explanation of behavioral dissociations, for example in infant looking behavior (Johnson & Munakata, 2005). As we understand more about how the brain builds cognitive representations from sensory input, our theories about cognitive development will inevitably change.

One relevant theoretical perspective, addressed in this volume, is neuroconstructivism (see Westermann, Thomas, & Karmiloff-Smith, chapter 28). As they demonstrate, a neuroscience perspective makes basic sensory processes more important in cognitive development than is traditionally acknowledged. Although provocative, it can be argued that young children's apparent tendency to seek hidden features to help them to understand what makes objects and events similar may not be a cognitive "bias" or a naïve "theory," but may rather reflect the operation of basic mammalian learning algorithms. The causal explanatory frameworks that are central to cognitive development may originate from statistical perceptual learning by the brain of spatio-temporal structure, enriched developmentally with information gained through sociocultural learning, imitation, analogy, and action. Using relatively simple learning mechanisms, the infant brain develops complex conceptual representations about how the world is (see Goswami, 2008). These conceptual representations originate in the sensory coding of the dynamic spatial and temporal behavior of objects, and are enriched as the infant distinguishes agents and their goal-directed actions, learns by imitation, and learns by analogy. Perceptual-cognitive representations are further enriched once the infant becomes capable of autonomous action. However, mental representations are transformed by the acquisition of language.

Currently, there are rather few sensory and neuroscience studies available to include in this new edition of the Handbook, but all the contributors comment on such studies when they are available. Therefore, this second edition is still focused on how different aspects of cognitive development unfold during the period of peak sensitivity for learning, infancy and childhood. The plasticity of the child's brain is often remarked upon, but equally remarkable is the similarity in cognitive development across cultures and social contexts. In the first section of the Handbook, on infancy, the authors focus on the basic kinds of knowledge that are central in human cognitive development. These are knowledge about the physical world of objects and events (Baillargeon, Li, Gertner, & Wu, chapter 1), knowledge about social cognition, self, and agency (Meltzoff, chapter 2; Gergely, chapter 3; Carpenter, chapter 4), and knowledge about the kinds of things in the world – conceptual knowledge (Quinn, chapter 5; Waxman & Leddon, chapter 7). These "foundational" domains (naïve physics, psychology, and biology) also depend on the development of memory (Bauer, Larkina, & Deocampo, chapter 6). Each chapter illustrates ways in which the foundational domains of cognition are functioning from the earliest months. Infants are characterized as active learners, equipped with certain innate expectations which, although quite primitive, enable them to benefit hugely from experience. Experience of the physical and social worlds allows infants to enrich and revise their initial expectations, so that they appear to be replaced with new understandings.

References

Goswami, U. (2008). *Cognitive development: The learning brain.* Hove, UK: Psychology Press.

Johnson, M. H., & Munakata, Y. (2005). Processes of change in brain and cognitive development. *Trends in Cognitive Sciences, 9,* 152–158.

Kaufman, J., Csibra, G., & Johnson, M. H. (2003). Representing occluded objects in the human infant brain. *Proceedings of the Royal Society of London B* (Suppl.), *270,* S140–S143.

Kaufman, J., Mareschal, D., & Johnson, M. H. (2003). Graspability and object processing in infants. *Infant Behavior and Development, 26,* 516–528.

Michotte, A. (1963). *The perception of causality.* Andover, UK: Methuen.

Munakata, Y. (2001). Graded representations in behavioral dissociations. *Trends in Cognitive Sciences,* 1, *5*(7), 309–315.

Rosch, E. (1978). Principles of categorization. In E. Rosch & B. B. Lloyd (Eds.), *Cognition and Categorization* (pp. 27–48). Hillsdale, NJ: Erlbaum.

Scholl, B. J., & Tremoulet, P. D. (2000). Perceptual causality and animacy. *Trends in Cognitive Sciences, 4,* 299–309.

Shultz, T. R. (1982). Rules of causal attribution. *Monographs of the Society for Research in Child Development, 47* (1, Serial No. 194).

Szűcs, D., & Goswami, U. (2007). Educational neuroscience: Defining a new discipline for the study of mental representations. *Mind, Brain and Education, 1*(3), 114–127.

Wellman, H. M., & Gelman, S. A. (1992). Cognitive development: Foundational theories of core domains. *Annual Review of Psychology, 43,* 337–375.

Wellman, H. M., & Gelman, S. A. (1998). Knowledge acquisition in foundational domains. In W. Damon, D. Kuhn, & R. Siegler (Eds.), *Handbook of child psychology: Vol 2. Cognition, perception and language* (5th ed., pp. 523–573). New York: Wiley.

PART I

Infancy
The Origins of Cognitive Development

The first section of the revised Handbook has been expanded to take account of recent developments in infancy research. One of the most remarkable findings from the last decade has been the statistical learning power of the infant brain. By processing sensory features of the input, and correlations and dependencies between these features, the infant brain basically learns about dynamic spatio-temporal structure, across modalities. Some relevant data are discussed in the chapters by Quinn; Baillargeon Li, Gertner, and Wu; Waxman and Leddon; and Bauer, Larkina, and Deocampo. Sensory statistical learning enables 2-month-old infants to learn visual transitional probabilities between abstract geometric shapes (Kirkham, Slemmer, & Johnson, 2002), and 3-month-old infants to learn to distinguish vehicles and animals on the basis of motion cues alone (when watching point light displays, Arterberry & Bornstein, 2001). Learning auditory conditional probabilities enables infants to extract structural properties from language input, for example the phonotactic patterns of language (the sounds that make up the language, and the orders in which they can be combined, see Tomasello, chapter 9), and the phonetic elements that comprise a particular language (e.g., Kuhl, 2004). Neural systems that can learn the patterns or regularities in environmental input captured by conditional probabilities can, in principle, acquire complex cognitive structures like language and concepts. On this kind of theoretical account, experience-dependent learning is the key to cognitive development, not the possession of innate "pre-knowledge." Theoretical constructs such as a "Language Acquisition Device" for acquiring syntax (Chomsky, 1957) are not required to explain the complexity of infant learning.

Machine learning studies show that statistical learning algorithms other than conditional probabilities can be extremely powerful. For example, research in machine learning has also discovered algorithms enabling *explanation-based learning*. As discussed by Baillargeon et al. (chapter 1), in explanation-based learning a machine can generalize from a single example by explaining to itself why the training example is an instantiation of a concept that is being learned (DeJong, 2006). The machine uses background knowledge (prior domain knowledge) to constrain the inferences made. In their chapter, Baillargeon and her colleagues illustrate that physical reasoning by infants follows similar principles. They argue that infants form distinct "event categories" (occlusion, containment, support) about the physical world, apparently learning about each category separately. The data show that perceptual variables such as height that are identified in one category (e.g., by 4-month-olds for occlusion) are not necessarily generalized to another category (e.g., height is only identified as an important variable for *covering* by 12-month-olds). This appears surprising, as the height variable is equally relevant to both categories.

On Baillargeon's data, infants appear to acquire event-specific expectations before event-general principles. However, this would be expected if a neural networks metaphor is applied. If the "physical reasoning system" of the infant is based on neural networks that are active in response to the sensory information experienced by the infant during each discrete event, then different types of "events" will be learned about separately. Other types of events will activate different neural networks, although there might be some overlap. Further, if infants are exposed to relevant discrete events purposely and incrementally within a category (as in the "teaching" experiments discussed by Baillargeon et al.), they will acquire event-specific knowledge earlier than if they lack such exposure. The experience-dependent construction of the neural networks responding to the spatio-temporal information in physical "events" such as covering will *in itself* yield this outcome.

The chapters by Meltzoff, Gergely, and Carpenter show that, when these perceptual learning mechanisms are supplemented with information gained by observing other agents and by acting oneself, then learning about the inner experiences or the mental life of others becomes possible. Meltzoff (chapter 2) argues that the first common code between self and other is the ability to map the actions of other people onto the actions of our own bodies. Action representation is the "supramodal" code enabling the infant to see others as "like me." Meltzoff suggests that the infant's experience with action productions and the consequences of actions enables a privileged understanding of people as distinct from other objects. A key developmental mechanism, available from birth, is imitation, which suggests an intrinsic link between action perception and production. Imitative ability depends on active intermodal mapping, the "supramodal code." The child, even the newborn, can watch the movements of other people and recognize that "those acts are like these acts" or "that looks the way this feels." Reciprocal imitation (e.g., copying games) enables further insight into intentionality. Meltzoff's view is that seeing others as "like me" enables bidirectional learning effects and is central to understanding persons within a framework involving goals and intentions. Via their own copying actions, infants gain understanding of the acts of others. By watching others copy them, infants learn about themselves and the consequences of their own potential actions. Meltzoff argues that the result is a child who discovers facets of other minds through analogy with his or her own mind, and who simultaneously discovers powers and possibilities of the self through observing and imitating others. He also makes the critical point that effective teaching and learning is linked to one's interpretation of the motivations and goals of others.

In chapter 3, on the early understanding of kinds of intentional agents, Gergely presents different evidence relevant to the same problem of knowing other minds. He suggests that being sensitive to information about what another "knows" on the basis of perceptual information about their line of regard is a basic and innate adaptation that has evolved in other social species as well (such as apes, crows, and scrub jays). For example, a bird may re-cache its food store having observed another bird see it. With respect to actually representing the content of the mind states of another, which appears to be specific to the human species, Gergely argues for two kinds of adaptations. One supports the recognition and interpretation of intentional agents performing goal-directed actions, and the second supports the recognition and interpretation of communicative agents performing acts of informational transfer (natural pedagogy). Gergely suggests that the developmental mechanisms enabling these adaptations include the ability to detect causal patterns of distal contingent reactivity between agents, such as taking turns; infants' preference for direct eye gaze; their sensitivity to ostensive cuing (e.g., eyebrow raising); and their sensitivity to "motherese" (the exaggerated prosodic register that we use to speak to babies). Intentional agents are those that babies perceive to make rational choices of action between multiple alternatives. Communicative agents are those that babies perceive as offering turn-taking patterns of communicative contingent reactivity. Gergely also argues that the system for detecting, interpreting, and learning about intentional agents may be developmentally independent of the separate system for mindreading, and that part of cognitive development might be the integration of these two systems.

Carpenter (chapter 4) addresses similar developmental issues from the complementary perspective that babies are motivated to share psychological states like attention and goals with others, and to do things the way that others do. This "shared intentionality" is what enables humans (and only humans) to engage in collaborative activities and to create cultural practices and institutions. Like Gergely, Carpenter invokes evidence from non-human species to show that some of infants' social cognition skills are not species specific. Both apes and babies can understand the goals and intentions of others, can understand others' perceptions, and can understand their knowledge or ignorance. The difference is that only babies participate in activities that require *shared* intentionality. The motivation to engage in joint attention, for example, is strong – infants will turn away from an engaging new event in order to draw their mother's attention to it so that they can attend to it together. Infant and adult *know together* that they are sharing attention and attitudes. Infants also keep track of the knowledge and experiences that they have shared with others in the past, what "we" know together, and comprehend and produce communicative gestures with this in mind. This enables joint collaborative activity, which is not found in the animal kingdom. Carpenter's thesis is that shared intentionality – the motivation to share psychological states and experiences – is unique to humans.

Quinn (chapter 5) considers the advantages of having a mind–brain system that categorizes experience. He argues that categorization is fundamental to cognition, enabling efficient learning and memory, and reducing the complexity of the external world. He considers evidence relevant to how infants go about the task of dividing the unlabeled world into like entities, which are then stored mentally as category representations. He explains Rosch's (1978) premise that the perceptual world has inbuilt structure in the form of bundles of statistically correlated attributes, to which the infant brain is sensitive. Quinn considers whether initial attention to correlation is at the "basic" categorical level of dogs and cars, or at the "superordinate" categorical level of animals and vehicles. He concludes that global categories emerge before basic categories because of cumulative instance-based learning. When a small number of exemplars has been experienced, the representation will be fairly general (global, for example that self-propelling animates with four legs are *animals*). When a large number of exemplars has been experienced, the representation can be more detailed (for example, enabling medium-sized four-legged animates to be divided into *cats* versus *dogs*). The key learning principle is exemplar-based and cumulative, which means that the number of exemplars experienced will produce changes in the inclusiveness of the category representations (global versus basic) and apparently qualitative changes in representation (from perceptual to conceptual). The similarities with Baillargeon's enrichment account and the developmental processes suggested by the neural networks metaphor are striking.

Bauer et al. (chapter 6) discuss the early development of declarative and non-declarative memory. They argue that this distinction is vital for developmental scientists, as the two types of memory rely on different neural substrates and develop in different ways. Non-declarative or implicit memory (such as learning habits and skills) involves non-conscious abilities and depends on incremental learning. Declarative or explicit memory involves what we usually mean by "remembering" – the conscious recall of places, dates, events, and so on. Declarative memory is fast (it can be formed on the basis of a single experience), can be fallible (because memory traces degrade and retrieval failures occur), and is flexible. Bauer et al. show that the development of new paradigms such as infant habituation and deferred imitation has enabled the documentation of really quite remarkable mnemonic capacities in infancy. They focus on event memory, as our memories of events define the self – who we are is who we were and what we did. Event memory becomes increasingly autobiographical across the early years of life, and experiments suggest that consolidation and storage processes, rather than retrieval processes, are the major sources of developmental change. An event that is not well encoded or stored cannot be retrieved. Bauer et al. also provide an overview of the neural structures supporting memory, as available neuroscience data are quite extensive here.

Waxman and Leddon (chapter 7) focus on early word learning and its critical impact on cognitive development. As infants learn words, they learn symbols that stand for or refer to something in the real world, and therefore they learn a code that they can use to manipulate their knowledge about the real world – a symbolic system. Waxman and Leddon describe the close interaction between early conceptual development and early linguistic development in detail. They argue that infants are born equipped with an innate expectation that words will refer to commonalities among objects. These commonalities can be of many kinds, for example taxonomic (dogs, cats), functional (pulls, cuts), thematic (bread goes with butter), or property-based (has wings, is red). As in Baillargeon's account, an initial core expectation is assumed to be fine-tuned via experience. As in the social cognition chapters, there is also a causal role for infants' innate propensity to attend to and interact with other people. Infants show a special interest in "people sounds" – the sounds of language. They rapidly become perceptually tuned to the phonologic, prosodic, and morphologic elements characterizing their native language, and, very soon, novel words guide attention to objects and highlight commonalities and differences between them. The ability to produce words oneself (naming) has powerful cognitive consequences, promoting the formation of object categories, and a means of tracing the identity of individual entities within these categories. Waxman and Leddon argue that words are powerful engines for conceptual development.

References

Arterberry, M. E., & Bornstein, M. H. (2001). Three-month-old infants' categorization of animals and vehicles based on static and dynamic attributes. *Journal of Experimental Child Psychology, 80*, 333–346.

Chomsky, N. (1957). *Syntactic structures.* The Hague/Paris: Mouton.

DeJong, G. (2006). Toward robust real-world inference: A new perspective on explanation-based learning. *ECML06, The Seventeenth European Conference on Machine Learning* (pp. 102–113).

Kirkham, N. Z., Slemmer, J. A., & Johnson, S. P. (2002). Visual statistical learning in infancy: Evidence for a domain general learning mechanism. *Cognition, 83*, B35–B42.

Kuhl, P. K. (2004). Early language acquisition: Cracking the speech code. *Nature Reviews Neuroscience, 5*, 831–843.

Rosch, E. (1978). Principles of categorization. In E. Rosch & B. B. Lloyd (Eds.), *Cognition and Categorization* (pp. 27–48). Hillsdale, NJ: Erlbaum.

CHAPTER ONE

How Do Infants Reason About Physical Events?

Renée Baillargeon, Jie Li, Yael Gertner, and Di Wu

Introduction

As adults, we possess a great deal of knowledge about the physical world: for example, we realize that an object continues to exist when hidden, that a wide object can fit inside a wide but not a narrow container, and that an object typically falls when released in midair. Piaget (1952, 1954) was the first researcher to systematically investigate the development of infants' physical knowledge. He examined infants' responses in various *action tasks* and concluded that young infants understand very little about physical events. For example, after observing that infants younger than 8 months do not search for objects they have watched being hidden, Piaget proposed that young infants lack a concept of *object permanence* and do not yet understand that objects continue to exist when hidden.

For the next several decades, Piaget's (1952, 1954) conclusion that young infants possess little or no knowledge about the physical world was generally accepted. (For reviews of this early research, see Bremner, 1985; Gratch, 1976; Harris, 1987). This state of affairs began to change in the 1980s, however, when researchers became concerned that exclusive reliance on action tasks as an investigative tool might underestimate young infants' physical knowledge. In order to search for an object hidden under a cloth, for example, infants must not only represent the existence and location of the object, but they must also plan and execute the appropriate means–end actions to retrieve it. Thus, young infants might represent the object but still fail to search for it because (a) they are unable to plan or execute the actions necessary to retrieve it (e.g., Baillargeon, Graber, DeVos, & Black, 1990; Diamond, 1991; Willatts, 1997), or (b) they can plan and execute these actions but lack sufficient information-processing resources to simultaneously represent the hidden object and carry out the actions required to retrieve it (e.g., Hespos &

The preparation of this chapter was supported by a grant from the National Institute of Child Health and Human Development to Renée Baillargeon (HD-21104). We would like to thank Jerry DeJong and Cindy Fisher for many helpful discussions.

Baillargeon, 2008; Keen & Berthier, 2004; Lockman, 1984; see also Munakata, McClelland, Johnson, & Siegler, 1997; Shinskey, 2002; Shinskey & Munakata, 2001).

These methodological concerns led investigators to seek alternative approaches for exploring young infants' physical knowledge. Their research efforts can be roughly organized into three successive, overlapping waves. The first wave established that, contrary to Piaget's (1952, 1954) claims, even young infants possess some expectations about physical events. The second wave began to systematically examine the development of infants' physical knowledge and brought to light striking patterns of successes and failures in infants' responses to physical events. Finally, the third, ongoing, wave builds on these preceding efforts and attempts to specify both how infants reason about physical events and what cognitive architecture makes this reasoning possible. In what follows, we first briefly review findings from the first and second waves. In the remainder of the chapter, we focus on the third wave and present a three-system account of how infants reason about physical events.

First Wave: The Competent Infant

One of the major alternative approaches used to explore young infants' physical knowledge relies on the long-established finding that infants (like older children and adults) tend to look longer at stimuli they perceive to be novel as opposed to familiar (e.g., Fantz, 1956). Looking-time tasks have two main advantages over action tasks: they can be administered to very young infants, and they can be modified endlessly to explore subtle facets of infants' responses to a wide array of physical events. The most commonly used looking-time task is the *violation of expectation* (VOE) task. In a typical experiment, infants see two test events: an expected event, which is consistent with the expectation being examined in the experiment, and an unexpected event, which violates this expectation. With appropriate controls, evidence that infants look reliably longer at the unexpected than at the expected event is taken to indicate that infants (a) possess the expectation under investigation; (b) detect the violation in the unexpected event; and (c) are "surprised" by this violation. The term surprise is used simply as a shorthand descriptor, to denote a state of heightened attention or interest caused by an expectation violation (for discussion, see Wang, Baillargeon, & Brueckner, 2004).

The first wave of looking-time experiments on infants' physical knowledge indicated that even young infants possess expectations about a number of physical events (e.g., Baillargeon, Spelke & Wasserman, 1985; Leslie, 1984; Leslie & Keeble, 1987; Needham & Baillargeon, 1993; Spelke, Breinlinger, Macomber, & Jacobson, 1992; Woodward, Phillips, & Spelke, 1993). For example, VOE experiments examining object permanence in infants aged 2.5–6 months (see figure 1.1) revealed that infants were surprised when an object was placed behind a screen which then rotated through the space occupied by the object (e.g., Baillargeon, 1987, 1991); when an object moved through an obstacle behind a screen (e.g., Baillargeon, 1986; Spelke et al., 1992); when an object disappeared from behind a screen or from under a cover (e.g., Leslie, 1995; Wynn, 1992); and when an object was hidden in one location and then retrieved from a different location (e.g.,

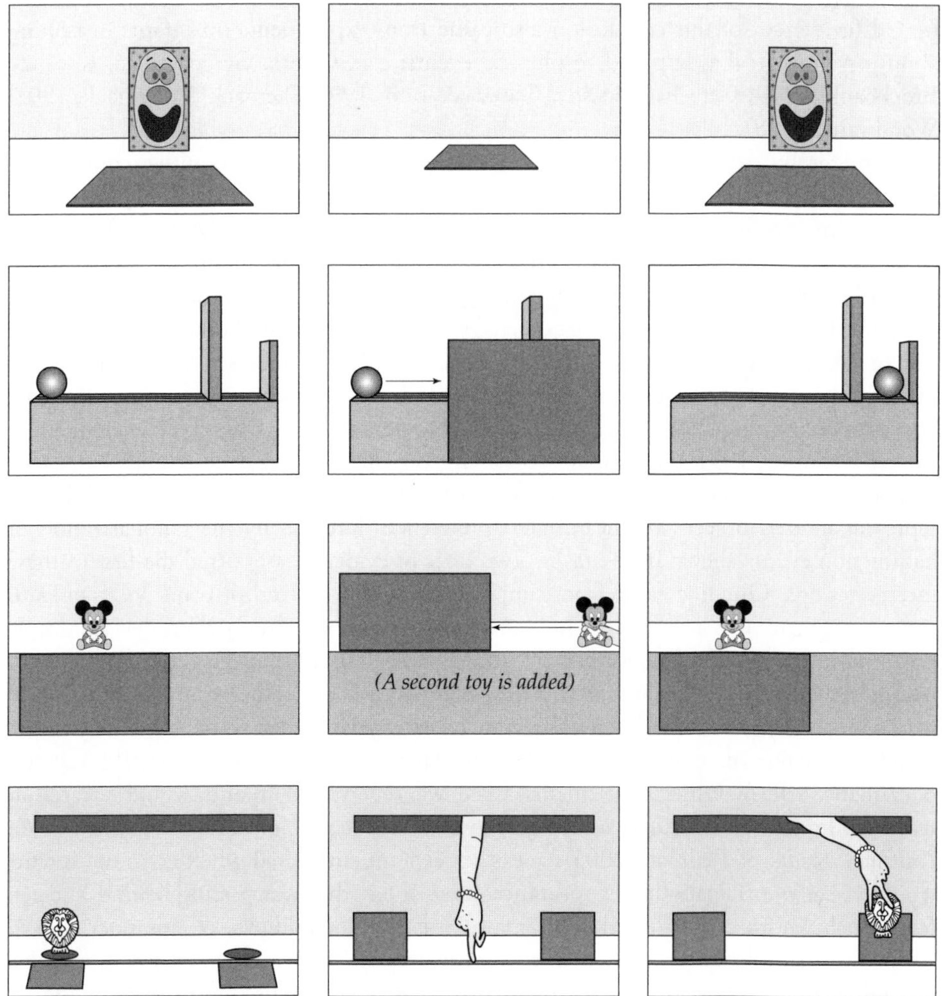

Figure 1.1 Examples of violations in experiments showing that young infants can represent hidden objects, as reported by Baillargeon (1987), Spelke et al. (1992), Wynn (1992), and Wilcox et al. (1996)

Newcombe, Huttenlocher, & Learmonth, 1999; Wilcox, Nadel, & Rosser, 1996). These and many other similar results provided consistent evidence that young infants realize that objects continue to exist when hidden. (For reviews, see Baillargeon, 1993; Spelke & Hespos, 2001).

The first wave of looking-time experiments on infants' physical knowledge helped bring about a revolution in researchers' characterization of young infants' cognitive abilities. For the greater part of the twentieth century, theoretical views had portrayed young infants as limited sensorimotor processors incapable of representation or thought (e.g., Bruner, 1968; Piaget, 1952, 1954). In marked contrast, these new experiments suggested that young infants were far more cognitively competent than had previously been suspected (evidence for this conclusion also came from experiments on infants' reasoning about psychological as opposed to physical events; e.g., Csibra, Gergely, Bíró, Koós, & Brockbank, 1999; Gergely, Nádasdy, Csibra, & Bíró, 1995; Premack & Premack, 1997; Woodward, 1998).

As might be expected, these groundbreaking claims of early cognitive competence were scrutinized in turn, and a heated controversy soon arose over the interpretation of looking-time findings (e.g., Baillargeon, 1999; Haith, 1998; Smith, 1999; Spelke, 1998). In particular, researchers offered deflationary accounts of young infants' apparent success in VOE object-permanence tasks. According to many of these accounts, infants looked longer at the unexpected than at the expected test event in each task because (a) familiarization or habituation events were used to introduce the task and (b) these events inadvertently induced a transient and superficial preference for the unexpected test event (e.g., Bogartz, Shinskey, & Schilling 2000; Bogartz, Shinskey, & Speaker, 1997; Cashon & Cohen, 2000; Thelen & Smith, 1994; for reviews, see Baillargeon, 2004; Wang et al., 2004).

Did infants' responses in VOE object-permanence tasks reflect a genuine ability to represent hidden objects, or meaningless preferences induced by the familiarization or habituation events shown in the tasks? Two lines of evidence supported the first of these interpretations. One line came from simple action tasks. Instead of using VOE tasks to explore young infants' responses to hidden objects, a number of researchers devised simple action tasks they had reason to believe would be less taxing than Piaget's (1952, 1954) manual search tasks. For example, some experiments asked whether young infants would search for an object that was "hidden" simply by extinguishing the room lights. The object could thus be recovered by a direct reach in the dark (e.g., Goubet & Clifton, 1998; Hood & Willatts, 1986). Other experiments asked whether young infants would succeed at searching for an object visually, as opposed to manually (e.g., Hofstader & Reznick, 1996; Ruffman, Slade, & Redman, 2005). Yet other experiments asked whether young infants would visually anticipate the reappearance of an object that was passing behind a screen (e.g., Kochukhova & Gredebäck, 2007; von Hofsten, Kochukhova, & Rosander, 2007). All of these simple action tasks yielded positive results with infants aged 4–6 months, providing converging evidence that young infants are able to represent hidden objects.

The other line of evidence came from experiments designed to test transient-preference accounts directly. According to these accounts, young infants should fail at VOE object-permanence tasks when given *no* familiarization or habituation trials: without such trials, infants could have no opportunity to form transient preferences, and they should therefore tend to look equally at the unexpected and expected test events. To test this prediction, young infants were given a VOE object-permanence task with test trials only (Wang et al., 2004). One experiment, for example, asked whether 4-month-olds realize that a wide object can be fully hidden inside a wide but not a narrow container (see figure 1.2). The infants saw a wide and a narrow test event. At the start of each event, an experimenter's gloved hand held a wide object above a wide (wide event) or a narrow (narrow event) container; the wide container was slightly wider than the object, and the narrow container was less than half as wide as the object. After a pause, a screen was raised to hide the container, and the hand then lowered the object into the container. Finally, the screen was lowered to reveal only the container; the object was not visible

Experimental condition

Wide event

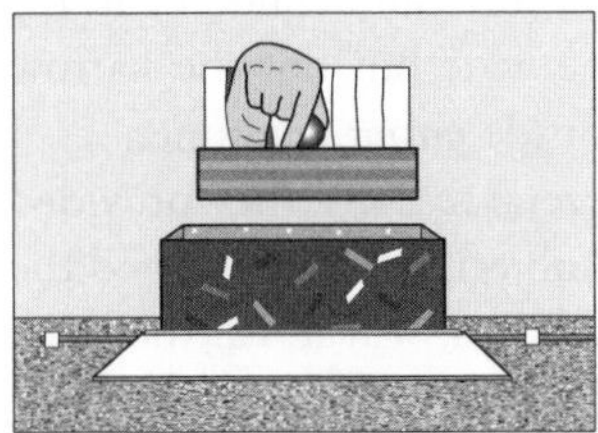
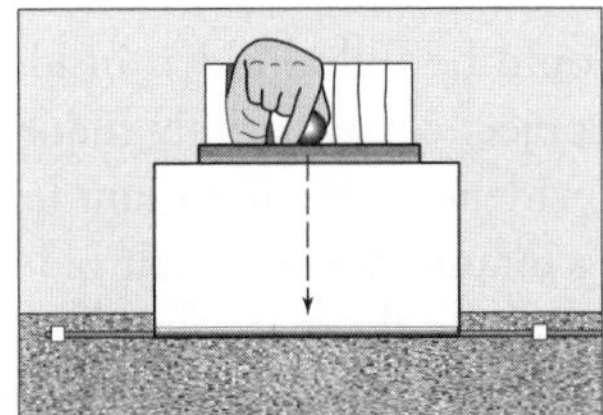

Narrow event

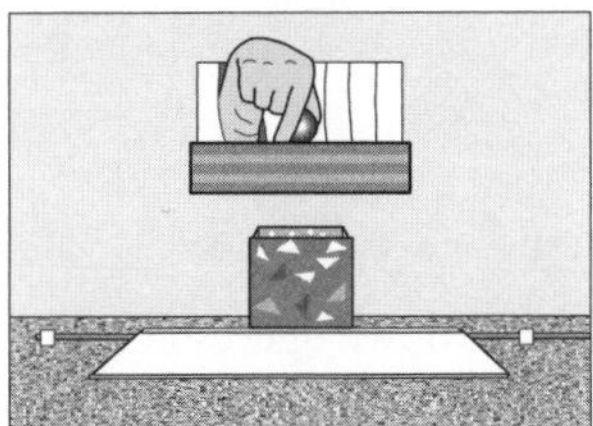
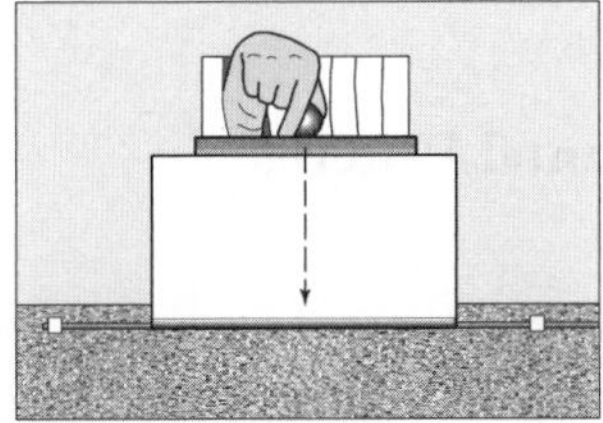

Control condition

Wide event

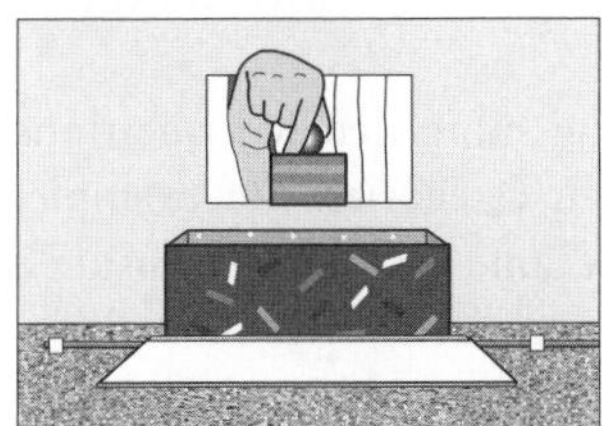
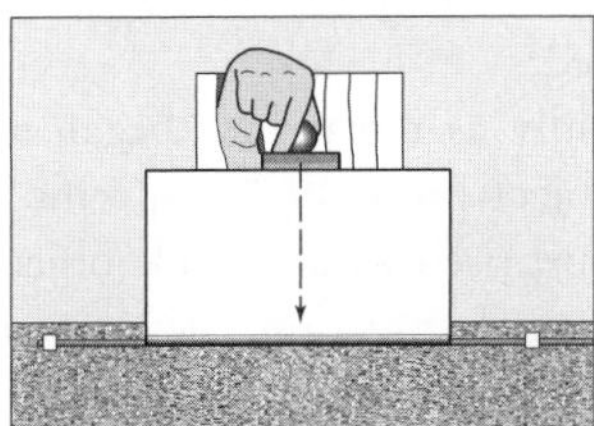

Narrow event

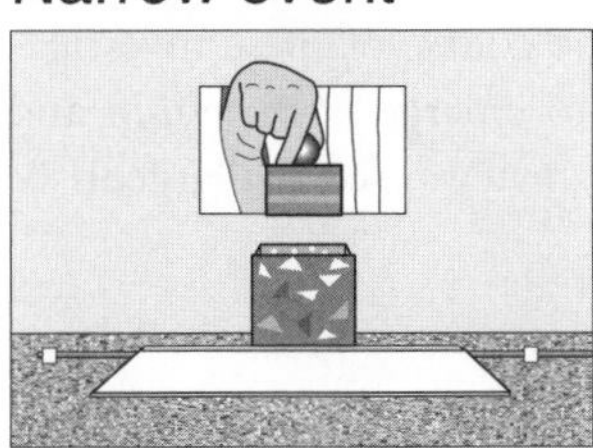
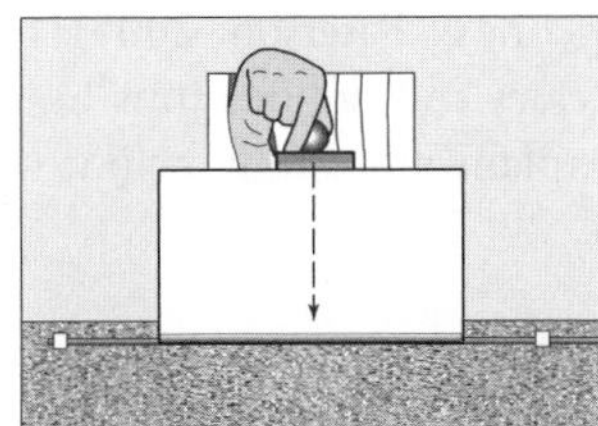

Figure 1.2 Test events used in the experimental and control conditions of Wang et al. (2004)

and was presumably hidden inside the container. This outcome was possible in the wide but not the narrow event: since the object was wider than the narrow container, it should have been impossible for the object to fit inside the narrow container. Infants in a control condition saw similar test events except that the object was much narrower and could be fully hidden inside either container. The infants in the experimental condition looked reliably longer at the narrow than at the wide event, whereas those in the control condition looked about equally at the two events. These results suggested that the infants (a) believed that the wide or narrow object continued to exist after it became hidden and (b) realized that the wide object could be fully hidden inside the wide but not the narrow container, whereas the narrow object could be fully hidden inside either container.

Together, these two lines of evidence were important for several reasons: they provided converging evidence that young infants can represent hidden objects; they supported the notion that infants who reveal a physical expectation in a VOE task will reveal the same expectation in an action task as long as the demands of the task do not overwhelm their limited information-processing resources; and they helped put to rest some of the concerns associated with VOE tasks.

Second Wave: Developmental Patterns

The first wave of looking-time experiments on infants' physical knowledge established that, contrary to traditional claims, even young infants possess expectations about physical events. However, little was known about how infants' physical knowledge *developed* during the first year of life. Initial investigations tended to focus on questions such as whether young infants are surprised if objects magically disappear, break apart, or pass through obstacles. Because the answers to these questions tended to be positive, no salient developmental patterns emerged.

The situation changed rapidly as researchers began asking more detailed questions about the effects of specific object properties in specific event categories. For example, although 4-month-olds were surprised when a wide object became fully hidden inside a narrow container, as we saw in the last section, they were *not* surprised when a tall object became fully hidden inside a short container (Hespos & Baillargeon, 2001a). By about 7.5 months of age, infants succeeded in detecting this violation – but they were *not* surprised if the tall object became fully hidden inside a short tube, instead of inside a short container (Wang, Baillargeon, & Paterson, 2005). In the course of these investigations, striking patterns of successes and failures thus began to emerge both *within* and *across* event categories, as we explain more fully below. (For reviews, see Baillargeon & Wang, 2002; Spelke & Hespos, 2002).

Developments Within Event Categories

As researchers began to study infants' expectations about specific event categories, it soon became apparent that whether infants succeeded or failed at detecting a violation in an event category depended on the particular expectation investigated. To illustrate, consider experiments on infants' expectations about occlusion events (i.e. events in which an object moves or is placed behind another object, or occluder). One series of experiments examined infants' ability to judge whether an object should be fully hidden when behind an occluder (see figure 1.3). At about 3 months of age, infants were surprised if an object

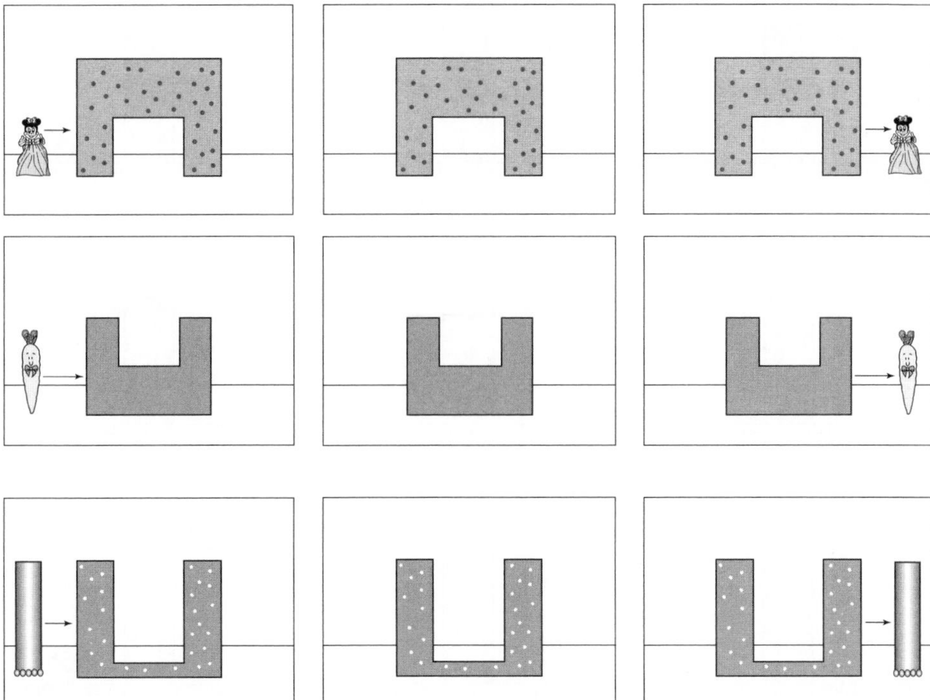

Figure 1.3 Examples of violations in experiments on young infants' ability to judge whether an object should remain hidden when passing behind an occluder, as reported by Aguiar and Baillargeon (2002), Baillargeon and DeVos (1991), and Luo and Baillargeon (2005)

remained hidden when passing behind a screen with a large opening extending from its lower edge (Aguiar & Baillargeon, 2002; Luo & Baillargeon, 2005). However, infants were not surprised if an object remained hidden when passing behind a screen with a large opening extending from its upper edge (Baillargeon & DeVos, 1991), and this held true even when the object was as tall as the screen, so that a large portion of the object should have become visible in the screen's opening (Luo & Baillargeon, 2005). By about 3.5 months of age, infants detected this violation, suggesting that they now attended to height information in occlusion events and expected tall objects to remain visible above short occluders (Baillargeon & DeVos, 1991; Hespos & Baillargeon, 2001a).

Another series of experiments on occlusion events examined infants' ability to notice impossible changes, or change violations, that took place while an object was briefly occluded (see figure 1.4). At about 4.5 months of age, infants were surprised if an object surreptitiously changed size or shape when passing behind a narrow screen (too narrow to hide two objects at once; Wilcox, 1999; Wilcox & Baillargeon, 1998). However, infants failed to detect other change violations: prior to about 7.5 months, infants were not surprised if an object changed pattern when passing behind a narrow screen (Wilcox, 1999; Wilcox & Chapa, 2004); furthermore, prior to about 11.5 months, infants were not surprised if an object changed color when passing behind a narrow screen (Wilcox, 1999; Wilcox & Chapa, 2004).[1]

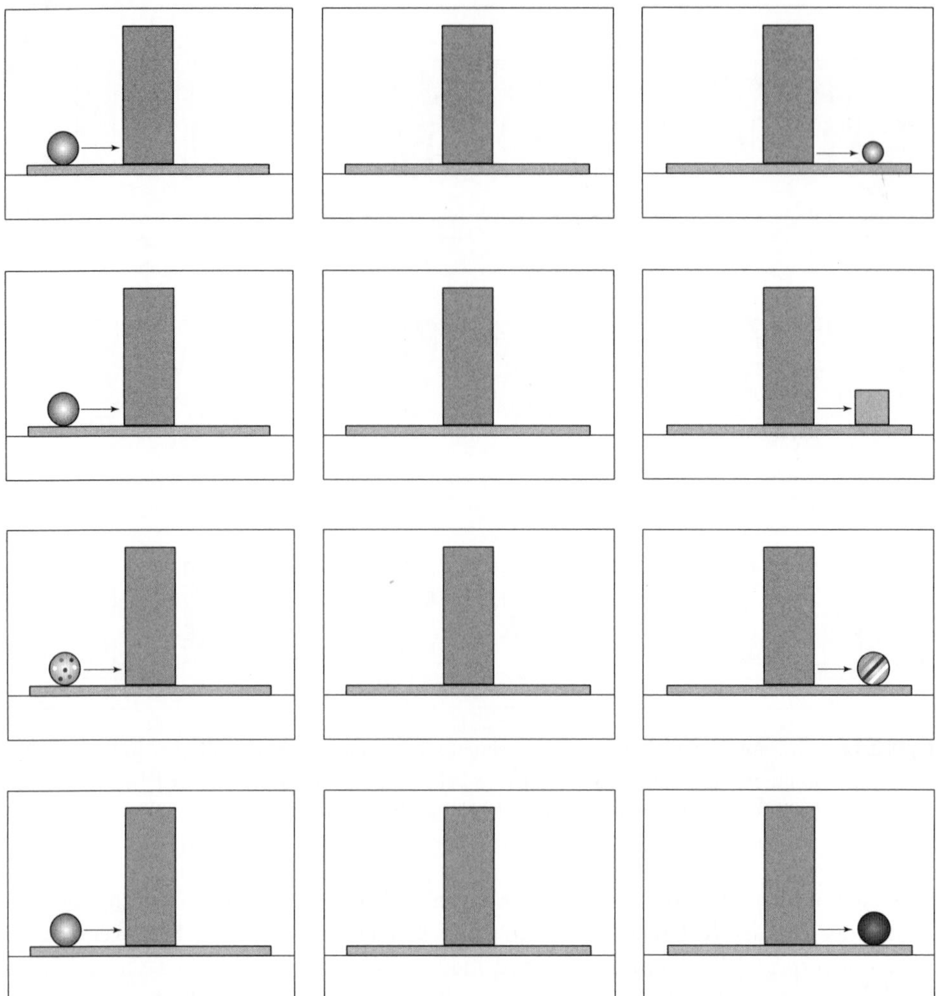

Figure 1.4 Examples of violations in experiments on young infants' ability to detect a surreptitious change to an object that is briefly occluded, as reported by Wilcox (1999)

Developments Across Event Categories

As researchers began to compare infants' physical expectations across event categories, further developmental patterns emerged. In some cases, infants seemed to acquire a physical expectation at about the same age in different event categories. To return to a previous example, 4-month-olds attended to width information in occlusion as well as in containment events: they were surprised if a wide object became fully hidden either behind a narrow occluder or inside a narrow container (Wang et al., 2004; see figure 1.2). In other cases, however, infants detected a violation in one event category, but failed to detect a similar violation in another event category. Thus, although 4.5-month-olds were surprised if an object changed shape when passing behind a narrow screen, as we just saw (Wilcox, 1999; Wilcox & Baillargeon, 1998), 5-month-olds were *not* surprised if an object changed shape when briefly buried in sand (Newcombe et al., 1999). These results suggested that there might be lags or *décalages* (to use a Piagetian term) in infants' acquisition of similar expectations in different event categories.

Of course, one difficulty with this conclusion was that the events being compared often differed in so many dimensions that it made it difficult to determine exactly why infants succeeded with one event category but failed with another. Subsequent investigations attempted to circumvent this difficulty by comparing infants' responses to *perceptually similar* events from different categories. In particular, a whole host of VOE experiments compared infants' responses to occlusion and containment events. In each experiment, the occluders used in the occlusion events were identical to the front walls of the containers used in the containment events, so that infants saw highly similar events in the two categories. These experiments revealed striking décalages in infants' acquisition of similar expectations in the two categories (see figure 1.5). Thus, although 4.5-month-olds were surprised if a tall object became almost fully hidden behind a short occluder, only infants aged 7.5 months and older were surprised if the object became almost fully hidden inside a short container (Hespos & Baillargeon, 2001a). Similarly, 7.5-month-olds detected a violation if an object became fully hidden behind a transparent occluder, but only infants aged 9.5 months and older detected a violation if the object became fully hidden inside a transparent container (Luo & Baillargeon, 2009). Finally, 12.5-month-olds were surprised if an object changed color when briefly hidden behind a small occluder (too small to hide more than one object), but they were not surprised if the object changed color when briefly hidden inside a small container (we still don't know at what age infants reliably detect this violation; Gertner, Baillargeon, Fisher, & Simons, 2009; Ng & Baillargeon, 2009).

Décalages were also observed in action tasks (e.g., Hespos & Baillargeon, 2006; Wang & Kohne, 2007). In one experiment, for example, 6- and 7.5-month-olds first played with a tall stuffed frog (see figure 1.6; Hespos & Baillargeon, 2006). Next, the frog was placed behind a large screen, which was then removed to reveal a tall and a short occluder (occlusion condition) or a tall and a short container (containment condition). The occluders were identical to the front halves of the containers; two frog feet protruded on either side of each occluder or through small holes at the bottom of each container. At both ages, infants were reliably more likely to search for the frog behind the tall as opposed to the short occluder; however, only the 7.5-month-olds were reliably more likely to search for the frog inside the tall as opposed to the short container (control infants who did not see the frog tended to reach about equally for the two occluders or containers).

The action results just described provided converging evidence for the décalage in infants' reasoning about height information in occlusion and containment events. Further experiments revealed that infants did not begin to attend to height information until about 12 months in covering events (e.g., events in which a cover, or inverted container, is placed over an object) and until about 14.5 months in tube events (e.g., events in which an object is placed inside a tube; e.g., Wang et al., 2005). In the case of tube events, for example, researchers found that, prior to about 14.5 months, infants were not surprised

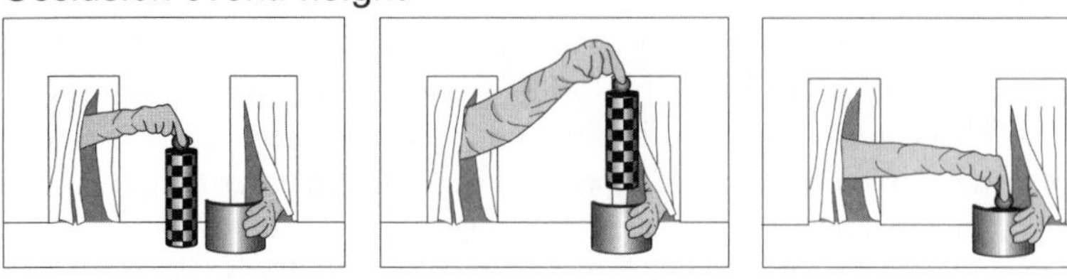

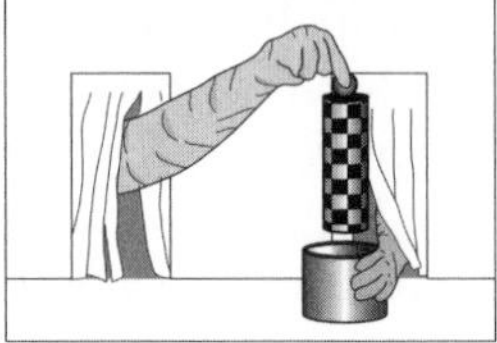
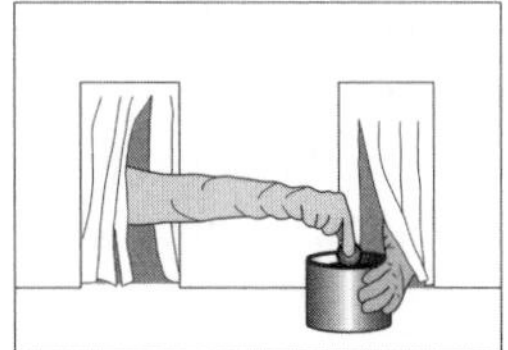

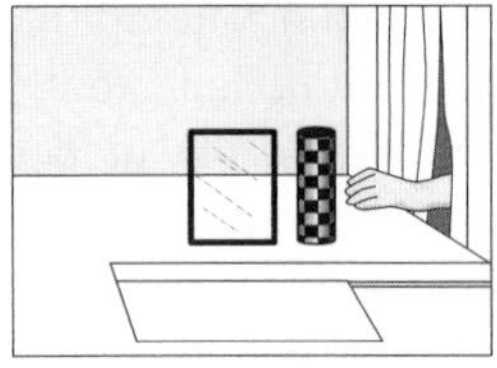

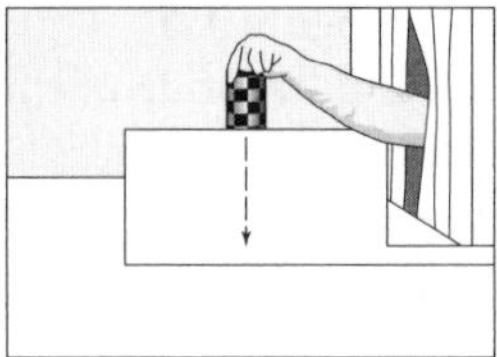
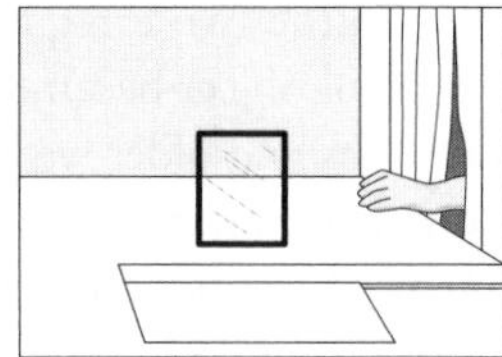

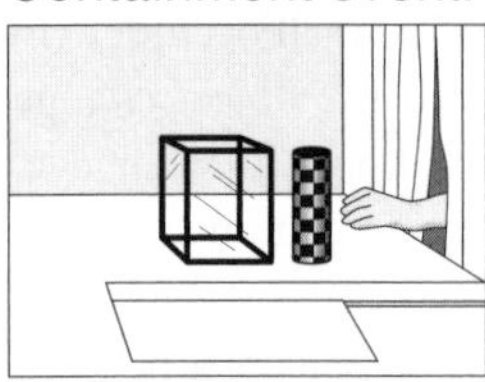

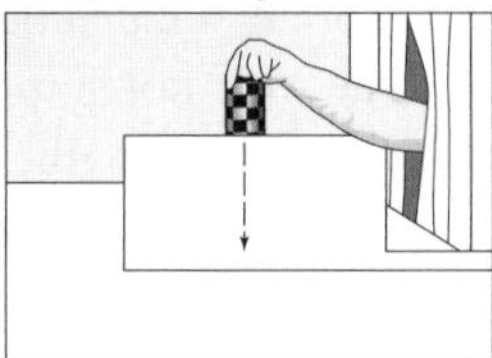
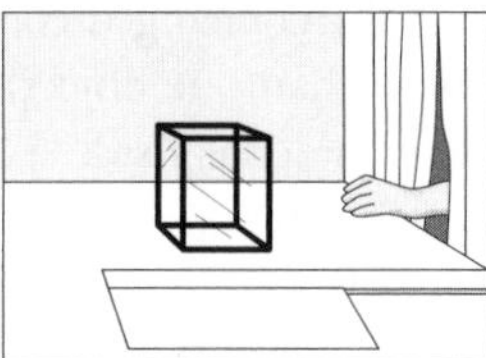

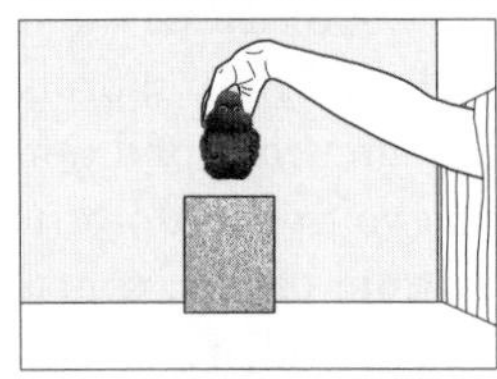

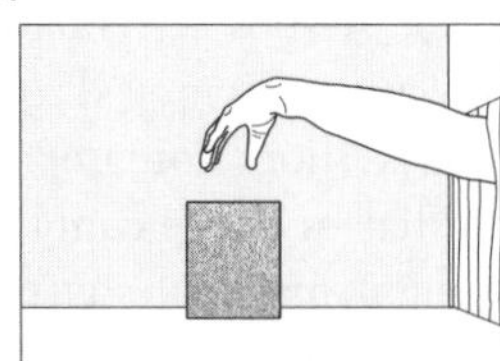
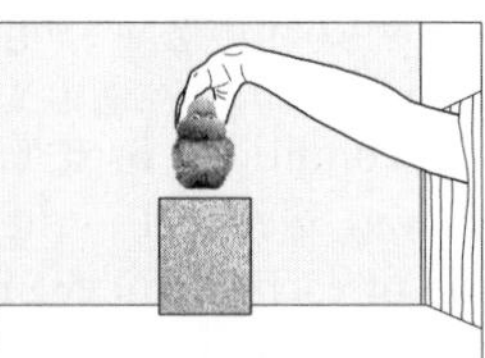

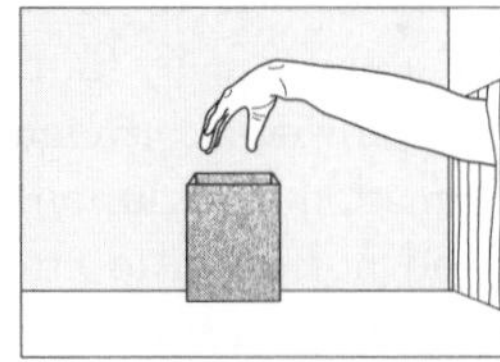
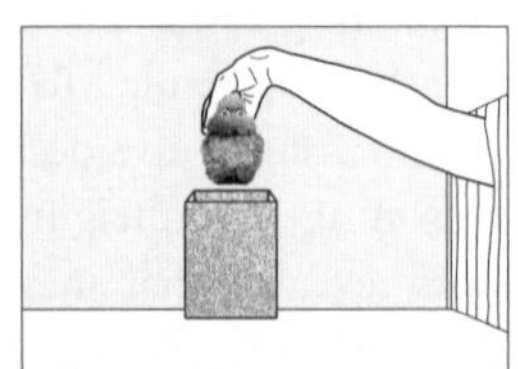

Figure 1.5 Décalages between occlusion and containment events in infants' reasoning about height information (Hespos & Baillargeon, 2001a), transparency information (Luo & Baillargeon, 2009), and color information (Ng & Baillargeon, 2009)

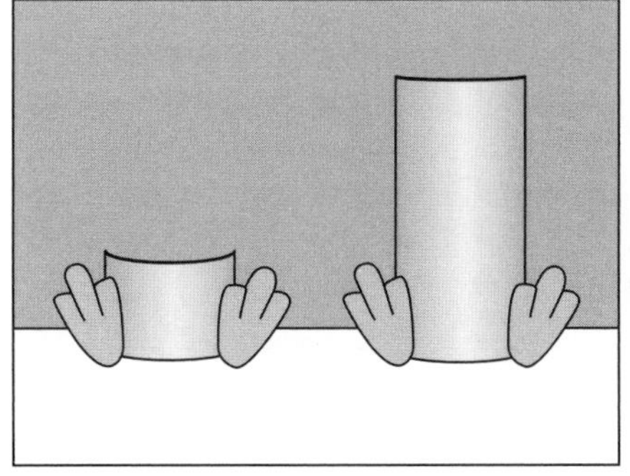

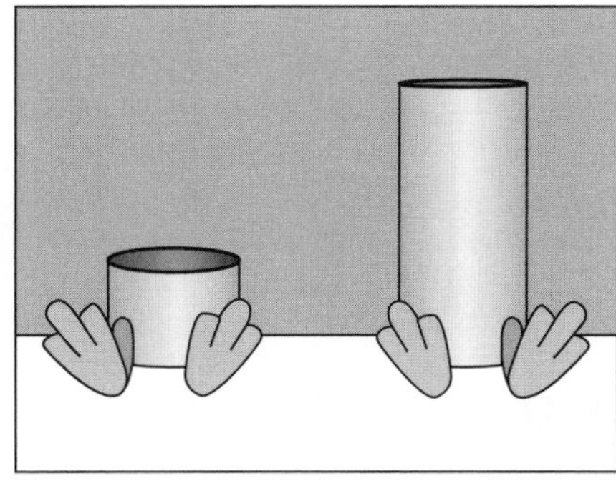

Figure 1.6 Test event used in Hespos and Baillargeon (2006)

if a tall object became fully hidden inside a short tube (Gertner et al., 2009; Wang et al., 2005), they were not surprised if an object changed height when briefly lowered inside a tall tube (Wang & Baillargeon, 2006), and they tended to search for a tall object inside either a tall or a short tube (Wang & Kohne, 2007).

Décalages With Perceptually Identical Events

In the last section, we saw that décalages can be observed in infants' responses to perceptually similar events from different categories. Remarkably, décalages have also been observed with *perceptually identical* events from different categories. These experiments took advantage of the findings (described above) that infants begin to attend to height information at about 7.5 months in containment events, but only at about 14.5 months in tube events.

In one experiment (Wang et al., 2005), 9-month-olds were presented in a brief orientation procedure with a tall and a short container (container condition) or a tall and a short tube (tube condition); the tubes were indistinguishable from the containers when standing upright. Next, the infants saw a tall and a short test event (see figure 1.7). At the start of each event, a tall object stood next to the tall (tall event) or the short (short

Containment and tube conditions

Tall event

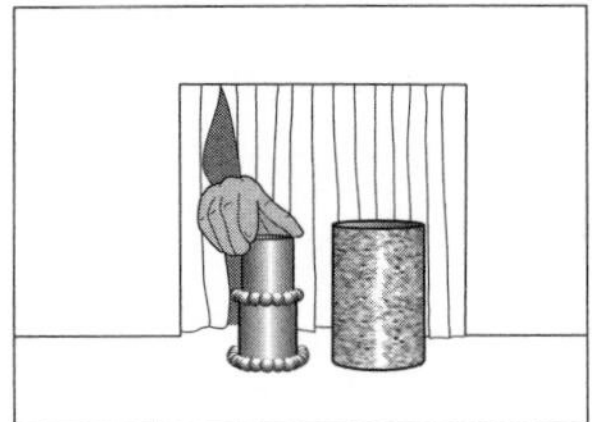
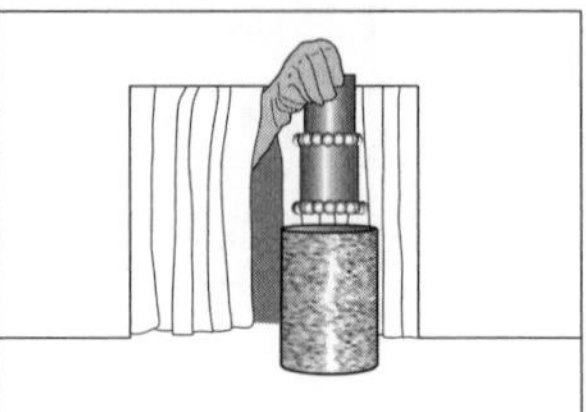

Short event

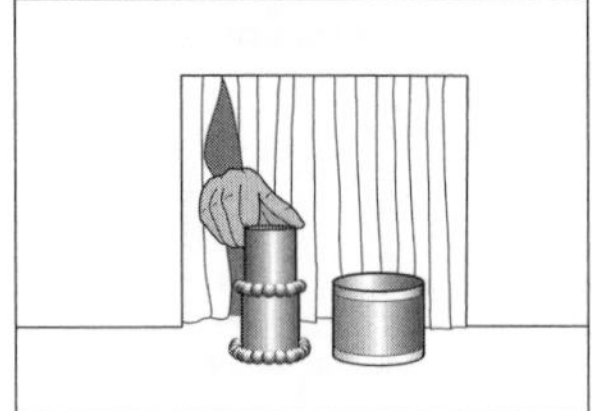
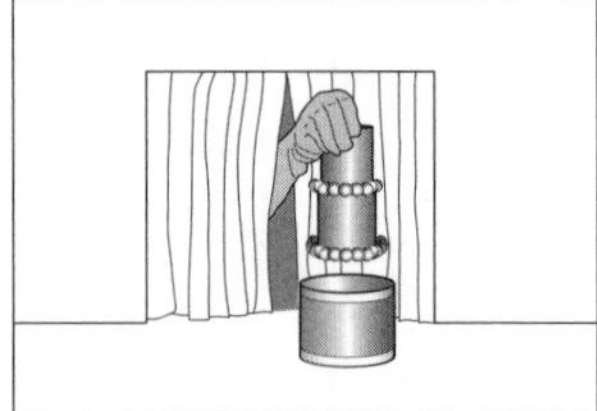

Figure 1.7 Test events used in Wang et al. (2005)

event) container/tube on the apparatus floor; the tall container/tube was slightly taller than the object, and the short container/tube was about half as tall as the object. In each event, an experimenter's gloved hand lifted the object and lowered it inside the container/tube until it became fully hidden. The infants in the container and tube conditions thus saw identical test events: only the information provided in the orientation procedure indicated to the infants in the tube condition that they were facing tubes rather than containers. The infants in the container condition looked reliably longer at the short than at the tall event, whereas those in the tube condition looked about equally at the two events. The infants thus detected the violation in the short event if they believed they were facing a container, but not if they believed they were facing a tube.

Décalages with perceptually identical containment and tube events have recently been observed in two other tasks (Li & Baillargeon, 2009). In a VOE task, 8-month-olds detected a violation if a tall object was much shorter after being briefly lowered inside a tall container, but they failed to detect a violation if the object was much shorter after being briefly lowered inside a tall tube. In an action task, 10-month-olds searched for a tall object inside a tall as opposed to a short container, but they searched for the same object inside either a tall or a short tube. In both tasks, the tubes were indistinguishable from the containers when upright, so that the infants saw perceptually identical test events.

The décalages discussed in this and in the previous section are not due to the fact that infants generally have more difficulty reasoning about containers as opposed to occluders, about covers as opposed to containers, or about tubes as opposed to covers and containers. In fact, even young infants can detect simple violations involving containers, covers, and tubes (e.g., Baillargeon, 1995; Hespos & Baillargeon, 2001b; Wang et al., 2005). What factors then, cause these décalages? Why do weeks or months sometimes separate infants' acquisition of similar expectations in different event categories? We return to this question in the next section.

Third Wave: An Account of Infants' Physical Reasoning

The first two waves of experiments on infants' physical knowledge painted a rather complex picture. Within each event category, some violations were detected at an early age, whereas others were not detected until much later. Across event categories, infants sometimes detected a violation when presented in the context of events from one category, but failed to detect the same violation when presented in the context of (perceptually similar or even identical) events from another category. Making sense of these intricate results required developing an account of infants' physical reasoning that made explicit (a) what information infants represent about physical events and (b) how infants interpret this information. Over the past few years, we have been working on developing such an account (e.g., Baillargeon, Li, Luo, & Wang, 2006; Baillargeon, Li, Ng, & Yuan, 2009).

Before we describe our account, two general comments may be helpful. First, our account focuses on very simple situations where infants reason about one or two successive events involving a small number of objects. This seems a reasonable starting point, because infants' performance often deteriorates when they are presented with two or more simultaneous events or with single events involving a large number of objects (e.g., Cheries, Wynn, & Scholl, 2006; Káldy & Leslie, 2005; Mareschal & Johnson, 2003; Sloane, Baillargeon, Simons, & Scholl, 2009). Second, the events we investigate are by and large simple everyday events that would have been familiar to our distant evolutionary ancestors (e.g., occlusion, containment, support, and collision events). At the present time, our account has little to say about events that involve complex cultural artifacts whose causal mechanisms are opaque to most adults – artifacts such as cell phones, computers, televisions, planes, or magic wands. Although infants may in some respects be prepared to learn how agents operate these complex artifacts (e.g., Csibra & Gergely, 2009; Muentener & Carey, 2009; Tomasello, Carpenter, Call, Behne, & Moll, 2005), these preparations are very different from those that concern us here.

Physical-Reasoning System and Causal Framework

Like several other researchers, we assume that infants are born equipped with a *physical-reasoning (PR) system* – an abstract, computational system that provides a skeletal causal framework for making sense of the displacements and interactions of objects and other physical entities (e.g., Carey & Spelke, 1994; Gelman, 1990; Leslie, 1995; Spelke et al.,

1992). The PR system operates without conscious awareness: infants are not aware of the causal framework they use when reasoning about physical events, any more than young children are aware of the grammar of their language as they begin to understand and produce sentences.

When infants watch a physical event, the PR system builds a specialized *physical representation* of the event. Any information included in this representation becomes subject to the system's causal framework. This framework includes a number of explanatory concepts (e.g., internal energy, force; Baillargeon, Wu, Yuan, Li, & Luo, 2009; Leslie, 1995) as well as core principles. Of most relevance to the research described in this chapter is the *principle of persistence*, which states that, all other things being equal, objects persist, as they are, in time and space (e.g., Baillargeon, 2008; Baillargeon et al., 2009). The persistence principle has many corollaries, including but not limited to those of continuity, solidity, cohesion, and boundedness (e.g., Spelke et al., 1992; Spelke, Phillips, & Woodward, 1995). It specifies that an object cannot spontaneously appear or disappear (continuity), occupy the same space as another object (solidity), break apart (cohesion), fuse with another object (boundedness), or change size, shape, pattern, or color. Thus, a wooden spoon cannot spontaneously disappear, pass through a table, break apart, fuse with a pot, or change into a noodle; all of these events represent persistence violations. (Of course, a wooden spoon could be painted red, burned, sawed into pieces, or glued to a pot; such events represent *object transformations* rather than persistence violations, because in each case there is a causal mechanism responsible for the change effected; e.g., Gelman, Bullock, & Meck, 1980; Goswami & Brown, 1990; Needham & Baillargeon, 1997; Tzelnic, Kuhlmeier, & Hauser, 2009).

Basic Information

When building a physical representation for an event, the PR system first represents the *basic* information about the event (see figure 1.8). This basic information includes both identity and spatio-temporal information. The *identity* information provides broad categorical descriptors for the objects in the event: in particular, it specifies whether the objects are inert or self-propelled, human or non-human, and closed or open (i.e. open at the top to form a container, open at the bottom to form a cover, or open at both ends to form a tube; e.g., Bonatti, Frot, Zangl, & Mehler, 2002; Hespos & Baillargeon, 2001b; Luo, Kaufman, & Baillargeon, 2009; Wang et al. 2005; Wu & Baillargeon, 2008; Yuan & Baillargeon, 2008). The *spatio-temporal* information specifies the spatial arrangement of the objects and how it changes as the event unfolds (e.g., Kestenbaum, Termine, & Spelke, 1987; Quinn, 2007; Slater, 1995; Yonas & Granrud, 1984).

Both the identity and the spatio-temporal information about an event help specify how many objects are involved in the event. For example, if a human disappears behind a large screen and a non-human object appears from behind it, the identity information will specify that two distinct objects are involved in the event, one human and one non-human (Bonatti et al., 2002; Wu & Baillargeon, 2008). Similarly, if two identical objects stand apart on an apparatus floor and a screen is then lifted to hide them, the

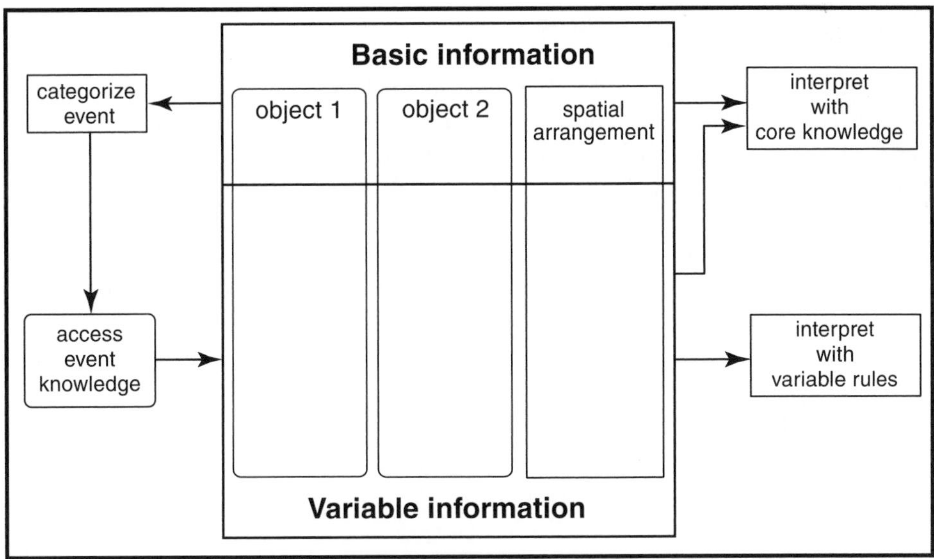

Figure 1.8 Schematic model of the physical-reasoning system: how infants represent and interpret the basic and the variable information about a physical event

spatio-temporal information will specify that two objects are present behind the screen (Aguiar & Baillargeon, 1999; Xu & Carey, 1996).

The PR system uses the identity and the spatio-temporal information about an event to *categorize* the event and to assign appropriate *roles* to the objects in the event (e.g., Leslie & Keeble, 1987; Onishi, 2009). Consider a simple event involving two identical blocks, block A and block B. If block A is used to hit block B, the event is categorized as a collision event, with block A as the hitter and block B as the object that is hit. If block B is lowered behind block A, the event is categorized as an occlusion event, with block A as the occluder and block B as the occluded object. After watching one of these events repeatedly, infants look reliably longer if the two objects change roles (e.g., if block A becomes the object that is hit in the collision event or the occluded object in the occlusion event).

The basic information about an event thus captures its essence: it specifies how many objects are involved in the event (e.g., two objects), what kinds of objects they are (e.g., inert, non-human, closed objects), what kind of event the objects are engaged in (e.g., a collision event), and what role each object plays in the event (object A is the hitter, object B is the object that is hit). (Note that, in our example, a simple sentence such as "It hit it" would map fairly well onto the basic description of the event, raising interesting questions about the links between language and basic event representations; for a discussion of structure-mapping between sentences and event representations in early language acquisition, see Fisher, 1996; Fisher, Gertner, Scott, & Yuan, in press).

Detecting basic persistence violations

In the first weeks of life, the PR system typically includes only basic information in its physical representation of an event. Although very limited, this information is nevertheless sufficient, when interpreted by the PR system's causal framework, to allow infants to detect several physical violations (e.g., Aguiar & Baillargeon, 1999; Baillargeon, 1987; Hespos & Baillargeon, 2001b; Lécuyer & Durand, 1998; Luo & Baillargeon, 2005; Spelke et al., 1992; Wang et al., 2005; Wilcox et al., 1996). These include the violations shown in figure 1.1 as well as those (from more recent experiments) shown in figure 1.9.

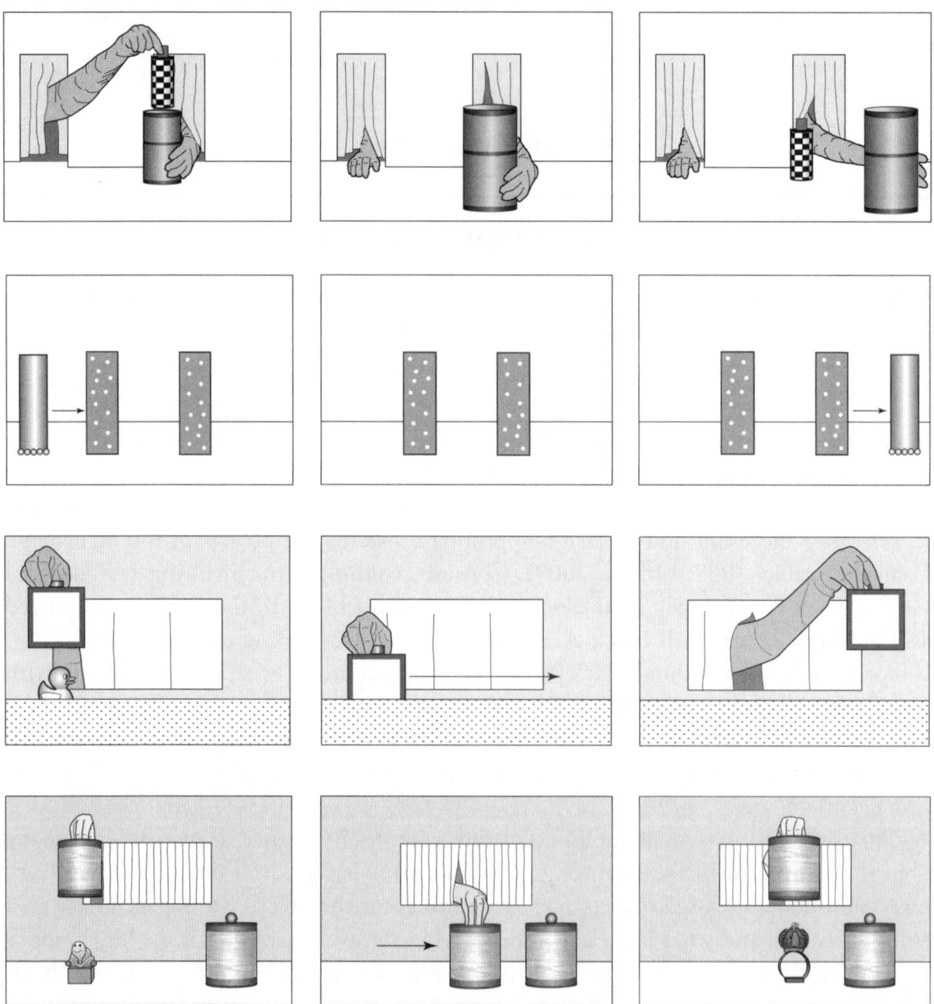

Figure 1.9 Examples of basic persistence violations that young infants are able to detect, as shown by Hespos and Baillargeon (2001b), Luo and Baillargeon (2005), Wang et al. (2005), and Wu et al. (2009b)

Focusing on the latter violations, 2.5- to 3-month-olds (the youngest infants tested successfully to date with the VOE method) are surprised when an object is lowered inside an open container which is then slid forward and to the side to reveal the object standing in the container's initial position (Hespos & Baillargeon, 2001b); when an object disappears behind one screen and then reappears from behind another screen without appearing in the gap between them (Luo & Baillargeon, 2005); when a cover is lowered over an object, slid to the side, and then lifted to reveal no object (Wang et al., 2005); and when a cover is lowered over a closed object, slid to the side, and then lifted to reveal an open object (Wu, Li, & Baillargeon, 2009).

All of these violations can be detected by very young infants because they involve only basic information (this is why we refer to them as *basic persistence violations*). In each case, the PR system represents the basic information about the event, applies the persistence principle to this information, and flags the event as a persistence violation. For example, consider once again the finding that infants are surprised when a cover is lowered over an object, slid to the side, and then lifted to reveal no object (Wang et al., 2005). As the event unfolds, the basic information represented by the PR system will include the following: (a) a cover is lowered over a closed object (the persistence principle will specify that the object continues to exist under the cover); (b) the cover is slid to the side (the persistence principle will specify that the object cannot pass through the sides of the cover and hence must have been displaced with the cover to its new location); and (c) the cover is lifted to reveal no object (the persistence principle will signal that a violation has occurred: the object should have been revealed when the cover was lifted).

Variable Information

We have just seen that, in the first few weeks of life, the PR system typically includes only basic information in its physical representation of an event. Although this information captures essential elements, it is still very limited. If a spoon is placed inside a pot, for example, the basic information will specify that an inert, non-human, closed object has been placed inside an inert, non-human, container. If a ball is placed on a block, the basic information will specify that an inert, non-human, closed object has been released in contact with another inert, non-human, closed object. In each case, the basic information thus leaves out many details: in particular, it does not specify the size, shape, pattern, or color of the objects, nor does it specify (in the second example) whether the ball is released on the top or against the side of the block. This more detailed information about the properties and arrangements of objects constitutes what we have termed *variable* information, and it is not included in physical representations until infants learn, with experience, that it is helpful for interpreting and predicting outcomes.

As infants observe physical events, they form distinct *event categories* (e.g., Aguiar & Baillargeon, 2003; Casasola, Cohen, & Chiarello, 2003; Hespos & Baillargeon, 2006; McDonough, Choi, & Mandler, 2003; Quinn, 2007; Wilcox & Chapa, 2002). For each category, infants identify *variables* that enable them to better interpret and predict outcomes (e.g., Aguiar & Baillargeon, 2002; Baillargeon, Needham, & DeVos, 1992; Hespos

& Baillargeon, 2008; Kotovsky & Baillargeon, 1998; Sitskoorn & Smitsman, 1995; Wang, Kaufman, Baillargeon, 2003; Wilcox, 1999). A variable both calls infants' attention to a certain type of information in an event (e.g., features of objects or their arrangements) and provides a causal rule for interpreting this information. To illustrate, by about 12 months of age, most infants have identified height as a relevant variable in covering events: when a cover is placed over an object, infants now attend to the relative heights of the cover and object. As a result, 12-month-olds look reliably longer if a tall object becomes fully hidden under a short cover (Wang et al., 2005); they look reliably longer if a short object is much taller after being briefly hidden under a tall cover (Wang & Baillargeon, 2006); and they are reliably more likely to search for a tall object under a tall as opposed to a short cover (Wang & Kohne, 2007). In contrast, infants younger than 12 months typically fail all of these tasks (Wang & Baillargeon, 2006; Wang & Kohne, 2007; Wang et al., 2005).

With the gradual identification of variables, infants' physical representations become increasingly richer (see figure 1.8). After representing the basic information about an event and using this information to categorize the event, the PR system accesses the list of variables that have been identified as relevant for predicting outcomes in the category selected. The PR system then gathers information about each variable and includes this information in the physical representation of the event. This variable information is then interpreted by the variable rules as well as by the PR system's causal framework.

To illustrate this process, consider what variable information 7.5-month-olds would include in their physical representation of a containment event in which a ball was lowered inside a box. By 7.5 months, width and height have typically been identified as containment variables, but container-surface and color have not (see figures 1.2, 1.5, and 1.6). Thus, infants should include information about the relative widths and heights of the ball and box in their physical representation of the event, but not information about the container's surface (e.g., whether it is transparent) or about the ball's color. As a rule, the PR system does not include information about variables that have not yet been identified in its physical representation of an event.

Detecting variable persistence violations

As may be obvious from the preceding description, infants can detect a persistence violation involving a specific variable (or a *variable persistence violation*) only if the PR system includes information about the variable in its physical representation of the event. Figures 1.3 to 1.7 present many examples of variable persistence violations that infants fail to detect because they have not yet identified the relevant variables and hence do not include the necessary information in their physical representations of the events. For instance, infants cannot be surprised if an object surreptitiously changes shape, pattern, or color when briefly hidden behind a narrow screen (Wilcox, 1999) or inside a small container (Ng & Baillargeon, 2009) if they do not include shape, pattern, and color information in their physical representations of the events (see figures 1.4 and 1.5). In the first year of life, whether a given variable persistence violation is detected will depend primarily on whether (a) the variable has been identified for the event category involved, and hence (b) information about the variable is included in the physical representation of the event.

The present account also helps explain the striking décalages discussed earlier in infants' VOE responses (see figures 1.5 and 1.7). In each case, the PR system will first represent the basic information about the event, categorize the event, and access the list of variables identified for the category. If height has been identified as a relevant variable for the category selected (e.g., a containment event), then height information will be included in the physical representation of the event, and violations involving this information will be detected. Conversely, if height has not yet been identified as a relevant variable for the category selected (e.g., a tube event), then height information will not be included in the physical representation of the event, and violations involving this information will obviously not be detected.

The same constraints apply to infants' responses in action tasks. Infants who have identified height as a containment variable will spontaneously attend to the heights of objects and containers and thus will search for a tall object inside a tall as opposed to a short container (see figure 1.6). In contrast, infants who have not yet identified height as a containment variable will fail to include height information in their physical representations and therefore will search for a tall object inside either a tall or a short container (Hespos & Baillargeon, 2006).

Identifying Variables: The Explanation-Based Learning Process

We suggested earlier that infants learn, with experience, what variables are helpful for interpreting and predicting outcomes in each event category. How does this learning process take place? Building on work in machine learning by DeJong (1993, 1997), we have proposed that the identification of a variable depends on an *explanation-based learning* (EBL) process that involves three main steps (e.g., Baillargeon et al., 2006; Baillargeon et al., 2009; Wang & Baillargeon, 2008a).

First, infants must notice *contrastive outcomes* relevant to the variable. This occurs when infants build similar physical representations for two or more events – and notice that the events have contrastive outcomes. For example, consider the variable height in covering events, which is typically identified at about 12 months of age (e.g., Wang et al., 2005; Wang & Kohne, 2007). We suppose that at some point prior to 12 months of age, infants begin to notice – as they manipulate covers and objects or as they observe others doing so – that when a cover is lowered over an object, the object sometimes remains partly visible beneath the cover and sometimes does not. Infants thus notice contrastive outcomes they cannot predict based on their current variable knowledge: similar physical representations ("cover lowered over object") lead to contrastive outcomes ("object remains partly visible beneath cover" versus "object becomes fully hidden"), suggesting that a crucial piece of information is missing from the representations.

At this point, infants begin to search for the *conditions* that map onto these contrastive outcomes. Specifically, infants attempt to determine under what condition one outcome is observed, and under what condition the other outcome is observed. Eventually, infants uncover a regularity linking each outcome with a distinct condition (we assume that infants' statistical learning mechanisms play a key role in detecting these regularities; e.g., Fiser & Aslin, 2002; Saffran, 2009). In the case of the variable height in covering events, infants detect that objects remain partly visible when placed under covers that are shorter than the objects, and become fully hidden when placed under covers that are as tall as or taller than the objects.

Finally, and most critically, infants attempt to generate an *explanation* for the condition–outcome regularity they have observed, based on their prior knowledge. According to the EBL process, *only* condition–outcome regularities for which explanations can be provided are recognized as new variables. These explanations are typically very limited and shallow (e.g., Keil, 1995; Luo et al., 2009; Wilson & Keil, 2000), but they still serve to integrate new variables with infants' existing causal knowledge (by the same token, explanations also prevent infants from learning incorrect or spurious variables). In the case of the variable height in covering events, infants' principle of persistence can provide a ready explanation for their observations: because an object continues to exist and retains its height when under a cover, it can become fully hidden only if its height is equal to, or shorter than, that of the cover.

After a new variable has been identified (i.e. is added to the list of variables relevant to an event category), infants begin to routinely include information about the variable in their physical representations of events from the category.

The EBL process thus helps make clear why infants learn separately about each event category. Infants do not compare arbitrary groups of events and look for invariants or critical variables that might explain similarities or differences among the events. The only situation that can trigger the identification of a variable is one where events with similar physical representations yield (as yet unpredicted or unexplained) contrastive outcomes. The learning process is thus highly constrained: it is designed to compare apples with apples, and not apples with rabbits or spoons.

Teaching experiments

The EBL process predicts that infants who have not yet identified a variable in an event category should be able to identify the variable – even several months before they would normally do so – if exposed in the laboratory (or the home) to appropriate observations for the variable. And indeed, a number of "teaching" experiments have now provided evidence for this prediction (e.g., Baillargeon, 2002; Wang & Baillargeon, 2008a; Wang & Kohne, 2007).

For example, in a recent series of experiments, Wang and her colleagues "taught" 9-month-old infants the variable *height* in covering events (recall that this variable is typically not identified until about 12 months of age; Wang & Baillargeon, 2006; Wang et al., 2005). Infants received three pairs of teaching trials. In each pair of trials, a tall and a short cover (that differed only in height) were lowered over a tall object; infants could see that the object remained partly visible beneath the short cover, but became fully hidden under the tall cover. Different covers were used in the three pairs of teaching trials. Following these trials, the infants received either a VOE or an action task involving novel covers and objects. In the VOE task, infants looked reliably longer (even after a 24-hour delay) when a tall object became fully hidden under a short as opposed to a tall cover (Wang & Baillargeon, 2008a; see figure 1.10). In the action task, infants

Teaching events

Tall event

Short event

Covers used in teaching trials

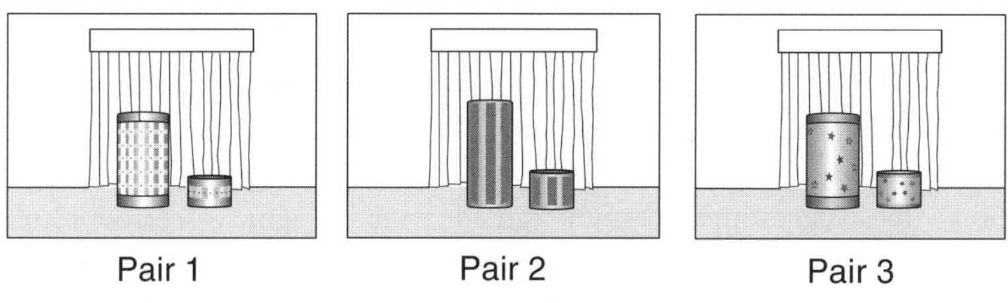

Test events

Tall event

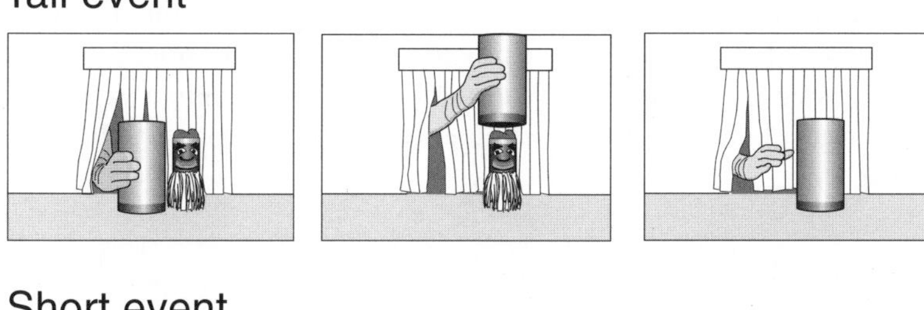

Short event

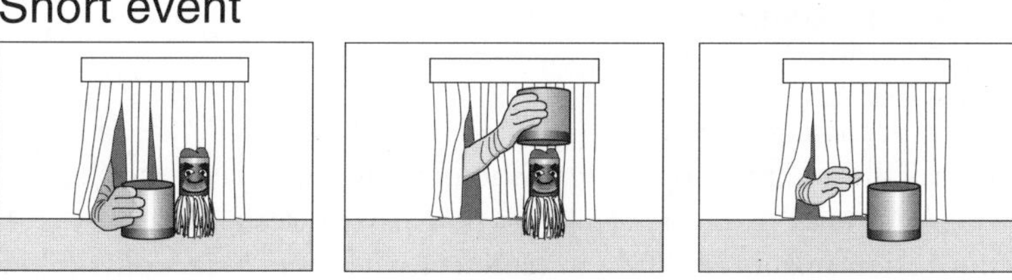

Figure 1.10 Teaching and test events used in Wang and Baillargeon (2008a)

searched correctly for a tall object under a tall as opposed to a short cover (Wang & Kohne, 2007).

From an EBL perspective, these results are readily interpretable. During the teaching trials, (a) the infants noticed that events with similar physical representations led to contrastive outcomes; (b) they uncovered the specific height conditions that mapped onto these outcomes; and (c) they built an explanation for this condition–outcome regularity using their prior knowledge. Height was then added to the list of variables identified as relevant to covering events. When the infants next encountered covering events, they attended to the height information in the events, which enabled them to detect the violation in the VOE task and to search correctly in the action task.

Two additional results supported this analysis. First, infants failed at the VOE task (indicating that they did not identify height as a covering variable) if they received inappropriate teaching trials for which no explanation was possible (Wang & Baillargeon, 2008a; see also Newcombe, Sluzenski, & Huttenlocher, 2005). In this experiment, false bottoms were inserted into the teaching covers, rendering them all 2.5 cm deep; when the covers were rotated forward to reveal their interiors, the infants could notice that they were all shallow. Thus, in each pair of teaching trials, the infants still observed that the tall object became fully hidden under the tall cover and partly hidden under the short cover – but they could no longer build an explanation for this condition–outcome regularity, because the tall and short covers were now equally shallow (i.e. it did not make sense that the tall object became fully hidden under the tall but shallow covers). Second, infants failed at the action task if they received appropriate teaching trials but were tested with tubes instead of covers (Wang & Kohne, 2007). When the tops of the tall and short covers were removed to form tubes, infants searched for the tall object in either the tall or the short tube, suggesting that they had identified height as a variable relevant to covering events and did not generalize this variable to tube events.

Together, the results summarized in this section suggest that infants can be taught a new variable in an event category through brief exposure to appropriate observations for the variable. Furthermore, infants who are taught a new variable immediately attend to information about the variable in situations presenting different stimuli and calling for different responses – but only when these situations involve events from the *same* category. The EBL process ensures broad, yet circumscribed, generalization: a variable identified in an event category is attended to in *any* event from the category – but *only* in events from the category.

A Three-System Account

In the previous section, we presented an account of how the PR system operates and reviewed some of the research supporting this account (for a detailed review, see Baillargeon et al., 2009). As a result of this research, we now have a clearer idea of what basic and variable information infants are likely to represent when watching a physical event, and how this information is likely to guide their responses in VOE and action tasks.

In this section, we begin to look *beyond* the PR system and consider how it relates to two other systems that have received a great deal of attention in the infant and adult visual cognition literature: the *object-tracking (OT) system* and another system that we have termed the *object-representation (OR) system* (e.g., Wang & Baillargeon, 2008b). Below, we first discuss these two systems and then describe new experiments that test possible links between the PR and the OR systems.

This is a truly exciting time in the field of infant cognition, as developments in different subfields are coming together to paint a much more detailed picture of the cognitive architecture that underlies infants' responses to physical events.

Object-Tracking System

Consider a simple situation in which infants see two objects standing apart on an apparatus floor. The object-tracking (OT) system assigns an index to each object, based on the available spatio-temporal information; because the objects occupy different locations in space, they are readily perceived as separate objects (e.g., Leslie, Xu, Tremoulet, & Scholl, 1998; Pylyshyn, 1989, 1994; Scholl & Leslie, 1999). Each index functions as an index finger or attentional pointer that "sticks" to its object as it moves, enabling infants to keep track of the object (i.e. to know where it is without having to search for it).

There is a sharp limit to the number of objects infants can track simultaneously. Initially, this limit was thought to be about three objects overall (e.g., Leslie et al., 1998; Scholl & Leslie, 1999), but seminal experiments by Feigenson and her colleagues have revealed that three is actually the limit *per set* of objects. In experiments using a manual search task (e.g., Feigenson & Carey, 2003, 2005; Feigenson & Halberda, 2004), for example, 12- to 14-month-olds were presented with a large box; in the front of the box was a spandex-filled opening with a slit (this arrangement made it possible for infants to reach into the box, but not to see into it). In each trial, an experimenter first placed objects such as balls on top of the box and then hid them inside the box; the infant was then allowed to search for the balls. Across trials, the researchers compared whether infants were more likely to continue searching when only some of the balls had been retrieved than when all of the balls had been retrieved. Results indicated that infants searched correctly when three but not four balls were hidden, suggesting that they could not keep track of more than three objects at a time. However, additional results indicated that infants could overcome this limit and search successfully when four and even six objects were hidden, as long as the objects were presented in spatially distinct subsets prior to hiding (Feigenson & Halberda, 2004, 2008). Thus, although 14-month-olds failed to search correctly when a single set of six balls was placed on top of the box at the start of the trial, they succeeded when the six balls were grouped into three spatially distinct sets of two balls. These results suggest that, in infancy, the OT system can simultaneously track as many as three sets of objects, provided that each set contains no more than three objects.

Object-Representation System

Let us return to our simple situation in which infants see two objects standing apart on an apparatus floor. As soon as the OT system assigns an index to each object, the object-representation (OR) system begins to build a detailed representation of each object, listing both individual (e.g., color) and relational (e.g., relative height) features (e.g., Huttenlocher, Duffy, & Levine, 2002; Kahneman, Treisman, & Gibbs, 1992; Needham, 2001; Rose, Gottfried, Melloy-Carminar, & Bridger, 1982). We assume that, under simple conditions, each object's representation is linked to its index, so that infants can keep track of which features belong to which object (e.g., Káldy & Leslie, 2003, 2005; Mareschal & Johnson, 2003; Oakes, Ross-Sheehy, & Luck, 2006).

A variety of segregation, recognition, and categorization processes can operate on the representations in the OR system, to highlight particular information or to include additional information (e.g., Feigenson & Halberda, 2008; Needham, 2001; Needham, Cantlon, & Ormsbee Holley, 2006; Needham, Dueker, & Lockhead, 2005). To illustrate, consider a situation in which two objects stand side by side (instead of apart) on an apparatus floor. Because the OT system relies primarily on spatio-temporal information, it will treat this *adjacent display* as a single object and will therefore assign a single index (e.g., Kestenbaum et al., 1987; Needham, 2000). However, if the OR system can determine that the display contains two separate objects, then (via communication between the OR and the OT systems) a second index will be assigned.

Experiments by Needham and her colleagues indicate that, beginning at 3–4 months of age, infants can sometimes use shape information to correctly segregate an adjacent display (e.g., Needham, 1998, 1999, 2000; for a review, see Needham, 2009). If infants cannot use shape information to parse the display (e.g., because the objects' shapes are too difficult for them to encode), they can still succeed if they recognize one of the objects in the display as one they have encountered previously (e.g., Needham, 2001; Needham & Baillargeon, 1998), or as one from a familiar object category (e.g., Needham et al., 2006). If neither object in the display is familiar or belongs to a familiar category, infants may still correctly parse the display if they are first induced to form a relevant category (e.g., Dueker, Modi, & Needham, 2003; Needham et al., 2005). In a seminal series of experiments, 4.5-month-olds were presented with an adjacent test display composed of a curved yellow cylinder and a tall blue rectangular block decorated with small white squares. Infants succeeded in parsing this display if they were briefly familiarized with a static array of three blocks that were similar in size and shape to the test block but differed in color and pattern. These results suggested that the infants (a) formed a category when shown the three familiarization blocks; (b) recognized that the test block was a novel exemplar of this category; and (c) perceived the cylinder and block in the test display as two separate objects.

Together, these results suggest that, when infants first see objects on an apparatus floor, they not only represent (many of) the features of each object, but they spontaneously engage in various processes including segregation, recognition, and categorization.

Physical-Reasoning System

Consider a simple situation in which infants see two distinct objects, a container and a block, standing apart on an apparatus floor (see figure 1.11). As infants attend to the

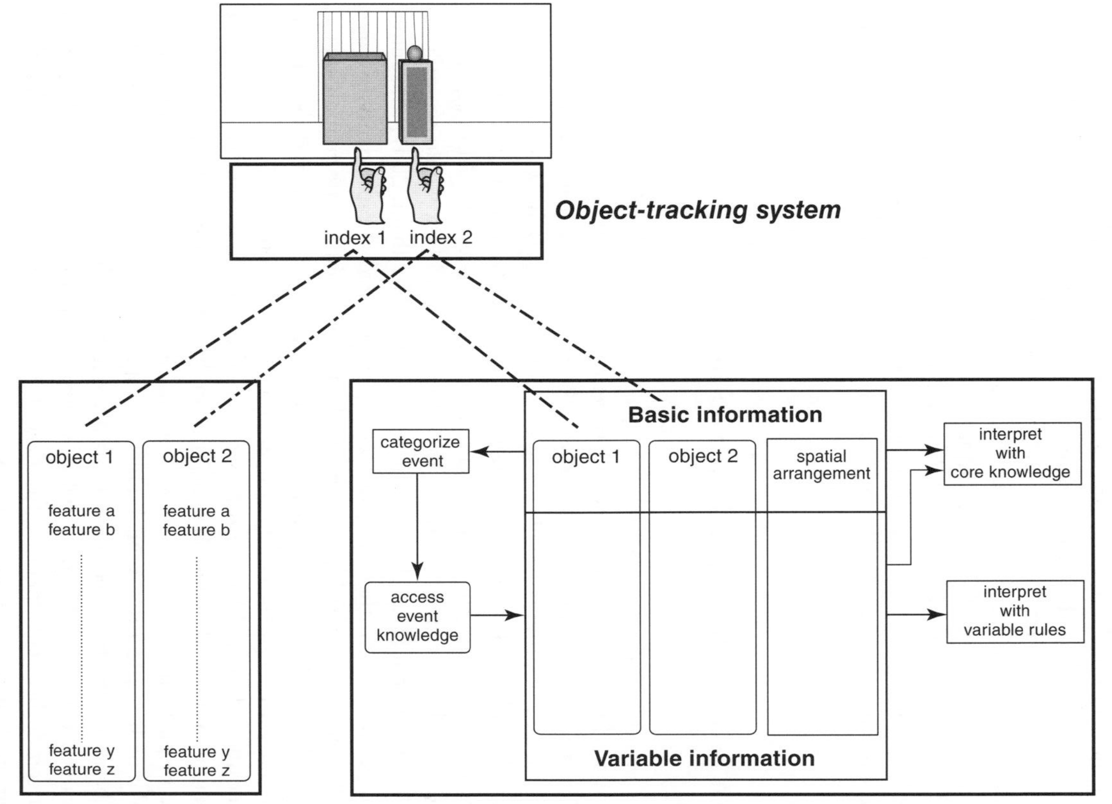

Figure 1.11 Schematic model of the object-tracking, object-representation, and physical-reasoning systems. The physical-reasoning system becomes involved when the objects interact (e.g., when an experimenter's hand lifts the block and lowers it inside the container)

objects, the OT system assigns an index to each object, and the OR system builds detailed representations of the objects. If an experimenter then places the block inside the container, the PR system also becomes involved: the objects are now engaged in an interaction, and the PR system's main purpose is that of interpreting and predicting the outcomes of such interactions.

As was explained previously, the PR system builds a specialized physical representation of the event: it (a) represents the basic information about the event; (b) uses this information to categorize the event; (c) accesses the list of variables that have been identified as relevant for the event category selected; and (d) includes information about each variable in the event's physical representation. The basic and variable information about each object is linked to its index, so that infants can keep track of the objects as they move and interact. Finally, the information included in the physical representation of the event is interpreted using the PR system's core knowledge and the applicable variable rules.

Dissociation between the OR and PR Systems

One striking consequence of the three-system account just outlined is that separate object representations are formed in the OR and PR systems, *with the OR representations often including information that is not included in the PR representations* (e.g., Gertner et al., 2009; Li, Baillargeon, & Simons, 2009; Wang & Baillargeon, 2008b; Wang & Mitroff, 2009; for related results with adults, see Simons, Chabris, Schnur, & Levin, 2002). To illustrate, consider once again the simple event depicted in figure 1.11. Although information about the color and height (say) of the container and block would typically be included in the OR system (e.g., Huttenlocher et al., 2002; Needham, 2001), this information would be included in the PR system *only* if infants had already identified color and height as containment variables (see figure 1.5). Thus, object information that is routinely included in the OR system may not be included in the PR system if the relevant variables have not yet been identified for the event category involved.

Why should the OR and PR systems be set up in this way? Why not have *all* of the object information in the OR system *also* included in the PR system? The answer to these questions, we suspect, mainly has to do with learnability. As we saw previously, in the first few weeks of life, the PR system builds very sparse physical representations that include only basic information; representations become gradually richer as infants learn, category by category and variable by variable, what information is causally relevant for predicting outcomes. If infants included from the start all of the object information from the OR system in their physical representations, they might have great difficulty sorting through all of that information to figure out what was helpful for predicting what. These learnability considerations loom even larger when one considers that (a) infants have limited information-processing resources and (b) the PR system (like the language-processing system, for example) must operate rapidly, online, as events unfold. Speed is critical: time spent sorting through irrelevant information is time ill-spent. To make sense of events as they occur in the world, infants must be able to keep up with them. Beginning with sparse blueprints and filling in additional information as it proves useful is thus a highly adaptive learning strategy.

Retrieving Object Information from the OR System

If separate object representations exist in the OR and PR systems, then it might be possible for the PR system to *query* the OR system for information about a variable when this information can no longer be gathered from inspection of the scene (e.g., because objects have become hidden). In other words, the OR system might serve as a generous neighbor who readily "passes on" object information when queried by the PR system (see figure 1.12).

To test this suggestion, we recently carried out an experiment with 6-month-olds (Li et al., 2009). This experiment examined infants' ability to detect a surreptitious change to the height of an object, and it built upon the findings that the variable height is identified at about 3.5 months in occlusion events, but only at about 7.5 months in containment events (e.g., Baillargeon & DeVos, 1991; Hespos & Baillargeon, 2001a). The infants were assigned to one of three conditions (see figure 1.13): an occlusion, a containment, and a no-event condition. We assumed that the occlusion and the containment conditions would involve both the OR and the PR systems, and that the no-event condition would involve only the OR system.

The infants in the *occlusion* condition received one trial presented in three successive "snapshots"; between snapshots, a large panel hid the interior of the apparatus. In snapshot 1 (which lasted about 5 s), a tall container stood next to a tall rectangular block with a knob at the top; the rectangular portion of the block was about the same height as the container. In snapshot 2 (which lasted about 4 s), an experimenter's gloved hand held the block *behind* the container, above the apparatus floor, and twisted it gently; only the knob and the very top of the block were visible, so that the infants could not determine the block's exact height. In snapshot 3, the block again stood next to the container, and was either the same height as before (no-change event) or much shorter (change event). Snapshot 3 lasted until the infant looked away and the trial ended.

We reasoned that, during snapshot 1, the OT system would assign an index to the container and block, and the OR system would form detailed representations of the objects, including their relative heights. During snapshot 2, the PR system would represent the basic information about the event, would categorize it as an occlusion event, and would access the list of variables identified as relevant for occlusion events. At 6 months of age, this list would include the variable height; although the infants could determine the container's height by inspecting the scene, they could not determine the block's height. At this point, the PR system would query the OR system for information about the relative heights of the container and block. The OR system would supply this information, which would become included in the PR system, allowing the infants to detect the change to the block's height in the change event. We thus predicted that, in the occlusion condition, the infants who saw the change event would look reliably longer than those who saw the no-change event.

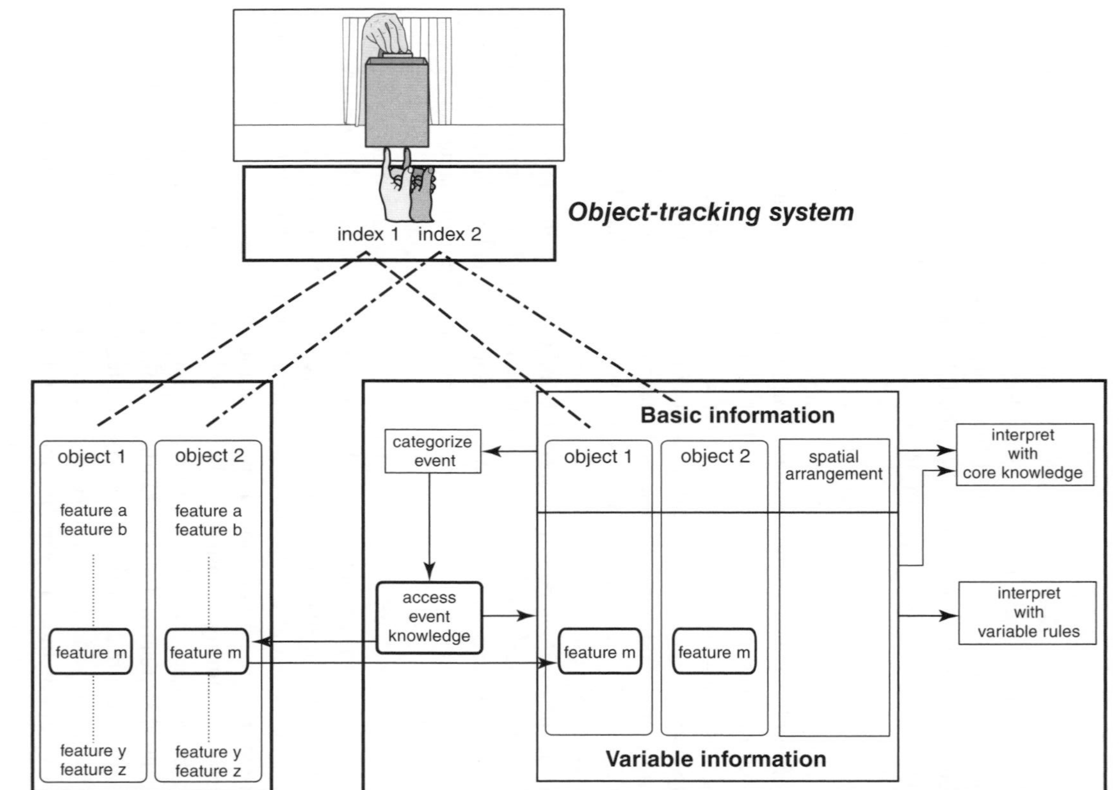

Figure 1.12 Schematic diagram of the retrieval of object information from the object-tracking system by the physical-reasoning system

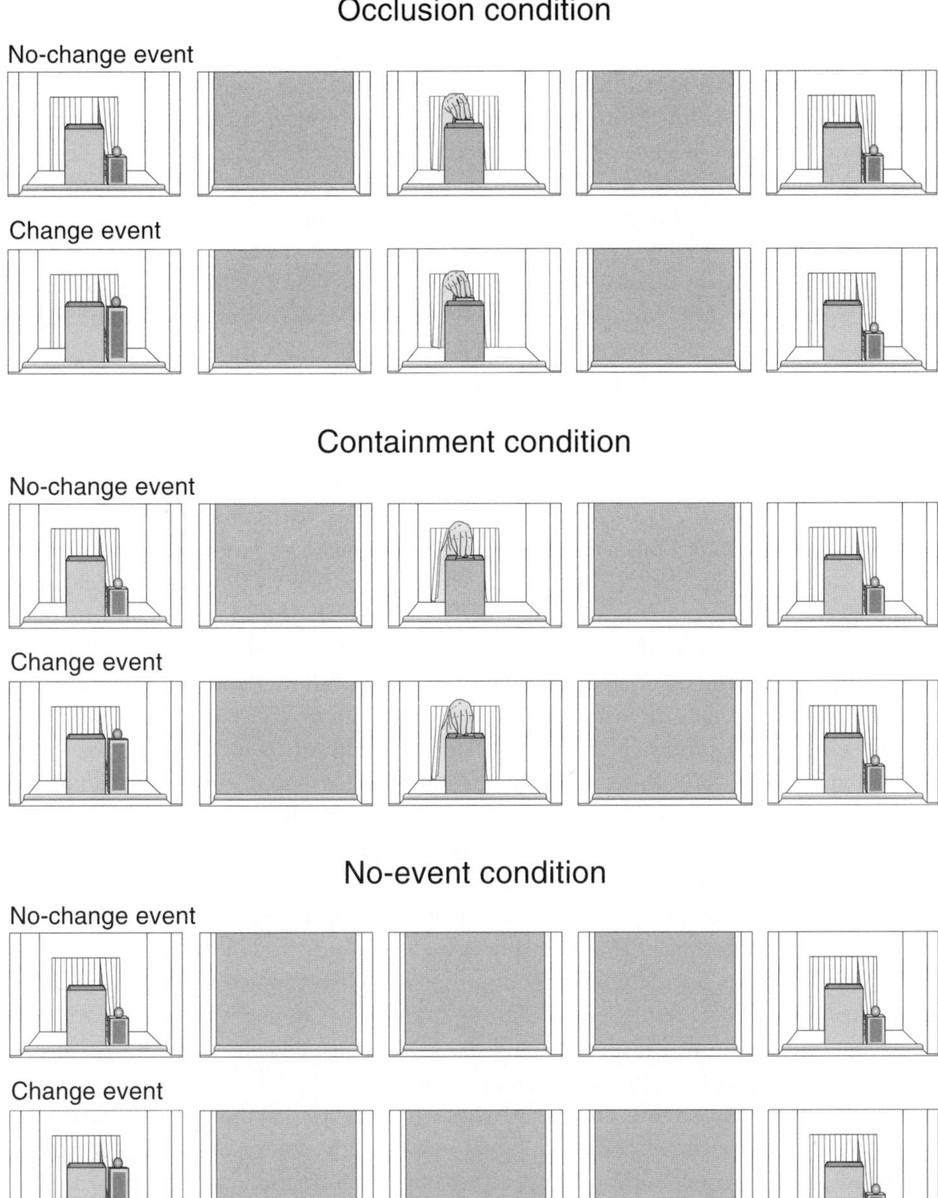

Figure 1.13 Test events used in the occlusion, containment, and no-event conditions of Li et al. (2009)

The infants in the *containment* condition received a similar trial except that in snapshot 2 the hand held the block *inside* the container, above its bottom surface; as before, the infants could not determine the block's exact height. Because at 6 months height has not yet been identified as a containment variable, we expected that the PR system would *not* query the OR system for information about the relative heights of the container and block. As a result, no height information would be included in the PR system, and the infants should fail to detect the violation in the change event. We thus predicted that, in the containment condition, the infants would look about equally whether they saw the change or the no-change event.

Finally, the infants in the *no-event* condition again received a similar trial, except that the panel remained shut throughout snapshot 2. We reasoned that, in snapshot 3, the OR system should readily detect that the block was no longer as tall as the container (after all, the no-event condition amounted to a simple recognition task). Interestingly, prior findings from the infant recognition literature suggested that, in the no-event condition, the infants would show the opposite pattern from that predicted in the occlusion condition. According to this prior research, infants presented with static visual stimuli typically show a *familiarity* preference under shorter familiarization conditions, and a *novelty* preference under longer familiarization conditions (e.g., Hunter & Ames, 1988; Hunter, Ross, & Ames, 1982; Rose et al., 1982). According to Rose et al. (1982), "as infants begin to process a stimulus, they prefer to look at that which is familiar; once processing is more advanced, their preference shifts to that which is novel" (p. 711). It seems adaptive that the OR system would be designed in this way, and that infants whose processing of an object is interrupted would "give priority to . . . consolidating information they are in the process of acquiring before moving on to make new discoveries" (Hunter et al., 1982, p. 528; see also Bauer, 2009). To return to our no-event condition, since snapshot 1 was very brief, we expected that the infants who saw the no-change event would look reliably longer than those who saw the change event.

Results were as predicted: in the occlusion condition, the infants who saw the change event looked reliably longer than those who saw the no-change event; in the containment condition, the infants looked about equally at the two events; and in the no-event condition, the infants who saw the no-change event looked reliably longer than those who saw the change event. These results provide strong support for our claim that separate object representations are formed in the OR and the PR systems, and that the PR system can query the OR system for information about a variable.

More generally, these results provide two pieces of evidence that the OR and PR systems constitute distinct systems with distinct signatures. First, the contrasting results of the no-event and containment conditions suggest that object information can be represented in the OR system and yet not be available to the PR system: the infants in the no-event condition detected the change to the block's height, but those in the containment condition did not. Second, the contrasting results of the no-event and occlusion conditions indicate that the OR and PR systems may respond differently to similar situations: although the infants in both conditions gave evidence that they detected the change to the block's height, they did so in different ways. In the no-event condition, the infants looked longer at the *familiar* block, as though they sought to complete or consolidate its representation. In contrast, the infants in the occlusion condition looked longer at the *novel* block, as though they were attempting to make sense of this persistence violation.

Concluding Remarks: We Have Come a Long Way!

As we saw at the start of this chapter, the questions that dominated investigations of infants' physical knowledge 25 years ago were broad questions such as whether infants realize that objects continue to exist when hidden. Today, as illustrated by the experiment discussed in the last section (Li et al., 2009), questions have become far more targeted and precise. We know a great deal more about what basic and variable information infants include in their physical representations of events and about how they interpret this information. We are discovering more and more ways of enhancing the information that infants represent about events, through teaching and other contextual manipulations (e.g., Feigenson & Halberda, 2008; Gertner et al, 2009; Li & Baillargeon, 2009; Wang & Baillargeon, 2005; Wang & Kohne, 2007; Wilcox & Chapa, 2004; Wilcox & Woods, 2009; Xu, 2002). Finally, we are beginning to understand the various cognitive systems that underlie infants' responses to events, and we are exploring the dynamic interplay between these systems.

Note

1 Young infants recognize that not all changes that occur while an object is briefly occluded are impossible changes (Wu, Baillargeon, & Gelman, 2009). In a series of experiments, 5-month-olds were first introduced to a novel self-propelled object with one or two prominent parts attached to its "body." In the test events, the object was briefly hidden by a screen; when the screen was removed, the object either was the same as before (no-change event) or had undergone some change (change event). This change was a change either in appearance (e.g., a jagged "tail" changed into a half-circle), in location (e.g., an "arm" moved from the left to the right side of the object's body), or in orientation (e.g., the object's "tail" changed from a horizontal to a vertical orientation). Infants detected a violation when the object's parts changed appearance or location, but not when they changed orientation (infants did view orientation changes as impossible, however, when the object was inert rather than self-propelled). By 5 months of age, infants thus believe that a self-propelled object can use its internal energy to reorient its parts, but not to alter their appearance or to reattach them at new locations.

References

Aguiar, A., & Baillargeon, R. (1999). 2.5-month-old infants' reasoning about when objects should and should not be occluded. *Cognitive Psychology, 39*, 116–157.

Aguiar, A., & Baillargeon, R. (2002). Developments in young infants' reasoning about occluded objects. *Cognitive Psychology, 45*, 267–336.

Aguiar, A., & Baillargeon, R. (2003). Perseverative responding in a violation-of-expectation task in 6.5-month-old infants. *Cognition, 88*, 277–316.

Baillargeon, R. (1986). Representing the existence and the location of hidden objects: Object permanence in 6- and 8-month-old infants. *Cognition, 23*, 21–41.

Baillargeon, R. (1987). Object permanence in 3.5- and 4.5-month-old infants. *Developmental Psychology, 23*, 655–664.

Baillargeon, R. (1991). Reasoning about the height and location of a hidden object in 4.5- and 6.5-month-old infants. *Cognition, 38*, 13–42.

Baillargeon, R. (1993). The object concept revisited: New directions in the investigation of infants' physical knowledge. In C. E. Granrud (Ed.), *Visual perception and cognition in infancy* (pp. 265–315). Hillsdale, NJ: Erlbaum.

Baillargeon, R. (1995). A model of physical reasoning in infancy. In C. Rovee-Collier & L. P. Lipsitt (Eds.), *Advances in infancy research* (Vol. *9*, pp. 305–371). Norwood, NJ: Ablex.

Baillargeon, R. (1999). Young infants' expectations about hidden objects: A reply to three challenges. *Developmental Science, 2*, 115–163.

Baillargeon, R. (2002). The acquisition of physical knowledge in infancy: A summary in eight lessons. In U. Goswami (Ed.), *Blackwell handbook of childhood cognitive development* (pp. 47–83). Oxford: Blackwell.

Baillargeon, R. (2004). Infants' reasoning about hidden objects: Evidence for event-general and event-specific expectations. *Developmental Science, 7*, 391–424.

Baillargeon, R. (2008). Innate ideas revisited: For a principle of persistence in infants' physical reasoning. *Perspectives on Psychological Science, 3*, 2–13.

Baillargeon, R., & DeVos, J. (1991). Object permanence in young infants: Further evidence. *Child Development, 62*, 1227–1246.

Baillargeon, R., Graber, M., DeVos, J., & Black, J. (1990). Why do young infants fail to search for hidden objects? *Cognition, 36*, 225–284.

Baillargeon, R., Li, J., Luo, Y., & Wang, S. (2006). Under what conditions do infants detect continuity violations? In M. H. Johnson & Y. Munakata (Eds.), *Attention and Performance XXI: Processes of change in brain and cognitive development* (pp. 163–188). Oxford: Oxford University Press.

Baillargeon, R., Li, J., Ng, W., & Yuan, S. (2009). An account of infants' physical reasoning. In A. Woodward & A. Needham (Eds.), *Learning and the infant mind* (pp. 66–116). New York: Oxford University Press.

Baillargeon, R., Needham, A., & DeVos, J. (1992). The development of young infants' intuitions about support. *Early development and parenting, 1*, 69–78.

Baillargeon, R., Spelke, E. S., & Wasserman, S. (1985). Object permanence in 5-month-old infants. *Cognition, 20*, 191–208.

Baillargeon, R., & Wang, S. (2002). Event categorization in infancy. *Trends in Cognitive Sciences, 6*, 85–93.

Baillargeon, R., Wu, D., Yuan, S., Li, J., & Luo, Y. (2009). Young infants' expectations about self-propelled objects. In B. M. Hood & L. R. Santos (Eds.), *The origins of object knowledge* (pp. 285–352). Oxford: Oxford University Press.

Bauer, P. J. (2009). Learning and memory: Like a horse and a carriage. In A. Woodward & A. Needham (Eds.), *Learning and the infant mind* (pp. 3–28). New York: Oxford University Press.

Bogartz, R. S., Shinskey, J. L., & Schilling, T. H. (2000). Object permanence in five-and-a half-month-old infants? *Infancy, 1*, 403–428.

Bogartz, R. S., Shinskey, J. L., & Speaker, C. J. (1997). Interpreting infant looking: The event set x event set design. *Developmental Psychology, 33*, 408–422.

Bonatti, L., Frot, E., Zangl, R., & Mehler, J. (2002). The human first hypothesis: Identification of conspecifics and individuation of objects in the young infant. *Cognitive Psychology, 44*, 388–426.

Bremner, J. G. (1985). Object tracking and search in infancy: A review of data and a theoretical evaluation. *Developmental Review, 5*, 371–396.

Bruner, J. S. (1968). *Processes of cognitive growth: Infancy*. Worcester, MA: Clark University Press and Barre Press.

Carey, S., & Spelke, E. S. (1994). Domain-specific knowledge and conceptual change. In L. A. Hirschfeld & S. A. Gelman (Eds.), *Mapping the mind: Domain specificity in cognition and culture* (pp. 169–200). New York: Cambridge University Press.

Casasola, M., Cohen, L., & Chiarello, E. (2003). Six-month-old infants' categorization of containment spatial relations. *Child Development, 74*, 679–693.

Cashon, C. H., & Cohen, L. B., (2000). Eight-month-old infants' perceptions of possible and impossible events. *Infancy, 1*, 429–446.

Cheries, E. W., Wynn, K., & Scholl, B. J. (2006). Interrupting infants' persisting object representations: An object-based limit? *Developmental Science, 9*, F50–F58.

Csibra, G., & Gergely, G. (2009). Natural pedagogy. *Trends in Cognitive Sciences, 13*, 148–153.

Csibra, G., Gergely, G., Bíró, S., Koós, O., & Brockbank, M. (1999). Goal attribution without agency cues: The perception of "pure reason" in infancy. *Cognition, 72*, 237–267.

DeJong, G. F. (1993). *Investigating explanation-based learning.* Boston: Kluwer Academic Press.

DeJong, G. F. (1997). Explanation-based learning. In A. Tucker (Ed.), *Encyclopedia of computer science* (pp. 499–520). Boca Raton, FL: CRC Press.

Diamond, A. (1991). Neuropsychological insights into the meaning of object concept development. In S. Carey & R. Gelman (Eds.), *The epigenesis of mind* (pp. 67–110). Hillsdale, NJ: Erlbaum.

Dueker, G., Modi, A., & Needham, A. (2003). 4.5-month-old infants' learning, retention, and use of object boundary information. *Infant Behavior and Development, 26*, 588–605.

Fantz, R. L. (1956). A method for studying early visual development. *Perceptual and Motor Skills, 6*, 13–15.

Feigenson, L., & Carey, S. (2003). Tracking individuals via object-files: Evidence from infants' manual search. *Developmental Science, 6*, 568–584.

Feigenson, L., & Carey, S. (2005). On the limits of infants' quantification of small object arrays. *Cognition, 97*, 295–313.

Feigenson, L., & Halberda, J. (2004). Infants chunk object arrays into sets of individuals. *Cognition, 91*, 173–190.

Feigenson, L., & Halberda, J. (2008). Conceptual knowledge increases infants' memory. *Proceedings of the National Academy of Sciences, 105*, 9926–9930.

Fiser, J., & Aslin, R. N. (2002) Statistical learning of new visual feature combinations by infants. *Proceedings of the National Academy of Sciences, 99*, 15822–15826.

Fisher, C. (1996). Structural limits on verb mapping: The role of analogy in children's interpretation of sentences. *Cognitive Psychology, 31*, 41–81.

Fisher, C., Gertner, Y., Scott, R., & Yuan, S. (in press). Syntactic bootstrapping. *Wiley Interdisciplinary Reviews: Cognitive Science.*

Gelman, R. (1990). First principles organize attention to and learning about relevant data: Number and the animate–inanimate distinction as examples. *Cognitive Science, 14*, 79–106.

Gelman, R., Bullock, M., & Meck, E. (1980). Preschoolers' understanding of simple object transformations. *Child Development, 51*, 691–699.

Gergely, G., Nádasdy, Z., Csibra, G., & Bíró, S. (1995). Taking the intentional stance at 12 months of age. *Cognition, 56*, 165–193.

Gertner, Y., Baillargeon, R., Fisher, C. L., & Simons, D. J. (2009, April). Language facilitates infants' physical reasoning. Paper presented at the Biennial Meeting of the Society for Research in Child Development, Denver, CO.

Goswami, U., & Brown, A. L. (1990). Higher-order structure and relational reasoning: contrasting analogical and thematic relations. *Cognition, 36*, 207–226.

Goubet, N., & Clifton, R. K. (1998). Object and event representation in 6.5-month-old infants. *Developmental Psychology, 34*, 63–76.

Gratch, G. (1976). A review of Piagetian infancy research: Object concept development. In W. F. Overton & J. M. Gallagher (Eds.), *Knowledge and development: Advances in research and theory* (pp. 59–91). New York: Plenum.

Haith, M. M. (1998). Who put the cog in infant cognition? Is rich interpretation too costly? *Infant Behavior and Development, 21*, 167–179.

Harris, P. L. (1987). The development of search. In P. Salapatek & L. B. Cohen (Eds.), *Handbook of infant perception* (Vol. *2*, pp. 155–207). New York: Academic Press.

Hespos, S. J., & Baillargeon, R. (2001a). Infants' knowledge about occlusion and containment events: A surprising discrepancy. *Psychological Science, 12*, 140–147.

Hespos, S. J., & Baillargeon, R. (2001b). Knowledge about containment events in very young infants. *Cognition, 78*, 204–245.

Hespos, S. J., & Baillargeon, R. (2006). Décalage in infants' knowledge about occlusion and containment events: Converging evidence from action tasks. *Cognition, 99*, B31–B41.

Hespos, S. J., & Baillargeon, R. (2008). Young infants' actions reveal their developing knowledge of support variables: Converging evidence for violation-of-expectation findings. *Cognition, 107*, 304–316.

Hofstadter, M., & Reznick, J. S. (1996). Response modality affects human infant delayed-response performance. *Child Development, 67*, 646–658.

Hood, B., & Willatts, P. (1986). Reaching in the dark to an object's remembered position: Evidence of object permanence in 5-month-old infants. *British Journal of Developmental Psychology, 4*, 57–65.

Hunter, M. A., & Ames, E. W. (1988). A multifactor model of infant preferences for novel and familiar stimuli. In C. Rovee-Collier & L. P. Lipsitt (Eds.), *Advances in infancy research* (Vol. *5*, pp. 69–95). Norwood, NJ: Ablex.

Hunter, M. A., Ross, H. S., & Ames, E. W. (1982). Preferences for familiar or novel toys: Effects of familiarization time in 1-year-olds. *Developmental Psychology, 18*, 519–529.

Huttenlocher, J., Duffy, S., & Levine, S. C. (2002). Infants and toddlers discriminate amount: Are they measuring? *Psychological Science, 13*, 244–249.

Kahneman, D., Treisman, A., & Gibbs, B. J. (1992). The reviewing of object files: Object-specific integration of information. *Cognitive Psychology, 24*, 174–219.

Káldy, Z. and Leslie, A. M. (2003) Identification of objects in 9-month-old infants: Integrating "what" and "where" information. *Developmental Science, 6*, 360–373.

Káldy, Z., & Leslie, A. M. (2005). A memory span of one? Object identification in 6.5-month-old infants. *Cognition, 97*, 153–177.

Keen, R. E., & Berthier, N. E. (2004). Continuities and discontinuities in infants' representation of objects and events. In R. V. Kail (Ed.), *Advances in child development and behavior* (Vol. *32*, pp. 243–279). San Diego: Elsevier Academic Press.

Keil, F. C. (1995). The growth of causal understandings of natural kinds. In D. Sperber, D. Premack, & A. J. Premack (Eds.), *Causal cognition: A multidisciplinary debate* (pp. 234–262). Oxford: Clarendon Press.

Kestenbaum, R., Termine, N., & Spelke, E. S. (1987). Perception of objects and object boundaries by 3-month-old infants. *British Journal of Developmental Psychology, 5*, 367–383.

Kochukhova, O., & Gredebäck, G. (2007). Learning about occlusion: Initial assumptions and rapid adjustments. *Cognition, 105*, 26–46.

Kotovsky, L., & Baillargeon, R. (1998). The development of calibration-based reasoning about collision events in young infants. *Cognition, 67*, 311–351.

Lécuyer, R., & Durand, K. (1998). Bi-dimensional representations of the third dimension and their perception by infants. *Perception, 27*, 465–472.

Leslie, A. M. (1984). Infant perception of a manual pick-up event. *British Journal of Developmental Psychology, 2*, 19–32.

Leslie, A. M. (1995). A theory of agency. In D. Sperber, D. Premack, & A. J. Premack (Eds.), *Causal cognition: A multidisciplinary debate* (pp. 121–149). Oxford: Clarendon Press.

Leslie, A. M., & Keeble, S. (1987). Do six-month-old infants perceive causality? *Cognition, 25*, 265–288.

Leslie, A. M., Xu, F., Tremoulet, P. D., & Scholl, B. J. (1998). Indexing and the object concept: Developing "what" and "where" system. *Trends in Cognitive Sciences, 2*, 10–18.

Li, J., & Baillargeon, R. (2009). Priming effects in infants' physical reasoning: Evidence from violation-of-expectation and action tasks. Manuscript in preparation.

Li, J., Baillargeon, R., & Simons, D. J. (2009, April). How do infants detect height changes? Double dissociations between infants' object-representation and physical-reasoning systems. Paper presented at the Biennial Meeting of the Society for Research in Child Development, Denver, CO.

Lockman, J. J. (1984). The development of detour ability during infancy. *Child Development, 55*, 482–491.

Luo, Y., & Baillargeon, R. (2005). When the ordinary seems unexpected: Evidence for rule-based physical reasoning in young infants. *Cognition, 95*, 297–328.

Luo, Y., & Baillargeon, R. (2009). Infants' reasoning about transparent occluders and containers. Manuscript in preparation.

Luo, Y., Kaufman, L., & Baillargeon, R. (2009). Young infants' reasoning about events involving inert and self-propelled objects. *Cognitive Psychology, 58*, 441–486.

Mareschal, D., & Johnson, M. H. (2003). The "what" and "where" of object representations in infancy. *Cognition, 88*, 259–276.

McDonough, L., Choi, S., & Mandler, J. M. (2003). Understanding spatial relations: Flexible infants, lexical adults. *Cognitive Psychology, 46*, 229–259.

Muentener. P., & Carey, S. (2009, April). The origin of causal representations in infancy. Paper presented at the Biennial Meeting of the Society for Research in Child Development, Denver, CO.

Munakata, Y., McClelland, J. L., Johnson, M. H., & Siegler, R. S. (1997). Rethinking infant knowledge: Toward an adaptive process account of successes and failures in object permanence tasks. *Psychological Review, 104*, 686–713.

Needham, A. (1998). Infants' use of featural information in the segregation of stationary objects. *Infant Behavior and Development, 21*, 47–76.

Needham, A. (1999). The role of shape in 4-month-old infants' segregation of adjacent objects. *Infant Behavior and Development, 22*, 161–178.

Needham, A. (2000). Improvements in object exploration skills may facilitate the development of object segregation in early infancy. *Journal of Cognition and Development, 1*, 131–156.

Needham, A. (2001). Object recognition and object segregation in 4.5-month-old infants. *Journal of Experimental Child Psychology, 78*, 3–24.

Needham, A. (2009). Learning in infants' object perception, object-directed action, and tool use. In A. Woodward & A. Needham (Eds.), *Learning and the infant mind* (pp. 208–226). New York: Oxford University Press.

Needham, A., & Baillargeon, R. (1993). Intuitions about support in 4.5-month-old infants. *Cognition, 47*, 121–148.

Needham, A., & Baillargeon, R. (1997). Object segregation in 8-month-old infants. *Cognition, 62*, 121–149.

Needham, A., & Baillargeon, R. (1998). Effects of prior experience on 4.5-month-old infants' object segregation. *Infant Behavior and Development, 21*, 1–24.

Needham, A., Cantlon, J. F., & Ormsbee Holley, S. M. (2006). Infants' use of category knowledge and object attributes when segregating objects at 8.5 months of age. *Cognitive Psychology, 53*, 345–360.

Needham, A., Dueker, G., & Lockhead, G. (2005). Infants' formation and use of categories to segregate objects. *Cognition, 94*, 215–240.
Newcombe, N., Huttenlocher, J., & Learmonth, A. (1999). Infants' coding of location in continuous space. *Infant Behavior and Development, 22*, 483–510.
Newcombe, N. S., Sluzenski, J., & Huttenlocher, J. (2005). Pre-existing knowledge versus on-line learning: What do infants really know about spatial location? *Psychological Science, 16*, 222–227.
Ng, W., & Baillargeon, R. (2009). Décalage in infants' reasoning about color information in occlusion and containment events. Manuscript in preparation.
Oakes, L. M., Ross-Sheehy, S., & Luck, S. J. (2006). Rapid development of feature binding in visual short-term memory. *Psychological Science, 17*, 781–787.
Onishi, K. H. (2009). Perception of event roles in infancy. Manuscript in preparation.
Piaget, J. (1952). The origins of intelligence in children. New York: International Universities Press.
Piaget, J. (1954). The construction of reality in the child. New York: Basic Books.
Premack, D., & Premack, A. J. (1997). Infants attribute value +/– to the goal-directed actions of self-propelled objects. *Journal of Cognitive Neuroscience, 9*, 848–856.
Pylyshyn, Z. W. (1989). The role of location indexes in spatial perception: A sketch of the FINST spatial index model. *Cognition, 32*, 65–97.
Pylyshyn, Z. W. (1994). Some primitive mechanisms of spatial attention. *Cognition, 50*, 363–384.
Quinn, P. C. (2007). On the infant's prelinguistic conception of spatial relations: Three developmental trends and their implications for spatial language learning. In J. M. Plumert & J. P. Spencer (Eds.), *The emerging spatial mind* (pp. 117–141). New York: Oxford University Press.
Rose, S. A., Gottfried, A. W., Melloy-Carminar, P., & Bridger, W. H. (1982). Familiarity and novelty preferences in infant recognition memory: Implications for information processing. *Developmental Psychology, 18*, 704–713.
Ruffman, T., Slade, L., & Redman, J. (2005). Young infants' expectations about hidden objects. *Cognition, 97*, B35–B43.
Saffran, J. R. (2009). What can statistical learning tell us about infant learning? In A. Woodward & A. Needham (Eds.), *Learning and the infant mind* (pp. 29–46). New York: Oxford University Press.
Scholl, B. J., & Leslie, A. M. (1999). Explaining the infant's object concept: Beyond the perception/cognition dichotomy. In E. Lepore & Z. Pylyshyn (Eds.), *What is cognitive science?* (pp. 26–73). Oxford: Blackwell.
Shinskey, J. L. (2002). Infants' object search: Effects of variable object visibility under constant means–end demands. *Journal of Cognition and Development, 3*, 119–142.
Shinskey, J. L., & Munakata, Y. (2001). Detecting transparent barriers: Clear evidence against the means–end deficit account of search failures. *Infancy 2*, 395–404.
Simons, D. J., Chabris, C. F., Schnur, T. T., & Levin, D. T. (2002). Evidence for preserved representations in change blindness. *Consciousness and Cognition, 11*, 78–97.
Sitskoorn, S. M., & Smitsman, A. W. (1995). Infants' perception of dynamic relations between objects: Passing through or support? *Developmental Psychology, 31*, 437–447.
Slater, A. (1995). Visual perception and memory at birth. In C. Rovee-Collier & L. P. Lipsitt (Eds.), *Advances in infancy research* (Vol. 9, pp. 107–162). Norwood: Ablex.
Sloane, S., Baillargeon, R., Simons, D. J., & Scholl, B. (2009, April). Can infants maintain their representations of hidden objects through an interrupting event? Paper presented at the Biennial Meeting of the Society for Research in Child Development, Denver, CO.
Smith, L. B. (1999). Do infants possess innate knowledge structures: The con side. *Developmental Science, 2*, 133–144.

Spelke, E. S. (1998). Nativism, empiricism, and the origins of knowledge. *Infant Behavior and Development, 21*, 181–200.

Spelke, E. S., Breinlinger, K., Macomber, J., & Jacobson, K. (1992). Origins of knowledge. *Psychological Review, 99*, 605–632.

Spelke, E. S., & Hespos, S. J. (2001). Continuity, competence, and the object concept. In E. Dupoux (Ed.), *Language, brain and cognitive development: Essays in honor of Jacques Mehler* (pp. 325–340). Cambridge, MA: MIT Press.

Spelke, E. S., & Hespos, S. J. (2002). Conceptual development in infancy: The case of containment. In N. L. Stein, P. Bauer, & M. Rabinowitch (Eds.), *Representation, memory, and development: Essays in honor of Jean Mandler* (pp. 223–246). Mahwah, NJ: Erlbaum.

Spelke, E. S., Phillips, A., & Woodward, A. L. (1995). Infants' knowledge of object motion and human action. In D. Sperber, D. Premack, & A. J. Premack (Eds.), *Causal cognition: A multidisciplinary debate* (pp. 44–78). Oxford: Clarendon Press.

Thelen, E., & Smith, L. B. (1994). *A dynamic systems approach to the development of cognition and action*. Cambridge, MA: MIT Press.

Tomasello, M., Carpenter, M., Call, J., Behne, T., & Moll, H. (2005). Understanding and sharing intentions: The origins of cultural cognition. *Behavioral and Brain Sciences, 28*, 675–735.

Tzelnic, T., Kuhlmeier, V. A., & Hauser, M. D. (2009, April). Nine-month-old infants understand sharpness as a causal property. Paper presented at the Biennial Meeting of the Society for Research in Child Development, Denver, CO.

Von Hofsten, C., Kochukhova, O., & Rosander, K. (2007). Predictive tracking over occlusions by 4-month-old infants. *Developmental Science, 10*, 625–640.

Wang, S., & Baillargeon, R. (2005). Inducing infants to detect a physical violation in a single trial. *Psychological Science, 16*, 542–549.

Wang, S., & Baillargeon, R. (2006). Infants' physical knowledge affects their change detection. *Developmental Science, 9*, 173–181.

Wang, S., & Baillargeon, R. (2008a). Can infants be "taught" to attend to a new physical variable in an event category? The case of height in covering events. *Cognitive Psychology, 56*, 284–326.

Wang, S., & Baillargeon, R. (2008b). Detecting impossible changes in infancy: A three-system account. *Trends in Cognitive Sciences, 12*, 17–23.

Wang, S., Baillargeon, R., & Brueckner, L. (2004). Young infants' reasoning about hidden objects: Evidence from violation-of-expectation tasks with test trials only. *Cognition, 93*, 167–198.

Wang, S., Baillargeon, R., Paterson, S. (2005). Detecting continuity and solidity violations in infancy: A new account and new evidence from covering events. *Cognition, 95*, 129–173.

Wang, S., Kaufman, L., & Baillargeon, R. (2003). Should all stationary objects move when hit? Developments in infants' causal and statistical expectations about collision events. *Infant Behavior and Development, 26*, 529–568.

Wang, S., & Kohne, L. (2007). Visual experience enhances infants' use of task-relevant information in an action task. *Developmental Psychology, 43*, 1513–1522.

Wang, S., & Mitroff, S. R. (2009). Preserved visual representations despite change blindness in 11-month-old infants. *Developmental Science, 12*, 681–687.

Wilcox, T. (1999). Object individuation: Infants' use of shape, size, pattern, and color. *Cognition, 72*, 125–166.

Wilcox, T., & Baillargeon, R. (1998). Object individuation in young infants: Further evidence with an event-monitoring task. *Developmental Science, 1*, 127–142.

Wilcox, T., & Chapa, C. (2002). Infants' reasoning about opaque and transparent occluders in an object individuation task. *Cognition, 85*, B1–B10.

Wilcox, T., & Chapa, C. (2004). Priming infants to attend to color and pattern information in an individuation task. *Cognition, 90*, 265–302.

Wilcox, T., Nadel, L., & Rosser, R. (1996). Location memory in healthy preterm and full-term infants. *Infant Behavior and Development, 19*, 309–323.

Wilcox, T., & Woods, R. (2009). Experience primes infants to individuate objects. In A. Woodward & A. Needham (Eds.), *Learning and the infant mind* (pp. 116–143). New York: Oxford University Press.

Willatts, P. (1997). Beyond the "couch potato" infant: How infants use their knowledge to regulate action, solve problems, and achieve goals. In J. G. Bremner, A. Slater, & G. Butterworth (Eds.), *Infant development: recent advances* (pp. 109–135). Hove, UK: Psychology Press.

Wilson, R. A., & Keil, F. C. (2000). The shadows and shallows of explanation. In F. C. Keil & R. A. Wilson (Eds.), *Explanation and cognition* (pp. 87–114). Cambridge, MA: MIT Press.

Woodward, A. L. (1998). Infants selectively encode the goal object of an actor's reach. *Cognition, 69*, 1–34.

Woodward, A. L., Phillips, A., & Spelke, E. S. (1993). Infants' expectations about the motion of animate versus inanimate objects. *Proceedings of the Fifteenth Annual Meeting of the Cognitive Science Society* (pp. 1087–1091). Hillsdale, NJ: Erlbaum.

Wu, D., & Baillargeon, R. (2008, March). One or two humans? 10-month-olds' use of ontological and featural information to individuate objects. Paper presented at the Biennial International Conference on Infant Studies, Vancouver, Canada.

Wu, D., Baillargeon, R., & Gelman, R. (2009, June). Infants' reasoning about the parts and insides of self-propelled objects. Paper presented at the International Conference on Biological Understanding and Theory of Mind, Reims, France.

Wu, D., Li, X., & Baillargeon, R. (2009). The 100-day milestone: Resolving conflicts between basic spatiotemporal and identity information. Manuscript in preparation.

Wynn, K. (1992). Addition and subtraction by human infants. *Nature, 358*, 749–750.

Xu, F. (2002). The role of language in acquiring object kind concepts in infancy. *Cognition, 85*, 223–250.

Xu, F., & Carey, S. (1996). Infants' metaphysics: The case of numerical identity. *Cognitive Psychology, 30*, 111–153.

Yonas, A., & Granrud, C. E. (1984). The development of sensitivity to kinetic, binocular, and pictorial depth information in human infants. In D. Engle, D. Lee, & M. Jeannerod (Eds.), *Brain mechanisms and spatial vision* (pp. 113–145). Dordrecht: Martinus Nijhoff.

Yuan, S., & Baillargeon, R. (2008, March). 2.5-month-olds hold different expectations about the support of inert and self-propelled objects. Paper presented at the Biennial International Conference on Infant Studies, Vancouver, Canada.

CHAPTER TWO

Social Cognition and the Origins of Imitation, Empathy, and Theory of Mind

Andrew N. Meltzoff

Scientists interested in social cognition investigate people's beliefs about thinking, feeling, and perceiving. This is differentiable from our knowledge of the physical world and logical-mathematical principles. Social cognition has deep roots in psychology (Heider, 1958), but was under-investigated by Piaget and Vygotsky. Piaget's *The Construction of Reality in the Child* contains brilliant chapters on objects, space, time, and causality. There are, however, none on people. His *Play Dreams and Imitation in Childhood* discusses people, but not how children come to understand the inner life of others. Even Vygotsky, whose *Mind in Society* highlights social interaction, does not focus on how children come to see others are thinking, feeling, and wanting beings.

Defining the Problem of Developing Social Cognition

What is the central problem of social cognition and why does it intrigue modern developmental theorists? The problem stems from the fact that persons are more than physical objects. When we describe a person's height, weight, and eye color, we do not exhaust

This research was supported by the National Institute of Child Health and Human Development (NICHD; HD-22514), the National Science Foundation (SBE-0354453), and the Tamaki Foundation. The thoughts expressed in the paper are those of the author and do not necessarily reflect the views of these agencies. I thank R. Brooks and U. Goswami for insightful comments on an earlier draft, K. Moore and A. Gopnik for useful discussions over the years, and C. Fisher for assistance.

Correspondence concerning this article should be addressed to Andrew N. Meltzoff, Institute for Learning and Brain Sciences, Box 357920, University of Washington, Seattle, WA 98195. Phone: 206-685-2045, fax: 206-221-6475, email: meltzoff@u.washington.edu.

our description of that person. We have omitted the individual's psychological makeup. If a self-mobile agent was devoid of psychological characteristics, we would not consider it a person but a robot, or to use a philosopher's favorite term, a zombie. A fundamental issue is how we come to know others as psychological agents like ourselves.

Each one of us has the phenomenological experience that he or she is not alone in the world, not the unique bearer of psychological properties. We know that we think, feel, and have intentions. We also find ourselves believing that others have similar psychological states, despite the fact that we do not experience others' states in the same way that we experience our own. Reflection on this gulf between self and other intrigues us. A robot with voice synthesis might cry out when pinched, but it does not feel pain. It can be programmed to wrinkle its elastic "brow" when its speech-recognition chip detects human sobbing, but we would not ascribe it empathy. Why, then, do we attribute psychological states to other humans?

Philosophers seek to justify the intuition that the sacks of skin we see around us are animated by psychological states like our own. Philosophers contemplate whether this is true and the criteria for knowing whether it is or is not – the problem of Other Minds (e.g., Campbell, 1994; Ryle, 1949; Strawson, 1959). This philosophical conundrum remains unsettled. Yet adults talk, act, and write in the hope of touching the minds and feelings of others. By 2–4 years of age all typically developing children treat others as intentional agents – having developed a practical solution to the problem of Other Minds. How does such a view take hold in children, whether it is justified or not?

Classical Theories of Childhood: The "Impossible Journey"

Classical theorists, including Freud, Piaget, and Skinner, all agree on one axiom: newborn infants have no inkling of the similarity between self and other. A primary task of psychosocial development is to build connections to others, so that the child realizes he is "one of us." The progression is from newborn solipsist to social intimate.

This is, I would argue, an impossible journey. But it was central in the classic literature. Freud and his followers proposed a distinction between a physical and psychological birth. When the baby is born there is a physical birth but not yet a birth of a social mind (Freud, 1911; Mahler, Pine, & Bergman, 1975). The baby is like an unhatched chick within an eggshell, incapable of interacting as a social being because a "barrier" leaves the newborn cut off from external reality:

> A neat example of a psychical system shut off from the stimuli of the external world … is afforded by a bird's egg with its food supply enclosed in its shell; for it, the care provided by its mother is limited to the provision of warmth. (Freud, 1911, p. 220)

This view deeply influenced psychiatry (Beebe, Knoblauch, Rustin, & Sorter, 2005; Beebe, Sorter, Rustin, & Knoblauch, 2003) and led psychoanalysts to postulate an early period of "normal autism" (Mahler et al., 1975, p. 42), which was only escaped via appropriate mothering.

Piaget's newborn is similar, but he drew on a philosophical metaphor. He believed that the baby is "radically egocentric" or "solipsistic" (Piaget, 1954, pp. 352–357). The neonate has only a few reflexes at his or her disposal (sucking, grasping), and other people are registered only inasmuch as they are assimilated to these action schemes:

> During the earliest stages the child perceives things like a solipsist ... This primitive relation between subject and object is a relation of undifferentiation ... when no distinction is made between the self and the non-self. (Piaget, 1954, p. 355)

The infant breaks free of solipsism by 18 months through cognitive development.

Skinner (1953) gave his blank-slate infant even less to work with. One cannot quote from Skinner about how children crack the puzzle of social cognition, because he does not think they ever do. To use Skinner's phrase, social cognition is largely a "matter of consequences" (Skinner, 1983) – we never really know others' minds, only their external behavioral reactions to us.

Two Types of Nativism

Modern research in developmental science changed these ideas. We now know that there is a much richer innate state than posited by Freud, Piaget, and Skinner. The nativists won the battle over the newborn's mind, but two distinct schools of nativism have emerged. The distinction is especially pronounced regarding social cognition. One view, *starting-state nativism*, argues for a rich innate state that undergoes conceptual change starting at birth, well before the influence of language (e.g., Gopnik & Meltzoff, 1997; Meltzoff & Moore, 1998). The other, *final-state nativism*, argues that the initial state is equivalent to the final state or is slightly enriched without qualitative transformations of the essential core knowledge (e.g., Spelke, Breinlinger, Macomber, & Jacobson, 1992). As a final-state nativist, Fodor believes that adult social cognition is innately specified:

> Here is what I would have done if I had been faced with this problem in designing *Homo sapiens*. I would have made a knowledge of commonsense *Homo sapiens* psychology innate; that way nobody would have to spend time learning it ... The empirical evidence that God did it the way I would have isn't, in fact, unimpressive. (Fodor, 1987, p. 132)

Fodor thinks the newborn innately possesses the mature theory of mind (see also Onishi & Baillargeon, 2005). Moreover, he says there are no alternatives: "I take the lack of a rival hypothesis ... to be a kind of empirical evidence" (Fodor, 1987, p. 132).

One of the goals of this chapter is to fill Fodor's gap and provide a rival hypothesis. In the starting-state view, infants have innate abstract knowledge, but the newborn does not innately possess the adult model. Evolution has provided newborns with powerful "discovery procedures," and genuine conceptual change starts in the prelinguistic period. The view is not standard Piaget, because the psychological primitives infants use to interpret their first encounters with people are different. Instead of Piaget's reflexes and action schemes, infants have abstract psychological structures that allow them to interpret others as "like me." This fundamental identification with others provides a toehold for developing social cognition.

The "Like-Me" Theory: Developing Social Cognition

Piagetian solipsism, Freudian eggs, and Skinner's contingencies will not get us from the newborn to the adult state because there is not enough innate structure to make use of the experience in social interaction. But this does not mean that the mature adult state is built in. Surely there is room for development, and the project is to specify the innate primitives and a plausible engine for social-cognitive change.

The Like-Me theory proposes three developmental phases for getting early social cognition off the ground (figure 2.1). It describes the infant's initial state (Developmental Phase 1) and also a process of change (phases 2 and 3). The older child and adult are not locked into the same understanding as the newborn.

Developmental Phase 1: starting state

The first phase is functional at birth. It concerns the representation of action. Newborn imitation provides evidence of an intrinsic link between the perception and production of human acts. When newborns see adult behavior, these acts are mapped onto the infant's body movements. Self and other are connected through an abstract representation of human acts, which we call a *supramodal representation* (Meltzoff & Moore, 1977, 1997), because it cuts across modalities. It is because of the infant's action representation – the supramodal code – that the movements of people are special to young babies. The child, even the newborn, processes the movements of other people and recognizes: "that looks the way this feels" or "those acts are like these acts." The fact that others are seen as "like me" provides an interpretive lens for infants' first social encounters. It is not learned, but provides the groundwork for learning, especially about people.

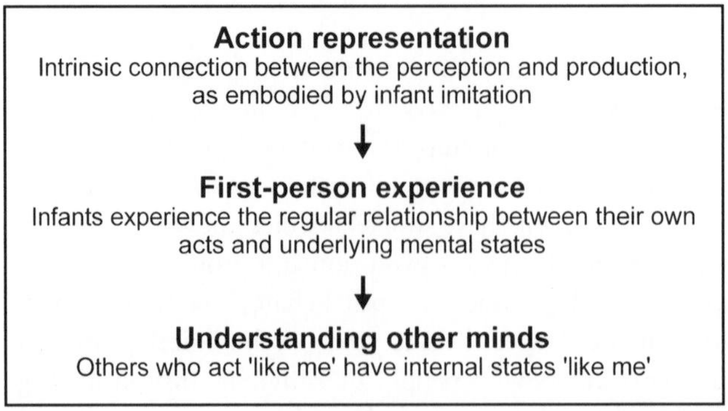

Action representation
Intrinsic connection between the perception and production, as embodied by infant imitation

↓

First-person experience
Infants experience the regular relationship between their own acts and underlying mental states

↓

Understanding other minds
Others who act 'like me' have internal states 'like me'

Figure 2.1 "Like-Me" theory for early social cognition (From Meltzoff, 2007b.)

Developmental Phase 2: first-person experience

The second phase is based on individual experience and provides an engine for developmental change. Through everyday experience infants map the relation between their own bodily states and mental experiences. For example, there is an intimate relation between striving to achieve a goal and the concomitant facial expression and effortful bodily acts. Infants experience their own unfulfilled desires and the simultaneous facial/postural behavior. From these experiences, they develop a detailed bidirectional map linking internal states and behavior (Meltzoff & Moore, 1997).

Developmental Phase 3: attributions to others

The third phase involves attribution. When infants see others acting similarly to how they have acted in the past – acting "like me" – they make an attribution. They ascribe the internal feelings that regularly go with those behaviors, based on their self-experience. This gives infants leverage for grasping other minds before language can be used. Infants' first-person experience could not be used in this way if they did not perceive the equivalence between their own acts and those of others (Phase 1, as indicated by imitation). Nor would it get very far if there was no systematic link between their own internal states and bodily acts (Phase 2). Humans, including preverbal infants, imbue the acts of others with felt meaning because the other is processed as "like me."

This attributes a good deal of machinery to infants, but it is not Fodorian (1987) nativism. Newborns do not have the adult theory of mind preloaded in their mind. The remainder of this chapter fleshes out this idea by showing how infants use the concept of "like me" in their social interactions.

Conceptual distinctions and caveats

Bidirectionality. Although the view proposed here is dubbed "Like Me," this is a shorthand, because the supramodal code supports *bidirectional* learning effects. Going in the direction of the inside out, infants' understanding of others' acts is enriched by performing similar acts themselves. Going from the outside in, infants learn about themselves and the consequences of their own potential actions by observing the acts of others (Meltzoff, 2007b). The result is a child who discovers facets of other minds through comparisons with his or her own mind and who simultaneously discovers powers and possibilities of the self through observing and imitating others (for example, infants learn novel acts from watching others, Meltzoff, 1988). The Like-Me framework suggests that the same underlying mechanism supports learning in both directions. Experiments in our laboratory have demonstrated this bidirectionality (Meltzoff, 1988, 2007a, 2007b; Repacholi, Meltzoff, & Olsen, 2008; Williamson, Jaswal, & Meltzoff, in press; Williamson, Meltzoff, & Markman 2008).

Theoretical terms. When writing about infants, English words are problematic. The words call up adult meanings, and infant concepts are not the same as adults'. The use of the words "me" and "self" in the Like-Me framework are not meant to imply that infants adopt the adult meanings. The "me" of the adult entails verbal self-reflection. It also involves appearances (what I see in the mirror) and moral values (I am a generous person). When I say that the infant construes another as "like me," what I mean is that the infant recognizes a cross-modal equivalence between acts that they observe in others and acts that they produce themselves: "That seen act is like this felt act." I am not appealing to a mature sense of "me" or "self," which I assume to be a developmental achievement.

Further development. The Like-Me framework provides only a partial story about how we come to understand others as intentional agents in the mature adult manner. The mental states most amenable to this analysis are desires, perceptions, emotions, and simple intentions. For these, there is a relatively close coupling between the internal mental states and their outward expression in bodily actions. When someone *sees* x or *desires* y, there are concomitant bodily movements (looking in the direction of, leaning towards, grasping, etc.). These bodily movements are observed in others, and they are produced by the self.

Other mental states have fewer behavioral markers. The "*belief* that x" can be held in the absence of telltale action. Although a person cannot visually inspect an object without bodily movements or become white-hot angry without behavioral leakage, he can certainly conjure up a belief while sitting stock-still. Moreover, people can silently hold beliefs that *conflict* with my own, for example, false beliefs (e.g., Astington & Gopnik, 1991; Flavell, 1999; Perner, 1991; Wellman, 1990; Wellman, chapter 10, this volume). The Like-Me framework provides the initial foothold for interpreting others as bearers of psychological properties *commensurate* with one's own, but further development is needed for acquiring the mature theory of mind encompassing beliefs that directly *conflict with/contradict* one's own.

Action measures. Infants may know more than they produce. This chapter focuses on infants' motor production for three reasons. First, there are comprehensive reviews of infants' parsing of human action based on looking-time response measures that do not require them to take action (Csibra, 2003; Csibra & Gergely, 2007; Gergely, chapter 3, this volume; Johnson, 2000, 2003; Sommerville & Woodward, 2005; Woodward, 2009). Second, infant action measures are important for developmental theory. The feedback infants receive from the social world is largely based on what they do (Rochat, 2009), not on what they do not express. Third, the transfer of goals and intentions from one actor to the next – the ability to carry out someone else's intentions – is crucial for seamless communication and interpersonal rapport.

Imitation and the Early Phases of Social Cognition

Starting-state nativists seek the origins of social cognition in the abstract representation of action available to human newborns – the supramodal code. The data from early imitation is well suited for exploring this perception–production expressway starting from the earliest stages of infancy. Imitation demonstrates that, at some level of processing, infants use the perceived behavior of others as a basis for producing similar behavior. Through imitation, infants make manifest a basic connection between self and other.

Meltzoff and Moore (1977) reported that 12- to 21-day-old infants imitate facial expressions. Subsequent studies revealed newborn imitation in a hospital setting (Meltzoff & Moore, 1983, 1989). The youngest infant was only 42 minutes old. Because of the theoretical tradition of Piaget, Freud, and Skinner, early imitation was at first considered surprising to developmental theorists, but it has now been replicated in 25 studies from 13 independent laboratories around the world. (For a review see Meltzoff & Moore, 1997). Today it is not as surprising that the perception and production of human acts are closely connected at birth.

Theoretical accounts of early imitation need to encompass three facts:

1. *Infant imitation entails specific matching, not global arousal.* The data demonstrate that imitative reactions are not a general arousal reaction. Rather infants' responses vary as a function of the act shown. Early imitative matching is specific in terms of both the *body part* used and the *action* evoked. Meltzoff and Moore (1977) found that infants move the same body part in different ways when they are shown two different actions with it (mouth opening versus lip protrusion). They also use two different body parts to produce the same movement (protrusion of the lips versus protrusion of the tongue). Infants even differentiate different types of tongue protrusions: straight tongue protrusion versus tongue out to the side of the mouth (Meltzoff & Moore, 1994, 1997). Such response specificity cannot be accounted for by general arousal. We need a theory that encompasses such specific mapping.
2. *Infants show temporal flexibility, not immediate mimicry.* The imitative response can be displaced in time and space from the demonstration. In one study, a pacifier was put in neonates' mouths as they watched the display. The adult then assumed a passive-face pose and removed the pacifier. Infants imitated the now-absent display based on memory (Meltzoff & Moore, 1977). In another study, 6-week-old infants were shown a gesture, and then left the laboratory for a 24-hour memory delay. The next day they were presented with the same adult sitting with a neutral facial expression. If the adult had shown mouth opening the day before, the infants initiated that gesture; if the adult had shown tongue protrusion, infants responded with that gesture (Meltzoff & Moore, 1994). Infants are not limited to duplicating the perceptual stimulus that is in front of them. Infants can imitate based on their stored representation of absent social stimuli.
3. *Infants correct their imitative efforts.* Early imitation is not rigidly fixed or stereotypic. From birth, infants correct their imitative attempts so that they more and more closely converge on the model demonstrated (Heimann, Nelson, & Schaller, 1989; Kugiumutzakis, 1998; Maratos, 1982; Meltzoff & Moore, 1983, 1994, 1997). For example, if the adult shows a novel gesture such as a tongue-protrusion-to-the-side-of-the-mouth, infants will begin with ordinary tongue protrusions before beginning to move it to the side. They use the proprioceptive feedback from their own actions as the basis for guiding their response to the target (Meltzoff & Moore, 1994, 1997). This is genuine imitation.

A Theoretical Model of Imitation: Connecting Self and Other

Meltzoff & Moore (1997) offered a theoretical model of the mechanism underlying imitation. We believe that imitation depends on a process of active intermodal mapping (AIM). The crux of the AIM hypothesis is that imitation, even early imitation, is a matching-to-target process. The goal or behavioral target is specified visually. Infants' self-produced movements provide proprioceptive feedback that can be compared to the visually specified target. AIM proposes that such comparison is possible because both perceived and performed human acts are represented within a common supramodal framework (figure 2.2).

Our account also specifies the metric of equivalence used by infants. The key insight is that an imitative act is not one indissociable unit. It can be differentiated into the *body part* used and the *movement* performed.

Organ identification

Regarding the former, the evidence suggests that neonates isolate what body part to use before determining how to move it. For example, when they see tongue protrusion, there is often a quieting of the movement of other body parts and an activation of the tongue. Infants don't necessarily protrude the tongue during this initial phase, but may elevate it or move it slightly in the oral cavity. The important point is that the tongue, rather than

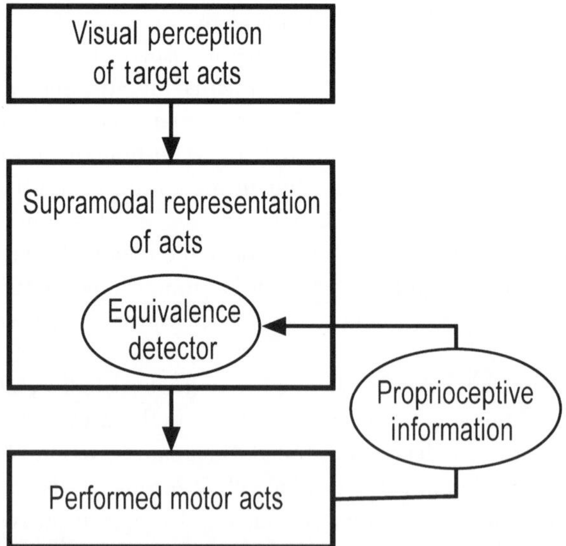

Figure 2.2 The AIM mechanism of imitation. According to AIM, imitation is a matching-to-target process. The imitator can correct errors by using proprioceptive feedback to compare their own actions to a visually specified target (From Meltzoff & Moore, 1997.)

the lips or fingers, is energized before the movement is isolated. We call this *organ identification.*

Neuroscience data show that visual displays of parts of the face and hands activate specific brain sites in monkeys (Desimone, 1991; Gross & Sergent, 1992; Jellema, Baker, Oram, & Perrett, 2002; Rolls, 1992) and humans (Buccino et al., 2001). These brain findings fit with the fast activation of a matching body part by neonates. Specific body parts could be neurally represented.

Body babbling and self-experience

Regarding the movement component, we don't think it is innately specified as to which muscle movements yield which particular body configurations. This could be the result of motor experience gained during motor play. Infants freely move their bodies including producing lip and tongue movements, both postnatally and also prenatally (Hooker, 1952; Patrick, Campbell, Carmichael, Natale, & Richardson, 1982; de Vries, Visser, & Prechtl, 1982; de Vries, Visser, & Prechtl, 1985). We call such self-generated motor experience *body babbling* (Meltzoff & Moore, 1997). Through body babbling, infants acquire a rich store of information about how their bodies work and the consequences of their muscle movements.

Body babbling provides experience linking muscle movements to resulting body configurations. Infants can appreciate the equivalence between the seen "tongue-to-lips" (an *organ relation*) and their own felt "tongue-to-lips," because they express the same arrangement of body parts. When they see such a body configuration they recognize what muscles to activate to achieve it, because they have learned how to reach that end state through previous body babbling. In this sense, body babbling works analogously to vocal play/babbling, which serves to link articulatory acts to auditory targets and supports vocal imitation (Kuhl & Meltzoff, 1982, 1996). In both the vocal and the action case, infants' prior motor experience – including *in utero* motor experience in the case of facial imitation – may play a crucial role in preparing them for later imitation. The AIM theoretical model is fleshed out in more detail in Meltzoff and Moore (1997).

Evidence from Neuroscience: Perception–Production Mappings and Mirror Neuron Systems

The idea of a supramodal representation of action that we used to explain behavioral imitation 30 years ago fits well with modern neuroscience discoveries. Neuroscientists have documented a striking overlap in the brain systems recruited for the perception and for the production of actions (e.g., Hari & Kujala, 2009). In a neuroscience study related to facial imitation, researchers showed adults articulatory movements and found neuronal activation in the cortical areas responsible for producing those articulations (Möttönen, Järveläinen, Sams, & Hari, 2004).

One crucial task for the future is to analyze the commonalities and the differences between the supramodal code, which is proposed at the psychological/personal level, and shared neural circuits, which encode activity at the sub-personal level. Analyses are beginning to emerge (e.g., Gallese, 2003; Hommel, Müsseler, Aschersleben, & Prinz, 2001; Iacoboni, 2005; Jackson, Meltzoff, & Decety, 2006; Meltzoff & Decety, 2003; Rizzolatti, Fogassi, & Gallese, 2001).

A second need is for *developmental* social-cognitive neuroscience studies to explore the neural machinery underlying infant perception–action links (Lepage & Théoret, 2007; Nyström, 2008). We know from the behavioral work on imitation that links exist, and this can help guide the neuroscience work. This is technically challenging work, however, because functional MRI is not suitable for newborns and EEG does not provide good localization data. The application of magnetoencephalography (MEG) technology to infants may provide a way past this roadblock. A MEG study traced changes in the neural network linking perception and production for speech stimuli in newborns, 6-month-olds, and 12-month-olds (Imada et al., 2006). The results at 6 months of age showed that listening to speech activates Broca's area, which controls speech production, although listening to non-speech sounds does not. Because MEG technology tolerates infant movements and provides excellent spatial and temporal resolution, it promises to be an ideal tool for studying perception–production couplings from infancy to adulthood.

Another area for needed work concerns animal studies from a developmental perspective. Despite a plethora of papers on mirror neurons in monkeys (Gallese, Fadiga, Fogassi & Rizzolatti, 1996; Rizzolatti & Craighero, 2004; Gallese, Fadiga, Fogassi, Rizzolatti, 1996), we currently lack the crucial *developmental* studies with newborn animals. Adult monkeys have repeatedly watched themselves grasp objects. The mirror neurons so far reported in adult monkeys could be formed based on such learning experiences. Developmental animal studies are needed to assure that we do not over-interpret the studies (for caveats about over-interpreting mirror neurons, see Hickok, 2009; Molenberghs, Cunnington, & Mattingley, 2009; Saxe, Carey, & Kanwisher, 2004).

Person Identity: Social-Communicative Functions of Imitation

We have seen that young infants recognize the similarity between self and other, which serves as a toehold for building social cognition. Nonetheless, there are some elementary aspects of social cognition that neonates don't grasp. One of the most surprising concerns the understanding of the identity of people. Keeping track of individuals is fundamental to adult social cognition. Social relations are not an oceanic feeling of connectedness with an undifferentiated universe of others. Adult social cognition involves specific others valued for their individuality.

In developmental science the complexities of tracing an individual's identity over time and space are usually discussed in relation to inanimate objects (Moore & Meltzoff, 2009; Spelke, Kestenbaum, Simons, & Wein, 1995; Xu & Carey, 1996). However, the same issues arise with people. People come and go: How do I know that this is the same person again – the same individual with whom I have a relationship?

In considering the role of identity in social cognition it is crucial to distinguish two meanings of identity or "sameness." One meaning is that of an entity being the self-same individual over different encounters in space and time. This is called "numerical identity." A different meaning of sameness concerns appearances. This is referred to as "qualitative" or "featural" identity. My can of Pepsi and yours differ in numerical identity but share the same qualitative or featural identity. Investigations of object permanence are concerned with numerical identity (Meltzoff & Moore, 1998; Moore & Meltzoff, 2004, 2008) – whether infants interpret the reappearing object as the same individual one that had disappeared; investigations of categorization are chiefly concerned with qualitative identity – "Is this exemplar the same kind as the other?" (Quinn, 2002).

Attachment and romantic love depend on distinguishing numerical and qualitative person identity. One stays in love with one's wife despite her new hairdo (same individual, different appearance). Each husband loves his own wife, even if she has an identical twin (same appearance, different individual). How do infants individuate one person from another and re-identify a person as the "same one" again after a break in perceptual contact? This can be posed as a baby-sized problem.

Infants use imitation to determine a person's identity

In one study, we presented 6-week-old infants with people who were coming and going in front of them, as would happen in real-world interaction (Meltzoff & Moore, 1992). The mother appeared and showed one gesture (say, mouth opening). Then she exited and was replaced by a stranger who showed a different gesture (say, tongue protrusion).

When infants visually tracked these people exchanges they imitated each person in turn. But we also discovered an interesting error. If the mother and stranger surreptitiously changed places without the infant visually tracking the movements, infants did not differentially imitate. Instead, infants stared at the new person ... paused ... and then intently produced the *previous* person's gesture. In the absence of clear spatio-temporal evidence of twoness (visual tracking of the entrances and exits), infants were faced with an ambiguity: Is it the same person with a different appearance, or a new person in the old place? Infants used action imitation to help address this question.

Meltzoff and Moore postulated that when infants are uncertain about person identity, they are motivated to test whether this person has the same behavioral properties as the old one – whether she acts the same – because body-actions and expressive behavior of people are identifiers of who they are. For young infants, actions serve a *social identity function.*

Much as infants shake a familiar rattle to see if it makes the same sound, infants probe an adult's distinctive actions to test whether this is the same person again. "Are you the same person I saw before? Are you the one who does x? Is this the game we played together?" Empirical work shows that we can motivate infant imitation by posing baby-sized problems of personal identity (Meltzoff & Moore, 1992, 1994). Thus one of the functions of imitation is social-communicative. Imitation is used as part of identifying specific others and testing their personal identity (Meltzoff & Moore, 1995, 1998).

Mutual Imitation Games Develop Social Cognition

Mutual imitation exchanges serve an interesting adaptive function. Both social psychologists (Bargh & Chartrand, 1999; van Baaren, Holland, Steenaert, & van Knippenberg, 2003) and psychotherapists (Ogden, 1982; Racker, 1968) note that being imitated has positive value – people feel comforted, liked, and an increased sense of rapport when others reflect their behavior back to them.

Mutual imitation has also been studied within the developmental literature (e.g., Nadel, 2002), but the chief focus has been on the temporal, turn-taking aspect of such games (Beebe et al., 2005; Brazelton & Tronick, 1980; Bruner, 1975, 1983; Stern, 1985; Trevarthen, 1979). I don't dispute that timing and contingencies are important to infants, but think that the special power of mutual imitation lies in the equivalence of the *form* of the participants' behavior. Physical objects may come under temporal control. Only people, indeed only people who are paying attention to you and acting intentionally, can systematically match the form of your behavior in a generative fashion. Mutual imitation games are emotionally engaging for infants (and adults), because the other is perceived to be acting "like me."

Value of being imitated

I designed a series of studies to test whether infants could recognize being imitated, and the emotional value they placed on it. In one study, 14-month-old infants sat across a table from two adults. There were two TV monitors behind the infant, one displaying the actions of the current infant, live, and the other displaying a video record of a previous infant. One adult imitated the actions of the current infant and the other adult imitated the previous infant (yoked-control procedure). The results showed that infants looked longer at the adult who was imitating them and also smiled more often at that person (Meltzoff, 2007a).

Timing versus form. Infants could have preferred the imitating adult based on either of two cues. First, they could have used *temporal* contingency information. According to this alternative, infants need only detect that when they do an action the adult responds. Infants need not recognize that the two acts are structurally congruent. The second alternative is that infants can recognize that the acts share the same *form*. According to this alternative, infants recognize that the adult is acting "just like me," not "just when I act."

In another study, the purely temporal aspects of the contingency were controlled by having both experimenters act at the same time (Meltzoff, 2007a). Both experimenters sat passively until the infant performed one of the target actions on a preset list. When the infant did one of these target actions, it launched both experimenters in unison, but one of the adults matched the infant and the other performed a mismatching response. Even under these conditions infants looked longer and smiled more at the adult who was imitating them. This shows that infants can recognize when another acts "like me."

Social hypothesis testing. There is also an interesting constellation of behaviors I call "testing behavior." Infants modulated their acts by performing sudden and unexpected movements while staring at the imitator, as if to check whether the adult was intentionally copying them. For example, the infant might look at the adult and then slowly slide the toy across the table, and then, very suddenly, go faster and faster, as if to check if the experimenter is shadowing. Or the infant might suddenly freeze and look specifically at the imitating adult to see if he also freezes. Infants directed significantly more of this testing behavior to the imitating adult. This goes beyond simple resonance and mirror neuron activity, because the infant is purposely acting *differently* from what they observe.

Generative matching games. We found this pattern of looking, smiling, and testing behavior very strongly exhibited at 14 months of age (and more weakly at ages down to about 9 months of age). However, this is not an innate reaction. We set up studies for 6-week-olds in which an adult matched the infant's mouth opening and closing. The baby's attention was attracted, but it did not lead the baby to systematically switch to tongue protrusion or another gesture. There was no testing. Young infants process specific behavior-to-behavior mapping, whereas the older infants go beyond this and treat the interaction as a generative matching game. Older infants abstract the notion that the game is "you will do what I do" with substitutable behaviors. It is no longer simply a behavior-to-behavior link as per the neonate, but a more abstract notion of "matching game" generalized across particular instances.

Mechanism for change in understanding other minds

There are two developmental consequences of reciprocal imitation games. First, in such biological mirroring, infants gain a sense of what his or her acts *look* like, because they are shown by the other. There are aspects of self that can only be known by seeing reflections of yourself as others see you. This is an advance, because early imitation is mediated by supramodal equivalence in which modality-specific information is not preserved. Neonates can successfully imitate without knowing what their acts *look* like in a purely visual sense, from the outside looking in. Classical developmental theory supposed that mirrors promote such development. However, not all cultures throughout history used mirrors. Being copied by caretakers and peers in mutual imitative games is a more culturally universal mechanism for coming to understand what one looks like from another's perspective.

Second, imitation games provide occasions for infants to go beyond surface behaviors to the *intentions* that generate behavior. Consider the information embedded in the interaction. At first, infants perform their own actions without concern for their effects on the adult (because they don't know they're in a mutual imitation encounter). When the infants notice the adult movement, they shift their attention and begin to vary their own behavior. If the adult continues to match, infants produce novel testing probes and smile as the adult follows suit. This interactive game carries four vital pieces of information: (a) the adult's behavior matches the infant's; (b) it is not a random congruence but is systematic; (c) the specific behaviors don't matter, because the invariant in this situation is "to match"; and (d) from the infant's viewpoint, the infant's own novel behaviors were intended acts.

This provides information for promoting change: "I intend my acts; the other systematically performs matching acts; perhaps the other also intends his or her acts." This inference would expand interpersonal understanding beyond the neonates'. Thus reciprocal imitation games are a tutorial in seeing self and other as producers of intended acts, instead of merely equivalent surface behaviors. Repetitive experiences with mutual imitation games help infants achieve Phase 3 in the Like-Me framework (figure 2.1), in which they make attributions about the internal states of others based on the behaviors they see.

Neuroscience evidence on mutual imitation. From a neuroscience point of view, mutual imitation games pose an interesting issue about *agency* and the ownership of action. When a person is being imitated, a very special event occurs. There is one intended action, but the action is performed twice over – by the self and also by the other. Neuroscience work has begun to examine mutual imitation and discovered that the right inferior parietal region is activated when a person is imitated by another (Decety, Chaminade, Grèzes, & Meltzoff, 2002). This makes sense because this region is known to be involved in determining the agency and authorship of action (Decety & Chaminade, 2005; Farrer & Frith, 2002).

We hypothesize that in mutual imitation the right inferior parietal lobe is activated, because it is involved in differentiating actions produced by the self from similar actions produced by others. More speculatively, mutual imitation games are providing children with input about self–other correspondences but also about *differentiating* self from other. That is what the infant "testing" behavior is all about. The other is "like me" but is *not* me. Others do not do everything I do exactly when I will it – they merely shadow me.

Primitive Perspective-Taking: Infant Gaze Following

Neonates enjoy something like a social Garden of Eden – populated by self and other paying attention to and imitating each other. But this Eden soon ends. The child becomes aware that their caretakers sometimes attend to third parties, inanimate objects. We are surrounded by objects, and many of our thoughts and wants are directed toward them. The Like-Me framework is useful for explaining how infants come to interpret behaviors as being about something beyond the motor movements themselves, as object-directed or referential.

Consider the case of visual perception. When others turn to look at an object we realize that they can pick up information about it from afar, despite the spatial gap between viewer and object. We ascribe intentionality to the gazer who turns his head. Do infants understand this body movement in the same way? Or are head turns interpreted as nothing more than physical motions with no notion that they are *directed toward* the external object – no referential value?

This is a key theoretical issue, much debated in the literature (Carpenter, Nagell, & Tomasello, 1998; Flom, Lee, & Muir, 2007; Moore, 2006; Tomasello, Carpenter, Call,

Behne, & Moll, 2005). One view is that adult looking behavior initially has no special value for young infants. In the leanest version, young infants simply are attracted by the salience of the adult's head movements. As the infant visually tracks the adult's head movement they are pulled to the correct hemifield where they accidently catch sight of the visual target object (Butterworth & Jarrett, 1991). Over time, infants then learn that the adult's head turn is a reliable cue indicating where an object can be seen (Moore, 1999, 2006). Conversely, Baron-Cohen (1995) offered a nativist view suggesting that infants have a built-in module that takes eye gaze as input and automatically makes attributions about seeing and visual experience in others. A third view is that infants' understanding of others' vision emerges developmentally. Meltzoff & Brooks (2008) propose that a mechanism of change is infants' experience with *their own vision*: infants develop an understanding of the vision of others, in part through their own acts of turning-in-order-to-see and opening/shutting of their eyes to cut off and reinstate visual experience.

Understanding eye closure as blocking perception

Crucial for sorting out the competing theories is determining whether infants are, as the lean view suggests, simply processing the salient physical movements in space caused by the head. Brooks and Meltzoff (2002, 2005) zeroed in on the importance of eyes in infant gaze following. The experimental manipulation was that the adult turned to the target with eyes *open* for one group and with eyes *closed* for the other group. If infants relied simply on head motions, as predicted by the lean view, they should turn in both cases. It is a step forward in social cognition for infants to put special emphasis on eyes as the organ of visual perception (something children with autism may not do; see Mundy & Newell, 2007), not only because this is necessary for understanding visual perception but also because it is important for showing, hiding, sharing, and deception.

Brooks and Meltzoff (2002) found that 12-, 14-, and 18-month-old infants followed the adult significantly more when the adult turned with open versus closed eyes. This runs against the leanest interpretation. We also found age-related developmental changes leading to this ability (Brooks & Meltzoff, 2005; Meltzoff & Brooks, 2007).

Understanding material things as blocking perception

Eye closure is only one way that a person's view can be blocked. Inanimate obstacles also can block one's view. Brooks and Meltzoff (2002, experiment 2) duplicated all aspects of the first study, using a headband and a blindfold. When the adult turns to look at a target with the headband on, she is visually attending to it; when she turns with a blindfold on, she is not.

The results showed that the 14- and 18-month-olds turned selectively to the target object in the headband case, but not the blindfold case. They seemed to grasp that the adult could not see in the latter case. In contrast, the 12-month-old infants did *not* distinguish between the two conditions. They systematically looked at the indicated target regardless of whether or not the adult's view was blocked by the blindfold or the headband. There is thus a puzzle: 12-month-olds understand that eye closure blocks the adult's view but not that blindfolds do. Why?

A Social-Cognition Training Study: Changing Infants' Understanding of Vision

The Like-Me theory offers a ready explanation. Eye closure is a biological motion with which infants have extensive first-person experience: infants control their own vision by closing their eyes when they do not want to look at something. The experience of turning off/on visual access through their own eye closing/opening serves as a framework for understanding the meaning of similar behaviors in others. Prediction: if infants are given extensive experience that blindfolds block their own view, they should make different attributions to others.

Accelerating social cognitive development

We designed an experimental intervention that provided blindfold experience to 12-month-old infants (Meltzoff & Brooks, 2008). Infants in the treatment group were provided objects on the table. When they turned to visually inspect an object, the experimenter held an opaque blindfold in between the object and the child's eyes (figure 2.3).

Two control groups were used. One used a windowed cloth. Infants received the same protocol but could peer through the slot. Infants in a baseline-control group were simply familiarized with the opaque blindfold (laying flat on the table).

At the end of training, infants in all three groups were presented with a blindfolded adult who turned toward the distal objects. The results showed that infants who had

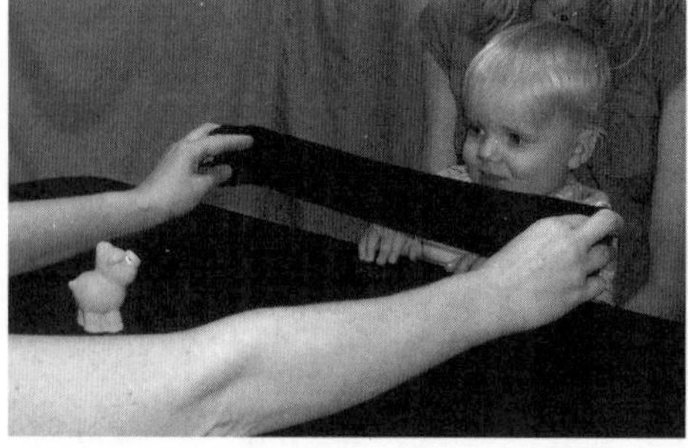
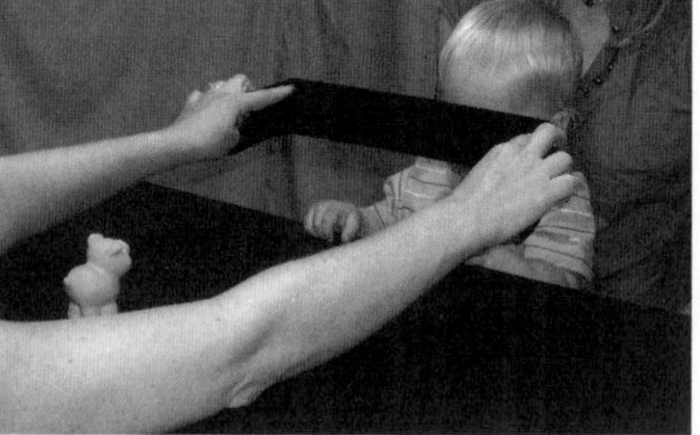

Figure 2.3 A 12-month-old boy in Meltzoff and Brooks' (2008) training study. Infants in the experimental group were given self-experience with a blindfold. Infants looked at interesting objects (left). The blindfold blocked their view (right). This was repeated over a 7.5-minute training session with different objects. Infants used this self-experience to make inferences about other people's perception in a gaze-following test

received first-person training on the opaque blindfold did *not* turn. Infants who had the windowed-cloth experience or were in the baseline group still mistakenly followed the blindfolded adult's "gaze" to the distal object (replicating Brooks & Meltzoff, 2002).

Learning novel information about perception

In the natural course of development, infants change their understanding of visual perception. By 14–18 months of age, infants do not act as though adults can see through opaque barriers and refrain from following if an opaque barrier blocks the adult's view (Brooks & Meltzoff, 2002; Butler, Caron, & Brooks, 2000; Dunphy-Lelii & Wellman, 2004).

Meltzoff and Brooks (2008, experiment 2) provided 18-month-olds with novel self-experience that countered this expectation about opaque occluders. We designed a trick blindfold that looked opaque from the outside but was made of special material that could be seen through when held close to the eyes. Infants were randomly assigned to one of three groups: (a) experience with this trick blindfold, (b) experience with the opaque blindfold, and (c) baseline control (familiarity with the blindfold laying flat on the table).

After training, infants saw the adult wear the blindfold in the standard test. The finding was that infants who had first-person experience with the trick see-through blindfold followed the adult's head turns significantly more than did infants in the two other groups (figure 2.4).

These training effects showcase the power of like-me attributions by infants. The information infants learned through self-experience is immediately applied to others. As

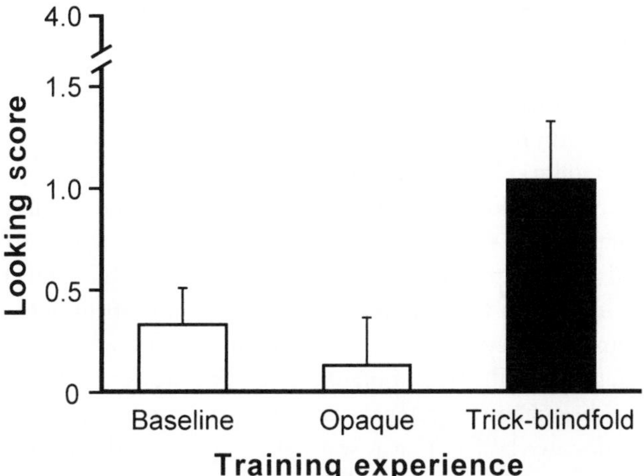

Figure 2.4 Infants learn new information through their own experience and immediately apply this to others. Infants who experienced the see-through, trick blindfold subsequently gaze-followed the blindfolded adult significantly more than controls. This is based on a "like-me" attribution (From Meltzoff & Brooks, 2008.)

they gain self-experience they flexibly transform their understanding of others *like me*: "If I can (or cannot) see in this situation, then another person in the same situation will have the same perceptual experiences." The child's understanding of others is thus not limited to what is preloaded in their mind; it changes as their own experience with the world increases.

Attributing Goals and Intentions

In adult social cognition, others are not only recognized as behaving "like me" and having perceptual experiences "like me," they also enjoy a palette of other mental states, including beliefs, emotions, and intentions just like my own (Searle, 1983; Stich, 1983).

Intentions are particularly interesting for developmentalists. A first question is whether infants have any inkling of the distinction between the actions someone performs and their goals and intentions in performing these actions. This is not an easy conceptual distinction. Wittgenstein (1953, p. 161) makes it clear: "What is left over if I subtract the fact that my arm goes up from the fact that I raise my arm?" Answer: Intention.

Intentions are mental states, and bodily movements are physical events in the world. The intentions themselves are not directly seen, heard, tasted, or smelled. Is there any evidence that infants read below the surface behavior and understand the intentions that lay behind them? How do they come to this (deep) interpretation of visible bodily acts?

Infant's understanding of others' unsuccessful attempts

The "behavioral re-enactment procedure" was designed to provide a non-verbal action measure for exploring infant intention reading (Meltzoff, 1995). The procedure capitalizes on children's natural tendency to re-enact or imitate, but uses it in a more abstract way to investigate whether infants can read below the literal surface behavior to something like the goal or intention of the actor (Bellagamba & Tomasello, 1999; Brandone & Wellman, 2009; Hamlin, Hallinan, & Woodward, 2008).

The experimental procedure involves showing infants an unsuccessful act. For example, the adult accidentally under- or overshoots his target, or he tries to pull apart a dumbbell-shaped toy but his hand slips off the ends and he is unsuccessful. Thus the goal-state is not achieved. To an adult, it is easy to read the actor's intentions although he never fulfills them. The experimental question is whether children read through the literal body movements to the underlying goal or intention of the act. The measure of how they interpreted the event is what they choose to re-enact, in particular whether they choose to produce the intended act despite the fact that it was never present to the senses. In a sense, the "correct answer" is not to copy the literal movement, but to copy the intended act that remains unfulfilled and invisible.

Meltzoff (1995) showed 18-month-old infants an unsuccessful attempt to reach a goal. The study compared infants' tendency to perform the target act in several situations: (a) after they saw the full-target act demonstrated, (b) after they saw the unsuccessful attempt to perform the act, and (c) after it was neither shown nor attempted. The results showed that 18-month-olds infer the unseen goals implied by unsuccessful attempts. Infants who saw the unsuccessful attempt and infants who saw the full-target act both produced target acts at a significantly higher rate than controls. Infants seemed to read through the surface behavior to the underlying goals or intentions of the actor. Evidently, toddlers can understand our goals even if we are unsuccessful in fulfilling them.

Infants understand goals not merely surface behavior. Another experiment underscored that infants in the behavioral re-enactment test are reading beyond the surface behavior of the adult. In this study, 18-month-olds were shown the unsuccessful-attempt display, and then handed a trick toy. The toy was surreptitiously glued shut (Meltzoff, 2007b). When children picked it up and attempted to pull it apart, their hands slipped off the ends of the cubes, matching the surface behavior of the adult. The question was whether this satisfied the children. It did not. They repeatedly grabbed the toy, yanked on it in different ways, and appealed to their mothers and the experimenter for help. They had matched the adult's surface behavior precisely, but were striving toward something else – the adult's goals, not his literal behavior. This work provides developmental roots for the centrality of goals in organizing imitative actions (Carpenter, Call, & Tomasello, 2005; Gattis, Bekkering, & Wohlschläger, 2002; Gleissner, Meltzoff, & Bekkering, 2000; Tomasello et al., 2005; Williamson et al., 2008).

Neuroscience evidence on goal-reading

Based in part on the developmental work, we designed brain-imaging work in adults to investigate the neural mechanisms involved in understanding other people's goals. In one study adults were shown (a) only the final step of an action sequence or (b) the means used by the adult, but with the film clip prematurely terminated, requiring participants to infer the unseen goal of the action sequence (Chaminade, Meltzoff, & Decety, 2002). The results showed that the medial prefrontal cortex was selectively activated when adults needed to infer the goal of the act. This fits well with the finding that this brain region is involved in other aspects of mentalizing or theory of mind (Blakemore & Decety, 2001; Frith & Frith, 1999; Liu, Meltzoff, & Wellman, 2009; Saxe et al., 2004).

Exploring what constitutes an intentional agent

Are there constraints on the types of entities that are interpreted to act in a goal-directed, intentional fashion? In the adult framework, only certain types of objects are ascribed intention. Chairs rock and boulders roll, but their motions are not seen as intentional. Most prototypically, human acts are the types of movement patterns that are seen as caused by intentions. (Animals and computers are borderline cases.) What do infants think?

Meltzoff (1995, experiment 2) tested how 18-month-olds responded to a mechanical device that mimicked the same movements as the actor in the failed-attempt condition.

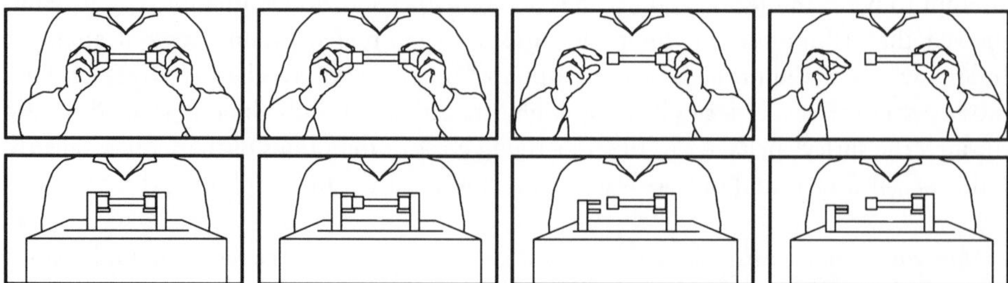

Figure 2.5 The events used to test infants' understanding of goals and intentions. The top row shows the unsuccessful attempt to separate the dumbbell by the human demonstrator. The bottom row shows a mechanical device tracing these same motions. Infants treated the former but not the latter within a psychological framework involving goals or intentions; see the text for details (From Meltzoff, 1995.)

An inanimate device was constructed that had poles for arms and mechanical pincers for hands. It did not look human but it could move very similarly to the human (figure 2.5, bottom panel). For the test, the pincers "grasped" the dumbbell at the two ends just as the human hands did. One mechanical arm was then moved outwards, just as in the human case, and its pincer slipped off the end of the dumbbell just as the human hand did. The movement patterns of machine and man were closely matched from a purely spatio-temporal description of movements in space.

Infants did not attribute a goal or intention to the movements of this mechanical device. Infants were no more (or less) likely to pull apart the toy after seeing the mechanical slippage of the inanimate device than in a baseline condition when they saw nothing.

Infants carefully watched the mechanical device and could learn certain things from it. This was demonstrated by another study in which the mechanical device succeeded (Meltzoff, 2007b). The device held the dumbbell from the two ends and successfully pulled it apart. When infants were given the dumbbell, they too pulled it apart. This makes sense because the infants then did not have to attribute goals or intentions. They simply had to reinstate what they saw – that the object was separated in two pieces. The important theoretical point is that infants only abstracted certain things (changes in the physical world) and not others (goals or intentions of the entity) from observing the behavior of the mechanical device.

I think 18-month-olds interpret the person's actions within a psychological framework that differentiates the surface behavior of people from a deeper level involving goals and intentions. When they see a person's hands slip off the ends of the dumbbell they infer what the adult was "trying" to do (which is different from what he did do). When they see the inanimate device slip off the end of the dumbbell, they see it as mechanical slippage with no implications for purposiveness. By 18 months of age and perhaps earlier, children have already adopted a fundamental aspect of a mature commonsense psychology – persons are understood within a framework involving goals and intentions.

Boundary conditions. It is possible that displays can be constructed that fool infants, as they do adults. Is a computer intentional? What about a goal-seeking robot?

We do not know the necessary and sufficient conditions for children's ascription of goals and intentions to entities, but research suggests that in certain circumstances infants ascribe goals to the movements of pretend humans (stuffed animals and puppets, Johnson, 2000; Johnson, Booth, & O'Hearn, 2001) and to dynamic displays that may be ambiguous as to whether they are of animate or mechanical origin (e.g., 2-D spots that leap, move spontaneously, and engage in mutual responsiveness, Gergely, chapter 3, this volume; Gergely, Nádasdy, Csibra, & Bíró, 1995).

This does not run against the thesis suggested here, but underscores the need for research on boundary conditions. The mechanical device used by Meltzoff (1995) gives a lower boundary (infants fail) and real people give an upper boundary (infants succeed). There is a lot of room in between for empirical research systematically manipulating relevant cues (e.g., Itakura et al., 2008).

Summary and Conclusions

Piaget (1952) argued that the infant is born a "solipsist." Fodor (1987) supposed that adult commonsense psychology was innately specified. Starting-state nativism offers a third way. My thesis is that a starting point for social cognition is that human acts are represented within a supramodal code that applies to self as well as others. Newborns bring this representation of human acts to their very first interactions with people. It provides an interpretive framework for understanding the behavior they see. Interpreting others as "like me" is our birthright.

It has long been thought that the commonality between self and other is integral to interpersonal relations (Husserl, 1977; Smith, 1976). Empathy, perspective-taking, and all manner of putting yourself in someone else's shoes rest on the connection between self and other (Jackson, Brunet, Meltzoff, & Decety, 2006; Lamm, Meltzoff, & Decety, in press). The way that the classic philosophers went wrong is that they thought the self–other equivalence was late to develop – emerging from language or complex cognitive analyses. The modern research on infancy stands this proposition on its head. It indicates that young infants can represent the acts of others and their own acts in commensurate terms. *The recognition of self–other equivalences is the starting point for social cognition, not its culmination.*

Given this facile self–other mapping, input from social encounters is more interpretable than supposed by Freud, Skinner, and Piaget. Infants have a storehouse of knowledge on which to draw: they can use the self as a framework for understanding the subjectivity of others. *Homo sapiens* begin the journey of social cognition armed with a common code, a *lingua franca*, that is more fundamental than spoken language.

We are not born social isolates. We are fundamentally connected to others right from the start, because they are seen as being "like me." This allows rapid and special learning from people (Meltzoff, Kuhl, Movellan, & Sejnowski, 2009). I can learn about myself and potential powers by watching the consequences of your acts, and can imbue your acts with felt meaning based on my own self-experience. As children's self-experience broadens, their appreciation of others' minds and behavior is enriched and refined. This propels infants beyond what they see or know innately. Social cognition rests on the fact that you are "like me," differentiable from me, but nonetheless enough like me to become my role model and I your interpreter.

References

Astington, J. W., & Gopnik, A. (1991). Theoretical explanations of children's understanding of the mind. *British Journal of Developmental Psychology, 9*, 7–31.

Bargh, J. A., & Chartrand, T. L. (1999). The unbearable automaticity of being. *American Psychologist, 54*, 462–479.

Baron-Cohen, S. (1995). *Mindblindness: An essay on autism and theory of mind.* Cambridge, MA: MIT Press.

Beebe, B., Knoblauch, S., Rustin, J., & Sorter, D. (2005). *Forms of intersubjectivity in infant research and adult treatment.* New York: Other Press.

Beebe, B., Sorter, D., Rustin, J., & Knoblauch, S. (2003). A comparison of Meltzoff, Trevarthen, and Stern. *Psychoanalytic Dialogues, 13*, 777–804.

Bellagamba, F., & Tomasello, M. (1999). Re-enacting intended acts: Comparing 12- and 18-month-olds. *Infant Behavior and Development, 22*, 277–282.

Blakemore, S.-J., & Decety, J. (2001). From the perception of action to the understanding of intention. *Nature Reviews Neuroscience, 2*, 561–567.

Brandone, A. C., & Wellman, H. M. (2009). You can't always get what you want. *Psychological Science, 20*, 85–91.

Brazelton, T. B., & Tronick, E. (1980). Preverbal communication between mothers and infants. In D. R. Olson (Ed.), *The social foundations of language and thought* (pp. 299–315). New York: Norton.

Brooks, R., & Meltzoff, A. N. (2002). The importance of eyes: How infants interpret adult looking behavior. *Developmental Psychology, 38*, 958–966.

Brooks, R., & Meltzoff, A. N. (2005). The development of gaze following and its relation to language. *Developmental Science, 8*, 535–543.

Bruner, J. S. (1975). From communication to language – A psychological perspective. *Cognition, 3*, 255–287.

Bruner, J. S. (1983). *Child's talk: Learning to use language.* New York: Norton.

Buccino, G., Binkofski, F., Fink, G. R., Fadiga, L., Fogassi, L., Gallese, V., Seitz, R. J., Zilles, K., Rizzolatti, G., & Freund, H.-J. (2001). Action observation activates premotor and parietal areas in a somatotopic manner: An fMRI study. *European Journal of Neuroscience, 13*, 400–404.

Butler, S. C., Caron, A. J., & Brooks, R. (2000). Infant understanding of the referential nature of looking. *Journal of Cognition and Development, 1*, 359–377.

Butterworth, G., & Jarrett, N. (1991). What minds have in common is space: Spatial mechanisms serving joint visual attention in infancy. *British Journal of Developmental Psychology, 9*, 55–72.

Campbell, J. (1994). *Past, space, and self.* Cambridge, MA: MIT Press.

Carpenter, M., Call, J., & Tomasello, M. (2005). Twelve- and 18-month-olds copy actions in terms of goals. *Developmental Science, 8*, F13–F20.

Carpenter, M., Nagell, K., & Tomasello, M. (1998). Social cognition, joint attention, and communicative competence from 9 to 15 months of age. *Monographs of the Society for Research in Child Development, 63*(4, Serial No. 255).

Chaminade, T., Meltzoff, A. N., & Decety, J. (2002). Does the end justify the means? A PET exploration of the mechanisms involved in human imitation. *NeuroImage, 15*, 318–328.

Csibra, G. (2003). Teleological and referential understanding of action in infancy. *Philosophical Transactions of the Royal Society of London. Series B, Biological Sciences, 358*, 447–458.

Csibra, G., & Gergely, G. (2007). "Obsessed with goals": Functions and mechanisms of teleological interpretation of actions in humans. *Acta Psychologica, 124*, 60–78.

De Vries, J. I. P., Visser, G. H. A., & Prechtl, H. F. R. (1982). The emergence of fetal behaviour. I. Qualitative aspects. *Early Human Development, 7*, 301–322.

De Vries, J. I. P., Visser, G. H. A., & Prechtl, H. F. R. (1985). The emergence of fetal behaviour. II. Quantitative aspects. *Early Human Development, 12*, 99–120.

Decety, J., & Chaminade, T. (2005). The neurophysiology of imitation and intersubjectivity. In S. Hurley & N. Chater (Eds.), *Perspectives on imitation: From neuroscience to social science* (Vol. *1*, pp. 119–140). Cambridge, MA: MIT Press.

Decety, J., Chaminade, T., Grèzes, J., & Meltzoff, A. N. (2002). A PET exploration of the neural mechanisms involved in reciprocal imitation. *NeuroImage, 15*, 265–272.

Desimone, R. (1991). Face-selective cells in the temporal cortex of monkeys. *Journal of Cognitive Neuroscience, 3*, 1–8.

Dunphy-Lelii, S., & Wellman, H. M. (2004). Infants' understanding of occlusion of others' line-of-sight: Implications for an emerging theory of mind. *European Journal of Developmental Psychology, 1*, 49–66.

Farrer, C., & Frith, C. D. (2002). Experiencing oneself vs. another person as being the cause of an action: The neural correlates of the experience of agency. *Neuroimage, 15*, 596–603.

Flavell, J. H. (1999). Cognitive development: Children's knowledge about the mind. *Annual Review of Psychology, 50*, 21–45.

Flom, R., Lee, K., & Muir, D. (Eds.). (2007). *Gaze-following: Its development and significance.* Mahwah, NJ: Erlbaum.

Fodor, J. A. (1987). *Psychosemantics: The problem of meaning in the philosophy of mind.* Cambridge, MA: MIT Press.

Freud, S. (1911). Formulations on the two principles of mental functioning. In J. Strachey (Ed.), *The standard edition of the complete psychological works of Sigmund Freud* (Vol. *12*, pp. 215–226). London: Hogarth Press.

Frith, C. D., & Frith, U. (1999). Interacting minds: A biological basis. *Science, 286*, 1692–1695.

Gallese, V. (2003). The manifold nature of interpersonal relations: The quest for a common mechanism. *Philosophical Transactions of the Royal Society of London. Series B, Biological Sciences, 358*, 517–528.

Gallese, V., Fadiga, L., Fogassi, L., & Rizzolatti, G. (1996). Action recognition in the premotor cortex. *Brain, 119*, 593–609.

Gattis, M., Bekkering, H., & Wohlschläger, A. (2002). Goal-directed imitation. In A. N. Meltzoff & W. Prinz (Eds.), *The imitative mind: Development, evolution, and brain bases* (pp. 183–205). Cambridge: Cambridge University Press.

Gergely, G., Nádasdy, Z., Csibra, G., & Bíró, S. (1995). Taking the intentional stance at 12 months of age. *Cognition, 56*, 165–193.

Gleissner, B., Meltzoff, A. N., & Bekkering, H. (2000). Children's coding of human action: Cognitive factors influencing imitation in 3-year-olds. *Developmental Science, 3*, 405–414.

Gopnik, A., & Meltzoff, A. N. (1997). *Words, thoughts, and theories.* Cambridge, MA: MIT Press.

Gross, C. G., & Sergent, J. (1992). Face recognition. *Current Opinion in Neurobiology, 2*, 156–161.

Hamlin, J. K., Hallinan, E. V., & Woodward, A. L. (2008). Do as I do: 7-month-old infants selectively reproduce others' goals. *Developmental Science, 11*, 487–494.

Hari, R., & Kujala, M. V. (2009). Brain basis of human social interaction: From concepts to brain imaging. *Physiological Reviews, 89*, 453–479.

Heider, F. (1958). *The psychology of interpersonal relations*. Hillsdale, NJ: Erlbaum.

Heimann, M., Nelson, K. E., & Schaller, J. (1989). Neonatal imitation of tongue protrusion and mouth opening: Methodological aspects and evidence of early individual differences. *Scandinavian Journal of Psychology, 30*, 90–101.

Hickok, G. (2009). Eight problems for the mirror neuron theory of action understanding in monkeys and humans. *Journal of Cognitive Neuroscience, 21*, 1229–1243.

Hommel, B., Müsseler, J., Aschersleben, G., & Prinz, W. (2001). The theory of event coding (TEC): A framework for perception and action planning. *Behavioral and Brain Sciences, 24*, 849–878.

Hooker, D. (1952). *The prenatal origin of behavior*. Lawrence, KS: University of Kansas Press.

Husserl, E. (1977). *Phenomenological Psychology: Lectures, summer semester, 1925 (J. Scanlon, Trans.)*. The Hague: Nijhoff. (Original work published 1962.)

Iacoboni, M. (2005). Neural mechanisms of imitation. *Current Opinion in Neurobiology, 15*, 632–637.

Imada, T., Zhang, Y., Cheour, M., Taulu, S., Ahonen, A., & Kuhl, P. K. (2006). Infant speech perception activates Broca's Area: A developmental MEG study. *NeuroReport, 17*, 957–962.

Itakura, S., Ishida, H., Kanda, T., Shimada, Y., Ishiguro, H., & Lee, K. (2008). How to build an intentional android: Infants' imitation of a robot's goal-directed actions. *Infancy, 13*, 519–532.

Jackson, P. L., Brunet, E., Meltzoff, A. N., & Decety, J. (2006). Empathy examined through the neural mechanisms involved in imagining how I feel versus how you feel pain. *Neuropsychologia, 44*, 752–761.

Jackson, P. L., Meltzoff, A. N., & Decety, J. (2006). Neural circuits involved in imitation and perspective-taking. *NeuroImage, 31*, 429–439.

Jellema, T., Baker, C. I., Oram, M. W., & Perrett, D. I. (2002). Cell populations in the banks of the superior temporal sulcus of the macaque and imitation. In A. N. Meltzoff & W. Prinz (Eds.), *The imitative mind: Development, evolution, and brain bases* (pp. 267–290). Cambridge: Cambridge University Press.

Johnson, S. C. (2000). The recognition of mentalistic agents in infancy. *Trends in Cognitive Sciences, 4*, 22–28.

Johnson, S. C. (2003). Detecting agents. *Philosophical Transactions of the Royal Society of London. Series B, Biological Sciences, 358*, 549–559.

Johnson, S. C., Booth, A., & O'Hearn, K. (2001). Inferring the goals of a nonhuman agent. *Cognitive Development, 16*, 637–656.

Kugiumutzakis, G. (1998). Neonatal imitation in the intersubjective companion space. In S. Bråten (Ed.), *Intersubjective communication and emotion in early ontogeny* (pp. 63–88). Cambridge: Cambridge University Press.

Kuhl, P. K., & Meltzoff, A. N. (1982). The bimodal perception of speech in infancy. *Science, 218*, 1138–1141.

Kuhl, P. K., & Meltzoff, A. N. (1996). Infant vocalizations in response to speech: Vocal imitation and developmental change. *Journal of the Acoustical Society of America, 100*, 2425–2438.

Lamm, C., Meltzoff, A. N., & Decety, J. (in press). How do we empathize with someone who is not like us? A functional magnetic resonance imaging study. *Journal of Cognitive Neuroscience*. doi:10.1162/jocn.2009.21186

Lepage, J.-F., & Théoret, H. (2007). The mirror neuron system: Grasping others' actions from birth? *Developmental Science, 10*, 513–523.

Liu, D., Meltzoff, A. N., & Wellman, H. M. (2009). Neural correlates of belief- and desire-reasoning. *Child Development, 80,* 1163–1171.

Mahler, M. S., Pine, F., & Bergman, A. (1975). *The psychological birth of the human infant.* New York: Basic Books.

Maratos, O. (1982). Trends in the development of imitation in early infancy. In T. G. Bever (Ed.), *Regressions in mental development: Basic phenomena and theories* (pp. 81–101). Hillsdale, NJ: Erlbaum.

Meltzoff, A. N. (1988). Infant imitation after a 1-week delay: Long-term memory for novel acts and multiple stimuli. *Developmental Psychology, 24,* 470–476.

Meltzoff, A. N. (1995). Understanding the intentions of others: Re-enactment of intended acts by 18-month-old children. *Developmental Psychology, 31,* 838–850.

Meltzoff, A. N. (2007a). "Like me": A foundation for social cognition. *Developmental Science, 10,* 126–134.

Meltzoff, A. N. (2007b). The "like me" framework for recognizing and becoming an intentional agent. *Acta Psychologica, 124,* 26–43.

Meltzoff, A. N., & Brooks, R. (2007). Eyes wide shut: The importance of eyes in infant gaze following and understanding other minds. In R. Flom, K. Lee, & D. Muir (Eds.), *Gaze following: Its development and significance,* pp. 217–241. Mahwah, NJ: Erlbaum.

Meltzoff, A. N., & Brooks, R. (2008). Self-experience as a mechanism for learning about others: A training study in social cognition. *Developmental Psychology, 44,* 1257–1265.

Meltzoff, A. N., & Decety, J. (2003). What imitation tells us about social cognition: A rapprochement between developmental psychology and cognitive neuroscience. *Philosophical Transactions of the Royal Society of London. Series B, Biological Sciences, 358,* 491–500.

Meltzoff, A. N., Kuhl, P. K., Movellan, J. R., & Sejnowski, T. J. (2009). Foundations for a new science of learning. *Science, 325,* 284–288.

Meltzoff, A. N., & Moore, M. K. (1977). Imitation of facial and manual gestures by human neonates. *Science, 198,* 75–78.

Meltzoff, A. N., & Moore, M. K. (1983). Newborn infants imitate adult facial gestures. *Child Development, 54,* 702–709.

Meltzoff, A. N., & Moore, M. K. (1989). Imitation in newborn infants: Exploring the range of gestures imitated and the underlying mechanisms. *Developmental Psychology, 25,* 954–962.

Meltzoff, A. N., & Moore, M. K. (1992). Early imitation within a functional framework: The importance of person identity, movement, and development. *Infant Behavior and Development, 15,* 479–505.

Meltzoff, A. N., & Moore, M. K. (1994). Imitation, memory, and the representation of persons. *Infant Behavior and Development, 17,* 83–99.

Meltzoff, A. N., & Moore, M. K. (1995). Infants' understanding of people and things: From body imitation to folk psychology. In J. L. Bermúdez, A. Marcel, & N. Eilan (Eds.), *The body and the self* (pp. 43–69). Cambridge, MA: MIT Press.

Meltzoff, A. N., & Moore, M. K. (1997). Explaining facial imitation: A theoretical model. *Early Development and Parenting, 6,* 179–192.

Meltzoff, A. N., & Moore, M. K. (1998). Object representation, identity, and the paradox of early permanence: Steps toward a new framework. *Infant Behavior and Development, 21,* 201–235.

Molenberghs, P., Cunnington, R., & Mattingley, J. B. (2009). Is the mirror neuron system involved in imitation? A short review and meta-analysis. *Neuroscience and Biobehavioral Reviews, 33,* 975–980.

Moore, C. (1999). Gaze following and the control of attention. In P. Rochat (Ed.), *Early social cognition: Understanding others in the first months of life* (pp. 241–256). Mahwah, NJ: Erlbaum.

Moore, C. (2006). *The development of commonsense psychology.* Mahwah, NJ: Erlbaum.

Moore, M. K., & Meltzoff, A. N. (2004). Object permanence after a 24-hr delay and leaving the locale of disappearance: The role of memory, space, and identity. *Developmental Psychology, 40,* 606–620.

Moore, M. K., & Meltzoff, A. N. (2008). Factors affecting infants' manual search for occluded objects and the genesis of object permanence. *Infant Behavior and Development, 31,* 168–180.

Moore, M. K., & Meltzoff, A. N. (2009). Numerical identity and the development of object permanence. In S. Johnson (Ed.), *Neo-constructivism* (pp. 61–83). New York: Oxford University Press.

Möttönen, R., Järveläinen, J., Sams, M., & Hari, R. (2004). Viewing speech modulates activity in the left SI mouth cortex. *NeuroImage, 24,* 731–737.

Mundy, P., & Newell, L. (2007). Attention, joint attention, and social cognition. *Current Directions in Psychological Science, 16,* 269–274.

Nadel, J. (2002). Imitation and imitation recognition: Functional use in preverbal infants and nonverbal children with autism. In A. N. Meltzoff & W. Prinz (Eds.), *The imitative mind: Development, evolution, and brain bases* (pp. 42–62). Cambridge: Cambridge University Press.

Nyström, P. (2008). The infant mirror neuron system studied with high density EEG. *Social Neuroscience, 3,* 334–347.

Ogden, T. H. (1982). *Projective identification and psychotherapeutic technique.* New York: Aronson.

Onishi, K. H., & Baillargeon, R. (2005). Do 15-month-old infants understand false beliefs? *Science, 308,* 255–258.

Patrick, J., Campbell, K., Carmichael, L., Natale, R., & Richardson, B. (1982). Patterns of gross fetal body movement over 24-hour observation intervals during the last 10 weeks of pregnancy. *American Journal of Obstetrics and Gynecology, 142,* 363–371.

Perner, J. (1991). *Understanding the representational mind.* Cambridge, MA: MIT Press.

Piaget, J. (1952). *The origins of intelligence in children (M. Cook, Trans.).* New York: International Universities Press.

Piaget, J. (1954). *The construction of reality in the child (M. Cook, Trans.).* New York: Basic Books.

Quinn, P. C. (2002). Early categorization: A new synthesis. In U. Goswami (Ed.), *Handbook of childhood cognitive development* (pp. 84–101). Oxford: Blackwell.

Racker, H. (1968). *Transference and countertransference.* New York: International Universities Press.

Repacholi, B. M., Meltzoff, A. N., & Olsen, B. (2008). Infants' understanding of the link between visual perception and emotion: "If she can't see me doing it, she won't get angry." *Developmental Psychology, 44,* 561–574.

Rizzolatti, G., & Craighero, L. (2004). The mirror-neuron system. *Annual Review of Neuroscience, 27,* 169–192.

Rizzolatti, G., Fadiga, L., Gallese, V., & Fogassi, L. (1996). Premotor cortex and the recognition of motor actions. *Cognitive Brain Research, 3,* 131–141.

Rizzolatti, G., Fogassi, L., & Gallese, V. (2001). Neurophysiological mechanisms underlying the understanding and imitation of action. *Nature Reviews Neuroscience, 2,* 661–670.

Rochat, P. (2009). *Others in mind: Social origins of self-consciousness.* New York: Cambridge University Press.

Rolls, E. T. (1992). Neurophysiological mechanisms underlying face processing within and beyond the temporal cortical visual areas. In V. Bruce, A. Cowey, A. W. Ellis, & D. Perrett (Eds.), *Processing the facial image* (pp. 11–21). New York: Oxford University Press.

Ryle, G. (1949). *The concept of mind.* London: Hutchinson.

Saxe, R., Carey, S., & Kanwisher, N. (2004). Understanding other minds: Linking developmental psychology and functional neuroimaging. *Annual Review of Psychology, 55,* 87–124.

Searle, J. R. (1983). *Intentionality: An essay in the philosophy of mind.* New York: Cambridge University Press.

Skinner, B. F. (1953). *Science and human behavior.* New York: Macmillan.

Skinner, B. F. (1983). *A matter of consequences.* New York: Alfred A. Knopf.

Smith, A. (1976). *The theory of moral sentiments.* New York: Oxford University Press. (Original work published 1759.)

Sommerville, J. A., & Woodward, A. L. (2005). Pulling out the intentional structure of action: The relation between action processing and action production in infancy. *Cognition, 95,* 1–30.

Spelke, E. S., Breinlinger, K., Macomber, J., & Jacobson, K. (1992). Origins of knowledge. *Psychological Review, 99,* 605–632.

Spelke, E. S., Kestenbaum, R., Simons, D. J., & Wein, D. (1995). Spatiotemporal continuity, smoothness of motion and object identity in infancy. *British Journal of Developmental Psychology, 13,* 113–142.

Stern, D. N. (1985). *The interpersonal world of the infant: A view from psychoanalysis and developmental psychology.* New York: Basic Books.

Stich, S. P. (1983). *From folk psychology to cognitive science: The case against belief.* Cambridge, MA: MIT Press.

Strawson, P. F. (1959). *Individuals: An essay in descriptive metaphysics.* London: Methuen.

Tomasello, M., Carpenter, M., Call, J., Behne, T., & Moll, H. (2005). Understanding and sharing intentions: The origins of cultural cognition. *Behavioral and Brain Sciences, 28,* 675–691.

Trevarthen, C. (1979). Communication and cooperation in early infancy: A description of primary intersubjectivity. In M. Bullowa (Ed.), *Before speech: The beginning of interpersonal communication* (pp. 321–347). New York: Cambridge University Press.

Van Baaren, R. B., Holland, R. W., Steenaert, B., & van Knippenberg, A. (2003). Mimicry for money: Behavioral consequences of imitation. *Journal of Experimental Social Psychology, 39,* 393–398.

Wellman, H. M. (1990). *The child's theory of mind.* Cambridge, MA: MIT Press.

Williamson, R. A., Jaswal, V. K., & Meltzoff, A. N. (in press). Learning the rules: Observation and imitation of a sorting strategy by 36-month-old children. *Developmental Psychology.*

Williamson, R. A., Meltzoff, A. N., & Markman, E. M. (2008). Prior experiences and perceived efficacy influence 3-year-olds' imitation. *Developmental Psychology, 44,* 275–285.

Wittgenstein, L. (1953). *Philosophical investigations (G. E. M. Anscombe, Trans.).* Oxford: Blackwell.

Woodward, A. (2009). Infants' learning about intentional action. In A. L. Woodward & A. Needham (Eds.), *Learning and the infant mind* (pp. 227– 248). Oxford: Oxford University Press.

Xu, F., & Carey, S. (1996). Infants' metaphysics: The case of numerical identity. *Cognitive Psychology, 30,* 111–153.

CHAPTER THREE

Kinds of Agents

The Origins of Understanding Instrumental and Communicative Agency

György Gergely

The Early Development of Understanding Intentional Agency and Representing Other Minds: A Brief Historical Introduction (1978–2005)

The systematic study of the early development of understanding intentional action and agency started some 30 years ago together with the sudden burst of research interest in the ontogenetic origins of understanding and representing other minds (Premack & Woodward, 1978; Wimmer & Perner, 1983). At that time the question of how and when children become able to interpret and predict the intentional actions of others was thought to be inherently related to (if not identical with) the issue of how and when children come to infer and represent other agents' causal intentional mental states (such as their beliefs, desires, and intentions). This is no coincidence, of course, given that the human ability to represent other agents' mental representations of the world and their intentional attitudes towards the contents of such representations (our "naïve theory of mind," Leslie, 1987) forms the very basis of adults' mature inferential capacity to predict, explain, and reason about the intentional actions of others.

The ensuing three decades of intensive research exploring the ontogenetic development of our mindreading ability (Wellman, Cross, & Watson, 2001), led to the – until very recently – widely shared belief that such an explicit mentalistic representational theory of mind is a rather late developmental achievement that emerges only around 4 years of age. This standard view has been based on a robust amount of converging evidence showing that while 3-year-olds massively fail the standard false-belief tasks (Wimmer & Perner, 1983), most 4- and 5-year-olds find it easy to predict others' actions based on their false (outdated) belief that was previously attributed to them (Wellman et al., 2001). In spite of the numerous methodological problems and – non-theory-of-mind-specific

– performance and pragmatic interpretational difficulties that these verbal false-belief tasks are now understood to be burdened with (e.g., Bloom & German, 2000), they have become widely used as the standard "litmus tests" for demonstrating the young child's mindreading ability.

During the same period, however, a growing body of evidence has also been accumulating that seemed to imply that infants during their second year (and in some cases even earlier) already understand important aspects of intentional agency in a variety of domains. These include goal attribution to agents and predicting their novel means–ends actions in changed situational contexts as early as 3–6 months of age (Bíró, Csibra, & Gergely, 2007; Csibra, 2008; Csibra, Bíró, Koós, & Gergely, 2003; Gergely & Csibra, 2003; Gergely, Nádasdy, Csibra, & Bíró, 1995; Luo, in press; Wagner & Carey, 2005); learning new goals and means–ends actions by imitative re-enactment from observing others' novel intentional actions from around 12 months (Gergely, Bekkering & Király, 2002; Király, 2008, 2009; Király, Csibra & Gergely, 2004; Meltzoff, 1988, 1995a); learning about the function and manner of use of novel artifacts in social communicative contexts during the second and third year (Casler & Kelemen, 2005; DiYanni & Kelemen, 2005; Hernik & Csibra, 2009) (and possibly as young as 10 months of age, Futó, Téglás, Csibra, & Gergely, 2009a, 2009b); establishing joint attention and reference in triadic interactions with others to request, share, or even provide relevant information from about 10–12 months (Liszkowski, Carpenter, Henning, Striano, & Tomasello, 2004; Liszkowski, Carpenter, Striano, & Tomasello, 2006; Tomasello, 2008; Tomasello, Carpenter, Call, Behne, & Moll, 2005), and learning about generalizable semantic properties of referent kinds from others' referent-directed action manifestations or emotion gestures in ostensive communicative contexts during the second year (Csibra & Gergely, 2009; Egyed, Király, & Gergely, 2007; Gergely, Király, & Egyed, 2007) and possibly as early as 8–10 months of age (Futó et al., 2009a, 2009b; Topál, Gergely, Erdőhegyi, Csibra, & Miklósi, 2009; Topál, Gergely, Miklósi, Erdőhegyi, & Csibra, 2008).

Clearly, however, given the apparently late emergence of the ability to represent other minds, these remarkably early indicators of understanding intentional agency represented a non-trivial theoretical challenge to the field. If the mindreading capacity is not yet available before 4 years, then how should one account for the evidence showing early understanding of numerous aspects of intentional agency already during the second and sometimes even the first year of life? This empirical dilemma provoked much theoretical debate and generated qualitatively different proposals to account for (and bridge) the apparent developmental gap between the early signs of understanding intentional action and agency on the one hand, and the relatively late emergence of mindreading on the other.

The modularist "theory-of-mind" account

Modularist theorists (Baron-Cohen, 1994; Fodor, 1992; Leslie, 1987, 1994; Premack, 1990) interpreted the 4-year-old's success in representing false beliefs as strong evidence for the existence of an innate domain-specific theory-of-mind system specialized to represent other agents' causal intentional mental states. They appealed to maturational factors to account for the relatively late emergence of representing others' epistemic mind states (such as false beliefs). They hypothesized that the specialized neural mechanisms supporting the meta-representational structures and computations (such as "decoupling") that are necessary for representing others' mental representations of counterfactual (false belief) or fictional (pretense) states of reality may have a late maturational onset somewhere around 18–24 months, as indicated by the emergence of understanding pretense in others (Leslie, 1987). Additionally, Leslie and his collaborators developed performance constraint models to explain the specific nature of the difficulty of the standard false-belief attribution tasks. They argued that children pass these tasks only around 4 years because of their difficulties with the inhibitory control requirements related to response selection processes rather than due to their lack of meta-representational competence (Leslie & Roth, 1993; Leslie, German, & Polizzi, 2005).

Experience-based motor-simulation accounts

In contrast, many researchers interpreted the lack of evidence for false-belief attribution until 4 years as providing strong reasons to reject the radical innatist proposals for a domain-specific capacity to represent invisible and abstract representational mind states of others. For example, experience-based simulationist approaches (Meltzoff, 1996, 2005; Rizzolatti & Craighero, 2004; Woodward, 1998; Woodward, Sommerville, & Guajardo, 2001) claimed to provide an alternative account for the early forms of intentional action understanding in terms of non-inferential, non-representational, and non-mentalistic processes. It was assumed that many "behaviorally more transparent" intentional states (for example, emotions) can be apprehended and simulated by non-inferential perceptual–motor "direct matching" mechanisms that map the observable behavioral correlates of the other's intentional states onto the corresponding motor representations of the self. According to the mirror neuron doctrine, for example, the understanding of goal-directed actions (as well as emotion expressions) is mediated by the direct and automatic activation and "motor resonance" of the self's corresponding motor action schemes or mirror-neuron emotion circuits (Rizzolatti & Craighero, 2004). Meltzoff (1996, 2005) conjectured that infants recognize other agents' behaviors as intentional actions by an innate "active intermodal mapping" mechanism that categorizes the other's actions as "like me" through the simulatory activation of the corresponding motor action programs of the self. This "like me" experience triggers an automatic process of identification with the other leading to the activation of a human-specific drive to imitate the other's actions. This is how Meltzoff accounts for human infants' precocious capacity to imitatively fast-learn novel means–ends actions as early as 14 months (Meltzoff, 1988, 1995a). Tomasello (1999) also assumed identification-based simulation processes as the basis for understanding others' goal-directed actions and underlying imitative learning of novel means–ends.

The teleological stance and natural pedagogy: separate and independent domain-specific adaptations to instrumental versus communicative agency

A third approach – that will be reviewed in more detail in the present chapter – proposes initially separate and independent systems of cognitive adaptations that are held accountable for different aspects of young infants' early abilities to recognize, interpret, and learn from the observed actions of two kinds of intentional agents: teleological or instrumental agents on the one hand, and communicative agents on the other. I'll use the term *instrumental agency* to identify the kinds of intentional agents whose actions are performed to realize specific change of states (goal states) in their environment.[1] Instrumental agency is distinguished here from *communicative agency*, the latter referring to the kind of intentional agents whose ostensively cued referential behavioral displays function as communicative acts to bring about a specific change in the epistemic contents of the addressee's mental representations of reality, generic knowledge about kinds, norms, and conventions, etc.

Instrumental agency: the infant's naïve "theory of rational action" and the teleological stance. As a domain-specific adaptation for instrumental agency, Gergely and Csibra (1997, 2003; Csibra & Gergely, 1998) hypothesized that infants are innately equipped with a *teleological action representation and interpretation system* (the "naïve theory of rational action" or the "teleological stance") that can account for infants' early ability to infer, represent, and predict the goal-directed actions that instrumental agents perform to realize some specific change of state in their environment (Bíró, Csibra, & Gergely, 2007; Csibra et al., 2003; Csibra, Gergely, Bíró, Koós, & Brockbank, 1999; Gergely et al., 1995). This system is hypothesized to be an adaptation to represent the teleological action properties of instrumental agents. The teleological stance is a context-sensitive and inferential system of action interpretation that is guided by the principle of rational action (figure 3.1). This inferential principle specifies the basic assumptions of rational agency and efficiency of action according to which instrumental agents are expected to perform the most efficient means–ends action available to them within their situational constraints to bring about the goal state. Attributing and representing the outcome of an observed action as the goal is, therefore, a function of evaluating whether the action satisfies the criterion of efficiency of goal approach given the physical constraints of the situation.

There is by now a significant amount of evidence indicating that when attributing goals to observed actions infants from as early as 3–6 months of age are sensitive to and evaluate the efficiency of the action in relation to its outcome and the relevant constraints of the situation (Bíró et al., 2007; Bíró & Leslie, 2007; Bíró & Verschoor, 2008; Csibra, 2008; Csibra et al., 2003; Csibra & Gergely, 2007; Csibra et al., 1999; Gergely, 2003; Gergely & Csibra, 2003; Gergely et al., 1995; Hernik & Southgate, 2010; Kamewari, Kato, Kanda, Ishiguro, & Hiraki, 2005; Király, 2008, 2009; Király, Jovanovic, Aschersleben, Prinz, & Gergely, 2003; Luo, in press; Luo & Baillargeon, 2005; Nielsen, 2006; Southgate, Johnson, & Csibra, 2008; Wagner & Carey, 2005).

Furthermore, some recent studies suggest that sensitivity to efficiency of goal-directed actions may be present in non-human primates also (Buttelmann, Carpenter, Call, & Tomasello, 2007, 2008; Rochat, Serra, Fadiga, & Gallese, 2008; Uller, 2004; Wood, Glynn, Phillips, & Hauser, 2007). This raises the possibility that the efficiency-based teleological action understanding is a phylogenetically ancient core cognitive adaptation (Carey, 2009; Spelke & Kinzler, 2007) that humans share with non-human primates.

Communicative agency: the natural pedagogy hypothesis. A noteworthy human-specific feature of our social-cultural environment (Gergely, 2007) is that, unlike other primates, humans routinely observe others' intentional actions in two qualitatively different input conditions: either in *non-communicative observation contexts* (say, when infants witness a goal-directed instrumental action such as "mother eating soup with a spoon"), or in *communicative demonstration contexts* (when mother demonstrates "*how to* eat soup with a spoon").

Humans seem naturally inclined to introduce and mark such communicative action displays by *ostensive behavioral signals* that are directed to the addressee (Sperber & Wilson, 1986). These ostensive cues indicate the agent's communicative intention to manifest relevant and new information about a referent "for" the child to selectively attend to and learn about (Csibra & Gergely, 2006). Human infants show species-unique innate sensitivity and preference for some ostensive signals such as eye contact, eyebrow raising, turn-taking contingent reactivity, or being addressed in "motherese" (Farroni, Csibra, Simion, & Johnson, 2002; Grossmann et al., 2008; Senju & Csibra, 2008; see Csibra & Gergely, 2006, 2009, for a review). In contrast, when adult primates perform a socially transmitted cultural skill (such as nut cracking) in front of onlooking naïve learners, they do not produce ostensive signals and do not (and possibly cannot) modify the primary functional pattern of efficient execution of their motor action scheme for purposes of demonstration (Gergely, 2007; Gergely & Csibra, 2006).

In communicative contexts ostensive cues are followed by deictic *referential gestures* (gaze-shift or pointing) designed to help the addressee to identify the referent about which relevant new knowledge is about to be manifested (Csibra, 2003; Csibra & Gergely, 2006, 2009). While primates also follow gaze, it is a uniquely human adaptation that spontaneous gaze-following in infants takes place *only if* the deictic referential cues were preceded by ostensive communicative framing cues. (For direct eye contact, see Farroni et al., 2002; Senju & Csibra, 2008; for motherese, see Senju & Csibra, 2008; for contingent reactivity, see Deligianni, Senju, Gergely, & Csibra, 2009; Johnson, Slaughter, & Carey, 1998; Movellan & Watson, 2002). Human communicative interactions also involve species-unique attention monitoring and visual checking-back behaviors to establish, direct, and maintain joint triadic attention between the communicating agent, the infant, and the referent (Tomasello et al., 2005; Tomasello, 2008).

Another species-unique feature that identifies communicative action manifestations is that they involve *marked motor transformations* of the primary functional execution pattern of the motor action schemes. Humans seem naturally inclined to produce such "marked" transformations of the execution of cultural skills when they are demonstrated in front of a naïve conspecific learner. Parents modify their actions when they ostensively demonstrate them to infants (Brand, Baldwin, & Ashburn, 2002) and infants prefer these "motionese" versions to adult-directed action demonstrations (Brand & Shallcross, 2008).

Such "manifestatively" transformed communicative action demonstrations involve schematized, partial, slowed down, repeated, or selectively exaggerated production of certain aspects of the primary motor routine. These transformations not only "mark" the action performance as a communicative demonstration (rather than primary functional use), but they are also used to background non-relevant and foreground relevant parts of the manifested skill in order to guide the naïve learner to identify and extract the relevant new information to be learned and retained (Gergely, 2007; Gergely & Unoka, 2008).

In contrast, the comparable input conditions available to primate learners of cultural skills are severely limited. The juvenile primate learner must acquire the cultural skills from conspecific users through unguided passive observation of their standard functional use and unguided attempts at their reproduction. Cultural learning in non-human primates must exclusively rely on individual observational learning mechanisms (such as associative learning, stimulus and response enhancement, emulation, or – possibly and controversially – rudimentary skills of "blind" imitation; see Gergely & Csibra, 2005, 2006 for a review).

To account for these differences, Csibra and Gergely (2006, 2009; Gergely et al., 2007) proposed that important aspects of human cultural knowledge transmission involve, and are made possible by, a *species-unique social communicative learning system* of mutual design, called *natural pedagogy*, which was selected as a domain-specific cognitive adaptation for communicative agency. The innate triggering inputs that activate this system consist of the set of ostensive cues that infants show innate sensitivity to and preference for (including direct eye contact, motherese, and turn-taking contingent reactivity). Ostensive signals are prewired to be interpreted by their addressee as indicating the agent's communicative intention to manifest new and relevant information about a referent for the infant to learn. This cue-driven social communicative learning system is hypothesized to account for infants' early recognition and functional interpretation of the kind of referent-directed action manifestations and emotion expressive gestures (as in social referencing, see Gergely et al., 2007) that agents with communicative intentions demonstrate in ostensively cued contexts of referential communication. Natural pedagogy is hypothesized to be a specialized social cognitive adaptation to enable fast and efficient social learning of *cognitively opaque cultural knowledge* that would be hard to acquire relying on purely observational learning mechanisms alone (Gergely & Csibra, 2006).

Natural pedagogy and referential communication: The "generic interpretation bias" hypothesis. A further proposal of natural pedagogy theory is that the species-unique human ability for communication is specifically adapted to fulfill the function of *transmitting generic knowledge about referent kinds* (Csibra & Gergely, 2009). This is, of course, not the only function that human communication serves: people also communicate about episodic facts to aid their cooperation (Tomasello, 2008), to manipulate each other (Sperber, 2006), to gossip (Dunbar, 1997), and for other reasons (Sperber & Wilson, 1986). Communication is a form of epistemic cooperation that can transfer relevant episodic information about specific referents as well as generic knowledge about referent kinds. To disambiguate the intended referent of a communicative act the addressee needs to rely on *pragmatic inferences* based on the other's referential signals, the already established common ground, world knowledge, or the inferred contents of the other's relevant beliefs, etc. (Sperber and Wilson, 1986).

The "generic interpretation bias" hypothesis (Csibra & Gergely, 2009) proposes that the innate ostensive cues trigger in infants a *default setting of the referential scope* of the communicative act, which is assumed to manifest new and relevant information about *generic properties of the referent kind* that the deictically indicated referent belongs to. This adaptation has two evolutionarily useful consequences. First, while non-verbal communication can only rely on deictic referential signals (gaze-shift or pointing), which by their very nature can pick out only particular referents, nevertheless, the innate default setting of the referential scope to apply to kinds allows for the fast and efficient "pedagogical" transfer of kind-generalizable information by means of ostensive- communicative referential knowledge manifestations even in preverbal infants. Second, due to its built-in "generic interpretation bias" natural pedagogy can support the communicative transfer and fast learning of generic knowledge about referent kinds (a) even when young infants may yet be unable to compute the pragmatic inferences necessary to disambiguate the intended referent, and (b) even if they cannot yet rely on their mindreading ability to infer the representational contents of the other agent's beliefs to help them in the referential disambiguation of the communicative act.

That being addressed by ostensive cues, indeed, triggers a generic interpretation bias has been demonstrated by a series of recent studies in a variety of domains showing that infants assign qualitatively different interpretations to the same intentional actions when these are presented in an ostensive communicative context versus being witnessed in non-communicative observation contexts (Csibra and Gergely, 2009). For example, selective imitative learning of cognitively "opaque" novel means actions is induced in 14-month-olds when the action demonstrations are accompanied by ostensive-referential cues (Gergely et al., 2002). However, when the same actions are observed in a non-communicative situation, infants showed no selective imitation of the "opaque" means actions (Király et al., 2004; for related findings, see Brugger, Lariviere, Mumme, & Bushnell, 2007; Király, 2008, 2009; Nielsen, 2006).

The robust perseverative search error in the classical A-not-B search task in 10-month-olds (Piaget, 1954) also turns out to be a function of the ostensive communicative context in which the object-hiding actions are typically presented in this paradigm (Topál et al., 2008; Topál et al., 2009). In the standard version of the task infants repeatedly succeed in retrieving an object that they observe being placed by a demonstrator under one of two containers (A trials). During subsequent B trials, however, when they observe the experimenter hiding the object in container B, infants continue to perseveratively (and erroneously) search at its previous hiding location (under the – now empty – container A). The perseverative error, however, is drastically reduced when the hiding actions are not accompanied by communicative cues (Topál et al., 2008; Topál et al., 2009) suggesting that the phenomenon is not due to factors such as insufficient memory or information processing skills, or lack of sufficient inhibitory control over the repeatedly primed and rewarded motor response as previously assumed (e. g., Diamond, 1985). Rather, the perseverative error seems to reflect the interpretation modulating influence of the communicative cuing context: the demonstrator's ostensive signals induce a pragmatic misinterpretation of this essentially episodic hide-and-search game as "teaching demonstrations" ("the illusion of being taught") to manifest new and relevant knowledge about some enduring functional property of the objects involved. This may have led infants to infer (and learn) from the A hiding trials that "the object 'belongs to' – is not just being presently hidden in – container A." This resulted in continued search for the object in container A (where it "ought to be") even during subsequent B trials.

In the domain of object processing, Yoon, Johnson, & Csibra (2008) demonstrated that ostensive referential gestures towards an object result in differentially inhibiting the processing of spatial information while resulting in better encoding of featural information about an object in a change detection violation-of-expectation looking time task. The opposite pattern was found, however, when the agent highlighted the object by performing a (non-communicative) goal-directed attempt to reach and grasp it with no ostensive and referential cues being present. Note that featural information (such as shape) is likely to be relevant for identifying kind-generalizable object properties, while spatial location is clearly irrelevant for that purpose. Therefore, the asymmetric pattern of processing may reflect a strategy to optimize the extraction of kind-generalizable information about the referent induced by the ostensively triggered generic interpretation bias of natural pedagogy. (Interestingly, the same effect has been recently demonstrated in adults' error patterns in a similar change-blindness object-monitoring paradigm, Marno, Csibra, & Davelaar, 2009).

In the domain of understanding artifact functions, Futó et al. (2009a, 2009b) recently applied the object individuation paradigm (Xu and Carey, 1996) to demonstrate that ostensive cuing (being addressed in motherese) can induce kind-based object individuation already in 10-month-olds. Two different novel artifacts were sequentially brought out at either one or the other side of an occluder by a hand that performed a different action on each resulting in the consequent display of a different sensory effect by the given artifact. When a female voice greeted the infant in motherese before the artifacts were brought out, infants interpreted the two different functional uses as providing generic information about separate kind-individuating functional properties specifying two different artifact kinds to which the particular artifacts were represented to belong. As a result, infants inferred that there must be *two* objects behind the occluder showing increased looking times when only one was revealed during the test phase. In contrast, in the non-ostensive cueing condition (where instead of motherese, a synthesized mechanical non-speech sound transform was presented) the 10-month-olds showed no object individuation (i.e., they did not expect two objects behind the screen). This suggests that they interpreted the two manual actions as different episodic functional uses of the *same* object when it appeared at one or the other side of the screen. Note that in this study the ostensively induced kind-based object individuation effect was demonstrated in 10-month-olds *without* the two objects being named by different linguistic labels when presented. This suggests that it is ostensive communicative reference that facilitates kind assignment under 12 months rather than linguistic labeling per se as was previously proposed (Xu, 2002, 2007).

In the domain of object-directed emotion expressions Gergely et al. (2007) found that when 14- month-olds observe others' ostensively cued object-referential emotion displays, they tend to interpret these emotion gestures as conveying valence information about the properties of the object rather than expressing the person-specific subjective attitude of the communicator towards the referent. In fact, Egyed et al. (2007) showed that 18-month-olds readily generalize the valence information that the agent communicatively displays about the object as being relevant to other people's object-directed actions as well. However, when they observe the agent's identical object-directed attitude expressions in a non-communicative context, they attribute it as her person-specific subjective preference, but do not interpret the valence information as a property of the referent object and do not generalize the displayed object-directed attitudes to others.

The developmental integration of the teleological stance and natural pedagogy with mindreading. Csibra and Gergely (2006) argue that in their early ontogenetic use (just as during the periods of evolutionary past when they originally became selected) both the infant's teleological stance and the system of natural pedagogy can function without having to rely on the infant's mindreading ability. In this view, the infant's naïve "theory of mind" can be considered as a biological adaptation that is *external* to the two specialized systems in question. As soon as the mindreading system comes online, however, its outputs can be made available to and can become used by either system. This can be expected to occur to the degree that the representational contents of the other's attributed mental states specify relevant types of information that are normally accessed by the two action interpretational systems and – by being added to their relevant database – their functional efficacy or scope of application is going to be increased.

For example, the infant's teleological stance (Gergely & Csibra, 2003) is hypothesized to be a non-mentalistic reality-based inferential and representational mechanism that assigns teleological representations to goal-directed actions of instrumental agents *without* making reference, or presupposing access to the representational contents of their mental states. The system identifies the teleological properties of goal-directed actions in terms of built-in basic assumptions about rational agency and the requirement of efficiency of goal approach. If the efficiency criterion is met by the observed behavior, the action becomes represented in terms of the domain-specific innate representational categories (agent, means action, and goal) that are assigned to the relevant *perceptible* aspects (actor, behavior, and outcome) of the observed action. Importantly, while the assignment of these built-in representational categories confers abstract conceptual content that captures the teleological properties of actions, it does so *without* presupposing the availability or necessarily relying on the contents of the agent's mental representations of reality.

It is assumed, however, that if and when the mindreading system starts to compute and deliver representations that specify relevant representational contents of the agent's epistemic mind states (such as her false beliefs about the relevant constraints of the situation), these mental representations of reality could become accessed and usefully integrated as part of the relevant database over which the agent's rational choice of means–ends action gets evaluated. To this degree the teleological stance will become transformed into a mentalistic intentional stance as illustrated by figure 3.1. (cf. Gergely & Csibra, 2003).

Criteria for an Adequate Developmental Theory of Understanding Intentional Agency

There are three main functional requirements that an adaptive developmental system specialized for representing intentional agency must be able to accomplish. First, it needs to be equipped with *perceptual input mechanisms* that allow for the identification of the range of entities that belong to its domain. Second it must be able to generate *inferences and predictions* on the basis of domain-specific principles about the behavior of such entities. Third, it must function as a *domain-specific learning device* that can extract and

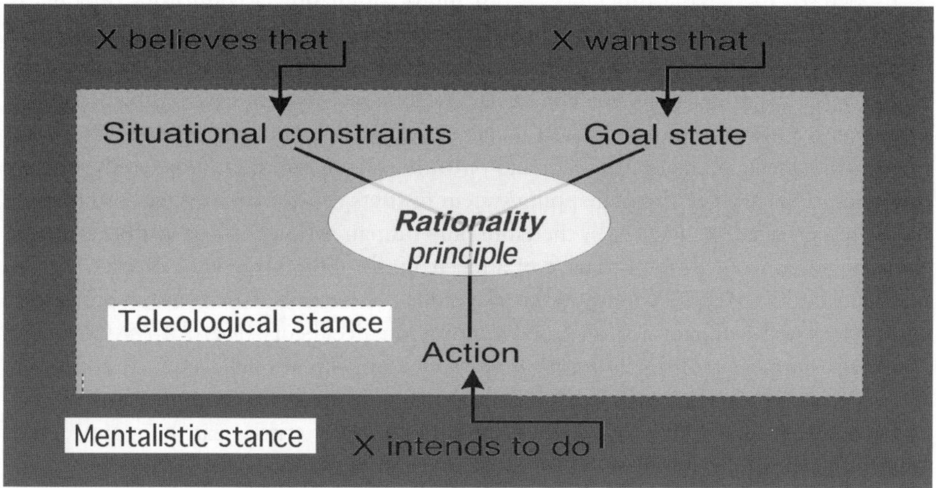

Figure 3.1 Teleological and mentalistic representations of actions. Teleological representations provide explanations and predictions for observed actions by relating three aspects of reality via the rationality principle. Mentalistic action representations involve three types of intentional mental states whose contents correspond to the representational elements of teleological action representations

represent the relevant properties of and accumulate generalizable knowledge about the entities and their kinds that constitute its domain. By now a large body of evidence indicates that human infants exhibit precocious competence in all these three areas of adaptive functioning in the domain of intentional agency already during the first 2 years of life. Below I shall examine how the different theoretical approaches to understanding intentional agency can account for these early signs of adaptedness and the rich range of competences that even young preverbal infants' demonstrate when interpreting the intentional actions of other agents they observe, react to, or interact with.

Identifying intentional agency: self-propulsion versus rational choice of action

How do infants identify the entities that belong to the domain of intentional agency? Carey and Spelke (1994) differentiated two types of models for how domain-specific perception and reasoning may be related in a given domain. The *feature-based approach* specifies domain-specific perceptual input systems sensitive to innate featural or behavioral cues identifying objects as belonging to the domain. In this view, cue-based identification and categorization of an object as belonging to the domain is a precondition for applying domain-specific principles of reasoning to interpret its behavior. In contrast, according to the *principle-based approach* the scope of a domain is not specified in terms of featural properties; rather, an object is identified as a member of a given domain by the successful *applicability of the principles of reasoning specific to the domain* (Csibra et al., 1999; Gergely & Csibra, 2003; Keil, 1994).

In spite of their basic differences, both motor-simulation accounts and modularist "theory of mind" approaches subscribe to the first alternative of cue-based identification of objects as intentional agents. However, the kinds of cues and input analyzer systems they propose are rather different. For Meltzoff's "like me" hypothesis, it is the perception of human features and biomechanical movements that generate the "like me" categorization of the object, by mapping such cues onto the corresponding motor representations of the self. This built-in direct mapping system restricts the domain of agency to humans (who are perceived as "like me"), therefore only human actions will be attributed intentionality (in contrast to the behavior of a mechanical robot, Meltzoff, 1995b).

Woodward's (1998; Woodward et al., 2001) experience-based motor-simulation approach as well as mirror neuron-based motor resonance theory (Rizzolatti & Craighero, 2004) also propose an initially *narrow-scope domain* of intentional agency. According to these accounts only those observed actions will be understood as intentional and goal-directed whose features and behavioral movement characteristics can be mapped by a "direct matching" mechanism onto already existing motor action schemes of the self. The set of actions recognizable as intentional increases only slowly and gradually with experience-based motor learning of new types of goal-directed actions.

In contrast to this narrow-scope view of the initial domain of agency, the abstract behavioral cue of *self-propelled movement* that the modularist theory-of-mind approach (Leslie, 1994; Premack, 1990; Premack & Premack, 1995; Baron-Cohen, 1994) proposes as the innate triggering condition for attributing agency is clearly compatible with a *wide-scope domain* of agency from the beginning. Leslie's (1994) domain-specific core cognitive "theory of agency" module includes an innate motion analyzer input mechanism that is triggered by objects exhibiting *self-initiated movement* inducing their categorization as mechanical agents possessing "internal and renewable energy, or FORCE." This representational output provides the input to the next subsystem that represents *intentional agents with teleological action properties* characterized by goal pursuit and the ability to act and re-act in relation to distal causal events. In the modularist models of Premack (1990) and Baron-Cohen (1994) the detection of self-propulsion directly triggers the categorization of the object as "intentional agent."

In contrast to these cue-based approaches, Gergely and Csibra's (2003) teleological-stance model assumes that objects are identified as goal-directed agents by the successful application of the same *principle-based inferential process* that attributes goals to actions based on evaluating their efficiency in bringing about their outcome states as a function of situational constraints. Thus, recognizing and representing an object as an agent and attributing a goal to its actions are part and parcel of the same efficiency-based teleological action interpretation process of which agency detection is not a precondition but a consequence. The development of the teleological-stance model was initially motivated by the realization that self-propulsion is not a sufficient basis for identifying intentional agents and attributing specific goals to their actions (Gergely & Csibra, 1997, 2003; Gergely et al., 1995). Csibra et al. (1999) and Bíró et al. (2007) directly tested the role of self-initiated movement as a cue to goal-attribution and found that self-propulsion is neither sufficient nor necessary for attributing goals to actions. These studies also show that apart from self-propulsion, other movement cues of animacy such as variability of movement, and even (unjustified) equifinal target approach also fail to provide sufficient grounds for goal attribution. For example, in spite of its familiarity, the hand action of grasping an object is *not* interpreted as goal-directed in the Woodward (1998) paradigm if this outcome (object grasped) is achieved as the end result of unnecessary and therefore unjustifiable and inefficient preceding actions, as when a hand first opens a transparent empty box before grasping the target object that is *in front of* the box (unjustifiable non-efficient target-approach condition). The same sequence of actions, however, does induce the goal-attribution effect when the object is *inside* the box (justifiable efficient means action condition) (Bíró & Verschoor, 2008; see also Hernik & Southgate, 2010).

In contrast, even 6- and 9-month-olds interpret a wide range of unfamiliar objects (such as a robot, a box, or abstract 2-D figures) as goal-directed agents as long as their behaviors exhibit rational sensitivity to relevant changes in their situational constraints by modifying their target-directed approach contingently and in a justifiable manner obeying the efficiency principle (Bíró et al., 2007; Csibra, 2008; Csibra et al., 2003; Csibra et al., 1999; Gergely, 2003; Gergely et al., 1995; Kamewari et al., 2005; Luo & Baillargeon, 2005; Wagner & Carey, 2005). These studies provide convergent evidence demonstrating that young infants are ready to interpret unfamiliar entities such as inanimate objects, abstract 2-D figures, humanoid robots, unfamiliar human actions, and even biomechanically impossible hand actions (Southgate et al., 2008) as goal-directed as long as they show evidence of context-sensitive justifiable variation of action obeying the principle of efficiency of goal approach. In other words, what seems to be criterial for attributing intentionality and goal-directedness is evidence indicating the ability for *rational choice* among the accessible action alternatives by reliably performing the most efficient action available to bring about the goal state across changing environmental constraints.

Goal attribution versus preference attribution: the role of perception of rational choice

A different kind of demonstration showing that evidence supporting the interpretation of *rational choice* of action is at the core of attributing intentionality comes from recent reinterpretations of the two-object Woodward (1998) paradigm as actually testing for *preference attribution* (Luo & Baillargeon, 2005) rather than goal attribution per se as previously thought (Woodward et al., 2001). As shown by both Luo and Baillargeon (2005) and Hernik and Southgate (2010), if in a modified version of the Woodward paradigm only one object A is present during the initial target approaches in familiarization trials and it is only during the test phase that the alternative target B is introduced (at which point the positions of the two objects are exchanged) infants do *not* show the "goal-attribution" effect found by Woodward (1998). This indicates that the initial presence of *two* alternative targets (A and B) in the Woodward paradigm invites the interpretation of the agent's repeated approach of one of them rather than the other as exhibiting "choice" or "preference" by the agent. Furthermore, to interpret the asymmetric target approach as a choice between the two alternative target objects that reflects the agent's preference for one of them, it seems to be a precondition to categorize the agent as being capable of rational choice on the basis of additional evidence such as previous relevant experience with the agent (as in the case of the hand-grasping actions presented by Woodward, 1998), or by the agent's exhibiting justifiable variation of the target approach that indicates choice of action based on efficiency and sensitivity to contextual constraints (Bíró & Verschoor, 2008; Hernik & Southgate, 2010), or, interestingly, on the basis of evidence that the agent is capable of engaging in *turn-taking contingent reactivity at a distance* (Johnson, Shimizu, & Ok, 2007). This latter cue can be hypothesized to provide a different kind of behavioral evidence for rational choice that relies not on the criterion of efficiency of goal-approach (that belongs to the proper domain of instrumental agency), but on the criterion of non-random variation of behavioral displays to establish a *distal causal contingency relation* (see Watson, 1995), such as the turn-taking contingent reactivity of Johnson et al. (2007). Note that according to natural pedagogy theory (Csibra & Gergely, 2006, 2009) the perception of turn-taking contingent reactivity at a distance is one of the innate ostensive cues triggering the recognition of communicative agency (Deligianni et al., 2009).

Preverbal Understanding of Other Minds: The Beginnings of a Paradigm Change? (2005–)

During the last few years the previously dominant view that representing others' representational mind states develops only by 4 years of age (as evidenced by passing the standard false-belief tasks) has become seriously challenged by the accumulation of significant new evidence generated by employing non-verbal versions of the false-belief paradigm. These studies suggest that infants during their second year of life and possibly even preverbal infants before their first birthday may be capable of representing other agents' false beliefs (Buttelmann, Carpenter, & Tomasello, 2009; Kovács, Téglás, & Endress, 2009a, 2009b; Onishi & Baillargeon, 2005; Scott & Baillargeon, in press; Song, Onishi, Baillargeon, & Fisher, 2008; Southgate, Chevallier, & Csibra, in press; Southgate, Senju, & Csibra, 2007; Surian, Caldi, & Sperber, 2007; see Caron, 2009, for a recent review). In a similar vein, a recent looking-time study indicated that even pretense actions can be understood mentalistically by 15-month-olds (i.e., before infants actively produce pretense actions themselves) (Onishi, Baillargeon, & Leslie, 2007).

Additional support for this newly emerging picture comes from studies showing that certain component competences presupposed by mindreading also show a much earlier onset than previously believed. For example, understanding the referential nature of gaze seems present already in 8-month-olds (Csibra & Volein, 2008; Senju, Csibra, & Johnson, 2008) as also indicated by converging neurological evidence from event-related potential (ERP) studies with 9-month-olds (Senju, Johnson, & Csibra, 2006). Further studies indicate that during the second year infants understand the seeing–knowing relation mentalistically as shown by attributing to others knowledge about some specific aspect of reality as a function of previous perceptual access (Luo & Baillargeon, 2007; Moll & Tomasello, 2007; Tomasello & Haberl, 2003).

Maybe the most striking evidence to date suggesting that the basic representational preconditions for false-belief attribution are present already at 7 months comes from the recent studies of Kovács et al. (2009a, 2009b) using a simple object-detection procedure (applied both to 7-month-olds and adults). While this paradigm does not require the subject to infer the belief states of others, the results nevertheless imply that the mere presence of another agent (who is potentially co-witnessing the event the subject observes) is sufficient to trigger an automatic process of computing that agent's representations of reality. The evidence suggests that after the agent leaves the scene, the contents of her representations of reality are maintained in the subject's memory and can be demonstrated to be present even when the states of affairs represented by the (now absent) agent no longer obtain (i.e., when there is a change in the event the subject is observing, which takes place after the agent has left). The subjects watch a video display in which in the presence of another agent a ball moves behind an occluding screen. By introducing subsequent changes in the event (e.g., the agent leaving the scene before or after the ball's rolling out of occlusion and disappearing), Kovács et al. could test whether – when the occluder was lowered to reveal the presence or absence of the ball – the adults' object-detection latencies or the 7-month-olds' looking times were influenced similarly when their own representation of reality was violated by the outcome, and when the representation of reality as the agent last saw it before leaving the scene was violated. The results indicate that both types of violation had a significant and similar effect on both the adults' detection latencies and the 7-month-olds' looking times, suggesting that the representation of the event as last witnessed by the agent before leaving was automatically computed and maintained and could exert an influence on the subject's behavior even when its contents mismatched the subject's own (updated) representation of the event.

Is the capacity to mindread non-human-specific?

A further contribution to the current atmosphere of paradigm change comes from the groundbreaking recent advances reported by comparative psychologists working with primate and avian minds as well as with dogs and goats. Not so long ago the generally shared view held that even chimpanzees lack the cognitive abilities involved in humans' understanding of goals, intentions, attention, and perception in others (Povinelli, 2000; Povinelli & Eddy, 1996; Tomasello & Call, 1997). This view has dramatically changed, however, as a result of recent findings that indicate an evolved sensitivity to gaze-direction and unobstructed line of regard, and an ability to infer referential information from other conspecifics' gaze-direction and perceptual access, not only in primates, but also in ravens, scrub-jays, goats, and dogs (Brauer, Kaminski, Riedel, Call, & Tomasello, 2006; Bugnyar & Heinrich, 2005; Bugnyar, Stowe, & Heinrich, 2004; Call & Tomasello, 2008; Clayton, Dally, & Emery, 2007; Clayton & Emery, 2008; Emery & Clayton, 2001; Flombaum & Santos, 2005; Hare, Call, Agnetta, & Tomasello, 2000; Hare, Call, & Tomasello, 2001; Kaminski, Call, & Tomasello, 2008; Kaminski, Riedel, Call, & Tomasello, 2005; Lakatos, Soproni, Doka, & Miklosi, 2009; Santos, Nissen, & Ferrugia, 2006; Tomasello et al., 2005). In particular, apes have been shown to follow gaze with referential expectations to find an object where the other is looking, and they also look behind barriers to find the object the other is gazing at (Call & Tomasello, 2008). Ravens monitor other conspecifics' presence and direction of gaze when they hide food, choosing hiding places that do not fall within the unobstructed line of regard of the onlooking competitor (Bugnyar & Heinrich, 2005; Bugnyar et al., 2004). Scrub-jays return to re-cache their food to a new location if they notice that their initial caching was observed by a conspecific (Clayton et al., 2007; Clayton & Emery, 2008; Emery & Clayton, 2001). Hare et al. (2000, 2001) demonstrated that subordinate chimps monitor whether a dominant chimp sees when a piece of food is hidden behind a barrier, and approach it in the dominant's presence only if the latter did not witness the hiding (or the later displacement) of the food.

These results have significantly transformed the current view about non-human species' abilities to understand intentional agency. This is well illustrated by the conclusion of Call and Tomasello's (2008) recent review of the primate literature: "there is solid evidence from several different experimental paradigms that chimpanzees understand the goals and intentions of others, as well as the perception and knowledge of others. Nevertheless … there is currently no evidence that chimpanzees understand false beliefs." (p. 6).

No doubt, in the light of these new developments many aspects of our recent theories about the origins of understanding intentional agency in humans may need to be reassessed. Below I shall consider some new theoretical questions raised by the recent evidence indicating preverbal mindreading abilities in human infants on the one hand, and the apparent presence of several component abilities for understanding intentional agency in non-human primates and other species on the other.

Do we share a core knowledge system of intentional agency with non-human primates?

The theory of "core knowledge systems" is a framework theory about the phylogenetic foundations of human cognition (Carey, 2009; Carey & Spelke, 1994; Spelke, 2000; Spelke & Kinzler, 2007). Its central assumption is that humans are innately endowed with a small number of domain-specific core knowledge systems for representing basic domains of cognition such as objects, actions, number, and space. These core cognitive systems are characterized by the common properties of having deep roots in phylogeny that humans share with other species, by the fact that they are active very early in life, and by the fact that they are prewired and modular systems whose built-in structural and functional architecture – such as their input analyzers, inferential principles, and output representations – remains unchanged and continues to function unmodified throughout the lifespan. The "strong" interpretation of the core knowledge approach, which assumes full phylogenetic continuity in the core domains across species, is well characterized by Spelke & Kinzler (2007), according to whom

> each system centers on a set of principles that serves to individuate the entities in its domain and to support inferences about the entities' behavior. Each system, moreover, is characterized by a set of signature limits that allow investigators to identify the system across tasks, ages, species, and human cultures. (p. 89)

The recent findings of the ontogenetically early emergence and probably cross-species presence of innate sensitivity to others' attentional and perceptual states and the capacity to attribute knowledge versus ignorance to others prompted leading theorists of the core cognitive systems approach to propose that humans share with non-human primates a domain-specific core system of phylogenetically ancient adaptations to represent intentional agency (Carey, 2009; Spelke & Kinzler, 2007). Spelke and Kinzler (2007) propose that the core properties of this system,

> goal directedness, efficiency, contingency, reciprocity, and gaze direction, provide signatures of agent representations that allow for their study in non-human animals and human adults. Newly hatched chicks, rhesus monkeys, and chimpanzees are sensitive to what their predators or competitors can and cannot see. (p. 90)

It seems clear that the core knowledge proposal makes a significant theoretical contribution in so far as it emphasizes that several aspects of our early understanding of intentional agency have their phylogenetic roots in the domain-specific cognitive adaptations of our primate ancestors. To focus on the ancient adaptations that we share with primates is entirely justified given that the competence of primates in understanding goal-directed actions and showing functional sensitivity to certain intentional agent–object relations involving attentional orientation and perceptual access have been seriously underestimated until recent advances in comparative primatology (see Call & Tomasello, 2008). This granted, I'll nevertheless argue that there are reasons to be cautious about extending the strong version of the phylogenetic continuity hypothesis to the domain of intentional agency by analogy with the other core domains of cognition. This principle (which forms the heart of the core knowledge approach, see Spelke & Kinzler, 2007) certainly rests on sufficiently firm empirical grounds in the other basic domains that core knowledge theory has been originally proposed for, such as physical objects (Spelke, Breilinger, Macomber, & Jacobsen, 1992) or numerosity (Carey, 2009; Dehaene, 2001). In comparison, given the current state of – clearly intriguing, but in important respects still meager – comparative evidence on the shared properties of understanding intentional mind states of others across human and non-human primate species, to postulate "a core system of agent representation that is evolutionarily ancient and that persists over human development" (Spelke & Kinzler, 2007, p. 90) may turn out to be a somewhat premature, and potentially more misleading than fruitful, theoretical strategy. The danger is that conceptualizing the phylogenetic groundedness of our mindreading ability in terms of a prewired and shared core knowledge system for representing agency may inadvertently lead us to underestimate the possibly significant modifications and enrichments in this domain that were selected only during hominid evolution. These later and human-specific adaptations may have resulted in qualitative transformations of the structural properties, representational power, and functional scope of the originally much more restricted concept of agency that we have inherited from our primate ancestors.

Carey (2009) was clearly aware of this problem when developing her own version of applying the core cognitive systems approach to the domain of intentional agency. Similarly to Spelke & Kinzler (2007) she also argues that "like object representations, core cognition of agency has a long evolutionary past" and hypothesizes that humans share a common core system of representing agency with their primate ancestors who "represent conspecifics and human beings as agents with goals, perceptions and attentional states." However, making reference to different recent proposals made by Tomasello et al. (2005) on the one hand, and by Gergely & Csibra (2006) on the other, Carey goes on to add that unlike in the case of object representations,

> it is likely that hominid evolution contributed to the enrichment of core cognition of intentional agency. It is true that primates do not generally establish joint attention, do not show and point out things to each other, do not teach, do not generally engage in cooperative problem solving, and do not analyze others' action in service of imitation. (Carey, 2009, p. 203)

Below I'll go a step further in emphasizing the potentially significant evolutionary *differences* between the evolved systems for understanding agency in non-human primates on the one hand, and human infants on the other. One reading of Carey's (2009) suggestion that more recent "hominid evolution contributed to the enrichment of core cognition of intentional agency" is that these "enrichments" correspond to the separate human-specific adaptations to communicative agency discussed earlier. These include our species-unique sensitivity to and functional reliance on an innate set of ostensive cues for identifying agents with communicative intentions; the human-specific competence to engage in epistemic communicative exchanges to transfer relevant and new information about referents and their kinds between conspecifics; and the capacity to interpret ostensive referential acts of communication through drawing pragmatic inferences to disambiguate and represent the referential intentions of communicative agents (as proposed by the theories of Csibra & Gergely, 2006, 2009; Sperber & Wilson, 1986; Tomasello, 2008; and Tomasello et al., 2005).

This would, of course, still allow for the other major component of the human core concept of agency, the efficiency-based teleological action interpretation mechanism (that may have evolved separately as an earlier adaptation to represent the goal-directed actions of instrumental agents, see Gergely & Csibra, 2003) to meet the strong criterion of the core knowledge hypothesis (Spelke & Kinzler, 2007) that requires full phylogenetic continuity of domain-specific systems that are shared and identical across human and non-human primate species. In contrast to this view, I shall argue below that even human infants' domain-specific "theory of rational action" (as implemented in their teleological stance for interpreting goal-directed actions, Gergely & Csibra, 1997, 2003) involves significant evolutionary transformations that have qualitatively changed the representational and inferential properties of human teleo-functional reasoning when compared to the system of "primate teleology" that forms its ancient phylogenetic roots that we inherited from our ancestors.

Teleology "Ungrounded": Differences Between Human and Primate Understanding of Instrumental Agency

As argued earlier, sensitivity to efficiency of goal-directed actions seems present in non-human primates (Buttelmann et al., 2007, 2008; Rochat et al., 2008; Uller, 2004; Wood et al., 2007). Primates also exhibit some level of teleo-functional understanding of means–end relations and physical affordance properties of objects that they use as temporary "tools." For example, from objects (such as stones or sticks) lying around a locally visible goal, they can choose as their "tool" the physically most affordant one to achieve the goal. Apes can also make simple functional modifications in the physical properties of such objects to make them more affordant when guided by the visible properties of a locally present goal (Boesch & Boesch, 1993; Goodall, 1986; Tomasello & Call, 1997). However, after having used the object to attain their goal, they tend to simply discard it. This can be considered evidence for a goal-activated, situationally restricted and temporally fleeting "teleological mode" of object construal.

This "primate teleology," however, is arguably severely restricted in at least three important respects when compared to the teleological action interpretation system of human infants (Gergely & Csibra, 2003) or, for that matter, to the teleo-functional reasoning skills and representational abilities of our hominid ancestors that we can reconstruct from the archeological evidence on hominid tool use and tool manufacturing practices (Gergely & Csibra, 2006; McGrew, 1996, 2004; Mithen, 1996, 2002; Schick & Toth, 1993; Semaw, 2000). First, *teleological inferencing is unidirectional* in primates: it is restricted to *goal-to-means inferences* that are guided by the visual properties of a locally present goal. Second, primate teleology has *restricted input conditions*: it is activated only in the visual presence of specific goals. Third, the representational contents of goals are likely to be *anchored to specific content-domains* such as food, mating partners, predator avoidance, etc.

In contrast, the archeological record implies that our hominid ancestors already possessed a teleo-functional reasoning system that was *inferentially multi-directional* allowing not only for goal-triggered local and transient inferences from *goal to means*, but also for applying the teleological stance in the absence of visible goals to examine and contemplate physical objects as potential tools. This required the "inverse" direction of teleological reasoning: *making inferences from means to goal.* The inverse inferential use of teleology entails that a remarkable cognitive transformation must have taken place in the implementation of our inherited teleological system during our hominid evolutionary past. This has "ungrounded" the ancient teleological system we shared with our primate ancestors, which had been evolutionarily anchored as a goal-triggered unidirectional inferential mechanism. In other words, the resulting systematization of teleological inferencing must have involved a cognitive *reversal of teleological perspective* that allowed our hominid ancestors to create new tools in the absence of locally visible goals and to represent such tools as having permanent functions (Csibra & Gergely, 2006).

As evidenced in the archaeological record, this led to the enduring teleo-functional conceptualization of objects *as* tools, which was manifested in routine behaviors such as keeping tools instead of discarding them after use, storing them at specific locations, or prefabricating the tools at one location and carrying them for long distances for their functional application at a different place). This apparently human-specific *systematization of teleological reasoning* allowed hominids to take an active teleo-functional stance towards novel physical objects and materials found at new and distant locations, whose sight could activate the question: "What purpose could I use this object for?" (Csibra & Gergely, 2007). This *inverse teleological inferencing* required imaginatively "conjuring up" memory representations of potential goals in relation to which the physical-causal properties of the object could be mentally evaluated in terms of the efficiency principle and represented as affordance properties of a potential tool.

The cognitive reversal of teleological perspective also provided the representational and inferential preconditions for the emergence of *recursive teleology* (Csibra & Gergely, 2006) in hominid artifact culture that involved *using tools to make other tools* without the visible presence of local goals (Schick & Toth, 1993). For this to come about a further significant cognitive transformation of teleology was necessary: *the representation of the concept of goals had to become ungrounded* from the domain-specific content constraints that the restricted range of goals representable by primate teleology had been evolutionarily anchored to. In other words, to conceptualize the hierarchical structure of complex chains of means–end skills that "recursive" tool use requires, and to flexibly generate and represent a variety of sub-goal-final-goal structural sequences, goal representations had to become *abstract and content free*. This allowed for the specific content represented as a goal state to be identified solely as a function of the successful application of the efficiency requirements of the teleological principle of rational action.

These non-trivial inferential and representational features that differentiate hominid from primate teleology seem also to characterize the teleological action interpretation system of 6–12-month-old preverbal infants as demonstrated in violation-of-expectation studies using visual presentation of incomplete goal-directed actions as stimuli (Csibra, 2008; Csibra et al., 2003; Csibra et al., 1999; Gergely & Csibra, 2003; Gergely et al., 1995; Luo, in press). As schematically depicted in figure 3.2, these studies provide evidence that young infants can draw all the three basic types of teleological inferences that are supported by their naïve "theory of rational action." Given perceptual information about the contents of any two of the three representational categories of their teleological action representational system (means action, goal, or situational constraints), they can make inferences to identify the likely content of the third (that is not directly observable in the action display) (see Gergely & Csibra, 2003). This *multidirectionality of teleological inferences indicates a systematization of the teleological action interpretation system* that is

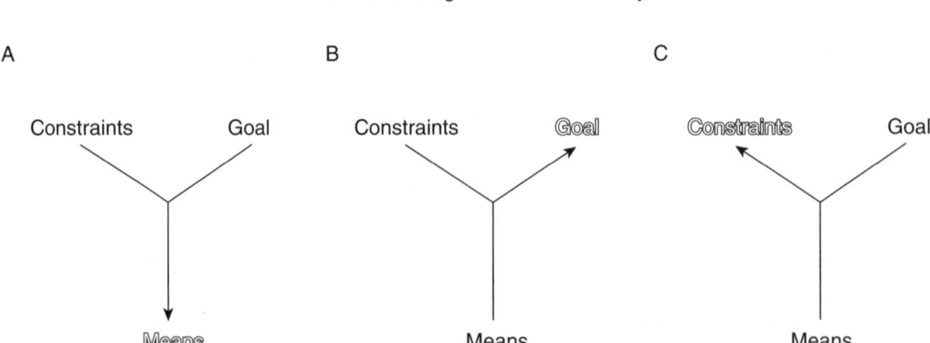

Figure 3.2 Types of inferences supported by the infant's naïve "theory of rational action": The inferential generativity and systematicity of the teleological stance in infancy

lacking from the more ancient primate teleology that forms our shared phylogenetic heritage. The experiments demonstrating such teleological inferences in young infants can be modeled and have been successfully simulated in a Bayesian probabilistic framework for goal inference based on the notion of inverse planning, in which observers invert a probabilistic generative model of goal-dependent plans to infer agents' goals (Baker, Tenenbaum, & Saxe, 2006, 2007). Evidence reviewed earlier demonstrating the "wide scope" of human infants' teleological stance (e. g., Csibra, 2008; Southgate et al., 2008) also suggests that humans apply from very early on an *ungrounded abstract and content-free goal concept* where the outcome states that can be represented as goals are identified solely as a function of the perceived efficiency of the goal approach within the relevant constraints of reality.

Food for thought: alternative ways of representing agent–object intentional relations in primates

Another area of apparently shared cross-species competence that is referred to as motivating the extension of the phylogenetic continuity hypothesis of the core knowledge approach to the domain of representing agency (Carey, 2009; Spelke & Kinzler, 2007) is the ability to attribute epistemic mental states (such as knowledge versus ignorance) to others. The evidence consists of the important discovery that non-human primates (as well as other phylogenetically unrelated social species including birds, dogs, and goats) have convergently evolved specialized mechanisms for detecting and representing the unobstructed (and invisible) line of regard that functionally connects conspecific agents to distal objects and events in their environment as a function of their attentional and perceptual orientation. Representing such distal agent–object relations, as well as the situational conditions under which they are established, remain maintained over time, or get reactivated, supports the highly adaptive capacity of these species to anticipate the functional consequences that their presence or reinstatement entails. Given the available evidence it certainly seems justified and uncontroversial, therefore, to suggest that the evolved mechanism that is sensitive to and represents the abstract cue of "unobstructed line of regard" as a functional connection between agents and distal objects is part of our phylogenetically ancient adaptation that we share with primates (and other species) and that forms the roots of our – possibly later emerging – human mindreading competence.

The core knowledge hypothesis, however, claims significantly more than that when it follows the theoretical strategy of collapsing these respective competences into one phylogenetically ancient hardwired core knowledge system that is proposed to underlie the basic capacity to monitor and represent the epistemic mind states of other agents both in non-human and human primate species. This strong hypothesis rests, however, solely on the intriguing functional similarities between some of the adaptive behaviors that are mediated by mental state attributions in humans and those recently demonstrated in several non-human species in relation to the attentional orientation and uninterrupted perceptual connectedness of conspecifics to distal states of reality. It should be emphasized though that the apparent functional equivalence of these adaptive behaviors in non-human species does not entail that they are necessarily mediated by the same domain-specific core representational mechanisms which underlie human infants' early emerging ability to infer and represent the mental contents of other agents' epistemic states.

First of all, in spite of a great deal of effort, no successful and replicable demonstration of false-belief attribution has been demonstrated in great apes (Call & Tomasello, 2008). Of course, it could still be proposed that – apart from this "small" difference – the rest of our mindreading abilities (such as monitoring, representing, and updating other agents' mental states of knowledge versus ignorance about specific aspects of reality in their distal environment) may, nevertheless, be shared with our primate ancestors consisting of ancient adaptations that are not only sensitive to other agents' attentional orientation and unobstructed perceptual access to distal states of reality, but also interpret these as the causal conditions and inferential bases for attributing knowledge representations to the other's mind.

Note, however, that this theoretical stance may turn out to be reinforcing an unjustified anthropomorphic over-attribution to our primate ancestors of our human-specific obsession with monitoring other minds in order to infer, represent, and update the epistemic contents of their belief representations. This cannot be ruled out as long as there remain other plausible mechanisms that have not yet been explored and empirically tested, but that could provide an alternative account for the apparent functional similarity of the adaptive reactions that non-human species exhibit when registering and representing the attentional and perceptual relatedness of other agents to distal aspects of their environment. (For a recent proposal in this direction, see Gómez, 2008).

To illustrate this point let us assume, for example, that non-human primates apply a *naïve theory of food* instead of a naïve theory of mind as an adaptive mechanism to deal with the contingencies of a social environment that is highly competitive over food resources. This could result from the selection of an adaptive strategy to monitor and represent the relevant properties of items (or sources) of food, such as their location, quantity, elapsed time of presence at location (the basis for attributing dispositional properties relevant for their palatability, such as rotting or drying out), and other relevant environmental constraints (such as being placed behind the south side of a barrier – say, a rock – which blocks uninterrupted line of regard becoming established between the food and a potential conspecific appearing from the north side). If the primate observer subsequently detects an onlooking conspecific located at the east side, it will register the uninterrupted line of regard between the food and the particular conspecific at that location. This distal relatedness between the food and the conspecific at their respective locations will become represented as a *dispositional property attributed to the monitored food item* (and *not* to the mind of the conspecific). Such a representation would imply that as long as the same environmental conditions continue to obtain or become reinstated in the future by the conspecific's return (given that the food item's location has not been changed in the meantime), the primate observer could (correctly) anticipate that the food will be approached and consumed by the conspecific. Whether the reader finds this a plausible interpretation or not (and why not?), it certainly identifies an alternative representational mechanism to attributing knowledge states to the minds of others that could account for the kinds of functional behavioral reactions exhibited, for example, by juvenile apes in the studies by Hare et al. (2000). The juvenile who observes the food item being hidden behind one of two barriers (barrier A) in the presence of an onlooking alpha male positioned on the opposite side, will represent the food as having become distally connected to the dominant male on the other side of the barriers. So when the same dominant conspecific later returns, the juvenile will be able to anticipate – based solely on its representation of the food item as being distally related the dominant – that it will be approached by the other. As a result, the juvenile itself will refrain from approaching the food. When, however, the food's location is later observed to be changed by being displaced from barrier A to its new position behind barrier B (when the dominant male is not present anymore), this spatial change in the location of the food will "erase" the representation of its previously attributed dispositional property of "being distally connected" to the dominant. Therefore, upon the latter's return the juvenile will feel safe to approach the food item at its new position.

This model of representing the detected uninterrupted line of regard between the monitored food item and a particular conspecific present as a dispositional property of the *food* could also account for the early return of the scrub-jay to re-cache a food item whose initial caching was observed to fall within the line of regard of an onlooking conspecific during its earlier caching (Clayton et al., 2007; Emery & Clayton, 2001). In this framework, the re-caching of the food item is carried out to change its dispositional state of being distally related to the other conspecific so that this outdated dispositional property will be erased from its representation, making it safe for the scrub-jay to return for the food later.

Note that the application of the naïve "theory of food" as it is outlined in the speculative account above could explain these highly adaptive functional reactions by monitoring and representing dispositional properties of food *without* involving a core mechanism that would monitor and represent the epistemic mind states of other conspecifics. My point is simply that this alternative – to my knowledge – has not yet been experimentally tested and ruled out, and before this kind of evidence becomes available it may be unwise to make the premature inferential leap to postulate ancient domain-specific core mechanisms of an implicit "theory of mind" to our primate ancestors (who may get around just as well using their own non-human naïve "theory of food").

In sum, given the current state of evidence it remains a distinct empirical possibility that important aspects of human theory of mind emerged only during hominid evolution resulting in a significant transformation and "enrichment" of the inferential and representational properties of our domain-specific phylogenetically ancient and shared adaptations for representing distal agent–object functional relations based on attentional orientation and unobstructed line of regard. Clearly, both joint cooperative actions and ostensive communicative acts of referential information exchange require humans to constantly monitor, infer, and update the representational contents of their communicative partners' mental states. This makes "other minds" the focal representational domain and target of systematic monitoring for humans. It is unclear, however, that non-human primates are equally obsessed with monitoring and representing others' mental states: after all, they engage neither in cooperation, nor in referential communication.

Conclusions

In this chapter I have explored the recent history and current state of the art of our scientific attempts to investigate the early development and phylogenetic origins of human infants' understanding of the domain of intentional agency and action. I have taken a historical stance in this selective review because the field is arguably facing a major paradigm change after having spent some thirty odd years under the methodological spell of the standard verbal false-belief tasks. These tasks have led most of us to share the collective false belief that a representational understanding of the intentional mind states of others is not achieved until about 4 years of age in ontogeny. These times, in my view, are coming to an end as a result of converging evidence suggesting that the domain-specific human adaptation for monitoring and representing the mental states of our conspecifics is fully operational already during the second year of life and probably even earlier. As a result, the field is in a healthy turmoil: a good time to stand back and reassess our theories of the developmental and phylogenetic origins of humans' domain-specific competence to understand the intentional actions and represent the causal intentional mind states of other agents.

Within this framework, I have argued for the merits of the view that assumes two basic and initially independent cognitive systems that have evolved as separate adaptations to two different kinds of intentional agency that constitute our uniquely human social-cultural environment, which I called instrumental and communicative agency. The two specialized systems of adaptation have distinct representational and inferential properties and input conditions and the entities belonging to their respective domains are only partially overlapping. While all communicative agents are also instrumental agents, the opposite is not the case and when we recognize instrumental agency, we do not automatically attribute communicative intentions or abilities to such agents. Clearly, however, during early development our core concepts of instrumental and communicative agency become integrated in intricate ways (see Carey, 2009) through the establishment of representations of the numerous shared properties that are possessed by both kinds of agents (such as, for example, their capacity for rational choice of action). Finally, in considering the representational and inferential properties of our human-specific cognitive adaptations to understand teleological versus communicative agency, I have emphasized the qualitative structural differences that characterize both of these systems when compared to their phylogenetically ancient evolutionary roots that we share with our primate ancestors.

Note

1 While such instrumental actions can involve the use of tools to bring about the goal state, this is not meant to be implied as a necessary condition by the present use of the terms "instrumental action" and "agency."

References

Baker, C. L., Tenenbaum, J. B., & Saxe, R. R. (2006). Bayesian models of human action understanding. *Advances in neural information processing systems* (Vol. *18*, pp. 99–106).

Baker, C. L., Tenenbaum, J. B., and Saxe, R. R. (2007). Goal inference as inverse planning. *Proceedings of the Twenty-Ninth Annual Conference of the Cognitive Science Society.*

Baron-Cohen, S. (1994). How to build a baby that can read minds: Cognitive mechanisms in mind reading. *Cahiers de Psychologie Cognitive/Current Psychology of Cognition, 13*, 513–552.

Bíró, S., & Leslie, A. M. (2007). Infants' perception of goal-directed actions: Development through cue-based bootstrapping. *Developmental Science, 10*(3), 379–398.

Bíró, S., Csibra, G., & Gergely, G. (2007). *The role of behavioral cues in understanding animacy, agency and goal-directed actions in infancy.* In C. von Hofsten & K. Rosander (Eds.), *Progress in brain research: From action to cognition* (Vol. *164*, pp. 303–322). Amsterdam: Elsevier.

Bíró, S., & Verschoor, S. (2008). The role of efficiency of action in infants' goal attribution. Poster session presented at the International Conference on Infant Studies, Vancouver.

Bloom, P., & German, T. P. (2000). Two reasons to abandon the false belief task as a test of theory of mind. *Cognition, 77*(1), B25–B31.

Boesch, C., & Boesch, H. (1993). Diversity of tool use and tool-making in wild chimpanzees. In A. Berthelet & J. Chavaillon (Eds.), *The use of tools by human and non-human primates* (pp.158–187). Oxford: Oxford University Press.

Brand, R. J., Baldwin, D. A., & Ashburn, L. A. (2002). Evidence for "motionese": Modifications in mothers' infant-directed action. *Developmental Science, 5*, 72–83.

Brand, R. J., & Shallcross, W. K. (2008). Infants prefer motionese to adult-directed action. *Developmental Science, 11*, 853–861.

Brauer, J., Kaminski, J. R., Riedel, J., Call, J., & Tomasello, M. (2006). Making inferences about the location of hidden food: Social dog, causal ape. *Journal of Comparative Psychology, 120*(1), 38–47.

Brugger, A., Lariviere, L. A., Mumme, D. L., & Bushnell, E. W. (2007). Doing the right thing: Infants' selection of actions to imitate from observed event sequences. *Child Development, 78*, 806–824.

Bugnyar, T., & Heinrich, B. (2005). Food-storing ravens differentiate between knowledgeable and ignorant competitors. *Proceedings of the Royal Society of London, Series B, 272*, 1641–1646.

Bugnyar, T., Stowe, M., & Heinrich, B. (2004). Ravens, Corvus corax, follow gaze direction of humans around obstacles. *Proceedings of the Royal Society of London, Series B, 271*, 1331–1336.

Buttelmann, D., Carpenter, M., Call, J., & Tomasello, M. (2007). Enculturated chimpanzees imitate rationally. *Developmental Science, 10*, F31–F38.

Buttelmann, D., Carpenter, M., Call, J., & Tomasello, M. (2008). Rational tool use and tool choice in human infants and great apes. *Child Development, 79*, 609–626.

Buttelmann, D., Carpenter, M., & Tomasello, M. (2009). Eighteen-month-old infants show false belief understanding in an active helping paradigm. *Cognition, 112*(2), 337–342.

Call, J., & Tomasello, M. (2008). Does the chimpanzee have a theory of mind? Thirty years later. *Trends in Cognitive Science, 12*, 187–192.

Carey, S. (2009). *The origins of concepts.* Oxford: Oxford University Press.

Carey, S., & Spelke, E. S. (1994). Domain-specific knowledge and conceptual change. In L. Hirschfeld & S. Gelman (Eds.), *Mapping the mind: Domain specificity in cognition and culture* (pp. 169–200). Cambridge: Cambridge University Press.

Caron. A. J. (2009). Comprehension of the representational mind in infancy. *Developmental Review*, *29*(2), 69–95.

Casler, K., & Kelemen, D. (2005). Young children's rapid learning about artifacts. *Developmental Science*, *8*(6), 472–480.

Clayton, N. S., Dally, J. M., & Emery, N. J. (2007). Social cognition of food-caching corvids. *Philosophical Transactions of the Royal Society of London B*, *362*, 507–522.

Clayton, N. S., & Emery, N. J. (2008). Canny corvids and political primates: A case for convergent evolution in intelligence. In S. Conway Morris (Ed.), *The deep structure of biology: Is convergence sufficiently ubiquitous to give a directional signal?* (pp. 128–142). West Conshohocken, PA: Templeton Foundation Press.

Csibra, G. (2003). Teleological and referential understanding of action in infancy. *Philosophical Transactions of the Royal Society of London B*, *358*, 447–458.

Csibra, G. (2008). Goal attribution to inanimate agents by 6.5-month-old infants. *Cognition*, *107*(70), 5–717.

Csibra, G., Bíró, S., Koós, O., & Gergely, G. (2003). One-year-old infants use teleological representations of actions productively. *Cognitive Science*, *27*(1), 111–133.

Csibra G., & Gergely, G. (1998). The teleological origins of mentalistic action explanations: A developmental hypothesis. *Developmental Science*, *1*(2), 255–259.

Csibra, G., & Gergely, G. (2006). Social learning and social cognition: The case of pedagogy. In M. H. Johnson & Y. M. Munakata (Eds.), Processes of change in brain and cognitive development. *Attention and Performance*, *21*, 249–274.

Csibra, G., & Gergely, G. (2007). "Obsessed with goals": Functions and mechanisms of teleological interpretation of actions in humans. In B. Hommel & S. Biro (Eds.), Becoming an intentional agent: The development of action control [Special issue]. *Acta Psychologica*, *124*, 60–78.

Csibra, G., & Gergely, G. (2009). Natural pedagogy. *Trends in Cognitive Sciences*, *13*(4 148–153.

Csibra, G., Gergely, G., Bíró, S., Koós, O., & Brockbank, M. (1999). Goal attribution without agency cues: The perception of "pure reason" in infancy. *Cognition*, *72*, 237–267.

Csibra, G., & Volein, A. (2008). Infants can infer the presence of hidden objects from referential gaze information. *British Journal of Developmental Psychology*, *26*, 1–11.

Dehaene, S. (2001). Précis of the number sense. *Mind and Language*, *16*, 16–36.

Deligianni, F., Senju, A., Gergely, G., & Csibra, G. (2009). *Gaze-contingent objects elicit the illusion of communication in preverbal infants.* Manuscript submitted for publication.

Diamond, A. (1985). Development of the ability to use recall to guide action, as indicated by infants' performance on AB. *Child Development*, *56*, 868–883.

DiYanni, C., & Kelemen, D. (2005). Using a bad tool with good intention: How preschoolers weigh physical and intentional cues when learning about artifacts. *Cognition*, *97*, 327–335.

Dunbar, R. (1997). *Grooming, gossip and the evolution of language.* Cambridge, MA: Harvard University Press.

Egyed, K., Király, I., & Gergely, G. (2007, August). *Understanding object-referential attitude expressions in 18-month-olds: The interpretation switching function of ostensive-communicative cues.* Poster session presented at the Biennial Meeting of the Society for Research in Child Development, Boston.

Emery, N. J., & Clayton, N. S. (2001). Effects of experience and social context on prospective caching strategies by scrub jays. *Nature*, *414*, 443–446.

Farroni, T., Csibra, G., Simion, F., & Johnson, M. H. (2002). Eye contact detection in humans from birth. *Proceedings of the National Academy of Sciences of the United States of America*, *99*, 9602–9605.

Flombaum, J., Santos, L. (2005). Rhesus monkeys attribute perceptions to others. *Current Biology, 15*, 447–452.

Fodor, J. A. (1992). A theory of the child's theory of mind. *Cognition, 44*, 283–296.

Futó, J., Téglás, E., Csibra, G., & Gergely, G. (2009a, April). *Object individuation in 10-month-olds: The role of ostensive cuing and function demonstration.* Poster session presented at the Biennial Meeting of the SRCD, Denver, CO.

Futó, J., Téglás, E., Csibra, G., & Gergely, G. (2009b). *Artifact representation in preverbal infants: Function overrides visual properties.* Manuscript submitted for publication.

Gergely, G. (2003). What should a robot learn from an infant? Mechanisms of action interpretation and observational learning in infancy. *Connection Science, 13*(4), 191–209.

Gergely, G. (2007). Learning "about" versus learning "from" other minds: Human pedagogy and its implications. In P. Carruthers, S. Laurence, & S. Stich (Eds.), *The innate mind: Foundations and the future* (pp. 170–198). Oxford: Oxford University Press.

Gergely, G., Bekkering, H., & Király, I. (2002). Rational imitation in preverbal infants. *Nature, 415*, 755.

Gergely, G., & Csibra, G. (1997). Teleological reasoning in infancy: The infant's naive theory of rational action. A reply to Premack and Premack. *Cognition, 63*, 227–233.

Gergely, G., & Csibra, G. (2003). Teleological reasoning about actions: The one-year-old's naïve theory of rational action. *Trends in Cognitive Sciences, 7*, 287–292.

Gergely, G. & Csibra, G. (2005). The social construction of the cultural mind: Imitative learning as a mechanism of human pedagogy. *Interaction Studies, 6*(3), 463–481.

Gergely, G., & Csibra, G. (2006). Sylvia's recipe: The role of imitation and pedagogy in the transmission of cultural knowledge. In S. Levenson & N. Enfield (Eds.), *Roots of human sociality: Culture, cognition, and human interaction* (pp. 229–255). Oxford: Berg Publishers.

Gergely, G., Király, I., & Egyed, K. (2007). On pedagogy. *Developmental Science, 10*(1), 139–146

Gergely, G., Nádasdy, Z., Csibra, G., & Bíró, S. (1995). Taking the intentional stance at 12 months of age. *Cognition, 56*, 165–193.

Gergely, G., & Unoka, Z. (2008). Attachment, affect-regulation and mentalization: The developmental origins of the representational affective self. In C. Sharpe, P. Fonagy, & I. Goodyer, (Eds.), *Social cognition and developmental psychopathology* (pp. 303–340). Oxford: Oxford University Press.

Gómez J. C. (2008).The evolution of pretence: From intentional availability to intentional non-existence. *Mind and Language, 23*(5), 586–606.

Goodall, J. (1986). *The chimpanzees of Gombe: Patterns of behavior.* Cambridge, MA: Harvard University Press, Belknap Press.

Grossmann, T., Johnson, M. H., Lloyd-Fox, S., Blasi, A., Deligianni, F., Elwell, C., & Csibra, G. (2008). Early cortical specialization for face-to-face communication in human infants. *Proceedings of the Royal Society of London, Series B, 275*, 2803–2811.

Hare, B., Call, J., Agnetta, B., & Tomasello, M. (2000). Chimpanzees know what conspecifics do and do not see. *Animal Behaviour, 59*, 771–85.

Hare, B., Call, J., & Tomasello, M. (2001). Do chimpanzees know what conspecifics know? *Animal Behaviour, 61*, 139–51.

Hernik, M., & Csibra, G. (2009). Functional understanding facilitates learning about tools in human children. *Current Opinion in Neurobiology, 19*, 34–38.

Hernik, M., & Southgate, V. (2010, March). *Nine-month-olds attribute goals to single-target events only if the action is efficiently related to the goal.* Poster session presented at Seventeenth Biennial International Conference on Infant Studies (ICIS), Baltimore, MD.

Johnson, S. C., Shimizu, Y. A., & Ok, S.-J. (2007). Actors and actions: The role of agent behavior in infants' attribution of goals. *Cognitive Development, 22*(3), 310–322.

Johnson, S. C., Slaughter, V., & Carey, S. (1998). Whose gaze would infants follow? The elicitation of gaze following in 12-month-olds. *Developmental Science, 1*, 233–238.

Kamewari, K., Kato, M., Kanda, T., Ishiguro, H., & Hiraki, K. (2005). Six-and-a-half-month-old children positively attribute goals to human action and to humanoid-robot motion. *Cognitive Development, 20*, 303–320.

Kaminski, J., Call, J., & Tomasello, M. (2008). Chimpanzees know what others know, but not what they believe. *Cognition, 109*, 224–234.

Kaminski, J., Riedel, J., Call, J., & Tomasello, M. (2005). Domestic goats (*Capra hircus*) follow gaze direction and use some cues in an object choice task. *Animal Behavior, 69*, 11–18.

Keil, F. C. (1994). The birth and nurturance of concepts by domains: The origins of concepts of living things. In L. Hirschfeld & S. Gelman, (Eds.), *Mapping the mind: Domain specificity in cognition and culture* (pp. 234–254). New York: Cambridge University Press.

Király I. (2008). Memories for events in infants: goal relevant action coding. In T. Striano & V. Reid (Eds.), *Social cognition: Development, neuroscience and autism* (pp. 113–128). Oxford: Wiley-Blackwell.

Király, I., (2009). The effect of the model's presence and of negative evidence on infants' selective imitation. *Journal of Experimental Child Psychology, 102*, 14–25.

Király, I., Csibra, G., & Gergely, G. (2004, May). *The role of communicative-referential cues in observational learning during the second year.* Poster session presented at the Fourteenth Biennial International Conference on Infant Studies, Chicago, IL.

Király, I., Jovanovic, B., Aschersleben, G., Prinz, W., & Gergely, G. (2003). Generality and perceptual constraints in understanding goal-directed actions in young infants. *Consciousness and Cognition, 12*(4), 752–769.

Kovács, Á. M., Téglás, E., & Endress, A. D. (2009a, April). *Seven-month-olds compute the beliefs of other agents.* Poster session presented at the Biennial Meeting of the SRCD, Denver, CO.

Kovács, Á. M., Téglás, E., & Endress, A. D. (2009b). *Automatic belief attribution to potential agents in adults and 7-month-old infants.* Manuscript submitted for publication.

Lakatos, G., Soproni, K., Doka, A., & Miklosi, A. (2009). A comparative approach to dogs' (*Canis familiaris*) and human infants' comprehension of various forms of pointing gestures. *Animal Cognition*, April 2009.

Leslie, A. M. (1987). Pretense and representation: The origins of "theory-of-mind." *Psychological Review, 94*, 412–426.

Leslie, A. M. (1994). ToMM, ToBy, and agency: Core architecture and domain specificity in cognition and culture. In L. Hirschfeld & S. Gelman (Eds.), *Mapping the mind: Domain specificity in cognition and culture* (pp. 119–148). New York: Cambridge University Press.

Leslie, A. M., German, T. P., & Polizzi, P. (2005). Belief-desire reasoning as a process of selection. *Cognitive Psychology, 50*, 45–85.

Leslie, A. M., & Roth, D. (1993). What autism teaches us about metarepresentation. In S. Baron-Cohen, H. Tager-Flusberg, & D. Cohen (Eds.), *Understanding other minds: Perspectives from autism* (pp. 83–111). Oxford: Oxford University Press.

Liszkowski, U., Carpenter, M., Henning, A., Striano, T., & Tomasello, M. (2004). Twelve-month-olds point to share attention and interest. *Developmental Science, 7*, 297–307.

Liszkowski, U., Carpenter, M., Striano, T., & Tomasello, M. (2006). 12- and 18- month-olds point to provide information for others. *Journal of Cognition and Development, 7*, 173–187.

Luo, Y. (in press). Three-month-old infants attribute goals to a human agent. *Developmental Science.*

Luo, Y., & Baillargeon, R. (2005). Can a self-propelled box have a goal? Psychological reasoning in 5-month-old infants. *Psychological Science, 16*(8), 601–608.

Luo, Y., & Baillargeon, R. (2007). Do 12.5-month-old infants consider what objects others can see when interpreting their actions? *Cognition, 105*, 489–512.

Marno, H., Csibra, G., & Davelaar, E. (2009, January). *Object perception in social-communicative context.* Paper presented at the Experimental Psychology Society meeting at University College London.

McGrew, W. C. (1996). *Chimpanzee material culture: Implications for human evolution.* New York: Cambridge University Press.

McGrew, W. C. (2004). *The cultured chimpanzee: Reflections on cultural primatology.* New York: Cambridge University Press.

Meltzoff, A. N. (1988). Infant imitation after a one week delay: Long-term memory for novel acts and multiple stimuli. *Developmental Psychology, 24*, 470–476.

Meltzoff, A. N. (1995a). What infant memory tells us about infantile amnesia: Long-term recall and deferred imitation. *Journal of Experimental Child Psychology, 59*: 497–515.

Meltzoff, A. N. (1995b). Understanding the intentions of others: Re-enactment of intended acts by 18-month-old children. *Developmental Psychology, 31*, 1–16.

Meltzoff, A. N. (1996). The human infant as imitative generalist: A 20-year progress report on infant imitation with implications for comparative psychology. In C. M. Heyes & B. G. Galef, (Eds), *Social learning in animals: The roots of culture* (pp. 347–370). New York: Academic Press.

Meltzoff, A. N. (2005). Imitation and other minds: The like-me hypothesis. In S. Hurley & N. Chater (Eds.), *Perspectives on imitation: From neuroscience to social science* (Vol. *2*, pp. 55–77). Cambridge, MA: MIT Press.

Mithen, S. (1996). *The prehistory of the mind.* London: Thames and Hudson.

Mithen, S. (2002). Mind, brain, and material culture: an archeological perspective In: P. Carruthers & A. Chamberlain (Eds.), *Evolution and the human mind* (pp. 207–217). Cambridge: Cambridge University Press.

Moll, H., & Tomasello, M. (2007). How 14- and 18-month-olds know what others have experienced. *Developmental Psychology, 43*, 309–317.

Movellan, J. R., & Watson, J. S. (2002). *The development of gaze following as a Bayesian systems identification problem.* University of California at San Diego Machine Perception Laboratory Technical Reports 2002.01.

Nielsen, M. (2006). Copying actions and copying outcomes: Social learning through the second year. *Developmental Psychology, 42*, 555–565.

Onishi, K. H., & Baillargeon, R. (2005). 15-month-old infants understand false beliefs. *Science, 308*(5719), 255–258.

Onishi, K. H., Baillargeon, R., & Leslie, A. M. (2007). 15-month-old infants detect violations in pretend scenarios. In B. Hommel & S. Biro, (Eds.), an intentional agent: The development of action control [Special issue]. *Acta Psychologica, 124*, 106–128.

Piaget, J. (1954). *The Construction of Reality in the Child.* New York: Basic Books.

Povinelli, D. J. (2000). *Folk physics for apes: The chimpanzee's theory of how the world works.* Oxford: Oxford University Press.

Povinelli, D. J. & Eddy, T. J. (1996). Chimpanzees: Joint visual attention. *Psychological Science, 7*, 129–135.

Premack, D. (1990). The infant's theory of self-propelled objects. *Cognition, 36*, 1–16.

Premack, D., & Premack, A. J. (1995). Origins of human social competence. In M. S. Gazzaniga (Ed.), *The cognitive neurosciences.* Cambridge, MA: MIT Press.

Premack, D., & Woodward, G. (1978). Does the chimpanzee have a theory of mind? *Behavioral and Brain Sciences, 4*, 515–526.

Rizzolatti, G., & Craighero, L. (2004). The mirror-neuron system. *Annual Review of Neuroscience, 27*, 169–192.

Rochat, M. J., Serra, E., Fadiga, L., & Gallese, V. (2008). The evolution of social cognition: goal familiarity shapes monkeys' action understanding. *Current Biology, 18*, 227–232.

Santos, L. R., Nissen, A. G., & Ferrugia, J. (2006). Rhesus monkeys (*Macaca mulatta*) know what others can and cannot hear. *Animal Behaviour, 71*(5), 1175–1181.

Schick, K. D., & Toth, N. (1993). *Making silent stones speak: Human evolution and the dawn of technology*. New York: Simon & Schuster.

Scott, R. M., & Baillargeon, R. (in press). Which penguin is this? Attributing false beliefs about object identity at 18 months [Special issue on developmental neuroscience]. *Child Development*.

Semaw, S. (2000). The world's oldest stone artefacts from Gona, Ethiopia: Their implications for understanding stone technology and patterns of human evolution between 2.6 and 1.5 million years ago. *Journal of Archaeological Science, 27*, 1197–1214.

Senju, A., & Csibra, G. (2008). Gaze following inhuman infants depends on communicative signals. *Current Biology, 18*, 668–671.

Senju, A. Csibra, G., & Johnson, M. H. (2008). Understanding the referential nature of looking: Infants' preference for object-directed gaze. *Cognition, 108*, 303–319.

Senju, A., Johnson, M. H., & Csibra, G. (2006). The development and neural basis of referential gaze perception. *Social Neuroscience, 1*, 220–234.

Song, H., Onishi, K. H., Baillargeon, R., & Fisher, C. (2008). Can an actor's false belief be corrected by an appropriate communication? Psychological reasoning in 18.5-month-old infants. *Cognition, 109*, 295–315.

Southgate,V., Chevallier, C., & Csibra, G. (in press). Seventeen-month-olds appeal to false beliefs to interpret others' referential communication. *Developmental Sciences*.

Southgate, V., Johnson, M. H., & Csibra, G. (2008). Infants attribute goals to even biologically impossible actions. *Cognition, 107*, 1059–1069.

Southgate, V., Senju, A., & Csibra, G. (2007). Action anticipation through attribution of false belief by 2-year-olds. *Psychological Science, 18*(7), 587–592.

Spelke, E. S. (2000). Core knowledge. *American Psychologist, 55*, 1233–1243.

Spelke, E. S., Breilinger, K., Macomber, J., & Jacobsen, K. (1992). Origins of knowledge. *Psychological Review, 99*, 605–632.

Spelke, E. S., & Kinzler, K. D. (2007). Core knowledge. *Developmental Science 10*(1) 89–96.

Sperber, D. (2006). An evolutionary perspective on testimony and argumentation. In Viale, R., Andler, D., and Hirschfeld, L. (Eds.), *Biological and cultural bases of human inference* (pp. 177–189). Mahwah, NJ: Erlbaum.

Sperber, D., & Wilson, D. (1986). *Relevance: Communication and cognition*. Oxford: Blackwell.

Surian, L., Caldi, S., & Sperber, D. (2007). Attribution of beliefs by 13-month-old infants. *Psychological Science 18*, 580–586.

Tomasello, M. (1999). *The cultural origins of human cognition*. Cambridge, MA: Harvard University Press.

Tomasello, M. (2008). *Origins of human communication*. Cambridge: MIT Press.

Tomasello, M., & Call, J. (1997). *Primate cognition*. Oxford: Oxford University Press.

Tomasello, M., Carpenter, M., Call, J., Behne, T., & Moll, H. (2005). Understanding and sharing intentions: The origins of cultural cognition. *Behavioral and Brain Sciences, 28*, 675–735.

Tomasello, M., & Haberl, K. (2003). Understanding attention: 12- and 18-month-olds know what is new for other persons. *Developmental Psychology, 39*, 906–12.

Topál, J., Gergely, G., Erdőhegyi, A., Csibra, G., & Miklósi, Á. (2009). Differential sensitivity to human communication in dogs, wolves and human infants. *Science, 325*, 1269–1272.

Topál, J., Gergely, G., Miklósi, Á., Erdőhegyi, Á., & Csibra, G. (2008) Infants' perseverative search errors are induced by pragmatic misinterpretation. *Science, 321*(5897), 831–1834.

Uller, C. (2004). Disposition to recognize goals in infant chimpanzees *(Pan troglodytes). Animal Cognition, 7*, 154–161.

Wagner, L. & Carey, S. (2005). 12-month-old infants represent probable ending of motion events. *Infancy, 7*, 73–83.

Watson, J. S. (2005). "Einstein's baby" could infer intentionality. Commentary on Tomasello, M., Carpenter, M., Call, J., Behne, T., & Moll, H. (2005). Understanding and sharing intentions: The origins of cultural cognition. *Behavioral and Brain Sciences, 28*, 719–720.

Wellman, H. M., Cross, D., & Watson, J. (2001). Meta-analysis of theory-of-mind development: The truth about false belief. *Child Development, 72*, 655–684.

Wimmer, H., & Perner, J. (1983). Beliefs about beliefs: Representation and constraining function of wrong beliefs in young children's understanding of deception. *Cognition, 13*, 103–128.

Wood, J. N., Glynn, D. D., Phillips, B. C., & Hauser, M. D. (2007). The perception of rational, goal-directed action in nonhuman primates. *Science, 317*(5843), 1402–1405.

Woodward, A. (1998). Infants selectively encode the goal object of an actor's reach. *Cognition, 69*, 1–34.

Woodward, A. L., Sommerville, J. A., & Guajardo, J. J. (2001). How infants make sense of intentional action. In B. F. Malle, L. J. Moses, & D. A. Baldwin (Eds.), *Intentions and intentionality: Foundations of social cognition* (pp. 149–171). Cambridge, MA: MIT Press.

Xu, F. (2002). The role of language in acquiring kind concepts in infancy. *Cognition, 85*, 223–250.

Xu, F. (2007). Sortal concepts, object individuation, and language. *Trends in Cognitive Sciences, 11*, 400–406.

Xu, F., & Carey, S. (1996). Infants' metaphysics: The case of numerical identity. *Cognitive Psychology, 30*(2), 111–153.

Yoon, J. M. D., Johnson, M. H., & Csibra, G. (2008). Communication-induced memory biases in preverbal infants. *Proceedings of the National Academy of Sciences of the United States of America, 105*, 13690–13695.

CHAPTER FOUR

Social Cognition and Social Motivations in Infancy

Malinda Carpenter

Humans build skyscrapers, play in symphony orchestras, use money, and show each other their vacation photos. They have thousands of different languages, participate in countless cultural rituals and practices, and attach much importance to the latest fads and fashions. Other animals, including our nearest primate relatives, chimpanzees, do none of these things. Why not? What do all of them have in common? There is something special about human social cognition – what is it?

We propose that this "something special" is shared intentionality, the skills and motivation to share goals, intentions, and other psychological states with others (Tomasello, Carpenter, Call, Behne, & Moll, 2005). Shared intentionality is what enables humans (and only humans) to engage in collaborative activities, to share experiences with each other, and to create cultural practices and institutions together. In this chapter I take a close look at human social cognition to show (a) where it is different from the social cognition of other animals and (b) by when in development this difference is apparent.

To do this we must consider social cognition from two different perspectives. First, there is social *cognition*, or cognition *about* one's social partners. Of particular interest here is cognition about others' cognition, especially what others want, intend, know, and believe. The other side to social cognition is *social* cognition, in the sense of joint cognition: one's ability to participate in shared cognition and activities *with* social partners. The two sides to social cognition are related, of course – one cannot engage in any complex way with others socially without understanding something about their minds. But they are also clearly separable, as we will see below when we compare humans' social cognition with that of apes. Furthermore, along with considering social cognition from these two perspectives, in order to get at the "something special" in humans we must also look beyond social cognition and consider social *motivations*, in particular the motivation to share psychological states like goals and attention with others, as well as the more general motivation to align oneself with others, and do things the way others do.

I discuss each of these three areas in turn. I start with social *cognition*, the understanding of others' psychological states, to make the point that infants and apes are not so different in this regard at all. I then show how a uniquely human motivation to share psychological states with others enables infants to participate in *social* cognition, for example joint attention, a special type of communication, and joint collaborative activities with others. Then I discuss evidence that infants and young children have the more general motivation to communicate to others that they are like them, and to conform to the way that "we" do things – a key factor in the development of conventional practices and social norms. In each section I first review findings on human infants and then mention briefly what is known about chimpanzees and other apes. I conclude with some suggestions for future research in this area.

Social *Cognition*: Understanding of Others' Psychological States

One of the most active fields in developmental psychology in the last few decades has been the study of what infants and young children understand about others' minds. Historically, the general consensus was that children younger than 3–5 years of age did not understand much about mental states such as intentions, knowledge, and beliefs (e.g., Wimmer, Hogrefe, & Perner, 1988; Wimmer & Perner, 1983). But recent advances in the design of novel, non-verbal tasks more suitable for younger children have resulted in quite a different developmental picture. These new studies suggest that the age estimates of the previous studies were off by several years – that infants as young as 1 year of age already understand others as possessing a variety of psychological states, including goals and intentions, perception and attention, knowledge/ignorance, and even false beliefs. (Note that there were those who spoke of "theory of mind" in infants, based on natural observations of infants in social interactions, but at the time there were few positive results from experimental studies to support these claims; see, e.g., Bretherton, McNew, & Beeghly-Smith, 1981; Trevarthen, 1979.) I will briefly review some of the new experimental evidence here.

Understanding of others' goals and intentions

There are now quite a few studies that show that 1-year-old (and even younger) infants understand something about the goals underlying others' actions. The most convincing evidence comes from tasks involving failed attempts and accidents, because in those tasks there is a mismatch between the actor's goal and her behavior so infants cannot simply use observable surface behavior instead of mental goals to succeed. For example, 9-month-old and older infants respond more patiently when an adult social partner is unable to give them a toy (due to failed attempts or accidents) than when she is unwilling to give them a toy (Behne, Carpenter, Call, & Tomasello, 2005). Younger infants – 6-month-olds – respond actively in Behne and colleagues' test but do so indiscriminately, without regard for the adult's differing goals. Similarly, in imitation tasks in which a model demonstrates a failed attempt, 15- and 18-month-old infants produce the action the model meant to perform instead of the action she actually did perform (Johnson, Booth, & O'Hearn, 2001; Meltzoff, 1995). And 14- to 18-month-olds are more likely to copy others' intentional actions than their accidental actions (Carpenter, Akhtar, & Tomasello, 1998; Olineck & Poulin-Dubois, 2005).

Along with an understanding of others' goals, infants around this age may also have some understanding of others' intentions: the means or plans for action others choose to use to achieve their goals (and why they have chosen those particular means). For example, 12- and 14-month-old infants imitate an unusual action more often when the actor freely chose to use that action than when she was forced to use the action by some constraint (Gergely, Bekkering, & Király, 2002; Schwier, van Maanen, Carpenter, & Tomasello, 2006). Tomasello et al. (2005) have taken these results as evidence that 1-year-old infants see others' behavior as governed by rational choices of action plans (intentions) that take into account the situation and the constraints on the actor.

Thus, by 9 months of age infants do not just perceive others' bodily motions on a surface level; instead they see others as persisting past failed attempts and accidents to achieve their goals. By 12 months of age, infants in addition are beginning to understand others' intentions, seeing others as choosing action plans for accomplishing their goals rationally in particular contexts.

Understanding of others' perception and attention

There are many studies showing that infants can follow others' gaze (see the chapters in Flom, Lee, & Muir, 2007, for recent reviews). However, as there is some doubt about whether the ability to follow gaze necessarily requires any understanding of others' psychological states – adult head turns could instead simply become associated with interesting sights in that direction over time (Moore & Corkum, 1994) – it is important to note that some recent findings suggest that infants do have some understanding that the adult whose gaze they are following actually sees something. For example, if an adult looks at something that infants cannot see because from their perspective it is behind a barrier, by 12 months of age infants will locomote to a new position so that they can see what the adult sees (Moll & Tomasello, 2004). By 14 months, infants have some understanding of the mechanisms of perception, that is, that people's eyes must be open and oriented toward things, with an unobstructed line of sight, in order for them to see things (Brooks & Meltzoff, 2002; Caron, Butler, & Brooks, 2002; Dunphy-Lelii & Wellman, 2004).

Along with an understanding of others' perception, infants around this age also apparently have some understanding of others' attention, the ability to focus on just one part of all the things in one's visual field. For example, if an adult gestures ambiguously toward three objects together on a tray, 12-month-olds can determine which one of the three objects the adult is attending (and referring) to based on the experiences the adult has previously had with each of the three objects (Tomasello & Haberl, 2003). Older infants can even determine whether an adult is focusing on an object as a whole versus on some particular aspect of that object, again based on the adult's prior experience with that object (Moll, Koring, Carpenter, & Tomasello, 2006).

Understanding of others' knowledge/ignorance

Twelve-month-old infants understand not just what others can see at the moment; they also understand something about what others have and have not seen or experienced in the past: their knowledge/ignorance. For example, 12-month-olds helpfully point out the location of a fallen object more often to an adult when the adult is ignorant about the object's location (she had not previously seen it fall) than when the adult is knowledgeable about the object's location (she had previously seen it fall; Liszkowski, Carpenter, & Tomasello, 2008). In some circumstances (see Moll & Tomasello, 2007), 12- and 14-month-olds can also keep track of which objects are known versus unknown to an adult in the sense of being familiar or not to her (i.e., experienced or not by her in the past; Tomasello & Haberl, 2003).

Understanding of others' false beliefs

Despite decades of research that consistently found no evidence of false-belief understanding in children under around 4 years of age (see Wellman, Cross, & Watson, 2001, for a meta-analysis), we now have evidence that even 1-year-old infants may understand something about others' false beliefs. The first studies of infants' understanding of false beliefs used infants' looking time to different displays as a measure of their understanding. For example, after an object's location was switched unbeknownst to a protagonist, 15-month-old infants looked longer when the protagonist searched for the object in the new location than in the old location, where she had seen it placed originally (e.g., Onishi & Baillargeon, 2005; see also Song, Onishi, Baillargeon, & Fisher, 2008; Surian, Caldi, & Sperber, 2007). More recent evidence suggests that infants can also actively use this understanding to make sense of adults' actions in real social interactions: by 16–18 months, infants can use an adult's true or false belief about the contents of a box to determine what the adult needs help with when he struggles unsuccessfully to open the box (Buttelmann, Carpenter, & Tomasello, in press).

By around their first birthdays, infants thus show evidence of having some understanding of a variety of psychological states in others, from goals and intentions to perception, attention, knowledge, and even false beliefs. But, perhaps surprisingly, we now have evidence that apes understand many of these psychological states as well. They understand others' goals and intentions (e.g., Buttelmann, Carpenter, Call, & Tomasello, 2007, 2008; Call, Hare, Carpenter, & Tomasello, 2004; Call & Tomasello, 1998), others' perception (e.g., Bräuer, Call, & Tomasello, 2005; Kaminski, Call, & Tomasello, 2004; Tomasello, Hare, & Agnetta, 1999), and others' knowledge/ignorance (e.g., Hare, Call, & Tomasello, 2001; Kaminski, Call, & Tomasello, 2008). However, they may have more difficulty understanding others' focus of attention (Tomasello & Carpenter, 2005) and false beliefs (e.g., Call & Tomasello, 1999; Kaminski et al., 2008 – although see Krachun, Carpenter, Call, & Tomasello, in press, for possible, weak evidence of some implicit understanding of false beliefs in chimpanzees).

Thus, apes, like infants, understand a variety of psychological states in others. Understanding others' goals, intentions, perception, and knowledge allows apes to engage in some complex social reasoning and interactions, as, in many cases, it enables them to explain others' behavior and even to predict what others will do in novel situations. It allows them to compete with, deceive, and even help others (e.g., Hare et al., 2001; Warneken & Tomasello, 2006; Whiten & Byrne, 1988). But alone it is not enough to enable them to participate in activities involving shared intentionality, for example, truly collaborative activities with joint goals and intentions, or sharing attention, attitudes, and experiences with others in joint attentional engagement. Humans are able to join forces with and align themselves with others in these ways, even as 1-year-old infants. What makes the difference is the motivation to *share* psychological states such as goals and attention with others. Now we get to the unique aspects of human social cognition.

Social Cognition and the Motivation to Share Psychological States with Others

Tomasello et al. (2005) proposed that the capacity for shared intentionality is a result of the interaction of two lines of development: infants' developing understanding of others' psychological states and their uniquely human motivation to share those psychological states with others. That is, the motivation to share psychological states with others transforms whatever social-cognitive understanding and skills infants have at any given age into a special, shared version of that understanding and its resulting skills: if infants understand others' emotions, they will be able and motivated to share emotions with others; if they understand others' goals, they will be able and motivated to share goals with others in joint action; and if they understand others' attention, they will be able and motivated to engage in joint attention. Next I will discuss three of the most important social-cognitive skills human infants acquire: joint attention, a special type of communication, and collaboration. These early-emerging skills are the foundation for most of human cultural cognition and are themselves unique to humans. For each skill, I will focus on recent studies that were designed to test the idea that infants are truly sharing psychological states with others against leaner, more egocentric explanations of the same behaviors.

Sharing attention and attitudes in joint attentional engagement

The motivation to share psychological states and activities with others is already evident very early in infancy in the delight with which young babies participate in face-to-face social interactions with their caregivers (e.g., Trevarthen, 1980). Somewhat later, by age 9 months, infants start coordinating their attention with others to objects of mutual interest outside the dyad, in joint attentional interactions (e.g., Bakeman & Adamson, 1984; Carpenter, Nagell, & Tomasello, 1998; Trevarthen & Hubley, 1978). The motivation to engage in joint attention is so strong that infants voluntarily turn away from interesting sights to engage in it – to "comment" to their partner on the sight or actively draw her attention to it so they can attend to it together.

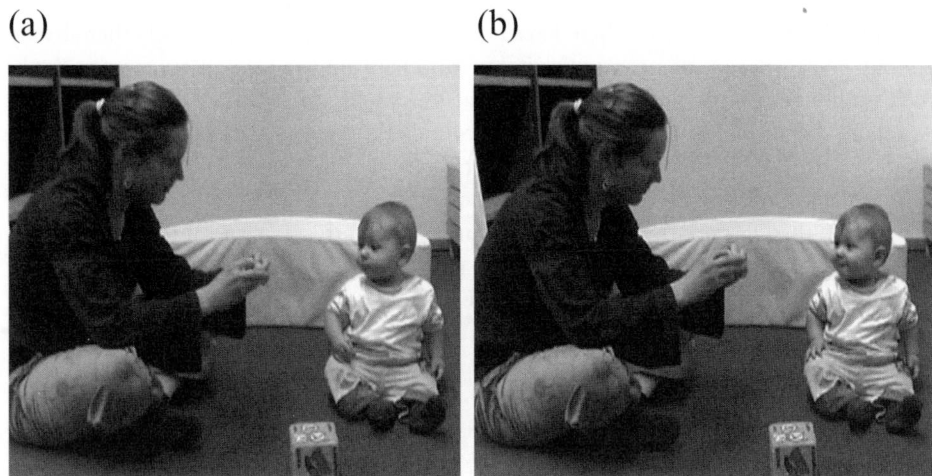

Figure 4.1 Sequential frames from a video of a 9-month-old initiating joint attention with his mother: (a) he watches as his mother makes a rubber duck squeak; (b) he smiles at the sound of the duck

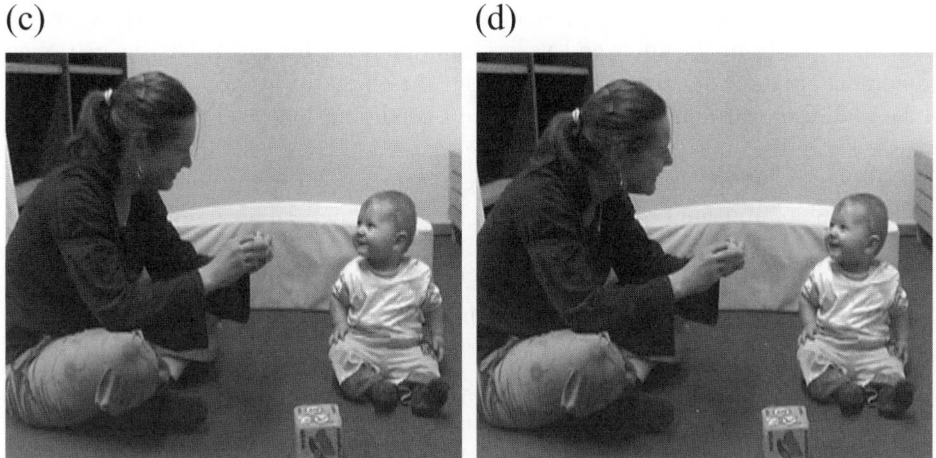

Figure 4.1 (c) and (d) he looks to his mother's face to share attention and interest with her

By 12 months of age, infants align their attention and attitudes with those of others in at least three ways. They look to others' faces to communicate that they are sharing attention, as in figure 4.1 (joint attentional engagement); they follow into others' focus of attention (gaze and point following); and they actively direct others to follow into their own focus of attention with communicative gestures (declarative showing and pointing) (Carpenter, Akhtar, et al., 1998). They thus seek to align themselves with others in both directions, by following into and directing others' attention. What makes all three types of behavior joint attention is that infant and adult *know together* that they are sharing attention and attitudes (Tomasello, 1995). Since this "knowing together" is crucial, but is a difficult thing to observe, there have been several studies to find out whether already around 1 year of age infants truly share attention in this way. I will review one set of such studies here, and another in the next section on communication.

Infants begin pointing "declaratively" around 12 months of age (e.g., Carpenter, Akhtar, et al., 1998). Most researchers see this behavior as a clear indication of infants' desire to share attention and interest about objects with a social partner. A leaner view, however, is that 12-month-olds do not point to share attention and interest but rather point for more egocentric reasons, simply to gain rewarding positive emotions to the self (Moore & D'Entremont, 2001). To test the rich against the lean view experimentally, Liszkowski, Carpenter, Henning, Striano, and Tomasello (2004) elicited declarative points from 12-month-old infants by having a series of puppets appear and move around from behind a screen at the far side of the room. We then manipulated the experimenter's reaction to infants' points to the puppets to test four different hypotheses about why infants point in this situation. To test the rich view that infants point to share attention and interest, in one condition the adult reacted by engaging in joint attention with infants about the object (i.e., alternating gaze between infants and the object and commenting about the object interestedly). To test Moore and colleagues' view that infants simply want the adult's attention and emotions on themselves, in another condition the adult responded with positive emotion just to infants (ignoring the object). And to test the other possibilities that infants just wanted the adult to look at the object, or wanted nothing at all from the adult and were simply pointing for themselves, in two other conditions the adult reacted by just looking at the object, or by ignoring infants' point. Infants' different patterns of responding across conditions indicated that they were only satisfied with the adult's response in the joint attention condition: when she reacted in any other way, infants were more likely to repeat their point to the object within a trial, and to stop pointing altogether across trials. Their point was an invitation to share attention to the object.

A further study by Liszkowski, Carpenter, and Tomasello (2007b) supports this interpretation by showing that it is important to infants both that the adult shares attention to the *specific* referent they are pointing to – not to some other random object in that general direction – and also that the adult shares their own attitude of interest to that object. In that study, if the adult misunderstood the referent of infants' point and "shared" to a different object nearby, infants repeated their point to the original referent. If the adult reacted in an uninterested way, infants stopped pointing altogether. Evidence that all this takes place on a mental level, about mutually imagined objects, comes from the finding that 12-month-old infants can point declaratively about absent referents – objects that were previously present but which have now disappeared – and that they do so selectively depending both on whether the adult knew about (had previously seen) the objects and how she had previously reacted to them (Liszkowski, Carpenter, & Tomasello, 2007a).

Apes do not share attention and interest with others in joint attentional engagement (e.g., Bard & Vauclair, 1984; Tomasello & Carpenter, 2005; Tomonaga et al., 2004), and they do not gesture declaratively to point out interesting objects or events for others (e.g., Gómez, Sarriá, & Tamarit, 1993; Tomasello & Carpenter, 2005). (They also do not point to make reference to absent referents, even imperatively; Liszkowski, Schäfer,

Carpenter, & Tomasello, in press.) They do follow others' gaze (e.g., Bräuer et al., 2005). However, although gaze following is often called "joint visual attention," it does not have to involve any "jointness" – any real coordination of attention – at all. Instead, it can be done in an exploitative manner, with the looker not even being aware that someone is following his gaze. In this type of gaze following, looker and follower end up looking at the same object but they do not necessarily know together that they are doing this. It can be difficult to distinguish between these two possibilities in gaze following but since apes do not participate in the other two types of joint attention at all we think it likely that gaze following reflects apes' desire to see what others see, not to see what others see and know this together. Thus, whereas already by their first birthdays infants show three different types of joint attentional behavior, there is little if any evidence of true joint attention in apes.

Use of shared experience in communication

Clark (1996) has pointed out that language is a type of joint action, one which relies on the common ground or knowledge the speaker and listener share in order to succeed. We would argue that the same can be said about prelinguistic communication as well, at least by 12–14 months of age – that human communication even in infancy is based on shared intentionality (Tomasello, Carpenter, & Liszkowski, 2007; Tomasello, 2008). The best evidence comes from infants' comprehension and production of the pointing gesture. For instance, by 14 months of age, when an adult points for infants, infants do not simply follow the point and make their own conclusions as to what the adult is trying to tell them based on whatever happens to grab their attention there. Instead, they take the adult as trying to tell them something relevant to their shared experience or common ground. For example, in one study, Liebal, Behne, Carpenter, and Tomasello (2009) had 14-month-old infants share a cleaning-up game with one adult, E1 (i.e., they threw a series of objects into a basket together), then that adult pointed to another target object and simply said, "There!" Infants picked up that object and threw it into the basket as well, apparently seeing E1's point as related to their joint activity. Infants' responses in a control condition ruled out the possibility that infants were responding egocentrically, based on what they themselves were doing, instead of what they were doing jointly with E1. In this condition, infants participated in the cleaning-up game with E1, exactly as before, but then another adult, E2, pointed at the target object instead. Infants rarely cleaned up the target object in this condition.

In another study, Moll, Richter, Carpenter, and Tomasello (2008) had 14-month-olds share (i.e., interact excitedly about) three objects with an adult in sequence, one of them in a special way (they encountered it several times on the way to the testing room). When later the adult gestured excitedly toward the three objects together on a tray and ambiguously requested, "Wow, look, can you give it to me please?", infants gave her the object they had shared in a special way. To test the possibility that infants simply gave her that object because it was special for them, individually (not because it was the one they had shared together), Moll et al. included a control condition in which infants shared the three objects with the adult exactly as before, one in a special way, but then a different adult ambiguously requested one of the objects. If infants were just choosing the special object because it was most interesting to them, they should have chosen it in this condition too, but they did not – they chose that object at chance levels. To test the possibility that infants gave the adult the special object because it was the object that was special for *her* (not because it was the one they had shared together in a special way), in another control condition infants watched as the adult experienced the objects individually (again, one in a special way) and then requested one of the objects from them ambiguously. Again, in this condition infants chose the special object at chance levels. In summary, infants responded not based on what they themselves knew individually about the objects, nor on what the adult knew individually, but instead on what they knew together. Thus infants use the common ground they share with others to interpret their communication. When they had not shared any relevant experiences with the requesting adult, they could not disambiguate her request (see also Saylor & Ganea, 2007, for another study on infants' use of common ground to interpret others' communication).

By 18 months of age, if not before (see the studies on declarative pointing by Liszkowski and colleagues discussed above), infants also tailor their own communication for others based on the common ground they share with them. Liebal, Carpenter, and Tomasello (2009) found that infants point differently for others depending on what particular experiences they have recently shared with the particular person for whom they are pointing.

Infants thus not only share attention and interest with others in joint attentional interactions, as we have seen above, they also keep track of the knowledge and experiences they have shared with others in the past, and use this common ground both to make sense of others' communication and to choose what to communicate about for others themselves. They know what "we" know together, and comprehend and produce communicative gestures with this in mind. A series of studies suggests that apes do not use common ground in this way. When, in the context of a hiding-finding game, a human points to a container containing hidden food, apes typically do not understand that the human is trying to tell them the food is there (see Call & Tomasello, 2005, and Miklósi & Soproni, 2006, for reviews). Human infants make this inference by age 14 months (Behne, Carpenter, & Tomasello, 2005). However, apes do succeed in a similar situation when non-communicative cues are provided – when the human simply reaches unsuccessfully for the food for himself (Hare & Tomasello, 2004). Tomasello (2006) suggests that apes' difficulty with the communicative version of this task is due in large part to their inability to take into account their common ground with the human when interpreting his point. Thus, whereas apes understand what others know, there is currently no evidence that they understand or use in communication what "we" know together.

Sharing goals in joint collaborative activities

Once infants are capable of understanding others' goals and intentions, they are able and motivated to pursue shared goals with others in joint collaborative activities. Methodologically, it is a challenge to identify instances of group activity that involve shared goals and intentions. True joint action is not just acting together, it is acting together with the mutual knowledge of a shared goal (e.g., Bratman, 1992; Tomasello et al., 2005) and a joint commitment to see the activity through (Gilbert, 1990). Next I discuss a series of studies designed to determine whether infants and young children participate in true joint action of this type.

In an initial study, Warneken, Chen, and Tomasello (2006) presented 18- and 24-month-old children with four tasks in which collaboration was needed in order to achieve a goal. Two of the tasks involved instrumental problem-solving (retrieving an object from an apparatus) and two were social games (e.g., bouncing a block on a small trampoline together). In the middle of each task, the adult partner suddenly stopped playing his role, and Warneken et al. coded communicative attempts by children to re-engage the adult in the activity. These adult interruption periods were included to see how joint children considered the activity to be: if children had formed a joint goal with the adult, and understood the commitment this entailed, then they should try to persuade the adult to recommit to the joint goal when he stopped instead of disengaging from the task or attempting to perform the activity individually. Warneken et al. also coded how well children coordinated actions with the adult before and after the interruption periods, during the joint activities.

They found that children at both ages succeeded in coordinating with the adult in at least some of the tasks, although 24-month-olds did this more skillfully than 18-month-olds. During the interruption periods, in about half the trials, children's predominate response was either to wait for the adult or to try to re-engage him communicatively (e.g., by pointing to the apparatus or pushing it toward the adult), and across trials all children at both ages attempted to re-engage the adult at least once. This suggests that children knew they had a shared goal with the adult, and that since the adult was committed to the shared goal, children had a right to expect that he would continue playing. Warneken and colleagues also noted two other findings that speak to the motivation children had to cooperate: (a) children participated enthusiastically in the social games, in which there was no material reward, and (b) once they had successfully retrieved the object from the apparatus in the problem-solving tasks, almost all the children replaced the object at some point and repeated the task. These findings indicate that the collaborative activity was an end in itself, not just a means to obtaining some material reward.

Warneken and Tomasello (2007) subsequently tested 14-month-old infants on two of the same tasks and found that they, too, showed some evidence both of coordination of actions and of re-engagement attempts during the interruption periods (see also, e.g., Brownell & Carriger, 1990; Eckerman & Didow, 1989; Hay, 1979; and Ross & Lollis, 1987, for other studies of collaboration in infants).

However, although the findings of Warneken et al. (2006) are consistent with the idea that children were engaging in truly joint action with shared goals and mutual commitments, this was not directly tested in their study. Because all the activities in their study required two players, it is possible that children re-engaged the adult simply as a means to achieving an *individual* goal, not a shared goal. That is, children could simply have wanted to achieve the effect (e.g., retrieving the object or seeing the block bounce) and needed the adult as a sort of "social tool" to make this happen. In two further studies we thus focused more directly on children's understanding of shared goals and joint commitments, while attempting to rule out the alternative "social tool" explanation of children's behavior.

In the first study, Gräfenhain, Behne, Carpenter, and Tomasello (in press, Study 1) tested 2- and 3-year-olds on a series of games which all could be played either jointly or individually. For example, in one game, each player could use a tool to press one of two levers to make two toy rabbits hop up inside a box, or else a single player could press the lever(s) individually. After the experimenter and an assistant demonstrated the games to children both jointly and individually, children were allowed to play the games too, in one of two ways. In the commitment condition, the experimenter invited children to play the game with her (and waited for them to accept her invitation), then played in a joint manner, making eye contact with children and playing contingently with them. In the no commitment condition, in contrast, children were told by the assistant that they could play the game; then as soon as they started playing, the experimenter approached and played in parallel with them on the same apparatus. After this brief play period, in both conditions there was an interruption period, as in Warneken and colleagues' (2006) study. We coded for waiting and re-engagement attempts during these interruption periods, expecting that children would show these behaviors more often in the commitment condition, in which there was a shared goal, than in the no commitment condition in which there was no shared goal.

The 3-year-olds showed the expected pattern of results: in the commitment condition, most children either waited for the experimenter or attempted to re-engage her into the game communicatively, whereas in the no commitment condition children mostly played the game alone. The fact that children waited for or attempted to re-engage the adult in the commitment condition, even in these types of games, when they could just as easily have played the games alone, suggests that they were not merely using the adult as a social tool to achieve their own individual ends – that instead they saw the game as a joint, committed activity.

The 2-year-olds also often waited for or attempted to re-engage the adult but, unexpectedly, they did this in *both* conditions. It is unclear whether these younger children do understand something about shared goals and joint commitments, but just over-attributed them in the no commitment condition, or whether instead in both conditions they simply preferred playing with a partner, even if they were only playing in parallel, and this is why they waited for or attempted to re-engage the adult. More research is needed on very young children's understanding of joint commitments in joint action.

To investigate the extent of the older children's understanding of joint commitments, Gräfenhain et al. (in press) conducted a second study in which we tested whether children themselves feel an obligation to their partner in a joint activity. In this study we measured how children took leave of a committed joint activity when they were done participating In the commitment condition, 3- and 4-year-olds were encouraged to invite the experimenter to play a game with them, and the experimenter accepted their invitation and began to play (basically in parallel to children, but with a verbal reminder halfway through that they were playing together). In the no commitment condition, the experimenter simply announced that she would like to play and started playing in parallel to children. After 30 seconds of play, the response period began: across the room, an assistant began playing another, highly attractive, game by herself. She gradually attempted to entice children to come play with her, first by simply playing loudly on her own, and eventually by asking children if they wanted to play too. The main measure was whether, upon leaving the first game for the second one, children would spontaneously acknowledge their leaving to the experimenter, their partner in the first game, for example by giving her the tool they had used in the game or telling her they wanted to leave.

We found that both 3- and 4-year-olds acknowledged their leaving to the experimenter significantly more often in the commitment condition than in the no commitment condition. Together, these studies show that by 3 years of age children are both sensitive to whether they are in a committed joint activity and also are beginning to know what obligations such committed activities engender.

By 14 to 18 months, infants are thus beginning to be able to coordinate actions with others in joint collaborative activities. There is evidence that is consistent with the idea that infants know they have a shared goal with their partner at this age, with much clearer evidence following by 3 years of age. By that age, children are also beginning to engage in much more complex – and even imaginary – joint actions, in their joint pretense with others. This sets the stage for some of the "bigger" uniquely human joint activities like social institutions and other forms of collective intentionality (Rakoczy, 2007).

There are many reports of cooperation in chimpanzees (e.g., Boesch, 2005; Melis, Hare, & Tomasello, 2006), but little if any evidence for shared goals (indeed see Warneken et al., 2006, for evidence against the idea that chimpanzees have shared goals with others). It appears that ape cooperation consists of apes simply using each other as social tools to obtain food that they cannot obtain on their own, or else accidental coordination of behavior when multiple apes pursue the same individual goal (Tomasello et al., 2005). Whereas human infants see collaboration as an end in itself, apes apparently see it only as a means to an individual goal.

Joint attention, communication about shared experiences, and true joint action all rely on a motivation to share psychological states and experiences together – a motivation that appears to be unique to humans. Together, these skills make possible a huge range of joint activities. However, to explain another set of uniquely human behaviors another social motivation is needed, as we will see next.

Broader Social Motivations

Beyond the motivation to share psychological states with others there is another strong social motivation in humans: the motivation to do things like others do – to *be like* others, and to let them know that "I am one of you." This tendency for humans to align themselves with group members, along with a complementary social pressure coming from the group to conform, ensures cultural transmission of conventional knowledge and shared values, and compliance with social norms. Since norms are, in effect, collectively shared beliefs about the "right" way to do things, again shared intentionality plays a major role in their formation. In the following section I review some evidence suggesting that these types of social motivations, too, are evident in infancy and early childhood.

Communicating mutuality and belongingness in social imitation

Engaging in joint attention is one way to communicate to others that you are sharing or want to share an experience with them. There is another way in which infants can communicate mutuality with others: by imitating them. Užgiris (1981, 1984) identified two functions of imitation in infancy: an instrumental function in which the infant learns something about the object or action in the demonstration, and a social function in which the focus is on the dyad and its interpersonal interaction. According to Užgiris, social imitation can communicate "mutuality or sharing of a feeling, understanding, or goal" and serves to "affirm a shared state" (Užgiris, 1984, p. 25; see also work by Nadel and colleagues, e.g., Nadel, Guérini, Pezé, & Rivet, 1999, for a similar view). Not only does it show that imitators understand that "you are *like me*" (Meltzoff, e.g., 2005), importantly, it also directly communicates to the model the message that "I am *like you*" (Carpenter & Call, in press). Indeed, children's copying of others' actions is related to their tendency to engage in joint attention with others, suggesting a common underlying motivation to communicatively share experiences with others (Carpenter, Tomasello, & Savage-Rumbaugh, 1995; Hobson & Meyer, 2006).

The social function of imitation is seen most clearly when children copy the particular way someone does something, even when that particular way is clearly not necessary to achieve the same effect. One can do this "in the moment," so to speak, just to convey to one's partner "I am like you," at a dyadic level. And one can also do it more lastingly and collectively, when one takes a modeled action to be a conventional action and thus learns it normatively as "this is the way *we* (as a group) do this." On the level of the dyad and its members' relationship, there is evidence that by 18–24 months of age, infants and toddlers often go out of their way to copy others' actions on objects closely, and do so more often in social than non-social situations (e.g., Nielsen, 2006; Nielsen, Simcock, & Jenkins, 2008; Tennie, Call, & Tomasello, 2006). Around the same age, infants also begin using imitation as a strategy to initiate and maintain communicative and socially coordinated interactions with peers (Eckerman, Davis, & Didow, 1989; Nadel, 2002). When they get older, children increase their copying behavior when their motivation to affiliate with others is heightened: 5-year-old children who have been primed with social exclusion (by watching videos in which one shape is ostracized by a group of other shapes) subsequently imitate a demonstrator's actions significantly more closely than children who have not been primed with social exclusion (Over & Carpenter, 2009) – reminiscent of findings in the adult social psychology literature showing that adults subconsciously mimic others when they have a goal to affiliate (e.g., Lakin & Chartrand, 2003).

On the level of conventional, normative understanding, at least by 2–3 years of age it is clear that children have a sense that when someone shows them something in a particular way, it marks the action as generalizable, cultural knowledge (see Gergely & Csibra, 2006). For example, when 2- and 3-year-olds are shown how to play a novel rule game, they learn it normatively, as "this is the way one must do this." They demonstrate this when they go so far as to protest when a puppet then comes in and performs the actions of the game in a different way – they enforce the norm (Rakoczy, Warneken, & Tomasello, 2008). This study, and the one on social exclusion above, thus go somewhat beyond the motivation to be like others and highlight the social pressure children feel to belong to the group, and to do things the way others do. Further evidence of this pressure comes from conformity studies: by 3 years of age, children often conform to majority opinions even when these opinions are clearly incorrect (e.g., Walker & Andrade, 1996).

It is unclear whether children younger than 2–3 years of age have this sense of social pressure to belong to the group, but they are sensitive to some aspects of group membership and affiliation. For example, even young infants have a preference for in-group members, at least in terms of people who speak their native language (Kinzler, Dupoux, & Spelke, 2007). And by 18 months, there are connections between affiliation and prosocial behavior: 18-month-old infants who are primed with affiliation (i.e., shown photographs of familiar household objects with two small dolls standing close to each other in the background) are significantly more likely to help an adult pick up her dropped belongings than infants who were primed with individuality (i.e., shown the same photographs but with only one doll in the background, or with the two dolls standing back-to-back; Over & Carpenter, in press).

A large literature has accumulated showing that apes typically do not copy others' actions – instead they learn something about the goal or results of the demonstration and achieve the goal or results using their own means, by emulation (see, e.g., Carpenter & Call, in press, for a review). It is thus likely that whereas children imitate for both social and instrumental functions (Užgiris, 1981), apes' "imitation" is only instrumental. This appears to be a matter of motivation rather than competence. For example, apes who have been trained to imitate can do so on command, but they do not then spontaneously imitate in novel contexts (Call & Tomasello, 1995; see Carpenter & Call, in press, and Nielsen, in press, for more on this). Finally, although much has been made recently of "ape culture," the tendency for different groups of apes to do things in different ways (e.g., van Schaik et al., 2003; Whiten et al., 1999), there are studies that suggest that at least some of these differences are simply due to differences in the ecological conditions of the different groups (e.g., Humle & Matsuzawa, 2002). There are also few reports of group differences in arbitrary behaviors like gestures – behaviors that can only be spread by convention (Carpenter & Call, in press). Thus, whereas apes, like all social animals, have a social motivation to be *with* others – to share company and simple activities with each other (grooming, rough-and-tumble play, etc.) – we currently have little clear evidence that they have the social motivation to be *like* others (see Carpenter, 2006, and Carpenter & Call, in press, for more on shared intentionality in infant and ape imitation).

Some questions for future research

The development of shared intentionality. Throughout this chapter I have focused on infants around 1 year of age, because that is when we have some of the strongest early evidence for each of the uniquely human skills and motivations I have discussed. Indeed, we think it is no coincidence that these behaviors all emerge at around the same time in development, as we see them as all related, and a result of the interweaving of the "sharing" and "understanding" lines of development at this age (Tomasello et al., 2005).

However, there are clearly precursors to these abilities in even younger infants, both in terms of social motivations and the two types of social cognition. For example, infants younger than 9 months of age may have some basic understanding of others' goals (e.g., Kamewari, Kato, Kanda, Ishiguro, & Hiraki, 2005; Woodward, 1998) and may be able to engage in some joint attention (Striano & Bertin, 2005). They also show some coordination (e.g., turn-taking and synchronization) in their interactions with adults (e.g., Trevarthen, 1980), and show responses to interruptions in social activity (the so-called "still-face effect") that at least on the surface have some commonalities with older children's waiting and re-engagement attempts in collaborative activities (see Adamson & Frick, 2003, for a review). It remains to be seen whether these early behaviors are already evidence of some early form of shared intentionality. For example, is early "joint attention" true coordination of attention or just alternation of attention between two interesting sights? Is the still-face effect evidence of babies' understanding of shared goals and joint commitments or just an expectation of contingency and a desire for social interaction? And does neonatal imitation (see, e.g., Meltzoff & Moore, 1983) already reflect infants' desire to be like others or is it even imitation at all (Jones, 1996)? More work needs to be done on the developmental emergence of all the uniquely human skills discussed here, as well as on interrelations among the different skills.

The neuropsychology of shared intentionality. There is currently much interest in the "social brain." From theory of mind to joint attention and joint action to empathy to mirror neurons, much research is currently focusing on the neuroscience of social cognition from both the perspectives discussed above: how we understand others' psychological states and how we share psychological states and activities with others. A detailed discussion of these topics is beyond the scope of this chapter (and my expertise); luckily there are many recent reviews of relevant literature, for example by Saxe (2006), Grossmann and Johnson (2007), Carrington and Bailey (in press), and Iacoboni and Dapretto (2006). All I wish to do here is bring up some suggestions for possible future directions in this area.

One suggestion is that it would be very helpful for neuroscientists to (somehow) target precisely what makes joint attention and joint action truly joint (and, apparently, unique to humans): the "knowing together" component. For example, several studies have used gaze following or gaze coordination procedures to attempt to investigate the neuropsychology of joint attention (e.g., Striano, Reid, & Hoehl, 2006; Williams, Waiter, Perra, Perrett, & Whiten, 2005). However, the "knowing together" component seems missing from these studies. In the Williams et al. (2005) study there is no indication of it and in the Striano et al. (2006) study it is not clear that it is there: the eye contact before the experimenter's head turn in the "joint attention" condition in that study likely serves as an attention getter or signal of communicative intent instead of a joint attention ("sharing") look. A simple first step that would help move these studies closer to investigating true joint attention might be to add or move the eye contact to *after* the participant and experimenter have looked at the same object. This might help "close" the joint attentional triangle (see figure 4.2) and evoke feelings of joint attention. It would also be interesting to look for relations between joint attention and joint action, as well as relations between these processes and motivation/reward centers of the brain (see, e.g., Henderson, Yoder,

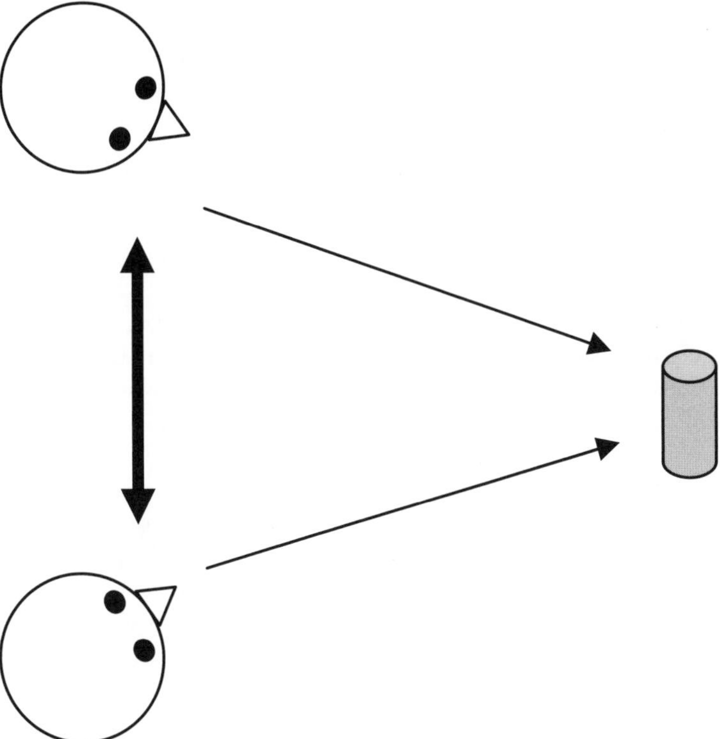

Figure 4.2 The "joint attention triangle." The double, bold arrow represents the crucial "knowing together" component of joint attention

Yale, & McDuffie, 2002, and forthcoming work by Leonhard Schilbach and colleagues). I would also predict that both joint attention and joint action should have something to do with basic communication areas, as to be sure that one is attending or acting jointly with someone else this must be communicated, even if just with a knowing look to the other.

Neuropsychological studies that investigate social cognition developmentally would also be helpful. For example, do 1-year-old infants who pass false-belief tests (see, e.g., Buttelmann et al., in press; Onishi & Baillargeon, 2005) do so using the same brain areas as 5-year-olds passing similar non-verbal tests? Do infants before and after the "social-cognitive revolution" at 9–12 months (Tomasello, 1995) process gaze, imitation, and other social interactions in the same way (see related questions above)? And are there brain explanations for developmental differences in social imitation (e.g., Nielson, 2006) and automatic mimicry (e.g., Anderson & Meno, 2003)?

Finally, there are many, far-reaching claims concerning the extensive role that mirror neurons are thought to play in various aspects of human social cognition, for example in imitation, empathy, theory of mind, cooperation, and language (see, e.g., Iacoboni & Dapretto, 2006). However, on both theoretical and methodological grounds, an increasing number of researchers are starting to question these claims (see, e.g., Csibra, 2007; Dinstein, Thomas, Behrmann, & Heeger, 2008; Jacob, 2008; Nielsen & Carpenter, 2008; Southgate, Gergely, & Csibra, 2008; Turella, Pierno, Tubaldi, & Castiello, 2009). It will be interesting to see whether these claims will stand the test of close empirical scrutiny.

Conclusion

Human social cognition is special. Humans, from very early in life, have a strong motivation to share experiences and activities with others, and to align themselves with and be like others. This motivation is what turns gaze following into joint attention, egocentric communication into communication about shared experiences, group activity into joint action, and social learning into conventional, cultural learning (Tomasello & Carpenter, 2007). It thus transforms individualistic skills (like those of chimpanzees) into the more collective counterparts of those skills which are the foundation for everything from declarative pointing and simple collaborative activities to fads and fashions, cultural practices, and social norms and institutions. This motivation for shared intentionality is so important, yet so basic it is seen in infants before they can walk. In infants' social cognition and social motivations, we see the social origins of cultural cognition.

References

Adamson, L. B., & Frick, J. E. (2003). The still face: A history of a shared experimental paradigm. *Infancy*, *4*, 451–473.

Anderson, J. R., & Meno, P. M. (2003). Psychological influences on yawning in children. *Current Psychology Letters: Behaviour, Brain and Cognition*, *11*. Retrieved from http://cpl.revues.org/document390.html

Bakeman, R., & Adamson, L. B. (1984). Coordinating attention to people and objects in mother–infant and peer–infant interaction. *Child Development*, *55*, 1278–1289.

Bard, K. A., & Vauclair, J. (1984). The communicative context of object manipulation in ape and human adult–infant pairs. *Journal of Human Evolution*, *13*, 181–190.

Behne, T., Carpenter, M., Call, J., & Tomasello, M. (2005). Unwilling versus unable: Infants' understanding of intentional action. *Developmental Psychology*, *41*, 328–337.

Behne, T., Carpenter, M., & Tomasello, M. (2005). One-year-olds comprehend the communicative intentions behind gestures in a hiding game. *Developmental Science*, *8*, 492–499.

Boesch, C. (2005). Joint cooperative hunting among wild chimpanzees: Taking natural observations seriously. *Behavioral and Brain Sciences*, *28*, 692–693.

Bratman, M. E. (1992). Shared cooperative activity. *The Philosophical Review*, *101*, 327–341.

Bräuer, J., Call, J., & Tomasello, M. (2005). All great ape species follow gaze to distant locations and around barriers. *Journal of Comparative Psychology*, *119*, 145–154.

Bretherton, I., McNew, S., & Beeghly-Smith, M. (1981). Early person knowledge as expressed in gestural and verbal communication: When do infants acquire a "theory of mind"? In M. E. Lamb & L. R. Sherrod (Eds.), *Infant social cognition: Empirical and theoretical considerations* (pp. 333–373). Hillsdale, NJ: Erlbaum.

Brooks, R., & Meltzoff, A. N. (2002). The importance of eyes: How infants interpret adult looking behavior. *Developmental Psychology, 38*, 958–966.

Brownell, C. A., & Carriger, M. S. (1990). Changes in cooperation and self–other differentiation during the second year. *Child Development, 61*, 1164–1174.

Buttelmann, D., Carpenter, M., Call, J., & Tomasello, M. (2007). Enculturated chimpanzees imitate rationally. *Developmental Science, 10*, F31–F38.

Buttelmann, D., Carpenter, M., Call, J., & Tomasello, M. (2008). Rational tool use and tool choice in human infants and great apes. *Child Development, 79*, 609–626.

Buttelmann, D., Carpenter, M., & Tomasello, M. (in press). Eighteen-month-old infants show false belief understanding in an active helping paradigm. *Cognition.*

Call, J., Hare, B., Carpenter, M., & Tomasello, M. (2004). "Unwilling" versus "unable": Chimpanzees' understanding of human intentions. *Developmental Science, 7*, 488–498.

Call, J. & Tomasello, M. (1995). The use of social information in the problem-solving of orangutans (*Pongo pygmaeus*) and human children (*Homo sapiens*). *Journal of Comparative Psychology, 109*, 308–320.

Call, J., & Tomasello, M. (1998). Distinguishing intentional from accidental actions in orangutans (*Pongo pygmaeus*), chimpanzees (*Pan troglodytes*), and human children (*Homo sapiens*). *Journal of Comparative Psychology, 112*, 192–206.

Call, J., & Tomasello, M. (1999). A nonverbal theory of mind test: The performance of children and great apes. *Child Development, 70*, 381–395.

Call, J., & Tomasello, M. (2005). What chimpanzees know about seeing, revisited: An explanation of the third kind. In N. Eilan, C. Hoerl, T. McCormack, & J. Roessler (Eds.), *Joint attention: Communication and other minds* (pp. 45–64). Oxford: Oxford University Press.

Caron, A. J., Butler, S., & Brooks, R. (2002). Gaze following at 12 and 14 months: Do the eyes matter? *British Journal of Developmental Psychology, 20*, 225–239.

Carpenter, M. (2006). Instrumental, social, and shared goals and intentions in imitation. In S. J. Rogers & J. Williams (Eds.), *Imitation and the development of the social mind: Lessons from typical development and autism* (pp. 48–70). New York: Guilford.

Carpenter, M., Akhtar, N., & Tomasello, M. (1998). Fourteen- to 18-month-old infants differentially imitate intentional and accidental actions. *Infant Behavior and Development, 21*, 315–330.

Carpenter, M., & Call, J. (in press). Comparing the imitative skills of children and nonhuman apes. *Revue de Primatologie.*

Carpenter, M., Nagell, K., & Tomasello, M. (1998). Social cognition, joint attention, and communicative competence from 9 to 15 months of age. *Monographs of the Society for Research in Child Development, 63* (4, Serial No. 255).

Carpenter, M., Tomasello, M., & Savage-Rumbaugh, S. (1995). Joint attention and imitative learning in children, chimpanzees, and enculturated chimpanzees. *Social Development, 4*, 217–237.

Carrington, S. J., & Bailey, A. J. (in press). Are there theory of mind regions in the brain? A review of the neuroimaging literature. *Human Brain Mapping.*

Clark, H. H. (1996). *Using language.* Cambridge: Cambridge University Press.

Csibra, G. (2007). Action mirroring and action understanding: An alternative account. In P. Haggard, Y. Rosetti, & M. Kawato (Eds.), *Attention and performance XXII: Sensorimotor foundations of higher cognition.* Oxford: Oxford University Press.

Dinstein, I., Thomas, C., Behrmann, M., & Heeger, D. J. (2008). A mirror up to nature. *Current Biology, 18*, R13–R18.

Dunphy-Lelii, S., & Wellman, H. M. (2004). Infants' understanding of occlusion of others' line-of-sight: Implications for an emerging theory of mind. *European Journal of Developmental Psychology, 1*, 49–66.

Eckerman, C. O., Davis, C. C., & Didow, S. M. (1989). Toddlers' emerging ways of achieving social coordinations with a peer. *Child Development, 60*, 440–453.

Eckerman, C. O., & Didow, S. M. (1989). Toddlers' social coordinations: Changing responses to another's invitation to play. *Developmental Psychology, 25*, 794–804.

Flom, R., Lee, K., & Muir, D. (Eds.). (2007). *Gaze following: Its development and significance.* Mahwah, NJ: Erlbaum.

Gergely, G., Bekkering, H., & Király, I. (2002). Rational imitation in preverbal infants. *Nature, 415*, 755.

Gergely, G., & Csibra, G. (2006). Sylvia's recipe: The role of imitation and pedagogy in the transmission of cultural knowledge. In N. Enfield & S. C. Levinson (Eds.), *Roots of human sociality: Culture, cognition, and interaction* (pp. 229–255). Oxford: Berg.

Gilbert, M. (1990). Walking together: A paradigmatic social phenomenon. *Midwest Studies in Philosophy, 15*, 1–14.

Gómez, J. C., Sarriá, E., & Tamarit, J. (1993). The comparative study of early communication and theories of mind: ontogeny, phylogeny, and pathology. In S. Baron-Cohen, H. Tager-Flusberg, & D. J. Cohen (Eds.), *Understanding other minds: Perspectives from autism* (pp. 397–426). Oxford: Oxford University Press.

Gräfenhain, M., Behne, T., Carpenter, M., & Tomasello, M. (in press). Young children's understanding of joint commitments to act jointly. *Developmental Psychology.*

Grossmann, T., & Johnson, M. (2007). The development of the social brain in human infancy. *European Journal of Neuroscience, 25*, 909–919.

Hare, B., Call, J., & Tomasello, M. (2001). Do chimpanzees know what conspecifics know and do not know? *Animal Behaviour, 61*, 139–151.

Hare, B., & Tomasello, M. (2004). Chimpanzees are more skillful in competitive than in cooperative cognitive tasks. *Animal Behaviour, 68*, 571–581.

Hay, D. F. (1979). Cooperative interactions and sharing between very young children and their parents. *Developmental Psychology, 15*, 647–653.

Henderson, L. M., Yoder, P. J., Yale, M. E., & McDuffie, A. (2002). Getting the point: electrophysiological correlates of protodeclarative pointing. *International Journal of Developmental Neuroscience, 20*, 449–458.

Hobson, R. P., & Meyer, J. (2006). Imitation, identification, and the shaping of mind: Insights from autism. In S. J. Rogers & J. Williams (Eds.), *Imitation and the development of the social mind: Lessons from typical development and autism* (pp. 198–224). New York: Guilford.

Humle, T. & Matsuzawa, T. (2002). Ant-dipping among the chimpanzees of Bossou, Guinea, and some comparisons with other sites. *American Journal of Primatology, 58*, 133–148.

Iacoboni, M., & Dapretto, M. (2006). The mirror neuron system and the consequences of its dysfunction. *Nature Reviews Neuroscience, 7*, 942–951.

Jacob, P. (2008). What do mirror neurons contribute to human social cognition? *Mind & Language, 23*, 190–223.

Johnson, S. C., Booth, A., & O'Hearn, K. (2001). Inferring the goals of a nonhuman agent. *Cognitive Development, 16*, 637–656.

Jones, S. S. (1996). Imitation or exploration? Young infants' matching of adults' oral gestures. *Child Development, 67*, 1952–1969.

Kamewari, K., Kato, M., Kanda, T., Ishiguro, H., & Hiraki, K. (2005). Six-and-a-half-month-old children positively attribute goals to human action and to humanoid-robot motion. *Cognitive Development, 20*, 303–320.

Kaminski, J., Call, J., & Tomasello, M. (2004). Body orientation and face orientation: Two factors controlling apes' begging behavior from humans. *Animal Cognition, 7*, 216–223.

Kaminski, J., Call, J., & Tomasello, M. (2008). Chimpanzees know what others know, but not what they believe. *Cognition, 109*, 224–234.

Kinzler, K. D., Dupoux, E., & Spelke, E. S. (2007). The native language of social cognition. *Proceedings of the National Academy of Sciences, 104*, 12577–12580.

Krachun, C., Carpenter, M., Call, J., & Tomasello, M. (in press). A competitive nonverbal false belief task for children and apes. *Developmental Science.*

Lakin, J. L., & Chartrand, T. L. (2003). Using nonconscious behavioral mimicry to create affiliation and rapport. *Psychological Science, 14*, 334–339.

Liebal, K., Behne, T., Carpenter, M., & Tomasello, M. (2009). Infants use shared experience to interpret pointing gestures. *Developmental Science, 12*, 264–271.

Liebal, K., Carpenter, M., & Tomasello, M. (2009). *Infants' use of shared experience in declarative pointing*. Manuscript submitted for publication.

Liszkowski, U., Carpenter, M., Henning, A., Striano, T., & Tomasello, M. (2004). Twelve-month-olds point to share attention and interest. *Developmental Science, 7*, 297–307.

Liszkowski, U., Carpenter, M., & Tomasello, M. (2007a). Pointing out new news, old news, and absent referents at 12 months of age. *Developmental Science, 10*, F1–F7.

Liszkowski, U., Carpenter, M., & Tomasello, M. (2007b). Reference and attitude in infant pointing. *Journal of Child Language, 34*, 1–20.

Liszkowski, U., Carpenter, M., & Tomasello, M. (2008). Twelve-month-olds communicate helpfully and appropriately for knowledgeable and ignorant partners. *Cognition, 108*, 732–739.

Liszkowski, U., Schäfer, M., Carpenter, M., & Tomasello, M. (in press). Prelinguistic infants, but not chimpanzees, communicate about absent entities. *Psychological Science.*

Melis, A. P., Hare, B., & Tomasello, M. (2006). Chimpanzees recruit the best collaborators. *Science, 311*, 1297–1300.

Meltzoff, A. N. (1995). Understanding the intentions of others: Re-enactment of intended acts by 18-month-old children. *Developmental Psychology, 31*, 838–850.

Meltzoff, A. N. (2005). Imitation and other minds: The "like me" hypothesis. In S. Hurley & N. Chater (Eds.), *Perspectives on imitation: From neuroscience to social science* (Vol. *2*, pp. 55–77). Cambridge, MA: MIT Press.

Meltzoff, A. N., & Moore, M. K. (1983). Newborn infants imitate adult facial gestures. *Child Development, 54*, 702–709.

Miklósi, Á., & Soproni, K. (2006). A comparative analysis of animals' understanding of the human pointing gesture. *Animal Cognition, 9*, 81–93.

Moll, H., Koring, C., Carpenter, M., & Tomasello, M. (2006). Infants determine others' focus of attention by pragmatics and exclusion. *Journal of Cognition and Development, 7*, 411–430.

Moll, H., Richter, N., Carpenter, M., & Tomasello, M. (2008). Fourteen-month-olds know what "we" have shared in a special way. *Infancy, 13*, 90–101.

Moll, H., & Tomasello, M. (2004). Twelve- and 18-month-old infants follow gaze to spaces behind barriers. *Developmental Science, 7*, F1–F9.

Moll, H., & Tomasello, M. (2007). How 14- and 18-month-olds know what others have experienced. *Developmental Psychology, 43*, 309–317.

Moore, C., & Corkum, V. (1994). Social understanding at the end of the first year of life. *Developmental Review, 14*, 349–372.

Moore, C., & D'Entremont, B. (2001). Developmental changes in pointing as a function of attentional focus. *Journal of Cognition and Development, 2*, 109–129.

Nadel, J. (2002). Imitation and imitation recognition: Functional use in preverbal infants and nonverbal children with autism. In A. N. Meltzoff & W. Prinz (Eds.), *The imitative mind: Development, evolution, and brain bases* (pp. 42–62). Cambridge: Cambridge University Press.

Nadel, J., Guérini, C., Pezé, A., & Rivet, C. (1999). The evolving nature of imitation as a format for communication. In J. Nadel & G. Butterworth (Eds.), *Imitation in infancy* (pp. 209–234. Cambridge: Cambridge University Press.

Nielsen, M. (2006). Copying actions and copying outcomes: Social learning through the second year. *Developmental Psychology, 42*, 555–565.

Nielsen, M. (in press). The imitative behaviour of children and chimpanzees: A window on the transmission of cultural traditions. *Revue de Primatologie.*

Nielsen, M., & Carpenter, M. (2008). Reflecting on imitation in autism: Introduction to the special issue. *Journal of Experimental Child Psychology, 101*, 165–169.

Nielsen, M., Simcock, G., & Jenkins, L. (2008). The effect of social engagement on 24-month-olds' imitation from live and televised models. *Developmental Science, 11*, 722–731.

Olineck, K. M., & Poulin-Dubois, D. (2005). Infants' ability to distinguish between intentional and accidental actions and its relation to internal state language. *Infancy, 8*, 91–100.

Onishi, K. H., & Baillargeon, R. (2005). Do 15-month-old infants understand false beliefs? *Science, 308*, 255–258.

Over, H., & Carpenter, M. (2009). Priming third-party ostracism increases affiliative imitation in children. *Developmental Science, 12*, F1–F8.

Over, H., & Carpenter, M. (in press). Eighteen-month-old infants show increased helping following priming with affiliation. *Psychological Science.*

Rakoczy, H. (2007). Play, games, and the development of collective intentionality. In C. Kalish & M. Sabbagh (Eds.), *Conventionality in cognitive development: How children acquire representations in language, thought and action. New Directions in Child and Adolescent Development.* No. 115 (pp. 53–67). San Francisco: Jossey-Bass.

Rakoczy, H., Warneken, F., & Tomasello, M. (2008). The sources of normativity: Young children's awareness of the normative structure of games. *Developmental Psychology, 44*, 875–881.

Ross, H. S., & Lollis, S. P. (1987). Communication within infant social games. *Developmental Psychology, 23*, 241–248.

Saxe, R. (2006). Uniquely human social cognition. *Current Opinion in Neurobiology, 16*, 235–239.

Saylor, M. M., & Ganea, P. (2007). Infants interpret ambiguous requests for absent objects. *Developmental Psychology, 43*, 696–704.

Schwier, C., van Maanen, C., Carpenter, M., & Tomasello, M. (2006). Rational imitation in 12-month-old infants. *Infancy, 10*, 303–311.

Song, H., Onishi, K. H., Baillargeon, R., & Fisher, C. (2008). Can an agent's false belief be corrected by an appropriate communication? Psychological reasoning in 18-month-old infants. *Cognition, 109*, 295–315.

Southgate, V., Gergely, G., & Csibra, G. (2008). Does the mirror neuron system and its impairment explain human imitation and autism? In J. A. Pineda (Ed.), *The role of mirroring processes in social cognition.* New York: Humana Press.

Striano, T., & Bertin, E. (2005). Coordinated affect with mothers and strangers: A longitudinal analysis of joint engagement between 5 and 9 months of age. *Cognition and Emotion, 19*, 781–790.

Striano, T., Reid, V. M., & Hoehl, S. (2006). Neural mechanisms of joint attention in infancy. *European Journal of Neuroscience, 23*, 2819–2823.

Surian, L., Caldi, S., & Sperber, D. (2007). Attribution of beliefs by 13-month-old infants. *Psychological Science, 18*, 580–586.

Tennie, C., Call, J., & Tomasello, M. (2006). Push or pull: imitation versus emulation in human children and great apes. *Ethology, 112*, 1159–1169.

Tomasello, M. (1995). Joint attention as social cognition. In C. Moore & P. J. Dunham (Eds.), *Joint attention: Its origins and role in development* (pp. 103–130). Hillsdale, NJ: Erlbaum.

Tomasello, M. (2006). Why don't apes point? In N. J. Enfield & S. C. Levinson (Eds.), *Roots of human sociality: Culture, cognition and interaction* (pp. 506–524). Oxford: Berg.

Tomasello, M. (2008). *Origins of human communication*. Cambridge, MA: MIT Press.

Tomasello, M., & Carpenter, M. (2005). The emergence of social cognition in three young chimpanzees. *Monographs of the Society for Research in Child Development, 70* (1, Serial No. 279).

Tomasello, M., & Carpenter M. (2007). Shared intentionality. *Developmental Science, 10*, 121–125.

Tomasello, M., Carpenter, M., Call, J., Behne, T., & Moll, H. (2005). Understanding and sharing intentions: The origins of cultural cognition. *Behavioral and Brain Sciences, 28*, 675–735.

Tomasello, M., Carpenter, M., & Liszkowski, U. (2007). A new look at infant pointing. *Child Development, 78*, 705–722.

Tomasello, M., & Haberl, K. (2003). Understanding attention: 12- and 18-month-olds know what's new for other persons. *Developmental Psychology, 39*, 906–912.

Tomasello, M., Hare, B., & Agnetta, B. (1999). Chimpanzees, *Pan troglodytes,* follow gaze direction geometrically. *Animal Behavior, 58*, 769–777.

Tomonaga, M., Tanaka, M., Matsuzawa, T., Myowa-Yamakoshi, M., Kosugi, D., Mizuno, Y., Okamoto, S., Yamaguchi, M. K., & Bard, K. A. (2004). Development of social cognition in infant chimpanzees (*Pan troglodytes*): Face recognition, smiling, gaze, and the lack of triadic interactions. *Japanese Psychological Research, 46*, 227–235.

Trevarthen, C. (1979). Instincts for human understanding and for cultural cooperation: Their development in infancy. In M. von Cranach, K. Foppa, W. Lepenies, & D. Ploog (Eds.), *Human ethology: Claims and limits of a new discipline* (pp. 530–571). Cambridge: Cambridge University Press.

Trevarthen, C. (1980). The foundations of intersubjectivity: Development of interpersonal and cooperative understanding in infants. In D. R. Olson (Ed.), *The social foundations of language and thought: Essays in honor of Jerome S. Bruner* (pp. 316–342). New York: Norton.

Trevarthen, C., & Hubley, P. (1978). Secondary intersubjectivity: Confidence, confiding and acts of meaning in the first year. In A. Lock (Ed.), *Action, gesture, and symbol* (pp. 183–229). London: Academic Press.

Turella, L., Pierno, A. C., Tubaldi, F., & Castiello, U. (2009). Mirror neurons in humans: Consisting or confounding evidence? *Brain and Language, 108*, 10–21.

Užgiris, I. C. (1981). Two functions of imitation during infancy. *International Journal of Behavioral Development, 4*, 1–12.

Užgiris, I. C. (1984). Imitation in infancy: Its interpersonal aspects. In M. Perlmutter (Ed.), *Parent–child interactions and parent–child relations in child development: The Minnesota symposia on child psychology* (Vol. *17*, pp. 1–32). Hillsdale, NJ: Erlbaum.

Van Schaik, C. P., Ancrenaz, M., Borgen, G., Galdikas, B., Knott, C. D., Singleton, I., Suzuki, A., Utami, S. S., & Merrill, M. (2003). Orangutan cultures and the evolution of material culture. *Science, 299*, 102–105.

Walker, M. B., & Andrade, M. G. (1996). Conformity in the Asch task as a function of age. *Journal of Social Psychology, 136*, 367–372.

Warneken, F., Chen, F., & Tomasello, M. (2006). Cooperative activities in young children and chimpanzees. *Child Development, 77*, 640–663.

Warneken, F., & Tomasello, M. (2006). Altruistic helping in human infants and young chimpanzees. *Science, 311*, 1301–1303.

Warneken, F., & Tomasello, M. (2007). Helping and cooperation at 14 months of age. *Infancy, 11*, 271–294.

Wellman, H. M., Cross, D., & Watson, J. (2001). Meta-analysis of theory-of-mind development: The truth about false belief. *Child Development, 72*, 655–684.

Whiten, A., & Byrne, R. W. (1988). Tactical deception in primates. *Behavioral and Brain Sciences, 11*, 233–273.

Whiten, A., Goodall, J., McGrew, W. C., Nishida, T., Reynolds, V., Sugiyama, Y., Tutin, C. E. G., Wrangham, R. W. & Boesch, C. (1999). Cultures in chimpanzees. *Nature, 399*, 682–685.

Williams, J. H. G., Waiter, G. D., Perra, O., Perrett, D. I., & Whiten, A. (2005). An fMRI study of joint attention experience. *NeuroImage, 25*, 133–140.

Wimmer, H., Hogrefe, G., & Perner, J. (1988). Children's understanding of informational access as source of knowledge. *Child Development, 59*, 386–396.

Wimmer, H., & Perner, J. (1983). Beliefs about beliefs: Representation and constraining function of wrong beliefs in young children's understanding of deception. *Cognition, 13*, 103–128.

Woodward, A. (1998). Infants selectively encode the goal object of an actor's reach. *Cognition, 69*, 1–34.

CHAPTER FIVE

Born to Categorize

Paul C. Quinn

This chapter will begin with an introduction to the concept of *categorization*, a mental ability that Thelen and Smith [(1994)] have described as "the primitive in all behavior and mental functioning" (p. 143). The discussion will focus on how categories get started, so the chapter will proceed to a description of some historical and more contemporary perspectives on how categories are initially formed. The historical perspectives include those from behaviorism (Hull, 1920), symbolic anthropology (Leach, 1964), and cognitive psychology (Rosch, 1978). The contemporary approaches include those of Mandler (1992) as well as reactions to the Mandler view of concept development (Madole & Oakes, 1999; Quinn & Eimas, 1997; Rakison & Poulin-Dubois, 2001; Younger, in press). In addition, the data that have been used to support one versus another position will be reviewed. The data center on a group of interrelated issues, including (a) whether there is a consistent order of emergence for category representations at different levels of inclusiveness (i.e., animal, cat, Siamese cat), (b) whether early categories are perceptually or conceptually based, (c) whether the tasks used to assess infant categorization are tapping into pre-existing concepts or simply inducing conceptual behavior that emerges in the context of the task, and (d) how the beginning categories of infants develop into the more mature concepts of children and adults. To address these issues, both behavioral and computational evidence will be considered. The ability of more recently developed technologies such as event-related potentials and eye tracking to inform our understanding of infant categorization performance will also be discussed.

Preparation of this chapter was supported by was supported by National Institutes of Health Grants HD-42451 and HD-46526. The author thanks Usha Goswami for comments on an earlier draft.

Correspondence concerning this chapter should be addressed to Paul C. Quinn, Department of Psychology, University of Delaware, Newark, DE 19716. Electronic mail may be sent to pquinn@udel.edu.

Categorization: A Foundation for Cognition

Gerald Edelman, a 1972 Nobel prizewinner for work in molecular immunology, turned his attention in the late 1980s to neuroscience and argued that ""One of the fundamental tasks of the nervous system is to carry out perceptual categorization in an unlabeled world"" (Edelman, 1987, p. 7). This observation certainly speaks to the task facing young infants who must at some point during development come to organize objects encountered in the environment into groupings or categories such as dog, animal, chair, and furniture. The term categorization as used in the modern cognitive sciences literature refers to the recognition of discriminably different entities as members of the same category based on some internalized representation of the category that has been called a schema (Kagan, 2008; Mandler, 1997) or concept (Murphy, 2002; Smith & Medin, 1981). In this chapter, the term category representation will be used to describe the mental structure under consideration (Quinn, 2002). Schema seems not powerful enough a label given that it describes a representation used to recognize objects experienced in the past, whereas category representations allow individuals to generalize to novel instances not previously experienced (Quinn, 2008). Likewise, concept may be too strong a label given that the infants at issue are less than a year of age and presumably do not have mental structures that are imbued with the abstract knowledge possessed by older children and adults. One can think of a category representation as a stored mental representation for like entities. A concrete way to think about category representations is to think about file folders. File folders are used to organize information, and many in the cognitive sciences believe that adult humans possess mental files or category representations to hold information about various object classes.

What are the advantages of having a mind–brain system that categorizes experience? First, categorization is important for reducing the diversity of the physical world. Color is a good example. It is estimated that there are 7,000,000 discriminable colors in our experience. Yet, most languages collapse the wavelength continuum into a dozen or fewer basic categories (Bruner, Goodnow, & Austin, 1956). Think about how complex child language acquisition would become if it included mapping 7,000,000 color terms onto 7,000,000 color experiences.

A second advantage of categorization is that it provides for organized storage and efficient retrieval of information from memory (Quinn & Bomba, 1986). If all human observers did was to throw individual items encountered in the natural environment into their memories in no particular arrangement in a kind of "garbage truck" or "laundry basket" model of storage, then recognition would be slow and error-prone because it would require comparing each new stimulus to a huge number of stored items on a trial-and-error basis. It would be a bit like searching for a needle in a haystack. That recognition is often fast and accurate is consistent with the idea that memory is organized and most likely in terms of categories.

A third advantage of categorization is our ability to respond equivalently to an indefinitely large number of examples from multiple categories including many instances never before experienced (Murphy, 2002; Smith & Medin, 1981). Our days can include encounters with novel stimuli, for example, new furry, four-legged creatures that bark, and new moving, elongated, metallic objects on rubber discs. Yet, human perceivers generally do not walk around the world saying "What is this?" or "How should I respond to that?" Rather, observers say "This is a dog and that is a car." In other words, categories allow individuals to respond to the novel as if it's familiar, thereby preserving cognitive resources for day-to-day mental activities including creative problem-solving, thinking, and reasoning.

Historical Perspective: Traditional Views

Because of the perceived importance of categories to mental life and the recognition that they have to start somewhere, there has been interest in how categories develop and there have been different historical perspectives on this issue. First, it needs to be acknowledged that Edelman (1987) may not have framed the problem correctly; maybe the world is labeled for the child. This in fact was the view taken by the behaviorist Clark Hull. According to Hull (1920):

> A young child finds himself in a certain situation … and hears it called "dog." After an indeterminate intervening period he finds himself in a somewhat different situation and hears that called "dog" also … The "dog" experiences appear at irregular intervals … At length the time arrives when the child has a meaning for the word "dog." (pp. 5–6)

Hull's view implies that a young child may not recognize a previously unseen dog as a member of the category dogs until hearing the label "dog" associated with different dogs over an extended period of time. So, for example, a young child might go for a walk with her parents, see a dog, and hear the parents label it as a dog. The repetition of this experience over time, Hull believed, prompted the child to seek out characteristics common to dogs that made them distinct from contrast categories such as cats, bears, and the like.

A second view about how categories emerge comes from the symbolic anthropology literature. Edmund Leach (1964) proposed that

> The physical and social environment of a young child is perceived as a continuum … The child, in due course, is taught to impose upon this environment a kind of discriminating grid which serves to distinguish the world as being composed of a large number of separate things, each labeled with a name. (p. 34)

According to Leach, the world has little or no natural order. To categorize, the child must learn through instruction to impose order on natural disorder.

These views are plausible, and there is certainly ample evidence that some of our skill at dividing experience into meaningful categories is derived from language and instruction (Anderson, 1991; Callanan, 1985; Carey, in press; Colunga & Smith, 2005; Gelman, Coley, Rosengren, Hartman, & Pappas, 1998; Gopnik & Meltzoff, 1997; Markman, 1989; Millikan, 1998; Waxman & Gelman, in press). The question is whether something even more fundamental might underlie the initial beginnings of categorization in young infants. An answer to this question emerges from examination of a third framework for understanding the emergence of categories, this one put forth by Eleanor Rosch and colleagues (Rosch, Mervis, Gray, Johnson, & Boyes-Braem, 1976). Rosch et al. advanced a position in between that of Edelman on the one hand, and Hull and Leach on the other. The major argument is that the world is not necessarily labeled for the child, but it does have structure, and that structure comes in the form of bundles of correlated attributes (Mervis & Rosch, 1981). In the Rosch view, categorization is highly determined because the world breaks down along lines of natural discontinuity. For example, objects like birds have feathers, beaks, two legs, and make chirping sounds, whereas objects like dogs have fur, snouts, four legs, and make barking sounds. Importantly, if the Rosch framework is correct, then an organism that can detect such regularities and correlations, and compile them into separate representations, is capable of categorization (e.g., Younger, 1990). And if that is true, then some of the abilities involved in categorizing may be present before the emergence of language and formal instruction. Thus, by the Rosch account, it becomes important to understand the abilities prelinguistic infants might have to categorize their environment, as it may be from these abilities that the complex categories of the adult will develop.

At the time of Rosch's writings, the mid- to late 1970s, the procedures available to study infant perception and cognition had not yet been adapted to study categorization. But Rosch (1978) did have a view of natural category development, and that was another major part of her overall theory. Rosch et al. (1976) had argued that category knowledge is organized hierarchically into various levels and the three that are most often discussed are the superordinate, basic, and subordinate levels. For example, subordinate categories like beagle and boxer are nested under the basic-level category of dog, which in turn lies below the superordinate categories of mammal and animal. Rosch et al. also claimed that the basic level in the hierarchy is the most functional: the level at which we do most of our thinking. Basic-level superiority occurs because members of basic-level categories tend to possess significant numbers of attributes in common, have similar shapes, and invoke similar motor movements.

Rosch et al. (1976) also suggested that basic-level categories might be the first to be acquired during development. Evidence supporting this suggestion came from a task in which 3-year-olds were asked to identify which two of three objects were alike. The key finding was that the children succeeded in the basic-level version of the task involving, for example, two airplanes and a dog, but performed poorly in the superordinate-level version of the task involving, for example, an airplane, a car, and a dog. On this basis, Rosch et al. argued that object categories were initially represented at the basic level. Development consisted of grouping together basic-level representations to form the superordinate level, and differentiating basic-level representations to form the subordinate level.

Evidence of Categorization by Infants

A methodology for studying categorization in young infants is called the familiarization/novelty-preference procedure and is based on the established preference that infants have for novel stimulation (e.g., Fantz, 1964). A number of stimuli, all of which belong to the same category, are presented during familiarization. Two new stimuli are then presented during a novel-category preference test – one is from the familiar category, and the other is from a novel category. If infants generalize familiarization to a novel discriminably different exemplar from the familiar category, and display a preference for an equally discriminable exemplar from a novel category, then this pattern of responding is taken as evidence to infer that the familiar exemplars have in some manner been grouped together or categorized and that the representation of this category excludes the novel-category exemplar.

Armed with the familiarization/novelty-preference procedure and with the Rosch view of basic-to-superordinate category development in mind, an initial investigation was undertaken to determine whether young infants, 3–4 months of age, could form separate category representations for cats, dogs, and birds chosen from the superordinate category animal (Quinn, Eimas, & Rosenkrantz, 1993). These categories seemed liked good candidates to begin the study of natural category formation by infants because some of the earliest words in the child's vocabulary refer to animals and include "dog," "kitty," and "bird" (Roberts & Cuff, 1989). The first question asked was whether infants could form separate category representations for dogs and cats that were sufficiently differentiated to exclude instances of birds. Half of the infants were exposed to a dozen cats, and the other half were shown a dozen dogs. Both groups were presented with a novel instance from the familiarized category versus a novel bird. It should be noted that the overall size of the images was equated across the categories. Infants that saw either cats or dogs looked predominantly to the novel birds. Control experiments indicated that there was no a priori preference for the birds and that the infants could discriminate among the exemplars within the dog and cat categories.

The next question asked was whether the infants could categorize cats versus dogs. Infants were familiarized with cats or dogs, and then tested with a novel cat versus a novel dog. Infants familiarized with cats preferred dogs over novel cats, and infants familiarized with dogs preferred cats over novel dogs. The latter result occurred with certain limitations related to the variability of the dog exemplars and their overlap (i.e., inclusion relation) with the cat exemplars (for further comment, see Mareschal, French, & Quinn, 2000; Oakes, Coppage, & Dingel, 1997). Nevertheless, the overall pattern of results indicated that young infants could form separate category representations for cats and dogs, each of which was sufficiently differentiated to exclude instances of the other as well as birds (for additional corroborating results of categorization of animal species by young infants, including a representation for horses that excluded cats, giraffes, and zebras, see Eimas & Quinn, 1994; Oakes & Ribar, 2005; Younger & Fearing, 1999; Younger & Furrer, 2005).

Neural Correlates as Evidenced with an Event-Related Potential Methodology

As a complement to the behavioral looking-time studies demonstrating category formation for various animal species by infants, Quinn, Westerlund, and Nelson (2006) asked whether neural correlates of category learning by infants might be measurable. They did so by developing an event-related potential (ERP) analogue of the behavioral looking-time procedure. Six-month-olds were familiarized with 36 cat images, and then tested with 20 novel cat images interspersed with 20 novel dog images. The results (i.e., the neural activations observed in different parts of the scalp up to a second and a half after stimulus presentation) were partitioned into four different conditions: cats 1–18, cats 19–36, novel cats, and novel dogs. The rationale is that if there is a neural signal that corresponds with category learning, then the responses to cats 1–18 and the novel dogs (reflecting initial experience with exemplars of a category) should be equivalent. The responses to cats 19–36 and the novel cats (reflecting a learned category of cats) should also be equivalent, but different from the responses to cats 1–18 and the novel dogs.

Of interest was a late-slow wave component, the amplitude of which has been associated with differentiation of familiarity and novelty in studies of recognition memory for individual stimuli by infants (Nelson, 1994; Reynolds & Richards, 2005). In particular, a slow wave that returns to baseline has been associated with recognition of familiarity, whereas a slow wave that deflects away from baseline in the negative direction is associated with detection of novelty. The results from Quinn et al. (2006) were that a negative slow wave was observed over left occipital parietal scalp in response to cats 1 through 18 and novel dogs, whereas a slow wave that returned to baseline was observed for cats 19–36 and novel cats. This analysis reveals that the infant's brain responded to novel cats with activity equivalent to that displayed for cats 19–36. More generally, it points to the neural instantiation of a key behavioral indicant of categorization: responding to the novel as if it's familiar.

Quinn et al. (2006) also reported an ERP component for preferring a novel contrast category. Specifically, a Negative central (Nc) component which has been linked with attentional responding to novelty in studies of recognition memory (Reynolds & Richards, 2005), was larger over left-central scalp for novel dogs relative to cats 1–18, cats 19–36, and novel cats. That there are distinct brain signals corresponding to the formation of a category representation for the exemplars presented during familiarization and the preferential responding to a novel contrast category during test provides convergent evidence with the looking-time studies and indicates a neural preparedness in the first half-year of life to represent category information.

Global-to-Basic Category Development: Two Systems of Category Representation?

Although the work described thus far is consistent with the Rosch et al. (1976) idea that basic-level category representations can be evidenced readily and early in development, another line of evidence questioned the developmental superiority of the basic level. Mandler and Bauer (1988) challenged the traditional view of category development by arguing that the critical sorting experiment of Rosch et al. (1976) was confounded in that the basic-level task could be solved on the basis of either basic-level knowledge (e.g., how much two airplanes are alike), superordinate-level knowledge (e.g., how much two airplanes are different from the dog), or both. The more appropriate test of the basic-to-superordinate hypothesis is to determine if children (or infants) can differentiate basic-level categories chosen from the same superordinate before they can differentiate two superordinates. Mandler's group reported a number of studies adopting this experimental design, and infants and toddlers between 7 and 24 months participating in both object-examining and sequential-touching procedures (Oakes, Madole, & Cohen, 1991; Riccuiti, 1965) more readily formed global representations differentiating between animals and vehicles than basic-level representations distinguishing horses from dogs or cars from trucks (reviewed in Mandler, 2004).

At this point in the discussion, the reader might note that Mandler and Bauer's (1988) argument concerning the experimental design of Rosch et al. (1976) would not be applicable to explaining the findings of Quinn et al. (1993) because the young infants in the Quinn et al. study were presented with basic-level categories chosen from the same superordinate structure (i.e., cats and dogs). The fact that older infants performing in the object-exploration procedures did not make use of the information that younger infants apparently used to form basic-level categories led Mandler and McDonough (1993) to suggest that the two outcomes can be explained if one assumes that the familiarization/novelty-preference procedure taps primarily a perceptual level of processing, whereas the object-exploration procedures tap a more conceptual level of processing. The suggestion is that cats and dogs can be categorically distinguished by young infants on a perceptual basis in the visual-recognition procedure (via attributes found on the surfaces of the stimuli), whereas animals and vehicles can be differentiated by older infants on a conceptual basis in the object-exploration procedures (via conceptual primitives – such as the recognition that animals are self-starters and vehicles are nonself-starters, Mandler, 1992). This suggestion makes the assumption that global or superordinate categories are too perceptually variable to be anchored by perceptual cues. On the basis of this reasoning, Mandler and McDonough (1993) speculated that, "Global categories such as animals and vehicles are highly perceptually variable, and it may not be possible to differentiate them by perceptual categorization … it should be difficult to show global categorization of animals and vehicles using the traditional looking time tests." (p. 315).

The dissociation prediction based on the two-process view of early category formation is contradicted by findings that young infants participating in familiarization-novelty preference tasks can form global category representations, and even do so more readily than they form basic-level representations (Behl-Chadha, 1996; Quinn & Eimas, 1998; Quinn & Johnson, 2000; Quinn, Slater, Brown, & Hayes, 2001; Turati, Simion, & Zanon, 2003; Younger & Fearing, 2000). In Behl-Chadha's study, for example, 3- and 4-month-olds formed a category representation for mammals that excluded nonmammalian animals (i.e., birds or fish) and furniture. Quinn and Johnson extended the Behl-Chadha findings by demonstrating that 2-month-olds (i.e., infants that were on average 6 weeks younger than those studied by Behl-Chadha) could form a global representation for mammals that excluded furniture, but did not form a basic-level representation for cats that excluded dogs, rabbits, or elephants. Given that 3- and 4-month-olds had been shown to form both global and child-basic category representations, the finding that 2-month-olds form only global category representations is consistent with a global-to-basic developmental trajectory in early category emergence. Younger and Fearing have also reported data supporting this conclusion: global-to-basic category development was observed in 3- to 10-month-olds presented with the animal versus vehicle contrast. Moreover, the ERP evidence described earlier in which 6-month-olds were simply provided with perceptual experience with visual images of cats and dogs also produced neural evidence for learning the more global category (cat + dog) prior to separating cats and dogs into distinct basic-level groupings (Quinn et al., 2006).

Quinn et al. (2001) further substantiated the broad-to-narrow trajectory of early category development in an investigation of the formation of geometric form categories (i.e., circles, crosses, squares, and triangles) by newborn versus 4-month-olds (see also Turati et al., 2003). Newborns formed category representations of open versus closed classes of forms (i.e., crosses vs. circles, squares, and triangles), whereas 4-month-olds formed more exclusive basic-like category representations (i.e., circles vs. crosses vs. squares vs. triangles). It should also be noted that 3- to 4-month-olds fail to show evidence of forming a subordinate-level representation for classes of cats and dogs (Quinn, 2004a). However, 6- to 7-month-olds have been shown to form subordinate-level representations for tabbies that exclude Siamese, and Saint Bernards that exclude Beagles (Quinn, 2004a; Quinn & Tanaka, 2007), suggesting that the full course of early category development proceeds from global to basic to subordinate representations.

The results from across the studies indicate that the trend from more global to more specific category representations is not exclusively found with certain age groups (i.e., older infants) participating in particular types of tasks (i.e., those involving object exploration). The broad-to-narrow trajectory is also found for young infants participating in looking-time and ERP tasks. The age of the infants (from birth to 10 months of age) and the nature of the stimuli (i.e., static pictorial instances of the categories) make it improbable that the participants relied on conceptual knowledge to perform successfully in the tasks. The findings thus cast doubt on the idea that global representations are necessarily conceptually based (see also Rakison & Butterworth, 1998), and the notion that broad-to-narrow category development is a signature for conceptually based responding. They also raise questions with the perceptual/conceptual dissociation view more generally. The studies actually support the alternative position that broad and narrow levels of category representation can be perceptually grounded, and that a broad-to-narrow trajectory of category development can have a perceptual basis.

A Continuity-Based Approach: Evidence from Computational Simulation

If a double dissociation model does not provide a proper account of the infant categorization data, then might an alternative model based on developmental continuity accommodate the evidence? In the tradition of differentiation theory (Gibson & Gibson, 1955; Werner, 1957), and in contrast to Rosch et al. (1976), this alternative account suggests that the early development of categorization may proceed from more general to more specific representations based on a single system of representation that becomes progressively differentiated during the course of experience (Quinn & Eimas, 2000; Quinn,

Johnson, Mareschal, Rakison, & Younger, 2000). The proposal is that the information that differentiates many global categories such as mammals and vehicles from each other may be the presence versus absence of perceptible surface features, such as faces, fur, and tails possessed by mammals and not by the vehicles, and wheels, windshields, and shiny exteriors possessed by the vehicles and not by the mammals (for related proposals and supportive evidence, see Rakison & Butterworth, 1998; Smith & Heise, 1992). This information may turn out to be more discriminable than the information that may be used to separate mammals from one another (or vehicles from one another), which may be the specific values of these same features. Such a suggestion is consistent with Murphy's (1982) argument that "superordinates … have more reliable cues than do the basic categories they include" (p. 176). Accordingly, global category distinctions may be more readily evidenced, whereas distinctions within a global category may be less likely. Although differentiation-based theories have sometimes been used to account for the development of conceptually based concepts (e.g., Keil, 1979; Mandler, 2004), the idea here is that global categories emerge before those at the basic (and subordinate) levels through the conjoint activity of perceptual systems which provide input to general learning processes.

Computational models have provided simulation-based evidence that is consistent with the idea that perceptual input systems combined with a general learning mechanism can account for the observed trends in the emergence of category representations in infants. Quinn and Johnson (1997, 2000) described a series of connectionist networks that were given the task of categorizing mammal and furniture stimuli at basic and global levels. Input included a number of dimensions measured from the surfaces of the mammal and furniture stimuli used in the familiarization-novelty preference experiments cited earlier. A majority of the simulations produced a common result, namely, that global categories preceded basic-level categories in order of appearance (see also McClelland, McNaughton, & O'Reilly, 1995; Rogers & McClelland, 2004; Rumelhart & Todd, 1993; Schyns, 1991). The strength of the modeling is that it provides an in-principle demonstration of the category representations that can be formed, their level of exclusiveness, and their relative time course of emergence, in a learning device that receives inputs measured directly from the surfaces of the stimuli – inputs that young infants might conceivably be sensitive to.

A global-to-basic sequence of category learning suggests that as infants are presented with increasing numbers of exemplars from a single basic-level category, the representation of these exemplars will initially be at the global level (for small numbers of exemplars), and only subsequently at the basic level (for larger numbers of exemplars). This time course of emergence helps to reconcile why older infants have been less likely to form basic-level categories in object-exploration procedures where a small number (n = 4) of exemplars are presented (e.g., Mandler & McDonough, 1993), while younger infants have been more likely to form basic-level categories in looking-time procedures where a larger number (n = 12) of exemplars are presented (e.g., Quinn et al., 1993). Note that this explanatory framework is very different from the perceptual/conceptual dissociation view discussed earlier. The overall pattern of findings may be more parsimoniously accommodated by a single representation that becomes progressively differentiated during the course of early experience.

It is important to recognize that changes in a single, quantitative variable like exemplar number can produce changes in the level of inclusiveness of the category representations formed (i.e., global vs. basic) – changes that lead to behavior that may on the surface appear to be qualitatively different (Mandler, 2000). However, the argument presented here is that the development of these representations need not be driven by dissociations or discontinuities in underlying mental processes or knowledge structures. Sophisticated category representations may grow from a gradual accrual of information provided by means of a variety of input systems (i.e., those based on perceptual experience, language, and instruction). Perhaps an analogy can be made between this process and the kinds of self-organizing processes described by Thelen and Smith (1994). For example, with respect to the gait of a horse, if one changes speed slightly, the nature of the gait appears to undergo a very considerable change in its nature. Although this example comes from the domain of locomotion, the principle remains the same – quantitative changes in input can lead to apparently qualitative changes in behavior, but without discontinuity of underlying process.

Out of Infancy – The Transition to Child and Adult Concepts

If one rejects the notion of a dissociation between perceptual and conceptual, and embraces the notion that category development can be explained via perceptual processes operating in conjunction with a general learning mechanism, then the question arises as to how the category representations of infants transition to the concepts possessed by older children and adults. The studies of infant learning of animal categories suggest that young infants divide the world of objects into perceptual clusters that later come to have conceptual significance for adults (i.e., mammals, cats, tabby cats). As such, the conceptual representations found later in development may be viewed as informational enrichments of the category representations that infants form on the basis of perceptual experience (Quinn & Eimas, 1997). For example, infants who are presented with exemplars of cats and dogs are not experiencing these exemplars as an undifferentiated mass, but rather as separate groups that fall into distinct representations. These representations might then serve as placeholders for the more abstract information that is acquired beyond infancy, through language and learning that occurs in both informal (e.g., home) and formal settings (e.g., school). Thus, over time, the perceptual placeholder representation for cats will come to include information that cats hunt mice, have cat DNA, give birth to kittens, and are labeled as "cats," whereas the representation for dogs will come to include information that dogs chew on bones, have dog DNA, give birth to puppies, and are labeled as "dogs." The acquisition of this additional information serves to enrich the original perceptually based category representations to the point that they attain the richness of the more mature conceptual representations of children and adults (Quinn & Eimas, 2000). By this view, what changes as concepts mature is the content of the representations, rather than the processes underlying their development (Madole & Oakes, 1999; Rakison & Poulin-Dubois, 2001).

It is important to acknowledge that this view does not imply that studies demonstrating concept formation by infants in the laboratory should be considered as evidence that infants are forming concepts that they leave the lab with and then carry around in their heads for everyday usage. The claim is more that infants are demonstrating perceptual grouping or clustering abilities in the laboratory that are presumably engaged when infants encounter cats and dogs in the course of experience in the world outside the laboratory (or images of them as depicted in videos and picture books). The latter representations are those believed to serve as supports for the acquisition of the nonobvious attributes that occurs beyond the infancy period.

This view of category development also acknowledges that one may distinguish between the perceptual competences of infants and the conceptual structures of children and adults (Kagan, 2008), but further maintains that qualitative change need not be the path to get from one to the other. More generally, the account disagrees with the idea that the physical features of events should be separated from their meaning. The view embraced here is that knowledge about the perceptible parts and properties of objects can be semantic knowledge (see also Murphy, 2002, in press). One could not have much of a concept of cats, for example, without knowing what they looked like and what parts they had. Concepts must include perceptual information, or else they would not be very helpful. It is hard to imagine how a child could learn to map the more abstract attributes onto their correct object referents without having category representations available from perceptual experience to serve as support structures. Even schoolchildren learning about the biological processes of cats and dogs must be able to recognize cats and dogs of multiple breeds, in different poses, and in various contexts in order for information about more theoretical life processes to be specifically linked with the appropriate categories.

By the enrichment view, it becomes difficult to envisage that the category representations formed by infants from perceptual experience are simply cast aside when a later concept that is instilled with more abstract information becomes available. This is not to deny that, in some instances, conceptual information can supplant perceptual information when the two sources of information are placed in competition as determinants of category identity (Keil, 1989; Plunkett, Hu, & Cohen, 2008). Such evidence has been used to support an "essentialist" view of concept development (Gelman, 2003). However, while "essentialist" arguments have been forceful in the literature, Hampton, Estes, and Simmons (2007) have reported scenarios in which a majority of adults weight characteristic perceptual features more heavily than defining essentialist features in decisions about category identity, thereby suggesting that at least in some cases information about perceptual properties is considered just as semantic as information about biology. Moreover, if one accepts the argument that perceptual information may be meaningful, then the difference between perceptually and conceptually based concepts is less clearly a qualitative one. Indeed, in nature, perceptual (form) and conceptual (function) information are often correlated, and investigations designed to tease apart whether perceptual or conceptual information is the more potent determinant of categorization behavior may serve only to perpetuate what is arguably a false dichotomy. Instead, the way to proceed would be to explain how perceptual and conceptual knowledge are integrated (not dissociated) to form mature concepts (Murphy, 2002, in press; Quinn, 2004c).

Is Category Learning Assisted by Biases? Evidence from Eye-Tracking

The account in the present chapter has attempted to provide a description of category development without invoking a separate mode of conceptual processing available to infants and without calling for a qualitative change between infancy and childhood. Nevertheless, it does recognize that there are likely to be constraints or biases of a general nature that help make the rapid development of categorization possible. Biases may assist infants in solving the non-trivial problem of determining which features should be selected for determining category membership (Rakison & Lupyan, 2008). And while the evidence reviewed indicates that young infants can learn category representations for various animal species from perceptual experience, it does not inform us as to the particular features the infants use to form the representations. The answer to this question is not obvious, given that exemplars of non-human animal categories such as cats and dogs possess a number of common attributes such as a head, torso, four legs, and a tail.

Quinn and Eimas (1996) examined infants' abilities to categorize cats versus dogs when provided with the whole stimuli, only the heads (bodies were occluded), or just the bodies (heads were occluded) during both familiarization and preference test. Infants categorized when presented with either the whole stimuli or the heads, but not with the bodies, indicating that the head provided a sufficient basis for categorization of cats versus dogs. Moreover, in an additional study in which infants were familiarized with whole cat or dog images and then preference tested with hybrid stimuli (i.e., cat head on dog body vs. dog head on cat body), infant preference during test was for the novel-category head (Spencer, Quinn, Johnson, & Karmiloff-Smith, 1997). Notably, adults also emphasize the head when representing animal species (Reed, McGoldrick, Shackelford, & Fidopiastis, 2004).

Use of the head could arise from a biasing mechanism that directs infant attention to the face information present in a visual display (Johnson & Morton, 1991). It is also possible that infants learn during the course of experience with the exemplars that the head is the most diagnostic part of the stimulus. In other words, the head feature may be flexibly created as the basis for the category representation in an online fashion (Quinn & Schyns, 2003). To determine whether infants use the head because of a bias or because of within-task learning, Quinn, Doran, Reiss, and Hoffman (2009) employed an eye-tracking methodology to measure the eye fixations of infants as they scanned the visual images presented in the categorization task. On the assumption that the stimulus regions used for categorization will be preferentially fixated over those not used (as is the case in adults, Rehder & Hoffman, 2005), it was reasoned that if the head preference reflects a biasing mechanism, then infants should fixate more on the heads than the bodies throughout the course of the familiarization portion of a category-learning procedure. Alternatively, if the infants learn that the head is the most diagnostic region of the stimulus, then the head preference should emerge during the course of the familiarization trials. The major finding was that the infants were shown to have a marked preference for fixating the head that was present on the very first familiarization trial and that remained in evidence through the whole of familiarization.

The results are consistent with the idea that reliance on the head for categorization of cats versus dogs arises from a biasing mechanism. However, one may still contend that infants are simply orienting to the head because it contains high-contrast internal features and infants are attracted to the most visible portion of the stimulus (Banks & Salapatek, 1981). To address this possibility, a control study was conducted that repeated the eye-tracking version of the category-familiarization procedure, but with inverted stimulus images (Quinn et al., 2009). If the head preference is an outcome of infants' orienting to the most visible portion of the stimulus, then it should still be present with inversion. However, if infants orient to the head because of a bias that is in place to facilitate face recognition, then one would not expect it to be observed with stimulus inversion, given that inversion changes the normal configuration of facial features, and faces are believed to be processed configurally, even by infants (Leo & Simion, in press; Quinn & Tanaka, in press). The critical finding from the control study was that fixations to the head were small when compared with fixations to the body. The inversion results provide evidence that infants use the head to categorize upright cat and dog images because of a biasing mechanism that responds to face information. A bias of this nature may aid infants in selecting from among various features that are potentially available in the input (i.e., head or body), and in this way "set the system on the trajectory of learning" (Thelen & Smith, 1994, p. 315).

A Role for Experience: Representations for Humans Versus Non-Human Animals

An issue that has not yet been addressed is whether investigations of categorization by infants are tapping into representations that existed prior to participation in the study or whether the representations are formed while participating in the study. When considering this issue, it is important to keep in mind the young age of the infants and the fact that for at least some of the category representations that have been observed, it is unlikely that many infants would have had the opportunity to form the category representation from prior experience (e.g., a representation for horses that excluded instances of giraffes and zebras). These observations suggest that the category representations for non-human animals that are manifested by infants in looking-time tasks reflect learning taking place during the course of the task. Findings from the ERP task are consistent with the conclusion that category learning is occurring within the context of the task inasmuch as the infants showed one response to the first set of cats that was also observed for the novel dogs, and a contrasting response to the second set of cats that was generalized to the novel cats (Quinn et al., 2006).

When it comes to the question of how infants represent other humans, however, the answer to the question of whether categorization tasks conducted in the laboratory tap category possession or formation is less clear. Because infants encounter instances of humans on a daily basis, it is conceivable that infant responsiveness to images of humans presented in the laboratory could reflect knowledge of humans acquired prior to arrival at the laboratory. In this regard, Quinn and Eimas (1998) reported differences in how infants represent information about humans versus non-human animals that may reflect differences in previously acquired knowledge and online learning. One difference is in the inclusivity of the representations that infants display for humans versus non-human animals. Specifically, 3- to 4-month-olds familiarized with humans generalize familiarization not only to novel humans, but also to cats, horses, and even fish, although they differentiate cars. By contrast, same-aged infants familiarized with horses generalize familiarization to novel horses, but differentiate humans, fish, and cars. A second difference that is observed is in the nature of the representation. In particular, infants represent humans as subordinate-level exemplars, but represent non-human animal species as basic-level category information.

The differences in how infants represent humans versus non-human animals have been attributed to infants' greater experience with humans inclusive of repeated encounters with parents, siblings, and caregivers. This experience leads to a larger representational space for humans, thereby allowing individual humans to be represented at the subordinate level and enabling generalization to non-human animals. The trends toward increased specificity and generality resonate with findings that experts recognize instances from their domain at more specific levels than novices (Tanaka, 2001), and are also better able to recognize commonalities across their domain (Murphy & Wright, 1984). These observations in turn suggest a sense in which infants' knowledge of humans may constitute an initial domain of expertise (Quinn, 2005). Consistent with this suggestion is the finding that infants' generalization from humans to non-human animals is rooted in holistic-configural structure, i.e., a head attached to an elongated body with skeletal appendages (Quinn, 2004b; Quinn, Lee, Pascalis, & Slater, 2007). Use of the whole when categorizing humans stands in contrast with the use of parts (e.g., the head) when categorizing non-human animals, and is in accord with the finding that experts perceive objects within their domain holistically (Gauthier & Tarr, 2002).

Evidence from computational simulations supports the account of the human–non-human animal categorization asymmetry that is based on prior knowledge about humans (Mermillod, French, Quinn, & Mareschal, 2004). A simple connectionist auto-encoder that was shown capable of accounting for how infants represent category distinctions between non-human animals (i.e., cats vs. dogs, Mareschal et al., 2000) was not able to simulate the human–non-human animal asymmetry. When the network of Mermillod et al. was trained on either horses or humans, and then tested on novel horses and novel humans, it produced consistently more error for images from the novel categories, irrespective of the trained category. However, when a long-term memory component that was pre-seeded with humans was added and coupled with the short-term memory component for learning about the images presented during familiarization, the human–non-human animal asymmetry was reproduced. That is, the "dual network" architecture, when trained on humans, produced equivalently small error for novel humans and novel horses; however, when trained on horses, the network produced small error for novel horses and more error for novel humans. The network simulations provide another source of evidence that the human–non-human animal asymmetry reflects the different knowledge-bases that infants have for humans versus non-human animals.

Additional evidence suggests that the contrast between how infants represent humans versus non-human animals is not a "special" phenomenon, and may reflect a more general property of learning systems that respond to frequency differences in experience. For example, Rogers and McClelland (2004) have described how increased experience with a particular category leads word learners to extend the label for that category to less familiar, similar categories, although not to less familiar, dissimilar categories. In a corresponding simulation, when a model was trained with dog patterns appearing more frequently than other mammals, early in learning, the model extended the label dog to goats and even robins, but not to trees. Rogers and McClelland have also described how increased experience with a category that has been linked with expertise acquisition leads to increased ability to differentiate within that category. A matching simulation demonstrated how birds (or fish) became more distinct for a model that was trained with birds (or fish) more frequently than other animals. Importantly, the different tendencies associated with increased experience, towards generalization and differentiation, were explained in a common framework in which the semantic space devoted to the more experienced class became larger than that allocated to less experienced classes.

Generalization from humans to non-human animals by infants may form a foundation for the construction of a broad, domain-level concept of animal, and may also be a precursor of how children first rely on a human prototype to reason about biological knowledge (Carey, 1985; Inagaki & Hatano, 2006). Thus, in accord with Rogers and McClelland (2004), differences in the frequency of exposure to different classes (humans vs. non-human animals), coupled with the similarity structure of those classes (attributes shared by humans and non-human animals, but not cars), are important determinants of the growth of category organization during early cognitive development.

Not All Humans Are Learned Equally: Further Evidence on the Role of Experience

Thus far in the chapter, it has been argued that the representation of humans by young infants is based on experience occurring prior to the experiment. In this section, direct evidence for this suggestion will be discussed. The studies to be reviewed examine how infants categorize two human attributes, namely, the gender and race of human faces. With regard to the processing of face gender, Quinn, Yahr, Kuhn, Slater, and Pascalis (2002) reported that 3- to 4-month-olds familiarized with male faces preferred novel female faces over novel male faces; however, infants familiarized with female faces exhibited a null preference between novel male and novel female faces. This asymmetrical pattern of outcomes had previously been observed in a study of 5- to 12-month-olds presented with male versus female faces in a habituation–dishabituation procedure (Leinbach & Fagot, 1993). To uncover the basis for the asymmetry, Quinn et al. (2002) investigated the possibility that infants might have a spontaneous preference for female faces. A female face preference would facilitate a novel-category preference for female faces after familiarization with male faces (thereby producing a robust preference) and it would interfere with a novel-category preference for male faces after familiarization with female faces (thus producing a null preference). To test the female face preference hypothesis, 3- to 4-month-olds were administered a series of paired preference trials with male versus female faces without a prior familiarization period. The infants preferred the female faces.

Subsequent experiments by Quinn et al. (2002) showed that the female face preference could not be attributed to longer length hair (i.e., infants still displayed a spontaneous preference for female faces when the male and female faces were presented without hair) or to higher-contrast internal features possibly related to greater cosmetic usage (i.e., the preference fell to chance when inverted male and female faces without hair cues were presented). With the low-level perceptual accounts failing to provide an explanation for the female face preference, Quinn et al. (2002) next considered a more cognitive hypothesis. Specifically, because all of the participants in their experiments had been reared by female primary caregivers, they hypothesized that infants might respond preferentially to female faces because they are more similar to the caregiver face than male faces. This reasoning is also consistent with the familiarity principle that infants follow in showing greater responsiveness to mother than stranger (Bushnell, 2001). If infants are responding preferentially to faces that are more similar to their caregiver, then infants reared with male caregivers should prefer male faces. In fact, although the base rate of such a caregiver population is small, Quinn and colleagues (see also Quinn, 2003) tested eight such infants on a spontaneous-preference test with upright male and female faces without hair, and seven of the eight displayed preferences for the male faces. The overall pattern of findings indicates that infant representation of the gender of human faces is strongly influenced by the gender of the primary caregiver's face – the face that infants are likely to have the most contact with on a day-to-day basis. More generally, it provides confirming evidence for the argument that infants' categorization of humans in laboratory tasks is influenced by experience occurring prior to participation in the tasks.

One point of comparison between the studies reported in Quinn and Eimas (1998) and Quinn et al. (2002) that deserves comment centers on the issue of spontaneous preference. In Quinn and Eimas, there was no spontaneous preference for the human over non-human animal stimuli. In Quinn et al., there was a spontaneous preference for female over male. This difference may reflect differences in the way the stimuli were presented. In Quinn and Eimas, the human stimuli were whole, fully clothed, and depicted with head, arms, legs, and the body torso in their correct spatial arrangement. In contrast, in Quinn et al., the human stimuli were enlarged faces, and may have tapped into a cognitive-emotional process related to attachment (i.e., similar to the one that gets activated when young infants prefer mother's to stranger's face). Such a process, when stimulated, may direct infants to maintain fixation on the triggering stimulus.

Kelly et al. (2005) sought to determine if the familiarity-based account that explains how infants respond to gender information in faces might be applicable to the question of how infants respond to race/ethnicity information from faces. Caucasian newborn and 3-month-olds exposed to predominantly Caucasian faces were presented with Caucasian-African, Caucasian-Asian, and Caucasian-Middle Eastern face pairings. Whereas the newborns did not display differential preferences for any of the face comparisons, the 3-month-olds preferred same-race faces in each of the pairings. Although one might interpret the null performance of the newborns by arguing for a biological limitation imposed by poor vision (e.g., Banks & Salapatek, 1981), this account is weakened by the finding that newborns can discriminate among faces from their own ethnic group (Pascalis & de Schonen, 1994; Turati, Cassia, Simion, & Leo, 2006). It follows that if infants can discriminate between faces from within their own ethnic category, then they should be able to discriminate between faces from different ethnic categories. These observations indicate that although sufficient sensitivity was available to the newborns to discriminate between faces from different ethnic groups, preference for faces from the same ethnic group was not present.

If sensory maturation is not responsible for the developmental difference between newborns and 3-month-olds in Kelly et al. (2005), the implication is that the predominant exposure that most infants have to same-race faces is driving the spontaneous preference for them. This experientially based interpretation has been bolstered by the follow-up studies of Bar-Haim, Ziv, Lamy, and Hodes (2006) and Kelly et al. (2007a). Bar-Haim et al. reported that 3-month-old Israeli infants exposed mostly to Caucasian faces preferred Caucasian to African faces, whereas Ethiopian infants exposed mainly to African faces preferred African to Caucasian faces. Moreover, a group of Ethiopian infants born in Israel and exposed to both African and Caucasian faces did not display a differential preference between Caucasian and African faces. Kelly et al. (2007a) provided evidence that cross-race preferences extend beyond the perceptually robust contrast between Caucasian and African faces by demonstrating that Chinese 3-month-olds prefer Asian faces over African, Caucasian, and Middle Eastern faces. The combined results indicate that differential exposure during the first 3 months to same- and other-race faces results in a consistent preference for same-race faces.

Even though the data from the spontaneous-preference studies implies a categorical partitioning between different race faces, it falls short of providing evidence that infants have formed a category representation for one race that includes novel instances of that race and excludes novel instances of another race. This is because based on spontaneous preference alone, there is no evidence that after familiarization with one race, infants will generalize to novel faces from that race, and respond differentially to novel faces from a novel race. To examine racial categorization of faces by infants, Anzures, Quinn, Pascalis, Slater, and Lee (2009) familiarized Caucasian 6- and 9-month-olds with different faces from a common ethnic background (i.e., either Caucasian or Asian) and then tested with novel faces from the familiarized category and novel faces from a novel race category. Performance of the 6-month-olds was consistent with the spontaneous preference for same-race faces. Infants familiarized with Caucasian faces generalized responsiveness to novel Caucasian faces, but did not respond differentially to Asian faces. By contrast, infants familiarized with Asian faces generalized responsiveness to novel Asian faces and responded differentially to Caucasian faces.

Performance of the 9-month-olds was more symmetrical. Infants familiarized with Caucasian or Asian faces generalized responsiveness to novel faces from the familiarized race and responded differentially to novel faces from the novel race. Of note is that when the within-category discrimination abilities of the 9-month-olds were assessed, performance was above chance for the same-race Caucasian faces, but not different from chance for the other-race Asian faces (see also Kelly et al., 2007b). This result suggests that same-race faces were categorized (i.e., responded to equivalently despite the ability to discriminate between them), but other-race faces were categorically perceived (i.e., the response equivalence was associated with lack of discriminability). In addition, the development change in performance between 6 and 9 months of age suggests a weaning away from categories based on spontaneous perceptual preference to categories that can overcome perceptual preference. Such a trend is in accord with the transition from perceptual to conceptual representations that has been proposed for the development of categories in general (Madole & Oakes, 1999; Quinn & Eimas, 1997; Rakison & Poulin-Dubois, 2001). The overall pattern of findings, moreover, provides further evidence for the role of differential experience in infant responses to social-category information in faces.

Summary and Conclusions

Although some traditional views of category development have suggested that categorization begins when the world becomes labeled and children are taught how to order classes of objects, the evidence reviewed in this chapter suggests that categorization begins in early infancy when core abilities can be used to organize perceptual experience. As such, current debates have centered around a set of interconnected issues including whether there is an order to the emergence of category representations formed by infants, whether early categories are based on perceptual or conceptual information, whether the tasks used to assess infant categorization are eliciting evidence of pre-existing concepts or inducing the formation of conceptual structures that emerge during administration of the task, and how the initial categories of infants transition to the more fully developed concepts of children and adults.

The data brought to bear on the issues have been forthcoming from different methodologies including looking time, ERPs, computational modeling, and eye-tracking. Despite the fact that one account of category development suggested that basic-level representations emerge before those at the superordinate level (Rosch et al., 1976), the evidence has indicated that global-category representations actually emerge before those at the basic and subordinate levels. Although this broad-to-narrow trajectory for category emergence was once thought to provide a distinctive signature for learning concepts separately from percepts (Mandler, 2000), subsequent behavioral and computational work has suggested that the broad-to-narrow developmental sequence may come about at least initially through the operation of perceptual learning processes (Quinn & Johnson, 2000). In addition, while the category representations that infants form for non-human animals are likely to be based on category learning of the stimuli presented in the laboratory, the category representations that infants form for humans seem to tap into representations that infants possess prior to arrival at the laboratory (Quinn, 2005). The latter is an important result because it indicates that cognitive processes like categorization, when put into operation in the developing infant, begin to yield functional knowledge within a short period of time.

The formation of category representations by young infants on the basis of perceptual experience has implications for the mechanisms of conceptual representation more generally. Infant performance is consistent with Malt's (1995) suggestion that many object categories "seem to be strongly influenced by regularities in the input that are recognized by the categorizer" (p. 130). In addition, Millikan (1998) has argued that many object concepts of adults begin with a process of perceptual tracking of object categories by infants. Furthermore, Xu, Tenenbaum, and Sorrentino (1998) have noted that "infants have a perceptual system that is similar to that of adults, so that infants carve up the world in more or less the same way adults do" (p. 89).

Given the observed correspondences between the category representations of infants and the concepts of adults, the account offered in the present chapter maintains that the perceptually based category representations of infants should not be dissociated from the knowledge-rich concepts of adults. Rather, the latter grow out of the former based on a process of enrichment in which category representations that are initially based on perceptual attributes come to incorporate non-obvious attributes acquired through informal and formal tuition, and language. From this perspective, infants begin to form categories based on core competencies consisting of functioning perceptual input systems (including that for language) and a general learning mechanism (that can represent within-category similarity and between-category dissimilarity) that is facilitated in its operation by biases to attend to some inputs more than others. Such competencies equip infants with the ability to form functional category representations that, although not adult-like in their initial form, will become adult-like during real-time development that occurs via interaction with a structured environment. Infants are thus endowed with the tools to build a foundation for conceptual development, rather than with a preconceptual form that will be discarded once metamorphosis provides mature concepts.

References

Anderson, J. R. (1991). The adaptive nature of human categorization. *Psychological Review, 3*, 409–429.

Anzures, G., Quinn, P. C., Pascalis, O., Slater, A. M., & Lee, K. (2009). *Racial categorization of faces in infancy: An extension of the other-race effect.* Manuscript submitted for publication.

Banks, M. S., & Salapatek, P. (1981). Infant pattern vision: A new approach based on the contrast sensitivity function. *Journal of Experimental Child Psychology, 31*, 1–45.

Bar-Haim, Y., Ziv, T., Lamy, D., & Hodes, R. M. (2006). Nature and nurture in own-race face processing. *Psychological Science, 17*, 159–163.

Behl-Chadha, G. (1996). Basic-level and superordinate-like categorical representations in early infancy. *Cognition, 60*, 105–141.

Bruner, J. S., Goodnow, J. J., & Austin, G. A. (1956). *A study of thinking.* New York: Wiley.

Bushnell, I. W. R. (2001). Mother's face recognition in newborn infants: Learning and memory. *Infant and Child Development, 10*, 67–74.

Callanan, M. A. (1985). How parents label objects for young children. *Child Development, 56*, 508–523.

Carey, S. (1985). *Conceptual change in childhood.* Cambridge, MA: MIT Press.

Carey, S. (in press). *The origin of concepts.* New York: Oxford University Press.

Colunga, E., & Smith, L. B. (2005). From the lexicon to expectations about kinds: A role for associative learning. *Psychological Review, 112*, 347–382.

Edelman, G. M. (1987). *Neural Darwinism.* New York: Basic Books.

Eimas, P. D., & Quinn, P. C. (1994). Studies on the formation of perceptually based basic-level categories in young infants. *Child Development, 65*, 903–917.

Fantz, R. L. (1964). Visual experience in infants: Decreased attention to familiar patterns relative to novel ones. *Science, 164*, 668–670.

Gauthier, I., & Tarr, M. J. (2002). Unraveling mechanisms for expert object recognition: Bridging brain activity and behavior. *Journal of Experimental Psychology: Human Perception and Performance, 28*, 431–446.

Gelman, S. A. (2003). *The essential child: Origins of essentialism in everyday thought*. Oxford: Oxford University Press.

Gelman, S. A., Coley, J. D., Rosengren, K., Hartman, E., & Pappas, A. (1998). Beyond labeling: The role of maternal input in the acquisition of richly-structured categories. *Monographs of the Society for Research in Child Development, 63*(1, Serial No. 253).

Gibson, J. J., & Gibson, E. J. (1955). Perceptual learning: Differentiation or enrichment? *Psychological Review, 62*, 32–41.

Gopnik, A., & Meltzoff, A. N. (1997). *Words, thoughts, and theories*. Cambridge, MA: MIT Press.

Hampton, J. A., Estes, Z., & Simmons, S. (2007). Metamorphosis: Essence, appearance, and behavior in the categorization of natural kinds. *Memory and Cognition, 35*, 1785–1800.

Hull, C. L. (1920). Quantitative aspects of the evolution of concepts. *Psychological Monographs* (Whole No. 123).

Inagaki, K., & Hatano, G. (2006). Young children's conception of the biological world. *Current Directions in Psychological Science, 15*, 177–181.

Johnson, M. H., & Morton, J. (1991). *Biology and cognitive development: The case of face recognition*. Cambridge, MA: Blackwell.

Kagan, J. (2008). In defense of qualitative changes in development. *Child Development, 79*, 1606–1624.

Keil, F. C. (1979). *Semantic and conceptual development: An ontological perspective*. Cambridge, MA: Harvard University Press.

Keil, F. C. (1989). *Concepts, kinds, and cognitive development*. Cambridge, MA: MIT Press.

Kelly, D. J., Liu, S., Ge, L., Quinn, P. C., Slater, A. M., Lee, K., Liu, Q., & Pascalis, O. (2007a). Cross-race preferences for same-race faces extend beyond the African versus Caucasian contrast in 3-month-old infants. *Infancy, 11*, 87–95.

Kelly, D. J., Quinn, P. C., Slater, A. M., Lee, K., Ge, L., & Pascalis, O. (2007b). The other-race effect develops during infancy: Evidence of perceptual narrowing. *Psychological Science, 18*, 1084–1089.

Kelly, D. J., Quinn, P. C., Slater, A. M., Lee, K., Gibson, A., Smith, M., Ge, L., & Pascalis, O. (2005). FAST TRACK REPORT: Three-month-olds, but not newborns, prefer own-race faces. *Developmental Science, 8*, F31–F36.

Leach, E. (1964). Anthropological aspects of language: Animal categories and verbal abuse. In E. H. Lenneberg (Ed.), *New directions in the study of language* (pp. 23–63). Cambridge, MA: MIT Press.

Leinbach, M. D., & Fagot, B. I. (1993). Categorical habituation to male and female faces: Gender schematic processing in infancy. *Infant Behavior and Development, 16*, 317–332.

Leo, I., & Simion, F. (in press). Face processing at birth: A Thatcher illusion study. *Developmental Science*.

Madole, K. L., & Oakes, L. M. (1999). Making sense of infant categorization: Stable processes and changing representations. *Developmental Review, 19*, 263–296.

Malt, B. C. (1995). Category coherence in cross cultural perspective. *Cognitive Psychology, 29*, 85–148.

Mandler, J. M. (1992). How to build a baby: II. Conceptual primitives. *Psychological Review, 99*, 587–604.

Mandler, J. M. (1997). Development of categorisation: Perceptual and conceptual categories. In G. Bremner, A. Slater, & G. Butterworth (Eds.), *Infant development: Recent advances* (pp. 163–189). Hove, UK: Psychology Press.

Mandler, J. M. (2000). Perceptual and conceptual processes. *Journal of Cognition and Development, 1*, 3–36.

Mandler, J. M. (2004). *The foundations of mind: Origins of conceptual thought.* New York: Oxford University Press.

Mandler, J. M., & Bauer, P. J. (1988). The cradle of categorization: Is the basic level basic? *Cognitive Development, 3*, 247–264.

Mandler, J. M., & McDonough, L. (1993). Concept formation in infancy. *Cognitive Development, 8*, 291–318.

Mareschal, D., French, R. M., & Quinn, P. C. (2000). A connectionist account of asymmetric category learning in early infancy. *Developmental Psychology, 36*, 635–645.

Markman, E. M. (1989). *Categorization and naming in children: Problems of induction.* Cambridge, MA: MIT Press.

McClelland, J. L., McNaughton, B. L., & O'Reilly, R. C. (1995). Why there are complementary learning systems in the hippocampus and neocortex: Insights from the successes and failures of connectionist models of learning and memory. *Psychological Review, 102*, 419–457.

Mermillod, M., French, R. M., Quinn, P. C., & Mareschal, D. (2004). The importance of long-term memory in infant perceptual categorization. In R. Alterman & D. Kirsh (Eds.), *Proceedings of the 25th annual conference of the Cognitive Science Society* (pp. 804–809). Mahwah, NJ: Erlbaum.

Mervis, C. B., & Rosch, E. (1981). Categorization of natural objects. *Annual Review of Psychology, 32*, 89–115.

Millikan, R. G. (1998). A common structure for concepts of individuals, stuffs, and real kinds: More mama, more milk, and more mouse. *Behavioral and Brain Sciences, 21*, 55–100.

Murphy, G. L. (1982). Cue validity and levels of categorization. *Psychological Bulletin, 91*, 174–177.

Murphy, G. L. (2002). *The big book of concepts.* Cambridge, MA: MIT Press.

Murphy, G. L. (in press). What are categories and concepts? In D. Mareschal, P. C. Quinn, & S. E. G. Lea (Eds.), *The making of human concepts.* Oxford: Oxford University Press.

Murphy, G. L., & Wright, J. C. (1984). Changes in conceptual structure with expertise: Differences between real-world experts and novices. *Journal of Experimental Psychology: Learning, Memory, and Cognition, 10*, 144–155.

Nelson, C. A. (1994). Neural correlates of recognition memory in the first postnatal year of life. In G. Dawson & K. Fischer (Eds.), *Human behavior and the developing brain* (pp. 269–313). New York: Guilford Press.

Oakes, L. M., Coppage, D. J., & Dingel, A. (1997). By land or by sea: The role of perceptual similarity in infants' categorization of animals. *Developmental Psychology, 33*, 396–407.

Oakes, L. M., Madole, K. L., & Cohen, L. B. (1991). Object examining: Habituation and categorization. *Cognitive Development, 6*, 377–392.

Oakes, L. M., & Ribar, R. J. (2005). A comparison of infants' categorization in paired and successive presentation familiarization tasks. *Infancy, 7*, 85–98.

Pascalis, O., & de Schonen, S. (1994). Recognition memory in 3- to 4-day-old human neonates. *NeuroReport, 5*, 1721–1724.

Plunkett, K., Hu, J. F., & Cohen, L. B. (2008). Labels can override perceptual categories in early infancy. *Cognition, 106*, 665–681.

Quinn, P. C. (2002). Category representation in infants. *Current Directions in Psychological Science, 11*, 66–70.

Quinn, P. C. (2003, April). Why do young infants prefer female faces? In M. S. Strauss (Organizer), *Development of facial expertise in infancy.* Symposium conducted at the meeting of the Society for Research in Child Development, Tampa, FL.

Quinn, P. C. (2004a). Development of subordinate-level categorization in 3- to 7-month-old infants. *Child Development, 75*, 886–899.

Quinn, P. C. (2004b). Is the asymmetry in young infants' categorization of humans versus nonhuman animals based on head, body, or global gestalt information? *Psychonomic Bulletin and Review, 11*, 92–97.

Quinn, P. C. (2004c). Multiple sources of information and their integration, not dissociation, as an organizing framework for understanding infant concept formation. *Developmental Science, 7*, 511–513.

Quinn, P. C. (2005). Young infants' categorization of humans versus nonhuman animals: Roles for knowledge access and perceptual process. In L. Gershkoff-Stowe & D. Rakison (Eds.), *Building object categories in developmental time: 32nd Carnegie symposium on cognition* (Vol. *32*, pp. 107–130). Mahwah, NJ: Erlbaum.

Quinn, P. C. (2008). In defense of core competencies, quantitative change, and continuity. *Child Development, 79*, 1633–1638.

Quinn, P. C., & Bomba, P. C. (1986). Evidence for a general category of oblique orientations in 4-month-old infants. *Journal of Experimental Child Psychology, 42*, 345–354.

Quinn, P. C., Doran, M. M., Reiss, J. E., & Hoffman, J. E. (2009). Time course of visual attention in infant categorization of cats versus dogs: Evidence for a head bias as revealed through eye tracking. *Child Development, 80*, 151–161.

Quinn, P. C., & Eimas, P. D. (1996). Perceptual cues that permit categorical differentiation of animal species by infants. *Journal of Experimental Child Psychology, 63*, 189–211.

Quinn, P. C., & Eimas, P. D. (1997). A reexamination of the perceptual to conceptual shift in mental representations. *Review of General Psychology, 1*, 271–287.

Quinn, P. C., & Eimas, P. D. (1998). Evidence for a global categorical representation for humans by young infants. *Journal of Experimental Child Psychology, 69*, 151–174.

Quinn, P. C., & Eimas, P. D. (2000). The emergence of category representations during infancy: Are separate perceptual and conceptual processes required? *Journal of Cognition and Development, 1*, 55–61.

Quinn, P. C., Eimas, P. D., & Rosenkrantz, S. L. (1993). Evidence for representations of perceptually similar natural categories by 3-month-old and 4-month-old infants. *Perception, 22*, 463–475.

Quinn, P. C., & Johnson, M. H. (1997). The emergence of perceptual category representations in young infants: A connectionist analysis. *Journal of Experimental Child Psychology, 66*, 236–263.

Quinn, P. C., & Johnson, M. H. (2000). Global-before-basic object categorization in connectionist networks and 2-month-old infants. *Infancy, 1*, 31–46.

Quinn, P. C., Johnson, M. H., Mareschal, D., Rakison, D. H., & Younger, B. A. (2000). Understanding early categorization: One process or two? *Infancy, 1*, 111–122.

Quinn, P. C., Lee, K., Pascalis, O., & Slater, A. M. (2007). In support of an expert–novice difference in the representation of humans versus non-human animals by infants: Generalization from persons to cats occurs only with upright whole images [Special issue on the development of categorization]. *Cognition, Brain, and Behavior, 11*, 679–694.

Quinn, P. C., & Schyns, P. G. (2003). What goes up may come down: Perceptual process and knowledge access in the organization of complex visual patterns by young infants. *Cognitive Science, 27*, 923–935.

Quinn, P. C., Slater, A. M., Brown, E., & Hayes, R. A. (2001). Developmental change in form categorization in early infancy. *British Journal of Developmental Psychology, 19*, 207–218.

Quinn, P. C., & Tanaka, J. W. (2007). Early development of perceptual expertise: Within-basic-level categorization experience facilitates the formation of subordinate-level category representations in 6- to 7-month-old infants. *Memory and Cognition, 35*, 1422–1431.

Quinn, P. C., & Tanaka, J. W. (in press). Infants' processing of featural and configural information in the upper and lower halves of the face. *Infancy*.

Quinn, P. C., Westerlund, A., & Nelson, C. A. (2006). Neural markers of categorization in 6-month-old infants. *Psychological Science, 17*, 59–66.

Quinn, P. C., Yahr, J., Kuhn, A., Slater, A. M., & Pascalis, O. (2002). Representation of the gender of human faces by infants: A preference for female. *Perception, 31*, 1109–1121.

Rakison, D., & Butterworth, G. (1998). Infants' use of object parts in early categorization. *Developmental Psychology, 34*, 49–62.

Rakison, D. H., & Lupyan, G. (2008). Developing object concepts in infancy: An associative learning perspective. *Monographs of the Society for Research in Child Development, 73*(1).

Rakison, D. H., & Poulin-Dubois, D. (2001). Developmental origin of the animate–inanimate distinction. *Psychological Bulletin, 127*, 209–228.

Reed, C. L., McGoldrick, J. E., Shackelford, R., & Fidopiastis, C. (2004). Are human bodies represented differently from other animate and inanimate objects? *Visual Cognition, 11*, 523–550.

Rehder, B., & Hoffman, A. B. (2005). Eyetracking and selective attention in category learning. *Cognitive Psychology, 51*, 1–41.

Reynolds, G. D., & Richards, J. E. (2005). Familiarization, attention, and recognition memory in infancy: An ERP and cortical source localization study. *Developmental Psychology, 41*, 598–615.

Riccuiti, H. N. (1965). Object grouping and selective ordering in infants 12 to 24 months. *Merrill-Palmer Quarterly, 11*, 129–148.

Roberts, K., & Cuff, M. D. (1989). Categorization studies of 9- to 15-month-old infants: Evidence for superordinate categorization? *Infant Behavior and Development, 12*, 265–288.

Rogers, T. T., & McClelland, J. L. (2004). *Semantic cognition: A parallel distributed processing approach*. Cambridge, MA: MIT Press.

Rosch, E. (1978). Principles of categorization. In E. Rosch & B. B. Lloyd (Eds.), *Cognition and categorization* (pp. 27–48). Hillsdale, NJ: Erlbaum.

Rosch, E., Mervis, C. B., Gray, W. D., Johnson, D. M., & Boyes-Braem, P. (1976). Basic objects in natural categories. *Cognitive Psychology, 8*, 382–439.

Rumelhart, D. E., & Todd, P. M. (1993). Learning and connectionist representations. *Attention and performance XIV: Synergies in experimental psychology, artificial intelligence, and cognitive neuroscience* (pp. 3–30). Cambridge, MA: MIT Press.

Schyns, P. G. (1991). A modular neural network of concept acquisition. *Cognitive Science, 15*, 461–508.

Smith, E. E., & Medin, D. L. (1981). *Categories and concepts*. Cambridge, MA: Harvard University Press.

Smith, L. B., & Heise, D. (1992). Perceptual similarity and conceptual structure. In B. Burns (Ed.), *Percepts, concepts and categories* (pp. 233–272). New York: North Holland.

Spencer, J., Quinn, P. C., Johnson, M. H., & Karmiloff-Smith, A. (1997). Heads you win, tails you lose: Evidence for young infants categorizing mammals by head and facial attributes [Special issue on perceptual development]. *Early Development and Parenting, 6*, 113–126.

Tanaka, J. W. (2001). The entry point of face recognition: Evidence for face expertise. *Journal of Experimental Psychology: General, 130*, 534–543.

Thelen, E., & Smith, L. B. (1994). *A dynamic systems approach to the development of cognition and action*. Cambridge, MA: MIT Press.

Turati, C., Cassia, V. M., Simion, F., & Leo, I. (2006). Newborns' face recognition: Role of inner and outer facial features. *Child Development, 77*, 297–311.

Turati C., Simion F., & Zanon, L. (2003). Newborns' perceptual categorization for closed and open geometric forms. *Infancy, 4*, 309–325.

Waxman, S. R., & Gelman, S. A. (in press). Different kinds of concepts and different kinds of words: What words do for human cognition. In D. Mareschal, P. C. Quinn, & S. E. G. Lea (Eds.), *The making of human concepts.* Oxford: Oxford University Press.

Werner, H. (1957). The concept of development from a comparative and organismic point of view. In D. B. Harris (Ed.), *The concept of development: An issue in the study of human behavior* (pp. 125–148). Minneapolis: University of Minnesota Press.

Xu, F., Tenenbaum, J. B., & Sorrentino, C. M. (1998). Concepts are not beliefs, but having concepts is having beliefs. *Behavioral and Brain Sciences, 21*, 89.

Younger, B. A. (1990). Infants' detection of correlations among feature categories. *Child Development, 61*, 614–620.

Younger, B. A. (in press). Categorization and concept formation in human infants. In D. Mareschal, P. C. Quinn, & S. E. G. Lea (Eds.), *The making of human concepts.* Oxford: Oxford University Press.

Younger, B. A., & Fearing, D. D. (1999). Parsing items into separate categories: Developmental change in infant categorization. *Child Development, 70*, 291–303.

Younger, B. A., & Fearing, D. D. (2000). A global-to-basic trend in early categorization: Evidence from a dual-category habituation task. *Infancy, 1*, 47–58.

Younger, B. A., & Furrer, S. D. (2005). Beyond the distributional input? A developmental investigation of asymmetry in infants' categorization of cats and dogs. *Developmental Science, 8*, 544–560.

CHAPTER SIX

Early Memory Development

Patricia J. Bauer, Marina Larkina, and Joanne Deocampo

The development of memory has been a topic of speculation at least since Freud's (1905/1953) observations of the "great intellectual accomplishments" (p. 64) of which infants and young children are capable. Yet, much of what we know about early memory has been learned since the 1980s. Prior to that time, it was widely assumed that infants were unable to encode, store, and subsequently retrieve memories of specific past events. Moreover, it was thought that, although children of preschool age could remember specific episodes, their memories were poorly organized and generally unremarkable. These perspectives held sway for both conceptual and methodological reasons.

As in so many areas of cognitive developmental science, the study of the development of memory got its start with Piaget (1952). Among the tenets of Piaget's theory of genetic epistemology was the suggestion that for the first 18–24 months of life, infants lacked symbolic capacity and thus, the ability to mentally *re-present* objects and events. Instead, they were thought to live in a world of physically present entities that had no past and no future. Even after they had constructed the capacity for mental representation, children were thought to be without the cognitive structures that would permit them to organize events along coherent dimensions that would make the events memorable. Consistent with this suggestion, in retelling fairy tales, children as old as 7 years made errors in temporal sequencing (Piaget, 1926, 1969).

Even as tenets attributed to Piagetian theory were being challenged on multiple fronts (e.g., Gelman & Baillargeon, 1983), the suggestion that infants were unable to remember the events of their lives went unexamined for want of suitable methodology. In older children and adults, memory is examined primarily through verbal report. For infants and young children, this is not a viable alternative: it is not until age 3 that children become reliable informants about the past. It was seen as more than coincidence that age 3 marks the end of the period of infantile amnesia (i.e., the relative paucity among adults of verbally expressible memories of specific events from the first years of life). Indeed, that the average age of earliest memory among adults is 3.5 (for reviews see Bauer, 2007; West & Bauer, 1999), and that age 3–3.5 marks the beginning of children's abilities to share past experiences verbally, "conspired" to create the impression that age 3 marked the onset of the ability to remember.

Methodological factors also contributed to the perspective that children of preschool age are poor mnemonists. Young children's memories often were tested using extensions of paradigms employed with adults, such as recall of lists of words or pictures. In such studies the youngest children did little to help themselves remember. In contrast to older children, they did not employ strategies to facilitate encoding or aid retrieval. Presumably as a consequence, they remembered fewer items (e.g., Flavell, Beach, & Chinsky, 1966). This pattern was replicated many times over, seemingly confirming the "fact" of young children's mnemonic incompetence (reviewed in Bjorklund, Dukes, & Brown, 2009).

In this chapter we summarize some of the research that has contributed to revision of the perspectives that infants are unable to remember the past and that preschoolers are not much better. Because questions of whether infants and young children are able to create, retain, and later retrieve coherent memories of specific past experiences have been the focus of much of the research attention, this type of memory (i.e., long-term memory for specific events or episodes) is featured. The review also includes discussion of the emergence of a particular type of episodic memory, namely, autobiographical or personal memory for events or experiences in which the individual has a sense of personal involvement.

Assessing Memory in Infancy

As summarized in the first edition of this volume (Bauer, 2002), it has long been clear that infants learn and otherwise benefit from past experience and thus, evidence memory of some sort. In fact, DeCasper and Spence (1986) suggest that even prenatal experiences may later manifest themselves in changes in behavior toward stimuli: mere hours after birth, infants distinguish between a novel story passage and one that their mothers read aloud during the last weeks of pregnancy. More common, however, are tests of memory for postnatal experiences using *visual paired comparison* or *habituation* and the operant conditioning paradigm of *mobile conjugate reinforcement*. Studies using these paradigms have revealed evidence of strikingly robust memory, from very young infants. Yet as discussed in Bauer (2006b), these findings were not what prompted revision of the suggestion that the first years of life were devoid of the ability to mentally re-present objects or events and thereby recall them. That distinction is reserved for findings from a third infant memory paradigm, *elicited* and *deferred imitation*, a non-verbal analogue to verbal report. Before summarizing some of the major findings from each of these paradigms, we introduce an important distinction in the memory literature – between declarative and non-declarative memory – that we believe is essential to adequate description of developmental changes, as well as their explanation.

Distinguishing declarative and non-declarative memory

Although it is not universally accepted, by both developmental and adult cognitive scientists, it is widely believed that memory is not a unitary trait but is comprised of different systems or processes, which serve distinct functions, and are characterized by fundamentally different rules of operation (e.g., Squire, 1992). The type of memory termed *declarative* (or explicit) captures most of what we think of when we refer to "memory" or "remembering" (Zola-Morgan & Squire, 1993). It involves the capacity for explicit recognition or recall of names, places, dates, events, and so on. In contrast, the type of memory termed *non-declarative* represents a variety of non-conscious abilities, including the capacity for learning habits and skills, priming, and some forms of conditioning (for reviews see Lloyd & Newcombe, 2009; Parkin, 1997). A defining feature of non-declarative memory is that the impact of experience is made evident through a change in behavior or performance, but the experience leading to the change is not consciously accessible (Zola-Morgan & Squire, 1993). Declarative memory is characterized as fast (e.g., supporting one-trial learning), fallible (e.g., memory traces degrade, retrieval failures occur), and flexible (i.e., not tied to a specific modality or context). Non-declarative memory is characterized as slow (i.e., with the exception of priming, it results from gradual or incremental learning), reliable, and inflexible (Squire, Knowlton, & Musen, 1993).

The distinction between different types of memory was originally derived from the adult cognitive and neuroscience literatures. Yet it is vitally important for developmental scientists because declarative and non-declarative memory rely on different neural substrates that have different courses of development. A variety of brain regions are implicated in support of non-declarative memory, including neocortex (priming), striatum (skill learning), and cerebellum (conditioning; for review see Toth, 2000). These regions are thought to develop early and, as a result, to support early emergence of non-declarative memory (for review see C. A. Nelson, 1997). In contrast, as described in more detail later, declarative memory depends on a multi-component neural network including temporal and cortical structures (e.g., Zola & Squire, 2000). Whereas most of the medial temporal lobe components of declarative memory develop early, other aspects of the network undergo a protracted developmental course. The entire circuit begins to coalesce near the end of the first year of life and continues to develop for years thereafter, contributing to pronounced changes in declarative memory (for reviews see Bachevalier & Mishkin, 1994; Bauer, 2007, 2009a; Nelson, de Haan, & Thomas, 2006; Richman & Nelson, 2008). The major findings from the three main infant memory paradigms are consistent with these expectations.

Visual paired comparison or habituation

Visual paired comparison was introduced by Fantz (1956). It involves exposing infants to pairs of pictures of a stimulus and then presenting the now "familiar" picture along with a novel one and observing at which infants look. A variant of the technique, visual habituation, involves sequentially exposing infants to numerous pictures of a stimulus and then, after some criterion is reached (typically, a 50% decrease in looking time), introducing a novel stimulus and noting changes in looking. In both techniques, differential looking to novel and familiar stimuli is taken as evidence of recognition memory. Typically, after short familiarization, infants look longer at familiar stimuli whereas after longer periods of familiarization (or habituation), they spend more time looking at novel stimuli (for a review see Bahrick & Pickens, 1995). The number of seconds of familiarization required to produce a novelty response interacts with age, with younger infants (e.g., 3.5-month-olds) requiring more encoding time to produce a novelty response, relative to older infants (e.g., 6.5-month-olds; Rose, Gottfried, Melloy-Carminar, & Bridger, 1982).

Changes in the distribution of looking to familiar and novel stimuli are typically examined over relatively short periods, with delays ranging from seconds to a few minutes. Rose, Feldman, and Jankowski (2007) reported that between 3 and 12 months, the length of time over which a novelty response was apparent increased from 5–10 seconds to 10 minutes. However, these delays do not represent the upper limit on infant recognition memory (for a review see Slater, 1995). For example, 5-month-olds recognize face stimuli after 2 weeks (Fagan, 1973). Visual attention also has been used to examine retention over as many as 1–3 months. Over such long intervals, the evidence for recognition changes, such that it is manifest as more visual attention to familiar stimuli (e.g., Bahrick & Pickens, 1995). The change in distribution of attention is taken as evidence of the differential status of mnemonic traces over time. The assumption is that on the basis of a "fresh" memory trace, infants need not spend time processing familiar stimuli and, consequently, spend more time attending to novel stimuli. As the memory fades, they devote attentional resources to reconstruction of the trace for the once-familiar stimulus (for discussion see Bahrick, Hernandez-Reif, & Pickens, 1997; Courage & Howe, 1998).

Whereas attentional preference techniques measure changes in infants' responses to previously encountered stimuli, it is unclear whether they measure the same type of recognition as evidenced when adults explicitly affirm that they have seen a particular stimulus before. Mandler (1998) suggested that infant recognition memory experiments are more analogous to adult priming than recognition memory studies. Adults suffering from amnesia show normal priming even as they evidence pronounced deficits in recognition memory (Warrington & Weiskrantz, 1974). In a similar vein, Snyder (2007) provided a compelling argument that greater attention to novel stimuli may result from a property of the visual system rather than a recognition response per se. She suggested that *repetition suppression* – a reduction of neuronal responses in the occipital-temporal visual pathway that occurs in response to stimulus repetition – is responsible for the shift in attention from an old to a new stimulus. This argument is consistent with one by C.A. Nelson (1995, 1997), who suggested that early in development, attention to novel stimuli may be driven by the frequency with which the stimuli are presented rather than their novelty per se (for discussion see Nelson & Collins, 1991, 1992). In sum, although changes in the distribution of infant attention as a result of prior exposure *may* be based on recognition memory, because such judgments are not required to produce the response (e.g., McKee & Squire, 1993), they should not be assumed, especially in light of several alternative candidate explanations.

Operant conditioning

The second major technique used to test retention in early infancy is conditioning in general and the operant conditioning paradigm of mobile conjugate reinforcement in particular. In this paradigm, an attractive mobile is suspended above an infant's crib or playpen. For a period of 1–3 minutes, researchers measure the baseline rate of infant kicking. They then "tether" the infant's leg to the mobile with a ribbon such that, as the infant kicks, the mobile moves. During a 3–9-minute acquisition period, infants learn the contingency between their kicking and the movement of the mobile. Once the conditional response is acquired, a delay is imposed, after which the mobile again is suspended above the infant; the infant's leg is not attached to the mobile. If the post-training rate of kicking is greater than the baseline rate of kicking (i.e., before the infant experienced the contingency), memory is inferred (see Rovee-Collier & Cuevas, 2009, for a description of this and related procedures).

The mobile conjugate reinforcement paradigm has been quite productive, yielding many important findings. With it, researchers have learned that infants 2 months of age remember the mobile for 1–3 days and that by 6 months, they remember for as many as 14 days (Hill, Borovsky, & Rovee-Collier, 1988). The length of time over which behavior toward the mobile is retained can be extended if infants are "reminded" of the mobile during the delay (Rovee-Collier, Sullivan, Enright, Lucas, & Fagen, 1980). A number of other factors also affect the time over which the conditioned response can be retained, including the amount of training that infants receive, the distribution of training, and the affect that they display during training (for a review see Rovee-Collier & Cuevas, 2009). One of the most striking characteristics of memory as evidenced by this paradigm is its specificity. For example, 2- and 3-month-olds fail to recognize the training mobile if even a single element of it is changed. Minor changes to the fabric that lines the crib or playpen (e.g., changing the shape of the figures on the liner) also disrupts performance (e.g., Borovsky & Rovee-Collier, 1990; Rovee-Collier, Schechter, Shyi, & Shields, 1992). Generalization from the stimulus or context associated with the learning episode to other similar stimuli occurs only as the details of the original stimulus are forgotten.

The specificity of memory in the mobile conjugate reinforcement paradigm is one feature that has led to the suggestion that the type of memory measured by this technique is different from that assessed through verbal report and other declarative memory paradigms. Indeed, as noted by Mandler (1998), the patterns of generalization, extinction, and reinstatement are similar to those observed across species in other operant conditioning paradigms (e.g., Campbell, 1984). In addition, although the neural substrate that supports the behavior has not been elucidated, C. A. Nelson's (1997) analysis of the paradigm implicates cerebellum and the hippocampus, but not the balance of the temporal-cortical network that supports declarative memory. For these reasons, the memory demonstrated in mobile conjugate reinforcement is thought to be reflective of implicit learning (e.g., Mandler, 1990; C.A. Nelson, 1997; Schneider & Bjorklund, 1998; Squire et al., 1993; although see Rovee-Collier, 1997, for a different view).

Deferred imitation

Deferred imitation was originally suggested by Piaget (1952) as a hallmark of the development of symbolic thought. Beginning in the mid-1980s, the technique was developed as a test of mnemonic ability in infants and young children (e.g., Bauer & Shore, 1987; Meltzoff, 1985). It involves using props to produce a single action or a multi-step sequence and then, either immediately (elicited imitation), after a delay (deferred imitation), or both, inviting the infant or young child to imitate.

As discussed in detail elsewhere (e.g., Bauer, 2007; Bauer, DeBoer, & Lukowski, 2007; Carver & Bauer, 2001; Mandler, 1990; Meltzoff, 1990; Squire et al., 1993), the conditions of learning and later testing in deferred imitation are conducive to formation of declarative memories but not non-declarative memories, and the resulting mnemonic behaviors share characteristics of declarative memories. First, although performance is facilitated by multiple experiences (e.g., Bauer, Hertsgaard, & Wewerka, 1995), infants learn and remember on the basis of a single experience (e.g., Bauer & Hertsgaard, 1993). Rapid learning is characteristic of declarative memory. Second, the contents of memories formed in imitation-based tasks are accessible to language. Once children acquire the linguistic capacity to do so, they talk about multi-step sequences they experienced as preverbal infants (e.g., Bauer, Kroupina, Schwade, Dropik, & Wewerka, 1998; Cheatham & Bauer, 2005; although see Simcock & Hayne, 2002, for a suggestion to the contrary, and Bauer et al., 2004, for discussion of possible reasons for the negative findings in Simcock & Hayne).

Third, the memory traces formed in imitation-based tasks are flexible. Infants show that they remember even when (a) the objects available at the time of retrieval differ in size, shape, color, and/or material composition from those encountered at the time of encoding (e.g., Bauer & Dow, 1994; Bauer & Fivush, 1992; Hudson, Sheffield, & Deocampo, 2006; Lechuga, Marcos-Ruiz, & Bauer, 2001; Sheffield, 2004); (b) the appearance of the room at the time of retrieval is different from that at the time of encoding (e.g., Barnat, Klein, & Meltzoff, 1996; Klein & Meltzoff, 1999); (c) encoding and retrieval take place in different settings (e.g., Hanna & Meltzoff, 1993; Klein & Meltzoff, 1999); and (d) the individual who elicits recall is different from the individual who demonstrated the actions (e.g., Hanna & Meltzoff, 1993). Evidence of flexible extension of event knowledge is apparent in infants as young as 9–11 months of age (e.g., Baldwin, Markman, & Melartin, 1993; Lukowski, Wiebe, & Bauer, in press; McDonough & Mandler, 1998).

Fourth, imitation-based tasks pass the "amnesia test." McDonough, Mandler, McKee, and Squire (1995) tested adults with amnesia (in whom declarative memory processes are impaired) and control participants in an imitation-based task using multi-step sequences. Whereas normal adults produced the model's actions even after a delay, patients with amnesia did poorly, performing no better than control participants who had never seen the events demonstrated. Older children and young adults who were rendered amnesic as a result of pre- or perinatal insults also show decreased performance on imitation-based tasks (Adlam, Vargha-Khadem, Mishkin, & de Haan, 2005). These findings strongly suggest that although imitation-based tasks are behavioral rather than verbal, they tap declarative memory.

Event and Autobiographical Memory

The remainder of this chapter is focused on early development of a particular type of declarative memory, namely, memory for events. The term "event" is broad, encompassing anything from a leaf fluttering in the breeze to something as complex and temporally extended as a world war. For present purposes, we borrow a definition from K. Nelson (1986): events "involve people in purposeful activities, and acting on objects and interacting with each other to achieve some result" (p. 11). This definition excludes simple physical transformations such as fluttering because they do not involve actors engaged in purposeful activity. In contrast, the definition includes the activities in which individuals engage as they move through a typical day as well as the unique experiences that ultimately define us as individuals. This definition also specifies what there is to be remembered about events, namely, actors, actions, objects, and the orders in which the elements combine to achieve specific goals.

We focus on the development of event memory because of its importance to the individual as well as the social group. For the individual, memories of past events shape current behavior and give us a guide for planning future behavior. Events and stories about them are also important instructional tools: we learn through reading and listening to stories of past events and how they have shaped the world. Finally, memories of the events in which we participated are self-defining: who we are is who we were and what we did. We use our past experiences to explain our present behavior and to motivate choices for the future. For these reasons and more, the ability to remember past events is important to the mature as well as the developing human.

The self-defining aspect of memories for past events is especially critical to a particular type of event memory known as *autobiographical*. As the name implies, autobiographical memories are about one's self. As argued by Bauer (2007), beyond the single defining feature of self-relevance, autobiographical memory can be treated as a "family resemblance" category and defined in terms of its characteristic features (Rosch & Mervis, 1975). Especially "good" or prototypical autobiographical memories are of clearly personally relevant specific past events that can be located in a particular time and place and are expressed verbally; retrieval of them involves a "re-living" of the experience as an event from the past. Memories that may also be autobiographical but can be considered less prototypical may lack one or more of the characteristic features: they might be of recurrent events (Lie & Newcombe, 1999), they might not be shared verbally (Bauer, 1993), they might be less vivid recollections, or there might not be awareness of the source of the memory (Howe & Courage, 1993, 1997a). When autobiographical memory is viewed in this way, as a "mental natural kind" (Brewer, 1996), it becomes possible to picture its development within the broader category of event memory. In the next section we review some of the major developmental changes in event and autobiographical memory throughout infancy and early childhood.

Developmental Changes Across Infancy and Early Childhood

There are numerous behavioral changes relevant to memory that occur across infancy and early childhood. Although changes for each of the behavioral domains occur to some extent across the entire period of interest, some are especially apparent in infancy whereas others are more salient during the preschool years. We focus on a subset of the most salient changes that serve to illustrate the increasing autobiographical nature of event memory across the early years of life (see Bauer, 2007, for a more extensive review).

Changes in temporal extent

The length of time over which events are remembered increases dramatically over the first two years of life. Importantly, because like any complex behavior, the length of time an episode is remembered is multiply determined, there is no "growth chart" function that specifies that children of a given age will remember for a particular length of time. Nevertheless, by comparing across studies with similar methodologies, it is possible to discern developmental trends. Early in the first year of life, the temporal extent of declarative memory is limited. For example, at 6 months of age, infants remember an average of one action of a three-step sequence (taking a mitten off a puppet's hand; shaking the mitten which, at the time of demonstration, held a bell that rang; and replacing the mitten) for 24 hours (Barr, Dowden, & Hayne, 1996). Collie and Hayne (1999) found that 6-month-olds remembered an average of one out of five possible actions over a 24-hour delay.

By 9–11 months of age, the length of time over which memory for events is apparent has increased substantially. Nine-month-olds remember individual actions over delays from 24 hours (Meltzoff, 1988) to 5 weeks (Carver & Bauer, 1999, 2001). By 10–11 months, infants remember over delays of 3 months (Carver & Bauer, 2001; Mandler & McDonough, 1995). Thirteen- to fourteen-month-olds remember actions over delays of 4–6 months (Bauer, Wenner, Dropik, & Wewerka, 2000; Meltzoff, 1995). By 20 months of age, children remember the actions of event sequences for as many as 12 months (Bauer et al., 2000). Thus, over the first two years of life, there are steady age-related increases in the length of time events are remembered. This change is a necessary prerequisite to development of a history of events over time.

Changes in robustness

The first two years of life also are witness to changes in the robustness of memories. One index of robustness has already been discussed, namely, the extent to which memory is disrupted by interference such as created by a change in context between encoding and retrieval. As noted earlier, infants demonstrate memory even when the materials, contexts, and examiners change between encoding and test. Yet there also are reports of developmental changes in the extent to which infants and very young children are sensitive to these types of contextual changes. For example, in research by Hayne, MacDonald, and Barr (1997), when 18-month-olds experienced the puppet sequence demonstrated on a cow puppet and then were tested with the same puppet, they showed robust retention over 24 hours. However, when they experienced the sequence modeled on a cow puppet and then were tested with a duck puppet, they did not show evidence of memory. Twenty-one-month-olds remembered the sequence whether tested with the same or a different puppet (see also Hayne, Boniface, & Barr, 2000; Herbert & Hayne, 2000).

Taken as a whole, this literature indicates that whereas from an early age infants' memories survive changes in context and stimuli, memory becomes more flexible with age.

Another index of the robustness of memory is an age-related reduction in the number of exposures to an event required for an infant to remember. Early in the first year, long-term recall seems dependent on multiple experiences. For example, in Barr et al. (1996), 6-month-olds who saw actions modeled six times remembered them for 24 hours whereas infants who saw the actions modeled only three times did not. By 9 months, three demonstrations are sufficient to support recall of individual actions over 24 hours (Meltzoff, 1988) and 1 week (Bauer, Wiebe, Waters, & Bangston, 2001). By early in the second year, a single exposure is sufficient for infants to recall it as many as 4 months later (Meltzoff, 1995). At least by 20 months of age, infants remember not only the individual actions but also the temporal order of actions months later, after only a single experience of them (Bauer, unpublished data). These developments are critical to the ability to remember unique episodes and events.

Changes in specificity

Another aspect of children's memory that increases across infancy and early childhood is the specificity with which events are remembered. Some of the findings reviewed in the section on the robustness of memory already suggested that infants remember the specific details of the objects used to produce events in elicited and deferred imitation paradigms. For example, the fact that 18-month-olds' recall can be disrupted by changes to the objects used to produce events (e.g., changing the puppet from a cow to a duck: Hayne et al., 1997), indicates that infants encode specific features. More direct evidence of memory for specific features in infancy comes from studies in which forced-choice selection procedures are used to test recognition of the props used to produce events. In Bauer and Dow (1994), 16- and 20-month-olds showed above-chance levels of selection of the props used to produce events, even when tested with functionally equivalent distracter props. By 20 months of age, memory for the specific objects used to produce multi-step sequences predicts how well the events will be remembered 1 month later (Bauer & Lukowski, 2009).

Memory for the specific details of events is apparent in children's verbal reports as well as their imitation, even after long delays. Age-related changes also are apparent. These trends are illustrated in an early study of long-term recall of naturally occurring events by Hamond and Fivush (1991). They interviewed 3- and 4-year-olds who had visited Disneyworld 6 months or 18 months earlier. Regardless of the children's age at the time of the trip, and the retention interval, the children recalled the event and reported specific activities in which they had engaged (e.g., riding particular rides). Yet the older children provided more descriptive detail about the events, relative to the younger children. Better memory for the specific details with age is also suggested by Pillemer (1992). Two weeks after an unexpected fire alarm at their school, Pillemer interviewed 3.5- and 4.5-year-olds about the event. The older children were more specific (and accurate) in their reports. They also seemed to have better appreciation of the cause and potential consequences of the event. For example, only the older children spontaneously mentioned the cause of the alarm (burning popcorn) and only they described a sense of urgency in leaving the building in response to the alarm. Although we cannot infer better *memory* based on more detailed verbal reports, there is reason to believe the two are related: When Pillemer and colleagues interviewed the children again 6 years later, when they were 9.5 and 10.5 years old, only the children who had been older at the time of the unexpected fire alarm provided detailed narratives about it (Pillemer, Picariello, & Pruett, 1994).

Changes in self-relevance

With development, children's memories become increasingly self-relevant and even defining of self. Some of the earliest evidence of the self-relevant nature of memories is from the middle of the second year of life, at about the time children show evidence of recognizing themselves in mirrors (for discussion see Howe & Courage, 1993). At roughly this time, children begin to reference themselves in talk about past events. These developments are related in that children who exhibit mirror self recognition have better event memory (Howe, 2003) and make faster progress in independent autobiographical reports, relative to children who do not yet exhibit self-recognition (Harley & Reese, 1999).

There are further developments in self-concept across the preschool years that are related to autobiographical narrative development in particular (see Welch-Ross, 2001). Children begin to evidence a sense of "temporally extended self" (Povinelli, 1995) or "self in time" (K. Nelson, 1989). This supports the realization that the self of their memories is the same self as that experienced in the present and thus makes possible establishment of a history of experiences of significance to the self. Over the preschool years children also show more and more evidence of a subjective or evaluative self, one who reflects on how an event made them think or feel. This perspective on experience facilitates inclusion of events in an autobiographical record: experiences are not just objective events that played out, but are events that influenced the self in one way or another. Finally, children develop a more coherent self-construct in which they begin to understand that they possess more or less stable psychological attributes that cause them to interpret and behave in the world in a similar manner across temporally disparate events. The net effect is that with development, memories become more and more prototypical on the dimension of self-relevance.

Explaining Age-Related Changes

Ultimately, several sources of variance will be implicated in the explanation of age-related changes in event and autobiographical memory. They will range from changes in the neural systems and basic mnemonic processes that permit memories to be formed, retained, and later retrieved, to the social forces that shape what children come to view as important to remember and even how they express their memories. In this section we illustrate some of these mechanisms of change. We begin with a brief review of the neural network thought to subserve event memory in the adult and what is known about its development. We then examine the basic mnemonic processes of encoding, consolidation, storage, and retrieval, and evaluate their contributions to age-related changes in long-term recall of events. Finally, we discuss how the social world of the child influences memory development and its expression.

The neural substrate of event memory and its development

In adult humans, the formation, maintenance, and retrieval of memories of events depends on a multi-component neural network involving temporal and cortical structures (e.g., Eichenbaum & Cohen, 2001; Markowitsch, 2000; Zola & Squire, 2000). Upon experience of an event, sensory and motor inputs from multiple brain regions distributed throughout the cortex converge on parahippocampal structures within the temporal lobes (e.g., entorhinal cortex). The work of binding the elements together to create a durable, integrated memory trace is carried out by another temporal lobe structure, the hippocampus. Cortical structures are the long-term storage sites for memories. Prefrontal structures are implicated in their retrieval after a delay. Thus, long-term recall requires multiple cortical regions, including prefrontal cortex; temporal structures; and intact connections between them.

In the human, aspects of the temporal structures in the temporal-cortical declarative memory network develop early. For instance, as reviewed by Seress and Abraham (2008), the cells that make up most of the hippocampus are formed in the first half of gestation and virtually all are in their adult locations by the end of the prenatal period. The neurons in most of the hippocampus also begin to connect early in development, with the adult number and density of synapses reached by approximately 6 postnatal months. Lagging behind in development is the dentate gyrus of the hippocampus (Seress & Abraham, 2008). At birth, this critical bridge between cortex and the hippocampus includes only about 70% of the adult number of cells and it is not until 12–15 postnatal months that the morphology of the structure appears adult-like. Maximum density of synaptic connections in the dentate gyrus is also delayed. Synaptic density increases dramatically (to well above adult levels) beginning at 8–12 postnatal months and reaches its peak at 16–20 months. After a period of relative stability, excess synapses are pruned until adult levels are reached at about 4–5 years of age (Eckenhoff & Rakic, 1991). As discussed elsewhere (e.g., Bauer, 2007, 2009a; C. A. Nelson, 1995, 1997, 2000), development of the dentate gyrus of the hippocampus may be a rate-limiting variable in memory early in life. Even beyond the preschool years there are increases in hippocampal volume and myelination that continue into adolescence (e.g., Arnold & Trojanowski, 1996; Benes, Turtle, Khan, & Farol, 1994; Giedd et al., 1999; Gogtay et al., 2004; Utsunomiya, Takano, Okazaki, & Mistudome, 1999).

The association areas also undergo a protracted course of development. It is not until the seventh prenatal month that all six cortical layers are apparent. The density of synapses in prefrontal cortex increases dramatically at 8 postnatal months and peaks between 15 and 24 months. Pruning to adult levels does not begin until late childhood; adult levels are not reached until late adolescence or early adulthood (Huttenlocher, 1979; Huttenlocher & Dabholkar, 1997; see Bourgeois, 2001, for discussion). In the years between, in some cortical layers there are changes in the size of cells and the lengths and branching of dendrites (Benes, 2001). There are also changes in glucose utilization and blood flow over the second half of the first year and into the second year (Chugani, Phelps, & Mazziotta, 1987). Other maturational changes in prefrontal cortex, such as myelination, continue into adolescence, and adult levels of some neurotransmitters are not seen until the second and third decades of life (Benes, 2001).

Changes in basic mnemonic processes

Developmental changes in the declarative memory network have implications for the efficacy and efficiency with which information is encoded and stabilized for long-term storage, for the reliability with which it is stored, and for the ease with which it is retrieved (see Bauer, 2004, 2006b, 2007, 2008, for expanded versions of this discussion). Late development of prefrontal cortex can be expected to impact all phases of the life of a memory trace from its initial encoding through consolidation to retrieval. Late development of the dentate gyrus is significant because it may lead to less effective and efficient consolidation of new information. As discussed in Bauer (2006a), the consequences of less effective and efficient early-stage processing are profound. If encoding is compromised, there is less to be consolidated. If consolidation is compromised and/or the information available for consolidation is degraded, less information will be stored. If less information is stored, there will be less to retrieve. Differences in the amount available for retrieval will become more apparent with the passage of time as interference and decay take their toll, further depleting the already degraded trace.

Encoding. Developmental changes in prefrontal cortex in particular may be expected to contribute to age-related changes in the efficiency with which young children encode information. Consistent with this suggestion, as mentioned earlier, 3-month-old infants require more time to encode a stimulus than 6-month-old infants (Rose et al., 1982). Researchers have also used event-related potentials (ERPs) to assess age-related changes in encoding processes. ERPs are electrical oscillations in the brain that are time-locked to presentation of a stimulus. Differences in the activity recorded to different classes of stimuli (familiar and novel stimuli, for example) can be interpreted as differential neural processing and recognition. In a longitudinal study of relations between encoding and long-term recall, Bauer and colleagues (Bauer et al., 2006) recorded infants' ERPs as they looked at photographs of props used in multi-step sequences to which they had just been exposed interspersed with photographs of props from novel sequences. The amplitudes of responses to newly encoded stimuli at 10 months were larger than those of the same infants at 9 months; there were no differences in responses to novel stimuli. The differences at encoding were related to differences at recall. One month after each ERP, imitation was used to test long-term recall of the sequences. The infants had higher rates of recall of the sequences to which they had been exposed at 10 months, relative to the sequences to which they had been exposed at 9 months.

Age-related differences in encoding do not end at 1 year of age. Relative to 15-month-olds, 12-month-olds require more trials to learn multi-step events to a criterion (learning to a criterion indicates that the material was fully encoded). In turn, 15-month-olds are slower to achieve the criterion, relative to 18-month-olds (Howe & Courage, 1997b). In the preschool years, age-related changes in encoding are suggested by changes in short-term memory "span," as measured by tests such as memory for digits or words. Whereas children 2 years of age are able to hold only about 2 units of information in mind, by the ages of 5 and 7, they can remember 4 and 5 units, respectively.

Consolidation and storage. Age-related differences in encoding are not the sole source of age trends in long-term declarative memory. Even with levels of encoding controlled statistically (Bauer et al., 2000), by matching (Bauer, 2005), or by bringing children of different ages to the same learning criterion (Howe & Courage, 1997b), older children have higher levels of long-term recall relative to younger children. This suggests that for younger children in particular, even once a memory has been successfully encoded, it remains vulnerable to forgetting. Greater vulnerability likely stems from the relative immaturity of the structures and connections required to consolidate memories for long-term storage (see Bauer, 2006a, 2009b, for discussion).

There are clear indications that consolidation and storage processes are a source of variance in long-term recall in the first year of life. For example, Bauer, Wiebe, Carver, Waters, and Nelson (2003) used ERPs and behavior to test (a) encoding of events via an immediate ERP, (b) consolidation and storage via an ERP 1 week later, and (c) long-term recall via deferred imitation 1 month later. As a group, the infants showed evidence of encoding (differential responses to the old and new stimuli) yet there was differential long-term recall that in turn related to differential consolidation and storage. Infants who did not recall the events after 1 month also did not recognize the familiar props after 1 week. Conversely, infants who recalled the events after 1 month showed successful consolidation and storage after 1 week. The two subgroups of infants did not differ at encoding, and individual variability in encoding was not a significant predictor of long-term recall. In contrast, successful consolidation and storage over 1 week accounted for 28% of the variance in recall 1 month later. Consolidation and storage processes continue to account for individual difference in recall in the second year of life. For infants 20 months of age, the amount of information retained after 48 hours following exposure to events explained 25% of variance in recall after 1 month (Bauer, Cheatham, Cary, & Van Abbema, 2002).

Changes in the processes by which memory representations are consolidated and stored can be expected throughout the preschool years. However, there are few data that can be brought to bear to evaluate the possibility. In most studies, children's recall is assessed only once, at the end of a retention interval. There is no opportunity to evaluate the amount of information in memory after some intermediate delay, and often there is no measure of the amount of information that was encoded originally. Moreover, neuroimaging studies (e.g., using ERPs) have not been conducted with preschool-age children to address this question. The relative contributions of encoding and consolidation and storage processes to long-term memory in the preschool years are an area for future research.

Retrieval. Retrieval of memories from long-term storage is thought to depend on prefrontal cortex, a neural structure that undergoes a protracted developmental course. In part for this reason, traditionally, retrieval processes have been considered to be the major source of developmental differences in long term-recall (e.g., Hayne et al., 2000; Liston & Kagan, 2002). However, there are actually few data with which to evaluate the contribution of retrieval processes because in most studies, there are alternative candidate sources of age-related differences. For instance, as implied earlier, unless the contributions of the early-stage processes of encoding and consolidation are evaluated, it is not appropriate to implicate retrieval-related processes as the major explanation for age-related differences in long-term recall (for discussion see Bauer, 2006a). Moreover, on the basis of a single recall test, it is difficult if not impossible to know whether a memory representation remains intact but is inaccessible given the cues provided (retrieval failure) or whether the trace has lost its integrity (consolidation/storage failure).

In the infant literature, one study in which measures of encoding and multiple recall tests are available is Bauer et al. (2000). Children of multiple ages (13, 16, 20 months) were tested over a range of delays (1–12 months). To eliminate encoding processes as a potential source of developmental differences in long-term recall, subsets of 13- and 16-month-olds and subsets of 16- and 20-month-olds were matched for levels of encoding (Bauer, 2005). In addition, at the time of test, the children were given two recall trials and also tested for relearning, thus allowing for assessment of the possibility of test-related increases in retrieval. Even under these conditions, the younger children remembered less than the older children. They also had lower levels of relearning. Together, the findings strongly implicate consolidation and storage as opposed to retrieval processes as the major source of developmental change.

Similar conclusions have been reached by Brainerd and colleagues (Brainerd & Reyna, 1990; Brainerd, Reyna, Howe, & Kingma, 1990) for children of preschool age and older. In this research, to eliminate encoding differences as a source of age-related effects, participants are brought to a criterion level of learning prior to imposition of a delay. Multiple test trials are administered, thereby allowing assessment of the contributions of storage versus retrieval failure. A consistent finding is that the largest proportion of age-related variance in children's recall is accounted for by memory failure at the level of consolidation and/or storage, as opposed to retrieval. Moreover, the results imply little change in retrieval failure rates throughout childhood in the face of declines in storage failure rates. These results thus implicate consolidation and storage processes as continued sources of developmental change throughout the period (for a review see Howe & O'Sullivan, 1997).

The suggestion that early-stage processes such as encoding and consolidation are major determinants of long-term recall should not be taken to imply that developmental changes in prefrontal cortex have nothing to do with memory development in infancy and childhood. A more productive conclusion is that the role played by developmental changes in prefrontal cortex is different than that previously assumed (Bauer, 2006a, 2007). Rather than on retrieval processes, a major effect of developments in prefrontal structures may be on the processes that precede it. Encoding and consolidation are interactive processes between cortical and medial temporal structures. As such, changes in both are important. Moreover, the ultimate storage sites for long-term memories are the association cortices. Prefrontal cortex is thought to play an especially significant role in storage of information about the *where* and *when* of events and experiences, the very features that distinguish episodes from one another. Thus, developmental changes in prefrontal cortex may play their primary role in supporting more effective and efficient encoding, consolidation, and storage; their role in improving retrieval processes may be secondary.

Socialization of memory

From some of its earliest manifestations, memory is influenced by the social world. Social influences from the family to the larger cultural group interact with the characteristics of the child to shape what children ultimately come to view as important to remember and even how they express their memories. We illustrate this interactional effect through examination of how one aspect of children's social context, namely, parental reminiscing style, is related to development of memory, especially for personal events.

Reminiscing style. Autobiographical memory is inherently social: individuals create stories about personally relevant events in their lives in part in order to share them with others. Young children learn to craft personal narratives by participating in conversations about past events with more skilled partners, typically their parents. Researchers have noted two different styles that adults exhibit when they engage in memory talk with their children (see K. Nelson, 1993). Parents who frequently engage in conversations about the past, provide rich descriptive information about previous experiences, and invite their children to "join in" the construction of stories about the past, are said to use an *elaborative* style. In contrast, parents who provide fewer details about past experiences and instead pose specific questions to their children (e.g., "What was the name of the restaurant where we had breakfast?"), are said to use a *repetitive* or *low elaborative* style. Both mothers and fathers exhibit these stylistic differences (Haden, Haine, & Fivush, 1997).

Stylistic differences have implications for children's memory narratives. Children of mothers using the elaborative style report more about past events than children of mothers using the repetitive or low elaborative style (e.g., Fivush & Fromhoff, 1988; Hudson, 1990; Tessler & Nelson, 1994). Interpreted within a social-constructivist perspective, the elaborative style is thought to provide the young child with, in effect, a "prototype" of the narrative frame into which information about the actors, actions, intentions, and affective experiences of those involved in an event is inserted. The advent of the narrative organization allows the child to begin to construct the personal history that is the hallmark of autobiographical or personal memory (for further discussion see, for example, Fivush, 1988; Hudson, 1990; K. Nelson, 1993). Consistent with this suggestion is evidence of cross-lag correlation from maternal style variables at 40 and 46 months to child verbal report variables at 58 and 70 months of age: maternal use of a more elaborative style facilitates children's independent narrative accounts (Reese, Haden, & Fivush, 1993).

Evidence from experimental studies provides additional support for the suggestion that maternal reminiscing style is a critical factor in the development of children's abilities to narrate their personal past experiences. For example, Reese and Newcombe (2007) instructed mothers of 21- to 29-month-old children to be more elaborative. Both concurrently and over time, their children provided more complete and higher-quality narratives, relative to children in a no-intervention group. The benefits were apparent in conversations with mothers and in children's independent narratives with an experimenter. In a study of low-income mothers and their 3-year-old children, the effect of reminiscing intervention was evident even 1 year later (Peterson, Jesso, & McCabe, 1999). Effects of elaborative style on children's narratives have also been found at the time of encoding of a to-be-remembered event (Bauer & Burch, 2004; Boland, Haden, & Ornstein, 2003; Haden, Ornstein, Eckerman, & Didow, 2001; Tessler & Nelson, 1994). They also extend beyond the reminiscing context to imitation-based tasks (Bauer & Burch, 2004). Analogous effects are observed in deliberate memory tasks (Larkina, Güler, Kleinknecht, & Bauer, 2008).

Interaction between children's characteristics and reminiscing style. There are numerous sources of individual differences to consider in evaluating how characteristics of the child who is doing the remembering might interact with the behavior of the conversational partner. Children's temperament, the dyadic quality of attachment, and children's gender all have been found to relate to parents' naturally occurring style of reminiscing (for detailed discussion see Bauer, 2007; Fivush, Haden, & Reese, 2006; K. Nelson & Fivush, 2004; Reese, 2002). For example, children who are rated as more interested and persistent (Bauer & Burch, 2004), more sociable and active (Lewis, 1999), and who are perceived as more attentive (Farrant & Reese, 2000), have mothers who are more elaborative. There are also relations between the quality of socio-emotional attachment and maternal elaboration concurrently (Fivush & Vasudeva, 2002; Laible, 2004) and longitudinally (Newcombe & Reese, 2004).

Children's gender is also associated with variability in reminiscing style. First, parents are more elaborative in conversations about past events with their daughters than with their sons (e.g., Fivush, Berlin, Sales, Mennuti-Washburn, & Cassidy, 2003; Reese et al., 1993; see Fivush & Buckner, 2003, for a review). Parents also more frequently confirm the participation of their daughters in conversations. Second, when talking about past events, parents use both a greater number and a greater variety of emotion words with daughters than sons (Adams, Kuebli, Boyle, & Fivush, 1995). These findings suggest that relative to boys, girls receive more reinforcement for participating in conversations about past events, and the conversations are more detailed and laden with emotion. Perhaps as a result, gender differences in children's narratives are observed as early as the elementary school years (Buckner & Fivush, 1998; Kuebli, Butler, & Fivush, 1995). Girls tend to produce longer, more coherent and more elaborate autobiographical narratives than boys of the same age (Bauer, Burch, Scholin, & Güler, 2007; Buckner & Fivush, 1998). Girls and boys also differ in use of emotion language. For example, in a longitudinal sample, between 40 and 70 months, girls showed increases in both the number and the variety of emotion words used. For boys, neither metric increased (Kuebli et al., 1995). These examples highlight the importance of consideration of interactions between the social environment in which memory skills are developing and the characteristics of the child who is doing the remembering.

Cultural factors

Just as important as differences in the child who is doing the remembering and in the familial environment in which memory for events is being shaped are differences in the larger cultural milieu of experience. Most of the research that makes this point has involved comparisons of children from Eastern and Western culture groups (although see MacDonald, Uesiliana, & Hayne, 2000). It has been found that the early autobiographical memory reports of children from Asian cultures include fewer references to themselves and fewer personal evaluations, relative to reports from children in the United States. In addition, the autobiographical narratives of children from Asian cultures tend to feature generic as opposed to specific events, and they are shorter and less detailed, relative to those provided by children in the United States (Han, Leichtman, & Wang, 1998; Wang, Leichtman, & Davies, 2000). These differences may be associated with variability in cultural perspectives on the value and goal of reminiscing (K. Nelson, 1988). If Asian cultures might foster a more communal sense of self in opposite to European and American cultures, which focus on the independent self, then these cultural expectations would influence early parent–child interaction. Indeed, Asian dyads engage in talk about the past less frequently and include fewer details than American dyads (Mullen & Yi, 1995). In addition, Asian mothers are less elaborative than American mothers, especially when talking about emotional experience (Fivush & Wang, 2005; Wang et al., 2000).

Infantile or Childhood Amnesia

Differences in socialization of autobiographical narratives might have direct implications for the variability in adults' autobiographical memories, particularly the age of first memory. As just reviewed, there is evidence that a more elaborative maternal reminiscing style leads to more organized, and therefore more accessible memories. Moreover, an elaborative style is thought to facilitate children's self-understanding and understanding of memory as representation (Bauer, 2007; K. Nelson & Fivush, 2004). Thus, we would expect gender and cultural differences in the age of first memory. Research has supported this expectation. Specifically, women have been found to have earlier first memories than men (e.g., Cowan & Davidson, 1984; Dudycha & Dudycha, 1941). There are also striking differences in the age of earliest autobiographical memory for European-Americans compared with Asian-Americans and Koreans living in America (e.g., MacDonald et al., 2000; Mullen, 1994; Wang, 2001; Wang, Conway, & Hou, 2004). The age of earliest memory for European-Americans is several months earlier than that of Asian-Americans or Koreans.

Although the relations between maternal style and later collaborative and independent narratives are correlational (not causal), the patterns suggest that exposure to an elaborative conversational style early in life has lasting effects that may work to increase memory for early life experiences. Consistent with this suggestion, Jack, MacDonald, Reese, and Hayne (2007) provide evidence that as adolescents, individuals whose mothers were more elaborative with them during the preschool years have earlier first memories than children of less elaborative mothers. This finding has been replicated in an independent sample in which it was found that adolescents whose mothers were highly elaborative in conversation in the preschool years provided earlier memories (M = 2.70 years) than children whose mothers were less elaborative (M = 3.33 years; Larkina, Merrill, Fivush, & Bauer,

2009). These studies indicate that maternal reminiscing style could be one of the critical factors that influences the "boundary" of childhood amnesia.

Participation in more elaborative conversations is seemingly related to the rate at which rich narrative descriptions of past events are formed and the efficacy with which they are retained. As discussed by Bauer (2007), the course of development of childhood amnesia is also related to the rate at which such memories are forgotten. Support for this suggestion came from a study in which a cue-word technique (reporting a memory in response to words such as *ice-cream* or *cup*) was used with children 7–10 years of age (Bauer, Burch, et al., 2007). The distribution of memories that the children provided in response to the cue words was well fit by an exponential function, implying a constant rate of forgetting over time (in contrast to decelerated forgetting among adults: e.g., Rubin, 1982). The consequence would be continued vulnerability to interference and decay, ultimately resulting in a smaller pool of early memories (relative to memories from later childhood and adulthood) from which to draw. Over time, the smaller pool would contribute to the appearance of "childhood amnesia" (Bauer, DeBoer, et al., 2007).

Conclusion

The study of the development of memory early in life has come a long way since its inception and even since the first edition of this volume (Bauer, 2002). The field has elaborated descriptions of changes in early memory and also made progress in explaining the course of development. The most salient advances are increased recognition of interactions as opposed to main effects, and of multiple determinants of developmental change. These have contributed to the richness of a field with a long and distinguished history. We look forward to further developments and the next "progress report."

References

Adams, S., Kuebli, J., Boyle, P. A., & Fivush, R. (1995). Gender differences in parent–child conversations about past emotions: A longitudinal investigation. *Sex Roles*, *33*, 309–323.

Adlam, A.-L. R., Vargha-Khadem, F., Mishkin, M., & de Haan, M. (2005). Deferred imitation of action sequences in developmental amnesia. *Journal of Cognitive Neuroscience*, *17*, 240–248.

Arnold, S. E., & Trojanowski, J. Q. (1996). Human fetal hippocampal development: I. Cytoarchitecture, myeloarchitecture, and neuronal morphologic features. *Journal of Comparative Neurology*, *367*, 274–292.

Bachevalier, J., & Mishkin, M. (1994). Effects of selective neonatal temporal lobe lesions on visual recognition memory in rhesus monkeys. *The Journal of Neuroscience*, *14*, 2128–2139.

Bahrick, L. E., & Pickens, J. N. (1995). Infant memory for object motion across a period of three months: Implications for a four-phase attention function. *Journal of Experimental Child Psychology*, *59*, 343–371.

Bahrick, L. E., Hernandez-Reif, M., & Pickens, J. N. (1997). The effect of retrieval cues on visual preferences and memory in infancy: Evidence for a four-phase attention function. *Journal of Experimental Child Psychology*, *67*, 1–20.

Baldwin, D. A., Markman, E. M., & Melartin, R. L. (1993). Infants' ability to draw inferences about nonobvious object properties: Evidence from exploratory play. *Child Development, 64,* 711–728.

Barnat, S. B., Klein, P. J., & Meltzoff, A. N. (1996). Deferred imitation across changes in context and object: Memory and generalization in 14-month-old children. *Infant Behavior and Development, 19,* 241–251.

Barr, R., Dowden, A., & Hayne, H. (1996). Developmental change in deferred imitation by 6- to 24-month-old infants. *Infant Behavior and Development, 19,* 159–170.

Bauer, P. J. (1993). Identifying subsystems of autobiographical memory: Commentary on Nelson. In C. A. Nelson (Ed.), *Memory and affect in development: The Minnesota Symposium on Child Psychology* (Vol. *26,* pp. 25–37). Hillsdale, NJ: Erlbaum.

Bauer, P. J. (2002). Early memory development. In U. Goswami (Ed.), *Blackwell Handbook of Childhood Cognitive Development* (pp. 127–146). Oxford: Blackwell.

Bauer, P. J. (2004). New developments in the study of infant memory. In D. M. Teti (Ed.), *Blackwell Handbook of Research Methods in Developmental Science* (pp. 467–488). Oxford: Blackwell.

Bauer, P. J. (2005). Developments in declarative memory: Decreasing susceptibility to storage failure over the second year of life. *Psychological Science, 16,* 41–47.

Bauer, P. J. (2006a). Constructing a past in infancy: A neuro-developmental account. *Trends in Cognitive Sciences, 10,* 175–181.

Bauer, P. J. (2006b). Event memory. In W. Damon & R. M. Lerner (Series Eds.), D. Kuhn & R. Siegler (Vol. Eds.), *Handbook of child psychology: Vol. 2. Cognition, perception, and language* (6th ed., pp. 373–425). Hoboken, NJ: Wiley.

Bauer, P. J. (2007). *Remembering the times of our lives: Memory in infancy and beyond.* Mahwah, NJ: Erlbaum.

Bauer, P. J. (2008). Toward a neuro-developmental account of the development of declarative memory. *Developmental Psychobiology, 50,* 19–31.

Bauer, P. J. (2009a). The cognitive neuroscience of the development of memory. In M. L. Courage and N. Cowan (Eds.), *The Development of Memory in Infancy and Childhood* (2nd ed., pp. 115–144). New York, NY: Psychology Press.

Bauer, P. J. (2009b). Neurodevelopmental changes in infancy and beyond: Implications for learning and memory. In O. A. Barbarin & B. H. Wasik (Eds.), *Handbook of child development and early education: Research to practice* (pp. 78–102). New York: Guilford.

Bauer, P. J., & Burch, M. M. (2004). Developments in early memory: Multiple mediators of foundational processes. In J. Lucariello, J. A. Hudson, R. Fivush, & P. J. Bauer (Eds), *Development of the mediated mind: Culture and cognitive development. Essays in honor of Katherine Nelson* (pp. 101–125). Mahwah, NJ: Erlbaum.

Bauer, P. J., Burch, M. M., Scholin, S. E., & Güler, O. E. (2007). Using cue words to investigate the distribution of autobiographical memories in childhood. *Psychological Science, 18,* 910–916.

Bauer, P. J., Cheatham, C. L., Cary, M. S., & Van Abbema, D. L. (2002). Short-term forgetting: Charting its course and its implications for long-term remembering. In S. P. Shohov (Ed.), *Advances in psychology research.* Huntington, NY: Nova Science Publishers. Reprinted in S. P. Shohov (Ed.), *Perspectives on cognitive psychology* (pp. 93–112). Huntington, NY: Nova Science Publishers.

Bauer, P. J., DeBoer, T., & Lukowski, A. F. (2007). In the language of multiple memory systems, defining and describing developments in long-term declarative memory. In L. M. Oakes and P. J. Bauer (Eds.), *Short- and long-term memory in infancy and early childhood: Taking the first steps toward remembering* (pp. 240–270). New York: Oxford University Press.

Bauer, P. J., & Dow, G. A. A. (1994). Episodic memory in 16- and 20-month-old children: Specifics are generalized, but not forgotten. *Developmental Psychology, 30*, 403–417.

Bauer, P. J., & Fivush, R. (1992). Constructing event representations: Building on a foundation of variation and enabling relations. *Cognitive Development, 7*, 381–401.

Bauer, P. J., & Hertsgaard, L. A. (1993). Increasing steps in recall of events: Factors facilitating immediate and long-term memory in 13.5- and 16.5-month-old children. *Child Development, 64*, 1204–1223.

Bauer, P. J., Hertsgaard, L. A., & Wewerka, S. S. (1995). Effects of experience and reminding on long-term recall in infancy: Remembering not to forget. *Journal of Experimental Child Psychology, 59*, 260–298.

Bauer, P. J., Kroupina, M. G., Schwade, J. A., Dropik, P., & Wewerka, S. S. (1998). If memory serves, will language? Later verbal accessibility of early memories. *Development and Psychopathology, 10*, 655–679.

Bauer, P. J., & Lukowski, A. F. (2009). *The memory is in the details: Relations between memory for the specific features of events and long-term recall in infancy*. Manuscript under review.

Bauer, P. J., & Shore, C. M. (1987). Making a memorable event: Effects of familiarity and organization on young children's recall of action sequences. *Cognitive Development, 2*, 327–338.

Bauer, P. J., Van Abbema, D. L., Wiebe, S. A., Strand Cary, M., Phill, C., & Burch, M. M. (2004). Props, not pictures, are worth a thousand words: Verbal accessibility of early memories under different conditions of contextual support. *Applied Cognitive Psychology, 18*, 373–392.

Bauer, P. J., Wenner, J. A., Dropik, P. L., & Wewerka, S. S. (2000). Parameters of remembering and forgetting in the transition from infancy to early childhood. *Monographs of the Society for Research in Child Development, 65* (4, Serial No. 263).

Bauer, P. J., Wiebe, S. A., Carver, L. J., Lukowski, A. F., Haight, J. C., Waters, J. M., & Nelson, C. A. (2006). Electrophysiological indices of encoding and behavioral indices of recall: Examining relations and developmental change late in the first year of life. *Developmental Neuropsychology, 29*, 293–320.

Bauer, P. J., Wiebe, S. A., Carver, L. J., Waters, J. M., & Nelson, C. A. (2003). Developments in long-term explicit memory late in the first year of life: Behavioral and electrophysiological indices. *Psychological Science, 14*, 629–635.

Bauer, P. J., Wiebe, S. A., Waters, J. M., & Bangston, S. K. (2001). Reexposure breeds recall: Effects of experience on 9-month-olds' ordered recall. *Journal of Experimental Child Psychology, 80*, 174–200.

Benes, F. M. (2001). The development of prefrontal cortex: The maturation of neurotransmitter systems and their interaction. In C. A. Nelson & M. Luciana (Eds.), *Handbook of developmental cognitive neuroscience* (pp. 79–92). Cambridge, MA: MIT Press.

Benes, F. M., Turtle, M., Khan, Y., & Farol, P. (1994). Myelination of a key relay zone in the hippocampal formation occurs in the human brain during childhood, adolescence, and adulthood. *Archives of General Psychiatry, 51*, 477–484.

Bjorklund, D. F., Dukes, C., & Brown, R. D. (2009). The development of memory strategies. In M. L. Courage & N. Cowan (Eds.), *The development of memory in infancy and childhood* (pp. 145–175). New York: Taylor & Francis.

Boland, A. M., Haden, C. A., & Ornstein, P. A. (2003). Boosting children's memory by training mothers in the use of an elaborative conversational style as an event unfolds. *Journal of Cognition and Development, 4*, 39–65.

Borovsky, D., & Rovee-Collier, C. (1990). Contextual constraints on memory retrieval at six months. *Child Development, 61*, 1569–1583.

Bourgeois, J.-P. (2001). Synaptogenesis in the neocortex of the newborn: The ultimate frontier for individuation? In C.A. Nelson & M. Luciana (Eds.), *Handbook of developmental cognitive neuroscience* (pp. 23–34). Cambridge, MA: The MIT Press.

Brainerd, C. J., & Reyna, V. F. (1990). Gist is the grist: Fuzzy-trace theory and the new intuitionism. *Developmental Review, 10,* 3–47.

Brainerd, C. J., Reyna, V. F., Howe, M. L., & Kingma, J. (1990). The development of forgetting and reminiscence. *Monographs of the Society for Research in Child Development, 55* (3–4, Serial No. 222).

Brewer, W. F. (1996). What is recollective memory? In D. C. Rubin (Ed.), *Remembering our past: Studies in autobiographical memory* (pp. 19–66). Cambridge: Cambridge University Press.

Buckner, J. P., & Fivush, R. (1998). Gender and self in children's autobiographical narratives. *Applied Cognitive Psychology, 12,* 407–429.

Campbell, B. A. (1984). Reflections on the ontogeny of learning and memory. In R. Kail & N. E. Spear (Eds.), *Comparative perspectives on the development of memory.* Hillsdale, NJ: Erlbaum.

Carver, L. J., & Bauer, P. J. (1999). When the event is more than the sum of its parts: Nine-month-olds' long-term ordered recall. *Memory, 7,* 147–174.

Carver, L. J., & Bauer, P. J. (2001). The dawning of a past: The emergence of long-term explicit memory in infancy. *Journal of Experimental Psychology: General, 130,* 726–745.

Cheatham, C. L., & Bauer, P. J. (2005). Construction of a more coherent story: Prior verbal recall predicts later verbal accessibility of early memories. *Memory, 13,* 516–532.

Chugani, H. T., Phelps, M., & Mazziotta, J. (1987). Positron emission tomography study of human brain functional development. *Annals of Neurology, 22,* 487–497.

Collie, R., & Hayne, H. (1999). Deferred imitation by 6- and 9-month-old infants: More evidence of declarative memory. *Developmental Psychobiology, 35,* 83–90.

Courage, M. L., & Howe, M. L. (1998). The ebb and flow of infant attentional preferences: Evidence for long-term recognition memory in 3-month-olds. *Journal of Experimental Child Psychology, 70,* 26–53.

Cowan, N., & Davidson, G. (1984). Salient childhood memories. *The Journal of Genetic Psychology, 145,* 101–107.

DeCasper, A. J., & Spence, M. J. (1986). Prenatal maternal speech influences newborns' perceptions of speech sounds. *Infant Behavior and Development, 9,* 133–150.

Dudycha, G. J., & Dudycha, M. M. (1941). Childhood memories: A review of the literature. *Psychological Review, 38,* 668–682.

Eckenhoff, M., & Rakic, P. (1991). A quantitative analysis of synaptogenesis in the molecular layer of the dentate gyrus in the rhesus monkey. *Developmental Brain Research, 64,* 129–135.

Eichenbaum, H., & Cohen, N. J. (2001). *From conditioning to conscious recollection: Memory systems of the brain.* New York: Oxford University Press.

Fagan, J. F. (1973). Infants' delayed recognition memory and forgetting. *Journal of Experimental Child Psychology, 16,* 425–450.

Fantz, R. L. (1956). A method for studying early visual development. *Perceptual and Motor Skills, 6,* 13–15.

Farrant, K., & Reese, E. (2000). Maternal style and children's participation in reminiscing: Stepping stones in children's autobiographical memory development. *Journal of Cognition and Development, 1,* 193–225.

Fivush, R. (1988). The functions of event memory. In U. Neisser & E. Winograd (Eds.), *Remembering reconsidered: Ecological and traditional approaches to the study of memory* (pp. 277–282). New York: Cambridge University Press.

Fivush, R., Berlin, L. J., Sales, J., Mennuti-Washburn, J., & Cassidy, J. (2003). Functions of parent–child reminiscing about emotionally negative events. *Memory, 11*, 179–192.

Fivush, R., & Buckner, J. P. (2003). Constructing gender and identity through autobiographical narratives. In R. Fivush & C. Haden (Eds.), *Autobiographical memory and the construction of a narrative self: Developmental and cultural perspectives*. Hillsdale, NJ: Erlbaum.

Fivush, R., & Fromhoff, F. (1988). Style and structure in mother–child conversations about the past. *Discourse Processes, 11*, 337–355.

Fivush, R., Haden, C. A., & Reese, E. (2006). Elaborating on elaborations: Role of maternal reminiscing style in cognitive and socioemotional development. *Child Development, 77*(6), 1568–1588.

Fivush, R., & Vasudeva, A. (2002). Remembering to relate: Socioemotional correlates of mother–child reminiscing. *Journal of Cognition and Development, 3*, 73–90.

Fivush, R., & Wang, Q. (2005). Emotion talk in mother–child conversations of the shared past: The effects of culture, gender, and event valence. *Journal of Cognition and Development, 6*(4), 489–506.

Flavell, J. H., Beach, D. R., & Chinsky, J. H. (1966). Spontaneous verbal rehearsal in a memory task as a function of age. *Child Development, 37*, 283–299.

Freud, S. (1905/1953). Three essays on the theory of sexuality. In J. Strachey (Ed.), *The standard edition of the complete psychological works of Sigmund Freud* (Vol. *7*, pp. 135–243). London: Hogarth Press.

Gelman, R., & Baillargeon, R. (1983). A review of some Piagetian concepts. In J. H. Flavell & E. M. Markman (Eds.), *Handbook of child psychology: Vol. 3. Cognitive development* (pp. 167–230). New York: Wiley.

Giedd, J. N., Blumenthal, J., Jeffries, N. O., Castellanos, F. X., Liu, H., Zijdenbos, A., Paus, T., Evans, A. C., & Rapoport, J. L. (1999). Brain development during childhood and adolescence: A longitudinal MRI study. *Nature Neuroscience, 2*, 861–863.

Gogtay, N., Giedd, J. N., Lusk, L., Hayashi, K. M., Greenstein, D., Vaituzis, A. C., … Thomson. P. M. (2004). Dynamic mapping of human cortical development during childhood through early adulthood. *PNAS, 101*, 8174–8179.

Haden, C., Haine, R., & Fivush, R. (1997). Development narrative structure in parent–child conversations about the past. *Developmental Psychology, 33*, 295–307.

Haden, C. A., Ornstein, P. A., Eckerman, C. O., & Didow, S. M. (2001). Mother–child conversational interactions as events unfold: Linkages to subsequent remembering. *Child Development, 72*, 1016–1031.

Hamond, N. R., & Fivush, R. (1991). Memories of Mickey Mouse: Young children recount their trip to Disneyworld. *Cognitive Development, 6*, 433–448.

Han, J. J., Leichtman, M. D., & Wang, Q. (1998). Autobiographical memory in Korean, Chinese, and American Children. *Developmental Psychology, 34*, 701–713.

Hanna, E., & Meltzoff, A. N. (1993). Peer imitation by toddlers in laboratory, home, and day-care contexts: Implications for social learning and memory. *Developmental Psychology, 29*, 702–710.

Harley, K., & Reese, E. (1999). Origins of autobiographical memory. *Developmental Psychology, 35*, 1338–1348.

Hayne, H., Boniface, J., & Barr, R. (2000). The development of declarative memory in human infants: Age-related changes in deferred imitation. *Behavioral Neuroscience, 114*, 77–83.

Hayne, H., MacDonald, S., & Barr, R. (1997). Developmental changes in the specificity of memory over the second year of life. *Infant Behavior and Development, 20*, 233–245.

Herbert, J., & Hayne, H. (2000). Memory retrieval by 18–30-month-olds: Age-related changes in representational flexibility. *Developmental Psychology, 36*, 473–484.

Hill, W. L., Borovsky, D., & Rovee-Collier, C. (1988). Continuities in infant memory development. *Developmental Psychobiology, 21*, 43–62.

Howe, M. L. (2003). Memories from the cradle. *Current Directions in Psychological Science, 12*, 62–65.

Howe, M. L., & Courage, M. L. (1993). On resolving the enigma of infantile amnesia. *Psychological Bulletin, 113*, 305–326.

Howe, M. L., & Courage, M. L. (1997a). The emergence and early development of autobiographical memory. *Psychological Review, 104*, 499–523.

Howe, M. L., & Courage, M. L. (1997b). Independent paths in the development of infant learning and forgetting. *Journal of Experimental Child Psychology, 67*, 131–163.

Howe, M. L., & O'Sullivan, J. T. (1997). What children's memories tell us about recalling our childhoods: A review of storage and retrieval processes in the development of long-term retention. *Developmental Review, 17*, 148–204.

Hudson, J. A. (1990). The emergence of autobiographical memory in mother–child conversation. In R. Fivush & J. A. Hudson (Eds.), *Knowing and remembering in young children* (pp. 166–196). Cambridge, MA: Cambridge University Press.

Hudson, J. A., Sheffield, E. G., & Deocampo, J. A. (2006). Effects of representational reminders on young children's recall: Implications for long-term memory development. In L. Balter & C. S. Tamis-LeMonda (Eds.), *Child psychology: A handbook of contemporary issues* (2nd ed., pp. 185–214). New York: Psychology Press.

Huttenlocher, P. R. (1979). Synaptic density in human frontal cortex: Developmental changes and effects of aging. *Brain Research, 163*, 195–205.

Huttenlocher, P. R., & Dabholkar, A. S. (1997). Regional differences in synaptogenesis in human cerebral cortex. *Journal of Comparative Neurology, 387*, 167–178.

Jack, F., MacDonald, S., Reese, E., & Hayne, H. (2007). Maternal reminiscing style during early childhood predicts the age of adolescents' earliest memories. *Child Development, 80*, 496–505.

Klein, P. J., & Meltzoff, A. N. (1999). Long-term memory, forgetting, and deferred imitation in 12-month-old infants. *Developmental Science, 2*, 102–113.

Kuebli, J., Butler, S., & Fivush, R. (1995). Mother–child talk about past emotions: Relations of maternal language and child gender over time. *Cognition and Emotion, 9*, 265–283.

Laible, D. (2004). Mother–child discourse in two contexts: Links with child temperament, attachment security, and socioemotional competence. *Developmental Psychology, 40*, 6, 979–992.

Larkina, M., Güler, O. E., Kleinknecht, E., & Bauer, P. J. (2008). Maternal provision of structure in a deliberate memory task in relation to their preschool children's recall. *Journal of Experimental Child Psychology, 100*, 235–251.

Larkina, M., Merrill, N., Fivush, R., & Bauer, P. J. (2009, October). *Linking children's earliest memories and maternal reminiscing style*. Poster session presented at the Cognitive Development Society, San Antonio, Texas.

Lechuga, M. T., Marcos-Ruiz, R., & Bauer, P. J. (2001). Episodic recall of specifics and generalisation coexist in 25-month-old children. *Memory, 9*, 117–132.

Lewis, K. D. (1999). Maternal style in reminiscing: Relations to child individual differences. *Cognitive Development, 14*, 381–399.

Lie, E., & Newcombe, N. S. (1999). Elementary school children's explicit and implicit memory for faces of preschool classmates. *Developmental Psychology, 35*, 102–112.

Liston, C., & Kagan, J. (2002). Memory enhancement in early childhood. *Nature, 419*, 896.

Lloyd, M. E., & Newcombe, N. S. (2009). Implicit memory in childhood: Reassessing developmental invariance. In M. L. Courage & N. Cowan (Eds.), *The development of memory in infancy and childhood* (93–113). New York: Taylor & Francis.

Lukowski, A. F., Wiebe, S. A., & Bauer, P. J. (in press). Going beyond the specifics: Generalization of single actions, but not temporal order, at nine months. *Infant Behavior and Development*.

MacDonald, S., Uesiliana, K., & Hayne, H. (2000). Cross-cultural and gender differences in childhood amnesia. *Memory, 8* (6), 365–376.

Mandler, J. M. (1990). Recall of events by preverbal children. In A. Diamond (Ed.), *The development and neural bases of higher cognitive functions* (pp. 485–516). New York: New York Academy of Science.

Mandler, J. M. (1998). Representation. In W. Damon (Series Ed.), D. Kuhn & R. Siegler (Vol. Eds.), *Handbook of Child Psychology: Vol. 2. Cognition, perception, and language* (pp. 255–308). New York: Wiley.

Mandler, J. M., & McDonough, L. (1995). Long-term recall of event sequences in infancy. *Journal of Experimental Child Psychology, 59*, 457–474.

Markowitsch, H. J. (2000). Neuroanatomy of memory. In E. Tulving and F. I. M. Craik (Eds.), *The Oxford handbook of memory* (pp. 465–484). New York: Oxford University Press.

McDonough, L., & Mandler, J. M. (1998). Inductive generalization in 9- and 11-month-olds. *Developmental Science, 1*, 227–232.

McDonough, L., Mandler, J. M., McKee, R. D., & Squire, L. R. (1995). The deferred imitation task as a nonverbal measure of declarative memory. *Proceedings of the National Academy of Sciences, 92*, 7580–7584.

McKee, R. D., & Squire, L. R. (1993). On the development of declarative memory. *Journal of Experimental Psychology: Learning, Memory, and Cognition, 19*, 397–404.

Meltzoff, A. N. (1985). Immediate and deferred imitation in fourteen- and twenty-four-month-old infants. *Child Development, 56*, 62–72.

Meltzoff, A. N. (1988). Infant imitation and memory: Nine-month-olds in immediate and deferred tests. *Child Development, 59*, 217–225.

Meltzoff, A. N. (1990). The implications of cross-modal matching and imitation for the development of representation and memory in infants. In A. Diamond (Ed.), *The development and neural bases of higher cognitive functions* (pp. 1–31). New York: New York Academy of Science.

Meltzoff, A. N. (1995). What infant memory tells us about infantile amnesia: Long-term recall and deferred imitation. *Journal of Experimental Child Psychology, 59*, 497–515.

Mullen, M. K. (1994). Earliest recollections of childhood: A demographic analysis. *Cognition, 52*, 55–79.

Mullen, M. K., & Yi, S. (1995). The cultural context of talk about the past: Implications for the development of autobiographical memory. *Cognitive Development, 10*, 407–419.

Nelson, C. A. (1995). The ontogeny of human memory: A cognitive neuroscience perspective. *Developmental Psychology, 31*, 723–738.

Nelson, C. A. (1997). The neurobiological basis of early memory development. In N. Cowan (Ed.), *The development of memory in childhood* (pp. 41–82). Hove, UK: Psychology Press.

Nelson, C. A. (2000). Neural plasticity and human development: The role of early experience in sculpting memory systems. *Developmental Science, 3*, 115–136.

Nelson, C. A, & Collins, P. F. (1991). Event-related potential and looking time analysis of infants' responses to familiar and novel events: Implications for visual recognition memory. *Developmental Psychology, 27*, 50–58.

Nelson, C. A., & Collins, P. F. (1992). Neural and behavioral correlates of recognition memory in 4- and 9-month-old infants. *Brain and Cognition, 19*, 105–121.

Nelson, C. A., de Haan, M., & Thomas, K. (2006). Neural bases of cognitive development. In W. Damon & R. M. Lerner (Series Eds.), D. Kuhn & R. Siegler (Eds.), *Handbook of Child Psychology: Vol. 2. Cognition, perception, and language* (6th ed., pp. 3–57). Hoboken, NJ: Wiley.

Nelson, K. (1986). *Event knowledge: Structure and function in development.* Hillsdale, NJ: Erlbaum.

Nelson, K. (1988). The ontogeny of memory for real events. In U. Neisser & E. Winograd (Eds.), *Remembering reconsidered: Ecological and traditional approaches to the study of memory* (pp. 244–276). New York: Cambridge University Press.

Nelson, K. (1989). *Narratives from the crib.* Cambridge, MA: Harvard University Press.

Nelson, K. (1993). The psychological and social origins of autobiographical memory. *Psychological Science, 4,* 7–14.

Nelson, K., & Fivush, R. (2004). The emergence of autobiographical memory: A social cultural developmental theory. *Psychological Review, 111,* 486–511.

Newcombe R., & Reese, E. (2004). Evaluations and orientations in mother–child narratives as a function of attachment security: A longitudinal investigation. *International Journal of Behavioral Development, 28,* 3, 230–245.

Parkin, A. J. (1997). The development of procedural and declarative memory. In N. Cowan (Ed.), *The development of memory in childhood* (pp. 113–137). Hove, UK: Psychology Press.

Peterson, C., Jesso, B., & McCabe, A. (1999). Encouraging narratives in preschoolers: An intervention study. *Journal of Child Language, 26,* 49–67.

Piaget, J. (1926). *The language and thought of the child.* New York: Harcourt Brace.

Piaget, J. (1952). *The origins of intelligence in children.* New York: International Universities Press.

Piaget, J. (1969). *The child's conception of time.* London: Routledge & Kegan Paul.

Pillemer, D. B. (1992). Remembering personal circumstances: A functional analysis. In E. Winograd, & U. Neisser (Eds.), *Affect and accuracy in recall: Studies of "flashbulb" memories* (pp. 236–264). New York: Cambridge University Press.

Pillemer, D. B., Picariello, M. L., & Pruett, J. C. (1994). Very long-term memories of a salient preschool event. *Applied Cognitive Psychology, 8,* 95–106.

Povinelli, D. J. (1995). The unduplicated self. In P. Rochat (Ed.), *The self in early infancy* (pp. 161–192). Amsterdam: Elsevier.

Reese, E. (2002). Social factors in the development of autobiographical memory: The state of art. *Social Development, 11,* 124–142.

Reese, E., Haden, C. A., & Fivush, R. (1993). Mother–child conversations about the past: Relationships of style and memory over time. *Cognitive Development, 8,* 403–430.

Reese, E., & Newcombe, R. (2007). Training mothers in elaborative reminiscing enhances children's autobiographical memory and narrative. *Child Development, 67,* 1153–1170.

Richman, J., & Nelson, C. A. (2008). Mechanisms of change: A cognitive neuroscience approach to declarative memory development. In C. A. Nelson & M. Luciana (Eds.), *Handbook of Developmental Cognitive Neuroscience* (2nd ed., pp. 541–552). Cambridge, MA: MIT Press.

Rosch, E. H., & Mervis, C. B. (1975). Family resemblances: Studies in the internal structure of categories. *Cognitive Psychology, 7,* 573–605.

Rose, S. A., Feldman, J. F., & Jankowski, J. J. (2007). Developmental aspects of visual recognition memory in infancy. In L. M. Oakes and P. J. Bauer (Eds.), *Short- and long-term memory in infancy and early childhood: Taking the first steps toward remembering* (pp. 153–178). New York: Oxford University Press.

Rose, S. A., Gottfried, A. W., Melloy-Carminar, P., & Bridger, W. H. (1982). Familiarity and novelty preferences in infant recognition memory: Implications for information processing. *Developmental Psychology, 18,* 704–713.

Rovee-Collier, C. (1997). Dissociations in infant memory: Rethinking the development of implicit and explicit memory. *Psychological Review, 104,* 467–498.

Rovee-Collier, C., & Cuevas, K. (2009). The development of infant memory. In M. L. Courage and N. Cowan (Eds.), *The Development of Memory in Infancy and Childhood* (2nd ed., pp. 11–41). New York: Psychology Press.

Rovee-Collier, C., Schechter, A., Shyi, G., & Shields, P. (1992). Perceptual identification of contextual attributes and infant memory retrieval. *Developmental Psychology, 28,* 307–318.

Rovee-Collier, C., Sullivan, M. W., Enright, M. K., Lucas, D., & Fagen, J. W. (1980). Reactivation of infant memory. *Science, 208,* 1159–1161.

Rubin, D. C. (1982). On the retention function for autobiographical memory. *Journal of Verbal Learning and Verbal Behavior, 21,* 21–38.

Schneider, W., & Bjorklund, D. F. (1998). Memory. In W. Damon (Series Ed.), D. Kuhn & R. S. Siegler (Eds.), *Handbook of child psychology: Vol. 2. Cognition, perception, and language* (5th ed., pp. 467–521). New York: Wiley.

Seress, L., & Abraham, H. (2008). Pre- and postnatal morphological development of the human hippocampal formation. In C. A. Nelson & M. Luciana (Eds.), *Handbook of developmental cognitive neuroscience* (2nd ed., pp. 187–212). Cambridge, MA: MIT Press.

Sheffield, E. G. (2004). But I thought it was Mickey Mouse: The effects of new post-event information on 18-month-olds' memory. *Journal of Experimental Child Psychology, 87*(3), 221–238.

Simcock, G., & Hayne, H. (2002). Breaking the barrier? Children fail to translate their preverbal memories into language. *Psychological Science, 13,* 225–231.

Slater, A. (1995). Visual perception and memory at birth. In C. Rovee-Collier & L. P. Lipsitt (Eds.), *Advances in Infancy Research* (Vol. *9,* pp. 107–162). Norwood, NJ: Ablex.

Snyder, K. A. (2007). Neural mechanisms of attention and memory in preferential looking tasks. In L. M. Oakes and P. J. Bauer (Eds.), *Short- and long-term memory in infancy and early childhood: Taking the first steps toward remembering* (pp. 179–208). New York: Oxford University Press.

Squire, L. R. (1992). Memory and the hippocampus: A synthesis from findings with rats, monkeys, and humans. *Psychological Review, 99,* 195–231.

Squire, L. R., Knowlton, B., & Musen, G. (1993). The structure and organization of memory. *Annual Review of Psychology, 44,* 453–495.

Tessler, M., & Nelson, K. (1994). Making memories: The influence of joint encoding on later recall by young children. *Consciousness and Cognition, 3,* 307–326.

Toth, J. P. (2000). Nonconscious forms of human memory. In E. Tulving & F. I. M. Craik (Eds.), *The Oxford handbook of memory* (pp. 245–261). New York: Oxford University Press.

Utsunomiya, H., Takano, K., Okazaki, M., & Mistudome, A. (1999). Development of the temporal lobe in infants and children: Analysis by MR-based volumetry. *American Journal of Neuroradiology, 20,* 717–723.

Wang, Q. (2001). Culture effects on adults' earliest childhood recollection and self-description: Implications for the relation between memory and the self. *Journal of Personality and Social Psychology, 81,* 220–233.

Wang, Q., Conway, M. A., & Hou, Y. (2004). Infantile amnesia: A cross-cultural investigation. *Cognitive Science, 1*(1), 123–135.

Wang, Q., Leichtman, M. D., & Davies, K. I. (2000). Sharing memories and telling stories: American and Chinese mothers and their 3-year-olds. *Memory, 8,* 159–177.

Warrington, E. K., & Weiskrantz, L. (1974). The effect of prior learning on subsequent retention in amnesic patients. *Neuropsychologia, 12,* 419–428.

Welch-Ross, M. (2001). Personalizing the temporally extended self: Evaluative self-awareness and the development of autobiographical memory. In C. Moore, & K. Lemmon (Eds.), *The self in time: Developmental perspectives* (pp. 97–120). Mahwah, NJ: Erlbaum.

West, T. A., and Bauer, P. J. (1999). Assumptions of infantile amnesia: Are there differences between early and later memories? *Memory*, *7*, 257–278.
Zola, S. M., & Squire, L. R. (2000). The medial temporal lobe and the hippocampus. In E. Tulving and F. I. M. Craik (Eds.), *The Oxford handbook of memory* (pp. 485–500). New York: Oxford University Press.
Zola-Morgan, S., & Squire, L. R. (1993). Neuroanatomy of memory. *Annual Review of Neuroscience*, *16*, 547–563.

CHAPTER SEVEN

Early Word-Learning and Conceptual Development

Everything Had a Name, and Each Name Gave Birth to a New Thought[1]

Sandra R. Waxman and Erin M. Leddon

Synopsis

Perhaps more than any other developmental achievement, word-learning stands at the very intersection of language and cognition. Early word-learning represents infants' entrance into a truly symbolic system and brings with it a means to establish reference. To succeed, infants must identify the relevant linguistic units, identify their corresponding concepts, and establish a mapping between the two. But how do infants begin to map words to concepts, and thus establish their meaning? How do they discover that different types of words – e.g., "dog" (noun), "fluffy" (adjective), "begging" (verb) – refer to different aspects of the same scene – e.g., a standard poodle, seated on its hind legs and holding its front paws in the air)? We have proposed that infants begin the task of word-learning with a broad, universal expectation linking novel words to a broad range of commonalities, and that this initial expectation is subsequently fine-tuned on the basis of their experience with the objects and events they encounter and the native language under acquisition. In this chapter, we examine this proposal, in light of recent evidence with infants and young children.

Introduction

Infants across the world's communities are exposed to vastly different experiences. Consider, for example, one infant being raised in a remote region of the Guatemalan rainforest, another growing up in the mountains of rural Switzerland, and a third being raised in Brooklyn, New York. Each infant will live in a world that is unimaginable to the other, surrounded by objects and events that are foreign to the other, and immersed in a language that the other cannot begin to understand. Yet despite these vast differences in experience, infants across the world display striking similarities in the most fundamental aspects of their conceptual and language development.

Within the first year of life, each of these infants will begin to establish systematic links between words and the concepts to which they refer. On the conceptual side, they will begin to form categories of objects that capture both the similarities and the differences among the objects they encounter. Most of these early object categories will be at the basic level (e.g., *dog*) and the more inclusive global level (e.g., *animal*). Infants will begin to use these early object categories as an inductive base to support inferences about new objects that they encounter. They will also begin to relate categories to one another, implicitly, on the basis of taxonomic (e.g., dogs are a kind of animal), thematic (e.g., dogs chase tennis balls), functional (e.g., dogs can pull children on sleds), and other relations. Infants' early object and event categories will provide a core of conceptual continuity from infancy through adulthood.

Concurrent with these conceptual advances, infants in each community will make remarkably rapid strides in language acquisition. Even before they begin to understand the words of their native language, infants show a special interest in the sounds of language. Newborns respond to the emotional tone carried by the melody of human speech (Fernald, 1992a, 1992b), and prefer speech sounds to other forms of auditory input (Jusczyk & Kemler Nelson, 1996; Vouloumanos & Werker, 2004, 2007). Within the first 6 months, infants become perceptually attuned to the distinct prosodic, morphologic, and phonologic elements that characterize their native language (Jusczyk & Kemler Nelson, 1996; Kemler Nelson, Hirsh-Pasek, Jusczyk, & Cassidy, 1989; Morgan & Demuth, 1996; Shi, Werker, & Morgan, 1999; Werker, Lloyd, Pegg, & Polka, 1996; see Saffran, Werker, & Werner, 2006 for a review). By their first birthdays, infants begin to produce their first words. These early words tend to refer to salient individual objects (e.g., "Mama"), categories of objects (e.g., "cup," "doggie"), social routines (e.g., "bye-bye"), and actions (e.g., "up"). Across languages, infants' earliest lexicons tend to show a "noun advantage," with nouns referring to basic-level object categories (e.g., cup, dog) being the predominant form (see Bornstein et al., 2004, for an excellent cross-linguistic developmental review). By their second birthdays, most infants have mastered hundreds of words of various grammatical forms (e.g., nouns, verbs, adjectives) and have begun to combine these into short, well-formed phrases that conform broadly to the syntactic properties of their native language.

This brief sketch illustrates several early milestones along the road of language and conceptual development. Infants naturally form *categories* to capture commonalities among objects and events and learn *words* to express them. What is perhaps even more intriguing is that these two advances do not proceed independently. Instead, there are powerful implicit links between them.

Links between early language and conceptual development: A view through the lens of word-learning

The links between early language and conceptual development are most clearly viewed through the lens of early word-learning. Word-learning supports infants' subsequent discovery of the fundamental syntactic properties of the native language (See Gillette, Gleitman, Gleitman, & Lederer, 1999; Pinker, 1984, 1989; Snedeker & Gleitman, 1999; Waxman, 1999a, 1999b) as well as the evolution of increasingly abstract conceptual representations. Moreover, from the onset of acquisition, the process of word-learning involves powerful, implicit links between the linguistic and conceptual systems. Even before infants begin to speak, novel words guide their attention to objects, and highlight commonalities and differences among them (Balaban & Waxman, 1997; Booth & Waxman, 2002; Fulkerson & Haaf, 2003, 2006; Fulkerson & Waxman, 2007; Graham, Kilbreath, & Welder, 2004; Keates & Graham, 2008; Waxman & Markow, 1995; Welder & Graham, 2006; Xu, 1999). But these links are not as precise as those held by older children and adults. How does their development proceed?

We have proposed that (a) infants across the world's language communities begin the task of word-learning equipped with an initially general and universal expectation, and (b) this early expectation is then shaped by the structure of the particular language under acquisition. In our most recent work, which will be reviewed here, we have sought to uncover the origin and unfolding of these links (Booth & Waxman, 2003; Fulkerson & Waxman, 2007; Klibanoff & Waxman, 2000; Waxman, 1998; Waxman & Booth, 2000; Waxman & Booth, 2001b; Waxman & Booth, in press; Waxman, Lidz, Braun, & Lavin, 2009; Waxman & Markow, 1995). To amplify this topic, we will discuss what it takes to learn a word, to establish a mapping between the linguistic entities that we call *words* and the corresponding entities and events in the *world*. We then go on to trace the origin and emergence of these links in infants.

What Does it Take to Learn a Word?

Perhaps the most celebrated example of word-learning comes from Helen Keller's autobiography. As Keller recounts:

> my teacher placed my hand under the spout. As the cool stream gushed over one hand she spelled into the other the word *water*, first slowly, then rapidly. I stood still, my whole attention fixed upon the motions of her fingers. Suddenly I felt a misty consciousness as of something forgotten – a thrill of returning thought; and somehow the mystery of language was revealed to me. I knew then that "w-a-t-e-r" meant the wonderful cool something that was flowing over my hand. That living word awakened my soul, gave it light, hope, joy, and set it free! … I left the well-house eager to learn. Everything had a name, and each name gave birth to a new thought. (Keller, 1904, p. 22–23)

This memorable passage poignantly conveys the obstacles in first establishing a correspondence between the abstract entities that we call *words* and their referents in the *world.* It also conveys the power of such *word-to-world* mappings, once they are attained. But the scenario in this passage differs in important ways from the more typical circumstances in which infants' first words are acquired. One important difference is the age of acquisition. Infants tend to produce their first words at approximately one year of age. Keller, in contrast, learned *water* at approximately seven years of age.[2] A second difference is the extent to which names are deliberately "taught." Psycholinguists and anthropologists have conducted detailed observations of naming practices across cultures. In some cultures (cf., Western, college-educated communities), caretakers do name objects deliberately for their infants, even before the infants themselves can speak. Yet in many other communities, (cf., Kahluli, see Ochs and Schieffelin, 1984), caretakers refrain from speaking directly to infants until the infants themselves have begun to speak. Clearly, then, infants can discover the meaning of novel words even in the absence of direct tutoring.

A third relevant difference is in the presentation of the new word. In the typical course of events, words are seldom, if ever, presented in isolation, as Keller's tutor presented the word *w-a-t-e-r*. Instead, words tend to be embedded in a fluent stream of continuous speech (e.g., "Look at the water! Oooh ... it's so cold. Isn't that cold water?"), leaving it to the infant to parse the novel word. How do they succeed in these cases? At a most general level, it helps that infants devote special attention to human speech, for this puts them in a good position to begin to single out the novel words (Jusczyk & Kemler Nelson, 1996). Moreover, in many cultures, caretakers use a special speech register (sometimes known as infant-directed speech or "motherese") when addressing infants and young children. Two characteristic features of this speech register – exaggerated pitch contours and phrase boundaries – help infants to identify words and phrases in the continuous speech stream (Gleitman & Wanner, 1988).

A fourth difference concerns the identification of the referent of the novel word. Unlike Keller, infants must identify the referent of a novel word amidst an ever-changing current of events. In many cases, the referent may be absent entirely (e.g., "Let's call Daddy," uttered as the caretaker picks up a phone), or may make only a fleeting appearance (e.g., "Look at the monkey," uttered as a monkey makes a brief appearance in its habitat at the zoo). And even if the referent is present throughout the naming episode, there is no guarantee that the infant will be attending to it at the time that the novel word is introduced (e.g., "Go find your teddy-bear," uttered as a caretaker tries (in vain) to pull the infant's attention away from the sleeping family cat).

The puzzle of word-learning

Thus, in the natural course of word-learning, an infant is faced with a difficult three-part puzzle: (a) parsing the relevant word from the ongoing stream of speech, (b) identifying the relevant entity in the ongoing stream of activity in the world, and (c) establishing a word-to-world correspondence. To put matters more formally, successful word-learning rests on the infant's ability to discover the relevant linguistic units, the relevant conceptual units, and the mappings between them.

Notice also that each piece in the word-learning puzzle is itself dependent on infants' ability to recruit other perceptual and psychological capacities. Consider, for example, the ability to parse words. We know that newborns prefer to listen to human speech – and particularly infant-directed speech – as compared to other sources of auditory stimulation. However, the function of infant-directed speech appears to change during the first year of life (Fernald, 1992b). Initially, infant-directed speech serves primarily to engage and modulate the infant's attention. Toward the end of the first year, "words begin to emerge from the melody" (Fernald, 1992a, p. 403). By approximately 9–10 months, infants become increasingly sensitive to the cues (morphologic, phonetic, and prosodic cues) that mark word and phrase boundaries (Jusczyk & Aslin, 1995; Kemler Nelson et al., 1989).

Infants' growing sensitivity to these perceptual cues permits them to distinguish two very broad classes of words: *open class* words (or *content* words, including nouns, adjectives, verbs) and *closed class* words (or *function* words, including determiners and prepositions). Research using a preferential listening task reveals that even 6-month-old infants prefer to listen to open class words (Gomez, 2002; Shi & Werker, 2003). This preference is likely related to the fact that such words are perceptually more salient: they receive greater stress and more interesting melodic contours than closed class words. Since this preference exists well before infants begin to map words systematically to meaning, it is reasonable to assume that it is perceptually based and independent of meaning. Yet this perceptually based preference represents an important step on the way to word-learning, for it insures that infants attend to just those words (the open class, content words) that are required if they are to anchor their first word-to-world mappings. (Jusczyk & Kemler Nelson, 1996; Morgan & Demuth, 1996; Werker et al., 1996).

Early word-learning also draws upon the infants' perceptual and conceptual ability to identify objects and events in their environment, and to notice commonalities among them. During the first year, infants demonstrate a great deal of core knowledge about objects (Baillargeon, 2000; Spelke, 2000). They also form a repertoire of prelinguistic concepts, including category-based (e.g., dog, bottle) and property-based (e.g., red, soft) commonalities. Since many of these concepts are formed before the advent of word-learning, it is reasonable to assume that they are independent of language and are universally available. Each object and concept is, in essence, a candidate for a word's meaning. The infant's task is to discover which candidate meaning maps to the word that they have parsed.

The third piece of the word-learning puzzle – grasping the symbolic and referential power of words – further requires infants to draw upon fundamental notions related to human behavior: inferring the goals and intentions of others (Waxman & Gelman, in press). For example, the ability to establish a mapping between a word and its referent is predicated upon infants' capacity to infer that the speaker *intended to name* the designated object. By the end of the first year of life, infants have begun to make such connections (Akhtar & Tomasello, 2000); for example, they spontaneously follow a speaker's line of regard to identify the object to which an adult speaker is attending (Baldwin & Baird, 1999; Guajardo & Woodward, 2000).

In addition to these three central elements, successful word-learning requires infants to go beyond a word-to-object mapping. To use a word consistently over time, infants must be able to store in memory the correspondence between a word and its intended referent. They must also be able to generalize a newly learned word appropriately beyond the individual on which it was taught. For example, to be able to apply the word *dog* to a new, and (as yet) unlabeled object, that child must make an inference regarding its extension. Infants' spontaneous extensions indicate that they do not merely map words to the objects on which they were introduced. Infants go beyond *word-to-object* mappings to establish *word-to-category* mappings (Gelman, 2006; Waxman & Lidz, 2006).

Different kinds of words highlight different aspects of a scene

To complicate matters further, many different words – indeed many different *types* of words – may be offered in a single naming episode. Importantly, each type of word highlights a different aspect of the same observed scene and supports a unique pattern of extension. For example, in English, count nouns ("Look, it's a *dog*") typically refer to the named object itself and are extended spontaneously to other members of the same object kind (other dogs); proper nouns ("Look, it's *Zeus*") also refer to the named individual, but these are not extended further. Adjectives can also be applied correctly to that individual ("Look, it's *furry*"); they refer to a property of the individual, and are extended to other objects sharing that property. Verbs, in contrast, are used to describe the event, or the relation in which the individual(s) are participating ("Look, it's running"), and are extended to other relations of the same type.

Considerable research has documented that by 2.5 to 3 years of age, children are sensitive to many of these links between kinds of words and kinds of relations among objects, and recruit these links in the process of word-learning (for a review, see Waxman & Lidz, 2006). This establishes that preschool-aged children have the *linguistic* capacity to distinguish among the relevant syntactic forms (e.g., count noun vs. adjective) and the *conceptual* or *perceptual* ability to appreciate many different kinds of relations among objects, and a tacit expectation that these linguistic and conceptual abilities are interwoven.

The proposal: The acquisition of word-to-world links

But how do infants acquire these specific word-to-world links? Which, if any, are available at the very onset of lexical acquisition, and how are these shaped over the course of development? The evidence discussed above suggests that infants begin with a perceptual preference for listening to open class words, with a repertoire of accessible perceptual and conceptual categories, and with a broad expectation that novel (open class) words, independent of their grammatical form, highlight commonalities among named objects. This initial link serves (at least) three essential functions. First, with words directing attention to commonalities, this link facilitates the formation of an expanding repertoire of concepts, concepts that may not have been detected in the absence of a novel word. Second, this initial expectation supports infants' first efforts to establish symbolic reference, to form a set of stable "word-to-world" mappings. Finally, and perhaps most radically, this initial expectation sets the stage for the evolution of the more specific expectations linking particular types of words (nouns, adjectives, verbs) to particular types of relations among objects (object categories, object properties, event categories) in the native language under acquisition (Waxman, 1999b).

How might this evolution come about? Infants' early expectation (that words refer to commonalities) supports the establishment of a rudimentary lexicon. This lexicon serves as a base upon which infants (a) begin to tease apart the various grammatical forms presented in the language under acquisition, and (b) begin to detect the correlations between these emerging forms and their meanings. We argue that infants' initial expectation (linking words in general) to commonalities (in general) will direct their attention to just the sorts of regularities in the input that will promote the rapid discovery of the distinct grammatical forms present in the language under acquisition, and will support the induction of more specific expectations.

The Evidence: The Evolution of Infants' Word-to-World Expectations

To test this proposal, we must identify the expectation(s) of infants on the threshold of word-learning, and observe how these are shaped in the course of acquiring their native language. The sections that follow describe the influence of language on categorization in infants and young children. The focus is on how infants and young children begin to map words to meaning, and how their expectations vary according to the word's grammatical category, be it noun, adjective, or verb. We examine the acquisition of words in each of these grammatical categories, considering evidence from a variety of measures, including time-course analyses of children's responses to a novel word. We conclude with a discussion of new avenues for research on word-learning.

The experiments described in this section all share several important features. Each is essentially a categorization task, tailored to suit the very different behavioral repertoires of infants versus young children. In each, the goal is to observe the influence of language on categorization. To do so, we compare subjects' performance in "neutral" conditions (involving no novel words), with their performance when they are introduced to novel words. Because our goal is to examine an abstract linkage between particular grammatical forms and particular types of relations, we introduce novel words (e.g., *blicket*), rather than familiar (e.g., *animal*) words. This insures that the words themselves carry no *a priori* meaning for the child. To examine the influence of grammatical form, we vary the frame in which the novel word is embedded. We use short, simple syntactic constructions that (a) are typical in infant- and child-directed speech, and that (b) provide unambiguous contextual evidence that the novel word is either a count noun, an adjective, or a verb. In all conditions, these constructions are presented to infants in a speech register known as "motherese" or infant-directed speech because infants find it especially engaging. In the *Novel Noun* conditions, we introduce the novel word, saying, for example, "This is a *blicket.*" In the *Novel Adjective* and *Novel Verb* conditions, we present the same word using a different frame, saying, for example, "This is a *blick-ish* one," or "She is *blicking* the cup." In the *No Word* control conditions, we engage the infants with infant-directed speech, but offer no novel word, simply saying, for example, "Do you like this?" or "Look at this." Performance in this *No Word* control condition assesses how readily subjects form the various categories presented in our tasks (e.g., dog, animal, purple, running). Performance in the *Noun*, *Adjective*, and *Verb* conditions assesses the role of naming in this important endeavor, and permits us to test the specificity of the relation between form and meaning. Because nouns, adjectives, and verbs alike can be used to describe different aspects of the very same scene, this is an important control.

Prelinguistic infants: cognitive consequences of naming

Recent research suggests that naming has several cognitive consequences, even for infants who have not yet begun to produce words on their own. For example, by 10 months, infants devote more attention to objects that have been named than to objects that have been presented in silence (Baldwin & Markman, 1989). This raises two further questions. First, does the increased attention stem from the general attention-engaging functions of auditory stimuli, or does it reflect something special about words? Second, does naming promote attention to a named individual only, or does it exert an influence beyond the named individual?

Several recent studies have compared the effect of novel words versus tone sequences on infants' categorization behavior, and these suggest that words are indeed special (Balaban & Waxman, 1997; Fulkerson & Haaf, 2003, 2006; Fulkerson & Waxman, 2007). In one study, Fulkerson and Waxman (2007) assessed 6-month-old infants' performance when presented with words versus tones in a novelty-preference task. During a familiarization phase, infants saw a sequence of colorful slides, each depicting a different member of a basic-level category (e.g., dinosaurs). To examine the influence of words, they randomly assigned infants to either a *Word* or a *Tone* condition. For infants in the *Word* condition, a naming phrase (e.g., "Oh look, it's a *toma*! Do you see the *toma*?") accompanied the familiarization trials. For infants in the *Tone* condition, a sine-wave tone (matched to the naming phrase in amplitude, duration, and pause length) accompanied the familiarization trials. Next, infants were presented with a *test* trial, including (a) a new member of the now-familiar category (e.g., another dinosaur) and (b) an object from a novel category (e.g., a fish). Test trials were presented in silence.

The authors reasoned that if words focus attention on commonalities among objects, then infants hearing words during familiarization should notice the commonalities among the familiarization objects. In that case, the infants should reveal a preference for the novel test-object (e.g., the fish). If this effect is specific to words, and not to auditory stimulation more generally, then infants hearing tones during familiarization should be less likely to notice these commonalities and less likely to reveal a novelty preference at test. This is precisely the pattern of results obtained. We can therefore conclude that for infants as young as 6 months of age, there is indeed something special about words, and that providing a shared name for distinct individuals highlights commonalities among them.

In addition to supporting object categories, naming supports the process of object individuation. Evidence suggests that 10-month-olds find it difficult to keep track of the unique identities of two distinct objects (e.g., a ball and a duck), especially if these objects are presented in constant motion, with one appearing and disappearing from one side of a screen, and the other appearing and disappearing from the other side of the same screen (Xu & Carey, 1996). However, infants' difficulty tracking these distinct objects diminishes dramatically if each is labeled with a distinct name as it emerges from behind the screen.

Together, these results reveal that naming has powerful cognitive consequences, even in prelinguistic infants. Naming supports the establishment of a repertoire of object categories and provides infants with a means of tracing the identity of individuals within these categories throughout development. These links appear before the advent of productive language.

Infants on the threshold of word-learning: changing expectations of word-to-world mappings

In the previous section, we established that words have a unique influence on prelinguistic infants' construals of individual objects and object categories. In this section, we trace the evolution of infants' expectations regarding word-to-world mappings as they cross the important developmental threshold of producing words on their own. At this developmental point, how do words influence infants' attention to individual objects and object categories?

Words as invitations to form categories. One series of experiments examined the influence of novel words on object categorization in 12- to 14-month old infants (see Waxman & Markow, 1995, for a complete description). We used a novelty-preference task (see figure 7.1 for a sample set of stimuli and introductory phrases). During a familiarization phase, an experimenter offered an infant four different toys from a given category (e.g., four animals) one at a time, in random order. This was immediately followed by a test phase, in which the experimenter simultaneously presented both (a) a new member of the now-familiar category (e.g., another animal) and (b) an object from a novel category (e.g., a fruit). Each infant completed this task with four different sets of objects. Two involved basic-level categories (e.g., horses vs. cats); two involved more abstract superordinate-level categories (e.g., animals vs. fruit). Infants manipulated the toys freely. Their manipulation served as the dependent measure.

To test the influence of novel words, we randomly assigned infants to one of three conditions. All infants heard infant-directed speech; what varied was the experimenter's comments during familiarization. (See figure 7.1.)

We reasoned as follows: if infants detect the presence of the novel word, and if novel words direct infants' attention to object categories, then infants who hear novel words during familiarization should be more likely than those in the No Word condition to form object categories. Including both a Novel Noun and Novel Adjective condition permitted us to test the specificity of infants' initial expectation. If the expectation is initially general, as we have proposed, then infants hearing either novel nouns or adjectives should be more likely than those hearing no novel words to form object categories.

For infants who had begun to produce words on their own, the data were entirely consistent with this prediction. Interestingly, the facilitative influence of novel words was

	Familiarization phase				Test phase	
	Trial 1	Trial 2	Trial 3	Trial 4		
Animal set	yellow duck	green raccoon	blue dog	orange lion	red cat	red apple
Noun	This one is. a(n) X	This one is a(n) X	See what I have?	This one is a(n)X	See what I have?	
Adjective	This one is X-ish	This one is X-ish	See what I have?	This one is X-ish	See what I have?	
No Word	Look at this.	Look at this.	See what I have?	Look at this.	See what I have?	

Figure 7.1 A schematic presentation of introductory phrases from Waxman and Markow (1995) and an example of a single stimulus set

most powerful on superordinate-level trials. On basic-level trials, all infants successfully formed categories. But on superordinate trials, infants in the No Word condition did not detect the commonalities. This difficulty is likely due to the fact that there is considerable variation among category members at superordinate levels, and, as a result, the commonalities among them can be difficult to trace. However, infants who heard novel words during familiarization (either count nouns or adjectives) detected the commonalities among objects and successfully formed superordinate-level object categories.

These results reveal that infants on the threshold of producing language can reliably detect novel words presented in fluent speech, and that these novel words (both adjectives and nouns) direct infants' attention to commonalities among objects. We have interpreted this finding as evidence that words serve as "invitations to form categories" and have pointed out that this invitation has several consequences. First, novel words invite infants to assemble together objects that might otherwise be perceived as disparate entities. We suggest that words promote comparison among objects, and that this process of comparison supports the discovery of other commonalities that might otherwise have gone unnoticed (Booth, 2006; Chambers, Graham, & Turner, 2008; Gelman, 2006; Gentner & Namy, 1999; Keates & Graham, 2008; Welder & Graham, 2006).

Naming may also have dramatic consequences in situations in which infants have already formed groupings and noticed (some of) the commonalities among objects. For example, although infants in this series successfully formed basic-level object categories (whether or not they were introduced to novel words), their knowledge about these categories is not on a par with the knowledge of an older child or adult. Even preschool-aged children lack detailed knowledge about most categories (Gelman, 1996; Keil, 1994). Nonetheless, despite their relative lack of information, children seem to expect that members of object categories share deep, non-obvious commonalities. Indeed, children depend upon these to support inference and induction. We suspect that novel words are instrumental in motivating infants and young children to discover the deeper commonalities that underlie our richly structured object categories (Ahn & Luhmann, 2004; Barsalou, 1983; Barsalou, Santos, Simmons, & Wilson, 2008; Gelman, 1996; Gelman, Coley, & Gottfried, 1994; Gelman & Kalish, 2006; Gelman & Medin, 1993; Kalish & Gelman, 1992; Keil, 1994; Landau, 1994; Landau, Smith, & Jones, 1988; Lassaline & Murphy, 1996; Macnamara, 1994; Markman, 1989; Medin & Heit, 1999; Murphy 2004). Most importantly, the results of this series of experiments document that a link between word-learning and conceptual organization is in place early enough to guide infants in their very first efforts to establish word-to-world mappings.

Specifying the scope of infants' word-to-world mappings. Having shown that words promote the formation of object categories, our next goal was to capture more precisely the scope, power, and evolution of infants' expectations in word-learning (Booth & Waxman, 2003; Waxman & Booth, 2001b, 2003). To do so, we extended the work described in the previous section in four ways. First, we included a developmental component, comparing the performance of 11-month-old infants on the very threshold of producing words with that of 14-month-olds whose lexicons already included a modest set of entries. Second, we expanded the range of commonalities under investigation. In the previously described studies (Waxman & Markow, 1995), the only commonality among objects was category based (e.g., four animals, all of a different color). Here, we asked whether infants link novel words specifically to category-based commonalities (e.g., animal), or whether they also link words to a wider range of groupings including, for example, property-based commonalities (e.g., pink things, lumpy things) (Waxman, 1999b).[3] Third, we considered the influence not only of nouns, but also of adjectives, on infants' categorization behavior.

A fourth goal in this series was methodological. All of the evidence reviewed thus far has been based entirely on infants' performance in novelty-preference tasks. In the current series, we asked whether infants' expectations would influence performance in a word-extension task. Our goal here was to bridge a methodological gap between research with infants and preschoolers. Novelty-preference tasks have been successful with infants, but beyond 18 months of age, infants lose interest in such tasks. Word-extension tasks have been successful with toddlers and preschoolers, but lack sensitivity with infants under 18-months, who have difficulty choosing systematically among objects in forced-choice tasks.

To bridge this methodological gap, we developed a new method, which weds features of the novelty-preference procedure with those of the word-extension paradigms. See figure 7.2 for a schematic description of the procedure and a summary of the instructions presented in each condition.

In the familiarization phase, an experimenter introduced infants in all conditions to four objects, all drawn from the *same object category* (e.g., horses or animals) and embodying the *same object property* (e.g., purple). These were presented in pairs, and infants manipulated them freely. During the contrast phase, the experimenter presented a new object (e.g., a brown rolling-pin), drawn from a contrastive object category and embodying a contrastive object property. In the test phase, infants were presented with one familiar object (e.g., a purple horse), and one novel object. For half of the infants in each condition (see below), this novel object was a member of a novel object-category, but embodied the same property (e.g., a purple plate). This constituted a category test. For the remaining infants, the novel object was a member of the same category as the familiarization objects, but embodied a novel property (e.g., a blue horse). This constituted a property test. Infants were first permitted to play freely with the two test objects. Then, to assess word extension, the experimenter removed the test objects. At this point, she introduced a target object, drawn from the familiarization set (e.g., a purple horse) and then re-presented the two test objects, asking the infant to give her one. (See figure 7.2). This word-extension task was presented a second time for each set of familiarization objects. This permitted us to observe the consistency of infants' responses. Infants completed this entire procedure four times, with four different sets of objects, two representing basic-level object categories and two representing superordinate-level categories.

To trace the proposed developmental trajectory from an initially general expectation linking open-class words (either count nouns or adjectives) to commonalities among objects (either category-based or property-based) to a more specific set of expectations, we compared the influence of novel nouns and adjectives in the performance of infants at 11 and 14 months of age. If infants begin the process of lexical acquisition with a broad expectation linking words (in general) to commonalities among objects (in general), then for 11-month-olds, both nouns and adjectives should highlight both category-based (e.g., animal) and property-based (e.g., purple things) commonalities.

	Familiarization		Contrast	Test	
	Trial 1	Trial 2		Category	Property
Purple animal set:	bear lion	elephant dog	red apple	purple horse vs. purple chair	purple horse vs. blue horse
Noun	These are blickets This one is a blicket & This one is a blicket	These are blickets This one is a blicket & This one is a blicket	Uh-oh, this one is not a blicket!	Can you give me the blicket?	Can you give me the blicket?
Adjective	These are blickish This one is blickish & This one is blickish	These are blickish This one is blickish & This one is blickish	Uh-oh, this one is not blickish!	Can you give me the blickish one?	Can you give me the blickish one?
No word	Look at these Look at this one & Look at this one	Look at these Look at this one & Look at this one	Uh-oh, look at this one!	Can you give me one?	Can you give me one?

Figure 7.2 A schematic presentation of introductory phrases from Waxman and Booth (2001) and an example of a single stimulus set

If this initial expectation is refined once the process of lexical acquisition is under way, then for more advanced learners, a different pattern should emerge. Different kinds of words should direct older infants' attention to different aspects of the same experience: naming objects (with either a count noun or adjective) should systematically influence infants' construals of the very *same* set of objects (e.g., purple animals) either as members of an *object category* (animals) or as embodying an *object property* (purple). Based on our previous work (Waxman, 1999b; Waxman & Booth, 2000), we expected that at 14 months, infants would have begun to distinguish count nouns (from among the other grammatical forms) and to map these specifically to category-based, but not property-based, commonalities. We expected that at this same developmental moment, infants' expectations for adjectives would still be quite general, directing their attention more broadly toward commonalities (be they category- or property-based).

The results were consistent with these predictions. At 11 months, infants hearing novel words (both nouns and adjectives) performed differently than those in the No Word condition. Infants extended both novel nouns and adjectives consistently to the familiar test object (e.g., the purple horse) on both category and property trials. This confirms that at the very onset of building a lexicon, (a) novel (open class) words direct infants' attention broadly to both category- and property-based commonalities among named objects, and (b) this link is sufficiently strong to support the extension of novel words. This outcome provides strong support for our proposal that infants on the very threshold of word-learning harbor a general expectation linking words (both nouns and adjectives) to commonalities (both category- and property-based) among objects.

We also proposed that once word-learning is underway, a more specific pattern should emerge. Evidence from 14-month-olds offers support for this developmental prediction. By 14 months, infants were sensitive to the distinction between novel words presented as nouns as compared to adjectives, and they recruited this distinction in mapping words to their meaning. They mapped nouns to category-based, rather than to property-based, commonalities. However, their expectations regarding the extension of novel adjectives were more general. Infants hearing adjectives were equally likely to select the familiar object on both types of test trials (see Waxman, 1999b; Waxman & Booth, 2000, for replications and extensions using various properties, e.g., color, texture). Clearly, by 14 months, infants have begun to distinguish among different kinds of words (nouns vs. adjectives) and recruit this distinction in the service of mapping words to their meaning.

Additional support for this developmental trajectory comes from a recent study using a precisely controlled automated method (Booth & Waxman, 2009). This method offers two advantages over the studies described above, which all involved direct interaction between an infant and an experimenter: (a) it allows for tight control over the presentation of stimuli, and (b) it permits us to trace the time-course of children's mapping of novel words to meaning (Fernald, Pinto, Swingley, Weinberg, & McRoberts, 1998; Fernald, Swingley, & Pinto, 2001; Golinkoff, Hirsh-Pasek, Cauley, & Gordon, 1987; Swingley, Pinto, & Fernald, 1999). In this study, 14- and 18-month-olds watched a video that mirrored the structure of the earlier studies. Their response was measured by examining the infants' eye movements during the test period. Examining which of two images the infant paid more attention to during this period provided an indirect measure of how they extended the novel noun or adjective.

Once again, infants at both ages in this study extended novel nouns to other members of the same category, as opposed to items sharing the same property. Moreover, the time-course of their extension was swift, occurring within 2 seconds of hearing the novel word. When the same words were presented as adjectives, infants revealed no preference for either category- or property-based extensions. This finding lines up with the results of previous studies, which suggest the adjective–property link may begin to emerge just after 18 months, or during the 18- to 21-month time frame (Waxman & Markow, 1998).

The convergence between performance in this automated procedure and in the live tasks is striking. Taken together, they show that, clearly, 14-month-olds are sensitive to (at least some of) the relevant cues (e.g., prosody, morphology, structural position within a phrase) that distinguish count nouns from adjectives. Cues like these are sufficiently rich to support an emerging distinction among major grammatical forms (Morgan & Demuth, 1996). Although infants' grammatical distinctions are certainly not as well-honed as those of adults, and although their knowledge of categories and properties of objects is certainly not as rich, 14-month-olds do appear to share with adults an expectation that different types of words (count nouns versus adjectives) refer to different types of relations among objects.

Talking two-year-olds: beyond nouns and adjectives

Having examined the trajectory of infants' mapping of novel nouns and adjectives, we turn our attention now to the acquisition of verbs. Verbs do not appear in appreciable number in infants' productive lexicons until several months after the appearance of nouns (between roughly 20 and 24 months: for recent reviews, see Gleitman, Cassidy, Nappa, Papafragou, & Trueswell, 2005; Waxman & Lidz, 2006). This developmental phenomenon, favoring the acquisition of nouns over verbs, suggests that these distinct grammatical forms differ not only in the kinds of meanings they convey, but also in their underlying course of acquisition. In the next series, we look at what it takes to learn a verb.

The conceptual underpinnings of verbs seem to be in place, at least in rudimentary ways, by the end of the first year of life. By 8–12 months, infants are sensitive to certain fundamental components of events, including animacy, agency, and cause (Buresh, Wilson-Brune, & Woodward, 2006; Casasola & Cohen, 2000; Gergely & Csibra, 2003; Gergely, Nádasdy, Csibra, & Bíró,1995; Gertner, Fisher, & Eisengart, 2006; Golinkoff & Hirsh-Pasek, 2006; Leslie & Keeble, 1987; Meltzoff, 2007; Muentener & Carey, 2006; Sommerville, Woodward, & Needham 2005; Wagner & Carey, 2005). Between 12 and 24 months, infants demonstrate sensitivity to other key elements of events, including changes of state, result, manner, and path of motion (Bunger, 2007; Bunger & Lidz, 2004; Pruden, Hirsh-Pasek, Maguire, & Meyer, 2004; Pulverman, Hirsh-Pasek, Pruden, & Golinkoff, 2006).

What this means is that infants' relatively delayed acquisition of verbs must be due, not to an inability to represent the kinds of concepts that underlie verb meaning, but rather to other factors. What might these factors be?

One possibility is that infants' relative delay in acquiring verbs reflects the fact that the meaning of a verb depends upon the arguments that it takes (and the relation among them). Simply put, to identify the event labeled by a verb, learners depend upon the noun phrases that represent the event participants and the linguistic relations among these phrases (Fisher, Hall, Rakowitz, & Gleitman, 1994; Gillette, Gleitman, Gleitman, & Lederer, 1999; Gleitman et al., 2005; Landau & Gleitman, 1985; Lidz, Gleitman, & Gleitman, 2003; Piccin & Waxman, 2007; Snedeker & Gleitman, 2004; Waxman & Lidz, 2006). Therefore, without the nouns, it should be difficult for learners to identify the arguments of a verb and impossible to identify the event labeled by the verb in that context. The acquisition of verbs must therefore follow the acquisition of nouns.

This trajectory is supported by studies of toddlers' vocabularies. Productive use of verbs to refer to actions, mental states, and relations is often not established until 24 months, well after the productive use of nouns (Fenson et al., 2000). Around this age, not only do toddlers produce verbs, but they seem to map novel verbs onto categories of events, taking into account syntactic information, including the number and types of frames in which novel verbs appear and the relations among the noun phrases in these frames, to narrow their hypotheses about possible verb meanings (Akhtar & Tomasello, 1996; Bunger & Lidz, 2004; Fernandes, Marcus, DiNubila, & Vouloumanos, 2006; Fisher, 2002; Gertner et al., 2006; Gleitman, 1990; Gleitman et al., 2005; Hirsch-Pasek, Golinkoff, & Naigles, 1996; Landau & Gleitman, 1985; Naigles, 1990, 1996; Naigles & Kako, 1993).

Nonetheless, the verb-learning literature also reveals some astonishing failures, many of which persist throughout the preschool years (Imai, Haryu, & Okada, 2005; Imai et al., 2008; see also Behrend, 1990; Kersten & Smith, 2002; Meyer et al., 2003). A review of the evidence suggests that infants and young children succeed in verb learning when the very same participant objects are present in all the events, but encounter difficulty when there is a change in the event participants. This suggests that infants and even young children are essentially "captured" by the participant objects and have difficulty extending verbs beyond them.

Interestingly, infants appear to be captured by participant objects in laboratory tasks, but not in real-world acquisition. Children are often observed extending verbs like "drink" to different beverages (e.g., milk, water), "run" to different actors (e.g., dogs, people), etc. outside of the laboratory. How can we account for this mismatch? What information is missing from laboratory tasks that hampers children's ability to learn novel verbs?

We examined infant verb learning using the automated procedure described above (Waxman et al., 2009). Videos of dynamic scenes (e.g., a man waving a balloon) were presented to 24-month-old infants. The study examined (a) whether infants could construe these scenes flexibly, noticing the consistent action (e.g., waving) as well as the consistent object (e.g., the balloon) and (b) whether their construals of the scenes were influenced by the grammatical form of a novel word used to describe them (verb or noun). Infants were presented with the scenes in a familiarization phase, where the accompanying audio varied as a function of condition. Afterward, during the test phase, infants saw two test scenes, presented simultaneously on either side of the screen. Both scenes featured the same actor (e.g., the man) and the same object (e.g., the balloon) as in familiarization; what varied was the event in which these two were involved. In the *familiar* test scene, the man performed the now-familiar action (e.g., man *waving* a balloon); in the *novel* test scene, he performed a novel action (e.g., man *tapping* a balloon). See figure 7.3 for the audio presented in each phase of each condition.

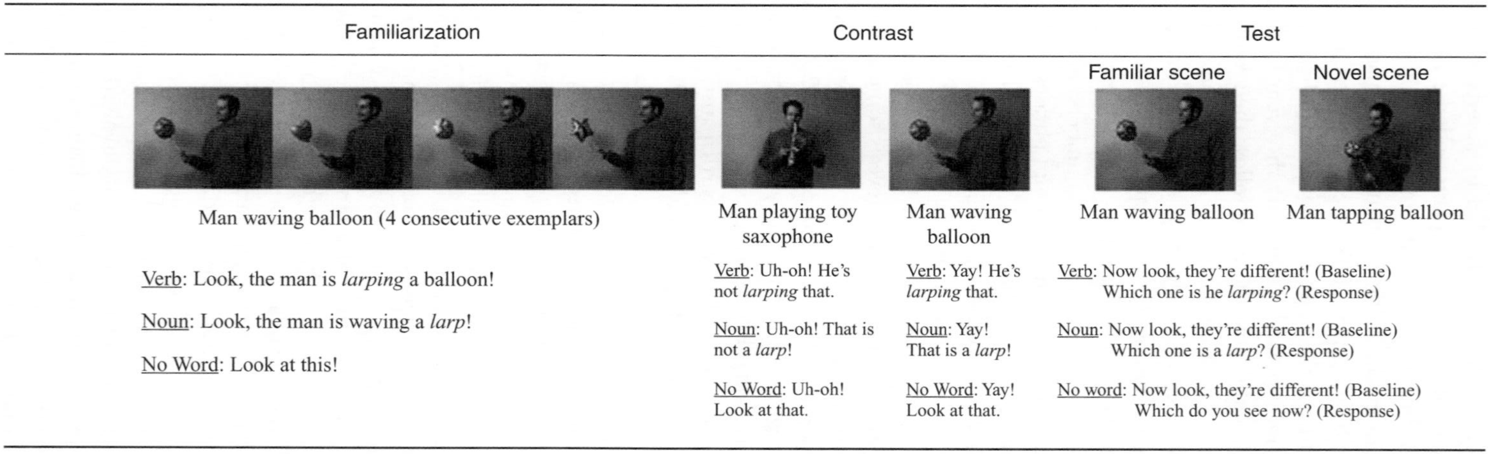

Familiarization	Contrast		Test	
			Familiar scene	Novel scene
Man waving balloon (4 consecutive exemplars)	Man playing toy saxophone	Man waving balloon	Man waving balloon	Man tapping balloon
Verb: Look, the man is *larping* a balloon!	Verb: Uh-oh! He's not *larping* that.	Verb: Yay! He's *larping* that.	Verb: Now look, they're different! (Baseline) Which one is he *larping*? (Response)	
Noun: Look, the man is waving a *larp*!	Noun: Uh-oh! That is not a *larp*!	Noun: Yay! That is a *larp*!	Noun: Now look, they're different! (Baseline) Which one is a *larp*? (Response)	
No Word: Look at this!	No Word: Uh-oh! Look at that.	No Word: Yay! Look at that.	No word: Now look, they're different! (Baseline) Which do you see now? (Response)	

Figure 7.3 A schematic presentation of introductory phrases from Waxman, Lidz, Braun, and Lavin (2009) and example of a single stimulus set

Infants' visual attention during each frame of the test phase was analyzed, measuring attention to the novel event (e.g. a man *tapping* a balloon) versus the familiar event (e.g. a man *waving* a balloon). These time-course results revealed that infants were sensitive to the consistent events shown during familiarization, as they exhibited a strong novelty preference (directing their attention to the novel event) before hearing the test sentence that varied by condition. Once the infants heard the test sentence (e.g., "Where's larping?"), their attention began to diverge. Children in the Verb condition reliably directed their attention back toward the familiar event, or the event labeled with the novel verb during familiarization (e.g. waving a balloon). Children in the Noun and No Word conditions maintained their visual attention on the novel event. Note that both the novel and familiar events included a balloon, making them both appropriate responses for the Noun condition. However, a subsequent experiment using the same familiarization phase, but changing the test phase to include events with the same action but different objects (e.g., waving a *balloon* versus waving a *rake*) revealed that children could indeed appropriately extend a novel noun and direct their attention back to the familiar object.

These results suggest that 24-month-olds' representations of novel words are sufficiently precise to permit them to map novel verbs to event categories (e.g., waving events) and novel nouns to object categories (e.g., balloons). Once again the time-course of their mapping is swift, occurring within about a second of hearing the novel word. These results beckon us to move beyond asking whether or not infants can represent verb meanings, and to consider instead the conditions that support their successful acquisition.

Avenues for future research

The evidence discussed above has significantly advanced our understanding of children's early word-learning, while simultaneously prompting myriad avenues for future research. Among them are questions concerning how word-learning proceeds in bilingual children, and what neuropsychological studies can contribute to theories of word-learning. We consider each of these in turn below.

Word-learning in bilingual environments. The previous sections highlight the many challenges word-learning presents to infants and young children. The task for bilingual children is even more complex, as they grapple with solving the puzzle of word-learning in more than one language. Nevertheless, the time-course of bilingual children's acquisition is similar to that of monolinguals (Holowka, Brosseau-Lapre, & Petitto, 2002; Oller, Eilers, Urbano, & Cobo-Lewis, 1997; Pearson, Fernandez, & Oller, 1993), and their early words and sentences closely resemble those of monolingual infants (Yip & Matthews, 2007).

Monolingual and bilingual word-learning nonetheless differ in important ways (see Fernald, 2006; Werker & Byers-Heinlein, 2008, for recent reviews). Bilingual infants must separate the linguistic input that they receive from their two languages, forming two distinct phonological systems and two lexicons. An active area of research is the way the two languages might be represented and processed in the brain. A recent neuropsychological study examined brain responses in 19- and 22-month-old bilingual infants as they listened to known and unknown words in both of their languages (Conboy & Mills, 2006). Differences were found not only in the infant brain responses to known and unknown words, but also in the infant brain responses to the two languages. Moreover, the timing and distribution of brain activity linked to word-meaning differed for children's dominant versus non-dominant language. These differences most likely reflect differences in the infants' experience with the two languages, rather than a general brain maturational mechanism.

The neuroscience of word-learning. Other recent neuropsychological studies contribute to our understanding of the neural processes underlying word-learning in both bilingual and monolingual environments, and support the behavioral findings detailed above in two main ways. First, neuropsychological evidence shows that the infant brain responds to speech in a special way, distinct from other auditory signals. This dovetails well with evidence that infants map words (but not non-speech stimuli like tones) to meaning (Fulkerson & Waxman, 2007). Second, there is evidence that the infant brain responds in a specific way not only to speech sounds in general, but also to words in particular. This specific response to the presentation of words provides the first neurological correlates of word-learning.

The evidence that even newborn infants process speech stimuli in a way that is distinct from non-speech stimuli suggests that the human brain comes prepared to process human speech. In particular, areas of activation observed in the newborn brain bear a striking resemblance to those for adults. Two recent studies examined areas of brain activation in neonates (Peña et al, 2003) and 3-month-olds (Dehaene-Lambertz, Dehaene, & Hertz-Pannier, 2002). These studies revealed that even in neonates there is a left hemisphere bias when listening to language, a bias that is not observed when listening to backwards speech or silence. Moreover, this left hemisphere bias was shown to emerge even when subjects were presented with a language other than their own (Hespos, Ferry, Cannistraci, Gore, & Park, 2009; Hespos, Park, Ferry, Lane, & Gore, 2009).

Recent work also shows that infants go beyond merely processing speech sounds in speech-specific ways, and that they can also detect speech patterns, like the repetition of syllables (Gervain, Macagno, Cogoi, Peña, & Mehler, 2008). Different patterns of brain responses emerged when neonates were presented with blocks of syllables with immediate repetition (e.g., ABB) versus no repetition. This indicates that the infant brain is sensitive to speech structure, and suggests at least one way in which neuropsychological capacities support the acquisition of words.

Beyond speech processing, neuropsychological research on word-learning primarily consists of event-related potential (ERP) studies that use the N400 as a method of testing children's knowledge. The N400 is an ERP response that is associated, in adults, with semantic integration. It is consistently observed after an unexpected stimulus, as when a picture is paired with a mismatching name (e.g., pairing the word "dog" with a picture of a banana). (See Werker & Yeung, 2005, for a terrific overview of ERP correlates to word-learning.)

The N400 response has been observed in several studies of infants and toddlers. In one study, 19-month-olds were presented with known words that either matched or did not match a sequentially presented picture (Friedrich & Friederici, 2004). The words referred to the basic-level name of the object or an incongruent basic-level name. As expected, the N400 emerged when the object names did not match the object pictures. A later study obtained this same result with 14-month-olds (Friedrich & Friederici, 2005). Studies featuring novel words have also revealed the N400 in infants and young children (Mills, Plunkett, Prat, & Schafer 2005; von Koss Torkildsen et al., 2008).

In conclusion, the neuropsychological evidence converges well with the behavioral evidence on word-learning. Recall that behavioral studies reveal that by 14 months, infants have mapped several nouns to objects and object kinds. Correspondingly, neuropsychological studies show that when a mismatch occurs between a known noun and picture of an object, the 14-month-old infant brain "notices" the mismatch. As research in this field progresses, it will be interesting to see if neuropsychological correlates are also evident in the infant brain's response to words from other grammatical categories, including adjectives and verbs.

Conclusions

In this chapter, we have focused on word-learning, asking what expectations, if any, infants recruit in the process of establishing their first word-to-world mappings, and how these evolve over development. We suggested that infants begin the task of word-learning equipped with a broad, initial, and universally available expectation that links novel open class words (independent of their grammatical form) to a wide range of commonalities among named objects. We suggested that this initially general expectation sets the stage for the evolution of more specific expectations, calibrated in accordance with the correlations between particular grammatical forms and their associated meanings in the language under acquisition.

Infants' performance provided clear support for this proposal. At 11 months, infants revealed a broad initial expectation, linking words (count nouns and adjectives) to commonalities (both category- and property-based) among named objects. By 14 months, infants' expectations have indeed become more fine-tuned. They distinguish nouns from adjectives, and treat this distinction as relevant when mapping words to their meaning (mapping count nouns specifically to category-based, but not property-based, commonalities among objects). Specific links between adjectives and properties of objects continue to emerge toward the end of the second year of life. By this age, infants also begin to map verbs to commonalities among events as well.

These results point to substantial continuity across development in the types of concepts we form, and in the influence of naming in their acquisition. We see this line of work as providing evidence that words are powerful engines for conceptual development: words advance us beyond our initial groupings, fueling the acquisition of the rich relations that characterize our most powerful concepts.

Finally, this developmental account has several distinct strengths. First, it embraces both the importance of the expectations imposed by the learner, as well as the shaping role of the environment. In the case of word-learning, this interplay between factors inherent in the child and factors within the environment is essential. Infants across the world will encounter different objects, will acquire different languages, and will be provided with different types of language input (Cole, Gay, Glick, & Sharp, 1971; Laboratory of Comparative Human Cognition, 1983).

Moreover, under our proposal, early acquisition is sufficiently constrained to permit infants to form fundamental categories of objects and to learn the words to express them, and sufficiently flexible to accommodate the systematic variations in the word-to-world mappings that occur across languages. Notice that our view of constraints on acquisition is not an argument based entirely on assumptions of innate knowledge. Neither is it a polarized argument that locates the engine of acquisition solely within the mind of the child. Rather, the idea is that in the process of word-learning, infants direct their attention toward precisely the sort of information and precisely the kinds of regularities in the environment that will support foundational concepts and the acquisition of words to describe them. Our proposal is flexible enough to account for the fact that infants naturally acquire a wide range of human languages, and that these differ in the ways in which they recruit the particular grammatical forms to convey particular types of meaning. We have suggested that the specific links between particular grammatical forms and their associated meanings are calibrated on the basis of correlations or regularities that are present in the language under acquisition. It therefore stands to reason that these more specific links would not be available at the onset of word-learning, but instead would emerge later, once the process of lexical acquisition is underway.

Finally, our proposal is a dynamic one: the initial expectations that we observe in infants at the outset of acquisition are not rigidly fixed, exerting a uniform influence throughout development. On the contrary, these expectations are shaped over the course of development in accordance with the observed regularities in the language under acquisition.

Notes

1 From Keller (1904).

2 Note that this was, in fact, Keller's second language. She had begun to acquire English before becoming deaf and blind.

3 This question itself hinges on there being a psychological distinction between object categories and object properties. Recent approaches in cognitive psychology distinguish object categories (sometimes known as *kinds* or *sortals*) from other types of groupings (e.g., *pink things, things to pull from a burning house*) on at least three (related) grounds: Object categories (a) are richly-structured, (b) capture many commonalities, including deep, non-obvious relations among properties (as opposed to isolated properties), and (c) serve as the basis for induction (Barsalou, 1983; Gelman & Medin, 1993; Kalish & Gelman, 1992; Macnamara, 1994; Medin & Heit, 1999; Murphy & Medin, 1985). Although infants and children lack detailed knowledge about most object categories, they clearly expect named object categories to serve these functions (Gelman, 1996; Keil, 1994). In addition, there is now evidence for a psychological distinction between individual properties and relations among properties in infancy (Bhatt & Rovee-Collier, 1997; Younger & Cohen, 1986). We selected color and texture because these

properties are perceptually salient to infants, and because these property-based commonalities typically do not underlie object categories. We suspect that an object's shape is more centrally related to category membership, particularly for simple artifacts and for animate objects (Waxman & Braig, 1996).

References

Ahn, W., & Luhmann, C. C. (2004). Demystifying theory-based categorization. In L. Gershkoff-Stowe & D. Rakison (Eds.), *Building object categories in developmental time* (pp. 277–300). Mahwah, NJ: Erlbaum.

Akhtar, N., & Tomasello, M. (1996). Two-year-olds learn words for absent objects and actions. *British Journal of Developmental Psychology, 14*, 79–93.

Akhtar, N., & Tomasello, M. (2000). The social nature of words and word learning. In M. Marschark (Series Ed.), *Counterpoints: Cognition, memory, and language. Becoming a word learner: A debate on lexical acquisition* (pp.115–35). New York: Oxford University Press.

Baillargeon, R. (2000). How do infants learn about the physical world? In D. Muir & A. Slater (Eds.), *Infant development: The essential readings. Essential readings in development psychology* (pp. 195–212). Malden, MA: Blackwell.

Balaban, M. T., & Waxman, S. R. (1997). Do words facilitate object categorization in 9-month-old infants? *Journal of Experimental Child Psychology, 64*(1), 3–26.

Baldwin, D. A., & Baird, J. A. (1999). Action analysis: A gateway to intentional inference. In P. Rochat (Ed.), *Early social cognition: Understanding others in the first months of life* (pp. 215–240). Mahwah, NJ: Erlbaum.

Baldwin, D. A., & Markman, E. M. (1989). Establishing word–object relations: A first step. *Child Development, 60*(2), 381–398.

Barsalou, L. W. (1983). Ad hoc categories. *Memory & Cognition, 11*(3), 211–227.

Barsalou, L.W., Santos, A., Simmons, W. K., & Wilson, C. D. (2008). Language and simulation in conceptual processing. In M. De Vega, A. M. Glenberg, & A. C. Graesser (Eds.), *Symbols, embodiment, and meaning* (pp. 245–283). Oxford: Oxford University Press.

Behrend, D. A. (1990). The development of verb concepts: Children's use of verbs to label familiar and novel events. *Child Development, 61*, 681–696.

Bhatt, R. S., & Rovee-Collier, C. (1997). Dissociation between features and feature relations in infant memory: Effects of memory load. *Journal of Experimental Child Psychology, 67*, 69–89.

Booth, A. E. (2006). Object function and categorization in infancy: Two mechanisms of facilitation. *Infancy, 10*(2), 145–169.

Booth, A. E., & Waxman, S. R. (2002). Object names and object functions serve as cues to categories for infants. *Developmental Psychology, 38*(6), 948–957.

Booth, A. E., & Waxman, S. R. (2003). Mapping words to the world in infancy: On the evolution of expectations for count nouns and adjectives. *Journal of Cognition and Development, 4*(3), 357–381.

Booth, A. E., & Waxman, S. R. (2009). A horse of a different color: Specifying with precision infants' mappings of novel nouns and adjectives. *Child Development, 80*(1), 15–22.

Booth, A. E., & Waxman, S. R. (2009). A horse of a different color: Specifying with precision infants' mappings of novel nouns and adjectives. *Child Development, 80*(1), 15–22.

Bornstein, M. H., Cote, L. R., Maital, S., Painter, K., Park, S.-Y., & Pascual, L. (2004). Cross-linguistic analysis of vocabulary in young children: Spanish, Dutch, French, Hebrew, Italian, Korean, and American English. *Child Development, 75*(4), 1115–1139.

Bunger, A. (2007). *How we learn to talk about events: linguistic andconceptual constraints on verb learning* (Unpublished doctoral dissertation). Northwestern University, Illinois.

Bunger, A., & Lidz, J. (2004). Syntactic bootstrapping and the internal structure of causative events. *Proceedings of the 28th Annual Boston University Conference on Language Development.* Boston, MA: Cascadilla Press.

Buresh, J., Wilson-Brune, C., & Woodward, A. L. (2006). Prelinguistic action knowledge and the birth of verbs. In K. Hirsh-Pasek & R. M Golinkoff (Eds.), *Action meets word* (pp. 208–227). Oxford: Oxford University Press.

Casasola, M., & Cohen, L. B. (2000). Infants' association of linguistic labels with causal actions. *Developmental Psychology, 36*(2), 155–168.

Caselli, M. C., Bates, E., Casadio, P., Fenson, L., Sanderl, L., & Weir, J. (1995). A cross-linguistic study of early lexical development. *Cognitive Development, 10*, 159–199.

Chambers, C. G., Graham, S. A., & Turner, J. (2008). When hearsay trumps evidence: How generic language guides preschoolers' inferences about unfamiliar things. *Language and Cognitive Processes, 23*(5), 749–766.

Cole, M., Gay, J., Glick, J. A., & Sharp, D. W. (1971). *The cultural context of learning and thinking*. New York: Basic Books.

Conboy, B. T., & Mills, D. L. (2006). Two languages, one developing brain: Effects of vocabulary size on bilingual toddlers' event-related potentials to auditory words. *Developmental Science, 9*(1), F1–F11.

Dehaene-Lambertz, G., Dehaene, S., & Hertz-Pannier, L. (2002). Functional neuroimaging of speech perception in infants. *Science, 298*(5600), 2013–2015.

Fenson, L., Bates, E., Dale, P., Goodman, J., Reznick, J. S., & Thal, D. (2000). Measuring variability in early child language: Don't shoot the messenger. *Child Development, 71*, 323–8.

Fernald, A. (1992a). Human maternal vocalizations to infants as biologically relevant signals: An evolutionary perspective. In J. H. Barkow, L. Cosmides, & J. Tooby (Eds.), *The adapted mind: Evolutionary psychology and the generation of culture* (pp. 391–428). New York: Oxford University Press.

Fernald, A. (1992b). Meaningful melodies in mothers' speech to infants. In H. Papousek, U. Jurgens, & M. Papousek (Eds.), *Nonverbal vocal communication: Comparative and developmental approaches. Studies in emotion and social interaction* (pp. 262–282). New York: Cambridge University Press.

Fernald, A. (2006). When infants hear two languages: Interpreting research on early speech perception by bilingual children. In P. McCardle & E. Hoff (Eds.), *Childhood bilingualism: Research on infancy through school-age*. Clevedon, UK: Multilingual Matters.

Fernald, A., Pinto, J. P., Swingley, D., Weinberg, A., & McRoberts, G. (1998). Rapid gains in speed of verbal processing by infants in the second year. *Psychological Science, 9*, 228–231.

Fernald, A., Swingley, D., & Pinto, J. P. (2001). When half a word is enough: infants can recognize spoken words using partial phonetic information. *Child Development, 72*, 1003–1015.

Fernandes, K. J., Marcus, G. F., DiNubila, J. A., & Vouloumanos, A. (2006). From semantics to syntax and back again: Argument structure in the third year of life. *Cognition, 100*, B10–20.

Fisher, C. (2002). Structural limits on verb mapping: The role of abstract structure in 2.5-year-olds' interpretations of novel verbs. *Developmental Science, 5*, 56–65.

Fisher, C., Hall, G., Rakowitz, S., & Gleitman, L. (1994). When it is better to receive than to give: structural and cognitive factors in acquiring a first vocabulary. *Lingua, 92*, 333–376.

Friedrich, M., & Friederici, A. D. (2004). N400-like semantic incongruity effect in 19-month-olds: Processing known words in picture contexts. *Journal of Cognitive Neuroscience, 16*(8), 1465–1477.

Friedrich, M., & Friederici, A. D. (2005). Lexical priming and semantic integration reflected in the event-related potential of 14-month-olds. *NeuroReport, 16*(6), 653–656.

Fulkerson, A. L., & Haaf, R. A. (2003). The influence of labels, non-labeling sounds, and source of auditory input on 9- and 15-month-olds' object categorization. *Infancy, 4*, 349–369.

Fulkerson, A. L., & Haaf, R. A. (2006). Does object naming aid 12-month-olds' formation of novel object categories? *First Language, 26*, 347–361.

Fulkerson, A. L., Waxman, S. R. (2007). Words (but not tones) facilitate object categorization: Evidence from 6- and 12-month-olds. *Cognition, 105*(1), 218–228.

Gelman, S. A. (1996). Concepts and theories. In R. Gelman & T. Kit-Fong (Eds.), *Perceptual and cognitive development. Handbook of perception and cognition*, 2nd ed. (pp. 117–150). San Diego, CA: Academic Press.

Gelman, S. A. (2006). Early conceptual development. In K. McCartney & D. Phillips (Eds.), *Blackwell handbook of early childhood development* (pp. 149–166). Malden, MA: Blackwell.

Gelman, S. A., Coley, J. D., & Gottfried, G. M. (1994). Essentialist beliefs in children: The acquisition of concepts and theories. In L. A. Hirschfeld & S. A. Gelman (Eds.), *Mapping the mind: Domain specificity in cognition and culture* (pp. 341–365). New York: Cambridge University Press.

Gelman, S. A., & Kalish, C. W. (2006). Conceptual development. In W. Damon & R. M. Lerner (Series Eds.), D. Kuhn & R. S. Siegler (Vol. Eds.), *Handbook of child psychology: Vol. 2. Cognition, perception, and language* (6th ed., pp. 687–733). Hoboken, NJ: Wiley.

Gelman, S. A., & Medin, D. L. (1993). What's so essential about essentialism? A different perspective on the interaction of perception, language, and conceptual knowledge. *Cognitive Development, 8*(2), 157–167.

Gelman, R., & Williams, E. M. (1999). Enabling constraints for cognitive development and learning: A domain-specific epigenetic theory. In W. Damon (Series Ed.), D. Kuhn & R. Siegler (Vol. Eds.), *Handbook of Child Psychology: Vol. 2. Cognition, perception, and language* (pp. 575–630). New York: Wiley.

Gentner, D., & Boroditsky, L. (2001). Individuation, relativity, and early word learning. In M. Bowerman & S. Levinson (Eds.), *Language Acquisition and Conceptual Development.* New York: Cambridge University Press.

Gentner, D., & Namy, L. (1999). Comparison in the development of categories. *Cognitive Development, 14*, 487–513.

Gergely, G., & Csibra, G. (2003). Teleological reasoning in infancy: the naive theory of rational action, *Trends in Cognitive Sciences, 7*, 287–292.

Gergely, G., Nádasdy, Z., Csibra, G., & Bíró, S. (1995). Taking the intentional stance at 12 months of age. *Cognition, 56*, 165–193.

Gerken, L., & McIntosh, B. J. (1993). Interplay of function morphemes and prosody in early language. *Developmental Psychology, 29*(3), 448–457.

Gertner, Y., Fisher, C., & Eisengart, J. (2006). Learning words and rules: Abstract knowledge of word order in early sentence comprehension. *Psychological Science, 17*, 684–691.

Gervain, J., Macagno, F., Cogoi, S., Peña, M., & Mehler, J. (2008) The neonate brain detects speech structure. *Proceedings of the National Academy of Sciences, 105*(37), 14222–14227.

Gillette, J., Gleitman, H., Gleitman, L., & Lederer, A. (1999). Human simulations of vocabulary learning. *Cognition, 73*(2), 135–176.

Gleitman, L. (1990). The structural sources of verb meanings. *Language Acquisition: A Journal of Developmental Linguistics, 1*(1), 3–55.

Gleitman, L. R., Cassidy, K., Nappa, R., Papafragou, A., & Trueswell, J. C. (2005). Hard Words. *Language Learning and Development, 1*(1), 23–64.

Gleitman, L. R., & Wanner, E. (1988). Current issues in language learning. In M. H. Bornstein & M. E. Lamb (Eds.), *Developmental psychology: An advanced textbook*, 2nd ed. (pp. 297–356). Hillsdale, NJ: Erlbaum.

Golinkoff, R. M., & Hirsh-Pasek, K. (2006). Introduction: Progress on the verb learning front. In K. Hirsh-Pasek & R. M. Golinkoff (Eds.), *Action meets word: How children learn verbs* (pp. 3–28). New York: Oxford University Press.

Golinkoff, R. M., Hirsh-Pasek, K., Cauley, K. M., & Gordon, L. (1987). The eyes have it: Lexical and syntactic comprehension in a new paradigm. *Journal of Child Language, 14*, 23–45.

Gomez, R. (2002). Variability and detection of invariant structure. *Psychological Science, 13*, 431–436.

Graham, S.A., Kilbreath, C. S., & Welder, A. N. (2004). 13-month-olds rely on shared labels and shape similarity for inductive inferences. *Child Development, 75*, 409–427.

Guajardo, J. J., & Woodward, A. L. (2000). *Using habituation to index infants' understanding of pointing*. Paper session presented at the Twelfth Biennial Meeting of the International Society for Infant Studies, Brighton, UK.

Hespos, S. J., Ferry, A. L., Cannistraci, C., Gore, J., Park, S. (2009) Optical imaging on human infants. In A.W. Roe (Ed.), *Imaging the brain with optical methods*. Springer: New York.

Hespos, S. J., Park, S., Ferry, A., Lane, A. P., & Gore, J. (2009). An optical imaging study of language recognition in the first year of life. Manuscript in preparation.

Hirsh-Pasek, K., Golinkoff, R., & Naigles, L. (1996). Young children's use of syntactic frames to derive meaning. In K. Hirsh-Pasek & R. M. Golinkoff, (Eds.), *The origins of grammar*. Cambridge, MA: MIT Press.

Holowka S., Brosseau-Lapre F., Petitto L. A. (2002). Semantic and conceptual knowledge underlying bilingual babies' first signs and words. *Language Learning, 52*(2), 205–262.

Huttenlocher, J. (1974). The origins of language comprehension. In R. L. Solso (Ed.), *Theories in cognitive psychology: The Loyola symposium* (pp. 331–368). Potomac, MD: Erlbaum.

Imai, M., Haryu, E., & Okada, H. (2005). Mapping novel nouns and verbs onto dynamic action events: Are verb meanings easier to learn than noun meanings for Japanese children? *Child Development, 76*(2), 340–355.

Imai, M., Lianjing, L., Haryu, E., Okada, H., Hirsh-Pasek, K., Golinkoff, R. M., & Shigematsu, J. (2008). Novel noun and verb learning in Chinese-, English-, and Japanese-speaking children. *Child Development, 79*, 979–1000.

Jusczyk, P., & Aslin, R. N. (1995). Infants' detection of the sound patterns of words in fluent speech. *Cognitive Psychology, 29*(1), 1–23.

Jusczyk, P. W., & Kemler Nelson, D. G. (1996). Syntactic units, prosody, and psychological reality during infancy. In J. L. Morgan & K. Demuth (Eds.), *Signal to syntax: Bootstrapping from speech to grammar in early acquisition* (pp. 389–408). Mahwah, NJ: Lawrence Erlbaum Associates, Inc.

Kalish, C. W., & Gelman, S. A. (1992). On wooden pillows: Multiple classification and children's category-based inductions. *Child Development, 63*(6), 1536–1557.

Keates, J., & Graham, S. A. (2008). Category labels or attributes: Why do labels guide infants' inductive inferences? *Psychological Science, 19*, 1287–1293.

Keil, F. C. (1994). The birth and nurturance of concepts by domains: The origins of concepts of living things. In L. A. Hirschfeld & S. A. Gelman (Eds.), *Mapping the mind: Domain specificity in cognition and culture* (pp. 234–254). New York: Cambridge University Press.

Keller, H. (1904). *The story of my life*. New York: Doubleday, Page, & Company.

Kemler Nelson, D. G., Hirsh-Pasek, K., Jusczyk, P. W., & Cassidy, K. W. (1989). How the prosodic cues in motherese might assist language learning. *Journal of Child Language, 16*(1), 55–68.

Kersten, A. W., & Smith, L. B. (2002). Attention to novel objects during verb learning. *Child Development, 73*(1), 93–109.

Klibanoff, R. S., & Waxman, S. R. (2000). Basic level object categories support the acquisition of novel adjectives: Evidence from preschool-aged children. *Child Development, 71*(3), 649–659.

Laboratory of Comparative Human Cognition (1983). Culture and cognitive development. In P. H. Mussen (Series Ed.), W. Kessen (Vol. Ed.), *Handbook of child psychology: Vol. 1. History, Theory, and Methods* (4th ed., pp. 295–356). New York: Wiley.

Landau, B. (1994). Object shape, object name, and object kind: Representation and development. In D. L. Medin (Ed.), *The psychology of learning and motivation: Advances in research and theory* (Vol. *31*, pp. 253–304). San Diego, CA: Academic Press.

Landau, B., & Gleitman, L. (1985). *Language and experience: Evidence from the blind child.* Cambridge, MA: Harvard University Press.

Landau, B., Smith, L. B., & Jones, S. S. (1988). The importance of shape in early lexical learning. *Cognitive Development, 3*(3), 299–321.

Lassaline, M. E., & Murphy, G. L. (1996). Induction and category coherence. *Psychonomic Bulletin and Review, 3*(1), 95–99.

Leslie, A. M., & Keeble, S. (1987). Do six-month-old infants perceive causality? *Cognition, 25*, 265–288.

Lidz, J., Gleitman, H., & Gleitman, L. (2003). understanding how input matters: The footprint of universal grammar on verb learning. *Cognition, 87*, 151–178.

Macnamara, J. (1994). Logic and cognition. In J. Macnamara & G. E. Reyes (Eds.), *The logical foundations of cognition. Vancouver studies in cognitive science* (Vol. *4*, pp. 11–34). New York: Oxford University Press.

Markman, E. M. (1989). *Categorization and naming in children: Problems of induction.* Cambridge, MA: MIT Press.

Medin, D. L., & Heit, E. (Eds.). (1999). Categorization. In D. Rumelhart & B. Martin (Eds.), *Handbook of cognition and perception* (pp. 99–143). San Diego, CA: Academic Press.

Meltzoff, A. N. (2007). The "like me" framework for recognizing and becoming an intentional agent. *Acta Psychologica, 124*(1), 26–43.

Meyer, M., Leonard, S., Hirsh-Pasek, K., Golinkoff, R. M., Imai, M., Haryu, R., Pulverman, R., & Addy, D. (2003). *Making a convincing argument: A cross-linguistic comparison of noun and verb learning in Japanese and English.* Poster session presented at the Boston University Conference on Language Development, Boston, MA.

Micciulla, L., & Smith, C. E. (Eds.), *Proceedings of the 28th Annual Boston University Conference on Language Development* (pp. 461–472). Somerville, MA: Cascadilla Press.

Mills, D. L., Plunkett, K., Prat, C., & Schafer, G. (2005). Watching the infant brain learn words: Effects of language and experience. *Cognitive Development, 20*, 19–31.

Morgan, J. L., & Demuth, K. (Eds.). (1996). *Signal to syntax: Bootstrapping from speech to grammar in early acquisition.* Mahwah, NJ: Erlbaum.

Muentener, P., & Carey, S. (2006). *Representations of agents affect infants' causal attributions.* Paper session presented at the annual meeting of the Fifteenth Biennial International Conference on Infant Studies, Westin Miyako, Kyoto, Japan.

Murphy, G. L. (2004). *The big book of concepts.* Cambridge, MA: MIT Press.

Murphy, G. L., & Medin, D. L. (1995). The role of theories in conceptual coherence. *Psychological Review, 92*, 289–316.

Naigles, L. (1990). Children use syntax to learn verb meanings. *Journal of Child Language, 17*, 357–374.

Naigles, L. (1996). The use of multiple frames in verb learning via syntactic bootstrapping. *Cognition, 58*, 221–251.

Naigles, L., & Kako, E. (1993). First contact in verb acquisition: Defining a role for syntax. *Child Development, 64*, 1665–1687.

Ochs, E., & Schieffelin, B. (1984). Language acquisition and socialization. In R. Shweder & R. LeVine (Eds.), *Culture Theory*. Cambridge: Cambridge University Press.

Oller, D. K., Eilers, R. E., Urbano, R., Cobo-Lewis, A. B. (1997). Development of precursors to speech in infants exposed to two languages. *Journal of Child Language, 24*(2), 407–425.

Pearson, B. Z., Fernandez, S. C., Oller, D. K. (1993). Lexical development in bilingual infants and toddlers: Comparison in monolingual terms. *Language Learning, 43*(1), 93–120.

Peña, M., Maki, A., Kovacic, D., Dehaene-Lambertz, G., Koizumi, H., Bouquet, F., & Mehler, J. (2003). Sounds and silence: An optical topography study of language recognition at birth. *Proceedings of the National Academy of Sciences of the United States of America, 100*(20), 11702–11705.

Piccin, T. B., & Waxman, S. R. (2007). Why nouns trump verbs in word learning: New evidence from children and adults in the Human Simulation Paradigm. *Language Learning and Development, 3*(4), 295–323.

Pinker, S. (1984). *Language learnability and language development*. Cambridge, MA: Harvard University Press.

Pinker, S. (1989) *Learnability and cognition: The acquisition of argument structure*. Cambridge, MA: MIT Press.

Pruden, S. M., Hirsh-Pasek, K., Maguire, M. J., & Meyer, M. A. (2004). Foundations of verb learning: Infants form categories of path and manner in motion events. In A. Brugos, L. Micciulla & C. E. Smith (Eds.), *Proceedings of the Annual Boston University Conference on Language Development* (pp. 461–472). Somerville, MA: Cascadilla Press.

Pulverman, R., Hirsh-Pasek, K., Pruden, S., & Golinkoff, R. M., (2006). Precursors to verb learning: Infant attention to manner and path. In K. Hirsh-Pasek & R. M. Golinkoff (Eds.), *Action meets word: How children learn verbs* (pp. 134–160). New York: Oxford Press.

Saffran, J. R., Werker, J. F., & Werner, L. A. (2006). The infant's auditory world: Hearing, speech, and the beginnings of language. In W. Damon & R. M. Lerner (Series Eds.), R. Siegler & D. Kuhn (Vol. Eds.), *Handbook of Child Psychology: Vol. 2. Cognition, perception and language* (6th ed., pp. 58–108). New York: Wiley.

Shi, R., & Werker, J. F. (2003). The basis of preference for lexical words in 6-month-old infants. *Developmental Science, 6*(5), 484–488.

Shi, R., Werker, J. F., & Morgan, J. L. (1999). Newborn infants' sensitivity to perceptual cues to lexical and grammatical words. *Cognition, 72*(2), B11–B21.

Snedeker, J., & Gleitman, L. (1999). Knowing what you know: Metacognitive monitoring and the origin of the object category bias. Paper session presented at the 24th annual Boston University Conference on Language Development, Somerville, MA.

Snedeker, J., & Gleitman, L. (2004). Why it is hard to label our concepts. In D. G. Hall & S. R. Waxman (Eds.), *Weaving a Lexicon* (pp. 257–294). Cambridge, MA: MIT Press.

Sommerville, J. A., Woodward, A. L., & Needham, A. (2005). Action experience alters 3-month-old infants' perception of others' actions. *Cognition, 96*, B1–B11.

Spelke, E. S. (2000). Nativism, empiricism, and the origins of knowledge. In D. Muir & A. Slater (Eds.), *Infant development: The essential readings. Essential readings in development psychology* (pp. 36–51). Malden, MA: Blackwell.

Swingley, D., Pinto, J. P., & Fernald, A. (1999). Continuous processing in word recognition at 24 months. *Cognition, 71*(2), 73–108.

Von Koss Torkildsen, J., Svangstu, J. M., Hansen, H. F., Smith, L., Simonsen, H. G., Moen, I., & Lindgren, M. (2008). Productive vocabulary size predicts event-related potential correlates of fast mapping in 20-month-olds. *Journal of Cognitive Neuroscience, 20*(7) 1266–1282.

Vouloumanos, A., & Werker, J. F. (2004). Tuned to the signal: The privileged status of speech for young infants. *Developmental Science, 7*, 270–276.

Vouloumanos, A., & Werker, J. F. (2007). Listening to language at birth: Evidence for a bias for speech in neonates. *Developmental Science, 10*, 159–164.

Wagner, L., & Carey, S. (2005). 12-month-old infants represent probable endings of motion events. *Infancy, 7*(1), 73–83.

Waxman, S. R. (1998). Linking object categorization and naming: Early expectations and the shaping role of language. In D. L. Medin (Ed.), *The Psychology of Learning and Motivation* (Vol. *38*, pp. 249–291). San Diego, CA: Academic Press.

Waxman, S. R. (1999a). The dubbing ceremony revisited: Object naming and categorization in infancy and early childhood. In D. L. Medin & S. Atran (Eds.), *Folkbiology* (pp. 233–284). Cambridge, MA: MIT Press.

Waxman, S. R. (1999b). Specifying the scope of 13-month-olds' expectations for novel words. *Cognition, 70*(3), B35–B50.

Waxman, S. R., & Booth, A. E. (2000). *Distinguishing count nouns from adjectives: Evidence from 14-month-olds' novelty preference and word extension.* Proceedings of the 24th Annual Boston University Conference on Language Development.

Waxman, S. R., & Booth, A. E. (2001a). On the insufficiency of domain-general accounts of word learning: A reply to Bloom and Markson. *Cognition, 78*, 277–279.

Waxman, S. R., & Booth, A. E. (2001b). Seeing pink elephants: Fourteen-month-olds' interpretations of novel nouns and adjectives. *Cognitive Psychology, 43*(3), 217–242.

Waxman, S. R., & Booth, A. E. (2003). The origins and evolution of links between word learning and conceptual organization: New evidence from 11-month-olds. *Developmental Science, 6*(2), 130–137.

Waxman, S.R., & Braig, B. (1996, April). *Stars and starfish: How far can shape take us?* Paper presented at the 10th Biennial Conference on Infant Studies, Providence, RI.

Waxman, S. R., & Gelman, S. A. (in press). Different kinds of concepts and different kinds of words: What words do for human cognition. In D. Mareschal, P. C. Quinn & S. E. G. Lea (Eds.), *The making of human concepts.* Oxford: Oxford University Press.

Waxman, S. R., & Lidz, J. (2006). Early word learning. In W. Damon & R. M. Lerner (Series Eds.), D. Kuhn & R. Siegler (Vol. Eds.), *Handbook of Child Psychology: Vol. 2. Cognition, perception, and language* (6th ed.). New York: Wiley.

Waxman, S. R., Lidz, J. L., Braun, I. E., & Lavin, T. (2009). 24-month-old infants' interpretations of novel verbs and nouns in dynamic scenes. *Cognitive Psychology, 59*, 67–95.

Waxman, S. R., & Markow, D. B. (1995). Words as invitations to form categories: Evidence from 12- to 13-month-old infants. *Cognitive Psychology, 29*(3), 257–302.

Waxman, S. R., & Markow, D. B. (1998). Object properties and object kind: Twenty-one-month-old infants' extension of novel adjectives. *Child Development, 69*(5), 1313–1329.

Welder, A. N., & Graham, S. A. (2006). Infants' categorization of novel objects with more or less obvious features. *Cognitive Psychology, 52*, 57–91.

Werker, J.F., & Byers-Heinlein, K. (2008). Bilingualism in infancy: first steps in perception and comprehension. *Trends in Cognitive Sciences, 12*(4), 144–151.

Werker, J. F., Lloyd, V. L., Pegg, J. E., & Polka, L. (1996). Putting the baby in the bootstraps: Toward a more complete understanding of the role of the input in infant speech processing. In J. L. Morgan & K. Demuth (Eds.), *Signal to syntax: Bootstrapping from speech to grammar in early acquisition* (pp. 427–447). Mahwah, NJ: Erlbaum.

Werker, J. F., & Yeung, H. H. (2005). Infant speech perception bootstraps word learning. *Trends in Cognitive Science*, *9*(11), 519–527.

Woodward, A. L., & Markman, E. M. (1998). Early word learning. In W. Damon (Series Ed.), D. Kuhn, & R. Siegler (Vol. Eds.), *Handbook of child psychology: Vol. 2. Cognition, perception and language* (pp. 371–420). New York: Wiley.

Xu, F. (1999). Object individuation and object identity in infancy: The role of spatiotemporal information, object property information, and language. *Acta Psychologica*, *102*(2–3), 113–136.

Xu, F., & Carey, S. (1996). Infants' metaphysics: The case of numerical identity. *Cognitive Psychology*, *30*(2), 111–153.

Yip, V., & Matthews, S. (2007). *The bilingual child: Early development and language contact.* Cambridge: Cambridge University Press.

Younger, B. A., & Cohen, L. B. (1986). Developmental change in infants' perception of correlations among attributes. *Child Development*, *57*, 803–815.

PART II

Cognitive Development in Early Childhood

This second section of the Handbook considers further development in the foundational domains of psychology and biology in early childhood. The development of principled biological knowledge is discussed by Opfer and Gelman, extending the work reported by Quinn. A concise view of language development is contributed by Tomasello, focusing on language as a system rather than on the learning of individual words. An overview of the development of psychological understanding (the child's acquisition of a "theory of mind") is presented by Wellman, extending the work discussed by Gergely, Carpenter, and Meltzoff. Lillard and her colleagues provide an exploration of pretend play and the development of the imagination, which is core to the development of psychological understanding and social cognition. A key mechanism for cognitive development in this period, the development of symbolic representational formats other than language, is considered by Deloache.

Opfer and Gelman (chapter 8) focus their discussion of the development of foundational biological knowledge around the animacy–inanimacy distinction. The animacy–inanimacy distinction is fundamental to the development of biological knowledge, and is cross-culturally universal. Opfer and Gelman argue for an enrichment account, again consistent with our neural networks metaphor encapsulating the exemplar-based, incremental, and continuous character of learning. Although incremental learning mechanisms can give rise to apparently radical reorganization of knowledge with age ("cognitive restructuring" or "conceptual change"), Opfer and Gelman show that in reality there is little substantive change with age. However, they are not convinced that developmental change can be reduced to the incremental acquisition of the correlations among environmental inputs. Rather, they favor innate organizing principles that constrain the child's developing conceptual system, such as attentional biases to animate faces and movement. In reality, however, these apparently distinct versions of continuity theory cannot be distinguished with behavioral data alone. The learning "biases" that characterize mammalian brains may in themselves arise from the way that neural coding works, thereby constraining how the incremental acquisition of sensory environmental correlations builds "conceptual knowledge." As Opfer and Gelman point out, the development of a core principle such as the animacy–inanimacy distinction has ramifications for many other aspects of cognitive development, for example categorization and language. It enables young children to integrate new conceptual knowledge to existing knowledge in a causally coherent way: learning can become "explanation based."

Tomasello's chapter on language acquisition (chapter 9) covers enormous ground and provides a clear demonstration of how difficult it is to study cognitive development of one kind in isolation from other kinds. Developing the core theme of *shared intentionality* discussed in the earlier chapter by Carpenter (chapter 4), he shows that the incremental learning of speech sounds and their meanings is constrained by the fact that all meanings are a form of *social agreement* that all speakers of a particular language share in common. Skills of intention-reading are fundamental to this enterprise, as all speakers of a particular language also "know" that they share these common social agreements. Prelinguistic forms of communication such as joint attention and gesture are part of the biological preparation for language acquisition, but only in general ways. Exposure to language and language use (i.e., incremental learning and action) are fundamental developmentally (a "usage" theory of acquisition). Children are exposed to individual utterances produced by individual speakers on individual occasions. An utterance is the smallest unit in which a person expresses a complete communicative intention, and is not necessarily a word. To become productive and creative speakers and users of their language, children must use general "pattern finding" cognitive processes such as categorization and analogy to reconstruct the linguistic abstractions of their speech communities for themselves. Tomasello argues that the fundamental mechanism in language acquisition is to comprehend utterances, which may require the child to determine the functional role that a particular word or a particular grammatical construction such as a noun phrase is playing in the utterance – which requires intention reading.

In chapter 10, Wellman also manages to condense a vast amount of empirical work, in this case into children's development of a theory of mind, into a clear summary of what children understand about the mind and when they understand it. He focuses in particular on areas that have been at the heart of research activity since the previous edition of this Handbook, such as false-belief understanding, and also draws on comparative data from other species. Wellman argues that theory of mind should be broadly conceived, encompassing human understanding of agents' mental states (intentions, desires, and thoughts), how action is shaped by mental states, and the development of our everyday "commonsense" psychological understandings. Wellman's thesis is that earlier developments focus on understanding that intentional agents behave in accordance with their desires, emotions, and perceptual experiences, while older children develop increasingly reflective ideas about minds, brains, and mental life. Again, the developmental thesis is one of continuity, and Wellman notes that infant attention to intentional action at 10- to 12-months is predictive of theory of mind understanding at 4 years of age. Finally, Wellman notes that although other species can understand action as intentional and can understand how the visual experiences of others can determine their knowledge, other species rarely if ever imitate, and their understanding of intentions falls far short of that of humans. He notes that neuroscience data regarding brain mechanisms have the potential to deepen our developmental understandings. Development of a theory of mind is experience-dependent, but the neural mechanisms available for acquiring the relevant information may differ in interesting ways (e.g., in children with autism).

Lillard, Pinkham, and Smith (chapter 11) tackle the important role of pretending and the imagination in cognitive development. As they note, pretend play has no obvious survival function, yet is ubiquitous across cultures and evolves in similar ways. The purpose of pretend play has been a mystery. Young children need to adapt to the world as it is, yet, in pretending, they contrive to make the world as it is not. As Lillard et al. point out, pretending is an early example of the child's symbolic capacity, a hallmark ability of the human species. Pretend play and imaginative games occupy a large portion of young children's unstructured time. As further research is required to understand the full developmental significance of pretend play, Lillard et al. focus instead on empirical data concerning how it develops. They show that pretending involves several important cognitive skills, including social referencing (using another person's response to a situation to guide one's own), interpretation of underlying intentions, "quarantining" of the pretend world from the real one, understanding alternative representations of the world, and, of course, symbolic understanding. Pretence activities focused on objects and props begin during the second year of life, sociodramatic pretending with caretakers and peers typically emerges at around 3–4 years, and the comprehension of pretence may not initially involve a symbolic capacity. Both language development and imitation interact in important ways with the development of pretending and the imagination, demonstrating again that cognitive development of one kind cannot be studied in isolation from cognitive development of other kinds.

As Deloache argues in chapter 12, humans are the symbolic species. A symbol can be defined as anything that someone intends to stand for or represent something other than itself. Human cultures create a variety of artifacts to serve symbolic functions (models, maps, pictures, religious artifacts), and young children learn gradually what these artifacts stand for. Symbols are inherently asymmetrical – a scale model of the Tower of London may represent the Tower of London, but the Tower of London does not represent the scale model. As Deloache makes clear, intentionality is critical to symbolic understanding. Nothing is inherently a symbol (the scale model may be simply a toy). What makes an entity a symbol is the intention of a person that it be so. Again, cognitive development concerning symbols does not occur in isolation from other developments. Intention-reading and language skills support symbolic development, just as symbolic artifacts impart new and useful information about the world that supports social-cognitive and cognitive development. The chapter focuses mainly on young children's ability to understand and use symbolic artifacts. For Deloache, the unique aspect of symbolic artifacts is that they have an inherently dual nature – they are both objects in their own right, and something entirely different. Deloache argues that the achievement of the "dual representation" is necessary for interpreting symbols, and demonstrates how this achievement goes through a number of developmental steps in early childhood. Many aspects of this understanding must be culturally acquired. Symbolic artifacts like pictures and videos are cultural inventions, hence cultural and social experiences are critical to their understanding and use. Representational insights are acquired artifact by artifact, as they depend on incremental individual experience.

Deloache's recognition of the importance of individual experience for symbolic development echoes the experience-dependence theme adopted by many other authors in the first two sections of the revised Handbook. The central role of individual experience in so many aspects of the cognitive development of young children again suggests that insights from cognitive neuroscience will have an important impact on developmental theorizing. The neural networks metaphor encapsulates the importance of individual, incremental, experience-dependent learning for building a cognitive system from sensory-perceptual and action experience. Indeed, the neural metaphor of pattern completion is drawn on by a number of authors. This is when neural networks respond to noise in the input, or partial information, by still activating the entire network. The cells that do fire perform a pattern-completion process and trigger the other cells that represent the percept or concept. Children are seen as pattern-completers, seeking and extracting patterns in the "input," for example via analogies and generalization. The highlighting of the central role of individual experience as a crucial mechanism of development also suggests that educators such as Maria Montessori (who stressed the important role of "doing" for learning) and theorists such as Jean Piaget (who argued that action is the source of knowledge) were tapping into something very important for young children's developing cognition. Education can transform the cognitive development of young children, by purposely manipulating the individual incremental experiences that they encounter.

CHAPTER EIGHT

Development of the Animate–Inanimate Distinction

John E. Opfer and Susan A. Gelman

Introduction: What Is the Animate–Inanimate Distinction and Why Is It Important?

A newborn looks longer at abstract shapes arranged in a face-like configuration than at the same shapes arranged randomly. An English-speaking 2-year-old appropriately uses word order in his sentences, so that the "doer" of an action appears before the verb. A 5-year-old claims that animals, but not plants, are living things. In each of these cases, children are making use of an animacy distinction (the distinction between animals and other sorts of entities) to sort the world and organize it into sensible categories.

Of the countless categorical distinctions available to humans – color, shape, size, texture, etc. – why a special interest in the animate–inanimate distinction? There are two primary reasons. First, the distinction is a fundamental, foundational one. The animate–inanimate distinction manifests early in infancy (Rakison & Poulin-Dubois, 2001), has distinct neurophysiological correlates (Caramazza & Shelton, 1998), is uniform across cultures (Atran, 1999) and languages (Diesendruck, 2003), and is central to a broad array of more complex abilities, including interpretations of causal events (Spelke, Phillips, & Woodward, 1995), word learning (Childers & Echols, 2004), and attributions of mental states (Baron-Cohen, 1995) and biological processes (Carey, 1985). Indeed, a creature incapable of distinguishing animates from inanimates would be severely impaired. Oliver Sacks (1985) describes a real-life example of a man who could not identify things as animate or inanimate on the basis of visual perception, thus, for example, mistaking his wife for a hat (and attempting to place her head on his own).

Support for writing the first-edition version of this chapter was provided by NICHD grant HD-36043 and NSF grant BCS-0817128 to the second author. Support for writing the current version was provided by NSF grant DRL-0909999 to the first author and by NICHD grant HD-36043 and NSF grant BCS-0817128 to the second author.

A second reason for special interest in the animate–inanimate distinction is that it sheds light on basic theoretical issues in cognitive development. Consider key issues such as the following: Are there innate concepts? Are cognitive systems modular? Can subtle and complex concepts emerge bottom-up on the basis of a perceptually based associative learning mechanism? How domain-general versus domain-specific is human cognition? Do children's concepts undergo qualitative reorganizations with age? At what age can children be said to have constructed a theory of psychology, or a theory of biology? All of these issues are informed by work on the animate–inanimate distinction.

Given the centrality of animacy as sketched out above, it is not surprising that the literature on children's understanding of this concept spans decades of scientific investigation, from numerous theoretical and methodological perspectives. The research includes non-verbal experimental methods with infants, interview studies with preschoolers, analyses of natural language, and a wide array of stimuli that manipulate both static and dynamic features that are central to the determination of animacy. In this chapter, we aim to reflect the breadth of this literature, but in a selective manner that recognizes the theoretical contexts motivating the work. We thus set forth the following central questions:

- What knowledge about animacy is present in infancy?
- What are the developmental paths by which this knowledge becomes enriched over time?
- When in development does this knowledge get recruited to build a framework theory of biology?
- How does an animacy distinction inform other aspects of cognitive development?

What Knowledge About Animacy Is Present in Infancy?

Four key issues arise in studies of animacy in infancy: (a) whether and at what age infants reliably distinguish animates from inanimates; (b) what information is used to decide whether something is animate or inanimate; (c) how and whether this distinction gets recruited in infants' *conceptual* understanding of the world (as measured by, for example, emotional responses, imitation, generalization, or causal attributions); and (d) by what mechanism the animacy distinction develops. For excellent reviews of these topics, see Legerstee (1992), Poulin-Dubois (1999), Rakison and Poulin-Dubois (2001), and Woodward and Needham (2007).

When in development do infants reliably distinguish animates from inanimates?

Of all the animals that infants must (eventually) differentiate from inanimate objects, the most important is the human animal – people. Humans care for infants, serve as potential models to imitate, and – unlike dolls and other inanimates – resist physical manipulation and instead engage in behaviors motivated by psychological processes. For these reasons, most studies examining the animate–inanimate distinction in infancy have focused on the person–object distinction.

The first signs of the person–object distinction appear quite early – much earlier than 8 months old, as Piaget (1952) had thought. By 12 weeks of age, infants show differences in looking time when presented with a person versus a musical mobile (Klein & Jennings, 1979), a person versus a toy monkey (Brazelton, Koslowski, & Main, 1974), a person versus a manikin (Carpenter, Tecce, Stechler, & Friedman, 1970), or a person versus a Raggedy Ann doll (Field, 1979). By 2 months of age, infants smile and coo when faced with a responsive adult, but not when faced with a toy monkey (Brazelton et al., 1974; Trevarthen, 1977; cited in Legerstee, Pomerleau, Malcuit, & Feider, 1987).

One potential concern is that infants may not be distinguishing between animate and inanimate so much as they are reacting differentially to other factors, such as the item's activity or familiarity. To address this issue, Legerstee et al. (1987) presented infants with both a doll and a person, manipulating both the familiarity of the item and its activity. Infants were studied longitudinally from 3–25 weeks of age. Results indicated that by age 9 weeks, infants smiled and cooed more at the person than the doll, when familiarity and activity were controlled. Later, at 4 months, the infants also reached significantly more for the doll than the person. Thus, the communication-like acts that infants direct toward people versus other objects suggest that infants are aware of differences between people and objects as young as 2 months of age.

Does infants' person–object distinction reflect a broader animate–inanimate distinction, or does it instead reflect the special status of people? For example, Klein and Jennings's (1979) finding that 12-week-old infants distinguish a human face from a rotating musical mobile is consistent with either interpretation. Studying this question is challenging. Ideally we would wish to know whether infants smile and coo at non-human animals, as they do for people, and whether they can imitate the behavior of non-human animals too (a point also noted by Rakison & Poulin-Dubois, 2001).

Perhaps not surprisingly, few relevant studies have been conducted on whether infants' socio-emotional behavior is constrained by the animate–inanimate distinction. One striking study, however, suggests that infants' imitation is *not* limited to imitating other humans. Beginning in the early 1930s, Wintrop and Luella Kellogg (1933) co-reared their 10-month-old son, Donald, with a 7-month-old female chimp, Gua, in an effort to examine Gua's ability to learn from Donald. What they found, however, was that Donald aped Gua more than the reverse: Donald imitated the chimp's knuckle-walking (even after he had learned to walk on his own), chewed on shoes and walls, and even acquired Gua's stereotypical food barks, including using one distinctive bark as a word for oranges when communicating with his mother.

Although non-human animals can elicit infant imitation, do non-animal agents also elicit imitation? This issue is important too because Donald's behavior is consistent with both possibilities. To test this, Meltzoff (1995) showed 18-month-olds an unsuccessful action (e.g., attempting to disassemble a dumbbell) that was modeled by a human and a robotic agent. Consistent with the idea that the animate–inanimate distinction constrains infants' imitation, Meltzoff found 18-month-olds were six times more likely to complete the action modeled by the human than the action modeled by the robot, a finding that has been replicated with infants as young as 10 months old (Legerstee and Markova,

2008). Thus, although it is not clear how broadly infants imitate non-human animals (e.g., whether they would imitate a spider), it appears that infants' selective imitation of human behavior can extend to encompass (non-human) animal behavior and exclude non-animal (robotic) behavior, which is consistent with the idea that the animate–inanimate distinction is present by at least 10 months of age.

What information is used to decide whether something is animate or inanimate?

Although research cited above documents an early-emerging distinction between some sorts of animates (such as people) and some sorts of inanimates (such as mobiles), it often leaves open the question of what cues infants are attending to. Typically, the experimental design does not allow one to determine precisely the basis of the distinction. As noted above, one gap in the literature concerns the extent to which the person–object distinction reflects a more general animal–object distinction. But even if this question were to be resolved, there is still the further question of what perceptual cues signal to the infant that an entity is animate, and whether neural mechanisms exist that are specialized for processing these cues.

Two broad classes of perceptual cues that could indicate that a given entity is either animate or inanimate include *featural* aspects of the object (e.g., whether or not it has a face; the texture of its contour) and *dynamic* aspects of the object's motion (e.g., whether or not it propels itself, whether or not it moves in the direction of another entity, whether or not it moves contingent on the movements of another). Some cues are arguably a combination of featural and dynamic information (e.g., a person's gaze has both characteristic static features [like shape and configuration of eyes] and characteristic motion properties [contingently following the gaze of another]).

Featural cues. Among featural qualities, one of the most reliable cues that something is an animal is that it possesses a face. Indeed, faces seem to be especially compelling to infants even in their first month after birth. During this period, although infants can only discern the schematic elements of faces (i.e., two dark areas above a mouth-shaped area; Maurer, 1985), when they are shown drawings of schematic faces, infants pay more attention to them than to drawings of non-faces (Fantz, Fagan, & Miranda, 1975). Indeed, neonates between 9 and 37 *minutes* old pay more attention to moving faces with a proper configuration (e.g., eyes level and above the nose) than those with scrambled configurations (Goren, Sarty, & Wu, 1975; Morton & Johnson, 1991). Moreover, eyes appear to be particularly attention-getting. An attentional bias toward faces could help even young infants begin to parse the world into animals and non-animals, and infants seem to develop specialized neural mechanisms (the fusiform face area) for processing faces visually if exposed to relevant stimuli within a sensitive period (de Haan & Nelson, 1999; Scherf, Behrmann, Humphreys, & Luna, 2007). (For reviews of this literature, see Johnson & Morton, 1991; Nelson, 2001.)

Rakison and Butterworth (1998) propose that another featural quality by which infants differentiate animals from non-animals is the presence of wheels versus legs. Not only do 18-month-olds distinguish toy animals (with legs) from toy vehicles (with wheels;

Mandler, Bauer, & McDonough, 1991), but also 14- and 18-month-olds violate the animal–vehicle distinction when toy animals are portrayed as having wheels rather than legs and toy vehicles are portrayed as having legs rather than wheels (Rakison & Butterworth, 1998). However, a problem with calling legs a perceptual feature is that only some legs are animate. For example, legs of a table or chair are inanimate, yet infants do not treat animals and furniture as a single group. Some inanimate legs even have feet and toes (e.g., the legs on a bathtub or statue). We suggest instead that infants are likely to be using other qualities, such as texture, contour, or material kind, to differentiate animals and inanimates.

Indeed Heise, Rivera, and Smith (cited in Smith & Heise, 1992) find that the contour of toy objects sufficiently distinguishes animals from inanimates by 12 months of age. Likewise, Van De Walle (1997) found that 9-month-olds use information about part structure (e.g., curvilinear vs. rectilinear contours, smooth vs. angular joints) to differentiate animals from vehicles.

There may be additional cues that are difficult to assess in experimental paradigms, and to which infants may be sensitive. We speculate that texture (e.g., metal vs. fur), odor, and sounds all provide important information in the real-world differentiation of animals versus inanimates, though none of these cues are defining or absolute. Certainly even young infants show exquisite sensitivity to differences in odor (Marlier, Schall, & Soussignan, 1998) and sound (e.g., Aslin, Jusczyk, & Pisoni, 1998), including differentiating and preferring the human voice from non-linguistic stimuli such as tones (Glenn, Cunningham, & Joyce, 1981) and preferring the odor of human milk to raw cow's milk (Russell, 1976). Like faces, these cues may also be processed by neurally specialized areas that are tuned for detecting animals (e.g., animal sounds; Suied, Viaud-Delmon, & Burr, 2009). Studies that use small-scale replicas or photos will be impoverished with respect to some of these cues.

Dynamic cues. Some researchers have proposed that entities are classified as animate or inanimate not solely by virtue of their static features, but also by virtue of dynamic information, such as animal-typical movement. Dynamic information is of particular theoretical interest because it seems to have the capacity to signal quite *abstract* conceptual information, such as agency, intentionality, or goal-directedness.

Central among such claims is the suggestion that animates can engage in self-generated and self-sustained motion, whereas inanimate objects typically cannot (Mandler, 1992, 2000; Premack, 1990; Rakison & Lupyan, 2008). By 7 months of age, infants reliably detect the difference between self-generated and other-generated movement (Cicchino & Rakison, 2008), and 7-month-olds also seem to appreciate that people – but not inanimate objects – can move on their own (Markson & Spelke, 2006; Spelke et al., 1995). In the study by Spelke et al. (1995), for example, 7-month-olds were assigned to one of two conditions: a person condition or an object condition. In both conditions, infants were habituated to a videotaped event. In the person condition, one person moved behind a screen and a second person emerged from the other side. In the object condition, an inanimate object moved behind a screen and a second inanimate object emerged from the other side. Infants in the *object* condition looked longer if the two inanimate objects failed to make contact before the second object moved. However, infants in the *person* condition looked longer if the two people did make contact before the second person moved. Thus, 7-month-olds seem to believe that people – but not inanimate objects – are capable of self-initiated movement. In further support of this interpretation, 9-month-olds become emotionally distressed on viewing inanimates moving on their own (Poulin-Dubois, Lepage, & Ferland, 1996).

In addition to self-generated movement, particular *patterns* of motion – such as walking or pursuing a goal – appear to be distinctively animate (see also Blythe, Todd, & Miller, 1999, for discussion of "biological motion"). One method used to study the perception of biological motion employs "point-light displays," in which a number of luminous dots are placed on the torso and joints of a person. The person is then filmed in the dark while moving about, such that these lights are the only visible stimuli. When adults view these displays, they can determine within a half-second that the moving entity is a person (Johansson, 1973). Several studies indicate that infants between 30 and 36 weeks of age perceive the difference between a person-based point-light display and an artificial display (Bertenthal, Proffit, & Cutting, 1984; Fox & McDaniel, 1982), and even 2-*day*-old newborns perceive the difference (Simion, Regolin, & Bulf, 2008). Finally, having seen a moving point-light display of a moving animal or a vehicle, 9-month-olds expect to see the same type of entity depicted in a picture (Arterberry & Bornstein, 2002), suggesting that biological motion is associated with the animate–inanimate distinction. Like perception of faces and goal-directed movement, adults' perception of biological movement in point-light displays relies on overlapping, specialized neural areas (posterior superior temporal sulcus and fusiform face areas; Blakemore & Decety, 2001; Grossman & Blake, 2002) that are activated by animates. Ongoing research finds that this specialization is present as early as 8 months of age (Reid, Hoehl, & Striano, 2006).

A third type of dynamic cue is that of goal-directed movement, of which all living things are capable – including animals (Carey, 1999) and insentient living things such as plants, amoebae, and leaves (Bargh, 1990; Opfer & Gelman, 1998; Opfer, 2002). Studies suggest that 9-month-olds expect goal-directed agents to move *directly* toward goals (i.e., taking the most direct path of motion; Csibra, Gergely, Bíró, Koos, & Brockbank, 1999; Gergely, Nadasdy, Csibra, & Bíró, 1995), and for 20-month-olds, this expectation about motion path is stronger for animals than non-animals (Rakison, Cicchino, & Hahn, 2007). As with perception of faces and biological movement in point-light displays, perception of goal-directed movement also relies on specialized neural areas (posterior superior temporal sulcus; Saxe, 2004; Wyk, Hudac, Carter, Sobel, & Pelphrey, 2009), in which activity is correlated with the degree to which the attended display is goal-directed and judged to be animate (Schultz, Friston, O'Doherty, Wolpert, & Frith, 2005). At least in adults, these areas are also disproportionately active when identifying the agent in a scene or sentence (Kuperberg, Sitnikova, & Lakshmanan, 2008). How early this specialization develops is an ongoing area of research (Pelphrey & Carter, 2008).

A final type of dynamic cue is *contingency* of behavior, in which the actions or behaviors of an entity are time-linked to those of another (e.g., an object that moves or vocalizes in response to a baby's movements or vocalizations) (Gergely & Watson, 1999; Johnson, Slaughter, & Carey, 1998). Watson (1972) presented 2-month-olds with both contingent caregivers and contingent mobiles over a period of 2 weeks, and found that the infants responded to each with an equal amount of smiling and cooing – thus treating the contingent mobiles in a "social" fashion. Watson and Ramey (1972) suggest that social responsiveness may have evolved to be elicited by contingent stimuli rather than by particular physical characteristics (such as the human face).

How the animate–inanimate distinction gets recruited in infants' conceptual understanding of the world

What meaning do infants attach to the animate–inanimate distinction? As noted earlier, some of the earliest evidence that infants distinguish people from inanimate objects comes from newborns' socio-emotional reactions, including gazing, smiling, cooing, and imitating the facial expressions of people (Field, Woodson, Greenberg, & Cohen, 1982; Meltzoff & Moore, 1983) but not objects (Legerstee et al., 1987; Legerstee, 1991; Legerstee, 1992). Furthermore, several researchers have proposed that infants imbue animates (particularly people) with important psychological characteristics. Baron-Cohen (1995), for example, credits infants with wired-in capacities to detect intentionality and eye-direction in other humans, and posits that these capacities are crucial components of a theory of mind. Likewise, research suggests that infants attribute psychological intent to objects that move spontaneously in a goal-directed fashion (Premack & Premack, 1997; Kuhlmeier, Wynn, & Bloom, 2003). Infants as young as 6 months also seem to expect that people but not objects pursue goals (Woodward, 1998). Older infants also seem to have different expectations for how objects and people act toward goals (Meltzoff, 1995).

Summary: animacy in infancy

The animate–inanimate distinction is well in place in the first year of life, with some sensitivity present immediately after birth. Infants make use of both featural information (e.g., faces, sounds) and dynamic information (e.g., biological and goal-directed movement) to determine which entities are animate versus inanimate, and specialized neural mechanisms for processing these cues function as early as 8 months old. At the same time, no single featural or dynamic cue seems to be necessary for treating an entity as if it were an animal (e.g., R. Gelman, Durgin, & Kaufman, 1995; Johnson et al., 1998; Watson, 1972), and infants appear to learn rich correlations among these cues as they parse animates from inanimates (Arterberry & Bornstein, 2002; Rakison, 2004; Rakison & Lupyan, 2008). This learning appears to be central to infants' later concept of animacy, guiding their socio-emotional understandings, theory of mind, and predictions of actions.

What Are the Developmental Paths by Which this Knowledge Becomes Enriched Over Time?

Although we have argued that the animate–inanimate distinction emerges in early infancy, it is far from complete at that point. How, then, does an understanding of animacy develop? We can coarsely characterize two major theoretical positions: (a) restructuring (qualitative change in children's understanding, with characteristic patterns of errors) and (b) continuity (core principles that undergo little or no change with development).

Restructuring

The classic restructuring position is Piaget's stage theory of cognitive development, which predicts radical reorganization of knowledge with age. Specifically, Piaget claimed that children progressed through a series of five levels of animacy understanding, from fundamental confusion (a chaotic mixing of animate and inanimate), to initial but flawed distinctions (e.g., linking animacy with the capacity to move, thus yielding the belief that clouds and bicycles are alive), to the eventual adult distinction (Piaget, 1929/1951). The Piagetian view predicts that children will display two sorts of errors until about 11 or 12 years of age: animacy errors, in which inanimate entities are imbued with life (e.g., thinking that anything that moves, including bicycles and clouds, is alive), and artificialism errors, in which all entities and events are viewed as the outcome of human intentional action (e.g., thinking that people made the rivers and mountains).

Piaget's initial work seemed to support the classic restructuring view. Relying on his "clinical interview" method, Piaget posed questions to children concerning which things are alive, could know, and could feel, and proposed 5 stages in children's understanding: (0) no understanding, (1) identifying life based on activity, (2) identifying life based on movement, (3) identifying life based on autonomous movement, and (4) correct (identifying either animals or animals and plants as alive). However, numerous scholars have noted methodological limitations of this work, including its reliance on verbal justifications, the use of anomalous questions, the scoring system, the choice of items (particularly remote or unfamiliar items), the wording of the interviews, etc. (e.g., Carey, 1985; R. Gelman & Baillargeon, 1983; Holland & Rohrman, 1979; Massey & Gelman, 1988; Richards & Siegler, 1984). Studies that corrected these shortcomings generally held that young children could not be characterized as "animistic" at any point in development (e.g., Massey & Gelman, 1988, for review).

A more recent radical restructuring view was advanced by Carey (1985, 1995), whose position differs importantly from that of Piaget. Carey suggested that children's errors resulted not from domain-general cognitive stage limitations, but rather from domain-specific misapplications of developing theories. Specifically, children were thought to misconstrue biological processes by inappropriately interpreting them within psychological framework theories (regarding naïve theories see Carey, 1985; Gopnik & Wellman, 1994). For example, children might understand eating as (psychologically) necessary to fulfill a person's desire for food and to assuage their hunger, but not understand eating as (biologically) necessary to maintain a person's health.

Evidence consistent with restructuring can be found in a broad array of studies showing that children have limited understanding of the body and of biological functioning (Au, Romo, & DeWitt, 1999; Carey, 1985; Siegal & Peterson, 1999; Slaughter, Jaakkola, & Carey, 1999). For example it is found in preschoolers' denial that plants are alive or can sensibly be grouped with animals (Carey, 1985; Hatano et al., 1993; Opfer & Siegler, 2004), in preschoolers' inferences of biological properties that rest on similarity to humans rather than on biological relatedness (Carey, 1985; Inagaki & Hatano, 1987, 1993), and in their difficulty grasping that humans are "one animal among many" (Carey, 1985; Coley, 1995; Johnson, Mervis, & Boster, 1992).

This theory-revision view has four implications for the animate–inanimate distinction. First, children appear to have difficulty grasping that humans are a type of animal (Carey, 1985; Johnson et al., 1992; Coley, 1995). Second, preschoolers fail to differentiate "not alive" from a variety of related (but distinct) concepts: dead, inactive, unreal, and absent (Carey, 1985; Slaughter, Jaakkola, & Carey, 1999). Third, preschoolers have persistent difficulties explaining animate processes, such as illness and contagion (Au & Romo, 1999; Solomon & Cassimatis, 1999). Finally, preschoolers treat inanimate bodily organs as agentive (a stance also known as vitalism; Inagaki & Hatano, 1993; Hatano & Inagaki, 1994; Miller & Bartsch, 1997; Morris, Taplin, & Gelman, 2000).

The notion of radical theory change in early childhood remains controversial. Competing data and arguments are brought to bear, both with respect to when conceptual change occurs (initial reports of radical change at around 10 years of age have been modified, placing the change much younger, between 4 and 6 years of age [Carey, 1995], though others suggest that no radical changes occur; see below), and with respect to whether such changes constitute fundamental misconstruals. Below we review evidence arguing that children's understanding of the biological realm is fairly continuous from age 3 or 4 years onward.

Continuity

In contrast to a theory of restructuring, a continuity theory posits little substantive change with age. Continuity views take at least two very different forms. On the one hand, continuity may reflect simply the accretion of facts stored in memory, as in connectionist accounts of conceptual development (e.g., French, Mareschal, Mermillod, & Quinn, 2004; Rakison & Lupyan, 2008; Rogers & McClelland, 2008; though see Marcus & Keil, 2008; Opfer & Doumas, 2008). According to this view, developmental change is best understood as resulting from the accumulation of correlations among environmental inputs. On the other hand, continuity may instead reflect innate organizing principles (e.g., attentional biases to animate faces and movement) that constrain the child's conceptual system and that do not change (or, change little) with age (Keil, 1979; R. Gelman, 1990). Here we focus on the latter type of continuity theory.

Several researchers have proposed that the animate–inanimate distinction is well-entrenched and essentially unchanging from the preschool years onward. Keil has argued that certain ontological distinctions, including the animate–inanimate distinction, are firmly established and innately constrained (1979, 1995). He initially studied this issue by noting that ontological distinctions can be gauged by "category errors" – statements in which the predicate cannot sensibly be applied to the subject noun. For example, "The cow is one hour long" is a category error, because the predicate "one hour long" does not sensibly apply to "the cow." In fact, physical objects (such as cows) do not have durations (such as an hour in length); only events have durations. Category errors contrast with run-of-the-mill false statements, such as "The cow is blue." False statements are sensible but depart from reality; category errors cannot even be interpreted in a literal way.

Keil (1979) successfully trained children of different ages to make judgments of category errors (e.g., reporting that "The cow is one hour long" is silly, but "The cow is blue" is not). Of particular interest to the animate–inanimate distinction, 4-year-olds recognized the inappropriateness of applying animate predicates to artifacts (e.g., "The chair is asleep" was judged as "silly"). Thus, by preschool age, children recognize an ontological partition between animate and inanimate.

Similarly, R. Gelman has suggested that the animate–inanimate distinction is one of the "skeletal principles" children possess, that organize experience, direct attention, guide learning, and promote conceptual coherence (R. Gelman, 1990). Indeed, preschool children (3 and 4 years of age) display remarkably accurate knowledge about the ways in which persons differ from inanimate objects (rocks and dolls), for example with respect to actions, parts, mental states, and reciprocal actions (e.g., talking to one another) (R. Gelman, Spelke, & Meck, 1983). Likewise, 3- and 4-year-olds have a rudimentary grasp that animal movement is governed by an "innards principle" (movement is self-generated), whereas the movement of inanimate objects is governed by an "external-agent principle" (movement is caused by an external agent) (R. Gelman, 1990; see also section on autonomous motion, below).

In large part motivated by the theoretical divide between Carey's (1985) claims regarding conceptual reorganization versus Keil's (1979, 1989) and R. Gelman's (1990) claims of unchanging skeletal principles, the last 20 years have seen an explosion of research examining children's biological understanding, with implications for the animate–inanimate distinction. For review, see S. A. Gelman (2003), Springer (1999), and Wellman and Gelman (1998). Topics of investigation include children's understanding of life, death, movement, growth, origins, reproduction, inheritance, germs and illness, organ transplants, teleology, and goal-directed action. Many of these topics are of inherent interest even apart from the larger theoretical issues, because of the pervasiveness of these issues in everyday life, their relevance to human actions, and their practical implications for education. We provide a selective review below, focusing on those studies and results most directly relevant to the animate–inanimate distinction.

What is "alive." The distinction between living and non-living kinds does not map directly onto the distinction between animate and inanimate kinds, because plants are living but inanimate. Nonetheless, the classic question for gathering evidence on children's animism came from asking children which of a variety of entities were alive, and children's errors raise questions regarding their capacity to distinguish animate from inanimate. As noted earlier, although children do make errors in life judgments, it is perhaps more striking how generally accurate even preschool children are, when questioned about animals and inanimate objects (Carey, 1985; Dolgin & Behrend, 1984; Hatano et al., 1993; Holland & Rohrman, 1979; Laurendeau & Pinard, 1962; Richards & Siegler, 1984, 1986). This finding contrasts with Piaget's (1929/1951) claim that children under 7 to 10 years initially adhered to "animism," that is, believing everything (including non-living things such as clouds and bicycles) to be alive.

Rather than being generally "animistic," preschoolers seem to associate life with animacy. Thus, 4–6-year-olds make very few animistic errors regarding non-moving things (e.g., rocks, dolls, household goods) or moving artifacts (e.g., cars, boats) (Dolgin & Behrend, 1984; R. Gelman, Spelke, & Meck, 1983; Hatano et al., 1993; Looft, 1974; Richards & Siegler, 1984; Sharp, Candy-Gibbs, Barlow-Elliot & Petrun, 1985). In contrast, moving natural kinds (e.g., clouds and rivers) elicit more animistic errors from young children (Carey, 1985; Laurendeau & Pinard, 1962; Smeets, 1973) and even from time-pressured adults and college biology professors (Goldberg & Thompson-Schill, 2009). Thus, it seems that animistic errors in life judgments partly reflect the animal-like properties (movement, natural kind status) that some non-living things may possess.

In addition to occasionally over-extending "alive" to animal-like non-living things, preschoolers are even more likely to under-extend "alive" by excluding non-animal living things (i.e., plants; Berzonsky, Miller, Woody-Ramsey, & Harris, 1987; Beveridge & Davies, 1983; Hatano et al., 1993; Opfer & Siegler, 2004). Preschoolers' errors about plants seem to have at least two causes. The first is that preschoolers are unaware of the animal-like, goal-directed movements that plants can engage in (e.g., growing toward sunlight; Opfer & Gelman, 2001). Thus, when preschoolers are taught that plants – like animals – can move in goal-directed ways, they immediately infer that plants – like animals – are living things, too (Opfer & Siegler, 2004). Another cause of preschoolers' errors seems to be ambiguity in the English words "alive" and "animal," which can mean more than just "living thing" and "human and non-human animals," respectively (e.g., the hills can be *alive* with the sound of music, but they can't be a *living thing* with the sound of music; Waxman & Medin, 2007). Preschoolers seem to interpret "alive" as referring to all and only animals (including people), and "animal" as ambiguous between including and excluding people. Consistent with this idea, preschoolers make fewer errors about plant life both when "living thing" is used instead of "alive" (Leddon, Waxman, & Medin, 2008) and when queried in languages (such as Indonesian) that use "animal" only to refer to non-human animals (Anggoro, Waxman, & Medin, 2008). Importantly, both causes of children's errors about the life status of plants share an important property – they each reflect a mapping of the concept alive onto the animacy concept, though in different ways.

Death. Although at first it might seem that concepts of death should reflect the same knowledge as concepts of life (i.e., those entities that can die are precisely the same as those entities that are alive), death concepts in fact warrant separate investigation. First, children are not wholly consistent, at times reporting different responses for what is alive and what can die (e.g., Berzonsky, 1987; Keil, 1979). Second, children could accurately report which entities live and die, without understanding the necessity and permanence of death (Slaughter et al., 1999). For present purposes, of interest is when children grasp that all animals can (and eventually must) die, whereas inanimate objects – with the exception of plants – do not.

Nguyen and Gelman (2000) presented 4-year-olds, 6-year-olds, and adults with displays of pictures of various plants, animals, and artifacts, and asked them to point to which of these would "have to die later on" and "stay dead after they die." Even

4-year-olds maintained a firm distinction between living and non-living things, with over 90% accuracy in reporting that artifacts do not undergo death. Similar results have been obtained in many cross-cultural studies (Barrett & Behne, 2005; Inagaki and Hatano, 1996; Hatano et al., 1993). Although clearly children's understanding of death undergoes considerable modifications over time (e.g., Slaughter et al., 1999), the animate–inanimate distinction appears to provide a fundamental basis for judgments of which things can die.

Autonomous motion. Although movement was one of the features that Piaget proposed children relied on *erroneously* (for example, treating clouds as alive), others have suggested that certain qualities of movement (such as autonomous movement) might be appropriately diagnostic of whether an entity is animate or inanimate. We have discussed some of this work in the infancy portion of the chapter, above. Here we focus on research with older children.

One especially clear-cut demonstration that the animate–inanimate distinction is linked to the presence or absence of autonomous motion comes from an elegant study by Massey and Gelman (1988). Three- and 4-year-olds were shown photographs of unfamiliar objects, and were asked whether or not each could move itself up and down a hill. There were a variety of items, including atypical animals (e.g., insects), complex artifacts, and statues with animal-like forms and parts. The children responded accurately in most cases, honoring the animate–inanimate distinction even with machines and statues. It is particularly noteworthy that children's excellent performance here was with *unfamiliar* items that in some cases were perceptually atypical (e.g., praying mantis, echidna, figurine). Thus, preschool children appropriately recognize that animates are capable of self-generated movement, in a way that inanimates are not.

Interestingly, autonomous movement alone may not be as diagnostic as *goal-directed movement* (Opfer, 2002). Goal-directed movement is a type of autonomous movement in which the agent contingently moves toward another object, state, or location (i.e., the agent's goal). Examples include an animal pursuing prey, or a plant growing toward the sun. Opfer (2002) found that children 5–10 years of age and adults use goal-directed movement to identify novel entities as living things. In one condition, the goal-directed movement condition, 4-, 5-, 7-, and 10-year-olds and adults viewed a set of unfamiliar, rather shapeless entities ("blobs") moving toward a goal. By 5 years of age, participants tended to attribute life, biological properties, and psychological capacities to these blobs. In contrast, in a control condition, participants viewed the same blobs moving identically, but without the presence of a goal. In this condition, no age group was likely to attribute life, biological properties, or psychological capacities to the blobs. Additionally, when asked what the blobs actually were, participants 5 years of age and older were more like to identify them as animals (such as a bug or a jellyfish) in the goal-directed movement condition than in the control condition (in which the blobs were more often identified as clouds, lava, or meteors). Like the identification of animacy with capacity for death, the identification of animacy with goal-directedness also appears to be cross-culturally uniform, apparent in young Americans, Germans, and Amazonian indigene (Shahar) (Barrett, Todd, Miller, & Blythe, 2005).

Biology-specific processes. Processes such as growth, metamorphosis, healing, reproduction, inheritance, illness, and contagion are specific to living things (see also Keil, 1994, pp. 236–237, for a list of some distinctive properties of living things). For example, animals predictably undergo increased size and complexity during maturation, but inanimate objects fail to undergo any analogous metamorphoses. At what age do children realize the domain-specificity of these processes? The answer, according to much research evidence, is that children grasp these distinctions by 4 years of age, at least with regard to prototypical living and prototypical non-living things.

Four-year-olds understand that an individual animal can change shape, color, and size over the course of growth, yet still keep the name and identity of its parents (Bulloch & Opfer, 2009; Opfer & Bulloch, 2007; Rosengren, Gelman, Kalish, & McCormick, 1991). In contrast, artifacts do not experience such predictable changes (Rosengren et al., 1991). Four- to 6-year-olds recognize that plants and animals grow whereas artifacts do not (Inagaki & Hatano, 1996). Preschoolers recognize that growth itself comes about due to natural processes (such as sunshine and rain), and not due to artificial processes (such as human activities) (Hickling & Gelman, 1995). Springer and Keil (1991) found that children 4–7 years of age preferred natural mechanisms for color inheritance in biological kinds, versus human intentions in producing the color of an artifact. They recognize that living things (both plants and animals) are capable of healing, whereas artifacts are not (Backscheider, Shatz, & Gelman, 1993). Thus, for example, a scratch on someone's hand will spontaneously heal, whereas a scratch on a table will not. They recognize that a range of biological properties apply to animals but not inanimate objects (Gutheil, Vera, & Keil, 1998). Interestingly, at least some of this knowledge seems to be derived from general expectations rather than specific facts, so that children for example have a general expectation that animals and artifacts will have different insides, before learning the particulars of how in fact their insides differ (Simons & Keil, 1995).

Causal explanations. Schult and Wellman (1997) and Wellman, Hickling, & Schult (1997) make the important point that when considering conceptual domains, modes of explanation are as central as type of entity, because the same entity can be construed from multiple perspectives. For example, a person can be understood as a physical object (e.g., subject to the forces of gravity), as a biological object (e.g., capable of life and death), and as a psychological object (e.g., possessing intentions, desires). With respect to the animate–inanimate distinction, the relevant point is that children need to distinguish not just between types of entities (animals vs. non-animals), but also between types of explanations (biological vs. non-biological). Furthermore, they need to learn that types of entities constrain the types of explanations (so that, for example, biological explanations cannot pertain to artifacts, whereas physics can pertain to animals; see also Gutheil, Vera, & Keil, 1998; Saxe, Tzelnic, & Carey, 2006).

As mentioned in an earlier section of this chapter, S. A. Gelman and Gottfried (1996) found that preschoolers provide different causal explanations for animate versus inanimate movement. Four-year-old children viewed brief videotapes in which unfamiliar animals and objects were moving, either autonomously or by means of a visible human agent. In several respects, children's causal explanations differed for the animals versus the inanimate objects. For the inanimates in the external-agent condition, children were much more likely to attribute the cause of motion to a person than to anything inside. With animals, however, the pattern was reversed. Children in the external-agent condition regularly denied that a person made the animals move. This result is striking, given that the animal was carried and that the human agent's hand was visible throughout the event. Instead, over 90% of the children in each condition claimed that the animals moved by themselves. For inanimates, only children in the autonomous-motion condition said the objects moved by themselves. The absence of an external agent led them to endorse an immanent cause. Interestingly, children maintain appropriate distinctions even when considering boundary cases, such as robots or computers (Jipson & Gelman, 2007; Koziol & Klahr, 2000; Van Duuren & Scaife, 1996).

Studies of natural language reveal similar domain distinctions in even younger children. Hickling and Wellman (2001) conducted a natural-language study, in which they examined the causal explanations that 2-, 3-, and 4-year-old children spontaneously produce, when discussing entities of different types. Importantly, they found that young children honor a clear distinction between living and non-living things, rarely using biological or psychological explanations in reference to inanimate objects. This was true even of the youngest age group (2-year-olds).

Summary

We propose that there is a potent animate–inanimate distinction by preschool age that serves readily as the center of a vast cluster of conceptual distinctions. There is a core distinction that is the seed of a naïve theory of biology. At the same time, it undergoes much change, including refinement (what is the scope of the distinction?), causal understanding (from framework to mechanistic; e.g., Au & Romo, 1999; Morris et al., 2000), and specificity (Simons & Keil, 1995).

How Does an Animacy Distinction Inform Other Aspects of Cognitive Development?

As noted earlier, animacy is an *ontological* distinction (Keil, 1979). Accordingly, we should expect the animate–inanimate distinction to have ramifications for other aspects of cognitive and linguistic development. There are potentially numerous such implications, for topics that include: categorization (Barrett, Abdi, Murphy, & Gallagher, 1993; Diesendruck & Gelman, 1999; Freeman & Sera, 1996; Keil, 1995), meta-linguistic judgments (Schwartz, 1980), metaphor (Gottfried, 1997), homonyms (Backscheider & Gelman, 1995), myth-making (Kelly & Keil, 1985), syntax (Croft, 1990; Lempert, 1989), theory of mind (Lillard, Zeljo, Curenton, & Kaugars, 2000), and physical reasoning (Heyman, Phillips, & Gelman, 2000). Below we focus briefly on just two areas of influence that have received sustained attention in the literature: word meanings and essentialist reasoning.

Animacy as constraint on word meanings

Not only are children *sensitive* to an animate–inanimate distinction, the distinction also guides children's word meanings and classifications. We cite just a few examples here. By 9 months old, infants sort together different basic-level animal categories (e.g., dogs and fish) and separate birds-with-outspread-wings from airplanes (Mandler & McDonough, 1993). By 2.5 months old, toddlers expect nouns to refer to animates when interpreting sentences describing events involving unfamiliar agents and patients (Childers & Echols, 2004). By 4 years old, children treat plants and animals as alike with respect to certain properties of growth and healing, despite the extreme differences in shape between, say, a cow and a tree (Backscheider et al., 1993; Hickling & Gelman, 1995). Conversely, children treat humans and apes as belonging to distinctly different categories, despite their greater similarity (as noted earlier; Coley, 1995; Johnson et al., 1992). Preschool children also overlook similarity in shape when making predictions about how statues versus live animals will move (Massey & Gelman, 1988). By age 7, children can sort objects into superordinate categories in ways that require overlooking shape (e.g., classifying a snake with other animals, or a sailboat with wheeled vehicles) (Sigel, 1953).

Nonetheless, the notion that words honor the ontological distinction between animate and inanimate has been called into question by studies suggesting that *shape* is a crucial component of children's semantic representations. On this view, children have a general shape bias in their interpretations of novel count nouns, such that a new word (e.g., "a dax") is assumed to refer to a set of objects that share a common shape (Imai, Gentner, & Uchida, 1994; Landau, Jones, & Smith, 1988, 1992). One interpretation of the bias is that ontological status is irrelevant, at least in naming and perhaps in conceptualization (e.g., toy bears and real bears are both "bears" because they have a common shape; Jones & Smith, 1993). In favor of this position, many studies indicate that shape is an important and salient feature for children, particularly in word-learning contexts (Baldwin, 1992; Samuelson & Smith, 2005).

However, a closer look at the evidence suggests that children attend to shape not because it is the basis on which words are extended, but rather because it is an indirect indicator of category membership; it correlates with and "is often … a good source of information about" what kind of thing an object is (Soja, Carey, & Spelke, 1992; see also Cimpian & Markman, 2005; S. A. Gelman & Diesendruck, 1999, but see Smith & Samuelson, 2006, for debate).

When shape is disentangled from taxonomic relatedness, we find that even 2-year-olds show no tendency to use shape more than taxonomic kind (S. A. Gelman, Croft, Fu, Clausner, & Gottfried, 1998). For example, when shape is crossed with animacy (i.e., children were asked whether the word "dog" applied to inanimate items of the same shape [e.g., dog-shaped chair], and animate distractors differing in shape [e.g,. chicken]), children are typically correct in comprehension. Moreover, when they did err, they typically over-extended to items that matched the target word in both shape *and* taxonomic relatedness (e.g., "dog" was more often extended to a cow [same kind and same shape] than to a chicken [same kind only] or a dog-shaped chair [same shape only]). Likewise, when learning words for novel items, children favor ontological information over shape (Booth & Waxman, 2005, 2008), and favor intended function over shape (Diesendruck, Markson, & Bloom, 2003).

To summarize, animacy is a powerful factor in children's naming and classification. Shape, although argued to be a strong contender, is not the sole or even primary factor. On tasks that provide information only about perceptual dimensions (e.g., sorting of simple, novel artifacts that vary only in shape, texture, and color), shape is an especially salient dimension. However, its salience derives largely from its value as an index or predictor of other information (Medin, 1989; Soja et al., 1992; Waxman & Braig, 1996). When ontological knowledge (including information about animacy) and theoretical beliefs are available, and when they conflict with shape, children often sort and name on the basis of these other factors.

Animacy and essentialist reasoning

Our last example comes from children's "essentialist" reasoning (also known as "psychological essentialism"). Essentialism is the view that categories have an underlying reality or true nature that one cannot observe directly but that gives an object its identity (S. A. Gelman, 2003; Locke, 1671/1959; Schwartz, 1977). In other words, according to essentialism, categories are real, in several senses: they are discovered (vs. invented), they are natural (vs. artificial), they predict other properties, and they point to natural discontinuities in the world. Essentialism requires no specialized knowledge, and people may possess an "essence placeholder" without knowing what the essence is (Medin, 1989). For example, a child might believe that girls have some inner, non-obvious quality that distinguishes them from boys and that is responsible for the many observable differences in appearance and behavior between boys and girls, before ever learning about chromosomes or human physiology.

Animacy appears to be particularly relevant, in that children assert essentialism almost exclusively in the domain of animals. One powerful example can be found in children's reasoning about identity across transformations (Keil, 1989). For even preschoolers, on some tasks, identity can change from one animal kind to another, but not from an animal kind to an inanimate kind (e.g., porcupine to cactus). For older children, identity can change from one artifact kind to another, but not from one animal kind to another. In this sense, animals are construed in essentialist terms, whereas artifacts are not.

Another indication comes from children's inductive inferences. Children draw a richer array of inferences from animals than from artifacts (S. A. Gelman, 1988). Heyman and Gelman (2000) found that category-based inferences differ for animate versus inanimate entities, even when controlling for outward appearances of the entities. In a procedure adapted from S. A. Gelman and Markman (1986), 4-year-old participants saw line drawings of three different faces that were described as depicting either children or dolls. Participants were asked to predict whether one of the children/dolls would share properties with a child/doll who has the same novel predicate (e.g. "is zav," which is never defined for participants) but is dissimilar in appearance, or with a child/doll who has a different novel predicate but is similar in appearance. Participants tended to use the novel predicates rather than superficial resemblance to guide their inferences about people. In contrast, when the line drawings were described as depicting dolls rather than children, participants showed no such emphasis on the novel predicate information. The results suggest that children have a general assumption that unfamiliar words hold rich inductive potential when applied to people, but not when applied to dolls.

In addition to inductive inferences, category-wide generalizations in language (generics) are also more frequent for animates than inanimates. For example, mothers are more likely to say something general about squirrels (e.g., "They like to eat nuts") than something general about shoes (S. A. Gelman, Coley, Rosengren, Hartman, & Pappas, 1998; S. A. Gelman, Goetz, Sarnecka, & Flukes, 2008), and this is true for both English- and Chinese-speaking mothers (S. A. Gelman & Tardif, 1998). Evidence suggests that children likewise honor the animate–inanimate distinction by 2 or 3 years of age (S. A. Gelman et al., 2008), and preschoolers are more likely to use generics when talking about novel animals than novel artifacts (Brandone & Gelman, 2009).

Summary and Conclusions

Developmental data suggest that the animate–inanimate distinction is fundamental, in the sense that it emerges early in infancy, robustly, and on a variety of tasks. Indeed, the early point at which the distinction develops contradicts traditional Piagetian analyses of animism, and suggests instead that the animate–inanimate distinction may be a "skeletal principle" (in R. Gelman's [1990] terms) that organizes children's experience from quite early on. This notion of "skeletal principles" seems to be instantiated biologically in neural mechanisms, such as the fusiform face area and posterior superior temporal sulcus, that are specialized for perceiving animates and representing them in higher cognition (e.g., in judging life status and comprehending sentences). What remains an open issue is the extent to which these mechanisms for representing animates are domain-specific and dependent on (presumably universal) experience with faces, biological motion, etc.

What is the basis of the distinction, at different ages? That is, what cues are used to determine whether an entity is animate or inanimate? Against radical restructuring theories such as Piaget's, we reviewed evidence that both featural properties (e.g., faces) and dynamic properties (e.g., autonomous motion, goal-directed action) are used from infancy onward, though no one cue appears to be conclusive. Interestingly, children appear to maintain a firm distinction even in the face of potentially ambiguous entities, such as computers and robots. As technology improves and robots become increasingly animal-like in appearance and capacities, it will be intriguing to examine if and/or how children interpret such entities.

References

Anggoro, F., Waxman, S., & Medin, D. (2008). Naming practices and the acquisition of key biological concepts: Evidence from English and Indonesian. *Psychological Science, 19*(4), 314–319.

Arterberry, M. E., & Bornstein, M. H. (2002). Variability and its sources in infant categorization. *Infant Behavior and Development, 25*, 515–528.

Aslin, R. N., Jusczyk, P. W., & Pisoni, D. B. (1998). Speech and auditory processing during infancy: Constraints on and precursors to language. In D. Kuhn & R. S. Siegler (Eds.), *Handbook of child psychology* (5th ed.): *Cognition, perception, and language* (pp. 147–198). New York: Wiley.

Atran, S. (1999). Itzaj Maya folkbiological taxonomy: Cognitive universals and cultural particulars. In D. L. Medin & S. Atran (Eds.), *Folkbiology* (pp. 119–213). Cambridge, MA: MIT Press.

Au, T. K., & Romo, L. F. (1999). Mechanical causality in children's "folkbiology." In D. L. Medin & S. Atran (Eds.), *Folkbiology* (pp. 119–213). Cambridge, MA: MIT Press.

Au, T., Romo, L., & DeWitt, J. (1999). Considering children's folkbiology in health education. In M. Siegal & C. C. Petersen (Eds.), *Children's Understanding of Biology and Health* (pp. 209–234). New York: Cambridge University Press.

Backscheider, A. G., & Gelman, S. A. (1995). Children's understanding of homonyms. *Journal of Child Language, 22*, 107–127.

Backsheider, A. G., Shatz, M., & Gelman, S. A. (1993). Preschoolers' ability to distinguish living kinds as a function of regrowth. *Child Development, 64*, 1242–1257.

Baldwin, D. A. (1992). Clarifying the role of shape in children's taxonomic assumption. *Journal of Experimental Child Psychology, 54*, 392–416.

Bargh, J. A. (1990). Goal ≠ intent: Goal-directed thought and behavior are often unintentional. *Psychological Inquiry, 1*, 248–277.

Baron-Cohen, S. (1995). *Mindblindness: An essay on autism and theory of mind.* Cambridge, MA: MIT Press.

Barrett, H., & Behne, T. (2005). Children's understanding of death as the cessation of agency: A test using sleep versus death. *Cognition, 96*, 93–108.

Barrett, H., Todd, P., Miller, G., & Blythe, P. (2005). Accurate judgments of intention from motion cues alone: A cross-cultural study. *Evolution and Human Behavior, 26*(4), 313–331.

Barrett, S. E., Abdi, H., Murphy, G. L., & Gallagher, J. M. (1993). Theory-based correlations and their role in children's concepts. *Child Development, 64*, 1595–1616.

Bertenthal, B. I., Proffitt, D. R., & Cutting, J. E. (1984). Infant sensitivity to figural coherence in biomechanical motions. *Journal of Experimental Child Psychology, 37*, 213–230.

Berzonsky, M. D. (1987). A preliminary investigation of children's conceptions of life and death. *Merrill-Palmer Quarterly, 33*, 505–513.

Berzonsky, M. D., Miller, P. H., Woody-Ramsey, J., & Harris, Y. (1987). The relationship between judgments of animacy and sentiency: Another look. *Journal of Genetic Psychology, 149*, 223–238.

Beveridge, M., & Davies, M. (1983). A picture-sorting approach to child animism. *Genetic Psychology Monographs, 107*, 211–231.

Blakemore, S. J., & Decety, J. (2001). From the perception of action to the understanding of intention. *Nature Reviews Neuroscience, 2*, 561–567.

Blythe, P. W., Todd, P. M., & Miller, G. F. (1999). How motion reveals intention: Categorizing social interactions. In G. Gigerenzer, P. M. Todd, & the ABC Research Group (Eds.), *Simple heuristics that make us smart* (pp. 257–285). New York: Oxford University Press.

Booth, A. E., & Waxman, S. R. (2005). Conceptual knowledge permeates word learning in infancy. *Developmental Psychology, 41*, 491–505.

Booth, A. E. & Waxman, S. R. (2008). Taking stock as theories of word learning take shape. *Developmental Science, 11*, 185–194.

Brandone, A., & Gelman, S. (2009). Differences in preschoolers' and adults' use of generics about novel animals and artifacts: A window onto a conceptual divide. *Cognition, 110*, 1–22.

Brazelton, T. B., Koslowski, B., & Main, M. (1974). The origins of reciprocity: The early mother–infant interaction. In M. Lewis & L. Rosenblum (Eds.), *The effect of the infant on the caregiver.* New York: Wiley.

Bulloch, M. J., & Opfer, J. E. (2009). What makes relational reasoning smart? Revisiting the perceptual-to-relational shift in the development of generalization. *Developmental Science, 12,* 114–122.

Caramazza, A., & Shelton, J. R. (1998). Domain-specific knowledge systems in the brain: The animate–inanimate distinction. *Journal of Cognitive Neuroscience, 10,* 1–34.

Carey, S. (1985). *Conceptual change in childhood.* Cambridge, MA: MIT Press.

Carey, S. (1995). On the origins of causal understanding. In S. Sperber, D. Premack, & A. Premack (Eds.), *Causal cognition: A multi-disciplinary debate* (pp. 268–308). Cambridge: Oxford University Press.

Carey, S. (1999). Sources of conceptual change. In E. K. Scholnick, K. Nelson, S. A. Gelman, & P. H. Miller (Eds.), *Conceptual development: Piaget's legacy* (pp. 293–326). Mahwah, NJ: Erlbaum.

Carpenter, G. C., Tecce, J. J., Stechler, G., & Friedman, S. (1970). Differential visual behavior to human and humanoid faces in early infancy. *Merrill-Palmer Quarterly, 16,* 91–108.

Childers, J., & Echols, C. (2004). 2 1/2-year-old children use animacy and syntax to learn a new noun. *Infancy, 5,* 109–125.

Cicchino, J., & Rakison, D. (2008). Producing and processing self-propelled motion in infancy. *Developmental Psychology, 44,* 1232–1241.

Cimpian, A., & Markman, E. M. (2005). The absence of a shape bias in children's word learning. *Developmental Psychology, 41,* 1003–1019.

Coley, J. (1995). Emerging differentiation of folkbiology and folkpsychology: Attributions of biological and psychological properties to living things. *Child Development, 66,* 1856–1874.

Croft, W. (1990). *Typology and universals.* New York: Cambridge University Press.

Csibra, G., Gergely, G., Bíró, S., Koos, O., & Brockbank, M. (1999). Goal attribution without agency cues: The perception of "pure reason" in infancy. *Cognition, 72,* 237–267.

De Haan, M., & Nelson, C. (1999). Brain activity differentiates face and object processing in 6-month-old infants. *Developmental Psychology, 35,* 1113–1121.

Diesendruck, G. (2003). Categories for names or names for categories? The interplay between domain-specific conceptual structure and language. *Language and Cognitive Processes, 18,* 759–787.

Diesendruck, G., & Gelman, S. A. (1999). Domain differences in absolute judgments of category membership: Evidence for an essentialist account of categorization. *Psychonomic Bulletin and Review, 6,* 338–346.

Diesendruck, G., Markson, L., & Bloom, P. (2003). Children's reliance on the creator's intent in extending names for artifacts. *Psychological Science, 14,* 164–168.

Dolgin, K., & Behrend, D. A. (1984). Children's knowledge about animates and inanimates. *Child Development, 55,* 1546–1650.

Fantz, R. L., Fagan, J. F., III, & Miranda, S. B. (1975). Early visual selectivity as a function of pattern variables, previous exposure, age from birth and conception, and expected cognitive deficit. In L. B. Cohen & P. Salapatek (Eds.), *Infant perception: From sensation to cognition. Vol. 1. Basic visual processes* (pp. 249–345). New York: Academic Press.

Field, T. M. (1979). Visual and cardiac responses to animate and inanimate faces by young term and preterm infants. *Child Development, 50,* 188–194.

Field, T., Woodson, R., Greenberg, R., & Cohen, D. (1982). Discrimination and imitation of facial expressions by neonates. *Science, 218,* 179–181.

Fox, R., & McDaniel, C. (1982). The perception of biological motion by human infants. *Science, 218*, 486–487.

Freeman, K. E., & Sera, M. D. (1996). Reliance on visual and verbal information across ontological kinds: What do children know about animals and machines? *Cognitive Development, 11*, 315–341.

French, R., Mareschal, D., Mermillod, M., & Quinn, P. (2004). The role of bottom-up processing in perceptual categorization by 3- to 4-month-old infants: Simulations and data. *Journal of Experimental Psychology: General, 133* (3), 382–397.

Gelman, R. (1990). First principles organize attention to and learning about relevant data: Number and the animate–inanimate distinction as examples. *Cognitive Science, 14*, 79–106. New York: Oxford University Press.

Gelman, R., & Baillargeon, R. (1983). A review of some Piagetian concepts. In J. H. Flavell & E. M. Markman (Eds.), *Handbook of Child Psychology: Vol. 3. Cognitive development*. New York: Wiley.

Gelman, R., Durgin, F., & Kaufman, L. (1995). Distinguishing between animates and inanimates: Not by motion alone. In D. Sperber, D. Premack, & A. J. Premack (Eds.), *Causal cognition: A multidisciplinary debate* (pp. 150–184). Cambridge University Press.

Gelman, R., Spelke, E. S., & Meck, E. (1983). What preschoolers know about animate and inanimate objects. In D. Rogers & J. A. Sloboda (Eds.), *The acquisition of symbolic skills* (pp. 297–324). New York: Plenum.

Gelman, S. A. (1988). The development of induction within natural kind and artifact categories. *Cognitive Psychology, 20*, 65–95.

Gelman, S. A. (2003). *The essential child: Origins of essentialism in everyday thought.*

Gelman, S. A., Coley, J. D., Rosengren, K. S., Hartman, E., & Pappas, A. (1998). Beyond labeling: The role of maternal input in the acquisition of richly structured categories. *Monographs of the Society for Research in Child Development, 63* v. 148.

Gelman, S. A., Croft, W., Fu, P., Clausner, T., & Gottfried, G. (1998). Why is a pomegranate an apple? The role of shape, taxonomic relatedness, and prior lexical knowledge in children's overextensions of apple and dog. *Journal of Child Language, 25*, 267–291.

Gelman, S. A., & Diesendruck, G. (1999). A reconsideration of concepts: On the compatibility of psychological essentialism and context sensitivity. In E. K. Scholnick, K. Nelson, S. A. Gelman, & P. H. Miller (Eds.), *Conceptual development: Piaget's legacy* (pp. 79–102). Mahwah, NJ: Erlbaum.

Gelman, S. A., Goetz, P. J., Sarnecka, B. W., & Flukes, J. (2008). Generic language in parent–child conversations. *Language Learning and Development, 4*, 1–31.

Gelman, S. A., & Gottfried, G. (1996). Children's causal explanations of animate and inanimate motion. *Child Development, 67*, 1970–1987.

Gelman, S. A., & Markman, E. M. (1986). Categories and induction in young children. *Cognition, 23*, 183–209.

Gelman, S. A., & Tardif, T. Z. (1998). Generic noun phrases in English and Mandarin: An examination of child-directed speech. *Cognition, 66*, 215–248.

Gergely, G., Nadasdy, Z. Z., Csibra, G., & Bíró, S. (1995). Taking the intentional stance at 12 months of age. *Cognition, 56*, 165–193.

Gergely, G., & Watson, J. S. (1999). Early socio-emotional development: Contingency perception and the social-biofeedback model. In P. Rochat (Ed.), *Early social cognition: Understanding others in the first months of life* (pp. 101–136). Mahwah, NJ: Erlbaum.

Glenn, S. M., Cunningham, C. C., & Joyce, P. F. (1981). A study of auditory preferences in non-handicapped infants and infants with Down's Syndrome. *Child Development, 52*, 1303–1307.

Goldberg, R. F., & Thompson-Schill, S. L. (2009). Developmental "roots" in mature biological knowledge. *Psychological Science, 20*, 480–487.

Gopnik, A., & Wellman, H. M. (1994). The theory theory. In L. A. Hirschfeld & S. A. Gelman (Eds.), *Mapping the mind: Domain-specificity in cognition and culture* (pp. 257–293). New York: Cambridge University Press.

Goren, C. C., Sarty, M., & Wu, P. Y. K. (1975). Visual following and pattern discrimination of face-like stimuli by newborn infants. *Pediatrics, 56*, 544–549.

Gottfried, G. M. (1997). Comprehending compounds: Evidence for metaphoric skill? *Journal of Child Language, 24*, 163–186.

Grossman, E. D., & Blake, R. (2002). Brain areas active during visual perception of biological motion. *Neuron, 35*, 1167–1175.

Gutheil, G., Vera, A., & Keil, F. C. (1998). Do houseflies think? Patterns of induction and biological beliefs in development. *Cognition, 66*, 33–49.

Hatano, G., & Inagaki, K. (1994). Young children's naïve theory of biology. *Cognition, 50*, 171–188.

Hatano, G., Siegler, R. S., Richards, D. D., Inagaki, K., Stavy, R., & Wax, N. (1993). The development of biological knowledge: A multi-national study. *Cognitive Development, 8*, 47–62.

Heyman, G. D., & Gelman, S. A. (2000). Preschool children's use of trait labels to make inductive inferences. *Journal of Experimental Child Psychology, 77*, 1–19.

Heyman, G., Phillips, A. T., & Gelman, S. A. (2000). *Animacy effects on children's reasoning about physics.* Unpublished data, University of Michigan.

Hickling, A. K., & Gelman, S. A. (1995). How does your garden grow? Evidence of an early conception of plants as biological kinds. *Child Development, 66*, 856–876.

Hickling, A., & Wellman, H. (2001). The emergence of children's causal explanations and theories: Evidence from everyday conversation. *Developmental Psychology, 37*(5), 668–683.

Holland, V. M., & Rohrman, N. L. (1979). Distribution of the feature [+animate] in the lexicon of the child. *Journal of Psycholinguistic Research, 8*, 267–378.

Imai, M., Gentner, D., & Uchida, N. (1994). Children's theories of word meaning: The role of shape similarity in early acquisition. *Cognitive Development, 9*, 45–75.

Inagaki, K., & Hatano, G. (1987). Young children's spontaneous personification as analogy. *Child Development, 58*, 1013–1020.

Inagaki, K., & Hatano, G. (1993). Young children's understanding of the mind–body distinction. *Child Development, 64*, 1534–1549.

Inagaki, K., & Hatano, G. (1996). Young children's recognition of commonalities between animals and plants. *Child Development, 67*, 2823–2840.

Jipson, J. L., & Gelman, S. A. (2007). Robots and rodents: Children's inferences about living and non-living kinds. *Child Development, 78*, 1675–1688.

Johansson, G. (1973). Visual perception of biological motion and a model for its analysis. *Perception and Psychophysics, 14*, 201–211.

Johnson, K. E., Mervis, C. B., & Boster, J. S. (1992). Developmental changes within the structure of the mammal domain. *Developmental Psychology, 28*, 74–83.

Johnson, M. H., & Morton, J. (1991). *Biology and cognitive development: The case of face recognition.* Oxford: Blackwell.

Johnson, S. C., Slaughter, V., & Carey, S. (1998). Whose gaze will infants follow? The elicitation of gaze following in 12-month-olds. *Developmental Science, 1*, 233–238.

Jones, S. S., & Smith, L. B. (1993). The place of perception in children's concepts. *Cognitive Development, 8*, 113–139.

Keil, F. C. (1979). *Semantic and conceptual development: An ontological perspective.* Cambridge, MA: MIT Press.

Keil, F. C. (1989). *Concepts, kinds, and cognitive development.* Cambridge, MA: MIT Press.

Keil, F. C. (1994). The birth and nurturance of concepts by domains: The origins and concepts of living things. In L. Hirschfeld & S. A. Gelman (Eds.), *Mapping the mind: Domain specificity in cognition and culture* (pp. 234–254). New York: Cambridge University Press.

Keil, F. C. (1995). The growth of causal understandings of natural kinds. In S. Sperber, D. Premack, & A. Premack (Eds.), *Causal cognition: A multi-disciplinary debate* (pp. 234–262). Cambridge: Oxford University Press.

Kellogg, W. N., & Kellogg, L. A. (1933). *The ape and the child: A study of environmental influence upon early behavior.* New York: McGraw-Hill.

Kelly, M. H., & Keil, F. C. (1985). The more things change … : Metamorphoses and conceptual structure. *Cognitive Science, 9*, 403–416.

Klein, R. P., & Jennings, K. D. (1979). Responses to social and inanimate stimuli in early infancy. *Journal of Genetic Psychology, 135*, 3–9.

Koziol, M. K., & Klahr, D. (2000, August). *If robots make choices, are they alive? Children's judgments of the animacy of intelligent artifacts.* Poster session presented at the Proceedings of the Society for Cognitive Science, Philadelphia, PA.

Kuhlmeier, V., Wynn, K., & Bloom, P. (2003). Attribution of dispositional states by 12-month-olds. *Psychological Science, 14*, 402–408.

Kuperberg, G. R., Sitnikova, T., & Lakshmanan, B. M. (2008). Neuroanatomical distinctions within the semantic system during sentence comprehension: Evidence from functional magnetic resonance imaging. *NeuroImage, 40*, 367–388.

Landau, B., Smith, L. B., & Jones, S. S. (1988). The importance of shape in early lexical learning. *Cognitive Development, 3*, 299–321.

Landau, B., Smith, L. B., & Jones, S. S. (1992). Perception, ontology, and naming in young children: Commentary on Soja, Carey, and Spelke. *Cognition, 43*, 85–91.

Laurendeau, M., & Pinard, A. (1962). *Causal thinking in the child: A genetic and experimental approach.* New York: International Universities Press.

Leddon, E. M., Waxman, S. R., & Medin, D. L. (2008). Unmasking "alive": Children's appreciation of a concept linking all living things. *Journal of Cognition and Development, 9*, 461–473.

Legerstee, M. (1991). The role of person and object in eliciting early imitation. *Journal of Experimental Child Psychology, 51*, 423–433.

Legerstee, M. (1992). A review of the animate–inanimate distinction in infancy: Implications for models of social and cognitive knowing. *Early Development and Parenting, 1*, 59–67.

Legerstee, M., & Markova, G. (2008). Variations in 10-month-old infant imitation of people and things. *Infant Behavior and Development, 31*, 81–91.

Legerstee, M., Pomerleau, A., Malcuit, G., & Feider, H. (1987). The development of infants' responses to people and a doll: Implications for research in communication. *Infant Behavior and Development, 10*, 81–95.

Lempert, H. (1989). Animacy constraints on preschool children's acquisition of syntax. *Child Development, 60*, 237–245.

Lillard, A. S., Zeljo, A., Curenton, S., & Kaugars, A. S. (2000). Children's understanding of the animacy constraint on pretense. *Merrill-Palmer Quarterly, 46*, 21–44.

Locke, J. (1671/1959). *An essay concerning human understanding: Vol. 2.* New York: Dover.

Looft, W. R. (1974). Animistic thought in children: Understanding of "living" across its associated attributes. *Journal of Genetic Psychology, 124*, 235–240.

Mandler, J. M. (1992). How to build a baby: II. Conceptual primitives. *Psychological Review, 99*, 587–604.

Mandler, J. M. (2000). Perceptual and conceptual processes in infancy. *Journal of Cognition and Development, 1*, 3–36.

Mandler, J. M., Bauer, P. L., & McDonough, L. (1991). Separating the sheep from the goats: Differentiating global categories. *Cognitive Psychology, 23*, 263–298.

Mandler, J. M., & McDonough, L. (1993). Concept formation in infancy. *Cognitive Development, 8*, 291–318.

Marcus, G. F., & Keil, F. C. (2008). Concepts, correlations, and some challenges for connectionist cognition. *Behavioral and Brain Sciences, 31*, 722–723.

Markson, L., & Spelke, E. S. (2006). Infants' rapid learning about self-propelled objects. *Infancy, 9*, 45–71.

Marlier, L., Schaal, B., & Soussignan, R. (1998). Neonatal responsiveness to the odor of amniotic and lacteal fluids: A test of perinatal chemosensory continuity. *Child Development, 69*, 611–623.

Massey, C., & Gelman, R. (1988). Preschoolers decide whether pictured unfamiliar objects can move themselves. *Developmental Psychology, 24*, 307–317.

Maurer, D. (1985). Infants' perception of facedness. In T. N. Field & N. Fox (Eds.), *Social perception in infants* (pp. 73–100). Norwood, NJ: Ablex.

Medin, D. (1989). Concepts and conceptual structure. *American Psychologist, 44*, 1469–1481.

Meltzoff, A. N. (1995). Understanding the intention of others: re-enactment of intended acts by 18-month-old children. *Developmental Psychology, 31*, 838–850.

Meltzoff, A. N., & Moore, M. K., (1983). Newborn infants imitate adult facial gestures. *Child Development, 54*, 702–709.

Miller, J. L., & Bartsch, K. (1997). The development of biological explanation: Are children vitalists? *Developmental Psychology, 33*, 156–164.

Morris, S. C., Taplin, J. E., & Gelman, S. A. (2000). Vitalism in naïve biological thinking. *Developmental Psychology, 36*, 582–595.

Morton, J., & Johnson, M. H. (1991). CONSPEC and CONLERN: A two-process theory of infant face recognition. *Psychological Review, 98*, 164–181.

Nelson, C. A. (2001). The development and neural bases of face recognition. *Infant and Child Development, 10*, 3–18.

Nguyen, S., & Gelman, S. A. (2000). *Children's understanding of death: The case of plants.* Unpublished data, University of Illinois.

Opfer, J. E. (2002). Identifying living and sentient kinds from dynamic information: The case of goal-directed versus autonomous movement in conceptual change. *Cognition, 86*, 97–122.

Opfer, J. E., & Bulloch, M. J. (2007). Causal relations drive young children's induction, naming, and categorization. *Cognition, 105*, 206–217.

Opfer, J. E., & Doumas, L. (2008). Analogy and conceptual change in childhood. *Behavioral and Brain Sciences, 31*, 723.

Opfer, J. E., & Gelman, S. A. (1998). *Children's and adults' models of teleological action: From psychology- to biology-based models.* Paper presented at the Jean Piaget Society Conference, Chicago.

Opfer, J. E., & Gelman, S. A. (2001). Children's and adults' models for predicting teleological action: The development of a biology-based model. *Child Development, 72*, 1367–1381.

Opfer, J. E., & Siegler, R. S. (2004). Revisiting preschooler's living things concept: A microgenetic analysis of conceptual change in basic biology. *Cognitive Psychology, 49*, 30 –332.

Pelphrey, K., & Carter, E. (2008). Charting the typical and atypical development of the social brain. *Development and Psychopathology, 20*, 1081–1102.

Piaget, J. (1929/1951). *The child's conception of the world.* Savage, MD: Littlefield Adams.

Piaget, J. (1952). *The origins of intelligence in children.* New York: Norton.

Poulin-Dubois, D. (1999). Infants' distinction between animate and inanimate objects: The origins of naïve psychology. In P. Rochat (Ed.), *Early social cognition: Understanding others in the first months of life* (pp. 257–280). Mahwah, NJ: Erlbaum.

Poulin-Dubois, D., Lepage, A., & Ferland, D. (1996). Infants' concept of animacy. *Cognitive Development, 11*, 19–36.

Premack, D. (1990). The infant's theory of self-propelled objects. *Cognition, 36*, 1–16.

Premack, D., & Premack, A. J. (1997). Infants attribute value ± to the goal-directed actions of self-propelled objects. *Journal of Cognitive Neuroscience, 9*, 848–856.

Rakison, D. (2004). Infants' sensitivity to correlations between static and dynamic features in a category context. *Journal of Experimental Child Psychology, 89*(1), 1–30.

Rakison, D. H., & Butterworth, G. E. (1998). Infants' use of object parts in early categorization. *Developmental Psychology, 34*, 49–62.

Rakison, D. H., Cicchino, J., & Hahn, E. (2007). Infants' knowledge of the path that animals take to reach a goal. *British Journal of Developmental Psychology, 25*, 461–470.

Rakison, D. H., & Lupyan, G. (2008). Developing object concepts in infancy: An associative learning perspective. *Monographs of the Society for Research in Child Development, 73*, 1–29.

Rakison, D. H., & Poulin-Dubois, D. (2001). The developmental origin of the animate–inanimate distinction. *Psychological Bulletin, 127*, 209–228.

Reid, V. M., Hoehl, S., & Striano, T. (2006). The perception of biological motion by infants: An event-related potential study. *Neuroscience Letters, 395*, 211–214.

Richards, D. D., & Siegler, R. S. (1984). The effects of task requirements on children's life judgments. *Child Development, 55*, 1687–1696.

Richards, D. D., & Siegler, R. S. (1986). Children's understandings of the attributes of life. *Journal of Experimental Child Psychology, 42*(1), 1–22.

Rogers, T., & McClelland, J. L. (2008). Précis of semantic cognition: A parallel distributed processing approach. *Behavioral and Brain Sciences, 31*, 689–749.

Rosengren, K. S., Gelman, S. A., Kalish, C. W., & McCormick, M. (1991). As time goes by: Children's early understanding of growth in animals. *Child Development, 62*, 1302–1320.

Russell, M. J. (1976). Human olfactory communication. *Nature, 260*, 520–522.

Sacks, O. (1985). *The man who mistook his wife for a hat and other clinical tales.* New York: Summit.

Samuelson, L. K., & Smith, L. B. (2005). They call it like they see it: Spontaneous naming and attention to shape. *Developmental Science, 8*, 182–198.

Saxe, R. (2004). A region of right posterior superior temporal sulcus responds to observed intentional actions. *Neuropsychologia, 42*(11), 1435–1446.

Saxe, R., Tzelnic, T., & Carey, S. (2006). Five-month-old infants know humans are solid, like inanimate objects. *Cognition, 101*(1), 1–8.

Scherf, K., Behrmann, M., Humphreys, K., & Luna, B. (2007). Visual category-selectivity for faces, places and objects emerges along different developmental trajectories. *Developmental Science, 10*(4), F15–F30.

Schult, C. A., & Wellman, H. M. (1997). Explaining human movements and actions. *Cognition, 62*, 291–324.

Schultz, J., Friston, K., O'Doherty, J., Wolpert, D., & Frith, C. (2005). Activation in posterior superior temporal sulcus parallels parameter inducing the percept of animacy. *Neuron, 45*(4), 625–635.

Schwartz, R. G. (1980). Presuppositions and children's metalinguistic judgments: Concepts of life and the awareness of animacy restrictions. *Child Development, 51*, 364–371.

Schwartz, S. P. (Ed.) (1977). *Naming, necessity, and natural kinds.* Ithaca, NY: Cornell University Press.

Sharp, K. C., Candy-Gibbs, S., Barlow-Elliot, L., & Petrun, C. J. (1985). Children's judgment and reasoning about aliveness: Effects of object, age, and cultural/social background. *Merrill-Palmer Quarterly, 31*, 47–65.

Siegal, M., & Peterson, C. (1999). *Children's understanding of biology and health*. Cambridge: Cambridge University Press.

Sigel, I. E. (1953). Developmental trends in the abstraction ability of children. *Child Development, 24*, 131–144.

Simion, F., Regolin, L., & Bulf, H. (2008). A predisposition for biological motion in the newborn baby. *Proceedings of the National Academy of Science, 105*, 809–813.

Simons, D. J., & Keil, F. C. (1995). An abstract to concrete shift in the development of biological thought: the "insides" story. *Cognition, 56*, 129–163.

Slaughter, V., Jaakkola, K., & Carey, S. (1999). Constructing a coherent theory: Children's biological understanding of life and death. In M. Siegal & C. Petersen (Eds.), *Children's understanding of biology and health*. Cambridge: Cambridge University Press.

Smeets, P. M. (1973). The animism controversy revisited: A probability analysis. *Journal of Genetic Psychology, 123*, 219–225.

Smith, L. B., & Heise, D. (1992). Perceptual similarity and conceptual structure. In B. Burns (Ed.), *Percepts, concepts, and categories* (pp. 233–271). Amsterdam: Elsevier.

Smith, L. B., & Samuelson, L. K. (2006). The shape bias: Different questions, fundamentally different answers: Reply to Cimpian & Markman (2005) and Booth, Waxman, & Huang (2005). *Developmental Psychology, 42*, 1339–1343.

Soja, N. N., Carey, S., & Spelke, E. S. (1992). Perception, ontology, and word meaning, *Cognition, 45*, 101–107.

Solomon, G. E. A., & Cassimatis, N. L. (1999). On facts and conceptual systems: Young children's integration of their understanding of germs and contagion. *Developmental Psychology, 35*, 113–126.

Spelke, E., Phillips, A., & Woodward, A. (1995). Infants' knowledge of object motion and human action. In D. Sperber, D. Premack, & A. J. Premack (Eds.), *Causal cognition: A multidisciplinary debate* (pp. 44–78). New York: Clarendon Press.

Springer, K. (1999). How a naive theory of biology is acquired. In M. Siegal & C. Petersen (Eds.), *Children's understanding of biology and health*. Cambridge: Cambridge University Press.

Springer, K., & Keil, F. C. (1991). Early differentiation of causal mechanisms appropriate to biological and nonbiological kinds. *Child Development, 62*, 767–781.

Suied, C., Viaud-Delmon, I., & Burr, D. (2009). Auditory-visual object recognition time suggests specific processing for animal sounds. *PLoS ONE, 4*(4), e5256.

Trevarthen, C. (1977). Descriptive analysis of infant communication behavior. In H. R. Schaffer (Ed.), *Studies on mother–infant interaction*. New York: Academic Press.

Van De Walle, G. A. (1997). *Perceptual foundations of categorization in infancy: The animal/vehicle distinction*. Unpublished doctoral dissertation, Cornell University.

Van Duuren, M., & Scaife, M. (1996). "Because a robot's brain hasn't got a brain, it just controls itself": Children's attributions of brain related behaviour to intelligent artifacts. *European Journal of Psychology of Education, 11*, 365–376.

Watson, J. S. (1972). Smiling, cooing, and "the game." *Merrill-Palmer Quarterly, 18*, 323–339.

Watson, J. S., & Ramey, C. T. (1972). Reactions to response-contingent stimulation in early infancy. *Merrill-Palmer Quarterly, 18*, 219–227.

Waxman, S. R., & Braig, B. (1996). *Stars and starfish: How far can shape take us?* Paper presented at the Tenth Biennial International Conference on Infant Studies, Providence, RI.

Waxman, S. R., & Medin, D. (2007). Experience and cultural models matter: Placing firm limits on childhood anthropocentrism. *Human Development, 50*, 23–30.

Wellman, H. M., & Gelman, S. A. (1998). Knowledge acquisition in foundational domains. In D. Kuhn & R. S. Siegler (Eds.), *Handbook of Child Psychology: Vol. 2* (5th ed.) (pp. 523–573). New York: Wiley.

Wellman, H. M., Hickling, A., & Schult, C. A. (1997). Young children's psychological, physical, and biological explanations. In H. M. Wellman & K. Inagaki (Eds.), *The emergence of core domains of thought* (pp. 7–25). San Francisco: Jossey-Bass.

Woodward, A. (1998). Infants selectively encode the goal object of an actor's reach. *Cognition, 69*, 1–34.

Woodward, A., & Needham, A. (2007). *Learning and the infant mind.* New York: Oxford University Press.

Wyk, B., Hudac, C., Carter, E., Sobel, D., & Pelphrey (2009). Action understanding in the superior temporal sulcus region. *Psychological Science, 20*(6), 771–777.

CHAPTER NINE

Language Development

Michael Tomasello

Human communication works in an utterly unique way. Other primates gesture and vocalize mostly selfishly, to get others to do what they want them to, but humans communicate cooperatively, to inform others of things helpfully and to share gossip with them freely (Tomasello, 2008). Human languages – there are approximately 6000 of them today – are sets of linguistic conventions for engaging in this kind of cooperative communication in especially powerful ways. And linguistic conventions add an extra dimension of cooperation to the process, in the sense that they are social "agreements" that all speakers of a particular language share in common, and know that they share in common, due to a shared history of learning and enculturation in the linguistic community. Other primate species mostly do not learn their communicative behaviors at all, and they certainly do not operate with communicative conventions.

Most of the learning involved in becoming a competent speaker of a language takes place during early childhood. But the way is prepared by various forms of prelinguistic communication that children employ beginning in the last few months of their first year of life. Most importantly, human infants at around 10–12 months of age begin engaging in cooperative communication by means of the pointing gesture. They not only point to request things, but they also point to share interest with others (*Look at that!*) and to inform others of things that might be useful to them (*There's the thing you are looking for.*). These forms of communication rely on infants' social-cognitive ability to direct the attention of others, and to understand the attention-directing intentions of others, so as to attend jointly to things with them. And then the infant must make inferences, or spur others to make inferences, about why they want joint attention to that entity in the first place; for example, they want the adult to fetch it for them or to be informed of its location (Bruner, 1983). These kinds of social-cognitive abilities are foundational to all forms of human communication, prelinguistic and linguistic, and are called by Tomasello (2003) skills of intention-reading.

This chapter is about how young children – who already have some sophisticated social-cognitive skills and can communicate cooperatively through gestures – acquire skills with a conventional language. The story begins at about 1 year of age, as infants make their first nascent attempts to produce the language they hear being used around them so that they can communicate more effectively with others. Within a few years they have built up a repertoire of many thousands, probably tens of thousands, of linguistic items, including small items like words and grammatical morphemes (e.g., the plural *-s*) as well as larger items like whole linguistic schemas and constructions.

Theory

The central theoretical issue in the study of language acquisition is whether and in what ways children are biologically prepared for the process. On the one hand are theories based mainly in adult formal linguistics, especially the approach pioneered by Chomsky (e.g., 1980). These theories emphasize the unique aspects of linguistic structures, as opposed to other types of cognitive structures, and so hypothesize that general-purpose cognitive skills and learning mechanisms are not sufficient for language acquisition. They also emphasize the gap between the language children hear and the abstract linguistic knowledge they seem to possess – again suggesting that normal processes of cognition and learning are not sufficient (e.g., Crain & Pietroski, 2001). The proposal is thus that children are born already possessing some type of innate universal grammar that structures and constrains language development (Roeper, 2007).

In contrast are theories based mainly in childhood cognitive development, sometimes called usage-based theories, or constructivist theories. These theories claim that children acquire competence with a language mainly through cultural learning and other general cognitive processes such as categorization and analogy (Tomasello, 2003; Goldberg, 2006). In usage-based theories, children are biologically prepared for language acquisition, but only in general ways. For example, humans have biologically evolved capacities for engaging in joint attention, for engaging in cooperative behavior and communication, for creating and using communicative conventions, for culturally learning things from others, for sequential learning, for generalizing over learned items to create more abstract categories and schemas, for processing vocal-auditory information in species-unique ways, and maybe others. But in this approach, there is no biologically evolved universal grammar. The abstract structures of language emerge from language use through the linguistic interaction of all the people in a linguistic community over historical time (e.g., through processes of grammaticalization; Heine & Kuteva, 2007) in combination with processes of child language acquisition.

The central fact facing all theories of language acquisition is that developing children do not encounter already created linguistic categories or constructions or other kinds of abstractions, but only individual utterances produced by individual speakers on particular occasions. To become productive and creative with the conventions of a language, therefore, children must, in a sense, reconstruct the linguistic abstractions of their speech community for themselves. They do this, in usage-based theories, using the general cognitive processes of categorization, analogy, schema formation, and distributional learning – what Tomasello (2003) calls cognitive skills of pattern-finding (to complement their skills of intention-reading, noted above).

Utterances and Words

It is widely thought that children begin language development by learning words. This has some truth to it, but it is also misleading. The fact is that the most basic unit of linguistic experience, and the one with which children begin, is not the word but the utterance. An utterance is the smallest unit in which a person expresses a complete communicative intention – that is, an intention that another person attend to something with them and so do something as a result – and it thus corresponds to prelinguistic communicative acts such as pointing. Like an act of pointing, an utterance is used both to direct a recipient's attention to something referentially, and also to express a communicative motive (imperative, declarative, informative, etc.), typically through some form of emotional expression in the face and/or voice. When the child either comprehends or produces an utterance such as *Birdie!* (to point it out) or *Give!* (to request this action), she understands a full communicative act, comprising both reference and motive – even though the form is simply a single adult word expressed with a certain intonation.

When an adult speaks to her, what the child is attempting to do most urgently is to comprehend the overall communicative intention behind the utterance: What does the adult intend for me to attend to and to do in this situation? At the same time, she is also attempting to determine the communicative function of particular constituents within the utterance. This is a kind of "blame assignment" procedure in which the child attempts to determine the functional role of a constituent in the utterance as a whole. This requires that the child determine, to some degree of specificity, the communicative intention of the whole utterance; one cannot determine a sub-function without knowing something about the overall function. Presumably, particular utterance constituents such as words are most easily identified – and emerge as independent units – when the same phonological form appears in different utterances over time with some functional consistency. Thus, if the child hears *There's the ball, Gimme my ball, The ball's rolling, The ball's bouncing, I want a ball, Throw the ball, That ball's Jeffery's, Where's your ball?* etc., the word *ball* comes to exist as a potential utterance constituent for future use when the child needs to indicate one of a certain class of objects as one sub-function of an utterance. One thing that facilitates this process is if the adult stresses the key word, as an indication of its referential newness, and its associated referent is indeed new to the situation (Grassman & Tomasello, 2007).

As a non-linguistic example, a child may see an adult use a stapler and understand that his goal is to staple together two pieces of paper. In some cases, the child may understand also that the sub-goal/function of placing the papers inside the stapler's jaws is to align them with the stapling mechanism inside the stapler, and that the sub-function of pressing down on the stapler is to eject the staple through the two papers – with both of these sub-functions being in the service of the overall goal of attaching the two sheets of paper. The child does not need to understand all of this to mimic an adult stapling papers with the same stapler over and over again (analogy: a child can say *There-ya-go* over and over again without understanding its internal constituents). But to the extent that the child does not understand these sub-functions, she will be lost when she encounters some new stapler in which the sub-functions are effected by a different means, for example, one whose stapling mechanism does not require pressing down but rather squeezing. Only to the extent that the child understands the relevant sub-functions, will she be able to adapt to new situations creatively by, for example, adjusting her behavior to effect the same outcome with the new stapling mechanism. In the same way, the child may hear an adult say *I stapled your papers* and comprehend not only the utterance and its overall communicative intention, but also, for example, the words *I* and *stapled* and their communicative sub-functions in the utterance (the contributions they are making to the utterance as a whole), along with the phrase *your papers* and its communicative sub-function in the utterance (and the sub-sub-functions of *your* and *papers*). As in the case of the stapler, it is only if the child performs some kind of blame assignment that she will be able to comprehend the constituent linguistic elements in a deep enough way to enable her in the future to use them creatively in novel utterances (Tomasello, 2003).

This is the way children learn words. That is, children do not try to learn words directly; they try to comprehend utterances and in doing so they often must comprehend a word in the sense of determining the functional role it is playing in the utterance – and they see commonalities in this functional role across utterances. This is true despite the fact that the process is sometimes obscured in Western middle-class culture because parents and children often establish highly frequent utterance schemas for naming objects (e.g., *That's a* ___; *It's a* ___; *Here's the* ___; etc.). Children understand quite well the overall function of these utterances as well as the function of the open slot, with the new word in the slot always serving to name the new object in the situation. This gives the impression that what children are doing is mapping a single word onto a single object or action, or concept thereof, as in most theories of word learning (e.g., Bloom, 2000; Markman, 1989). But if "mapping" means simply associative learning, this is clearly not how things work. Children are attempting to understand how the adult is using an utterance (and its constituents as sub-elements) to direct their attention. The process is not one of association or mapping but of intention-reading and blame assignment.

We may use children's learning of new words in an experiment as an example. Akhtar and Tomasello (1996) had an adult set up a joint attentional game with 24-month-old children in which a novel action was performed always and only with a particular toy character on a particular substrate (e.g., Big Bird on a swing, with other character-action pairings demonstrated as well). The adult then picked up Big Bird and announced to the child *Let's meek Big Bird*, but the swing was nowhere to be found – so the action was not performed. Children thus never saw the new word *meek* paired with the corresponding action. But later, when the adult handed them a new toy and told them to *Meek it*, they searched for (and found) the swing and used it to swing the new toy, thus demonstrating their understanding of the action intended. The only way they could do this was to understand the adult's intentions with respect to the key objects and actions in this jointly understood situation when she originally said *Let's meek Big Bird* – and something of the particular intentions behind the use of *meek* – even though she never actually did it. That is to say, the child had to identify the aspect of the adult's overall communicative intention not covered by the known parts of the utterance *Let's* and *Big Bird* and connect it to the unknown word *meek*. To learn a new word, children must extract it from a larger utterance and connect it with the relevant aspect of the current situation.

In many ways this process is even clearer for word types other than nouns and verbs. Thus, many function words can *only* be learned through efforts to isolate their functional contribution in some large and not-so-predictable set of phrases. For example, Tomasello (1987) reports that his daughter learned the preposition *of* from such expressions as *piece of ice*, *piece of bread*, *scared of that*, and *scared of monsters*. It is hard to conceive of any method of acquisition in this case other than some process of extracting *of* from larger expressions and attempting to discern its function in the overall utterance. Levy and Nelson (1994) make a similar argument about children's earliest uses of causal and temporal terms such as *because*, *so*, *since*, *and*, *but*, *before*, and *if*. And, of course, there can be no question of mapping or association when what is involved is not learning a word per se, but rather learning which referential term of several to choose for a given referent – for example, *the chair* or *Daddy's chair* or *the chair in my room* or simply *it* – in different communicative situations. Learning to make these pragmatic choices in the conventional manner – for example, learning when to use a pronoun versus a lexical noun phrase – requires children to understand why a person chose one means of expression rather than another, that is, her intentions in making the choice (Matthews, Lieven, Theakston, & Tomasello, 2006).

Schemas and Constructions

This communication-based, usage-based way of looking at things means we cannot explain children's acquisition of grammatical competence by starting with individual words, learned in isolation, and then gluing them together with abstract meaningless rules, as in the very common "words and rules" approach (Pinker, 1999). Instead, we must begin with children's comprehension and production of whole, meaningful utterances. We then investigate how children *extract* words from utterances and, at the same time, how they find analogical patterns across utterances and thereby *abstract* meaningful grammatical constructions.

A linguistic construction is prototypically a unit of language that comprises multiple linguistic elements used together for a relatively coherent communicative function, with sub-functions being performed by the elements as well. Consequently, constructions may vary in their complexity depending on the number of elements involved and their interrelations. For example, the English regular plural construction (N+*s*) is relatively simple, whereas the passive construction (NP *was* VERB*ed by* NP) is relatively complex. Constructions also vary in their abstractness, from abstract constructions such as the English plural and passive, to various concrete idioms such as *kick the bucket* and *paint the town*. Importantly, even the most abstract constructions are still meaningful, as they possess a coherent, if abstract, meaning in relative independence of the lexical items involved (Goldberg, 1995). Thus, we know the general profile of the event when we hear *The dax got mibbed by the gazzer* (the gazzer did something to the dax), even though we know none of the individual content words involved.

Children begin, as noted above, by producing holophrases – one-unit utterances with an intonational contour expressing communicative motive. Their earliest multi-unit utterances soon follow and form schemas or constructions. But initially these schemas and constructions are very concrete, not abstract; that is, they are organized around particular words and phrases not abstract categories. From the point of view of linguistic form, the utterance-level constructions underlying children's earliest multi-word utterances come in three types: word combinations, pivot schemas, and item-based constructions.

Word combinations

Beginning at around 18 months of age, many children combine two words or holophrases in situations in which they both are relevant – with both words having roughly equivalent status. For example, a child has learned to name a ball and a table and then spies a ball on a table and says, *Ball table*. Utterances of this type include both "successive single-word utterances" (with a pause between them; Bloom, 1973) and "word combinations" (under a single intonational contour). The defining feature of word combinations is that they partition the experiential scene into multiple symbolic units – in a way that holophrases obviously (by definition) do not – and they are totally concrete in the sense that they are comprised only of concrete pieces of language, such as words, not abstract categories such as nouns and verbs.

Pivot schemas

Beginning at around this same age, however, many of children's multi-word productions show a more systematic pattern. Often there is one word or phrase that seems to structure the utterance in the sense that it determines the speech-act function of the utterance as a whole (often with help from an intonational contour), with the other linguistic item(s) simply filling in variable slot(s) – the first type of linguistic abstraction. Thus, in many of these early utterances one event-word is used with a wide variety of object labels (e.g., *More milk*, *More grapes*, *More juice*) yielding a schema such as *More* ___. Following Braine (1963), we may call these pivot schemas or constructions (see also Lieven, Behrens, Speares, & Tomasello, 2003; Lieven, Pine, & Baldwin, 1997), and they characterize children learning many different types of languages.

Pivot schemas are organized concretely and locally, around particular words, with only one slot that is abstract. Moreover, they do not have syntax; that is, *Gone juice* does not mean something different from *Juice gone*, and there is no other marking (e.g., no case marking) to indicate syntactic roles for elements in pivot schemas. The consistent ordering patterns in many pivot schemas (e.g., it is always "More + X" in that order) are very likely direct reproductions of the ordering patterns children have heard most often in adult speech, with no communicative significance. This means that although young children are using their early pivot schemas to partition scenes conceptually with different words, and typically following a consistent ordering pattern, they are not using syntactic symbols – such as word order or case marking – to indicate the different roles being played by different participants in the referential scene.

Item-based constructions

Item-based constructions go beyond pivot schemas in having syntactic marking as an integral part of the construction. For example, children barely 2 years of age respond appropriately to requests that they *Make the bunny push the horse* (reversible transitives) that depend crucially and exclusively on a knowledge of canonical English word order (e.g., DeVilliers & DeVilliers, 1973; Hirsh-Pasek & Golinkoff, 1996). However, the syntactic marking in these item-based constructions is still verb-specific, depending on how a child has heard a particular verb being used – and so they are often called verb-island constructions. Evidence for this proposal was provided by Tomasello (1992), who found that almost all of his daughter's early multi-word utterances during her second year of life revolved around the specific verbs or predicate terms involved. Thus, during exactly the same developmental period some verbs were used in only one type of construction and that construction was quite simple (e.g., *Cut* ___), whereas other verbs were used in more complex frames of several different types (e.g., *Draw*___; *Draw*___ *on*___; *Draw*___ *for* ___; ___*draw on*___). Interestingly and importantly, within any given verb's development over time, there was great continuity such that new uses of a given verb almost always replicated previous uses and then made one small addition or modification (e.g., the marking of tense or the adding of a new argument). In general, by far the best predictor of this child's use of a given verb on a given day was not her use of other verbs on that same day, but rather her use of that same verb on immediately preceding days.

Experimental evidence for the item-specific nature of children's early grammatical productions has come from many different studies. As one example, Tomasello and Brooks (1998) exposed 2–3-year-old children to a novel verb used to refer to a highly transitive and novel action in which an agent was doing something to a patient. In the key condition the novel verb was used in an intransitive sentence frame such as *The sock is tamming* (to refer to a situation in which, for example, a bear was doing something that caused a sock to *tam* – similar to the verb *roll* or *spin*). Then, with novel characters performing the target action, the adult asked children the question: *What is the doggie doing?* (when the dog was causing some new character to tam). Agent questions of this type encourage a transitive reply such as *He's tamming the car* – which would be creative since the child has heard this verb only in an intransitive sentence frame. The result was that very few children at either age produced a full transitive utterance with the novel verb; instead they tended to produce the novel verb in the way that they had heard it being modeled by the experimenter (i.e., in an intransitive construction such as *The bird is tamming*). Importantly, as a control, children also heard another novel verb introduced in a transitive sentence frame, and in this case virtually all of them produced a transitive utterance – demonstrating that they could use a novel verb in a subject-verb-object construction when they had heard it used in that way. It is also important to note that it is not the case that young children are simply reluctant to use newly learned words in novel ways; when even younger children (22 months) are taught novel nouns, they use them quite freely in already established pivot schema slots (Tomasello et al., 1997).

The generality of this finding is demonstrated by a number of similar studies using different modeled constructions and measurement procedures – and the finding holds in comprehension as well (Akhtar & Tomasello, 1997). Children begin to perform more productively in these kinds of experiments – and so to provide evidence that they have gone beyond the verb-island manner of organization – typically sometime after their third birthdays (see Tomasello, 2000, 2003, for reviews). What little experimental evidence we have from nonce-verb studies of case-marking languages (e.g., Berman, 1993; Dittmar, Abbot-Smith, Lieven, & Tomasello, 2008; Wittek & Tomasello, 2005) is in general accord with this developmental pattern.

The main point is that unlike in pivot schemas, in item-based constructions children use syntactic symbols such as word order and case marking to syntactically mark the roles participants are playing in these events, including generalized "slots" that include whole categories of entities as participants. But all of this is done on an item-specific basis; that is, the child does not generalize to syntactically mark similar participant roles in similar ways without having heard those participants used and marked in adult discourse for each verb specifically. This limited generality is presumably due to the difficulty of categorizing or schematizing entire utterances, including reference to both the event and the participant roles involved, into more abstract constructions – especially given the many different kinds of utterances children hear and must sort through. Early syntactic competence is therefore best characterized as a semi-structured inventory of relatively independent verb-island constructions that pair a scene of experience and an item-based construction, with very few structural relationships among these constructional islands.

Abstract constructions

Between two and three years of age, children begin the process of constructing some more abstract constructions, with fewer particular lexical items necessary. However, despite their abstractness, each of these has a particular communicative function in terms of the communicative contexts in which it is appropriately used. Examples of some early abstract constructions in English are as follows:

Identificationals, attributives, and possessives. Serve to identify an object or to attribute to it some property. Most common for the identification function: *It's a/the X*; *That's a/the X*; or *This is a/the X.* Most common for the attributive function: *It's X*; *That's X.* Most common for the possessive function: (*It's*) *X's* ___; *That's X's/my* ___; *This is X's/your* ___.

Simple transitives and intransitives. Serve to indicate or request an activity or state of affairs. Transitives (NP + V + NP): prototype is a scene in which there are two participants and one acts on the other (e.g., *Daddy cut the grass*). Intransitives (NP + V): prototype is activities involving a single participant; either an actor does something (e.g., *Mommy smiled*; unergatives) or something happens to something (e.g., *The vase broke*; unaccusatives).

Datives, ditransitives, and benefactives. Serve to indicate or request the transfer of objects (and other things) between people. Dative (NP + V + NP *to* NP): *He gave it to Mommy.* Ditransitive (NP + V + NP + NP): *Daddy sent her a present* or *Daddy told me a story.* Benefactive (NP + V + NP *for* NP): *She did it for me.*

Locatives, resultatives, and causatives. Serve to indicate or request spatial or causal relations. Early locatives include such things as: *Put NP in/on/ the NP*; *Take NP off my shirt*; *NP's under the NP*; etc. Resultatives indicate outcomes of actions and include such things as: *NP eat NP all up*; *NP wash it off*; *NP push it down*; etc. Causatives prototypically involve as a first verb *make, let*, or *help*, as in: *Make NP do it*; *Help NP do it*; or *Let NP do it*.

Passives and reflexives. Serve to indicate things happening to people or things, who are not active agents. Children's early passives (NP + *be/get* + V + by NP) are such things as: *Spot got hit by a car*; *Mommy got sick*; or *It was taken by a bear*. Reflexives are such things as *I hurt myself*.

Imperatives and questions. Many of the above construction types can be used as imperatives to request certain kinds of actions, typically without a subject as in: *Push it here*; *Smile*; *Don't do that*; etc. Many of the above construction types can be used as questions to request certain kinds of information. While mature questions are quite complex, two very common formulae early on are: *What NP doing?* and *Where NP (going)?* Slightly later they start with such things as: *How do … ?*; *What are … ?*; and *Where is … ?*.

The key theoretical point is that when we conceptualize children's early grammatical competence not in terms of abstract rules with no semantic content, but rather in terms of constructional patterns conventionally associated with particular communicative functions, the acquisition processes needed are not so different from those we need for word learning. The child needs, first of all, to see that when the adult produces an utterance that fits a particular linguistic pattern (construction), she intends a particular kind of meaning. Then to see similarities among different utterances, young children need skills of schematization and analogy to make the appropriate abstraction – skills they also use in other domains of cognitive activity (Goswami, 1992; Gentner & Markman, 1997).

Later Development

Many more formally oriented theorists agree that the kind of account given above works for the very earliest stages of language acquisition – for very simple constructions – but they object that it does not work for more syntactically complex constructions. Recent research has found, however, that complex constructions may not be so different if children's actual productions are looked at more carefully (Diessel, 2004).

For example, among the more complex constructions in English are sentential complement constructions. The prototype is utterances with two verbs such as *I <u>know</u> she <u>hit</u> him*, and *I <u>think</u> I can <u>do</u> it*. Diessel and Tomasello (2001) looked at young English-speaking children's earliest utterances with sentential complements from 2–5 years of age. They found that virtually all of them were composed of a simple sentence schema that the child had already mastered combined with one of a delimited set of fixed phrases containing a complement-taking matrix verb (see also Bloom 1992). The matrix verbs were of two types. First were epistemic verbs such as *think* and *know*. As one example, in almost all cases children used *I think* to indicate their own uncertainty about something, and they basically never used the verb *think* in anything but this first-person, present-tense form. That is, there were virtually no examples of *He thinks* … , *She thinks* … , etc.; virtually no examples of *I don't think* … , *I can't think* … , etc.; and virtually no examples of *I thought* … , *I didn't think* … , etc. And there were almost no uses with a complementizer (virtually no examples of *I think that* …). It thus appears that for many young children *I think* is a relatively fixed phrase meaning something like *Maybe*. The child then pieces together this fixed phrase (or one of the other similar phrases like *I hope* … *I bet* … , etc.) with a full proposition, with its function being as a sort of evidential marker (not as a matrix clause that embeds another as in traditional analyses). The second kind of matrix verbs were attention-getting verbs like *Look* and *See*, used in conjunction with full finite clauses. In this case, children used these "matrix" verbs almost exclusively in imperative form (again almost no negations, no non-present tenses, no complementizers), as in *See the dog eating a bone*, suggesting again an item-based approach not involving syntactic embedding.

A second example is relative clauses. Textbook descriptions focus on so-called restrictive relative clauses – e.g., *The dog that barked all night died this morning* – in which the relative clause serves to identify a noun by using presupposed information (both speaker and listener already know that there was barking all night – that's why it can be used as identifying information). Because relative clauses are a part of a noun phrase argument, they are classically characterized as embedded clauses. Diessel and Tomasello (2000) studied four English-speaking children aged from 1 year and 9 months to 5 years and 2 months in quantitative detail and made a surprising discovery: virtually all of these children's earliest relative clauses were of the same general form, and this form was not the form typically described in textbooks. Examples would be:

Here's the toy that spins around.
That's the sugar that goes in there.

What is noteworthy here is: (a) the main clause is a presentational construction (predicate nominal or closely related), basically introducing a new topic using a previously mastered fixed presentational phrase such as *Here's the* … , *That's the* … ; and (b) the information in the relative clause is not presupposed, as in textbook (restrictive) relative clauses, but rather is new information about the just-introduced referent. Again, the main point is that, when examined closely, even this very complex construction is firmly based in a set of simpler constructions (copular presentationals) that children have mastered as item-based constructions some time before relative clauses are first acquired and produced. Even in German, where relative clauses have a different word order from simple main clauses, this same basic acquisition pattern is found (Brandt, Diesel, & Tomasello, 2008).

Finally are questions. A particularly interesting phenomenon is so-called inversion errors. English-speaking children sometimes invert the subject and auxiliary in Wh- questions and sometimes not – leading to errors such as *Why they can't go?* A number of fairly complex and abstract rule-based accounts have been proposed to account for these errors, but in a more detailed analysis Rowland and Pine (2000) discovered the surprising fact that the child they studied from age 2–4 consistently inverted or failed to invert particular Wh-word–auxiliary combinations on an item-specific basis. He thus consistently said such incorrect things as *Why I can … ?*, *What she will … ?*, *What you can … ?*, but at the same time he also said such correct things as *How did … ?*, *How do … ?*, *What do … ?*. In a recent experiment, Ambridge, Rowland, Theakston, and Tomasello (2006) elicited inversion errors from 4-year-old English children and confirmed this pattern. Young children do not seem to have an overall rule for forming questions, or even Wh-questions, but rather they have a collection of more item-based schemas that presumably will become a set of more coherent and abstract constructions later in ontogeny.

Processes of Language Acquisition

In usage-based theories of language acquisition, children acquire language using their general cognitive and social-cognitive abilities (along with some specialized skills of vocal-auditory processing). Tomasello (2003) proposed two broad sets of these general skills, alluded to above: (a) intention-reading skills for determining the meaning and communicative function of concrete pieces of language, and (b) pattern-finding skills for detecting and constructing abstract grammatical patterns of these meaningful uses of language. But these very general processes actually are best described at a slightly more specific level, as they are used for specific aspects of the language-acquisition process.

Intention reading and cultural learning

Because natural languages are conventional, the most fundamental process of language acquisition is the ability to do things the way that other people do them. But this does not mean simply mimicking, without understanding, the language that other people are using. Because linguistic items are essentially tools for directing the attention and mental states of others, the imitative learning (cultural learning) that takes place in language acquisition requires an understanding of the communicative function of a piece of language, that is, the communicative intentions with which a person uses that piece of language (skills of intention-reading). Thus, although cultural/imitative learning cannot account for children's acquisition of the more abstract, grammatical dimensions of language, it is the fundamental process for learning concrete pieces of language such as words and the better part of pivot schemas and item-based constructions.

Schematization and analogy

Young children hear and use – on a numbingly regular basis – the same utterances repeated over and over but with systematic variation, for example, as instantiated in item-based constructions such as *Where's-the X?*, *I wanna X*, *Let's X*, *Can you X?*, *Gimme X*, *I'm Xing it*. Forming schemas of this type means imitatively learning the recurrent concrete pieces of language for concrete functions, as well as forming a relatively abstract slot designating a relatively abstract function. This process is called *schematization*, and its roots may be observed in various primates who schematize everything from food-processing skills to arbitrary sequences in the laboratory. In grammatical development, schematization yields what we have called item-based constructions, which can be seen as a combination of constant item(s) plus slot(s), where slots represent functional categories for the child.

Key factors that are likely to affect the formation of slots relative to constant items are *token* and *type frequency*. Consider the following sample of three sentences:

Where's the dog? *Where's daddy?* *Where's your spoon?*

Token frequency refers to the frequency with which a specific form is heard in a sample. In the above sample the token frequency of *where's* is 3 and the token frequency of *dog* is 1. Token frequency should predict the selection of a constant item in a schema. This is simply because the more often a word occurs, the more easily it can be picked out as a constant. Type frequency refers to the frequency with which different items of the same type (e.g. nouns referring to sought things) are heard. In the above sample the type frequency of "sought after objects" is 3. Type frequency should predict where slots are formed in relation to constant items. That is, one needs to witness a certain amount of variability before or after a constant item in order to realize that different forms can slot in around it. This variability, however, cannot be completely random. Rather the variables will all bear a common relation to the constant item (i.e. they will be of one *type*). Slot formation is therefore an instance of category formation.

In order to move from item-based constructions to abstract constructions, children need to form schemas that have no concrete items in common. We will refer to the learning process that achieves this as *analogy*, a form of schematization that places heavy emphasis on commonalities in relational structure (because there are no recurrent items). For example, despite the different number of words in the sentences below, the two may be functionally aligned in that they both encode the roles of agent, action, and patient. Drawing an analogy between the two would thus give an abstract transitive construction, perhaps of the form [agent causes-motion patient].

I kicked the ball. *Daddy threw his keys.*

As is the case for schematization, the coherence of the category of variables that enters into each role (e.g., agent: *I* and *Daddy*) is proposed to affect the ease of analogizing. This means that analogies will be formed more easily if certain items always tend to fill certain roles (e.g., if the patient role is predominantly filled by nouns denoting inanimate objects and the agent role is predominantly filled by first- and second-person pronouns in both constructions).

The only experimental study of children's formation of an abstract linguistic construction (as tested by their ability to assimilate a nonce verb to it) was conducted by Childers and Tomasello (2001). In this training study, 2.5-year-old English-speaking children heard several hundred transitive utterances, such as *He's kicking it*, involving 16 different verbs across three separate sessions. Half the children learned new English verbs (and so increased their transitive verb vocabularies during training – toward a critical mass) whereas the other half heard only verbs they already knew. Within these groups, some children heard all the utterances with full nouns as agent and patient, whereas others heard utterances with both pronouns (i.e., *He's VERB-ing it*) and also full nouns as agent and patient. They were then tested to see if they could creatively produce a transitive utterance with a nonce verb. The main finding was that children were best at generalizing the transitive construction to the nonce verb if they had been trained with pronouns and nouns, regardless of the familiarity of the trained verbs (and few children in a control condition generalized to the novel verb at all). That is, the consistent pronoun frame *He's VERB-ing it* (in combination with type variation in the form of nouns as well) seemed to facilitate children's formation of a verb-general transitive construction to a greater degree than the learning of additional transitive verbs with nouns alone, in the absence of such a stabilizing pronominal frame.

These results show three interesting things. First, they show that children can make generalizations, perhaps based on analogy, across different item-based constructions. Second and more specifically, they also show that the material that goes in the slots, in this case NP slots, plays an important role (see also Dodson & Tomasello, 1998). In English, the pronoun *he* only goes in the preverbal position, and, although the pronoun *it* may occur in either position in spontaneous speech, it occurs most frequently in postverbal position in child-directed speech, and that is the only position in which the children heard it during training. Third, the way all of this is done in language is very similar to the way it is done in non-linguistic cognition: specifically, schematization (with concrete items in common across exemplars) precedes fully abstract analogy-making (see reviews in Goswami, 1992; Gentner & Markman, 1997) – providing evidence for the usage-based view that specifically linguistic abstractions are created by general cognitive processes.

The key skill involved in analogy formation is the ability to focus on detecting similarities in relational structure. This is central to the acquisition of grammar because surface similarities between utterances often need to be glossed over in order to form complex, abstract constructions. To actually use abstract constructions, though, children need to fill abstract slots with concrete words and this requires selecting words from relevant categories. For example, in the transitive construction [subject verb object] the verb slot can be filled with any word that falls into the category of transitive verbs. We now consider how children cluster words into these categories.

Distributional analysis

In order to cluster words and morphemes into categories, such as *noun*, *pronoun*, *verb*, *adjective*, children must draw upon information about the word's *distribution* and its *function*. The term distribution simply refers to the types of neighborhoods a word tends to inhabit. For example, English nouns (e.g. *dog*) are often found after determiners (*the dog*, *a dog*) and before a plural suffix (dog–*s*). So children might form rough categories by clustering together words that often share the same distribution. They could also notice functional regularities pertaining to a given class of words (e.g. that nouns tend to denote entities whereas verbs tend to denote actions). However, neither distributional nor functional cues used alone would be likely to yield a very satisfactory taxonomy. Studies that have used distributional analyses to categorize English words have typically only correctly classified a certain percentage of words, mostly only nouns and verbs. Functional analysis, on the other hand, does not explain children's early use of words such as the non-object nouns *breakfast* and *night* and dual-category words such as *kiss* and *hug*, which may be used as nouns or verbs (*a kiss* vs. *to kiss*). Rather it would seem that only a combination of formal and functional cues is sufficient, and these would have to be understood in the context of each word's role in the wider communicative attempt – the whole construction or discourse turn. We refer to this combination of distributional and functional cues as *functionally based distributional analysis*, which can be seen as the identification of items in a category on the grounds that they occur in the same formal contexts and perform the same communicative function within an utterance.

It is important to emphasize that this same process of functionally based distributional analysis also operates on units of language larger than words. For example, what is typically called a noun phrase may be constituted by anything from a proper name (*Mary*) to a pronoun (*she*) to a common noun with a determiner and a relative clause hanging off it (*the girl who sold me the bike*). But for many syntactic purposes these may all be treated as the same kind of unit (e.g., they may all be the subject of a sentence). How can this be – given their very different surface forms? The only reasonable answer is that they are treated as units of the same type because they all do the same job in utterances: in this case they all identify a particular girl playing a role in the scene being depicted. Indeed, given the very different form of the different expressions involved, it is difficult to even think of an alternative to this functionally based account.

Mechanisms for constraining generalizations

In all theories of language acquisition, there must be some constraints on children's linguistic generalizations and abstractions. Classically, a major problem for formal theories is that as the rules and principles are made more elegant and powerful through theoretical analyses, they become so abstract that they generate too large a set of grammatical utterances – and so constraints (e.g., the subjacency constraint) must be posited to restore empirical accuracy. In usage-based theories children are abstracting as they learn, but they cannot do this indiscriminately; they must make just those generalizations that are conventional in the language they are learning and not others. It is thus clear that any serious theory of syntactic development, whatever its basic assumptions, must address the question of why children make just the generalizations they do and not others.

We may illustrate the basic problem with so-called dative alternation constructions. The situation is that some verbs can felicitously appear in both ditransitive and prepositional dative constructions, but others cannot; for example:

He gave/sent/bequeathed/donated his books to the library.
*He gave/sent/bequeathed/*donated the library his books.*

Why should the other three verbs be felicitous in both constructions, but *donate* be felicitous only in the prepositional dative? The three verbs have very similar meanings, and so it would seem likely that they should all behave the same. Another example is:

She said/told something to her mother.
*She *said/told her mother something.*

Again, the meanings of the verbs are very close, and so the difference of behavior seems unprincipled and unpredictable (Bowerman, 1988, 1996). Other similar alternations are the causative alternation (*I rolled the ball*; *The ball rolled*) and the locative alternation (*I sprayed paint on the wall*; *I sprayed the wall with paint*) – both of which also apply only to limited sets of verbs.

One solution is quite simple. Perhaps children only learn verbs for the constructions in which they have heard them. Based on all of the evidence reviewed above, this is very likely the case at the earliest stages of development. But it is not true later in development, especially in the 3–5-year age period. Children at this age overgeneralize with some regularity, as documented most systematically by Bowerman (1982, 1988; see Pinker, 1989, for a summary of evidence): "Don't giggle me" (at age 3) and "I said her no" (at age 3 years and 1 month). It is thus not the case that children are totally conservative throughout development, and so this cannot be the whole answer. A second simple but untrue solution is that when children make overgeneralization errors adults correct them, and so children's overgeneralization tendencies are constrained by the linguistic environment. But this is not true in the sense that adults do not explicitly correct the grammar of child utterances with any frequency (Brown & Hanlon, 1970). Adults, at least Western middle-class adults, do respond differently to well-formed and ill-formed child utterances (e.g., Farrar, 1992; Bohannon & Stanowicz, 1988), but this kind of indirect feedback is generally not considered by most theorists sufficient to constrain children's overgeneralization tendencies, and it is far from consistent.

Given the inadequacy of these simple solutions, three factors have been most widely discussed. First, Pinker (1989) proposed that there are certain very specific and (mostly) semantic constraints that apply to particular English constructions and to the verbs that may or may not be conventionally used in them. For example, a verb can be used felicitously with the English transitive construction if it denotes "manner of locomotion" (e.g., *walk* and *drive* as in *I walked the dog at midnight* or *I drove my car to New York*), but not if it denotes a "motion in a lexically specified direction" (e.g., *come* and *fall* as in **He came her to school* or **She falled him down*). How children learn these verb classes – and they must learn them since they differ across languages – is unknown at this time. Second, it has also been proposed that the more frequently children hear a verb used in a particular construction (the more firmly its usage is entrenched), the less likely they will be to extend that verb to any novel construction with which they have not heard it used (Bates & MacWhinney, 1989; Braine & Brooks, 1995; Clark, 1987; Goldberg, 1995). And third, if children hear a verb used in a linguistic construction that serves the same communicative function as some possible generalization, they may infer that the generalization is not conventional – the heard construction preempts the generalization. For example, if a child hears *He made the rabbit disappear*, when she might have expected *He disappeared the* *rabbit*, she may infer that *disappear* does not occur in a simple transitive construction – since the adult seems to be going to some lengths to avoid using it in this way (the periphrastic causative being a more marked construction).

Two experimental studies provide evidence that indeed all three of these constraining processes – entrenchment, preemption, and knowledge of semantic sub-classes of verbs – are at work. First, Brooks, Tomasello, Lewis, and Dodson (1999) modeled the use of a number of fixed-transitivity English verbs for children from 3 years and 5 months to 8 years – verbs such as *disappear* that are exclusively intransitive and verbs such as *hit* that are exclusively transitive. There were four pairs of verbs, one member of each pair typically learned early by children and typically used often by adults (and so presumably more entrenched) and one member of each pair typically learned later by children and typically used less frequently by adults (less entrenched). The four pairs were: *come–arrive, take–remove, hit–strike, disappear–vanish* (the first member of each pair being more entrenched). The finding was that, in the face of adult questions attempting to induce them to overgeneralize, children of all ages were less likely to overgeneralize the strongly entrenched verbs than the weakly entrenched verbs; that is, they were more likely to produce *I arrived it* than *I comed it.*

Second, Brooks and Tomasello (1999) taught novel verbs to children 2.5, 4.5, and 7 years of age. They then attempted to induce children to generalize these novel verbs to new constructions. Some of these verbs conformed to Pinker's (1989) semantic criteria, and some did not. Additionally, in some cases experimenters attempted to preempt generalizations by providing children with alternative ways of using the new verb (thus providing them with the possibility of answering *What's the boy doing?* with *He's making the ball tam* – which allows the verb to stay intransitive). In brief, the study found that both of these constraining factors worked, but only from age 4.5. Children from 4.5 showed a tendency to generalize or not generalize a verb in line with its membership in one of the key semantic sub-classes, and they were less likely to generalize a verb to a novel construction if the adult provided them with a preempting alternative construction. But the younger children showed no such tendency.

Overall, entrenchment seems to work early, from 3 years old or before, as particular verb-island constructions become either more or less entrenched depending on usage. Preemption and semantic sub-classes begin to work sometime later, perhaps not until 4 years of age or later, as children learn more about the conventional uses of verbs and about all of the alternative linguistic constructions at their disposal in different communicative circumstances. Thus, just as verb–argument constructions become more abstract only gradually, so also are they constrained only gradually.

Conclusions

The usage-based theory of language acquisition makes the fundamental claim that language structure emerges from language use. This applies at the level of individual words, as their communicative function derives from their use, as well as at the level of grammar, as structure emerges from patterns of use of multi-unit utterances. Historically, the structure of a language emerges through processes of grammaticalization. Ontogenetically, children hear individual utterances and then (re-)construct the abstract constructions of a language. All of this is done with general cognitive processes, and universals of linguistic structure derive from the fact that people everywhere have the same set of general cognitive processes and communicative needs. We may segregate these general cognitive processes into the two overall headings of: (a) intention-reading, comprising the species-unique social-cognitive skills responsible for joint attention, communicative intentions, symbol acquisition, and in general the functional dimensions of language; and (b) pattern-finding, the primate-wide cognitive skills involved in the abstraction process, including categorization, analogy, distributional analysis, and others. These then actually manifest themselves more specifically in skills of cultural learning, schematization and analogy, distributional analysis, and constraints on generalization.

Together these processes account for how children construct a language – that is, a structured inventory of linguistic constructions – from the language they hear being used around them. Further insights into how these processes work in detail are given in Lieven and Tomasello (2008) and Abbot-Smith and Tomasello (2006), mainly in the form of patterns of linguistic input that facilitate these processes – for example, type frequency for analogy, token frequency for creating item-based constructions, statistical patterns leading to paradigmatic categories, and many other aspects of the role of linguistic input – as well as processes of exemplar-based learning and categorization. Tomasello (2003) also argues that connectionist accounts in which almost everything is based on distributional analysis (and with no account of communicative function or analogy) are not sufficient to account for language acquisition because they neglect important aspects of the process. Human languages emerged evolutionarily and historically from a complex set of processes, and children acquire competence with a particular language through a complex set of cognitive and learning processes as well. A complete account must recognize all of these processes, and then show how they work in concrete instances of language acquisition.

References

Abbot-Smith, K., & Tomasello, M. (2006). Exemplar-learning and schematization in a usage-based account of syntactic acquisition. *The Linguistic Review*, *23*, 275–290.

Akhtar, N., & Tomasello, M. (1996). Two-year-olds learn words for absent objects and actions. *British Journal of Developmental Psychology*, *14*, 79–93.

Akhtar, N., & Tomasello, M. (1997). Young children's productivity with word order and verb morphology. *Developmental Psychology*, *33*, 952–965.

Ambridge, B., Rowland, C., Theakston, A., & Tomasello, M. (2006). Comparing different accounts of auxiliary inversion errors. *Journal of Child Language*, *33*, 519–557.

Bates, E., & MacWhinney, B. (1989). Functionalism and the competition model. In B. MacWhinney, & E. Bates (Eds.), *The cross-linguistic study of sentence processing*. Cambridge: Cambridge University Press.

Berman, R. (1993). Marking verb transitivity in Hebrew-speaking children. *Journal of Child Language*, *20*, 641–670.

Bloom, L. (1973). *One word at a time*. The Hague: Mouton.

Bloom, L. (1992). *Language development from two to three.* Cambridge: Cambridge University Press.

Bloom, P. (2000). *How children learn the meanings of words.* Cambridge, MA: MIT Press.

Bohannon, N., & Stanowicz, L. (1988). The issue of negative evidence: Adult responses to children's language errors. *Developmental Psychology 24*, 684–689.

Bowerman, M. (1982). Reorganizational processes in lexical and syntactic development. In Wanner & Gleitman (Eds.), *Language acquisition: The state of the art.* Cambridge: Cambridge University Press.

Bowerman, M. (1988). The "no negative evidence" problem. How do children avoid constructing an overgeneral grammar? In J. A. Hawkins (Ed.), *Explaining language universals.* Oxford: Blackwell.

Bowerman, M. (1996). Learning how to structure space for language: A cross-linguistic perspective. In P. Bloom, M. Peterson, L. Nadel, & M. Garret (Eds.), *Language and space.* Cambridge, MA: MIT Press.

Braine, M. (1963). The ontogeny of English phrase structure. *Language, 39*, 1–14.

Braine, M., & Brooks, P. (1995). Verb–argument structure and the problem of avoiding an overgeneral grammar. In M. Tomasello & W. E. Merriman (Eds.), *Beyond names of things: Young children's acquisition of verbs* (pp. 353–376). Hillsdale, NJ: Erlbaum.

Brandt, S., Diessel, H., Tomasello, M. (2008). The acquisition of German relative clauses: A case study. *Journal of Child Language, 35*(2), 325–349.

Brooks, P., & Tomasello, M. (1999). How young children constrain their argument structure constructions. *Language, 75*, 720–738.

Brooks, P., Tomasello, M., Lewis, L., & Dodson, K. (1999). Children's overgeneralization of fixed transitivity verbs: The entrenchment hypothesis. *Child Development, 70*, 1325–1337.

Brown, R., & Hanlon, C. (1970). Derivational complexity and order of acquisition in child speech. In J. R. Hayes (Ed.), *Cognition and the development of language.* New York: Wiley.

Bruner, J. (1983). *Child's talk.* New York: Norton.

Childers, J. & Tomasello, M. (2001). The role of pronouns in young children's acquisition of the English transitive construction. *Developmental Psychology, 37*, 739–748.

Chomsky, N. (1980). Rules and representations. *Behavioral and Brain Sciences, 3*, 1–61.

Clark, E. (1987). The principle of contrast: A constraint on language acquisition. In B. MacWhinney (Ed.), *Mechanisms of language acquisition.* Hillsdale, NJ: Erlbaum.

Crain, S., & Pietroski, P. (2001). Nature, nurture and universal grammar. *Linguistics and Philosophy, 24*, 138–185.

DeVilliers, J., & DeVilliers, P. (1973). Development of the use of word order in comprehension. *Journal of Psycholinguistic Research, 2*, 331–341.

Diessel, H. (2004). *The acquisition of complex sentences.* Cambridge: Cambridge University Press.

Diessel, H., & Tomasello, M. (2000). The development of relative constructions in early child speech. *Cognitive Linguistics, 11*, 131–152.

Diessel, H., & Tomasello, M. (2001). The acquisition of finite complement clauses in English: A usage-based approach to the development of grammatical constructions. *Cognitive Linguistics, 12*, 97–141.

Dittmar, M., Abbot-Smith, K., Lieven, E., & Tomasello, M. (2008). Comprehension of case marking and word order cues by German children. *Child Development, 79*, 1152–1167.

Dodson, K. & Tomasello, M. (1998). Acquiring the transitive construction in English: The role of animacy and pronouns. *Journal of Child Language, 25*, 555–574.

Farrar, J. (1992). Negative evidence and grammatical morpheme acquisition. *Developmental Psychology, 28*, 90–98.

Gentner, D., & Markman, A. (1997). Structure mapping in analogy and similarity. *American Psychologist, 52*, 45–56.

Goldberg, A. (1995). *Constructions: A construction grammar approach to argument structure*. Chicago: University of Chicago Press.

Goldberg, A. (2006). *Constructions at work*. Oxford: Oxford University Press.

Goswami, U. (1992). *Analogical reasoning in children*. Hillsdale, NJ: Erlbaum.

Grassman, S., & Tomasello, M. (2007). Two-year-olds use primary sentence accent to learn new words. *Journal of Child Language, 34*, 677–687.

Heine, B., & Kuteva, T. (2007). *The genesis of grammar: A reconstruction*. Oxford: Oxford University Press.

Hirsh-Pasek, K., & Golinkoff, R. M. (1996). *The origins of grammar: Evidence from early language comprehension*. Cambridge, MA: MIT Press.

Levy, E., & Nelson, K. (1994). Words in discourse: A dialectical approach to the acquisition of meaning and use. *Journal of Child Language, 21*, 367–389.

Lieven, E., Behrens, H., Speares, J., & Tomasello, M., (2003). Early syntactic creativity: A usage-based approach. *Journal of Child Language, 30*, 333–370.

Lieven, E., Pine, J., & Baldwin, G. (1997). Lexically-based learning and early grammatical development. *Journal of Child Language, 24*, 187–220.

Lieven, E., & Tomasello, M. (2008). Children's first language acquisition from a usage-based perspective. In P. Robinson and N. C. Ellis (Eds.), *Handbook of Cognitive Linguistics and Second Language Acquisition*. London: Routledge.

Markman, E. (1989). *Categorization and naming in children*. Cambridge, MA: MIT Press.

Matthews, D., Lieven, E. V., Theakston, A. L., & Tomasello, M. (2006). The effect of perceptual availability and prior discourse on young children's use or referring expressions. *Applied Psycholinguistics, 27*, 403–422.

Pinker, S. (1989). *Learnability and cognition: The acquisition of verb–argument structure*. Cambridge, MA: Harvard University Press.

Pinker, S. (1999). *Words and rules*. New York: Morrow Press.

Roeper, T. (2007) *The Prism of Grammar*. Cambridge, MA: MIT Press.

Rowland, C., & Pine, J. M. (2000). Subject–auxiliary inversion errors and wh-question acquisition: "What children do know?" *Journal of Child Language 27*, 157–181.

Tomasello, M. (1987). Learning to use prepositions: A case study. *Journal of Child Language, 14*, 79–98.

Tomasello, M. (1992). *First verbs: A case study of early grammatical development*. Cambridge: Cambridge University Press.

Tomasello, M. (2000). Do young children have adult syntactic competence? *Cognition, 74*, 209–253.

Tomasello, M. (2003). *Constructing a language: A usage-based theory of language acquisition*. Cambridge, MA: Harvard University Press.

Tomasello, M. (2008). *Origins of human communication*. Cambridge, MA: MIT Press.

Tomasello, M., Akhtar, N., Dodson, K., & Rekau, L. (1997). Differential productivity in young children's use of nouns and verbs. *Journal of Child Language, 24*, 373–387.

Tomasello, M., & Brooks, P. (1998). Young children's earliest transitive and intransitive constructions. *Cognitive Linguistics, 9*, 379–395.

Wittek, A., & Tomasello, M. (2005). German-speaking children's productivity with syntactic constructions and case morphology: Local cues help locally. *First Language, 25*, 103–125.

CHAPTER TEN

Developing a Theory of Mind

Henry M. Wellman

The question of how people come to understand their own and other minds has a long history in philosophy and psychology. It is a vigorous contemporary question as well – phrased as "What is the nature and development of theory of mind?" Cognizing about mind is a ubiquitous human activity; we consistently construe each other as agents undertaking intentional action based on our underlying beliefs and desires (and not as "bags of skin stuffed into pieces of cloth … that move in unpredictable ways," Gopnik , Meltzoff, & Kuhl, [2001], pp. 4–5.) Yet, acquisition of this theory of mind may be one of the most impressive intellectual accomplishments of human development. Much like human language, theory of mind is notably abstract, but accomplished in basic forms rapidly by young children everywhere. And, again like language, both intriguing early competences and striking developments are apparent: infants closely attend to other humans; 2-year-olds talk about wants and feelings; 3- and 4-year-olds talk about thoughts and begin to engage in lies and trickery; and nuanced theories of mind – in "folk psychologies" – are apparent in (and dramatically differ) across cultural communities worldwide.

There is some consensus about key milestones of theory-of-mind development, but there are radically different perspectives on the basic character of this achievement and how it is acquired. For some scholars, theory of mind and its development are the product of learning processes (with resulting debates about what processes are involved – perhaps bottom-up expertise-building, perhaps domain-specific "theory building"). A prominent alternative to such generally experience-dependent views is much more nativist – understanding of agents' mental states is the product of an evolved theory-of-mind module (ToMM). Such a module "comes online" early in life and it is other, performance factors (e.g., increasing language capacities, increasing capacities for cognitive complexity or control) that account for the changes apparent in childhood. All agree, however, that developmental differences of some sort exist and that developmental data reveal, and must constrain accounts of, the nature and acquisition of theory of mind.

Preparation of this chapter was supported in part by grant HD-22149 to Wellman form NICHD.

Indeed, rich developmental data showing near-universal attribution by young children of mental states to self and other has prompted a variety of disciplines to embrace the task of accounting for theory of mind: Evolutionary scientists consider how theory of mind evolved, the extent to which it is uniquely human, and whether it was the breeding ground for advances in human intelligence and cultural learning. Clinicians consider the extent to which deficits in theory of mind account for various social impairments, especially in autism. Neuroscientists now address whether and how mentalizing is specially supported in the human brain. Religious scholars have suggested that an everyday theory of mind provides the foundation for a universal human interest in god and the supernatural.

In this chapter I review a subset of topics within the study of theory-of-mind development, emphasizing topics where there are considerable data, recent progress, and continuing debate. I begin with an overview of the course of childhood theory of mind. Then I address in more detail: infancy; understanding false beliefs; atypical development in autism and deafness; developmental sequences in understanding theory of mind; mentalizing in primates; and brain bases for theory of mind. Throughout I address alternative theoretical positions, essentially modular versus "theory-theory" accounts. As a preface it is important to note that sometimes theory of mind is described as a preschool achievement equated with children's performance on false-belief tasks. I advocate a much broader (and more interesting) construal, both conceptually and developmentally. Theory of mind describes our wide-ranging human understanding of agents' mental states like intentions, desires and thoughts, and how action is shaped by such states. It refers to our everyday psychology, appropriately emphasizing the mentalism that so strongly characterizes our everyday, "commonsense" psychological understandings.

The Course of Theory-of-Mind Development

Developing an understanding of people begins at birth. Infants who are only a few days old prefer to look at people and faces, imitate people but not inanimate devices, listen to human voices, and so on. Nothing in the data for early infancy convincingly demonstrates that such young infants penetrate to a deeper "internal," "psychological" sense of persons beyond apparent, surface features. But it has now become uncontroversial that older infants do so; by the end of the first year children begin to treat themselves and others as intentional agents and experiencers.

Box 10.1 provides one example of a paradigm used to demonstrate intention understanding in infants (from Brandone & Wellman, 2009; Phillips & Wellman, 2005). In the initial demonstrations using something like this paradigm, infants saw an animated circle "jumping" over a barrier to reach its goal-object. Just as they do for intentional human acts, 9- and 12-month-olds look longer at the indirect test event, showing an abstract, generalized understanding of intentional agency (Csibra, Gergely, Bíró, Koós, & Brockbank, 1999).

Persons not only engage in intentional action, they subjectively experience the world. Potentially, gaze following, where infants follow an agent's line of sight (or head

Box 10.1 A paradigm used to demonstrate intention understanding in infants

Habituation event

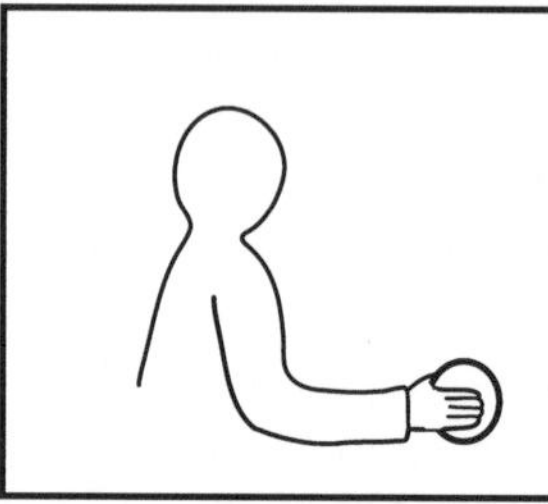
Direct reach test event

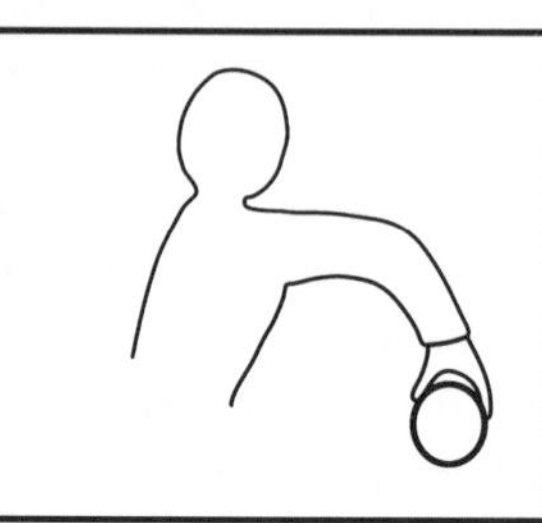
Indirect reach test event

Habituation-test (or familiarization-test) paradigms set the infant up so that he/she will then look longer at novel, unexpected test events. In the reaching paradigm (above), infants view multiple trials of the barrier-reaching event in habituation. Then, the barrier is *removed* and the test events contrast two different construals of the person's actions, one in terms of intentions and one in terms of physical motions of the body. Suppose during habituation the infant construes the agent's action in terms of its physical movement (the arm and hand up and then down in an arc), then the indirect-reach test event should be expected (as it repeats the same movement) whereas the direct reach will stand out as novel and so specially attention-worthy. In contrast, if the infant initially construes the action as goal directed, then when the barrier is removed the direct reach is the expected action because the agent continues to directly seek the goal. Under this second construal, the indirect reach would be more attention-worthy because (although the agent's arm movement remains the same as during habituation) the agent no longer seems straightforwardly directed to the goal. Eight-, nine-, ten-, and 12-month-olds consistently look longer at the *indirect*-reach test event.

Infants look equally to both test events in control conditions where they are first habituated to a display with no barrier, *or* first habituated to the exact same over-the-barrier arm movements but where there is no goal-object.

orientation) toward an object, would be produced by an understanding that the agent sees something – the person has a visual experience of some sort. But infant gaze following could be more "behavioral," tracking others' head-eye orientations might simply yield for the infant interesting sights without a recognition of the agent's visual experience (Baldwin & Moses, 1996). However, by 12–14 months infants also follow an adult's gaze around a barrier – even if this requires leaning or moving behind the barrier on their own – coupled with visual checking back and forth, apparently to verify that they and the agent are seeing the same thing (Dunphy-Lelii & Wellman, 2004; Moll & Tomasello, 2004). Indeed, by 20–24 months children orient an object away from themselves (depriving themselves of the interesting sight) to ensure others will see it (Lempers, Flavell, & Flavell, 1977).

Initial infant insights about intention culminate in their understanding that intentional agents behave according to their desires and emotions, constrained by their perceptual experiences. This desire-emotion-perception understanding of persons encompasses a rudimentary but impressive sense of agents' awareness or unawareness (knowledge or ignorance) of events, a recognition that if persons' experiences of situations are not updated as events change then they can be unaware of key circumstances (and thus act in ignorance).

To be ignorant about something (event X) is *not* the same as to have a false belief about it. As depicted in box 10.2 an agent might have a false belief about (for example) where an object is – think it is in the drawer – beyond just being ignorant of its location. Beliefs thus more definitively focus on a person's mental "contents." Understanding the possibility of an internal realm of mental contents (ideas, thoughts, images) is the hallmark of a "representational" theory of mind. False beliefs, when contents of the world (object-in-cupboard) are seen to contradict contents of thought (object-in-drawer), provide a powerful, yet everyday, illustration of such representational understanding.

This is one reason there has been so much research on children's understanding of false belief (hundreds of studies in meta-analyses by Liu, Wellman, Tardif, & Sabbagh, 2008; Milligan, Astington, & Dack, 2007; Wellman, Cross, & Watson, 2001). Another reason for this voluminous research, is that when researchers were first becoming interested in theory of mind, several easy-to-use, "standard" false-belief tasks were developed (box 10.2) and these have proved nicely revealing. For one, they consistently show an important developmental transition. Indeed, as shown in box 10.2, because they have been used worldwide, false-belief tasks reveal a universal childhood theory-of-mind achievement.

While false belief has proven empirically useful in several fashions, a focus on a single task or achievement is limited and misleading. So, it is important that by 3–4 years children expect people not only to act in accord with their beliefs, even when those are mistaken or false, but also to experience "internal," immaterial ideas, thoughts, and dreams. Thus, at about the same time that children consistently pass false-belief tests, they judge mental entities (thoughts, dreams) as not-real (Harris, Brown, Marriot, Whithall, & Harmer, 1991; Wellman & Estes, 1986): if told about someone who has a dog versus someone thinking about a dog, children at this age know who can pet and see "her dog," and which dog is just made up or "in the mind." They understand that thought-bubbles (an external representation) show a person's thoughts (internal, mental representations) (Wellman, Hollander, & Schult, 1996). They come to understand about lies and deception (Peterson & Siegal, 2002), appearances versus reality (Flavell, Flavell, & Green, 1987) and that someone's external expressions or actions need not display their internal feelings (Harris, Donnelly, Guz, & Pitt-Watson, 1986).

Still-older children develop increasingly reflective ideas about minds, brains, and mental life. Children's understanding of thinking, for example, shows considerable development. While 3- and 4-year-olds know that thinking is an internal mental event (different from looking, talking, or touching) and that the contents of one's thoughts (e.g., a thought about a dog) are not public or tangible, they fail to recognize the constant flow of ideas and thoughts experienced in everyday life and involved in actively, consciously thinking. Thus, 7-year-olds and adults assert that a person sitting quietly with

Box 10.2 False-belief tasks

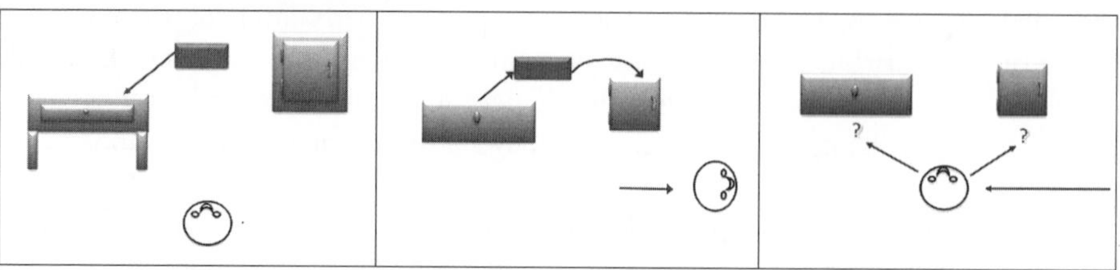

False-belief tasks have children reason about an agent whose actions should be controlled by a false belief. Such tasks have many forms, but a common task employs a change in locations, as depicted above. The child (not shown above) sees the character, Jill, put her candy in one of two locations. The character leaves and, while she cannot see, the candy gets moved. The character returns, wants her candy, and the child is asked "Where will Jill look for her candy?" or "Where does Jill think her candy is?" Older children answer correctly, like adults. Younger children answer incorrectly. They are not just random: they consistently say Jill will search in the cupboard (where it really is). Note that the task taps more than just attribution of ignorance (Jill doesn't know); rather it assess attribution of false belief (Jill thinks – falsely – her candy is in the drawer).

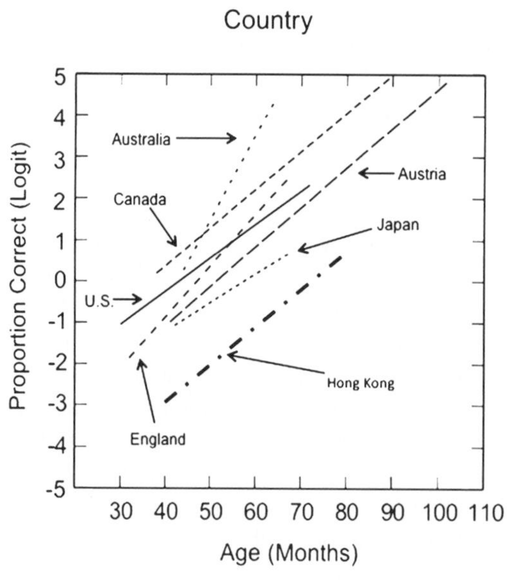

A frequently used alternative task uses deceptive contents (rather than a change of location). For example, children see a crayon box and say they think it holds crayons. Then, upon opening it, they see that it holds candies. They are asked what someone else who has never looked inside will think the box holds – crayons or candies.

Several task factors make such tasks harder or easier, but nonetheless children go from below-chance to above-chance performance, typically in the preschool years. Moreover, as shown in the graph (combining results from Wellman et al., 2001, and Liu et al., 2008), children in different cultural-linguistic communities can achieve false-belief understanding more quickly or more slowly, yet in all locales they evidence the same trajectory – from below-chance to above-chance performance in early to late childhood. This is true even for children growing up in non-Western cultural communities speaking non-Indo-European language. And it is true even for children in traditional, non-literate societies.

blank expression is still experiencing "some thoughts and ideas" and that it is nearly impossible to have a mind completely "empty of thoughts and ideas"; but children 5 and younger do not share these intuitions (Flavell, Green, & Flavell, 1993, 1995). Coming to recognize that thinking streams constantly along develops on the heels of initial preschool understandings of mental contents.

Older children also come to understand how mind and brain interrelate (Johnson & Wellman, 1982; Richert & Harris, 2006). Moreover they wrestle with the possibilities of extraordinary mental capacities. Thus, early understandings of mind established in the preschool years allow children to begin to think about how mind is embodied or, potentially, disembodied; about mental-spiritual activity beyond the confines of the body (e.g., life after death) and beyond the limits of ordinary human thought (e.g., the possibility of superhuman capabilities and agents, including God, that might be all-knowing or all-seeing in contrast to human fallibility). (See Wellman & Johnson, 2008, for a recent review.)

Several topics embedded in this overview are particularly rich in data or debate. They reveal more precisely how theory of mind develops, and allow deeper consideration of competing accounts of that development.

Infants' Intention Understandings

How does theory of mind originate? The earliest examples of psychological construals of persons appear in the intention understandings of infants. In common parlance "intentional" means goal-directed and applies to action, but in the wider philosophic sense "intentionality" marks a distinctive kind of subjective orientation of beings to the world. The infant intention-understandings to be addressed, therefore, encompass understanding of action and experience. An ever-present issue for methodological consideration and theoretical debate is whether infants' achieve intention understanding at all, or rather impressive yet nonetheless surface-behavioral analyses of human action.

Understanding intentional actions

As the stimuli outlined in box 10.1 show, intentional actions are amenable to research with non-verbal infants because they are easily observable by infants. Yet, such acts potentially manifest an actor's psychological states – her goals, desires, intentions. Results like those in box 10.1 provide evidence of infant understandings that go beyond attention to surface behaviors. Other such tasks provide converging results, including an often-used paradigm developed by Woodward (1998) where infants see a person (or inanimate device; Luo & Baillargeon, 2005) contacting, grasping (pointing to, etc.) one of two objects adjacent to each other.

In the Woodward paradigm as well as the one in box 10.1, the actions presented to infants are pre-packaged and carefully segmented in various ways – for example, infants are habituated to a single reaching behavior shown for multiple trials. In everyday behavior, however, intentional actions merge seamlessly in ongoing streams (e.g., mother goes to closet, gets mop, mops floor, rinses mop, and so on). Baldwin, Baird, Saylor, & Clark (2001) filmed such everyday streams of action and then asked adults to identify portions that were "meaningful in terms of understanding the actor's intentions." Infants aged 10–11 months were then shown such videos in *intention-completing* versions (a pause was inserted in the video at a point that adults identified as the endpoint of an intentional-action segment) and *intention-disrupting* versions (pause inserted in the middle of an intentional-action segment). Infants looked longer at the *intention-disrupting* videos: behavior segments that contradict the intentional boundaries that adults recognize seem "funny" to infants. Apparently, infants not only identify agents' goals in simple, discreet acts, they can extract goal-directed acts from ongoing behavior.

Infant understandings of intentional action appear in looking-time research, but also in more active-interactive paradigms. For example, Behne, Carpenter, Call, & Tomasello (2005) engaged infants in a game where a woman gave them toys across a table. Interspersed were trials where she held up a toy but did not give it over, sometimes because she was "unwilling" to do so and sometimes because she was "unable" (e.g., could not extract the toy from a transparent container). Infants aged 9–18 months (but not 6-month-olds) behaved more impatiently (e.g., reaching, turning away) when the woman willfully kept the toy than when she was making good-faith efforts to pass it along. Infants thus appreciated something of the intentional differences between "unable" and "unwilling" scenarios, although the surface behaviors and outcomes were parallel in both.

Relatedly, intentional action is not only directed toward specific goals, it is non-accidental. Thus, in Carpenter, Akhtar, & Tomasello (1998), 14- and 18-month-old infants watched an adult model several two-action sequences on complex objects (e.g., pushing a button and then moving a lever). One action was marked vocally by the adult as intentional ("There!"), and one as accidental ("Whoops!"). Infants imitated almost twice as many intentional as accidental actions and only very rarely imitated the entire two-action sequences (see also Olineck & Poulin-Dubois, 2005).

When viewing actions such as those in box 10.1 or such as pushing buttons and moving levers, infants might conceivably identify only the spatial-directedness and objective efficiency of the overt behavior toward its overt target – a teleological or behavioral rather than intentional understanding (Gergley & Csibra, 2003). However, inferring a goal when it is unfulfilled, and thus non-overt in the actor's movements or outcomes, demonstrates an understanding that intentions exist beyond the surface actions performed. So, in a seminal study (Meltzoff, 1995) 18-month-olds witnessed an adult try but fail to fulfill several novel, object-directed goals (e.g., trying to hang a ring on a hook). Although infants never saw the actions successfully modeled, when given a chance to act on the objects themselves they "imitated" the successful action much more than the failed (actually witnessed) actions. Fifteen-, but not 12-month-olds also display this pattern (Carpenter et al., 1998). Of course, motoric imitation is arguably a demanding response system, more so than attentive looking. So, consider a version of the displays in box 10.1 where now the actor reaches for but falls short of successfully grasping the target object. If habituated to such unsuccessful actions 10- and 12-month-olds, but *not* 8-month-olds, interpret the actions in terms of the (never actually seen) intentional goal of grasping the object (Brandone & Wellman, 2009).

Understanding intentional experiences

Recall that by about the first birthday infants gaze-follow and even move to follow a person's gaze around barriers, visually checking back and forth. However, even in appropriately gazing around barriers, infants could be responding to the agent's eyeball (or head-nose) orientation without a deeper sense of her intentional experience (Moore & Corkum, 1994). For example, at 12 months, infants often "gaze-follow" the head turns of adults who wear blindfolds. But recent data confirm a deeper understanding of visual experience. In Meltzoff and Brooks (2008) 12-month-olds were given advance experience with blindfolds occluding their own vision. After such experiences they were significantly less likely to "gaze-follow" a blindfolded adult, suggesting that their sense of what the adult can see – visually experience – guided infants' actions. Eighteen-month-olds do not often gaze-follow a blindfolded adult – probably because they have come to understand that blindfolds occlude vision. But in this same study 18-month-olds were given experience with a special blindfold that looked opaque yet was easily seen through when worn. After experience with that blindfold, 18-month-olds did gaze-follow the head turn of a blindfolded adult. Thus, by 12–18 months it is infants' sense of the person's visual experience (not just overt eye- or head-directedness) that often controls their gaze following.

Persons not only can have intentional experiences about some here-and-now event, their experiences can accumulate and update (or fail to update) over time. Tomasello and Haberl (2003) examined this with 12- and 18-month-old infants who interacted with three objects. Critically, a target adult joined in these interactions for two of the objects, but was absent for the third. After these interactions, the target adult saw all three objects displayed on a tray, and said to the infant, "Wow! That's cool! Can you give it to me?" while gesturing ambiguously in the direction of the objects. Three objects were now familiar for the infant, but one was new (and so "cool") to the target adult. Infants gave the target adult the object that was new for her. Thus, they tracked the adult's experiences sufficiently to know that (a) her experience was not updated when theirs was (a recognition of the subjectivity of experience) and (b) she was previously unaware of (ignorant of) the third object.

Infant intention understandings predict later theory of mind

As outlined earlier and in box 10.2, children in the preschool years evidence many further theory-of-mind achievements including but not limited to a robust, explicit understanding of false belief. Arguably, these later understandings represent increasingly rich and deep intention understandings continuous with precursory infant understandings. Indeed, several studies now show that infant attention to intentional action in looking-time studies predicts later theory of mind (Aschersleben, Hofer, & Jovanovic, 2008; Wellman, Phillips, Dunphy-Lelii, & LaLonde, 2004). In essence, how long infants attend to intentional action, in displays very much like those in box 10.1, predicts their later performance on false belief as well other preschool theory-of-mind tasks.

However, infant attention to perceptual-object displays (such as familiar vs. novel objects and images) in looking-time studies predicts later IQ (Bornstein & Sigman,

1986). These perceptual-attention findings are consistently interpreted as demonstrating developmental continuity in general information processing, such as memory-encoding or executive function. Do the intention-understanding findings simply tap continuity in such general cognitive processing, or are they more specific to a domain of social cognition? In the most comprehensive study to date, infant attention to intentional action at 10- to 12-months predicted later theory-of-mind understanding at 4-years (essentially false-belief understanding on standard tasks) even when IQ, language competence (vocabulary), and executive functioning at 4-years were factored out (Wellman, Lopez-Duran, LaBounty, & Hamilton, 2008). Moreover, in one recent study infant attention to physical-action displays did not predict later theory of mind (Yamaguchi, Kuhlmeier, Wynn, & vanMarle, 2009). Thus, intention understanding evidences distinctive infant-to-preschool continuities; infant intention understanding is not only early achieved, it is formative for further developmental advances in theory of mind.

In sum, infant intention understandings are deep and generative, encompassing intentional action and experience and yielding an initial sense of persons' knowledge and ignorance that predicts later, preschool, theory of mind. If anything, this summary may underestimate the full extent of infants' early understanding of mental states: some now claim infants understand false belief, as I address within the next section.

False Belief within Belief–Desire Reasoning

False-belief tasks, as outlined at the top of box 10.2 encompass mentalistic reasoning about others but also the self. Young children are as incorrect about their own false beliefs as they are for others; the trajectories for preschool self-understanding exactly parallel those shown for other-understanding in box 10.2 (see Wellman et al., 2001). False-belief tasks also encompass reasoning about more than just beliefs. The character *wants* her toy, she did not *see* it move, when she looks for it in the drawer she will be *disappointed*.

Philosophers and psychologists often characterize our everyday system of reasoning about mind, world, and behavior as a belief–desire psychology (D'Andrade, 1987; Fodor, 1987; Wellman, 1990). Such an everyday psychology provides explanations and predictions of action by appeal to what the person thinks, knows, and expects coupled with what he or she wants, intends, and hopes for. Why did Jill go to the drawer: she *wanted* her chocolate and *thought* it was in the drawer. Everyday psychological reasoning also includes reasoning about the origins of mental states (Jill wants candy because she is *hungry*; Jill thinks it is in the drawer where she last *saw* it). That is, naïve psychology incorporates a variety of related constructs such as drives and preferences that ground one's desires, and perceptual-historical experiences that ground one's beliefs. It also includes emotional reactions that result from these desires, beliefs, preferences, and perceptions: happiness at fulfilled desires, frustration at unfulfilled desires, surprise when events contradict one's firmly held beliefs. As follows from this quick outline of everyday psychological reasoning, considerable research has charted children's understanding of beliefs, desires, perceptions, emotions, and how these relate to real-world actions, situations, and objects (see Harris, 2006). Children's performance on false-belief tasks stands as a marker of important developments in this network of belief–desire reasoning about self and others.

Amid the consistent trajectories shown in box 10.2, from below-chance incorrect judgment to above-chance correct judgments in the years from 2 to 6 or 7, there is also obvious variation in the timetable across countries. There is considerable variation across individuals too. Although almost all normally developing children eventually master false belief, some children (in any cultural-language community) come to this understanding earlier and some later. This variation is important for identifying factors that impact the achievement of theory-of-mind understandings and outcomes that are influenced by theory-of-mind insights.

For antecedents, conversations with parents about mental states, about emotions, about the causes of action, influence how quickly children come to theory-of-mind milestones (e.g. false belief) (Dunn & Brown, 1993; Ruffman, Slade, & Crowe, 2002). Language competence more generally also impacts theory-of-mind achievement (Astington & Baird, 2005). Living in social networks, such as having siblings or larger social kin groups, also enhances preschool theory of mind (e.g., Perner, Ruffman, & Leekam, 1994).

Regarding outcomes, differences in false-belief understanding as measured in the preschool years predict several key childhood competences, such as how and how much children talk about people in everyday conversation, their engagement in pretense, their social interactional skills and consequently their interactions with and popularity with peers (Astington & Jenkins, 1995; Lalonde & Chandler, 1995; Watson, Nixon, Wilson, & Capage, 1999). These findings are important for confirming theory of mind's real-life relevance. But the links are neither as strong nor as direct as some have assumed. Astington (2003) puts this nicely by saying that theory of mind is "sometimes necessary but never sufficient" to guide children's social-communicative interactions.

All these findings suggest something definite and important is happening in children's theory-of-mind understandings in the preschool years. But what? Recent research claims infants – at 10–15 months – already recognize that actors act on the basis of their beliefs, and false beliefs. If accurate, such findings would argue that coming to an awareness of false belief (and relatedly a representational theory of mind) is not as central a part of the preschool transition as it once seemed.

Box 10.3 presents the essence of the initial influential task and findings from Onishi & Baillargeon (2005). Several other demonstrations are on offer (Scott & Baillargeon, in press; Surian, Caldi, & Sperber, 2007) with more sure to follow. I believe these studies confirm, in important fashions, that infants understand actors as goal-directed, that infants track the changing experiences of other persons that yield for them awareness or unawareness of key events (at least in simplified scenarios), and that infants expect aware and unaware agents to act differently. Thus these findings help underwrite the description above that infants achieve a desire–emotion–perception understanding of persons that encompasses an initial sense of knowledge and ignorance (or more precisely, awareness and unawareness). As outlined in box 10.3, however, I do not believe the data demonstrate an infant recognition of false belief (and hence of an internal world of mental contents). Instead, to repeat, infants track and rely on awareness (knowledge) and unawareness (ignorance).

Box 10.3 Onishi and Baillargeon's (2005) demonstration of false-belief understanding

Recent research claims that the intention understanding of one-year-old infants also includes false belief understanding. The initial and most well-known demonstration comes from Onishi and Baillargeon (2005), in a familiarization-test paradigm schematized here. In essence, paralleling standard tasks (see Box 10.2), infants see that the agent places the object in one location and does not see the object switch locations. If infants expect the agent to search in the prior location (on the basis of a false belief), they should look longer at the Light box test event (not expecting her to search at the correct, new location). 15-month-old infants do consistently look longer at Light box test events.

Onishi & Baillargeon also use several other carefully contrasting conditions. For example, in a True-belief condition infants see the same events except that in phase B they see the agent watch the object move to the lighter box. In that condition, infants look longer at the Dark box test event (rather than the Light box).

A. Familiarization: Agent puts toy in dark box

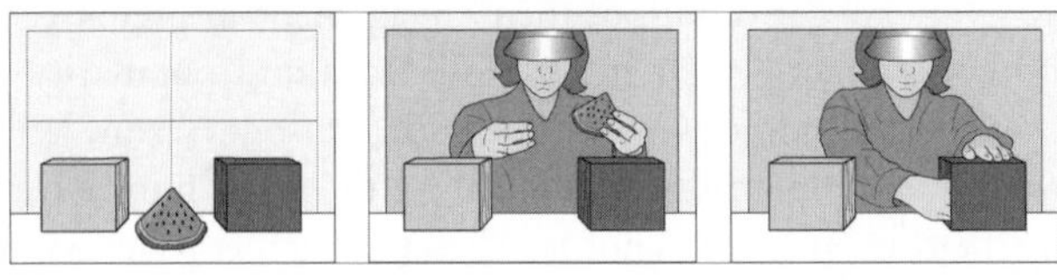

B. Change: Agent doesn't see toy move to lighter box

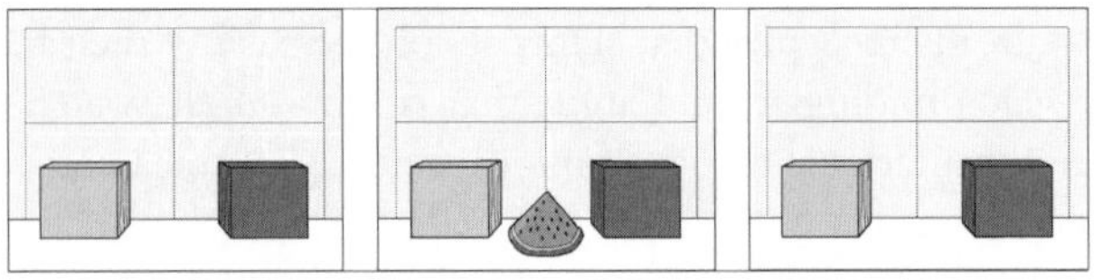

C. Test events: Infant sees agent search, in either:

Light box

Dark box

Note, again, however, that understanding false belief requires more than just understanding ignorance. So, alternative interpretations are possible based on an infant understanding of ignorance rather than false belief. For example, if infants understand the agent is unaware (and thus ignorant of the location of the object), that understanding would be sufficient for them to see the Light box test event (in the events shown to the left) as novel or unexpected (e.g., if the agent is ignorant, she might search in neither place, she might search in both places, she might search incorrectly, but in any event it would be novel/unexpected to see her search directly in only the correct location.)

Part of the force of this argument comes from a deeper consideration of infant looking-time methods. We can assume for now that such "violation of expectation" methods (Baillargeon, Li, Gertner, & Wu, chapter 1, this volume) do help reveal something like infants' expectations (although whether such methods reveal expectancies is hotly debated (Haith, 1998). The question remains: *what* expectations? Baillargeon et al. reason that by looking longer at Light-box (new location) events (in the focal condition shown in box 10.3) the infant shows he was expecting the agent to reach to the prior location instead, because of the agent's un-updated, and hence false, belief about where the object is. However, looking-time tasks such as these have a powerful asymmetry to them. If the infant looks longer at event A than event B (given proper familiarization and control conditions) we can infer that he did *not* expect A. We cannot infer that, in contrast, he did expect B; the infant might have no expectation about B, but still look longer at A because he did not expect *that*. We have no evidence as to the infant's expectation about B, because the increased infant looking time is toward A. That is, in tasks like those in box 10.3 we do not know the infant expects the agent to search at the prior location, only that the infant did not expect her to search at the new location.

This is importantly related to whether the infant is attributing ignorance (unawareness) or something more belief-like. By looking longer at the Light-box (new location) test event the infant signals he did not expect (or was puzzled by) the unaware (ignorant) agent searching (directly, unhesitatingly) at the new location – why should she do that when she was unaware where it was? On this more critical analysis the data fall crucially short of demonstrating that the infant recognizes (as you or I might) that the agent *believes* the object is in the prior location. It is sufficient that the infant recognizes that the agent is unaware where the object is.

Admittedly, infants' understanding of mental states (beyond intentions and emotions) is both contested and still unclear. It is being vigorously researched because the resolution of this issue is important to competing accounts for characterizing the nature of theory-of-mind cognition and its development. To illustrate, consider two important and contrasting positions.

Theory-theories

One account of theory-of-mind development takes the term "theory" quite seriously. This theory-theory account (e.g., Gopnik & Meltzoff, 1997; Wellman, 1990) claims that young children's psychological understandings are demonstrably theory-like in that unobservable constructs – such as beliefs and desires – are used to explain, predict, and understand human behavior and experience. A theory-theory account is a constructivist account (albeit a domain-specific one): the basic claim is that children achieve a coherent understanding of persons via everyday theoretical *constructs*. Developmentally, theory-theory contends that an initial theory of mind is revised into later understandings, because accumulating data and information lead to theory change. According to this position, the progression of observable developmental changes – from understanding intentions, then desires and emotions and even ignorance but not beliefs, to understanding of beliefs but rarely considering them in everyday understandings of persons' lives and actions, to later more comprehensive appreciation of the role of mental contents in many, many human actions and experiences (a representational theory of mind) – closely mimics a process of theory change whereby a conception of belief is first absent, and then developed only as a marginal auxiliary hypothesis, before becoming theoretically central to children's understanding (Gopnik & Wellman, 1994).

Mental modules

In contrast, other theorists contend that "theory of mind" is misnamed, and psychological understandings are achieved via the computations of an innate mental module. Mental modules, as described initially by Fodor (1983), generate representations of perceptual inputs, as in the 3-D representations of spatial layout achieved by the visual system (Marr, 1982). Such modules are innately specified, their processing is mandatory and encapsulated, and thus they are essentially unrevisable – no amount of training or counter-experiences would cause us to perceive the world in terms of two dimensions rather than three. On analogy to such perceptual modules, Leslie (1987, 1994) in particular, but also others (Baron-Cohen 1995; Fodor 1992), propose there is a distinct theory-of-mind module that produces representations of human activity in terms of a person's mental attitudes toward events, such as his beliefs about X, desires about X, emotions about X. As detailed by Leslie (1987, 1994) this module – ToMM – enables the child to represent not just actions, but also representational states themselves (e.g., a person's belief about the world). The rapid development of person-understandings apparent in normal children, such as the acquisition of an understanding of false-belief, depends on this specialized mental module "coming online" (Scholl & Leslie, 1999).

Obviously, for Leslie's position it is troublesome that understanding beliefs and false beliefs appears to come after clear understanding of desires and emotions. If ToMM automatically computes mental attitudes – desires, emotions, but also beliefs – these should come online together. Leslie proposes that ToMM comes online in late infancy (Leslie, 1994), so it is also problematic if there is no evidence of understanding beliefs and false beliefs until later in the preschool years. But, of course, demonstrations of infant recognition that actions can be shaped and constrained by false beliefs, if accurate, are completely consistent with his position. They would be a welcome confirmation of his originally theoretical proposals (Leslie, 2005).

Conversely for theory-theories, demonstrations of infant recognition that actions can be shaped and constrained by false beliefs, if true, undermine an account based on the progressive construction of new concepts built from a process of evidence-based revision of prior less-complete conceptual networks. And demonstrations of early, infant understanding of false belief, if accurate, would overthrow the more specific proposal that early intentional understanding is bereft of an understanding of belief (Wellman et al., 2001). This would then undermine the assertion that understanding of belief and false belief represent a clear case of genuine conceptual change within children's developing theories of mind (Gopnik & Wellman, 1994). So, data on potential infant understanding of false belief is of keen import to our understanding of theory of mind and its development. Stay tuned.

That said, not everything, or even most things, turns on properly characterizing infants' understandings.

Autism and Deafness

Modular theorists proposed that the social and communicative deficits of autism reflect neurological impairment to the theory-of-mind module (Baron-Cohen, Leslie, & Frith, 1985; Leslie, 1987). Many studies now show impairment in reasoning about mental states in high-functioning individuals with autism (see Baron-Cohen, 1995). These sorts of deficits in psychological reasoning are not apparent in control groups of subjects with Down's syndrome, general retardation, or specific language delays.

This research has helped address the question of whether theory of mind is domain-specific or rather the result of domain-general cognitions applied to the task of understanding persons. Connectionist modeling of various forms of knowledge and cognition, among other analyses, helps underwrite the possible power of more domain-general processes and accounts of conceptual development in general, and conceivably of theory of mind more specifically. However, most scholars now believe that understanding of persons is advantaged or prepared by more specialized domain-specific processing as well.

In this regard, high-functioning autistics' performance with false photographs versus false beliefs has proved revealing. False-belief tasks are outlined in box 10.2; false-photograph tasks are comparable in format but target not mental representational devices but rather physical representational devices. High-functioning autistics consistently fail false-belief tasks, yet consistently pass parallel false-photo tasks (Leekam & Perner, 1991; Leslie & Thaiss, 1992). Because these individuals' memory, attention, learning, or executive functioning are sufficient to understand false photos, such domain-general processing factors fail to account for the parallel difficulties with false beliefs. Data such as these lend support to more domain-specific accounts of psychological understandings. So do the data reviewed earlier, showing that early infant intention understandings predict later theory of mind even when IQ, language competence, and executive functioning are controlled for. Still, to be clear, none of this requires that theory-of-mind reasoning reflect the working of an innate ToMM, although that sort of position first inspired research on theory of mind and autism.

Indeed, one implication of positing ToMMs is that individuals who are not impaired in the relevant modules – for example, are not autistic – should achieve mental-state understandings on a roughly standard maturational timetable. Yet, in many studies deaf preschool children raised by hearing parents show delays and deficiencies on theory-of-mind tasks comparable to those of children with autism (Gale, deVilliers, deVilliers, & Pyers, 1996; Peterson & Siegal, 1995, 1997; see Peterson, 2004, for a review). These deaf children have not suffered the same sort of neurological damage that autistics have, as evidenced by the fact that deaf children raised by deaf parents do not show theory-of-mind delays. Findings such as these challenge accounts of theory-of-mind development relying solely on neurological-maturational mechanisms; as do the data reviewed earlier on individual and cultural differences in preschool theories of mind that highlight a sizable role for experience-based learning about the mind.

Progressions in Theory-of-Mind Understandings

Theory-theorists have focused more on charting the extended progression of conceptions that children achieve in their early years. An extended series of developmental achievements in infants', young children's, and older children's mental-state understandings fits a theory-construction perspective that expects children to achieve a progression of intermediate understandings as initial conceptions fail to adequately explain behavior and thus get progressively revised in the face of counter-evidence.

Consider the overview of developmental progressions with which I began this chapter. Within such broad progressions are several more precise ones. The best-established progression concerns comparisons between children's understanding of desires and intentions versus beliefs. When tested in closely comparable tasks toddlers evidence an understanding that people can have differing desires for the exact same object or event but not that they may have differing beliefs (Wellman & Liu, 2004, provide a meta-analytic review). Comparisons on closely comparable tasks also show preschool understanding of knowledge and ignorance in the face of failing to understand false belief (Wellman & Liu, 2004).

A progression from reasoning about desires (as well as perceptual awareness and emotional experience) to later reasoning about beliefs is also revealed in children's everyday conversations. In the research reviewed thus far, infants and children mostly make elicited responses and judgments in tasks that guide their attention to mental states. If children's ordinary construal of persons is mentalistic, however, these conceptions should be apparent in their everyday life, as in everyday references to people.

Children produce such words as *happy*, *sad*, *want*, and *like* by late in the second year of life (e.g., Bretherton & Beeghly, 1982; Brown & Dunn, 1991). Systematic analyses show that young children use these terms to refer to persons' internal experiential states distinct from their external behaviors, physical features, and facial expressions. These conceptual distinctions are nicely clear when young children explicitly contrast desires and reality, or two individuals' different desires or preferences, as in the following conversational exchanges, all from 2-year-old children (Bartsch & Wellman, 1995; Wellman, Harris, Bannerjee, & Sinclair, 1995).

Father: Marky's mad at your Daddy. [Mark is Ross's brother.]
Ross: But I'm happy at my Daddy!

Adult: You don't like it?
Abe: No … You like it?
Adult: Yes, I do.
Abe: But I don't like it.

Peter: I wanna come out. But I can't come out.

Abe: I like Michael. I like Michael, Mommy.

Mother: Do you want to go outside and play with Michael?
Abe: No. Not right now.

Child: "I was sad. But I didn't cry."

In these contrastive discourses children make several subjective distinctions. Some contrast one person's subjective experience with that of another – one person is mad but another is happy about the exact same physical object (e.g., Daddy). Others contrast desire or emotion with overt action: "I wanna come out; but I can't come out"; "I was sad; but I didn't cry."

These everyday conversations also evidence a shift from early references to desire and emotion to a later reference to beliefs and thoughts. Early on, children use words like *want* and *like* to refer to desires, and begin to say "I don't *know*," but they do not use words such as *think* and *wish* to refer to thoughts or beliefs until about 3 years of age or older (Bartsch & Wellman, 1995; Brown & Dunn, 1991). This shift is also apparent for children in China acquiring Mandarin or Cantonese (Tardif & Wellman, 2000), and for deaf children acquiring sign language (Anderson & Reilly, 2002). Absence of references to thinking in very young preschoolers is striking considering that their parents talk to them about beliefs and thoughts as well as desires and emotions (Bartsch & Wellman, 1995).

A more detailed, extended progression of understandings that characterize theory of mind has been recently established in a theory-of-mind scale (Wellman & Liu, 2004) that encompasses carefully constructed tasks assessing childhood understanding of: (a) diverse desires (people can have different desires for the same thing); (b) diverse beliefs (people can have different beliefs about the same situation); (c) knowledge-ignorance (something can be true, but someone can be ignorant of that); (d) false belief (something can be true, but someone might believe something different); and (e) hidden emotion (someone can feel one way but display a different emotion). The tasks are similar in procedures, language, and format, yet US preschoolers evidence a clear order of difficulty (as listed above), with understanding diverse desires being easiest and understanding hidden emotion being hardest. The same 5-step progression also characterizes Australian (Peterson, Wellman, & Liu, 2005) and German (Kristen, Thoermer, Hofer, Aschersleben, & Sodian, 2006) preschoolers, and a very similar progression characterizes Chinese children (Wellman, Fang, Liu, Zhu, & Liu, 2006). Moreover, Harris, Pons, and colleagues (Harris, Rosnay, & Pons, 2006; Pons, Harris, & Rosnay, 2003) report a related scale-like progression in children's understanding of emotion.

Consider the scale findings that children become aware that two persons can have different desires for the same object (diverse desires) before they become aware that two persons can have different beliefs about the same object (diverse beliefs), and that both diverse-desire awareness and diverse-belief awareness are achieved before children achieve understanding of false beliefs. Modular accounts (e.g., Leslie, 1994, 2005) claim that preschool children equally understand beliefs and desires; it is false belief that is peculiarly and distinctively difficult. In contrast, the scaling data show that understanding beliefs is more difficult than desires, even when understanding false belief is not at issue: The diverse-belief task does not require understanding false belief, but is nonetheless significantly more difficult than understanding diverse desires in spite of being almost identical in format, materials, and so on. Alternatively, executive-function accounts (or more precisely what Carlson & Moses, 2001, called executive-function expression accounts) suggest that children's difficulty with mental states in general, and false belief in particular, stems from difficulties in inhibiting a pre-potent response to generate a different response. For example, responding correctly to a false-belief task requires not stating what one knows is true but stating instead what the other person thinks is true. However, both diverse desires and diverse beliefs are similar in requiring inhibition of one's own point of view to answer in terms of the other person's point of view. Performance in belief tasks is nonetheless still worse than performance in desire tasks.

Of course executive-functioning skills undoubtedly impact children's understanding of mental states as well as performance on specific theory-of-mind tasks (Carlson & Moses, 2001; Leslie, German, & Polizzi, 2005), as does the child's developing language competence (Astington & Baird, 2005). But the scale data, and other data as well (e.g., see Sabbagh, Xu, Carlson, Moses, & Lee, 2006), show that executive-function developments and developing language competencies fall short of explaining theory-of-mind development. Something more specific to an understanding of persons and minds is also crucial.

Recall the research showing that children with autism evidence severe delays in understanding theory of mind as measured by false-belief tasks, as do children with deafness (more precisely deaf children of hearing parents). To what extent do such differences reflect severe delays along a "standard" theory-of-mind trajectory and/or altogether different developmental trajectories? Investigators have now used scaling methods (the theory-of-mind scale described above) to address this question (Peterson & Wellman, in press; Peterson et al., 2005). The short and intriguing answer is that children with deafness represent a case of severe delay whereas high-functioning children with autism represent a case of alternative, non-standard trajectory. Moreover, high-functioning autistic children are characterized by special difficulties understanding cognitive mental states (ideas, thoughts) and in particular belief and false belief. Findings like these help disentangle the contributing factors to theory-of-mind development that stem from (a) basic mentalizing capacities coupled with (b) conversational, social-interactive experiences and inputs.

In sum, theory-of-mind development is laced with more specific conceptual progressions that are informative in their own right and that provide more precise developmental data to inform theoretical accounts, as well as to better compare children across cultural contexts and across typical versus atypical development.

Primate Intention Understanding

Until recently it seemed that non-human primates (primates for short in what follows) construed agents in social-behavioral ways with very little, if any, understanding of them as intentional agents (Tomasello & Call, 1997). However, understanding of intentional action has been increasingly confirmed in primates (see Rosati, Hare, & Santos, in press, for a review). As one example, reconsider box 10.1. Following familiarization with events in which a human agent reaches in an arcing path over a barrier that separates it from a goal object, macaque monkeys looked longer at the indirect than the direct test event (Rochat, Serra, Fadiga, & Gallese, 2008). In control conditions, after familiarization with actors displaying the same acts with no barrier, macaques looked equally at the indirect and direct test events. These findings support the view that, like human infants, primates possess a basic understanding of the goal-directedness of action.

Complementary data again come from more active-interactive paradigms. In extensions of the unwilling–unable paradigm described earlier for infants, chimpanzees produced more begging behaviors and left the testing room earlier when an experimenter was unwilling to give them food (e.g., offering and withdrawing a grape teasingly) than when she was unable but trying to give them food (e.g., repeatedly dropping the grape) (Call, Hare, Carpenter, & Tomasello, 2004). Similarly, capuchins left the testing station sooner in response to the actions of an unwilling compared to an unable experimenter (Phillips, Barnes, Mahajan, Yamaguchi, & Santos, in press). Although the experimenter's actions were nearly identical at the surface, chimpanzees and capuchins recognized a difference between the underlying intentions.

Primates' understanding of intentional experiences, such as seeing, has also been studied. Many primates spontaneously follow the gaze or head orientation of conspecifics or humans. Although it is unlikely that most primate species follow gaze because they understand the nature of visual experience, great apes probably do. In controlled situations chimpanzees, bonobos, gorillas, and orangutans all follow gaze to distant locations and around barriers (even when it requires physically reorienting their bodies), and visually check back to verify the direction of the looker's gaze (Rosati et al., in press).

Data on primate understanding of visual experience is particularly strong for chimpanzees and in contexts of food competition. In early research using cooperative-communicative paradigms (in which an experimenter's goal was to share food with the chimpanzee), primates performed poorly and failed to demonstrate awareness of the intentional experience of others (e.g. Povinelli & Eddy, 1996). In paradigms involving competition for food, however, chimpanzees perform much better (Hare & Tomasello, 2004).

Consider: A piece of food is hidden between a dominant and a subordinate chimpanzee and, as a result of certain obstacles, the chimpanzees have different visual access to the food. When the subordinate could see two pieces of food and the dominant could see only one, the subordinate preferentially targeted the less-risky food that the dominant could not see (Hare, Call, Agnetta, & Tomasello, 2000). Further studies suggest that chimpanzees demonstrate these preferences because they understand something about the link between seeing and knowing: subordinates preferentially targeted an occluded piece of food that the dominant was ignorant of (had never seen and so was unaware of) or misinformed about (had seen in one place but had not seen moved) (Hare, Call, & Tomasello, 2001).

These abilities are probably not unique to chimpanzees. Rhesus monkeys also show impressive sensitivity to experimenters' perception and perceptual experiences in competitive situations (Flombaum & Santos, 2005).

Although chimpanzees (and some monkeys) understand action as intentional and understand something about the visual experience and even knowledge of others, primates' intention understanding falls short of children's. First, primates' understanding may be limited to competitive contexts, not more broadly applicable (e.g., to cooperative situations), as in children. Second, there is no evidence that primates go beyond the distinction between knowledge and ignorance to represent the false beliefs of others, even in competitive situations (Call & Tomasello, 2008; Rosati et al., in press). Finally, in the human case, intention understanding and theory of mind are revealed in numerous acts of pointing, showing, and teaching (Gergely, Egyed, & Kiraly, 2007); yet there is little if any evidence for anything like teaching in non-human primates.

In the human case, cognitive neuroscientists have been identifying a network of brain regions associated with theory of mind and intention understanding, as I address in the next section. Some of these systems appear to be uniquely human. But some overlap. For example, a related system of "mirror neurons" seems evident in both humans and primates; indeed this system was first discovered with non-human primates. These are called mirror neurons because they often fire if animals watch an action take place (enacted by someone else) *or* enact that action themselves. The exact role of mirror neurons in primates and humans is under debate. Possibly, they underlie imitative responding specifically, and by extension underlie a capacity for action/mental simulation (Rizzolatti, Fadiga, Fogassi, & Gallese, 2002) – whereby people understand others' states only "through" a sense of their own actions and states, by projecting or simulating others' actions and states from their own. One challenge for that interpretation is that non-human primates rarely if ever imitate (Rosati et al., in press), although imitation is rampant in very young children, even in infants and neonates (Bauer, 2002; Meltzoff & Moore, 1977). So an alternative intriguing possibility is that mirror neurons enable intention understanding (rather than imitative behavior or simulative reactions more specifically) (Lyons, Santos, & Keil, 2006; Rizzolatti & Fabbri-Destro, 2008).

Brain Bases

Characterizing and understanding the development of theory of mind requires not only research on infancy, sequential progressions, impairment, cultural–parental–child interactions, and conceptual learning, but also understanding the brain mechanisms involved. Indeed, functional neuroimaging, neurophysiology, and brain lesion studies with normal and autistic adults have begun to identify a network of brain regions associated with theory of mind and thus critical to smooth navigation of the social world (Gallagher & Frith, 2003; Saxe, Carey, & Kanwisher, 2004); these regions include the medial prefrontal cortex, the temporo-parietal junction, the superior temporal sulcus, and the temporal poles.

The extant research is intriguing and informative but far from definitive. One gap seems especially important: neuroimaging or neurophysiological studies of theory of mind have almost never examined children. Specialization of functions in the mature brain could, of course, come about in several ways – e.g., perhaps representing innate modularized functions or perhaps representing acquired specializations due to increasing expertise and conceptual learning. In general, from a *developmental cognitive neuroscience* perspective (e.g., Nelson & Luciana, 2001; Westermann et al., 2007), investigating developmental processes is critical for a complete understanding of human cognition and brain functioning.

Liu, Sabbagh, et al. (2009) provide initial developmental data about how theory of mind and the brain develop together. Because rapid theory-of-mind developments occur in the preschool years (see box 10.2) and because functional MRI and PET are not easily feasible for examining online cognitive functioning in children younger than 7or 8, they used ERP (event-related potentials) methodology (a form of EEG recording that is time-locked to specific events). Liu et al. recorded ERPs while children 3.5 to 6.5 years of age and adults made mental-state (false-belief) judgments and reality judgments. Children were divided into false-belief *passers* and *failers*. A characteristic late slow wave (LSW) with distinctive frontal scalp distribution appeared for adults when participants reasoned about beliefs in comparison to reality, consistent with other work (e.g. Sabbagh & Taylor, 2000) and consistent with other methods identifying medial prefrontal cortex as particularly recruited for theory-of-mind reasoning (e.g. Gallagher & Frith, 2003).

Two informative developmental changes emerged: (a) frontal brain substrates were recruited with increasing age for belief-judgments (they were apparent for child passers not failers, and for older more than younger children); (b) there was also a progression from a more diffuse frontal activation for child passers versus more specifically left-frontal activations for adults. A consistent finding in developmental cognitive neuroscience is that the neural activity associated with children's cognitive functioning may be more diffuse than that of adults (Casey, Giedd, & Thomas, 2000; Johnson, 1999); here, increased cortical specialization came with greater theory-of-mind development. These results begin to demonstrate the crucial developmental emergence of neural activity associated with the ability to reason about mental states.

Mature theory of mind requires understanding both beliefs and desires, and children can reason about desires and intentions well before beliefs. What about the neurocognitive underpinnings of desire reasoning, and relatedly this developmental lag? Liu, Meltzoff, and Wellman (2009) used ERP methodology to compare adults on three carefully matched tasks: desire-reasoning (essentially diverse-desire reasoning from the theory-of-mind scale), belief-reasoning (essentially diverse-belief reasoning from that scale), and reality-reasoning (a task with parallel format and stimuli, but requiring judgments about where two different physical objects go rather than what two different protagonists desire or think).

Adults' mental-state judgments were again characterized by LSW activations; in comparison to reasoning about reality, *both* belief- and desire-reasoning were characterized by LSW *frontal* activations. In addition, a LSW with *right posterior* scalp distribution was associated only with belief-reasoning.

To reiterate, neuroscience research increasingly suggests a network of brain regions associated with theory of mind that include not only the medial prefrontal cortex, but also the right temporo-parietal junction (RTPJ). In particular, functional MRI research with adults now indicates that the RTPJ is especially recruited for reasoning about beliefs and false beliefs in comparison to reasoning about pains or bodily actions or physical appearances (Saxe & Powell, 2006). The desire versus belief ERP data showing LSW right posterior activations for belief reasoning are thus consistent with research suggesting a special role for RTPJ in reasoning specifically about beliefs.

These results are especially intriguing in suggesting that desire-reasoning and belief-reasoning, while related, are probably not the product of a single ToMM at least at the neurological level. Moreover, they provide an explanation for a crucial developmental lag in theory-of-mind understandings: children need to recruit additional neural processes for reasoning about beliefs beyond an initial neural system for reasoning about mental states more generally (and common to reasoning about desires and beliefs). Such an interpretation could help explain the progression outlined earlier in behavioral studies showing a developmental sequence from understanding desires to understanding beliefs. Of course, such findings require confirmation; further *developmental* data will best test a hypothesis that children recruit two sets of neural processes to reason about mental states: an initial neural system (system 1) that encompasses, for example, reasoning about desires and intentions but that is supplemented (system 2) to reason about beliefs and false belief.

Conclusions

Researchers in this area now believe that theory of mind (a) is rapidly acquired in the normal case, (b) is acquired in an extended series of developmental accomplishments, (c) encompasses several basic insights that are acquired worldwide on a roughly similar trajectory (but not timetable), (d) requires considerable learning and development based on an infant set of prepared abilities to attend to and represent persons, (e) is severely impaired in autism, (f) is severely delayed in deaf children of hearing parents, and (g) results from but also contributes to specialized neural substrates associated with reasoning about agency, experience, and mind. Not all researchers would agree with all these points, but nonetheless this list represents an important consensus regarding theory of mind, based on considerable empirical knowledge garnered from 20 years of research effort by developmental scientists across a range of disciplines and countries.

At the same time, researchers in this area remain in serious dispute about how to characterize the nature of and the acquisition of theory of mind. In this chapter I use a contrast between modular and theory-theory positions as a way to capture some of the ongoing differences, but there are additional voices in the debate as well (see Harris, 2000, for a simulationist perspective, and Carlson & Moses, 2001, or Leslie et al., 2005, who emphasize the role of executive functioning in theory-of-mind development). These debates lead to a further conclusion of import for future research: we need enhanced developmental data and models. All comprehensive accounts of theory of mind have developmental components and expectations. This is obvious for theory-theory that, for example, predicts and receives support from findings such as the following: (a) theory-of-mind understandings unfold in a progression of developmental insights; (b) theory-of-mind achievements are attained at different times by children with different social-communicative experiences (sometimes dramatically different timetables, as in deafness), including growing up in different cultural communities; (c) even individuals with autism achieve, developmentally, some theory-of-mind advances; and (d) (as prediction) specialized brain circuitry dedicated to theory-of-mind reasoning is, in important part, the *outcome* of experience-dependent development. But the importance of developmental data also holds for nativist modular positions (Scholl & Leslie, 1999), that predict and receive support from findings such as the following: (a) typically developing children robustly achieve theory-of-mind understandings (e.g., false belief); (b) they do so across all cultures and languages, despite wide differences in social experiences; (c) individuals with autism are specifically impaired in theory-of-mind understandings, notably false belief (in comparison to other individuals with other impairments including, probably, even deafness); and (d) (as prediction) specialized brain circuitry dedicated to theory-of-mind reasoning is, in important part, the *cause* of experience-expectant development.

In very real senses, therefore, all accounts predict patterns of change and stability over a number of years as theory of mind is achieved. Indeed, although they approach the task in different ways, modular and theory-theory perspectives can both be described as attempting to characterize and understand complex learning mechanisms (Scholl & Leslie, 1999). Thus, a comprehensive understanding of theory of mind must be constrained by data as to how development actually progresses – which initial states lead to which intermediate and asymptotic states, influenced by which mechanisms. That sort of data (encompassing normally developing *and* atypically developing individuals across a variety of social-cultural experiences and backgrounds, with regard to sequences and progressions and not merely age groupings), while emerging, is still in short supply.

References

Anderson, D., & Reilly, J. (2002). The McArthur developmental inventory: Data for American sign language. *Journal of Deaf Studies and Deaf Education, 1*, 83–104.

Aschersleben, G., Hofer, T., & Jovanovic, B. (2008). The link between infant attention to goal-directed action and later theory of mind abilities. *Developmental Science, 11*, 862–868.

Astington, J. W. (2003). Sometimes necessary, never sufficient: False belief understanding and social competence. In B. Repacholi, & V. Slaughter (Eds.), *Individual differences in theory of mind: Implications for typical and atypical development* (pp. 13–38). New York: Psychology Press.

Astington, J. W., & Baird, J. A. (2005). *Why language matters for theory of mind.* New York: Oxford University Press.

Astington, J. W., & Jenkins, J. M. (1995). Theory of mind development and social understanding. *Cognition and Emotion, 9*(2–3), 151–165.

Baldwin, D. A., Baird, J. A., Saylor, M., & Clark, M. A. (2001). Infants parse dynamic action. *Child Development, 72*, 708–717.

Baldwin, D. A., & Moses, L. J. (1996). The ontogeny of social information gathering. *Child Development, 67*, 1915–1939.

Baron-Cohen, S. (1995). *Mindblindness: An essay on autism and theory of mind.* Cambridge, MA: MIT Press.

Baron-Cohen, S., Leslie, A. M., & Frith, U. (1985). Does the autistic child have a "theory of mind?" *Cognition, 21*, 37–46.

Bartsch, K., & Wellman, H. M. (1995). *Children talk about the mind.* New York: Oxford University Press.

Bauer, P. J. (2002). Early memory development. In U. Goswami (Ed.), *Blackwell Handbook of Cognitive Development* (pp. 127–146). Oxford: Blackwell.

Behne, T., Carpenter, M., Call, J., & Tomasello, M. (2005). Unwilling versus unable: Infants' understanding of intentional action. *Developmental Psychology, 41*, 328–337.

Bornstein, M. H., & Sigman, M. D. (1986). Continuity in mental development from infancy. *Child Development, 57*, 251–274.

Brandone, A. C., & Wellman, H. M. (2009). You can't always get what you want: Infants understand failed goal-directed actions. *Psychological Science, 20*(1), 85–91.

Bretherton, I., & Beeghly, M. (1982). Talking about internal states: The acquisition of an explicit theory of mind. *Developmental Psychology, 18*, 906–921.

Brown, J. R., & Dunn, J. (1991). "You can cry, mum": The social and developmental implications of talk about internal states. *British Journal of Developmental Psychology, 9*, 237–256.

Call, J., Hare, B., Carpenter, M., & Tomasello, M. (2004). "Unwilling" versus "unable": Chimpanzees' understanding of human intentional action. *Developmental Science, 7*, 488–498.

Call, J., & Tomasello, M. (2008). Does the chimpanzee have a theory of mind? 30 years later. *Trends in Cognitive Science, 12*, 187–192.

Carlson, S. M., & Moses, L. J. (2001). Individual differences in inhibitory control and children's theory of mind. *Child Development, 72*, 1032–1053.

Carpenter, M., Aktar, N., & Tomasello, M. (1998). 14- to 18-month-old infants differentially imitate intentional and accidental actions. *Infant Behavior and Development, 21*, 315–330.

Casey, B. J., Giedd, J. N., & Thomas, K. M. (2000). Structural and functional brain development and its relation to cognitive development. *Biological Psychology, 54*(1–3), 241–257.

Chi, M. T. H. (1978). Knowledge structure and memory development. In R. Siegler (Ed.), *Children's thinking: What develops?* (pp. 73–96). Hillsdale, NJ: Erlbaum.

Cosmides, L., & Tooby, J. (1994). Origins of domain specificity: The evolution of functional organization. In L. A. Hirschfeld & S. A. Gelman (Eds.), *Mapping the mind: Domain specificity in cognition and culture.* New York: Cambridge University Press.

Csibra, G., Gergely, G., Bíró, S., Koós, O., & Brockbank, M. (1999). Goal attribution without agency cues: The perception of "pure reason" in infancy. *Cognition, 72*, 237–267.

D'Andrade, R. (1987). A folk model of the mind. In D. Holland & N. Quinn (Eds.), *Cultural models in language and thought* (pp. 112–148). Cambridge: Cambridge University Press.

Dunn, J., & Brown, J. (1993). Early conversations about causality: Content, pragmatics and developmental change. *British Journal of Developmental Psychology, 11*, 107–123.

Dunphy-Lelii, S., & Wellman, H. M. (2004). Infants' understanding of occlusion of others' line-of-sight: Implications for an emerging theory of mind. *European Journal of Developmental Psychology, 1*, 49–66.

Flavell, J. H., Flavell, E. R., & Green, F. L. (1987). Young children's knowledge about apparent–real and pretend–real distinctions. *Developmental Psychology, 23*, 816–822.

Flavell, J. H., Green, F. L., & Flavell, E. R. (1993). Children's understanding of the stream of consciousness. *Child Development, 64*, 387–398.

Flavell, J. H., Green, F. L., & Flavell, E. R. (1995). Young children's knowledge of thinking. *Monographs of the Society for Research in Child Development* (Serial No. 243).

Flombaum, J. I., & Santos, L. R. (2005). Rhesus monkeys attribute perceptions to others. *Current Biology, 15*, 447–452.

Fodor, J. A. (1983). *Modularity of mind.* Cambridge, MA: MIT Press.

Fodor, J. A. (1987). *Psychosemantics: The problem of meaning in the philosophy of mind.* Cambridge, MA: Bradford Books/MIT Press.

Fodor, J. A. (1992). A theory of the child's theory of mind. *Cognition, 44*, 283–296.

Gale, E., deVilliers, P., deVilliers, J., & Pyers, J. (1996). *Language and theory of mind in oral deaf children.* Paper presented at the Boston University Conference on Language Development, Boston, MA.

Gallagher, H. L., & Frith, C. D. (2003). Functional imaging of theory of mind. *Trends in Cognitive Science, 7*, 77–83.

Gergely, G., & Csibra, G. (2003). Teleological reasoning in infancy. The naïve theory of rational action. *Trends in Cognitive Sciences, 7*, 287–292.

Gergely, G., Egyed, K., & Kiraly, I. (2007). On pedagogy. *Developmental Science, 10*, 139–146.

Gergely, G., Nádasdy, Z., Csibra, G., & Bíró, S. (1995). Taking the intentional stance at 12 months of age. *Cognition, 56*(2), 165–193.

Gopnik, A., & Meltzoff, A. N. (1997). *Words, thoughts and theories.* Cambridge, MA: MIT Press.

Gopnik, A., Meltzoff, A. N., & Kuhl, P. K. (2001). *The scientist in the crib: What early learning tells us about the mind.* New York: HarperCollins.

Gopnik, A., & Wellman, H. M. (1994). The theory theory. In L. Hirschfeld & S. Gelman (Eds.), *Domain specificity in cognition and culture* (pp. 257–293). New York: Cambridge University Press.

Haith, M. M. (1998). Who put the cog in infant cognition? Is rich interpretation too costly? *Infant Behavior and Development, 21*(2), 167–179.

Hamlin, J. K., Hallinan, E. V., & Woodward, A. L. (2008). Do as I do: 7-month-old infants selectively reproduce others' goals. *Developmental Science, 11*, 487–494.

Hare, B., Call, J., Agnetta, B., & Tomasello, M. (2000). Chimpanzees know what conspecifics do and do not see. *Animal Behaviour, 59*, 771–785.

Hare, B., Call, J., & Tomasello, M. (2001). Do chimpanzees know what conspecifics know? *Animal Behaviour, 61*, 139–151.

Hare, B., & Tomasello, M. (2004). Chimpanzees are more skillful in competitive than in cooperative cognitive tasks. *Animal Behaviour, 68*(3), 571–581.

Harris, P. L. (2000). *The work of the imagination.* Oxford: Blackwell.

Harris, P. L. (2006) Social cognition. In D. Kuhn & R. Siegler (Eds.), *Handbook of child psychology* (5th ed., pp. 811–858). NY: Wiley.

Harris, P. L., Brown, E., Marriot, C., Whithall, S., & Harmer, S. (1991). Monsters, ghosts and witches: Testing the limits of the fantasy–reality distinction in young children. *British Journal of Developmental Psychology, 9*, 105–123.

Harris P. L., de Rosnay, M., & Pons, F. (2006) Language and children's understanding of mental states. *Current Directions in Psychological Science, 14*, 69–73.

Harris, P. L., Donnelly, K., Guz, G. R., Pitt-Watson, R. (1986). Children's understanding of the distinction between real and apparent emotion. *Child Development, 57*, 895–909.

Hickling, A. K., & Wellman, H. M. (2001). The emergence of children's causal explanations and theories: Evidence from everyday conversation. *Developmental Psychology, 37*, 668–683.

Johnson, C. N., & Wellman, H. M. (1982). Children's developing conceptions of the mind and brain. *Child Development, 53*, 222–234.

Johnson, M. A. (1999). Developmental cognitive neuroscience. In M. Bennett (Ed.), *Developmental psychology: Achievements and prospects* (pp. 147–164). Philadelphia, PA: Psychology Press.

Kristen, S., Thoermer, C., Hofer, T., Aschersleben, G., & Sodian, B. (2006). Skalierung von "theory of mind" aufgaben (Scaling of theory of mind tasks). *Zeitschrift fur Entwicklungspsychologie und Padagogische Psychologie, 38*, 186–195.

Lalonde, C. E., & Chandler, M. J. (1995). False belief understanding goes to school: On the social-emotional consequences of coming early or late to a first theory of mind. *Cognition & Emotion, 9*(2–3), 167–185.

Leekam, S., & Perner, J. (1991). Does the autistic child have a "metarepresentational" deficit? *Cognition, 40*, 203–218.

Lempers, J. D., Flavell, E. R., & Flavell, J. H. (1977). The development in very young children of tacit knowledge concerning visual perception. *Genetic Psychology Monographs, 95*(1), 3–53.

Leslie, A. M. (1987). Pretense and representation: The origins of "theory of mind." *Psychological Review, 94*, 412–426.

Leslie, A. M. (1994). ToMM, ToBy, and agency: Core architecture and domain specificity in cognition and culture. In L. Hirschfeld & S. Gelman (Eds.), *Mapping the mind: Domain specificity in cognition and culture* (pp. 119–148). New York: Cambridge University Press.

Leslie, A. M. (2005). Developmental parallels in understanding minds and bodies. *Trends in Cognitive Sciences, 9*, 459–462.

Leslie, A. M., German, T. P., & Polizzi, P. (2005). Belief–desire reasoning as a process of selection. *Cognitive Psychology, 50*(1), 45–85.

Leslie, A. M., & Thaiss, L. (1992). Domain specificity in conceptual development: Neuropsychological evidence from autism. *Cognition, 43*, 225–251.

Liu, D., Meltzoff, A. N., & Wellman, H. M. (2009). Neural correlates of belief- and desire-reasoning. *Child Development, 80*, 1163–1171.

Liu, D., Sabbagh, M. A., Gehring, W. J., & Wellman, H. M. (2009). Neural correlates of children's theory of mind. *Child Development, 80*, 318–326.

Liu, D., Wellman, H. M., Tardif, T., & Sabbagh, M. A. (2008). Theory of mind development in Chinese children: A meta-analysis of false-belief understanding across cultures. *Developmental Psychology, 44*, 523–531.

Luo, Y., & Baillargeon, R. (2005). Can a self-propelled box have a goal? Psychological reasoning in 5-month-old infants. *Psychological Science, 16*, 601–608.

Lyons, D. E., Santos, L. R., & Keil, F. C. (2006). Reflections of other minds: How primate social cognition can inform the function of mirror neurons. *Current Opinion in Neurobiology, 16*, 1–5.

Marr, D. (1982). *Vision*. New York: W. H. Freeman.

Meltzoff, A. N. (1995). Understanding the intentions of others: Re-enactment of intended acts by 18-month-old children. *Developmental Psychology, 31*, 838–850.

Meltzoff, A. N., & Brooks, R. (2008). Self-experience as a mechanism for learning about others: A training study in social cognition. *Developmental Psychology, 44*(5), 1257–1265.

Meltzoff, A. N., & Moore, M. K. (1977). Imitation of facial and manual gestures by human neonates. *Science, 198*, 75–78.

Milligan, K., Astington, J. W., & Dack, L. A. (2007). Language and theory of mind: Meta-analysis of the relation between language ability and false-belief understanding. Preview. *Child Development, 78*(2), 622–646.

Moll, H., & Tomasello, M. (2004). 12- and 18-month-old infants follow gaze to spaces behind barriers. *Developmental Science, 7*, F1–F9.

Moore, C., & Corkum, V. (1994). Social understanding at the end of the first year of life. *Developmental Review, 14*, 349–372.

Nelson, C. A., & Luciana, M. (2001). *Handbook of developmental cognitive neuroscience*. Cambridge, MA: MIT Press.

Olineck, K. M., & Poulin-Dubois, D. (2005). Infants' ability to distinguish between intentional and accidental actions and its relation to internal state language. *Infancy, 8*, 91–100.

Onishi, K. H., & Baillargeon, R. (2005). Do 15-month-old infants understand false beliefs? *Science, 308*(5719), 255–258.

Perner, J., Ruffman, T., & Leekam, S. R. (1994). Theory of mind is contagious: You catch it from your sibs. *Child Development, 65*, 1228–1238.

Peterson, C. C. (2004) Theory of mind development in oral deaf children with cochlear implants or hearing aids. *Journal of Child Psychology and Psychiatry, 45*, 1096–1106.

Peterson, C. C., & Siegal, M. (1995). Deafness, conversation and theory of mind. *Journal of Child Psychology and Psychiatry, 36*, 459–474.

Peterson, C. C., & Siegal, M. (1997). Domain specificity and everyday biological, physical, and psychological thinking in normal, autistic, and deaf children. *New Directions for Child Development, 75*, 55–70.

Peterson, C. C., & Siegal, M. (2002). Mindreading and moral awareness in popular and rejected preschoolers. *British Journal of Developmental Psychology, 20*, 205–224.

Peterson, C. C., & Wellman, H. M. (in press). From fancy to reason: Scaling deaf and hearing children's understanding of theory of mind and pretence. *British Journal of Developmental Psychology.*

Peterson, C. C., Wellman, H. M., & Liu, D. (2005). Steps in theory of mind development for children with autism and deafness. *Child Development, 76*, 502–517.

Phillips, W., Barnes, J. L., Mahajan, N., Yamaguchi, M., & Santos, L. R. (in press). Unwilling versus unable: Capuchins' (*Cebus paella*) understanding of human intentional action. *Developmental Science.*

Phillips, A. T., & Wellman, H. M. (2005). Infants' understanding of object-directed reaching. *Cognition, 98*, 137–155.

Pons, F., Harris, P. L., & de Rosnay, M. (2003). Emotion comprehension between 3 and 11 years: Developmental periods and hierarchical organization. *European Journal of Developmental Psychology, 2*, 127–152.

Povinelli, D. J., & Eddy, T. J. (1996). What young chimpanzees know about seeing. *Monographs of the Society for Research in Child Development, 61* (Serial No. 247).

Richert, R. A., & Harris, P. L. (2006). The ghost in my body: Children's developing concept of the soul. *Journal of Cognition and Culture, 6*(3–4), 409–427.

Rizzolatti, G., Fabbri-Destro, M. (2008). The mirror system and its role in social cognition. *Current Opinion in Neurobiology, 18*(2), 179–184.

Rizzolatti, G., Fadiga, L., Fogassi, L., & Gallese, V. (2002). From mirror neurons to imitation: Facts and speculations. In A. N. Meltzoff & W. Prinz (Eds.), *The imitative mind: Development, evolution, and brain bases* (pp. 247–266). New York: Cambridge University Press.

Rochat, M. J., Serra, E., Fadiga, L., & Gallese, V. (2008). The evolution of social cognition: Goal familiarity shapes monkeys' action understanding. *Current Biology, 18*, 1–6.

Rosati, A., Hare, B. A., & Santos, L. R. (in press). Primate social cognition: Thirty years after Premack and Woodruff. In M. Platt & A. A. Ghazanfar (Eds.), *Primate Neuroethology.* Oxford: Oxford University Press.

Ruffman, T., Slade, L., & Crowe, E. (2002). The relation between children's and mothers' mental state language and theory-of-mind understanding. *Child Development, 73*, 734–751.

Sabbagh, M. A., & Taylor, M. (2000). Neural correlates of theory-of-mind reasoning: An event-related potential study. *Psychological Science, 11*, 46–50.

Sabbagh, M. A., Xu, F., Carlson, S. M., Moses, L. J., & Lee, K. (2006). The development of executive functioning and theory of mind: A comparison of Chinese and US preschoolers. *Psychological Science, 17*, 74–81.

Saxe, R., Carey, S., & Kanwisher, N. (2004). Understanding other minds: Linking developmental psychology and functional neuroimaging. *Annual Review of Psychology, 55*, 87–124.

Saxe, R., & Powell, L. J. (2006). It's the thought that counts: Specific brain regions for one component of theory of mind. *Psychological Science, 17*, 692–699.

Scholl, B. J., & Leslie, A. M. (1999). Modularity, development and "theory of mind." *Mind and Language, 14*(1), 131–153.

Scott, R. M., & Baillargeon, R. (in press). Which penguin in this? Attributing false beliefs about object identity at 18 months. *Child Development.*

Surian, L., Caldi, S., & Sperber, D. (2007). Attribution of beliefs by 13-month-old infants. *Psychological Science, 18*(7), 580–586.

Tardif, T., & Wellman, H. M. (2000). Acquisition of mental state language in Mandarin- and Cantonese-speaking children. *Developmental Psychology, 36*, 25–43.

Tomasello, M., & Call, J. (1997). *Primate cognition.* New York: Oxford University Press.

Tomasello, M., & Haberl, K. (2003). Understanding attention: 12- and 18-month-olds know what is new for other persons. *Developmental Psychology, 39*, 906–912.

Watson, A. C., Nixon, C. L., Wilson, A., & Capage, L. (1999). Social interaction skills and theory of mind in young children. *Developmental Psychology, 35*(2), 386–391.

Wellman, H. M. (1990). *The child's theory of mind.* Cambridge: MIT Press.

Wellman, H. M., Cross, D., & Watson, J. (2001). Meta-analysis of theory of mind development: The truth about false belief. *Child Development, 72*, 655–684.

Wellman, H. M., & Estes, D. (1986). Early understanding of mental entities: A reexamination of childhood realism. *Child Development, 57*, 910–923.

Wellman, H. M., Fang, F., Liu, D., Zhu, L., & Liu, G. (2006). Scaling of theory of mind understanding in Chinese children. *Psychological Sciences, 17*, 1075–1081.

Wellman, H. M., & Gelman, S. A. (1998). Knowledge acquisition in foundational domains. In D. Kuhn & R. Siegler (Eds.), *Handbook of child psychology (5th ed.): Vol. 2. Cognition, perception, and language* (pp. 523–573). New York: Wiley.

Wellman, H. M., Harris, P. L., Banerjee, M., & Sinclair, A. (1995). Early understanding of emotion: Evidence from natural language. *Cognition and Emotion, 9*, 117–149.

Wellman, H. M., Hollander, M., & Schult, C. A. (1996). Young children's understanding of thought-bubbles and of thoughts. *Child Development, 67*, 768–788.

Wellman, H. M., & Johnson, C. N. (2008). Developing dualism: From intuitive understanding to transcendental ideas. In A. Antonietti, A. Corradini, & E. Lowe (Eds.), *Psychophysical dualism today: An interdisciplinary approach* (pp. 3–35). Lanham, MD: Lexington Books.

Wellman, H. M., & Lagattuta, K. H. (2004). Theory of mind for learning and teaching: The nature and role of explanation. *Cognitive Development, 19*, 479–497.

Wellman, H. M., & Liu, D. (2004). Scaling of theory of mind tasks. *Child Development, 75*, 523–541.

Wellman, H. M., Lopez-Duran, S., LaBounty, J., & Hamilton, B. (2008). Infant attention to intentional action predicts preschool theory of mind. *Developmental Psychology, 44*(2), 618–623.

Wellman, H. M., Phillips, A. T., Dunphy-Lelii, S., & LaLonde, N. (2004). Infant social attention predicts preschool social cognition. *Developmental Science, 7*, 283–288.

Westermann, G., Mareschal, D., Johnson, M. H., Sirois, S., Spraling, M. W., & Thomas, M. S. C. (2007) Neuroconstructivism. *Developmental Science, 10*, 75–83.

Woodward, A. (1998). Infants selectively encode the goal object of an actor's reach. *Cognition, 69*, 1–34.

Yamaguchi, M., Kuhlmeier, V. A., Wynn, K., & vanMarle, K. (2009). Continuity in social cognition from infancy to childhood. *Developmental Science, 12*, 746–752.

CHAPTER ELEVEN

Pretend Play and Cognitive Development

Angeline Lillard, Ashley M. Pinkham, and Eric Smith

Introduction

Pretending is among the most interesting activities of childhood. As many have noted, pretending appears to be an early expression of the child's ability to use and understand symbols (Piaget, 1945/1962). Using symbols is one of the human species' major achievements; some would argue that it is the hallmark of our uniqueness among animals. Yet in contrast to other activities in which the symbolic function is central, like language and theory of mind, relatively little scholarly attention is accorded to pretend play. Until the first edition of this volume (see also Goncu, Patt, & Kouba, 2004), it received only one major handbook review, in the *Handbook of Child Development* (Rubin, Fein, & Vandenberg, 1983).

Pretending holds a mysterious place amongst apparently innate activities. Pretending is judged to be innate in part because it is universal and emerges like clockwork at 18–24 months of age (Eibl-Eibesfeldt, 1989). Pretending appears even when it is not modeled and even where parents discourage it, suggesting a biological basis (Carlson, Taylor, & Levin, 1998; Danziger, 2006; Gaskins, 1999; Haight, Wang, Fung, Williams, & Mintz, 1999; Schwartzman, 1978; Taylor & Carlson, 2000). Another criterion for innate behaviors is stereotypy: pretending begins with simple self-directed object substitutions, and evolves through predictable forms to complex role-play.

Yet unlike many other innate behaviors, pretend play does not serve any obvious survival function. Innate behaviors are normally phylogenetic adaptations to the environment (Eibl-Eibesfeldt, 1989). Even human babbling serves apparent developmental purposes. Human babies babble from 3 months to 12 months of age, the world over. Accumulating evidence suggests that the selective value of this behavior is to exercise and tune vocal chords to prepare them for speaking (Levit & Utman, 1992; Locke, 1993).

We are grateful to Patricia Ganea, Rebekah Richert, Lori Skibbe, Young-Joo Song, Peter Smith, David Witherington, and Jessi Witt for comments on an earlier draft of this chapter.

Babbling also serves protoconversations, because parents (at least in many cultures) tend to "talk back" with their babbling infants (Snow, 1988). Such protoconversations set infants up for understanding the back and forth nature of verbal exchange (Bruner, 1983), as well as promoting attachment and intersubjectivity (Isabella & Belsky, 1991). In contrast, pretend play's purpose is a mystery. The mystery is this: young children need to adapt to the world as it is, yet in pretend play they contrive the world to be as it is not.

Below we briefly review the history of the study of pretend play, the developmental course of pretend play, and literature on cultural universals and variations. The bulk of the chapter then reviews cognitive skills that are involved in pretend play.

History of study

The first wave of scholarly interest in pretend play occurred in the 1920s–1930s (Fein, 1981). Parten (1932,1933), an early chronicler of the naturalistic appearance of different forms of children's play, made the most lasting contributions. A second wave of interest occurred in the 1940s, stimulated by personality theorists and play therapy (Fein, 1981). A third wave of interest was stimulated by Piaget's (1945/1962) writing on the emergence of pretending in his own children. Experimental methods of studying pretend play emerged from this movement, although Piaget himself used naturalistic observations.

Piaget designated pretending a major hallmark of the sixth stage of the sensorimotor period; along with language and deferred imitation, pretense was considered evidence of representational capacity (Miller, chapter 25, this volume). For Piaget, pretending revealed children's inability to accommodate cognitive structures to the world: a mature cognitive system does not need to twist reality to its own ends. In addition, Piaget considered pretending to be an individual process, suggesting that each child invented and used symbols (Smolucha & Smolucha, 1998), although he noted that "obviously social life plays an essential role in the elaboration of concepts and of the representational schemas" (Piaget, 1945/1962, p. 4). The view that pretending emerges as an asocial activity has dominated the field, although many scholars have recently taken the Vygotskian perspective that pretense arises through social interaction (Goncu, 1993; Haight & Miller, 1993; Howes, Unger, & Matheson, 1992; Lillard & Witherington, 2004; Tomasello & Rakoczy, 2003).

Along with other research inspired by Piaget, during the 1970s pretend play research was lively. Studies emerged detailing the stages of pretending, as well as how children engage in object substitutions and apply agency to pretend entities (Fein, 1975; McCune-Nicholich, 1977; Nicolich, 1977; Watson & Fischer, 1977). The relationship between pretend play and language, another major hallmark of the symbolic capacity, was also intensively investigated (Bates, Benigni, Bretherton, Camaioni, & Volterra, 1979; Bretherton et al., 1981). In addition, pretend play training was used to determine if it would facilitate children's performance on other cognitive tasks, such as conservation. This was done because pretending appears to involve a form of Piagetian decentration (Miller, chapter 25, this volume): the separation of symbol and referent. These training studies did not, in the end, produce definitive results, largely due to methodological problems (Rubin et al., 1983; Smith, 1988). As is too often the case in training studies, the control groups were generally not treated appropriately (e.g., all things equal except the pretending). Another common problem was that post-test experimenters were rarely blind to condition. In the wake of the 1970s surge of activity, pretend play research declined until the 1990s, when it was infused with new vigor as a possible early marker of a theory of mind, as discussed later and in Wellman (chapter 10, this volume).

Developmental course

Many excellent reviews describe the developmental course of pretend play (Fein, 1981; Nicolich, 1977; Piaget, 1945/1962; Rubin et al., 1983); a short summary is provided here. Studies of pretense have primarily involved middle-class European and Euro-American children, although there is emerging interest in cultural differences and similarities.

The earliest instances of pretending are usually noted in the second year (Fein, 1981). In one classic example, Piaget (1945/1962) described 15-month-old Jacquelyn putting a blanket under her head, blinking her eyes, laughing, and saying "Nono" (Obs. 64A). Jacquelyn's activities suggested she was pretending to go to sleep, the blanket symbolizing her pillow. A dramatic increase in symbolic acts occurs between 15 and 18 months (Rubin et al., 1983), with pretending in full swing by approximately 24 months (Bates et al., 1979; Bretherton, 1984; Dunn & Wooding, 1977; Fein, 1981; Nicolich, 1977; Tamis-LeMonda & Bornstein, 1991). Two-year-olds spend 5–20% of their playtime engaged in pretense activities (Dunn & Dale, 1984; Dunn & Wooding, 1977; Haight & Miller, 1993; Miller & Garvey, 1984) and can interpret and respond to others' pretense acts in some circumstances (Harris & Kavanaugh, 1993; Walker-Andrews & Kahana-Kalman, 1999).

Sociodramatic pretending with peers emerges around 4 years of age, or earlier in the context of a more proficient partner such as an older sibling or the mother (Dale, 1989; DeLoache & Plaetzer, 1985; Dunn & Dale, 1984; Fiese, 1990; Haight & Miller, 1993; Howes et al., 1992; Kavanaugh, Whittington, & Cerbone, 1983; Miller & Garvey, 1984; O'Connell & Betherton, 1984), or the father (Farver & Wimbarti, 1995). Although Piaget claimed that pretending is replaced by games with rules when children enter the concrete operational stage, recent evidence suggests that the average age at which people claim to have stopped pretending is 12, and a fair proportion of adults say they have not stopped at all (Smith, Lillard, & Sorensen, 2009). Some theorists maintain that all counterfactual and hypothetical thinking (Hofstaeder, 1979), as well as engaging with art, can be thought of as a form of pretense (Walton, 1990).

As mentioned earlier, pretend play does appear to be universal; the developmental patterns just mentioned have been observed in a variety of communities around the world. Haight et al. (1999) have proposed that what is universal is not merely the fact and early appearance of pretense, but extends even to how pretense is conducted. For example, they speculate that all children use objects in their pretend play, and that pretend play takes place largely in a social context. However, there are also variations across cultures in pretend play.

Cultural variation in pretense

Cultural differences in pretend play include its topics and the frequency of different forms. These differences appear to stem from the values and practices of the adult community and ecological features (e.g., availability of toys). For example, Haight et al. (1999) found that American preschoolers enacted more fantasy themes than did Taiwanese children; by contrast, Taiwanese children engaged in more social routine and proper conduct themes in pretense. Similarly, Farver (1999) found that Korean-American preschoolers' play emphasized family roles, whereas European-Americans emphasized danger and fantasy themes. Gosso, Morais, and Otta (2007) obtained similar findings in Brazil, where high socioeconomic-status (SES) children's play included some fantasy (e.g., witches, mermaids, *Pokemon*), and that of reservation-dwelling American Indians and other low-SES children lacked fantasy themes altogether.

Other cultural differences concern the amount and ages of particular forms of pretense. In one study, American toddlers engaged in more pretend play than did Mexican children (Farver & Howes, 1993). American and Turkish children engaged in more pretend play than did Guatemalan and Indian children (Goncu, Tuermer, Jain, & Johnson, 1999). Gaskins (1999) noted very few instances of pretend play among Mayan children. Regarding level of pretense, the symbolic play of Japanese 1-year-olds was more advanced than that of their American counterparts, in a manner that directly corresponded to the level of play of their mothers (Tamis-LeMonda et al., 1992). As compared with French 20-month-olds, American 20-month-olds tended to engage in more symbolic pretend play, and the amount they engaged in was correlated with how much their mothers (all of European origin) tended to elicit that play (Suizzo & Bornstein, 2006). Gosso et al. (2007) found more symbolic transformations among high-SES children as contrasted with several other cultural groups within Brazil.

Importantly, in all these communities some pretending did occur, and the sequence and level of its occurrence was consistent with the review studies (of mainly Euro-American and European children) mentioned in the prior section. Changes in the frequency of children's pretense at different ages vary with parental attitudes and engagement. Where pretense was more frequent, adults believed it was important to development and engaged in it themselves with children. Where pretense was less frequent, parental attitudes ranged from mildly accepting to discouraging, and parents did not engage in it with children. Gaskins (1999) noted that when Mayan parents stopped children's pretense it was often because children were inappropriately using household objects (e.g., placing fruit on a wheelbarrow and turning its wheel as if to grind corn). However, Taylor and Carlson (2000) note that for some parents religious beliefs lead to discouraging of pretend because it is "false"; Danziger (2006) has reported a similar reason for discouraging pretending among the Mopan Maya, although the admonition has abated over the decades she has studied them.

Pretense play connects with several important cognitive skills: social referencing, reading intentions, quarantine of hypothetical and real worlds, the symbolic function, and role-taking. These connections are examined in the remainder of this chapter.

Social Referencing

In the United States, adults pretend for very young children. Haight and Miller (1993) reported that all of the mothers they studied pretended in front of their 12-month-olds; Kavanaugh et al. (1983) noted 75 distinct pretense utterances by eight mothers playing with 12- to 15-month-olds during 40-minute sessions; and Tamis-LeMonda and Bornstein (1991) found that 36% of mothers pretended with their 13-month-olds during a 15-minute observation (see also Crawley & Sherrod, 1984). How do young children understand acts of pretense?

Knowledge about what is real could be an important cue. A child might understand that a person talking into a banana must be pretending it is a telephone since people do not typically talk into bananas otherwise. By age 4, children also seem to understand that deviation from what is real is an important marker of pretense. When asked to judge whether people in videotaped clips were pretending to eat or really eating, 4- and 5-year-olds frequently justified their judgments with reference to whether food was actually present (Ma & Lillard, 2009; Richert & Lillard, 2004). But how do children determine whether an act is pretend or real when this obvious external cue is not present?

In addition, very young children might not even know when an act is real, since they are relatively ignorant; when someone is pretending about something novel to an infant, the ability to interpret the act as pretense may be especially puzzling. Babies witness new events every day. Why shouldn't talking into bananas be yet another new, real event? One might expect that young children immediately interpret pretend events as symbols of known real events, yet their symbolizing abilities do not seem sufficient to do so at such young ages (DeLoache & Smith, 1999; Tomasello, Striano, & Rochat, 1999).

One possibility is that social referencing abilities enable children to categorize new pretense events as pretense rather than real. Social referencing is using another person's response to an ambiguous situation as a guide for one's own response (Campos, 1980; Feinman, 1992). In the classic experiments, 12-month-olds chose not to venture across an illusory drop-off (the visual cliff) when their mother expressed fear but did when she seemed happy and encouraging (see also Mumme, Fernald, & Herrera, 1996). In such situations, children appear to adopt the parent's emotional response to an ambiguous situation, and act accordingly. Novel pretense events may present infants with a similarly ambiguous situation: what is one to make of talking into a banana? The infant can properly respond to this novel event if she adopts the parent's emotional stance (e.g., "goofy"). If the child fails to adopt the adult's stance towards the pretend event, the child could become confused and embed the pretend relations in her representation of the real world (discussed later). It is quite plausible that the ability to reference adults for appropriate attitudes is a key reason that young children are not generally confused by pretense acts.

Indeed, the times when children do get confused by pretense may be ones in which "silly" signals are not given.

Recent research has supported the possibility that infants engage in social referencing when observing adults pretending. When Lillard and Witherington (2004) asked mothers to have a real snack and a pretend snack with their 18-month-olds, two differences were observed in mothers' behavior that are relevant to social referencing. First, mothers smiled more frequently during pretense episodes relative to real ones; these smiles were frequently placed just after a pretend action and perhaps signaled a "goofy" interpretation. Second, mothers looked more often at their infants during pretense, and each look was of longer duration. Importantly, when mothers looked at their children during a pretend action and smiled, children were more apt to also smile and engage in pretend behaviors themselves.

Nishida and Lillard (2007) conducted a more refined analysis of this data pertinent to the social referencing hypothesis of pretense understanding. Data from 32 mother–child pairs were subjected to sequential analysis to determine if children's smiles and snack behaviors (suggesting a correct pretense interpretation) were significantly more likely to occur after a "social referencing sequence" (i.e., mother looks at child, acts, then smiles as if to comment on the action) during pretense than real snacking episodes. Results were positive. Alternative interpretations like imitation and affective mirroring were not consistent with the data. Parents appear to provide cues that may help 18-month-olds interpret pretense as pretense.

A further study examined maternal pretense behavior with younger (15-month-old) and older (24-month-old) children to investigate if the signs of pretense change with age, and also to examine other possible cues like voice and exaggerated movements (Lillard et al., 2007). Parents did not appear to change signs across this age span, but they did exaggerate gestures (like pouring at a much wider angle) and vary their pitch more while pretending. A second experiment moved beyond the snacking paradigm to examine pretend grooming. Results were consistent, with mothers tending to look at their children and smile more during pretense, particularly just before engaging in a pretend action. Children appeared to interpret this sequence of behavior as a signal of pretense. In sum, results from studies of mother–toddler pretending are consistent with the idea that adult cues assist early pretense interpretation.

Reading Intentions

In interpreting pretense one must also read through the pretender's actions to his or her intentions. For example, if a pretender is flying a pen around through the air and pretending the pen is an airplane, children must realize that the actor means that the pen is an airplane. The child must cognitively insert a "real" airplane into the scene, in place of the pen. Likewise, if a pretender is holding a stick at her mouth and miming eating actions, children must complete the goal, reading her behavior as "eating" even though the pretender is not actually eating. Pretense acts are instances of ellipsis: something is left out of a scene and must be filled in.

By the second year, infants are able to attribute intentions or goals to actors even when the intended outcomes are not achieved or directly observable. For example, Carpenter, Akhtar, & Tomasello (1998) used verbal signs to indicate that some acts were intentional (by having the actor say "There!") and others were mistakes (by having the actor say "Whoops!"). Even many 14-month-olds imitated the "There!" but not the "Whoops!" acts, thereby appearing to read which acts were intentional. Meltzoff (1995) goes a step further, requiring that children infer an actor's intention despite only observing unsuccessful attempts at achieving that goal. For example, 18-month-olds observed someone trying to pull apart the ends of a barbell, but not succeeding. When later given the barbell, children executed the intended acts rather than the behaviors they had actually observed. Recent research suggests infants as young as 10 months of age can interpret intentions (Brandone & Wellman, 2009).

What is being pretended must sometimes be read from incomplete acts or scenarios. Children can read pretense intention in such contexts by at least 2 years of age. For example, when shown a hammering motion, incomplete in that it lacked a hammer and an object being hit, many 18-month olds correctly identified the missing object as a hammer and by implication that the actor was pretending to hammer (Tomasello et al., 1999). In another study, after watching an experimenter pour pretend tea on one of two pigs, young 2-year-olds (but not old 1-year-olds) correctly dried the one who had been "made wet," suggesting they correctly understood what the experimenter "intended" by her pretense actions, at least when aided by language (Harris & Kavanaugh, 1993).

Ma and Lillard (2006) examined children's inference of pretense intentions when given behavioral cues but not pretense content (i.e., "reality cues"). Toddlers watched videotapes of two actors side-by-side. The first actor pretended to eat from a covered bowl and then the other actor really ate from a different covered bowl (or vice versa). In both cases, the presence or absence of food was concealed and both actors said, "Mmm, [food item]" after eating. However, the behavioral cues in the two events differed. For example, the pretend eater made more eye contact and burst into a large smile after completing the eating actions. After viewing the videos, children were presented with two covered bowls that matched the ones on the television screen and asked, "Where's the [food item]? Can you get the [food item]?" Surprisingly, not until 2.5 years of age did children reliably choose the correct bowl, indicating that they understood that one person was pretending and the other was really eating. Interestingly, children's behavior (e.g., lip smacking) suggested that younger children knew which person was really eating versus pretend eating although their explicit choices did not reflect such an understanding.

Further experiments (Ma & Lillard, 2009) examined whether children's errors on the explicit choice task were due to a problem inferring that only real eaters would have real content in their bowls; perhaps children believed pretend eaters had real food in their bowls, but simply were not eating it. To test this, in one experiment before the bowls were covered, the child saw that one bowl was empty and the other contained food. Performance in this condition improved slightly for 24-month-olds, but was not impressive overall (2.7 correct of 4 trials, with chance being 2 of 4). A second experiment examined whether children would do better were they not being asked to point to an *empty* bowl; perhaps the draw to point to *something* was masking competence. For this, the pretend bowl contained some toys and for the test question children were asked to state which bowl had toys; performance was again only slightly above chance for 2-year-olds (2.6 correct of 4 trials). In a third experiment, children were asked to point to which bowl was empty. This was difficult: even 36-month-olds were at chance. Interestingly, in all these experiments, children performed much better on the first trial than the subsequent three, suggesting fragile understandings that were easily overwhelmed. In addition, in each experiment implicit behaviors like lip smacking suggested understanding at some level that only the real eater had food across all trials. In sum, although children appear to understand failed intentions in real domains by the middle of the second year, their ability to read pretend intentions and reason from them to real-world content is quite limited even at age 2.

Onishi, Baillargeon, and Leslie (2007) also examined young children's understanding of pretend action sequences, and found apparent implicit understanding much earlier. In one experiment, 15-month-olds watched a person pretend to pour into one of two cups, and then pretend to drink from the same (expected) or other (unexpected) cup. Infants looked longer after the unexpected event, suggesting they might understand pretense. An alternative explanation is that infants simply glossed both events as pouring and drinking without even noticing the lack of liquid, and looked longer because a different object was being acted on. Further research is needed to shed more light on this issue.

Quarantine

A third cognitive skill involved in interpreting pretense is to quarantine the pretend situation from the real situation, to prevent representational abuse. Several theorists have noted this separation. For example, Bateson (1955/1972) pointed out that pretending is a special frame that organizes the activities within it, a concept developed later by Goffman (1974); Ryle (1949) suggested that pretense episodes occur in quotes; Vygotsky (1978) noted that, "The child at play operates with meanings detached from their usual objects and actions" (p. 98); and Leslie (1987) described the separation as "decoupling."

Unlike social referencing and reading intentions, which young children engage in for both real and pretend contexts, quarantining does not appear in non-pretense domains until older ages. For example, hypothetical reasoning requires quarantining reality from the hypothesized world. Young children's ability to reason hypothetically is relatively poor, but, interestingly, it improves when the hypothetical premises are placed in a fantasy context (Dias & Harris, 1988, 1990; Hawkins, Pea, Glick, & Scribner, 1984; Kuczaj, 1981; Scott, Baron-Cohen, & Leslie, 1999; but see Richert, Shager, Hoffman, & Taylor, 2009). Recent research shows that pretending is one of several ways to get children to step back from real-world circumstances to engage in hypothetical thinking (Harris, 2000).

Pretense requires reasoning about a hypothetical world. If children did not separate pretense worlds from the real one, they would become confused; thus, pretend acts must be marked as unserious and not reflecting the real world. As Leslie (1987) pointed out, the developing cognitive system's ability to do this is amazing. One would expect that a cognitive system that misrepresents reality would be suboptimal and that natural selection would instead favor a cognitive system that only constructs models of how the world actually is. How do children purposefully construct, reason about, and act upon a misrepresentation of the world?

One pertinent issue is the extent to which young children actually keep pretend and real systems separate. Logic suggests that children observing pretense must usually quarantine pretense events from real ones (Leslie, 1987). If young children instead interpreted pretense and real events as being of the same kind, then having viewed someone pretending a banana is a telephone, children might no longer have a distinct representation of bananas as bananas and might later attempt to answer the banana when the phone rings. Although we know of no systematic studies, the infrequency of reported errors of this kind suggests rarity. Some studies suggest that more frequent pretenders are even better at discerning reality from fantasy (Sharon & Woolley, 2004; but see Woolley, Boerger, & Markman, 2004). At times, however, young children do appear to mistake pretense for real, thereby failing to maintain the real–pretense boundary (Scarlett & Wolf, 1979). Three types of situations in which confusion has been noted are discussed next. Some of these involve simply asking children if some event is real, raising important methodological issues. First, researchers have tended to opt for a binary classification although children will often take a "maybe" option if offered. For example, when given a "not sure" option, only 35% of 4-year-olds claimed that the Easter Bunny was real, whereas 35% were not sure and 29% claimed he was not (Sharon & Woolley, 2004); this contrasts with the 74% of parents who claimed their children believed in the Easter Bunny (Rosengren, Kalish, Hickling, & Gelman, 1994). Second, children are more likely to use the word *real* to refer to the authenticity of an object (i.e., not a fake) than its existence (Bunce & Harris, 2008). These studies suggest that some standard techniques to determine whether children quarantine pretend from real are problematic. Bearing this in mind, consider three cases in which we see a breakdown of the real–pretense boundary.

Describing events or entities as pretense or real

When asked to describe pictures, verbally described events, or television events, children sometimes appear confused about the reality status of pretense versus real events. Errors particularly occur under three circumstances. First, children sometimes claim the pretense entities are real when those entities are marginal ones about which adults intentionally deceive children (e.g., Santa Claus or the Tooth Fairy; Clark, 1995). Indeed, 76% of 4-year-olds tested by Sharon and Woolley (2004) made this claim. This is not really surprising given the orchestrated cultural hoax involved, and given that children can easily be made to believe things. In one fascinating study, researchers told children about the Candy Witch, who replaces children's candy with a toy on Halloween night. After just two presentations, 66% of children claimed the Candy Witch was real; children who were also visited by the witch at home, 4-year-olds (in contrast to 3-year-olds), and children who believed in other fantastical figures were all more likely to believe in the Candy Witch (Woolley et al., 2004). In fact, even 8-year-olds who had been introduced to the Candy Witch concept a year earlier often professed belief (Boerger, Tullos, & Woolley, in press).

Children also err when asked to classify entities that "walk the boundary" even for adults. For example, many otherwise sane-seeming adults believe witches are real; Luhrman (1989) offers a fascinating account of witchcraft cults in modern-day London. Although researchers might comfortably assert that witches should be classified as pretense (Morison & Gardner, 1978), children's reduced level of certainty may not reflect a specifically developmental cognitive deficit.

A third circumstance in which children may err is when they have little or no real-world experience with the entity (Samuels & Taylor, 1994). Preschoolers who heard a story about a train with feelings and a family were significantly more likely to endorse the idea that trains really had such things than were preschoolers who heard about real trains (Ganea, Richert, Bean, & DeLoache, 2004). Likewise, children may be confused about the reality status of television events (Downs, 1990), although this may also be due to not understanding the concept of acting.

Children generally maintain boundaries not just between pretend and real, but also between different pretense worlds. For example, 5-year-olds were significantly more likely to claim that Batman would interact with Robin than with Sponge Bob (Skolnick & Bloom, 2006; see also Skolnick, Weisberg, & Bloom, in press).

In sum, some purported cases of pretense–reality boundary breakdown involve classes of entities about which children lack knowledge, coupled at times with deliberate attempts by adults to make the pretense seem real. These mistakes seem quite different from being mistaken about whether a parent flying a pen with her hand is flying a pretend or a real airplane.

Scary pretense episodes

Children's behavioral responses to scary pretend situations sometimes suggest that they think pretense is real. They occasionally appear truly frightened during scary pretense play, such as pretending to be monsters, and have even asked to cease playing (Garvey & Berndt, 1975; Scarlett & Wolf, 1979). Consistent with these observations, Harris and colleagues found that preschoolers avoided a box after having imagined it contained a scary creature (Harris, Brown, Marriott, Whittall, & Harmer, 1991; Johnson & Harris, 1994). They suggested that preschoolers sometimes believe that what they imagine can become true and entities can cross the boundary from pretend into real. In fact, when Kavanaugh and Harris put pairs of children alone in the room with the box in which they had imagined a monster, the children discussed, with apparent seriousness, the possible existence of the monster (P. L. Harris, personal communication, September 2000).

Children's avoidance of scary pretense does not mean they are *generally* susceptible to pretense–reality breakdown; indeed, Woolley and Phelps (1994) reported that preschoolers were also reluctant to approach a box in which they had imagined a non-scary object. Scary pretense elicits emotions, and emotions are usually reliable cues to reality (Damasio, 1994; Zajonc, 1980). But because physiological reactions to real and imagined scary events are similar (Lang, 1984), children might interpret the physiological signs of fear as a cue to reality (see Harris, 2000). Further, children are notoriously poor at monitoring sources (Foley, Harris, & Hermann, 1994; Foley & Ratner, 1998) and may fail to note that the source of fear is purely their own imagination. Interestingly, there is a high degree of individual variability in the tendency to think what one has imagined has become real (Bourchier & Davis, 2000; Johnson & Harris, 1994).

In short, when it comes to pretense involving frightening entities, pretend–real boundary problems certainly do exist. Yet even adults are not immune to such problems: emotions from pretend events, such as dreams or fantasies, frequently color our real-world behavior and possibly even our representations. Although such cases are very interesting, they may not be relevant to more everyday pretense.

Non-scary pretense episodes

The third circumstance concerns whether children who are engaged in everyday, non-frightening pretense behave as though their pretense is real. Research suggests that even 5-year-olds might have this problem, seeming disoriented when an adult changed the status of a pretend prop in the middle of a pretend game (DiLalla & Watson, 1988); however, more tightly controlled experiments indicated that by age 4, children are not typically disrupted by such interventions (Golomb & Kuersten, 1996). Moreover, Taylor (1999) reported that 4-year-olds sometimes expressed concern that the experimenter was taking their imaginary companions too seriously; one child reminded her, "It's only pretend, you know." Even 3-year-olds appear very clear in their understanding of the differences between pretend and real entities. When told about one boy who had a cookie and another who was just pretending to have a cookie, 3-year-olds were quite accurate about which boy could eat the cookie, touch the cookie, see the cookie, and so on (Wellman & Estes, 1986). In a review of this area, Woolley (1997) concluded that children are not fundamentally different from adults in their separation of real and pretense.

It is less clear whether younger children keep everyday pretense and real episodes separate. Harris and Kavanaugh's (1993) results suggest that by age 2, children can usually follow pretense episodes even when substitute objects are involved. In another study, 2-year-olds protested more when an experimenter violated a pretense identity (e.g., eating what had been a pretend knife) than when the experimenter behaved in accordance with the pretense assignments (e.g., eating a pretend carrot; Rakoczy, 2008a). However, in examining mother–child pretend play at ages 15 through 30 months, DeLoache and Plaetzer (1985) saw clear examples of pretense–reality confusion in a quarter of the children studied. For example, when a mother asked a child to wipe up some spilled "tea," the child searched around as though looking for real tea. DeLoache and Plaetzer suggested that the mother's pretense was too elaborate for the child's current level. Closer analysis of the types of pretense adults engage in with young children, the length of those episodes, and the degree to which the mothers signal pretense may provide further clues.

The appearance–reality distinction

A special case of quarantine involves the appearance–reality distinction (Flavell, Green, & Flavell, 1986), in which one understands that an object can look like one thing but really be something else. Flavell and colleagues hypothesized that children might have a precocious ability to discriminate reality from representation in the realm of pretense (Flavell, Flavell, & Green, 1987). To test this, the first experimenter pretended to eat an apple-candle and the second experimenter asked, "Is she pretending that thing is a candle or pretending it's an apple?" and, "Right now, does that thing look like an apple or look like a candle?" Children performed significantly better on the pretense question than on the appearance question, suggesting that pretense is an area of early competence for understanding mental representation.

However, an alternative explanation is that children might have interpreted pretense as false action rather than false representation (Lillard, 1993). For example, the experimenter was engaging in "pretend-to-eat-an-apple" actions, not actions that would really be directed at candles. When asked if she was pretending it was an apple or a candle, children could answer correctly simply by reading her false behavior, a suggestion which has been empirically supported (Sodian & Huelsken, 1999; Sodian, Huelsken, Ebner, & Thoermer, 1998). Similarly, Abelev and Markman (2006) argued children perform better on the pretense version of the appearance–reality task because they do not need to contrast an object's essential nature with its superficial nature; instead, they must only differentiate between what an object really is and its temporary function. Children's quarantining of pretense and real seems dependent on the actions that go along with pretending (Harris & Kavanaugh, 1993; Lillard, 2001a; Tomasello et al., 1999), which has important implications for children's understanding of symbols in pretend play, as discussed in the next section.

Pretense Play as Symbolic

In interpreting pretense, children must keep pretense separate from real as well as understand what real objects and events the pretense objects and events symbolize. When children pretend or watch others pretend, to what extent do they perceive the pretense as symbolizing real objects and events?

Language has often been considered a parallel development to pretense, as both appear to involve the use and comprehension of symbols (Bates et al., 1979; Piaget, 1945/1962; Werner & Kaplan, 1963). For children younger than 18 months (i.e., before the typical vocabulary spurt), pretense and language production are significantly correlated (Bates et al., 1979; Nicolich, 1977; Tamis-LeMonda et al., 1992). Moreover, children with productive language delays are less successful at engaging in symbolic play than are age-matched children with normally developing language (Beeghly, 1998). Although the notion that early word or pretense productions are symbolic is not uncontroversial (Huttenlocher & Higgins, 1978; Piaget, 1945/1962; Tomasello et al., 1999), the observed correlations suggest some common underlying function.

In addition to being parallel developments, children's pretense and language production may be mutually influential. During joint parent–child symbolic play, parents often provide explicit narratives related to children's pretense behaviors and ask children to elaborate on those narratives (Kavanaugh & Engel, 1998). Such conversation may help highlight the symbolic nature of pretense. In one recent study, children who received explicit training about the phrase "pretend that" showed greater improvement in identifying what was symbolized by pretense acts than untrained controls (Rakoczy, Tomasello, & Striano, 2006).

Pretense comprehension is often measured by imitation. For instance, researchers demonstrate pretense acts and note if children imitate those acts (Bates, Bretherton, Snyder, Shore, & Volterra, 1980; Fenson & Ramsay, 1981; Nielsen & Dissanayake, 2004; Ungerer, Zelazo, Kearsley, & O'Leary, 1981). Such imitation measures suggest pretense comprehension as early as 13 months (Bates et al., 1980), the same approximate age of onset as pretense and language production. However, assuming that such imitation indicates symbolic understanding is clearly problematic, as children's behaviors might involve imitation without comprehension of what the actions and objects symbolize. Not until 2 years of age do children imitate observed behaviors in a way that shows sensitivity to the underlying intention (e.g., trying but failing to really write with a pen versus pretending to write with a pen; Rakoczy, Tomasello, & Striano, 2004; Rakoczy & Tomasello, 2006).

Harris and Kavanaugh (1993) traded this imitation problem for a linguistic one. Children were shown a yellow block and a teddy and told that the yellow block was Teddy's sandwich. When asked to show what Teddy does with his sandwich, 18-month-olds correctly had Teddy display eating behaviors toward the block on 50% of trials; 28-month-olds did so on 75% of trials. Although this eliminated the possibility that children were merely imitating an action, they may have responded based upon language rather than an underlying understanding of the symbol. Indeed, research by DeLoache (chapter 12, this volume) suggests that symbolic understanding emerges between 2.5 and 3 years of age, not earlier.

Children's understanding of what pretense symbolizes appears to develop gradually and involves much scaffolding by more competent play partners. This scaffolding occurs in two main ways. First, as may be the case in the aforementioned Harris and Kavanaugh experiment, language can scaffold pretense comprehension. Kavanaugh et al. (1983) found that parents of 12- to 21-month-olds initiated nearly all pretense episodes by verbally attributing pretend identities to objects, thereby facilitating the symbolic mapping task (see also Rakoczy et al., 2006).

Second, play partners' pretense gestures may also facilitate symbolic mapping. Cognition is very much influenced by action (Campos et al., 2000; Glenberg, Gutierrez, Levin, Japuntich, & Kaschak, 2004), an insight implicit in Montessori's notion that the hand leads the mind (Lillard, 2005) and in Piaget's idea – credited to Montessori (Piaget, 1970, pp. 147–8) – of action as the source of knowledge (Flavell, 1963). Perhaps gesture leads to the appreciation of symbols in pretense; several lines of research support this suggestion. For example, Tomasello et al. (1999) showed that young children's understanding of pretense may be guided by their ability to read gestures rather than their symbolic understanding. Such results are particularly interesting in light of Goldin-Meadow (2003) and colleagues' work showing that children's gestures may reveal new cognitive advances before they are revealed in other ways.

Even once children have a rudimentary symbolic understanding of pretense, their ability to manipulate and reason with pretense symbols remains fragile. In a recent series of experiments, Ma and Lillard (2009) pretended with three different objects; two were acted on in the same manner, suggesting they symbolized a single object, while the other was used in a different manner. When asked which two "go together," 3-year-olds sorted the objects at random although they appeared to understand the pretense gestures (e.g., they spontaneously described them). However, if one of the three objects was a miniature (e.g., a tiny toy telephone) or the symbolic demands were minimized (by using plain blocks as substitute objects), 3-year-olds sorted correctly.

Findings such as these suggest that pretense comprehension might not initially involve a symbolic capacity. Children's ability to comprehend pretense symbols lags considerably behind pretense production as well as language comprehension and production; this should not be the case if a single ability to see one object as signifying another underlies all four capacities. In addition, an opposing acquisition pattern is seen in language and pretense. While comprehension precedes production in language (Benedict, 1979), the opposite is true for pretense. Furthermore, children's comprehension also varies as a function of the iconicity of the pretense behavior: the more similar in form and function an object or action is to its referent, the more easily children appear to comprehend the pretense (Bigham & Bourchier-Sutton, 2007; Mizuguchi & Sugai, 2002); the same is not true for language (Clark, 2003).

Pretend Play and Social Cognition

Recent research on children's theory of mind (Wellman, chapter 10, this volume) suggests a relationship between pretend play and mental-state understanding, such that frequent or high-level pretenders also have advanced understandings of others' mental states (Astington & Jenkins, 1995; Connolly & Doyle, 1984; Dunn & Cutting, 1999; Gleason, 2004; Hughes & Dunn, 1997; Lalonde & Chandler, 1995; Lillard, 2001b; Schwebel, Rosen, & Singer, 1999; Taylor & Carlson, 1997; Youngblade & Dunn, 1995). Although the direction of effects for this relation is uncertain, at least one study supports the possibility that pretense drives social understanding. Youngblade and Dunn (1995) found that children's level of pretense at 33 months was positively related to their mental-state understanding at 40 months. It is also possible that the reverse relation occurs, such that advanced social skills enable pretense, or that a third underlying variable drives both pretend play and social cognition. This section explores various means by which the two domains might be related.

Meta-representation

Pretend play might drive social understanding via meta-representation, such that pretending would provide early insight into mental representations (Wellman, chapter 10, this volume). While children are engaged in pretend play, they might reflect on the fact that they are entertaining mental ideas, and this understanding could then be applied outside of pretense (Taylor & Carlson, 1997; Taylor, Carlson, Maring, Gerow, & Charley,

2004). Some studies support this argument, whereas others do not (see review in Lillard, 2001a). One problem with the early-insight-in-pretense account is that, were it true, all pretend play should be associated with precocious theory-of-mind task performance. However, only social forms of pretending (including imaginary companions; Taylor, 1999) are consistently related with theory of mind, making a link via meta-representation unlikely. Gomez (2008) also notes that there is increasing evidence for some meta-representational capacity in primates, yet little evidence that they engage in anything like pretend play. Although this could be a result of equifinality, or arriving at the same end via a different path (Gottlieb, Wahlsten, & Lickliter, 1998), it seems unlikely.

Decentration

Pretending might also assist social understanding via decentration, or moving away from a single viewpoint to take other perspectives into account (Piaget, 1945/1962). Pretend play seems to require decentration because a child must decenter from one view of an object as what it really is to entertain what else that object could be. This same skill is involved in perspective-taking (Wellman, chapter 10, this volume), which may be positively correlated with pretend play (Rubin et al., 1983). As with meta-representation, however, this view is weakened by the fact that social but not solitary pretend play is linked to social cognition.

Role-taking

Role-taking is another skill that might promote social cognition. Children may become, emotionally and mentally, like the characters that they impersonate (Harris, 2000). Practice at taking others' perspectives in non-pretense contexts is associated with social understanding. For example, children whose parents discipline by asking them to imagine how it must feel to be someone else are precocious at understanding beliefs (Ruffman, Perner, & Parkin, 1999). One important issue is whether young children's pretending involves experiencing the feelings of the characters, or simply playing their roles. Historically, the practice of acting has been a practice of playing roles, not adopting the psychological characteristics of enacted characters. Around the turn of the last century, Stanislavsky (1922/1984) contributed the insight that one could act by "becoming," in a psychological sense, the characters that one played. Whether children naturally act in a Stanislavskian manner during sociodramatic play is a pertinent topic of inquiry.

Social pretend play themes

Social pretense might also lead to understanding minds via pretend themes, which are frequently emotional in nature and include discussion of mental states (Fein, 1989; Haight & Miller, 1993). Several theorists have even argued that a fundamental drive to pretend is the need to work out emotional issues (Bretherton, 1989; Fein, 1989). Indeed, children use more internal state words while pretending than not (Hughes & Dunn, 1997), and children who pretend frequently use more internal state words than children who pretend less (Howe, Petrakos, & Rinaldi, 1998). Children who engage in more discussion about emotions pass theory-of-mind tasks earlier (Dunn, Brown, & Beardsall, 1991) and children practice event schemas related to internal states while enacting emotional plots (Bretherton, 1989; Nelson & Seidman, 1984; Schank & Abelson, 1977), so it might be simply that role-play pretense provides a context for such learning.

Negotiation

The aforementioned possibilities all concern "in-frame" pretending, or the events and discussions that occur while children play at being others. But when children pretend, they sometimes step out of their pretense to negotiate turns of the plot, object entities, and so forth (Giffin, 1984; Howe, Petrakos, Rinaldi, & LeFebvre, 2005). Indeed, pretend play is often prefaced by several minutes of such negotiations; as children grow older, an increasing proportion of playtime is devoted to out-of-frame negotiation. Sociodramatic pretend play may engender social-cognitive skills by forcing children to negotiate their viewpoints and wishes with those of other players (Cutting & Dunn, 2006; Nelson & Seidman, 1984; Rakoczy, 2008b). Supporting this, children engage in more internal state talk during out-of-frame pretense negotiations than during pretense itself (Brown, Donelan-McCall, & Dunn, 1996; Howe et al., 1998; Howe et al., 2005; cf. Wolf et al., 1985, as cited in Bretherton, 1989), and sibling pairs who frequently engage in pretense negotiate their play at higher levels as compared to less frequent pretenders (Howe et al., 1998; Howe, Rinaldi, Jennings, & Petrakos, 2002). Moreover, sociodramatic pretend play is linked to children's social competence (Lindsay & Mize, 2000), with well-liked children engaging in more pretense negotiations with peers than disliked children (Black, 1992). Hence, cognitive skills related to understanding minds might be required for what occurs around the pretend frame.

Attachment

Secure attachment is associated with earlier pretend play (Howes & Rodning, 1992; Meins & Russell, 1997) and better theory-of-mind performance (Fonagy, 1996; Meins, Fernyhough, Russell, & Clark-Carter, 1997). Secure attachment is also associated with parent–child discourse in which parents frequently discuss feelings and use reason, both of which are positively associated with theory-of-mind skills (Ruffman et al., 1999).

Older peers

Research has shown that children with older siblings acquire theory-of-mind skills relatively early (e.g., Jenkins & Astington, 1996; Lewis, Freeman, Kyriakidou, Maridaki-Kassotaki, & Berridge, 1996; McAlister & Peterson, 2006; Ruffman, Perner, Naito,

Parkin, & Clements, 1998; but see Cutting & Dunn, 1999), and older siblings also lead younger ones to early engagement in sociodramatic play (e.g., Dunn, 1988; Dunn & Dale, 1984). For example, the age of a first-born child is positively related to the likelihood that the second-born child engages in pretend role-play (Youngblade & Dunn, 1995), and second-borns are more likely to extend their play partner's ideas during dyadic pretend play than first-borns or only children (Howe et al., 2005). Even extrafamilial daily peer contacts can produce such effects (Fein, Moorin, & Enslein, 1982; Kowalski, Wyver, Masselos, & de Lacey, 2005). In addition, children who regularly engaged in pretend play with older peers showed higher levels of empathy and emotional regulation than children who did not (Galyer & Evans, 2001).

Social competence

Social competence might also underlie both theory-of-mind skills and sociodramatic play. Negotiating pretense with others requires a certain level of competence. Several studies reported relationships between social competence and sociodramatic play (Connolly & Doyle, 1984; Howes & Matheson, 1992). For example, Black (1992) showed that more-popular children engaged in more pretend play and behaved in more socially competent ways during pretense. They were also more likely to provide explanations about ongoing play and to include peers' ideas in their pretense negotiations. Researchers have also shown relations between sociometric status and theory-of-mind skills (Dockett & Degotardi, 1997; Dunn & Cutting, 1999).

Personality

Another possible reason for the link between sociodramatic play and theory of mind is an underlying personality dimension. Wolf, Rygh, and Altshuler (1984) identified two main types of pretenders: dramatists and patterners. Dramatists frequently enacted plots involving other people, whereas patterners' play was more object-dependent and tended not to involve social or communicative exchanges. Children's pretense styles emerged at 1 year of age and remained distinct well into the preschool years. It is possible that children's interest in people influences their play styles, and this interest might also lead to earlier theory-of-mind development (Lillard, 1998). Although "hard to manage" preschoolers, such as children exhibiting antisocial behavior and personality traits, engaged in comparable amounts of sociodramatic play to that of their peers, the content of their pretense episodes was often characterized by violent fantasizing, and they exhibited relatively poor theory-of-mind skills (Dunn & Hughes, 2001; but see Nelson, Hart, & Evans, 2008).

Summary

Researchers have noted correlations between various forms of social pretend play and children's understanding of others' minds. There are several possible reasons for the link between social pretend play and social-cognitive skills, some of which are directional and others of which involve third variables that could reasonably account for both. Future work should further explore the direction and possible sources of the relations between young children's pretend play and social-cognitive skills.

Pretense and Cognitive Neuroscience

By 2–3 years of age, children can differentiate whether an actor's intention was to really perform an action or to pretend to do so (Rakoczy et al., 2004; Rakoczy & Tomasello, 2006); however, relatively little is known about the neural correlates of understanding such pretense behaviors, and the available evidence is limited to research with adults. Schubotz and von Cramon (in press) argue that the interpretation of real behaviors and the interpretation of pretend behaviors require similar neural processes. Indeed, recent functional MRI research demonstrates that the neural regions implicated in making mental state judgments (German, Niehaus, Roarty, Giesbrecht, & Miller, 2004) and goal inferences (Schubotz & von Cramon, in press) are similarly activated when observing real and pretend actions.

There are, however, also some differences in neural activity across the two types of actions. For example, when participants were asked to judge the possibility that scenarios involving real people could be real, neural regions associated with episodic memory were activated; in contrast, when the scenarios involved fictional characters, like Cinderella, regions associated with semantic memory were activated (Abraham, von Cramon, & Schubotz, 2008). Other research suggests that the performance of real versus pantomimed actions involves overlapping but not identical neural mechanisms (Imazu, Sugio, Tanaka, & Inui, 2007; Króliczak, Cavina-Pratesi, Goodman, & Culham, 2007; Westwood, Chapman, & Roy, 2000). Furthermore, a growing literature shows that when people imagine themselves or another person performing an action or experiencing a psychological state, the neural activation occurs in the same areas of the brain as when one actually performs that action or experiences that state (see discussion in Decety & Grèzes, 2006). This suggests interesting possibilities for how children interpret and learn via pretense.

Conclusion

Pretending is a fascinating development in young children. Pretend play emerges early and consumes a large portion of young children's unstructured time (Haight & Miller, 1993). It involves a remarkable cognitive feat: the child's mind purposely thwarts reality, making things other than they are, at an age when the child is just learning what reality is. Pretending apparently involves several important cognitive skills, including social referencing, interpretation of underlying intentions, quarantining of a pretend world, symbolic understanding, and understanding alternative representations of the world. Although researchers have made progress towards understanding these interesting relations, many puzzles remain. Is early pretense symbolic, and when? How does the cognitive system manage to quarantine pretense acts? Why do we see correlations between pretending and theory of mind? These questions call out for more research, enabling deeper understanding of this hallmark ability of the human species.

References

Abelev, M., & Markman, E. (2006). Young children's understanding of multiple object identity: Appearance, pretense and function. *Developmental Science, 9*, 590–596.

Abraham, A., von Cramon, D. Y., & Schubotz, R. I. (2008). Meeting George Bush versus meeting Cinderella: The neural response when telling apart what is real from what is fictional in the context of our reality. *Journal of Cognitive Neuroscience, 20*(6), 965–976.

Astington, J. W., & Jenkins, J. M. (1995). Theory of mind development and social understanding. *Cognition and Emotion, 9*, 151–165.

Bates, E., Benigni, L., Bretherton, I., Camaioni, L., & Volterra, V. (1979). Cognition and communication from nine to thirteen months: Correlational findings. In E. Bates (Ed.), *The emergence of symbols: Cognition and communication in infancy*. New York: Academic Press.

Bates, E., Bretherton, I., Snyder, L., Shore, C., & Volterra, V. (1980). Vocal and gestural symbols at 13 months. *Merrill-Palmer Quarterly, 26*, 407–423.

Bateson, G. A. (1955/1972). A theory of play and fantasy. In G. A. Bateson (Ed.), *Steps to an ecology of mind* (pp. 39–51). New York: Chandler. (Reprinted from American Psychiatric Association Research Reports, 1955, II.)

Beeghly, M. (1998). Emergence of symbolic play: Perspectives from typical and atypical development. In J. Burack, R. M. Hodapp, & E. Zigler (Eds.), *Handbook of mental retardation and development* (pp. 240–289). New York: Cambridge University Press.

Benedict, H. (1979). Early lexical development: Comprehension and production. *Journal of Child Language, 6*, 183–200.

Bigham, S., & Bourchier-Sutton, A. (2007). The decontextualization of form and function in the development of pretence. *British Journal of Developmental Psychology, 25*, 335–351.

Black, B. (1992). Negotiating social pretend play: Communication differences related to social status and sex. *Merrill-Palmer Quarterly, 38*(2), 212–232.

Boerger, E. A., Tullos, A., & Woolley, J. D. (in press). Return of the Candy Witch: Individual differences in acceptance and stability of belief in a novel fantastical being. *British Journal of Developmental Psychology.*

Bourchier, A., & Davis, A. (2000). The influence of availability and affect on children's pretence. *British Journal of Developmental Psychology, 18*, 137–156.

Brandone, A. C., & Wellman, H. M. (2009). You can't always get what you want: Infants understand failed goal-directed actions. *Psychological Science, 20*(1), 85–91.

Bretherton, I. (Ed.). (1984). *Symbolic play: The development of social understanding.* Orlando: Academic Press.

Bretherton, I. (1989). Pretense: The form and function of make-believe play. *Developmental Review, 9*, 383–401.

Bretherton, I., Bates, E., McNew, S., Shore, C., Williamson, C., & Beeghly-Smith, M. (1981). Comprehension and production of symbols in infancy: An experimental study. *Developmental Psychology, 17*, 728–736.

Brown, J. R., Donelan-McCall, N., & Dunn, J. (1996). Why talk about mental states? The significance of children's conversations with friends, siblings, and mothers. *Child Development, 67*, 836–849.

Bruner, J. (1983). *Child's talk: Learning to use language*. New York: Norton.

Bunce, L., & Harris, M. (2008). "I saw the real Father Christmas!" Children's everyday uses of the words real, really, and pretend. *British Journal of Developmental Psychology, 26*, 445–455.

Campos, J. J. (1980). Human emotions: Their new importance and their role in social referencing. *Research and Clinical Center for Child Development. Annual Report*, 1–7.

Campos, J. J., Anderson, D. I., Barbu-Roth, M. A., Hubbard, E. M., Hertenstein, M. J., & Witherington, D. (2000). Travel broadens the mind. *Infancy, 1*(2), 149–219.

Carlson, S. M., Taylor, M., & Levin, G. (1998). The influence of culture on pretend play: The case of Mennonite children. *Merrill-Palmer Quarterly, 44*, 538–565.

Carpenter, M., Akhtar, N., & Tomasello, M. (1998). Fourteen- through 18-month-old infants differentially imitate intentional and accidental actions. *Infant Behavior and Development, 21*, 315–330.

Clark, C. D. (1995). *Flights of fancy, leaps of faith*. Chicago: University of Chicago Press.

Clark, E. V. (2003). *First language acquisition*. New York: Cambridge University Press.

Connolly, J. A., & Doyle, A. (1984). Relation of social fantasy play to social competence in preschoolers. *Developmental Psychology, 20*, 597–608.

Crawley, S. B., & Sherrod, K. B. (1984). Parent–infant play during the first year of life. *Infant Behavior and Development, 7*, 65–75.

Cutting, A. L., & Dunn, J. (2006). Conversations with siblings and with friends: Links between relationship quality and social understanding. *British Journal of Developmental Psychology, 24*, 73–87.

Dale, N. (1989). Pretend play with mothers and siblings: Relations between early performance and partners. *Journal of Psychology and Psychiatry, 30*, 751–759.

Damasio, A. R. (1994). *Descartes' error : Emotion, reason, and the human brain*. New York: G. P. Putnam.

Danziger, E. (2006). The thought that counts: Understanding variation in cultural theories of interaction. In S. Levinson & N. Enfield (Eds.), *The roots of human sociality: Culture, cognition and human interaction* (pp. 259–278): Oxford: Berg Press.

Decety, J., & Grèzes, J. (2006). The power of simulation: Imagining one's own and other's behavior. *Brain Research, 1079*(1), 4–14.

DeLoache, J. S., & Plaetzer, B. (1985). *Tea for two: Joint mother–child symbolic play*. Paper presented at Biennial meeting for the Society for Research in Child Development, Toronto.

DeLoache, J. S., & Smith, C. M. (1999). Early symbolic representation. In I. E. Sigel (Ed.), *Development of mental representation: Theories and applications* (pp. 61–86). Mahwah, NJ: Erlbaum.

Dias, M. G., & Harris, P. L. (1988). The effect of make-believe play on deductive reasoning. *British Journal of Developmental Psychology, 6*, 207–221.

Dias, M. G., & Harris, P. L. (1990). The influence of the imagination on reasoning by young children. *British Journal of Developmental Psychology, 8*, 305–318.

DiLalla, L. F., & Watson, M. W. (1988). Differentiation of fantasy and reality: Preschoolers' reactions to interruptions in their play. *Developmental Psychology, 24*, 286–291.

Dockett, S., & Degotardi, S. (1997). Some implications of popularity at age four. *Journal of Australian Research in Early Childhood Education, 1*, 21–31.

Downs, A. C. (1990). Children's judgments of televised events: The real versus pretend distinction. *Perceptual and Motor Skills, 70*, 779–782.

Dunn, J. (1988). *The beginnings of social understanding*. Cambridge, MA: Harvard University Press.

Dunn, J., Brown, J., & Beardsall, L. (1991). Family talk about feeling states and children's later understanding of others' emotions. *Developmental Psychology, 27*, 448–455.

Dunn, J., & Cutting, A. L. (1999). Understanding others, and individual differences in friendship interactions in young children. *Social Development, 8*, 201–219.

Dunn, J., & Dale, N. (1984). I a daddy: 2-year-olds collaboration in joint pretend play with sibling and with mother. In I. Bretherton (Ed.), *Symbolic Play* (pp. 131–158). London: Academic Press.

Dunn, J., & Hughes, C. (2001). "I got some swords and you're dead!": Violent fantasy, antisocial behavior, friendship, and moral sensibility in young children. *Child Development, 72*(2), 491–505.

Dunn, J., & Wooding, C. (1977). Play in the home and its implications for learning. In B. Tizard & D. Harvey (Eds.), *Biology of play*. London: Spastics International.

Eibl-Eibesfeldt, I. (1989). *Human Ethology*. New York: Aldine de Gruyter.

Farver, J. A. M. (1999). Activity setting analysis: A model for reexamining the role of culture in development. In A. Goncu (Ed.), *Children's engagement in the world: Sociocultural perspectives* (pp. 99–127). New York: Cambridge University Press.

Farver, J. A. M., & Howes, C. (1993). Cultural differences in American and Mexican mother–child pretend play. *Merrill-Palmer Quarterly, 39*, 344–358.

Farver, J. A. M., & Wimbarti, S. (1995). Paternal participation in toddler's pretend play. *Social Development, 4*, 17–31.

Fein, G. G. (1975). A transformational analysis of pretending. *Developmental Psychology, 11*, 291–296.

Fein, G. G. (1981). Pretend play in childhood: An integrative review. *Child Development, 52*, 1095–1118.

Fein, G. G. (1989). Mind, meaning, and affect: Proposals for a theory of pretense. *Developmental Review, 9*, 345–363.

Fein, G. G., Moorin, E. R., & Enslein, J. (1982). Pretense and peer behavior: An intersectoral analysis. *Human Development, 25*, 392–406.

Feinman, S. (Ed.). (1992). *Social referencing and the social construction of reality in infancy*. New York: Plenum Press.

Fenson, L., & Ramsay, D. S. (1981). Effects of modeling action sequences on the play of twelve-, fifteen-, and nineteen-month-old children. *Child Development, 52*, 1028–1036.

Fiese, B. H. (1990). Playful relationships: A contextual analysis of mother–toddler interaction and symbolic play. *Child Development, 61*, 1648–1656.

Flavell, J. H. (1963). *The developmental psychology of Jean Piaget*. New York: D. Van Nostrand Co.

Flavell, J. H., Green, F. L., & Flavell, E. R. (1986). Development of knowledge about the appearance–reality distinction. *Monographs of the Society for Research in Child Development, 51*, (1, Serial No. 212).

Flavell, J. H., Flavell, E. R., & Green, F. L. (1987). Young children's knowledge about the apparent–real and pretend–real distinctions. *Developmental Psychology, 23*, 816–822.

Foley, M. A., Harris, J. F., & Hermann, S. (1994). Developmental comparisons of the ability to discriminate between memories for symbolic play enactments. *Developmental Psychology, 30*, 206–217.

Foley, M. A., & Ratner, H. H. (1998). Children's recoding memory for collaboration: A way of learning from others. *Cognitive Development, 13*, 91–108.

Fonagy, P. (1996). The significance of the development of metacognitive control over mental representations in parenting and infant development. *Journal of Clinical Psychoanalysis, 5*, 67–86.

Galyer, K. T., & Evans, I. M. (2001). Pretend play and the development of emotional regulation in preschool children. *Early Child Development and Care, 166*, 93–108.

Ganea, P. A., Richert, R. A., Bean, E., & DeLoache, J. S. (2004). *Fantasy books and children's conceptions about reality*. Unpublished manuscript, University of Virginia.

Garvey, C., & Berndt, R. (1975). *Organization in pretend play*. Paper presented at the meeting of the American Psychological Association, Chicago.

Gaskins, S. (1999). Children's daily lives in a Mayan village: A case study of culturally constructed roles and activities. In A. Goncue (Ed.), *Children's engagement in the world: Sociocultural perspectives* (pp. 25–60). New York: Cambridge University Press.

German, T. P., Niehaus, J. L., Roarty, M. P., Giesbrecht, B., & Miller, M. B. (2004). Neural correlates of detecting pretense: Automatic engagement of the intentional stance under covert conditions. *Journal of Cognitive Neuroscience, 16*(10), 1805–1817.

Giffin, H. (1984). The coordination of meaning in the creation of shared make-believe play. In I. Bretherton (Ed.), *Symbolic play* (pp. 73–100). Orlando: Academic Press.

Gleason, T. R. (2004). Imaginary companions and peer acceptance. *International Journal of Behavioral Development, 28*(3), 204–209.

Glenberg, A., Gutierrez, T., Levin, J., Japuntich, S., & Kaschak, M. (2004). Activity and imagined activity can enhance young children's reading comprehension. *Journal of Educational Psychology, 96*(3), 424–436.

Goffman, E. (1974). *Frame analysis: An essay on the organization of experience*. Cambridge, MA: Harvard University Press.

Goldin-Meadow, S. (2003). *Hearing gesture: How our hands help us think*. Cambridge, MA: Harvard University Press.

Golomb, C., & Kuersten, R. (1996). On the transition from pretence play to reality: What are the rules of the game? *British Journal of Developmental Psychology, 14*, 203–217.

Gomez, J.-C. (2008). The evolution of pretence: From intentional availability to intentional non-existence. *Mind and Language, 23*(5), 586–606.

Goncu, A. (1993). Development of intersubjectivity in the social pretend play of preschool children. *Human Development, 36*, 185–198.

Goncu, A., Patt, M., & Kouba, E. (2004). Understanding young children's pretend play in context. In P. Smith (Ed.), *Handbook of childhood social development* (pp. 418–437). London: Blackwell.

Goncu, A., Tuermer, U., Jain, J., & Johnson, D. (1999). Children's play as cultural activity. In A. Goncue (Ed.), *Children's engagement in the world: Sociocultural perspectives* (pp. 148–170). New York: Cambridge University Press.

Gosso, Y., Morais, M. L. S., & Otta, E. (2007). Pretend play of Brazilian children: A window into different cultural worlds. *Journal of Cross-Cultural Psychology, 38*(5), 539–558.

Gottlieb, G., Wahlsten, D., & Lickliter, R. (1998). The significance of biology for human development: A developmental psychobiological systems view. In R. Lerner (Ed.), *Handbook of child psychology: Vol. 1. Theoretical models of child development* (pp. 233–273). New York: Wiley.

Haight, W. L., & Miller, P. J. (1993). *Pretending at home*. Albany: SUNY Press.

Haight, W. L., Wang, X.-l., Fung, H. H.-t., Williams, K., & Mintz, J. (1999). Universal, developmental, and variable aspects of young children's play: A cross-cultural comparison of pretending at home. *Child Development, 70*, 1477–1488.

Harris, P. L. (2000). *The work of the imagination*. Oxford: Blackwell.

Harris, P. L., Brown, E., Marriott, C., Whittall, S., & Harmer, S. (1991). Monsters, ghosts, and witches: Testing the limits of the fantasy–reality distinction in young children. *British Journal of Developmental Psychology, 9*, 105–124.

Harris, P. L., & Kavanaugh, R. D. (1993). Young children's understanding of pretense. *Monographs of the Society for Research in Child Development, 58*, (1, Serial No. 231).

Hawkins, J., Pea, R. D., Glick, J., & Scribner, S. (1984). Merds that don't like mushrooms: Evidence for deductive reasoning by preschoolers. *Developmental Psychology, 20*, 584–589.

Hofstaeder, D. (1979). *Godel, Escher, Bach: An eternal golden brain*. New York: Basic Books.

Howe, N., Petrakos, H., & Rinaldi, C. (1998). "All the sheeps are dead. He murdered them": Sibling pretense, negotiation, internal state language, and relationship quality. *Child Development, 69*, 182–191.

Howe, N., Petrakos, H., Rinaldi, C. M., & LeFebvre, R. (2005). "This is a bad dog, you know ...": Constructing shared meanings during sibling pretend play. *Child Development, 76*(4), 783–794.

Howe, N., Rinaldi, C. M., Jennings, M., & Petrakos, H. (2002). "No! The lambs can stay out because they got cozies": Constructive and destructive sibling conflict, pretend play, and social understanding. *Child Development, 73*(5), 1460–1473.

Howes, C., & Matheson, C.C. (1992). Sequences in the development of competent play with peers: Social and social pretend play. *Developmental Psychology, 28*, 961–974.

Howes, C., & Rodning, C. (1992). Attachment security and social pretend play negotiations. In C. Howes, O. Unger, & C. C. Matheson (Eds.), *The collaborative construction of pretend: Social pretend play functions* (pp. 89–98). Albany: State University of New York Press.

Howes, C., Unger, O. A., & Matheson, C. C. (1992). *The collaborative construction of pretend: Social pretend play functions.* Albany: State University of New York Press.

Hughes, C., & Dunn, J. (1997). "Pretend you didn't know": Preschoolers' talk about mental states in pretend play. *Cognitive Development, 12*, 381–403.

Huttenlocher, J., & Higgins, E. T. (1978). Issues in the study of symbolic development. In W. A. Collins (Ed.), *Minnesota Symposia on Child Psychology* (Vol. *11*, pp. 98–140). Hillsdale, NJ: Earlbaum.

Imazu, S., Sugio, T., Tanaka, S., & Inui, T. (2007). Differences between actual and imagined usage of chopsticks: An fMRI study. *Cortex, 43*, 301–307.

Isabella, R. A., & Belsky, J. (1991). Interactional synchrony and the origins of mother–infant attachment: A replication study. *Child Development, 62*, 373–384.

Jenkins, J. M., & Astington, J. W. (1996). Cognitive factors and family structure associated with theory of mind development in young children. *Developmental Psychology, 32*, 70–78.

Johnson, C., & Harris, P. L. (1994). Magic: Special but not excluded. *British Journal of Developmental Psychology, 12*, 35–51.

Kavanaugh, R. D., & Engel, S. (1998). The development of pretense and narrative in early childhood. In O. Saracho & B. Spodek (Eds.), *Multiple perspectives of play in early childhood* (pp. 80–99). Albany, NY: State University of New York Press.

Kavanaugh, R. D., Whittington, S., & Cerbone, M. J. (1983). Mother's use of fantasy speech to young children. *Journal of Child Language, 10*, 45–55.

Kowalski, H. S., Wyver, S. R., Masselos, G., & de Lacey, P. (2005). The long-day childcare context: Implications for toddlers' pretend play. *Early Years: An International Journal of Research and Development, 25*(1), 55–65.

Króliczak, G., Cavina-Pratesi, C., Goodman, D. A., & Culham, J. C. (2007). What does the brain do when you fake it? An fMRI study of pantomimed and real grasping. *Journal of Neurophysiology, 9*(7), 2410–2422.

Kuczaj, S. A. (1981). Factors influencing children's hypothetical reference. *Journal of Child Language, 8*, 131–137.

Lalonde, C. E., & Chandler, M. J. (1995). False belief understanding goes to school: On the social-emotional consequences of coming early or late to a first theory of mind. *Cognition and Emotion, 9*, 167–185.

Lang, P. J. (1984). Cognition in emotion: Concept and action. In C. E. Izard, J. Kagan, & R. B. Zajonc (Eds.), *Emotions, cognition, and behavior* (pp. 192–228). Cambridge: Cambridge University Press.

Leslie, A. M. (1987). Pretense and representation: The origins of "theory of mind." *Psychological Review, 94*, 412–426.

Levit, A. G., & Utman, J. G. A. (1992). From babbling towards the sound systems of English and French: A longitudinal two-case study. *Journal of Child Language, 19,* 19–49.

Lewis, C., Freeman, N., Kyriakidou, C., Maridaki-Kassotaki, K., & Berridge, D. (1996). Social influences on false belief access: Specific sibling influences or general apprenticeship? *Child Development, 67,* 2930–2947.

Lillard, A. S. (1993). Pretend play skills and the child's theory of mind. *Child Development, 64,* 348–371.

Lillard, A. S. (1998). Playing with a theory of mind. In O. Saracho & B. Spodek (Eds.), *Multiple perspectives on play in early childhood education* (pp. 11–33). New York: SUNY Press.

Lillard, A. S. (2001a). Pretend play as Twin Earth. *Developmental Review, 21,* 1–33.

Lillard, A. S. (2001b). Pretending, understanding pretense, and understanding minds. In S. Reifel (Ed.), *Play and culture studies* (Vol. *3,* pp. 233–254). Westport, CT: Ablex.

Lillard, A. S. (2005). *Montessori: The science behind the genius.* New York: Oxford University Press.

Lillard, A. S., Nishida, T., Massaro, D., Vaish, A., Ma, L., & McRoberts, G. (2007). Signs of pretense across age and scenario. *Infancy, 11*(1), 1–30.

Lillard, A. S., & Witherington, D. (2004). Mothers' behavior modifications during pretense snacks and their possible signal value for toddlers. *Developmental Psychology, 40*(1), 95–113.

Lindsay, E. W., & Mize, J. (2000). Parent–child physical pretense play: Links to children's social competence. *Merrill-Palmer Quarterly, 46*(4), 565–591.

Locke, J. L. (1993). *The child's path to spoken language.* Cambridge, MA: Harvard.

Luhrman, T. M. (1989). *Persuasions of the witch's craft.* Cambridge, MA: Harvard University Press.

Ma, L., & Lillard, A. S. (2006). Where is the real cheese? Young children's ability to discriminate between real and pretend acts. *Child Development, 77*(6), 1762–1777.

Ma, L., & Lillard, A. S. (2009). What makes an act a pretense one? Young children's pretend–real judgments and explanations. Unpublished manuscript, University of Virginia.

McAlister, A., & Peterson, C. C. (2006). Mental playmates: Siblings, executive functioning and theory of mind. *British Journal of Developmental Psychology, 24,* 733–751.

McCune-Nicholich, L. (1977). Beyond sensorimotor intelligence: Assessment of symbolic maturity through analysis of pretend play. *Merrill-Palmer Quarterly, 23,* 89–99.

Meins, E., Fernyhough, C., Russell, J., & Clark-Carter, D. (1997). *Security of attachment as a predictor of symbolic and mentalising abilities: A longitudinal study.* Unpublished manuscript, University of Cambridge.

Meins, E., & Russell, J. (1997). Security and symbolic play: the relation between security of attachment and executive capacity. *British Journal of Developmental Psychology, 15,* 63–76.

Meltzoff, A. (1995). Understanding the intentions of others: Re-enactment of intended acts by 18-month-old children. *Developmental Psychology, 31,* 838–850.

Miller, P., & Garvey, C. (1984). Mother–baby role play: Its origins in social support. In I. Bretherton (Ed.), *Symbolic Play* (pp. 101–158). London: Academic Press.

Mizuguchi, T., & Sugai, K. (2002). Object-related knowledge and the production of gestures with imagined objects by preschool children. *Perceptual and Motor Skills, 94*(1), 71–79.

Morison, P., & Gardner, H. (1978). Dragons and dinosaurs: The child's capacity to differentiate fantasy from reality. *Child Development, 49,* 642–648.

Mumme, D. L., Fernald, A., & Herrera, C. (1996). Infants' responses to facial and vocal emotional signals in a social referencing paradigm. *Child Development, 67,* 3219–3237.

Nelson, K., & Seidman, S. (1984). Playing with scripts. In I. Bretherton (Ed.), *Symbolic play* (pp. 45–72). London: Academic Press.

Nelson, L. J., Hart, C. H., & Evans, C. A. (2008). Solitary-functional play and solitary-pretend play: Another look at the construct of solitary-active behavior using playground observations. *Social Development, 17*(4), 812–831.

Nicolich, L. M. (1977). Beyond sensorimotor intelligence: Assessment of symbolic maturity through analysis of pretend play. *Merrill-Palmer Quarterly, 23*, 89–99.

Nielsen, M., & Dissanayake, C. (2004). Pretend play, mirror self-recognition and imitation: A longitudinal investigation through the second year. *Infant Behavior and Development, 27*, 342–365.

Nishida, T., & Lillard, A. S. (2007). The informative value of emotional expressions: Social referencing in mother–infant pretense. *Developmental Science, 10*(2), 205–212.

O'Connell, B., & Betherton, I. (1984). Toddler's play, alone and with mother: The role of maternal guidance. In I. Bretherton (Ed.), *Symbolic Play* (pp. 337–368). London: Academic Press.

Onishi, K. H., Baillargeon, R., & Leslie, A. M. (2007). 15-month-old infants detect violations in pretend scenarios. *Acta Psychologica, 124*(1), 106–128.

Parten, M. B. (1932). Social participation among preschool children. *Child Development, 27*, 243–269.

Parten, M. B. (1933). Social play among preschool children. *Journal of Abnormal and Social Psychology, 28*, 136–147.

Piaget, J. (1945/1962). *Play, dreams, and imitation in childhood.* New York: Norton.

Piaget, J. (1970). *Science of education and the psychology of the child* (D. Coltman, Trans.). New York: Orion Press.

Rakoczy, H. (2008a). Taking fiction seriously: Young children understand the normative structure of joint pretence games. *Developmental Psychology, 44*(4), 1195–1201.

Rakoczy, H. (2008b). Pretence as individual and collective intentionality. *Mind and Language, 23*(5), 499–517.

Rakoczy, H., & Tomasello, M. (2006). Two-year-olds grasp the intentional structure of pretense acts. *Developmental Science, 9*(6), 557–564.

Rakoczy, H., Tomasello, M., & Striano, T. (2004). Young children know that trying is not pretending: A test of the "behaving-as-if" construal of children's early concept of pretense. *Developmental Psychology, 40*(3), 388–399.

Rakoczy, H., Tomasello, M., & Striano, T. (2006). The role of experience and discourse in children's developing understanding of pretend play actions. *British Journal of Developmental Psychology, 24*, 305–335.

Richert, R. A., & Lillard, A. S. (2004). Observers' proficiency at identifying pretense acts based on behavioral cues. *Cognitive Development, 19*, 223–240.

Richert, R. A., Shager, A. B., Hoffman, R. E., & Taylor, M. (2009). Learning from fantasy and real characters in preschool and kindergarten. Unpublished manuscript, University of California, Riverside.

Rosengren, K. S., Kalish, C. W., Hickling, A. K., & Gelman, S. A. (1994). Exploring the relation between preschool children's magical beliefs and causal thinking. *British Journal of Developmental Psychology, 12*, 69–82.

Rubin, K. H., Fein, G. G., & Vandenberg, B. (1983). Play. In P. H. Mussen (General Ed.), E. M. Hetherington (Vol. Ed.), *Handbook of child psychology: Vol. 4. Socialization, personality, and social development.* (4th ed., pp. 693–774). New York: Wiley.

Ruffman, T., Perner, J., Naito, M., Parkin, L., & Clements, W. (1998). Older (but not younger) siblings facilitate false belief understanding. *Developmental Psychology, 34*, 161–174.

Ruffman, T., Perner, J., & Parkin, L. (1999). How parenting style affects false belief understanding. *Social Development, 8*, 395–411.

Ryle, G. (1949). *The concept of mind.* Chicago: University of Chicago Press.

Samuels, A., & Taylor, M. (1994). Children's ability to distinguish fantasy events from real-life events. *British Journal of Developmental Psychology, 12*, 417–427.

Scarlett, W. G., & Wolf, D. (1979). When it's only make-believe: The construction of a boundary between fantasy and reality. In E. Winner & H. Gardner (Eds.), *Fact, fiction, and fantasy in childhood* (Vol. *6*, pp. 29–40). San Francisco: Jossey-Bass.

Schank, R. C., & Abelson, R. P. (1977). *Scripts, plans, goals and understanding.* Hillsdale, NJ: Erlbaum.

Schubotz, R. I., & von Cramon, D. Y. (in press). The case of pretense: Observing actions and inferring goals. *Journal of Cognitive Neuroscience.*

Schwartzman, H. B. (1978). *Transformations: The anthropology of children's play.* New York: Plenum.

Schwebel, D. C., Rosen, C. S., & Singer, J. L. (1999). Preschoolers' pretend play and theory of mind: The role of jointly constructed pretence. *British Journal of Developmental Psychology, 17,* 333–348.

Scott, F. J., Baron-Cohen, S., & Leslie, A. (1999). "If pigs could fly": A test of counterfactual reasoning and pretence in children with autism. *British Journal of Developmental Psychology, 17,* 349–362.

Sharon, T., & Woolley, J. (2004). Do monsters dream? Young children's understanding of the fantasy/reality distinction. *British Journal of Developmental Psychology, 22,* 293–310.

Skolnick, D., & Bloom, P. (2006). What does Batman think about SpongeBob? Children's understanding of the fantasy/fantasy distinction. *Cognition, 101*(1), B9–B18.

Skolnick Weisberg, D., & Bloom, P. (in press). Young children separate multiple pretend worlds. *Developmental Science.*

Smith, E., Lillard, A. S., & Sorenson, L. (2009). When pretending ends: Undergraduates' retrospective accounts of pretending. University of Virginia.

Smith, P. K. (1988). Children's play and its role in early development: A re-evaluation of the "play ethos." In A. D. Pellegrini (Ed.), *Psychological bases for early education* (pp. 207–226). Chichester, UK: Wiley.

Smolucha, L., & Smolucha, F. (1998). The social origins of mind: Post-Piagetian perspectives on pretend play. In O. N. Saracho & S. Bernard (Eds.), *Multiple perspectives on play in early childhood education.* SUNY series, early childhood education: Inquiries and insights (pp. 34–58). Albany, NY: State University of New York Press.

Snow, C. (1988). The development of conversations between mothers and babies. In M. B. Franklin & S. S. Barten (Eds.), *Child language: A reader* (pp. 20–35). New York: Oxford University Press.

Sodian, B., & Huelsken. (1999, April). *Young children's ability to differentiate pretense from reality.* Paper presented at the Biennial Meeting of the Society for Research in Child Development, Albuquerque.

Sodian, B., Huelsken, C., Ebner, C., & Thoermer, C. (1998). Children's differentiation of mentality and reality in pretense-precursor to a theory of mind? *Sprache & Kognition, 17,* 199–213.

Stanislavsky, K. (1922/1984). On various trends in the theatrical arts. In O. C. Korneva (Ed.), *Konstantini Stanislavsky: Selected works* (pp. 133–191). Moscow: Raduga Publishers.

Suizzo, M., & Bornstein, M. (2006). French and European American child–mother play: Culture and gender considerations. *International Journal of Behavioral Development, 30*(6), 498–508.

Tamis-LeMonda, C. S., & Bornstein, M. H. (1991). Individual variation, correspondence, stability, and change in mother and toddler play. *Infant Behavior and Development, 14,* 143–162.

Tamis-LeMonda, C. S., Bornstein, M. H., Cyphers, L., Toda, S., et al. (1992). Language and play at one year: A comparison of toddlers and mothers in the United States and Japan. *International Journal of Behavioral Development, 15,* 19–42.

Taylor, M. (1999). *Imaginary companions and the children who create them.* Oxford: Oxford University Press.

Taylor, M., & Carlson, S. (1997). The relation between individual differences in fantasy and theory of mind. *Child Development, 68*, 436–455.

Taylor, M., & Carlson, S. (2000). The influence of religious beliefs on parent's attitudes about children's fantasy behavior. In K. S. Rosengren, C. N. Johnson, & P. L. Harris (Eds.), *Imagining the impossible: Magical, scientific, and religious thinking in children* (pp. 247–268). Cambridge: Cambridge University Press.

Taylor, M., Carlson, S., Maring, B., Gerow, L., Charley, C. (2004). The characteristics and correlates of fantasy in school-age children: Imaginary companions, impersonation, and social understanding. *Developmental Psychology, 40*, 1173–1187.

Tomasello, M., & Rakoczy, H. (2003). What makes human cognition unique? From individual to shared to collective intentionality. *Mind and Language, 18*(2), 121–147.

Tomasello, M., Striano, T., & Rochat, P. (1999). Do young children use objects as symbols? *British Journal of Developmental Psychology, 17*, 563–584.

Ungerer, J., Zelazo, P. R., Kearsley, R. B., & O'Leary, K. (1981). Developmental changes in the representation of objects in symbolic play from 18 to 34 months of age. *Child Development, 52*, 186–195.

Vygotsky, L. S. (1978). *Mind in society*. Cambridge, MA: Harvard University Press.

Walker-Andrews, A., & Kahana-Kalman, R. (1999). The understanding of pretense across the second year of life. *British Journal of Developmental Psychology, 17*, 523–536.

Walton, K. L. (1990). *Mimesis as make-believe*. Cambridge, MA: Harvard University Press.

Watson, M. W., & Fischer, K. W. (1977). A developmental sequence of agent use in late infancy. *Child Development, 48*, 828–836.

Wellman, H. M., & Estes, D. (1986). Early understanding of mental entities: A re-examination of childhood realism. *Child Development, 57*, 910–923.

Werner, H., & Kaplan, B. (1963). *Symbol formation*. New York: Wiley.

Westwood, D. A., Chapman, C. D., & Roy, E. A. (2000). Pantomimed actions may be controlled by the ventral visual stream. *Experimental Brain Research, 130*, 545–548.

Wolf, D. P., Rygh, J., & Altshuler, J. (1984). Agency and experience: Actions and states in play narratives. In I. Bretherton (Ed.), *Symbolic Play*. Cambridge: Academic Press.

Woolley, J. D. (1997). Thinking about fantasy: Are children fundamentally different thinkers and believers from adults? *Child Development, 6*, 991–1011.

Woolley, J. D., Boerger, E. A., & Markman, A. B. (2004). A visit from the Candy Witch: Factors influencing young children's belief in a novel fantastical being. *Developmental Science, 7*(4), 456–468.

Woolley, J. D., & Phelps, K. E. (1994). Young children's practical reasoning about imagination. *British Journal of Developmental Psychology* [Special issue: Magic], *12*, 53–67.

Youngblade, L. M., & Dunn, J. (1995). Individual differences in young children's pretend play with mother and sibling: Links to relationships and understanding of other people's feelings and beliefs. *Child Development, 66*, 1472–1492.

Zajonc, R. B. (1980). Feeling and thinking: Preferences need no inferences. *American Psychologist, 35*, 151–175.

CHAPTER TWELVE

Early Development of the Understanding and Use of Symbolic Artifacts

Judy S. DeLoache

a rose is a rose is a rose.

In this famous statement, Gertrude Stein emphasizes that any given rose is incontrovertibly a singular object. Ironically, this oft-quoted line also draws our attention to the fact that a rose can also be something other than a rose. For example, these flowers have traditionally served as symbols of love, death, and success. Roses are not alone; virtually any natural object can be used to stand for something other than itself. Consider the meanings we project onto rainbows, majestic peaks, and dark, dank swamps.

Artifacts can also serve as symbols; indeed, our world is replete with objects that have been specifically designed to fulfill a symbolic function. Symbolic artifacts are a ubiquitous and vital feature of modern life. This fact is well illustrated by William Ittelson's (1996) description of the wealth of pictorial media present in his breakfast room one morning:

> As I sit here at my breakfast table, my morning newspaper has **printing** on it; it has a **graph** telling me how the national budget will be spent, a **map** trying to tell me something about the weather; a table of baseball **statistics**, an engineering **drawing** with which I can build a garden chair, **photographs** of distant places and people, a **caricature** expressing what the editor thinks of a political figure … On the wall in front of me hangs … a **calendar** [and above it] is a **clock**. All this and more, and I haven't even turned on the **TV** or the **computer** … (p. 171)

Before proceeding further, we should note that the term "symbol" has been used in many different ways in psychology, as well as in other disciplines. The word has also been

Preparation of this manuscript was supported in part by Grant HD25271 from the National Institutes of Health.

used for language and certain gestures. Indeed, most of the scholars who have written about symbolization – from Peirce (1903) to Langer (1942) to Deacon (1997) – have been primarily interested in language. In addition, "symbol" is used to refer to purely internal, mental representations – the coding of experience in memory (e.g., Newell & Simon, 1972). A third use – the one of primary relevance to this chapter – is to refer to a variety of artifacts created to serve a referential function. Unlike mental representations or words, many symbolic artifacts are *iconic* representations: they bear some physical resemblance to what they stand for, whereas others have only an abstract relation to what they represent. Although some theorists reserve the term "symbol" for arbitrary, non-iconic representations (e.g., Bruner, Olver, & Greenfield, 1966; Peirce, 1903), others argue persuasively that iconicity per se is irrelevant to whether something serves a symbolic function (e.g., Goodman, 1976; Huttenlocher & Higgins, 1978; Ittelson, 1996).

I have offered this definition: *A symbol is something that someone intends to stand for or represent something other than itself* (DeLoache, 1995a). The foremost of the four components of the definition is *someone*. Humans are the "symbolic species" (Deacon, 1997); symbolization is the "most characteristic mental trait of mankind" that "makes [us] lord of the earth" (Langer, 1942, pp. 72, 26). Although some non-human primates have been trained to recognize and use symbols to an impressive degree (e.g., Boysen & Berntson, 1990), their symbolic acumen never approaches that of very young humans (DeLoache & Bloom-Pickard, 2008). The second element – the very indefinite term *something* – is used quite deliberately in this definition to signify that almost anything can serve as a symbol for almost anything else. The third element is *representation*. A symbol *represents*, refers to, denotes, something other than itself. As a consequence, symbols are inherently asymmetrical, even when symbol and referent resemble one another. A scale model of the Tower of London represents that structure, but the tower does not represent the model. One important source of this asymmetry is that symbol and referent typically have different action affordances: one can, for example, climb the steps of the real tower, but not the model of it.

The last, but certainly not the least, element of the definition is *intention*: one entity stands for another only if some person *intends* for it to do so. Intention is both necessary and sufficient to establish a symbolic relation. Thus, nothing is inherently a symbol; only as a result of someone using it with the goal of denoting or referring does it become a symbol. A dozen long-stemmed red roses can simply be a bunch of flowers. But, presented by a lover to his beloved, the same roses serve as a symbol of love and devotion.

A unique aspect of symbolic objects is that they have an inherently dual or double nature (Kennedy, 1974; Potter, 1979; Sigel, 1978; Werner & Kaplan, 1963). An object, such as a picture, that is created and/or used to serve a symbolic function is seen both as itself and as something entirely different (Gregory, 1970).

> A picture, no matter how "realistic" or "representational," always presents two broad classes of visual information: (1) information that would be provided by viewing the pictured real-world scene … and (2) information that is unrelated to the pictured scene but comes from the real-world surface on which the picture appears … These two types of information can be analyzed separately by the psychologist, and they can be decoupled by the observer, but they are always encountered together. (Ittelson, 1996, pp. 175–176)

Because of the dual nature of symbolic objects, both aspects of their reality must be mentally represented to use them. *Dual representation* must be achieved; one must think about both the concrete object itself and its abstract relation to what it stands for. As we shall see, the need for dual representation presents a substantial challenge to young children's understanding and use of symbolic objects. They tend to focus either on the conceptual referent or on the symbolic object itself, missing the relation between them (DeLoache, 1995a; Potter, 1960).

A crucial role that symbolic artifacts play in our everyday lives is as a source of information. Interaction with symbols expands our intellectual horizons in both time and space. Because of our access to books, pictures, models, maps, and other media, we can indirectly experience and learn about events, objects, and people we have never directly encountered. From an infant on her father's lap looking at a picture book of zoo animals she has never seen to an adult studying the diagrams in an instruction manual on car repair, we acquire new and useful information about the world from a variety of symbolic artifacts. A sailing chart is invaluable for getting from one port to another. A scale model of the Rotunda designed by Thomas Jefferson can provide useful clues for understanding Palladian architecture.

Given the important informational role of symbolic artifacts and the degree to which our world knowledge is symbolically mediated rather than acquired through direct experience, the process of coming to understand and use symbols as a source of information is a vital part of early cognitive development. All children, everywhere in the world, must master the symbols and symbol systems that are important in their society. In spite of the importance of learning from symbols, we know relatively little about how children develop the ability to do so.

There is, of course, an enormous body of research on symbolic development, with by far the most work on language development. With respect to symbolic artifacts, researchers have investigated children's developing abilities to interpret and produce instances of various media. Substantial attention has been paid to children's ability to interpret pictures (Freeman, 1993; Preissler & Carey, 2004; Robinson, Nye, & Thomas, 1994; Thomas, Nye, & Robinson, 1994), as well as children's interpretation of television (Barr, Muentener, Garcia, Fujimoto, & Chávez, 2007; Kirkorian & Anderson, 2008; Strouse & Troseth, 2008; Troseth, 2003). Pretend play has also been the focus of a substantial amount of research (see Lillard, Pinkham, & Smith, chapter 11, this volume). However, other than research on maps (Liben, 2003; Liben & Christensen, chapter 17, this volume; Uttal, 2000), little attention has been paid to young children's ability to acquire information via symbols. And virtually no research has examined the emergence and very early development of children's use of symbol-mediated information. The research that is the focus of this chapter concerns infants' and very young children's interaction with a variety of symbolic artifacts and replica objects.

Symbol-Mediated Problem Solving

We begin with research on very young children's ability to understand and use symbolic artifacts to solve a problem. If the children appreciate the relevance of the symbol, the problem is easy to solve using the symbol-mediated information. If they do not understand the relevance of the symbol to the problem at hand, they have absolutely no means of solving it.

The basic problem is retrieving a hidden object. Finding an object that they have observed being hidden is well within the competence of infants and very young children: after watching as an attractive toy is hidden somewhere in a natural environment, children as young as 18 months of age are very successful at retrieving it, even after relatively long delays (e.g., DeLoache & Brown, 1979, 1983). Thus, children younger than 2 years of age who directly observe a hiding event are able to use that information to guide their search for a hidden toy. The question addressed in the first line of research described here is whether children can remember and use information that they experience *indirectly*, that is, information presented to them via a symbolic medium. The underlying question is the degree to which very young children understand the relevant *symbol–referent relation*.

Scale-model task

The majority of the research that I and my colleagues have conducted investigating this question has employed a scale model as the source of information about the present state of reality, that is, about the current location of a hidden object (see DeLoache, 1995a, 2002, for reviews of this work). Typically, the model is a realistic scale model of a regular room containing miniature items of furniture corresponding to the items of furniture in the room itself. The miniature items are highly similar in surface appearance to their larger counterparts in the room, and they are in the same spatial arrangement. The children in these studies typically receive an extensive orientation in which the relation between the model and room and all the individual items contained in them is described in detail and demonstrated by the experimenter. A crucial part of the orientation is that the experimenter takes each of the miniature items of model furniture into the room and explicitly compares it to its larger counterpart.

On each of the retrieval trials, children watch as the experimenter hides a miniature toy ("Little Snoopy" – a toy dog – or "Little Terry" – a troll doll) somewhere in the model (behind the couch, under a chair, etc.). They are told that a larger toy ("Big Snoopy," "Big Terry") will be hidden in the corresponding place in the room itself, and they are instructed to remember where the smaller one is hidden in the model so they will know where to find the larger one in the room. The only way they know where to search for the large toy in the room is if (a) they remember where the small one is in the model, and (b) they understand the relation between the model and room and between the hiding events in the two spaces.

After searching in the room, the children return to the model to find the miniature toy they had originally observed being hidden. This serves as a memory and motivation check. If the children can find the toy in the model, it tells us that they remember the hiding event they observed earlier and are motivated to find it. Thus, if they fail to retrieve the larger toy in the room, it must be for some other reason than memory or motivational problems.

Picture and video tasks

The same symbolic object-retrieval task has also been used with pictures and video. Various types of pictures have been used, ranging from highly realistic photographs of single items of furniture in the room to colored line drawings of the entire room. As in the model task, children again receive an extensive orientation to the relation between the picture or pictures and the room. On each trial, the experimenter points to the appropriate picture or to a location on a picture to communicate to the children the location of the toy in the room In the case of video, children again receive an extensive orientation, designed to demonstrate to the child that what they see on a monitor is being filmed at the same time. They see themselves, their parent, and the room on the monitor as the experimenter talks about what they are looking at and how it is being filmed by the camera. On the retrieval trials, the child watches on the video monitor as the experimenter goes into the room and hides the toy. The child is then invited to search for it. Again, the question is whether children are able to use the relevant symbol–referent relation to solve the problem, with successful retrieval taken as evidence that the children appreciate something about the nature of that relation.

Our symbol-mediated object-retrieval tasks are thus essentially analogical reasoning problems, in which children must reason from a base to a target problem (Goswami, chapter 15, this volume). The target problem is finding the toy that is hidden in the room. To solve it, the child has to use the base information he or she has been given via a symbol to construct a mental model of the location of the toy. The unique element is that the base information is provided via a symbolic artifact.

Advantages of the symbolic object-retrieval task

There are several advantages to this format for investigating the early development of symbolic understanding (Marzolf & DeLoache, 1997). An important one has to do with the relatively low verbal demands made by this task. Children do, of course, have to understand the simple instructions they are given, but they are not required to respond verbally. Therefore, performance in these search tasks is unlikely to be confounded by limited verbal ability, a perennial problem in research with young children.

A related advantage is that we can be reasonably confident that even very young children will encode and remember the base information. Young children generally perform much more competently on memory tests that require them to retrieve a hidden object than they do in standard verbal-memory tasks (e.g., Myers & Perlmutter, 1978), and their memory-based retrieval performance is very good. For example, after observing a toy being hidden somewhere in a room, 18- to 24-month-old children retrieve it over 80% of the time (DeLoache & Brown, 1983).

Furthermore, because the dependent variable is searching for a hidden object, children's performance is unambiguous: either they find the toy in the first location they search, or they do not. (Our results are typically reported only in terms of children's first search.) Because very young children's behavior is often difficult to interpret, the relatively straightforward nature of the relevant response is another benefit of object-retrieval tasks.

Another beneficial feature of search tasks for studying toddlers is that these tasks are highly motivating. One of the major challenges in doing research with young children is designing tasks that will engage and hold their attention. By capitalizing on young children's natural enjoyment of searching for hidden objects, we can obtain reliable and consistent data, even from such a notoriously uncooperative age group.

Finally, object-retrieval tasks have relatively high ecological validity. Searching for objects is ubiquitous in everyday life, and children are frequently faced with the need to retrieve misplaced shoes and mittens and to locate items needed for play. Thus, this part of the task is highly familiar to young children. The only unfamiliar part is receiving the information about where to search from a symbol. The set of advantages of search tasks means that we do not have to worry that our results will be caused by something other than what we wish to study – children's understanding of symbol–referent relations. As it turns out, the simplicity of our task has revealed a wealth of complexity in young children's developing symbolic abilities.

Young Children's Performance in Symbolic Object-Retrieval Tasks

The original scale-model study resulted in the pattern of results shown in figure 12.1 (DeLoache, 1987). This study was based on the *standard model task*, in which the room was a large room with basic living-room furniture, and the model contained miniature items of furniture that were in the same spatial positions and that were highly similar in appearance to those in the room. The older children in this study were 3-year-olds, and the younger ones were 2.5-year-olds. Retrieval 1 refers to finding the larger toy in the

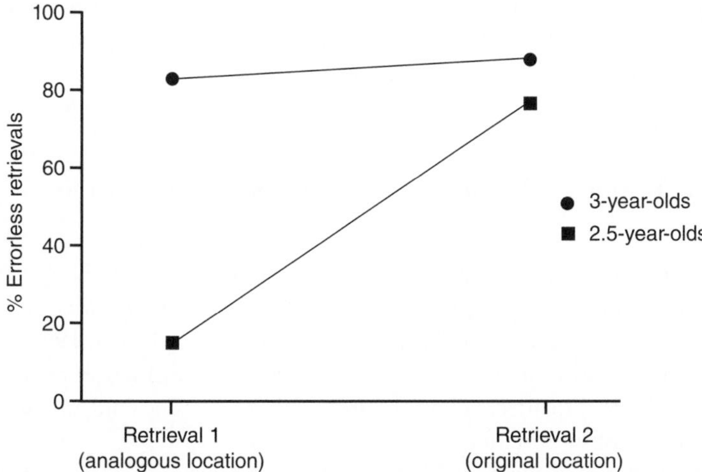

Figure 12.1 The performance of 2.5- and 3-year-old children in the standard model task. Both age groups are successful on the memory-based retrieval 2, but only the 3-year-olds succeed on the symbol-mediated retrieval 1

room, based on the hiding event the children had seen in the model; hence, this search is symbol-mediated. Retrieval 2 is finding the miniature toy in the model; hence, this search is based on direct experience.

As is apparent in the figure, both the older and younger children were highly successful at retrieving the miniature toy that they had observed being hidden in the model. Having directly observed a hiding event, they remembered the location of the toy and successfully retrieved it. The older children, the 3-year-olds, were equally successful in the symbol-mediated retrieval. They used their memory representation of the location of the miniature toy in the model to figure out where to search for the larger toy in the room. They achieved the same high level of success in the retrievals based on direct and symbol-mediated experience. In contrast, the younger children, the 2.5-year-olds, had virtually no idea where to search in the room. They failed to use their memory for where the miniature toy was in the model to infer where to find the larger toy in the room.

This pattern of results reveals a large difference in the understanding of the two age groups of the relation between the model and the room, that is, the symbol–referent relation. The difference apparent in the mean levels of performance shown in figure 12.1 is equally evident in the performance of the individual children: The great majority of 3-year-olds are successful in the retrieval task (i.e., they are over 75% correct on Retrieval 1); in stark contrast, the great majority of 2.5-year-olds are markedly unsuccessful. Thus, the older children clearly appreciated the symbol–referent relation and used it to succeed in the task. The younger children gave no evidence of understanding anything about the model–room relation.

This basic pattern of performance has been replicated many times, both in our lab and in others (Dow & Pick, 1992; O'Sullivan, Mitchell, & Daehler, 1999; Sharon, 1999). Across a large number of studies that have been performed using various versions of the standard scale-model task, as well as other symbolic object-retrieval tasks, the performance of children of 2.0, 2.5, 3.0, and 3.5 years of age has been shown to vary dramatically as a function of age and several task factors. A consistent but complex pattern of results has emerged. Accounting for this complex pattern of performance requires consideration of the interaction of several different variables.

A Model of Young Children's Symbol Use and Understanding

A substantial amount of research using the scale model and other symbolic-retrieval tasks led to the formulation of a conceptual *model of symbol understanding and use*. The model in figure 12.2 is a revision of one published earlier (DeLoache, 1995a, 1995b). Note that this is not a formal path model; rather it is a heuristic representation of several factors known or hypothesized to affect young children's ability to understand and use a symbolic artifact as a source of information.

The pivotal element in the model is *representational insight*. This component concerns children's insight into the existence of a symbol–referent relation in a particular task. Thus, the model represents the factors that combine to determine the likelihood that young children will achieve representational insight and hence be successful in a specific

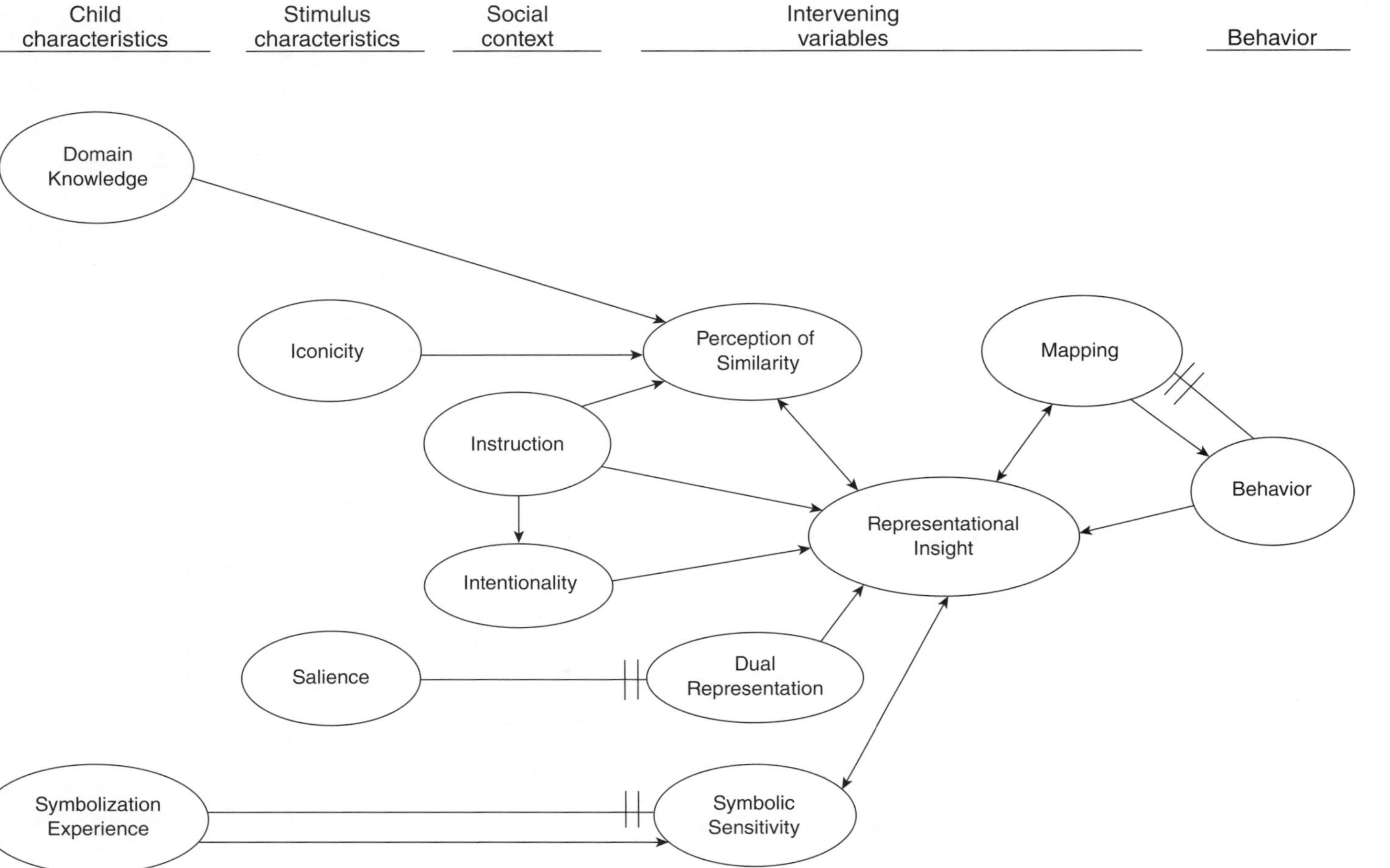

Figure 12.2 A model of young children's understanding and use of symbols (An earlier version appeared in DeLoache, 1995a, 1995b.)

situation. It is important to appreciate that representational insight does *not* refer to children's ability to understand and use symbols *in general*, although their general symbolic ability does, as will be discussed later, influence the likelihood of achieving representational insight in any specific task. We will briefly describe the components of the model and then focus in detail on some of the evidence for each of them. We will particularly highlight some relatively recent results regarding intentionality that motivated revision of the original model.

Behavior and mapping

Starting at the end point, the *behavior* in question in this research is, of course, retrieving a hidden object, based on a mental representation of the correct location. *Mapping* is the process of constructing and using a mental representation of the current location of the toy in the room based on what was observed via the symbolic artifact (model, picture, or video image). To map from symbol to referent, children must draw on their memory representation of the location of the small toy in the model, and based on insight into the general model–room relation, infer the location of the large toy in the room. Their mental representation of that inferred location must then serve as the guide for their search behavior in the room.

The perception of similarity

Physical similarity always makes it easier to detect the relation between two entities, and it plays an important role in relational reasoning of various sorts (DeLoache, Miller, & Pierroutsakos, 1998). The more two things resemble each other, the more likely it is that one will suppose that they belong to the same conceptual category. In analogical reasoning problems, higher levels of surface similarity between base and target increase the likelihood that the relation between them will be detected.

The same is true for symbolic retrieval tasks. A high level of iconicity between symbol and referent facilitates reasoning between them. In the standard model task, there is a high level of surface similarity between model and room, including similar surface appearance (color, fabric, material) of the miniature and full-sized items of furniture. The importance of this similarity is shown by the fact that the high level of performance achieved by 3-year-olds in this task (see figure 12.1) can be seriously disrupted by decreasing the level of physical similarity between the scale model and the room. When the items of furniture in the two spaces do not look so similar, 3-year-olds perform at the same low level as 2.5-year-olds do with high similarity. With age, children become able to cope with this lower level of similarity: 3.5-year-olds are highly successful in the low-similarity task that is so difficult for 3-year-olds.

Increasing similarity has an equally strong effect in the opposite direction for 2.5-year-olds. If the larger space is only twice as large as the scale model (rather than 16 times as large, as in the standard model task), 2.5-year-olds are reasonably successful, achieving a retrieval rate of around 70% (DeLoache, Kolstad, & Anderson, 1991; Marzolf & DeLoache, 1994).

Although iconicity has a strong effect on young children's performance in symbolic retrieval tasks, the perception of similarity between symbol and referent is not enough for success. For example, in one study, the experimenter pointed to one of the items in the model and asked 2.5-year-old children to show her one just like it in the room. The children readily matched the individual items of furniture in the two spaces. However, when tested in the standard model task minutes later, they failed. Although they knew that the little couch was like the big couch, they still failed to realize that the fact that the miniature toy was hidden behind the small couch meant/told them that the larger toy was hidden behind the large couch. Thus, appreciating the correspondence between the individual items of furniture in the two spaces is *necessary, but not sufficient* for success in the task.

Dual representation

Representational insight – and successful symbol use – requires *dual representation.* To use a symbolic artifact as a source of information, children must mentally represent both the concrete entity itself and, at the same time, its abstract relation to its referent. Achieving dual representation is a major challenge to young children's symbolic understanding and use. One reason, which is not at all specific to symbols, is that it is generally difficult for young children to have two active representations of a single entity (Zelazo & Frye, 1996). Specifically with respect to symbol use, the concrete features of a symbolic artifact can interfere with young children's ability to notice its relation to what it stands for. A realistic scale model like those used in our research is a highly salient, attractive, interesting object in and of itself. It affords and even invites direct physical activity – playing with the items of furniture contained in it, for example. This makes it hard for young children to treat it as standing for something other than itself. The younger the child, the more difficult it is to notice and think about both the concrete model itself and its relation to the room it stands for.

A picture or video image is much less physically salient than a model, and it has no competing affordances; there is little one can do with a 2-dimensional representation other than look at it, talk about it, or think about its relation to what it represents. Thus, it should be easier to achieve dual representation with pictorial images than with real objects.

This hypothesis was confirmed in a series of studies in which the experimenter pointed to a photograph of the room while telling the child, "This is where Snoopy's hiding." In every comparison, 2.5-year-olds have succeeded in a variety of picture tasks but not in the model task (DeLoache, 1987; DeLoache, 1991; Marzolf & DeLoache, 1994). The superior performance by 2.5-year-old children with pictures versus real objects is strong evidence for the concept of dual representation, because such a result is counterintuitive on any other basis. Children typically perform better when real objects are used in a wide variety of cognitive tasks (such as memory or categorization tasks) than when pictures serve as stimuli.

The importance of dual representation in young children's use of symbols has received substantial empirical support from the confirmation of a series of other theoretically motivated, but similarly counterintuitive, predictions. *Decreasing* the salience of a model by placing it behind a window enables 2.5-year-olds to succeed in the model task, whereas *increasing* the physical salience of a model by letting 3-year-olds play with it for several minutes before the retrieval task leads to significantly poorer performance (DeLoache, 2000). *Eliminating* the need for dual representation altogether also enhances performance. After 2.5-year-olds were led to believe that a scale model was actually a room that had been shrunk by a "shrinking machine," they successfully retrieved the miniature toy based on where they had seen the larger toy being hidden in the room (DeLoache, Miller, & Rosengren, 1997).

The challenge that achieving dual representation presents for young children is not limited to symbolic retrieval tasks. For example, Tomasello and his colleagues have shown that young children can interpret gestural symbols earlier than object symbols (Tomasello, Striano, & Rochat, 1999). When an experimenter used either a symbolic gesture or a replica object to communicate which of a set of objects was the correct one, children below 2 years of age more often selected the object indicated by a gesture than the one the experimenter denoted by holding up a replica of it. Thus, the replica objects, which require dual representation, were more difficult for these young children to interpret symbolically than were gestures, which do not require dual representation.

Other examples of dual-representation problems come from the work of Liben and Downs (1992; Liben & Christensen, chapter 17, this volume), who have documented a number of cases in which young children misinterpret the relation between a map and the space it represents. For example, when told that a red line on a highway map was a road, one child argued that it could not be because roads are not red, and another rejected the line on the basis that it was too narrow for a car. These children are responding in an overly literal way to the map, confusing its concrete and abstract nature.

Symbolic sensitivity

The only specific element in the model (shown in figure 12.2) having to do with why children exploit symbolic artifacts more successfully with age is *symbolic sensitivity*. Adults readily assume that any novel entity they encounter may have a symbolic function, but children do not make this assumption so easily. As they gain experience with symbols, children develop a general expectation or readiness to look for and detect symbolic relations among entities. Thus, *symbolization experience* generally increases their readiness to respond to novel entities in an abstract rather than concrete mode. This view is consistent with Sigel's (1970) concept of *distancing*: in common is the notion that children become increasingly able to achieve psychological distance from concrete entities, enabling them to think about those entities more abstractly. Young children who are given an opportunity to explore a scale model with calm detachment rather than an overwhelming desire to get their hands on it are more likely to appreciate its relation to the room it stands for.

Support for the importance of experience in performance in the symbolic-retrieval task comes from a series of transfer studies in which children of a given age are first given experience with a task on which they can succeed – and in which they presumably achieve representational insight. When subsequently presented with a task their age group normally fails, they now succeed. For example, in one study, 3.0-year-olds first successfully transferred from a high-similarity (standard) model task to a low-similarity one. In another study, 2.5-year-olds who had first performed well in a similar-scale model task later did equally well in the more difficult different-scale (standard) task (Marzolf & DeLoache, 1994). Similarly, 2.5-year-olds show substantial transfer from a picture or video task to the scale model task (DeLoache, 1991; Troseth & DeLoache, 1998). (Additional transfer studies will be discussed later.)

The social context

The social context of the symbolic-retrieval task is of great importance. The nature and extent of the *instructions* that children receive about the symbol–referent relation profoundly affect their performance (DeLoache, 1989). The success of 3-year-olds depends critically on receiving very extensive instructions and demonstrations of the model–room relation. Their performance, and even that of 3.5-year-olds, is dramatically disrupted by slightly less complete instructions (such as leaving out the *explicit comparison* of all the individual items of furniture in the two spaces). Not until 4 years of age can children detect the model–room relation with less than the standard extensive orientation to the task, and not until 5–6 years are they able to figure it out with no instructions about the relation at all (DeLoache, DeMendoza, & Anderson, 1999).

Another aspect of the social context of the task is *intentionality*. As discussed above, an inherent aspect of any symbol–referent relation is the intention of the creator and/or user of that relation. A hiding event in a scale model is informative about a hiding event in a different space only because someone makes it so. There is no direct causal link; it is only by virtue of the adult's intention to hide the toys in corresponding locations that the hiding event in the model has significance for the unseen event in the room. Presumably, a mature understanding of the symbol–referent relation in our symbolic object-retrieval tasks includes some recognition of the intention that establishes it.

Very young children are sensitive to adult intention and use it as a guide in many ways. One clear demonstration of this is research by Meltzoff (1995; chapter 2, this volume) in which 18-month-old infants observe an adult apparently *trying*, but failing, to do something to a toy. When children are later given the toy, they imitate what they assumed the adult wanted to do to the toy, rather than what he actually did. Children also rely on an adult's apparent intention in learning new words. For example, after hearing an adult announce her intention to "dax" a toy, children assumed that "dax" referred to an action that apparently produced an intended result but not to an action that appeared to result in the same outcome accidentally (Tomasello & Barton, 1994).

Intentionality is also important in young children's judgments about pictures. For example, Bloom and Markson (1998) reported that 3- and 4-year-old children believe that a drawing is of whatever the person who drew it intended it to be. Thus, even though someone's drawing of *X* may look at least as much like *Y*, it is a drawing of *X* if that's what the individual intended to draw. Similarly, research by Gelman and Ebeling (1998) shows that young children regard a picture that looks like some particular entity (e.g., a bear) to be a picture *of* that entity only if it was produced intentionally, not accidentally.

Emphasizing the intentional nature of the model–room relation

The performance of young children can be improved by highlighting the intentional nature of the model–room relation. In a series of studies, we modified the standard task in several ways. First, the children were given a "blind" trial in which they were told that Snoopy was hidden in the room and they should try to find him. The point was to make them realize that they had no way of knowing where the toy was. Next a "helpful" assistant to the experimenter indicated that she could help the child know how to find the toy. She then proceeded to assemble the model of the room, commenting on the similarity between the two spaces and explaining how the model would help the child know where Snoopy was hidden. On the first hiding trial, after the experimenter entered the room to hide the larger toy, the "helper" assumed a conspiratorial stance, peeking through the door as the experimenter was hiding the toy. She then hid the miniature toy in the model, telling the child this would help her know where Snoopy was hiding in the room. Finally, the child searched in the room.

A group of 3-year-old children received this assistance in the context of the low-similarity task that their age group typically fails. Their success rate of 52% indicates that they benefitted to some degree from the "helpful" experimenter's efforts to clue them in to the model–room relation. However, a group of 2.5-year-olds, who were given the standard task that their age group typically fails, showed less benefit from the helpful assistant's conspiratorial behavior (only 31%). Thus, we find that emphasizing the intentional nature of the adults' actions in the task can assist 3-year-olds to appreciate the model–room relation, but, at least in this initial study, 2.5-year-olds were less receptive to the intervention.

Children's explicit awareness of the model–room relation

In another recent study, we asked whether young children's understanding of the intentional nature of the model–room relation is explicit enough to enable them to ignore irrelevant information. A group of 3.5-year-olds participated in the standard model task, with two very non-standard trials interpolated among four regular ones. On the two "accidental hiding" trials, the children watched as the experimenter hid the miniature toy in the model as usual and then went into the room to hide the larger toy. At this point, a second, "clumsy" experimenter "accidentally" kicked the model, dislodging its contents. She replaced all the furniture in the correct locations. Then, picking up the miniature toy, she said, "Hmm, I don't know where this was; I'll just put it here." She proceeded to put the toy in a different place from where the experimenter had hidden it.

The question was whether the children would realize that the "accidental" hiding was irrelevant to where the larger toy was hidden in the room. In other words, would they realize that the intention of the first experimenter determined its location, not the last hiding event that had actually taken place in the model?

The results were quite clear. The children in both age groups ignored the "accidental" hiding to the extent that their retrieval performance did not suffer at all. Performance was 80% on the standard trials and 75% on the accidental trials. Thus, these children recognized the importance – and information value – of the experimenter's intentions in hiding the two toys. We are currently examining whether younger children (3-year-olds) are similarly sensitive to the intentional basis for the model–room relation.

Representational insight

As noted before, the pivotal element in the *model* is *representational insight*, the recognition of the existence of a symbol–referent relation. As figure 12.2 shows, mapping occurs in a particular task only if representational insight is achieved in that task. In the symbolic object-retrieval task, only if children appreciate the way that the model (or picture or video) is related to the room it stands for do they transfer their knowledge from the symbol to the referent. Although previous versions of the model in figure 12.2 showed some other factors as having a direct impact on mapping, it has become clear that successful performance is always mediated by representational insight.

The level of awareness involved in this insight can obviously be explicit knowledge of the relation that is accessible to conscious reflection and verbalizable, such as an adult or older child would have. However, it can also be some implicit form of insight that enables young children to successfully exploit the symbol–referent relation in our retrieval tasks even though they do not show evidence of awareness of that relation.

There are three aspects of children's performance in the scale model and other retrieval tasks that provide strong support for the idea that the key factor is whether or not children achieve representational insight.

The difficulty of improving performance

Another form of support for the idea that children must achieve representational insight is the great difficulty we have experienced trying to improve children's performance in our tasks. Over the years, we have tried a very large number of manipulations designed, often with great optimism and enthusiasm, to raise the performance of 2.5-year-olds in the scale-model task. Although a few have succeeded (most notably the various transfer procedures), most have not. We very recently added some more unsuccessful interventions to the long list.

One was designed to highlight the idea that corresponding hiding events take place in the two spaces. In the orientation to this study, 2.5-year-olds watched two simultaneous hiding events, one in the model and one in the room. The model was positioned so the children could readily see into both it and the room. In the orientation to the task, two experimenters (one near the model and the other in the room) drew the children's attention to their hiding of the miniature and larger toys in the model and room, inviting them to look back and forth between the two events. Then the children searched – successfully – for both toys. Following this orientation, the children were given the standard model task in which they observed a hiding event in the model and then searched in the room. In spite of the orientation in which they saw the analogous hiding events taking place in the two spaces and searched successfully in both of them, the children now failed to use the hiding event they observed in the model as a guide for searching in the room.

Another unsuccessful effort was based on modeling. Strong evidence exists for imitation by toddlers and even infants (e.g., Barr & Hayne, 2000; Heimann & Meltzoff, 1996; Meltzoff, chapter 2, this volume). We thought that if 2.5-year-old children observed another person successfully performing in the model task, it might help them appreciate the basis for that person's success – especially if she explained what she was doing (Troseth, 2001). For this study, the child and an adult assistant observed the experimenter hide two miniature toys together in the same location in the model. The experimenter then hid two large toys in the corresponding location in the room. Then the child watched as the assistant retrieved one of the larger toys in the room, narrating her thought processes: "Let's see, I know Kathy hid Little Snoopy behind the couch, so that means she hid Big Snoopy behind his big couch. I'm going to look there." Next the child was given the opportunity to search for the remaining hidden toy. At this point, the child had observed the experimenter perform the original hiding event at a location in the model and the assistant search successfully at that same location in the room. Performance was 28%. Watching someone else use the model as a source of information clearly did not make these children aware of its relevance and usefulness. Exactly the same result occurred for a group of 2.0-year-olds in an analogous version of the video task. After watching on a monitor as the experimenter hid two toys in the room and the assistant successfully retrieved one of them, the children still failed to use the video-based information to find the remaining toy.

One other recent series of studies provided further evidence of the difficulty of improving the performance of very young children in our tasks (although in this particular case, we actually expected a negative result). This time the goal was to see if increasing children's motivation to find the hidden object would improve their retrieval performance. In a series of studies referred to in our lab as "Hide-a-Mom," the hidden object was something we could be certain any child would be extremely highly motivated to find – his or her own mother or father. To do this study, we added some hiding places to the room large enough to conceal an adult (e.g., a card table covered with a floor-length tablecloth, a curtain across a corner of the room). Corresponding features were of course added to the model. On each trial, the child's parent – usually mother – hid in the room. A doll was placed in the model to show the child where Mom was waiting. The children loved the task; they were excited to search for their mothers and were filled with glee when – typically with the experimenter's assistance – they were reunited. They did not, however, know where their mothers were; the level of correct retrievals was only 38%, no significant improvement over the standard level. Again, exactly the same pattern was found in a video study in which 2.0-year-olds watched on a monitor as their mother went into the room and hid herself. Thus, heightened motivation does not increase young children's use of symbol-mediated information in object-retrieval tasks.

These recent failures to improve young children's performance (and the many that preceded them) testify to the imperviousness of young children to manipulations that any reasonable person might expect would help them. This long list of failures makes all the more remarkable the interventions that have succeeded.

Successful transfer

We have been extremely successful in improving children's performance via transfer (Marzolf & DeLoache, 1994). As described earlier, these studies show that an appreciation of one symbol–referent relation can help children recognize a more difficult one that children their age do not typically grasp. In other words, the attainment of representational insight in one task increases greatly the likelihood that they will achieve representational insight in another one.

A transfer study conducted by Marzolf, Pascha, & DeLoache (1996) provides further evidence that success in the model task involves an appreciation of the higher-order model–room relation. In that study, 2.5-year-old children were first given the easy similar-scale task described previously. This task was administered by two experimenters in a lab in one building using one set of toys as hidden objects. As expected, the children's performance was reasonably good (63%). A full week later, the same children were given the more difficult dissimilar-scale (standard) task by two different experimenters in a different lab in a different building using a second set of toys. A control group received the difficult task twice with only one day intervening. Thus, the only thing that was the same over the two sessions was the underlying structure of the tasks – using a model as a source of information about the location of a toy in a larger space. As expected, the control group performed poorly on both days (16% and 31%). The transfer group performed significantly better than the control group on the difficult task (69%): Their success with the easy model–room relation helped them recognize a similar but more difficult relation a full week later, even with very little contextual support. Thus, these results indicate that transfer was supported by a relatively abstract representation of the relevant symbol–referent relations.

Troseth (2000) found dramatic levels of transfer using the video task in which 2.0-year-old children typically perform relatively poorly (around 40–45% correct). In this series of studies, 2.0-year-olds were given experience with live video in their own homes before being tested in the lab. The goal was to help the children realize that what they observe on a television screen can have relevance for current reality. In our laboratory studies (Troseth & DeLoache, 1998), children have always been given experience seeing themselves, their parent(s), the experimenters, and the room on live video. However, this orientation typically lasts for only 5–10 minutes. In the new study, the children's parents were asked to film them several times over a 2-week period. The film was simultaneously shown live on their television set, and the parents drew the children's attention to the relation between what they were doing and what they saw on the screen. Thus, the children received extensive experience with the relation between their own and others' behavior and images they saw on television.

The children were then brought into the laboratory where they participated in the standard video task in which they watched on video as the experimenter hid the toy in the room next door. They successfully retrieved the toy 77% of the time, significantly more often than a control group (approximately 40%). Thus, experience with live video at home facilitated these children's insight into the relation between the hiding event they saw on the monitor and the unseen hiding event in the other room. Furthermore, these children were then given a second transfer test – they were tested in the standard picture study. Recall that 2.0-year-old children have been markedly unsuccessful (usually around 15%) in the picture task. However, the group of children who had the home video experience and who had then performed well on the video task also performed well on the picture task (60% correct). Their success in the picture task could have been based on their home video experience, their success in the video retrieval task, or – more likely – on both.

These and many other transfer studies we have performed using various media provide strong evidence that young children's early understanding of the correspondence between a symbolic artifact and the space it stands for involves insight into the higher-order symbol–referent relation. Once children gain representational insight into one type of symbolic relation, they readily detect another symbol–referent relation of which they would otherwise remain unaware.

Inhibitory control hypothesis

An alternative account of young children's difficulty in the basic model task has recently been ruled out. This alternative is the idea that poor inhibitory control, manifested as a strong tendency for response perseveration, causes young children to perform poorly. In the model task (and in object-retrieval tasks generally), the predominant error children make is to perseverate, that is, to return to the location where they found the toy (usually with the experimenter's assistance) on the previous trial. Across many studies and multiple labs, over half of all errors in symbolic retrieval tasks are perseverative (e.g., DeLoache, 1999; DeLoache & Burns, 1994; O'Sullivan et al., 1999; Sharon, 1999; Solomon, 1999).

It is possible that this high level of perseverative responding masks insight into the basic symbol–referent relation; even if children had some understanding of the model–room relation, for example, they might perform poorly because of difficulty inhibiting a prepotent (previously rewarded) response. Thus, on a given trial, the child might have a representation of the location of the toy, but fail to search there because of being drawn to repeat his or her previous response. Support for this idea comes from some studies in which performance was significantly better on the first trial than on subsequent ones (Schmitt, 1997; Sharon, 1999; Troseth & DeLoache, 1998).

The possible importance of perseveration as a cause of poor performance in the model task was evaluated in two ways. First, Sharon and DeLoache (2000) analyzed existing data from 13 separate groups of 2.5-year-olds in the standard model task. The results did not support the idea that 2.5-year-old children know more about the model–room relation than their performance reveals. Although performance on the first trial was significantly better than on the second trial, the difference was quite small, and performance subsequently improved. In addition, the level of perseveration actually decreased over trials, exactly the opposite of what one would expect if perseveration were a significant factor in children's performance. Finally, the children almost never corrected their search errors; if children have a mental representation of the correct location but cannot resist repeating their previous response, one would expect that they would go to the correct place after performing an incorrect search.

The second way the limited inhibitory control hypothesis was evaluated was by an experiment designed specifically to address this issue (Sharon & DeLoache, 2000). Following pilot work by Sharon (1999), the standard model task was modified to make it less likely children would repeat their previous response. The question was whether decreasing the level of perseverative responding would lead to an increase in correct responding; if 2.5-year-olds' typically poor performance is caused by inadequate inhibitory control, then removing the need for inhibitory control should enable them to be more successful. Accordingly, after every trial, the location that the child had just searched was modified to make it clear that it was no longer a potential hiding place, and it was left that way for the remaining trials. For example, after the child searched in the basket, it was turned over and left on its side to reveal its empty interior, and the tablecloth on the table was pulled up to show nothing was beneath it. This manipulation did, as expected, reduce the level of perseverative searching. However, there was no concomitant increase in correct responding.

A very similar study that was simultaneously designed and conducted in another lab (O'Sullivan et al., 1999) produced the same result. In this case, the item of furniture that had served as the hiding place on a given trial was actually removed (from both model and room). As a consequence, it was impossible to search perseveratively on subsequent trials. In spite of the impossibility of searching where they had looked before, the children still failed to search correctly.

Taken together, the results of our analysis of existing data and the two independently conducted experiments provide strong evidence that the typical poor performance of young children in the model task is not due to difficulty inhibiting a previous response. Perseveration is a consequence, not a cause, of young children's deficient performance. Thus, there is no evidence that 2.5-year-olds have representational insight into the model task but are prevented from succeeding by perseveration. Rather, the preponderance of the evidence indicates their failure is due to a lack of representational insight in the first place.

Having made the case that success in symbolic object-retrieval tasks is based on insight into the symbol–referent relation, it is important to emphasize again that this insight is not necessarily accessible or verbalizable. Even children who perform successfully in the model task have difficulty explaining what they know about the model–room relation. For example, in one study, 3-year-olds who had participated successfully in the standard model task were asked to choose which of two models of the room was better (i.e., "which one is just like Snoopy's room"). The items of furniture were either highly similar or quite dissimilar in appearance to those in the room, and they were either arranged in the same spatial organization or in a discrepant array. In spite of having exploited the model–room relation to find the toy in the retrieval task, the children chose randomly among the models. In another study, 3-year-olds were given the standard model task, except that on two trials, the toy was not in the correct location in the room; that is, it was not in the location corresponding to the hiding place of the miniature toy in the model. Although most of the children indicated that the toy should have been in that location, they could not explain how they knew it should be there.

Development in Young Children's Symbolic Functioning

The research we have reviewed here reveals that progress in young children's use of symbolic artifacts as a source of information is relatively rapid. Although 2.0-year-old children fail miserably at our basic picture task, 2.5-year-olds are very successful in it. Similarly, 2.5-year-olds generally perform extremely badly in the basic model task, whereas 3.0-year-olds perform extremely well. What accounts for the fact that children who find a task very difficult at one age find it trivially simple only 6 months later?

But age changes in our symbolic object-retrieval tasks are not all that must be explained. A full account must also address the fact that children of a given age who fail a task find that same task simple after experience with a related one, as well as the fact that children of a given age may be highly successful in one task but fail a *very* similar one.

Our review makes it clear that there is substantial complexity involved in the understanding and use of simple symbol–referent relations. Therefore, it should not be surprising if the developmental story is similarly complex, involving changes in numerous domains. We think this is exactly the case. It is unlikely that any one or two factors are by themselves responsible for the rapid development we have documented. Some of the likely factors appear in the model shown in figure 12.2.

One course of developmental progress has to do with the ease of achieving *dual representation*. This development is presumably facilitated by increasing inhibitory control. Although we ruled out response perseveration as a result of poor inhibitory control as a cause of young children's poor performance in the model task, it may very well be important in a different way. To achieve dual representation in the first place, a child has to inhibit responding to a symbolic artifact exclusively or primarily as an object. The more young children respond to a scale model as an interesting toy, the less likely they are to appreciate its role as a representation of something else. General inhibitory control is known to increase during the first several years (e.g., Harnishfeger & Bjorklund, 1993). This improvement is believed to be due in part to frontal lobe development, which is proceeding rapidly throughout this period (Diamond, 1990; Welsh & Pennington, 1991). Thus, basic brain development, leading to improved ability to inhibit their natural response to symbolic artifacts as objects, may underlie children's increased success in symbolic retrieval tasks with age.

The model in figure 12.2 explicitly specifies symbolic experience as an important source of development. The idea, as described earlier, is that experience with symbols would contribute to the development of symbolic sensitivity – a general readiness to assume that a novel entity may have a symbolic function, that is, that it may be used to stand for something other than itself. This increased symbolic sensitivity results in part from repeated experience achieving dual representation. Presumably, the more experience children have mentally representing the dual nature of symbolic artifacts, the easier it becomes to do so with a novel entity.

There is no question that the mostly middle-class American children who have participated in our research receive an enormous amount of exposure to a wide variety of symbolic artifacts in their early years. From very young ages, they enjoy daily picture-book interactions with their parents and others (Gelman, Coley, Rosengren, Hartman, &

Pappas, 1998). Joint picture-book reading has been shown to promote vocabulary development (Whitehurst et al., 1988), so it is reasonable to suppose that experience with pictures contributes to symbolic sensitivity. So might the many hours that young children spend watching television and videos.

Young children are not just consumers of ready-made symbols; 2- to 3-year-olds also begin to create symbolic mappings. Although their scribbles may not be decipherable to anyone else, evidence is accumulating that at least some of very young children's earliest artistic products do involve representational intent (Bloom & Markson, 1998). A large literature documents very young children's use of representational toys in pretend or symbolic play, as well as their increasing ability to perform object substitutions (Lillard, Pinkham, & Smith, chapter 11, this volume). Increasing facility with drawing and pretense presumably contributes to symbolic sensitivity.

We should note that none of these experiences involves the use of symbolic artifacts to solve problems based on current reality, as is required in our symbolic retrieval tasks. To use a model, picture, or video as a source of information about reality, children need to have the cognitive flexibility to treat a familiar kind of artifact in a novel way. Part of what is involved in the development of symbolic sensitivity is increased cognitive flexibility, the ability to achieve psychological distance from something and respond to it abstractly (Sigel, 1970).

The model in figure 12.2 includes intentionality as a key element. An increasing body of research is establishing impressive levels of understanding of intention by infants and young children (e.g., Gergely, chapter 3, this volume), and such understanding expands dramatically during this period and for years to come. Paying attention to and thinking about the reasons for another person's behavior would presumably help young children figure out the basic nature of the symbolic object-retrieval task. There is no evidence, however, that success in these tasks requires full or even substantial understanding of intentionality.

Several other important aspects of early development that are likely to affect performance in symbolic retrieval tasks are not formally represented in the figure 12.2 model. One is the large increase that takes place in the first years of life in the basic amount of information that children can mentally represent. Our symbolic object-retrieval tasks require children to represent and coordinate multiple relations. In the model task, for example, the children must use their representation of the model–room relation to infer from the relation between the miniature toy and its hiding place in the model what relation must hold between the larger toy and a location in the room. They also have to remember both the hiding event *and* the model–room relation; delays between seeing the miniature object hidden in the model and the opportunity to retrieve the larger one in the room cause substantial deficits in children's performance (Uttal, Schreiber, & DeLoache, 1995). Their steadily increasing speed of information processing and resulting increases in working memory (Kail, 1995) no doubt help young children cope with these cognitive demands. Similarly, their growing ability to represent multiple relations simultaneously would also make developmental progress possible (Case, 1992; Halford, 1993; Halford & Andrews, chapter 27, this volume). Any symbolic-retrieval task has, at a minimum, one more relation – the relation between symbol and referent – to represent than does any task based on direct experience (Marzolf & DeLoache, 1997; Troseth & DeLoache, 2001).

In addition, between the ages of 2 and 3, children undergo extensive language development. At a minimum, their increased language skills should make it easier for them to apprehend our instructions. Young children also show substantial improvement in their ability to reason by analogy. Although even infants and toddlers can use information from a base to solve a simple target problem (Brown, 1990; Chen, 1996; Chen & Siegler, 2000), with age they more readily gain access to analogies and are able to solve increasingly complex problems (Gentner, Ratterman, Markman, & Kotovsky, 1995; Goswami, 1992, chapter 15, this volume). Young children's increasingly successful performance in symbolic retrieval tasks is presumably supported by more general analogical reasoning skills.

This list of factors known or assumed to contribute to the development of symbolic functioning is by no means intended to be complete; rather, it serves to emphasize that the rapid developmental improvement that occurs in our symbolic object-retrieval tasks is almost certainly attributable to several interacting and converging lines of development.

Conclusion

Children in Western societies are encountering an ever-wider variety of media and symbolic artifacts, and their exposure to these media begins at increasingly younger ages. Parents begin picture-book interactions with increasingly younger infants. Television programming is now designed specifically for toddlers and even infants, and children begin learning numbers and letters in preschool and sometimes even from television. Computers have become ubiquitous, and children are being exposed to them increasingly early. Consequently, full participation in society requires that children begin to understand several kinds of symbolic media quite early in life.

The increasing prominence of symbolic artifacts in the lives of very young children and the importance of symbolic literacy throughout life means that it is more important than ever to increase our knowledge about the developmental processes involved in coming to understand and interpret symbols.

References

Barr, R., & Hayne, H. (2000). Age-related changes in imitation: Implications for memory development. In C. Rovee-Collier & L. P. Lipsitt (Eds.), *Progress in infancy research* (pp. 21–67). Mahwah, NJ: Erlbaum.

Barr, R., Muentener, P., Garcia, A., Fujimoto, M., & Chávez, V. (2007). The effect of repetition on imitation from television during infancy. *Developmental Psychobiology*, *49*, 2, 196–207.

Barr, R., & Wyss, N. (2008). Reenactment of televised content by 2-year olds: Toddlers use language learned from television to solve a difficult imitation problem. *Infant Behavior and Development*, *31*(4), 696–703.

Bloom, P., & Markson, L. (1998). Intention and analogy in children's naming of pictorial representations. *Psychological Science*, *9*, 200–204.

Boysen, S. T. & Berntson, G. G. (1990). The emergence of numerical competence in the chimpanzee (*Pan troglodytes*). In S. T. Parker & K. R. Gibson (Eds.), *Language and intelligence in animals: Developmental perspectives*. Cambridge: Cambridge University Press.

Brown, A. L. (1990). Domain-specific principles affect learning and transfer in children. *Cognitive Science, 14*, 107–133.

Bruner, J. S., Olver, R. R., & Greenfield, P. M. (1966). *Studies in cognitive growth*. New York: Wiley.

Case, R. (1992). *The mind's staircase*. Hillsdale, NJ: Erlbaum.

Chen, Z. (1996). Children's analogical problem solving: The effects of superficial, structural, and procedural similarity. *Journal of Experimental Child Psychology, 62*, 410–431.

Chen, Z., & Siegler, R. S. (2000). Across the great divide: Bridging the gap between understanding of toddlers' and other children's thinking. *Monographs of the Society for Research in Child Development, 65* (Serial No. 261).

Deacon, T. W. (1997). *The symbolic species: The co-evolution of language and the brain*. NY: Norton.

DeLoache, J. S. (1987). Rapid change in the symbolic functioning of very young children. *Science, 238*, 1556–1557.

DeLoache, J. S. (1989). Young children's understanding of the correspondence between a scale model and a larger space. *Cognitive Development, 4*, 121–129.

DeLoache, J. S. (1991). Symbolic functioning in very young children: Understanding of pictures and models. *Child Development, 62*, 736–752.

DeLoache, J. S. (1995a). Early symbol understanding and use. In D. Medin (Ed.), *The psychology of learning and motivation* (Vol. *33*, pp. 65–114). New York: Academic Press.

DeLoache, J. S. (1995b). Early understanding and use of symbols: The model model. *Current Directions in Psychological Science, 4*, 109–113.

DeLoache, J. S. (1999, March). *The role of inhibitory control in early symbol use*. Paper presented at the Society for Research in Child Development, Albuquerque.

DeLoache, J. S. (2000). Dual representation and young children's use of scale models. *Child Development, 71*, 329–338.

DeLoache, J. S. (2002). Early development of the understanding and use of symbolic artifacts. In U. Goswami (Ed.), *Blackwell handbook of childhood cognitive development* (pp. 206–226). Malden, MA: Blackwell.

DeLoache, J. S., & Bloom-Pickard, M. (2008). Of chimps and children: Use of spatial symbols by two species. In R. Mitchell & F. Dolins (Eds.), *Spatial perception, spatial cognition: Mapping the self and space*. New York: Cambridge University Press.

DeLoache, J. S., & Brown, A. L. (1979). Looking for Big Bird: Studies of memory in very young children. *The Quarterly Newsletter of the Laboratory of Comparative Human Cognition, 1*, 53–57.

DeLoache, J. S., & Brown, A.L. (1983). Very young children's memory for the location of objects in a large scale environment. *Child Development, 54*, 888–897.

DeLoache, J. S., & Burns, N. M. (1994). Early understanding of the representational function of pictures. *Cognition, 52*, 83–110.

DeLoache, J. S., DeMendoza, O. A. P., & Anderson, K. N. (1999). Multiple factors in early symbol use: The effect of instructions, similarity, and age in understanding a symbol–referent relation. *Cognitive Development, 14*, 299–312.

DeLoache, J. S., Kolstad, V. & Anderson, K. N. (1991). Physical similarity and young children's understanding of scale models. *Child Development, 62*, 111–126.

DeLoache, J. S., Miller, K. F., & Pierroutsakos, S. L. (1998). Reasoning and problem solving. In D. Kuhn & R. Siegler (Eds.), *Handbook of child psychology: Vol. 2. Cognition, perception, and language* (5th ed., pp. 801–850). New York: Wiley.

DeLoache, J. S., Miller, K. F., & Rosengren, K. S. (1997). The credible shrinking room: Very young children's performance with symbolic and non-symbolic relations. *Psychological Science, 8*, 308–313.

DeLoache, J. S., & Sharon, T. (2004). Symbols and similarity: You can get too much of a good thing. *Journal of Cognition and Development, 6*, 33–49.

Diamond, A. (1990). Developmental time course in human infants and infant monkeys, and the neural bases, of inhibitory control in reaching. In A. Diamond (Ed.), *The development and neural bases of higher cognitive functions. Annals of the New York Academy of Sciences, 608*, 637–676.

Dow, G. A., & Pick, H. L. (1992). Young children's use of models and photographs as spatial representations. *Cognitive Development, 7*, 351–363.

Freeman, N. H. (1993). Drawing: The representation of public representations. In C. Pratt & A. F. Garton (Eds.), *Systems of representation in children* (pp. 113–132). New York: Wiley.

Gelman, S. A., Coley, J. D., Rosengren, K. S., Hartman, E. E., & Pappas, A. S. (1998). Beyond labeling: The role of parental input in the acquisition of richly structured categories. *Monographs of the Society for Research in Child Development, 63* (1, Serial No. 253).

Gelman, S. A., & Ebeling, K. S. (1998). Shape and representational status in children's early naming. *Cognition, 66*, 35–47.

Gentner, D., Rattermann, M. J., Markman, A., & Kotovsky, L. (1995). Two forces in the development of relational similarity. In T. J. Simon & G. S. Halford (Eds.), *Developing cognitive competence: New approaches to process modeling*, Hillsdale, NJ: Erlbaum.

Goodman, N. (1976). *Languages of art: An approach to a theory of symbols* (2nd ed.). Indianapolis, IN: Hackett Publishing.

Goswami, U. (1992). *Analogical reasoning in children.* Hillsdale, NJ: Erlbaum.

Gregory, R. L. (1970). *The intelligent eye.* New York: McGraw-Hill.

Halford, G. S. (1993). *Children's understanding: The development of mental models.* Hillsdale, NJ: Erlbaum.

Harnishfeger, K. K., & Bjorklund, D. F. (1993). The ontogeny of inhibition mechanisms: A renewed approach to cognitive development. In M. L. Howe & R. Pasnak (Eds.), *Emerging themes in cognitive development: Vol 1. Foundations* (pp. 28–49). New York: Springer-Verlag.

Heimann, M., & Meltzoff, A. N. (1996). Deferred imitation in 9- and 14-month-old infants: A longitudinal study of a Swedish sample. *British Journal of Developmental Psychology, 14*, 55–64.

Huston, A., & Wright, J. (1998). Mass media and children's development. In I. E. Sigel & K. A. Renninger (Eds.), *Handbook of child psychology: Vol. 4. Child psychology in practice* (5th ed.). New York: Wiley.

Huttenlocher, J., & Higgins, E. T. (1978). Issues in the study of symbolic development. In W. A. Collins (Ed.), *Minnesota symposia on child psychology* (Vol. *11*, pp. 98–140). Hillsdale, NJ: Erlbaum.

Ittelson, W. H. (1996). Visual perception of markings. *Psychonomic Bulletin and Review, 3*, 171–187.

Kail, R. (1995). Processing speed, memory, and cognition. In F. E. Weinert & W. Schneider (Eds). *Memory performance and competencies: Issues in growth and development* (pp. 71–88). Mahwah, NJ: Erlbaum.

Kennedy, J. M. (1974). *A psychology of picture perception.* San Francisco: Jossey-Bass.

Kirkorian, H. L., & Anderson, D. R. (2008). Learning from educational media. In S. L. Calvert & B. J. Wilson (Eds.), *The handbook of children, media, and development* (pp. 188–213). Chichester, UK: Blackwell

Langer, S. K. (1942). *Philosophy in a new key.* Cambridge, MA: Harvard University Press.

Liben, L. S. (1999). Developing an understanding of external spatial representations. In I. E. Sigel (Ed.), *Development of mental representation: Theories and applications* (pp. 297–321). Mahwah, NJ: Erlbaum.

Liben, L. S. (2003). Beyond point and shoot: Children's developing understanding of photographs as spatial and expressive representations. In R. V. Kail (Ed.), *Advances in child development and behavior* (Vol. *31*, pp. 1–42). San Diego: Elsevier.

Liben, L. S., & Downs, R. M. (1992). Developing an understanding of graphic representations in children and adults: The case of GEO-graphics. *Cognitive Development, 7*, 331–349.

Marzolf, D. P., & DeLoache, J. S. (1994). Transfer in young children's understanding of spatial relations. *Child Development, 64*, 1–15.

Marzolf, D. P., & DeLoache, J. S. (1997). Search tests as measures of cognitive development. In N. Foreman & R. Gillett (Eds.), *Interacting with the environment: A handbook of spatial research paradigms and methodologies* (pp. 131–152). Hove, UK: Erlbaum.

Marzolf, D. P., Pascha, P. T., & DeLoache, J. S. (1996). *Transfer of a symbolic relation by young children.* Poster session presented at the International Conference on Infant Studies, Providence, RI.

Meltzoff, A. N. (1995). Understanding the intentions of others: Re-enactment of intended acts by 18-month-old children. *Developmental Psychology, 31*, 838–850.

Myers, N., & Perlmutter, M. (1978). Memory in the years from two to five. In P. A. Ornstein (Ed.), *Memory development in children.* Hillsdale, NJ: Erlbaum.

Newell, A., & Simon, H. A. (1972). *Human problem solving.* Englewood Cliffs, NJ: Prentice-Hall.

O'Sullivan, L. P., Mitchell, L. L., & Daehler, M. W. (1999). Representation and perseveration: Influences on young children's symbolic functioning. Unpublished manuscript.

Peirce, C. S. (1903/1955). Logic as semiotic: The theory of signs. In J. Buchler (Ed.), *The philosophical writings of Peirce* (pp. 98–119). New York: Dover Books.

Potter, M. C. (1979). Mundane symbolism: The relations among objects, names, and ideas. In N. R. Smith & M. B. Franklin (Eds.), *Symbolic functioning in childhood* (pp. 41–65). Hillsdale, NJ: Erlbaum.

Preissler, M. A., & Carey, S. (2004). Do pictures and words function as symbols for 18- and 24-month-old children? *Journal of Cognition and Development, 5*(2), 185–212.

Robinson, E. J., Nye, R., & Thomas, G. V. (1994). Children's conceptions of the relationship between pictures and their referents. *Cognitive Development, 9*, 165–191.

Schmitt, K. L. (1997). *Two- to three-year-olds' understanding of the correspondence between television and reality* (Unpublished doctoral dissertation). University of Massachusetts, Amherst.

Sharon, T. (1999, October). *Avenues into symbolic understanding: The role of intentionality.* Paper presented at the meeting of the Cognitive Development Society, Chapel Hill, NC.

Sharon, T., & DeLoache, J. S. (2003). The role of perseveration in children's symbolic understanding and skill. *Developmental Science, 6*, 289–297.

Sigel, I. E. (1970). The distancing hypothesis: A causal hypothesis for the acquisition of representational thought. In M. R. Jones (Ed.), *Miami Symposium on the prediction of behavior, 1968: Effect of early experiences* (pp. 99–118). Coral Gables, FL: University of Miami Press.

Sigel, I. E. (1978). The development of pictorial comprehension. In B. S. Randhawa & W. E. Coffman (Eds.), *Visual learning, thinking, and communication* (pp. 93–111). New York: Academic Press.

Solomon, T. L. (1999). The effect of enriched instructions on 2.5-year-olds' understanding of scale models. Poster session presented at the Society for Research in Child Development, Albuquerque, NM.

Strouse, A., & Troseth, G. L. (2008). "Don't try this at home": Toddlers' imitation of new skills from people on video. *Journal of Experimental Child Psychology, 101*, 4, 262–280.

Thomas, G. V., Nye, R., & Robinson, E. J. (1994). How children view pictures: Children's responses to pictures as things in themselves and as representations of something else. *Cognitive Development, 9*, 141–164.

Tomasello, M., & Barton, M. (1994). Learning words in non-ostensive contexts. *Developmental Psychology, 30*, 639–650.

Tomasello, M., Striano, T., & Rochat, P. (1999). Do young children use objects as symbols? *British Journal of Developmental Psychology, 17*, 563–584.

Troseth, G. L. (2000). *TV guide: Learning to use video as a source of information* (Unpublished doctoral dissertation). University of Illinois, Urbana-Champaign.

Troseth, G. L. (2001). *Getting a clear picture: Young children's understanding of a televised image.* Unpublished manuscript.

Troseth, G. L. (2003). TV guide: Two-year-old children learn to use video as a source of information. *Developmental Psychology, 39*, 1, 140–150.

Troseth, G. L., & DeLoache, J. S. (1998). The medium can obscure the message: Young children's understanding of video. *Child Development, 69*, 950–965.

Troseth, G. L., & DeLoache, J. S. (2001). Now you "see" it, now you don't: Young children's use of directly-experienced versus symbol-mediated information. Unpublished manuscript.

Troseth, G., Pierroutsakos, S. L., & DeLoache, J. S. (2004). From the innocent to the intelligent eye: The early development of pictorial competence. In R. V. Kail (Ed.), *Advances in Child Behavior and Development* (Vol. *32*). New York: Academic Press.

Uttal, D. H. (2000). Maps and spatial thinking: A two-way street. *Developmental Science, 3*, 283–286.

Uttal, D. H., Schreiber, J. C., & DeLoache, J. S. (1995). Waiting to use a symbol: The effects of delay on children's use of models. *Child Development, 66*, 1875–1891.

Welsh, M., & Pennington, B. (1991). Assessing frontal lobe functioning in children: views from developmental psychology. *Developmental Neuropsychology, 4*, 199–230.

Werner, H., & Kaplan, H. (1963). *Symbol formation.* New York: Wiley.

Whitehurst, G. J., Falco, F. L., Lonigan, C. J., Fischel, J. E., DeBaryshe, B. D., Valdez-Menchaca, M. C., & Caulfield, M. (1988). Accelerating language development through picture book reading. *Developmental Psychology, 24*, 552–559.

Zelazo, P. D., & Frye, D. (1996). Cognitive complexity and control: A theory of the development of deliberate reasoning and intentional action. In M. Stamenov (Ed.), *Language structure, discourse, and the access to consciousness* (pp 113–153). Philadelphia: John Benjamins.

PART III

Topics in Cognitive Development in Childhood

As in the first edition, the third section of the Handbook is less closely themed than the first two sections. Having achieved certain core developments in understanding their psychological, biological, and physical worlds, children's cognition in relatively unrelated domains such as moral development, spatial reasoning, physics, scientific reasoning, reading, and mathematics progresses in fairly independent fashion. There are of course considerable continuities in cognitive development across these domains, for example via contributions from relatively domain-general mechanisms such as the incremental growth of stored knowledge in long-term memory, the improved capacity of working memory, the development of more efficient inhibitory processes, and the development of executive functions. In some domains of enquiry, such as inductive reasoning and deductive reasoning, research since the first edition of the Handbook has focused almost exclusively on the developmental contributions of these more basic mechanisms. Nevertheless, each domain also has its own, sometimes fairly specific, developmental mechanisms. These include phonological awareness for the development of decoding skills in reading, understanding sharing and one-to-many correspondence for the development of multiplicative reasoning in mathematics, and the distinction between morality and convention that all children make as moral development unfolds. The functioning of even these relatively specific developmental mechanisms, however, is of course influenced by the social, emotional, and cultural context in which learning takes place.

Memory development is one of the most studied topics in all psychology, the field of childhood cognitive development included, and in chapter 13 Schneider again does a remarkable job of distilling this vast literature into a clear account of what develops and when. He notes the growth of a "computer" metaphor in memory research, with a research focus on either "hardware" (the capacity of memory systems, the speed with which information is processed) or "software" (the use of strategies). In line with current neuroscience perspectives, he argues that the brain systems mediating perceptual and conceptual implicit memory are fully developed early in life. The neural structures supporting implicit memory are also different from those that support the explicit memory system, which develops continuously throughout the lifespan. Here, social and cultural factors inevitably play a role, as for example in autobiographical memory, where social interactions and long-term knowledge affect what is encoded at the time of the autobiographical experience. Importantly, even apparently independent memory systems, such as working memory, are affected by the type of information to be remembered. Memory span is not a domain-general phenomenon that is essentially identical irrespective of what is being remembered. When age differences in task-relevant knowledge are controlled experimentally, age differences in memory span are no longer found. Children's prior knowledge of related content also affects their execution of basic mnemonic strategies, their metacognitive knowledge, and their acquisition of new strategies. For example, experts learn "new" knowledge faster in their domain of expertise compared to novices.

Koslowski and Masnick (chapter 14) focus on the importance of background knowledge, explanation, and information about mechanism in the development of causal reasoning. They point out that current algorithms for modeling causal reasoning, such as Bayes nets, share the drawbacks of older approaches, such as the Humean indices of causation (e.g., covariation information). This is because such algorithms do not include the background knowledge that children will bring with them to the reasoning task, which will affect how they treat the different causal variables with which they are presented. Indeed, much recent research utilizes "knowledge-lean" tasks to study causal reasoning, using unfamiliar events. As Koslowski and Masnick note, this research demonstrates clearly that children do take account of Bayesian and Humean indicators in situations where little other causal information is present. However, much of human reasoning is not like this. Prior knowledge will mean that some types of causal event are more plausible than others, and that some types of causal mechanism are more plausible than others. As causal reasoning is always embedded in context, prior knowledge will always play a role, and so causal reasoning is heuristic rather than formal. Implausible agents are more likely to be treated as causal if mechanism information is available, and frequent covariations suggest the presence of an undiscovered mechanism that might be responsible for the covariations. When there is anomalous (disconfirming) data, causal theories may only be modified if there is a plausible mechanism linking the anomalies – when the anomalies appear to follow a pattern. Koslowski and Masnick demonstrate consistencies between their approach and current approaches in philosophy, such as "inference to the best explanation." Causal explanations are evaluated with respect to other competing explanations, and an explanation is judged with respect to the extent to which it is causally consistent with what else the child knows about the world. As will be seen, similar factors affect the development of inductive and deductive reasoning by children.

In my own chapter (Goswami, chapter 15), I show that recent research in deductive and inductive reasoning by children, like the study of causal reasoning, has taken greater account of the importance of stored real-world knowledge. If children are able to access and retrieve relevant real-world knowledge for a particular problem, then both inductive and deductive reasoning are facilitated. Research in reasoning has also focused particularly on the role of inhibitory processes in successful reasoning – the ability to inhibit irrelevant or competing knowledge that will interfere with successful solution of a particular problem. Indeed, sometimes younger children can be more successful in reasoning tasks, because their more limited real-world knowledge means that they have less irrelevant or competing knowledge to inhibit. Recent research has also begun to focus on the role of working memory capacity in successful inductive and deductive reasoning. Working memory capacity refers to the mental "workspace" where premises and real-world knowledge must be interrelated. This research has yet to consider the important point about working memory capacity made by Schneider (chapter 13) – that working memory capacity is itself affected by task-relevant knowledge. Rather, in the reasoning literature working memory capacity is assumed to always increase with age. Interesting demonstrations that inductive reasoning, for example, may be affected by children's decisions about which cues are most valid (which is of course affected by their background knowledge, Bulloch & Opfer, 2009) suggest that this state of affairs may not be stable. The availability of background knowledge will always interact with the efficiency of inhibitory processes, and will also interact with working memory capacity, and future research in reasoning needs to address these developmental interactions.

The moral domain is a broad one, encompassing philosophy as well as psychology. Understanding moral development involves understanding the structure of moral cognition, the generality of moral concepts, and the complementary roles of judgment and emotion. As Nucci and Gingo (chapter 16) demonstrate, historically the development of moral reasoning was thought to progress through a series of universal stages that transcended culture and context (e.g., Kohlberg, 1969; Piaget, 1932). Nucci and Gingo make it clear that moral concepts are not really general, and that it is very difficult to divorce moral cognition from context and culture. Many moral issues are matters of convention, based on contextually dependent and agreed-upon social rules. These social rules naturally vary with social context, and social structure has a big impact on how morality is experienced and thought about in everyday life. Even young children differentiate between matters of convention and matters of morality, for example judging unprovoked harm as wrong. As they get older, they begin to understand fairness as reciprocity, and to incorporate notions of human welfare, benevolence, equity, and equality. The increased ability to handle complexity with age partly underpins these developments. As we also saw for inductive and deductive reasoning, however, lack of real-world knowledge can in some cases facilitate moral judgments. Whereas 8-year-old children judge that it is wrong to keep money that has been dropped unknowingly by someone else, 13-year-olds are less sure, recognizing that there is some moral ambiguity. After all, the keeper did not take the money directly, and in the absence of an observer the money would have been lost in any case. By age 16, children judge that notwithstanding these complexities, the act of *observing* renders the bystander obligated to return the money. Neuroscience has also entered the field of moral development, with demonstrations that reasoning and emotions activate different areas of the brain. Nucci and Gingo show that the neuroanatomy suggests to some moral theorists that intuitive emotional responses drive moral *reactions*, with slower cognitive control processes then sometimes (not always) controlling moral *judgments*. The essential claim is that moral judgments are non-rational. Nucci and Gingo offer a number of cogent criticisms of this position, which appears mistakenly to assume that affective and cognitive processes can be disaggregated in human decision-making. Nevertheless, they point out that issues of morality are viewed by children as rife with emotional content, an area of human conduct associated with "hot" affect (see also Zelazo & Müller, chapter 22). Sociomoral affect may provide the raw data from which children form more general abstract moral principles, using a variety of cognitive abilities and depending on the affective climate within their families. For example, unprovoked harm has intrinsic emotional content, and children may have quite different experiences of unprovoked harm depending on adults' behavior to them. The moral reasoning and behavior of a child who has grown up in an affectively supportive environment may thus be rather different from the moral reasoning and behavior of a child who has grown up in an aggressive and affectively unsupportive environment.

Liben and Christensen's chapter on spatial development (chapter 17) also evokes the philosophical roots of psychology as a discipline. In classic empiricism, people have to learn about space via experiences such as those generated by vision and touch. Biological approaches to spatial development focus instead on innate endowments for perceiving and representing space, such as the role of the dorsal visual stream in establishing spatial location and the developmental role of the hormone testosterone. Clearly, both perspectives contribute to development, and Liben and Christensen show how children develop an understanding of space in areas of investigation as diverse as environmental space (the space we live and move about in), representational space (our referents for space, such as maps and models), and perceptual space (we see objects in space, we see space itself, we get spatial information from hearing and touch, and all this perceptual information guides our actions and understandings about where objects are in relation to ourselves). Liben and Christensen identify current areas of intensive research activity, such as the neural substrates of the memory for spatial location and the neuropsychological bases of spatial development, and illustrate how developments in experimental methodology, particularly for testing infants, have led to changes in our understanding of spatial development. Infants are remarkably aware of many spatial features of their environments. Action is particularly important for spatial development, and crawling, climbing, and walking all aid the development of external, proximal, and distal frames of reference. As they grow older, children's environments (their "home ranges") expand greatly, and children who are given more personal control over their travel through environments have relatively more spatial knowledge about these environments. The knowledge and understanding of representational space (such as maps) develops more slowly, presumably because many of the conventions of representational space (e.g., red lines on a map correspond to roads) must be learned. Liben and Christensen cite Deloache's work (chapter 12) as evidence that a basic understanding of representational correspondences emerges early, with even 3-year-olds able to demonstrate some basic map skills. They then demonstrate how gradual mastery of spatial relations such as scale and viewing angle contribute to a deeper and more principled understanding of representational space. They also touch on recent technological developments that are bound to affect the development of knowledge about space, such as Google Earth and satellite navigation systems, and technology that can transform experiments on spatial understanding, such as virtual realities (computer-generated spaces that feel three-dimensional). As they state, our daily lives are being profoundly affected by current space-related technologies, which seem likely to affect the ways in which children represent, think about, and manipulate their spatial worlds.

In chapter 18, on the development of intuitive physics, Wilkening and Cacchione focus on the variability of children's intuitive knowledge. Covering research in a multitude of domains, including time, speed, force, buoyancy, temperature, and color intensity, they show that intuitive physical knowledge is largely experience-dependent. At the same time, everyday perceptual experience yields some intuitions that are physically wrong – such as that objects falling from a moving carrier will fall straight down. For such intuitions, formal instruction in physics is necessary, as perceptual experience by itself will never overcome these wrong intuitions: direct perceptual experience is itself the source of the error. Therefore, general cognitive mechanisms such as improved inhibitory processes play an important role in the development of intuitive physics. Wilkening and Cacchione also discuss two theoretical perspectives currently popular in the field of intuitive physics. One is the idea that children's developing knowledge structures are equivalent to scientific concepts, and are theory-like and coherent (e.g., Carey, 1999). The coexistence of potentially contradictory or empirically unfounded beliefs is thus expected to culminate in conceptual change, or radical theory revision. The other is that children's physical knowledge is so dependent on experience that it is fragmentary and completely unintegrated, and tied to the specific context in which it was acquired (diSessa, Gillespie, & Esterly, 2004). Neither framework is particularly satisfactory. Wilkening and Cacchione conclude that variability in children's intuitive physics is the norm, and cannot be eliminated by choosing the "right" experimental methods. Rather, this variability is an intrinsic part of children's adaptive physical concepts, and needs to be a focus of systematic study in its own right. From the perspective of a neural networks metaphor, what is needed is a systematic research strategy for exploring how incremental sensory and perceptual physical experiences and actions build an integrated system of physical knowledge.

Kuhn's chapter on the development of scientific thinking (chapter 19) also rejects the idea that there is a restricted set of "right" methods that will enable the accurate documentation of development. As she points out, scientific thinking is really knowledge seeking. Any purposeful thinking that aims to enhance the thinker's knowledge is scientific. Scientific thinking is distinct from scientific understanding, which does not always result from knowledge seeking by individuals. Nevertheless, Kuhn endorses the view that children are constructing implicit scientific theories from their earliest years to make sense of their experiences, leading to theory revision in the face of new evidence – conceptual change. Kuhn then focuses her chapter on the processes that children use to revise their theories. She identifies the coordination of theory and evidence as particularly important developmentally, especially when new evidence is not consistent with a currently held theory. In such cases, children can either form a distinct mental representation of the discrepant evidence, enabling them to contemplate the implications for their current theory, or the discrepant evidence can go unrecognized. Identifying the new evidence as a source of knowledge is important for theory revision. Yet even adolescents and adults experience difficulties in coordinating theories and evidence, particularly when there is complexity involved.

Kuhn then explores the phases of scientific thinking, namely inquiry, analysis, inference, and argument. The prototypical form of scientific inquiry is a situation in which a number of variables have potential casual connections to an outcome, and the child must choose examples for investigation that will enable the identification of those that are causal and those that are non-causal. As children's knowledge of the network of collateral or background information in which these variables are embedded necessarily affects the success of the inquiry process, scientific thinking, like causal, moral, and deductive reasoning, cannot be divorced from the context in which it takes place (see Koslowski & Masnick, chapter 14). Kuhn argues that meta-level strategies are important for theory change: children need purposely to select the relevant knowledge-seeking strategies to apply. Epistemological understanding regarding what knowledge is and what it means to "know" something is also important. This means that children will not become scientific thinkers simply by interacting with materials and phenomena. Instead, good science education requires a focus on knowledge seeking and argument – transmitting the understanding of what questions are worth asking, and why.

In chapter 20, Snowling and Göbel consider the burgeoning area of reading research. Reading is a critical aspect of cognitive development, because in later childhood so much information about the world comes via the written word, especially in the age of the internet. However, reading is also a somewhat unique cognitive skill, as our brains were not designed for reading. Our brains were designed to process spoken language. As Snowling and Göbel demonstrate, this fundamental insight is very important for understanding the cognitive skills that underpin efficient reading acquisition. Preschool children's *phonological awareness* skills, namely their ability to reflect upon the sound patterning and phonological structure of their spoken language, is the most important precursor skill to acquiring the alphabetic principle. Snowling and Göbel also look beyond phonology, at the skills related to achieving reading fluency, and at environmental and genetic factors. Learning to read also depends on the language of learning, and accordingly a consideration of reading acquisition in different languages is provided. Atypical development of reading skills (developmental dyslexia) can be very serious for those children affected, typically around 7% of children in any population, and its primary cognitive cause is an impairment in phonological processing. Finally, reading is one area of cognitive development where neuroscientists have been very active. Neuroimaging data suggest that the reading system comprises three overlapping systems: a neural network responsive to the low-level visual features of words, a neural network responsive to phonology and to orthography–phonology mappings, and a neural network for semantics. These neural networks are not discrete, and parts of these networks are also used in other cognitive tasks such as object recognition. As might be expected, specialized activity related to reading in these networks is dependent on incremental word-learning experiences – the neural systems for reading are experience-dependent. One interesting developmental idea is that of neuronal recycling (Dehaene, 2004) – the idea that the brain areas recruited for reading have several other functions as well, which may be evolutionarily older (such as object recognition). This may serve as a good analogy for other higher-level cognitive systems, such as the deductive reasoning system – which also seems likely to draw on several functions (such as working memory and declarative memory) that are not specialized to deductive reasoning per se.

Mathematical knowledge is another critical aspect of cognitive development, and in chapter 21, Bryant and Nuñes point out that most people rely heavily on mathematics in their daily lives. In contrast to reading development, however, some researchers have suggested that there is a "mathematical brain," a neural substrate that is specialized for number. This neural system is an analogue system, representing the number of items in an array in terms of the amount of neural activity. It is postulated to enable numerical behavior in preverbal infants, although its role in learning formal school mathematics is unclear. Some form of preverbal numerical abilities are even thought to be present in other species. Bryant and Nuñes question the idea that infants have an innate understanding of number. They argue instead that mathematical knowledge, like knowledge about reading, develops over time. They show that children learn a lot about the underlying logic of mathematics through their own experiences, a hypothesis first proposed by Piaget. According to their analysis, cardinal and ordinal knowledge of number – the understanding that all sets with the same number are qualitatively equivalent, and that numbers come in an ordered scale of magnitude – develops relatively slowly during the first years of life. Children can learn to count at a young age, but this is not the same thing as understanding ordinal number. In fact, a number of research studies (including some of Piaget's studies about conservation) suggest that children at first count without understanding what they are doing. Further, although children do have some understanding of basic principles underpinning the number system, such as one-to-one correspondence (they are quite good at sharing), they do not seem to extend this knowledge to counting. Learning about the arithmetical operations of adding, subtracting, dividing, and multiplying also requires considerable development. An understanding of addition develops first, at about 3 years. However, being able to add two numbers is not the same thing as additive reasoning, which requires understanding the inverse relation between adding and subtracting. This takes a bit longer to develop, emerging at around 5 years. Similarly, sharing and an understanding of one-to-many correspondence develop relatively early, at around 4 and 5 years, but full multiplicative reasoning develops quite a bit later, and much of it requires formal teaching. Bryant and Nuñes end their chapter by stressing the importance of teaching in all areas of mathematical development. The counting system is based partly on logic and partly on human invention. It is unreasonable to expect each child to reinvent or intuitively understand symbol systems such as counting that required extensive cultural invention. Mathematics, like reading, must be taught, and it must be taught in ways that are meaningful to the young child.

In chapter 22, Zelazo and Müller consider the role of executive function in typical and atypical development. They define executive function as a behavioral construct with a specific goal, namely deliberate problem-solving. It is a complex function encompassing aspects of problem-solving such as goal selection and planning, and relies on a variety of processes including inhibitory control, working memory, reflection, and the ability to handle rule complexity. Executive function undergoes protracted developmental change, and continues to develop in adolescence and early adulthood. Although research into the development of executive function has been strongly influenced by research on the prefrontal cortex (PFC) of the brain and its development, Zelazo and Müller stress that executive function should not be conceived as synonymous with PFC function. Nevertheless, PFC comprises between a quarter and a third of the brain, and is intimately involved in executive function; therefore Zelazo and Müller provide an overview of its structure and development. They also distinguish the affective ("hot") aspects of executive function, from the cognitive ("cool") aspects, showing how these relate to different parts of PFC. Hot executive function is required for problems that have high affective involvement, such as social problems, or for problems that involve appraising the affective significance of stimuli. Cool executive function is elicited by relatively abstract and decontextualized problems. The complexity of the cognitive processes that a task requires is important (see also Halford & Andrews, chapter 27), and Zelazo's functional problem-solving framework is offered as one means of assessing developmental change systematically. Finally, a brief analysis of executive function in atypical development is offered.

As we saw in the chapters by Waxman and Leddon in part I and by Tomasello in part II, language development and cognitive development are intimately related. In chapter 23, Dodd and Crosbie consider the relationship between language and cognition from the perspective of communication disorders. As many as 15% of children will fail to acquire language milestones at the appropriate ages, and their use of language may be socially inappropriate. The etiology of their difficulties is usually difficult to identify and is the source of considerable theoretical debate. Dodd and Crosbie argue that research that seeks to identify specific linguistic and cognitive skills has the greatest potential to elucidate relationships between cognition and language. In the absence of this type of research, they focus their chapter on two key questions: whether children with cognitive (intellectual) disabilities are necessarily language-disordered, and whether children with language disorders show specific cognitive deficits. In fact, children with intellectual impairments may have surprisingly good language skills, and children with poor language skills less frequently can have preserved cognitive skills. The documentation of language "savants" shows that children with very severe cognitive impairments because of factors such as perinatal brain damage can develop into adults who speak 16 different languages. However, the developmental picture is complex, and the "preserved skills" are rarely fully intact. Furthermore, most children with language impairments are receiving intensive language therapy, and so their linguistic profiles are very unstable over time and their patterns of impairment on linguistic versus cognitive tasks are continually changing. Dodd and Crosbie also consider different theories of specific language impairment. They conclude that there is no one cause of specific language impairment, and no single linguistic profile associated with cognitive impairment. The links between language and cognition are developmentally complex.

In his chapter on autism (chapter 24), Baron-Cohen gives a concise account of his empathizing-systemizing (E-S) theory of autism. He argues that the "triad" of impairments that are used to diagnose autism (atypical social development, atypical development of communication, and repetitive behavior/narrow and obsessive interests) may arise from a primary cognitive impairment in this E-S system. On Baron-Cohen's theory, the key cognitive impairment in autism is a deficit in *empathizing*. Empathizing encompasses the abilities that enable us to make sense of the behavior of other agents, to predict what they might do next and how they might feel, and to adjust our own behavior accordingly. Empathy requires both mindreading abilities and an emotional response to another's state of mind. Baron-Cohen analyzes the developmental roots of empathizing behavior, namely skills such as joint attention and pretend play, the building blocks of social cognition (see the chapters by Gergely, Meltzoff, and Carpenter in part I). He also suggests that individuals with autism have superior *systemizing* skills. Systemizing is defined as the drive to analyze or construct systems, for example mechanical systems like video recorders and abstract systems such as the grammar of a natural language. Baron-Cohen suggests that the developmental roots of systemizing lie in the development of physical knowledge (see Baillargeon et al., chapter 1; Wilkening & Cacchione, chapter 18), the development of causal and logical reasoning (see Koslowski & Masnick, chapter 14; Goswami, chapter 15), the development of scientific thinking (see Kuhn, chapter 19), and executive function (Zelazo & Müller, chapter 22). Being excellent at systemizing offers a number of advantages, including facilitating the development of superior engineering and mathematical skills when other cognitive skills are intact (i.e., in high-functioning autism). As systemizing skills are usually better in males, while empathizing skills are better in females, Baron-Cohen ends his chapter by proposing an "extreme male brain" theory of autism. He suggests that this theory, for which he notes some neurobiological support, may ultimately explain why autism is more prevalent in males than in females.

As will be clear, many of the topics discussed in part III draw on the same core developmental mechanisms to explain age-related change, for example working memory capacity and inhibitory processes. The authors of the chapters also consider similar theoretical explanations, such as metacognitive evaluation, choice of strategies, or assessment of plausibility. In many of these topic areas, earlier research guided by theories about universal laws of cognitive development has been replaced by research studying the developmental importance of social and contextual information and incremental knowledge. Research strategies have changed accordingly. Instead of seeking to describe cognitive change in terms of the discovery of assumed formal universal laws, research in many areas of cognitive development has converged on theoretical models that depend on experience-specific learning. As noted, such theoretical models are consistent with the models of learning that inform developmental cognitive neuroscience.

Therefore, developments in developmental cognitive neuroscience seem likely to change our cognitive theories. One example is developmental assumptions about conceptual change. If knowledge acquisition is incremental and experience-dependent, with neural networks changing and enriching their activation patterns as the child has more and more relevant experiences, then a sudden and radical restructuring of the neural network ("conceptual change") seems the wrong metaphor. Of course, conceptual development is not purely deterministic, as children will actively seek knowledge to enrich their concepts, and teachers will purposely contribute knowledge designed to change children's understandings. Therefore, we may eventually explain conceptual change in terms of changes in the spatial configurations of neural networks driven by perceptual and sensory experiences, coupled with "top-down" input gained via language, action, direct teaching, and being part of a community. Metaphors from cognitive neuroscience make it more likely that conceptual development is gradual and cumulative, rather than prone to sudden radical change and restructuring.

References

Bulloch, M. J., & Opfer, J. E. (2009). What makes relational reasoning so smart? Revisiting the relational shift in cognitive development. *Developmental Science, 12*, 114–122.

Carey, S. (1999). Knowledge acquisition: Enrichment or conceptual change? In E. Margolis & S. Laurence (Eds.), *Concepts: core readings* (pp. 459–487). Cambridge, MA: MIT Press.

Dehaene, S. (2008). Cerebral constraints in reading and arithmetic: Education as a "neuronal recycling" process. In A. M. Battro, K. W. Fischer, & P. J. Lena (Eds.), *The educated brain: Essays in neuroeducation* (pp. 232–247). New York: Cambridge University Press.

Di Sessa, A. A., Gillespie, N. M., & Esterly, J. B. (2004). Coherence vs. fragmentation in the development of the concept of force. *Cognitive Science, 28*, 843–900.

Kohlberg, L. (1969). Stage and sequence: The cognitive-developmental approach to socialization. In D. Goslin (Ed.), *Handbook of socialization theory and research* (pp. 347–480). Chicago: Rand McNally.

Piaget, J. (1932). *The moral judgment of the child.* New York: Free Press.

CHAPTER THIRTEEN

Memory Development in Childhood

Wolfgang Schneider

In their comprehensive review of children's memory development, Schneider and Bjorklund (1998) emphasized that memory development has been one of the most studied topics in all of cognitive development, and deservedly so. In fact, an impressive amount of scientific studies on this issue have been published within the last four decades, stimulated by a shift away from the behaviorist theories to information-processing considerations. Given the extent and diversity of the memory-development literature, this overview will be restricted to major trends in the field, thereby focusing on the age period between early and late childhood (i.e., approximately ages 3–12). Memory development in very young children will not be discussed because it is already addressed in a separate chapter (see Bauer, Larkina, & Deocampo, chapter 6, this volume). Before getting to the bulk of memory research carried out with children, major historical developments are briefly summarized (for extended reviews, see Schneider, 2000a; Schneider & Pressley, 1997).

Early Investigations of Memory Development

Experimental studies of memory are as old as scientific psychology. When Ebbinghaus (1885) started with his classic experiments on memory and forgetting in 1879, Wundt founded the first psychological laboratory. Although this is widely known, it is not equally well known that research on memory *development* also started at about that time. Around the turn of the century, numerous studies were carried out in Europe to investigate developmental and individual differences in children's memory. There were three rather independent lines of research that contributed to this early trend.

I wish to thank David Bjorklund, Usha Goswami, Ulman Lindenberger, and Yee Lee Shing for their valuable comments on a previous version of this chapter.

First, carefully conducted case studies of young children's development (which also included systematic observations of memory development in early childhood) received a lot of attention, leading to the scientific foundation of child psychology in Germany.

A second line of research was directly derived from memory experiments with adults. Some of these studies explored whether findings obtained for adult populations could be easily generalized to children of different ages. Other investigations were less basic in nature and were driven by educational interests. These studies tested common (mis)conceptions held at that time, for example, that children, because they practice their memory skills in school almost every day, are better at remembering verbal material than adults. Also, many of these studies examined the popular assumption that boys have a better memory than girls. As the issue of co-education was at stake in Germany around the turn of the century, this question was of high practical relevance.

The third line of research on children's memory was even more applied, focusing on children and adults' testimonial competence. The prevailing legal attitude had been one of scepticism about the testimony of child witnesses. Nonetheless, interest in children's eyewitness memory competencies was particularly strong in Germany and France, where systematic research on this issue flourished at the start of the twentieth century (e.g., Stern, 1910; Whipple, 1909, 1911). Most studies focused on children's suggestibility, developing methodologies that are still in use in modern research on the topic.

One of the major insights concerning the "general" course of memory development stems from a classic large-scale study conducted by Brunswik, Goldscheider, and Pilek (1932) in the early 1930s. This developmental study aimed at providing a general description of short-term and long-term memory in school-age children and adolescents and differed from earlier investigations in that the issues addressed were directly derived from truly developmental theory, that is, Charlotte and Karl Bühler's doctrine of phases and stages (e.g., Bühler, 1930). A large variety of memory tasks were presented to a sample of about 700 participants, ranging from 6 to 18 years of age. Tests involved short- and long-term memory for nonsense and meaningful words, colors, and numbers, as well as memory for poems. Moreover, several non-verbal memory tasks such as memory for motor actions and their correct sequence were included. As a main result, reliable age differences were observed for most short-term memory tasks. Six- to 13-year-olds required more practice to learn nonsense syllables than words or numbers. This difference was particularly marked for the youngest children. The findings for short-term memory in the older students were not clear-cut because performance differences between the 14- and 18-year-olds were not consistently observed. A curve of the general development of immediate memory ("memory strength") constructed by Brunswik and colleagues, based on an aggregation of all memory scores, indicated linear and steep rises in memory performance for participants from 6 to 11 years of age, followed by a plateau in performance during pre- and early adolescence. The developmental curve regarding general improvements in memory performance was in accord with several other studies of the early period and also validated in modern longitudinal work (e.g., the Munich Longitudinal Study: see Schneider, Knopf, & Sodian, 2009).

Current Trends in Research on Memory Development

How does modern research on memory development differ from the historical approaches outlined above? One of the crucial differences concerns a shift from an emphasis on describing developmental differences in memory to an emphasis on identifying the underlying mechanisms of change. Another difference concerns the theoretical framework used. Since the mid-1960s, research on memory development has been influenced strongly by theoretical models derived from information-processing and neuroscience approaches (see the reviews by Bauer, 2006; Kail, 1990; Schneider & Bjorklund, 1998, 2003; Schneider & Pressley, 1997). Developmental psychologists began looking at changes in children's thinking in terms of a computer metaphor. From this perspective, memory development can be seen as reflecting either *hardware* (the capacity of memory systems and the speed at which information can be processed) or *software* (e.g., use of strategies). Developmental research on memory was strongly influenced by multistore memory models that distinguished between a sensory register, a short-term store, and a long-term store.

Regarding the content of the long-term store, it was proposed that information can be represented in two ways. *Explicit*, or *declarative*, memory refers to our capacity for conscious recollection of names, places, dates, or events and comes in two types, episodic and semantic. Whereas episodic memory concerns events and experiences that can be consciously retrieved, semantic memory refers to our knowledge of language, rules, and concepts. In contrast, *implicit* or *procedural* memory represents a variety of non-conscious abilities, including the capacity for learning habits and skills, and some forms of classical conditioning.

The distinction between implicit and explicit memory was proposed by Graf and Schacter (1985), and is more than one of conceptual convenience. There is evidence that different areas of the brain are involved in declarative and procedural memory (Schacter, 1992), suggesting that memory is not a single phenomenon but a set of domain-specific operations that may show different patterns of developmental function. Research on adult memory has shown clear dissociations between explicit and implicit memory. For instance, some brain-damaged patients were found to be seriously impaired with explicit memory compared to normals but did not show implicit memory impairment (see Roediger & McDermott, 1993). Although the distinction has been questioned in several scientific debates, it seems to have withstood the test of time (Lloyd & Newcombe, 2009).

Given that the focus of this chapter is on the development of deliberate, explicit memory, only a brief summary of developmental trends in implicit memory will be given below. Please note that under ordinary circumstances, explicit and implicit memory operate in parallel, and also co-exist in situations where behavior no longer requires conscious awareness (Bauer, 2006). Accordingly, implicit memory may also contribute to performance in tasks aiming to assess deliberate memory.

The Development of Implicit Memory

By definition, implicit memory is "memory without awareness." Developmentally, it has been claimed that implicit memory is present from the start of life, and does not change much over the years (Parkin, 1998; Reber, 1989). This conclusion was drawn from studies focusing on perceptual priming. Most of these developmental studies involved the use of fragmented pictures, perhaps pictures of a dog, which should be identified by the participants. This is very difficult to do initially, but as more of the picture is completed, it becomes increasingly easier to identify the pictures. After a series of such picture-identification tasks has been given, children are provided with degraded pictures of both previously-seen versus unseen objects. The typical finding is that repetition priming is observed. That is, children identify fragmented pictures of previously seen pictures much faster than fragmented pictures of previously unseen objects (see Ausley & Guttentag, 1993). Interestingly, most developmental studies failed to find age differences in implicit picture-fragment completion tasks (for reviews, see Lloyd & Newcombe, 2009; Parkin, 1998; Rovier-Collier, Hayne, & Colombo, 2002). Thus perceptual priming effects seem comparable for older and younger participants, even though findings by Cycowicz, Friedman, Snodgrass, and Rothstein (2000) on age differences in perceptual priming suggest that processes such as encoding and storage may show (slight) age-related improvements. Given that perceptual priming at younger ages has not been extensively studied, it is difficult to prove that the system is as early appearing as has been claimed (see Lloyd & Newcombe, 2009).

As noted above, most developmental studies have focused on a single type of implicit memory, that is, *perceptual priming*. In order to draw firm conclusions about the developmental invariance of priming, other types of implicit memory testing such as *conceptual priming* are needed. For instance, a conceptual measure of implicit memory provides participants with a list of category names and requires them to produce the first exemplars of the categories that come to mind. The typical finding from studies with adults is that prior presentation of a category exemplar increases the likelihood of that word being named as a category instance (Schumann-Hengsteler, 1995).

Given that these tests emphasize the semantic relationships between studied and tested items and thus require conceptually driven processing, one should expect age differences in conceptual priming. That is, older children should show more priming because the semantic categories are more meaningful to them than to younger children. However, the research situation is not clear. Some of the few studies that examined developmental trends in conceptual priming indicate that priming is age-invariant (see Anooshian, 1997; Perez, Peynircioglu, & Blaxton, 1998). Other researchers have argued that the unexpected finding of age-invariant conceptual priming could be due either to the rather narrow age ranges or to the predominance of familiar semantic categories in those studies (Mecklenbräuker, Hupbach, & Wippich, 2003; Perruchet, Frazier, & Lautrey, 1995). In fact, both Mecklenbräuker et al. (2003) and Perruchet et al. (1995) found reliable age differences in conceptual priming for atypical but not for typical category exemplars. Accordingly, although there is substantial evidence for the age invariance of priming effects, performance on conceptual priming tasks changes with age. However, these changes seem related to changes in conceptual knowledge rather than caused by changes in the priming mechanism per se (see Lloyd & Newcombe, 2009). More studies using novel materials are needed to examine this issue further.

Overall, the implicit memory results to date point to an independent memory system. It seems that the brain systems mediating perceptual and conceptual priming are fully developed early in life, which clearly contrasts with the continuous development of the explicit memory system (cf. Squire, Knowlton, & Musen, 1993). There is substantial evidence in cognitive neuroscience that perceptual and conceptual priming do not depend upon the medial-temporal and diencephalic brain structures that mediate intentional declarative memory. Although early Russian research already pointed to young children's surprisingly well-developed "involuntary" memory, contemporary findings on implicit memory provide a convincing explanation for dissociations between involuntary and voluntary memory that are found throughout the lifespan.

The Development of Episodic Memory

Unlike implicit memory, episodic memory involves conscious awareness. This memory system usually refers to memory for episodes and events in one's life. Research from the last three decades indicates that children and adults organize memory for recurring events in the form of "scripts" or general event representations (Nelson, 1986). Whereas this topic was only briefly addressed in Mandler's (1983) chapter in the fourth edition of the *Handbook of Child Psychology*, it was devoted a whole chapter in the handbook's sixth edition (Bauer, 2006; see also Hudson & Mayhew, 2009; Nelson & Fivush, 2004, for reviews of the literature). The most important findings concerning the development of children's event memory are summarized next.

Event memory

To study children's memory for recurring events, a suitable method is to ask young children questions about familiar routines such as attending birthday parties and going grocery shopping. This is exactly what Nelson and her colleagues (e.g., Nelson, 1986; Nelson & Gruendel, 1981) did in their pioneering research on scripts. Children were asked to tell the experimenters what happens during such events, and were then prompted when necessary. Nelson and colleagues found that children as young as 3 years had general and temporally organized knowledge for recurring events. This groundbreaking discovery illustrated the importance of familiarity with a domain or event for memory performance, challenging the prevailing assumption of that time that young children's event memories were unorganized and idiosyncratic. Instead, this research showed that children's episodic memory is organized around general event representations from a very early age. As demonstrated by Bauer and her colleagues (Bauer, Wenner, Dropik, & Wewerka, 2000), even younger, preverbal children show long-term ordered recall for events. In this impressive study, memory for action sequences was tested in 360 children aged from 1 to 3 years. Bauer et al. found that whereas almost 80% of the 1-year-olds could retain temporally ordered memories for about 1 month, most older children of the sample were able to retain these memories for more than 6 months (for confirming evidence, see also Meltzoff, 1985; Rovier-Collier, 1997). As noted by Bauer (2006, 2009), changes in basic mnemonic processes such as encoding, consolidation, storage, and retrieval are associated with this accomplishment, with consolidation and storage contributing most to the observed developmental changes.

Other studies with young children have demonstrated that novel and unusual events also can be remembered over longer periods of time, indicating that episodic memory is not constrained to routines and recurring events. For instance, Fivush and Fromhoff (1988) interviewed 2- to 3-year-old children about events that had occurred in the recent past. As a main result, they found that all children in the sample recalled at least one event that had happened 6 months or more in the past. This study thus demonstrated that children quite young at the time of experience of unique events are able to remember them over longer periods of time, a finding confirmed by a subsequent study dealing with slightly older children's memories of a trip to Disneyworld (Hamond & Fivush, 1991). Although the ability to remember specific events for a longer period of time is already evident at this early age, it undergoes further changes with development, affecting both the number of events remembered and the robustness of memories for specific events (for a review of relevant studies, see Bauer, 2006).

There are only a few studies that directly compared young children's memory for script-based versus unfamiliar information. Children in the Munich Longitudinal Study were presented with several narratives that dealt with familiar and less familiar events (e.g., birthday party, moving to another town). As a main result, substantial increases in text recall were observed for most familiar stories, with 4-year-olds freely recalling about 20%, and 8-year-olds recalling about 50% of the information provided in the texts. Although text recall was better for script-like information than for unfamiliar stories, the difference was not pronounced. Individual differences in text recall were rather stable over time from the very beginning of the longitudinal study, regardless of text (see Knopf, 1999; Schneider, Knopf, & Sodian, 2009). The authors concluded that the ability to learn, store, and recall text information develops rather early in childhood, and progresses at a similar pace for the majority of children.

Autobiographical memory

There is a widespread view in the adult literature that event knowledge is hierarchically organized in a general autobiographical memory system (see Barsalou, 1988; Conway, 2005; Hudson & Mayhew, 2009). Although we know a lot about the characteristics and functions of autobiographical memory in adolescence and adulthood, considerably less is known about its genesis and early development. Although the neural "hardware" necessary to encode, store, and retrieve information is present at birth (and before), very young children's memory is rather fragile. This frailty of early memory has been assumed to cause "infantile amnesia," that is, the fact that adults seem unable to recall events that happened to them in their infancy and toddler years, a finding repeatedly documented in the literature (see Bauer, 2006; Courage & Howe, 2004; Howe & Courage, 1993, 1997). The general absence of autobiographical memory before the age of about 3 years has stimulated numerous explanatory attempts (for reviews, see Howe, Courage, & Rooksby, 2009; Nelson, 1993; Schneider & Pressley, 1997). As emphasized by Howe et al. (2009), there is reason to assume that the factor most important to the emergence of autobiographical memory is the emergence of the cognitive self late in the second year of life. This cognitive self enables a new knowledge structure whereby new experiences can be organized as personal.

Alternative hypotheses about the delayed onset of autobiographical memory focus on the role of emerging language and social interaction, in particular, the sharing of experiences with others linguistically (for reviews see Fivush, 2009; Nelson & Fivush, 2004; Reese, 2002). According to this argument, the lack of early memories is not the result of basic structural changes in the memory system with development, but due to the absence of abstract knowledge structures for describing the temporal and causal sequences of events.

There is growing evidence that talking about past experiences with one's parents and family facilitates the construction of a personal history (e.g., Haden, Ornstein, Rudek, & Cameron, 2009; Hudson, 1990; Reese, Haden, & Fivush, 1993). Simply talking about the past with one's parents may increase memory of observed events. Longitudinal studies on autobiographical memory provide evidence for this hypothesis. For instance, the longitudinal study carried out by Reese et al. (1993) allowed an estimate of rehearsal frequency, thus enabling researchers to investigate the effects of family rehearsal on the construction of personal histories. It could be shown that highly distinctive events (e.g., going to Disneyworld) were well remembered several years later (Fivush & Schwarzmüller, 1998). Interestingly, a large proportion of the information remembered at a later point in time was new (and accurate, as confirmed by the mothers). Fivush and Schwarzmüller concluded from this that much more information had been encoded and retained by the children than was evident from their first reports immediately after the experiences.

Overall, these and other developmental studies indicate that the primary function of autobiographical memory is to develop a life history in time, and to do that by telling others about events of the past. Representing events of one's life is clearly a social process that begins early in development (Fivush, 2009). The capacity to organize information more coherently in memory is critical to most memory advances in childhood, and seems closely related to the emergence of the cognitive self (see Howe et al., 2009). Subsequent advances in language and social cognition seem very important for developmental changes in autobiographical memory. An interesting aspect of autobiographical memories is that they simultaneously reflect elements of the original experience as well as interpretations of those events that occurred during dialogues with significant others. Given that autobiographical memory is reconstructive memory, with social interactions and long-term knowledge affecting original encodings, there is always the risk of memory errors. The accuracy of autobiographical memory is crucial in the context of forensic investigations, and numerous studies have been carried out to investigate developmental trends in children's eyewitness memory.

Eyewitness memory

Eyewitness memory represents one specific form of event memory that emphasizes the accuracy rather than the amount of information recalled about an experienced event. In most experimental studies, children either witnessed events staged at their schools, or videotaped events, or were asked to recollect some potentially traumatic experiences, such as visits to the doctor or dentist. During the interview period following the event, children were typically first questioned using general prompts, usually followed by more specific questions.

With children being increasingly called upon to provide testimony in legal cases, issues about how much and how accurately they remember, and the degree to which they are influenced by suggestion, have become a high-priority research interest (for reviews, see Bruck & Ceci, 1999; Ceci & Bruck, 1998; Pipe & Salmon, 2009).

In general, the developmental patterns for episodic memory and eyewitness memory are highly similar in that older children can generally provide more detailed and narratively coherent memories (Ceci & Bruck, 1993). Regarding *age differences* in eyewitness memory, most investigations revealed that levels of recall to general questions are generally low, and that free recall increases with age (e.g., Cassel & Bjorklund, 1995; Poole & Lindsay, 1995; Roebers, 2002). However, despite low levels of free recall, what preschoolers and kindergarteners do recall is usually accurate. Thus, despite age differences, most young children possess the cognitive capacity necessary for accurate testimony. Age differences may diminish or even disappear under certain conditions – for instance, if an event is particularly salient or personally meaningful to young children. In most studies, levels of correct recall increased when more specific cues were provided, unfortunately in most cases also accompanied by an increase in the number of inaccurate responses, which reduced overall accuracy particularly in younger children. See the parallel findings in research on aging (e.g., Shing, Werkle-Bergner, Li, & Lindenberger, 2008). However, even young schoolchildren can enhance the accuracy of their testimony by screening out wrong answers when given explicit incentives for accuracy (Koriat, Goldsmith, Schneider, & Nakash-Dura, 2001; Roebers & Schneider, 2005). This finding indicates that young children can regulate their memory reporting to produce a more accurate record of past events when they are allowed and encouraged to screen out wrong answers (e.g., by saying "I don't know") and when they are explicitly motivated to do so. Although eyewitness memory improves with age, differences seem most pronounced for the period between 4 and 7 years of age. Most studies that included samples of adults illustrated that older elementary schoolchildren's free recall of witnessed events is comparable to that of adults (e.g., Cassel, Roebers, & Bjorklund, 1996).

An important topic in children's eyewitness memory concerns *age differences in susceptibility to suggestion*. In most suggestibility paradigms, participants witness an event and are later asked sets of misleading questions, suggesting an inaccurate "fact." Most studies that have looked for developmental differences in suggestibility have found them, with preschool children being particularly prone to suggestion, much more than schoolchildren and adults (Pipe & Salmon, 2009). It appears that young children's erroneous answers do not always reflect an actual change in memory representation. It is likely that some of the young children's compliance with misleading questions is related to the social demand characteristics of the situation. However, other research suggests that misleading questions actually result in changes in the underlying memory representations, with young children being more likely to make such changes than older children (Ceci & Bruck, 1998; Leichtman & Ceci, 1995).

How long do memories of witnessed events last? Are there developmental differences in long-term recall and forgetting rates? This seems like an important question given that in forensic interviews children are asked to recall experiences or events they witnessed weeks, months, or even years earlier (Paz-Alonso, Larson, Castelli, Alley, & Goodman, 2009; Pipe & Salmon, 2009). Several studies investigated children's memories of specific events for periods ranging from several weeks to 2 years. Although the results of these studies are not totally consistent, they indicate that age differences in the accuracy of recall increase with increasing delays, at least when delays are longer than 1 month. This finding is in accord with the experimental research on long-term retention and forgetting conducted by Brainerd, Howe, Reyna, and colleagues (e.g., Brainerd, Reyna, Harnishfeger, & Howe, 1993), and may be explained by fuzzy trace theory (Brainerd & Reyna, 1993, 2005; Reyna & Brainerd, 1995). That is, given that verbatim traces, favored by young children, deteriorate more rapidly than the gist, or fuzzy traces, preferred by older children, greater losses of information over delays should be expected for younger as compared to older children.

Developmental studies on recall of *stressful and traumatic events* have shown that developmental differences are typically evident, with older children tending to be more accurate and complete than younger ones in their reports for non-stressful and stressful events (for a review, see Paz-Alonso et al., 2009). Young children's memories of stressful experiences such as a visit to the doctor for a physical examination seem quite accurate (see Baker-Ward, Gordon, Ornstein, Larus, & Clubb, 1993; Goodman & Quas, 1997; Ornstein, Baker-Ward, Gordon, & Merritt, 1997; Ornstein et al., 2006), with higher levels of distress frequently associated with better memory, even though findings are not totally consistent. Direct comparisons of reports of traumatic and non-traumatic events revealed that narratives about traumatic events such as a devastating tornado were about twice as long as those referring to non-traumatic events experienced at about the same time, regardless of age (Ackil, Van Abbema, & Bauer, 2003). Although the range in ages of the children participating in the study was large, age differences in recall were not pronounced. The results of this research and other studies (e.g., Fivush, Hazzard, Sales, Sarfati, & Brown, 2003) suggest that the memory reports about traumatic and non-traumatic experiences differ qualitatively, with narratives about traumatic events being more complete and better integrated (Bauer, 2006).

Overall, the findings of recent eyewitness memory research confirm several findings of the early period (e.g., Whipple, 1911), such as age differences in recall of events and the particularly large effects of misleading questions and repeated questioning on young children's memory reports. On the other hand, however, recent studies do not support the assumption held by the early eyewitness memory researchers that young children are generally unreliable witnesses. One merit of contemporary research is that conditions have been identified that increase the probability for obtaining accurate memory reports from young children. For instance, new and promising interview techniques have been developed that avoid the problems of previous interrogations and provide the conditions for optimal recall, particularly in young children. Adults interviewing young children need to establish good rapports, use a neutral tone, and avoid social demand characteristics as well as leading questioning (Pipe & Salmon, 2009).

Important Determinants of Memory Development

The vast majority of studies on memory development since the mid-1960s have been carried out with older children, mainly dealing with explicit memory, that is, conscious remembering of facts and events. It was repeatedly found that particular clear improvements in declarative memory can be observed for the age range between 6 and 12 years, which roughly corresponds to the elementary school period in most countries. In order to explain these rapid increases in memory performance over time, different sources or determinants of memory development have been identified. According to most contemporary memory researchers, changes in *basic capacities, memory strategies, metacognitive knowledge*, and *domain knowledge* all contribute to developmental changes in memory performance. There is also broad agreement that some of these sources of development contribute more than others, and that some play an important role in certain periods of childhood but not in others (see Schneider & Pressley, 1997; Siegler, 1998). In the following, evidence concerning the relevance of these sources for memory development will be summarized.

The role of basic capacities and working memory

Development of short-term memory. One of the oldest and most controversial issues concerning children's information processing is whether the amount of information they can actively process at one time changes with age (see also Halford & Andrews, chapter 27, this volume). Age differences in the capacity of the short-term store (STS) were typically found in developmental studies that used *memory span tasks*. Such tasks require that participants must repeat, in exact order, a series of rapidly presented items such as digits or words. Age differences in memory span are very stable. In an extensive review of the literature, Dempster (1981) reported that the memory span of 2-year-olds is about two items; of 5-year-olds about four items; of 7-year-olds about five items, and of 9-year-olds about six items. The average memory span of adults is about seven items. Recent longitudinal work using the same sentence span measure for the same participants from age 4 to age 23 showed continuous span increases until the age of 18, but no increases thereafter (Schneider, Knopf, & Sodian, 2009). Individual stability over time was generally high, with test–retest correlations ranging between .57 (for ages 6–18), and .75 (between ages 8–10).

The robustness of these span differences makes very attractive the interpretation that the actual capacity of the STS is increasing with age. As appealing as this is, however, it is too simple. Research over the past three decades has made it clear that memory span is *not* a domain-general phenomenon that is essentially identical regardless of what type of information is being remembered. Rather, how much a person knows about the stimuli he or she is remembering definitively affects memory span, with knowledge presumably having its effect by influencing speed of processing. The impact of knowledge on memory span has been demonstrated in studies assessing the memory span of child chess experts and adult chess novices for chess positions on a chessboard and for other types of items, such as digits (Chi, 1978; Schneider, Gruber, Gold, & Opwis, 1993). Although the adults outperformed the children on the digit-span task, the children excelled when tested on the chess-span task. This suggests that memory span is domain-specific, varying with the person's knowledge about the to-be-remembered material.

However, there is also indication that age differences in memory span (and increases in processing speed) are due to a presumably domain-general mechanism. One reason for the regular age-related improvements observed on most memory-span tasks is that older children typically have a larger vocabulary and know more about most domains under investigation. For instance, when age differences in task-relevant knowledge are experimentally controlled for, age differences in memory span no longer occur (cf. Dempster, 1985). It has been well established by now that speed of information processing increases with age across a wide range of tasks (cf. Case, 1985; Dempster, 1981; Kail & Miller, 2006; Kail & Salthouse, 1994).

Development of working memory. A popular model of working memory that accounts for age differences in memory span primarily in terms of speed of processing has been developed by Baddeley and Hitch (Baddeley, 1986, 2000; Baddeley & Hitch, 1974; Hitch & Towse, 1995). Working memory as conceived of by Baddeley, Hitch, and colleagues has at least three subcomponents. These are the *central executive*, the *visuo-spatial sketchpad*, and the *articulatory or phonological loop*. Whereas the central executive represents an attentional control system, coordinating the various working memory activities, the visuo-spatial sketchpad is thought to process and retain visual and spatial information, and also to hold any verbal information stored as an image. The articulatory loop is a temporary phonological store which maintains and processes verbal and acoustic information (speech sounds), lasting about 1–2 seconds. As decay in this store is rapid, verbal information needs to be rehearsed by sub-vocal articulation. There is evidence that the basic modular structure of this working-memory model is present from 6 years of age and possible earlier (Gathercole, Pickering, Ambridge, & Wearing, 2004). Another model quite attractive for developmentalists was introduced by Cowan (1999; for more detailed reviews of these models, see Cowan & Alloway, 2009; Gathercole, 1998; Towse & Cowan, 2005), and focuses on the *span of apprehension*, that is, the amount of information people can attend to at a single time. Tests of working memory are similar to memory-span tasks in that participants must remember a series of items in exact order, but they are embedded in an additional task in which participants must transform information held in the STS. In general, children's performance on working-memory tasks shows the same age-related increase in their performance as their performance on memory-span tasks, although the absolute level is somewhat reduced in working-memory tasks.

The working memory models described above emphasize the fact that information processing is restricted by capacity limits *and* time limits. Accordingly, they place substantial emphasis on speed of verbal processes. Several studies on the development of working memory have reported age differences in the speed with which words can be articulated and corresponding differences in memory span and working-memory span (e.g., Hitch & Towse, 1995; Hulme, Thompson, Muir, & Lawrence, 1984). For instance, given that number words vary in length in different languages, Chinese children have longer digit spans than American children, and American children in turn have longer digit spans than Welsh children. This is because Chinese number words are much shorter than English number words, and Welsh number words are much longer than English number words (Chen & Stevenson, 1988; Ellis & Hennelly, 1980).

Overall, there is converging evidence that developmental changes in memory capacity are due to significant increases in information processing speed which are most obvious in early ages, with the rate of changes slowing thereafter. Age differences in speed of processing influence a wide range of tasks and may represent a cognitive primitive (see Kail, 1991, 1993, 2007; Kail & Salthouse, 1994). However, considerable controversy has arisen over whether the increased speed is due to greater use of strategies, to greater familiarity with the items used, or to speed per se. There is evidence suggesting that age differences in speed of processing are primarily influenced by maturational factors (e.g., Cowan, Nugent, Elliott, Ponomarev, & Saults, 1999). Cowan and his colleagues evaluated age differences in the *span of apprehension*, which refers to the amount of information that people can attend to at a single time or the number of items that people can keep in mind at any one time. They found that the average span of apprehension increased significantly with age, and interpreted these differences as reflecting a true developmental difference in the capacity of the STS.

Overall, then, age differences in speed of processing are influenced by maturational and experiential factors. Maturational factors place biological limits on how quickly children can process information and retain items in their STS. However, speed of processing is also influenced by experiential factors (e.g., knowledge base), making it clear that development of basic memory abilities is a result of the dynamic interaction between biological and experiential factors that vary over time.

Effects of memory strategies

Memory strategies have been defined as mental or behavioral activities that achieve cognitive purposes and are effort-consuming, potentially conscious, and controllable (Bjorklund, Muir-Broaddus, & Schneider, 1990; Flavell, Miller, & Miller, 1993; Pressley & Van Meter, 1993). Since the mid-1960s numerous studies have investigated the role of strategies in memory development. Strategic memory was at the center of early investigations in this area (see Harnishfeger & Bjorklund, 1990, for a historical sketch) and continues to be so today, although the topic no longer dominates the field as it once did. One reason for this development is that a lot has been learned about memory strategy development in about 40 years of research (Pressley & Hilden, 2006). Research interest in strategies such as rehearsal and semantic organization was partially motivated by the crucial role of such control processes in general multistore memory models, and by John Flavell's work establishing rehearsal and organization as strategies that develop between 5 and 10 years of age (e.g., Flavell, Beach, & Chinsky, 1966).

Strategies can be executed either at the time of learning (encoding) or later on when information is accessed in long-term memory (retrieval). The example of organizational strategies will be used to illustrate the case. Typically, the development of such strategies is explored in sort-recall tasks that involve organizing pictures or words into semantic categories. Children are given a randomly ordered list of categorizable items (e.g., animals, furniture, and the like). They are then told that their task is to remember the items later on, and that they are free to do anything with the materials that may help their recall. Following a short study period, children are asked to recall as many stimuli as they can. Children's organization of items during study (sorting) and recall (clustering) has been measured using various clustering indices. For most of these measures, values close to 1 represent almost perfect organization of stimuli, whereas values close to 0 indicate random responding.

Early research by Flavell and colleagues as well as subsequent studies confirmed a specific trend in strategy development (for reviews, see Bjorklund, Dukes, & Brown, 2009; Schneider & Pressley, 1997). Typically, deliberate strategies were not observed in children younger than 5 or 6 years of age. The lack of strategic behaviors in very young children was labeled *mediation deficiency*, indicating that children of a particular (preschool) age do not benefit from memory strategies, even after having been instructed how to use them. Although slightly older children such as kindergarteners and young schoolchildren also did not utilize strategies spontaneously, their problem was different. These children were shown to suffer from a *production deficiency*. That is, they failed to use (or to produce) strategies when given "neutral" instructions but could be easily trained to do so, usually with corresponding improvements in memory performance. Much research in strategy development has concerned the factors responsible for production deficiencies, the subsequent failure to transfer an acquired strategy to a new situation, and ways in which to improve children's strategy effectiveness (for reviews, see Bjorklund et al., 2009; Pressley & Van Meter, 1993; Schneider & Pressley, 1997). This research demonstrated that insufficient mental capacity was partially responsible for production deficiencies in young children. Research based on dual-task procedures in which children are asked to perform two tasks, both separately and together, demonstrated that young children require more mental effort than older ones in order to implement and execute memory strategies (e.g., Bjorklund & Harnishfeger, 1987; Guttentag, 1984; Kee & Davies, 1990). Moreover, individual differences in domain knowledge contribute to the age differences in strategy use (Bjorklund & Schneider, 1996). As noted above, rich knowledge influences the speed with which children can process domain-related information. As a consequence, less mental energy is needed to execute a strategy based on this information.

Numerous studies showed that memory strategies develop most rapidly over the elementary school years. Older children are more likely to actively rehearse items (Guttentag, Ornstein, & Siemens, 1987; Ornstein, Naus, & Liberty, 1975), and to group items on the basis of meaning and study same-category items together, with higher levels of sorting and clustering yielding higher levels of recall (e.g., Hasselhorn, 1992; Schneider, 1986). However, the ages of strategy acquisition are relative, and variable within and between strategies. Even preschoolers and kindergarten children are able to use intentional strategies, both in ecologically valid settings such as hide-and-seek tasks, and in the context of a laboratory task (e.g., Schneider & Sodian, 1988). There is also no doubt that memory strategies can be effectively taught to young children. For example, young children trained to use an active (cumulative) rehearsal strategy increased levels of recall substantially (Cox, Ornstein, Naus, Maxfield, & Zimler, 1989), and even preschool children use organizational strategies and demonstrate enhanced levels of recall when instructions emphasize the importance of grouping (Carr & Schneider, 1991; Lange & Pierce, 1992).

More recently, research on strategy development has focused on at least three interesting phenomena. First, memory researchers have observed that higher levels of organization are not always accompanied by higher levels of recall. Such *utilization deficiencies* (UD) have been shown in several studies with both preschoolers and elementary schoolchildren (for reviews, see Bjorklund & Coyle, 1995; Bjorklund, Miller, Coyle, & Slawinski, 1997; Miller & Seier, 1994). It appears from this research that using a strategy such as organization is only a first step. Once the mechanics of the strategy are learned, children need more time before they can execute it proficiently. Converging evidence also comes from lifespan training studies (e.g. Brehmer et al., 2008; Shing et al., 2008). Although there is plenty of evidence supporting the UD paradigm (cf. Bjorklund & Coyle, 1995; Hasselhorn, 1995; Miller, 1994, 2000), it is important to note that findings are not always consistent, depending on the particular definition and on certain characteristics of the task (Schneider & Sodian, 1997; Waters, 2000). Research findings concerning UD with regard to organizational strategies are particularly difficult to reconcile, given that the UD phenomenon was found for some children but not for others (e.g., Schneider, Kron, Hünnerkopf, & Krajewski, 2004; Schlagmüller & Schneider, 2002; Schwenck, Bjorklund, & Schneider, 2007, in press). There seems reason to conclude from recent research that UD are context dependent and only one of several patterns of strategy use/recall relations (Bjorklund et al., 2009).

A second relatively new line of research explored whether children use more than one strategy for remembering at a time, and whether the use of multiple strategies can benefit children's recall (e.g., Coyle & Bjorklund, 1997; DeMarie & Ferron, 2003; DeMarie, Miller, Ferron, & Cunningham, 2004; Schneider, Kron-Sperl, & Hünnerkopf, 2009; Schwenck et al., 2007; Shin, Bjorklund, & Beck, 2007). Several studies revealed that even young children (kindergarteners) may use more than one strategy when dealing with a memory task (e.g., DeMarie & Ferron, 2003; Schneider et al., 2004). Other studies demonstrated that children are more likely to use multiple strategies with age, and that the number of strategies children used on a memory task was related with amount recalled (e.g., Cox et al., 1989; Coyle & Bjorklund, 1997; DeMarie et al., 2004). Moreover, recent longitudinal research indicated that those first graders who used two or more strategies in a sort-recall task at the beginning of the longitudinal study outperformed those who used no or only a single strategy (Schneider et al., 2004). Subsequent assessments of strategy use on the sort-recall task showed that using only one strategy (either sorting or clustering or rehearsal) led to worse recall performance, as compared to using two or more strategies (see Schneider et al., 2009).

A third line of research based on longitudinal data has also broadened our knowledge concerning the nature of developmental changes in memory strategies. In particular, this research showed that findings based on cross-sectional studies and analyses of group data do not tell us the whole story about individual developmental trends. Using data from the Munich Longitudinal Study, Schneider and Sodian (1997; Sodian & Schneider, 1999) explored the issue of whether the impression of gradual developmental increases in strategy use and recall derived from cross-sectional studies could be confirmed by longitudinal data. Although Schneider and Sodian first confirmed earlier results on the group level (which suggested gradual increases of strategy use and recall over time), they were struck by low individual stabilities for the strategy and recall variables over time; their closer inspection of individual change data revealed that gradual, steady increases were rarely observed. Whereas only about 8% of the children showed a gradual improvement in the use of organizational strategies (sorting and clustering), as suggested by the group data, about 81% of the children "jumped" from chance level to near perfection between subsequent measurement points. These findings thus confirm that children go from chance levels of sorting to perfection, but they do it at different points in time. Subsequent analyses based on data of the Würzburg-Göttingen longitudinal memory study (Kron-Sperl, Schneider, & Hasselhorn, 2008; Lehmann & Hasselhorn, 2007; Schneider et al., 2009) basically confirmed this pattern of result, even though the percentage of children "jumping" from chance level to near perfection was somewhat lower and that showing gradual increase was higher than that observed in the Munich Longitudinal Study. Overall, the data seem to square well with other evidence of substantial inter- and intrasubject variability in strategy use, with children using different strategies and combinations of strategies on any given memory problem (Siegler, 1996).

A drawback of longitudinal studies for assessing patterns of strategy change is that a lot can happen within 6 months (the time interval between adjacent waves in the Würzburg-Göttingen study), and it may be that developmental change in strategy use is more gradual than abrupt when shorter time intervals are chosen (Ornstein, 1999). This was addressed in a *microgenetic study* by Schlagmüller and Schneider (2002). In this study, 8- to 12-year-old children (non-strategists at the beginning) performed a series of sort-recall tasks over 11 consecutive weeks. Patterns of change in strategy use and recall were then assessed. Consistent with the findings of the two longitudinal studies described above, it was shown that the transition from non-strategic to strategic occurred quickly, not gradually. Once children started to use an organizational strategy, they also improved their recall performance.

Taken together, research conducted during the last four decades has shown convincingly that age-related effects in the frequency of use and quality of children's strategies play a large role in memory development between the early school years and adolescence. However, there is now an increasing realization that the use of encoding and retrieval strategies largely depends on children's strategic as well as non-strategic knowledge and binding processes. There is broad consensus that the narrow focus on developmental changes in strategy use should be replaced by an approach that takes into account the effects of various forms of knowledge on strategy execution.

The impact of metacognitive knowledge

Almost 40 years ago, John Flavell (1971) introduced the term *metamemory* to refer to knowledge about memory processes and contents. From a developmental perspective, this concept seemed well-suited to explain young children's production deficiencies on a broad variety of tasks. Whereas young children do not learn much about the advantages of memory strategies, schoolchildren are regularly confronted with various memory tasks that eventually help them discover the advantages of strategies and improve their metamemory.

Two broad categories of metacognitive knowledge have been distinguished in the literature (Flavell & Wellman, 1977). *Declarative metacognitive knowledge* refers to what children factually know about their memory. This type of knowledge is explicit and verbalizable and includes knowledge about the importance of person variables (e.g., age or IQ), task characteristics such as task difficulty, and strategy knowledge. In comparison, *procedural metacognitive knowledge* is mostly implicit (subconscious) and refers to children's self-monitoring and self-regulation activities while solving memory problems.

Empirical research exploring the development of declarative metamemory revealed that children's knowledge of facts about memory increases considerably over the primary-grade years, but is still incomplete by the end of childhood. Recent studies also showed that increases in knowledge about strategies are paralleled by the acquisition of strategies, and that metamemory–memory behavior relationships tend to be moderately strong (cf. reviews by Joyner & Kurtz-Costes, 1997; Schneider, in press; Schneider & Lockl, 2002). Thus, what children know about their memory frequently influences how they try to remember. However, although late-grade-schoolchildren know much about common strategies, there is increasing evidence that many adolescents and adults (including college students) have little or no knowledge of some more complex, important, and powerful memory strategies such as those related to the processing of text information.

The situation regarding developmental trends in procedural metacognitive knowledge is not entirely clear (Schneider & Lockl, 2008). Several studies explored how children use their knowledge to monitor their own memory status and regulate their memory activities. There is evidence that older children are better able to predict future performance on memory tasks than younger children (Schneider, 1998; Shin et al., 2007), and that there are similar age trends when the task is to judge performance accuracy after the test has been taken. Also, older children seem better able to judge whether the name of an object that they currently cannot recall would be recognized later if the experimenter provided it (feeling-of-knowing judgments).

However, although monitoring skills seem to improve continuously across childhood and adolescence, it is important to note that developmental trends in self-monitoring are less pronounced than those observed for declarative metamemory. Contrary to earlier assumptions, recent research shows that even young children are well able to monitor their progress in memory tasks (cf. Butterfield, Nelson, & Peck, 1988; Schneider, Visé, Lockl, & Nelson, 2000). It appears that the considerable developmental improvements in procedural metamemory observable in elementary schoolchildren are mainly due to an increasingly better interplay between monitoring and self-regulatory activities. That is, even though young children may be as capable of identifying memory problems as older ones, in most cases only the older children will effectively regulate their behavior in order to overcome these problems.

One conclusion drawn from the developmental studies described above is that self-regulated learning behavior is based on monitoring processes. In this sense item difficulty is monitored before actually investing study time. The outcome of monitoring processes then serves as a basis for subsequent study-time allocation. Contrary to this view, more recent developmental studies demonstrated that the sequence of monitoring and control may also be reversed. Koriat, Ackerman, Lockl, and Schneider (in press a, in press b) investigated what they labeled the "data-driven function" of study time: According to this approach, learners use self-paced study time as a basis for subsequent judgments of learning (JOLs). Consistent with this view, in self-paced learning, older elementary schoolchildren's JOLs (but not younger one's) made at the end of each study trial *decreased* with the amount of time spent studying the item, suggesting that older children's JOLs are based on the memorizing-effort heuristic that easily learned items are more likely to be remembered.

Metamemory–memory relations. One of the main motivations to study metamemory has been the assumption that there are important relationships between knowing about memory and memory behaviors (cf. Brown, 1978; Flavell & Wellman, 1977; Weinert, 1986). However, early investigations did not find substantial links between the two components (Cavanaugh & Perlmutter, 1982). More recent research has shown that the relation one finds between memory and metamemory is considerably stronger than previously assumed. For example, in a meta-analysis based on about 60 studies and more than 7000 participants, Schneider and Pressley (1997) reported a correlation of .41 between metamemory and memory behavior. The strength of relation varied as a function of type of task (e.g., organizational strategies or memory monitoring), task difficulty, when metamemory was assessed (before or after the memory task), age, and the interaction of these various factors.

A typical feature of more recent studies is that they do not limit themselves to analyses of simple intercorrelations but they also use causal modeling procedures. For instance, Schneider, Schlagmüller, and Visé (1998) used such multivariate analyses to show that in a sort-recall paradigm metamemory had a substantial indirect effect on recall (via strategic behavior). As a consequence, individual differences in metamemory explained a large proportion in the variance of the recall data. These findings are in accord with theoretical assumptions that emphasize a bidirectional relationship between metamemory and memory behavior (e.g., Brown, 1978; Hasselhorn, 1995). Accordingly, metamemory can influence memory behavior, which in turn leads to enhanced metamemory (see also DeMarie & Ferron, 2003; DeMarie et al., 2004, for confirming evidence).

Taken together, research on the role of metamemory in memory development has created a large body of evidence supporting the utility of the concept. Mainly due to methodological improvements, more recent work on the metamemory–memory link has provided evidence for rather strong relations among metamemory, memory behavior, and memory performance (see Schneider, in press, for a review of this literature).

Effects of domain knowledge. Surprisingly, one of the most obvious sources of individual differences in memory performance, prior knowledge of task-related content, was discovered relatively recently. Since the late seventies, however, a large number of developmental studies have demonstrated that the amount of knowledge in a particular domain such as chess, physics, or sports determines how much new information from the same domain can be stored and retrieved (see the reviews by Bjorklund & Schneider, 1996; Chi & Ceci, 1987; Schneider & Bjorklund, 1998).

Prior knowledge of related content affects memory in several ways. It not only influences how much and what children recall, but also affects their execution of basic processes and strategies, their metacognitive knowledge, and their acquisition of new strategies. Rich domain knowledge can also have non-strategic effects, that is, diminish the need for strategy activation. Interestingly, domain knowledge can serve as an explanation for other memory changes. Increasing domain knowledge improves efficiency of basic processes, acquisition and execution of strategies, and metacognitive knowledge (cf. Hasselhorn, 1995).

Evidence for the powerful effects of domain knowledge on memory performance comes from studies using the *expert–novice paradigm*. These studies compared experts and novices in a given domain (e.g., baseball, chess, or soccer) on a memory task related to that domain. From a developmental perspective, the major advantage of the expert–novice paradigm is that knowledge and chronological age are not necessarily confounded, a problem inherent in most studies addressing knowledge-base effects. Several studies demonstrated that rich domain knowledge enabled a child expert to perform much like an adult expert and better than an adult novice – thus showing a disappearance and sometimes reversal of usual developmental trends (e.g., Chi, 1978; Schneider, Gruber, Gold, & Opwis, 1993). Experts and novices not only differed with regard to quantity of knowledge but also regarding the quality of knowledge; that is, in the way their knowledge is represented in the mind. Moreover, several studies also confirmed the assumption that rich domain knowledge can compensate for low overall aptitude on domain-related memory tasks, as no differences were found between high- and low-aptitude experts on various recall and comprehension measures (for a review, see Bjorklund & Schneider, 1996). Perhaps the most robust finding in the literature on knowledge effects is that experts in an area learn faster and more when studying "new" information in their domain of expertise than do novices.

How is such a rich knowledge-base acquired? The few available longitudinal studies indicate that expertise is based on a long-lasting process of motivated learning. Building up a rich knowledge-base requires not only cognitive abilities but also high levels of interest and motivation. In several domains, it is the amount of practice and not so much the level of general aptitude that determines exceptional performance (see Ericsson, Krampe, & Tesch-Roemer, 1993, for a review). However, even though most available developmental studies on expertise highlight the importance of deliberate practice in developing domain-specific expertise, they do not support the assumption that individual differences in basic abilities (such as memory capacity) can be completely neglected when it comes to predicting the development of exceptional performance (for a review, see Schneider, 2000b).

Overall, research on the effects of domain knowledge conducted during the last 30 years has shown convincingly that any explanation of memory development must reserve a large place for increasing knowledge of specific content (Siegler, 1998). Domain knowledge is a powerful determinant of memory and learning. It increases steadily from infancy to adulthood and contributes to the development of other sources of memory competencies, such as basic capacities, strategies, and metacognitive knowledge. Research on the development of domain knowledge has illustrated the fact that the sources of memory development interact in numerous ways, which sometimes makes it very difficult to disentangle the effects of specific sources from those of other influences. The importance of these interactions was highlighted in the *model of good information processing* (Pressley, Borkowski, & Schneider, 1989; Pressley & Hilden, 2006) which emphasizes the interplay of intact neurology (basic capacities), strategic, knowledge-base, and motivational components in determining cognitive performance.

Future Directions for Memory Development Research

Although memory development is a rather mature field, there is still much to learn, and the centrality of memory to all other aspects of cognition makes it likely that the ontogeny of memory, in one form or another, will continue to be a primary focus of cognitive development. Examples of much-studied topics that require more in-depth investigation in the years ahead include children's metacognitive development and their autobiographical memory.

Many cognitive developmentalists meanwhile have recognized that the development of information processing cannot be isolated from development of the brain (Bauer, 2009; Cycowicz, 2000; Johnson, 1998; Schneider & Bjorklund, 1998). In the field of memory development, there is an increasing emphasis on the need for greater awareness of and interaction with neuroscience perspectives (e.g., Gathercole, 1998; Nelson, 1997). However, we still know very little about the neuropsychology of memory development, both at the level of description and explanation.

Neuropsychological research can influence memory development research in a number of ways. For instance, De Haan, Mishkin, Baldeweg, and Vargha-Khadem (2006) investigated memory development following bilateral hippocampal damage early in life. Individuals with such damage did not show the severe deficits in semantic memory that might be expected if the hippocampus was crucial for both episodic and semantic memory. However, their performance on episodic memory tasks such as delayed recall of information was markedly impaired. One explanation for the relative preservation of semantic memory following early hippocampal injury is that transient projections exist during normal development between the rhinal cortex and hippocampus that are retained because the hippocampus lesions occurred before the time when these projections are usually retracted. This explanation thus reflects the plasticity of developing memory systems. De Haan and colleagues concluded from their research that the hippocampus and related medial temporal lobe (MTL) structures contribute significantly to memory development in infancy and childhood. They propose that normal memory development involves a sequence in which semantic-like memory emerges first, whereas episodic memory develops only later with progressive development of the hippocampus. Accordingly, development of memory abilities appears to unfold in a sequence, beginning with novelty preferences and/or familiarity based recognition, followed by recall, then by flexible memory, and ultimately by source memory. See de Chastelaine, Friedman, and Cycowicz (2007) for an interesting event-related potential study on the development of source memory from childhood to adulthood, and Ofen et al. (2007) for the involvement of posterior parietal cortex (PPC) and MTL in the development of declarative memory.

Another line of research that already shows great promise (at least in the area of implicit memory) is to conduct parallel memory studies with human infants and age-matched non-human primates, or to develop tasks with infants that are based on tasks already being used with human adults (cf. Nelson, 1997). Although it seems important for memory development researchers to become familiar with neuropsychological techniques and research findings, it is also important not to lose sight of the cognitive and behavioral levels while examining brain functions. Accordingly, biological levels of explication should not replace psychological-level theories, but be integrated with them to yield a proper perspective of memory development (Bjorklund, 1997). As noted by Bauer (2009), the young field of the cognitive neuroscience of memory development has already proven the potential to move beyond description to explanation.

Another promising line of research on memory development that does not focus on biological but on social factors has already been described above in detail. Research by Fivush, Haden, Nelson, Reese, and their colleagues has convincingly illustrated that early memory skills develop in the context of social interaction (for a review, see Fivush, 2009). This research has shown that differences in parents' reminiscing styles (low elaborative vs. high elaborative) observed in children's early years are associated with later differences in children's ability to recall personally experienced events (e.g., Haden et al., 2009). Recent research by Ornstein, Coffman, and their colleagues (Coffman, Ornstein, McCall, & Curran, 2008; Ornstein, Grammar, & Coffman, in press) supplemented this work on the social origins of memory skills, focusing on the classroom setting. They observed that first-grade teachers engage in "memory talk," including strategy suggestions, and metacognitive questioning (see also Moely, Hart, Leal, Santulli, Rao, Johnson, et al., 1992). First-grade children taught by "high mnemonic" teachers who used more of this type of memory talk benefitted more from a memory-strategy training than those children with "low mnemonic" teachers (Coffman et al., 2008). Interestingly, the long-term impact of the first-grade teachers was still observed in second grade when children were taught by other teachers (Ornstein et al., in press). Thus this work suggests that "teacher talk" may be relevant for the emergence of mnemonic skills.

On a more general level, an interesting question is whether the study of memory needs to be situated in a number of broader conceptual and research contexts, or whether future research activities should focus on more specific memory functions. The position that future research on memory development should be embedded within the context of broader topics such as comprehension, knowledge, context, and strategy has been proposed by Kuhn (2000; chapter 19, this volume). The basic claim is that although memory research has contributed significantly to our understanding in each of these four areas, the study of memory development in turn needs to profit from what has been accomplished in each of those areas and to be enriched by integration with each of them. Kuhn votes for an approach that connects the studies of memories and memorizing to the four broader topics described above, and that interprets the results within the frameworks that those topics provide.

On the other hand, there is also research indicating that the assumption of general memory concepts may oversimplify the case. For instance, several studies concerned the issue of whether the concept of verbal memory represents a domain-general skill or consists of domain-specific verbal abilities (for a review, see Schneider & Bjorklund, 1998).

The way to assess this question empirically is to administer different verbal memory tasks and assess the intertask correlations. Overall, both cross-sectional and longitudinal studies showed that intertask correlations were rather low, regardless of children's age, and that the low correlations were not due to reliability problems (Schneider & Weinert, 1995). Recent findings from the Munich Longitudinal Study indicate that relations among various facets of verbal memory such as strategic memory, memory capacity, and text recall are only moderate in early childhood and continue to be so until early adulthood (Schneider, Knopf, & Sodian, 2009). These findings are consistent with the position that there is no "unitary" verbal memory construct, and that deliberate verbal memory may be better thought of as a set of specific abilities ("modules") rather than a domain-general concept.

Overall, although the field of memory development constitutes one of the oldest and most active research areas in the field of cognitive development, there are still many open issues that need to be clarified in future research. We still need more precise cross-sectional experimental studies to better understand the role of mediators of memory development, but also more longitudinal studies which should be combined, when possible, with parallel experimental studies that bring hypothesized mediators of developmental change under experimental control. As emphasized by Ornstein and Haden (2009), it should be possible to study both *memory* development and the *development* of memory by this integration of methods.

References

Ackil, J. K., Van Abbema, D. L., & Bauer, P. J. (2003). After the storm: Enduring differences in mother–child recollections of traumatic and nontraumatic events. *Journal of Experimental Child Psychology, 84*, 286–309.

Anooshian, L. J. (1997). Distinctions between implicit and explicit memory: Significance for understanding cognitive development. *International Journal of Behavioral Development, 21*, 453–478.

Ausley, J. A., & Guttentag, R. E. (1993). Direct and indirect assessments of memory: Implications for the study of memory development during childhood. In M. L. Howe & R. Pasnak (Eds.), *Emerging themes in cognitive development: Vol. 1. Foundations* (pp. 234–264). New York: Springer-Verlag.

Baddeley, A. (1986). *Working memory*. Oxford: Clarendon Press.

Baddeley, A. (2000). The episodic buffer: A new component of working memory? *Trends in cognitive Sciences, 4*, 417–423.

Baddeley, A. D., & Hitch, G. J. (1974). Working memory. In G. Bower (Ed.), *The psychology of learning and motivation: Advances in research and theory* (Vol. *8*, pp. 47–89). New York: Academic Press.

Baker-Ward, L., Gordon, B. N., Ornstein, P. A., Larus, D. M., & Clubb, P. A. (1993). Young children's long-term retention of a pediatric examination. *Child Development, 64*, 1519–1533.

Barsalou, L. W. (1988). The content and organization of autobiographical memories. In U. Neisser & E. Winograd (Eds.), *Real events remembered: Ecologica and traditional approaches to the study of memory* (pp. 193–243). Cambridge: Cambridge University Press.

Bauer, P. J. (2006). Event memory. In W. Damon & R. M. Lerner (General Eds.), D. Kuhn & R. Siegler (Vol. Eds.), *Handbook of child psychology: Vol. 2. Cognition, perception, and language* (6th ed., pp. 373–425). Hoboken, NJ: John Wiley.

Bauer, P. J. (2009). The cognitive neuroscience of the development of memory. In M. L. Courage & N. Cowan (Eds.), *The development of memory in infancy and childhood* (pp. 115–144). Hove, UK: Psychology Press.

Bauer, P. J., Wenner, J. A., Dropik, P. L., & Wewerka, S. S. (2000). Parameters of remembering and forgetting in the transition from infancy to early childhood. *Monographs of the Society for Research in Child Development, 65* (4, Serial No. 263).

Bisanz, J., Vesonder, B., & Voss, J. (1978). Knowledge of one's own responding and the relation of such knowing to learning. *Journal of Experimental Child Psychology, 25*, 116–128.

Bjorklund, D. F. (1997). The role of immaturity in human development. *Psychological Bulletin, 122*, 153–169.

Bjorklund, D. F., & Coyle, T. R. (1995). Utilization deficiencies in the development of memory strategies. In F. E. Weinert & W. Schneider (Eds.), *Memory performance and competencies: Issues in growth and development* (pp. 161–180). Hillsdale, NJ: Erlbaum.

Bjorklund, D. F., Dukes, Ch., & Brown, R. D. (2009). The development of memory strategies. In M. L. Courage & N. Cowan (Eds.), *The development of memory in infancy and childhood* (pp. 145–175). Hove, UK: Psychology Press.

Bjorklund, D. F., & Harnishfeger, K. K. (1987). Developmental differences in the mental effort requirements for the use of an organizational strategy in free recall. *Journal of Experimental Child Psychology, 44*, 109–125.

Bjorklund, D. F., Miller, P. H., Coyle, T. R., & Slawinski, J. L. (1997). Instructing children to use memory strategies: Evidence of utilization deficiencies in memory training studies. *Developmental Review, 17*, 411–442.

Bjorklund, D. F., Muir-Broaddus, J. E., & Schneider, W. (1990). The role of knowledge in the development of strategies. In D. F. Bjorklund (Ed.), *Children's strategies: Contemporary views of cognitive development* (pp. 93–128). Hillsdale, NJ: Erlbaum.

Bjorklund, D. F., & Schneider, W. (1996). The interaction of knowledge, aptitude, and strategies in children's memory performance. In H. W. Reese (Ed.), *Advances in child development and behavior* (Vol. *26*, pp. 59–89). San Diego: Academic Press.

Brainerd, C. J., & Reyna, V. F. (1993). Domains of fuzzy-trace theory. In M. L. Howe & R. Pasnak (Eds.), *Emerging themes in cognitive development: Vol. 1: Foundations* (pp. 50–93). New York: Springer-Verlag.

Brainerd, C. J., & Reyna, V. F. (2005). *The science of false memory: An integrative approach*. Oxford: Oxford University Press.

Brainerd, C. J., Reyna, V. F., Harnishfeger, K. K., & Howe, M. L. (1993). Is retrievability grouping good for recall? *Journal of Experimental Psychology: General, 122*, 249–268.

Brehmer, Y., Li, S.-C., Straube, B., Stoll, G., von Oertzen, T., Müller, V., & Lindenberger, U. (2008). Comparing memory skill maintenance across the life span: Preservation in adults, increase in children. *Psychology and Aging, 23*(2), 227–238.

Brown, A. L. (1978). Knowing when, where, and how to remember: A problem of metacognition. In R. Glaser (Ed.), *Advances in instructional psychology* (pp. 77–165). Hillsdale, NJ: Erlbaum.

Bruck, M., & Ceci, S. J. (1999). The suggestibility of children's memory. *Annual Review of Psychology, 50*, 419–439.

Brunswik, E., Goldscheider, L., & Pilek, E. (1932). Untersuchungen zur Entwicklung des Gedächtnisses [Studies on the development of memory]. In W. Stern & O. Lippmann (Eds.), *Beihefte zur Zeitschrift für angewandte Psychologie* (Beiheft 64). Leipzig: Ambrosius Barth.

Bühler, K. (1930). Die Erinnerungen des Kindes [Memories of children]. In K. Bühler (Ed.), *Die geistige Entwicklung des Kindes* (6th ed., pp. 318–329). Jena: Gustav Fischer.

Butterfield, E., Nelson, T., & Peck, J. (1998). Developmental aspects of the feeling of knowing. *Developmental Psychology, 24*, 654–663.

Carr, M., & Schneider, W. (1991). Long-term maintenance of organizational strategies in kindergarten children. *Contemporary Educational Psychology, 16*, 61–72.

Case, R. (1985). *Intellectual development: A systematic reinterpretation.* New York: Academic Press.

Cassel, W. S., & Bjorklund, D. F. (1995). Developmental patterns of eyewitness memory and suggestibility: An ecologically based short-term longitudinal study. *Law and Human Behavior, 19*, 507–532.

Cassel, W. S., Roebers, C. E. M., & Bjorklund, D. F. (1996). Developmental patterns of eyewitness responses to increasingly suggestive questions. *Journal of Experimental Child Psychology, 61*, 116–133.

Cavanaugh, J. C., & Perlmutter, M. (1982). Metamemory: A critical examination. *Child Development, 53*, 11–28.

Ceci, S. J., & Bruck, M. (1993). Suggestibility of the child witness: A historical review and synthesis. *Psychological Bulletin, 113*(3), 403–439.

Ceci, S. J., & Bruck, M. (1998). Children's testimony: Applied and basic issues. In W. Damon (General Ed.) & I. Sigel & K. A. Renninger (Vol. Eds.), *Handbook of child psychology: Vol. 4. Child psychology in practice* (5th ed., pp. 713–774). New York: Wiley.

Chen, C., & Stevenson, H. W. (1988). Cross-linguistic differences in digit span of preschool children. *Journal of Experimental Child Psychology, 46*, 150–158.

Chi, M. T. H. (1978). Knowledge structures and memory development. In R. Siegler (Ed.), *Children's thinking: What develops* (pp.73–96)? Hillsdale, NJ: Erlbaum.

Chi, M. T. H., & Ceci, S. J. (1987). Content knowledge: Its role, representation, and restructuring in memory development. In H. W. Reese (Ed.), *Advances in child development and behavior* (Vol. *20*, pp. 91–142). Orlando, FL: Academic Press.

Coffman, J. L., Ornstein, P., McCall, L., & Curran, P. (2008). Linking teachers' memory-relevant language and the development of children's memory skills. *Developmental Psychology, 44*, 1640–1654.

Conway, M. A. (2005). Memory and the self. *Journal of Memory and Language, 53*, 594–628.

Courage, M. L., & Howe, M. L. (2004). Advances in early memory development research: Insights about the dark side of the moon. *Developmental Review, 24*, 6–32.

Cowan, N. (1999). An embedded-processes model of working memory. In A. Miyake & P. Shah (Eds.), *Models of working memory: Mechanisms of active maintenance and executive control* (pp. 62–101). Cambridge: Cambridge University Press.

Cowan, N., & Alloway, T. (2009). Development of working memory in childhood. In M. L. Courage & N. Cowan (Eds.), *The development of memory in infancy and childhood* (pp. 303–342). Hove, UK: Psychology Press.

Cowan, N., Nugent, L., Elliott, E., Ponomarev, I., & Saults, J. (1999). The role of attention in the development of short-term memory: Age differerences in the verbal span of apprehension. *Child Development, 70*, 1082–1097.

Cox, B. D., Ornstein, P. A., Naus, M. J., Maxfield, D., & Zimler, J. (1989). Children's concurrent use of rehearsal and organizational strategies. *Developmental Psychology, 25*, 619–627.

Coyle, T. R., & Bjorklund, D. F. (1997). Age differences in, and consequences of, multiple- and variable-strategy use on a multitrial sort-recall task. *Developmental Psychology, 33*(2), 372–380.

Cycowicz, Y. M. (2000). Memory development and event-related brain potentials in children. *Biological Psychology, 54*, 145–174.

Cycowicz, Y. M., Friedman, D., Snodgrass, J. G., & Rothstein, M. (2000). A developmental trajectory in implicit memory is revealed by picture fragment completion. *Memory, 8*, 19–35.

De Chastelaine, M., Friedman, D., & Cycowicz, Y. M. (2007). The development of control processes supporting source memory discrimination as revealed by event-related potentials. *Journal of Cognitive Neuroscience, 19*, 1286–1301.

De Haan, M., Mishkin, M., Baldeweg, T., & Vargha-Khadem, F. (2006). Human memory development and its dysfunction after early hippocampal injury. *Trends in Neuroscience, 29*, 374–381.

DeMarie, D., & Ferron, J. (2003). Capacity, strategies, and metamemory: Tests of a three-factor model of memory development. *Journal of Experimental Child Psychology, 84*, 167–193.

DeMarie, D., Miller, P. H., Ferron, J., & Cunningham, W. R. (2004). Path analysis tests for theoretical models of children's memory performance. *Journal of Cognition and Development, 5*, 461–492.

Dempster, F. N. (1981). Memory span: Sources of individual and developmental differences. *Psychological Bulletin, 89*, 63–100.

Dempster, F. N. (1985). Short-term memory development in childhood and adolescence. In C. J. Brainerd & M. Pressley (Eds.), *Basic processes in memory development: Progress in cognitive development research* (pp. 209–248). New York: Springer-Verlag.

Dufresne, A., & Kobasigawa, A. (1989). Children's spontaneous allocation of study time: Differential and sufficient aspects. *Journal of Experimental Child Psychology, 47*, 274–296.

Ebbinghaus, H. (1885). *Über das Gedächtnis.* [On memory]. Darmstadt: Wissenschaftliche Buchgesellschaft.

Ellis, N. C., & Hennelly, R. A. (1980). A bilingual wordlength effect: Implications for intelligence testing and the relative ease of mental calculation in Welsh and English. *British Journal of Psychology, 71*, 43–52.

Ericsson, K. A., Krampe, R., & Tesch-Roemer, C. (1993). The role of deliberate practice in the acquisition of expert performance. *Psychological Review, 100*, 363–406.

Fivush, R. (2009). Sociocultural perspectives on autobiographical memory. In M. L. Courage & N. Cowan (Eds.), *The development of memory in infancy and childhood* (pp. 283–301). Hove, UK: Psychology Press.

Fivush, R., & Fromhoff, F. (1988). Style and structure in mother–child conversations about the past. *Discourse Processes, 11*, 337–355.

Fivush, R., Hazzard, A., Sales, J. M., Sarfati, D., & Brown, T. (2003). Creating coherence out of chaos? Children's narratives of emotionally positive and negative events. *Applied Cognitive Psychology, 17*, 1–19.

Fivush, R., & Schwarzmüller, A. (1998). Children remember childhood: Implications for childhood amnesia. *Applied Cognitive Psychology, 12*, 455–473.

Flavell, J. H. (1971). First discussant's comments: What is memory development the development of? *Human Development, 14*, 272–278.

Flavell, J. H., Beach, D. H., & Chinsky, J. M. (1966). Spontaneous verbal rehearsal in a memory task as a function of age. *Child Development, 37*, 283–299.

Flavell, J. H., Miller, P. H., & Miller, S. A. (1993). *Cognitive development* (3rd ed.). Englewood Cliffs, NJ: Prentice Hall.

Flavell, J. H., & Wellman, H. M. (1977). Metamemory. In R. V. Kail & J. W. Hagen (Eds.), *Perspectives on the development of memory and cognition* (pp. 3–33). Hillsdale, NJ: Erlbaum.

Gathercole, S. E. (1998). The development of memory. *Journal of Child Psychology and Psychiatry, 39*, 3–27.

Gathercole, E. S., Pickering, S. J., Ambridge, B., & Wearing, H. (2004). The structure of working memory from 4 to 15 years of age. *Developmental Psychology, 40*, 177–190.

Goodman, G. S., & Quas, J. A. (1997). Trauma and memory: Individual differences in children's recounting of a stressful experience. In N. L. Stein, P. A. Ornstein, B. Tversky, & C. Brainerd (Eds.), *Memory for everyday and emotional events* (pp. 267–294). Mahwah, NJ: Erlbaum.

Graf, P., & Schacter, D. L. (1985). Implicit and explicit memory for new associations in normal and amnesic subjects. *Journal of Experimental Psychology: Learning, Memory, and Cognition, 11*, 501–518.

Guttentag, R. E. (1984). The mental effort requirement of cumulative rehearsal: A developmental study. *Journal of Experimental Child Psychology, 37*, 92–106.

Guttentag, R. E., Ornstein, P. A., & Siemens, L. (1987). Children's spontaneous rehearsal: Transitions in strategy acquisition. *Cognitive Development, 2*, 307–326.

Haden, C. A., Ornstein, P. A., Rudek, D. J., & Cameron, D. (2009). Reminiscing in the early years: Patterns of maternal elaborativeness and children's remembering. *International Journal of Behavioural Development, 33*, 118–130.

Hamond, N. R., & Fivush, R. (1991). Memories of Mickey Mouse: Young children recount their trip to Disneyworld. *Cognitive Development, 6*, 433–448.

Harnishfeger, K. K., & Bjorklund, D. F. (1990). Children's strategies: A brief history. In D. F. Bjorklund (Ed.), *Children's strategies: Contemporary views of cognitive development* (pp. 1–22). Hillsdale, NJ: Erlbaum.

Hasselhorn, M. (1992). Task dependency and the role of category typicality and metamemory in the development of an organizational strategy. *Child Development, 63*, 202–214.

Hasselhorn, M. (1995). Beyond production deficiency and utilization inefficiency: Mechanisms of the emergence of strategic categorization in episodic memory tasks. In F. E. Weinert & W. Schneider (Eds.), *Memory performance and competencies: Issues in growth and development* (pp. 141–159). Hillsdale, NJ: Erlbaum.

Hitch, G. J., & Towse, J. (1995). Working memory: What develops? In F. Weinert & W. Schneider (Eds.), *Memory performance and competencies: Issues in growth and development* (pp. 3–22). Mahwah, NJ: Erlbaum.

Howe, M. L., & Courage, M. L. (1993). On resolving the enigma of infantile amnesia. *Psychological Bulletin, 113*, 305–326.

Howe, M. L., & Courage, M. L. (1997). Independent paths in the development of infant learning and forgetting. *Journal of Experimental Child Psychology, 67*, 131–163.

Howe, M. L., Courage, M. L., & Rooksby, M. (2009). The genesis and development of autobiographical memory. In M. L. Courage & N. Cowan (Eds.), *The development of memory in infancy and childhood* (pp. 177–196). Hove, UK: Psychology Press.

Hudson, J. A. (1990). The emergence of autobiographical memory in mother–child conversation. In R. Fivush & J. A. Hudson (Eds.), *Knowing and remembering in young children* (pp. 166–196). Cambridge: Cambridge University Press.

Hudson, J. A., & Mayhew, E. M. (2009). The development of memory for recurring events. In M. L. Courage & N. Cowan (Eds.), *The development of memory in infancy and childhood* (pp. 69–91). Hove, UK: Psychology Press.

Hulme, C., Thompson, N., Muir, C., & Lawrence, A. (1984). Speech rate and the development of spoken words: The role of rehearsal and item identification processes. *Journal of Experimental Child Psychology, 38*, 241–253.

Johnson, M. H. (1998). The neural basis of cognitive development. In W. Damon (General Ed.) & D. Kuhn & R. S. Siegler (Vol. Eds.), *Handbook of child psychology: Vol. 2 Cognition, perception, and language* (5th ed., pp. 1–49). New York: Wiley.

Joyner, M. H., & Kurtz-Costes, B. (1997). Metamemory development. In N. Cowan (Ed.), *The development of memory in childhood* (pp. 275–300). London: London University College Press.

Kail, R. V. (1990). *The development of memory in children* (3rd ed.). New York: W. H. Freeman and Company.

Kail, R. V. (1991). Processing time declines exponentially during childhood and adolescence. *Developmental Psychology, 27*(2), 259–266.

Kail, R. V. (1993). The role of a global mechanism in developmental change in speed of processing. In M. L. Howe & R. Pasnak (Eds.), *Emerging themes in cognitive development: Vol.1. Foundations* (pp. 97–119). New York: Springer-Verlag.

Kail, R. V. (2007). Longitudinal evidence that increases in processing speed and working memory enhance children's reasoning. *Psychological Science. 18*, 312–313.

Kail, R. V., & Miller, C. A. (2006). Developmental change in processing speed: Domain specifity and stability during childhood and adolescence. *Journal of Cognition and Development, 7*, 119–137.

Kail, R. V., & Salthouse, T. A. (1994). Processing speed as a mental capacity. *Acta Psychologica, 86*, 199–225.

Kane, M. J., & Engle, R. W. (2003). The role of prefrontal cortex in working-memory capacity, executive attention, and general fluid intelligence: An individual-differences perspective. *Psychonomic Bulletin and Review, 9*, 637–671.

Kee, D. W., & Davies, L. (1990). Mental effort and elaboration: Effects of accessibility and instruction. *Journal of Experimental Child Psychology, 49*, 264–274.

Klingberg, T., Forssberg, H., & Westerberg, H. (2002). Increased brain activity in frontal and parietal cortex underlies the development of visuospatial working memory capacity during childhood. *Journal of Cognitive Neuroscience, 14*, 1–10.

Knopf, M. (1999). Development of memory for texts. In F. E. Weinert & W. Schneider (Eds.), *Individual development from 3 to 12: Findings from the Munich Longitudinal Study* (pp. 106–122). Cambridge: Cambridge University Press.

Koriat, A., Ackerman, R., Lockl, K., & Schneider, W. (in press a). The memorizing-effort heuristic in judgments of learning: A developmental perspective. *Journal of Experimental Child Psychology.*

Koriat, A., Ackerman, R., Lockl, K., & Schneider, W. (in press b). The easily learned, easily remembered heuristic in children. *Cognitive Development.*

Koriat, A., Goldsmith, M., Schneider, W., & Nakash-Dura, M. (2001). The credibility of children's testimony: Can children control the accuracy of their memory reports? *Journal of Experimental Child Psychology, 79*, 405–437.

Kron-Sperl, V., Schneider, W., & Hasselhorn, M. (2008). The development and effectiveness of memory strategies in kindergarten and elementary school: Findings from the Würzburg and Göttingen longitudinal studies. *Cognitive Development, 23*, 79–104.

Kuhn, D. (2000). Does memory development belong on an endangered topic list? *Child development, 71*, 21–25.

Lange, G., & Pierce, S. H. (1992). Memory-strategy learning and maintenance in preschool children. *Developmental Psychology, 28*, 453–462.

Lehmann, M., & Hasselhorn, M. (2007). Variable memory strategy use in children's adaptive intratask learning behavior: Developmental changes and working memory influences in free recall. *Child Development, 78*, 1068–1082.

Leichtman, M. D., & Ceci, S. J. (1995). The effects of stereotypes and suggestions on preschoolers' reports. *Developmental Psychology, 31*, 568–578.

Lloyd, M., & Newcombe, N. S. (2009). Implicit memory in childhood: reassessing developmental invariance. In M. L. Courage & N. Cowan (Eds.), *The development of memory in infancy and childhood* (pp. 93–113). Hove, UK: Psychology Press.

Lockl, K., & Schneider, W. (2004). The effects of incentives and instructions on children's allocation of study time. *European Journal of Developmental Psychology, 1*, 153–169.

Mandler, J. M. (1983). Representation. In J. H. Flavell & E. M. Markman (Eds.), *Handbook of child psychology* (Vol. *3*, pp. 420–493). New York: Wiley.

McDonough, L., Mandler, J., McKee, R., & Squire, L. (1995). The deferred imitation task as a nonverbal measure of declarative memory. *Proceedings of the National Academy of Science, 92*, 7580–7584.

Mecklenbräuker, S., Hupbach, A., & Wippich, W. (2003). Age-related improvements in a conceptual implicit memory test. *Memory and Cognition, 31*, 1208–1217.

Meltzoff, A. N. (1985). Immediate and deferred imitation in fourteen and twenty-four-month-old infants. *Child Development, 56*, 62–72.

Miller, P. H. (1994). Individual differences in children's strategic behavior: Utilization deficiencies. *Learning and Individual Differences, 6*, 285–307.

Miller, P. H. (2000). How best to utilize a deficiency: A commentary on Waters' "Memory strategy development." *Child Development, 71*, 1013–1017.

Miller, P. H., & Seier, W. L. (1994). Strategy utilization deficiencies in children: When, where, and why. In H. W. Reese (Ed.), *Advances in child development and behavior* (Vol. *25*, pp. 107–156). San Diego: Academic Press.

Moely, B. E., Hart, S. S., Leal, L., Santulli, K. A., Rao, N., Johnson, T., & Hamilton, L. B. (1992). The teacher's role in facilitating memory and study strategy development in the elementary school classroom. *Child Development, 63*, 653–672.

Nelson, C. A. (1997). The neurobiological basis of early memory development. In N. Cowan (Ed.), *The development of memory in childhood* (pp. 41–82). Hove, UK: Psychology Press.

Nelson, K. (1986). *Event knowledge: Structure and function in development.* Hillsdale, NJ: Erlbaum.

Nelson, K. (1993). The psychological and social origins of autobiographical memory. *Psychological Science, 4*, 7–14.

Nelson, K., & Fivush, R. (2004). The emergence of autobiographical memory: A social cultural developmental theory. *Psychological Review, 111*, 486–511.

Nelson, K., & Gruendel, J. (1981). Generalized event representations: Basic building blocks of cognitive development. In M. E. Lamb & A. L. Brown (Eds.), *Advances in Developmental Psychology* (Vol. *1*, pp. 21–46). Hillsdale, NJ: Erlbaum.

Ornstein, P. A. (1999). Comments: Toward an understanding of the development of memory. In F. E Weinert & W. Schneider (Eds.), *Individual development from 3 to 12: Findings from the Munich Longitudinal Study* (pp. 94–105). Cambridge: Cambridge University Press.

Ornstein, P. A., Baker-Ward, L., Gordon, B. N., & Merritt, K. A. (1997). Children's memory for medical experiences: Implications for testimony. *Applied Cognitive Psychology, 11*, 87–104.

Ornstein, P. A., Baker-Ward, L., Gordon, B. N., Pelphrey, K. A., Tyler, C. S., & Gramzow, E. (2006). The influence of prior knowledge and repeated questioning on children's long-term retention on the details of a pediatric examination. *Developmental Psychology, 42*, 332–344.

Ornstein, P. A., Grammar, J. K., & Coffman, J. L. (in press). Teachers' "mnemonic style" and the development of skilled memory. In H. S. Waters & W. Schneider (Eds.), *Metacognition, strategy use, and instruction.* New York: Guilford.

Ornstein, P. A., & Haden, C. A. (2009). Developments in the study of memory development. In M. L. Courage & N. Cowan (Eds.), *The development of memory in infancy and childhood* (pp. 367–385). Hove, UK: Psychology Press.

Ornstein, P. A., Naus, M. J., & Liberty, C. (1975). Rehearsal and organizational processes in children's memory. *Child Development, 46*, 818–830.

Parkin, A. J. (1998). The development of procedural and declarative memory. In N. Cowan (Ed.), *The development of memory in childhood* (pp. 113–137). Hove, UK: Psychology Press.

Paz-Alonso, P. M., Larson, R. P., Castelli, P., Alley, D., & Goodman, G. S. (2009). Memory development: emotion, stress, and trauma. In M. L. Courage & N. Cowan (Eds.), *The development of memory in infancy and childhood* (pp. 197–239). Hove, UK: Psychology Press.

Perez, L. A., Peynircioglu, Z. F., & Blaxton, T. A. (1998). Developmental differences in implicit and explicit memory performance. *Journal of Experimental Child Psychology, 70*, 167–185.

Perruchet, P., Frazier, N., & Lautrey, J. (1995). Conceptual implicit memory: A developmental study. *Psychological Research, 57*, 220–228.

Pipe, M.-E., & Salmon, K. (2009). Memory development and the forensic context. In M. L. Courage & N. Cowan (Eds.), *The development of memory in infancy and childhood* (pp. 241–282). Hove, UK: Psychology Press.

Poole, D. A., & Lindsay, D. S. (1995). Interviewing preschoolers: Effects of nonsuggestive techniques, parental coaching and leading questions on reports of nonexperienced events. *Journal of Experimental Child Psychology, 60*, 129–154.

Pressley, M., Borkowski, J. G., & Schneider, W. (1989). Good information processing: What it is and how education can promote it. *Journal of Educational Research, 14*, 857–867.

Pressley, M., & Hilden, K. R. (2006). Memory strategies. In W. Damon & R. M. Lerner (General Eds.) & D. Kuhn & R. Siegler (Vol. Eds.), *Handbook of child psychology: Vol. 2. Cognition, perception, and language* (6th ed., pp. 511–556). Hoboken, NJ: John Wiley.

Pressley, M., & Van Meter, P. (1993). Memory strategies: Natural development and use following instruction. In R. Pasnak & M. L. Howe (Eds.), *Emerging themes in cognitive development: Vol. 2. Competencies* (pp. 128–165). New York: Springer-Verlag.

Reber, A. S. (1989). Implicit learning and tacit knowledge. *Journal of Experimental Psychology: General, 118*, 219–235.

Reese, E. (2002). Social factors in the development of autobiographical memory: The state of the art. *Social Development, 11*, 124–142.

Reese, E., Haden, C. A., & Fivush, R. (1993). Mother–child conversations about the past: Relationships of style and memory over time. *Cognitive Development, 8*, 403–430.

Reyna, V. F., & Brainerd, C. J. (1995). Fuzzy-trace theory: An interim synthesis. *Learning and Individual Differences, 7*, 1–75.

Roebers, C. M. (2002). Confidence judgments in children's and adults' event recall and suggestibility. *Developmental Psychology, 38*, 1052–1067.

Roebers, C. M., & Schneider, W. (2005). The strategic regulation of children's memory performance and suggestibility. *Journal of Experimental Child Psychology, 91*, 24–44.

Roediger, H. L., & McDermott, K. B. (1993). Implicit memory in normal human subjects. In H. Spinnler & F. Boller (Eds.), *Handbook of neuropsychology* (Vol. *8*, pp. 63–131). Amsterdam: Elsevier.

Rovier-Collier, C. (1997). Dissociations in infant memory: Rethinking the development of implicit and explicit memory. *Psychological Review, 104*, 467–498.

Rovier-Collier, C., Hayne, H., & Colombo, M. (2002). *The development of implicit and explicit memory*. Philadelphia: John Benjamin.

Schacter, D. L. (1992). Understanding implicit memory: A cognitive neuroscience perspective. *American Psychologist, 47*, 559–569.

Schlagmüller, M., & Schneider, W. (2002). The development of organizational strategies in children: Evidence from a microgenetic longitudinal study. *Journal of Experimental Child Psychology, 81*, 298–319.

Schneider, W. (1986). The role of conceptual knowledge and metamemory in the development of organizational processes in memory. *Journal of Experimental Child Psychology, 42*, 218–236.

Schneider, W. (1998). The development of procedural metamemory in childhood and adolescence. In G. Mazzoni & T. O. Nelson (Eds.), *Monitoring and control processes in metacognition and cognitive neuropsychology* (pp. 1–21). Mahwah, NJ: Erlbaum.

Schneider, W. (2000a). Research on memory development: Historical trends and current themes. *International Journal of Behavioral Development, 24*, 407–420.

Schneider, W. (2000b). Giftedness, expertise, and (exceptional) performance: A developmental perspective. In K. A. Heller, F. J. Mönks, R. J. Sternberg, & R. F. Subotnik (Eds.), *International handbook of research and development of giftedness and talent* (2nd ed., pp. 165–178). London: Elsevier

Schneider, W. (in press). Metacognition and memory development in childhood and adolescence. In H. S. Waters & W. Schneider (Eds.), *Metacognition, strategy use, and instruction.* New York: Guilford Press.

Schneider, W., & Bjorklund, D. F. (1998). Memory. In W. Damon (General Ed.), & D. Kuhn & R. S. Siegler (Vol. Eds.), *Handbook of child psychology: Vol. 2. Cognition, perception, and language* (5th ed., pp. 467–521). New York: Wiley.

Schneider, W., & Bjorklund, D. F. (2003). Memory and knowledge development. In J. Valsiner & K. Connolly (Eds.), *Handbook of developmental psychology* (pp. 370–403). London: Sage.

Schneider, W., Gruber, H., Gold, A., & Opwis, K. (1993). Chess expertise and memory for chess positions in children and adults. *Journal of Experimental Child Psychology, 56*, 328–349.

Schneider, W., Knopf, M., & Sodian, B. (2009). Verbal memory development from early childhood to early adulthood. In W. Schneider & M. Bullock (Eds.), *Human development from early childhood to early adulthood: Findings from a 20 year longitudinal study* (pp. 63– 90). New York: Psychology Press.

Schneider, W., Kron, V., Hünnerkopf, M., & Krajewski, K. (2004). The development of young children's memory strategies: Findings from the Würzburg Longitudinal Memory Study. *Journal of Experimental Child Psychology, 88*, 193–209.

Schneider, W., Kron-Sperl, V., & Hünnerkopf, M. (2009). The development of young children's memory strategies: Evidence from the Würzburg Longitudinal Memory Study. *European Journal of Developmental Psychology, 6*, 70–99.

Schneider, W., & Lockl, K. (2002). The development of metacognitive knowledge in children and adolescents. In T. Perfect & B. Schwartz (Eds.), *Applied metacognition* (pp. 224–257). Cambridge: Cambridge University Press.

Schneider, W., & Lockl, K. (2008). Procedural metacognition in children: Evidence for developmental trends. In J. Dunlosky & B. Bjork (Eds.), *A handbook of memory and metacognition.* Mahwah, NY: Erlbaum.

Schneider, W., & Pressley, M. (1997). *Memory development between two and twenty* (2nd ed.). Mahwah, NJ: Erlbaum.

Schneider, W., Schlagmüller, M., & Visé, M. (1998). The impact of metamemory and domain-specific knowledge on memory performance. *European Journal of Psychology of Education, 13*, 91–103.

Schneider, W., & Sodian, B. (1988). Metamemory–memory behavior relationships in young children: Evidence from a memory-for-location task. *Journal of Experimental Child Psychology, 45*, 209–233.

Schneider, W., & Sodian, B. (1997). Memory strategy development: Lessons from longitudinal research. *Developmental Review, 17*, 442–461.

Schneider, W., Visé, M., Lockl, K., & Nelson, T. O. (2000). Developmental trends in children's memory monitoring: Evidence from a judgment-of-learning task. *Cognitive Development, 15*, 115–134.

Schneider, W., & Weinert, F. E. (1995). Memory development during early and middle childhood: Findings from the Munich Longitudinal Study (LOGIC). In W. Schneider & F. E. Weinert (Eds.), *Memory performance and competencies: Issues in growth and development* (pp. 263–279). Mahwah, NJ: Erlbaum.

Schumann-Hengsteler, R. (1992). The development of visuo-spatial memory: How to remember location. *International Journal of Behavioral Development, 15*, 445–471.

Schumann-Hengsteler, R. (1995). *Die Entwicklung des visuo-räumlichen Gedächtnisses [Development of visuo-spatial memory]*. Göttingen: Hogrefe.

Schwenck, C., Bjorklund, D. F., & Schneider, W. (2007). Factors influencing the incidence of utilization deficiencies and other patterns of recall/strategy-use relations in a strategic memory task. *Child Development, 78*, 1771–1787.

Schwenck, C., Bjorklund, D. F., & Schneider, W. (in press). Developmental and individual differences in young children's use and maintenance of a selective memory strategy. *Developmental Psychology*.

Shin, H.-E., Bjorklund, D. F., & Beck, E. F. (2007). The adaptive nature of children's overestimation in a strategic memory task. *Cognitive Development, 22*, 197–212.

Shing, Y. L., Werkle-Bergner, M., Li, S.-C., & Lindenberger, U. (2008). Associative and strategic components of episodic memory: A life-span dissociation. *Journal of Experimental Psychology: General, 137*, 495–513.

Siegler, R. S. (1996). *Emerging minds: The process of change in children's thinking*. New York: Oxford University Press.

Siegler, R. S. (1998). *Children's thinking* (3rd ed.). Upper Saddle River, NJ: Prentice Hall.

Sodian, B., & Schneider, W. (1999). Memory strategy development – Gradual increase, sudden insight or roller coaster? In Weinert, F. E. & Schneider, W. (Eds.), *Individual development from 3 to 12: Findings from the Munich Longitudinal Study* (pp. 61–77). Cambridge: Cambridge University Press.

Squire, L., Knowlton, B., & Musen, G. (1993). The structure and organization of memory. *Annual Review of Psychology, 44*, 453–495.

Stern, W. (1910). Abstracts of lectures on the psychology of testimony and on the study of individuality. *American Journal of Psychology, 21*, 270–282.

Towse, J., & Cowan, N. (2005). Working memory and its relevance for cognitive development. In W. Schneider, R. Schumann-Hengsteler, & B. Sodian (Eds.), *Young children's cognitive development: Interrelationships among executive functioning, working memory, verbal ability, and theory of mind*. (pp. 9–38). Mahwah, NJ: Erlbaum.

Van Abbema, D. L., & Bauer, P. J. (2005). Autobiographical memory in middle childhood: Recollections of the recent and distant past. *Memory, 13*, 829–845.

Van der Molen, M. W., & Ridderinkhof, K. R. (1998). The growing and aging brain: Life-span changes in brain and cognitive functioning. In A. Demetriou, W. Doise, & C. van Lieshout (Eds.), *Life-span developmental psychology* (pp. 35–99). New York: Wiley.

Waters, H. S. (2000). Memory strategy development: Do we need yet another deficiency? *Child Development, 71*, 1004–1012.

Weinert, F. E. (1986). Developmental variations of memory performance and memory-related knowledge across the life-span. In A. Sörensen, F. E. Weinert, & L. R. Sherrod (Eds.), *Human development: Multidisciplinary perspectives* (pp. 535–554). Hillsdale, NJ: Erlbaum.

Whipple, G. M. (1909). The observer as reporter: A survey of the "psychology of testimony." *Psychological Bulletin, 6*, 153–170.

Whipple, G. M. (1911). The psychology of testimony. *Psychological Bulletin, 8*, 307–309.

CHAPTER FOURTEEN

Causal Reasoning and Explanation

Barbara Koslowski and Amy Masnick

Introduction and Overview

There is an interesting and somewhat puzzling disconnect in the psychological literature. Much of the psychological research on causal reasoning (including probabilistic reasoning) has operationally defined causation in terms of the Humean indices (Hume, 1973) of temporal priority, contiguity, and – most typically – covariation. However, one of the most basic principles of causal reasoning – mentioned prominently in every methods text and emphasized to students – is that correlation (the most stringent Humean index) does not necessarily indicate causation, even when subsumed under probabilistic models. Thus, research participants have been said to engage in accurate causal reasoning when they rely on the very indices that experimenters acknowledge to be either limited or genuinely flawed.

However, although covariation does not guarantee causation, there is no question that it is useful and ought to be taken into account; when causation is present, covariation can typically be found as an indicator. The tension between covariation as a limited indicator of cause and, implicitly, as the sole indicator has been acknowledged, at least tacitly, in research that examines the interdependence of covariation and background knowledge (especially information about theory or mechanism or explanation). On the interdependence view, covariation information and information about mechanism or explanation each inform the other.

However, while generating some sort of mechanism or explanation can be fairly easy, deciding whether the explanation is plausible can be more difficult. Thus, although the present chapter briefly describes the work on Humean indices, it focuses on the role of explanation in causal reasoning and on the interdependence of information about covariation and information about mechanism or explanation. (The chapter in the first edition of this Handbook that corresponds to the present chapter provides more

We thank Tamar Kushnir for her contributions to the section on causal Bayes nets.

extensive coverage of research conducted in a Humean framework; see Koslowski & Masnick, 2002.)

We will describe several strategies that people rely on and argue that the interdependence of covariation and explanation makes the strategies heuristics rather than algorithms. Furthermore, when we decide that one explanation is the more plausible of two, the end result is that we treat the other as having been undermined. Thus, we will also describe some research on explanation that has implications for the literature on confirmation bias, as well as on causal reasoning (including scientific reasoning).

Finally, although, historically, psychological studies of causal reasoning have focused on perceptual and mechanical causation, the emphasis in the present chapter is on non-mechanical causation. (Space limitations do not permit us to cover the large literature on causal attribution in social psychology.)

Perceptual and Mechanical Causation

For the most part, research on perceptual and mechanical causation has examined whether and, if so, to what extent, people base their causal judgments on the Humean indices of priority, contiguity, and covariation. This research fails to acknowledge classic criticisms of the Humean account of causation. The conceptual criticism is that Humean indices alone do not account for why some covariations are taken seriously and others not. The psychological criticism is that, given humans' information processing limitations, it is unlikely that individual people could keep track of the many covariations in the world and compute the relative likelihood that one event covaries with another. When research does demonstrate that people take account of Humean indices, it is often because the tasks involve unfamiliar events designed so that the only information available relates to the Humean indices. When this happens, then even children do indeed take account of Humean indices in making causal judgments.

Sensitivity to Humean indices

Early on, Michotte (1963) demonstrated that, when presented with films of abstract figures, adults rely on Humean indicators to decide whether one moving figure is "causing" the other to move. For example, if a ball rolls towards a stationary square and the square then moves, people are more likely to infer causation if the time interval between the two events is short and if the ball actually contacts the square rather than stopping short of it. Research on infants used much the same procedure in assessing their reactions to a "launching event," in which an agent object (such as a red brick) moves across a screen, either does or does not contact a recipient object (such as a green brick), and the recipient moves after varying lengths of time. Conclusions from the infant research are a matter of debate. (See Koslowski & Masnick, 2002, for a summary of this debate.)

Recent neurological studies of adults performing Michotte's perceptual task suggest different activations when viewing a causal version of the task (with no temporal delay or spatial gap between objects on the screen) as compared to a non-causal version (with either a temporal delay or a spatial gap). Specifically, the right middle frontal gyrus and right inferior parietal lobule were more activated when participants watched a causal task (Fugelsang, Roser, Corballis, Gazzaniga, & Dunbar, 2005). The authors note these findings suggest the involvement of executive functioning systems in reasoning, beyond simple perception of stimuli.

Several researchers examined elementary schoolchildren's sensitivity to Humean indices by presenting them with tasks in which one unfamiliar event was followed by another event either all or only half of the time, and after either a long or a short delay (Siegler, 1976; Siegler & Liebert, 1974). Other tasks also included a facilitatory-inhibitory covariate, such as a small toy car placed on the side of the box used in the task (Shultz & Mendelson, 1975). It is not clear what one ought to conclude from these studies; although children were sometimes told not "to worry about the way the wires and the electricity cause the light to go on," they might well have had trouble ignoring this injunction or might have already learned, in interactions outside of the laboratory, that the proximity of toy cars has no effect on whether pulling down a lever is likely to make a light go on. That is, the children might well have based their judgments on the interaction of Humean information and causal information about how things work that they brought to the laboratory situation.

As already noted, there is a long tradition of studying people's (including children's and infant's) ability to detect and base causal judgments on Humean indices. A recent approach frames children's causal reasoning (especially sensitivity to Humean indices) in terms of causal Bayes nets. (For a non-technical overview of the assumptions behind this approach, see Gopnik & Schulz, 2007, pp. 3–8). The causal Bayes nets approach models situations in which one predicts the outcomes of hypothetical interventions on variables (priors) by, for example, predicting that changing diet might increase susceptibility to disease but that changing susceptibility to disease will not likely change diet. Research with young children has shown that consistent with the assumptions of causal Bayes nets, young children can (a) discriminate between interventions and observed correlations, (b) reason about conditional independence and dependence and (c) use patterns of interventions and conditional probabilities to learn causal structure (Schulz, Kushnir, & Gopnik, 2007).

As models of how individual people engage in causal reasoning, Bayesian models are subject to the same criticisms as Humean models (and as general models of induction): how do we decide in the first place which priors to include in the model and how do we assign probabilities to the models? (Why, for example, consider diet rather than musical preferences, and how do individual people keep track of the extent to which diet and disease in fact covary?) Some researchers suggest that one way of making decisions about which variables are relevant in the first place is by relying on innate core domains that can serve as organizing frameworks for new information, and therefore aid in establishing prior probabilities (Hirschfeld & Gelman, 1994; Roberts, 2007). These include the domains of physics (Kushnir & Gopnik, 2007); biology (Schulz & Gopnik, 2004; Schulz, Kushnir, et al., 2007) and psychology (Schultz, Kushnir, et al., 2007; Kushnir, Wellman, & Gelman, 2007).

However, much research in the causal Bayes net framework has relied on knowledge-lean tasks, using unfamiliar events, in which the priors (and their probabilities) are provided in the experimental task itself (for example, Sobel et al., 1991). Thus, part of the reason people in such tasks are able to make probabilistic judgments based on Humean indices is that the tasks are designed so that the only indicators of causation that are present (or that are arranged to be salient) are the Humean indices presented in the restricted experimental situation. Moreover, recent connectionist approaches also suggest competing frameworks for modeling children's causal inferences (McClelland & Thompson, 2007).

Regardless of the criticisms of the causal Bayes net approach, research done in this paradigm corroborates, as already noted, earlier findings that children have the capacity to detect and to base causal judgments on probabilistic data. For example, extracting statistical patterns from the environment might allow infants to develop inductive prior beliefs that lead to simple causal hypotheses (Sobel & Kirkham, 2007). Furthermore, preschoolers preferentially explore confounded rather than non-confounded causal situations, thus displaying the ability, at least tacitly, to distinguish the two (Schulz & Bonawitz, 2007). In addition, researchers in this paradigm have documented the role of intervention in causal reasoning, noting that, if pushing a button is followed by an effect, then regardless of whether children identify a mechanism, they are more likely to infer that pushing the button causes the event (rather than vice versa) when human intervention depresses the button, rather than when the human intervention is not seen (Gopnik et al., 2004; Schulz, Gopnik, & Glymour, 2007; Kushnir, Wellman & Gelman, 2009). Furthermore, some researchers have been using the basic task to examine other issues, such as the way in which social input affects causal reasoning (Kushnir, Wellman, & Gelman, 2008).

To summarize: Several researchers have documented that even young children take account of Humean indicators, including indicators presented in a probabilistic way, at least in situations where little if any other causal information is present. However, this research does not typically address questions of how Humean information is integrated with, and in some cases overridden by, other information, including information about mechanism or explanation – a question that will be discussed in more detail below.

Non-Humean considerations

Despite the early emphasis on Humean indices of cause, there were also indications that children and adults do not always treat Humean indicators as conclusive and also consider information about mediating mechanisms. Some of the research was prompted by Piaget's conclusion that children believe in action at a distance – that mediating connections between cause and effect are not necessary. Piaget's conclusion was based on children's answers to questions about potential causes of an effect. Children often mentioned agent and effect without noting anything about the mediating connection between the two; for example, "You push the pedals and the wheels turn." (Piaget, 1930). Subsequent research has called this conclusion into question.

For example, Bullock and Gelman (1979) asked preschoolers to choose whether a "rolling" light (phi phenomenon) or a rolling marble caused a jack to pop up. They found that 5- but not 3-year-olds proposed mediating mechanisms for whichever causal agent they chose that could mediate between cause and effect (for example, a hidden pathway for the marble and electricity for the light). Koslowski, Spilton, & Snipper (1981) found similar explanations when preschool children explained whether a battery would make a bell ring if the connecting electrical wire from battery to bell was disconnected. Children who predicted it would work argued, for example, that the "electric stuff" would "whoosh" through the end of the wire and hit the bell; those who predicted it would not work noted, for example, that the electric stuff would dribble out of the end of the wire and not reach the bell. That is, both predictions invoked a mediating mechanism.

In a temporal contiguity task, Mendelson and Shultz (1976) included a condition in which a tube ran from a potentially causal event to the effect. When the tube was present rather than absent, children were less troubled by a long temporal delay, seemingly because the tube provided a rationale for the delay. Although not interpreted this way, the finding suggested that children interpret covariation in light of information about mediating mechanisms. In addition, if anything the results suggested a tendency to avoid, rather than believe in, action at a distance.

Recall the 3-year-olds in Bullock & Gelman's study, who were least likely to mention a mediating mechanism. Their behavior might have reflected, not a belief in action at a distance, but rather an early step in the acquisition of causal knowledge about a particular situation. For example, in a separate study (Koslowski et al., 1981), 3- and 4-year-olds were allowed to operate a pulley in which two pulley wheels were connected by a rubber band, so that turning the handle on one pulley wheel caused the connected wheel to turn. Their explanations were consistent with action at a distance; for example, "You turn this wheel and this one turns." And, when the connecting band was removed, children predicted that the pulley would continue to work – a prediction also consistent with action at a distance. However, the children's justifications for their predictions noted, for example, that nothing had been broken, it wasn't dirty or "gunked up," or that they could still reach the handle, etc. Thus, although the experimenters were asking about the effect of removing the mediating band, the children were still focused on whether the causal agent/event (the first pulley wheel) was still in good condition. Only when allowed to continue to explore the pulley system did the children come to concern themselves with the mediating band and to predict correctly that the pulley would fail to work without the connecting band.

This finding raises the question of whether an adult who was learning, for example, how to operate complicated machinery, might also focus initially on identifying the causal agent and only later concern herself with mechanism. Indeed, as many adults cannot describe the mediating mechanisms in admittedly complicated machinery such as helicopters (Mills & Keil, 2004), one might infer that in some situations many adults either do not reach the point of being concerned about mechanism or, if they do, do not concern themselves about it deeply enough to try to learn about it.

Non-Mechanical Causation

Identifying causal agents or events

In this section, we summarize research on reasoning about two sorts of possibly causal events: initially plausible and initially implausible.

Ruling out confounded, alternative causes that are plausible. Simpler than the ability to change one variable while holding others constant is the ability to realize that some sort of contrast is necessary to test a hypothesis. Most children at even the third- or fourth-grade level do realize, for example, that to find out whether the position of a rudder affects the fuel efficiency of a plane, they would need to vary the position of the rudder. By grade six, almost all children (and adults) propose changing the possible causal variable to test whether it is actually causal, and by sixth grade, at least a third of the children also note that at least one other variable ought to remain the same, that is, to be controlled (Bullock & Ziegler, 1999).

In addition, as already noted, even young children at least tacitly distinguish controlled and confounded contrasts, preferentially exploring confounded rather than controlled situations (Schulz & Bonawitz, 2007). Furthermore, even preschoolers can extract information in a way that is sensitive to confounding. When shown that a tulip and a daisy and later a tulip and a violet, but not a daisy and a violet induce sneezing, preschoolers inferred that it was the tulip that was the causal culprit (Schulz & Gopnik, 2004). Similarly, even sixth graders treat controlled data as more likely to reflect causation than confounded data (Koslowski, 1996, chapter 6). Furthermore, when presented with various options, more than a third of the third graders, about 60% of the fourth- and fifth-graders, close to 80% of the sixth-graders, and almost all the adults could choose or recognize a controlled test to answer a causal question (Bullock, 1991; Bullock & Ziegler, 1999).

Nevertheless, children's understanding of control and confounding is constrained. One constraint involves consistency with background beliefs. When choosing possible contrasts, children are more likely to vary a possible cause (and hold other factors constant) when they think that doing so will eliminate an undesirable result, but hold the possible cause constant (and vary the other factors) when they think that doing so will maintain a good outcome (Tschirgi, 1980). Similarly, 4- to 10-year-olds are likely to choose controlled tests when the hypothesis being tested matches their prior beliefs and has led to a good outcome (healthy teeth) rather than when information was inconsistent with their beliefs and led to a bad outcome (unhealthy teeth) (Croker and Buchanan, 2008). However, although preschoolers' ability to evaluate patterns of covariation is affected by their pre-existing causal beliefs, even 4-year-olds can bracket their beliefs and realize that available evidence supports a belief different from theirs (Koerber, Sodian, Thoermer, & Nett, 2005.) (On a different but related note, this finding as well as others – Sodian et al., 1991; Ruffman, Perner, Olson, & Doherty, 1993 – also suggests an early ability to distinguish theory and evidence, which has sometimes been held to be absent in both children and adults; Kuhn, Amsel, & O'Loughlin, 1988.)

Children's understanding of control is also constrained by whether the goal is scientific (in which variables are tested systematically to determine their effects, such as which size wheel leads to a faster car) or engineering (in which variables are manipulated to bring about a particular effect, such as a car that is as fast as possible) (Schauble, Klopfer, & Raghavan, 1991; Masnick, Klahr, & Knowles, 2009). Furthermore, the effect of type of goal may depend in part on the causal relation being tested; children and adults are more likely to change beliefs from non-causal to causal after seeing evidence than vice versa

(Amsel, Goodman, Savoie, & Clark, 1996; Kanari & Millar, 2004; Klahr, Triona, & Williams, 2007; Kuhn, Schauble, & Garcia-Mila, 1992). Given that causal and non-causal beliefs were operationalized as beliefs about covariation and non-covariation respectively, the greater difficulty in changing from causal to non-causal beliefs (than vice versa) might reflect the more general difficulty that preschoolers have in dealing with non-covariation rather than covariation evidence (Koerber et al., 2005).

Instruction also facilitates understanding of control and confounding. After appropriate instruction, even preschoolers choose a contrastive over a non-contrastive test, deciding for example that contrasting a blue with a yellow car is more informative than comparing two yellow cars to determine whether blue or yellow cars are faster (Brenneman et al., 2007). Bullock & Ziegler (1999), in the research described above, also induced children to generate all the variable dimensions and combinations of variables used in the story task. After this intervention, children's production of controlled tests more than doubled. Similarly, 7- to 10-year olds who could not always spontaneously design controlled comparisons, could be taught to do so (Chen & Klahr, 1999), and children benefit more from explicit instruction than from exploring on their own (Klahr & Nigam, 2004; Strand-Cary & Klahr, 2008). (However, how children learned this skill was less effective than how well they had mastered it in enabling them to transfer their knowledge.)

Two additional points are worth noting. The effect of prior beliefs and of goals suggests that children's understanding of control and confounding is not a formal one; that is, it is not an algorithm applied across situations. Rather, it is embedded in context and thus a heuristic. This is directly demonstrated by the finding that, when only two variables are involved, children fail to realize that varying either one of the variables amounts to holding the other constant (Tschirgi, 1980). The second point is that recognizing good tests does not guarantee being able to design or produce, rather than recognize or choose one. For example, in the study mentioned above, when Bullock and Ziegler (1999) asked children what to do to test whether, for example, rudder position affected the fuel efficiency of a plane, many fewer children (and adults) were able to produce a controlled test than had been able to recognize one. Similarly, when adolescents and college students are asked to find out whether hospitalized children recover faster when their parents are allowed to stay overnight with them, they spontaneously proposed the appropriate contrast (have some parents stay and others not) (Koslowski, 1996, chapter 12; Koslowski, Susman, & Serling, 1991). However, when even college students are presented with actual sets of data, there is no guarantee that they will compute and contrast the mean length of hospital stays for the two groups, often preferring instead, for example, to "eyeball" the data, consider which group had the largest outlier, etc. (Koslowski, Cohen, Spund, & Fleury, 2009) We suggest that even when participants have the *conceptual* knowledge that contrasts are important, they often lack the *technical* skills to arrange the appropriate contrasts.

To summarize: Children's understanding of control and confounding is constrained by their pre-existing causal beliefs and by their goals. That is, their understanding is not formal. In addition, it can be facilitated by instruction. Furthermore, a conceptual understanding of contrast and control does not guarantee the technical ability to arrange or produce the appropriate contrasts.

Beliefs about implausible causal events and implausible mechanisms

For many situations that require identifying a causal event, even 11-year-olds have at least a limited "catalogue of likely causes" that they invoke to account for effects, noting for example that children might recover faster if they have good doctors, are in good hospitals, etc. But what about potential causes that are initially *im*plausible? Scientific inquiry, which arguably includes many good examples of causal reasoning (Zimmerman, 2000, 2007), suggests that plausibility judgments take into account (at least) three considerations: the status of possible alternative causes, information about mechanism or explanation, and frequency of occurrence.

As with plausible potential causes, *im*plausible potential causes are also increasingly likely to be treated as actually causal, by 11-year-olds as well as college students, when plausible potential causes are controlled for and thus ruled out. (For example, car color as a possible – though implausible – cause of differences in gas mileage becomes increasingly likely if one has controlled for year, model, brand of gasoline, etc.) (Koslowski, 1996, chapter 7). Note, though, that the content of the story problems in these studies dealt with fairly everyday things, such as gas mileage, hospital recovery rates, book sales, etc.

As in scientific inquiry, for both 11-year-olds and college students, plausibility judgments are also affected by mechanism information. Not surprisingly, providing mechanism information to an already plausible cause does little to make it appear increasingly plausible, likely because what makes something plausible in the first place is being able to generate a possible mechanism, however undeveloped it may be. However, the addition of a possible mechanism does make an *im*plausible cause appear increasingly plausible for adolescents and college students. Thus, where a car was built is no more likely to be seen as a cause of differences in gas mileage if participants are told that new factories likely mean better assembly and thus better mileage; where a car was built is already a plausible cause. However, car color is more likely to be seen as affecting gas mileage if participants are told that red cars lead to alertness which in turn leads to gas-conserving driving; car color is an initially implausible cause that is rendered increasingly plausible by mechanism information (Koslowski, 1996, chapter 8). Similarly, for undergraduates, probability assessments depend on explanation, so that being able to explain a set of characteristics in a causally plausible way makes the characteristics seem more probable and thus, in some cases, more normal (Ahn, Novick, & Kim, 2003; Koehler, 1991).

Furthermore, when reasoning about causation, 11-year-olds as well as college students not only take account of, but also invoke mechanism information. Recall the study, mentioned earlier, that asked participants about hospitalized children. In this study, at least 94% of adolescents as young as 11 years of age and college students considered mechanism information on their own, when, for example, generating alternative causes or considering external validity, offering such explanations as, "You could have some parents stay overnight and some not, because parents might help their kids by telling the doctors if there were problems" or "It might not work with teenagers, because a lot of teenagers don't get along with their parents and having a parent around would just stress them out" (Koslowski, 1996, chapter 12).

In addition, when assessing mechanisms that others provided to account for covariations, 11-year-olds and college students are still comparable so long as the covariations are plausible. However, when the covariations are *im*plausible, there is a trend for the sixth-graders to believe that a mechanism currently unknown to experts will eventually be discovered to explain the implausible covariations. Furthermore, although age groups are comparable in rating plausible mechanisms that are generated by others, they differ when asked to rate *im*plausible mechanisms; sixth- and ninth-graders find mechanisms to be plausible that college students find to be dubious (Koslowski, 1996, chapter 5).

Age differences in treatment of mechanisms also affect the mechanisms the participants generate on their own. Again, for plausible covariations, the age groups are comparably likely to generate reasonable mechanisms and to rate them as reasonable. However, when asked to explain *im*plausible covariations, age differences became apparent because, we suggest, implausible covariations call for implausible mechanisms. In response to implausible covariations, college students restrict the number of mechanisms they propose (likely because they are reluctant to propose dubious mechanisms), while 11-year-olds do propose dubious mechanisms (for example, longer visiting hours will make people in a hospital heal faster, because "they'd keep awake more and keep their blood flowing; they wouldn't get too much sleep.") We suggest that sixth-graders' inflated belief in the range of plausible mechanisms reflects a knowledge-base deficit that limits their awareness that some mechanisms, though possible, are simply not very likely (Koslowski, 1996, chapter 5).

Furthermore, as well as relying on whether alternative causes have been ruled out and on mechanism information, 11-year-olds and college students also take into account frequency of covariation, treating implausible causal agents as increasingly likely to be actually causal if the variable has covaried with the effect a sufficiently large number of times. Car color is treated as an implausible cause of differences in mileage, but it warrants a second look if it occurs repeatedly – and especially if other, more likely, causes have been controlled for (Koslowski, 1996, chapter 8). That is, covariation and mechanism information are interdependent; just as the presence of a mechanism can render a covariation causal, the presence of repeated covariations can signal that a mechanism may exist, even though it has yet to be discovered.

We are not arguing that explicit consideration of mechanism underwrites every causal judgment. About many things, preschoolers have only a catalogue of likely causes, and likely do not understand (or are not even at that point thinking about) the mechanisms by which the causes operate (Koslowski et al., 1981). And, as Mills and Keil (2004) note, sometimes even adults have only a very rudimentary or shallow understanding of particular mechanisms. However, it is worth noting that Mills and Keil typically asked their participants about fairly complicated entities, such as helicopters, etc. In addition, we often base our judgments on distributed cognition, or a division of cognitive labor, believing that penicillin kills germs not because we understand the mechanism involved, but because experts have told us that it does (Giere, 2002; Koenig & Harris, 2005; Lutz & Keil, 2002). Thus although people may not be able to explain the mechanism by which complicated things such as helicopters work, they doubtless believe that there is a mechanism that makes them work and that some expert knows what the mechanism is. What we are arguing is that, in addition to a catalogue of likely causes – whether or not based on other people's expertise – background information about mechanisms as well as about alternative causes does play some role in causal judgments – especially when the possible causes in question are, at first glance, improbable.

In addition, there appear to be differences in brain activation when adults evaluate covariation results that are consistent, rather than inconsistent, with a plausible causal mechanism (Fugelsang & Dunbar, 2005). Reasoning about data when participants were provided with a plausible theory activated the parahippocampal gyrus, an area associated with executive processing, more than when there was no plausible theory. It appears that the brain processes evidence differently based on the presence or absence of a plausible causal mechanism, and that the presence or absence of such a mechanism is important to consider in understanding such reasoning.

To summarize: Initially implausible causes are increasingly likely to be treated as causal when alternative possible causes have been controlled for or ruled out and when there is a possible mechanism that could have mediated between the possible cause and the effect. However, 11-year-olds are more likely than college students to generate dubious mechanisms and to rate them as reasonable. Finally, mechanism information and covariation information are interdependent, with mechanism information making covariations seem increasingly causal, and frequent covariations suggesting a possibly undiscovered mechanism that might be responsible for the covariations.

Evaluating causal explanations or mechanisms

Explanation or mechanism is crucial to distinguishing between covariations that are genuinely causal and those likely to be merely artifactual. However, explanations can be wrong or, at least, incomplete or misleading. For example, considerations of mechanism can make it difficult to acknowledge data inconsistent with a causal belief in 7- to 12-year-olds (e.g., Masnick, Klahr, & Morris, 2007); in preschoolers (Karmiloff-Smith & Inhelder, 1974/75); and in 10- to 12-year-olds (Chinn & Malhotra, 2002). Furthermore, even when presented with sets of numbers to compare with limited context, college students as well as 9- to 12-year-olds often not only attend to the data, but also seek explanations at least partly based on causal mechanisms – which can be misleading (Masnick & Morris, 2008). Thus, it is not sufficient simply to generate or rely on explanations; it is also crucial to evaluate them. (See Keil & Wilson, 2000; Lombrozo, 2006; Lombrozo & Carey, 2006, for additional work on explanation.)

In this section we discuss how explanations are evaluated in response to anomalous data, in terms of metaconceptual criteria, and in terms of consistency with networks of related information.

Theory modification versus rejection in response to anomalous data. One of the most basic points about changing beliefs in response to anomalous data is that the belief in question must be activated or called to mind before the relevant evidence can have an effect; without that framework, the anomalous evidence has less of an effect (Kloos & Somerville, 2001). When the belief in question is activated, and when anomalous or disconfirming evidence accumulates, people (including even preschoolers in some situations) do eventually change their causal beliefs, sometimes rejecting them and sometimes modifying them to take account of the anomalies (Abelson, 1959; Chinn & Brewer, 1998; Karmiloff-Smith & Inhelder, 1974/75; Klahr, Faye, & Dunbar, 1993; Kloos & van Orden, 2005; Schauble, 1990). The question is, when are anomalies more or less likely to result in preserving an explanation by modifying it to take account of the anomalous data? (The importance of activation of beliefs may well continue into adulthood and will also be addressed again, below.)

Insofar as scientific inquiry is a model of sound causal reasoning, there is a tension between responding to anomalous data by rejecting the claim as opposed to modifying it to take account of the anomalies. It is often legitimate in scientific (and, thus, causal) reasoning to modify an explanation or theory as additional data become available. However, modifying an explanation in response to all anomalous data runs the risk of maintaining an explanation that should, in fact, be rejected. (The distinction between legitimate and unwarranted modification is often marked by the distinction between theory modification – when changing a theory in response to additional data is seen as warranted – and what is pejoratively called "*ad hoc* theorizing" – when changes to a theory in response to additional data are seen as merely opportunistic strategies for trying to preserve a theory that ought to be rejected.)

One way to recognize that modifying a theory or explanation is often appropriate is to note that many hypotheses are initially advanced (and treated) as working hypotheses that do not specify, often because they have not yet been discovered, all the variables that might constrain the effect of a target cause. For example, the working hypothesis that drug X cures cancer would probably not specify, initially, the dosage required, whether it will be effective in all stages of the illness, etc., and might be able to add such refinements only after additional (often seemingly anomalous) data have been gathered. For example, if the drug works for only some patients, it might later be discovered that those patients were in different stages of the illness, etc. We suggest that most scientists would consider it reasonable, in this case, to modify the initial causal claim to take account of the disconfirming data, by concluding that drug X cures cancer but only in certain stages of the illness.

However, this raises the question of when it is that modifying a theory is likely to be warranted. One situation in which modification seems to be warranted occurs when the anomalies form a pattern, because patterns often indicate that the anomalies reflect a systematic mechanism rather than statistical noise. For example, if drug X fails to work for two populations and both populations are anemic, we would suspect some (possibly unknown) mechanism associated with anemia that prevents the drug from operating. Other times, theory modification seems warranted when there is a known mechanism that accounts for how each of the anomalies came to be. For example, we would lean towards modification if the drug fails to work for two types of people, the anemic and those who have high blood pressure, if we also learn that too little iron prevents absorption of the drug and that the negative effects of high blood pressure override the beneficial effects of the drug.

Even 11-year-olds as well as college students treated anomalies as less problematic (that is, as more likely to warrant modification) when the anomalies were characterized by common rather than separate features or if accompanied by mechanisms that could explain how the anomalies came to be. That is, these age groups tailored their decisions to take account of the characteristics of the anomalies (Koslowski, 1996, chapter 9).

However, in a separate study, when 11-year-olds and college students were provided with no information about mechanism but were told only that two anomalies to a causal claim were characterized by either separate features or by a common feature, the overwhelming response was to assume that the anomalies had something in common. Thus, participants were likely to assume a pattern that would have been consistent with modifying the causal claim. Whether this assumption was a cognitive bookkeeping strategy or a genuine preference for modification over rejection is not clear (Koslowski, 1996, chapter 9).

Finally, the response to anomalous (or disconfirming) data takes account of the fact that a causal belief often consists of two components: a belief that two things covary (eating high- rather than low-sugar causes sleeplessness) and a belief that there is a mechanism that might make the covariation causal (sugar "revs kids up" or "makes them hyper"). Thus, to disconfirm a belief, one might need to disconfirm both components. Depending on the condition, we either disconfirmed or confirmed either the causal belief about sugar and sleeplessness or the non-causal belief that consuming high- rather than low-fat milk has no effect on sleeplessness. In addition, we confirmed (or disconfirmed) either the covariation component alone or both the covariation and the mechanism components. For 11-year-olds as well as for college students, covariation plus mechanism evidence (in contrast to covariation evidence alone) had a greater effect on a causal belief (which included a belief about mechanism) than on a non-causal belief (which included no belief about mechanism). This was not surprising, as the confirming condition simply reinforced a belief that participants already held. What was surprising, because of the assumed prevalence of confirmation bias (Chapman & Chapman, 1969; Koslowski & Maqueda, 1993; Nickerson, 1998) was the fact that it did not matter whether the evidence confirmed the initial belief or disconfirmed it (Koslowski, 1996, chapter 10). That is, this finding has implications for why people often fail to reject theories in light of anomalous data (Kuhn et al., 1988).

To summarize: In actual scientific practice, it is sometimes legitimate to modify or refine a causal explanation to account for anomalous information (because some causal explanations are rudimentary working hypotheses), but doing so sometimes preserves explanations that ought to be replaced. It is also sometimes legitimate to reject it. What is important is to try to identify when the responses are differentially warranted. Congruent with suggestions from scientific inquiry, children as young as 11 years of age as well as college students are more likely to modify rather than reject an explanation when anomalies form a pattern and when there is a possible mechanism that can account for why the anomalies failed to conform to the explanatory rule. Rejection is also more likely to occur when both the mechanism and the covariation components of a causal claim are called into question.

Metaconceptual criteria. Samarapungavan (1992) found that even first-graders preferred explanations (about chemistry and astronomy) that satisfied certain metaconceptual criteria by accounting for a broad range of data, and by being logically and empirically consistent. Fifth-graders also preferred non-*ad hoc* theories (which provided a single explanation for initial as well as anomalous data) to *ad hoc* theories (which offered a different explanation for each). Note that, for the first- through third-graders, reliance on metaconceptual criteria was especially likely when the theories were neutral with respect to the child's prior beliefs or when the theories were consistent with the child's prior beliefs. That is, just as understanding of control and confounding is affected by preexisting beliefs or information, theoretical preferences were also informed by beliefs and by related information, as well as by metaconceptual criteria. Brewer, Chinn, and Samarapungavan (1998) discuss a more detailed account of how explanations develop and the similarities between children's explanations and those of adults.

Lombrozo (2007) found that, all other things being equal, undergraduates prefer explanations that are more probable and that are simpler, in the sense that they invoke fewer causes. In addition, 6-year-olds also prefer simpler to complex explanations (Bonawitz & Lombrozo, 2009). However, preference for simpler explanations is also affected by contextual information. That is, preference for simplicity appears to be a heuristic, rather than an algorithm. Finally, as already noted in the previous section, regardless of whether anomalies are characterized by either separate features or by a common feature, children as young as 11 years of age, as well as older adolescents and college students, are overwhelmingly likely to assume that the anomalies have something in common. Whether this is a preference for simplicity or a cognitive bookkeeping strategy is not clear (Koslowski, 1996, chapter 9).

Consistency or "consilience" with the network of related information: inference to the best explanation. Inference to the best explanation (IBE) captures several points relevant to evaluating causal explanations and also illustrates the interdependence of theory (or explanation) and evidence. IBE (often called "abduction") argues that, in actual scientific practice (which includes causal explanation) one explanation is chosen over its competitor(s) because it provides a better causal account of the data (Lipton, 1991; Magnani, 2001; Thagard, 1989; Thagard & Verbeurgt, 1998). Two points about IBE are especially relevant to the present chapter: an explanation is evaluated with respect to other, competing explanations and an explanation is embedded in, and judged with respect to, the extent to which it is causally consistent (or "unified" or "consilient") with a network of well-established background beliefs, or what else we know about the world – what Quine & Ullian (1970) referred to as a "web of belief." Thus, evolutionary theory as an explanation for speciation is widely accepted because it provides a better explanation than does the competing explanation that different species arose spontaneously, of such things as the presence of intermediate fossil forms, the fact that particular adaptations depend on the type of environmental niche that the animal lives in, etc. That is, evolutionary theory (in contrast to the competing account) renders information evidential, because it makes causal sense of it and, in doing so, the theory itself becomes increasingly compelling. Therefore, according to IBE, whether we treat information as evidence depends on whether there is an explanation that can incorporate it into a causal framework. In addition evolutionary theory is also causally consistent with the web of related information, about, for example, plate tectonics, population genetics, and animal breeding. To what extent does IBE characterize the way in which non-scientists evaluate explanations that are less momentous than that of evolution?

When children reason about explanations, they take account of consistency with the network of related information. However, it may not always seem apparent to the adult mind, because adults have so thoroughly incorporated the relevant information, and it is so widely shared, that we no longer make explicit how our reasoning is based on it; it seems obvious. For example, children had to decide whether to put cheese in a house with either a small or a large opening to decide whether a mouse was large or small. Even young children chose the small opening, reasoning that only mice that were small could fit through it (Sodian et al., 1991). Though it may not seem obvious to an adult, the children's choice took into account the fact that the opening in the house was likely to be fixed in size (rather than, for example, made of rubber and thus expandable) and that mice cannot change their size (as some snakes do, for example, by disconnecting their jaws).

Children also rely on the network of related information that might bear on an event when they either generate explanations of their own or ask questions. For example, consider a preschool child who has been told that a friend's dead cat went up to heaven. The child responds that the cat "did not go *up* to heaven when it died, because bones are heavy and clouds are just water and bones are heavy and would fall right through the clouds" (Koslowski & Pierce, 1981). This child made explicit several pieces of information (about the composition of clouds, the relative weight of bones with respect to clouds, etc.) to draw the conclusion that he did. Similarly, consider the child who asked, "Why do angels never fall down to earth, when there is no floor to heaven?" (Isaacs, 1930, cited in Harris, 2000).

Of course, adults, too, when reasoning about causal explanations, invoke a network of information that is less obvious (or in some cases, that has only recently been acquired or retrieved from memory). For example, Chinn & Brewer (1998) asked college students to assess the theory that dinosaurs were cold-blooded in light of data anomalous to the theory, namely, that the bone density of dinosaurs was comparable to the bone density of extant warm-blooded animals. In reasoning about the anomalies, the students relied on their related knowledge of, for example, the effects of calcium on bones.

Note that it is difficult to reduce such reasoning to a Humean model (including one based on causal Bayes nets). Some of the covariations that might conceivably be relevant would involve events unlikely to have been encountered (such as the ease with which heavy objects, such as cats, fall through clouds). Rather, people rely on assessments of how the causal mechanisms involved in various events are related to one another.

We have already noted that the seemingly obvious reasoning that children engage in (about, for example, what size house can best assess the size of a mouse) does, in fact, rely on a network of related information that has already been acquired. However, in some cases, development involves acquiring new information. If reasoning about explanations relies on networks of related information, then development (at least in the very short run) should depend on the information that is acquired. Furthermore, in some cases, development (again, at least in the short run) might involve reminding people to consider information that they already have, but to see it in a new light.

In this regard, recall that IBE draws attention to the fact that information is evidence, not in an absolute sense, but because there is a theory (or explanation) that can make causal sense of it. College students were asked to decide, for example, why inhabitants in a particular village are of smaller stature than those of neighboring villages and were given two pieces of potentially relevant information: that the pipes in the target village are old and that the language in the target village has different grammatical structures from the languages in the neighboring villages. When told that polluted water is one possible explanation for short stature, participants judged the old pipes as relevant to explaining the stature differences (presumably, because old pipes can allow pollutants to seep in from the ground). In contrast, when told that different gene pools can also result in different statures, participants judged the grammatical differences to be relevant (presumably, because different language groups might have resulted from different gene pools). Thus, whether information was treated as evidence depended on whether an explanation was present that could incorporate the information into a broader causal framework (Koslowski, Marasia, Chelenza, & Dublin, 2008). Thus, the distinction between theory and evidence may not be as clean-cut as one might suppose. However, although college students' decisions about relevance are affected by the explanations or theories to which they have access, students are not necessarily aware of this on a metacognitive level; development from college through the advanced years of graduate school shows no evidence of development in awareness of the extent to which theories provide a framework for the process of scientific research (Thoermer & Sodian, 2002).

To return to the topic of IBE, recall that IBE argues that any single explanation is evaluated, not in isolation, but with respect to competing explanations. Competing explanations can, in turn, affect judgments about which information is relevant to explaining an event. For example, in a subsequent study, college students were again presented with the polluted water explanation and the two possibly relevant pieces of information. When told to undermine (disconfirm) the pollution explanation, participants were more likely than when told to support (confirm) it to cite as relevant the information about different grammatical structures (arguing, for example, that different languages might go along with different practices regarding sanitary conditions). However, participants were less likely to do this when the pollution explanation was presented along with the alternative gene pools explanation. That is, the presence of an alternative provided a competing causal framework that enabled participants to realize that, although the information could be contrived to be consistent with the pollution account, it was in fact more plausibly consistent with the alternative, gene pools explanation. Put differently, the causal consistency of the information with the target was evaluated, not in isolation, but with respect to a particular explanation, in this case, an alternative explanation (Koslowski, Marasia, & Liang, 2008).

College students also take account of consistency or consilience in deciding which information will be useful in deciding between explanations. Students rated diagnostic information (causally consistent with one but not the other of two competing explanations) as more useful in distinguishing between the two explanations than either non-diagnostic information (compatible with both explanations) or neutral information (Koslowski, Beckmann, et al., 2008). This might shed some light on one of the findings of Jeong, Songer, and Lee (2007) regarding evidentiary competence in sixth-graders, namely that the students had difficulty distinguishing relevant from irrelevant evidence. For example, children who were asked how the distance from the equator affected the daily high temperature of a city during winter had difficulty realizing that the month of data collection was relevant. This may well have been because the students lacked a theoretical (broadly understood) understanding of how it is that temperature is affected by season. That is, it may be that learning to differentiate relevant from irrelevant evidence is a function of having and understanding the related background information as well as having a domain-general skill of the sort connoted by "the scientific method." Knowing that the scientific method should be applied is one thing; having the relevant background knowledge to be able to do so may well be quite another.

These results regarding the importance of consilience with related background information also illustrate the more general point that beliefs are not judged in isolation. Rather, they are embedded in and judged with respect to a network of related information or beliefs (Koslowski & Thompson, 2002). In line with this argument, Masnick (1999) and Swiderek (1999) asked college students about their opinions on affirmative action and capital punishment, respectively. Participants were also interviewed about several subsidiary beliefs that underlie the general beliefs (for example, whether capital punishment in fact reduces the incidence of capital crimes, is cost-effective, applied in a non-biased way). Regardless of whether participants subscribed to each of the sub-beliefs, they had their beliefs challenged or were presented with disconfirming evidence. For example, participants who believed that capital punishment did not reduce the incidence of capital crimes were shown data that the rate of capital crimes was reduced after a state introduced capital punishment. Those who believed it did reduce capital crimes were given the same information but told that the decrease only held for the first three months after capital punishment was introduced.

Participants were brought back for a second interview 2 weeks after the first interview and were asked again about their general belief as well as about the sub-beliefs. The sum of the change on the individual sub-beliefs predicted 79% of the variance in change in the general belief about affirmative action when beliefs were challenged, and 85% of the variance of the change in the general belief in capital punishment when participants saw disconfirming data. The results echo the point that explanations are embedded in a network of related information and, thus, to change any particular belief, one must also change the related beliefs in which it is embedded.

To summarize: Explanations are embedded in and judged with respect to a network of related information, including information about competing alternative explanations. Thus, when evaluating complex explanations, people treat information as evidence if there is a mechanism that can incorporate it into a broader causal framework; they consider consilience or consistency with both the explanation and what else they know about the world; and they reduce their support of a general belief to the extent that the sub-beliefs that underwrite the general belief have been undermined.

General Summary and Implications

Even young children have an appreciation of many of the considerations relevant to making sound causal judgments. When allowed to choose, they prefer assessing causal relations with contrasts rather than simple demonstrations and with controlled rather than confounded designs. At least by 11 years of age, they make it clear, even without prompting, that they consider possible alternative causes. However, appreciation of control and confounding is embedded in the context of prior beliefs, background information, and goals. Children (including preschoolers) also treat Humean indices in making causal judgments, but at least by 11 years of age, they temper such conclusions with considerations of theory (or mechanism or explanation), relying on theory to determine: when covariations are likely to be causal rather than artifactual; when implausible possible causes might actually be plausible; when anomalies are more or less likely to call for refining (and keeping) an existing explanation rather than rejecting it. Moreover, at least by 11 years of age, people treat covariation and mechanism information as interdependent, relying on mechanism or explanation to make decisions about whether information is evidentially relevant, etc., and relying on information about covariation to identify possible mechanisms that might as yet be undiscovered. Furthermore, with increasing age, people come to be increasingly discerning about the plausibility of particular mechanisms and the likelihood that unknown mechanisms will be discovered. Finally, when assessing mechanisms or explanations, even preschoolers (as well as 11-year-olds and college students) take account of consilience or consistency with what else is known about the world.

We draw attention to several implications of this research. First, for better or worse, causal reasoning (like scientific reasoning) does not consist of the application of formal rules. Although various rules (for example, consider alternative possible causes; covariation indicates cause) can be formulated as though they were formal (and thus applicable in all situations), the likelihood that they will be deployed depends on context, including information about mechanism. That is, the principles of causal reasoning are heuristics rather than algorithms. Thus, to assume that sound causal reasoning can be taught by teaching a set of formal rules will be misguided. Second, considerations of mechanism or explanation can be both useful (in allowing us to realize that some information is evidential and that some implausible covariations may be worth a second look) as well as detrimental (in preventing us from arranging the appropriate controls). Put differently, the distinction between theory and evidence may not be clean-cut; we may need theory to realize that information is evidence and we need evidence to point the way to mechanisms or explanations that have yet to be discovered. Third, people's seeming reluctance to relinquish causal beliefs (confirmation bias) might depend, in part, on whether the disconfirming data take account of theoretical considerations. If people do not have access to an alternative explanation, they might well not realize that evidence inconsistent with an existing explanation is in fact consistent with the alternative. Most generally, causal relations and explanations are embedded in and judged with respect to a network of related information, and consilience with the information affects how children as well as adults reason about causation and, thus, about scientific reasoning as well.

References

Abelson, R. P. (1959). Modes of resolution of belief dilemmas. *Journal of Conflict Resolution, 3*, 343–352.

Ahn, W-K, Novick, L., & Kim, N. S. (2003). Understanding behavior makes it more normal. *Psychonomic Bulletin and Review, 10*, 746–752.

Amsel, E., Goodman, G., Savoie, D., & Clark, M. (1996). The development of reasoning about causal and noncausal influences on levers. *Child Development, 67*, 1624–1646.

Bonawitz, E. B., & Lombrozo, T. (2009). Occam's Rattle: Children's use of simplicity and probability to constrain inference. Manuscript under review.

Brenneman, K., Gelman, R., Massey, C., Roth, Z., Nayfield, I., & Downs, L. (2007, October). Preschool pathways to science: Fostering and assessing scientific reasoning in preschoolers. Paper presented at the meeting of the Cognitive Development Society, Santa Fe, NM.

Brewer, W. F., Chinn, C. A., & Samarapungavan, A. (1998). Explanation in scientists and children. *Minds and Machines, 8*, 119–136.

Bullock, M., (1991). Scientific reasoning in elementary school: Developmental and individual differences. Paper presented at the Biennial Meeting of the Society for Research in Child Development, Seattle, Washington.

Bullock, M., & Gelman, R. (1979). Preschool children's assumptions about cause and effect: Temporal ordering. *Child Development, 50*(1), 89–96.

Bullock, M., & Ziegler, A. (1999). Scientific reasoning: Developmental and individual differences. In. F. E. Weinert & W. Schneider (Eds.), *Individual development from 3 to 12: Findings from the Munich Longitudinal Study* (pp. 38–54). Cambridge: Cambridge University Press.

Chapman, L., & Chapman, J. (1969). Illusory correlation as an obstacle to the use of valid psychodiagnostic signs. *Journal of Abnormal Psychology, 74*, 271–280.

Chen, Z., & Klahr, D., (1999). All other things being equal: Children's acquisition of the control of variables strategy, *Child Development, 70*, 1098–1120.

Chinn, C. A., & Brewer, W. F. (1998). An empirical test of a taxonomy of responses to anomalous data in science. *Journal of Research in Science Teaching, 35*, 623–654.

Chinn, C. A., & Malhotra, B. A. (2002). Children's responses to anomalous scientific data: How is conceptual change impeded? *Journal of Educational Psychology, 94*, 327–343.

Croker, S., & Buchanan, H. (2008, July). Context and plausibility of evidence affects scientific reasoning in children and adults. Paper presented at the meeting of the International Society of the Psychology of Science and Technology, Berlin.

Fugelsang, J. A., & Dunbar, K. N. (2005). Brain-based mechanisms underlying complex causal thinking. *Neuropsychologia, 43*, 1204–1213.

Fugelsang, J. A., Roser, M. E., Corballis, P. M., Gazzaniga, M. S., & Dunbar, K. N. (2005). Brain mechanisms underlying perceptual causality. *Cognitive Brain Research, 24*(1), 41–47.

Giere, R. (2002). Scientific cognition as distributed cognition. In P. Carruthers, S. Stich, & M. Siegel (Eds.), *The cognitive basis of science: Multidisciplinary approaches*. Cambridge: Cambridge University Press.

Gopnik, A., Glymour, C., Sobel, D., Schulz, L., Kushnir, T., & Danks, D. (2004). A theory of causal learning in children: Causal maps and Bayes nets. *Psychological Review, 111*, 1, 1–31.

Gopnik, A., & Schulz, L. (Eds.) (2007). *Causal learning: Psychology, philosophy, and computation.* New York: Oxford University Press.

Harris, P. L. (2000). Children's metaphysical questions. In K. S. Rosengren, C. N. Johnson, & P. L. Harris, *Imagining the impossible: Magical, scientific, and religious thinking in children.* Cambridge: Cambridge University Press.

Hirschfeld, L., & Gelman, S. (Eds.) (1994). *Mapping the mind: Domain specificity in cognition and culture.* New York: Cambridge University Press.

Hume, D., (1973). *A Treatise of Human Nature* (2nd ed.) L. A. Selby-Bigge and P. H. Nidditch, Eds. Oxford: Oxford University Press.

Jeong, H., Songer, N. B., & Lee, S-Y. (2007). Evidentiary competence: Sixth graders' understanding for gathering and interpreting evidence in scientific investigations. *Research in Science Education, 37*, 75–97.

Kanari, Z., & Millar, R. (2004). Reasoning from data: How students collect and interpret data in science investigations. *Journal of Research in Science Teaching, 41*, 748–769.

Karmiloff-Smith, A., & Inhelder, B. (1974/1975). If you want to get ahead, get a theory. *Cognition, 3*, 195–212.

Keil, F. C., & Wilson, R. A. (Eds.) (2000). *Explanation and cognition*. Cambridge, MA: MIT Press.

Klahr, D., Fay, A. L., & Dunbar, K. (1993). Heuristics for scientific experimentation: A developmental study. *Cognitive Psychology, 25*(1), 111–146.

Klahr, D., & Nigam, M. (2004). The equivalence of learning paths in early science instruction: Effects of direct instruction and discovery learning. *Psychological Science, 15*, 661–667.

Klahr, D., Triona, L. M., & Williams, C. (2007). Hands on what? The relative effectiveness of physical versus virtual materials in an engineering design project by middle school children. *Journal of Research in Science Teaching, 44*, 183–203.

Kloos, H., & Somerville, S. C. (2001). Providing impetus for conceptual change: The effect of organizing the input. *Cognitive Development, 16*, 737–759.

Kloos, H., & Van Orden, G. C. (2005). Can a preschooler's mistaken belief benefit learning? *Swiss Journal of Psychology, 64*, 195–205.

Koehler, D. J. (1991). Explanation, imagination, and confidence in judgment. *Psychological Bulletin, 110*, 499–519.

Koenig, M., & Harris, P. L. (2005). The role of social cognition in early trust. *Trends in Cognitive Science, 9*, 457–459.

Koerber, S., Sodian, B., Thoermer, C., & Nett, U. (2005). Scientific reasoning in young children: Preschoolers' ability to evaluate covariation evidence. *Swiss Journal of Psychology, 64*, 2005, 141–152.

Koslowski, B., (1996). *Theory and evidence: The development of scientific reasoning*. Cambridge, MA: MIT Press.

Koslowski, B., Beckmann, L., Bowers, E., DeVito, J., Wonderly, B., Vermeylan, F. (2008, July). The cognitive basis for confirmation bias is more nuanced than one might expect. Paper presented at the meeting of the International Society of the Psychology of Science and Technology, Berlin.

Koslowski, B., Cohen, L., Spund, & Fleury, J. (2009). The conceptual understanding of ruling out alternatives does not guarantee the technical ability to do so. Manuscript in preparation.

Koslowski, B., & Maqueda, M. (1993). What is confirmation bias and when do people have it? *Merrill-Palmer Quarterly* [Special issue: The development of rationality and critical thinking], *39*(1) 104–130.

Koslowski, B., Marasia, J., Chelenza, M., & Dublin, R. (2008). Information becomes evidence when an explanation can incorporate it into a causal framework. *Cognitive Development, 23*, 472–487.

Koslowski, B., Marasia, J., & Liang, V. (2008, July). Confirming a belief is not necessarily problematic; disconfirming a belief is not necessarily good. Paper presented at the meeting of the International Congress of Psychology, Berlin.

Koslowski, B., & Masnick, A. (2002). The development of causal reasoning. In U. Goswami (Ed.), *Blackwell handbook of childhood cognitive development*. Oxford: Blackwell.

Koslowski, B., & Pierce, A. (1981, April). Children's spontaneous explanations and requests for explanations. Paper presented to the Society for Research in Child Development.

Koslowski, B., Spilton, D., & Snipper, A. (1981). Children's beliefs about instances of mechanical and electrical causation. *Journal of Applied Developmental Psychology, 2*, 189–210.

Koslowski, B., Susman, A., & Serling, J. (1991, April). Conceptual vs. technical understanding of evidence in scientific reasoning. Paper presented at the Biennial Meeting of the Society for Research in Child Development. Seattle, WA.

Koslowski, B., & Thompson, S. L. (2002). Theorizing is important, and collateral information constrains how well it is done. In P. Carruthers, S. Stitch, & M. Siegal (Eds.), *The cognitive bases of science: Multidisciplinary approaches*. Cambridge: Cambridge University Press.

Kuhn, D., Amsel, E., & O'Loughlin, M. (1988). *The development of scientific thinking skills*. Orlando, FL: Academic Press.

Kuhn, D., Schauble, L., & Garcia-Mila, M. (1992). Cross-domain development of scientific reasoning. *Cognition and Instruction, 9*, 285–327.

Kushnir, T., & Gopnik, A. (2007). Conditional probability versus spatial contiguity in causal learning: Preschoolers use new contingency evidence to overcome prior spatial assumptions. *Developmental Psychology. 43*, 1, 186–196.

Kushnir, T., Wellman, H. M., & Gelman, S. A. (2008). The role of preschoolers' social understanding in evaluating the informativeness of causal interventions. *Cognition, 107*(3), 1084–1092.

Kushnir, T., Wellman, H., & Gelman, S. (2009). A self-agency bias in preschoolers' causal inferences. *Developmental Psychology, 45*, 2, 597–603.

Lipton, P. (1991). *Inference to the best explanation*. London: Routledge.

Lombrozo, T. (2006). The structure and function of explanations. *Trends in Cognitive Sciences, 10*, 464–470.

Lombrozo, T. (2007). Simplicity and probability in causal explanation. *Cognitive Psychology, 55*(3), 232–257.

Lombrozo, T., & Carey, S. (2006). Functional explanation and the function of explanation. *Cognition, 99*(2), 167–204.

Lutz, D., & Keil, F. C. (2002). Early understanding of the division of cognitive labor. *Child Development, 73*, 1073–1084.

Magnani, L. (2001). *Abduction, reason, and science: Processes of discovery and explanation*. Dordrecht: Kluwer.

Masnick, A. M. (1999). *Belief patterns and the intersection of cognitive and social factors* (Unpublished doctoral thesis). Cornell University.

Masnick, A. M., Klahr, D., & Knowles, E. R. (2009). Learning from pendulum data with systematic and exploratory testing. Manuscript in preparation.

Masnick, A. M., Klahr, D., & Morris, B. J. (2007). Separating signal from noise: Children's understanding of error and variability in experimental outcomes. In M. Lovett & P. Shah (Eds.), *Thinking with Data* (pp. 3–26). New York: Erlbaum.

Masnick, A. M., & Morris, B. J. (2008). Investigating the development of data evaluation: The role of data characteristics. *Child Development, 79*, 1032–1048.

McClelland, J. L., & Thompson, R. M. (2007). Using domain-general principles to explain children's causal reasoning abilities. *Developmental Science, 10*, 333–356.

Mendelson, R., & Shultz, T. R. (1976). Covariation and temporal contiguity as principles of causal inference in young children. *Journal of Experimental Child Psychology, 22*(3), 408–412.

Michotte, A. (1963). *The perception of causality*. Oxford: Basic Books.

Mills, C. M., & Keil, F. C. (2004). Knowing the limits of one's understanding: The development of an awareness of an illusion of explanatory depth. *Journal of Experimental Child Psychology, 87*, 1–32.

Nickerson, R. S. (1998). Confirmation bias: A ubiquitous phenomenon in many guises. *Review of General Psychology, 2*, 175–220.

Piaget, J. (1930). *The child's conception of physical causality*. London: Routledge & Kegan Paul.

Quine, W., & Ullian, J. (1970). *The web of belief.* New York: Random House.

Roberts, M. J. (Ed.). (2007). *Integrating the mind: Domain general vs. domain specific processes in higher cognition*. New York: Psychology Press.

Ruffman, T., Perner, J., Olson, D. R., & Doherty, M. (1993). Reflecting on scientific thinking: Children's understanding of the hypothesis–evidence relation. *Child Development, 64*, 1617–1636.

Samarapungavan, A. (1992). Children's judgments in theory choice tasks: Scientific rationality in childhood. *Cognition, 45*, 1–32.

Schauble, L. (1990). Belief revision in children: The role of prior knowledge and strategies for generating evidence. *Journal of Experimental Child Psychology, 49*, 31–57.

Schauble, L., Klopfer, L., & Raghavan, K. (1991). Students' transition from an engineering model to a science model of experimentation. *Journal of Research in Science Teaching, 18*, 859–882.

Schulz, L. E., & Bonawitz, E. B. (2007). Serious fun: Preschoolers engage in more exploratory play when evidence is confounded. *Developmental Psychology, 43*, 1045–1050.

Schulz, L. E., & Gopnik, A. (2004). Causal learning across domains. *Developmental Psychology, 40*, 162–176.

Schulz, L. E., Gopnik, A., & Glymour, C. (2007). Preschool children learn about causal structure from conditional interventions. *Developmental Science, 10*, 322–332.

Schulz, L. E., Kushnir, T., & Gopnik, A. (2007). Learning from doing: Interventions and causal inference. In A. Gopnik & L. E. Schulz (Eds.), *Causal learning: Psychology, philosophy and computation*. Oxford: Oxford University Press.

Shultz, T. R., & Mendelson, R. (1975). The use of covariation as a principle of causal analysis. *Child Development, 46*, 394–399.

Siegler, R. S. (1976). The effects of simple necessity and sufficiency relationships on children's causal inferences. *Child Development, 17*, 1058–1063.

Siegler, R. S., & Liebert, R. M. (1974). Effects of contiguity, regularity, and age on children's causal inferences. *Developmental Psychology, 10*, 574–579.

Sobel, D. M., & Kirkham, N. Z. (2007). Interactions between causal and statistical learning approaches. In A. Gopnik & L. Schulz (Eds.), *Causal learning: Psychology, philosophy, and computation* (pp. 139–153). New York: Oxford University Press.

Sobel, D. M., & Kushnir, T. (2006). The importance of decision making in causal learning from interventions. *Memory and Cognition, 34*(2), 411–419.

Sodian, B., Zaitchik, D., & Carey, S. (1991). Young children's differentiation of hypothetical beliefs from evidence. *Child Development, 62*(4), 753–766.

Strand-Cary, M., & Klahr, D. (2008). Developing elementary science skills: Instructional effectiveness and path independence. *Cognitive Development, 23*, 488–511.

Swiderek, M. R. (1999). *Beliefs can change in response to disconfirming evidence and can do so in complicated ways, but only if collateral beliefs are disconfirmed* (Unpublished doctoral dissertation). Cornell University.

Thagard, P. (1989). Explanatory coherence. *Behavioral and Brain Sciences, 12*, 435–502.

Thagard, P., & Verbeurgt, K. (1998). Coherence as constraint satisfaction. *Cognitive Science, 22*, 1–24.

Thoermer, C., & Sodian, B. (2002). Science undergraduates' and graduates' epistemologies of science: The notion of interpretive frameworks. *New Ideas in Psychology, 20*, 263–283.

Tschirgi, J. E. (1980). Sensible reasoning: A hypothesis about hypotheses. *Child Development, 51*(1), 1–10.

Zimmerman, C. (2000). The development of scientific reasoning skills. *Developmental Review, 20*, 99–149.

Zimmerman, C. (2007). The development of scientific thinking skills in elementary and middle school. *Developmental Review, 27*, 172–223.

CHAPTER FIFTEEN

Inductive and Deductive Reasoning

Usha Goswami

Human reasoning can be defined as mental activity that involves the manipulation of given information to reach new conclusions. Two kinds of reasoning are frequently identified, inductive reasoning and deductive reasoning. In inductive reasoning, adults and children are required to "go beyond the information given" and make inferences that may not be deductively valid. Examples of inductive reasoning include generalizing on the basis of a known example, making an inductive inference from a particular premise, and drawing an analogy. Inductive reasoning is ubiquitous in human thinking. Deductive reasoning can also reach new conclusions. In contrast to inductive reasoning, however, in a deductive reasoning problem there is only one logically valid answer. Deductive reasoning is usually measured by the ability to apply deductive logic to known information that is given (e.g., logical syllogisms). For example, if a child is given the two premises "All dogs bark" and "Rex is a dog," there is only one logical deduction. Rex is a dog, all dogs bark, therefore Rex must also bark. Deductive reasoning includes conditional reasoning ("if A, then B"), counterfactual reasoning, and transitive reasoning (linear syllogisms).

One important difference between inductive and deductive reasoning is that deductive reasoning problems can be solved without (or despite) real-world knowledge. In the example of Rex the dog, a child can make a logical deduction about Rex barking even if "barking" is a totally unfamiliar activity. If the child had been told instead "Rex is a cat. All cats bark. Does Rex bark?", then the correct deduction would again be that Rex must also bark, even though in the real world cats do not bark (thus the logical deduction is counterfactual and in conflict with real-world beliefs). Counterfactual deductions are still logically valid. Both inductive and deductive reasoning are subject to certain constraints, some of which arise from real-world knowledge, which can both facilitate and impede reasoning efficiency. Since the previous edition of this Handbook, new research on reasoning has focused in particular on the importance of the child being able to access and retrieve the stored real-world knowledge relevant to a particular reasoning problem. Knowledge retrieval affects reasoning in both children and adults. Research has also focused on the importance of the inhibition of competing or irrelevant information, for both induction and deduction. A third focus of inquiry has been the developmental effects of working-memory capacity, the mental "workspace" where premises and real-world knowledge must be interrelated. Brain-imaging studies of reasoning in children are just beginning to appear.

Indeed, it is now accepted that both inductive and deductive reasoning show remarkable continuity across the lifespan. Inductive reasoning and deductive reasoning are influenced by similar factors and are subject to similar heuristics and biases, in both children and adults. This current view of developmental continuity stands in sharp contrast to the historical view, which was that reasoning is age-dependent and content-independent (see Brown, 1990). Historically, it was thought that children gradually became increasingly efficient all-purpose learning machines, acquiring and applying general reasoning strategies irrespective of domain knowledge. Traditionally, developmental textbooks had separate sections for "problem solving" and "concept formation." Problem solving was about the acquisition of logical rules, and was usually studied by seeing whether children could acquire isolated rules in completely unfamiliar situations – which they were typically bad at. Conceptual development was about the growth of real-world knowledge, and the need for transfer of learning by induction was taken for granted – after all, even toddlers could do it. The focus in conceptual development was on the extent and organization of knowledge that determined transfer. The obvious connection between the two topics was widely ignored. The importance of the existing state of the conceptual system, the context in which the new concept is first encountered, and the availability of real-world knowledge for both types of reasoning is now recognized. As young children typically have less relevant real-world information to retrieve compared to adults, and are less efficient at inhibiting irrelevant factors, both deductive and inductive reasoning show age-related effects.

Inductive Reasoning

Inductive reasoning in children has been studied in a variety of ways. Many studies of categorization and conceptual development involve inductive reasoning. For example, children may be told that sparrows can fly, and then asked whether eagles can fly. There are many examples of such studies in this book (see chapters by Opfer & Gelman, Quinn, and Waxman & Leddon, for examples of experiments in which even infants and toddlers make inductive inferences). This aspect of induction will therefore be covered extremely briefly. Studies of "insight" are also studies of inductive reasoning. "Insight" refers to the apparently spontaneous solution of a difficult problem without the application of any conscious reasoning strategies. It was first studied in detail by the Gestalt psychologists (e.g., Maier, 1931), who focused on adults. Insight has not been studied widely in young children. Thirdly, inductive reasoning in children has been studied by investigating analogical development. Studies of analogical reasoning are widely available, and there are recent developmental brain-imaging studies (for reviews, see Goswami, 1991, 1992, 1996, 2001). Analogical reasoning can also be described as the study of similarity-based or relational reasoning. As we will see, all inductive reasoning in humans appears to be similarity-based. Hence analogical reasoning is a useful paradigm within which to explore the development of inductive reasoning more generally.

Inductive inferences

Inductive inferences are made surprisingly readily by very young children. For example, Gelman and Coley (1990) asked 2-year-old children questions about the properties of typical and atypical members of familiar categories like birds. The children were shown a picture of a typical category member, such as a robin, and were asked "This is a bird. Does it live in a nest?" They were then shown more pictures of birds, such as a dodo (atypical category member) and a bluebird (typical category member). For each picture, they were asked the same question ("Does it live in a nest?"). The category label "bird" was not repeated. Gelman and Coley found that the children ascribed the relevant properties (lives in a nest) to the typical category members (bluebird) 76% of the time, and to the atypical category members (dodo) 42% of the time. Similar results for 3- and 4-year-olds were reported by Gelman and Markman (1986). Such studies show that children, like adults, make inductive inferences on the basis of *typicality*. When the premise category is very typical (a robin is a very typical bird), children are ready to reason inductively. Further, when the premise and conclusion categories are very similar (as in robin and bluebird), inductive reasoning is promoted. This similarity effect is also found in adults.

Two other factors also appear to promote inductive reasoning in adults. These are the number of observations upon which the induction is based, and the nature of the property being projected. For example, if you are told that dogs, cats, bears, monkeys, bees, horses, and blackbirds have spleens, you should be more likely to judge that rabbits have spleens than if you are told only that dogs and bees have spleens (the sample-size effect). However, if you are told that a coat "smells yucky," you are unlikely to project this property to other coats, as "smelling yucky" should be treated as an idiosyncratic property of a particular coat rather than as a general property of coats. Real-world knowledge tells you that "smelling yucky" is not an enduring property in the way that "having a spleen" is.

There is a small amount of evidence that children's inductive reasoning is subject to the same effects. Gutheil and Gelman (1997) asked children aged from 8 to 10 years to make inductions based on varying sample sizes. For example, the children were shown pictures of butterflies and told "Here is one butterfly. This butterfly has blue eyes." "Here are five other butterflies. These five butterflies have grey eyes." The experimenter then looked at another picture card that wasn't shown to the child, and said "I'm looking at another butterfly. Do you think this butterfly has blue eyes like this butterfly (single exemplar) or grey eyes like these butterflies (many exemplars)?" The children chose to project the properties of the larger sample (e.g., grey eyes) at rates significantly above chance. Gelman (1988) explored the nature of the properties that children will use as a basis for inductive inferences. She examined whether preschool children (aged on average 4 years 8 months) and second-graders (aged on average 8 years) would differentiate between generalizable and non-generalizable properties in their inductive inferences. Generalizable properties were deliberately unfamiliar, such as "likes to eat alfalfa" for rabbits, and "needs CO_2 to grow" for flowers. Non-generalizable properties were chosen to be familiar, as a strong test of whether the children realized that inductive inferences about these properties were non-legitimate, and included "smells yucky" for a coat, "has a little scratch" for a clock, or "has a piece of grass stuck to it" for a fish. Gelman found that all of the children were sensitive to the generalizable nature of the different properties. Even the preschoolers differentiated clearly between the generalizable properties (such as eating alfalfa) and the non-generalizable properties (such as smelling yucky). They seemed to realize that these properties were temporary or accidental, and, like adults, they took the nature of the property into account when making inductive inferences. Although the systematic manipulation of all the factors that affect inductive reasoning in adults is currently lacking in the developmental literature (see Heit, 2000), in general inductive inferences seem to be affected by similar factors throughout development.

Insight

Another form of inductive reasoning is a sudden "insight" into how to solve an apparently intractable problem. The reasoner is conscious of no inductive inferences in reaching the solution, which seems to appear spontaneously "in mind." This form of inventive or creative reasoning was first studied by the Gestalt psychologists (e.g., Duncker, 1945; Maier, 1931), who focused their investigations on adults. A classic "insight" problem is the following. In the "matchbox" problem (Duncker, 1945), participants are required to fix a candle to a vertical surface so that it can burn properly. Various tools such as string and drawing pins (tacks) are provided to assist them. The drawing pins are in a small box. The solution is to empty the box and pin it to the vertical surface, thereby creating a horizontal shelf on which to stand the candle. Many participants did not think of this solution, because the box was seen only in terms of its function of containing the drawing pins. This constraint on reasoning was described as "functional fixedness." In fact, rather than studying how insight could be promoted, the paradigms invented by the Gestalt psychologists led to the study of how insight was impeded.

To investigate how insight could be supported, Ann Brown and her colleagues invented a number of paradigms for promoting cognitive flexibility in young children (see Brown, 1990). For example, to overcome functional fixedness in young children, Brown and her colleagues used the genie analogy paradigm, originally developed by Holyoak, Junn, and Billman (1984). The child had to help a genie to move his jewels from one bottle to another without breaking them and without moving his feet, which had been glued into the first bottle by a wicked witch (Brown, 1989). Various tools were available to solve this problem, including glue, string, tape, and a sheet of paper. The solution was to use the paper to make a tube, through which the jewels could then be rolled. Children aged 5 and 9 years were tested on the genie problem in two conditions. In the Functional Fixedness condition, the children were first asked to make drawings on 3 sheets of paper prior to receiving the genie problem. In the Cognitive Flexibility condition, the children used the 3 sheets of paper to make a tent, to make a drawing and for a communication game. Only 20% of the 5-year-olds and 35% of the 9-year-olds who had spent time making 3 drawings prior to the test thought of rolling the paper into a tube to help the genie. In contrast, 75% of the 5-year-olds and 80% of the 9-year-olds spontaneously generated the rolling solution in the Cognitive Flexibility condition. Brown and Kane (1988) argued that the experience of using the paper for drawing fixed its function for the former group, impeding inductive reasoning. Experimenting with a variety of uses for the paper freed it from a specific role for the Cognitive Flexibility group, making it available for other creative solutions.

German and Defeyter (2000) produced the interesting argument that younger children might actually be *less* susceptible to functional fixedness than older children, because they have a more fluid notion of function than older children. German and Defeyter explored this possibility by giving a variant of Duncker's candle problem to children aged from 5 to 7 years. The children were introduced to Bobo, a toy bear with short legs who wanted to reach his toy down from a shelf. They were told that he couldn't jump to reach it because of his short legs, and were asked to help him. Various tools were available, including toy blocks, a magnet, a ball, and a car, all presented inside a small box. The toy blocks could be used to build a tower, but it was too short to enable Bobo to reach his toy. The solution was to empty the box and turn it over, and then to build the tower on top of the box. In a control condition, the box was given to the children empty. German and Defeyter found that the 5-year-olds were equally fast at using the box as a support for the tower in the Functional Fixedness condition and the control condition, whereas the 6- and 7-year-olds were significantly slower in the Functional Fixedness condition than in the control condition. They were also significantly slower than the younger children, taking on average 120 seconds to think of the box solution compared to 40 seconds for the 5-year-olds.

This suggested greater cognitive flexibility concerning notions of function in the younger children. Defeyter and German (2003) followed this up by teaching children aged 5 to 7 years novel functions for two artifacts. These were a "light stick," which completed a circuit when touched to a switch, enabling lights to come on, and a "music stick," which made a tone sound when inserted into a hole in a box. The children were then given a novel problem, which was to remove a soft toy from the centre of a transparent plastic tube. The solution was to use a stick, but other distracter objects were also present (e.g., a ruler, a tennis ball). Defeyter and German found that 75% of 5-year-olds correctly selected the stick for their first solution attempt, regardless of whether it had previously been demonstrated to have a certain function (light switching on, music switching on). In contrast, only 35% of 6-year-olds first selected the stick in the function demonstration condition, even though 95% of this age group selected the stick if no function had been demonstrated. Comparable figures for the 7-year-olds were 40% and 80%. Again, functional fixedness was present in the older children but not the younger children. Although Defeyter and German proposed an explanation based on the developmental understanding of the intended purpose of an artifact, it also seems plausible that younger children had less real-world knowledge about how switches work. Hence cognitive flexibility is partly a result of how much information one has, with in some situations, less information enabling superior reasoning.

Analogical reasoning

In contrast to inductive inferences, believed to be present from early in development, the standard view of analogy was that it was a content-independent reasoning strategy characteristic of the later stages of cognitive development (Piaget, Montangero, & Billeter, 1977). There was also a belief that younger children were "perceptually bound" and relied on surface similarity to solve analogies (Gentner, 1989). Currently, the dominant view is that analogy is an early-developing form of inductive reasoning that is probably available from infancy (Goswami, 1992, 1996), but is subject to constraints connected to information retrieval and inhibition (Richland, Morrison, & Holyoak, 2006). In fact, the constraints on induction discussed in the preceding sections apply to analogical reasoning as well. Children's analogies are supported by the similarity of premise and conclusion categories (at the levels of both surface and relational similarity), by the number of exemplars on which the analogy is based, and by the nature of the relations in the analogy. Analogical reasoning is also impeded by factors such as functional fixedness, cognitive embeddedness, the inability to retrieve relevant information, and the inability to inhibit competing irrelevant information. When children are reasoning in familiar domains, they can go beyond surface features and make analogies on the basis of structural or relational similarity. However, younger children may not be as efficient as older children if, for example, they have to inhibit competing information.

The relational similarity constraint. The hallmark of analogical reasoning is its dependence on structural or relational similarity (the "relational similarity constraint," Goswami, 1992). A striking example of this constraint in action comes from the analogy that led to Kekule's (1865) theory about the molecular structure of benzene (see Holyoak & Thagard, 1995). In a dream, Kekule had a visual image of a snake biting its own tail. This gave him the idea that the carbon atoms in benzene could be arranged in a ring. The similarity between the snake and the carbon atoms was at a purely structural/relational level – circular arrangement.

Classic investigations of analogical development have focused on when children become able to reason according to the relational similarity constraint. Formal tests of analogical reasoning skills in children are usually based on "item analogies." In item analogies, two items A and B are presented to the child, a third item C is presented, and the child is required to generate a D term that has the same relation to C as B has to A. Successful generation of a D term requires the use of the relational similarity constraint. For example, if the child is given the items *horse is to foal as cat is to* ?, she is expected to generate the solution term "kitten." The response "dog," which is a strong associate of "cat," would be an error. Another test of understanding of the relational similarity constraint is to offer an apparently successful child alternative completion terms or "countersuggestions" to the analogy that they have just formed. For example, a child who accepted "bird" as the completion term for the analogy "*horse : foal :: cat :?*" would not be credited with understanding the relational similarity constraint.

sThe first developmental psychologist to study analogical reasoning, Piaget, used both of these tests. He designed a pictorial version of the item-analogy task suitable for children aged from 5 to 13 years of age (Piaget et al., 1977). The analogies were largely based on functional and causal relations, such as *bicycle : handlebars :: ship :?* and *dog : hair :: bird :?* Younger children (5- to 7-year-olds) tested by Piaget offered solutions like "bird" to the *bicycle/ship* analogy, giving reasons like "both birds and ships are found on the lake." Piaget concluded that younger children solved analogies on the basis of associative reasoning (see also Sternberg & Nigro, 1980). Slightly older children, approximately aged 7 to 12 years, were very susceptible to counter-suggestions from the experimenter. They were happy to accept a D term such as "pump" to complete the ship/bicycle analogy (*ship : ship's wheel :: bicycle : pump*). Piaget thus argued that understanding of the relational similarity constraint did not develop until early adolescence, during the formal operational period (Miller, chapter 25, this volume). This conclusion was accepted in developmental psychology for many years.

The role of relational familiarity in analogical development. One problem with Piaget's methodology, however, was that he did not check whether the younger children in his experiments understood the functional and causal relations on which his analogies were based (for example, the relation "steering mechanism" in the bicycle/ship analogy). Some of these relations may not yet have been specified in the child's conceptual system. As noted earlier, in the absence of the requisite knowledge, it is difficult to reason by induction. In such circumstances, novice learners are likely to fall back on simpler solution strategies such as associative reasoning and matching on the basis of surface similarity. Item analogies based on *unfamiliar* relations will obviously *underestimate* analogical ability.

One way to test this idea is to design analogies based on relations that are known to be highly familiar to younger children from other cognitive developmental research, such as family relations (Goswami & Pauen, 2005), thematic relations (Goswami & Brown, 1990; see figure 15.1), and causal relations (Goswami & Brown, 1989). For example, Goswami and Brown (1989) designed a series of item analogies based on causal relations. Causal relations were chosen because children understand simple causal relations like cutting, wetting, and melting by at least the age of 3–4 (Koslowski & Masnick, chapter 14, this volume). Children aged from 3 to 6 years were shown causal relations instantiated in familiar entities, such as *chocolate is to melted chocolate as snowman is to ?*, and *playdoh is to cut playdoh as apple is to* ? Five different solution options were then presented, such as the wrong object undergoing the correct causal transformation, a perceptual similarity match, or the correct object undergoing the incorrect causal transformation. Knowledge of the causal relations required to solve the analogies was measured in a control condition. In this control, the children were shown three pictures of items that had been causally transformed (e.g., cut playdoh, cut bread, cut apple), and were asked to select the causal agent responsible for the transformation from a set of pictures of possible agents (e.g., a knife, water, the sun). The results showed that both analogical success and causal relational knowledge increased with age. The 3-year-olds solved 52% of the analogies and 52% of the control sequences, the 4-year-olds solved 89% of the analogies and 80% of the control sequences, and the 6-year-olds solved 99% of the analogies and 100% of the control sequences. There was also a significant *conditional* relationship between performance in the analogy condition and performance in the control condition, as would be expected if successful inductive reasoning depends on the existing state of

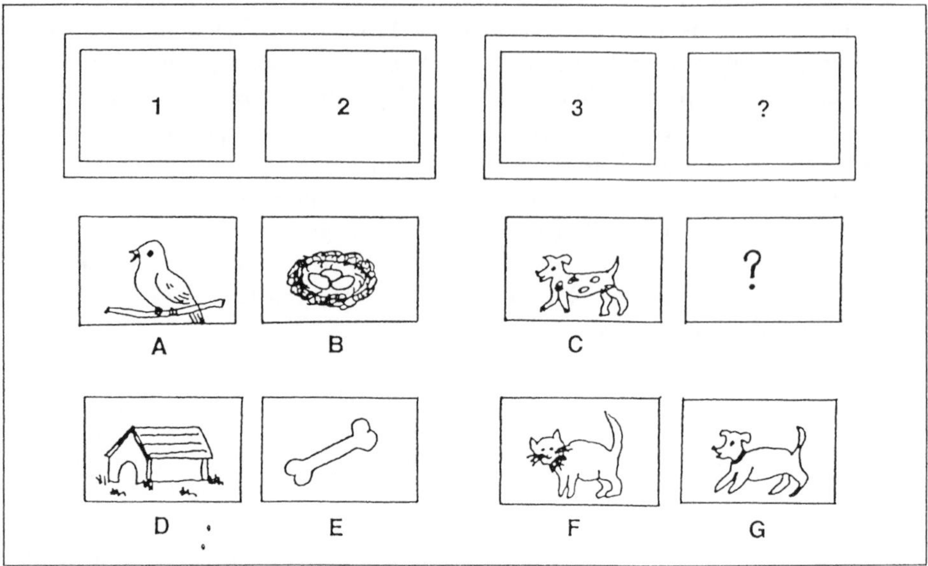

Figure 15.1 Schematic depiction of the pictorial analogy dog : doghouse :: bird : nest and the incorrect solution choices. Reprinted from U. Goswami and A. L. Brown (1990). Higher-order structure and relational reasoning: Contrasting analogical and thematic relations. *Cognition, 36*, 207–226, with permission from Excerpta Medica Inc.

the child's conceptual system. There was no evidence of matching on the basis of surface similarity (perceptual features). Goswami and Brown argued that analogical reasoning in children is highly dependent on relational knowledge.

In fact, relational knowledge is frequently an integral part of how objects behave or are used, and is not necessarily acquired later than perceptual knowledge (Goswami, 2008a). This was demonstrated by a recent connectionist simulation of the development of analogical reasoning. Leech, Mareschal, and Cooper (2008) used Goswami and Brown's (1989) causal relations data to demonstrate that analogical completion is an emergent property of the way that relational information is represented in a (neural) network that learns perceptual instances such as "apple," "cut apple," and "knife." The connectionist model learned how to complete analogies very successfully from instance-based learning. Further, it did not show a "relational shift" as it developed (a shift from object matching to relational matching in analogical solution; see Gentner, 1989). Sensory information is clearly rich in relational information as well as information about perceptual features. Indeed, for some relations, children might show an initial bias for relations over objects (Goswami, 2008b).

A study by Bulloch and Opfer (2009) with children aged 3 to 5 years showed exactly this effect. Bulloch and Opfer demonstrated that the "relational shift" was actually an epiphenomenon of children's developing sensitivity to the predictive accuracy of different similarity types. In their study, children had to generalize novel information in two types of problems, *offspring* problems and *prey* problems. In offspring problems, the children might have to decide whether a particular baby bug was the same kind as another baby bug that looked different. The different-looking baby had parents that were similar to the target baby. Here relational similarity was important, as the identity of a baby can generally be identified on the basis of its parentage (the baby's current appearance is not important, as in the Ugly Duckling story). In prey problems, the children might have to decide whether this same baby bug was likely to be the prey of a particular pair of larger bugs. This time a similar-looking baby bug, who was the prey of the target pair of bugs, had very different-looking parents. Here perceptual similarity was important, as the identity of prey is better predicted by what it looks like (e.g., an owl predator may eat many types of mice). Bulloch and Opfer were able to demonstrate increasing relational matches with age in the offspring condition, and increasing perceptual matches with age in the prey condition. They argued that even young children can be cognitively flexible, as long as they have a sufficient knowledge base.

Inhibition and analogical development. Richland and her colleagues (Richland et al., 2006; Morrison, Doumas, & Richland, 2006) made a different point about the causal reasoning data collected by Goswami and Brown (1989). They also discussed a related study by Goswami, Leevers, Pressley, and Wheelwright (1998), who studied item analogies based on two causal relations. Richland et al. (2006) pointed out that for two causal relations, younger children were not always as successful as older children, even when they appeared to have the same amount of relational knowledge (see Goswami et al., 1998). Richland et al. (2006) argued that the differential success rates with age could depend on general factors such as the ability to hold and integrate relations in working memory and the ability to inhibit competing irrelevant distractors. Accordingly, they designed a series of item analogies to test these ideas.

The item analogies involved relations based on familiar motion verbs, such as "kiss," "chase" and "feed." For example, an analogy could be *cat chases mouse :: boy chases girl*, or *dog chases cat chases mouse :: mum chases boy chases girl.* The latter type of analogy involved two relations, and was expected to require more working-memory capacity, which was expected to be present in older but not younger children. Inhibitory skills were tested in each kind of analogy by the presence of object distractors (e.g., for "boy chases girl," a cat was present in the scene as a distractor). Richland et al. found that all children tested (3- to 4-year-olds, 6- to 7-year-olds, 9- to 11-year-olds, and 13- to 14-year-olds) solved more single-relation analogies than two-relation analogies, but that only the 13- to 14-year-olds showed no effect of distraction. They suggested that maturational changes in the availability of inhibitory control (i.e., the ability to inhibit erroneously selecting the cat picture) explained these developmental effects.

In order to investigate possible neurocognitive changes in relational reasoning, Bunge and her colleagues carried out a functional magnetic resonance imaging (fMRI) study with children aged 8 to 12 years and adults (Crone et al., 2008). The fMRI imaging technique measures changes in blood flow, and shows which areas of the brain are most active during particular mental functions such as reasoning. The participants were asked to solve the Ravens Progressive Matrices, which depict increasingly complex visuo-spatial relations and are thought to provide a culture-free measure of fluid intelligence (see Sternberg, chapter 29, this volume). In adults, prefrontal cortex (PFC) is activated during relational reasoning, with rostrolateral PFC thought to be involved in relational integration and dorsolateral PFC thought to be involved in working-memory processes (see also Zelazo & Müller, chapter 22, this volume). Crone et al. speculated that children might show immature activation in one or both neural areas during relational reasoning. The data were complex, and interpretation was complicated by the fact that children made more errors than adults in all conditions (the conditions were, no relation, 1 relation, 2 relations). A major difference was that children engaged dorsolateral PFC even for the simpler 1-relation matrices, whereas adults did not. For rostrolateral PFC, children showed more activity in this region for the more complex 2-relation problems, as did adults, but unlike adults did not show *sustained* activity in this area. Crone et al. suggested that the children were failing in relational integration in these more complex problems, and were choosing a response without considering all the relations. Rostrolateral PFC specialization for relational integration was not yet complete. In order to be secure in this conclusion, a task is required in which children and adults can integrate relations *to the same extent* in the behavioral task. Once task difficulty is equated, the hypothesis that rostrolateral PFC specialization is not yet complete can be examined with more confidence.

The early availability of analogy? All analogy studies discussed so far have relied on the item-analogy task (A : B :: C : D). It is difficult to use the item-analogy task with children younger than 3 years of age, because of its formal nature. For this reason, problem-solving paradigms ("problem analogies") are more useful. Children are shown a problem A, and are also shown its solution. A different problem, B, is then presented. The measure of analogy is whether the child solves problem B by analogy to problem A.

A number of problem-analogy paradigms have been used with children aged 3 years and younger. For example, Chen, Sanchez, and Campbell (1997) devised a way of giving analogies to infants as young as 10 months of age, using a procedure first developed by Brown (1989) for 1.5- to 2-year-olds. In Chen et al.'s procedure, the infants came into the laboratory and were presented with an Ernie doll that was out of their reach. The Ernie doll was also behind a barrier (a box), and had a string attached to it that was lying on a cloth. In order to bring the doll within reach, the infants needed to learn to perform a series of actions. They had to remove the barrier, to pull on the cloth so that the string attached to the toy came within their grasp, and then to pull on the string itself so that they could reach Ernie. Following success on the first trial, two different toy problem scenarios were presented, each using identical tools (cloths, boxes, and strings). However, each problem appeared to be different to the problems that preceded it, as the cloths, boxes, and strings were always perceptually dissimilar to those encountered before. In addition, in each problem *two* strings and *two* cloths were provided, although only one pair could be used to reach the toy.

Chen et al. tested infants aged 10 and 13 months in the Ernie paradigm. They found spontaneous analogical reasoning in the 13-month group. Most infants of this age needed their parents to model the solution to the first toy-acquisition problem for them, but once the solution had been modeled they readily transferred it to the second and third problems. The younger infants (10 months) needed more salient perceptual support in order for reasoning by analogy to occur. They only showed spontaneous evidence of using analogies when the perceptual similarity between the problems was increased (for example, by using the same goal toy, such as the Ernie doll, in all three problems). This is not surprising, as the younger infants have less experience of the underlying causal structure in the different situations (e.g., box moving, string pulling), and so would be expected to need surface similarity cues to guide their inductions. Further examples of very young children reasoning by analogy are given in Goswami (1992, 2001).

Problem analogies have also been used to investigate how to support better analogical reasoning by young children. As sample size affects inductive inferences, one important factor is likely to be experiencing multiple exemplars. Brown and Kane (1988) designed some animal defense-mechanism analogies for 3-year-olds, comparing analogical transfer on the first analogy with transfer after three different analogies. The design depended on three pairs of biological analogies, one based on camouflage by color change, one based on camouflage by shape change, and one based on mimicry of a more dangerous animal. For example, the children were first told about the arctic fox, who changes color in winter, and the chameleon, who changes color to match his surroundings. They were then told about the walking stick insect, which can resemble a twig or leaf, and the pipe fish, which can resemble a reed. Finally, they were told about the crested rat, which can part its hair to show skunk-like markings, and the hawkmoth caterpillar, which has underside markings like a poisonous snake. The measure of analogical reasoning was performance on the final problem pair. Children were asked "How could the hawkmoth caterpillar stop the big bird that wants to eat him?"

In this context of multiple analogies (which Brown calls the A_1A_2, B_1B_2, C_1C_2 or "learning to learn" paradigm), 70–80% of the 3-year-olds reasoned by analogy on the final problem pair (i.e., unaided solution of C_2). In contrast, successful solution of the first problem pair (i.e., solution of A_2) was around 25%. The provision of multiple analogies was clearly important in fostering this high level of performance, but so was the children's interest in the biological relations on which the analogies were based. In a different study, Brown and Kane gave 3-year-olds the same manipulation (three pairs of analogies in the order A_1A_2, B_1B_2, C_1C_2), but instead of setting the analogies in the biological domain, they used story scenarios with toy characters. These characters had to solve problems based on stacking real objects or pulling real objects. Although these should also be familiar relations to young children, analogical reasoning on the third problem pair was much lower in this study, at around 40% correct. One possibility is that the relations necessary to the analogy (stacking, etc.) were not part of a causally relevant conceptual system in the same way that animal defense mechanisms were. In this sense they were quite different from the arguably less familiar but more systematically constrained relations about how biological kinds can avoid predation.

Summary

Inductive reasoning in children is facilitated by the nature of the function to be transferred, the existing state of the child's conceptual system, and the context in which the new function is first encountered. It is also affected by the efficiency of retrieval and inhibition processes. Inductive reasoning is similarity-based, and factors that facilitate or impede the recognition of which cues are most valid for similarity-based reasoning will facilitate or impede inductive reasoning. Some kinds of knowledge (e.g. about natural kinds) are acquired very early, enabling the development of a relatively sophisticated conceptual system at a young age (e.g., some children's dinosaur knowledge) and new knowledge is easily absorbed into the system, particularly in certain contexts (e.g., those promoting cognitive flexibility, such as experiencing a multitude of uses for a tool, or experiencing multiple exemplars for a new concept). In such circumstances, inductive reasoning will be difficult to impede (Brown, 1990).

Deductive Reasoning

Similar to inductive reasoning, recent research in deductive reasoning has also recognized the importance of inhibitory processes, the importance of working memory, and the importance of the mediation of background knowledge in constraining successful reasoning. As in inductive reasoning, younger children are assumed to have poorer inhibitory processes, to have less working-memory capacity, and to have less background knowledge. Hence, when other factors are not equal, deductive reasoning by younger children will be less successful.

The simplest form of deductive reasoning is the *syllogism*. In a syllogism, the reasoner is presented with two premises that allow only one logical conclusion. An example is: "All cats bark. Rex is a cat. Does Rex bark?" Deductive reasoning has also been studied via the selection task, which can also be called a *conditional syllogism*. The selection task is based on the logical implication "If *p* then *q*." Participants are asked to work out the minimum number of pieces of evidence that they need in order to decide whether the statement "If *p* then *q*" (i.e., if *p* is true, then *q* is true) is correct. Syllogistic reasoning and the selection task have been fairly widely used with young children, and will be discussed in some detail. The kinds of deductive reasoning considered by Piaget will not be discussed (see Miller, chapter 25, this volume). However, it is worth noting that studying a mental operation such as transitivity ("A is greater than B, B is greater than C, therefore A is greater than C") is also a study of deductive reasoning, as a transitive problem is a linear syllogism. The deduction that "A is greater than C" must follow given the premises "A is greater than B" and "B is greater than C." Physical reasoning (Wilkening and Cacchione, chapter 18, this volume), scientific reasoning (Kuhn, chapter 19, this volume), and causal reasoning (Koslowski & Masnick, chapter 14, this volume) can also involve deductive logic. Because these forms of deductive reasoning are extensively covered in other chapters, they will not be considered here.

Traditionally, deductive reasoning was thought to develop rather slowly in children. For example, Piaget thought that certain mental operations could only be applied to information by children older than around 6 to 7 years (the concrete operations, such as transitivity and class inclusion; see Miller, chapter 25, this volume). It was thought that more complex mental operations could only be applied by adolescents (such as scientific reasoning and hypothesis testing; see Kuhn, chapter 19, this volume). This is no longer the case. Instead, broadly speaking, age differences in the successful application of deductive reasoning are thought to depend on developmental differences in working-memory capacity, the availability and efficiency of the retrieval of long-term knowledge, and the efficiency of inhibitory processes.

Syllogistic reasoning

Aristotle apparently claimed that syllogistic reasoning represented the highest achievement in human rational thought (see Mayer, 1992). Perhaps unsurprisingly given this particular premise, young children and adults from non-Westernized cultures were for a long time thought to be very poor at syllogistic reasoning. The critical test upon which this conclusion was based involved syllogisms utilizing unfamiliar information. For example, peasants from Uzbekistan (a hot, plains region of Russia) were given syllogisms such as "In the Far North, where there is snow, all bears are white. Novaya Zemla is in the Far North. What color are the bears there?" (Luria, 1977). Snow was completely unfamiliar to these villagers, who performed rather poorly on such syllogisms. However, they did well on syllogisms that were based on familiar information, such as the factors that affect the growth of cotton. The same peasants could make logical deductions from premises such as "Cotton grows well where it is hot and dry. England is cold and damp. Can cotton grow there or not?"

The tendency of adults from traditional societies to reason poorly with unfamiliar premises was labeled the "empirical bias" by Scribner (1977). She found that west African Kpelle tribes people showed good syllogistic reasoning when given premises that they could empirically verify as being true, such as paying a house tax. However, when given premises that they could not verify as true, such as whether "Mr Smith" was a Kpelle man given that he was not a rice farmer and that all Kpelle men are rice farmers, they performed poorly or even refused to reason ("I don't know the man in person … I cannot answer that question"). Schooling had a remarkable effect on these adults' ability to make deductive inferences about unfamiliar premises (see also Ventura et al., 2008). Scribner argued that this was because education enables participants to set empirical considerations aside, and to utilize the premises as stated, independently of their plausibility. As young children are typically relatively unschooled, the assumption that young children were incapable of syllogistic reasoning about unfamiliar premises followed quite naturally from the cross-cultural studies.

For example, Hawkins, Pea, Glick, and Scribner (1984) gave 4- and 5-year-old preschoolers syllogistic reasoning problems that were either based on familiar knowledge ("bears have big teeth") or unfamiliar (incongruent) knowledge ("everything that flies has wheels"). The children did poorly with the incongruent problems, displaying an empirical bias. However, they did relatively well with fantasy premises ("Pogs wear blue boots. Tom is a pog. Does Tom wear blue boots?"). This prompted Dias and Harris (1988, 1990) to explore whether preschoolers can reason syllogistically about incongruent premises when the reasoning task is presented in a "fantasy" mode. The fantasy mode was created by telling the children that they should pretend that the experimenter was on another planet, and that everything on that planet was different from how it was in the world. For example, the experimenter would say "All cats bark. On that planet I saw that all cats bark," using a "make-believe" intonation, and would then verbally present the syllogism "All cats bark. Rex is a cat. Does Rex bark?" In these fantasy conditions, the levels of syllogistic reasoning shown by these young children approached ceiling levels. The "fantasy" effect was robust whether the premises were presented as referring to another planet, were presented using a make-believe intonation, or were presented using visual imagery ("Make a picture in your head"). Dias and Harris concluded that young children were capable of deductive reasoning, even about counterfactual premises, as long as logical problems were presented in a context that clearly marked for the child that the situation was make-believe.

Later work by Leevers and Harris (1999, 2000) extended these findings, and showed that the "make-believe" nature of the situation was not the critical factor in determining whether children showed deductive logic or an "empirical bias." Rather, the important feature was the *pragmatic aspects* of the reasoning situation. Situations that enabled young children to set empirical considerations aside, and to utilize the premises as stated, independently of their plausibility, facilitated the application of deductive reasoning. The manipulation used by Leevers and Harris was simply to ask the children to *think* about the problems ("I want you to *think about* what things would be like if it was true ... are you *thinking about* x?"). They then gave them counterfactual syllogisms of the type used by Dias and Harris, such as "All snow is black. Tom sees some snow. Is it black?" and "All ladybirds have stripes on their backs. Daisy sees a ladybird. Is it spotty?" Leevers and Harris found that "thinking about" the empirically incongruent premises facilitated syllogistic reasoning just as much as fantasy presentation of the same premises.

Conditional syllogisms: the selection task

The selection task provides a different measure of deductive reasoning, as the task is presented in such a way that participants do not have to make a logically valid inference. Rather, they have to choose the conditions that would enable a valid inference to be made. In the selection task, the participant is usually told about a certain state of affairs "If *p* then *q*." For example, the participant might be shown a pack of cards which all have a letter on one side and a number on the other side, and told the rule "If a card has a vowel on one side, then it has an even number on the other side" (Wason & Johnson-Laird, 1972). Four cards are then presented, showing respectively A, D, 4, 7. The participant's task is to decide the minimum number of cards that must be selected in order to validate the rule. The correct solution (A and 7, or *p* and *not-q*), is typically selected rather rarely (only 5 out of 128 adults selected this pair of cards in the original studies). However, it was soon discovered that this apparently massive failure in deductive logic could be reduced or eradicated by changing *pragmatic* aspects of the reasoning situation.

One of the first demonstrations of this was in an experiment that set the selection task in the context of a post office. Participants were told to imagine that they were postal workers sorting letters on a conveyor belt. They had to make sure that the post did not violate the rule "If a letter is sealed, then it has a 5p stamp on it." The pieces of evidence available were *p* (a sealed letter, shown face-down), *q* (a letter with a 5p stamp, shown face-up), *not-p* (an unsealed letter, shown face-down), and *not-q* (a letter with a 4p stamp, shown face-up). Most adult participants easily solved this version of the selection task, correctly selecting the sealed envelope and the envelope with the 4p stamp (Johnson-Laird, Legrenzi, & Sonino-Legrenzi, 1972). Following other demonstrations of successful reasoning in the selection task when presented in more familiar contexts, Wason and colleagues realized that difficulties in deductive reasoning are not usually determined by the intrinsic logical structure of the task. Rather, they are determined by the problem content or mode of presentation of the problem itself.

This conclusion about *deductive* reasoning in adults is obviously very similar to the conclusions that we reached about *inductive* reasoning in young children. If inductive reasoning is affected by problem content (is it familiar to children?) and by mode of presentation (the context in which the problem is encountered), then presumably deductive reasoning in children will be affected by the same parameters. A series of experiments utilizing "permission schemas" suggest that this is indeed the case. Children encounter permission rules all the time ("If you want to stay up late, you must finish your homework and have your bath," "If you are outside school premises, you must wear your blazer and your cap"). Harris and Nunez (1996) have shown that even 3- and 4-year-olds are sensitive to the pragmatics of permission and inhibition in the selection task. Harris and Nunez used a story-based format to present children with a variety of permission rules, and presented the conclusions via pictures, asking the children to select the picture that depicted a breach of the rule (the *p*, *not-q* picture). For example, in one study the children were told "This is a story about Sally. One day Sally wants to play outside. Her mum says that if she plays outside, she must put her coat on." The children were then shown 4 pictures: a picture of Sally outside with her coat on (*p*, *q*), a picture of Sally outside without her coat on (*p*, *not-q*), a picture of Sally inside with her coat on (*not-p*, *q*), and a picture of Sally inside without her coat on (*not-p*, *not-q*). The children were asked "Show me the picture of where Sally is being naughty and not doing what her mum told her." The correct answer was Sally outside without her coat on, the combination of *p* and *not-q*.

The majority of 3- and 4-year-old children were able to choose the picture of Sally outside without her coat on. This is presumably a familiar situation for young children, who often fail to see the need to wear a coat when going outside. Hence in principle it could be solved without making a logical deduction. However, Harris and Nunez were able to demonstrate that the children were also successful with novel permission rules tapping scenarios that they had not experienced, such as "Carol's mum says if she does some painting she should put her helmet on" and "Carol's mum says if she rides her bicycle she should put her apron on." Harris and Nunez's paradigm may be less demanding than the traditional selection task, as the children had to select the picture that depicted the combination of *p* and *not-q* rather than independently identify *p* and *not-q*. Nevertheless, their conclusion that 3- and 4-year-old children are quite capable of identifying breaches of a permission rule seems convincing.

The role of inhibitory and retrieval processes

More recent work on both conditional and syllogistic reasoning has considered the important developmental roles of the retrieval of background knowledge about the conditional or the premises in the syllogism, and the need to inhibit inappropriate or irrelevant information in order to make a successful deduction. For example, it has been suggested that there is a curvilinear age trend in the success of deductive reasoning. With development, there are firstly age-related increases in reasoning success as children get better at inhibiting competing information, and then there is a decline in success at older ages (65-plus) as inhibitory processes become less efficient (e.g., De Neys & Van Gelder, 2009). This interesting idea was first proposed by Stanovich and West (2000). They pointed out that some forms of logical deduction require the inhibition of beliefs based on real-world knowledge (e.g., the inhibition of prior background knowledge, such as the belief that cats do not bark), and that belief inhibition is likely to be more successful in older than in younger children. The critical test of belief inhibition is when belief and logic conflict (as in "All mammals can walk. Whales are mammals. Therefore, whales can walk"). In these "conflict" syllogisms, the conclusion is logically valid, but it is unbelievable (Kokis, Macpherson, Toplak, West, & Stanovich, 2002).

In a recent study, De Neys and Van Gelder (2009) used such "conflict" syllogisms to explore whether curvilinear age trends would be found when comparing 12-year-old children, university students in their twenties, and older adults (aged 65 or older). They confirmed that when given syllogisms where beliefs and logic were in conflict, as in "All mammals can walk. Whales are mammals. Therefore, whales can walk," reasoning success increased from childhood to early adulthood, but then declined later in life. A control condition tested syllogistic reasoning when beliefs and logic were not in conflict (e.g., "All mammals can walk. Apes are mammals. Therefore, apes can walk"). For these syllogisms, no curvilinear age trend was found. Instead, all groups performed close to ceiling. De Neys and Van Gelder concluded that although inhibitory capacities do not always mediate reasoning performance, inhibitory processing plays an important role in successful deductive reasoning.

Houde and his colleagues used a different method to investigate the role of inhibition in deductive reasoning, *negative priming* (Moutier, Plagne-Cayeux, Melot, & Houde, 2006). They also used "conflict" syllogisms as a critical test, so that children had to inhibit "unbelievable = invalid" reasoning strategies and reason logically on the basis of the premises. For example, in a conflict syllogism such as "All elephants are hay eaters. All hay eaters are light. All elephants are light," the conclusion is deductively valid, but unbelievable. This unbelievability means that the child must inhibit real-world knowledge about elephants being heavy in order to judge the syllogism as valid. In the experiment, these "conflict" syllogisms were followed immediately by "non-conflict" syllogisms in which the deduction was both believable and valid. In these non-conflict syllogisms, the opposite deduction was required (e.g., in the non-conflict syllogism, children had to confirm that all elephants are heavy). The experimenters argued that a role for inhibitory control in syllogistic reasoning would be revealed by a significant drop in reasoning success on the non-conflict syllogisms when preceded by the conflict syllogisms (a negative priming effect). The study tested children aged 8 to 10 years, and indeed found a strong negative priming effect. The authors concluded that the inhibitory and logical components of syllogistic reasoning were to some extent dissociated. Note that this theoretical position also predicts that when a young child does not have to inhibit a belief, perhaps because their real-world knowledge is not yet extensive enough to include this belief, then their syllogistic reasoning performance may be *better* than that of older children and adults. Jacobs and Potenza (1991) have indeed shown that 6-year-old children out-perform adults on statistical base rate problems where beliefs about salient social stereotypes impede logical reasoning. For example, when told that a sample of 30 girls contained 10 girls trying out to be cheerleaders and 20 trying out for the school band, and given a stereotypical description of a popular and pretty girl who loved people, the young children were more successful at concluding that the person selected was more likely to be trying for the band. This was assumed to be because they lacked a strong social stereotype for cheerleaders.

Clearly, when children are reasoning about pragmatically plausible content, then their deductive reasoning can be as efficient as that of adults. Difficulties in deductive reasoning do not usually appear to be determined by the intrinsic logical structure of a particular task. Rather, they are determined by the problem content or mode of presentation, by the availability of relevant background knowledge, and by the efficiency with which irrelevant background knowledge can be inhibited – which itself interacts with availability. When children lack relevant background knowledge, they may actually reason *more* efficiently than adults in certain circumstances.

Summary

Deductive reasoning in children is affected by the nature of the problem to be solved and the context in which the problem is first encountered. As long as deductive reasoning is tested using content that is represented in the child's existing conceptual system (e.g., permission rules about familiar activities), then young children can perform successfully in deductive reasoning tasks. The same is true of adults, who for example are impaired in reasoning about permission rules that instantiate very abstract concepts (the A, D, 4, 7 study). Similarly, the context of problem presentation can impede the application of deductive logic by both children and adults. If syllogisms based on unfamiliar premises are presented to unschooled adults, if schooled adults are given logical problems where there is highly salient real-world knowledge to be inhibited, and if counterfactual syllogisms are presented to children in ways that fail to signal that they should reason about the premises as given, then children and adults show poor deductive reasoning. However, if children and adults recognize that they must utilize the premises as stated, irrespective of their truth value, and ignore their prior beliefs, then deductive reasoning is successful.

Conclusion

As long as children are reasoning in familiar domains, they are capable of inductive reasoning, and as long as they are reasoning in pragmatically acceptable scenarios, they are capable of deductive reasoning. Both inductive and deductive reasoning are available early in development. Children are not inductively "perceptually bound," as was believed for so long, able to transfer knowledge only when surface appearances suggest that transfer is appropriate. Children can go beyond surface features and transfer knowledge on the basis of relational similarity, even when perceptual attributes are pitted against category membership (e.g., Gelman & Markman, 1987). Indeed, in some circumstances children may privilege relations over perceptual attributes (Bulloch & Opfer, 2009). The key to successful induction is recognizing which cues are most valid for similarity-based reasoning. For deductive reasoning, children are not bound by the "empirical bias," able only to reason about premises that they know from personal experience to be true. They can make deductive inferences about fantasy premises or about premises that are contrary to their real-world knowledge, as long as they understand that the premises should be accepted as valid for the purpose of deduction (Harris & Leevers, 2000). They can also reason validly about conditional syllogisms, and inhibit beliefs that conflict with logic under certain circumstances. However, as both inhibitory processes and working-memory capacity increase with age, in general older children will reason more successfully than younger children.

There is thus considerable continuity across the lifespan in both inductive and deductive reasoning. In both children and adults, successful inductive and deductive reasoning appears to be influenced by similar factors and subject to similar constraints. It is easy to make children perform poorly in reasoning experiments. The experimenter simply has to give them unsuitable tasks based on unfamiliar concepts. It is also possible to make adults perform poorly in reasoning experiments. Of course, it would be absurd to argue that there are no developmental differences between children and adults (or between younger and older children). There are considerable differences in many experimental paradigms. The key point is that these differences are not linked to the intrinsic logical requirements of the reasoning tasks instantiated in these paradigms. Rather, they reflect a variety of general factors such as working-memory capacity (see also Halford & Andrews, chapter 27, this volume). Children become able to learn almost anything with appropriate effort, tuition, skill, and strategies as they get older. The important point for developmental analyses is that while factors such as working-memory capacity and inhibition affect performance, their effects do not demonstrate the unavailability of basic competence.

References

Brown, A. L. (1989). Analogical learning and transfer: What develops? In S. Vosniadou & A. Ortony (Eds.), *Similarity and analogical reasoning* (pp. 369–412). Cambridge: Cambridge University Press.

Brown, A. L. (1990). Domain-specific principles affect learning and transfer in children. *Cognitive Science, 14*, 107–133.

Brown, A. L., & Kane, M. J. (1988). Preschool children can learn to transfer: Learning to learn and learning by example. *Cognitive Psychology, 20*, 493–523.

Bulloch, M. J., & Opfer, J. E. (2009). What makes relational reasoning smart? Revisiting the perceptual-to-relational shift in the development of generalization. *Developmental Science, 12*, 114–122.

Chen, Z., Sanchez, R. P., & Campbell, T. (1997). From beyond to within their grasp: Analogical problem solving in 10- and 13-month-olds. *Developmental Psychology, 33*, 790–801.

Crone, E. A., Wendelken, C., van Leijenhorst, L., Honomichl, R. D., Christoff, K., & Bunge, S. A. (2008). Neurocognitive development of relational reasoning. *Developmental Science, 12*, 55–66.

Defeyter, M. A., & German, T. P. (2003). Acquiring an understanding of design: Evidence from children's insight problem solving. *Cognition, 89*, 133–155.

De Neys, W., & Van Gelder, E. (2009). Logic and belief across the lifespan: The rise and fall of belief inhibition during syllogistic reasoning. *Developmental Science, 12*, 123–130.

Dias, M. G., & Harris, P. L. (1988). The effect of make-believe play on deductive reasoning. *British Journal of Developmental Psychology, 6*, 207–221.

Dias, M. G., & Harris, P. L. (1990). The influence of the imagination on reasoning by young children. *British Journal of Developmental Psychology, 8*, 305–318.

Duncker, K. (1945). On problem solving. *Psychological Monographs, 58* (whole No. 270). Washington, DC: American Psychological Association.

Gelman, S. A. (1988). The development of induction within natural kind and artifact properties. *Cognitive Psychology, 20*, 65–95.

Gelman, S. A., & Coley, J. D. (1990). The importance of knowing a dodo is a bird: Categories and inferences in 2-year-old children. *Developmental Psychology, 26*, 796–804.

Gelman, S. A., & Markman, E. M. (1986). Categories and induction in young children. *Cognition, 23*, 183–209.

Gelman, S. A., & Markman, E. M. (1987). Young children's inductions from natural kinds: The role of categories and appearances. *Child Development, 58*, 1532–1541.

Gentner, D. (1989). The mechanisms of analogical learning. In S. Vosniadou & A. Ortony (Eds.), *Similarity and analogical reasoning*, (pp. 199–241). London: Cambridge University Press.

German, T. P., & Defeyter, M. A. (2000). Immunity to "functional fixedness" in young children. *Psychonomic Bulletin and Review, 7*, 707–712.

Goswami, U. (1991). Analogical reasoning: What develops? A review of research and theory. *Child Development, 62*, 1–22.

Goswami, U. (1992). *Analogical reasoning in children*. Hillsdale, NJ: Erlbaum.

Goswami, U. (1996). Analogical reasoning and cognitive development. *Advances in Child Development and Behaviour, 26*, pp. 91–138. San Diego, CA: Academic Press.

Goswami, U. (2001). Analogical reasoning in children. In D. Gentner, K. Holyoak, & B. Kokinov (Eds.), *Analogy: Interdisciplinary perspectives*. Cambridge, MA: MIT Press.

Goswami, U. (2008a). *Cognitive development: The learning brain*. Philadelphia, PA: Psychology Press of Taylor & Francis.

Goswami, U. (2008b). Analogy and the brain: A new perspective on relational primacy. *Behavioural and Brain Sciences, 31*, 387–8.

Goswami, U., & Brown, A. L. (1989). Melting chocolate and melting snowmen: Analogical reasoning and causal relations. *Cognition, 35*, 69–95.

Goswami, U., & Brown, A. L. (1990). Higher-order structure and relational reasoning: Contrasting analogical and thematic relations. *Cognition, 36*, 207–226.

Goswami, U., Leevers, H., Pressley, S., & Wheelwright, S. (1998). Causal reasoning about pairs of relations and analogical reasoning in young children. *British Journal of Developmental Psychology, 16*, 553–569.

Goswami, U., & Pauen, S. (2005). The effects of a "family" analogy on class inclusion reasoning by young children. *Swiss Journal of Psychology, 64*, 115–124.

Gutheil, G., & Gelman, S. A. (1997). Children's use of sample size and diversity information within basic-level categories. *Journal of Experimental Child Psychology, 64*, 159–174.

Harris, P. L., & Leevers, H. J. (2000). Reasoning from false premises. In P. Mitchell & K. J. Riggs (Eds), *Children's reasoning and the mind* (pp. 67–86). Hove, UK: Psychology Press.

Harris, P. L., & Nunez, M. (1996). Understanding of permission rules by preschool children. *Child Development, 67*, 1572–1591.

Hawkins, J., Pea, R. D., Glick, J., & Scribner, S. (1984). "Merds that laugh don't like mushrooms": Evidence for deductive reasoning by preschoolers. *Developmental Psychology, 20*, 584–594.

Heit, E. (2000). Properties of inductive reasoning. *Psychonomic Bulletin and Review, 7*, 569–592.

Holyoak, K. J., Junn, E. N., & Billman, D. O. (1984). Development of analogical problem-solving skill. *Child Development, 55*, 2042–2055.

Holyoak, K. J., & Thagard, P. (1995). *Mental leaps*. Cambridge, MA: MIT Press.

Jacobs, J. E. & Potenza, M. (1991). The use of judgement heuristics to make social and object decisions: A developmental perspective. *Child Development, 62*, 166–178.

Johnson-Laird, P. N., Legrenzi, P., & Sonino-Legrenzi, M. (1972). Reasoning and a sense of reality. *British Journal of Psychology, 63*, 395–400.

Kalish, C. W., & Gelman, S. A. (1992). On wooden pillows: Multiple classifications and children's category-based inductions. *Child Development, 63*, 1536–1557.

Kokis, J. V., Macpherson, R., Toplak, M. E., West, R. F., & Stanovich, K. E. (2002). Heuristic and analytic processing: Age trends and associations with cognitive ability and cognitive styles. *Journal of Experimental Child Psychology, 83*, 26–52.

Leech, R., Mareschal, D., & Cooper, R. P. (2008). Analogy as relational priming: A developmental and computational perspective on the origins of a complex cognitive skill. *Behavioural and Brain Sciences, 31*, 357–378.

Leevers, H. J., & Harris, P. L. (1999). Persisting effects of instruction on young children's syllogistic reasoning with incongruent and abstract premises. *Thinking and Reasoning, 5*, 145–173.

Leevers, H. J., & Harris, P. L. (2000). Counterfactual syllogistic reasoning in normal 4-year-olds, children with learning disabilities and children with autism. *Journal of Experimental Child Psychology, 76*, 64–87.

Luria, A. R. (1977). *Cognitive development: Its cultural and social foundations*. Cambridge, MA: Harvard University Press.

Maier, N. R. F. (1931). Reasoning in humans II: The solution of a problem and its appearance in consciousness. *Journal of Comparative Psychology, 12*, 181–194.

Mayer, R. E. (1992). *Thinking, problem solving, cognition* (2nd ed.). New York: W. H. Freeman and Co.

Morrison, R. G., Doumas, L. A. A., & Richland, L. E. (2006). *The development of analogical reasoning in children: A computational account*. Proceedings of the Twenty-Ninth Annual Conference of the Cognitive Science Society. Mahwah, NJ: Erlbaum.

Moutier, S., Plagne-Cayeux, S., Melot, A-M., & Houde, O. (2006). Syllogistic reasoning and belief-bias inhibition in schoolchildren: Evidence from a negative priming paradigm. *Developmental Science, 9*, 166–172.

Piaget, J., Montangero, J., & Billeter, J. (1977). La formation des corrélats. In J. Piaget (Ed.), *Recherches sur L'abstraction réfléchissante I* (pp. 115–129). Paris: Presses Universitaires de France.

Richland, L. E., Morrison, R. G., & Holyoak, K. J. (2006). Children's development of analogical reasoning: Insights from scene analogy problems. *Journal of Experimental Child Psychology, 94*, 249–273.

Scribner, S. (1977). Modes of thinking and ways of speaking: Culture and logic reconsidered. In P. N. Johnson-Laird and P. C. Wason (Eds.), *Thinking: Readings in cognitive science* (pp. 483–500). Cambridge: Cambridge University Press.

Stanovich, K. E., & West, R. F. (2000). Individual differences in reasoning: Implications for the rationality debate. *Behavioural and Brain Sciences, 23*, 645–726.

Sternberg, R. J., & Nigro, G. (1980). Developmental patterns in the solution of verbal analogies. *Child Development*, *51*, 27–38.

Wason, P. C., & Johnson-Laird, P. N. (1972). *Psychology of Reasoning: Structure and Content*. Cambridge, MA: Harvard University Press.

Ventura, P., Pattamadilok, C., Fernandes, T., Klein, O., Morais, J., Kolinsky, R. (2008). Schooling in Western culture promotes context-free processing. *Journal of Experimental Child Psychology*, *100*, 215–224.

CHAPTER SIXTEEN

The Development of Moral Reasoning

Larry P. Nucci and Matthew Gingo

The contemporary study of the development of moral reasoning originated with the account provided by Piaget (1932), subsequently extended by Kohlberg (1963/2008). While differing in their details, both explanations held that moral reasoning progresses through a universal sequence of stages eventuating in conceptualizations of morality that transcend the particulars of culture and context. Over the past several decades, the study of moral reasoning has largely been about challenges and responses to the basic story contained in the Piaget/Kohlberg theory. These challenges and revisions have led to a serious reworking of our notions of moral development, and have left a number of issues unresolved. Moreover, what had once been largely a developmental psychological enterprise is now home to a variety of subfields of psychology and philosophy, including neuropsychology, as well as philosophy of mind, and experimental moral philosophy. This chapter will review some of those challenges, and the attendant changes they have brought to our view of moral development.

Recent work on moral development can be viewed in terms of three main interrelated issues. The first has to do with the structure of moral cognition. Questions have been raised in terms of the breadth of what should be included within the moral domain, whether morality can be defined in terms of a single developmental progression, and whether age-related changes in moral cognition constitute a stage-like sequence. The second set of questions has to do with the generality of moral concepts, and how moral cognition interacts with context and culture. Questions have been raised regarding the degree of internal consistency displayed by individuals in their moral judgments across contexts, and whether morality can be viewed as independent of cultural norms. Finally, questions have been raised regarding whether morality is a function of judgment at all, or whether it is instead the result of non-rational factors such as emotion and socialization. While theorists and researchers often address more than one of these issues in a single paradigm, as a heuristic this chapter will examine each of these three major sets of issues separately.

The Structure and Scope of Morality

The moral domain

For both Piaget (1932) and Kohlberg (1963/2008), moral development moves from earlier stages, in which morality is intertwined with self-interest and social norms, to later more mature stages, in which morality as justice is differentiated from and displaces social convention as the basis for moral judgments. During the 1960s and early 1970s a considerable amount of evidence was generated in support of the six-stage sequence of moral development described by Kohlberg (1963/2008). However in the late 1960s, results from longitudinal studies began to turn up evidence that was in conflict with the assumptions of Kohlberg's stage theory. In particular, researchers uncovered that a number of young adults appeared to move from Kohlberg's stage 4 (a developmental period in which morality is defined by the laws of society) to what looked to be a less mature form of reasoning based on the immediate context and self-interest typical of children at Kohlberg's stage 2 (Kohlberg & Kramer, 1969). This apparent adolescent regression went contrary to the basic assumptions of structuralist stage theory, and posed a major challenge to the Kohlbergian account.

Kohlberg and Kramer (1969) initially explained these results as a temporary regression brought on either by the pressures of college life, or as regression "in the service of the ego" (Turiel, 1974, p. 16) that would lead to developmental progress. This assumption was buttressed by findings that their young adult subjects did not long remain at stage 2, but moved on to the next stage (5) within Kohlberg's framework (Kohlberg & Kramer, 1969). On closer examination, however, the moral reasoning of these young adults turned out not to have matched the instrumentalist thinking of stage 2 children (Turiel, 1974). Instead, the apparent regression reflected a conflation of an understanding of convention as the particular construction of a given social system with morality itself. In the thinking of these young relativists, there was no particular force to the morality of any given system of conventions, and thus no reason to favor the morality of one system over another. More importantly, no one, according to the line of reasoning employed by these subjects, had the moral right to privilege one conventional system of laws over those of another. Thus, morality had to be worked out by individuals within each situation as best as one could based upon one's reading of what was right in the context. Behind this relativism, however, there appeared to be a moral principle of mutual respect, and just reciprocity. Following this thread, researchers committed to Kohlberg's sequence felt that they had accounted for the apparent developmental discrepancy uncovered in their longitudinal studies (Turiel, 1974). This period of relativism was explained as a transition in which the conventional basis of stage 4 reasoning was replaced by post-conventional (stage 5) principled moral thought.

While the above explanations seemed to satisfy many in the Kohlberg camp (Colby, Kohlberg, Gibbs, & Lieberman, 1983), others began to explore whether in fact the distinctions between convention and moral issues of justice being made by young adults in the midst of their apparent period of relativism was particular to that period of development, or if it reflected a manifestation of conceptual frameworks from earlier ages.

The latter seemed to be a likely possibility since all developmental theories presuppose that concepts do not simply appear out of nowhere, but have a developmental history. Following up on that hunch has led to one of the most fruitful lines of inquiry in the field (for a discussion of this early history see Turiel, 2008).

Domain theory: distinguishing morality from the conventional and personal. Following his analysis of the reasoning of the relativists uncovered in Kohlberg's longitudinal work, Turiel (1975) and his colleagues began to explore whether young children also maintain a set of conceptual distinctions between morality (non-arbitrary and unavoidable features of social relations pertaining to matters of human welfare and fairness) and matters of convention (contextually dependent and agreed-upon social rules). What they discovered was that very young children differentiate between matters of convention and morality, employing criteria consistent with the formalist properties of these two types of social regulation (Turiel, 1978). Since then, numerous studies have been conducted that have reported results concordant with these initial findings (for recent reviews see Smetana, 2006; Turiel, 2002). This research has indicated that the differentiation between morality and convention emerges at very young ages (as young as age 3; Smetana & Braeges, 1990) and is maintained by individuals across cultures (Turiel, 2002). With some variations in specific findings regarding convention, the distinction between morality and convention has been reported in each of the cultures examined. In all cases, children and adolescents have been found to treat moral issues entailing harm and injustice in much the same way. Children across cultural groups and social classes have been found to treat moral transgressions, such as unprovoked harm, as wrong regardless of the presence or absence of rules, and have viewed the wrongness of such moral transgressions as holding universally for children in other cultures or settings, and not just for their own group. The basic finding of a conceptual distinction between morality and convention has proven to be among the most robust phenomena uncovered by psychological research. Most recently, it has been discovered that this basic distinction is maintained even by children with autism (James & Blair, 2005; Leslie, Mallon, & Dicorcia, 2006).

The domains of morality and convention are further differentiated from conceptions of personal matters of privacy and individual discretion (Nucci, 1996). While morality and convention deal with aspects of interpersonal regulation, concepts of personal issues refer to actions that comprise the private aspects of one's life, such as the contents of a diary, and issues that are matters of preference and choice (e.g., friends, music, hairstyle) rather than right or wrong. It has been proposed that the establishment of control over the personal domain emerges from the need to establish boundaries between the self and others, and is critical to the establishment of personal autonomy and individual identity (Nucci, 1996). Studies conducted in northeastern Brazil (Lins Dyer & Nucci, 2007; Milnitsky-Sapiro, Turiel, & Nucci, 2006; Nucci, Camino, & Sapiro, 1996), Colombia (Ardilla-Rey & Killen, 2001), Hong Kong (Yau & Smetana, 2003a), China (Helwig, Yang, Nucci, Yun, & To, 2009; Yau & Smetana, 2003b), and Japan (Hasebe, Nucci, & Nucci, 2004) as well as the United States (cf. Nucci, 2001) have shown that children and adolescents judge personal issues to be within their jurisdiction. Evidence has been presented that parents within the United States (Nucci & Smetana, 1996; Nucci & Weber, 1995), China (Yau & Smetana, 2003b), and Brazil (Nucci & Milnitsky Sapiro,

1995) provide for a zone of personal discretion and privacy with children as young as 3- to 4-years-of-age. Justifications that children and their parents provide for why behaviors and decisions should be treated as personal and within the child's jurisdiction focus on the role of such choices in developing the child's autonomy and personal identity, and the child or adolescent's moral right to have such discretion (for reviews see Nucci, 1996; Smetana, 2005).

This set of results has led to a reconceptualization of the breadth and scope of what falls within moral judgment. Rather than entailing a process of gradual differentiation of morality out of convention and personal preference as envisioned by Kohlberg (1969), social-domain theory posits that conceptions of morality, convention, and other social concepts are structured within what Piaget (1985) referred to as partial systems or subsystems. On this account, each partial system forms an internally equilibrated structure that in certain contexts may interact with other systems requiring interdomain equilibration or coordination. These partial systems are thought to correspond to qualitatively different aspects of social interaction, and to follow discrete, identifiable courses of development (Turiel, 1978, 1979).

Observational research has reported that the patterns of social interactions associated with moral events among children and between children and adults focus on features intrinsic to the acts such as the harm that is caused or the fairness or unfairness of actions. Interactions surrounding conventional events, on the other hand, focus upon aspects of the social order such as the governing rules, social expectations, wishes of authority, and elements of the social structure and hierarchy. Finally, social interactions involving personal-domain issues focus on claims made by children and adolescents that actions involve matters of choice or privacy. Often these exchanges with adults include conflict and/or resistance to adult authority (for reviews see Nucci, 2001; Smetana, 2006).

Development within domains: morality and convention. Conceptual development within each of the domains just described follows a distinctive pattern. Development of morality is structured by changes in underlying conceptualizations of justice and human welfare (Damon, 1977; Nucci & Turiel, 2007). Development of convention is structured by underlying conceptualizations of social systems and social organization (Turiel, 1983). Finally, development of concepts about the personal is structured by underlying conceptions of self, identity, and personhood (Nucci, 1996). It is beyond the scope of this chapter to present a detailed description of each developmental sequence. What follows are descriptions of general patterns for development of morality and convention with references to sources where detailed descriptions can be found. A summary of the levels of development of social convention along with age-related changes in the moral domain is presented in table 16.1.

Moral development. Morality begins in early childhood with a focus upon issues of harm to the self and others. Davidson, Turiel, and Black (1983) found that up to about age 7 moral judgment is primarily regulated by concerns for maintaining welfare and avoiding harm and is limited to directly accessible acts. Young children's morality is not yet structured by understandings of fairness as reciprocity. Thus, young children have a difficult time making moral judgments when the needs of more than one person are at stake

Table 16.1 Age-Related Changes in Moral and Conventional Development

Ages	*Moral (harm/helping)*	*Conceptual framework*	
		Moral (distributive justice)	*Convention*
5–7	Recognition of prima facie obligations (e.g., not to hit and hurt others).	Keeping all common goods (e.g., toys) is wrong. Keeping favored goods while sharing non-favored is "fair."	Conventions tied to observed regularities in social interaction. Gender roles, table manners, modes of dress all should conform to general patterns defined by convention.
8–10	Harm viewed as wrong and helping as "right" in most contexts. Non-moral elements generally not taken into account. "Self-defense" viewed in direct reciprocity tit-for-tat terms. Indirect harm "not returning lost money" viewed in same terms as direct harm "stealing."	What is fair is equal distribution. Direct reciprocity means equal pay for equal output.	Negation of convention is based on observed inconsistencies and exceptions to conventional norms (e.g., some women wear pants).
10–12		Concerns for equity (taking into account special needs or capacities of others) now coordinated with reciprocity in structuring decisions about distribution of goods.	Affirmation of convention is based on concrete understanding that conventional rules maintain order (keep people from running in the halls). Top-down conception of social authority and rules. People in charge make rules that preserve order. No understanding that conventions help structure social systems.

12–14	Increased attention to multiple factors in moral situations. Inability to coordinate these multiple factors leads to ambiguity. Not returning lost money not same as stealing since the protagonist did not actively cause the loss. Tit-for-tat response seen as wrong, but to do otherwise is unsatisfying since there is no "revenge." Confusion between personal choice and a right to not act in a moral direction.	Consolidation of the relations between equity and equality in conceptions of what is fair and caring in social relations.	Negation of conventions as "nothing but" the expectations or the dictates of authority. The arbitrary nature of convention is viewed as undercutting the force of a rule. Acts are evaluated independent of rules.
16–18	Ability to coordinate multiple factors allows for resolution in moral direction. Not returning lost money not same as theft. However, keeping the money has the same consequence as theft and is therefore wrong. To help a former antagonist does not allow for "revenge," however, compassion should take priority in a case of obvious need. A personal choice is clearly differentiated from a moral right.		Emergence of systematic concepts of social structure. Conventions are understood as helping to maintain social systems and also symbolically reflect the social organization and social hierarchy. Conventions are viewed as normative and binding within social system of fixed roles and hierarchical organization. Members of a social group are expected to adhere to conventions.

(Damon, 1977). In addition, there is little subtlety in young children's concepts of moral harm, and in their moral evaluations of situations involving helping others (Eisenberg, 1986; Nucci & Turiel, 2007).

Research on children's distributive and retributive justice reasoning shows that as they develop, children form increased understandings of benevolence, equality, reciprocity, and equity (Damon, 1977, 1980; Lapsley, 1982). With respect to sharing, for example, the 4-year-olds' premise that they should be allowed to have more of a desired good (e.g., candies) as long as they don't keep all of it, is replaced by the idea that distributive decisions should be based on strict equality or reciprocity. This strict reciprocity is replaced in turn by an attention to equity as well as equality such that those with special needs, such as poor or handicapped people, deserve special attention (Damon, 1977, 1980). The pattern of development reflects an increased ability of children to coordinate elements of moral situations within their justice reasoning. In the case of distributive justice this increased capacity to handle complexity leads to a linear growth pattern of steady incremental changes in moral thinking. When it comes to reasoning about issues of human welfare, however, the developmental pattern is more complex.

Recent studies of children's reasoning about situations involving harm or helping behavior have indicated that development of concepts about moral culpability and obligation with regard to such issues follows a U-shaped pattern rather than a linear one. As we saw above, very young children understand that unprovoked hitting and hurting someone is morally wrong. As one would expect, reasoning about this straightforward moral transgression does not change with age (Nucci & Turiel, 2007). What do appear to change, however, are children's concepts about indirect forms of harm, such as not letting another person know that they have dropped some money and keeping it for oneself instead. When this situation is placed in a real-life context, 8-year-old children and 16-year-old adolescents are more likely to judge keeping the money as wrong than are 13-year olds. Moreover, 13-year-olds are far more likely to claim that they would have a right to keep the money than are 8-year-olds or 16-year-olds (Nucci & Turiel, 2007). Interestingly, 13-year-old children are as likely to return the money as 8- and 16-year-olds when the person who drops the money is described as handicapped. Across ages nearly all children agree that it would be wrong to keep the money in that case. Thus, the reasoning of the 13-year-olds does not fit a pattern of purely instrumentalist moral thinking. Instead, several factors related to their increased understanding of the social world are converging to make the moral evaluation of the situation more variable. Development is allowing young adolescents to recognize the moral ambiguity of non-prototypical situations. In this case, the loss of the money did not occur because of an action taken by the observer; the observer did not reach in and take it from the other person's pocket. What is more, in the absence of an observer the money would have been lost in any case. To quote one of the adolescents in this ongoing study "It's [the money] in never land." Added to this moral ambiguity is the confusion adolescents experience as they sort out the differences in meaning among free will, personal choice (as in the personal domain), and a moral right to do something. For the 8-year-olds, the situation holds no ambiguity. There is a simple line drawn between the money and its owner. Hence there is no problem. By age 16, most of the adolescents in the study had resolved the complexities identified by the 13-year-olds, and after acknowledging the ambiguities inherent in the situation, judged that the act of observing rendered the bystander obligated to return the money.

Similar U-shaped developmental patterns were found for helping behavior in early adolescents (Nucci & Turiel, 2007), and again in young adulthood (early 20s) (Eisenberg, Cumberland, Guthrie, Murphy, & Shephard, 2005). These fluctuating patterns of development signal periods of increased attention to new elements of moral situations and mark transitions to more complex integrations of moral thought.

Social convention. The development of concepts about convention also presents an oscillating pattern between periods affirming the importance of convention, and phases negating the basis of the affirmations of the prior phase. Seven levels of development have been described from early childhood to early adulthood (Turiel, 1983). Evidence for these levels comes from cross-sectional (Nucci, Becker, & Horn, 2004; Turiel, 1975), cross-cultural (Hollos, Lies, & Turiel, 1986), experimental (Nucci & Weber, 1991), and longitudinal studies (see Turiel, 1998). Concepts about convention reflect the person's underlying conceptions of social organization. Within the school years, for example, the typical 10-year-old affirms convention as serving to maintain social order. Along with this is a concrete sense of social hierarchy. People in charge of schools make up rules to keep everyone from running in the hallways. At the next level of development, typical of early adolescence, children enter into a negation phase in which the prior basis for affirming convention, now becomes viewed through the lens of the arbitrariness of the norms, and their status as "simply" the dictates of authority. Later in middle adolescence, the dismissal of convention is replaced by an understanding that conventions have meaning within a larger framework. Thus, conventions are seen as normative and binding within a social system of fixed roles and obligations. The oscillating pattern of development of convention indicates the difficulty children have in accounting for the function of arbitrary social norms and illustrates the slow process of reflection and construction that precedes the adolescents' view of convention as important to the structuring of social systems.

General issues of development. The oscillating or U-shaped patterns of development being ascribed to morality and convention in this more recent work would appear to be at variance with more long-standing depictions of development as entailing a succession of improvements as children move from one developmental stage to the next (Colby & Kohlberg, 1987). However, U-shaped growth patterns appear to be normative across developmental domains including language, cognition, and physical abilities, and may be a general property of all dynamic systems (Gershkoff & Thelen, 2004).

Moral development and inter-domain interactions

Work demonstrating the conceptual independence of morality and convention has focused on children's and adults' reasoning about prototypical issues. Unprovoked harm is an example of a prototypical moral issue, while addressing teachers by their titles rather than first names is an example of a prototypical conventional issue. Many everyday social judgments, however, involve overlap across domains necessitating the sorts of interdomain equilibrations envisioned in Piaget's (1985) theory. When overlaps occur an individual's reasoning will reflect both the degree to which the individual attends to the domain-salient features of the given issue and the degree to which an individual is able to bring elements across domains into coordination or harmony. In some cases conventions merely codify, or are consistent with, morality. In other cases conventions that serve to maintain social organization are in conflict with moral concerns for what might be objectively considered fair or just. An example of such conventions is gender norms that describe roles in such a way that members of one sex are accorded privileges not given to the other. In such cases people either subordinate the issue to a single domain (viewing it either as an issue of fairness or as an issue of custom, convention, and tradition), are conflicted as to how to think about the issue, or arrive at a coordinated integration of the need for conventional organization and moral requirements of equitable and beneficent treatment of persons. What this analysis suggests is that we should anticipate variance across and within individuals' applications of moral reasoning in context.

This is in fact what the data on moral reasoning indicate (Bandura, 1991; Keller, Eckensberger, & von Rosen, 1989; Rest, Narvaez, Bebeau, & Thoma, 1999; Turiel, 2002). For example, adult tendencies to display conventional (stage 4) or post-conventional, principled (stage 5) moral reasoning as defined within the Kohlberg framework are significantly associated with whether one has a conservative or liberal political ideology (Emler, Plamer-Canton, & St James, 1998; Emler & Stace, 1999). These latter findings lead to either the questionable assumption that people on the political left are more morally developed than people on the political right, or to an alternative interpretation that political affiliation tends to raise the salience of either moral or social-organizational concerns in one's interpretation of complex social and political issues.

Multiple moral orientations: justice and care

A different challenge to the Piaget/Kohlberg framework has been offered by Carol Gilligan (1982; Gilligan & Wiggins, 1987) who makes a distinction between a morality of justice and a morality of care. These two moral orientations according to Gilligan correspond to different, compelling moral injunctions. The morality of justice corresponds to the injunction not to treat others unfairly, while the morality of care corresponds to the injunction not to turn away from someone in need. In her initial work, Gilligan saw these two moral orientations as strongly linked to gender, and viewed Kohlberg's moral theory as gender biased resulting from an under-representation of females in his original research sample (Gilligan, 1982). Gilligan's (Gilligan & Wiggins, 1987) theorizing about the origins of the gender differences in morality employed the neo-Freudian characterizations of family relations offered by the feminist sociologist Nancy Chodorow (1978). The morality of care as characterized by Gilligan emphasizes interconnectedness and presumably emerges to a greater degree in girls owing to their early connection in identity formation with their mothers. The morality of justice, on the other hand, is said to emerge within the context of coordinating the interactions of autonomous individuals. A moral orientation based on justice was proposed as more prevalent among boys because their attachment relations with the mother, and subsequent masculine identity formation entailed that boys separate from that relationship and individuate from the mother. For boys, this separation also heightens their awareness of the difference in power relations between themselves and the adult, and hence purportedly engenders an intense set of concerns over inequalities. Girls, however, because of their continued attachment to their mothers, are not as keenly aware of such inequalities, and are, hence, said to be less concerned with fairness as an issue.

While Gilligan's (1982) initial studies were consistent with her strong gender-based hypotheses, further research has indicated, that moral reasoning does not follow the distinct gender lines that Gilligan originally reported. The preponderance of evidence is that both males and females reason based on justice and care (Walker, 2006). A recent meta-analysis (Jaffee & Hyde, 2000) examining more than 180 published studies revealed a small difference in the care orientation favoring women and a small difference in the justice orientation favoring men. Overall, gender accounted for less than 17% of the variance in effect sizes for justice and care reasoning, leading the authors to conclude that the findings do not offer strong support for a linkage between moral orientation and gender. Although the strong gender-based claims of Gilligan's (1982) original theory have not been sustained, the notion of an ethic of care continues to inform the work of many educators. Nel Noddings in particular has offered a philosophical analysis of an ethic of care (Noddings, 1984) along with detailed prescriptions for how to construct what she refers to as caring classrooms and schools (Noddings, 2002, 2008).

Morality and Culture

The previous section on the structure of morality also raised questions regarding the relations between cultural experiences and moral development. One of the primary influences upon the ways in which people read social situations is the cultural frame in which they live. It is a truism that values differ across cultures, and that people from different cultures tend to express the values of their cultures. What is less clear is the extent to which such variations represent fundamental differences in human morality. Nor is it self-evident that such differences reflect a direct mapping between cultural norms and individual moral cognition. Culture theorists, however, have tended toward the view that individual morality is a reflection of the norms of the person's culture (Miller, 1994; Shweder, 1990; Wellman & Miller, 2008). Central to their position is a tendency to define cultures in ways that emphasize their internal consistency (Geertz, 1984). Cultures are said to be shared systems of values and symbols with origins in collective activity (Geertz, 1984). Individuals, according to this view, construct their social values through a reconstruction at an individual level of the normative social constructions of their respective cultures (Shweder, Mahapatra, & Miller, 1987; Wellman & Miller, 2008). Thus, the process of moral socialization involves the child's active construction at an individual level of an internal value system through the personal interpretation of overt and tacit social messages transmitted by the agents of the culture such as parents, family members, and elders. The structure and content of these social values is thought to be constrained by the formal properties of justice (Shweder et al., 1987). However, these formal constraints are minimal since they gain meaning only through their operation within the context of variations within sets of moral qualities corresponding to notions of rights, duties, autonomy, interdependence, and sanctity (Shweder et al., 1987; Turiel, 1998, 2002). These patterns of variation correspond to cultural types that differ in terms of their definitions of personhood and community. Some cultures are thought to operate in terms of moralities emphasizing rights and equality of persons, while others are thought to emphasize interdependence, duties, hierarchy, and respect for authority (Shweder, 1990; Wellman & Miller, 2008).

These broad classifications of cultures lead to a set of interesting predictions about the moral and social reasoning of their members. One would expect that children and adults reared in a collectivist culture would place a higher priority on social convention than would individuals reared in so-called individualist cultures such as the United States. That expectation is born out in some of the cross-cultural data on children's judgments about social convention. Ijo children and adolescents in Nigeria (Hollos et al., 1986), Arab children in Israel (Nisan, 1987), and lower-class children in northeastern Brazil (Haidt, Koller, & Dias, 1993; Nucci et al., 1996) tend to affirm the importance of customs and tradition to a greater degree than American children. Children within the more traditional cultures are less likely to view the conventional norms of their society as alterable, and more likely to generalize their conventions to other cultural settings than are American children. One probable consequence of these differences is that individuals in more traditional cultures would be more sensitive to the salience of custom and convention in contexts where convention and morality (justice, human welfare) overlap. There is some indirect evidence that this is the case. It comes from the cross-cultural work done using the Kohlberg stage sequence (Snarey, 1985). One of the striking findings of this cross-cultural work is that post-conventional reasoning (as defined within the Kohlberg framework) is almost absent among the adult population of traditional cultural groups.

Such findings, however, are not conclusive evidence that the morality of persons within collectivist or traditional cultures is markedly different from that of others. Nor does it show that individual morality is reducible to the acquisition of shared cultural norms. We have already discussed some of the contradictory evidence in the previous section. Children and adults across a wide range of cultures, including those used as evidence in support of the contentions of culture theorists, have been shown to treat moral issues of fairness and human welfare as independent of the presence of cultural norms, and as obligatory and binding for all persons (Shweder et al., 1987; Turiel, 1998, 2002). A second challenge to the assumptions of culture theory are findings indicating (a) that cultures themselves are internally heterogeneous, and (b) that conceptions of personal autonomy and interdependence exist side-by-side within members of all cultures.

Part of the evidence comes from research on a third domain of social judgments described above, having to do with what people consider to be legitimate areas of personal discretion and privacy (Nucci, 1996; Nucci & Turiel, 2000). As such, these actions are not subject to considerations of right and wrong. Control over such actions permits the individual to establish a unique, bounded social identity. Thus, individuals endeavor to control areas of conduct that permit them opportunities to engage in self-expression, personal growth, selection of intimates, and zones of privacy. The view of the personal as just outlined is not in accord with the views of culture theorists who consider such a construct with its links to notions of individual identity and autonomy to hold only for members of so-called individualist cultures (Geertz, 1984). Recent work, however, has documented that efforts to establish a personal domain are made by children and adolescents in cultures presumed to be collectivist (Triandis, 1988), and that the reasons subjects employ to justify their treatment of issues as personal matters center on efforts to maintain a sense of individuality, autonomy, and rights (Ardilla-Rey & Killen, 2001; Hasebe et al., 2004; Helwig et al., 2009; Lins Dyer & Nucci, 2007; Nucci et al., 1996; Milnitsky-Sapiro et al., 2006; Yau & Smetana, 2003a; Yau & Smetana, 2003b). These same studies have also shown that children and adolescents, while staking claim to a set of behaviors as personal and private, also maintain the legitimacy of conventional regulation and moral obligation. In other words, children and adolescents in purportedly collectivist cultures hold social values that are simultaneously collectivist and individualist. This evidence of heterogeneity in children's social reasoning is similar to what was uncovered in studies of the supposed dichotomy between justice and care orientations in moral judgment, and suggests that such pigeonholing of people and cultures is the result of the misreading of dimensions of social judgment as evidence of cultural or individual types.

In sum, the work that has been done on culture and moral reasoning indicates that cultures, like individuals, are multifaceted and complex. The lesson to be gained from such cross-cultural research is that social structure may have considerable impact on the ways in which morality is experienced and thought about in everyday life. This is something different, however, from asserting that culture determines individual morality, or that morality is culturally divergent in some incommensurate or fundamental respect. The ways in which cultures structure the conventions and customs of society are often the accidents of history resulting from collective efforts to structure and coordinate the social interactions of a particular group of people. But, in many cases, these norms are also informed by the factual assumptions people make about the world, and/or the presumed relations between humanity and the cosmos. For example, some of the norms people establish to structure male–female relations are based on factual assumptions people make about the differing nature and capacities of members of each gender. We will close this discussion of the ways in which our moral judgment is affected by cultural setting by looking at the ways in which factual assumptions may enter into the picture (Wainryb, 2004).

Imagine a situation in which a surgeon fails to scrub up prior to engaging in an elective abdominal surgery on a patient. Most people, and we can assume the reader, would judge such an action by the surgeon to be immoral. This is because we all assume that by failing to engage in proper cleansing procedures, the doctor is likely to introduce micro-organisms into the patient and place him/her in severe risk of infection and possible death. Very few of us, however, have ever actually seen a germ or virus presumed to cause such an infection, and our certainty about the risks of the doctor's actions are taken on faith that our sources of scientific information about the nature of the world are accurate. In fact, at the beginning of the nineteenth century doctors were unaware of the existence of germs, and did not take the same precautions prior to surgery as do the doctors of today. Because of this, surgeons were often themselves the cause of illness and death among their own patients. Nonetheless, we would hardly engage in the same moral condemnation of their actions as we would of the surgeon described at the beginning of the paragraph. This is because of the differences in assumptions about the facts of the world that we can attribute to the early and modern-day surgeons.

The issues raised in the above illustration may help us to account for some of the findings of apparent cultural variability in morality reported by anthropologists. As an example, let's consider the rather shocking findings reported in an anthropological study of the moral values of devout Hindus living in the Temple community of Bhubaneswar, Orissa, India (Shweder et al., 1987). In one part of this study, Shweder and his colleagues presented their subjects with descriptions of 39 different behaviors entailing breaches of their community norms and asked them to judge them in terms of their "seriousness." The act rated as the most serious breach was for the eldest son in a family to get a haircut and eat chicken the day after his father died. Rated thirty-fifth in seriousness among the 39 behaviors was a man beating his disobedient wife black and blue. Certainly, on the face of it, these data would appear to be evidence that this community of Hindus has a very different way of conceptualizing morality from what is generally considered moral in the West. Shweder and his colleagues (1987), however, provide additional information in their report, which helps to account for the ways in which the subjects in their study reasoned about these issues. As it turns out, the Hindu judgments of the actions of the eldest son getting a haircut and eating chicken the day after his father's death, while morally neutral from a Western point of view, take on a different meaning within the context of the Hindu subjects' beliefs about the impact of these actions upon the father. In particular, the judgments of these subjects must be seen from within the context of their beliefs about the ways in which events in the natural world operate in relation to *unobserved entities*, such as souls and spirits of deceased ancestors. In this case, the father's soul would not receive salvation if the norm prohibiting the eating of chicken was not observed.

If we allow ourselves to role-take for a moment, and imagine that we are in the son's position, we can see how the act of eating chicken becomes a serious matter of causing grave harm to another being. We don't need to assume a new set of *moral* understandings, but rather to apply our moral conceptions of harm and fairness to this situation once the *facts* of the matter are understood. Our relation to Shweder's Hindu subjects is quite analogous to that of the twentieth-century surgeon to his nineteenth-century counterpart with respect to germ theory, and the morality of maintaining a sterile environment for surgical procedures. Now, it might be argued that knowledge derived from science has a different epistemic claim to validity than knowledge provided by religious belief. What cannot be argued, however, is that the assumptions one has about the natural world, however arrived at, have an impact on our moral evaluations of actions.

Morality and Emotion

Up to this point, our discussion has focused on the structure of moral reasoning. Some have argued, however, that the emphasis on moral judgment is wrongheaded since morality is primarily a function of responses to moral emotion, and the playing out of moral habits (Wilson, 1993). The focus on emotion has gained renewed impetus from recent studies suggesting that moral decisions can be traced to the emotion centers of the brain (Greene, 2005; Greene, Sommerville, Nystrom, Darley, & Cohen, 2001). As we will discuss below, these discoveries of potential neuronal correlates of morality are being conjoined with evolutionary scenarios to form a rather reductionist account of moral functioning (Greene, 2007; Haidt, 2001, 2007; Hauser, 2006a). Although the role of emotion in morality has garnered new attention, the arguments for emotional primacy can be traced back to Hume's (1751/1983) foundational positions advanced in the eighteenth century.

> There has been a controversy started of late ... worth examination, concerning the general foundation of Morals; whether they be derived from Reason, or from Sentiment; whether we attain the knowledge of them by chain of argument and induction, or by an immediate feeling and finer internal sense; whether like all sound judgments of truth and falsehood, they should be the same to every rational intelligent being; or whether like the perception of beauty and deformity, they be found entirely on the particular fabric and constitution of the human species. (p. 13)

Contemporary reductionist perspectives

The current reductionist view of emotion and moral functioning asserts that "affect-laden intuitions" (Greene & Haidt, 2002, p. 517) automatically and unconsciously produce moral judgments, while reasoning is employed for *post hoc* justification of these judgments. In rare situations, that allow for longer periods of reflection, moral reasoning may override emotional responses. Greene (2007) summarizes the relationship of emotion and reason in moral judgment by explaining that "intuitive emotional responses drive prepotent moral intuitions while 'cognitive' control processes sometimes rein them in" (p. 56). At the neuroanatomical level of analysis, reasoning and emotions are different processes because they purportedly engage different brain areas. Their disaggregation and dichotomization, which is premised on evolutionary assumptions and regionalized cognitive functioning, affords claims of primacy (Haidt, 2007) and competition between cognition and prepotent emotions (Greene, 2007). In this view emotion and cognition are "two different kinds of psychological process" (Greene, 2007, p. 41); "emotions are very reliable, quick, and efficient responses ... whereas reasoning is unreliable, slow, and inefficient" (p. 60).

The basic paradigm for this recent neuroscience research involves presenting adult participants with dilemmas presumed to differentially tap into emotional and rational regions of the brain, and recording their brain activity through processes of neural imaging (fMRI). The dilemmas presumed to tap into the emotional centers of the brain are also expected to generate the phenomenon of "moral dumfounding," a term coined by Jonathan Haidt (2001) to capture instances in which people seem unable to articulate reasons for their objections to actions such as incest between two adult consenting siblings. The most popular of these situations in the moral neuroscience literature are the trolley-car dilemmas, which originate in the virtuist philosophy of Philippa Foot (1967). These stories, which require judgment about two supposedly similar cases, have become known as the "push scenario" and the "switch scenario." In each, the lives of five individuals are pitted against the life of one other, as is the act of pushing an individual or pushing a lever. Characteristic examples are taken from recent empirical investigations:

> Switch scenario:
>
> A trolley is hurtling down the tracks. There are five innocent people on the track ahead of the trolley, and they will be killed if the trolley continues going straight ahead. There is a spur of track leading off to the side. There is one innocent person on that spur of track. The brakes of the trolley have failed and there is a switch which can be activated to cause the trolley to go to the side track. You are an innocent bystander (that is, not an employee of the railroad, etc.). You can throw the switch saving the five innocent people, which will result in the death of the one innocent person on the side track. What would you do? (Petrinovich, O'Neill, & Jorgensen, 1993, p. 468)
>
> Push scenario
>
> A runaway trolley is heading down the tracks toward five workmen who will be killed if the trolley proceeds on its present course. You are on a footbridge over the tracks, in between the approaching trolley and the five workmen. Next to you on this footbridge is a stranger who happens to be very large. The only way to save the lives of the five workmen is to push this stranger off the bridge and onto the tracks below where his large body will stop the trolley. The stranger will die if you do this, but the five workmen will be saved. Is it appropriate for you to push the stranger onto the tracks in order to save the five workmen? (Greene et al., 2001, supplementary material)

Though numerous variations have been developed, these represent the general tenor and circumstance of these studies. Each pits the lives of individuals against each other, and asks study participants to determine if it is morally permissible to push the lever, or to push the individual, in order to save five by killing one. Reliably, participants in these studies find pushing the lever to save five and kill one acceptable, but reject pushing the stranger to his death in order to save five (Cushman, Young, & Hauser, 2006; Greene, Nystrom, Engell, Darley, & Cohen, 2004; Hauser, Cushman, Young, Jin, & Mikhail, 2007; Lombrozo, 2009). Noting that the consequences for each action are identical, while the moral judgments are opposite, many of these neuroscientists conclude that the moral judgments are non-rational (Hauser, 2006b). This line of reasoning suggests that an individual's judgments should be consistent across both situations, that is, they should push the stranger off the footbridge because it will have similar positive net results (five-over-one) to the switch scenario.

In support of this conclusion are findings from fMRI studies suggesting that moral judgments can be traced to the emotion centers of the brain (Green et al., 2001; Green et al., 2004). In a frequently cited fMRI study of individuals engaged in judging dilemmas such as the trolley-car scenarios, Greene et al. (2001) reported that differential activation in brain regions known to be responsible for different sorts of cognition were correlated with two kinds of moral judgments. Greene and colleagues interpreted these results to mean that the up-close nature of the "push" scenario made it more personal and thus resulted in greater activation in the emotion processing regions. Whereas, the relative distance from victim(s) in the "switch" scenario was "more intuitively impersonal" resulting in both diminished emotional activation and increased activation in the reasoning centers of the brain (p. 2106). In summarizing his position, Greene (2003) stated that "people who are 'up close and personal' push our emotional buttons, whereas those who are out of sight languish out of mind" (p. 848). The importance of this claim was particularly tied to the causal inference it reported. Greene (2007; Greene et al., 2001) concluded that activation of the emotion processing regions of the brain demonstrated that moral judgments of an up-close and personal nature were based upon emotion, rather than reason. Greene (2007) went on to explain that "when a harm is *impersonal*, it should fail to trigger this alarm-like emotional response, allowing people to respond in a more 'cognitive' way, perhaps employing a cost-benefit analysis" (p. 43).

The strength of this account relies on two key assumptions. The first is that the regions being tracked are directly linked to emotional or rational processes, and the second is that these are causally responsible for particular reactions that lead to moral judgment. Speaking to the first point, Miller (2008) noted that the regions suggested to be responsible for emotional reasoning are also known to engage in memory and language processing. Whether Greene et al.'s (2001) fMRI revealed the processing of emotion, memory, or language is debatable (Mikhail, 2007), and one could certainly argue that each of the three processes were involved in their participants' judgments.

The appeal of explaining the organization of cognitive phenomena in a one-to-one correspondence with its neurological substrates is not particular to moral neuroscience. In explaining what they termed the "category error in neuroscience," Cacioppo et al. (2003, p. 654) noted that other fields of neuroimaging made similar mistakes in their infancy: "memories, emotions, and beliefs … were each once thought to be localized in a single site in the brain. Current evidence, however, suggests that most complex psychological or behavior concepts do not map into a single center in the brain" (p. 654).

With regard to the second of the two key assumptions mentioned above, Miller (2008) cited a group of 16 neuroscientists who object to causal inferences like those made by Greene et al. (2001), noting that "it's not possible to infer a particular mental state (such as anxiety) from the activation of a particular brain region" (p. 1412).

Whereas neural activation in several neuroimaging studies has shown a fairly consistent association between brain regions (ventromedial prefrontal cortex, or VMPC) involved in emotional processing and moral judgments (Harenski & Hamann, 2006; Moll et al., 2002), the fact that the VMPC is also implicated in other cognitive processes limits the conclusions we can draw. And the questions of what we could conclude about moral judgment if we were able to pinpoint the brain's "moral organ" (Hauser, 2006a) remain. Would this help us understand the process through which social knowledge emerges and develops, or the origins and sources of influence that structure our moral judgments?

The major contribution of Greene's (2001) study is that it putatively demonstrated that individuals do make judgments about their acts, not just the consequences of those acts. However, there are also several problems in coming to this conclusion. We have no evidence indicating whether these differential activations are causes of, or are caused by, the moral judgments. Along these lines, neuroscientists Young and Koenigs (2007) note that Greene's studies "do not settle the question of whether emotional processing plays a systematic role in moral judgment, driving some kinds of moral judgments over others" (p. 74). Similarly, this study neglects to consider the possibility that individuals are evaluating not only the consequences of these acts for the individuals who will be harmed in the scenario, but also for themselves. In the case of physically overpowering the stranger on the footbridge and forcing him to his death, the act is surely more hands-on and emotionally laden that the act of pulling the lever. But, this may be the result of complex reasoning that coordinates concerns about saving lives, killing innocent people, and interfering in the natural order of events with considerations such as "How will I feel after pushing him?" "What will happen to me if I push him?" and "Can I justify this as the best course of action?" Thus, the differential emotional activation may be a result of complex evaluation and coordination of the acts and possible consequences.

Another more general criticism comes from Turiel (in press) and Sunstein (2005), who note that neither the push nor the switch scenario presents common, or everyday, moral choices; they are extreme, exotic cases. Turiel's argument continues by suggesting that the "push" and "switch" scenario each "constitutes a different context of evaluation" (p. 18); by being made to directly "execute" the stranger in the push scenario, participants must coordinate more concerns and more complex features than in the switch scenario.

These issues of complexity and abnormality become even more apparent when considering the larger corpus of scenarios that Greene et al. (2001, 2004; Greene & Haidt, 2002) use to make generalized claims about moral judgments. These scenarios include judgments about exotic cases, such as torturing an innocent child to save several others, choosing which of your two children you will allow to be tortured and killed, and smothering your crying infant to prevent being caught and killed by enemy soldiers occupying your home. It would seem that none of these scenarios are typical of people's moral experiences, and that such forced-choice scenarios, which offer only two courses of action, unrealistically constrain moral choice.

The inseparability of emotion and cognition

Ultimately, the basic flaw in this effort to reduce morality to non-rational emotional processes is that it mistakenly assumes that affective and cognitive processes can be disaggregated in human decision-making. Interestingly, Piaget (1981) rejected the dualism between cognition and affect inherent in such positions. As Bearison and Zimiles (1986) summarize, "for Piaget, the dichotomy between intelligence and affectivity has been artificially created by analytic abstractions to serve as an axiomatic device for the convenience of exposition, whereas in reality, neither can function without the other" (p. 4). The construction of any cognitive scheme, such as the simple means–end relationships involved in reaching and grasping a ball, don't only involve the generation of computational sub-routines (as would be employed by a computer), but also incorporate the associated affect (e.g., desire for the ball, joy at grasping it). Cognitive scientists who share Piaget's position on this issue have ascribed to affect the role of weighting various schemata that may be evoked in a problem space, thereby serving as a heuristic selection device for honing in on a plausible "right" answer when consideration of all rational possibilities would render practical decision-making impossible (Pugh, 1977). Such heuristics are not in place of reasoning, but are instead part and parcel of everyday cognition (Kahneman, Slovic, & Tversky, 1982). Thus, a moral judgment may be reflective of extensive deliberation and reasoning, though it is veiled by apparent automaticity (Pizarro & Bloom, 2003).

A question we might ask regarding the relations between emotion and the child's construction of moral understandings is whether morality is associated with particular emotions. There are at least two ways to understand this question. The first is whether there are particular kinds of emotional experience that lead to moral constructions, rather than the development of knowledge about other social-cultural rules such as conventions. The second, related, question is whether certain kinds of feelings help to motivate and direct moral behavior. A good place to begin consideration of the issues raised in these questions is the work of William Arsenio (Arsenio, 1988; Arsenio, Gold, & Adams, 2006). Arsenio set out to discover whether social events that involve moral forms of "right and wrong" elicit different emotions than events that have to do with conventional or personal matters. In his initial studies, Arsenio (1988) presented kindergarten, third-, and fifth-grade children with drawings depicting children engaged in actions that fit within conventional or moral rule systems.

Children were asked to indicate how three actors in each of the scenarios would feel. These three were the child engaged in the action, the person who was the recipient of the action, and a third-person observer. The drawings depicting each of the scenarios presented the characters with neutral facial expressions so that the children would have to infer what the characters felt from their own personal experiences and understandings of these situations, rather than by reading the facial expressions of characters.

Findings were that with respect to violations of convention (e.g., wearing inappropriate attire to school), children judged that the child violating a convention would be neither happy nor sad about it and would experience essentially neutral affect. They also expected neutral affect from a child third-person observer, and thought they (the child subjects) would themselves have neutral affect if they were to observe the situation. On the other hand they expected the adult governing the convention (the teacher) to be upset about the violation and to experience some degree of negative affect. In terms of conventional rules governing personal issues, the children expected the governing adult and the third-person observers to have relatively neutral affect, but expected the main actor in the personal scenarios to experience negative affect such as anger or sadness at having his/her personal forms of conduct controlled by an adult authority. This latter reaction is consistent with children's and adolescents' views that the personal domain constitutes a zone in which it is illegitimate for adults to intercede or regulate.

With respect to the four moral scenarios, the results were as follows. In the case of inhibitive morality (acts one should refrain from, e.g., causing harm or unfairness), children judged all parties, including themselves, to experience considerable negative affect (sadness, anger, fear) in the face of such events, with the exception of the perpetrator of the act, who was judged to experience positive affect (happiness) with his/her behavior. In contrast with the findings regarding inhibitive morality, they expected all parties involved to experience positive affect (happiness) in response to acts that entailed distributive justice or prosocial conduct. Not only were the recipients of such actions thought to be happy, but so were the actors themselves.

Arsenio (1988) then investigated whether children would use emotional information conveyed by drawings of people's emotional expressions to make inferences about what sort of interaction produced the depicted emotions. Specifically, children were presented with drawings of individual characters displaying various emotional expressions that the children had attributed to the actors depicted in the first part of the study. They were then presented with two storyboards. One depicted a scenario consistent with the emotions shown in the individual character drawings, the other did not. Findings were that children, including preschoolers, accurately matched the emotional displays of the actors with the scenario most likely to have produced the depicted emotions.

As Arsenio's work demonstrates, children associate different feelings with different domains of social events. Issues of social convention generally elicit "cool" affect on the part of children who expect both compliance and violations of conventional norms to elicit neutral affect from children. To the extent that emotion is generated by convention, children see it as emerging on the part of adults who might become upset at the violation of such norms. Thus, it would appear that children do not experience the conventions of society as containing much in the way of intrinsic emotional content (but see Nucci et al., 1996 and Shweder et al., 1987).

Issues of morality, however, are viewed by children as rife with emotional content. All parties to moral interactions, not just the guardians of the social order, as with convention, are thought by children to experience identifiable emotional responses to moral events. This is the case whether the moral behavior is positive or negative in impact. In Arsenio's (1988) study, children described the participants in distributive-justice situations as experiencing happiness – or a sense of satisfaction that things turned out fairly. They likewise attributed positive emotions to all participants in prosocial moral situations. In contrast, moral transgressions entailing violations of inhibitive morality were seen by children as arousing feelings of anger, sadness, and fear in victims and bystanders alike. Only the perpetrators were viewed by young children as having positive feelings in the context of moral transgressions.

Morality, then, is an area of human conduct associated with "hot" affect. In addition to the emotions identified in Arsenio's (Arsenio & Lover, 1995; Arsenio et al., 2006) work, prosocial morality has been associated with feelings of care (Carlo, 2006; Gilligan, 1982), and empathy (Eisenberg, Spinrad, & Sadovsky, 2006; Hoffman, 1981). Inhibitive morality has been associated with shame, guilt (Ferguson, Stegge, & Damhuis, 1991), and disgust (Haidt, 2001; Haidt et al., 1994). And the victims of moral transgression are said to respond not simply with anger, but with outrage.

As Arsenio explains "emotions appear to be routinely stored as a part of our basic cognitive and social-cognitive representations" (Arsenio & Lover, 1995, p. 90). Children extract different affect–event links depending on the particular nature of the acts. Repeated experience with events with similar emotional outcomes allows children to form generalized scripts. The automatic reactions to familiar events, or events of similar type, result from the affective triggering of these scripts or habits. Thus, we begin to see how the basic connections between affect and cognition play out in the domain of morality.

Arsenio (Arsenio & Lover, 1995) adds an additional step to the processes of moral knowledge formation. He states "Children coordinate their knowledge of sociomoral affect to form more general sociomoral principles. For example, commonalties in the expected emotional outcomes of being a target of theft, a target of undeserved aggression, and a target of verbal abuse might all be combined to form a concept of unfair victimization" (Arsenio & Lover, 1995, p. 91).

The work of Arsenio and others has provided a plausible portrait of the developmental connections between morality and affect. In Arsenio's view, sociomoral affect provides the raw data from which more general abstract principles are formed using a variety of cognitive abilities. Beginning in infancy we initiate the process of constructing the schemata that form our social and moral values. Incorporated within those schemata are the emotions associated with particular event-types, including the affect associated with adult reactions to children's compliance with or violation of social norms (Hoffman, 1983; Kochanska, 1993; Lagattuta, 2005; Zahn-Waxler, Radke-Yarrow, & King, 1979). The development of these early social and moral schemata form the substrate of our moral habits, and, in the view of some researchers, the beginnings of our moral character (Kochanska & Aksan, 2006). Variations in the nature of these interactions stemming from such things as differences in children's temperament (Kochanska, 1993), the degree of anger displayed by adults in reaction to children's transgressions, or warmth in reaction to children's prosocial conduct (Emde, Biringen, Clyman, & Oppenheim, 1991), and the overall affective climate of the household (Katz & Gottman, 1991; Zahn-Waxler & Kochanska, 1990) appear to impact the ways in which young children construct the basic underpinnings of their concepts of how to react within interpersonal situations. The cross-cultural consensus that we observe in the meaning of moral acts may be accounted for, according to Arsenio, because of the basic similarities in meanings people attribute to the emotions that accompany moral events.

The developmental work on children's affective development has demonstrated the process by which normal affective experiences are integrated into the child's moral constructions. Morality is not simply guided by "feelings" as the emotivist philosophers (Hume, 1751/1983; Moore, 1903) would have it. Nor is it cold-blooded rationality as depicted in some misreadings of cognitive accounts of morality (e.g., MacIntyre, 1984). Our feelings are an integral part of the very schemes that constitute the whole of our so-called moral habits. Our moral reasoning and processes of reflection are in reciprocal relation with the schemes that generate our moral behaviors.

Conclusion

The picture that emerges from our current understanding of the development of moral reasoning is both clearer and more complex than the one we once held. What has become clarified is that the domain of morality constitutes a basic knowledge system for regulating social interactions around issues of fairness and human welfare. This basic knowledge system stems from patterns of social interaction that are inherent to social relations, and appear to have connection to a common set of affective experiences. Social judgments that involve a moral component, however, are more variable and heterogeneous than we once supposed. This is because morality is but one component involved in the generation of social judgments in context. Such contextual social judgments entail the application of multiple knowledge systems that may be coordinated in a variety of ways. Part of what enters into such variation are the factual assumptions, customs, and social conventions of the person's culture and society. These factors, however, are themselves reflections of systematic and basic elements of social life. What is more, the relation between cultural values and norms, and those of the individual are reciprocal and interactive rather than unidirectional. The process of moral development involves the progressive generation of regulatory structures of justice and human welfare. These non-arbitrary aspects of morality form part of the dynamic tension that exists both within individuals and within social systems inasmuch as each must balance and trade-off the needs of persons and the requirements of social structure and organization. What this means for future research on moral development is that we must look not only at the progression of transformations within the moral domain, but also at the ways in which children and adolescents coordinate morality with other social knowledge systems in generating judgments in context.

References

Ardilla-Rey, A., & Killen, M. (2001). Middle class Colombian children's evaluations of personal, moral, and social-conventional interactions in the classroom. *International Journal of Behavioral Development, 25*, 246–255.

Arsenio, W. (1988). Children's conceptions of the situational affective consequences of sociomoral events. *Child Development, 59*, 1611–1622.

Arsenio, W. F., Gold, J., & Adams, E. (2006). Children's conceptions and displays of moral emotions. In M. Killen & J. G. Smetana (Eds.), *Handbook of moral development* (pp. 581–609). Mahwah, NJ: Erlbaum.

Arsenio, W., & Lover, A. (1995). Children's conceptions of socio-moral affect: Happy victimizers, mixed emotions, and other expectancies. In M. Killen & D. Hart (Eds.), *Morality in everyday life* (pp. 87–130). New York: Cambridge University Press.

Bandura, A. (1991). Social cognitive theory of moral thought and action. In W. Kurtines & J. Gewirtz (Eds.), *Handbook of moral behavior and development: Vol. 1. Theory* (pp. 45–104). Hillsdale, NJ: Erlbaum.

Bearison, D., & Zimiles, H. (1986). Developmental perspectives of thought and emotion: An introduction. In D. Bearison & H. Zimiles (Eds.), *Thought and emotion: Developmental perspectives* (pp. 1–10). Hillsdale, NJ: Erlbaum.

Cacioppo, J. T., Bernston, G. G., Lorig, T. S., Norris, C. J., Rickett, E., & Nusbaum, H. (2003). Just because you're imaging the brain doesn't mean you can stop using your head: A primer and set of first principles. *Journal of Personality and Social Psychology, 85*, 650–661.

Carlo, G. (2006). Care-based and altruistically-based morality. In M. Killen & J. G. Smetana (Eds.), *Handbook of moral development* (pp. 551–580). Mahwah, NJ: Erlbaum.

Chodorow, N. (1978). *The reproduction of mothering.* Berkeley: University of California press.

Colby, A., & Kohlberg, L. (1987). *The measurement of moral judgment: Vol. 1. Theoretical foundations and research validation; Vol. 2. Standard issue scoring manual.* New York: Cambridge University Press.

Colby, A., Kohlberg, L., Gibbs, J., & Lieberman, M. (1983). A longitudinal study of moral judgment. *Monographs of the Society for Research in Child Development, 48* (Serial No. 200).

Cushman, F., Young, L., & Hauser, M. (2006). The role of conscious reasoning and intuition in moral judgment: Testing three principles of harm. *Psychological Science, 17*, 1082–1089.

Damon, W. (1977). *The social world of the child.* San Francisco: Jossey-Bass.

Damon, W. (1980). Patterns of change in children's social reasoning: A two-year longitudinal study. *Child Development, 51*, 1010–1017.

Davidson, P., Turiel, E., & Black, A. (1983). The effect of stimulus familiarity on the use of criteria and justifications in children's social reasoning. *British journal of developmental psychology, 1*, 46–65.

Eisenberg, N. (1986). *Altruistic emotion, cognition and behavior*. Hillsdale, NJ: Erlbaum.

Eisenberg N., Cumberland A., Guthrie I. K., Murphy, B. C., Shepard, S. A. (2005). Age changes in prosocial responding and moral reasoning in adolescence and early adulthood. *Journal of Research on Adolescence, 15*, 235–260.

Eisenberg, N., Spinrad, T., & Sadovsky, A. (2006). Empathy-related responding in children. In M. Killen & J. G. Smetana (Eds.), *Handbook of moral development* (pp. 517–550). Mahwah, NJ: Erlbaum.

Emde, R. N., Biringen, Z., Clyman, R. B., & Oppenheim, D. (1991). The moral self of infancy: Affective core and procedural knowledge. *Developmental Review, 11*(3), 251–270.

Emler, N., Palmer-Canton, E., & St James, A. (1998). Politics, moral reasoning and the Defining Issues Test: A reply to Barnett et al. (1995). *British Journal of Social Psychology, 37*, 457–476.

Emler, N., & Stace, K. (1999). What does principled moral versus conventional moral reasoning convey to others about the politics and psychology of the reasoner? *European Journal of Social Psychology, 29*, 455–468.

Ferguson, T. J., Stegge, H., & Damhuis, I. (1991). Children's understandings of guilt and shame. *Child Development, 62*, 827–839.

Foot, P. (1967). The problem of abortion and the doctrine of double effect. *Oxford Review, 5*, 5–15.

Geertz, C. (1984). From the natives' point of view: On the nature of anthropological understanding. In R. A. Shweder & R. Levine (Eds.), *Culture theory* (pp. 123–136). Cambridge: Cambridge University Press.

Gershkoff, L., & Thelen, E. (2004). U-shaped changes in behavior: a dynamic systems perspective. *Journal of Cognition and Development, 5*, 11–36.

Gilligan, C. (1982). *In a different voice: Psychological theory and women's development*. Cambridge, MA: Harvard University Press.

Gilligan, C., & Wiggins, G. (1987). The origins of morality in early childhood relationships. In J. Kagan & S. Lamb (Eds.), *The emergence of morality in young children* (pp. 277–305). Chicago: University of Chicago Press.

Greene, J. (2003). From neural "is" to moral "ought": what are the moral implications of neuroscientific moral psychology? *Nature, 4*, 847–851.

Greene, J. (2005). Cognitive neuroscience and the structure of the moral mind. In P. Carruthers, S. Laurence, & S. Stich (Eds.), *The innate mind: Structure and content*. New York: Oxford University Press.

Greene, J. (2007). The secret joke of Kant's soul. In W. Sinnott-Armstrong (Ed.), *Moral psychology: The neuroscience of morality, emotion, brain disorders, and development* (pp. 35–80). Cambridge, MA: MIT Press.

Greene, J., & Haidt, J. (2002). How (and where) does moral judgment work? *Trends in Cognitive Science, 6*, 516–523.

Greene, J., Nystrom, L. E., Engell, A. D., Darley, J. M., & Cohen, J. D. (2004). The neural bases of cognitive conflict and control in moral judgment. *Neuron, 44*, 389–400.

Greene, J., Sommerville, R. B., Nystrom, L. E., Darley, J. M., & Cohen, J. D. (2001). An fMRI investigation of emotional engagement in moral judgment. *Science, 293*, 2105–2108.

Haidt, J. (2001). The emotional dog and its rational tail: A social intuitionist approach to moral judgment. *Psychological Review, 108*, 814–834.

Haidt, J. (2007). The new synthesis in moral psychology. *Science, 316*, 998–1002.

Haidt, J., Koller, S. H., & Dias, M. G. (1994). Affect, culture, and the morality of harmless offenses. *Journal of Personality and Social Psychology, 65*, 613–629.

Harenski, C. L., & Hamann, S. (2006). Neural correlates of regulating emotions related to moral violations. *NeuroImage, 30*(1), 313–324.

Hasebe, Y., Nucci, L., & Nucci, M. (2004). Parental control of the personal domain and adolescent symptoms of psychopathology: A cross-national study in the U.S. and Japan. *Child Development, 75*, 1–14.

Hauser, M. D. (2006a). The liver and the moral organ. *Scan, 1*, 214–220.

Hauser, M. D. (2006b). *Moral minds: How nature designed our universal sense of right and wrong.* New York: HarperCollins.

Hauser, M. D., Cushman, F., Young, L., Jin, R., & Mikhail, J. (2007). A dissociation between moral judgment and justification. *Mind and Language, 22*, 1–21.

Helwig, C., Yang, S., Nucci, L., Yun, K., & To, S. (2009). *Parental control of the personal domain and adolescent symptoms of psychopathology in urban and rural China.* Paper presented at the biennial meeting of the Society for Research in Child Development, Denver, CO.

Hoffman, M. L. (1981). Is altruism part of human nature? *Journal of Personality and Social Psychology, 40*, 121–137.

Hoffman, M. L. (1983). Affective and cognitive processes in moral internalization. In E. Higgins, A. Ruble, & W. Hartup. (Eds.), *Social cognition and social development: A sociocultural perspective.* (pp. 236–274). Cambridge: Cambridge University Press.

Hollos, M., Leis, P., & Turiel, E. (1986). Social reasoning in Ijo children and adolescents in Nigerian communities. *Journal of Cross-Cultural Psychology, 17*, 352–376.

Hume, D. (1751/1983). *An enquiry concerning the principles of morals.* J. B. Schneewind (Ed.). Indianapolis, IN: Hackett.

Jaffee, S., & Hyde, J. (2000). Gender differences in moral orientation: A meta-analysis. *Psychological Bulletin, 126*, 703–726.

James, R., & Blair, R. (2005). Morality in the autistic child. *Journal of autism and developmental disorders, 26*, 571–579.

Kahneman, D., Slovic, P., & Tversky, A. (Eds.) (1982). *Judgment under uncertainty: Heuristics and biases.* Cambridge: Cambridge University Press.

Katz, L. F., & Gottman, J. M. (1991). Marital discord and child outcomes: A social psychophysiological approach. In J. Garber & K. A. Dodge (Eds.), *The development of emotion regulation and dysregulation* (pp. 129–155). Cambridge: Cambridge University Press.

Keller, M., Eckensberger, L., & von Rosen, K. (1989). A critical note on the conception of preconventional morality: The case of stage 2 in Kohlberg's theory. *International Journal of Behavioral Development, 12*, 57–69.

Kochanska, K. (1993). Toward a synthesis of parental socialization and child temperament in early development of conscience. *Child Development, 64*, 325–347.

Kochanska, G., & Aksan, N. (2006). Children's conscience and self-regulation. *Journal of Personality, 74*, 1587–1617.

Kohlberg, L. (1963/2008). The development of children's orientations toward a moral order. I: Sequence in the development of moral thought. *Human Development, 51*, 8–20.

Kohlberg, L. (1969). Stage and sequence: The cognitive-developmental approach to socialization. In D. Goslin (Ed.), *Handbook of socialization theory and research* (pp. 347–480). Chicago: Rand McNally.

Kohlberg, L., & Kramer, (1969). Continuities and discontinuities in childhood and adult moral development. *Human Development, 12*, 93–120.

Lagattuta, K. H. (2005). When you shouldn't do what you want to do: Young children's understanding of desires, rules, and emotions. *Child Development, 76*, 713–733.

Lapsley, D. (1982). *The development of retributive justice in children (Unpublished doctoral dissertation).* University of Wisconsin, Madison.

Leslie, A., Mallon, R., Dicorcia, J. (2006). Transgressors, victims, and cry babies: Is basic moral judgment spared in autism? *Social neurosciences, 1*, 270–283.

Lins-Dyer, T., & Nucci, L. (2007). The impact of social class and social cognitive domain on northeastern Brazilian mothers' and daughters' conceptions of parental control. *International Journal of Behavioral Development. 31*, 105–114.

Lombrozo, T. (2009). The role of moral commitments in moral judgment. *Cognitive Science, 33*, 273–286.

MacIntyre, A. (1984). *After virtue* (2nd ed.). Notre Dame, IN: University of Notre Dame Press.

Mikhail, J. (2007). Moral cognition and computational theory. In W. Sinnott-Armstrong (Ed.), *Moral psychology: The neuroscience of morality, emotion, brain disorders, and development* (pp. 81–91). Cambridge, MA: MIT Press.

Miller, G. (2008). Growing pains for fMRI. *Science, 320*, 1412–1414.

Miller, J. G. (1994). Cultural diversity in the morality of caring: Individually-oriented versus duty-based interpersonal moral codes. *Cross-Cultural Research, 28*, 3–39.

Milnitsky-Sapiro, C., Turiel, E., & Nucci, L. (2006). Brazilian adolescents' concepts of autonomy and parental authority. *Cognitive Development, 21*, 317–331.

Moll, J., de Oliveira-Souza, R., Eslinger, P. J., Bramati, I., Mourao-Miranda, J., Andreiuolo, P. A., Pessoa, L. (2002). The neural correlates of moral sensitivity: A functional magnetic resonance imagining investigation of basic and moral emotions. *The Journal of Neuroscience, 22*(7), 2730–2736.

Moore, G. E. (1903). *Principia ethica*. Cambridge: Cambridge University Press.

Nisan, M. (1987). Moral norms and social conventions: A cross-cultural comparison. *Developmental Psychology, 23*, 719–725.

Noddings, N. (1984). *Caring, a feminine approach to ethics and moral education*. Berkeley: University of California Press.

Noddings, N. (2002). *Educating moral people: A caring alternative to character*. New York: Teachers College Press.

Noddings, N. (2008). Caring and moral education. In L. Nucci & D. Narvaez (Eds.), *Handbook of moral and character education*. (pp. 161–174). New York: Routledge.

Nucci, L. (1996). Morality and the personal sphere of actions. In E. Reed, E. Turiel, & T. Brown (Eds.), *Values and knowledge* (pp. 41–60). Hillsdale, NJ: Erlbaum.

Nucci, L. (2001). *Education in the moral domain*. Cambridge: Cambridge University Press.

Nucci, L., Becker, K., & Horn, S. (2004). *Assessing the development of adolescent concepts of social convention*. Paper presented at the annual meeting of the Jean Piaget Society, Toronto.

Nucci, L., Camino, C., & Sapiro, C. (1996). Social class effects on Northeastern Brazilian children's conceptions of areas of personal choice and social regulation. *Child Development, 67*, 1223–1242.

Nucci, L., & Milnitsky Sapiro, C. (1995). *The impact of region and social class on Brazilian mothers' conceptions of children's areas of personal choice*. Unpublished manuscript, University of Illinois at Chicago.

Nucci, L., & Smetana, J. (1996). Mothers' concepts of young children's areas of personal freedom. *Child Development, 67*, 1870–1886.

Nucci, L., & Turiel, E. (2000). The moral and the personal: Sources of social conflicts. In L. Nucci, E. Turiel, & G. Saxe (Eds.), *Culture, thought and development* (pp. 115–140). Mahwah, NJ: Erlbaum.

Nucci, L., & Turiel, E. (2007). *Development in the moral domain: The role of conflict and relationships in children's and adolescents' welfare and harm judgments*. Paper presented as part of the symposium "Moral development within domain and within context" at the biennial meeting of the Society for Research in Child Development, Boston.

Nucci, L., & Weber, E. K. (1991). Research on classroom applications of the domain approach to values education. In W. Kurtines & J. Gewirtz (eds.) *Handbook of moral behavior and development: Vol. 3. Applications* (pp. 251–266). Hillsdale, NJ: Erlbaum.

Nucci, L., & Weber, E. K. (1995). Social interactions in the home and the development of young children's conceptions within the personal domain. *Child Development, 66*, 1438–1452.

Petrinovich, L., O'Neill, P., & Jorgensen, M. J. (1993). An empirical study of moral intuitions: Towards an evolutionary ethics. *Journal of Personality and Social Psychology. 64*, 467– 478.

Piaget, J. (1932). *The moral judgment of the child.* New York: Free Press.

Piaget, J. (1981). *Intelligence and affectivity: Their relationship during child development* (T. Brown & C. Kaegi, Trans. and Eds.). Palo Alto, CA: Annual Reviews Monographs.

Piaget, J. (1985). *The equilibration of cognitive structures.* Chicago: University of Chicago Press.

Pizarro, D. A., & Bloom, P. (2003). The intelligence of moral intuitions: Comment on Haidt (2001). *Psychological Review, 110*, 193–196.

Pugh, G. E. (1977). *The biological origin of human values.* New York: Basic Books.

Rest, J., Narvaez, D., Bebeau, M., & Thoma, S. (1999). *Postconventional moral thinking: A neo-Kohlbergian approach.* Mahwah, NJ: Erlbaum.

Searle, J. R. (1969). *Speech acts.* London: Cambridge University Press.

Shweder, R. A. (1990). In defense of moral realism: Reply to Gabennesch. *Child Development, 61*, 2060–2067.

Shweder, R., Mahapatra, M., & Miller, J. (1987). Culture and moral development. In J. Kagan & S. Lamb (Eds.), *The emergence of morality in young children.* Chicago: University of Chicago Press.

Smetana, J. G. (2005). Adolescent–parent conflict: Resistance and subversion as developmental process. In L. Nucci (Ed.), *Conflict, contradiction and contrarian elements in moral development and education.* (pp. 69–91). Mahwah, NJ: Erlbaum.

Smetana, J. G. (2006). Social-cognitive domain theory: Consistencies and variations in children's moral and social judgments. In M. Killen & J. G. Smetana (Eds.), *Handbook of moral development* (pp. 119–154). Mahwah, NJ: Erlbaum.

Smetana, J., & Braeges, J. L. (1990). The development of toddlers' moral and conventional judgments. *Merrill-Palmer Quarterly, 36*, 329–346.

Snarey, J. (1985). Cross-cultural universality of social-moral development: A critical review of Kohlbergian research. *Psychological Bulletin, 97*, 202–232.

Sunstein, C. R. (2005). Moral heuristics. *Behavioral and Brain Sciences, 28*, 531–573.

Triandis, H. C. (1988). Collectivism vs. individualism: A reconceptualization of a basic concept in cross-cultural social psychology. In C. Bagley & G. K. Verma (Eds.), *Personality cognition and values: Cross-cultural perspectives of childhood and adolescence.* London: MacMillan.

Turiel, E. (1974). Conflict and transition in adolescent moral development. *Child Development, 45*, 14–29.

Turiel, E. (1975). Domains and categories in social-cognitive development. In W. Overton (Ed.), *The relationship between social and cognitive development* (53–90). Hillsdale, NJ: Erlbaum.

Turiel, E. (1978). The development of concepts of social structure: Social convention. In J. Glick and K. Alison Clarke-Stewart (Eds.), *The development of social understanding.* New York: Gardner Press.

Turiel, E. (1979). Distinct conceptual and developmental domains: Social convention and morality. In H. Howe and G. Keasy (Eds.), *Nebraska symposium on motivation: 1977: Vol. 25. Social cognitive development* (pp. 77–116). Lincoln: University of Nebraska.

Turiel, E. (1983). *The development of social knowledge: Morality and convention.* Cambridge: Cambridge University Press.

Turiel, E. (1998). The development of morality. In W. Damon (General Ed.), N. Eisenberg (Vol. Ed.), *Handbook of child psychology: Vol. 3. Social, emotional, and personality development* (5th ed., pp. 863–932). New York: Academic Press.

Turiel, E. (2002). *The culture of morality: Social development, context, and conflict.* Cambridge: Cambridge University Press.

Turiel, E. (2008). The development of children's orientations toward moral, social and personal orders: More than a sequence of development. *Human Development, 51,* 21–39.

Turiel, E. (in press). The relevance of moral epistemology and psychology. In P. Zelazo, M. Chandler, & E. Crone (Eds.), *Developmental social cognitive neuroscience.* New York: Taylor & Francis.

Wainryb, C. (2004). Is and ought: Moral judgments about the world as understood. In J. Baird & B. Sokol (Eds.), *Mind, morals, and action* (pp. 3–18). San Francisco: Jossey-Bass.

Walker, L. (2006). Gender and morality. In M. Killen & J. G. Smetana (Eds.), *Handbook of moral development* (pp. 93–118). Mahwah, NJ: Erlbaum.

Wellman, H., & Miller, J. (2008). Including deontic reasoning as fundamental to theory of mind. *Human Development, 51,* 105–135.

Wilson, J. Q. (1993). *The moral sense.* New York: The Free Press.

Yau, J., & Smetana, J. G. (2003a). Adolescent–parent conflict among Chinese adolescents in Hong Kong. *Child Development, 67,* 1262–1275.

Yau J., Smetana J. G. (2003b). Adolescent–parent conflict in Hong Kong and Shenzhen: A comparison of youth in two cultural contexts. *International Journal of Behavioral Development, 27,* 201–211.

Young, L., & Koenigs, M. (2007). Investigating emotion in moral cognition: A review of evidence from functional neuroimaging and neuropsychology. *British Medical Bulletin, 84,* 69–79.

Zahn-Waxler, C., & Kochanska, G. (1990). The origins of guilt. In R. Thompson (Ed.), *Nebraska symposium on motivation: Socioemotional development 1988* (Vol. *36,* pp. 183–258). Lincoln, University of Nebraska Press.

Zahn-Waxler, C., Radke-Yarrow, M., & King, R. (1979). Child rearing and children's prosocial initiations toward victims of distress. *Child Development, 50,* 319–330.

CHAPTER SEVENTEEN

Spatial Development

Evolving Approaches to Enduring Questions

Lynn S. Liben and Adam E. Christensen

Introduction

Space and spatial cognition pervade our daily lives. The alarm rings and we reach out to hit the snooze button in the dark, adjusting arm angle, distance, and hand position by knowing our location in bed, the position of the clock, and the shape of the button. Still in the dark, we head directly to the bathroom, using our knowledge of the layout of the house to avoid bumping into walls. In the kitchen, we go directly to the right cupboards for a mug, coffee, and cereal by drawing on our location memory. As we eat, we read the newspaper, extracting information about economics, wars, and the visual arts by using our skills in interpreting graphic representations. Driving to work, we detour around a traffic jam by consulting our cognitive map of the city. In addition to their centrality for daily life, space and spatial cognition are central to disciplines as diverse as physics, mathematics, geography, biology, geoscience, and chemistry (National Research Council, 2006). They are increasingly central to developmental psychology. Illustratively, the current edition of the *Handbook of Child Psychology* (Damon & Lerner, 2006), often taken as the hallmark of the field, includes two chapters on spatial development (Liben, 2006; Newcombe & Huttenlocher, 2006); in contrast, the prior five editions included none.

What is the path to these spatial competencies? In this chapter, we begin by highlighting the major ways that the field of spatial development has been or could be organized. Our goal is to offer readers an idea of the structure of the topic, a sense of the broad questions that have been studied, and a brief look at alternative theoretical approaches. We then describe illustrative empirical research on several enduring topics in spatial development. In the third section, we offer brief remarks about the value of examining group and individual differences and about emerging technologies that affect both research design and everyday spatial lives.

Organizing Spatial Development

Historical lenses

One organizational approach, taken by Eliot (1987), is historical. Eliot divided the study of spatial development into three eras. The first (1900–1960) focused primarily on assembling normative data on topics such as age-linked advances in children's drawings of people and objects, left and right in relation to the child's own body, and geographic environments and their representations (e.g., maps). The next phase (1960–1974) concerned many of the same substantive topics, but now scholarship turned away from normative description and toward understanding how developing spatial behaviors are linked to underlying conceptual advances. Research during this period was dominated by theorists who sought to explain cognitive development via children's self-motivated interactions with the environment (Piaget's cognitive-constructive approach) and via socially influenced interactions with the world (Vygotsky's sociocultural approach). In the final phase (1974 to the "present"), the developmental study of psychological space had "become less the subject of broadly conceived models of spatial development, and more the focus of fragmented or isolated topics of interest" (p. 113). Eliot identified several research areas that had become research domains in their own right (e.g., infants' spatial competence, spatial-skill training, sex differences in spatial behavior), adding that it had become "increasingly difficult to envision how such diverse strands will ever be re-united or integrated into a comprehensive explanation of spatial development throughout the lifespan" (p. 113). Given the publication date of the book, the "present" was roughly three decades ago, but Eliot's characterization might well still hold.

Theoretical traditions and developmental mechanisms

It is also possible to organize spatial development by reference to the traditional nature, nurture, and interactional approaches taken to developmental phenomena more broadly. Scholars of biological foundations of spatial development (a) attempt to identify the ways in which humans as a species are biologically endowed – apart from experience – to perceive and represent space (the nativist approach; see Spelke & Newport, 1998); (b) propose ways in which the process of natural selection may account for different traits in different groups (as in the evolutionary argument that contemporary sex differences in spatial traits reflect millennia of sex-differentiated roles in obtaining food and mating behaviors; see Cosmides & Tooby, 1992; Gaulin, 1992); and (c) identify individual-level biological mechanisms that may lead to different spatial outcomes (e.g., studying the role of prenatal or pubertal testosterone in relation to spatial performance; see Hines, 2000; Liben et al., 2002). At the other end of the theoretical continuum is the empiricist tradition, emphasizing the role of experience. The most extreme version of this approach is classic empiricism epitomized by seventeenth- to eighteenth-century philosophers such as Locke and Berkeley. In this view, people learn what space is by accumulating experiences from sight and touch (see reviews in Eliot, 1987; Jammer,

1954; Spelke & Newport, 1998), and what is known about space is presumed to be a copy of the physical environment. There is little contemporary support for either pure biological or pure environmental approaches: any scholar of biological factors recognizes the role of experience, and any scholar of experience recognizes that what is afforded by the environment differs radically depending on the individual encountering that environment.

Interactionist approaches attempt to go beyond additive contributions of biology and experience, focusing instead on their transactions. In such theories, self- and socially-directed transactions lead to the *construction* of spatial knowledge which does not merely mimic or internalize the external physical or social world. Within the family of constructivist theories, different theorists emphasize different transactional components. For example, Piaget focused on the individual's self-motivated interactions with the physical environment which in infancy lead to a practical, action-based understanding of space (Piaget, 1954) and in childhood lead to a conceptual, representational understanding of space (Piaget & Inhelder, 1956). Vygotsky (1962, 1978) focused on the social environment, emphasizing how knowledgeable adults guide children's learning, and how language influences cognition. Although Vygotsky (unlike Piaget) did not focus explicitly on spatial development, later researchers in this tradition have studied related topics including how parents guide their children's map-based route planning (Radziszewska & Rogoff, 1988), understanding of spatial graphics (Szechter & Liben, 2004), and graphic-based problem solving (Gauvain, 1993).

Levels of analysis

Scholarship on spatial cognition may also be organized by levels of analysis. Most empirical work on spatial development has been at what might be called the meso- or middle-level of analysis, and it is work at this level that we focus on later in this chapter. Meso-level research concerns spatial actions and behaviors of a scope described by everyday language; for example, routes children take to navigate to a target location or actions they take to fit pieces of a puzzle together. Increasingly, there has also been research at the micro-level, primarily as part of the contemporary attempt to understand the neurological substrates of human behavior. Much of this research has been with adults, aimed at cataloguing brain regions activated by various spatial tasks. Developmental work asks whether (and how early) similar patterns are found in children. For example, neuroimaging studies in adults have associated object recognition and spatial location with, respectively, ventral and dorsal streams (McIntosh & Schenk, 2009) and have mapped brain locations associated with specific tasks (e.g., mental rotation; Nelson, de Haan, & Thomas, 2006). Developmental work has shown dorsal/ventral specialization prior to puberty (Nelson, Monk, Lin, Carver, Thomas, & Truwit, 2000) and that right-lateralization of spatial processing occurs as early as 5 years of age for some tasks, but considerably later for others (Boles, Barth, & Merrill, 2008). Although we include some findings from this level of analysis in our review, we have not attempted to provide detailed reviews of neurological work on spatial development given that this research approach is still in its infancy.

At the other end is work at the molar level of analysis which involves the bottom-up inference of constructs from empirical data (e.g., factor analyses), or the top-down application of constructs formulated by conceptual analysis (e.g., models of space drawn from mathematics). Illustrative of a bottom-up approach is Linn and Petersen's (1985) meta-analysis through which they identified three spatial skills – spatial perception, mental rotation, and spatial visualization (see also Carroll, 1993; Hegarty & Waller, 2005; Uttal, Hand, & Newcombe, 2009, for alternative factor structures). Illustrative of the top-down approach is Piagetian theory (Piaget, 1964; Piaget & Inhelder, 1956) proposing that spatial development begins during infancy at a perceptual, sensorimotor, or action level and continues during childhood at a representational level, first (early childhood) characterized by topological concepts (e.g., "on" and "between"), and later (middle childhood) by projective concepts (e.g., vantage-point dependent left vs. right) and Euclidean concepts (e.g., Cartesian coordinates).

Research has addressed connections within and across levels. Within-level research is aimed primarily at expanding descriptive data (e.g., learning more about what regions of the brain are involved in which spatial tasks and how these change with age; see Kwon, Reiss, & Menon, 2002), identifying component foundations of a spatial skill (e.g., examining the role of working memory in mental rotation; see Fitzhugh, Morrison, Shipley, Chein, & Newcombe, 2008), or evaluating the internal coherence of a theoretical model (e.g., testing the within-child consistency in solving Piagetian projective and Euclidean tasks; see Dodwell, 1963). Between-level research is aimed at linking constructs across levels, as in linking brain activation patterns to their concurrent performance on mental rotation (e.g., Weiss et al., 2003), students' spatial skills to success in science and mathematics (e.g., Casey, Nuttall, & Pezaris, 2001), or performance on projective and Euclidean tasks to performance on mapping tasks (e.g., Liben & Downs, 1993).

Substantive domains

Finally, an organizational strategy used in contemporary work is topical. Illustratively, in their introductory chapter to an edited book on *The Emerging Spatial Mind*, Plumert and Spencer (2007) note that the chapters cover three themes: memory for spatial location, self- and other-directed communication about spatial relations, and neuropsychological bases of spatial development, themes they selected "because they represent 'hot' areas within the field of spatial cognition, areas within which researchers are making serious progress on the question of how spatial skills develop" (p. xiv). Other recent reviews (e.g., Newcombe & Huttenlocher, 2000, 2006) are likewise organized by particular topics (e.g., infant location coding, models and maps, space and language). In one sense, these topical organizations appear to fit Eliot's suggestion that the field has moved to studying "isolated topics of interest." However, contemporary scholars have explicitly attempted to weave the topics together. For example, Plumert and Spencer (2007) asked each contributor to address developmental mechanisms and included integrative commentaries; Newcombe and Huttenlocher (2000) conclude their monograph with an interactionist approach which links topics within spatial development and places spatial development within a context of general developmental mechanisms and phenomena.

Illustrative Empirical Research

Empirical research on spatial development: an eclectic approach to enduring themes

The preceding section demonstrates the diversity and complexity of how spatial development has been conceptualized. We now turn to sampling empirical research. Rather than selecting any one tradition to organize our review, we have taken a more eclectic approach by discussing four topics, each of which has attracted sustained attention over time, is relevant to a range of theoretical traditions, and has been addressed at more than one level of analysis: (a) early visual perception of space; (b) coding locations in space; (c) representing and acquiring environmental knowledge; and (d) interpreting representations of space.

Early visual perception of space

Historically, infants were thought to be oblivious to their perceptual spatial worlds. Almost every introductory textbook in developmental psychology quotes William James's description of the infant's world as a "blooming, buzzing confusion" (James, 1890, p. 462). These generalizations stemmed from infants' inability to demonstrate their perception of a variety of stimuli or events. With the development of more sensitive methodologies (see Adolph & Berger, 2006; Cohen & Cashon, 2006; Kellman & Arterberry, 2006; Nelson, Thomas, & de Haan, 2006), data have shown that even very young infants perceive spatial qualities like depth, distance, size, shape, and position.

Depth. The classic study of infants' depth perception was by Gibson and Walk (1960) who placed infants (about 6 months old) at one side of a platform and asked their parents to beckon them. Moving toward their parents would take them over a "cliff" (in actuality covered by a transparent sheet). Babies with minimal crawling experience generally moved forward despite the apparent cliff; those with more crawling experience generally refused to budge. Early researchers inferred that only the latter infants had perceived depth. However, later methods revealed earlier depth sensitivity. For example, 2-month-olds showed different heart rates when held over the deep versus shallow side (Campos, Langer, & Krowitz, 1970) and made different kinds of anticipatory actions when lowered to the shallow versus deep sides (Campos, Bertenthal, & Kermoian, 1992).

Distance. Ability to perceive distance has been studied by examining infants' responses to looming objects. Even 1- or 2-month-old infants show startle responses to an expanding optical array like that seen when an object approaches the face rapidly (e.g., Ball & Tronick, 1971). Infants also show motor responses to moving objects suggesting distance sensitivity. In one illustrative study (Ronnqvist & von Hofsen, 1994), objects were moved quickly in front of 2-day-old infants. Although infants could not actually catch the objects, they swept their hands toward the objects in synchrony with the objects' trajectories, suggesting sensitivity to objects' changing distance. Older infants demonstrate sensitivity to distance in different paradigms. Granrud, Haake, and Yonas (1985), for example, found that 7- but not 5-month-old infants used prior tactile knowledge about objects' sizes to infer objects' distances under binocular viewing conditions. Yonas and Granrud (2006) showed that 7- month-olds used information from objects' cast shadows to determine which of two objects was closer.

Size and shape. Related to depth and distance perception is shape and size constancy – perceiving actual sizes and shapes of objects despite changes in sizes and shapes of retinal images that accompany changes in viewing distance and angle. To test constancy, Caron, Caron, and Carlson (1979) repeatedly showed 3-month-olds either rectangular or trapezoidal solids at different angle tilts. After infants became bored or "habituated" (indexed by short looking-times), they were shown either the shape used during habituation trials or the other (novel) object. Both objects were positioned so that the retinal images would differ from those experienced during habituation trials. Infants showed renewed interest (i.e., dishabituated or looked longer) only when the novel shape was shown, implying that 3-month-olds had developed size and shape constancy. Infants as young as 2 months are able to extract shape solely from seeing differences in motion between the contours of figures versus that of the background against which the figure moves (Johnson & Mason, 2002), and even newborns can perceive shape from stroboscopic motion which eliminates the need for smooth visual gaze for following moving objects (Valenza & Bulf, 2007). Recent research has also demonstrated that even during the first half-year of life, infants (especially males) respond to shapes they had seen earlier – but in different rotations – as if they were familiar. This sensitivity to rotation has been demonstrated in 3- to 4-month-old infants with 2-dimensional stimuli (Quinn & Liben, 2008) and in 5-month-old infants with 3-dimensional stimuli (Moore & Johnson, 2008).

Position. We end by sampling research on infants' recognition of position (a topic we revisit later when discussing more complex location tasks). In early work, Antell and Caron (1985) reported that newborns were sensitive to changes in the relative positions (above vs. below) of two simple geometric forms. In later work, Quinn (1994) studied sensitivity to more abstract spatial relations. During familiarization trials, 3-month-old infants repeatedly saw images in which a dot was positioned above a bar. During test trials, infants looked longer when the dot was below the bar than when it was in a novel location above the bar. Infants responded to increasingly abstract relations with age: at 3–4 months, infants' concepts were tied to the specific objects seen during familiarization; by 6–7 months, their spatial categories generalized across objects (Quinn, 1996). Another line of research has explored infants' sensitivity to absolute location. Newcombe and colleagues (Newcombe, Huttenlocher, & Learmonth, 1999; Newcombe, Sluzenski, & Huttenlocher, 2005) found that even by 5 months, infants recognize a disparity between where a toy had been buried in a sandbox and where it reappeared, in some cases only 8 in. (20.3 cm) away.

Taken together, a wealth of empirical research employing diverse tasks suggests that infants are remarkably sensitive to many spatial features of their environments. Although their skills are not full blown, and although much remains to be discovered, there is little question that infants do not experience space as the "blooming, buzzing confusion" described by William James over a century ago.

Coding locations in space

Having established that even very young infants are sensitive to basic qualities of space, we now turn to how infants and children use these qualities to organize spatial locations. We discuss, in turn, whether children code locations in relation to their own bodies (*egocentric* coding) or to the external environment (*allocentric* coding), which environmental features children use (geometric qualities or feature cues like color), and whether children's coding is affected by physical action.

Egocentric versus allocentric frames of reference. The study of egocentric versus allocentric coding may be traced back to research with animals well over half a century ago. In a now classic study by Tolman, Ritchie, and Kalish (1946), rats were placed at the beginning of a maze and learned to make a series of turns to reach a goal box containing food. The initial alley was then blocked. Would rats enter a nearby alley, or instead execute a more dissimilar motor response and choose an alley that was oriented directly toward the goal box? Rats did the latter, demonstrating "place learning," and leading Tolman (1948) to posit that rats rely on a "cognitive map" rather than a motor sequence ("response learning"). Are infants as clever?

One reason researchers thought infants might *not* be as clever comes from Piaget's (1954) suggestion that infants' general inability to differentiate their own bodily actions from the surrounding world would lead them to encode space in relation to their own bodies. Findings from early research using an anticipation paradigm were consistent with this idea (Acredolo, 1978; Acredolo & Evans, 1980). Infants were placed in a seat in the middle of a room that had identical windows in the walls on either side. A buzzer sounded, followed immediately by the appearance of a smiling, talking person in the window to the infant's right. After several trials, as soon as the buzzer sounded, infants looked at the right window in anticipation of the interesting event. The critical question was whether the infant had learned the event's location in relation to *body* space or in relation to *room* space.

To answer this question, the child was moved to a position directly opposite the original one and the buzzer was sounded. Infants at all ages (6, 9, and 11 months) responded egocentrically by turning to their right (now the incorrect window). However, when windows were marked, performance changed, but differently with age. With a minor landmark (star) above the window, room-based (correct) responses increased among only the 11-month infants; with salient cues (flashing lights and stripes), room-based responses were common at all ages. However, whereas most infants in the older two groups looked immediately to the correct window, those in the youngest group tended to look back and forth between windows, seemingly torn between egocentric and allocentric strategies.

A second method commonly used to study body-based versus environment-based encoding is a search task in which an interesting object is hidden in one of multiple containers arrayed in front of the child (Bremner, 1978; Bremner & Bryant, 1977).

Between the time that the object is hidden and the child is permitted to look for it, the child is moved to the opposite side of the array. As in the anticipation task, if children encode location egocentrically, they should search in the incorrect container; if they use an allocentric frame of reference, they should search correctly. Findings from this search paradigm are similar to those from the anticipation paradigm: infants have difficulty finding the environmentally defined locations when the containers are identical, but are more likely to respond correctly with additional external cues. For example, although painting the opposing ends of the table different colors has little effect, using different colored cloths to hide objects led infants as young as 9 months to search in the correct container (e.g. Butterworth, Jarrett, & Hicks, 1982).

Both anticipation and search paradigms have been used under many conditions (see Acredolo, 1981; Bremner, 1993; Newcombe & Huttenlocher, 2000; Pick & Lockman, 1981; Wellman, Cross, & Bartsch, 1986). Overall, egocentric responding is more common in unfamiliar environments, when environments lack geometric or otherwise salient cues, and when there are fewer opportunities for children to keep track of their own movements in the space. In general, young infants are more likely to use egocentric than allocentric coding, but under some conditions, they, too, can use environmental frames of reference.

Geometric and landmark cues. Once children begin attending to cues outside their own bodies, to *which* external cues do children attend? From the perspective of spatial development, of particular interest is whether children are predisposed to rely on the geometry of a space. A method originally developed to test rats' reliance on geometry (Cheng & Gallistel, 1984) has been adapted for children: the child is placed in a small rectangular room, watching as something is hidden in one of the four identical containers located in each corner (see figure 17.1). The child's eyes are covered, and the child is then turned around a few times. Once disoriented, the child is set back down and allowed to search for the object. The key finding reported initially by Cheng and Gallistel for rats, and later by Hermer and Spelke (1994, 1996) for 18- to 24-month-old children, is that after disorientation, participants typically search in a container at one of the two geometrically correct corners (figure 17.1). Within these corners, searches are usually divided about equally, even when wall colors offer cues to disambiguate correct from incorrect corners. From these data, Hermer and Spelke proposed a biologically given "geometric module" for reorientation that is impenetrable to landmark (here color) information.

Subsequent researchers have demonstrated that children rely on both landmark and geometric information under some conditions. For example, Huttenlocher and Lourenco (2007) found that toddlers used some kinds of non-geometric cues (size and density of dots) and Learmonth, Nadel, and Newcombe (2002) showed that toddlers can disambiguate locations by using stable landmark information (e.g., a bookcase or door marking one of the walls). Nardini, Atkinson, and Burgess (2008) have shown that in a square room which does not provide geometric information (because all walls are of equal length), young children use the simple color distinctions that they ignore in rectangular rooms.

Other researchers have taken issue with the artificial nature of the testing environments. One simple change that makes the space feel less artificial is to increase its size,

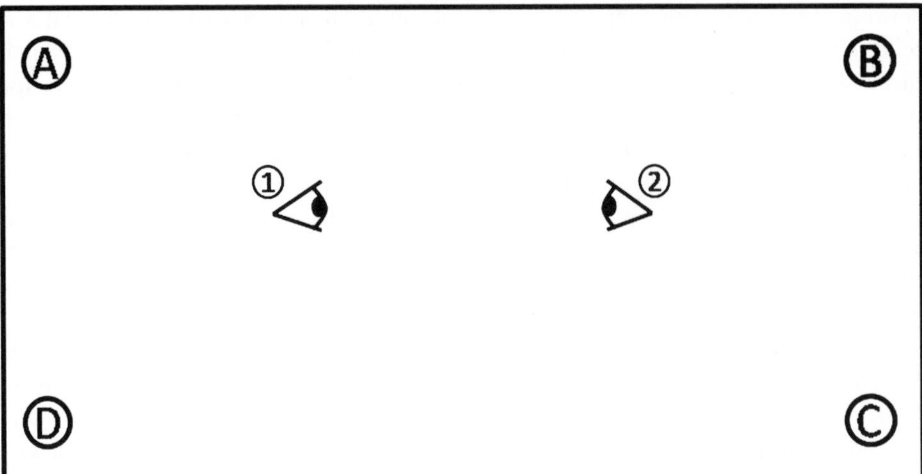

Figure 17.1 Layout of the space used in testing toddlers' use of geometric cues in a search task used by Hermer and Spelke (1994, 1996). For example, the child watches (position 1) as something is hidden in the container at location B. The child is disoriented and placed back down (position 2) to look for the hidden object. Most children search in either B or D with searches roughly divided between the two locations. Both these locations are geometrically correct and equivalent in the sense that when searching in either B or D, the long wall is to the left

and indeed, enlarging the space has increased children's use of featural (landmark) information (Learmonth; Newcombe, & Huttenlocher, 2001; Learmonth, Newcombe, Sheridan, & Jones, 2008). Others have argued for the importance of more naturalistic environments. Smith, Gilchrist, Cater, Ikram, Nott, and Hood (2008), for example, tested children in an outside grassy area that provided both natural and built landmarks. Children (3, 5, and 7 years) saw a sticker hidden beneath one of four buckets that were arrayed in a square configuration. Children were disoriented, and asked to find the sticker. Under some conditions the buckets were identical; under others, the buckets were of different colors. The scale of the configuration within the grassy area was also varied. Findings showed that the youngest children did better with the larger configuration and distinct buckets whereas older children managed even with the smaller configuration and identical buckets. Although these investigators contrast their findings with those of Hermer and Spelke (1996), it is important to note that they were studying considerably older children, with non-trivial differences in procedures (including a square rather than rectangular configuration). Thus, questions concerning the use of landmarks versus geometry are far from settled.

The role of action in spatial coding. The studies just reviewed show many circumstances in which children encode locations in relation to their own position in space. As children acquire the ability to move independently, they have many opportunities to learn that objects' positions relative to their own body change with movement. These opportunities should lead to a greater reliance on allocentric rather than egocentric codes. Consistent with this reasoning, investigators have found that children who can self-locomote are better able to identify locations in relation to the environment than are chronologically matched children who still depend on others to move them (Bai & Bertenthal, 1992; Clearfield, 2004; Horobin & Acredolo, 1986; Kermoian & Campos, 1988).

Variations in experimental conditions have also demonstrated the importance of children's actions on the way they encode spatial locations. For example, Newcombe and Ratliff (2007) observed that in reorientation tasks, restricting young children's actions decreased their tendency to draw on featural (landmark) information in identifying target locations: feature information was used by 18 months when action was unrestricted but not until 4 years when action was restricted.

Other investigators have given children either free or restricted access to environments such as room-sized model towns and then tested their cognitive maps of the spaces. Herman, Kolker, and Shaw (1982), for example, found that kindergarten children were increasingly accurate in reconstructing a model town in relation to how actively they had initially explored the town. Children who simply stood at a single location did worst, those taken passively through the town (on a wagon) did better, and those who walked through the model town under their own power did best. More recent investigators (e.g., Foreman, Gillett, & Jones, 1994; McComas, Dulberg, & Latter, 1997) have attempted to pinpoint whether the advantage from the active-movement condition derives from physical movement through the space and/or from active control over the route taken through the space, but the data do not yet allow definitive conclusions.

Investigators have also studied whether knowledge about the relation between two locations is controlled by physical experience of moving between the locations or by the perceptual experience of looking from one location to the other. Kosslyn, Pick, and Fariello (1974) placed 10 objects in a square room that had been divided into quadrants by two barriers, one opaque (preventing both travel and vision), and the other transparent (preventing only travel). Critical object pairs were separated by either 3 ft. or 5 ft. and were either within a single quadrant or located on either side of a barrier. Children (5 years) and adults first learned (to criterion) to go from a home position to place each object in its correct location. Respondents were then taken to a test location, given one object, and asked which of the remaining nine had been closest in the room, which next closest, and so on, until all were ranked. Each of the 10 objects served once as the referent, and for each, the participant was asked to rank the distances of the other nine items. The data showed that relative to objects pairs falling *within* a single quadrant, both children and adults exaggerated distances between pairs that had been separated by opaque barriers, but only children also exaggerated distance between objects separated by transparent barriers, leading Kosslyn et al. to conclude that physical movement was important for children but not adults. Subsequent work, though, suggests that these effects vary depending on how participants are asked to externalize their knowledge of the layout (Newcombe & Liben, 1982), an issue that is pervasive in the study of spatial representation (see Liben, 1981, 1988).

Using a similar paradigm, Hund, Plumert, and Benney (2002) have shown that when a space is divided by opaque walls or lines, there is category bias (i.e., a tendency to place objects closer to the center and therefore closer together within a region), but this effect varies with age in interaction with learning conditions. Adults showed category bias for all boundary types, and irrespective of whether objects' locations were learned all at once or region by region. Older children (9 and 11 years) showed category bias under the former learning condition only; younger children (7 years) showed bias under neither condition. In summarizing research on category effects, Plumert, Hund, and Recker (2007) correctly point out the critical importance of studying the "interactions of the cognitive system and environmental structure over time to fully understand how thinking emerges over short and long time scales" (p. 49).

Representing and acquiring environmental knowledge

Thus far we have shown that even infants are sensitive to many features of space, and that, with age, these sensitivities develop and the range of spatial strategies expands. Development also brings an increasing range of opportunities to interact with the environment. Newborns can control only their gaze, and even that is possible only within a limited focal range. They gradually master movement (head lifting, head turning, body turning, sitting, crawling, walking), and develop into children, adolescents, and adults who can bike, drive, and perhaps fly. Each new means of locomotion – in interaction with a host of cognitive and social factors – expands individuals' ecological worlds. What do children learn about these worlds?

Stored environmental knowledge. One question of interest is what children learn naturally about their everyday environments. In early research, Piaget and Inhelder (1956) asked children to draw maps of their home and school. Preschoolers typically represented isolated buildings, perhaps including clusters of nearby locations, but with little integration across areas. Older children produced more integrated representations, improvement taken as a sign of spatial conceptual development. Later investigators using similar tasks have shown that young children typically use inconsistent scales, inconsistent viewing perspectives (e.g., showing some objects from overhead and others from an eye-level viewing angle), and incorrect links among neighborhoods even when spatial relationships are reasonably accurate within them (e.g., Gerber, 1981, 1984; see reviews in Liben, Patterson, & Newcombe, 1981; Ottosson, 1987; Spencer, Blades, & Morsley, 1989; Wiegand, 2006).

Recognizing that children's difficulties might reflect an inability to create sketch maps rather than their ignorance of the environment, some investigators have used other methodologies to externalize children's environmental knowledge. In one illustrative study, Siegel and Schadler (1977) asked preschool children to use blocks to create a tabletop model of their classroom layout. Some models were very accurate; others bore no similarity to the real classroom. To reduce representational demands even further, Liben, Moore, and Golbeck (1982) included a task devoid of symbolic demands: furniture was removed from the child's familiar classroom, and the child was asked to help the experimenter move the furniture back so that it would be "exactly where it usually is when you come to school in the morning" (p. 1278). As predicted, children performed significantly better in the real room than on the model. Interestingly, though, several children were grossly inaccurate even on the full-scale task, suggesting that at least some children fail to encode, store, or retrieve basic information about the layout of their everyday environments, even under minimally demanding task requirements.

In research designed to study children's knowledge of their larger communities, Hart (1981) asked 4- to 9-year-olds to create floor-sized models of all of the places in the town that they knew, and asked them questions about where they played, how they traveled between home and school, and where they were allowed to go without supervision (i.e., their "free range"). Children tended to show the highest levels of spatial organization in the regions near their homes, emphasized places in their models that had high personal value (e.g., a candy store), but, again, often failed to integrate clusters of known neighborhoods. Greater free range was correlated with greater environmental knowledge. Data from other research suggests that it is not only the size of free range that matters, it is also the way it is experienced. Children who travel to school independently evidence greater environmental knowledge than children typically driven to school by an adult (Hart & Berzok, 1982; Ottosson, 1987; Rissotto & Tonucci, 2002; Spencer & Darvizeh, 1981), although the correlational nature of these findings does not allow conclusions about causality.

Acquiring new environmental knowledge. The research discussed thus far establishes that, in general, older children know more than younger children about their environments and are able to represent their environmental knowledge more completely and systematically, but also that there are considerable differences among children of the same age. Data from both correlational and experimental studies are consistent with the hypothesis that experiences in environments – particularly experiences that involve physical action and self-direction – are important for developing environmental knowledge and integrated representations. In addition to cross-sectional studies of children's performance in relation to age and experience, investigators have also looked at microgenetic change within individual children.

The classic paper on the emergence of children's environmental knowledge and representation was written over three decades ago by Siegel and White (1975) who suggested that children first encode landmarks, later represent routes linking landmarks, and finally integrate routes into an overall framework or configuration something akin to a survey map. This progression is compatible with Piaget's suggestion that children begin with topological concepts (e.g., the candy store is next to the theatre) and only gradually develop projective and Euclidean concepts (e.g., knowing whether to turn right or left at a particular intersection depending on heading direction; understanding how to represent the length of roads and angles of intersections).

One empirical approach to studying children's changing environmental knowledge has been to ask the same children to produce representations of an environment as they become familiar with it. For example, Wapner, Kaplan, and Ciottone (1981) examined sketch maps produced by children soon after they had arrived in a new town, and then again over the ensuing 9 months. Figure 17.2 shows drawings made by one child over a 6-month period that are compatible with the landmark–route-survey sequence suggested by Siegel and White (1975). More recent research, though, suggests that there may not be a fixed sequence either with respect to age, or with respect to increasing familiarity with the environment (see, e.g., Allen, 1999; Montello, 1998).

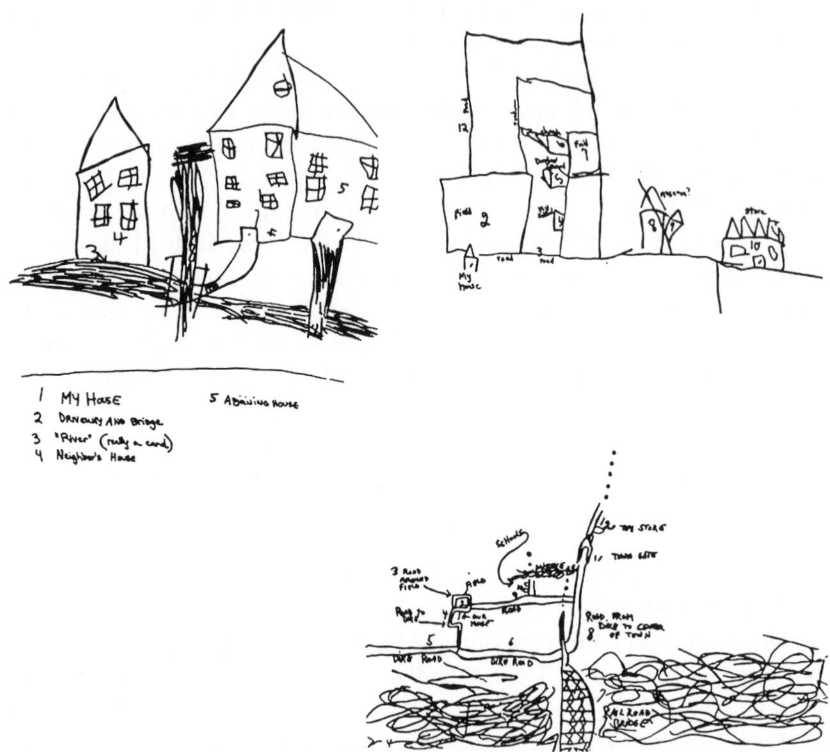

Figure 17.2 Sketch maps drawn by a 6.5-year-old soon after arriving in a new community and then again during the following 6 months. (From Wapner, Kaplan, and Ciottone, 1981.)

An important component of research on children's acquisition of knowledge about environments is aimed at identifying specific processes that are involved. Illustrative is an early study by Allen, Kirasic, Siegel, and Herman (1979) designed to study age-linked differences in skill at identifying informative cues from the environment. Children (grades 2 and 5) and adults were asked to select which locations along a walk (shown as a series of slides) would be particularly good for helping them remember "where they were along the walk" (p. 1064). In a second study, new participants of the same ages judged distances between the starting point and each of nine scenes identified in Study 1 as having high landmark potential. Children were worse than adults in selecting informative scenes (e.g., corners where turns were necessary) and at answering questions about distances. However, older (but not younger) children profited from being given adults' scene selections. Similar findings were reported in actual outdoor environments with 8- versus 12-year-olds: older children more commonly used permanent references as landmarks, younger children more commonly used transient objects such as animals or vehicles (Cornell, Hadley, Sterling, Chan, & Boechler, 2001). Others (Allen & Kirasic, 2003) have directly examined specific visual-attention processes (e.g., monitoring eye movements to study where and how long participants look at different parts of the images), although, to our knowledge, thus far this work has been limited to adults.

The role of attentional strategies has also been tested with intervention designs. For example, Cornell and colleagues (e.g., Cornell, Heth, & Broda, 1989; Cornell, Heth, & Rowat, 1992) reported that environmental knowledge is enhanced by suggesting to children that they "look back" as they travel, or by pointing out landmarks that are useful choice points for a return journey. Interestingly, the success of such interventions interacts markedly with age: salutary effects on performance are typically found for children in late, but not early, childhood.

Interpreting representations of space

The research just discussed was focused first on environmental knowledge that children acquire naturally (and incidentally) from direct interactions in home, school, and play environments. Knowledge about environments can also be acquired via environmental representations such as maps. Before turning to research on children's understanding and use of such representations, it is important to distinguish between research in which external representations like maps are used as tools to study some construct of interest (e.g., how children conceptualize their home neighborhood) versus research in which maps are the focus of interest in their own right (Liben, 1981). Much early research using maps was the former; more recent work (and our focus here) is the latter (e.g., Liben & Myers, 2007; Uttal, 2000; Wiegand, 2006). The goal of this work is to learn how children develop their understanding (or production) of symbolic and spatial information in maps.

It is also useful to provide some introductory comments about maps themselves to address the common misconception that maps are essentially flattened miniaturizations (or *re*-presentations) of reality as it exists. Instead, and as discussed in far greater detail elsewhere (Downs, 1981; Liben, 2001, 2006; Liben & Downs, 1989, 1992), maps are selective, symbolic communications about the referent. A mapmaker (whether a professional cartographer or a layperson drawing a sketch map for a tourist) selects only some information to represent (e.g., perhaps major buildings, roads, traffic signals, but not sidewalks, trees, bus stops); chooses specific symbols to represent the selected referents (e.g., rectangles, lines, double circles); and makes decisions about the spatial qualities of the map (e.g., drawing it at a small or large scale, or perhaps not to scale at all). Maps thus require the user to understand both the symbolic and the spatial correspondences between the referent space and the map, the two topics used to organize our empirical review below.

Interpreting symbolic meaning of maps. A foundational skill in interpreting place representations is extracting referential meaning from marks on paper or screen. Infants interpret referential content of representations very early. DeLoache, Strauss, and Maynard (1979), for example, found that 5-month-old infants who had been habituated to an actual object did not dishabituate when shown a photograph of the same object, but did dishabituate when shown a novel object irrespective of whether it was shown as an object or picture. These data show that infants were attending to the semantic meaning, not to the medium of presentation. Anecdotes suggest that infants approach pictures as though they are actual objects (as when infants attempt to lift patterns off fabric or paper; Liben

& Downs, 1992; Ninio & Bruner, 1978) and research has shown that infants grasp at photographs with hand positions that would be needed to grasp the depicted objects (DeLoache, Pierroutsakos, Uttal, Rosengren, & Gottlieb, 1998).

By roughly 3 years, toddlers understand the basic "stand for" link between representations (e.g., scale models) and their environmental referents (objects in a room; see DeLoache, 1987). But even after children have come to understand the basic idea that one thing can be used to stand for another, and thus to appreciate representational correspondences in general, there is still much to learn. Some charming examples of the challenges of symbolic understanding come from an interview study of 3- to 6-year-old children (Liben & Downs, 1989, 1991). When shown various place representations, even the youngest children understood that representations depicted environments (e.g., indentifying an aerial photograph of Chicago as "a city" or "buildings and roads"), but were confused with respect to referential scope (e.g., identifying it as "the United States," "Africa," and "the whole world"). Preschoolers also tend to assume that qualities of the symbol are necessarily informative about the analogous qualities of the referent, as in suggesting that a red line on a road map stood for a road that was really red, or that the yellow areas (cities) showed "eggs" or "firecrackers." More recent research (Myers & Liben, 2008) has demonstrated that even 6- to 8-year-olds struggle against the assumption that referent and symbol color necessarily match.

Understanding the spatial meaning of maps. As discussed in more detail elsewhere (Liben, 2001, 2006), maps are designed for particular purposes, and these influence cartographic decisions. Every map represents its referential space at a particular scale (e.g., large scale as in a map of a zoo vs. small scale as in a state road map), from a particular viewing angle (e.g., vertical as in a room plan vs. oblique as in a tourist map with perspective drawings of buildings), and from a particular viewing direction or azimuth (e.g., facing north or east). Below we use these three map qualities – scale, viewing angle, and viewing azimuth – to organize our empirical review. We emphasize studies employing large- or medium-scale maps of everyday settings such as classrooms and campuses. Before turning to those studies, however, we mention briefly some illustrative findings from developmental mapping research that uses maps of simple layouts (sometimes with as few as one or two objects) in small spaces (such as table tops, small laboratory rooms, or playrooms erected within them). Such research is designed to test component skills under tightly controlled circumstances.

Under these conditions, very young children demonstrate basic map skills. To illustrate, under some conditions, 4-year-olds can use a picture of an isosceles triangle to place an object in the appropriate corner of a tabletop triangle (Vasilyeva & Bowers, 2006; Vasilyeva & Huttenlocher, 2004) and can use geometric information from a simple map to place objects into appropriate bins (Shusterman, Lee, & Spelke, 2008). By 4 (and sometimes by 3) years, children can use dots placed on a small strip of paper to guide their placement of objects in a larger sandbox (Huttenlocher, Newcombe, & Vasilyeva, 1999). Studies like these suggest that rudimentary representational and spatial skills needed for map reading appear early. However, studies using more natural maps and spaces paint a more protracted picture of development with respect to scale, viewing angle, and viewing direction.

Scale confusions have been observed in young children in several studies. Preschoolers, shown an aerial photograph, interpreted boats as fish, a river as a snake, and roads as ropes. In some cases they rejected a line as showing a road because it was "too skinny" or "not fat enough for two cars to go on" (Liben & Downs, 1989). In another study, 3- and 4-year-olds, having just identified the sea on an aerial photograph, proceeded to identify neighboring hills as "pebbles" (Spencer, Harrison, & Darvizeh, 1980). Findings reported by Uttal (1996) are also indicative of young children's difficulty with scale. Using a plan map of a room, he taught 4- to 6-year-old children the locations of toys, and then took children to the actual room to place the toys. Although children were quite good at reproducing the configural relations among the toys, they were not good at scaling up the configuration accurately, sometimes simply clustering the configuration of toys in a small corner of the room. Also demonstrating the challenges of metrics are data from studies in which elementary schoolchildren are asked to place stickers on maps to show the locations of people in classrooms (Liben & Downs, 1993), toy flags on a 3-dimensional model of the local terrain (Liben & Downs, 1989), and large flags hung at various locations on a campus (Kastens & Liben, 2007). Many of the children who managed to place their sticker on the correct type of symbol or even the correct token (e.g., the symbol for the correct table or building) were inaccurate with respect to the precise metric location. The metric imprecision seen in these older children suggests that the evidence of metric sensitivity in infancy described earlier (see, e.g., Huttenlocher et al., 1999; Shusterman et al., 2008) represents the emergence but not the mastery of relevant spatial concepts and skills.

Viewing angle is another aspect of maps that is mastered only gradually. Part of the challenge stems from the contrast between the straight-ahead eye-level angle seen when moving around the real environment versus the overhead angle of the prototypical plan-view map. Consistent with the proposed importance of embodied experience (Liben, 2008a), preschool children interpret vertical views on photographs or maps as if they were eye-level views. For example, preschoolers shown aerial photographs identified trains lined up in parallel as bookshelves, a triangular-shaped parking area as a hill (Liben & Downs, 1991), and tennis courts as doors (Spencer et al., 1980). When asked to draw their school from directly overhead, many first- and second-grade children drew or selected elevation views (Liben & Downs, 1989). In another study in which preschoolers were asked to place stickers on maps of their classroom to show the locations of objects (Liben & Yekel, 1996), children performed significantly worse on a plan (overhead) view map than on an oblique perspective map. Performance was particularly poor on the plan map if it was used first.

The third cartographic feature is viewing direction or azimuth, expressed as degrees (clockwise) from true north. Importantly, despite common contemporary beliefs, maps need not place north at the top of the page. To make this point one need only recall that during the Middle Ages, maps were conventionally drawn facing east – the orient – hence the term "orientation." Azimuth may also be selected based on environmental layout. For example, for graphic convenience, maps of New York City are typically oriented with avenues running straight up and down the page even though the avenues do not actually run north/south.

Assuming a paper map (rather than a GPS-controlled navigational device), the map user must understand the self–map–space relation illustrated in figure 17.3. In this

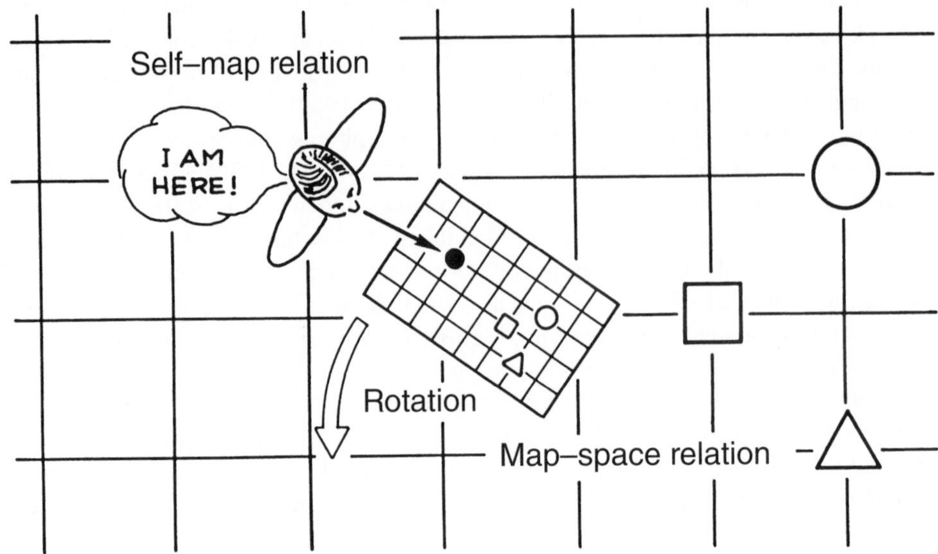

Figure 17.3 Illustration of self–map–space relationship. When using a map for navigational purposes, the user needs to determine self-location and facing direction on the map and, in addition, understand the relation between map and space. In this figure, the map is unaligned with the space and would have to be rotated approximately 35° counterclockwise to bring it into alignment. (From Liben, 2006.)

example, map and space are not perfectly aligned: to bring the map into alignment, it must be rotated approximately 35° counterclockwise (see arrow labeled "Rotation"). When an individual is using a map within the depicted space, it is also necessary to identify self-location ("I am here" or IAH) within the space and map (see black dot in figure 17.3). When the space and map are unaligned, the user's facing direction in the space (room) differs from the facing direction on the map. Thus, in the example shown, if a user's target were the location represented by the open circle, the user would need to turn about 35° counterclockwise before walking forward (even though on the map, the circle-target is directly ahead of the IAH starting location).

A considerable body of research has examined children's ability to respond to challenges raised by unaligned maps. In one early study (Bluestein & Acredolo, 1979), a square room contained four identical boxes in each corner. A toy elephant was hidden in one box and an elephant sticker was placed on that box's symbol on a room map. The child was then asked to find the elephant. When map and room were aligned, the elephant was found by most 4- and 5-year-olds, and by about half the 3-year-olds. When the map was misaligned, success was common (>80%) in only the oldest group. Success was rare in both 3- and 4-year-old children (<20% correct; see Liben & Downs, 1989). In another early study, Presson (1982) showed that kindergarten and first-grade children were virtually always able to go correctly to one of four identical containers in a room after seeing the location indicated on one of four identical symbols on a map. However, success rates dropped to 33% and 50% respectively when the map was misaligned with the space. Similarly, Liben and Downs (1993) asked children (kindergarteners, first- and second-graders, and fifth/sixth-graders) to place arrows on classroom maps to show where someone was standing, and which direction he was pointing. Performance was worse on both location and direction tasks under unaligned conditions. Even many adults find it difficult to understand the relation between representations and spaces when the map and space are unaligned. For example, Levine, Marchon, and Hanley (1984) found that college students who consulted a floor plan of a university library took longer to study the map and were less likely to reach the target when the map was rotated 180° than when it was aligned with the space.

In the studies just described, participants were forced to use a misaligned map, either because the experimenter fixed the map in an unaligned position or because the map was posted on the wall out of alignment. What happens when map users are free to move the map at will? Among college students asked to indicate their position on a campus map, those who spontaneously turned the map as they worked (rather than leaving it in a fixed position) were more accurate (Liben, Myers, & Kastens, 2008). A similar advantage held when students were asked to show their own location and the direction they were facing, and to point toward a target building (Liben, Myers, & Christensen, in press). Data from 8- to 10-year-olds show a similar pattern: children who tended to align their maps were more accurate in placing stickers on a map to show flags' locations (Liben, 2008b). Additional research is underway to test whether students who do not spontaneously align the map are able to do so, and, if so, whether their accuracy improves accordingly.

Taken together, studies on map understanding have provided evidence that all major spatial qualities of maps (scale, angle, and azimuth) present significant challenges to users. Normative developmental data show improvement with age, but data from studies examining individual difference reveal that some people have difficulty with graphic representations even during adulthood. Although we have focused our review on representations in relation to environmental knowledge, there is also a large body of work on developmental changes and individual differences in understanding other forms of spatial–graphic representations (e.g., graphs, diagrams; see Lehrer & Schauble, 2006).

Concluding Comments

This chapter has only scratched the surface of concepts and empirical research related to spatial development. We began by discussing a variety of approaches to organizing the study of spatial development, each of which is informative in a somewhat different way. We devoted the bulk of the chapter to discussing four enduring topics and to a sample of research addressed to each. The work to date leads us to paint a picture of the infant who begins with some rudimentary skills, and who, with age, develops increasingly diverse and more flexible strategies that can be applied to a range of spatial challenges. Our closing comments are necessarily brief, and offer more questions than answers. We hope that these ideas, combined with the literature already reviewed, will tantalize readers to consult other resources and perhaps even to join the community of scholars who study spatial development.

Group and individual differences

Implied by the earlier comparisons across age groups is the importance of normative cognitive development, the accumulation of experience, and the unfolding of biologically controlled maturation. It is noteworthy, though, that most extant spatial-development research is cross-sectional rather than longitudinal, and that researchers rarely assess those factors assumed to account for differences across chronological age (itself only a marker variable). It is also notable that, in contemporary scholarship, probably what have attracted the most attention are the very early spatial competencies revealed by new infant methodologies. What is arguably equally newsworthy and potentially problematic for a theory of normative spatial development is the accumulating evidence that some cognitively intact adults have significant difficulty on spatial tasks designed for children. A second relevant grouping variable mentioned briefly in earlier portions of this chapter is participant sex. Although the vast literature on sex-related differences was not discussed here, there is compelling evidence of sex differences on a range of spatial tasks (see National Research Council, 2006). Such differences have proven useful in suggesting both biological and experiential factors that contribute to spatial development.

In addition to age and sex, there are many other grouping variables that should continue to be explored in relation to spatial cognition. For example, there are effects associated with how space is encoded in the language of one's native tongue (Choi & McDonough, 2007) or in the art of one's culture (Hagen, 1986). And, apart from differences in spatial outcomes that appear to be linked to the consequences of group membership, there are differences that appear to be linked to the combination of biological and experiential histories which makes every individual unique.

In short, for full understanding of spatial development, it will be important that future lifespan researchers study the origins and educational implications of significant differences in spatial cognition not only across age, but also between males and females, across cultures, languages, and different family and educational histories.

Methodological advances

The study of spatial development is likely to be enhanced not only by expanding the range of studies using traditional methodologies, but also by employing new methodologies. One particularly promising methodology involves virtual realities (VRs) or environments (VEs) which are computer-generated spaces that appear (or even feel) 3-dimensional. Some VRs are presented on desktops; others are presented with goggles and permit the user to act on objects in space or even walk among them. An important advantage of VRs is that they can allow researchers to control or manipulate environmental features in ways that would be impossible in real space. Ongoing research is studying the degree to which VR methods can substitute for methods traditionally used to study spatial development (e.g., presenting environmental data with still photographs or film or in the real field). For example, early developmental VR work (e.g., Jansen-Osmann & Wiedenbauer, 2004) has replicated some but not all findings using more traditional methods. In addition to holding promise as a research tool, VR has already demonstrated its utility for helping physically disabled children learn real-world layouts (Foreman, Stanton, Wilson, & Duffy, 2003). Other new technologies are also providing powerful ways to record spatial behaviors. For example, the GPS-enabled WayTracer (Kuhnmünch & Strube, 2009) allows researchers to track participants' locations and strategies during navigation and map use. Eye-tracking devices and head-mounted cameras can likewise serve as useful tools for recording behaviors in natural environments. Advances in neuroimaging also promise to help illuminate some of the nuances of spatial development. While developmental neurological research on spatial cognition has thus far been relatively limited and has been focused largely on mapping brain areas associated with different tasks, we anticipate that future work will address questions about how maturation and experience work together to shape the child's spatial thought and behaviors.

The evolving spatial world

It is not only the world of researchers that is changing. Daily lives are being profoundly affected by the ever faster, smaller, cheaper, and more pervasive space-related technologies which allow people to access, communicate, and manipulate vast quantities of data instantaneously. Individual GPS devices, car navigational systems, and programs such as Google Earth allow people to maintain an egocentric frame of reference as they move through space. Computer-assisted design programs enable users to see (rather than just imagine) how a new addition will look on a building. Various scientific visualization tools allow scientists to catalogue and study terabytes of information and allow children to learn about a wide range of scientific phenomena. An important question raised by these new technologies is whether their ready availability will come to affect the ways people represent, think about, and manipulate their spatial worlds. The evolution of spatial tools will probably challenge us as developmental scientists at least as much as it challenges the developing children we study.

References

Acredolo, L. P. (1978). Development of spatial orientation in infancy. *Developmental Psychology*, *14*, 224–234.

Acredolo, L. P. (1981). Small- and large-scale spatial concepts in infancy and childhood. In L. S. Liben, A. H. Patterson, & N. Newcombe (Eds.), *Spatial representation and behavior across the life span: Theory and application* (pp. 63–81). New York: Academic Press.

Acredolo, L. P., & Evans, D. (1980). Developmental changes in the effects of landmarks on infant spatial behavior. *Developmental Psychology*, *16*, 312–318.

Adolph, K. E., & Berger, S. E. (2006). Motor development. In W. Damon & R. M. Lerner (Series Eds.), D. Kuhn & R. S. Sigler (Vol. Eds.), *Handbook of child psychology: Vol 2. Cognition, perception, and language* (6th ed., pp. 161–213). Hoboken, NJ: Wiley.

Allen, G. L. (1999). Spatial abilities, cognitive maps, and wayfinding. In R. G. Golledge (Ed.), *Wayfinding behavior: Cognitive mapping and other spatial processes* (pp. 46–80). Baltimore: Johns Hopkins University Press.

Allen, G. L., & Kirasic, K. C. (2003). Visual attention during route learning: A look at selection and engagement. In W. Kuhn, M. F. Worboys, & S. Timpf (Eds.), *Lecture notes in computer science* (Vol. *2825*, pp. 390–398). Heidelberg: Springer Berlin.

Allen, G. L., Kirasic, K. C., Siegel, A. W., & Herman, J. F. (1979). Developmental issues in cognitive mapping: The selection and utilization of environmental landmarks. *Child Development, 50*, 1062–1070.

Antell, S. E. G., & Caron, A. J. (1985). Neonatal perception of spatial relationships. *Infant Behavior and Development, 8*, 15–23.

Bai, D. L., & Bertenthal, B. I. (1992). Locomotor status and the development of spatial search skills. *Child Development, 63*, 215–226.

Ball, W., & Tronick, E. (1971). Infant responses to impending collision: Optical and real. *Science, 171*, 818–820.

Bluestein, N., & Acredolo, L. (1979). Developmental changes in map-reading skills. *Child Development, 50*, 691–697.

Boles, D. B., Barth, J. M., Merrill, E. C. (2008). Asymmetry and performance: Toward a neurodevelopmental theory. *Brain and Cognition, 66*, 124–139.

Bremner, J. G. (1978). Egocentric versus allocentric coding in nine-month-old infants: Factors influencing the choice of code. *Developmental Psychology, 14*, 346–355.

Bremner, J. G. (1993). Spatial representation in infancy and early childhood. In C. Pratt & A. F. Garton (Eds.), *Systems of representation in children* (pp. 67–89). New York: Wiley.

Bremner, J. G., & Bryant, P. E. (1977). Place versus response as the basis of spatial errors made by young infants. *Journal of Experimental Child Psychology, 23*, 162–171.

Butterworth, G., Jarret, N., & Hicks, L. (1982). Spatiotemporal identity in infancy: Perceptual competence or conceptual deficit? *Developmental Psychology, 18*, 435–449.

Campos, J. J., Bertenthal, B. I., Kermoian, R. (1992). Early experience and emotional development: The emergence of wariness of heights. *Psychological Science, 3*, 61–64.

Campos, J. J., Langer, A., & Krowitz, A. (1970). Cardiac responses on the visual cliff in prelocomotor human infants. *Science, 9*, 196–197.

Caron, A. J., Caron, R. F., & Carlson, V. R. (1979). Infant perception of the invariant shape of objects varying in slant. *Child Development, 50*, 716–721.

Carroll, J. B. (1993). *Human cognitive abilities: A survey of factor-analytic studies.* New York: Cambridge University Press.

Casey, M. B., Nuttall, R. L., & Pezaris, E. (2001). Spatial-mechanical reasoning skills versus mathematics self-confidence as mediators of gender differences on mathematics subtests using cross-national gender-based items. *Journal of Research in Mathematics Education, 32*, 28–57.

Cheng, K., & Gallistel, C. R. (1984). Testing the geometric power of an animal's spatial representation. In H. L. Roitblat, T. G. Bever, & H. S. Terrace (Eds.), *Animal cognition: Proceedings of the Harry Frank Guggenheim Conference, June 2–4, 1982* (pp. 409–423). Hillsdale, NJ: Erlbaum.

Choi, S., & McDonough, L. (2007). Adapting spatial concepts for different languages. In J. M. Plumert & J. P. Spencer (Eds.), *The emerging spatial mind* (pp. 142–167). New York: Oxford.

Clearfield, M. W. (2004). The role of crawling and walking experience in infant spatial memory. *Journal of Experimental Child Psychology, 89*, 214–241.

Cohen, L. B., & Cashon, C. H. (2006). Infant cognition. In W. Damon & R. M. Lerner (Series Eds.), D. Kuhn & R. S. Sigler (Vol. Eds.), *Handbook of child psychology: Vol 2. Cognition, perception, and language* (6th ed., pp. 214–251). Hoboken, NJ: Wiley.

Cornell, E. H., Hadley, D. C., Sterling, T. M., Chan, M. A., & Boechler, P. (2001). Adventure as a stimulus for cognitive development. *Journal of Environmental Psychology, 21*, 219–231.

Cornell, E. H., Heth, C. D., & Broda, L. S. (1989). Children's wayfinding: Response to instructions to use environmental landmarks. *Developmental Psychology, 25*, 755–764.

Cornell, E. H., Heth, C. D., & Rowat, W. L., (1992). Wayfinding by children and adults: Response to instructions to use look-back and retrace strategies. *Developmental Psychology, 28*, 328–336.

Cosmides, L., & Tooby, J. (1992). Cognitive adaptations for social exchange. In J. Barkow, L. Cosmides, & J. Tooby (Eds.), *The adapted mind: Evolutionary psychology and the generation of culture* (pp. 163–228). New York: Oxford University Press.

Damon, W., & Lerner, R. M. (Eds.) (2006). *Handbook of child psychology* (6th ed.). Hoboken, NJ: Wiley.

DeLoache, J. S. (1987). Rapid change in the symbolic functioning of very young children. *Science, 238*, 1556–1557.

DeLoache, J. S., Pierroutsakos, S. L., Uttal, D. H., Rosengren, K. S., & Gottlieb, A. (1998). Grasping the nature of pictures. *Psychological Science, 9*, 205–210.

DeLoache, J. S., Strauss, M. S., & Maynard, J. (1979). Picture perception in infancy. *Infant Behavior and Development, 2*, 77–89.

Dodwell, P. C. (1963). Children's understanding of spatial concepts. *Canadian Journal of Psychology, 17*, 141–161.

Downs, R. M. (1981). Maps and mappings as metaphors for spatial representation. In L. S. Liben, A. H. Patterson, & N. Newcombe (Eds.), *Spatial representation and behavior across the life span: Theory and application* (pp. 143–166). New York: Academic Press.

Eliot, J. (1987). *Models of psychological space, psychometric, developmental, and experimental approaches*. New York: Springer-Verlag.

Fitzhugh, S., Morrison, A., Shipley, T. F., Chein, J., Newcombe, N. (2008, June). *The effects of working memory training versus spatial visualization training on general intelligence measures, spatial intelligence measures and eye movements*. Paper presented at the Conference on Research and Training in Spatial Intelligence, Evanston, IL.

Foreman, N., Gillett, R., & Jones, S. (1994). Choice autonomy and memory for spatial locations in six-year-old children. *British Journal of Psychology, 85*, 17–27.

Foreman, N., Stanton, D., Wilson, P., & Duffy, H. (2003). Spatial knowledge of a real school environment acquired from virtual or physical models by able-bodied children and children with physical disabilities. *Journal of Experimental Psychology: Applied, 9*, 67–74.

Gaulin, S. J. C. (1992). Evolution of sex difference in spatial ability. *American Journal of Physical Anthropology, 35*, 125–151.

Gauvain, M. (1993). The development of spatial thinking in everyday activity. *Developmental Review, 13*, 92–121.

Gerber, R. (1981). Young children's understanding of the elements of maps. *Teaching Geography, 6*, 128–133.

Gerber, R. (1984). The development of competence and performance in cartographic language by children at the concrete level of map-reasoning. *Cartographica, 21*, 98–119.

Gibson, E. J., & Walk, R. D. (1960). The "visual cliff." *Scientific American, 202*, 64–71.

Granrud, C. E., Haake, R. J., & Yonas, A. (1985). Infants' sensitivity to familiar size: The effect of memory on spatial perception. *Perception and Psychophysics, 37*, 459–466.

Hagen, M. A. (1986). *Varieties of realism: Geometries of representational art.* New York: Cambridge University Press.

Hart, R. A. (1981). Children's spatial representation of the landscape: Lessons and questions from a field study. In L. S. Liben, A. H. Patterson, & N. Newcombe (Eds.), *Spatial representation and behavior across the life span: Theory and application* (pp. 195–233). New York: Academic Press.

Hart, R. A., & Berzok, M. (1982). Children's strategies for mapping the geographic-scale environment. In M. Potegal (Ed.), *Spatial abilities: Development and physiological foundations* (pp. 147–169). New York: Academic Press.

Hegarty, M., & Waller, D. A. (2005). Individual differences in spatial abilities. In P. Shah & A. Miyake (Eds.), *The Cambridge handbook of visuospatial thinking* (pp. 121–169). New York: Cambridge University Press.

Herman, J. F., Kolker, R. G., & Shaw, M. L. (1982). Effects of motor activity on children's intentional and incidental memory for spatial locations. *Child Development, 53,* 239–244.

Hermer, L., & Spelke, E. S. (1994). A geometric process for spatial reorientation in young children. *Nature, 370,* 57–59.

Hermer, L., & Spelke, E. S. (1996). Modularity and development: The case of spatial reorientation, *Cognition, 61,*195–232.

Hines, M. (2000). Gonadal hormones and sexual differentiation of human behavior: Effects on psychosexual and cognitive development. In A. Matsumoto (Ed.), *Sexual differentiation of the brain* (pp. 257–278). Boca Raton, FL: CRC Press.

Horobin, K., & Acredolo, L. (1986). The role of attentiveness, mobility history and separation of hiding sites on Stage IV behavior. *Journal of Experimental Child Psychology, 41,* 114–127.

Hund, A. M., Plumert, J. M., & Benney, C. J. (2002). Experiencing nearby locations together in time: The role of spatiotemporal contiguity in children's memory for location. *Journal of Experimental Child Psychology, 82,* 200–225.

Huttenlocher, J., & Lourenco, S. F. (2007). Coding location in enclosed spaces: Is geometry the principle? *Developmental Science, 10,* 741–756.

Huttenlocher, J. Newcombe, N., & Vasilyeva, M. (1999). Spatial scaling in young children. *Psychological Science, 10,* 393–398.

Jammer, M. (1954). *Concepts of space.* Cambridge, MA: Harvard University Press.

Jansen-Osmann, P., & Wiedenbauer, G. (2004). The representation of landmarks and routes in children and adults: A study in a virtual environment. *Journal of Environmental Psychology, 24,* 347–357.

Johnson, S. P., & Mason, U. (2002). Perception of kinetic illusory contours by two-month-old infants. *Child Development, 73,* 22–34.

Kastens, K. A., & Liben, L. S. (2007). Eliciting self-explanations improves children's performance on a field-based map skills task. *Cognition and Instruction, 25,* 45–74.

Kellman, P. J., & Arterberry, M. E. (2006). Infant visual perception. In W. Damon & R. M. Lerner (Series Eds.), D. Kuhn & R. S. Siegler (Vol. Eds.), *Handbook of child psychology: Vol 2. Cognition, perception, and language* (6th ed., pp. 109–160). Hoboken, NJ: Wiley.

Kermoian, R., & Campos, J. J. (1988). Locomotor experience: A facilitator of spatial cognitive development. *Child Development, 59,* 908–917.

Kosslyn, S. M., Pick, H. L., & Fariello, G. R. (1974). Cognitive maps in children and men. *Child Development, 45,* 707–716.

Kuhnmünch, G., & Strube, G. (2009). WayTracer: A mobile assistant for real-time logging of events and related positions, *Computers in Human Behavior, 25,* 1156–1164.

Kwon, H., Reiss, A. L., & Menon, V. (2002). Neural basis of protracted developmental changes in visuo-spatial working memory. *Proceedings of the National Academy of Sciences, 99,* 13336–13341.

Learmonth, A. E., Nadel, L., & Newcombe, N. S. (2002). Children's use of landmarks: Implications for modularity theory. *Psychological Science, 13*, 337–341.

Learmonth, A. E., Newcombe, N., & Huttenlocher, J. (2001). Toddlers' use of metric information and landmarks to reorient. *Journal of Experimental Child Psychology, 80*, 225–244.

Learmonth, A. E., Newcombe, N. S., Sheridan, N., & Jones, M. (2008). Why size counts: Children's spatial reorientation in large and small enclosures. *Developmental Science, 11*, 414–426.

Lehrer, R., & Schauble, L. (2006). Scientific thinking and science literacy. In W. Damon & R. M. Lerner (Series Eds.), K. A. Renninger, & I. E. Sigel (Vol. Eds.), *Handbook of child psychology: Vol. 4. Child psychology in practice* (6th ed., pp. 153–196). Hoboken, NJ: Wiley.

Levine, M., Marchon, I., & Hanley, G. (1984). The placement and misplacement of you-are-here maps. *Environment and Behavior, 16*, 139–158.

Liben, L. S. (1981). Spatial representation and behavior: Multiple perspectives. In L. S. Liben, A. H. Patterson, & N. Newcombe (Eds.), *Spatial representation and behavior across the life span: Theory and application* (pp. 3–36). New York: Academic Press.

Liben, L. S. (1988). Conceptual issues in the development of spatial cognition. In J. Stiles-Davis, M. Kritchevsky, & U. Bellugi (Eds.), *Spatial cognition: Brain bases and development* (pp. 167–194). Hillsdale, NJ: Erlbaum.

Liben, L. S. (2001). Thinking through maps. In M. Gattis (Ed.), *Spatial schemas and abstract thought* (pp. 44–77). Cambridge, MA: MIT Press.

Liben, L. S. (2006). Education for spatial thinking. In W. Damon & R. M. Lerner (Series Eds.), K. A. Renninger & I. E. Sigel (Vol. Eds.), *Handbook of child psychology: Vol 4. Child psychology in practice* (6th ed., pp. 197–247). Hoboken, NJ: Wiley.

Liben, L. S. (2008a). Embodiment and children's understanding of the real and representational world. In W. Overton, U. Mueller, & J. Newman (Eds.), *Developmental perspectives on embodiment and consciousness* (pp. 191–224). Mahwah, NJ: Erlbaum.

Liben, L. S. (2008b, September). *Putting oneself on a map: A developmental psychologist's perspective.* Keynote address in Workshop on You-Are-Here Maps, Conference on Spatial Cognition 2008, Freiburg, Germany.

Liben, L. S., & Downs, R. M. (1989). Understanding maps as symbols: The development of map concepts in children. In H. W. Reese (Ed.), *Advances in child development and behavior* (Vol. *22*, pp. 145–201). New York: Academic Press.

Liben, L. S., & Downs, R. M. (1991). The role of graphic representations in understanding the world. In R. M. Downs, L. S. Liben, & D. S. Palermo (Eds.), *Visions of aesthetics, the environment, and development: The legacy of Joachim Wohlwill* (pp. 139–180). Hillsdale, NJ: Erlbaum.

Liben, L. S., & Downs, R. M. (1992). Developing an understanding of graphic representations in children and adults: The case of GEO-graphics. *Cognitive Development, 7*, 331–349.

Liben, L. S., & Downs, R. M. (1993). Understanding person–space–map relations: Cartographic and developmental perspectives. *Developmental Psychology, 29*, 739–752.

Liben, L. S., Moore, M. L., & Golbeck, S. L. (1982). Preschoolers' knowledge of their classroom environment: Evidence from small-scale and life-size spatial tasks. *Child Development, 53*, 1275–1284.

Liben, L. S., & Myers, L. J. (2007). Children's understanding of maps: What develops? In J. Plumert & J. Spencer (Eds.), *The emerging spatial mind* (pp. 193–218). Oxford: Oxford University Press.

Liben, L. S., Myers, L. J., & Christensen, A. E. (in press). Identifying locations and directions on field and representational mapping tasks: Predictors of success. *Spatial Cognition and Computation.*

Liben, L. S., Myers, L. J., & Kastens, K. A. (2008). Locating oneself on a map in relation to person qualities and map characteristics. In C. Freksa, N. S. Newcombe, P. Gärdenfors, & S. Wölfl (Eds.), *Proceedings of the International Conference on Spatial Cognition VI: Learning, reasoning, and talking about space*. Berlin: Springer-Verlag.

Liben, L. S., Patterson, A. H. & Newcombe, N. (Eds.) (1981). *Spatial representation and behavior across the life span: Theory and application*. New York: Academic Press.

Liben, L. S., Susman, E. J., Finkelstein, J. W., Chinchilli, V. M., Kunselman, S., Schwab, J., … Kulin, H. E. (2002). The effects of sex steroids on spatial performance: A review and an experimental clinical investigation. *Developmental Psychology, 38*, 236–253.

Liben, L. S., & Yekel, C. A. (1996). Preschoolers' understanding of plan and oblique maps: The role of geometric and representational correspondence. *Child Development, 67*, 2780–2796.

Linn, M. C., & Petersen, A. C. (1985). Emergence and characterization of sex differences in spatial ability: A meta-analysis. *Child Development, 56*, 1479–1498.

McComas, J., Dulberg, C., Latter, J. (1997). Children's memory for locations visited: Importance of movement and choice. *Journal of Motor Behavior, 29*, 223–230.

McIntosh, R. D., & Schenk, T. (2009). Two visual streams for perception and action: Current trends. *Neuropsychologia, 47*, 1391–1396.

Montello, D. R. (1998). A new framework for understanding the acquisition of spatial knowledge in large-scale environments. In M. J. Egenhofer & R. G. Golledge (Eds.), *Spatial and temporal reasoning in geographic information systems* (pp. 143–154). New York: Oxford University Press.

Moore, D. S., & Johnson, S. P. (2008). Mental rotation in human infants: A sex difference. *Psychological Science, 19*, 1063–1066.

Myers, L. J., & Liben, L. S. (2008). The role of intentionality and iconicity in children's developing comprehension and production of cartographic symbols. *Child Development, 79*, 668–684.

Nardini, M., Atkinson, J., & Burgess, N. (2008). Children reorient using the left/right sense of coloured landmarks at 18–24 months. *Cognition, 106*, 519–527.

National Research Council (2006). *Learning to think spatially: GIS as a support system in the K–12 curriculum*. Washington DC: National Academy Press.

Nelson, C. A., de Haan, M., Thomas, K. M. (2006). *Neuroscience of cognitive development: The role of experience and the developing brain*. Hoboken, NJ: Wiley.

Nelson, C. A., Monk, C. S., Lin, J., Carver, L. C., Thomas, K. M., & Truwit, C. (2000). Functional neuroanatomy of spatial working memory in children. *Developmental Psychology, 36*, 109–116.

Nelson, C. A., Thomas, K. M., & de Haan, M. (2006). Neural bases of cognitive development. In W. Damon, R. M. Lerner (Series Eds.), D. Kuhn & R. Siegler (Vol. Eds.), *Handbook of child psychology: Vol. 2. Cognition, perception, and language* (6th ed., pp. 3–57). Hoboken. NJ: Wiley.

Newcombe, N., & Huttenlocher, J. (2000). *Making space*. Cambridge, MA: MIT Press.

Newcombe, N. S., Huttenlocher, J. (2006). Development of spatial cognition. In W. Damon & R. M. Lerner (Series Eds.), D. Kuhn & R. S. Siegler (Vol. Eds.), *Handbook of child psychology: Vol 2. Cognition, perception and language* (6th ed., pp. 734–776). Hoboken, NJ: Wiley.

Newcombe, N., Huttenlocher, J., & Learmonth, A. (1999). Infants' coding of location in continuous space. *Infant Behavior and Development, 22*, 483–510.

Newcombe, N., & Liben, L. S. (1982). Barrier effects in the cognitive maps of children and adults. *Journal of Experimental Child Psychology, 34*, 46–58.

Newcombe, N. S., & Ratliff, K. R. (2007). Explaining the development of spatial reorientation: Modularity-plus-language versus the emergence of adaptive combination. In J. M. Plumert & J. P. Spencer (Eds.), *The emerging spatial mind.* (pp. 53–76). New York, Oxford.

Newcombe, N. S., Sluzenski, J., & Huttenlocher, J. (2005). Preexisting knowledge versus on-line learning: What do young infants really know about spatial location? *Psychological Science, 16*, 222–227.

Ninio, A., & Bruner, J. (1978). The achievements and antecedents of labeling. *Journal of Child Language, 5*, 1–15.

Ottosson, T. (1987). Map-reading and wayfinding. *Göteborg Studies in Educational Sciences, 65* [Whole issue].

Piaget, J. (1954). *The construction of reality in the child.* New York: Ballantine Books.

Piaget, J., & Inhelder, B. (1956). *The child's conception of space.* New York: Norton.

Pick, H. L., & Lockman, J. J. (1981). From frames of reference to spatial representations. In L. S. Liben, A. H. Patterson, & N. Newcombe (Eds.), *Spatial representation and behavior across the life span: Theory and application* (pp. 39–61). New York: Academic Press.

Plumert, J. M., Hund, A. M., & Recker, K. M. (2007). Organism–environment interaction in spatial development: Explaining categorical bias in memory for location. In J. M. Plumert & J. P. Spencer (Eds.), *The emerging spatial mind* (pp. 25–52). New York, Oxford.

Plumert, J. M., & Spencer, J. P. (2007). *The emerging spatial mind.* New York: Oxford University Press.

Presson, C. C. (1982). The development of map-reading skills. *Child Development, 53*, 196–199.

Quinn, P. C. (1994). The categorization of *above* and *below* spatial relations by young infants. *Child Development, 65*, 58–69.

Quinn, P. C. (1996). Development of categorical representations for *above* and *below* spatial relations in 3- to 7-month-old infants. *Developmental Psychology, 32*, 942–950.

Quinn, P. C., & Liben, L. S. (2008). A sex difference in mental rotation in young infants. *Psychological Science, 19*, 1067–1070.

Radziszewska, B., & Rogoff, B. (1988). Influence of adult and peer collaborators on children's planning skills. *Developmental Psychology, 24*, 840–848.

Rissotto, A., & Tonucci, F. (2002). Freedom of movement and environmental knowledge in elementary school children. *Journal of Environmental Psychology, 22*, 65–77.

Ronnqvist, L., & von Hofsen, C. (1994). Neonatal finger and arm movements as determined by a social and an object context. *Early Development and Parenting, 3*, 81–94.

Shusterman, A., Lee, S. A., & Spelke, E. S. (2008). Young children's spontaneous use of geometry in maps. *Developmental Science, 11*, F1–F7.

Siegel, A. W., & Schadler, M. (1977). Young children's cognitive maps of their classroom. *Child Development, 48*, 388–394.

Siegel, A. W., & White, S. H. (1975). The development of spatial representations of large-scale environments. In H. W. Reese (Ed.), *Advances in child development and behavior* (Vol. *10*, pp. 9–55). New York: Academic Press.

Smith, A. D., Gilchrist, I. D., Cater, K., Ikram, N., Nott, K., & Hood, B. M. (2008). Reorientation in the real world: The development of landmark use and integration in a natural environment. *Cognition, 107*, 1102–1111.

Spelke, E. S., & Newport, E. L. (1998). Nativism, empiricism, and the development of knowledge. In W. Damon (Series Ed.) & R. M. Lerner (Vol. Ed.), *Handbook of child psychology: Vol 1. Theoretical models of human development* (5th ed., pp. 275–340). New York: Wiley.

Spencer, C., Blades, M., & Morsley, K. (1989). *The child in the physical environment.* New York: Wiley.

Spencer, C., & Darvizeh, Z. (1981). Young children's descriptions of their local environment: A comparison of information elicited by recall, recognition and performance techniques of investigation. *Environmental Education and Information, 1*, 275–284.

Spencer, C., Harrison, N., & Darvizeh, Z. (1980). The development of iconic mapping ability in young children. *International Journal of Early Childhood, 12*, 57–64.

Szechter, L. E., Liben, L. S. (2004). Parental guidance in preschoolers' understanding of spatial–graphic representations. *Child Development, 75*, 869–885.

Tolman, E. C. (1948). Cognitive maps in rats and men. *Psychological Review, 55*, 189–208.

Tolman, E. C., Ritchie, B. F., & Kalish, D. (1946). Studies in spatial learning: Orientation and the short cut. *Journal of Experimental Psychology, 36*, 13–34.

Uttal, D. H. (1996). Angles and distances: Children's and adults' reconstructions and scaling of spatial configurations. *Child Development 67*, 2763–2779.

Uttal, D. H. (2000). Seeing the big picture: Map use and the development of spatial cognition. *Developmental Science, 3*, 247–286.

Uttal, D. H., Hand, L. L., & Newcombe, N. S. (2009, April). *Malleability of spatial cognition: Results of a meta-analysis*. Paper presented at "How malleable is spatial skill? What we can change and what we can't," symposium conducted at the meeting of the Society for Research in Child Development, Denver, Co.

Valenza, E., & Bulf, H. (2007). The role of kinetic information in newborns' perception of illusory contours. *Developmental Science, 10*, 492–501.

Vasilyeva, M., & Bowers, E. (2006). Children's use of geometric information in mapping tasks. *Journal of Experimental Child Psychology, 95*, 255–277.

Vasilyeva, M., & Huttenlocher, J. (2004). Early development of scaling ability. *Developmental Psychology, 40*, 682–690.

Vygotsky, L. S. (1962). *Thought and language* (E. Hanfmann & G. Vakar, Trans.). Cambridge, MA: MIT Press.

Vygotsky, L. S. (1978). *Mind in society: The development of higher psychological processes*. Cambridge, MA: Harvard University Press.

Wapner, S., Kaplan, B., & Ciottone, R. (1981). Self–world relationships in critical environmental transitions: Childhood and beyond. In L. S. Liben, A. H. Patterson, and N. Newcombe (Eds.), *Spatial representation and behavior across the life span: Theory and application* (pp. 251–280). New York: Academic Press.

Weiss, E., Siedentopf, C. M., Hofer, A., Deisenhammer, E. A., Hoptman, M. J., Kremser, C., … Delazer , M. (2003). Sex differences in brain activation pattern during a visuospatial cognitive task: A functional magnetic resonance imaging study in healthy volunteers. *Neuroscience Letters, 344*, 169–172.

Wellman, H. M., Cross, D., & Bartsch, K. (1986). Infant search and object permanence: A meta-analysis of the A-not-B error. *Monographs of the Society for Research in Child Development, 51*, 1–51.

Wiegand, P. (2006). *Learning and teaching with maps*. New York: Routledge.

Yonas, A., & Granrud, C. E. (2006). Infants' perception of depth from cast shadows. *Perception and Psychophysics, 68*, 154–160.

CHAPTER EIGHTEEN

Children's Intuitive Physics

Friedrich Wilkening and Trix Cacchione

Children in all cultures have some knowledge about the physical world, long before they get formal instruction about physics in school. Phenomena of the physical environment such as time, force, and temperature are ecologically relevant entities and appropriate knowledge in these elementary domains has a high survival value. In addition, studying children's intuitive physics has for a long time been considered the *via regia* to the investigation of cognitive development in general, an idea going back to the seminal work of Piaget (1929). His goal of a genetic epistemology led quite naturally to his predominant interest in the development of children's physical knowledge. With his fascinating discoveries of children's understanding of the physical world, Piaget not only opened this field to developmental research, but also motivated subsequent generations of scholars to study the questions raised by him in greater detail. In recent decades, the interest in researching children's intuitive physics appears to have increased even further. The field continues to be recognized as a "foundational domain" in the study of general issues of knowledge acquisition (Wellman & Gelman, 1998).

Intuitive physics is a rich field, with something to offer nearly every branch of psychology (Anderson & Wilkening, 1991). It is at the core of perception, cognition, and goal-directed action. It includes innate aspects, our perceptual-motor skills and even our higher-level cognitive abilities rooting in a long evolutionary history. At the same time, it is a prime field to study learning during ontogeny, with our ever-present environment having the potential of both confronting us with natural tasks of variable difficulty, and of providing permanent feedback, usually in precise and strict terms. Much of intuitive physics can be studied via non-verbal tasks, which is of great advantage for comparisons across ages, across cultures, and even across species. This feature also allows the joint study of non-verbal behavior and conscious reflection, and thus comparisons of different levels or forms of knowledge, implicit and explicit. Finally, a question of special interest for educational psychology is how – if ever – our commonsense knowledge can be translated into the concepts of textbook physics.

For a long time, the richness of the field of intuitive physics was not fully acknowledged. Piagetian theory, which guided the research until at least the 1970s, took quite a narrow look at children's intuitive physics. Development of children's knowledge about the physical world was studied by reference to a presumed adult conceptual structure that was thought to mirror the laws of physics. The less mature knowledge structures in the earlier stages, it was held, ought to be revealed in their pure form. This chapter will show that this traditional approach largely misled developmental inquiry and failed to capture vital facets of children's intuitive physics.

Interest in the field was renewed in the early 1980s. Most influential was McCloskey's (1983) *Scientific American* paper titled "Intuitive Physics," which – besides popularizing the term for a broad scientific community – pointed to the fact that many well-educated adults hold beliefs about simple phenomena of motion that are astonishingly at variance with physically correct Newtonian theory (thus labeled *misconceptions*; see Chi, 2005, for a review). According to McCloskey the beliefs of these adults were not just local misconceptions but formed a coherent theory, in this case a theory of motion that was held in the Middle Ages. In fact, many researchers likened conceptual development to the construction and revision of naïve, commonsense, or folk theories (Carey, 1985; Gopnik & Meltzoff, 1997; Keil, 1989; Vosniadou, Ioannides, Dimitrakopoulou, & Papademetriou, 2001; Wellman & Gelman, 1998). A common characteristic of naïve theories is that they provide good approximations of external reality. Naïve theories, however, are not isomorphic to physical laws, as had been postulated by Piaget for the final stage of cognitive development. Moreover, they appear to be highly domain-specific, even within the field of intuitive physics. Because of its distinct domain-specifity some researchers even deny that naïve knowledge is at all theory-like and coherent. Instead, they describe naïve ideas as a collection of diverse relatively independent explanatory facets which are not theoretical in any deep sense (e.g., diSessa, 1993; diSessa, Gillespie, & Esterly, 2004; Hunt & Minstrell, 1994; Minstrell & Stimpson, 1996).

For cognitive-developmental research, this new way of looking at intuitive physics had the effect that researchers regained interest in intuitive physics in itself, focusing on issues that in traditional developmental theory would have been devalued as surface phenomena. Among these new issues of research were questions of learning (Anderson, 1983), of intra- and interindividual variability (Siegler, 1995), and of children's adaptive capabilities in tasks involving intuitive physics and emphasizing goal-directed action (Anderson & Wilkening, 1991). Probably most remarkably, the past decades have seen a revival of the study of the perceptual-motor aspects of intuitive physics – with children who, according to the traditional view, are far beyond the so-called sensorimotor stage. Since the early work of Krist, Fieberg, and Wilkening (1993) in this field, several studies found interesting interrelations and also dissociations of sensorimotor, perceptual, and cognitive components of children's physical knowledge. The focus in these studies shifted away from diagnosing the correctness or incorrectness of the responses, to investigating how well they are approximated to physical reality, and under which circumstances these approximations change. It seems, thus, that the richness of the field of intuitive physics has been rediscovered in recent years and has become more and more represented in contemporary research.

In the following sections of this chapter, we will give an account of the progress the field has seen during the past years. We will do this separately for each of the various domains – time, speed, force, mass, and so on – with focusing on those that have received the greatest attention in recent research. In a final section, we will try to integrate the findings under common themes of cognitive development and also point to questions that are still unanswered. As to the age dimension, the chapter will focus on children from preschool age onward. Findings obtained with adults will sometimes be mentioned, but mainly as a standard of reference. Infancy will be largely excluded, because a separate chapter is devoted to this rapidly expanding field (Baillargeon, Li, Gertner, & Wu, chapter 1, this volume).

Time and Speed

As reported by Piaget, the impetus for this line of research came from a question Albert Einstein had posed him in the 1920s: When we look at children, which concept develops first, time or speed? Piaget's answer, published about 20 years later (Piaget, 1946a, 1946b), was somewhat surprising and proved to be more complex than he had originally anticipated: the acquisition of the concepts of time and speed was found to undergo a lengthy developmental progression, and when one of the two concepts develops first, if at all, it seemed to be speed, not time. This finding was counterintuitive because, according to Newtonian theory (and Kantian philosophy), one would have expected that time as a basic entity would be grasped first, and that an understanding of speed, an entity that can be conceptualized as derived from time (and distance), would appear later in the course of development.

The evidence for Piaget's conclusions came from his choice tasks. In the prototypical task, two trains moved on parallel tracks at the same or different speeds, covering the same or different distances. Children between 4 and 11 years of age were asked which train travelled for the longer time, at the higher speed, or for the greater distance; or whether the two durations, speeds, or distances, respectively, had been the same. The general finding was that correct answers for speed (and also for distance) were given at an earlier age than those for time. For Piaget, the data from these and similar studies suggested that speed and distance are the primitive concepts and that the concept of time is derived from them.

Virtually all of the early follow-up studies kept the task format introduced by Piaget and more or less supported his conclusions concerning the developmental sequence of the concepts of time and speed (e.g., Acredolo & Schmid, 1981; Crépault, 1979; Montangero, 1979; Richards, 1982; Weinreb & Brainerd, 1975). Most notable is the often-cited work of Siegler and Richards (1979), a first attempt to apply Siegler's rule-assessment methodology in this domain of intuitive physics. After having systematized Piaget's task format these authors still found the same developmental sequence, the major difference to Piaget's conclusions being that the age of mastery of the concept of time was set "somewhere between 11 years and adulthood" and thus even higher than in the original studies (Siegler & Richards, 1979, p. 297).

The finding of such a late mastery of the concept of time was challenged by Levin (1977, 1982). She showed that even young children have the capacity for comparing durations, if they are not confused by interfering cues. Presenting time problems without movement cues, which in one of Levin's studies was done via sleeping times of dolls, or presenting time information in rotational instead of linear movements, she found that children's capability to judge time deteriorates with the number of interfering cues. This seems to be true for relevant cues such as speed and distance, as well as for irrelevant ones such as the intensity of a light in judging the duration of its burning (Levin, 1982).

A different approach to studying children's knowledge about time–speed–distance interrelations, was developed by Wilkening (1981, 1982). Rather than using the choice task, which tends to confound the relevant variables and asks for qualitative judgments only, he presented information on two of the dimensions in the time–speed–distance triad separately and asked the children to infer the quantitative value of the third. In one of the tasks, for example, children made judgments about how far an animal would have fled from a barking dog for various levels of time (how long the dog barked) and speed (fleetness of the animal; e.g., turtle, guinea pig, cat). Information integration theory and functional measurement (Anderson, 1996) served as the theoretical and methodological framework.

In these studies 10-year-olds – as well as adults – combined the information in agreement with the normative multiplicative or ratio rules, whereas 5-year-olds' judgments followed an additive rule if the initial possibility of an eye-movement strategy was eliminated (or a subtractive rule for distance and speed integration, as if Time = Distance – Speed). Although the additive and subtractive integration rules are wrong from a normative point of view, the results reveal a quantitative, functional understanding of time and speed even at 5 years of age, in sharp contrast to Piagetian theory and the conclusions drawn by others in the follow-up work using the Piagetian choice task.

The contrast comes out clearly if one considers the implications of an algebraic rule for information integration. First, an additive rule – even more than a multiplicative rule – suggests that dimensions from which the information is integrated are conceptualized as separate variables, independent from each other. Five-year-olds, thus, appear to see time and speed as different entities and do not confound them. Second, time and speed are obviously grasped as entities that have a metric, at an age which is far below the so-called stage of formal operations. Third, concepts of time and speed were found to be interrelated in a sensible way even in 5-year-olds. Taking all this together, the integration rules revealed a knowledge system that appears to be fundamentally different from that envisaged in the Piagetian and post-Piagetian studies.

It is interesting to note that in connectionist simulations of children's acquisition of concepts of time, speed, and distance, rules and networks emerged that were consistent with those that had been found in Wilkening's experiments (Buckingham & Shultz, 2000). Of course, the data from connectionist modeling cannot be taken as a proof of the integration rules. However, the simulation data are no less compelling than the results from other recent experiments that tried to expand upon the traditional choice paradigm and/or to somehow combine it with the information integration approach (Acredolo, 1989; Albert, Kickmeier-Rust, & Matsuda, 2008; Matsuda, 1994, 1996, 2001; Zhou, Peverly, Boehm, & Chongde, 2000). Rather than elucidating the acquisition of concepts of time and speed, the results from these studies further obscured the problem. All these attempts to elaborate on the choice method did not lead to a convergence of the conclusions – contrary to what the authors had expected – but made the data even harder to interpret. As Zhou et al. (2000) rightly acknowledge, a serious limitation of the choice format in these tasks is that it is not suited to what the tasks are designed to assess: the integration of concepts. Although, in information integration experiments, children from 5 years on were found to have virtually perfect function knowledge about time–speed–distance interrelations, this does not mean that they can apply it in all contexts. Even in tasks that are quite simple from a formal point of view, children and even adults give judgments that are wrong in an amazing way. The basic problem addressed by Wilkening and Martin (2004) and Huber, Krist, and Wilkening (2003) can be exemplified as follows: if drivers of two cars travel the same distance, one with a constant speed of 100 km/h over the whole distance and the other with a (constant) lower speed for the first half – say 75 km/h – how fast does the second driver have to be for the second half to compensate for the time loss experienced in the first half and so arrive at the same time as the first one? The correct answer, by the way, is 150 km/h, not 125 km/h which appears to be the standard response even in adults.

In the experiment by Wilkening and Martin, this problem was presented in the following task. Two toy cars travelled on parallel tracks, one always at the same speed over the whole track, the other starting at one of three slower speeds. Exactly halfway along the track, the first car went into a tunnel that covered it from view for the second half of the distance. For each of the slower speeds of the second car, the question was how fast it had to travel to catch up exactly with the other car at the end of the track. The second car, children were told, could change its speed either halfway along the track (non-linear condition), or when the first car entered the tunnel, that is, when half of the total time had elapsed (linear condition). Children could give their responses either on a quasi-numerical, graphic rating-scale (judgment condition), or by actually pushing the second car (action condition) and thus producing the speeds, which could be recorded by photometers.

In the judgment part of the non-linear condition, the same misconception appeared in all age groups, from 6-year-olds to adults: instead of grading the required speeds in a non-linear fashion, participants gave "linear" responses by just adding the speed differences – as in the numerical example above. Thus, virtually all children and adults were unable to differentiate between the two situations and gave the same linear responses in both linear and non-linear conditions. Interestingly, this differentiation was found to emerge in the *actions* of children around 10 years of age and was clearly there in adulthood. In action tasks, the produced speeds were in correspondence with physical laws, linear in the linear condition and non-linear in the non-linear condition – a result indicating that knowledge in this domain may be dissociated.

This was corroborated in the follow-up study by Huber et al., which implemented the Wilkening and Martin task in a virtual environment, with respect to both the visual and the haptic sense, and at the same time reduced the imagery demands. Even more 10-year-olds acted according to physical laws, as could be seen from their speed productions, while still adhering to the wrong linear rule in their judgments. Many adults, on the other hand, now also judged according to physical laws, as had been found to hold for their actions. In other words, by varying the task while keeping its logical structure, the knowledge dissociation was found to decrease in adults and to increase in children. Thus, instead of asking which of the tasks is the more adequate to assess children's "real" knowledge, the phenomenon of knowledge dissociation may be worth studying in itself.

Trajectories of Moving Objects and the Straight Throw

Although the physical principles governing motions have been well known since Newton, many adults still seem to believe that objects behave otherwise. One of the most striking misconceptions found by McCloskey (1983) – and certainly the most extensively studied – is the so-called straight-down belief. Most children, and even about half of well-educated adults, predict that an object dropped from a moving carrier – from a running person or from an airplane – will fall in a straight vertical path and land directly beneath the point of release. Based on these observations and findings in similar tasks, McCloskey offered an interesting interpretation of children's and adults' misconceptions. They are consistent with a pre-Newtonian, medieval theory of motion: the impetus theory. According to this theory, each motion must have a cause. In the case of a thrown ball, the cause is the force (impetus) that the thrower implants into it, which steadily diminishes until the ball falls down. In the case of an object's "passive" release from a moving carrier, there is no longer a force acting horizontally on the object, so according to the impetus theory, it will fall straight down, by the shortest path.

Would the same children who adhere to the straight-down belief (and presumably to the impetus theory) in the moving-carrier task predict that a ball pushed from a table – with more or less speed – will fall straight down from the edge of the table to the floor? Intuitively, the two situations may seem quite different, a view that would be in line with the medieval impetus theory. According to Newtonian physics, however, the two situations are formally equivalent. How are these problems represented and conceptualized in children's intuitive physics?

A first attempt to investigate this question was made by Kaiser, Proffitt, and McCloskey (1985). They asked children from preschool to sixth grade to predict where a ball would land if (a) rolled off a table, or (b) dropped from a toy train travelling at the same speed as the rolling speed of the ball on the table and at the same height above the floor. In the first task, the percentage of children who correctly predicted that the ball would continue to move forward (for a while) increased continuously with age. In the second task, by contrast, there was no age trend: the great majority of children predicted that the ball would fall straight down.

Kaiser et al. conjectured that the straight-down belief, corresponding with the impetus theory, is a developmentally basic one. As children get older, they revise this belief only in the light of perceptual counter-evidence. However, in the case of objects falling from moving carriers, a visual illusion is normally involved: the falling object is seen as taking a straight-down path – or even a backward path if there is an air drag. Thus, Kaiser et al. concluded that the straight-down belief for carried objects cannot be overcome via perceptual experience but only via formal instruction in physics.

All these considerations refer to children's judgments concerning hypothetical, imagined events. What can we say about children's actions? Watching children when they are throwing balls, stones, and sticks, or when they are trying to bring about or prevent collisions of moving objects, one may get the impression that they are quite proficient in this domain. Are their beliefs as expressed in their judgments reflected in their actions, and vice versa? Krist et al. (1993) investigated children's knowledge about the role of two factors influencing an object's movement in the so-called straight throw: the (horizontal) target distance and the (vertical) height of release. To this end, children from 5 years on had to determine the speed a tennis ball should have on a horizontal platform to hit a target on the ground. Height of the platform and target distance each were varied by multiple levels and factorially combined. For each height–distance combination, the speed of the ball could either (a) be judged on a graphic rating-scale or (b) be produced by actually pushing the ball.

According to the laws of physics, speed in this situation is a direct function of distance (the farther, the faster), and an inverse function of height (the higher, the slower). Moreover, distance and height interact according to a multiplicative rule in determining the launch speed. All these principles were mirrored in the patterns of the speed productions, that is, in children's actions, with virtually no age trend from the youngest children investigated up to adults. The judgment condition, however, yielded a very different picture: the 5-year-olds now failed to integrate the relevant dimensions, and many 10-year-olds (and even several adults) showed striking misconceptions. According to their judgments, most of these children seemed to hold an inverse-height belief: that the ball should fall faster the higher the level of release.

Follow-up work has provided interesting additional information. On the action side, children's intuitive physics regarding the straight throw seems to be highly effector-specific (Krist, 2003; Krist, Loskill, & Schwarz, 1996). Despite effector-specifity, a recent study of Daum and Krist (2009) suggests that both adults and children can even access action knowledge when "throwing" objects in a virtual environment. As to the judgment side, children's predictions for the case of the upward throw were found to be no less deficient than those for the straight throw (Krist, 1992). Further, similar action/judgment dissociations were also observed when, instead of the horizontal speed, an object's flight time had to be estimated or produced (Huber & Krist, 2004).

In an in-depth developmental analysis of the straight-down belief in action and judgment, Krist (2001) found that, in contrast to the earlier conjectures by Kaiser et al., many children are able to revise the misconception, without formal instruction, between 8 and 12 years of age. Moreover, the data of these experiments suggest that the straight-down belief is not rooted in a perceptual illusion, which could be demonstrated by ingenious variations of the task. And most interestingly, the experiments provided clear converging evidence for an early assumption put forward by McCloskey and his associates: that people use their naïve beliefs to plan their actions. When asked to hit a target on the floor by dropping a ball while moving, those children who held the straight-down belief in a judgment condition dropped the ball significantly later (above the target) than those who exhibited correct judgmental knowledge; they seemed to realize that the ball should clearly be released before being exactly above the target.

It would be a misinterpretation of Krist's findings to say that, by 12 years of age, children have a full-fledged understanding of the inertia of moving objects. The knowledge of even the oldest children in his study seemed to be fragile, and to have developed in a slow and piecemeal fashion. These conclusions are reminiscent of those drawn by Kim and Spelke (1999), who studied the development of the understanding of gravity and inertia on object motion at much younger ages, from 7-month-old infants to 6-year-old children. Of particular interest in the present context are the changes in understanding beyond infancy. In the final experiment in the Kim and Spelke study, children had to predict where a ball would land if rolled off a slightly downward slanted ramp. Three possible landing locations were shown: one consistent with the straight-down belief, one corresponding to the correct parabolic path, and one that would result if there were no gravity.

Whereas children up to 4 years of age predicted that the ball would land in the straight-down location, 6-year-olds consistently judged that the ball would land in the location prescribed by a parabolic path. The younger children seemed to be sensitive to gravity only. The 6-year-olds, by contrast, who expected the ball to move both downward and forward, appeared to be sensitive to both gravity and inertia. However, if children were given the opportunity to view the three fully visible motions and had to judge their "naturalness," even the 3- and 4-year-olds reliably chose the parabolic path as the normal one, now showing a sensitivity to both gravity and inertia which, in the prediction task, did not appear before 6 years of age. The developmental patterns observed in the different tasks thus provide further evidence for a dissociation in children's performance, in this study even in the case of judgments only (Kim & Spelke, 1999).

Considered together, the findings by Krist and his associates and by Kim and Spelke allow two general conclusions. First, children's developing understanding of object motion is a complex, multifaceted process. It has now repeatedly been shown that some aspects of knowledge may be expressed in – and are revealed by – a particular task but not another, without either of them necessarily being the more adequate or sensitive for diagnosing the "true" concept in question. Second, following from the above, children's knowledge about object motion reveals itself and can be studied in a broad array of contexts.

A further compelling example is the so called "gravity error" demonstrated by Hood (1995). He studied young children's understanding of object motion by contrasting aspects of gravity and solidity. Children from 2 to 3 years of age were asked to find a ball that was dropped down one of three opaque tubes that could be interwoven. Most of the children searched in the wrong location: beneath the point where the ball was dropped, not at the lower exit of the tube into which the ball was dropped. For these children, gravity obviously outperformed solidity. The error did not occur when transparent tubes were used (Hood, 1995), or when upward or horizontal motion was presented (Hood, 1998; Hood, Santos, & Fieselman, 2000). Neither was it found in tasks involving vertical trajectories if they were substantially less demanding (Hood, Carey, & Prasada, 2000). However, in contrast to the straight-down belief in older children and adults, the gravity error may not be associated with naïve beliefs, but occur as a consequence of immature inhibitory abilities. For example, Hood, Wilson, and Dyson (2006) showed that the gravity bias reappears in 4-year-old children if the recruitment of inhibitory mechanisms is hindered. Further, recent comparative research strongly suggests that gravity errors root in more encapsulated mechanisms, and that they increase and decrease as a function of inhibitory control (Cacchione, Call, & Zingg, 2009; Cacchione & Call, in press).

Force and Weight

In this third section, we will focus on force and weight, dimensions that partly were involved already in the past sections, but only in an implicit and peripheral way. In the domain of weight, the instrument most extensively used has been the balance scale, originally designed by Inhelder & Piaget (1958) as a means of studying formal operational reasoning. Since then, the balance-scale task has developed into a paradigm per se, a sort of *drosophila* in research on children's intuitive physics, if not on cognitive development in general. The task exists in several variations and has been studied across all ages: in infants (Case, 1985), preschoolers (Halford, Andrews, Dalton, Boag, & Zielinski, 2002; Siegler, 1978; Siegler & Chen, 1998), schoolchildren (Amsel, Goodman, Savoie, & Clark, 1996; Ferretti & Butterfield, 1986; Krist, Bach, Öndül, & Huber, 2004), and adults (Hardiman, Pollatsek, & Well, 1986). It has been used to gather evidence for a variety of theories in accounting for developmental data: Piagetian (Inhelder & Piaget, 1958; Karmiloff-Smith & Inhelder, 1974), neo-Piagetian (Case, 1985; Marini, 1992; Marini & Case, 1994) cultural-contextualist (Tudge, 1992; Weir & Seacrest, 2000), symbolic information processing (Klahr & Siegler, 1978; Langley, 1987; Newell, 1990), information integration (Surber & Gzesh, 1984; Wilkening & Anderson, 1982, 1991), connectionist (McClelland, 1995; Schapiro & McClelland, 2009), and psychometric approaches (Jansen & van der Maas, 1997, 2002; Wilson, 1989). It has also been used to examine a large range of issues concerning factors that may determine rule use (Amsel et al., 1996; Andrews, Halford, Murphy, & Knox, 2009; Ferretti, Butterfield, Cahn, & Kerkman, 1985; Halford, Wilson, & Phillips, 1998; Tudge, 1992; Wilkening & Anderson, 1982, 1991).

Siegler's (1976) account of children's reasoning about the balance-scale problem, which entered into many textbooks and served as a point of reference for a vast amount of follow-up research in various fields of cognitive development, has certainly been the most influential in the past decades. He used a very common version of the task: different or same numbers of weights are placed on each side of a horizontal, two-arm balance beam, the weights being at different or the same distances from the fulcrum, and the child is asked to predict which side would go down if the beam, which initially is presented as being fixed, were left free.

In an attempt to systematize the notions put forward by Piaget, Siegler postulated that children, in the course of development, use four different rules in solving the balance-scale problem, each rule representing a different level of knowledge. Each rule is based on binary decisions, and the rules are usually represented as binary decision trees, resembling simple computer programs. To diagnose the rule a child uses in solving the task and, at the same time, to diagnose his or her pre-existing knowledge, Siegler developed the so-called rule-assessment methodology. This requires the presentation of a carefully selected series of problems, with different combinations of weights on the balance beam and distances from the fulcrum, so that the different rules yield unique performance patterns that can be attributed to the operation of one of the four rules.

From the data in these tasks, Siegler (1976) concluded that children, in the course of development, progress through a sequence of rules, these rules being hierarchically ordered in a quite simple way. In accordance with Piaget, the physically correct, normative rule was postulated as the endpoint of development. Because each of the developmentally "lower" rules is included in the decision-tree representation of the one above, the question of rule learning has received particular interest in this approach (Siegler, 1976, 1978; Siegler & Chen, 1998). In a series of training studies, the more recent using the microgenetic method, Siegler and his co-workers showed that young children can learn higher rules when four components of the learning process are mastered: noticing potential explanatory variables, formulating predictive rules, applying the rules to new problems, and maintaining them under less supportive conditions.

Amsel et al. (1996) took this research one step further, by investigating children's reasoning about causal and non-causal influences on the behavior of the balance scale – and on levers in general. In addition to the well-investigated causal factors – weight and distance from the fulcrum – non-causal factors were varied, for example the color of the weights and/or their orientation, and whether they were standing on the beam or hanging from it. These authors found that in the course of development children appear to pay attention primarily to salient physical features – causal and non-causal – such as the weight and color of the objects, and only thereafter consider spatial features, again both causal and non-causal, such as distance from the fulcrum and the particular orientation or mounting of the objects. These data show that the selection of cues that a child considers to be relevant does not necessarily follow principles that could be derived from the normative laws of physics, as held in traditional views.

Wilkening and Anderson (1991) varied the standard approach by not only asking the choice question but also asking the child, after he or she had said that one side would go down, to adjust the weight and/or distance on one side so that the scale would come into balance. These production responses, embedded in an alternative rule-assessment methodology, yielded quite different results than those to be expected if Siegler's rule sequence were a true account of children's knowledge in this domain. Most importantly, many children were found to integrate the relevant information, weight and distance, according to a non-normative adding-type of rule. These children showed integration although in terms of the rule sequence according to Siegler's analysis they should not have. These findings point to serious problems of knowledge representation, which had been raised earlier by Wilkening and Anderson (1982).

Recently, Andrews et al. (2009) assessed children's integration of weight and distance information using a new methodology that combines a single-armed apparatus with functional measurement. Three- to seven-year-old children had to assess how far the beam would tilt when different weights were placed at different distances from the pivot. Results reveal a developmental progression: while the majority of 3-year-olds responded nonsystematically, 4-year-olds based their judgments on a single variable (usually weight). Five to seven-year-olds integrated weight and distance information, with individual analyses revealing both additive and multiplicative integration rules.

Tasks related to the balance-scale problem have been studied by Pauen (1996). These experiments investigated children's knowledge of the addition of force vectors. In a king-on-the-ice game, two unequal forces were pulling at the target object, a toy king fixed to the center of a circular platform. The forces were weights positioned on small plates that hung from two cords, thereby pulling the target towards the edge of the platform.

Children were asked to predict in which direction the target would be moving if released. The vast majority of first- to third-graders, and almost half of fourth-graders, erroneously predicted that the object would always be pulled straight in the direction of the stronger force (one-force-only rule), in contrast to the correct integration rule, which requires not only the consideration of which force is the stronger, but the taking into account of both forces and the integration of the quantities and directions of the force vectors. The correct resulting direction is given by the vector addition of the two force vectors.

Verbal reports of the children gave hints of their use of analogical reasoning, which happened to be misleading in this case: many children appeared to employ their already-existing knowledge about the behavior of balance scales to derive the answers for the vector-addition problem. This assumption was corroborated in a follow-up experiment (Pauen & Wilkening, 1997). Children who were about to overcome their false beliefs in the original task were presented with two different types of balance scales and trained to use either the one-force-only rule or the correct rule, depending on the kind of balance scale. One of them was the common balance scale, for which the stronger-force-only rule provides a perfect prediction. The other had an uncommon swing suspension of the beam, providing a correct analogy for the force-interaction problem in Pauen's original task. The training had a clear effect: the majority of children trained on the swing-suspension balance beam integrated the relevant forces in the vector-addition problem almost perfectly, whereas all of the children who were trained on the common balance scale adhered to the one-force-only rule. It appears, thus, that at least some misconceptions about the interaction of forces may have their roots in false analogies.

In closing the discussion of children's intuitive physics of force and weight, the fact that research in this domain has strongly focused on explicit knowledge deserves mention. A notable exception is the early study by Karmiloff-Smith and Inhelder (1974), who investigated children's implicit knowledge when balancing weight-symmetric and weight-asymmetric objects. They found that 4- and 8-year-olds performed better on this action task than 6-year-olds, whose performance seemed to be derived from their naïve theory that all objects balance at their geometric center. Only when asked to close their eyes, which prevented the implementation of the naïve geometric-center rule in a simple way, did 6-year-olds attain the same level of behavioral mastery as the younger children who relied on proprioceptive feedback. However, in a recent study of Krist, Horz, and Schönfeld (2005) children between 4 and 8 years of age showed a quasi-linear performance improvement which complicates the view that children redescribe their initial implicit knowledge on an explicit level. Overall, it appears that in this domain, too, children's intuitive physics is a non-trivial blend of sensorimotor action and operational thought, to use Piagetian terms.

Matter, Mass, Weight, Volume, and Density

We now turn from dynamic and kinetic aspects to more static phenomena of the physical environment: to the fundamental domain of matter, the stuff from which our world is built. In the physicist's framework, on the macroscopic level matter is defined by its mass, volume, and density. Density is defined quite simply: the ratio of mass and volume. People's ordinary understanding of density, however, seems to be complicated by their difficulties in grasping the difference between mass and weight. This is probably due to the fact that under normal, constant gravitational conditions mass and weight are directly proportional. However, as textbook physics tells us, weight – in contrast to mass – can change under certain physical transformations, such as heating, deformation, and pressure. The same holds for volume and density. To what extent are these principles and concepts reflected in our intuitive physics, and how did they develop?

To study these questions, children have been asked about matter, weight, and related quantities before and after certain transformations of stimuli (Andersson, 1990; Driver, 1985; Galili & Bar, 1997; Liu & Lesniak, 2006; Piaget, 1974). Do children know that increases of heat and pressure lead to an increase and decrease of volume and a decrease and increase of density, respectively, but do not affect mass?

Many psychologists and educators have noted that the relation of mass, volume, and density is extremely difficult to understand for children – and therefore very difficult to teach (Smith, Maclin, Grosslight, & Davis, 1997; Smith, Snir, & Grosslight, 1992). Questions of interest have been why this should be so, and how learning procedures may facilitate the understanding of these relations. As to children's concepts of matter, it appears that their knowledge system, although highly adapted to their everyday needs, differs substantially from the definitional system of physics. For instance, preschool children do differentiate between physical objects on one side and dreams or wishes on the other, but they seem to do so on an axis of reality instead of a material–immaterial axis (Estes, Wellman, & Woolley, 1989). Between 4 and 11 years of age, almost all children who categorize solids, liquids, and gases as matter also say that electricity, temperature, light, echo, or shadow are of material kind (Carey, 1991; DeVries, 1987; Lautrey & Mazens, 2004; Mazens & Lautrey, 2003; Piaget, 1960).

Children's concept of weight has been studied mainly in conservation tasks (Driver, 1985; Galili & Bar, 1997; Piaget & Szeminska, 1939; Smedslund, 1961; Stavy & Stachel, 1985). Much data suggests that younger children have a concept of weight that is highly influenced by the felt weight of an object. For instance, more than half of 4-year-olds, and half of 6-year-olds, have been found to judge that a small rice corn or even a sizable piece of Styrofoam weighs nothing (Smith, Carey, & Wiser, 1985). Only at around 9 years of age, children begin to relate weight with the amount of matter, and to realize that neither matter nor weight ever disappear if an object is divided into smaller and smaller pieces. At around the same age they develop the analogous insight for the case of transparent gases, if water is transformed into vapor, for instance (Carey, 1991). It appears, thus, that children start out with diverse concepts of weight, and that it takes them a long time to integrate them into one, coherent concept that finally, if ever, becomes isomorphic to the concept of weight held in physics.

Conceptualizing density appears to be even more difficult for children. This has been found in a large variety of studies, including tasks on sorting objects according to material kind, judging effects of thermal expansion, and predicting the floating or sinking of objects. A general conclusion has been that children's problems arise due to an undifferentiated weight–density concept (Hewson, 1986; Piaget & Inhelder, 1974; Smith et al., 1985; Smith, Snir, & Grosslight, 1992). A second hypothesis was lately added by

Kloos (2007). She proposes that children's difficulty in understanding density is not caused by their inability to differentiate between mass and density, but because of the inherent logical incongruence of the concept of density itself (i.e., children fail to understand that mass and volume have opposite effects on density). Finally, it has also been suggested that the concept of density is difficult because it requires, in a more general sense, the understanding of ratio and proportionality which, according to the Piagetian view, is not fully developed before children enter the stage of formal-operational reasoning. We will first look at studies focusing on the first two hypotheses and come back to the latter one in the following section.

In a series of experiments, including both verbal and non-verbal tasks, Smith et al. (1985) investigated children's distinctions of weight and size as well as of weight and material-type (or density). They asked children to compare the weight, the size, or the material of objects, and to respond verbally or non-verbally. In the non-verbal tasks, children had to sort the objects into steel and aluminum families, for instance (density being the relevant factor), make a sponge bridge collapse (weight being the relevant factor), or judge whether a piece of matter would fit into a box (size being the relevant factor). Children as young as 3 years of age did not have any problems in differentiating between size and weight, but they were unable to discriminate weight and density, which was found to remain a major difficulty for much older children, up to middle-school age.

In the search for alternative non-verbal tasks suitable for investigating weight–density differentiation, phenomena of flotation and buoyancy came into focus – buoyancy being the more general concept because it relates to both the floating and sinking of a solid object in a liquid with a given density. If the density of a solid is less than the density of the liquid, the object will float; and the object will sink if its density is greater than that of the liquid.

The studies by Halford, Brown, and McThompson (1986) and Smith et al. (1992) deserve special mention in this context. Children between 8 and 13 years of age had to judge whether cubes of different size and weight would sink or float. Most of these children had a clear tendency to focus on weight and to disregard density as the primary relevant variable. Kohn (1993) devised a flotation prediction task capable of finding earlier forms of understanding of density. Preschool children, as well as adults, made floating–sinking predictions concerning a set of objects with systematic variations in density, weight, and volume. From the age of 4 years onward a rudimentary understanding in this domain seemed to emerge. However, irrelevant weight and volume information still interfered in systematic ways. The children at even younger ages, in comparison, gave very inconsistent responses, indicating that they did not have any idea about density as a factor relevant to an object's floating or sinking.

Penner and Klahr (1996) tested 10-, 12-, and 14-year-old children's knowledge about a more specific aspect: the sinking time of various objects. These authors were particularly interested in the question of if and how children use self-designed experimental strategies to test and revise their *a priori* beliefs. Most children initially held the belief that weight alone determines which one of two objects will sink faster. After having experimented, however, all children came to realize that other factors such as object shape and material also had an effect on the sinking speed. The main difference between the age groups appeared to be their belief that experimentation can help to identify the relevant factors and the corresponding effects – which was typically held by the older children but was virtually absent at younger ages. The ability to revise erroneous belief about an objects' sinking time was also addressed by Kloos and colleagues (Kloos, 2007; Kloos & Somerville, 2001; Kloos & Van Orden, 2005). Kloos and Sommerville (2001) presented 3 to 6-year-old children with demonstrations conveying the relation between volume and sinking speed. They found that calling to mind initial beliefs (i.e., that heavier/larger objects sink faster) and presenting information challenging them may bring about a replacement of erroneous beliefs. This was true even if the relevant dimension was not deliberately pointed out (Kloos & Van Orden, 2005). A recent example for how children may revise their misconceptions in this domain is reported by Hardy, Jonen, Möller, and Stern (2006) who investigated the effects of instructional support on 9-year-old children's understanding of floating and sinking. Based on their findings the authors argue that high instructional support fosters a long-term reduction of misconceptions and facilitates the adoption of scientific explanations.

Janke (1995) studied children's intuitive physics of flotation by applying principles of functional measurement. Like in the previous studies, children were presented with objects varying in volume and weight. However, instead of asking for verbal explanations and for binary choices as to whether the objects would float or sink, children had to give fine-graded quantitative ratings. These were judgments about the maximum load that boats differing in volume and weight could carry. Although the integration of the relevant variables was found to improve with age, in children between the ages of 8 and 12 there was still a strong tendency to overvalue the role of weight. However, this misconception largely disappeared in a task in which the unloaded boats were presented floating on water (with different amounts of dip) and thus the effects of both volume and weight were perceptually accessible. It appears, thus, that children's concepts of flotation and buoyancy do not develop in an all-or-none fashion. In this micro-domain, in particular, a complete understanding seems to take a long time (see also Esterly & Barbu, 1999). This is one reason why it is especially suited for studies on learning and belief revision (Hardy et al., 2006; Kloos & Sommerville, 2001; Kloos & Van Orden, 2005; Penner & Klahr, 1996), with many possibilities for future research.

Density, Temperature, Sweetness, and Other Intensive Quantities

Why do children fail to understand the concept of density? Do they have specific problems with this particular concept, or do they have a general problem with intensive quantities, perhaps due to a general lack of the ability to perform the logical operations necessary for proportional thinking? Nunes, Desli, and Bell (2003) propose that, among others, inverse proportional reasoning is a major obstacle to children's understanding of intensive quantities. The sweetness of a drink, for example, may be judged by comparing the amount of water with the amount of sugar dissolved in it, according to principles of proportionality and ratio rules. However, as data from several studies suggest, children appear to have considerable difficulties attaining a deep understanding of these principles, sometimes even up to adolescence (Hart, 1988; Karplus, Pulos, & Stage, 1983).

Several micro-domains studied by various researchers are of interest in the present context: sugar or acid concentrations in water; viscosity; color brightness; and temperature (Jäger & Wilkening, 2001; Moore, Dixon, & Haines, 1991; Reed & Evans, 1987; Stavy, Strauss, Orpaz, & Carmi, 1982; Stavy & Tirosh, 2000; Strauss & Stavy, 1982). These are all instances of intensive quantities: Their values remain unchanged under the variation of matter, which is an extensive quantity.

In the pioneering studies by Sidney Strauss and his colleagues, for example, children were asked about the sweetness of a mixture that resulted from two glasses filled with water, and with the same or different numbers of pieces of sugar dissolved in them. These authors found that children younger than 5 years of age arrived at (qualitatively) correct answers by relying on their experience-based intuitive understanding of intensive quantities. Children between 6 and 10 years of age, in contrast, typically tried to apply quantitative rules, but chose the incorrect one, which led to a drop in their performance. Most of the children predicted that the mixture would become sweeter than the sweetest of the two initial components. Children seemed to add the values of one extensive quantity (amount of sugar) without taking into account that the other extensive quantity (water) also increased. The correct answer re-appeared in children from about 10 years on who, as concluded by the authors, understood the role of both relevant extensive quantities and were able to integrate them.

Colleen Moore and her colleagues (Ahl, Moore, & Dixon, 1992; Dixon & Moore, 1996; Moore, Dixon, & Haines, 1991) were particularly interested in the development of function knowledge in tasks involving intensive quantities. They investigated children's understanding of temperature mixture so as to study their self-initiated generation of mathematical strategies. A general conclusion from these studies was that children up to the age of 8 years tend to understand the domain quite poorly, and even fifth- and eighth-graders were far from showing a perfect understanding. Such an understanding would require the grasp of different principles, as has been pointed out by detailed task-analyses in these studies. Children appear to have difficulties even with the seemingly simplest of these, the range principle, stating that the value of the mixture of intensive quantities must always fall between those of the two initial components, or at least cannot lie above or below either of them.

Recently, Howe, Nunes, and Bryant (in press) presented strong evidence for the claim that two factors – termed "variable salience" and "relational focus" – heavily influence reasoning about intensive quantities in 7- to 12-year-old children. Effects of variable salience arise from pragmatic consequences of how quantities are represented in language (i.e., language use highlights specific variables). Further, difficulties may be connected to the particular relational focus presented in a problem (i.e., children have greater difficulty in reasoning about part–whole relations than about part–part relations). Both factors stem from the fact that intensive quantities are constituted from proportional relations.

All these studies have presented the intensive quantities in some symbolized form. Temperature and sweetness, for example, were not perceivable, in contrast to the extensive quantity of the stimuli, volume in these cases. Therefore, Jäger and Wilkening (2001) speculated that children's errors might result from their difficulties with inferring the intensive quantity, and that these might disappear when the intensities are directly visible. For this reason, color intensity was used as a variable. Surprisingly, this study replicated previous findings in important respects. For instance, children predicted that a mixture of two liquids, one light red and the other a red of a middle intensity, would become darker than that of the darkest initial component. Even half of the children in the 10-year-old group gave these "additive" responses. Besides putting into question the hypothesis that children's problems in the previous studies were due to the fact that the intensive quantities were not accessible to perception, the results found by Jäger and Wilkening indicate that children's problems in this domain cannot simply be attributed to their inability to take both relevant extensive quantities (e.g., sugar and water) into account and to integrate them appropriately (Strauss, Ankori, Orpaz, & Stavy, 1977). The problem seems to be a different one: Lacking a specific rule for these quantities, children seem to resort to a sort of general-purpose adding rule – a rule that at young ages has already proven its worth in the case of extensive quantities. An *extensitivity bias* (Jäger & Wilkening, 2001) seems thus to operate in children's concepts of intensive quantities.

Although young children seem to have a strong bias in favor of additive rules – exceptions have been observed. Dixon and Tuccillo (2001) asked children and college students to predict what would happen when quantities of a substance were combined. Two of these questions were about familiar properties: weight and sweetness. The third question was about a fictitious property, the "hemriness" of the resulting matter, which could be liquids (drinks) or eatable solids. Would children be more likely to conceptualize the fictitious property as an extensive or an intensive one, after having answered the weight and sweetness questions? That is, would the hemriness of the two initial components be added or averaged? Although there was a clear developmental shift from adding to averaging in this study, the adding rule was not always used as the default. Even some of the youngest children tested, 10-year-olds, were transferring principles from their averaging model, the appropriate one for sweetness, to make judgments about the fictitious property. These results suggest that the extensitivity bias discussed by Jäger and Wilkening is not so strong that it cannot be overcome in middle-school age, at least in some domains.

Conclusions

As a result of a change of emphasis in studying children's intuitive physics, the field has become richer than originally anticipated. In the traditional view, founded by Piaget, children's knowledge of the physical world was of relatively little interest per se. The major reason why it was studied was that this promised to be the *via regia* to the uncovering of cognitive structures and their development. The physical world was chosen because it seemed to have a heuristic advantage: it has a logical structure, much more – so was the belief – than the social and mental world, and the child was thought to be able to internalize this structure through active explorations in everyday life. Many laws of elementary physics can be expressed via simple algebraic rules that are structurally identical. This feature made the field attractive for stage theorists. In a strict domain-general stage theory of cognitive development, it would suffice to determine for each stage the nature of one concept, say time. All other concepts for which the physical law is structurally isomorphic would then have to be the same.

It is well known that this is not what was found over decades of intensive research. The concepts that were assessed in many studies were more or less advanced between and within different domains and often proved to be highly task dependent. But this was seen more as a methodological embarrassment than as a natural fact. The goal had been to find the pure concepts in tasks uncontaminated by demands not related to the logical structure in question. As a consequence, the research largely went off in side issues of methodology. This view, looking at children's intuitive physics mainly as an instrument to attain the higher goal of revealing cognitive structures, had almost necessarily lead to a narrowing of the field.

The new look as presented in this chapter opens the field and makes it interesting for more branches within psychology and beyond. The variability in children's intuitive physics observed in every domain discussed here, ranging from time and speed over force and buoyancy to temperature and color intensity, is now seen as an inherent characteristic of developing knowledge and not as extraneous noise that should be eliminated by choosing the right methods. Currently, two diverging theoretical perspectives try to capture the variability of children's concepts and the frequently observed knowledge dissociations. Contextualist theories adhere to the view that much of our knowledge is in fact tied to the specific context in which it was acquired. These theories picture naïve physical knowledge as a more or less fragmentary collection of myriads of unintegrated pieces of knowledge (e.g., diSessa, 1993; diSessa, Gillespie, & Esterly, 2004; Hunt & Minstrell, 1994; Minstrell & Stimpson, 1996). On the other hand, children's developing knowledge structures are proposed to be equivalent to scientific concepts. In this view, children's naïve beliefs are described as coherent and theory-like. Further, it is assumed that the coexistence of potentially contradictory or empirically unfounded beliefs eventually culminates in a conceptual change analogous to the revolution in scientific thought (Carey, 1999; Carey & Smith, 1995; Gopnik & Wellman, 1994). A challenge for future research will be to narrow down the scope of *contextuality* and to identify the conditions that facilitate the revision of erroneous beliefs. As Sophian (2006) puts it: "To accept contradictory beliefs would jeopardize cognitive development itself . . . as children would have no way of evaluating existing beliefs in the light of new experiences" (Sophian, 2006, p. 1556). At any rate, to better approximate children's naïve beliefs must be a major concern of scientific education: if intuitive beliefs are best described as erroneous theories or misconceptions they should be entirely replaced by formal physics. On the other hand, formal education could offer a coherent frame to integrate the productive elements of children's intuitive physics.

These conclusions necessarily lead to a new research tactic. It seems obsolete – and would seriously mislead the direction of inquiry – to look for entities that are probably not there: pure, naked concepts of intuitive physics operative in a context-free world. The findings discussed in the present chapter show that the attempts to construct the one and only "ideal" task for such an endeavor have to run idle. What is needed instead is a stronger focus on performance in different contexts and, accordingly, the use of batteries of tasks of varying content, of varying information-processing demands, of varying shares of cognition and action, and of varying motivational appeal, thus to do justice to the wide range of children's possible goals (Sophian, 1997). Such a strategy, to be sure, requires much more work than originally envisaged but, seen in a more positive light, opens a horn of plenty for future research. And if this strategy is already necessary for getting an adequate account of children's intuitive physics from the point of view of basic research, it will all the more be required for all attempts to derive consequences for educational applications from that basic knowledge.

References

Acredolo, C. (1989). Assessing children's understanding of time, speed, and distance interrelations. In I. Levin & D. Zakay (Eds.), *Time and human cognition: A life-span perspective* (pp. 219–257). Amsterdam: North-Holland.

Acredolo, C., & Schmid, J. (1981). The understanding of relative speeds, distances, and durations of movement. *Developmental Psychology, 17*, 490–493.

Ahl, V. A., Moore, C. F., & Dixon, J. A. (1992). *Development* of intuitive and numerical proportional reasoning. *Cognitive Development, 7*, 81–108.

Albert, D., Kickmeier-Rust, M. D., & Matsuda, F. (2008). A formal framework for modelling the developmental course of competence and performance in the distance, speed, and time domain. *Developmental Review, 28*, 401–420.

Amsel, E., Goodman, G., Savoie, D., & Clark, M. (1996). The development of reasoning about causal and noncausal influences on levers. *Child Development, 67*, 1624–1646.

Anderson, N. H. (1983). Intuitive physics: Understanding and learning of physical relations. In T. J. Tighe & B. E. Shepp (Eds.), *Perception, cognition, and development: Interactional analyses* (pp. 231–265). Hillsdale, NJ: Erlbaum.

Anderson, N. H. (1996). *A functional theory of cognition*. Mahwah, NJ: Erlbaum.

Anderson, N. H., & Wilkening, F. (1991). Adaptive thinking in intuitive physics. In N. H. Anderson (Ed.), *Contributions to information integration theory: Vol. 3. Developmental* (pp. 1–42). Hillsdale, NJ: Erlbaum.

Andersson, B. (1990). Pupils' conceptions of matter and its transformation (age 12–16). *Studies in Science Education, 18*, 53–88.

Andrews, G., Halford, G. S., Murphy, K., & Knox, K. (2009). Integration of weight and distance information in young children: The role of relational complexity. *Cognitive Development, 24*, 49–60.

Buckingham, D., & Shultz, T. R. (2000). The developmental course of distance, time, and velocity concepts: A generative connectionist model. *Journal of Cognition and Development, 1*, 305–345.

Cacchione, T., & Call, J. (in press). Intuitions about gravity and solidity in great apes: The tubes task. *Developmental Science.*

Cacchione, T., Call, J., & Zingg, R. (2009). Gravity and solidity in four great ape species (*Gorilla gorilla, Pongo pygmaeus, Pan troglodytes, Pan paniscus*): Vertical and horizontal variations of the table task. *Journal of Comparative Psychology, 123*(2), 168–80.

Carey, S. (1985). *Conceptual change in childhood.* Cambridge, MA: MIT Press.

Carey, S. (1991). Knowledge acquisition: Enrichment or conceptual change? In S. Carey & R. Gelman (Eds.), *The epigenesis of mind: Essays on biology and cognition* (pp. 257–291). Hillsdale, NJ: Erlbaum.

Case, R. (1985). *Intellectual development: A systematic reinterpretation.* New York: Academic Press.

Chi, M. T. H. (2005). Commonsense conceptions of emergent processes: Why some misconceptions are robust. *Journal of the Learning Sciences, 14*, 161–199.

Crépault J. (1979). Influence du repérage sur la durée: Etude génétique des inférences cinématiques. *L'Anée Psychologique, 79*, 43–64.

Daum, M. M., & Krist, H. (2009). Dynamic action in virtual environments: Constraints on the accessibility of action knowledge in children and adults. *Quarterly Journal of Experimental Psychology, 62*(2), 335–351.

DeVries, R (1987). Children's conceptions of shadow phenomena. *Genetic Psychology Monographs, 112*, 479–530.

diSessa, A. A. (1993). Toward an epistemology of physics. *Cognition and Instruction, 10*, 105–225.

diSessa, A. A., Gillespie, N. M., & Esterly, J. B. (2004). Coherence versus fragmentation in the development of the concept of force. *Cognitive Science, 28*, 834–900.

Dixon, J. A., & Moore, C. F. (1996). The developmental role of intuitive principles in choosing mathematical strategies. *Developmental Psychology, 32*, 241–253.

Dixon, J. A., & Tuccillo, F. (2001). Generating initial models for reasoning. *Journal of Experimental Child Psychology, 78*, 178–212.

Driver, R. (1985). Beyond appearance: The conservation of matter. In R. Driver, E. Guesne, & A. Tiberghien (Eds.), *Children's ideas in science* (pp. 145–169). Milton Keynes: Open University Press.

Esterly, J. B., & Barbu, M. (1999). *The role of size, weight, density, and material in children's developing understanding of buoyancy*. Poster session presented at the Biennial Meetings of the Society for Research in Child Development, Albuquerque, NM.

Estes, D., Wellman, H. M., & Woolley, J. D. (1989). Children's understanding of mental phenomena. In H. Reese (Ed.), *Advances in child development and behavior* (pp. 41–87). New York: Academic Press.

Ferretti, R. P., & Butterfield, E. C. (1986). Are children's rule-assessment classifications invariant across instances of problem types? *Child Development, 57*, 1419–1428.

Ferretti, R. P., Butterfield, E. C., Cahn, A., & Kerkman, D. (1985). The classification of children's knowledge: Development on the balance-scale and inclined-plane tasks. *Journal of Experimental Child Psychology, 39*, 131–160.

Galili, I., & Bar, V. (1997). Children's operational knowledge about weight. *International Journal of Science Education, 19*, 317–340.

Gopnik, A. & Meltzoff, A. N. (1997). *Words, thoughts, and theories*. Cambridge, MA: MIT Press.

Gopnik, A., & Wellman, H. (1994). The theory theory. In L. Hirschfield & S. Gelman (Eds.), *Mapping the mind: Domain specificity in culture and cognition* (pp. 257–293). New York: Cambridge University Press.

Halford, G. S., Andrews, G., Dalton, C., Boag, C., & Zielinski, T. (2002). Young children's performance on the balance scale: The influence of relational complexity. *Journal of Experimental Child Psychology, 81*, 417–445.

Halford, G. S., Brown, C. A., & McThompson, R. M. (1986). Children's concepts of volume and flotation. *Developmental Psychology, 22*, 218–222.

Halford, G. S., Wilson, W. H., & Phillips, S. (1998). Processing capacity defined by relational complexity: Implications for comparative, developmental, and cognitive psychology. *Behavioral and Brain Sciences, 21*, 803–831.

Hardiman, P. T., Pollatsek, A., & Well, A. D. (1986). Learning to understand the balance beam. *Cognition and Instruction, 3*, 63–86.

Hardy, I., Jonen, A., Möller, K., & Stern, E. (2006). Effects of instructional support within constructivist learning environments for elementary school students' understanding of "floating and sinking." *Journal of Educational Psychology, 98*, 307–326.

Hart, K. (1988). Ratio and proportion. In J. Hiebert & M. Behr (Eds.), *Number concepts and operations in middle grades* (pp. 198–219). Hillsdale, NJ: Erlbaum.

Hewson, M. G. (1986). The acquisition of scientific knowledge: Analysis and representation of student conceptions concerning density. *Science Education, 70*, 159–170.

Hood, B. M. (1995). Gravity rules for 2- to 4-year-olds? *Cognitive Development, 10*, 577–598.

Hood, B. M. (1998). Gravity does rule for falling events. *Developmental Science, 1*, 59–64.

Hood, B. M., Carey, S., & Prasada, S. (2000). Predicting the outcomes of physical events. *Child Development, 71*, 1540–1554.

Hood, B. M., Santos, L., & Fieselman, S. (2000). Two year-olds' naïve predictions for horizontal trajectories. *Developmental Science, 3*, 328–332.

Hood, B. M., Wilson, A., & Dyson, S. (2006). The effect of divided attention on inhibiting the gravity error. *Developmental Science, 9*, 303–308.

Howe, C., Nunes, T., & Bryant, P. (in press). Intensive quantities: Why they matter to developmental research. *British Journal of Developmental Psychology.*

Huber, S., & Krist, H. (2004). When is the ball going to hit the ground? Duration estimates, eye movements, and mental imagery of object motion. *Journal of Experimental Psychology: Human Perception and Performance, 30*, 431–444.

Huber, S., Krist, H., & Wilkening, F. (2003). Judgment and action knowledge in speed adjustment tasks: Experiments in a virtual environment. *Developmental Science, 6*, 197–210.

Hunt, E., & Minstrell, J. (1994). A cognitive approach to the teaching of physics. In K. McGilly (Ed.), *Classroom lessons: Integrating cognitive theory and classroom practice* (pp. 51–74). Cambridge, MA: MIT Press.

Inhelder, B., & Piaget, J. (1958). *The growth of logical thinking from childhood to adolescence: An essay on the construction of formal operational structures.* New York: Basic Books.

Jäger, S., & Wilkening, F. (2001). Development of cognitive averaging: When light and light make dark. *Journal of Experimental Child Psychology, 79*(4), 323–345.

Janke, B. (1995). Entwicklung naiven Wissens über den physikalischen Auftrieb: Warum schwimmen Schiffe? *Zeitschrift für Entwicklungspsychologie und Pädagogische Psychologie, 27*, 122–138.

Jansen, B. R. J., & van der Maas, H. L. J. (1997). Statistical test of the rule assessment methodology by latent class analysis. *Developmental Review, 17*, 321–357.

Jansen, B. R. J., & van der Maas, H. L. J. (2002). The development of children's rule use on the balance scale task. *Journal of Experimental Child Psychology, 81*, 383–416.

Kaiser, M. K., Proffitt, D. R., & McCloskey, M. (1985). The development of beliefs about falling objects. *Perception and Psychophysics, 38*, 533–539.

Karmiloff-Smith, A., & Inhelder, B. (1974). If you want to get ahead, get a theory. *Cognition, 3*, 195–212.

Karplus, R., Pulos, S., & Stage, E. K. (1983). Proportional reasoning of early adolescents. In R. Lesh & M. Landau (Eds.), *Acquisition of mathematics concepts and processes* (pp. 45–91). New York: Academic Press.

Keil, F. (1989). *Concepts, kinds, and cognitive development.* Cambridge, MA: MIT Press.

Kim, I. K., & Spelke, E. S. (1999). Perception and understanding of effects of gravity and inertia on object motion. *Developmental Science, 2*, 339–362.

Klahr, D., & Siegler, R. S. (1978). The representation of children's knowledge. In H. W. Reese & L. W. Lipsitt (Eds.), *Advances in child development* (Vol. 12, pp. 61–116). New York: Academic Press.

Kloos, H. (2007). Interlinking physical beliefs: Children's bias towards logical congruence. *Cognition, 103*, 227–252.

Kloos, H., & Somerville, S. C. (2001). Providing impetus for conceptual change: The effect of organizing the input. *Cognitive Development, 16*, 737–759.

Kloos, H., & Van Orden, G. C. (2005). Can a preschooler's mistaken belief benefit learning? *Swiss Journal of Psychology, 64*, 195–205.

Kohn, A. S. (1993). Preschoolers' reasoning about density: Will it float? *Child Development, 64*, 1637–1650.

Krist, H. (1992). Development of naive concepts of motion: The lower the angle, the further the throw? *Zeitschrift für Entwicklungspsychologie und Pädagogische Psychologie, 24*, 171–183.

Krist, H. (2001). Development of naive beliefs about moving objects: The straight-down belief in action. *Cognitive Development, 15*, 397–424.

Krist H. (2003). Knowing how to project objects: probing the generality of children's action knowledge. *Journal of Cognition and Development, 4*(4), 383–414.

Krist, H., Bach, S., Öndül, S., & Huber, S. (2004). Mikrogenetische Studien zum physikalischen Wissenserwerb von Kindern: Neue Trainingsstudien mit der Balkenwaage. *Zeitschrift für Entwicklungspsychologie und Pädagogische Psychologie, 36*, 119–129.

Krist, H., Fieberg, E. L., & Wilkening, F. (1993). Intuitive physics in action and judgment: The development of knowledge about projectile motion. *Journal of Experimental Psychology: Learning, Memory, and Cognition, 19*, 952–966.

Krist, H., Horz, H., & Schönfeld, T. (2005). Children's block balancing revisited: No evidence for representational redescription. *Swiss Journal of Psychology, 64*, 183–193.

Krist, H., Loskill, J., & Schwarz, S. (1996). Intuitive physics in action: Perceptual-motor knowledge about projectile motion in 5–7-year-old children. *Zeitschrift für Psychologie, 204*, 339–366.

Langley, P. (1987). A general theory of discrimination in learning. In D. Klahr, P. Langley, & R. Neches (Eds.), *Production system models of learning and development* (pp. 99–161). Cambridge, MA: MIT Press.

Lautrey, J., & Mazens, K. (2004). Is children's naïve knowledge consistent? A comparison of the concepts of sound and heat. *Learning and Instruction, 14*, 399–423.

Levin, I. (1977). The development of time concepts in young children: Reasoning about duration. *Child Development, 48*, 435–444.

Levin, I. (1982). The nature and development of time concepts in children: The effect of interfering cues. In W. J. Friedman (Ed.), *The developmental psychology of time* (pp. 47–85). New York: Academic Press.

Liu, X., & Lesniak, K. (2006). Progression in children's understanding of the matter concept from elementary to high school. *Journal of Research in Science Teaching, 43*, 320–347.

Marini, Z. A. (1992). Synchrony and asynchrony in the development of children's scientific reasoning. In R. Case (Ed.), *The mind's staircase: Exploring the conceptual underpinnings of children's thought and knowledge* (pp. 55–73). Hillsdale, NJ: Erlbaum.

Marini, Z. A., & Case, R. (1994). The development of abstract reasoning about the physical and social world. *Child Development, 65*, 147–159.

Matsuda, F. (1994). Concepts about interrelations among duration, distance, and speed in young children. *International Journal of Behavioral Development, 17*, 553–576.

Matsuda, F. (1996). Duration, distance, and speed judgments of two moving objects by 4- to 11-year-olds. *Journal of Experimental Child Psychology, 63*, 286–311.

Matsuda, F. (2001). Development of concepts of interrelationship among duration, distance, and speed. *International Journal of Behavioral Development, 25*, 466–480.

Mazens, K., & Lautrey, J. (2003). Conceptual change in physics: Children's naïve representations of sound. *Cognitive Development, 18*, 159–176.

McClelland, J. L. (1995). A connectionist perspective on knowledge and development. In T. J. Simon & G. S. Halford (Eds.), *Developing cognitive competence: New approaches to process modeling* (pp. 157–204). Hillsdale, NJ: Erlbaum.

McCloskey, M. (1983). Intuitive physics. *Scientific American, 248*(4), 122–130.

Minstrell, J., & Stimpson, V. (1996). A classroom environment for learning: Guiding students' reconstruction of understanding and reasoning. In L. Schauble & R. Glaser, (Eds.), *Innovations in learning: New environments for education* (pp. 175–202). Mahwah, NJ: Erlbaum.

Montangero, J. (1979). Les relations du temps, de la vitesse et de l'espace parcouru chez le jeune enfant. *L'Année Psychologique, 79*, 23–42.

Moore, C. F., Dixon, J. A., & Haines, B. A. (1991). Components of understanding in proportional reasoning: A fuzzy set representation of developmental progression. *Child Development, 62*, 441–459.

Newell A. (1990). *Unified theories of cognition.* Cambridge, MA: Harvard University Press.

Nunes, T., Desli, D., & Bell, D. (2003). The development of children's understanding of intensive quantities. *International Journal of Educational Research, 39*, 651–675.

Pauen, S. (1996). Children's reasoning about the interaction of forces. *Child Development, 67*, 2728–2742.

Pauen, S., & Wilkening, F. (1997). Children's analogical reasoning about natural phenomena. *Journal of Experimental Child Psychology, 67*, 90–113.

Penner, D. E., & Klahr, D. (1996). The interaction of domain-specific knowledge and domain-general discovery strategies: A study with sinking objects. *Child Development, 67*, 2709–2727.

Piaget, J. (1929). *The child's conception of the world.* London: Routledge & Kegan.

Piaget, J. (1946a). *Le développement de la notion de temps chez l'enfant.* Paris: Presses Universitaires de France.

Piaget, J. (1946b). *Les notions de mouvement et de vitesse chez l'enfant.* Paris: Presses Universitaires de France.

Piaget, J. (1960). *The child's conception of physical causality.* Paterson, NJ: Littlefield, Adams, and Co.

Piaget, J. (1974). *Understanding causality.* New York: Norton.

Piaget, J., & Inhelder, B. (1974). *The child's construction of quantities.* London: Routledge & Keagan Paul.

Piaget, J., & Szeminska, A. (1939). Experiences of children in the conservation of quantities. *Journal of Normal Psychology, 36*, 36–65.

Reed, S. K., & Evans, A. C. (1987). Learning functional relations: A theoretical and instructional analysis. *Journal of Experimental Psychology: General, 116*, 106–108.

Richards, D. D. (1982). Children's time concepts: Going the distance. In W. J. Friedman (Ed.), *The developmental psychology of time* (pp. 13–45). New York: Academic Press.

Schapiro, A. C., & McClelland, J. L. (2009). A connectionist model of continuous developmental transition in the balance scale task. *Cognition, 110*, 395–411.

Siegler, R. S. (1976). Three aspects of cognitive development. *Cognitive Psychology, 8*, 481–520.

Siegler, R. S. (1978). The origins of scientific reasoning. In R. S. Siegler (Ed.), *Children's thinking: What develops?* (pp. 109–149). Hillsdale, NJ: Erlbaum.

Siegler, R. S. (1995). Children's thinking: How does change occur? In F. E. Weinert & W. Schneider (Eds.), *Memory performance and competencies: Issues in growth and development* (pp. 405–430). Mahwah, NJ: Erlbaum.

Siegler, R. S., & Chen, Z. (1998). Developmental differences in rule learning: A microgenetic analysis. *Cognitive Psychology, 36*, 273–310.

Siegler, R. S., & Richards, D. D. (1979). Development of time, speed, and distance concepts. *Developmental Psychology, 15*, 288–298.

Smedslund, J. (1961). The acquisition of conservation of substance and weight in children: III. Extinction of conservation acquired "normally" and by means of empirical controls on a balance scale. *Scandinavian Journal of Psychology, 2*, 85–87.

Smith, C., Carey, S., & Wiser, M. (1985). On differentiation: A case study of the development of the concepts of size, weight, and density, *Cognition, 21*, 177–237.

Smith, C., Maclin, D., Grosslight, L., & Davis, H. (1997). Teaching for understanding. A study of students' pre-instruction theories of matter and a comparison of the effectiveness of two approaches to teaching about matter and density. *Cognition and Instruction, 15*, 317–393.

Smith, C., Snir, J., & Grosslight, L. (1992). Using conceptual models to facilitate conceptual change: The case of weight–density differentiation. *Cognition and Instruction, 9*, 221–283.

Sophian, C. (1997). Beyond competence: The significance of performance for conceptual development. *Cognitive Development, 12*, 281–303.

Sophian, C. (2006). Variability is the norm in performance, but not in beliefs. *Child Development, 77*, 1554–1556.

Stavy, R., & Stachel, D. (1985). Children's conception of changes in the state of matter: From solid to liquid. *Archives de Psychologie, 53*, 331–344.

Stavy, R., Strauss S., Orpaz, N., & Carmi, G. (1982). U-shaped behavioral growth in ratio comparisons. In S. Strauss (Ed.), *U-shaped behavioral growth* (pp. 11–36). New York: Academic Press.

Stavy, R., & Tirosh, D. (2000). *How students (mis-) understand science and mathematics. Intuitive rules*. New York: Teachers College Press.

Strauss, S., Ankori, M., Orpaz, N., & Stavy, R. (1977). Schooling effects on the development of proportional reasoning. In Y. H. Poortinga (Ed.), *Basic problems in cross-cultural psychology* (pp. 129–137). Amsterdam: Swets & Zeitlinger.

Strauss, S., & Stavy, R. (1982). U-shaped behavioral growth: Implications for the theories of development. In W. W. Hartup (Ed.), *Review of child development research* (Vol. *6*, pp. 547–599). Chicago: University of Chicago Press.

Surber, C. F., & Gzesh, S. M. (1984). Reversible operations in the balance scale task. *Journal of Experimental Child Psychology, 38*, 254–274.

Tudge, J. (1992). Processes and consequences of peer collaboration. A Vygotskian analysis. *Child Development, 63*, 1364–1379.

Vosniadou, S., Ioannides, C., Dimitrakopoulou, A., & Papademetriou, E. (2001). Designing learning environments to promote conceptual change in science. *Learning and Instruction, 15*, 317–419.

Weinreb, N., & Brainerd, C. J. (1975). A developmental study of Piaget's groupment model of the emergence of speed and time concepts. *Child Development, 46*, 176–185.

Weir, C., & Seacrest, M. (2000). Developmental differences in understanding of balance scales in the United States and Zimbabwe. *Journal of Genetic Psychology, 161*, 5–22.

Wellman, H. M., & Gelman, S. A. (1998). Knowledge acquisition in foundational domains. In W. Damon (Series Ed.), D. Kuhn, & R. S. Siegler (Vol. Eds.), *Handbook of child development: Vol. 2. Cognition, perception, and language* (pp. 523–573). New York: Wiley.

Wilkening, F. (1981). Integrating velocity, time, and distance information: A developmental study. *Cognitive Psychology, 13*, 231–247.

Wilkening, F. (1982). Children's knowledge about time, distance, and velocity interrelations. In W. J. Friedman (Ed.), *The developmental psychology of time* (pp. 87–112). New York: Academic Press.

Wilkening, F., Anderson, N. H. (1982). Comparison of the two rule-assessment methodologies for studying cognitive development and knowledge structure, *Psychological Bulletin*, *92*, 215–237.

Wilkening, F., & Anderson, N. H. (1991). Representation and diagnosis of knowledge structures in developmental psychology. In N. H. Anderson (Ed.), *Contributions to information integration theory: Vol. 3. Developmental* (pp. 45–80). Hillsdale, NJ: Erlbaum.

Wilkening, F., & Martin, C. (2004). How to speed up to be in time: Action–judgment dissociations in children and adults. *Swiss Journal of Psychology*, *63*, 17–29.

Wilson, M. (1989). Saltus: A psychometric model of discontinuity in cognitive development. *Psychological Bulletin*, *105*, 276–289.

Zhou, Z., Peverly, S. T., Boehm, A. E., & Chongde, L. (2000). American and Chinese children's understanding of distance, time, and speed interrelations. *Cognitive Development*, *15*, 215–240.

CHAPTER NINETEEN

What is Scientific Thinking and How Does it Develop?

Deanna Kuhn

What does it mean to think scientifically? We might label a preschooler's curious question, a high-school student's answer on a physics exam, and scientists' progress in mapping the human genome as instances of scientific thinking. But if we are to classify such disparate phenomena under a single heading, it is essential that we specify what it is that they have in common. Alternatively, we might define scientific thinking narrowly, as a specific reasoning strategy (such as the control-of-variables strategy that has dominated research on the development of scientific thinking), or as the thinking characteristic of a narrow population (scientific thinking is what scientists do). But to do so is to seriously limit the interest and significance the phenomenon holds. This chapter begins, then, with an attempt to define scientific thinking in an inclusive way that encompasses not only the preceding examples, but numerous other instances of thinking, including many not typically associated with science.

What is Scientific Thinking?

Scientific thinking as knowledge seeking

Is scientific thinking of any relevance outside of science? In this chapter I answer this question with an emphatic *yes* and portray scientific thinking as a human activity engaged in by most people, rather than a rarefied few. As such, it connects to other forms of thinking studied by cognitive psychologists, such as inference and problem-solving. In particular, I highlight its connection to argumentive thinking (Kuhn, 1991) and characterize its goals and purposes as more closely aligned with argument than with experimentation (Kuhn, 1993; Lehrer, Schauble, & Petrosino, 2001). Scientific thinking is most often social in nature, rather than a phenomenon that occurs only inside people's heads. A group of people may rely jointly on scientific thinking in pursuing their goals.

To fully appreciate scientific thinking, it must be situated in a developmental framework, with a goal of identifying both its origins and endpoints. These endpoints are more general than the practices and standards of professional science. The most skilled, highly developed thinking that we identify here is essential to science, but not specific to it.

The definition of scientific thinking adopted in this chapter is *knowledge seeking*. This definition encompasses any instance of purposeful thinking that has the objective of enhancing the seeker's knowledge. One consequence that follows from this definition is that scientific thinking is something people *do*, not something they *have*. The latter we will refer to as *scientific understanding*. When conditions are favorable, the process of scientific thinking may lead to scientific understanding as its product. Indeed, it is the desire for scientific understanding – for explanation – that drives the process of scientific thinking.

Scientific thinking and scientific understanding

The distinction between scientific thinking and scientific understanding is an important one, since there has arisen in recent years an extensive literature on children's developing understandings in the domains of physics, biology, and psychology (see Gelman & Kalish, 2006, for review). From their earliest years, children construct implicit theories that enable them to make sense of and organize their experience. These early theories are most often incorrect, as well as incomplete. In a process that has come to be referred to as *conceptual change*, these theories are revised as new evidence is encountered bearing on them. Knowledge acquisition, then, is not the accumulation of isolated bits of knowledge, but, rather, this process of conceptual change.

In contrast to the sizable body of knowledge that has accrued regarding the content of children's evolving theories within specific domains, less is known about the process by means of which theory revision is accomplished. It is this process that is the concern of the present chapter. How is theory revision possible, is there a single process by means of which it occurs, and where does scientific thinking come into this picture? From an applied, educational perspective, as well as a theoretical one, the process of theory revision assumes particular significance. Enhanced understandings of scientific phenomena are certainly a goal of science education. But it is the *ability to advance these understandings* that depends on scientific thinking and is at least as important as an educational goal.

On the grounds that there is no rigid dividing line between informal and formal theories (Kuhn & Pearsall, 2000), we refer here to any cognitive representation of the way things are, no matter how simple, implicit, or fragmentary, as a theory, rather than reserve the latter term for theories meeting various formal criteria that might be invoked (Brewer & Samarapungavan, 1991). We can claim, then, that in the early years of life, theories and theory revision are common, as children seek to make sense of a widening array of experience. This early theory revision shares two important attributes with scientific thinking. First, both involve the coordination of theory and evidence – a characterization of scientific thinking common to most contemporary accounts of it (Bullock, Sodian, &

Koerber, in press; Klahr, 2000; Klahr, Fay, & Dunbar, 1993; Klahr & Simon, 1999; Koslowski, 1996; Kuhn, 1989; Kuhn, Amsel, & O'Loughlin, 1988; Lehrer & Schauble, 2006; Zimmerman, 2000, 2007). Second, both can lead to enhanced understanding. There is one important difference, however, between the two. Unlike scientific thinking, early theory revision occurs implicitly and effortlessly, without conscious awareness or intent. Young children think *with* their theories, rather than about them. In the course of so doing they may revise these theories, but they are not aware that they are doing so.

The modern view of scientific thinking as theory–evidence coordination, note, can be contrasted to the pioneering work on scientific thinking by Inhelder and Piaget (1958). Despite the centrality of meaning-making in much of Piaget's writing, in this work Inhelder and Piaget conceptualized scientific reasoning strategies largely as logic-driven devices to be applied independently of any context of understanding of the phenomena being investigated. In the modern view, in contrast, theories are integral to knowledge seeking at every phase of the process, a view consonant with modern philosophy of science (Kitcher, 1993).

Knowledge seeking as the intentional coordination of theory and evidence

It is the intention to seek knowledge that transforms implicit theory revision into scientific thinking. Theory revision becomes something one *does*, rather than something that happens to one outside of conscious awareness. To seek knowledge is to acknowledge that one's existing knowledge is incomplete, possibly incorrect – that there is something new to know. The process of theory–evidence coordination accordingly becomes explicit and intentional. Newly available evidence is examined with regard to its implications for a theory, with awareness that the theory is susceptible to revision.

The coordination of theory and evidence entailed in scientific thinking may yield either of two broad categories of outcomes – congruence or discrepancy. In the first case, the new evidence that is encountered is entirely compatible with existing theories, and no new understanding results. A new instance is simply absorbed into existing understanding. In the second, more interesting, case, some discrepancy between theory and evidence exists and relations between the two need to be constructed. It is possible that the discrepancy will go unrecognized, because the theory, the new evidence, or both have not been adequately represented in a manner that allows relations between them to be constructed. In this case, a likely outcome is that the evidence is ignored or distorted to allow assimilation to existing theoretical understanding. If we decide to include this as a case of scientific thinking at all, it can only be labeled as faulty scientific thinking, since one's existing understandings have been exposed to no test. No knowledge seeking occurs, nor is the possibility of new knowledge even allowed.

Alternatively, in a process we can refer to as "data reading" (Kuhn & Katz, in press), a mental representation of discrepant evidence may be formed – a representation distinct from the theory – and its implications for the theory identified. Such cases may vary vastly in the complexity of thinking involved, but they have in common encoding and representation of the evidence distinct from the theory, which is also explicitly represented as an object of cognition, and contemplation of its implications for the theory. It is important to note that the outcome of this process remains open. It is not necessary that the theory be revised in light of the evidence, nor certainly that theory be ignored in favor of evidence, which is a misunderstanding of what is meant by theory–evidence coordination. The criterion is only that the evidence be represented in its own right and its implications for the theory contemplated. Skilled scientific thinking always entails the coordination of theories and evidence, but coordination cannot occur unless the two are encoded and represented as distinguishable entities.

We turn now to tracing the developmental origins of these capacities and then go on to examine them in their more sophisticated forms. Note that none of the processes identified above restricts scientific thinking to traditional scientific content. We are tracing, then, the development of a broad way of thinking and acquiring knowledge about the world, rather than an ability to reason about "scientific" phenomena narrowly conceived.

Developmental Origins of Scientific Thinking

A now sizeable literature on children's theory of mind (Flavell, 1999; Wellman, 1988; Wellman, chapter 10, this volume) affords insight into the origins of scientific thinking because it identifies the earliest forms of a child's thinking about thinking. Thinking about thinking is not delayed until adolescence, as Inhelder and Piaget's (1958) account of formal operations might suggest. Rather, it is identifiable in the early forms of awareness preschool children display regarding their own and others' thinking. By age 3, they show some awareness of their own thinking processes and distinguish thinking about an object from perceiving it (Flavell, Green, & Flavell, 1995). They also begin to use mental-state concepts such as desire and intention in describing their own and others' behavior.

Differentiating claims from evidence

Not until about age 4, however, does a child understand that mental representations, as products of the human mind, do not necessarily duplicate external reality. Before children achieve this concept of false belief, they show unwillingness to attribute to another person a belief that they themselves know to be false (Perner, 1991). Children of this young age hold a naïve epistemological theory of beliefs as mental copies of reality. Mental representations are confined to a single reality defined by what the individual takes to be true. The world is thus a simple one of objects and events that we can characterize for ourselves and others. There are no inaccurate renderings of events.

At this level of mental development, the evaluation of falsifiable claims that is central to science cannot occur (Kuhn, Cheney, & Weinstock, 2000). The early theory-of-mind achievement that occurs at least by age 4 – in which assertions come to be understood as generating from human minds and are recognized as potentially discrepant with an external reality to which they can be compared – is thus a milestone of foundational status in the development of scientific thinking. Assertions become susceptible to evaluation vis-à-vis the reality from which they are now distinguished. The complexity of claims that a 4-year-old is able to evaluate as potentially false is extremely limited. A child of this age is capable of little more, really, than determining whether a claim regarding some physical state of affairs does or does not correspond to a reality the child can directly observe. Yet, this differentiation of assertion and evidence sets the stage for the coordinations between more complex theoretical claims and forms of evidence that are more readily recognizable as scientific thinking.

A related development during this preschool period is the ability to recognize indeterminacy; that is, to recognize situations in which two or more alternative reality states are possible and it is not known which is true, and to discriminate these indeterminate situations from determinate ones. Fay and Klahr (1996), and before them Pieraut-Le Bonniec (1980), report development in this respect beginning in early childhood (but continuing through adolescence), as do Sodian, Zaitchik, and Carey (1991). Sodian et al. found that by age 7, children were able to choose a determinate over an indeterminate test to find out if a mouse was large or small by placing food in a box overnight. The indeterminate option was a box with a large opening (able to accommodate a large or small mouse) and the determinate option a box with a small opening (big enough for only the small mouse). In choosing the latter, 7-year-olds also show some rudimentary skill in investigative strategy, an aspect of inquiry we discuss at length later.

An early competency that is less compelling as an origin of scientific thinking is identification of correspondences between theory and data (Ruffman, Perner, Olson, & Doherty,1993). Connecting the two does not imply their differentiation, as Ruffman et al. claim, based on findings that 5- to 7-year-olds make inferences from evidence (e.g., dolls who choose red food over green food) to theory (the dolls prefer red food to green), and vice versa. Instead, theory and evidence fit together into a coherent depiction of a state of affairs. In neither the Ruffman et al. nor the Sodian et al. studies, however, is there reason to assume that the child recognizes the differing epistemological status of theory and evidence. (See Kuhn & Pearsall, 2000, for further discussion of these studies.)

Identifying evidence as a source of knowledge

Once assertions are differentiated from evidence that bears on their truth value, it becomes possible for evidence to be appreciated as a source of support for a theory and for relations between evidence and theory to be constructed. To appreciate the epistemological status of evidence, one must be sensitive to the issue of how one knows – to the sources of one's knowledge. Several researchers have reported increasing sensitivity to the sources of knowledge during the preschool years, for example in distinguishing imagining from perceiving (Woolley & Bruell, 1996), seeing from being told (Gopnik & Graf, 1988), and something just learned from something known for a long time (Taylor, Esbensen, & Bennett, 1994).

In a study of 4- to 6-year-olds, Pearsall and I (Kuhn & Pearsall, 2000) investigated specifically whether children of this age were sensitive to evidence as a source of knowledge to support the truth of a claim, distinguishable from theory that enhances plausibility of the claim. Participants were shown a sequence of pictures in which, for example, two runners compete in a race. Certain cues suggest a theory as to why one will win; for example, one has fancy running shoes and the other does not. The final picture in the sequence provides evidence of the outcome – one runner holds a trophy and exhibits a wide grin. When asked to indicate the outcome and to justify this knowledge, 4-year-olds show a fragile distinction between the two kinds of justification – "How do you know?" and "Why is it so?" – in other words, the evidence for the claim (the outcome cue in this case) versus an explanation for it (the initial theory-generating cue). Rather, the two merge into a single representation of what happened, and the child tends to choose as evidence of what happened the cue having greater explanatory value as to why it happened. Thus, children often answered the "How do you know [he won]?" question, not with evidence ("He's holding the trophy") but with a theory of why this state of affairs makes sense ("Because he has fast sneakers"). A follow-up probe, "How can you be sure this is what happened?" elicited a shift from theory-based to evidence-based responses in some cases, but, even with this prompt, 4-year-olds gave evidence-based responses on average to less than a third of the items. At age 6, confusions between theory and evidence still occurred, but children of this age were correct a majority of the time. A group of adults, in contrast, made no errors.

Development of theory–evidence coordination skill as a continuing process

By the end of the preschool years, when children have begun to show an appreciation of the role of evidence in supporting a falsifiable claim, do they confront further challenges in coordinating theories and evidence? The research on older children and adolescents that we turn to now contains substantial evidence of difficulties in this respect, with degree of difficulty influenced by the number and level of complexity of the theoretical alternatives, as well as by the complexity of the evidence. Thus, as Klahr (2000) similarly concludes, coordination of theory and evidence is not a discrete skill that emerges at a single point in cognitive development. Rather, it must be achieved at successively greater levels of complexity, over an extended period of development. This is especially so if it is to keep pace with increasingly complex models of scientific understanding that are encountered with increasing age. In evaluating such models, requisite skills are invoked: What data support or contradict this piece of the model? How can we test whether particular segments of the model are correct? In such contexts, even able adults' limitations in coordinating theory and evidence become evident. The range and variability in the scientific thinking skills of adults is in fact striking (Kuhn et al., 1988, 1995; Kuhn & Pease, 2006).

Phases of Scientific Thinking: Inquiry, Analysis, Inference, and Argument

Preschool children, we noted, are able to coordinate a simple event claim and evidence regarding its truth, e.g., they can verify whether the claim that candy is in the pencil box is true or false. More complex claims, however, which begin to assume greater similarity to genuine theories, cause difficulty among school-age children. One such form of rudimentary theory is the imposition of a categorization scheme on a set of instances. Categorization constitutes a theory, in stipulating that some instances are identical to others but different from a third set with respect to some defining attribute(s). Lehrer and Romberg (1996) describe the conceptual obstacles young school-age children encounter in representing theory and data as they engage in such seemingly simple tasks as categorizing classmates' favorite activities and representing their findings. Another series of studies shows only gradually developing skills in children's making appropriate inductive inferences regarding category definition based on a sample of exemplars (Lo, Sides, Rozelle, & Osherson, 2002; Rhodes, Brickman, & Gelman, 2008). We turn now to this coordination process in the more complex forms characteristic of scientific thinking.

As Klahr (2000) notes, very few studies of scientific thinking encompass the entire cycle of scientific investigation, a cycle I characterize here as consisting of four major phases: inquiry, analysis, inference, and argument. A number of researchers have confined their studies to only a portion of the cycle, most often the evaluation of evidence (Amsel & Brock, 1996; Klaczynski, 2000; Koslowski, 1996; Masnick & Morris, 2008), a research design that links the study of scientific reasoning to research on inductive causal inference (Gopnik & Schultz, 2007; Koslowski & Masnick, chapter 14, this volume). Many of the studies in which participants acquire their own data, following the lead of Inhelder and Piaget (1958), have focused their attention on the control-of-variables strategy (in which a focal variable is manipulated to assess its effect, while all other variables are held constant), as an isolated cognitive strategy divorced from a context of the theoretical meaning of the phenomena being investigated or the goals of the investigations conducted. In the remainder of this chapter, as well as focusing on research that examines strategies in a context of theoretical understanding, we focus on more recent studies that encompass the entire cycle of inquiry, analysis, inference, and argument. These studies offer a picture of how the strategies associated with each phase of scientific investigation are situated within a context of all the others and how they influence one another.

The microgenetic method

We also focus in this chapter on *microgenetic* research (Kuhn, 1995; Kuhn & Phelps, 1982; Siegler, 2006; Siegler & Crowley, 1991), that is, studies in which an individual engages in the same essential task over multiple sessions, allowing the researcher to observe a dynamic process of change in the strategies that are applied to the task. Participants in microgenetic studies are observed in the process of acquiring new knowledge over time. Knowledge acquisition is best conceptualized as a process of theory–evidence coordination, rather than an accumulation of facts (Kuhn, 2000). A major finding from microgenetic research has been that an individual applies a range of alternative strategies in knowledge-acquisition tasks. The selection of strategies chosen for application evolves over time, toward more frequent use of more developmentally advanced strategies. The theory–evidence coordination process of concern to us here, then, while itself dynamic, is likely to undergo modifications in its own nature as it is applied over time. Microgenetic change can thus be observed at two levels: knowledge (or understanding) changes, but so do the strategies by means of which this knowledge is acquired. Indeed, the latter is a primary thesis of this chapter: the process of theory–evidence coordination shows developmental change. The microgenetic method offers insight into how this change occurs.

The studies by Klahr and his associates (Klahr, 2000; Klahr et al., 1993; Klahr, Triona, & Williams, 2007; Masnick & Klahr, 2003) have followed children and adults asked to conduct scientific investigations, for example of the function of a particular key in controlling the behavior of an electronic robot toy, or, in another version, the behavior of a dancer who performs various movements in a computer simulation. To do this, individuals need to coordinate hypotheses about this function with data they generate, or, in Klahr's (2000) terminology, to coordinate searches of an hypothesis space and an experiment space. Consistent with the findings reported in this chapter, Klahr and his associates find younger children less able to meet this challenge than are older children or adults.

My own microgenetic studies (Kuhn, Black, Keselman, & Kaplan, 2000; Kuhn, Garcia-Mila, Zohar, & Andersen, 1995; Kuhn & Pease, 2008; Kuhn & Phelps, 1982; Kuhn, Schauble, & Garcia-Mila, 1992), as well as studies by Schauble (1990, 1996), Echevarria, (2003), and Penner and Klahr (1996), address what we have regarded as a prototypical form of scientific inquiry – the situation in which a number of variables have potential causal connections to an outcome and the investigative task is choose instances for examination and on this basis to identify causal and non-causal variables, with the goals of predicting and explaining variations in outcome. Considered here in their simplest, most generic form, these are common objectives of professional scientists engaged in authentic scientific inquiry.

Following our initial assessment of their own theories regarding the presence and direction of causal effects and the mechanisms underlying them, participants in our studies engage in repeated investigative cycles (within a session and across multiple sessions) in which they identify a question, select instances for examination, analyze and make comparisons, and draw conclusions. They also make predictions regarding outcomes and justify these predictions, allowing us to compare implicit causal theories regarding effects of the variables with the earlier-voiced explicit theories regarding these effects. We have conducted these studies in a variety of physical and social domains involving, for example, the speed of cars travelling around a computerized racetrack, the speed of toy boats travelling down a makeshift canal, the variables influencing the popularity of children's TV programs, the variables affecting children's school achievement, the variables affecting a teacher-aide's performance in the classroom, and the variables influencing several kinds of natural disasters – floods, earthquakes, and avalanches.

The illustrations in this chapter are drawn from preadolescent boys' investigations of a single domain (earthquakes), to facilitate comparison and to highlight differences in performance. The earthquake problem is presented as a computer simulation in which five dichotomous features have potential causal effects on the risk of earthquake (portrayed on a "risk meter" with four gradations from lowest to highest risk). Two of the features – type of bedrock (igneous or sedimentary) and speed of S-waves (slow or fast) in fact have no effect on outcome, while the other three – water quality (good or poor), radon gas levels (light or heavy), and snake activity (high or low) – have simple additive effects. (A version of the problem can be examined at educationforthinking.org.)

The inquiry phase

We begin with an excerpt from the investigations of 10-year-old Brad, who does not see the goal of the task as analysis. In identifying the second instance he wishes to examine, he commented:

> Last time, the [sedimentary] rock was like white. This one [igneous] is sort of like not. It looks like it's going to just blow up any second. This [sedimentary] one looks like it's okay. [So which one do you want to choose to investigate?] Sedimentary. [Why?] Because last time I chose sedimentary as well and it seemed to work out pretty good. The igneous looks like it's about to explode any second.

Brad's primary objective, it appears, is to achieve a "good" outcome, rather than to understand the role of the different features in producing different kinds of outcomes. Another approach common among students of Brad's age is to have no other goal than to "experiment," to "try different stuff and see what happens," with no particular intention or organization shaping their investigations. These students, we find, rarely go on to make any informative comparisons in the analysis phase.

The *inquiry* phase of scientific investigation (figure 19.1) is a crucial one in which the goals of the activity are formulated, the questions to be asked identified, and the remaining phases thereby shaped (see left side of figure 19.1, which lists the tasks that characterize the inquiry phase). The ovals in the upper center of figure 19.1 portray the meta-task and metastrategic knowledge associated with this phase.

The most fundamental challenge of the inquiry phase is to recognize that the database I have the opportunity to access yields information that bears on the theories I hold – a recognition that eludes many young investigators. The issue is not how heavily such data

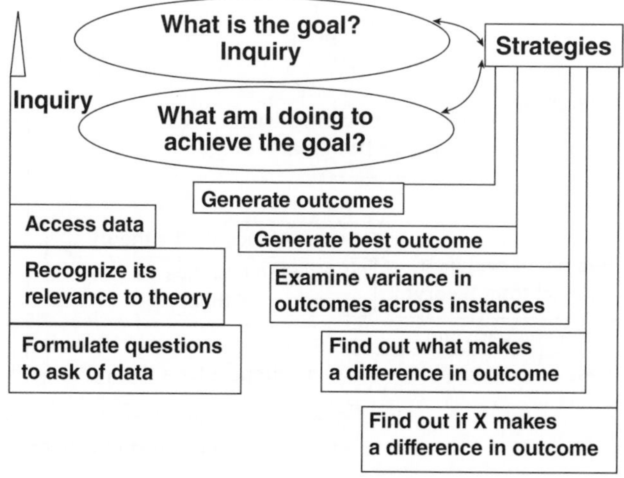

Figure 19.1 The inquiry phase

are weighed relative to pre-existing theories, but simply to recognize that these data stand independently of and *speak to* a claim being made. Once the relevance of the data in this respect is recognized, questions can be formulated of a form that is productive in connecting data and theory.

The various strategies that can be observed in response to the tasks of the inquiry phase are portrayed on the right side of figure 19.1. Here (in contrast to the left side of figure 19.1, where objectives are compatible), there appears a set of competing strategies which overlap in their usage and are of varying degrees of adequacy (with more adequate strategies appearing further down in the figure). At the lowest level, a strategy for some individuals (or for a particular individual some of the time) may be the simple one of activity, i.e., choosing instances and generating outcomes. Later, after the phenomenon has been observed a number of times, the dominant strategy may become one of producing the most desirable or interesting outcome, as Brad illustrates. The major developmental shift is one from strategies of activity to genuine inquiry, which in its most rudimentary appearance takes the form of "What is making a difference?" or "What will enable me to predict outcomes?" In more advanced forms, inquiry becomes focused on the specific features in terms of which there is variability, and, ultimately, on the effect of a specific feature, "Does X make a difference?"

Analysis and inference phases

The *analysis* phase of scientific inquiry is depicted in figure 19.2. To engage in productive analysis (left side of figure 19.2), some segment of the database must be accessed, attended to, processed, and represented as such, i.e., as evidence to which one's theory can be related, and these data must be operated on (through comparison and pattern detection), in order to reach the third phase, which yields the product of these operations – *inference*.

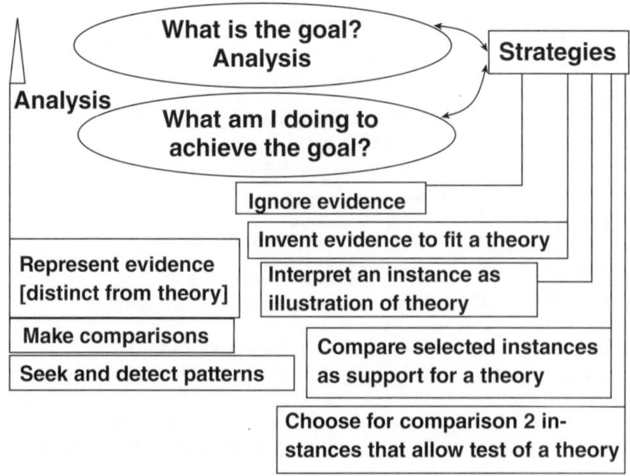

Figure 19.2 The analysis phase

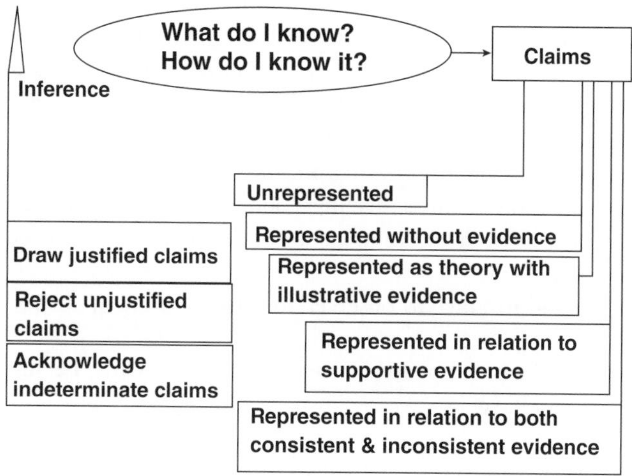

Figure 19.3 The inference phase

The strategies that can be observed being applied to this task reflect the struggle to coordinate theories and evidence. As seen on the right side of figure 19.2, theory predominates in the lower-level strategies, and only with the gradually more advanced strategies does evidence acquire the power to influence theory.

In moving from the analysis to the *inference* phase, we move from procedural strategies to declarative claims. As shown on the left side of figure 19.3, the inference phase involves inhibiting claims that are not justified, as well as making those that are. The inferential processes that may be applied to this task (right side of figure 19.3) range in adequacy from no processing of the evidence and no conscious awareness of one's theories (so-called "theories in action") to the skilled coordination of theory and evidence, which entails understanding the implications of evidence as supporting or disconfirming one's theories.

In contrast to Brad, 11-year-old Tom exhibits a more advanced level of investigation in which he sets out to identify effects of individual features. Two characteristics, however, limit the effectiveness of Tom's investigations. First, he believes he can find out the effects of all features at one time and hence does not focus his inquiry on any particular feature. Second, his investigations are theory-dominated to the undesirable extent that the evidence he generates he does not mentally represent in a form that is distinct from his theories.

In response to the first instance he chose to examine, Tom noted the outcome of highest risk level, but, contrary to Brad, he regarded this result favorably and commented:

> I'm feeling really good about this. [Why?] Like I said before on everything. The water quality being poor. Obviously the earthquake would contaminate the water in some way. The S-waves would go fast because logically thinking even big earthquakes happen pretty quickly. Gas, I figured it'd be kind of hard to breathe in an earthquake. Like I said before about the snakes, in the '86 earthquake, dogs started howling before it happened.

Tom, then, appeared quite ready to interpret multiple variables as causally implicated in an outcome, based on a single co-occurrence of one level of the variable and an outcome. We have referred to the mental model of causality underlying this stance as a *co-occurrence* model (Kuhn, Black, et al., 2000). Typically, the single-instance inferences deriving from this model are theory-laden in the sense that the empirical observation is seen not so much as a test of, or even evidence bearing on, the theory, as it is simply an "illustration" of the theory in operation. Tom is "feeling good" because his theories have, from his perspective, withstood the test of empirical verification. In reality, of course, they have not been tested at all.

In choosing a second instance to observe, Tom used a strategy that is also common:

> I'm going to do everything the opposite of what I did before. [Why?] Because I want to see if there's risk or no risk involved.

Tom went on to declare, however, "Actually, I'm going to mix it up kind of," and after several alternations back and forth he ended up changing bedrock from igneous (chosen for the first instance he examined) to sedimentary, water quality from poor to good, and S-wave rate from fast to slow. Gas levels he left unchanged at heavy, and snake activity unchanged at high.

Tom then observed the outcome fall to medium-high risk and made this interpretation:

> Bedrock makes no difference. No actually it makes a difference. Snake activity makes a difference. And water quality … hmm, yeah it brought it down. That was probably half the reason that lowered [the risk] down, with the bedrock and the S-wave. Bedrock made a difference I think because it lowered it down because … well, it [sedimentary rock] seemed less threatening, so I figured it lowered it down. Snake activity, like I said before, animals act up before disasters happen.

Note the predominant role that theory plays in Tom's implicating bedrock as affecting the outcome. Snake activity, note, Tom implicated as causal even though it remained at an unchanged high level in both of the instances he has observed to this point. The interviewer probed Tom about this feature:

> [Suppose someone disagreed and said that snake activity makes no difference. What would you tell them? Could you tell them that you found out here that it did make a difference?] Well, if you did it low, probably everything's normal because the snakes wouldn't be acting up in some odd way.

Thus, Tom's claim rests on evidence (regarding low snake activity) that he does not in fact have. Tom and the interviewer go on to have a similar exchange regarding gas level, which also has remained at the same (heavy) level across the two instances, and, this time, Tom did not even make reference to evidence:

> The gas makes a difference because the heavier it is, the harder it would be to breathe. [Suppose someone disagreed and said that gas level makes no difference. How could you

show them that you're right? Did you see anything here that shows you that it does make a difference?] Well, I think it makes a difference because … let me summarize this up. When it's heavy there are more things in the air to clog up your lungs.

Finally, based on the two instances available, Tom again implicated water quality, which has covaried with outcome, as causal. He changed his mind about S-wave rates, however, which also covaried with outcome, now claiming this feature to be non-causal:

> Water quality makes a big difference. If it's good it wouldn't be contaminated by an earthquake, which also brought [risk] down. And the S-waves, they're going slowly, always moving. So they don't really make a difference.

These excerpts from Tom's investigative activity suggest that when data are not represented in their own right distinct from theory, the potential for scientific analysis remains limited. It should be emphasized again, however, that the scientific thinking tasks described here are *not* ones that ask individuals to cast aside their own beliefs about the world in favor of some arbitrary new information. Rather, they assess the ability to access and represent new evidence and to appreciate the relation it bears to different theoretical claims. Skilled scientific thinking always entails the coordination of theories and evidence, and this coordination requires that the two be clearly distinguished. Someone could say, "This is what this evidence implies for these theories, although other sources of support I have for some of these theories lead me to maintain belief in them in the face of your disconfirming evidence." This individual would do perfectly well in our tasks. More troubling are those whose beliefs *are* influenced by the evidence but who remain metacognitively unaware that this has happened and, more broadly, of why they claim what they do.

Mental models of causality and their implications for scientific investigation

Mark, also aged 11, does better than Tom in representing data separately from his theories and drawing on these data as a basis for his inferences. In other respects, however, his approach is like Tom's. Mark implicates features as causal based on a single co-occurrence of variable level and outcome. In choosing an instance for observation, he intended, "to try to find out about everything," and in choosing a second instance, he decided to "do the opposite of each one." Mark saw risk level drop (from instance 1 to 2) from medium-high to low risk. In interpreting the second outcome, he implicated four of the five varying features as causal (with the justification that they covaried with outcome) and yet dismissed the fifth (for which evidence was identical) on the basis of his theory that it doesn't matter.

The performance of both Mark and Tom is consistent with the interpretation of their causal analysis and inference as based on the co-occurrence mental model. Both boys falsely include as causal a variable that either co-occurs with outcome in a single instance or covaries with outcome over two instances. Mark also shows an even more interesting inferential error, which (following Inhelder & Piaget, 1958) we have called *false exclusion* (in contrast to the *false inclusion* errors just noted). In choosing a third instance for examination, Mark changed some features and left others the same and observed a low-risk outcome. Following causal inferences for several features, Mark made two non-causal inferences, using false exclusion to justify each. Water quality, he said, made no difference because

> before [instance 1] it was good and had medium-high risk. This time it's good and has low risk. [What does that tell you?] It probably doesn't matter.

The implication is that another feature has produced variation showing that feature's causal power in affecting the outcome, and the feature in question can therefore be discounted. Mark's inference regarding snake activity was identical in form. Both of these features, note, he had earlier implicated as causal, illustrating the vacillation in claims that our microgenetic studies have shown to be common.

Both false exclusion and false inclusion are consistent with a co-occurrence criterion for inferring causality. The co-occurrence of a level of one variable and an outcome is sufficient to explain that outcome. The potential causal influence of a second variable, therefore, need not be treated as additive. Instead, it can be invoked as a different explanation for a later outcome, or it can be discounted because the first feature explains the outcome (false exclusion, if the discounted variable has not been varied). Accordingly, then, the co-occurrence mental model treats causal influences as neither consistent nor additive.

Computing the consistent effects of multiple variables on an outcome rests on a different, more advanced model of causality. Identification of an individual effect ("Does X make a difference?") is only one step in explaining the causal structure of a domain. The broader task is to identify the effect of each of the varying features, and then – a part of the task that has received little attention – consider their joint effects on outcome. Doing so is of course the only way to achieve the goal of accurate prediction of outcomes. It requires that a different mental model of causality replace the co-occurrence model, one in which multiple causes operate individually in a consistent fashion, simultaneously and additively producing an outcome. (Interactive effects require a further level of understanding.)

In our research, we have observed an association between the goal of identifying effects of individual features and use of controlled comparison as an analysis strategy (Kuhn, Black, et al., 2000). Arguably this is so because both rest on the mature mental model of causality in which multiple individual variables additively influence an outcome. In the absence of this model, one's task goal is unlikely to be identification of the effect of each of the individual variables. Accordingly, neither attribute of the controlled comparison strategy will be compelling. The "comparison" attribute is not compelling, given it entails comparing the outcomes associated with different levels of an individual variable to assess its effect. And the "controlled" attribute is even less compelling, since it is the individual effects of other variables that need to be controlled.

The immature mental model of causality underlying Tom's and Mark's performance, then, limits adoption of either the goals or the strategies that make for effective scientific investigation. Unsurprisingly, neither Mark's nor Tom's investigations led to judgments of any greater than chance correctness. Mark, for example, concluded (after examining 4 instances) that all features except water quality are causal. He was thus wrong about 3 of the 5 features. Moreover, when asked how sure he was that he had found out which features were and weren't making a difference, on a 1–10 scale, Mark rated his certainty as "9."

The performance of 12-year-old Robbie can be contrasted to that of Tom and Mark. Robbie's approach initially does not look that different. He chose as the second instance "the opposite of what I did last time." When asked for his inferences, however, he initially implicated S-wave rates, but then said:

> Well, I should … I can do a test to find out actually.

Robbie then said:

> I am going to keep everything the same as last time and just change the igneous to sedimentary to see if it alters the thing.

In response to the interviewer's question, "Why are you keeping the others the same?" Robbie responded:

> If you alter one thing and it's different, that means it has to be the difference. So the type of bedrock does not make a difference. [How do you know?] Because it [the outcome] didn't change. If it had changed, it would mean that it mattered.

Robbie proceeded in an identical manner to assess effects of the remaining features and was able to explain his strategy explicitly:

> I'm doing the same thing as last time. I'll keep everything the same except for gas level, which I am changing to the opposite, light.

After satisfying himself that he had discovered which features did or did not make a difference, Robbie went on to the next phase of the activity, in which he is asked to make predictions about outcomes and then to indicate (as an assessment of implicit causal judgments) which features had influenced the prediction. For each of his predictions, Robbie implicated the same three features. The interviewer asked, "Would it always be these three for every prediction, or would it be different for some predictions?", to which Robbie replied:

> It would always be these three for all predictions, because [the other two] didn't matter. It was only these three that actually mattered.

With this awareness of what and how he knows, Robbie would be well equipped to defend his claims in discussion with others. This is an important achievement, since a final *argument* phase of scientific thinking consists of debate of the claims that are the product of the earlier phases, in a framework of alternatives and evidence (see figure 19.4). Again, a range of strategies can be identified, strategies that an individual draws on with

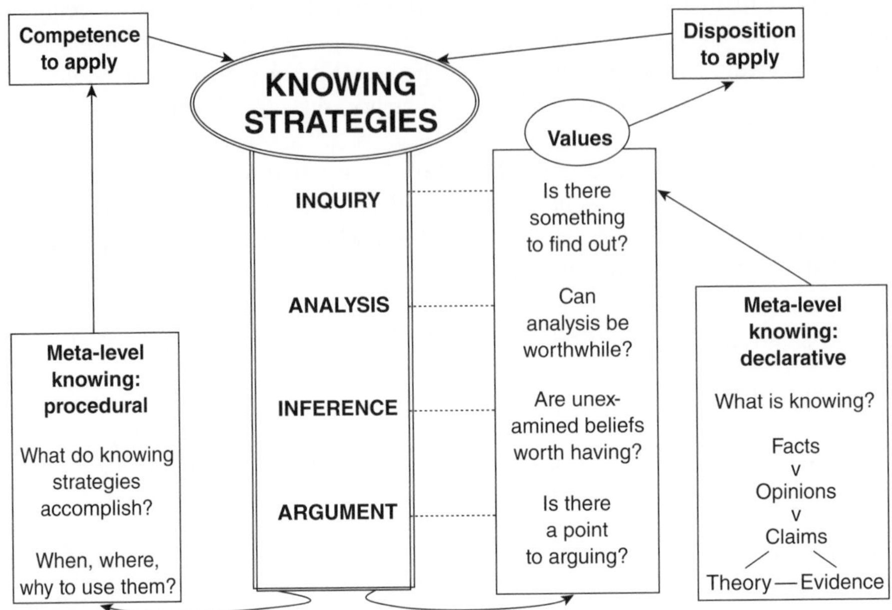

Figure 19.4 The role of meta-level operators in scientific thinking. (From Kuhn, 2001.)

varying degrees of probability. Given sustained exercise, these argumentive strategies undergo development (Felton, 2004; Kuhn, 1991; Kuhn, Goh, Iordanou, & Shaenfield, 2008; Kuhn, Shaw, & Felton, 1997; Kuhn & Udell, 2003; Udell, 2007). The products of the argumentive process are revised and strengthened *claims*, strengthened in the sense of being better supported as an outcome of the argumentive process.

The progression from absence of an analysis goal on the part of 10-year-old Brad to 12-year-old Robbie's explicit awareness of the effective analysis strategies he used should not be taken as implying an orderly age-related progression in the development of scientific thinking skills. To the contrary, the norm is wide inter-individual variability. As often as 12-year-olds like Robbie, we see children of similar age and even adults, reported in our earlier research (Kuhn et al., 1995), who over 7 or 8 weekly sessions examine a database that provides no support for a theory and yet maintain to the end not just the correctness of their theory, but, more importantly, that the data they have examined *shows* that it is correct.

Recognizing the centrality of argument to scientific thinking extends scientific thinking beyond traditional science and into the realm of everyday thinking. People typically hold entrenched beliefs, supported by contextually rich representations and sometimes significant affect. This richness may facilitate thinking about such topics, but it may also make it more difficult to think well about them. This was the finding of a comparison of inquiry processes in social science versus physical science domains (Kuhn et al., 1995). Thus, while it would be hard to contest that "valid experimentation strategies support the development of more accurate and complete knowledge" (Schauble, 1996, p. 118), it is less clear that rich knowledge necessarily enhances the selection of valid experimentation strategies.

Coordinating effects of multiple variables – an overlooked aspect of scientific thinking

Tom and Mark, we noted, were constrained by their satisfaction with a single factor as sufficient in explanatory power to discourage investigation of additional factors acting on the outcome. In further work (Kuhn & Dean, 2004; Kuhn, Iordanou, Pease, & Wirkala, 2008; Kuhn, Pease, & Wirkala, in press), we have in fact found that coordination of the effects of multiple factors on an outcome is a skill in its own right that is by no means implied by the ability to identify the effect of each individual feature. This skill is called upon when individuals are asked to predict outcomes on the basis of multiple features that they have identified as causal and to explain the basis for their predictions. Typical among preadolescents (and even many adults) is inconsistent causal attribution across consecutive predictions, for example implicating variable A as the sole basis for an outcome prediction for one case and variable B as the basis for the prediction in the next case. Moreover, they typically implicate fewer variables (and very often only one) as having affected the prediction than they earlier identified as causal variables.

These behaviors cannot be attributed to failure to maintain mental representations of the multiple effective variables. Even when we provided pictorial memory aides depicting the various effects, these response patterns persisted (Kuhn, Iordanou, et al., 2008). Performance does improve with practice over time (Kuhn et al., in press), but the weaknesses are persistent and do not disappear entirely. In particular, we observed a common conceptual error that is crucial in scientific reasoning, a confusion between the levels of a variable and the variable itself. Thus, a frequent response to the question of which variables had affected a prediction judgment was, for example, "I considered the snake activity, because it's high and that increases risk, but I didn't consider any of the others because they were all low so they wouldn't matter." What the student in this case does not recognize is that, unlike the non-causal variables, the other two causal variables of course had to be considered, or she would not have been able to categorize their levels as ones associated with lower risk. They could not be ignored.

Students of this age, appear to have at best a fragile concept of what a variable is, without which it is difficult to reason explicitly or with precision about the effect of one variable on another. In particular, the concept that under consistent conditions a variable operates in a consistent way across occasions is fundamental to science, and yet it is a concept that children appear to only gradually acquire and one therefore that cannot be assumed to be in place. Equally fundamental to science is the assumption that to be adequately explained most events require that a confluence of multiple causes be invoked. In the absence of this assumption, scientific thinking is severely constrained. Variables and multiple causation are the bread and butter of science. Despite their often being taken for granted in the design of science curricula, our studies suggest that neither of these assumptions is easily come by.

The Role of Meta-Level Processes in Scientific Thinking

Fully as important as the inter-individual variability portrayed by the preceding examples is the intra-individual variability that microgenetic studies have found to be the norm: individuals typically have available a range of different strategies of differing levels of advancement and effectiveness (Kuhn, 1995; Siegler, 1996). Development consists of shifts in the frequencies with which different strategies are chosen for application. To explain development, we therefore need to turn to a meta-level of functioning (Kuhn, 2000, 2001; Kuhn & Pease, 2009) – the level at which strategies are selected and their use monitored. The meta-level involves knowing about knowing. Strong meta-level processes afford Robbie the certainty that he has drawn correct conclusions, while insufficiently developed meta-level processes are implicated in Tom and Mark's false certainty that their inferences are correct.

Figure 19.4 places the strategies and phases of knowledge seeking in the context of meta-level processes that regulate them. On the left side is the *procedural* meta-level that selects knowledge-seeking strategies to apply, in relation to task goals, and manages and monitors their application. Feedback from this application is directed back to the meta-level. This feedback leads to enhanced awareness of the task goal and the extent to which it is being met by different strategies, as well as enhanced awareness of the strategies themselves (in particular, increased recognition of the power and the limitations associated with each). These enhancements at the meta-level lead to revised strategy selection and hence changes in the distribution of strategies observed at the performance level. In a continuous process, this modified usage in turn feeds back to enhanced understanding at the meta-level, eventually getting the individual to the performance goal of consistent use of the more powerful strategies (Kuhn, 2000).

A notable feature of this model is that it accounts for the common finding that efforts to induce change directly at the performance level have only limited success, reflected in failures to transfer outside a specific context. As the figure 19.4 model predicts, if nothing has been done to influence the meta-level, new behavior will quickly disappear once the instructional context is withdrawn and individuals resume meta-level management of their own behavior. This limitation applies to many of the studies that have undertaken to improve scientific thinking simply by teaching strategies ("do this"), and, if meta-level understanding is addressed at all, by assessing children's knowledge that this is what they should do. The meta-level understanding that is critical, in contrast, is *why* this is what to do and why other strategies are less effective or wrong. In one of the most meticulously designed training studies, for example, Chen and Klahr (1999) explained to second- to fourth-graders that some (confounded) comparisons were bad comparisons while other (unconfounded) comparisons were good comparisons because just one feature changed. In post-tests in new contexts, many children were able to choose a good comparison over a bad one and to justify it as good because only one feature changed. Indicative of their fragile meta-level knowledge, however, was the continued mixture of correct and incorrect strategies shown by a majority of children in conducting their own investigations.

The right side of figure 19.4 depicts *declarative* meta-level understanding regarding what it means to know something. Epistemological understanding regarding knowledge and knowing is a crucial underpinning of scientific thinking. What is science and scientific knowledge? Most children bring an *absolutist* understanding to their study of science (Hofer & Pintrich, 1997; Kuhn, Cheney, et al., 2000; Smith, Maclin, Houghton, & Hennessey, 2000): scientific knowledge is an accumulating set of certain facts. By adolescence, most have made the radical shift to a *multiplist* epistemology that embraces an awareness of the uncertain, subjective nature of knowing. This awareness initially assumes such proportions, however, that it overpowers any objective standard that could serve as a basis for evaluating conflicting claims. Because claims are subjective opinions freely chosen by their holders and everyone has a right to their opinion, all opinions are equally right. By adulthood, many, though by no means all, people have reintegrated the objective dimension of knowing and espouse the *evaluativist* understanding that some claims are superior to others to the extent they are better supported by argument and evidence. Only at this level is the coordination of theories and evidence that marks authentic science fully understood. If facts can be readily ascertained with certainty, as the absolutist understands, or if any claim is as valid as any other, as the multiplist understands, scientific inquiry has little purpose.

Values are the final component that figures importantly in figure 19.4. Epistemic understanding informs intellectual values (Kuhn & Park, 2005), in connection with each of the four knowledge-seeking phases; values in turn affect disposition to action. Meta-level procedural knowing is necessary if one is to be able to apply knowing strategies effectively, but it is the intellectual values depicted in figure 19.4 that determine whether one regards knowledge seeking as worthwhile and is therefore disposed to engage in it. Our earlier definition of scientific thinking as knowledge seeking thus accords values a central place in conceptions of scientific thinking.

Scientific Thinking as Argument

Meta-level understanding is a crucial part of what needs to develop in scientific thinking. Fortunately, like performance, it shows improvement over time, when thinking is exercised, and correspondences are apparent in the improvements that occur at the two levels (Kuhn & Pearsall, 1998). Returning scientific thinking to its real-life social context is one approach to strengthening the meta-level components of scientific thinking. When students find themselves having to justify claims and strategies to one another, normally implicit meta-level cognitive processes become externalized, making them more available. Social scaffolding, then, may assist a less-able collaborator to monitor and manage strategic operations in a way that he or she cannot yet do alone, as in this example from two girls working on the problem of what variables affect the speed that model boats travel down an improvised canal (Kuhn, 2000):

S: We found out about the weight.
N: No, about the boat size, that's all.
S: Oh, the boat size.
N: Just talk about the boat size.

Peer collaboration can be highly variable, however, in its form and effects. The interchange in box 19.1 (which occurs just after a second instance of evidence has been observed), comes from a single segment of a session with the earthquake problem in which 10-year-old Brad is working together with 11-year-old Tod (Kuhn, unpublished). In discussing the gas-level feature, Tod supports and strengthens Brad's theory-based claim by drawing on evidence. With respect to the snake-activity and water-quality features, the boys disagree and we see Tod vacillate between endorsement and rejection of Brad's incorrect inference strategies. In one case, Tod ends up succumbing to Brad's inferior reasoning. In the other, he does not and the disagreement stands. It is clear, nonetheless, that both boys' scientific thinking has been exercised by the exchange.

The excerpt in box 19.1 brings individual reasoning strategies into the richer context of social discourse or argument. Increasingly, contributors to both the cognitive development and science education fields have emphasized scientific thinking as a form of discourse (Berland & Reiser, 2009; Bricker & Bell, 2008; Duschl, 2008; Duschl, Schweingruber, & Shouse, 2007; Erduran, Simon, & Osborne, 2004; Garcia-Mila & Andersen, 2007; Iordanou, 2009; Lehrer, Schauble, & Lucas, 2008; Zimmerman, 2007). This is of course the richest and most authentic context in which to examine scientific thinking, as long as the mistake is not made of regarding these discourse forms as exclusive to science. Scientific discourse asks, most importantly, "How do you know?" or "What is the support for your statement?" When children participate in discourse that poses these questions, they acquire the skills and values that lead them to pose the same questions to themselves (Olson & Astington, 1993). Although central to science, this critical development extends far beyond the borders of traditional scientific disciplines.

Box 19.1 Excerpt of discussion of Brad and Tod in the earthquake problem

GAS LEVEL

B [Brad]: Gas level makes a difference because if an earthquake is coming the level of oxygen would decrease I think because the earthquake is taking up all the oxygen.

T [Tod]: Can I say something? We also know that by trial and error. Last time we had heavy gas and got low-medium risk. Since we changed the gas to low, we found out gas did make a difference.

SNAKE ACTIVITY

T: Brad, before you move on, how do you know snake activity makes a difference?

B: It makes no difference.

T: Okay, okay.

I [Interviewer]: Well, let's talk about this a minute. One of you says it makes a difference, the other that it doesn't. Did you find that out, Brad, by looking at these cases?

B: Yes.

I: How did you know?

B: Well, last time I kept snake activity the same and I only changed two things, and I believe those were the ones that made a difference. Now I'm just gonna keep snake activity the same, because it does not make any difference.

I: Tod, do you disagree?
T: No. I was asking him the same question; how did he know?
I: Well, he's told you how he knows; what do you think of his answer?
T: I think it's correct, because he just made some changes [itemizes] … and all those changes made it go to low. But if he'd changed snake activity, it may have made a difference and it may have not.
I: But he didn't change snake activity.
T: Right, he didn't and that's why he said that snake activity didn't make a difference.
I: So, do we know then that snake activity makes no difference?
B: No, not positively, but it's a good estimate.
T: If we changed it to heavy next time, and keep all of these [other features the same], we may find out if it makes a difference.
I: But I thought before you were both telling me you'd already found out it does not.
B: That's my good estimate.
T: I agree. But just to make sure, change it to heavy. If risk went back to low, we'd know it would make a difference.
I: And what do we know now about snake activity?
T: We are pretty sure it makes no difference.
I: Why is that?
T: Because he made changes in everything else and he kept snake activity the same and it went to the lowest.

WATER QUALITY

B: Water quality made a difference because last time I kept it good. I think it made a difference because the water would be sinking down if there was an earthquake coming.
I: Do the records show whether it made a difference?
B: Yes. Because last time it was good and this time it was good too. I think it should be good because I got the lowest risk and last time I got medium-low risk. I changed two [others] and it got me down to the lowest risk. So I think the water quality should be good.
I: And how do you know water quality makes a difference?
B: Because last time it was good and this time it was good and [both times] we got the lowest risk.
I: Tod, what do you think?
T: Last time it was good and this time good. I say it wouldn't really make a difference. They were both the same and how would you see that it made a difference if they were both the same, if they were both good?
I: Brad, what do you think?
B: It makes a difference, because I kept it good and I got a medium-low risk; this time I got a [even] lower risk.
I: So what does that tell you again?
B: Two of my answers were wrong last time. And I think I changed them to the right answers this time.
I: And so does water quality make a difference?
B: It makes a difference.
I: Tod, what do you think?
T: We don't know if it does.

Educating Scientific Thinking and Thinkers

Science education does not necessarily involve scientific thinking. In the kinds of learning experiences that are commonplace in much of science education, information may be presented or a phenomenon demonstrated, with the questions the new information is intended to answer either left unclear or externally imposed. Students may, in such cases, respond in routinized ways that avoid scientific thinking entirely.

In addition to what they may undertake to teach children about science, science educators hope that the educational activities they design will develop the scientific thinking skills that have been the subject of the present chapter. Much educational practice in preschool and early elementary years rests on the idea of young children's "natural curiosity." Practices that encourage children to ask questions, to observe, and to express their ideas in response to teachers' questions have been accepted as sufficient components to define good "constructivist" teaching practice. It becomes clear, however, by the middle elementary-school years, that these practices do not by themselves constitute an adequate instructional model. Palincsar and Magnusson (2001) note "the impossibility that children will come to meaningful understandings of the nature of scientific thinking simply through the process of interacting with materials and phenomena." Video-based teacher-training material of a constructivist bent commonly features a teacher asking a bright-eyed, appealing youngster, "What do you think, Tommy?", making a minimal acknowledgment ("Okay, good."), and then turning to the next child with the same query. The richness of inquiry teaching and learning depends on the teacher's *doing something* with that child's response, in a way that leaves the child with a richer, more elaborated conceptual representation than the child had previously. Such conceptual representations encompass far more than specific content, extending, for example, to understandings of what kinds of questions are worth asking and why. To develop these instructional skills, teachers need to understand what the child is bringing to the instructional situation and exactly what kinds of process skills are in the process of developing (Kuhn, 2005; Kuhn & Pease, 2008; Lehrer et al., 2008).

With respect to the process skills of investigation and inference that lie at the heart of authentic scientific thinking, there is a divergence of opinion as to the most productive instructional methods. Klahr and colleagues (Chen & Klahr, 1999; Klahr & Nigam, 2004), have focused their efforts on single-session direct instruction, specifically of the control-of-variables strategy, whereas others have engaged children in the practice of scientific inquiry over longer periods of time (Kuhn & Pease, 2008; Lehrer et al., 2008). (See educationforthinking.org for examples of the Kuhn & Pease software-based curriculum.) When evaluation is extended over time, a study by Strand-Cary & Klahr (2008) and a study by Dean and Kuhn (2007) nonetheless show very similar results. Direct instruction with respect to the control-of-variables strategy confers a temporary benefit. This benefit recedes over time and in transfer assessments, however, unless, as in the Dean and Kuhn (2007) study, it is accompanied by sustained practice with problems requiring the strategy. Moreover, in a direct comparison, Dean and Kuhn (2007) found that a group engaged in practice alone performed as well after several months as the group who in addition had initially received direct instruction.

Most needed now are studies examining the mechanisms by means of which thinking improves as it is practiced. From an educational perspective, the importance of doing so is undeniable, for it has become clear that most of the thinking skills, as well as dispositions, examined in this chapter develop only in environments conducive to them (Bullock et al., in press; Lehrer et al., 2008). As highlighted in this chapter through its emphasis on meta-level understanding, perhaps most important for teachers to convey to children about science is less the *what* or the *how* but the *why*, including, ultimately, why inquiry and analysis are worth the effort they entail. These values, as shown in figure 19.4, are supported by epistemological understanding of what scientific knowing entails (Kuhn & Park, 2005). It is here that the variance emerges with respect to whether learned skills will be used.

If we can clearly identify what the cognitive skills are and how they develop, we are in the best position to learn how to promote understanding of their value. Thus, science educators need to base their efforts on a sound understanding of the entire complex of skills and meta-skills that have the potential to develop during the childhood and adolescent years. Educators who are informed developmentalists stand to bring the strengths of both traditions to the challenge that science education poses.

References

Amsel, E., & Brock, S. (1996). The development of evidence evaluation skills. *Cognitive Development, 11*, 523–550.

Berland, L., & Reiser, B. (2009). Making sense of argumentation and explanation. *Science Education, 93*, 26–55.

Brewer, W., & Samarapungavan, A. (1991). Children's theories vs. scientific theories: Differences in reasoning or differences in knowledge. In R. Hoffman & D. Palermo (Eds.), *Cognition and the symbolic processes* (pp. 209–232). Hillsdale NJ: Erlbaum.

Bricker, L., & Bell, P. (2009). Conceptualizations of argumentation from science studies and the learning sciences and their implications for the practices of science education. *Science Education, 92*, 473–498.

Bullock, M., Sodian, B., & Koerber, S. (in press). Doing experiments and understanding science: Development of scientific reasoning from childhood to adulthood. In W. Schneider & M. Bullock (Eds.), *Human development from early childhood to early adulthood: Findings from a 20-year longitudinal study*. Mahwah NJ: Erlbaum.

Chen, Z., & Klahr, D. (1999). All other things being equal: Children's acquisition of the control of variables strategy. *Child Development, 70*, 1098–1120.

Dean, D., & Kuhn, D. (2007). Direct instruction vs. discovery: The long view. *Science Education, 91*, 384–397.

Duschl, R. (2008). Science education in three-part harmony: Balancing conceptual, epistemic, and social learning goals. *Review of Research in Education, 32*, 268–291.

Duschl, R., Schweingruber, H., & Shouse, A. (2007). *Taking science to school: Learning and teaching science in grades K-8*. Washington DC: National Academies Press.

Echevarria, M. (2003). Anomalies as a catalyst for middle school students' knowledge construction and scientific reasoning during science inquiry. *Journal of Educational Psychology, 95*, 357–374.

Erduran, S., Simon, S., & Osborne, J. (2004). TAPing into argumentation: Developments in the application of Toulmin's argument pattern for studying science discourse. *Science Education, 88*, 915–933.

Fay, A., & Klahr, D. (1996). Knowing about guessing and guessing about knowing: Preschoolers' understanding of indeterminacy. *Child Development. 67*, 689–716.

Felton, M. (2004). The development of discourse strategies in adolescent argumentation. *Cognitive Development, 19*, 35–52.

Flavell, J. (1999). Cognitive development: Children's knowledge about the mind. *Annual Review of Psychology*. Palo Alto, CA: Annual Reviews.

Flavell, J., Green, F., & Flavell, E. (1995). Young children's knowledge about thinking. *Society for Research in Child Development Monographs, 60*(1), (Serial No. 243).

Garcia-Mila, M., & Andersen, C. (2007). Cognitive foundations of learning argumentation. In S. Erduran & M. P. Jimenez-Aleixandre (Eds.), *Argumentation in science education: Perspectives from classroom-based research*. New York: Springer.

Gelman, S., & Kalish, C. (2006). Conceptual development. In W. Damon & R. M. Lerner (Series Eds.), D. Kuhn & R. Siegler (Vol. Eds.), *Handbook of child psychology: Vol. 2. Cognition, perception, and language*. (6th edition). Hoboken NJ: Wiley.

Gopnik, A., & Graf, P. (1988). Knowing how you know: Young children's ability to identify and remember the sources of their beliefs. *Child Development, 59*, 1366–1371.

Gopnik, A., & Schultz, L. (2007). *Causal learning: Psychology, philosophy, and computation*. New York: Oxford University Press.

Hofer, B., & Pintrich, P. (1997). The development of epistemological theories: Beliefs about knowledge and knowing and their relation to learning. *Review of Educational Research, 67*, 88–140.

Inhelder, B., & Piaget, J. (1958). *The growth of logical thinking from childhood to adolescence*. New York: Basic Books.

Iordanou, K. (2009). *Developing argument skills across scientific and social domains*. Unpublished manuscript.

Kitcher, P. (1993). *The advancement of science*. New York: Oxford University Press.

Klaczynski, P. (2000). Motivated scientific reasoning biases, epistemological beliefs, and theory polarization: A two-process approach to adolescent cognition. *Child Development, 71*, 1347–1366.

Klahr, D. (2000). *Exploring science: The cognition and development of discovery processes*. Cambridge, MA: MIT Press.

Klahr, D., Fay, A., & Dunbar, K. (1993). Heuristics for scientific experimentation: A developmental study. *Cognitive Psychology, 25*, 111–146.

Klahr, D., & Nigam, M. (2004). The equivalence of learning paths in early science instruction: Effects of direct instruction and discovery learning. *Psychological Science, 15*, 661–667.

Klahr, D., & Simon, H. (1999). Studies of scientific discovery: Complementary approaches and convergent findings. *Psychological Bulletin, 125*, 524–543.

Klahr, D., Triona, L., & Williams, C. (2007). Hands on what? The relative effectiveness of physical vs. virtual materials in an engineering design project by middle school children. *Journal of Research in Science Teaching, 44*, 183–203.

Koslowski, B. (1996). *Theory and evidence: The development of scientific reasoning*. Cambridge, MA: MIT Press.

Kuhn, D. (1989). Children and adults as intuitive scientists. *Psychological Review, 96*, 674–689.

Kuhn, D. (1991). *The skills of argument*. New York: Cambridge University Press.

Kuhn, D. (1993). Science as argument: Implications for teaching and learning scientific thinking. *Science Education, 77*, 319–337.

Kuhn, D. (1995). Microgenetic study of change: What has it told us? *Psychological Science, 6*, 133–139.

Kuhn, D. (2000). Why development does (and doesn't) occur: Evidence from the domain of inductive reasoning. In R. Siegler & J. McClelland (Eds.), *Mechanisms of cognitive development: Neural and behavioral perspectives* (pp. 221–249). Mahwah, NJ: Erlbaum.

Kuhn, D. (2001). How do people know? *Psychological Science, 12*, 1–8.

Kuhn, D. (2005). *Education for thinking*. Cambridge, MA: Harvard University Press.

Kuhn, D., Amsel, E., & O'Loughlin, M. (1988). *The development of scientific thinking skills*. Orlando, FL: Academic Press.

Kuhn, D., Black, J., Keselman, A., & Kaplan, D. (2000). The development of cognitive skills that support inquiry learning. *Cognition and Instruction, 18*, 495–523.

Kuhn, D., Cheney, R., & Weinstock, M. (2000). The development of epistemological understanding. *Cognitive Development, 15*, 309–328.

Kuhn, D., & Dean, D. (2004). Connecting scientific reasoning and causal inference. *Journal of Cognition & Development, 5*, 261–288.

Kuhn, D., Garcia-Mila, M., Zohar, A., & Andersen, C. (1995). Strategies of knowledge acquisition. *Society for Research in Child Development Monographs, 60*(4), (Serial No. 245).

Kuhn, D., Goh, W., Iordanou, K., & Shaenfield, D. (2008). Arguing on the computer: A microgenetic study of developing argument skills in a computer-supported environment. *Child Development, 79*, 1311–1329.

Kuhn, D., Iordanou, K., Pease, M., & Wirkala, C. (2008). Beyond control of variables: What needs to develop to achieve skilled scientific thinking? *Cognitive Development, 23*, 435–451. [Special issue, The Development of Scientific Thinking, B. Sodian & M. Bullock, Eds.]

Kuhn, D., & Katz, J. (in press). Are self-explanations always beneficial? *Journal of Experimental Child Psychology*.

Kuhn, D., & Park, S. H. (2005). Epistemological understanding and the development of intellectual values. *International Journal of Educational Research, 43*, 111–124.

Kuhn, D., & Pearsall, S. (1998). Relations between metastrategic knowledge and strategic performance. *Cognitive Development, 13*, 227–247.

Kuhn, D., & Pearsall, S. (2000). Developmental origins of scientific thinking. *Journal of Cognition and Development, 1*, 113–129.

Kuhn, D., & Pease, M. (2006). Do children and adults learn differently? *Journal of Cognition and Development, 7*, 279–293.

Kuhn, D., & Pease, M. (2008). What needs to develop in the development of inquiry skills? *Cognition and Instruction, 26*, 512–559.

Kuhn, D., & Pease, M. (2009). The dual components of developing strategy use: Production and inhibition. In H. S. Waters & W. Schneider (Eds.), *Metacognition, strategy use, and instruction*. New York: Guilford Press.

Kuhn, D., Pease, M., & Wirkala, C. (in press). Coordinating effects of multiple variables: A skill fundamental to causal and scientific reasoning. *Journal of Experimental Child Psychology*.

Kuhn, D., & Phelps, E. (1982). The development of problem-solving strategies. In H. Reese (Ed.), *Advances in child development and behavior* (Vol. *17*). New York: Academic Press.

Kuhn, D., Schauble, L., & Garcia-Mila, M. (1992). Cross-domain development of scientific reasoning. *Cognition and Instruction, 9*, 285–32.

Kuhn, D., Shaw, V., & Felton, M. (1997). Effects of dyadic interaction on argumentive reasoning. *Cognition and Instruction, 15*, 287–315.

Kuhn, D., & Udell, W. (2003). The development of argument skills. *Child Development, 74*(5), 1245–1260.

Lehrer, R., & Romberg, T. (1996). Exploring children's data modeling. *Cognition and Instruction, 14*, 69–108.

Lehrer, R., & Schauble, L. (2006). Scientific thinking and scientific literacy: Supporting development in learning contexts. In K. A. Renninger & I. Sigel (Eds.), *Handbook of child psychology* (Vol. *4*). Hoboken, NJ: Wiley.

Lehrer, R., Schauble, L., & Lucas, D. (2008). Supporting development of the epistemology of inquiry. *Cognitive Development, 23*, 512–529. [Special issue, The Development of Scientific Thinking, B. Sodian & M. Bullock, Eds.]

Lehrer, R., Schauble, L., & Petrosino, A. (2001). Reconsidering the role of experiment in science education. In K. Crowley, C. Schunn, & T. Okada (Eds.). *Designing for science: Implications from everyday, classroom, and professional settings* (pp. 251–277). Mahwah, NJ: Erlbaum.

Lo, Y., Sides, A., Rozelle, J., & Osherson, D. (2002). Evidential diversity and premise probability in young children's inductive judgment. *Cognitive Science, 26*, 181–206.

Masnick, A. M., & Klahr, D. (2003). Error matters: An initial exploration of elementary school children's understanding of experimental error. *Journal of Cognition and Development, 4*, 67–98.

Masnick, A., & Morris, B. (2008). Investigating the development of data evaluation: The role of data characteristics. *Child Development, 79*, 1032–1048.

Olson, D., & Astington, J. (1993). Thinking about thinking: Learning how to take statement and hold beliefs. *Educational Psychologist, 28*, 7–23.

Palincsar, A., & Magnusson, S. (2001). The interplay of first-hand and second-hand investigations to model and support the development of scientific knowledge and reasoning. In S. Carver & D. Klahr (Eds.), *Cognition and instruction: Twenty-five years of progress*. Mahwah, NJ: Erlbaum.

Penner, D., & Klahr, D. (1996). The interaction of domain-specific knowledge and domain-general discovery strategies: A study with sinking objects. *Child Development, 67*, 2709–2727.

Perner, J. (1991). *Understanding the representational mind*. Cambridge MA: MIT Press.

Pieraut-Le Bonniec, G. (1980). *The development of modal reasoning*. New York: Academic Press.

Rhodes, M., Brickman, D., & Gelman, S. (2008). Sample diversity and premise typicality in inductive reasoning: Evidence for developmental change. *Cognition, 108*, 543–556.

Ruffman, T., Perner, J., Olson, D., & Doherty, M. (1993). Reflecting on scientific thinking: Children's understanding of the hypothesis–evidence relation. *Child Development, 64*, 1617–1636.

Schauble, L. (1990). Belief revision in children: The role of prior knowledge and strategies for generating evidence. *Journal of Experimental Child Psychology, 49*, 31–57.

Schauble, L. (1996). The development of scientific reasoning in knowledge-rich contexts. *Developmental Psychology, 32*, 102–119.

Siegler, R. (1996). *Emerging minds: The process of change in children's thinking*. New York: Oxford University Press.

Siegler, R., & Crowley, K. (1991). The microgenetic method: A direct means for studying cognitive development. *American Psychologist, 46*, 606–620.

Smith, C., Maclin, D., Houghton, C., & Hennessey, M. G. (2000). Sixth-grade students' epistemologies of science: The impact of school science experiences on epistemological development. *Cognition and Instruction, 18*, 349–422.

Sodian, B., Zaitchik, D., & Carey, S. (1991). Young children's differentiation of hypothetical beliefs from evidence. *Child Development, 62*, 753–766.

Strand-Cary, M., & Klahr, D. (2008). Developing elementary science skills: Instructional effectiveness and path independence. *Cognitive Development, 23*, 435–451. [Special issue, The Development of Scientific Thinking, B. Sodian & M. Bullock, Eds.]

Taylor, M., Esbensen, B., & Bennett, R. (1994). Children's understanding of knowledge acquisition: The tendency for children to report they have always known what they have just learned. *Child Development, 65*, 1581–1604.

Udell, W. (2007). Enhancing adolescent girls' argument skills in reasoning about personal and non-personal decisions. *Cognitive Development, 22*, 341–352.

Wellman, H. (1988). First steps in the child's theorizing about the mind. In J. Astington, P. Harris, & D. Olson (Eds.), *Developing theories of mind* (pp. 64–92). Cambridge: Cambridge University Press.

Woolley, J., & Bruell, M. (1996). Young children's awareness of the origins of their mental representations. *Developmental Psychology, 32*, 335–346.

Zimmerman, C. (2000). The development of scientific reasoning skills. *Developmental Review, 20*, 99–149.

Zimmerman, C. (2007). The development of scientific thinking skills in elementary and middle school. *Developmental Review, 27*, 172–223.

CHAPTER TWENTY

Reading Development and Dyslexia

Margaret J. Snowling and Silke M. Göbel

The scientific study of reading is now well established and theories of how children learn to read are increasingly used to guide research on reading difficulties and reading instruction. Learning to read depends on the language of learning; it is easier to learn in transparent languages with consistent relationships between letters and sounds than in opaque languages, such as English, in which letter–sound relationships are inconsistent. However, in all languages learning to read is a challenge and a child's ability to process the sound structure of words is a strong predictor of how well they will succeed in learning to decode print efficiently. But there is more to reading than decoding (Gough & Tunmer, 1986) and reading for meaning depends upon a broad range of language and metacognitive resources (see Kintsch & Rawson, 2005). It follows that children with oral language difficulties are at high risk of reading difficulties. More generally, reading depends upon motivation and practice, and hence both print exposure and instructional factors play a role in determining the literacy outcomes for typically developing children as well as for those with learning difficulties.

This chapter begins by discussing the process of learning to read before describing the cognitive and linguistic processes that predict its growth. In the past 10 years reading research has burgeoned, therefore it will be necessary to focus on decoding rather than comprehension aspects of reading, and we will also make reference to spelling to illustrate specific points about the development of orthographic competence. Against this backdrop we will consider individual differences in reading development, specifically dyslexia, and their neural correlates. By necessity the chapter is selective; we will primarily consider reading development in alphabetic languages. The bulk of research has focused on English. (For discussion of reading development in non-alphabetic languages see Hanley, 2005; McBride-Chang, 2004).

This chapter was prepared with the support of Wellcome program grant 082036 to Margaret J. Snowling and a University of York Anniversary Lectureship to Silke M. Göbel.

The Task of Learning to Read

The English writing system represents spoken language via two main systems of "rules," more accurately described as "mappings." In common with all alphabetic languages, its core is a system of grapheme–phoneme correspondences. Within this system there are basic mappings, many of which are explicitly taught in school, including correspondences between phonemes and single letters, e.g., /t/ maps to "t," consonant digraphs, e.g., /tz/ maps to "ch," and vowel digraphs, e.g., /E/ maps to "ee." There are also conditional or "hierarchical" rules. These include the "silent e" rule (a final "e" following a consonant lengthens the pronunciation of the medial vowel as in *g*A*te*; *t*U*be*) and the "soft c" rule ("c" is pronounced /s/ rather than /k/ when followed by "e," "i," or "y" as in "city") (Marsh, Friedman, Welch, & Desberg 1980).

In addition to connections between orthography and phonology, there are also mappings between orthography and meaning: this is well illustrated by the case of homophones, words with the same phonology but different meanings (e.g., leak–leek), the spellings of which have to be learned on a word-by-word basis. Importantly, there are also mappings at the level of morphology – the meaning components of words that are reflected in the grammar. Some of these mappings are to phonemes while others are at the level of the larger unit or syllable. There are also formal constraints on letter position in English; for example, the letter string "ck" can only occur at the end (and not the beginning) of the word and the letter "j" cannot occur in final position.

In the Western world, children begin formal reading instruction at around 5–6 years and at least by age 7, though they will have been exposed to print in the environment for many years. In addition, some will have received informal instruction in their homes and in preschool settings. The crux of the matter is that the child must learn how strings of letters correspond to spoken words. Children's initial reading attempts underline the fact that they do not know about the intricacies of the mapping process. Although from a remarkably young age children can read the names of local stores and advertising logos, such print recognition uses non-conventional cues (Gough & Hillinger, 1980) and depends heavily on the context in which it is seen (Masonheimer, Drum, & Ehri, 1984; Seymour & Elder, 1986). To become a proficient reader a child needs to build up a set of orthographic "rules" which will enable him or her to decode new words, as well as a set of word-specific connections between printed words and whole-word phonology.

Predictors of learning to read: the early stages

In order to develop a generative reading system, children must gain insights into how printed words map to spoken words – the "alphabetic principle" (Byrne, 1996, 1998) To do so requires both awareness of phonemes (phoneme identity) and knowledge of the letters representing the phonemes. Once they have acquired this "alphabetic principle" children have a so-called "self-teaching" device which they can use to "work out" the pronunciations of words they have not seen before (Share, 1995, 2008).

A number of studies have now followed the progress of children in reading and spelling through the early years. Muter, Hulme, Snowling, and Stevenson (2004) assessed some 90 4-year-old children in UK nurseries, reassessing their reading and reading-related skills 1 and 2 years later. At Time 1, the children were assessed on tests of word reading, letter-sound knowledge, vocabulary, and phonological awareness. One year later these tests were repeated together with two grammatical tests; a morphological awareness task (in which children were required to generate the inflected forms of a series of target words) and a test in which they had to rearrange a jumbled sentence orally to produce a grammatically correct form. Reading accuracy and reading comprehension were the outcome measures assessed after a further year at Time 3.

The findings of this study were very clear. There were two early predictors of reading accuracy after 2 years in school: children's ability to manipulate phonemes in spoken words and their letter knowledge. These findings replicate and extend other studies of English-speaking children (Wagner, Torgesen, Laughan, Simmons, & Rashotte, 1993), and are consistent with the view that phoneme awareness and letter knowledge are co-requisites (Share, 1995) or co-determinants (Bowey, 2005) of alphabetic literacy. In contrast, reading comprehension at Time 3 was predicted by earlier measures of vocabulary and grammatical skills when the effects of word-level reading were controlled.

The development of spelling skills

A remarkably similar picture emerges with respect to the early development of spelling skills. Caravolas, Hulme, and Snowling (2001) analyzed the spelling attempts of UK children as they progressed through the first years of reading instruction, from age 4 to age 6 years. Children's early spelling attempts mostly consisted of one or two letters from the target word or a partial phonetic rendering of it. Spelling errors were analyzed using a scoring procedure that reflected the phonemic accuracy of the attempt in relation to the target word, as well as for conventional spelling accuracy. The investigators went on to use measures of children's early reading, letter-sound knowledge, phoneme awareness, speed of processing, and non-verbal IQ to predict their emergent spelling skills.

During the first 6 months of this study, there were just two clear predictors of children's ability to spell words phonemically: letter-sound knowledge and phoneme awareness. Early reading did not contribute to the prediction of spelling at this stage and nor did it during the ensuing 12 months when the pattern of prediction remained the same. Thus, children's spelling attempts during the first 18 months of schooling appear to depend upon their knowledge of letter-sounds and their ability to segment spoken words at the level of the phoneme (Goswami & Bryant, 1990).

However, the inconsistencies of English spelling, together with its many irregularities (e.g., yacht, colonel), provide prima facie evidence that accurate spelling cannot be accomplished on the basis of phonemic analysis alone – rather children must become aware of the orthographic consistencies that characterize their language (Nuñes & Bryant, 2009). According to Caravolas et al. (2001) it is only during the second year of reading instruction that reading begins to influence spelling. Children then develop sensitivity to the consistencies within the grapheme–phoneme mapping system (Treiman & Kessler, 2005; Caravolas, Kessler, et al., 2005).

Increasing reading experience also brings with it sensitivity to morphological structure; for example, children begin to represent the regular past-tense ending of verbs ("-ed") when they still use a predominantly phonetic approach to their spelling (Nuñes, Bryant, & Bindman, 1997). Morphological boundaries can also give information about phonological inconsistencies. Treiman et al. (1994) asked children to spell words containing medial /t/ phonemes which, in American English, are typically flapped so that phonetically they are articulated [d]. The children were more likely to write the medial sound correctly as a "t" if it marked a morpheme boundary (as in *dirty*) than if it did not (as in *attic*) when it would be transcribed as "d." In similar vein, Treiman and Cassar (1997) showed that young reader/spellers of American English were more likely to spell the first consonant of a cluster correctly if it marked the end of a morpheme (i.e., the "s" in *kissed*) than in a phonetically equivalent monomorphemic word (*lost*).

But how exactly do children learn spelling rules and when to apply them in a language which permits many alternatives? Building on a theory of rule induction proposed by Holland, Holyoak, Nisbett, and Thagard (1986), Nuñes and Bryant (2009) propose that when more than one rule fits the context there is competition. Resolution of this conflict depends upon a number of factors – namely, match, strength, specificity, and support.

To take the example of how to spell the word "missed," *specificity* refers to the fact that the past-tense inflection (marked in the orthography by "-ed") signals that the verb is in past tense; *match* refers to the fact that the spelling matches that of the uninflected form; *support* refers to the fact that the inflection is added to a related word-form ("miss") which is itself a root morpheme; and *strength* refers to the frequency with which this rule has fitted on previous occasions. In short, feedback is important for inducing new rules and improving performance; it can be internally generated or come from outside (for example from a teacher). Within this same framework it can be seen how important print exposure is to learning conditional rules. For example, early in development the simple grapheme–phoneme rule, "c" maps to /k/ may be well established while the conditional "soft c" rule will still be only weak in strength. The young reader will continue to revert to the basic rule until he or she has experienced sufficient exposure to the alternate spelling pattern. Whether or not the child needs to be consciously aware of the "rules" or simply sensitive to the statistical regularities of the orthographic system in order to progress is open to question.

Learning to read in transparent languages

The foregoing discussion has focused on English. Despite a blossoming of research on reading development in other languages, English remains the best studied of the alphabetic languages. Yet English is an "outlier" orthography (Share, 2008). Languages differ in the regularity or transparency of their orthographies and therefore in the task they pose to children learning to read (Harris & Hatano, 1999). German and Italian are two of the more transparent European orthographies and in these languages letters generally correspond to single phonemes. The same is true for Greek though the script is different.

In contrast, the English writing system is much more opaque, and very frequently a grapheme may correspond to more than one phoneme. For example, the grapheme e may correspond to /E/ as in *bed*, to /i/ as in *eve* and to "schwa" as in *believe*. In particular, the way in which vowels are represented in English is much less consistent than in regular languages (Frith, Wimmer, & Landerl, 1998).

Phonological development follows its own developmental course at least up until the point at which a child starts to learn to read, when phonological awareness proceeds from an awareness of large units (such as syllables) to awareness of small units (phonemes) (Carroll, Snowling, Hulme, & Stevenson, 2003; Liberman & Shankweiler, 1979; Treiman & Breaux, 1982). However, it is clear from studies of children learning in other languages that the rate and sequence of phonological development, and hence of phonological awareness, may be subject to variation associated with linguistic factors. Studies of children learning to read in languages with simple syllable structures, such as French, show high levels of syllable awareness (Bruck, Genesee, & Caravolas, 1997), whereas children learning in languages with complex syllable structures that include a preponderance of consonant clusters show well-developed phoneme awareness even from a relatively young age (Caravolas & Bruck, 1993).

Caravolas and Landerl (in press) extended these findings in a direct comparison of phoneme awareness in German and Czech first-grade children. The comparison is important because German and Czech are languages from the same group but, whereas Czech contains many consonantal onsets, German favors consonantal codas. In line with the view that the phonological characteristics of a language (e.g., its syllable structure) play a role in shaping phoneme awareness from early on in development, pre-reading Czech children were better at segmenting onsets while German pre-readers were better at segmenting codas. More generally, de Cara and Goswami (2003) have proposed that the phonological neighborhood statistics of a language play a role in determining the course of phoneme awareness. In turn, it is reasonable to expect that differences in the accessibility of different phonological units will influence the nature of the mappings that are created between orthography and phonology.

Thus, it is important not to rely exclusively on findings from English when building a theory of reading development. What then can studies of reading in languages other than English tell us? First, there is unequivocal evidence that learning to read proceeds faster in transparent orthographies than in English. In the most comprehensive study to date, Seymour, Aro, and Erskine (2003) investigated early reading in 14 European nations; in the majority of these countries, children were proficient decoders by the end of first grade, reading about 87% of high-frequency words correctly. In contrast, English children were only about 34% accurate at the same time-point (even though they had been in school for an additional year); the next-worst outcome being for Danish children, who scored 71% correct.

Second, there is evidence that this difference in the rate of reading development is not just quantitative, there are qualitative differences too. A number of studies highlight the fact that children reading English rely more on whole-word phonology in non-word reading than do children reading in transparent orthographies (Goswami, Ziegler, Dalton, & Schneider, 2001) whereas exhaustive letter-by-letter decoding strategies are more evident in readers of transparent orthographies, as revealed by behavioral studies (in German; Landerl, 2000) as well as by studies of eye movements during reading (in Italian; Zoccolotti et al., 1999).

Third, these cross-language differences in reading strategy pattern with differences in emergent phoneme awareness. Mann and Wimmer (2002) compared US and German kindergartners on tests of phoneme awareness, letter knowledge, and word reading. The US children showed a significant advantage at this stage in their development; however this advantage diminished when the German children entered formal schooling, and by the end of first grade the German children equaled the American in phoneme skills.

Data such as these have sometimes been used to argue that the predictors of reading skills are different in different languages. Whereas phoneme awareness is a robust predictor of reading in English, rapid automatized naming (RAN – the rate at which familiar stimuli, such as objects, letters, and digits, can be named; Wolf & Bowers, 1999) is a stronger predictor in transparent languages (de Jong & van der Leij, 1999; Ho & Bryant, 1997). However, it needs to be borne in mind that most English research has focused on explaining individual differences in reading accuracy while studies of transparent languages have tended to focus on reading fluency.

In a direct cross-linguistic comparison of Dutch (a transparent language) and English, using identical measures of reading accuracy and rate and a timed measure of phoneme awareness, Patel, Snowling, and de Jong (2004) found an identical pattern of prediction in the two languages. Thus, RAN predicted reading rate for words and non-words in each language and, interestingly, so did phoneme awareness when a timed measure of the speed at which a child could delete a phoneme from a non-word was used. In similar vein, Caravolas, Volín, and Hulme (2005) assessed children in grades 2 to 7 in a direct comparison of Czech (which has a highly consistent orthography) and English speakers. Phoneme awareness predicted individual differences in reading and spelling skills in both languages, and, further, it played an equally important predictive role.

Drawing together findings from studies of reading in different languages, Ziegler and Goswami (2005) proposed the *psycholinguistic grain size theory*. According to this theory, reading development is shaped by three factors: the availability (or accessibility) of different phonological units prior to reading, the consistency of the orthography–phonology mappings in the language that the child is learning, and the granularity of the orthography, specifically whether mappings are at the level of smaller or larger units, or both as in English. Within this model, the successful development of phonological recoding requires the child "to find shared grain sizes in the symbol system and the phonology of their language that allow an … unambiguous mapping between the two domains" (Ziegler & Goswami, 2005, p. 3). Ziegler and Goswami (2005) further propose that differences in these early mappings are not "transitory phenomena but leave developmental 'footprints' across the entire reading life-span."

Predictors of learning to read and spell: beyond phonology

Arguably, the bulk of research on reading development has focused on the early stages and the important factors that enable a child to move from being a novice to an expert reader have been relatively neglected (Share, 2008). As Perfetti (1995) stated, the essence of reading skill is high-speed retrieval yet relatively little is understood about the predictors of reading fluency, defined as the ability to read aloud accurately with appropriate speed and intonation.

In this section we consider three themes in recent research which address aspects of the development of reading proficiency, the basic idea being that the reader must be able to access high-quality orthographic representations to become a fluent reader (Ehri, 2005; Perfetti & Hart, 2001). The first approach has developed from Share's (1995) self-teaching hypothesis which proposes that "every successful decoding encounter with an unfamiliar word provides an opportunity to acquire word-specific orthographic information that is critical to the development of skilled word recognition." As the child develops more orthographic knowledge, the phonological recoding mechanism itself becomes increasingly "lexicalized," taking it beyond its basic function of translating letters into sounds, for use in deciphering words containing a wide range of spelling patterns.

To test this hypothesis, Share (1999) asked children to read target pseudo-words which were embedded in short texts between 4 and 6 times. After three days, the children's knowledge of the orthographic forms of the target words (compared with homophones) was assessed three different ways. First, in an orthographic choice task, children chose the correct target word 73.5% of the time compared to 16.8% for the homophone foil; second the average response-time (RT) for the target words was 816 ms compared with 874 ms for the homophones; and finally on a spelling test the children made considerably fewer errors on target words (2%) compared with homophones (13%). Together these findings show that within a relatively short space of time, children can build up detailed orthographic representations of words which they can initially read only by phonological decoding (Ehri, 1995). In English such orthographic learning processes are likely to be particularly critical for learning about irregular or inconsistent words that cannot be read by relying on a phonological decoding mechanism (Ricketts, Bishop, & Nation, 2008).

A number of studies have considered whether, independent of phonological awareness, children's propensity to develop mappings between visual and phonological (word) forms contributes to their orthographic skill. Hulme, Goetz, Gooch, Adams, and Snowling (2007) investigated the significance of three paired-associate learning (PAL) measures (learning of visual–visual, verbal–verbal, visual–verbal connections) alongside phoneme awareness as concurrent predictors of single word reading and non-word reading ability in 8- to 9-year-old readers. Both phoneme deletion and visual–verbal PAL were unique predictors of a composite word reading measure, and also of the ability to read irregular words. Interestingly, however, only phoneme deletion, and not visual–verbal PAL, was a significant predictor of non-word reading. These results are consistent with the view that learning mappings between visual (orthography) and verbal (phonological) attributes of words is an important skill for developing word-recognition skills in reading, and that individual differences in this ability may underpin variations in orthographic skills (Windfuhr & Snowling, 2001). In contrast, the findings suggest that word decoding depends primarily upon phonological skills.

One widely used task that taps the integrity of mappings between visual and verbal domains is RAN. This point was made forcibly by Bowey (2005) who argued that alphanumeric RAN depends on letter-name knowledge and, hence, individual differences in RAN relate to variations in the rate at which children have been able to learn such mappings. Along similar lines, Price et al. (2006) have suggested that the reading system builds on a more general system of object naming but places greater demands on speech output mechanisms. For this reason, it is perhaps not surprising that performance on the RAN task is highly predictive of reading fluency across languages. Nonetheless, the processes tapped by RAN remain unclear (Clarke, Hulme, & Snowling, 2005; Powell, Stainthorp, Stuart, Garwood, & Quinlan, 2007); although its relationship with processing speed has often been emphasized, it seems increasingly clear that RAN may engage the processes required for new word learning, which hence underpin the development of fully specified orthographic representations (Lervåg & Hulme, in press).

Finally, the role of environmental factors in determining children's reading achievement should not be forgotten. Recent evidence suggests that social class accounts for substantial amounts of variance in the growth of reading skills between first grade and fourth grade, even when the effects of intelligence and phonological skills in kindergarten are accounted for (Hecht, Burgess, Torgesen, Wagner, & Rashotte, 2000). Furthermore, reading practice is particularly important for ensuring progress in an opaque reading system such as English, because many of its words cannot be decoded using spelling-sound rules. Tests of print exposure in which readers are required to discriminate between real versus fictitious names of authors and titles of books provide a metric for reading practice. Importantly, print exposure accounts for variations in reading skills, even when the effects of phonological awareness are controlled (Cunningham & Stanovich, 1991; Griffiths & Snowling, 2001).

Individual Differences in Reading Development

Dyslexia

Dyslexia is a specific learning disorder that primarily affects the development of reading and spelling but also has adverse effects on other cognitive skills (Snowling, 2008). Although in a minority of cases, problems of word identification (sometimes referred to as surface dyslexia) can be dissociated from problems of phonological decoding (phonological dyslexia), the majority of children with reading difficulties have phonological difficulties (Manis, Seidenberg, Doi, McBride-Chang, & Petersen, 1996; Vellutino & Scanlon, 1991). In the first place, these difficulties cause delayed reading development (Gallagher, Frith, & Snowling, 2000). In the longer term, problems with the generalization of word-specific lexical knowledge are marked by deficits in non-word reading (Rack, Snowling, & Olson, 1992), although both exception word reading (Griffiths & Snowling, 2002; Metsala, Stanovich, & Brown, 1998) and reading comprehension (Frith & Snowling, 1983) may be commensurate with reading age. Dyslexia is a life-persistent disorder and follow-up studies suggest a striking similarity in the cognitive profile of dyslexia across the lifespan (Bruck, 1990, 1992; Maughan et al., 2009).

The predominant theoretical account of dyslexia views its primary cognitive cause as a phonological processing impairment. According to this hypothesis, children with dyslexia have poorly specified phonological representations (Snowling, 2000; Swan &

Goswami, 1997). Put simply, the part of their language system that maps between word meanings and speech sounds is impaired. Deficits in phonological representation explain why people with dyslexia have difficulties with tasks that engage phonological processes. The most consistently reported difficulties are problems of phonological awareness and limitations of verbal short-term memory. However, children with dyslexia also have difficulties with verbal learning (Mayringer & Wimmer, 2000; Messbauer & de Jong, 2003; Vellutino, Scanlon, & Spearing, 1995) and with the retrieval of phonological information from long-term memory for the purpose of naming (Bowers & Wolf, 1993; Griffiths & Snowling, 2001; Swan & Goswami, 1997).

The strength of the evidence pointing to phonological deficits in dyslexia led to the proposal that dyslexia should be defined as a "core" phonological deficit. Within the *phonological core-variable difference* model of dyslexia (Stanovich & Siegel, 1994), poor phonology is related to poor reading performance, irrespective of IQ. Skills close to the "core" of dyslexia include phonological awareness; all poor readers will tend to differ from normal readers in these skills. Children with specific reading difficulties differ from generally poor readers in skills further from the core, notably in their performance on working-memory and listening-comprehension tasks.

Various theories have implicated deficits in low-level visual or auditory processing in dyslexia. Although research findings are mixed, and typically only a proportion of people with dyslexia are affected (Ramus et al., 2003), it is difficult to interpret current findings because studies have been done at a late developmental stage when such deficits could be compensated. One interesting proposal is that low-level auditory impairments in the preschool years are developmental antecedents of the phonological deficits that underlie dyslexia (Benasich, Curtiss, & Tallal, 1993; Richardson, Thomson, Scott, & Goswami, 2004). Preliminary evidence for this hypothesis comes from a study of infants at high risk of dyslexia (Lyytinen et al., 2006) who showed abnormal electrophysiological responses to auditory tones (suggesting an insensitivity to duration). This finding is of considerable theoretical interest suggesting that abnormal auditory processing may be causally linked to dyslexia.

Children at family risk of dyslexia

There are now a number of family studies of dyslexia investigating differences between children from dyslexic and non-dyslexic families before they learn to read; such studies have the potential for investigating developmental precursors of learning disorders. Scarborough (1990) followed the development of children of 2 to 7 years who were "at risk" of dyslexia by virtue of having one dyslexic parent. When the children were 7 and their reading skills could be assessed, it was possible to compare retrospectively the preschool data of children who went on to become dyslexic with children who did not develop reading difficulties. An important difference between the groups was in their early language skills. Although the dyslexic children used as large a range of vocabulary as their non-dyslexic peers at 2.5 years, they made more speech errors and used simpler sentence structures. At 3 years, the dyslexic children had more difficulty with object naming and at 5, their difficulties extended to problems with phonological awareness. Their emerging literacy skills were also poorer; they were less familiar with the letters of the alphabet and worse at matching pictures with print.

Gallagher et al. (2000) reported converging findings from a study in which at-risk children were worse at repeating novel words at 45 months, especially those with phonological structures comprising late-acquired forms. In addition, their knowledge of nursery rhymes, a test known to predict reading achievement, was poorer and they already knew fewer letters. When followed through to 8 years, the at-risk children as a group showed an elevated rate of literacy impairments (Snowling, Gallagher, & Frith, 2003). Comparing at-risk "dyslexic" children with at-risk "typical" readers, this study revealed that those children who had experienced delayed language development at 3 years and 9 months went on at 6 years to show difficulties in phonological awareness. In contrast, the high-risk but normally reading group was indistinguishable from controls on oral language tests. However there were also interesting similarities between the dyslexic and the unimpaired high-risk children – both groups showed poorer letter knowledge and spelling skills at 6 years than controls, highlighting the genetic liability.

This finding suggests that family risk of dyslexia is continuous rather than discrete, as argued by Pennington and Lefly (2001), who found shared deficits between impaired and unimpaired children on a phoneme-awareness task. It is not appropriate, therefore, to think of "dyslexia" as a discrete category of impairment; some children are slow in the early stages of reading but may compensate and proceed to be normal readers. Lyytinen et al. (2006) described four different developmental trajectories to literacy in a Finnish family-risk sample. In addition to those whose reading development was normal and those who showed a typically discrepant profile (with selective reading impairment), some children followed a "declining" trajectory in all skills domains and others a "dysfluent" pathway with severe impairments in rapid naming. More research is required to clarify the different pathways that children at risk of dyslexia follow on the way to literacy.

In summary, there are strong reasons to suggest that children at risk of dyslexia are delayed in their phonological development. A reasonable hypothesis is that these children come to the task of learning to read with poorly specified phonological representations. According to this view, poor phonology compromises literacy development by placing limitations on children's ability to form the mappings between letter strings and the phonological units that are critical for learning to read. Arguably, in other alphabetic languages, the impact of a phonological deficit on reading might be expected to be milder given that learning is so much easier. However, in our present state of knowledge, there is no strong evidence that that is the case and even in Chinese, children with dyslexia experience phonological deficits accompanying their reading problems (see Caravolas, 2005, for a review). What does differ is the behavioral manifestation of dyslexia. In English, the child with dyslexia is identified early because of difficulties with reading accuracy, whereas in transparent languages, dyslexia is characterized by a slow rate of reading (in fact a slow rate of reading is an additional feature of dyslexia in English; Bonifacci & Snowling, 2008). Moreover, whereas in English it would be most unusual to find a poor reader who was not also a poor speller, Moll and Landerl (in press, 2009) have described just such children among German poor readers.

Genetic and environmental contributions to individual differences in reading

We have seen that prospective studies following the development of children born to parents with dyslexia reveal a heightened risk of literacy impairment. Twin studies now show that reading skills are highly heritable and, furthermore, individual differences in word-decoding skills are closely related to individual differences in phoneme awareness, with genetic correlations in the region of .70 (Gayan & Olson, 2001; Petrill, Deater-Deckard, Thompson, DeThorne, & Schatschneider, 2006).

Longitudinal studies from a behavior-genetic perspective allow us to investigate whether the same genetic and environmental factors influence early emerging as well as later literacy skills. In a cross-nation twin study, Byrne and colleagues (Byrne et al., 2005) assessed preschool, kindergarten, and first-grade children in Australia, the US, and Norway. Initial assessments comprised tests of oral language skills (vocabulary and grammar), phonological awareness, rapid naming (RAN), and a composite measure of print awareness (including letter knowledge). One year later, in kindergarten, children were assessed on a similar battery of tests, and also on word and non-word reading and spelling measures, with subsequent data collected in first grade including tests of reading comprehension.

Consistent with the idea that the strong link between phonology and reading is specified genetically, most of the genetic factors affecting phonological awareness in preschool also influenced reading scores in kindergarten (Byrne et al., 2005). Moreover, when children were aged 6, the amount of variance attributable to environmental factors was small and genetic factors accounted for most of the individual variability in phonology. In addition to these continuous effects, there were also new genetic effects that came into play at kindergarten, once formal reading instruction had begun; it is possible that these additional effects were mediated by letter knowledge (Byrne et al., 2005). Furthermore, at both preschool and kindergarten, the shared genetic factors affecting phonological awareness and reading were also involved in other phonological tasks, such as RAN, and, to a lesser extent, they accounted for variance in print awareness. These results are consistent with a perspective emphasizing the rather general influence that any particular set of genes is likely to have on cognitive processes (Plomin & Kovas, 2005).

Notable progress has been made in understanding the molecular basis of genetic influences on reading and reading difficulties (Fisher & DeFries, 2002; Paracchini et al., 2008). To date, the strongest evidence for linkage with dyslexia is a site on the short arm of chromosome 6, with others replicated on chromosomes 1, 2, 3, 11, 15, and 18 (Grigorenko, 2005). Recently, candidate susceptibility genes have been identified within these chromosomal regions but it is important to emphasize that genetic influences are probabilistic; complex disorders depend on the combined influence of many genes of small effect, as well as on environmental influences.

Indeed many school and home environmental factors contribute to reading development (Petrill, Deater-Deckard, Schatschneider, & Davis, 2005; Phillips & Lonigan, 2005) and hence to a child's risk of developing dyslexia. Reading disorders show a strong social gradient, and poor readers often come from large families (Snowling & Maughan, 2006). Where parents themselves have literacy problems, they may provide less than optimal reading-related experiences in the home (though in practice many parents with dyslexia are acutely aware of the need to support their children's literacy development). Reading disorders primarily become apparent at school, and school experiences are influential. If texts are too difficult, reading becomes an unrewarding experience and the cumulative impact of such processes leads to variations in children's "exposure to print" (Snowling, Muter, & Carroll, 2007) which, as we have seen, has an independent effect on reading progress. This needs to be borne in mind when considering genetic findings.

Neural Correlates of Reading and Dyslexia

Despite its significance for daily life, literacy has only been a key skill for the last few hundred years and therefore there can be no brain system dedicated solely to reading. Rather, as argued by Dehaene (2004) in his "neuronal recycling hypothesis," brain areas employed when reading are bound to support several other (evolutionarily older) functions, such as for example the recognition of objects (Price et al., 2006). It is unfortunately not straightforward to understand the brain systems involved in learning to read. Primarily this is because there is something of a disjunction between the rich developmental literature on reading and the much younger research on neural correlates of reading. Most neuroscientific studies have focused on reading in the adult brain and only recently has brain imaging of emergent readers begun. We will first summarize what is known about the neural underpinnings of reading in skilled adult readers, then focus on differences in brain activations between skilled and beginning readers, before discussing potential abnormalities in the brain systems used for reading in dyslexia.

The most common method that has been used to investigate neural correlates of reading is functional magnetic resonance imaging (fMRI) (earlier brain-imaging studies have used a method called PET which will not be reviewed here). In fMRI participants are typically asked to perform both the task of interest (e.g., reading a word silently) and a baseline task (e.g., looking at a blank screen). A signal called the BOLD (blood oxygenation-level dependent) signal, that varies with activity in the brain, is measured while participants are performing the tasks lying in the scanner. Typically the difference in BOLD signal between the task of interest and the control task is calculated for several brain regions (this method is called subtraction). Brain regions that have significantly higher BOLD signal during the task of interest than during the control task are considered to be "activated," in contrast, brain regions with significantly lower BOLD response during the task of interest than during the control task are described as being "deactivated." Thus in this type of analysis the choice of the control task is crucial. Given this methodological consideration, most neuroimaging approaches study components of reading (such as single-word reading) or reading-related tasks (such as rhyme judgment) rather than prose reading.

Neural system in skilled readers

At a basic level of description, the reading system can be thought of as consisting of three overlapping subsystems: brain areas responding to changes in the low-level visual features

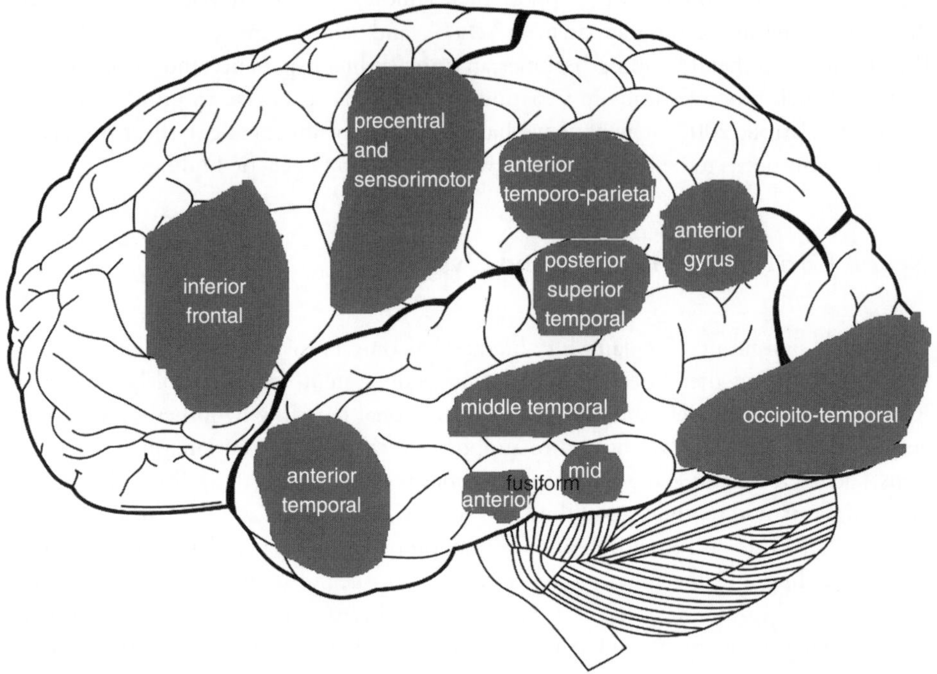

Figure 20.1 A schematic version of the reading system of skilled readers (fusiform areas projected onto the surface), adapted from Price and McCrory, 2005 with permission

of words; areas that support mapping from orthography to phonology (possibly including areas for speech production and perception); and a semantic system (see figure 20.1).To investigate the fine-grained structures involved in the visual processing of printed words, a number of studies have compared feature detection in real words versus false fonts (as a baseline). Three areas have been identified that respond more to the presentation of words than to false fonts: the left mid-fusiform, the left anterior fusiform and the left posterior superior temporal cortex. These areas have sometimes been described as the *ventral* reading circuit (Pugh et al., 2001). The left mid-fusiform area is also activated when reading aloud a word compared to viewing a false font and saying "okay" and has been referred to as the visual word form area (Cohen et al., 2000). It has been suggested that this area is specialized for recognizing letter strings and extracting the identity of visual words from a variety of different visual presentation formats (Dehaene, 2004).

Arguably, the specialization of the "visual word form area" might be shaped by learning to read in a specific script. However, whether the function of this area really changes during reading acquisition is controversial (Price & Devlin, 2004). There is clear evidence that this region is involved not only in reading but also in object naming, a finding which might speak to the link between RAN and reading (McCrory, Mechelli, Frith, & Price, 2005). The activation found in the more anterior region of the left fusiform when comparing feature detection in real words versus false fonts is possibly related to amodal semantic word processing. Additional areas that are more strongly activated during single-word reading relate to speech production (left precentral cortex, anterior cingulate, and the supplementary motor cortex). In studies using a comparison of reading aloud single words versus resting with closed eyes, there is typically brain activation in regions at the junction of the occipital and temporal lobes and in the superior temporal lobe in both hemispheres. These activations are possibly related to the mapping from orthography to phonology and can be observed even in the absence of overt speech. In addition, sensorimotor areas and central regions of the superior temporal cortex are often activated. These activations might be more related to articulation and hearing the sound of a spoken response.

Pugh et al. (2001) have also suggested that a *dorsal* reading circuit comprising the precentral cortex and anterior parts of temporo-parietal cortex is involved in phonological processing, though these regions are not typically activated during reading aloud. Interestingly, and in contrast to expectations from patient studies, the left angular gyrus in particular is not activated during reading aloud. Activations here are found when tasks entail semantic associations. Other brain areas involved in retrieving semantic information are regions in the temporal lobe (anterior temporal region and a middle temporal area) and the left inferior frontal gyrus.

Reading development and brain imaging

Researchers have only recently started to investigate how the network of regions underpinning skilled reading might emerge during reading acquisition. It is likely that the semantic system will only be automatically recruited in response to written words once early stages of word recognition are mastered. So far, the debate has therefore been mainly focused on the emergence of the visual word form area, the systems for grapheme–phoneme mapping, and the relationship between those two during development. Pugh et al. (2001) for example suggested that during reading development, the grapheme–phoneme mapping system dominates at first, and that the reliance on the visual word form area is late-developing and related to word fluency.

Most studies have looked at developmental changes in the reading network with chronological age as a proxy for reading development. Arguably, a better method would be to benchmark processing changes to changes in measured skill. In the absence of such data, figure 20.2 provides an overview of brain regions for which age-related increases or decreases in activation during reading-related tasks have been reported. For example, Turkeltaub, Gareau, Flowers, Zeffiro, and Eden (2003) used an implicit word processing task (visual feature detection within words and false fonts) in a cross-sectional study with participants aged 6 to 22 years. Better reading was associated with increased activity in the left middle temporal gyrus and the left inferior frontal gyrus and decreased activity in right inferotemporal cortical areas. These findings could indicate a stronger reliance on the grapheme-to-phoneme mapping and the semantic system with age. In the same study they also found that the amount of activity in left posterior superior temporal sulcus of the youngest readers (9 years and younger) was associated with their phonological processing abilities.

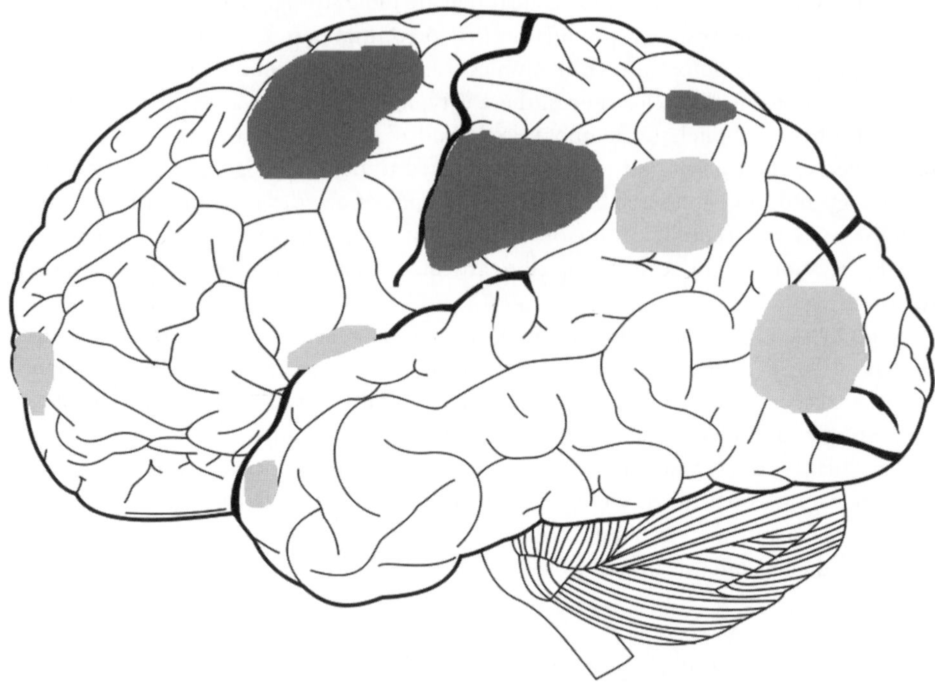

Figure 20.2 A schematic version of age-related changes in the reading system (dark = activity increases with age, pale = activity decreases with age), adapted from Schlaggar and Church, 2009, with permission

Using a lexical decision task in a study of 7- to 32-year-olds, Schlaggar and Church (2009) showed that activity increased with age in lateral frontal and parietal cortical regions and decreased in medial frontal, occipital, and temporal cortical regions. They interpreted those developmental changes as indicative of decreasing reliance on phonological mechanisms and increasing reliance on top-down control. Furthermore, they suggested that during development, the function of the bilateral occipital-temporal cortex shifts from being used for auditory and lexical processing tasks to being more specialized for visual than for auditory processing.

In contrast to this proposal, Shaywitz et al. (2002) studied 70 children with dyslexia and 74 typically developing children and found that as reading skill increased in children, activation in left occipito-temporal cortex increased, whereas activation in right occipito-temporal cortex decreased. However, as Price and Devlin (2004) remark, the correlations between activation and age do not provide conclusive evidence that the *function* of the left occipito-temporal cortex changes during reading development – the correlations could just indicate that the same function is used to a greater extent in older readers. A possible way to test whether the function of the left occipito-temporal cortex changes with reading development would be to investigate whether with reading experience the activation gets tuned to the grain size (Ziegler & Goswami, 2005) that is optimal for the language in which the child learns to read.

In summary, it is clear that there are dynamic changes in the functional anatomy of the reading system during development, with an increasing involvement of the semantic system. It is however less clear how far responses of the visual word form area are shaped by reading development. Furthermore, there is conflicting evidence as to whether there is less reliance on grapheme-to-phoneme mapping and a growing reliance on visual processing with age. Comparative studies are needed, in particular in transparent orthographies, to investigate the extent to which an emerging reading system is shaped by linguistic factors.

Dyslexia and brain imaging

Brain imaging has also been used to identify which brain systems might be impaired in reading disorders. Although this line of research holds great promise there are some serious methodological issues to face: the comparison of interest is not within the same participants between different tasks but between different participants on the same tasks. So a major issue is how, and on which skills, to equate participants. If one group suffers from a reading disorder and the other group does not, clearly their performance on reading tasks will differ as well as their reading experience. How to best control for these performance confounds is a matter of debate. In addition, any differential activation found could be the consequence rather than the cause of slow and inefficient reading. Observed differences between skilled and impaired readers may reflect primary cognitive deficits, secondary consequences of those deficits, compensatory processing, or differences in other parameters such as intelligence (Price & McCrory, 2005). Careful matching is essential and longitudinal studies are needed. Given that dyslexia often co-occurs with other developmental disorders such as attention deficit hyperactivity disorder (ADHD), and that few imaging studies have controlled for co-morbidities, many reported differences found between groups with and without dyslexia could theoretically be due to a co-morbid disorder. Furthermore, most brain-imaging studies on dyslexia so far have focused on university-educated adults, i.e. probably "compensated" adults, and it can be questioned how representative their reading system is for classic dyslexia.

With the above methodological issues in mind, we turn now to consider what is known about the neural correlates of dyslexia. Here, as in studies of typical development, there is evidence of both increased and reduced brain activation. Reduced left posterior inferior and middle temporal activation has been reported in participants with dyslexia when reading aloud and silently, as well as when making phonological or semantic decisions. There is some evidence that activation in left posterior inferior temporal lobe might index reading ability irrespective of dyslexia. Reduced activation in participants with dyslexia has been found also in left temporo-parietal cortex and the angular gyrus during semantic decisions and letter rhyming. Activation in these areas correlates with reading skill during semantic decisions and reading. Price and McCrory (2005) suggest that these activation differences may reflect reduced access to semantic processing as a consequence of deficits at an earlier stage in the reading system. Within this view, reduced temporo-parietal activation is likely to be a consequence not cause of dyslexia.

Adults with dyslexia have also been reported to show increased left pre-motor and inferior frontal activation during explicit but not implicit reading tasks, correlated positively with age (Shaywitz et al., 2002). There is also higher activation in right inferior frontal regions in participants with dyslexia during phonological decision tasks which could be related to strategic processes, working memory, and memory-retrieval demands. So far the evidence suggests that individuals with dyslexia use brain areas involved in grapheme-to-phoneme mapping and semantic areas to a lesser degree during reading than controls. There is also evidence for lower activation in the visual word form area during word reading in participants with dyslexia (McCrory, Mechelli, Frith, & Price, 2005). Reduced activation was also found in this area for participants with dyslexia during picture naming. Increases in frontal activation might be related to compensatory processes in dyslexia.

Recent fMRI studies have tried to identify brain regions that might fulfill compensatory functions in individuals with dyslexia by comparing their reading system to that of both age-matched and reading-age-matched controls. Hoeft et al. (2007), for example, suggest that the increased activation they found in left inferior and middle frontal gyri in individuals with dyslexia is related to their level of current reading, while the decreased activation found in left parietal and bilateral fusiform gyri reflect functional abnormalities possibly related to atypical brain morphology.

Indeed, any differences in brain activation found could be due to structural brain differences between brains of skilled readers and those with dyslexia.

Galaburda (1992) reported reduced leftward asymmetry and cellular abnormalities in auditory and visual areas. However, later studies (e.g., Leonard et al., 2001; Leonard et al., 1993) have found the opposite trend – an increased leftward asymmetry in individuals with dyslexia. Recent voxel-based morphometry studies have reported less temporo-parietal grey matter, in particular in the left parietal region and in pre-motor cortex, and less cerebellar grey matter (Brambati et al., 2004; Hoeft et al., 2007). Leonard and Eckert (2008) suggest that there might be two types of structural abnormalities found in dyslexia: individuals with a broader phenotype of dyslexia (with deficits in multiple domains of written and oral language) are more likely to have small symmetrical brain structures; in contrast, larger asymmetrical structures are more likely to be found in adults with compensated dyslexia with isolated phonological deficits.

Furthermore, connectivity among regions of the reading system might vary with differences in structural anatomy. According to Paulesu et al. (1996) there is a functional disconnection between areas involved in speech perception and speech production in dyslexia. This hypothesis predicts altered connectivity within the language system of adults with dyslexia. Subsequent studies have indeed reported significant reduction of white-matter density (indexing connectivity) within the arcuate fasciculus, the fiber bundle linking temporo-parietal and frontal regions (Klingberg et al., 2000; Silani et al., 2005).

As for studies using functional imaging, most of the anatomical studies have been done on adults, leaving open the thorny issue of what is the cause and what the effect of reading disability. However, it is clear that early brain abnormalities could lead to an impairment in reading. In a recent review discussing genetic models of dyslexia, Galaburda, LoTurco, Ramus, Fitch, and Rosen (2006) provide evidence that the current candidate genes for a susceptibility to develop dyslexia are also responsible for subtle cortical abnormalities that are related to neuronal migration and axon growth (Paracchini et al., 2006). In summary, differences in brain structure have been found in individuals with dyslexia. Future research will shed light on whether these observed differences are consequences of having dyslexia, reflect aberrant gene function, or evolve from the interaction of subtle brain abnormalities with altered reading experiences.

A Final Word on Reading Instruction

It is now well established that intervention programs that promote phonological skills in the context of reading are effective methods of instruction (National Reading Panel, 2000). For children with dyslexia, such programs are best delivered by trained teachers who understand how to tune a program to a child's specific needs (Brooks, 2002; Torgesen, 2005; Hatcher et al., 2006). In contrast to what is known about how to teach poor readers, there is limited evidence regarding preventative programs. Preliminary evidence suggests that theoretically motivated programs to promote phonological skills and letter knowledge at school entry can bring the literacy skills of at-risk children within the normal range (Bowyer-Crane et al., 2008) but the longer-term impact of such interventions is unknown.

However, it is important to emphasize that children with dyslexia are "hard to teach" and can respond very slowly even to the most effective of teaching approaches (Hindson et al., 2005). An important issue is the problem of children who despite high-quality intervention, continue to have persistent reading impairments. These "treatment non-responders" tend to have the most severe phonological deficits, are often socially disadvantaged, and many experience emotional and behavioral difficulties (Torgesen, 2000; Duff et al., 2008).

Recently the effect of reading intervention on the reading system has been investigated in several neuroimaging studies (Eden et al., 2004; Simos et al., 2002). Phonological training resulted in increased activation in left parietal regions and the left fusiform gyrus in individuals with dyslexia, which could be interpreted as a normalization of their activation patterns. In addition, after training, increased activity was observed in regions in the right hemisphere (temporo-parietal and frontal regions). Interestingly, the left hemisphere homologues of those regions play an important role in normal reading and it has been suggested that those right hemisphere activations reflect compensatory processes. There is some evidence that abnormal functional connectivity between brain regions can also be normalized by intervention (Richards & Berninger, 2008).

Conclusions

In the past decade, the study of reading development has matured and begun to guide not only reading intervention but also neuroscientific investigations of emergent reading processes. Increasingly, the agenda is turning to the foundations of reading development in the preschool years. The stage is therefore set for investigations of the precursors of reading, how these relate to brain-based processes, and what can be done to ensure they are properly fostered.

References

Benasich, A. A., Curtiss, S., & Tallal, P. (1993). Language, learning, and behavioral disturbances in childhood: A longitudinal perspective. *Journal of American Academy Child Adolescence Psychiatry*, *32*(3), 585–594.

Bonifacci, P., & Snowling, M. J. (2008). Speed of information processing in children with dyslexia and children of low-IQ: A test of the modular hypothesis. *Cognition*, *107*, 999–1017.

Bowers, P. G., & Wolf, M. (1993). Theoretical links among naming speed, precise timing mechanisms and orthographic skill in dyslexia. *Reading and Writing*, *5*, 69–85.

Bowey, J. A. (2005). Predicting individual differences in learning to read. In M. J. Snowling & C. Hulme (Eds.), *The science of reading: A handbook* (pp. 155–172). Oxford: Blackwell.

Bowyer-Crane, C., Snowling, M., Duff, F., Carroll, J., Fieldsend, E., Miles, J., Gotz, K., & Hulme, C. (2008). Improving early language and literacy skills: Differential effects of an oral language versus a phonology with reading intervention. *Journal of Child Psychology and Psychiatry*, *49*, 422–432.

Brambati, S. M., Termine, C., Ruffino, M., Stella, G., Fazio, F., Cappa, S. F., & Perani, D. (2004). Regional reductions of gray matter volume in familial dyslexia. *Neurology*, *63*, 742–745.

Brooks, G. (2002). *What works for children with literacy difficulties? The effectiveness of intervention schemes*. UK Department for Education & Skills. Retrieved from www.dfes.gov.uk/research.

Bruck, M. (1990). Word recognition skills of adults with childhood diagnoses of dyslexia. *Developmental Psychology*, *26*, 439–454.

Bruck, M. (1992). Persistence of dyslexics' phonological awareness deficits. *Development Psychology*, *28*, 874–886.

Bruck, M., Genesee, F., & Caravolas, M. (1997). A cross-linguistic study of early literacy acquisition. In B. Blachman (Ed.), *Foundations of reading acquisition and dyslexia: Implications for early intervention* (pp. 145–162). Mahwah, NJ: Erlbaum.

Byrne, B. (1996). The learnability of the alphabetic principle: Children's initial hypotheses about how print represents spoken language. *Applied Psycholinguistics*, *17*, 1469–1817.

Byrne, B. (1998). *The foundation of literacy: The child's acquisition of the alphabetic principle.* Hove, UK: Psychology Press.

Byrne, B., Wadsworth, S., Corley, R., Samuelsson, S., Quain, P., DeFries, J. C., Willcutt, E., & Olson, R. K. (2005). Longitudinal twin study of early literacy development: Preschool and kindergarten phases. *Scientific Studies of Reading*, *9*, 219–235.

Caravolas, M. (2005). The nature and causes of dyslexia in different languages. In M. J. Snowling & C. Hulme (Eds.), *The science of reading: A handbook* (pp. 336–356). Oxford: Blackwell.

Caravolas, M., & Bruck, M. (1993). The effect of oral and written language input on children's phonological awareness: A cross-linguistic study. *Journal of Experimental Child Psychology*, *55*, 1–30.

Caravolas, M., Hulme, C., & Snowling, M. J. (2001). The foundations of spelling ability: Evidence from a 3-year longitudinal study. *Journal of Memory and Language*, *45*, 751–774.

Caravolas, M., Kessler, B., Hulme, C., & Snowling, M. J. (2005). Effects of orthographic consistency, frequency and letter knowledge on children's vowel spelling development. *Journal of Experimental Child Psychology*, *92*, 307–321.

Caravolas, M., & Landerl, K. (in press). The influences of syllable structure and reading ability on the development of phoneme awareness: A longitudinal, cross-linguistic study. *Scientific Studies of Reading.*

Caravolas, M., Volín, J., & Hulme, C. (2005). Phoneme awareness is a key component of alphabetic literacy skills in consistent and inconsistent orthographies: Evidence from Czech and English children. *Journal of Experimental Child Psychology, 92,* 107–139.

Carroll, J., Snowling, M. J., Hulme, C., & Stevenson, J. (2003). The development of phonological awareness in pre-school children. *Developmental Psychology, 39,* 913–923.

Clarke, P., Hulme, C., & Snowling, M. J. (2005). Individual differences in RAN and reading: A response timing analysis. *Journal of Research in Reading, 28,* 73–86.

Cohen, L., Dehaene, S., Naccache, L., Lehéricy, S., Dehaene-Lambertz, G., Hénaff, M., & Michel, F. (2000). The visual word form area: Spatial and temporal characterization of an initial stage of reading in normal subjects and posterior split-brain patients. *Brain, 123,* 291–307.

Cunningham, A. E., & Stanovich, K. E. (1991). Tracking the unique effects of print exposure in children: Associations with vocabulary, general knowledge and spelling. *Journal of Educational Psychology, 83,* 264–274.

De Cara, B., & Goswami, U. (2003). Phonological neighbourhood density: Effects in a rhyme awareness task in five-year-old children. *Journal of Child Language, 30,* 695–710.

De Jong, P. F., & van der Leij, A. (1999). Specific contributions of phonological abilities to early reading acquisition: Results from a Dutch latent variable longitudinal study. *Journal of Educational Psychology, 9*(3), 450–476.

Dehaene, S. (2004). Evolution of human cortical circuits for reading and arithmetic: The "neuronal recycling" hypothesis. In S. Dehaene, J. R. Duhamel, M. Hauser, & G. Rizzolatti (Eds.), *From monkey brain to human brain.* Cambridge, MA: MIT Press.

Duff, F., Fieldsend, E., Bowyer-Crane, C., Hulme, C., Smith, G., Gibbs, S., & Snowling, M. J. (2008). Reading with vocabulary intervention: Evaluation of an instruction for children with poor response to reading intervention. *Journal of Research in Reading, 31,* 319–336.

Eden, G. F., Jones, K. M., Cappell, K., Gareau, L., Wood, F. B., Zeffiro, T. A., … Flowers, D. L. (2004). Neural changes following remediation in adult developmental dyslexia. *Neuron, 44,* 411–422.

Ehri, L. C. (1995). Phases of development in learning to read words by sight. *Journal of Research in Reading, 18,* 116–125.

Ehri, L. C. (2005). Development of sight word reading: Phases and findings. In M. J. Snowling & C. Hulme (Eds.), *The science of reading: A handbook* (pp. 135–154). Oxford: Blackwell.

Fisher, S. E., & DeFries, J. C. (2002). Developmental dyslexia: Genetic dissection of a complex cognitive trait. *Nature Reviews Neuroscience, 3,* 767–780.

Frith, U., & Snowling, M. J. (1983). Reading for meaning and reading for sound in autistic and dyslexic children. *British Journal of Developmental Psychology, 1,* 329–342.

Frith, U., Wimmer, H., & Landerl, K. (1998). Differences in phonological recoding in German and English speaking children. *Scientific Studies of Reading, 2*(1), 31–54.

Galaburda, A. M. (1992). Neurology of developmental dyslexia. *Current Opinions in Neurology and Neurosurgery, 5,* 71–76.

Galaburda, A. M., LoTurco, J., Ramus, R. F., Fitch, R. H., & Rosen, G. D. (2006). From genes to behavior in developmental dyslexia. *Nature Neuroscience, 9,* 1213–1217.

Gallagher, A., Frith, U., & Snowling, M. J. (2000). Precursors of literacy-delay among children at genetic risk of dyslexia. *Journal of Child Psychology and Psychiatry, 41,* 203–213.

Gayan, J., & Olson, R. K. (2001). Genetic and environmental influences on orthographic and phonological skills in children with reading disabilities. *Developmental Neuropsychology, 20*(2), 483–507.

Goswami, U., & Bryant, P. E. (1990). *Phonological skills and learning to read.* London: Erlbaum.

Goswami, U., Ziegler, J., Dalton, L., & Schneider, W. (2001). Pseudohomophone effects and phonological recoding procedures in reading development in English and German. *Journal of Memory and Language, 45*, 648–664.

Gough, P. B., & Hillinger, M. (1980). Learning to read: An unnatural act. *Bulletin of the Orton Society, 30*, 179–196.

Gough, P. B., & Tunmer, W. E. (1986). Decoding, reading and reading disability. *Remedial and Special Education, 7*, 6–10.

Griffiths, Y. M., & Snowling, M. J. (2001). Auditory word identification and phonological skills in dyslexic and average readers. *Applied Psycholinguistics, 22*, 419–439.

Griffiths, Y. M., & Snowling, M. J. (2002). Predictors of exception word and nonword reading in dyslexic children: The severity hypothesis. *Journal of Educational Psychology, 94*(1), 34–43.

Grigorenko, E. L. (2005). A conservative meta-analysis of linkage and linkage-association studies of developmental dyslexia. *Scientific Studies of Reading, 9*, 285–316.

Hanley, R. (2005). Learning to read in Chinese. In M. Snowling & C. Hulme (Eds.), *The science of reading: A handbook* (pp. 316–335). Oxford: Blackwell.

Harris, M., & Hatano, G. (Eds.) (1999). *Learning to read and write: A cross-linguistic perspective.* Cambridge: Cambridge University Press.

Hatcher, P. J., Hulme, C., Miles, J. N. V., Carroll, J. M., Hatcher, J., Gibbs, S., … Snowling, M. J. (2006). Efficacy of small group reading intervention for beginning readers with reading-delay: A randomized controlled trial. *Journal of Child Psychology and Psychiatry, 47*, 820–827.

Hecht, S. A., Burgess, S. R., Torgesen, J. K., Wagner, R. K., & Rashotte, C. A. (2000). Explaining social class differences in growth of reading skills from beginning kindergarten through fourth-grade: The role of phonological awareness, rate of access, and print knowledge. *Reading and Writing, 12*(1–2), 99–127.

Hindson, B., Byrne, B., Fielding-Barnsley, R., Newman, C., Hine, D. W., & Shankweiler, D. (2005). Assessment and early instruction of pre-school children at risk for reading disability. *Journal of Educational Psychology, 97*, 687–704.

Ho, C. S. H., & Bryant, P. (1997). Phonological skills are important in learning to read Chinese. *Developmental Psychology, 33*, 946–951.

Hoeft, F., Meyler, A., Hernandez, A., Juel, C., Taylor-Hill, H., Martindale, J. L., … Gabrieli, J. D. E. (2007). Functional and morphometric brain dissociation between dyslexia and reading ability. *Proceedings of the National Academy of Sciences, 104*, 4234–4239.

Holland, J. H., Holyoak, K. J., Nisbett, R. E., & Thagard, P. R. (1986). *Induction. Processes of inference, learning, and discovery.* Cambridge, MA: MIT Press.

Hulme, C., Goetz, K., Gooch, D., Adams, J., & Snowling, M. J. (2007). Paired-associate learning, phoneme awareness and learning to read. *Journal of Experimental Child Psychology, 96*, 150–166.

Klingberg, T., Hedehus, M., Temple, E., Salz, T., Gabrieli, J. D. E., Moseley, M. E., & Poldrack, R. A. (2000). Microstructure of temporo-parietal white matter as a basis for reading ability: Evidence from diffusion tensor magnetic resonance imaging. *Neuron, 25*, 493–500.

Kintsch, W., & Rawson, K. (2005). Comprehension. In M. J. Snowling & C. Hulme (Eds.), *The science of reading: A handbook* (pp. 209–226). Oxford: Blackwell.

Landerl, K. (2000). Influences of orthographic consistency and reading instruction on the development of nonword reading skills. *European Journal of Psychology of Education, 15*, 239–257.

Leonard, C. M., & Eckert, M. A. (2008). Asymmetry and Dyslexia. *Developmental Neuropsychology, 33*(6), 663–681.

Leonard, C. M., Eckert, M. A., Lombardino, L. J., Oakland, T., Kranzler, J., Mohr, C. M., King, W. M., & Freeman, A. (2001). Anatomical risk factors for phonological dyslexia. *Cerebral Cortex, 11*, 148–157.

Leonard, C. M., Voeller, K. K., Lombardino, L. J., Morris, M. K., Hynd, G. W., Alexander, A. W., … Staab, E. V. (1993). Anomalous cerebral structure in dyslexia revealed with magnetic resonance imaging. *Archives of Neurology, 50*(5), 461–469.

Lervåg, A., & Hulme, C. (in press). Rapid naming (RAN) taps a basic constraint on the development of early reading fluency. *Psychological Science.*

Liberman, I. Y., & Shankweiler, D. (1979). Speech, the alphabet, and teaching to read. In L. Resnick & P. Weaver (Eds.), *Theory and practice of early reading.* Hillsdale, NJ: Erlbaum.

Lyytinen, H., Erskine, J. M., Tolvanen, A., Torppa, M., Poikkeus, A.-M., & Lyytinen, P. (2006). Trajectories of reading development: A follow-up from birth to school age of children with and without risk for dyslexia. *Merril-Palmer Quarterly, 52*(3), 514–546.

Manis, F. R., Seidenberg, M. S., Doi, L. M., McBride-Chang, C., & Petersen, A. (1996). On the bases of two subtypes of developmental dyslexia. *Cognition, 58*(2), 157–195.

Mann, V., & Wimmer, H. (2002). Phoneme awareness and pathways to literacy: A comparison of German and American children. *Reading and Writing, 17*, 653–682.

Marsh, G., Friedman, M., Welch, V., & Desberg, P. (1980). The development of strategies in spelling. In U. Frith (Ed.), *Cognitive processes in spelling.* London: Academic Press.

Masonheimer, P. E., Drum, P. A., & Ehri, L. C. (1984). Does environmental print identification lead children into word reading? *Journal of Reading Behavior, 16*, 257–271.

Maughan, B., Messer, J., Collishaw, S., Snowling, M. J., Yule, W., & Rutter, M. (2009). Persistence of literacy problems: Spelling in adolescence and at mid-life. *Journal of Child Psychology and Psychiatry, 50*, 893–901.

Mayringer, H., & Wimmer, H. (2000). Pseudoname learning by German-speaking children with dyslexia: Evidence for a phonological learning deficit. *Journal of Experimental Child Psychology, 75*, 116–133.

McBride-Chang, C. (2004). *Children's Literacy Development.* Cambridge: Cambridge University Press.

McCrory, E. J., Mechelli, A., Frith, U., & Price, C. J. (2005). More than words: A common neural basis for reading and naming deficits in developmental dyslexia? *Brain, 128*, 261–267.

Messbauer, V., & de Jong, P. (2003). Word, nonword, and visual paired associate learning in Dutch dyslexic children. *Journal of Experimental Child Psychology, 84*, 77–96.

Metsala, J. L., Stanovich, K. E., & Brown, G. D. A. (1998). Regularity effects and the phonological deficit model of reading disabilities: A meta-analytic review. *Journal of Experimental Psychology, 90*(2), 279–293.

Moll, K., & Landerl, K. (in press). Double dissociation between reading and spelling deficits. *Scientific Studies of Reading.*

Muter, V., Hulme, C., Snowling, M. J., & Stevenson, J. (2004). Phonemes, rimes, vocabulary, and grammatical skills as foundations of early reading development: Evidence from a longitudinal study. *Developmental Psychology, 40*, 663–681.

National Reading Panel (2000). Teaching children to read: An evidence-based assessment of the scientific research literature on reading and its implications for reading instruction. Reports of subgroups. National Institute of Child Health and Human Development.

Nuñes, T., & Bryant, P. (2009). *Children's reading and spelling: Beyond the first steps.* Oxford: Wiley-Blackwell.

Nuñes, T., Bryant, P., & Bindman, M. (1997). Morphological spelling strategies: Developmental stages and processes. *Developmental Psychology, 33*, 637–649.

Paracchini, S., Steer, C., Buckingham, L.-L., Morris, A., Ring, S., Scerri, T., ... Monaco, A. P. (2008). Association of the KIAA0319 dyslexia susceptibility gene with reading skills in the general population. *American Journal of Psychiatry, 165*, 1576–1584.

Paracchini, S., Thomas, A., Castro, S., Lai, C. S., Paramsivam, M., Wang, Y., ... Monaco, A. P. (2006). The chromosome 6p22 haplotype associated with dyslexia reduces the expression of KIAA0319, a novel gene involved in neuronal migration. *Human Molecular Genetics, 15*, 1659–1666.

Patel, T. K., Snowling, M. J., & De Jong, P. F. (2004). Learning to read in Dutch and English: A cross-linguistic comparison. *Journal of Educational Psychology, 96*, 785–797.

Paulesu, E., Frith, U., Snowling, M. J., Gallagher, A., Morton, J., Frackowiak, F. S. J., & Frith, C. D. (1996). Is developmental dyslexia a disconnection syndrome? Evidence from PET scanning. *Brain, 119*, 143–157.

Pennington, B. F., & Lefly, D. L. (2001). Early reading development in children at family risk for dyslexia. *Child Development, 72*, 816–833.

Perfetti, C. A. (1995). Cognitive research can inform reading education. *Journal of Research in Reading, 18*, 106–115.

Perfetti, C. A., & Hart, L. (2001). The lexical bases of comprehension skill. In D. Gorfien (Ed.), *On the consequences of meaning selection* (pp. 67–86). Washington DC: American Psychological Association.

Petrill, S. A., Deater-Deckard, K., Schatschneider, C., & Davis, C. (2005). Measured environmental influences on early reading: Evidence from an adoption study. *Scientific Studies of Reading, 9*, 237–259.

Petrill, S. A., Deater-Deckard, K., Thompson, L. A., DeThorne, L. S., & Schatschneider, C. (2006). Genetic and environmental effects of serial naming and phonological awareness on early reading outcomes. *Journal of Educational Psychology, 98*, 112–121.

Phillips, B. M., & Lonigan, C. J. (2005). Social correlates of emergent literacy. In M. J. Snowling & C. Hulme (Eds.), *The science of reading: A handbook* (pp. 173–187). Oxford: Blackwell.

Plomin, R., & Kovas, Y. (2005). Generalist genes and learning disabilities. *Psychological Bulletin, 131*(4), 592–617.

Powell, D., Stainthorp, R., Stuart, M., Garwood, H., & Quinlan, P. (2007). An experimental comparison between rival theories of rapid automatized naming performance and its relationship to reading. *Journal of Experimental Child Psychology, 98*(1), 46–68.

Price, C. J., & Devlin, J. T. (2004). Reply to letter to the editor. *NeuroImage, 22*, 477–479.

Price, C. J., & McCrory, E. (2005). Functional brain imaging studies of skilled reading and developmental dyslexia. In M. J. Snowling & C. Hulme (Eds.), *The science of reading: A handbook* (pp. 473–496). Oxford, Blackwell.

Price, C. J., McCrory, E., Noppeney, U., Mechelli, A., Moore, C. J., Biggio, N., Devlin, J. T. (2006). How reading differs from object naming at the neuronal level. *NeuroImage, 29*, 643–648.

Pugh, K. R., Einer, W. E., Jenner, A. R., Katz, L., Frost, S. J., Lee, J. R., Shaywitz, S. E., & Shaywitz, B. A. (2001). Neurobiological studies of reading and reading disability. *Journal of Communication Disorders, 34*, 479–492.

Rack, J., Snowling, M. J., & Olson, R. (1992). The nonword reading deficit in dyslexia: A review. *Reading Research Quarterly, 27*, 28–53.

Ramus, F., Rosen, S., Dakin, S. C., Day, B. L., Castellote, J. M., White, S., & Frith, U. (2003). Theories of developmental dyslexia: Insights from a multiple case study of dyslexic adults. *Brain, 126*, 1–25.

Richards, T., & Berninger, V. (2008). Abnormal fMRI connectivity in children with dyslexia during a phoneme task: Before but not after treatment. *Journal of Neurolinguistics, 21*, 294–304.

Richardson, U., Thomson, J., Scott, S. K., & Goswami, U. (2004). Auditory processing skills and phonological representation in dyslexic children. *Dyslexia, 10,* 215–233.

Ricketts, J., Bishop, D., & Nation, K. (2008). Investigating orthographic and semantic aspects of word learning in poor comprehenders. *Journal of Research in Reading, 31,* 117–135.

Scarborough, H. S. (1990). Very early language deficits in dyslexic children. *Child Development, 61,* 1728–1743.

Schlaggar, B. L., & Church, J. A. (2009). Functional neuroimaging insights into the developmental of skilled reading. *Current Directions in Psychological Science, 18,* 21–26.

Seymour, P. H. K., Aro, M., & Erskine, J. M. (2003). Foundation literacy acquisition in European orthographies. *British Journal of Psychology, 94,* 143–174.

Seymour, P. H. K., & Elder, L. (1986). Beginning reading without phonology. *Cognitive Neuropsychology, 1,* 43–82.

Share, D. L. (1995). Phonological recoding and self-teaching: Sine qua non of reading acquisition. *Cognition, 55,* 151–218.

Share, D. L. (1999). Phonological recoding and orthographic learning: A direct test of the self-teaching hypothesis. *Journal of Experimental Child Psychology, 72,* 95–129.

Share, D. L. (2008). Orthographic learning, phonological recoding, and self-teaching. *Advances in child development and behavior, 36,* 31–82.

Shaywitz, B. A., Shaywitz, S. E., Pugh, K. R., Mencl, W. E., Fulbright, R. K., Skudlarski, P., … Gore, J. C. (2002). Disruption of posterior brain systems for reading in children with developmental dyslexia. *Biological Psychiatry, 52,* 101–110.

Silani, G., Frith, U., Demonet, J.-F., Fazio, F., Perani, D., Price, C., Frith, C. D., and Paulesu, E. (2005). Brain abnormalities underlying altered activation in dyslexia: a voxel based morphometry study. *Brain, 128,* 2453–2461.

Simos, P. G., Fletcher, J. M., Bergman, E., Breier, J. I., Foorman, B. R., Castillo, E. M. … Papanicolaou, A. C. (2002). Dyslexia-specific brain activation profile becomes normal following successful remedial training. *Neurology, 58,* 1203–1213.

Snowling, M. J. (2000). *Dyslexia.* Oxford: Blackwell.

Snowling, M. J. (2008). Specific disorders and broader phenotypes: The case of dyslexia. *Quarterly Journal of Experimental Psychology, 61,* 142–156.

Snowling, M. J., Gallagher, A., & Frith, U. (2003). Family risk of dyslexia is continuous: Individual differences in the precursors of reading skill. *Child Development, 74,* 358–373.

Snowling, M. J., & Maughan, B. (2006). Reading and other learning disabilities. In C. Gillberg, R. Harrington, & H.-C. Steinhausen (Eds.), *Clinician's deskbook of child and adolescent psychiatry.* Cambridge: Cambridge University Press.

Snowling, M. J., Muter, V., & Carroll, J. M. (2007). Children at family risk of dyslexia: A follow-up in adolescence. *Journal of Child Psychology and Psychiatry, 48,* 609–618.

Stanovich, K. E., & Siegel, L. S. (1994). The phenotypic performance profile of reading-disabled children: A regression-based test of the phonological-core variable-difference model. *Journal of Educational Psychology, 86,* 24–53.

Swan, D., & Goswami, U. (1997). Phonological awareness deficits in developmental dyslexia and the phonological representations hypothesis. *Journal of Experimental Child Psychology, 60,* 334–353.

Torgesen, J. K. (2000). Individual differences in response to early interventions in reading: The lingering problem of treatment registers. *Learning Disabilities Research and Practice, 15,* 55–64.

Torgesen, J. K. (2005). Recent discoveries on remedial interventions for children with dyslexia. In M. J. Snowling & C. Hulme (Eds.), *The science of reading: A handbook* (pp. 521–537). Oxford: Blackwell.

Treiman, R., & Breaux, A. M. (1982). Common phoneme and overall similarity relations among spoken syllables: Their use by children and adults. *Journal of Psycholinguistic Research, 11*(6), 569–598.

Treiman, R., & Cassar, M. (1997). Effects of morphology on children's spelling of final consonant clusters. *Journal of Experimental Child Psychology, 63*, 141–170.

Treiman, R., Cassar, M., & Zukowski, A. (1994). What types of linguistic information do children use in spelling? The case of flaps. *Child Development, 65*(5), 1318–1337.

Treiman, R., & Kessler, B. (2005). Writing systems and spelling development. In M. J. Snowling & C. Hulme (Eds.), *The science of reading: A handbook* (pp. 120–134). Oxford: Blackwell.

Turkeltaub, P. E., Gareau, L., Flowers, D. L., Zeffiro, T. A., & Eden, G. F. (2003). Development of neural mechanisms for reading. *Nature Neuroscience, 6*, 767–773.

Vellutino, F. R., & Scanlon, D. M. (1991). The pre-eminence of phonologically based skills in learning to read. In S. Brady & D. Shanweiler (Eds.), *Phonological processes in literacy: A tribute to Isabelle Liberman*. Hillsdale, NJ: Erlbaum.

Vellutino, F. R., Scanlon, D. M., & Spearing, D. (1995). Semantic and phonological coding in poor and normal readers. *Journal of Experimental Child Psychology, 59*, 76–123.

Wagner, R. K., Torgesen, J. K., Laughan, P., Simmons, K., & Rashotte, C. A. (1993). The development of young readers' phonological processing abilities. *Journal of Educational Psychology, 85*, 1–20.

Windfuhr, K., & Snowling, M. J. (2001). The relationship between paired associate learning and phonological skills in normally developing readers. *Journal of Experimental Child Psychology, 80*, 160–173.

Wolf, M., & Bowers, P. G. (1999). The double-deficit hypothesis for the developmental dyslexias. *Journal of Educational Psychology, 91*(3), 415–438.

Ziegler, J. C., & Goswami, U. (2005). Reading acquisition, developmental dyslexia and skilled reading across languages: A psycholinguistic grain size theory. *Psychological Bulletin, 131*(1), 3–29.

Zoccolotti, P., De Luca, M., Di Pace, E., Judica, A., Orlandi, M., & Spinelli, D. (1999). Markers of developmental surface dyslexia in a language (Italian) with high grapheme–phoneme correspondence. *Applied Psycholinguistics, 20*, 191–216.

CHAPTER TWENTY-ONE

Children's Understanding of Mathematics

Peter Bryant and Terezinha Nuñes

Mathematics poses many interesting and rewarding questions for developmental psychologists. The crux of the psychological problem is the variety of forms that mathematical knowledge takes. Some sophisticated and abstract mathematical concepts require much formal teaching, which puts them outside the experience of most people. Yet, most people rely heavily on mathematics in their everyday life. People have to deal with money, calculate distances, work out times, and think about speeds, and if they do not manage these calculations well their lives will be harder and less predictable as a result.

The sources of mathematical knowledge also vary. Formal teaching is essential for some kinds of knowledge, such as trigonometry, but it is quite likely that, as Piaget (1952, 1953) claimed, children also learn a lot of the underlying logic of mathematics through their informal experiences. People also can acquire mathematical techniques by imitating other people's solutions or by learning informally from them. Lately, too, some psychologists have broached the idea that people are born with an understanding of number and of addition and subtraction.

Numbers, Quantities, and Relations

Mathematics is the study of quantitative relations. Usually these relations can be expressed numerically, and numbers make it possible for people to understand and manipulate relations between quantities in powerful and precise ways.

At school, children's first formal mathematical experiences tend to be about counting and numbers. However, knowing how to count is of little intellectual value to them unless they also grasp how numbers are connected to quantities and quantitative relations. Numbers have no genuine mathematical meaning for children who do not realize that each child can have one book when there are 20 pupils and 20 exercise books in a classroom, and that there would not be enough books to go round if there were 15 books there.

Knowing that a set of 20 items has the same number of items in it as another set of 20 items and that a set of 20 items is more numerous than one of 15 items is relational knowledge. "Cardinality" is the correct term for the first of these relations and "ordinality" for the second. Cardinality means that a set with a particular number of items contains the same number of items as any other set with that number. Ordinality means that numbers come in an ordered series: 3 is a larger number than 2 and 2 than 1, and it follows that 3 is also larger than 1.

The distinctions that we have drawn between quantities, relations, and numbers are not new. Piaget stressed the importance of children learning not just about counting but also about numerical relations, and in particular about cardinal and ordinal number. More recently, Thompson (1993) argued that people must be able to connect numbers, quantities, and relations in order to reason mathematically. Nevertheless, many recent psychological studies of children's mathematical learning have bypassed Piaget's and Thompson's injunctions about quantitative relations. With this caveat in mind, we can now consider the relevant research.

Infants' knowledge of number: does it exist?

Some psychologists (Butterworth, 1999; Dehaene, 1997; Gelman & Gallistel, 1978) suggest that children have the help of a formidable resource, an innate understanding of number, when they start to learn about mathematics. The evidence for this claim comes mainly from experiments with babies.

Most of these were habituation experiments which exploited the fact that babies seem more interested in novel than in familiar stimuli. Starkey and Cooper (1980) used habituation to find out whether 4-month-old babies discriminate different numbers. Their study consisted of two phases, as figure 21.1 demonstrates. In the first, the babies were shown, over series of trials, cards with a certain number of dots on them. In each trial, the baby saw the same number of dots. Some babies were shown "small" numbers, i.e., less than 4; others saw "large" numbers, i.e., 4 or more. During this first phase, the babies' attention to the number displays usually flagged, and the point of the second phase was to measure if their interest revived when the number of dots was changed. In this phase, all the babies were shown cards with a new number of dots on them.

Starkey and Cooper found that, when the new number of dots was introduced, there was a clear jump in the amount of time spent looking at the displays by the babies in the small-number group but not by the large-number group. The babies in the former group clearly recognized the change, and Starkey and Cooper argued that this meant that they are able to discriminate small numbers. These results have been repeated many times. They apply to neonates as well as to older babies (Antell & Keating, 1983), and the same pattern emerged in a study in which the objects in the displays were in constant movement (van Loosbroek & Smitsman, 1990). However, their significance can be questioned.

The main question is whether the experiments really are about number. One team of researchers (Clearfield & Mix, 1999; Mix, Huttenlocher, & Levine, 2002; Mix, Levine, & Huttenlocher, 1997; Mix, Levine, & Huttenlocher, 2002) claims that in all these

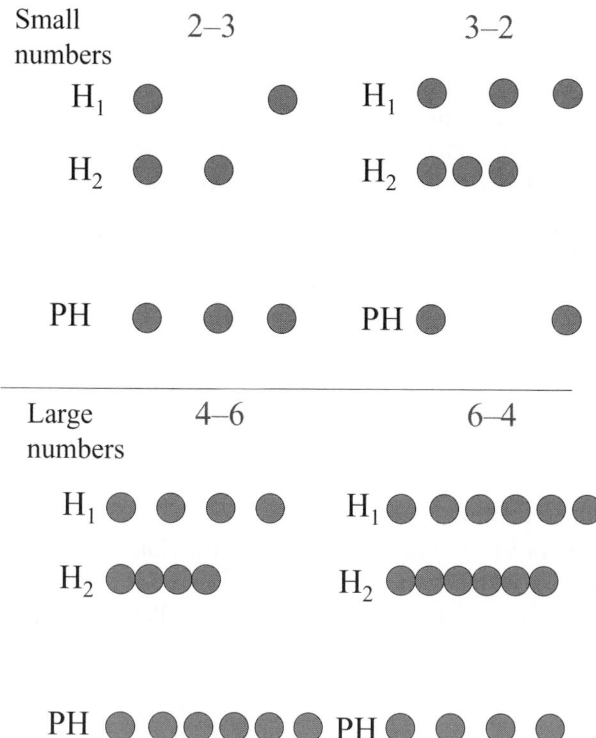

Figure 21.1 The kinds of displays used in Starkey and Cooper's study. H displays were presented in the habituation period of the experiment, and PH displays were presented in the post-habituation period. In the habituation period the babies saw the H_1 display on some trials and the H_2 display on others

studies the babies were making discriminations not of number but of continuous quantities like the total amount of space taken up by the objects or their total contour. Clearfield and Mix (1999) produced the clearest evidence for this alternative hypothesis. They varied both the number of objects and the total amount of the contour of the objects independently and found that the babies responded to a change in the total amount of object contour when the number of objects remained the same in the post-habituation as in the habituation phase. However, they did not respond to a change in number when the total amount of object contour on the stimuli shown to them was the same in both phases of the experiment. Thus, the infant experiments on number may have been about continuous rather than discontinuous numerical quantities.

This is not the only concern. Most infant studies, and all those that we have mentioned so far, do not follow Piaget's and Thompson's requirement that you must study children's grasp of quantitative relations, and in particular of cardinal and ordinal relations, in order to tap their understanding of number. These studies, however, are about the detection of single quantities, not about mathematical relations.

Ordering numbers

An important part of the case that young babies have a powerful "number sense" is the claim by Brannon (2002) that they grasp ordinality. She devised a habituation study in which, on each trial, she showed 11-month-old infants sequences of three cards, each of which depicted a different number of squares. In the habituation phase of the experiment, some babies were repeatedly shown increasing three-card-sequences (e.g. 2, then 4, then 8; and 3, then 6, then 12) and others decreasing sequences (e.g. 16, then 8, then 4). In the second phase, all were shown some decreasing and some increasing sequences.

The infants did discriminate the two kinds of sequence. After seeing several increasing sequences, they were more interested in looking at a decreasing than at yet another increasing sequence, and vice versa. Brannon concluded that infants have some understanding of ordinal number.

This, however, was a weak test of the understanding of ordinality. It probably shows that children of this age are aware to some extent of the relations "more" and "less," but it does not establish that the children were acting on the relation between all three quantities in each sequence. In order to understand ordinality the child must be able to coordinate a set of "more" and "less" relations. This means understanding that B is smaller than A and at the same time larger than C in an A>B>C series. Brannon did not show whether the young children in her study could or could not grasp these two-way relations.

Principles before skills: a theory about an innate sense of number

The significance of children's counting is a hugely controversial issue. Some (Nuñes & Bryant, 1996; Piaget, 1952; Thompson, 1993Nuñes) take the position, which we have already described, that just knowing how to count has very little mathematical importance unless this knowledge is firmly linked to quantitative relations. Others, (Carey, 2004; Gelman & Gallistel, 1978) study children's understanding of the counting system without considering quantitative relations.

Gelman, who was a colleague and co-author in some of Starkey's research with babies, also worked with older children who could speak and were beginning to learn to count. She and Gallistel (1978) started from the position that any viable number system must have five characteristics, which they called "principles." They claimed that an understanding of these universal principles was an innate part of the structure of the human mind.

The first three principles were about "how to count." We can consider first the one-to-one principle which is that one must count all the objects in a set once and once only: each one must be given just one number tag. Another principle is the stable-order principle, which means that we must count in a set order and in the same order each time. The final "how to count" principle is the cardinal principle. In Gelman's terms the cardinal principle is that the last number counted represents the value of the set.

The other two principles were the abstraction principle and the order-irrelevance principle. The first of these states that the number in a set is quite independent of any of the qualities of the members in that set: the rules for counting a heterogeneous set of objects are the same as for counting a homogeneous one. The order-irrelevance principle is that the order in which members of a set are counted makes no difference: you get the same answer counting from the right as from the left.

Gelman and Gallistel set out to find out how well children aged between 2 and 5 years count single sets of objects, varying in number from 2 to 19. They found that the children seemed to respect the five principles with small number sets, although they often failed to do so with larger sets. They reasoned that the children did understand counting principles since they consistently respected them with the smaller sets. Their mistakes with the larger sets were due not to a failure in understanding, but to difficulties in carrying out procedures in difficult circumstances. One-to-one counting is hard, for example, with large sets because one is more likely to forget which items have already been counted in a large set. So Gelman and Gallistel's hypothesis is that children start with the right principles, but only gradually acquire the skills to apply them effectively.

In other studies Gelman and her colleagues (Gelman & Meck, 1983; Gelman, Meck, & Merkin, 1986) asked preschool children to make judgments about a puppet counting. The puppet occasionally violated the "how to count" principles, and the aim was to see whether children spot these violations. The results supported Gelman's contention that preschool children do understand these principles.

This research demonstrated that young children have some knowledge about how to count, but this does not mean that they know about number. The gap in the research is that it ignores relations between sets. Gelman and Gallistel's criterion for the cardinal principle (the last number counted) is adequate for the counting of one set of objects, but cardinality, being the principle that any set of a particular number is the same in quantity as any other set with that same number, is about relations between sets.

The scheme also omits ordinal relations. The nearest that the data get to these is in the use of the stable-order principle – the use of count words in the same order on different occasions. This is an essential feature of any counting system, but it is not necessarily relevant to the understanding that successive numbers represent an ascending quantitative scale.

Carey's hypothesis about individuation

Susan Carey's (2004) central claim is that children have to learn about number. Carey's definition of cardinality seems much the same as Gelman's, but she has different ideas about how children acquire this principle.

Carey claims that initially in the first 3 years of life young children represent number in at least two different ways (LeCorre & Carey, 2007). First, she claims that infants have access to an inexact but powerful "analog" system, which represents the number of items in a display by the size of its signal: the greater the number, the bigger is the signal. The system allows infants, as well as older children and adults, to make approximate judgments about numerical quantities, in exactly the way that they judge other continua, such as distance, loudness, and brightness. The evidence for this analog system being an innate one comes largely from studies of infants (McCrink & Wynn, 2004; Xu & Spelke, 2000) and to a certain extent of animals too. However, although Carey may be right that this system plays a part in people's informal experiences of quantity, she does not give it a role in children's learning of mathematics at school.

Carey argues that another system, which she called "parallel individuation," allows children to learn about the counting system. The system makes it possible for infants to recognize and represent very small numbers exactly (not approximately like the analog system). The system only operates for sets of 1, 2, and 3 objects and, even within this restricted scope, there are sharp developmental changes in the first 3 years of life.

Initially the system allows very young children to recognize sets of 1 as having a distinct quantity, though they do not know at first that the word "one" applies to this quantity. Later on the child is able "to individuate" – in other words to discriminate and recognize – sets of 1 and 2 objects. Later still, by the age of 3 to 4 years, most children have individuated sets of 1, 2, and 3 objects as distinct quantities. They start as "one-knowers" and become "two-knowers" and then "three-knowers."

At roughly the same time, these children also learn number words and manage to associate the right count words ("one," "two," and "three") with the right quantities. The association between parallel individuation and the count list eventually leads to what Carey (2004) calls "bootstrapping." With the help of the constant order of number words in the count list, the children begin to learn about the ordinal properties of numbers: 2 always comes after 1 in the count list and is always more numerous than 1, and 3 is more numerous than 2 and always follows 2. They eventually infer that the number words represent a continuum of distinct quantities that stretches beyond "three." Carey calls this new understanding "enriched parallel individuation" (Carey, 2004, p. 65).

To test these claims she used the "Give a number" task. The experimenter asks the child to give her a certain number of objects: "Could you take two elephants out of the bowl and place them on the table?" Carey showed that different 3-, 4-, and 5-year-old children can be classified as "one-," "two-," or "three-knowers," or as "counting-principle-knowers." The one-knowers do well when asked to provide one object but not when asked the other numbers, while the two- and three-knowers can respectively provide up to two and three objects successfully. "Counting-principle-knowers" count quantities above three or four as well.

Carey's research demonstrates interesting developmental changes in counting, but it does not include a measure of children's understanding of cardinality in full. The criterion that the child should realize that the last number that he or she counted is the number of the set is, as we explained before, incomplete.

Carey's theory has also been criticized for the role that it gives to induction or analogy in the use of the "next" principle and to language. Rips, Asmuth, and Bloomfield (2006, 2008) argue that the bootstrapping hypothesis presupposes the knowledge of number that it attempts to explain. In order to apply the "next number" principle, children would have to know already that 1 is a set included in 2, 2 in 3, and 3 in 4. If they know this already, then they do not need to use the "next number" principle to infer the meanings of number words.

Piaget's hypothesis about logic and number

Piaget's (1952) theory still provides a more coherent explanation than any other of children's solutions to mathematical problems. It is a theory of learning, and the most exciting part of the theory is about the steps that children take in order to conquer the complexities of mathematics.

For Piaget, young children's counting was a clear instance of children using words without understanding what they mean. They learn to count objects and actions, and yet for several years they do not have the slightest idea of the meaning of number words.

In order to grasp these meanings, Piaget argued, children must understand the cardinal and the ordinal properties of number. He based his striking conclusion that at first children count without understanding counting on evidence from his well-known conservation, transitivity, and seriation experiments. Conservation experiments convinced him that children do not understand one-to-one correspondence in the preschool years and therefore have no grasp of cardinality. Seriation and transitivity experiments provided the basis for Piaget's claim that children cannot deal with a series of relations: they are perfectly capable of understanding that A is more than B at one time and at another that B is more than C, but they cannot coordinate these two pieces of information to reach the conclusion that A is more than C, according to Piaget, and this means that they are unable to understand the number sequence as a sequence of ascending magnitude.

Of these two claims, the first (failure in cardinality) is easier to assess than the second (failure in ordinality), at any rate as far as children's counting is concerned, because Piaget's work on seriation and transitivity was done with continuous quantities and the children did not have to count to solve these problems. In contrast, some conservation studies, and particularly those done by Piaget's colleague Pierre Greco, are directly concerned with children's use and understanding of number words.

Greco (1962) gave children of 4 to 8 years three different versions of the conservation of number task. One was the traditional conservation problem, in which children saw two identical-looking sets, judged correctly that the two sets were equal, then saw the appearance of one of the sets being altered, and were asked once again to compare the quantity of the two sets. The second task took roughly the same form except that after the transformation the children were required to count one of the sets and were then asked to infer the number of the second set. In the third task, the children were required to count both sets after the transformation and then were asked whether they were equal in quantity.

Two results are important here. Most children younger than 6 years failed all three tasks: the point to grasp about these children is that in the third task they counted both sets in the final part of the task, arrived at the same number, and yet still said that the more spread-out of the two sets had more objects in it than the other one did. They judged that one set with "eight" objects in it was more numerous than another set, also with "eight" objects, and that meant, according to Piaget and to Greco, that they really could not know what the word "eight" means.

The second important result was that slightly older children tended to get the first task (the traditional conservation problem) wrong and yet were right in the second task in which they counted one set and then were asked to infer the number of objects in the second set. These children therefore judged that spreading out a set of objects alters its quantity (their mistaken judgment in the traditional task) but not its number in the sense of the number one would reach if one were to count the set.

Piaget and Greco's explanation of these results took the form of a distinction between *quantité* and *quotité*. *Quotité* describes the understanding of the children who realize that two sets of objects have the same number, in the sense that counting each one leads to the same number word, and yet think that there are more objects in the more spread-out set. These children grasped the fact that the number words (*quotité*) stayed the same despite the perceptual transformation of one of the sets, and yet did not realize that the numerosity (*quantité*) was also quite unchanged by this irrelevant, perceptual change.

Virtually all the other evidence on children making number comparisons supports the idea that preschool children do not yet have a well-developed understanding of number. There is, for example, some striking evidence that young children who count quite proficiently still do not know how to use numbers to compare two different sets. Both Michie (1984) and Saxe (1979) found a marked reluctance in young children, whom they asked to compare two sets of objects quantitatively, to count the two sets. They could have counted them and it would have been the right thing to do, but they did not.

Children's reluctance to use number as a comparative measure was confirmed in a striking experiment by Sophian (1988) who asked 3- and 4-year-old children to judge whether a puppet who counted was doing the right thing. The puppet was given two sets of objects and was told in some trials to compare the two sets and in others to find out how many objects there were in front of it altogether. In the first kind of trial the right thing to do was to count the two sets separately while in the second it was to count them together. Sometimes the puppet got it right but at other times not.

The younger children did particularly badly (below chance) in the trials in which the puppet was asked to compare two different sets. They clearly had no idea that one must count two rows separately in order to compare them, and this suggests that they had not yet grasped the cardinal properties of the numbers that they were counting.

Similar difficulties can even be found in tasks where children have to count single quantities. Several "Give a number" studies (Frye, Braisby, Lowe, Maroudas, & Nicholls, 1989; Wynn, 1990) have shown that children often fail to count and simply grab a handful of objects when asked to give someone a certain number of objects. Again they do not seem to understand the significance of counting.

Another look at one-to-one correspondence

Piaget argued that young children do not understand one-to-one correspondence. He based this conclusion on the results of his conservation studies. The main purpose of the conservation experiments was to test children's understanding of the invariance of quantity, a question about which there has been a great deal of controversy (Donaldson, 1978, 1982; Light, Buckingham, & Robbins, 1979; McGarrigle & Donaldson, 1974). Nevertheless conservation experiments also produced evidence to support Piaget's claim about one-to-one correspondence, at any rate when the correspondences are spatially defined.

When two sets of objects are put side-by-side, it is quite easy to see whether each item has its pair in the other set. Of course, these spatial comparisons are much easier with some spatial arrangements than with others. It is easier to compare two ranks of soldiers in this way than two football teams in action on a football ground. Yet 6-year-old children seem unable to use one-to-one correspondence even with displays where it should be easy to do so. Piaget, for example, showed children a row of objects and asked them to lay out another row with the same number. The younger children plainly did not pair the items and usually equated the rows in terms of their length rather than their number. Piaget and Inhelder (1966) and also Cowan and Daniels (1989) have shown that many children fail to use one-to-one correspondence to compare the number of items in two straight rows of counters laid side by side, even when the individual counters in each set are themselves connected by straight lines.

It would be easy to decide from results such as these that young children have no understanding at all of one-to-one correspondence, but there is at least one good reason for not rushing to this negative conclusion. It is that children often share, and sharing is an activity that seems to depend on one-to-one correspondence. Three separate studies (Desforges & Desforges, 1980; Frydman & Bryant, 1988; Miller, 1984) showed that many children as young as 4 years share numbers of things equally between two or more recipients rather successfully, and usually do so on a repetitive "one for A, one for B" basis. This looks like a temporal form of one-to-one correspondence.

If that is so, we have to ask the same question that we asked with counting. Children often count without understanding counting. Perhaps, they also share without understanding sharing. They may know that sharing in a one-to-one way is the right thing to do in certain circumstances, and yet have no clear idea why. Frydman and Bryant (1988) tried to find out more about children's understanding of sharing with a task in which children who share without understanding one-to-one correspondence would behave in one way, and children who understand the basis of one-to-one sharing would respond quite differently. We gave the children "chocolates" which were either single or double chocolates: in fact these were plastic Unifix bricks, all of the same color, which could be stuck together. We asked the children to share the chocolates out to two recipients, so that each recipient ended up with the same total amount, as figure 21.2 demonstrates. We also told the children that one of the recipients only accepted doubles and the other only singles. So the child's problem was to work out that for every double that she gave one recipient, she now had to give two singles to the other one. We reasoned that a child who had shared on a one-to-one basis in a rote fashion would not be able to make this adjustment, whereas a child who understood the basis for one-to-one sharing would see the reason for changing to a pattern of one (double) for A, two (singles) for B.

This study produced a sharp developmental difference. Most 4-year-old children did not make the adjustment, and typically ended up giving the recipient who accepted doubles twice as many chocolates in all as the recipient who accepted singles. These children continued sharing in a one-to-one manner, which meant that for every single that they gave one recipient they handed out a double to the other. In contrast most of the 5-year-olds did manage to make the necessary adjustment. These children usually gave a double to one recipient and then immediately two singles to the other, and so on. The reason for the difference between the two age groups is unclear to us, but at the very least the study establishes that 5-year-old children have a clear and flexible understanding of the mathematical basis of one-to-one sharing. They know how it works.

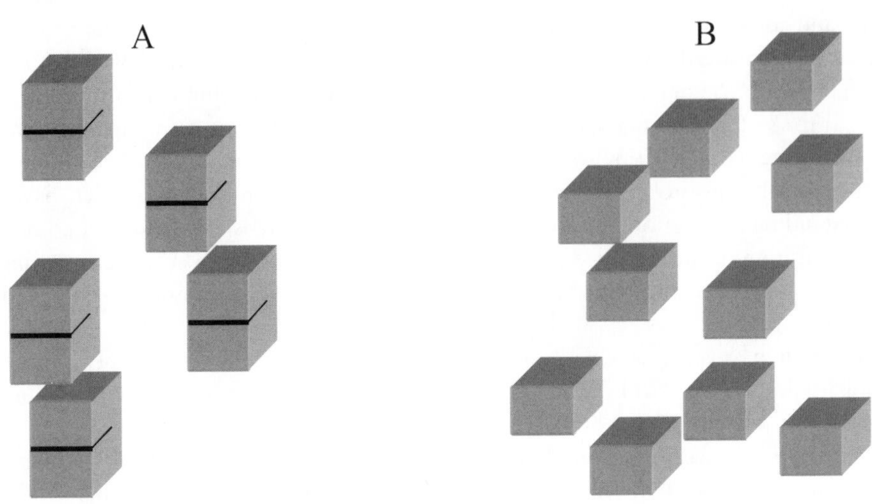
Sharing doubles and singles
A
B
"Give doubles to A and singles to B, but make sure that A and B have the same amount."

Figure 21.2 The doubles and singles condition in Frydman and Bryant's (1988) experiment

The 4-year-olds certainly hit a barrier in our new version of the sharing task, but we still had no idea how formidable that barrier was for them. In a later study we devised a new version of the singles/doubles task in which we introduced bricks of different colors. This is illustrated in figure 21.3.

Our aim was to use color cues to emphasize one-to-one correspondence. In this new task each double consisted of a yellow and a blue brick joined together, and half the singles were blue and half yellow. This was the only change, and yet it had a dramatic effect. Nearly all the 4-year-old children solved the problem, and they did so because they could now see how to use one-to-one correspondence to solve the problem. The typical pattern of sharing was to give a double (consisting of course of one yellow and one blue brick) to one recipient and then to give a yellow and a blue single to the other one. They adapted the one-to-one strategy successfully when the one-to-one cues were emphasized. They also learned a great deal from this experience, because when later on we gave the same children the single/doubles task with bricks of one color only (as in the original experiment) these children did extremely well. They had surmounted the barrier that we identified in the first study, and we conclude from this that even four-year-old children have a basic understanding of the reason why one-to-one sharing leads to equal quantities. It follows that they do have a respectable grasp of temporal

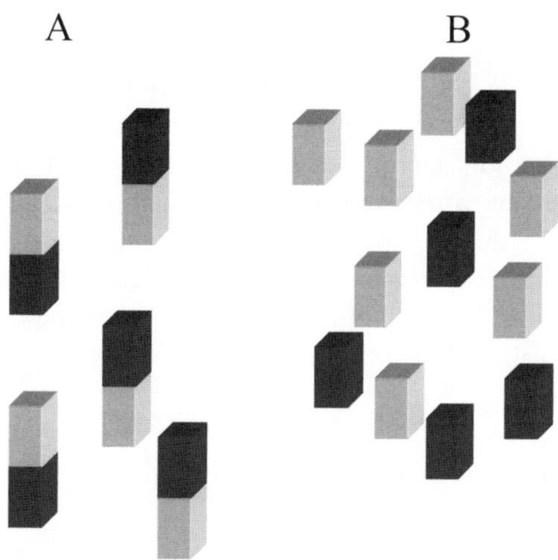
Intervention: sharing singles and doubles
Experimental group's task
A
B
"Give singles to A and doubles to B, but make sure that A and B have the same amount."

Figure 21.3 The material given to the experimental group in the intervention experiment on sharing singles and doubles

one-to-one correspondence and therefore a basis for understanding the cardinal properties of number.

Do they extend this understanding to number words? We looked at this question in another study. In this we took a group of 4-year-old children who could share quite well, and we asked them to share out some "sweets" (again Unifix bricks) between two recipients. When this was done, we counted out aloud the number of sweets that the children had given to one recipient, and then asked them how many had been given to the other recipient. None of the children straightaway made the correct inference that the other recipient had the same number of sweets even though they had meticulously shared the sweets out on a one-to-one basis: instead all of them tried to count the second lot of sweets. We stopped them doing so, and asked the question again. Even then slightly less than half the children made the correct inference about the second recipient's sweets.

Thus, some, though not all, 4-year-old children fail to extend their considerable understanding of sharing to counting. We conclude from this that young children do grasp the cardinality of number in sharing and yet do not at first apply this understanding to number words. Here, it could be said, is an example of *quantité* without *quotité*. The children understand temporal one-to-one correspondence, but do not apply this knowledge to number words.

Conclusions about the beginnings of the understanding of number

Which is the right theory? The answer depends on your criteria for mathematical knowledge. In our view, the criterion is whether children understand that numbers represent quantities and quantitative relations. If that is so, Piaget's approach is undoubtedly the winner.

The case for effective innate structures especially tuned to mathematical rules is not strong. Tasks, in which young children have to compare quantities, show genuine gaps in the young children's understanding of basic and essential number concepts. They do not see counting as a way to measure the relative quantities of two different sets, and they are happy to assert that two sets with the same number are different in quantity. Even when they know that two sets are equal in quantity and they also know the number of items in one set, some young children often fail to infer the number of items in the uncounted set. They plainly have a lot to learn.

Learning About Arithmetical Operations

Now we must turn to the operations that children perform on numbers. There are four of these, but we have good grounds for dividing them into two broad categories and two forms of reasoning, additive and multiplicative reasoning. Additive reasoning includes addition and subtraction, which are inverse operations. Multiplicative reasoning includes multiplication and division, which are also the inverse of each other.

Adding and subtracting

Just how early children begin to reason additively is a matter of strong contention. In 1992, Wynn, an American psychologist, made the striking claim that babies as young as 6 months add and subtract, and thereby started a controversy which still rages today (see also Wynn, 1998).

Wynn argued that if babies can add and subtract they should be surprised and their attention should be caught by additions and subtractions that apparently end in the wrong result. She therefore enacted additions and subtractions, which sometimes led to the correct and sometimes to the incorrect outcome. The addition was always 1 + 1, which she enacted by putting a Mickey Mouse on a platform in front of the child, then raising a screen between this toy and the child so that the toy was now out of sight, and finally ostentatiously placing another Mickey Mouse behind the screen, so that there were now two of these toys but both hidden from the child. At this point she lowered the screen, and the child could see how many Mickey Mouses there were on the platform. On half the trials two toys were there, but on the other half, by trickery, only one toy was left.

The subtraction trials (2 – 1) took the same form. Wynn started these by showing the child two Mickey Mouses on the platform and continued by blocking the child's view of these with the screen: then, in full view of the child, she put her hand behind the screen and removed one of the two toys. Finally, the screen was lowered, revealing one Mickey Mouse on some trials, and on other trials, again by artifice, two of them.

Wynn argued that any baby who can add 1 to 1, or subtract 1 from 2 should be surprised, and should look longer, at the two incorrect outcomes. Her results supported this idea. The babies looked longer at the wrong than at the right outcomes, and Wynn concluded that they had added and subtracted.

This study did not exclude an alternative explanation. The incorrect outcome was always the same as the starting point in each problem (1 in the addition and 2 in the subtraction problems). Perhaps the babies had expected a change – any change – as a result of the addition or subtraction, and were simply surprised to see the status quo.

To rule out this alternative, Wynn did another study, this time just with the 1 + 1 addition. Again she compared the babies' looking time to correct and incorrect outcomes, but this time the incorrect outcome was 3. Thus both outcomes, correct and incorrect, were different from the starting point. Again the babies looked longer at the incorrect outcome (1 + 1 = 3) than at the correct one. Wynn concluded that babies reason additively.

There are reasons for doubting this striking conclusion. One is that Wynn apparently did not carry out the same further test with subtraction. She could, for example, have given babies trials in which 3 – 1 led to the incorrect outcome of 1, but she did not. So, one cannot be sure that babies have any understanding of subtraction (Bryant, 1992). Another problem is that the babies' greater interest in the 1 + 1 = 3 than in the 1 + 1 = 2 outcome could simply be due to them being more interested in the larger number, or just taking more time to process 3 than 2 objects. So, the apparently crucial result of the second study could be spurious, and again the acid test would be to introduce the 3 – 1 = 1 outcome.

This was the starting point for an experiment by Wakeley, Rivera, and Langer (2000a, 2000b) that introduced the 3 – 1 = 1 and 3 – 1 = 2 events, and also repeated all four conditions of Wynn's first study. These experimenters found no significant difference in looking time at the 3 – 1 = 1 and the 3 – 1 = 2 outcomes, and also failed to repeat the differences in the attention that babies spent on trials with correct and trials with incorrect outcomes that Wynn reported in her first study. This double failure was a serious blow for Wynn's hypothesis. It is hard at the moment for an impartial observer to conclude anything much, except that there is a need for extreme caution. Babies may add and subtract, but, then again, they may not.

Preschool children: adding, counting all, counting on

Children are able to perform simple additions and subtractions with concrete objects long before they go to school (Hughes, 1981, 1986), and probably by the age of 3 years or so (Huttenlocher, Levine, & Jordan, 1994). There are some interesting details here, in particular Hughes' observation of a large discrepancy between children's success in additions and subtractions with concrete objects (2 + 2 toys), even imagined objects, and with abstract numbers (just 2 + 2). As with sharing, so too with adding: children have great difficulty in translating a basic, effective mathematical procedure into the conventional counting system.

Again Piaget (1952; Piaget & Inhelder, 1974) provided the most convincing conceptual framework for studying children's additive reasoning. He argued that children do not understand the nature of additive reasoning until they have grasped the inverse relations between adding and subtracting. It is not enough, he claimed, for them to know, or to be able to work out, that 4 + 3 = 7 and that 7 – 4 = 3. They must also understand why each of these two sums automatically follows from the other. They must realize how one operation cancels out the other.

He went further, for he also claimed that children's understanding of number itself depends on this knowledge. Here, he invoked the notion of the additive composition of number, which is an important, but underrated, idea in the study of children's mathematics. It means that numbers consist, or are made up, of other numbers. So 7 is made up of 4 and 3 or 5 and 2, and it follows that if you subtract 3 from 7 you will be left with 4. Thus Piaget (1952, 2001) argued that children's understanding of the inverse relations between adding and subtracting will revolutionize their thinking about the nature of number itself.

It is strange that Piaget and his colleagues did very little empirical research on this stimulating idea, but others have. The main evidence about it comes from three rather different types of experiment: one is the study of children's use of counting to solve simple addition problems, another is research on word problems, and the final one involves direct experiments on the study of inversion.

Counting and adding. Most adults use their well-rehearsed knowledge of simple facts to solve addition and subtraction problems. We all know that 4 + 3 = 7 and we can use this knowledge without having to add three units to four. It takes some time before young children have this sort of knowledge at their fingertips, and so they actually have to do the addition. The way that they do so changes as they grow older and the change is directly relevant to the question of the additive composition of number.

In the relevant task children are first given a set of objects and are told its number; then another set is added and again the children are told its number. The question that they are asked is: How many there are altogether? The sharp developmental difference in children's reaction to this question (Fuson, 1988) is simple to tell. Thus, if the children are dealing with a set of 4 and a set of 3, the younger ones will count one set (1-2-3-4) and then the other (5-6-7) whereas the older children will, more economically, start where the first set leaves off (5-6-7).

The success of the older children in finding an economic, and usually quite untaught, strategy suggests that they have begun to realize that the total number is made up of different component numbers, and that the difference between one component (4) and the total is the other component (3).

Word problems: missing addends and subtrahends. Word problems are sums that are couched in fictional events. Some time ago, Vergnaud (1982), a French psychologist, showed that children who easily solve a direct addition word problem (Tom had 5 apples, and Bill gave him 3 more. How many does he have now?) are nevertheless in great difficulty when they face the same sum as a "missing subtrahend" problem (Bob had some apples: Bill ate 4 of them. There were 3 apples left. How many did Bob have to start off with?). Why is one so much more difficult than the other?

The main difficulty is in transforming a story that is about subtraction (Bob took and ate some apples) into an addition problem. Nuñes and Bryant (1996) showed this by giving children calculators to help them solve the problem: most children who failed to find the right solution actually performed the wrong operation (addition when it should have been subtraction and vice versa) on the calculator.

Children who make this mistake do so because they apparently cannot move quickly from information about addition to subtracting, and vice versa. To solve the missing subtrahend problem that I have just described, you must know that if a – b = c, then c + b = a: you must understand inversion.

Experiments on inversion. 254 + 178 – 178 is an easy sum because one can solve it by cancelling the addition with the subtraction. However, children who do not grasp the inverse relation between adding and subtracting should not find it easy or easier than any other similar additive problem. Yet there is evidence that some, though not all, children between the ages of 5 and 8 years do find a + b – b problems easier than standard adding and subtracting problems, and therefore seem to be taking advantage of inversion (Bisanz & Lefevre, 1992; Bryant, Christie, & Rendu, 1999; Stern, 1993).

One potential problem with this positive conclusion is that children could solve the inversion problems just on the basis of identity rather than in a quantitative sense. If you get a shirt muddy and then the mud is washed off, the shirt is as clean as before. One physical change is cancelled out by the other, but to work this out is not to make a quantitative judgment.

However, Bryant et al. (1999) produced evidence that some young children do make genuinely quantitative judgments about inversion problems. Our study is illustrated in figure 21.4. We gave children a + b – b and a – b + b as well as control (a + a – b and a – b + a) problems with concrete material under two conditions. In one (identity) the same bricks were added and then taken away, or taken away and then added. In the other (non-identity) the same amount of bricks was added and then subtracted or vice versa in the inversion problems, but they were different bricks. Bricks were added to one end of the tower and subtracted from the other. Thus the use of inversion here would have nothing to do with identity: it had to be quantitative. We found that even many 5-year-old children were able to take advantage of inversion in the non-identity condition, and therefore were making a genuinely quantitative judgment about inversion.

These last results do not fit well with Piaget's idea that young children fail to grasp the inversion principle, and yet studies of counting all and counting on and of missing addend/subtrahend problems certainly support that idea. Can these two sets of results be reconciled?

The solution, it seems to us, is to make a distinction between understanding a principle and using it to solve problems. It looks as though even 5-year-old children do have some understanding, in a quantitative sense, of the way in which an addition cancels out a subtraction, but do not at first use this knowledge to grasp the additive composition of number. The understanding of inversion is, as Piaget pointed out, absolutely necessary

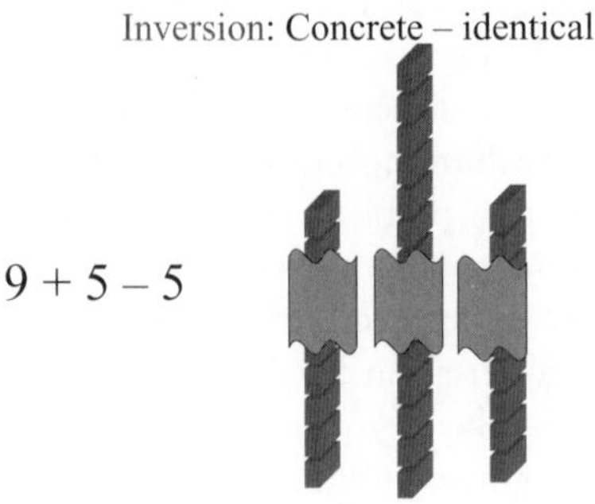

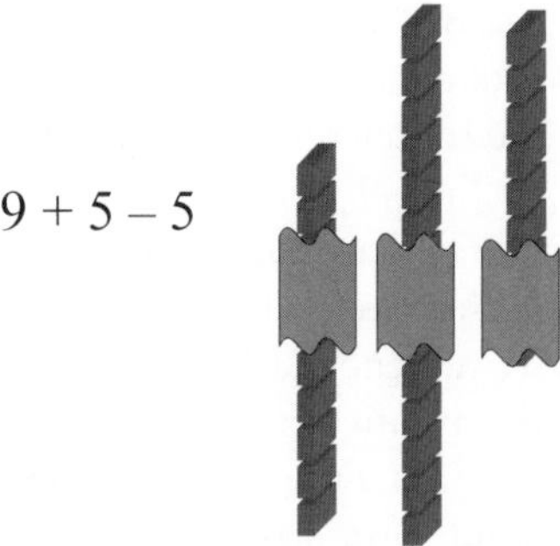

Figure 21.4 The two kinds of inversion task with concrete material. In the identical task the same items are added and subtracted to the tower. In the different task different items are added and subtracted. The tower is partially covered by a cloth to prevent the children solving the problem by counting

for grasping additive composition, but it seems that it is not immediately sufficient. It takes time for children to work out the implications of inversion.

Since the inversion principle is so important, it is worth considering whether children's grasp of it can be strengthened. Siegler and Stern (1998), gave 8-year-old children inversion problems in eight successive sessions in order to see whether practice improves children's use of the inversion principle. The children were also exposed to other traditional scholastic problems (e.g., a + b − c) for which the inversion principle was not appropriate for solution. The children, who were given lots of inversion problems in the first seven sessions, tended to get better at solving these problems over these sessions, but in the final session in which they were given control as well as inversion problems they often, quite inappropriately, overgeneralized the inversion strategy to the control sums: they would give a as the answer in a + b + b control problems as well as in inverse a + b − b problems. Their relatively good performance with the inversion problems in the previous sessions, therefore, was probably not the result of an increasing understanding of inversion. They learned some lower-level, inadequate strategy, such as "If the first number (a) is followed by another number (b) which is then repeated, the answer must be a."

Another study with 8-year-olds (Nuñes, Bryant, Hallett, Bell, & Evans, 2009) was more successful. It compared teaching children about inversion with concrete materials with teaching them in the context of verbally presented sums. Both groups were given inversion problems in the pre- and post-test. We also included tasks, called "complement tasks" in the pre- and post-tests in this study. In this kind of task children are first shown the results of a simple inversion problem and then immediately asked the complementary question, c – a = ? (Baroody, Ginsburg, & Waxman, 1983; Baroody & Tiilikainen, 2003; Putnam, de Bettencourt, & Leinhardt, 1990; Resnick, 1983). Both taught groups made more progress from the pre-test to the post-test in solving inversion problems than an untaught control group. The group taught with concrete material made more progress than the control group in the transfer problems. We conclude that it is quite easy to improve children's understanding of inversion, particularly by working with concrete materials.

Additive composition and the decimal system

It is easy to see that an understanding of the decimal system must be heavily dependent on a good understanding of the additive composition of number. This link is essential, because the whole system depends on our knowing that 12 is composed of 10 and 2, and that 53 is composed of five 10s and a 3. So, it is not surprising given the results that we have already presented that 5- and 6-year-old children often do have difficulty in constructing numbers by combining 10s and units.

One task that shows this difficulty is the Shop Task, described in Nuñes and Bryant (1996). Children are given money by the experimenters and are charged for items that they want to buy in a shop set-up. In some trials, they can pay in one denomination only – just in pence or just in 10p coins. In others, they must mix denominations – 10ps and pence to reach the right price. These mixed trials are the hardest for 5- and 6-year-old children. It is possible that their difficulty in the mixed denomination trials is really a difficulty in additive composition of number. They do not see clearly enough that the number 19 can be decomposed into a 10 and a 9.

There is another explanation, which is that their difficulty with the decimal system is a linguistic one. Words like "eleven" and "thirteen" are not transparent: they do not make it explicitly clear that they stand for 10 + 1 and 10 + 3. *Quatre-vingt-dix*, the French term for 90, is hardly better, and German children have to contend with numbers between 20 and 99 that start with the larger unit when written, but with the smaller unit when spoken.

The evidence that these linguistic obscurities might be a serious obstacle comes from a series of studies that show that children in Asian countries are better at composing quantities by combining 10s and units than children from European countries (Miura, Kim, Chang, & Okamoto, 1988; Miura et al., 1994). In Chinese and Japanese (the Asian countries represented in these studies) the teen and decade words are more transparent than in European languages. They do not have words like "eleven," "twelve," "thirteen": they say the equivalent of "ten-one," "ten-two," "ten-three."

However, the Asian superiority may not be due to linguistic differences (Towse & Saxton, 1997). There is plenty of evidence that children from the countries represented in these studies do better in mathematics generally than children from the West (Stevenson et al., 1990). Thus, they may understand the additive composition of number well before their Western peers. This, and not the linguistic variable, could be the reason for the differences between Asian and Western children in the effective use of the decimal system.

Multiplicative reasoning

Multiplication and proportions. If you add 5 to 17 or to 23 or to 41, the ensuing change is the same with each addition: in each case there is an increase of 5. But if you multiply 17, 23 and 41 by 5 the change depends not just on the size of the multiplier but also on the size of the multiplicand: the change will be greater when 42 is multiplied by 5 than when 17 is multiplied by 5. Multiplicative problems require a kind of double-entry thinking, and there is no doubt that this causes even quite old children a great deal of difficulty. Inhelder and Piaget (1958) certainly showed this in a series of problems in which two variables covary multiplicatively. Their tasks were about the understanding of proportions, mostly in scientific demonstrations, such as tests of children's understanding of equilibrium and of probability. It could be argued that the context of these problems was unfamiliar and off-putting, but the same difficulties have been documented in tasks that use mundane everyday material.

Karplus, Pulos and Stage (1983), for example, gave 12- and 14-year-old children a task in which there were two characters, Mr Tall and Mr Short. The first measured 6 buttons in height and the second 4 buttons. Having shown the children this, the experimenters then measured Mr Short's height with paperclips, and showed that he was 6 paperclips high. The children then had to work out Mr Tall's height in paperclips. Karplus and his colleagues found some stubborn difficulties among their teenage participants, many of whom made the additive error: they argued that Mr Tall was 8 paperclips high. Presumably, these children assumed that because there was a difference of 2 buttons, there would also be a difference of 2 paperclips.

These errors suggest that proportional reasoning comes late to most children, but it is not as simple as that. There are often different ways to solve the same proportional problems, and there is evidence that some of them come more easily to children than others. Piaget (1952) himself demonstrated that 5- to 6-year-old children can solve proportional problems on the basis of one-to-many correspondence: for example he showed that they could work out how many flowers could go in a certain number of vases when each vase took two flowers. One-to-many correspondences are in effect ratios, and the intriguing possibility here is that children first solve proportional problems on the basis of ratios and only later are able to understand and work out functions. This has to be the subject of future research, but there is already some evidence, though mainly so far with adults, that it is easier for people to use ratios than to use functions to solve proportional problems (see Nuñes, Schliemann, & Carraher, 1993, for a discussion of the distinction between scalar and functional solutions to such problems).

Division. We now must consider whether children's understanding of division can be analyzed in the same way. In fact, there are relatively few studies of children and division, but the data that we have suggest that sharing is a starting point for understanding division. Children share at quite a young age which means that, in practical terms, they divide, because that is what sharing equal portions to different recipients amounts to. However, there is a crucial difference in the intellectual demands made by sharing and by division. When sharing, one only has to be sure that everyone receives an equal portion. How much that portion (the quotient) is and how it is affected by the number of recipients (the divisor) is not essential information. One can share without knowing anything about either the quotient or the divisor.

The relation between divisor and quotient is an inverse one: the more recipients there are the smaller is the portion that each recipient gets. We (Correa, Nuñes, & Bryant, 1998) have shown that young children who share perfectly well are nevertheless very unclear about this inverse relation. We tested this understanding by showing each child two groups of toy rabbits, as figure 21.5 shows, and explaining that we were going to share out a certain quantity of sets – always the same quantity for each group – among the rabbits in the two groups. Then we asked the children whether the individual rabbits in one group had been given the same amount as the rabbits in the other group.

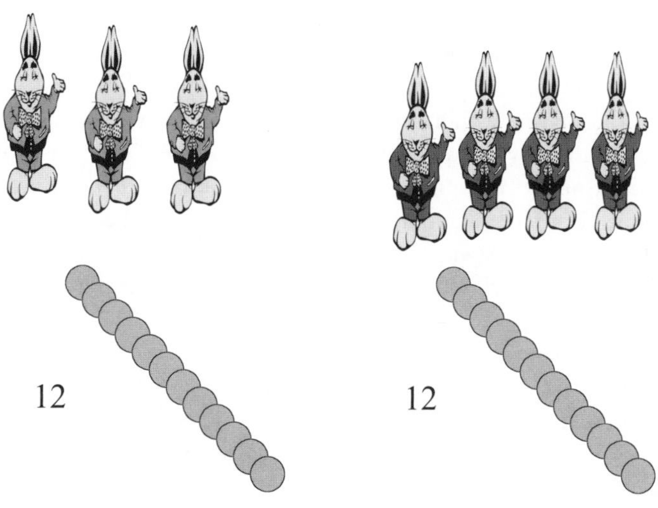

"Will each rabbit in A get the same as each one in B, or will the rabbits in one group get more than those in the other?"

Figure 21.5 The different condition in Correa, Nunes and Bryant's (1998) division task. The same quantity is shared out among the two groups, but one group is less numerous than the other

On some trials the number of rabbits in the two groups was the same, which meant that the portions shared out were the same for both groups. In other trials, there were more rabbits in one group than in the other. We wanted to discover whether children would understand that the rabbits in the larger group would get a smaller portion than those in the smaller group – the inverse divisor–quotient relationship.

Most children in the 5-year group and many in the 6- and 7-year groups seemed unaware of this relation. They all did well when the size of the two groups of rabbits was the same, but rather badly when it was different. In this more difficult condition the younger children tended still to say that the rabbits in each group would get the same amounts. They did not understand that the size of the divisor makes a difference. In contrast, when the older children erred in this condition, they tended to say that the rabbits in the larger group would each get more than the rabbits in the smaller group: so these children realized that the divisor made a difference, but still had not grasped the inverse relationship.

This developmental pattern is robust. It was repeated in several experiments by Correa (1994), and by Sophian, Garyantes, and Chang (1997). The reason for it, we argue, is that the origins of children's understanding of division lies in their experience of sharing, and that while sharing leads them to grasp some aspects of division, it does not in any way depend on knowledge about the inverse divisor–quotient relationship.

This argument is bolstered by some further research by Squire and Bryant, (2002, 2003) who looked at children's reactions to concrete representations of division. There are two ways in which you can represent a division in concrete terms. One is to group the object by the divisor. If 15 sweets, say, have to be divided among 5 rabbits, grouping by the divisor would mean forming 5 sets of sweets – one for each rabbit. The other is to group by the quotient: in this case, we would form 3 groups of 5 sweets, which would mean that there is a sweet for each rabbit in each of the groups. In mathematical terms, both representations of this 15/3 division are equally valid, but the first, grouping by the divisor, is what happens when we share. If children base their ideas of division on sharing they should find this concrete representation the more comprehensible one.

In a series of experiments, illustrated in figure 21.6, with children ranging from 5 to 7 years in age, we have shown that the grouping by divisor condition is, indeed, far the easier of the two. This pattern of results is highly consistent. It occurs over several different kinds of spatial representation, and is impervious to variations in the relative size of the divisor and quotient. It suggests that children take some time to enlarge on the limited framework of sharing when they are learning about division.

Conclusions

This mention of teaching takes us back to the questions that we started with. Where does children's mathematical knowledge come from? How do they find out about quantities, numbers and relations? The research reviewed in this chapter suggests that there are three bases to children's mathematical knowledge.

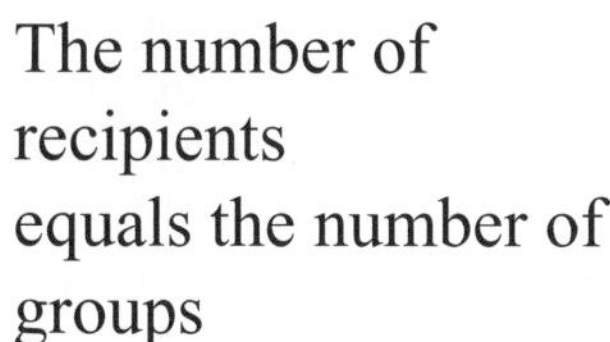
The number of
recipients
equals the number of
groups

The number of
recipients
equals the number of
items in each group

Figure 21.6 An example of the two conditions in the Squire and Bryant (2002) studies

One is logic and logical development. Additive and multiplicative reasoning both depend on the use of logic, and it is clear that, as Piaget originally suggested, children do not at first apply some basic logical principles to the solution of mathematical problems. It takes them quite a time to understand the additive composition of number, for example, and to apply the inversion principle when they are dealing with additive problems. We cannot take these and other basic logical principles for granted. They are a source of genuine difficulty for children, and the idea that they come as an innate and universal gift is misguided and actually harmful, for it distracts us from giving help to children where they need it.

The second is the teaching of conventional systems. Counting systems are based partly on logic and partly on human invention. The decimal system is an invention and, linguistically, it varies from culture to culture. Inventions, by and large, have to be taught, either formally or informally. One cannot expect children to reinvent them. Children certainly have to be taught their counting systems, and how to use them. Some of the evidence that we have presented shows that children learn to count before they really know what counting means and before they apply the logic of one-to-one correspondence to number words. It is as though they have to learn, and to become used to, number words for quite a while before they can connect them with their existing mathematical knowledge.

The third factor is meaning. The evidence suggests that children learn most about mathematics on the basis of experiences with situations and actions that mean something to them. These meaningful situations affect and sometimes restrict what they learn at first. We have seen this with multiplicative reasoning. Children's ideas of multiplication seem to be based on their understanding of one-to-many correspondence, and this almost certainly accounts for the fact that they understand ratios before fractions, and adopt scalar before functional reasoning. The origins of their understanding of division seem to be in their experiences of sharing, which certainly affect the shape of their knowledge about this mathematical operation. Even before they go to school they are quite sophisticated at dividing quantities into equal shares, but have hardly any grasp of the inverse divisor–quotient relationship.

The importance of meaning in mathematical learning is illustrated by the work of Nuñes et al. (1993) on street mathematics. They showed that children who work in the informal economy in Brazil are able to make quite complex calculations when buying and selling in the most flexible ways. These calculations often involve combinations of different arithmetical operations and also quite sophisticated maneuvers like decomposing numbers in order to perform complex additions and subtractions. Yet, these same children make very little headway with the algorithms and procedures that they are taught at school, which mean little to them and which they do not really understand. Their mathematical world is determined by meaning. At a time when there is renewed pressure to concentrate mathematical teaching on drills and on facts, we should remember that children learn best when they understand the meaning of what they are taught.

References

Antell, S. E., & Keating, D. P. (1983). Perception of numerical invariance in neonates. *Child Development, 54*, 695–701.

Baroody, A. J., Ginsburg, H. P., & Waxman, B. (1983). Children's use of mathematical structure. *Journal for Research in Mathematics Education, 14*, 156–168.

Baroody, A. J., & Tiilikainen, S. H. (2003). Two perspectives on addition development. In A. J. Baroody & A. Dowker (Eds.), *The development of arithmetic concepts and skills* (pp. 75–126). Mahwah, NJ: Erlbaum.

Bisanz, J., & Lefevre, J.-A. (1992). Understanding elementary mathematics. In J. I. D. Campbell (Ed.), *The nature and origins of mathematical skills* (pp. 113–136). Amsterdam: Elsevier.

Brannon, E. M. (2002). The development of ordinal numerical knowledge in infancy. *Cognition, 83*, 223–240.

Bryant, P. E. (1992). Arithmetic in the cradle. *Nature, 358*, 712–713.

Bryant, P., Christie, C., & Rendu, A. (1999). Children's understanding of the relation between addition and subtraction: Inversion, identity and decomposition. *Journal of Experimental Child Psychology, 74*, 194–212.

Bryant, P., & Squire, S. (2001). Children's mathematics: Lost and found in space. In M. Gattis (Ed.), *Spatial schemas and abstract thought* (pp. 175–200). Cambridge, MA: MIT Press.

Butterworth, B. (1999). *The mathematical brain.* London: Macmillan.

Carey, S. (2004). Bootstrapping and the origin of concepts. *Daedalus, 133*, 59–69.

Carraher, T. N., Carraher, D. W., & Schliemann, A. D. (1985). Mathematics in the streets and in school. *British Journal of Developmental Psychology, 3*, 21–29.

Chomsky, N. (1986). *Knowledge of language: Its nature, origins and use*. New York: Praeger.

Clearfield, M. W., & Mix, K. S. (1999). Number vs. contour length in infants' discrimination of small visual sets. *Psychological Science, 10*, 408–411.

Correa, J. (1994). *Young children's understanding of the division concept* (Unpublished doctoral dissertation). Oxford University.

Correa, J., Nuñes, T., & Bryant, P. (1998). Young children's understanding of division: The relationship between division terms in a noncomputational task. *Journal of Educational Psychology, 90*, 321–329.

Cowan, R., & Daniels, H. (1989). Children's use of counting and guidelines in judging relative number. *British Journal of Educational Psychology, 59*, 200–210.

Dehaene, S. (1997). *The number sense*. London: Penguin.

Desforges, A., & Desforges, G. (1980). Number-based strategies of sharing in young children. *Educational Studies, 6*, 97–109.

Donaldson, M. (1978). *Children's minds*. London: Fontana.

Donaldson, M. (1982). Conservation: what is the question? *British Journal of Psychology, 73*, 199–207.

Frydman, O., & Bryant, P. E. (1988). Sharing and the understanding of number equivalence by young children. *Cognitive Development, 3*, 323–339.

Frye, D., Braisby, N., Lowe, J., Maroudas, C., & Nicholls, J. (1989). Young children's understanding of counting and cardinality. *Child Development, 60*, 1158–1171.

Fuson, K. C. (1988). *Children's counting and concepts of number*. New York: Springer Verlag.

Gelman, R., & Gallistel, C. R. (1978). *The child's understanding of number*. Cambridge, MA: Harvard University Press.

Gelman, R., & Meck, E. (1983). Preschoolers' counting: Principles before skill. *Cognition, 13*, 343–360.

Gelman, R., Meck, E., & Merkin, S. (1986). Young children's numerical competence. *Cognitive Development, 1*, 1–30.

Greco, P. (1962). Quantité et quotité: Nouvelles recherches sur la correspondance terme-a-terme et la conservation des ensembles. In P. Greco & A. Morf (Eds.), *Structures numeriques elementaires: Etudes d'epistemologie genetique* (Vol. 13., pp. 35–52). Paris: Presses Universitaires de France.

Hart, K. (1981). *Children's understanding of mathematics:* 11–16. London: John Murray.

Hughes, M. (1981). Can preschool children add and subtract? *Educational Psychology, 3*, 207–219.

Hughes, M. (1986). *Children and number*. Oxford: Blackwell.

Huttenlocher, J., Levine, S. C., & Jordan, N. (1994). A mental model of early arithmetic. *Journal of Experimental Psychology: General, 123*, 284–296.

Inhelder, B., & Piaget, J. (1958). *The growth of logical thinking from childhood to adolescence*. New York: Basic books.

Karplus, R., Pulos, S., & Stage, E. K. (1983). Proportional reasoning of early adolescents. In R. Lesh & M. Landau (Eds.), *Acquisition of mathematics concepts and processes* (pp. 45–90). London: Academic Press.

Le Corre, M., & Carey, S. (2007). One, two, three, nothing more: An investigation of the conceptual sources of verbal number principles. *Cognition, 105*, 395–438.

Light, P. H., Buckingham, N., & Robbins, A. H. (1979). The conservation task as an interactional setting. *British Journal of Educational Psychology, 49*, 304–310.

McCrink, K., & Wynn, K. (2004). Large number addition and subtraction by 9-month-old infants. *Psychological Science, 15*, 776–781.

McGarrigle, J., & Donaldson, M. (1974). Conservation accidents. *Cognition, 3*, 341–350.

Michie, S. (1984). Why preschoolers are reluctant to count spontaneously. *British Journal of Developmental Psychology, 2*, 347–358.

Miller, K. (1984). The child as the measurer of all things: Measurement procedures and the development of quantitative concepts. In C. Sophian (Ed.), *Origins of cognitive skills* (pp. 193–228). Hillsdale, NJ: Erlbaum.

Miura, I. T., Kim, C. C., Chang, C. M., & Okamoto, Y. (1988). Effects of language characteristics on children's cognitive representation of number: Cross-national comparisons. *Child Development, 59*, 1445–1450.

Miura, I. T., Okamoto, Y., Kim, C. C., Chang, C. M., Steere, M., & Fayol, M. (1994). Comparisons of children's cognitive representation of number: China, France, Japan, Korea, Sweden and the United States. *International Journal of Behavioural Development, 17*, 401–411.

Mix, K. S., Huttenlocher, J., & Levine, S. C. (2002). Multiple cues for quantification in infancy: Is number one of them? *Psychological Bulletin, 128*, 278–294.

Mix, K. S., Levine, S. C., & Huttenlocher, J. (1997). Numerical abstraction in infants: Another look. *Developmental Psychology, 35*, 423–428.

Mix, K. S., Levine, S. C., & Huttenlocher, J. (2002). *Quantitative development in infancy and early childhood.* New York: Oxford University Press.

Nuñes, T., & Bryant, P. (1996). *Children doing mathematics.* Oxford: Blackwell.

Nuñes, T., Bryant, P., Hallett, D., Bell, D., & Evans, D. (2009). Teaching children about the inverse relation between addition and subtraction. *Mathematical Thinking and Learning, 11*(1–2), 61–78.

Nuñes, T., Schliemann, A.-L., & Carraher, D. (1993). *Street mathematics and school mathematics.* New York: Cambridge University Press.

Piaget, J. (1952). *The child's conception of number.* London: Routledge & Kegan Paul.

Piaget, J. (1953). How children form mathematical concepts. *Scientific American*, November.

Piaget, J. (2001). *Studies in reflecting abstraction* (R. Campbell, Trans.). Hove, UK: Psychology Press.

Piaget, J., & Inhelder, B. (1966). *Mental imagery in the child.* London: Routledge & Kegan Paul.

Piaget, J., & Inhelder, B. (1974). *The child's construction of quantities.* London: Routledge & Kegan Paul.

Putnam, R., de Bettencourt, L. U., & Leinhardt, G. (1990). Understanding of derived fact strategies in addition and subtraction. *Cognition and Instruction, 7*, 245–285.

Resnick, L. B. (1983). A developmental theory of number understanding. In H. P. Ginsburg (Ed.), *The development of mathematical thinking* (pp. 110–152). New York: Academic Press.

Rips, L. J., Asmuth, J., & Bloomfield, A. (2006). Giving the boot to the bootstrap: How not to learn the natural numbers. *Cognition, 101*, B51–B60.

Rips, L. J., Asmuth, J., & Bloomfield, A. (2008). Discussion. Do children learn the integers by induction? *Cognition, 106*, 940–951.

Saxe, G. (1979). A developmental analysis of notational counting. *Child Development, 48*, 1512–1520.

Siegler, R. S., & Stern, E. (1998). Conscious and unconscious strategy discoveries: A microgenetic analysis. *Journal of Experimental Psychology: General, 127*, 377–397.

Sophian, C. (1988). Limitations on preschool children's knowledge about counting: Using counting to compare two sets. *Developmental Psychology, 24*, 634–640.

Sophian, C., Garyantes, D., & Chang, C. (1997). When three is less than two: Early developments in children's understanding of fractional quantities. *Developmental Psychology, 33*, 731–744.

Squire, S., & Bryant, P. (2002). The influence of sharing on children's initial concept of division. *Journal of Experimental Child Psychology, 81*, 1–43.

Squire, S., & Bryant, P. (2003). Children's models of division. *Cognitive Development, 18*, 355–376.

Starkey, P., & Cooper, R. (1980). Perception of numbers by human infants. *Science, 210*, 1033–1034.

Starkey, P., Spelke, E. S., & Gelman, R. (1990). Numerical abstraction by human infants. *Cognition, 36*, 97–128.

Stern, E. (1993). What makes certain arithmetic word problems involving the comparison of sets so difficult for children? *Journal of Educational Psychology, 85*, 7–23.

Stevenson, H. W., Lee, S.-Y., Chen, C., Lummis, M., Stigler, J., Fan, L., & Ge, F. (1990). Mathematics achievement of children in China and the United States. *Child Development, 61*, 1053–1066.

Thompson, P. W. (1993). Quantitative reasoning, complexity, and additive structures. *Educational Studies in Mathematics, 3*, 165–208.

Towse, J. N., & Saxton, M. (1997). Linguistic influences on children's number concepts: methodological and theoretical considerations. *Journal of Experimental Child Psychology, 66*, 362–375.

Van Loosbroek, E., & Smitsman, A.W. (1990). Visual perception of numerosity in infancy. *Developmental Psychology, 26*, 916–922.

Vergnaud, G. (1982). A classification of cognitive tasks and operations of thought involved in addition and subtraction problems. In T. P. Carpenter, J. M. Moser, & T. A. Romberg (Eds.), *Addition and subtraction: A cognitive perspective* (pp. 60–67). Hillsdale, NJ: Erlbaum.

Wakeley, A., Rivera, S., & Langer, J. (2000a). Can young infants add and subtract? *Child Development, 71*, 1525–1534.

Wakeley, A., Rivera, S., & Langer, J. (2000b). Not proved: Reply to Wynn. *Child Development, 71*, 1537–1539.

Wynn, K. (1990). Children's understanding of counting. *Cognition, 36*, 155–193.

Wynn, K. (1992). Addition and subtraction by human infants. *Nature, 358*, 749–750.

Wynn, K. (1998). Psychological foundations of number: Numerical competence in human infants. *Trends in Cognitive Science, 2*, 296–303.

Wynn, K. (2000). Findings of addition and subtraction in infants are robust and consistent: Reply to Wakeley, Rivera and Langer. *Child Development, 71*, 1535–1536.

Xu, F., & Spelke, E. (2000). Large number discrimination in 6-month-old infants. *Cognition, 74*, B1–B11.

CHAPTER TWENTY-TWO

Executive Function in Typical and Atypical Development

Philip David Zelazo and Ulrich Müller

Introduction

Executive function (EF) is an ill-defined but important construct that refers generally to the psychological processes involved in the conscious control of thought and action. Although EF has long been studied from a neuropsychological perspective, with researchers seeking to map function onto neurological structure, it is now the focus of intensive research from a variety of other perspectives, including the perspectives of developmental psychology, developmental psychopathology, and educational psychology. Developmental research on EF has revealed that: (a) EF first emerges early in development, probably around the end of the first year of life; (b) EF develops across a wide range of ages, with important changes occurring between about 2 and 5 years of age, adult-level performance on many standard tests of EF being reached at about 12 years of age, and performance on some measures continuing to change into adulthood; (c) failures of EF occur in different situations at different ages, and these situations can be ordered according to the complexity of the inferences required; (d) although EF can be understood in fairly domain-general terms, a distinction can be made between the development of relatively "hot" affective aspects of EF more associated with ventral and medial parts of prefrontal cortex (VM-PFC) and the development of relatively "cool" cognitive aspects more associated with lateral prefrontal cortex (L-PFC); (e) EF difficulties may be a common consequence of many different perturbations of the epigenetic process; and (f) different developmental disorders may involve impairments in different aspects of EF.

We would like to thank Keith Happaney and Sophie Jacques for helpful comments on an earlier draft of this manuscript. Please address correspondence to: Philip David Zelazo, Institute of Child Development, University of Minnesota, 51 East River Parkway, Minneapolis, MN 55455. Email: zelazo@umn.edu.

In the following sections, we will first address definitional issues surrounding the construct of EF, and then consider research on prefrontal cortex (PFC) and its development. Although EF can be studied in purely functional terms, consideration of concomitant neurological systems provides an important source of constraints on functional models of EF. Our review of research on the development of EF in typically developing children proceeds according to the problem solving (PS) framework introduced by Zelazo, Carter, Reznick, and Frye (1997). In light of this review, we then briefly consider the role of EF in psychiatric conditions with childhood onset. Finally, we conclude with several generalizations about the development of EF, including recommendations for future research.

Definitional Issues

Historically, the construct of EF has been derived from analysis of the consequences of PFC damage. These consequences are numerous and diverse, and often described as a list of partially overlapping deficits – deficits that have family resemblance structure. Wise, Murray, and Gerfen (1996, p. 325) provide one such list:

> Lesions of PF in humans yield a constellation of neuropsychological deficits that have been described variously as difficulties with planning, concept formation, abstract thinking, decision making, cognitive flexibility, use of feedback, temporal ordering of events, fluid or general intelligence, and monitoring one's own actions.

The construct of EF is intended to capture the psychological abilities whose impairment is presumed to underlie these manifest deficits, but again, researchers often rely on what amounts to a list: the ability to plan, the ability to form concepts, etc. After reviewing several such lists, Tranel, Anderson, and Benton (1994, p. 130) attempted "to distil a fairly cohesive notion of what is meant by the term executive functions," and suggested that EF corresponds to the following: planning, decision-making, judgment, and self-perception.

An alternative approach to the characterization of EF is to emphasize just one aspect of EF, such as inhibitory control, and attempt to explain various behavioral deficits in terms of this aspect (e.g., Barkley, 1997; Dempster, 1992). Generally, however, and as we discuss later, this approach to EF is too simple to provide an adequate characterization of the complex strategic and metacognitive processes involved in EF.

Another alternative is to treat EF as a higher-order unitary cognitive mechanism or ability. Denckla and Reiss (1997, p. 283), for example, follow an influential line of authors (e.g., Baddeley, 1996; Norman & Shallice, 1986) when they suggest that "*Executive function* refers to a cognitive module consisting of effector output elements involving inhibition, working memory, and organisational strategies necessary to prepare a response." Unfortunately, this approach essentially invokes a homunculus and leaves unanswered questions about how EF is accomplished and about functional relations among aspects of EF such as planning and self-perception.

Table 22.1 Confirmatory factor analytic studies of EF in children

Study, N, ages (in years), factors (and tasks)
Lehto, Juujarvi, Kooistra, & Pulkkinen (2003), N = 108, ages = 8 to 13 years 1. Working memory (Mazes, Spatial Working Memory [Between Search Errors], Spatial Span, Auditory Attention and Response Set) 2. Shifting (Trail Making B, Word Fluency) 3. Inhibition (Matching Familiar Figures Test, Tower of London)
Huizinga, Dolan, & van der Molen (2006), N = 384, ages = 7 to 21 years Confirmatory factor analysis corrected for basic speed 1. Working memory (Tic Tac Toe Task, Mental Counters Task) 2. Shifting (Local–Global task, Dots–Triangles Task, Smiling Faces Task) Failure to find a common inhibitory factor (Stop-Signal Task, Eriksen Flanker Task, Stroop Task)
van der Sluis, de Jong, & van der Leij (2007), N = 172, ages = 4th- to 5th-graders Confirmatory factor analysis corrected for naming speed 1. Working memory or updating (Keep Track, Letter Memory, Digit Memory) 2. Shifting (Object Shifting, Symbol Shifting, Place Shifting, Trail Making B) Failure to find a common inhibition factor (Quantity inhibition, Object inhibition, Stroop, Numerical Size inhibition)
Wiebe, Espy, & Charak (2008), N = 243, ages = 2.3 to 6 years Tested multiple models (inhibition and components of inhibition, working memory); one-factor model was sufficient to explain data (Delayed Alternation, Digit Span, Six Boxes, Delayed Response, NEPSY Statue, Whisper, Continuous Performance Test, Shape School [inhibit condition], NEPSY Visual Attention, Tower of Hanoi)

Miyake, Friedman, Emerson, Witzki, Howerter, and Wager (2000) provided an influential characterization of EF as involving "separable but moderately correlated constructs, thus indicating both unity and diversity of executive functions" (p. 87). Based on a literature review and confirmatory factor analysis of adults' performance on selected measures of EF, Miyake and colleagues identified three aspects of EF: inhibition of prepotent responses, shifting between mental sets (or flexibility), and updating and monitoring of representations in working memory. Factor analytic studies with children have generally also revealed several factors (see Garon, Bryson, & Smith, 2008, for a review). As shown in table 22.1, some of these studies have encountered difficulties in finding a unitary inhibition factor (see also Friedman & Miyake, 2004), and there is some suggestion that the factor structure may become more differentiated between childhood and adulthood.

A potential problem with this approach, however, is that the simple EF tasks designed to probe one specific aspect of EF may, in fact, tap into multiple component processes (see Lehto, Juujäarvi, Kooistra, & Pulkkinen, 2003). Moreover, providing labels for factors may lead to the impression that researchers understand the cognitive processes underlying performance on various tasks, but this is rarely the case. Note that the same tasks are sometimes clustered with different tasks, and characterized by different labels. Thus, for example, the Wisconsin Card Sorting Test (WCST) is considered part of a "Perseveration/Disinhibition" factor by Levin et al. (1991) and part of a "Set Shifting or Cognitive Flexibility" factor by Pennington (1997). In the absence of an understanding of underlying cognitive processes, it is unclear what this approach can tell us about the structure of EF. For example, does flexibility rely on inhibitory control or is inhibition an outgrowth of flexibility? It is also impossible to determine the extent to which correlations among tasks are due to shared method variance, or influenced by differential sensitivity to individual differences at different ages. Nonetheless, this approach can provide an empirical characterization of correlations among tasks, as opposed to processes, and it can be used to generate hypotheses about EF processes that can then be tested experimentally.

Luria's (e.g., 1973) approach to neurological systems suggests a way to characterize EF that avoids these limitations. For Luria, PFC and other neurological systems consist of *interactive functional systems* that involve the integration of subsystems. Subsystems have specific roles to play, but cannot be considered outside of the larger systems of which they are a part. Zelazo et al. (1997) took seriously Luria's suggestion that EF is a function, and not a mechanism or cognitive structure. Functions are essentially behavioral constructs defined in terms of their outcome – what they accomplish. In the case of EF, the outcome is deliberate PS. To a large extent, the task of characterizing a complex function such as EF is a matter of describing its hierarchical structure, characterizing its subfunctions, and organizing these subfunctions around their constant common outcome. In the case of EF, functionally distinct phases of PS can be organized around the constant outcome of solving a problem, and we can attempt to show how these phases contribute to that outcome. Figure 22.1 presents a familiar looking flowchart.

For example, consider the WCST (Grant & Berg, 1948; see table 22.2), widely regarded as "the prototypical EF task in neuropsychology" (Pennington & Ozonoff, 1996, p. 55). The WCST taps numerous aspects of EF, and, as a result, the origin of errors on this task is difficult to determine (e.g., see Delis, Squire, Bihrle, & Massman, 1992). To perform correctly on the WCST, one must first construct a representation of the problem space, which includes identifying the relevant dimensions. Then, one must choose a promising plan – for example, sorting according to shape. After selecting a plan, one must (a) keep the plan in mind long enough for it to guide one's thought or action, and (b) actually carry out the prescribed behavior. Keeping a plan in mind to control behavior is referred to as *intending*; translating a plan into action is *rule use*. Finally, after acting, one must evaluate one's behavior, which includes both error detection and error correction.

According to the PS framework, inflexibility can occur at each phase so there are several possible explanations of perseverative performance on the WCST – and on global EF tasks more generally. For example, perseveration could occur after a rule change in the WCST either because a new plan was not formed (one type of *representational inflexibility*; Zelazo, Reznick, & Piñon, 1995) or because the plan was formed but not carried out (an example of *lack of response control*; Zelazo et al., 1995). As a descriptive framework, the delineation of PS phases does not *explain* EF, but it does allow us to ask more precisely

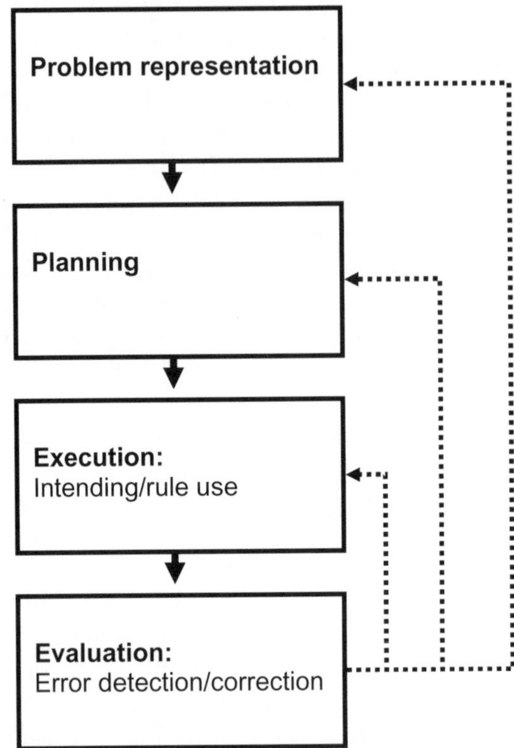

Figure 22.1 A problem-solving framework for understanding EF as a functional construct. (Reprinted with permission from Zelazo, Carter, Reznick, & Frye, 1997.)

when in the process of PS performance breaks down. In addition, the framework accomplishes the following: (a) it clarifies the way in which diverse aspects of EF work together to fulfill the higher-order function of PS; (b) it avoids conceptualizing EF as a homuncular ability (e.g., as a central executive; Baddeley, 1996); (c) it suggests relatively well-defined measures of EF (e.g., measures of rule use for which problem representation, planning, and evaluation are not required); (d) it allows us to capture key aspects of EF, including goal selection, conceptual fluency, and planning in novel situations (e.g., Tranel et al., 1994), that occur even in situations that do *not* demand resistance to interference; and (e) it permits the formulation of specific hypotheses regarding the role of more basic cognitive processes (e.g., negative priming, procedural memory) in different aspects of EF.

Structure–Function Mapping

Although EF can be studied in purely functional terms, consideration of concomitant neurological systems provides an important source of constraints on functional models

Table 22.2 Selected measures of EF in children

A-not-B. Based on Piaget's work with infants. An object is conspicuously hidden at one location, location A, and an infant (or child) is allowed to retrieve it. Then, the object is hidden at another location, location B, and the infant is allowed to search for it. Infants often persist in searching at location A (the A-not-B error). The key dependent measures are performance on the first B trial and number of post-switch perseverative errors at B prior to success on a B trial (error run). The A-not-B task has been used in infants and preschoolers.

Children's Gambling Task. From Kerr and Zelazo (2004), based on Bechara et al. (1994). This task consists of two decks of cards that, when turned, display a number of happy and sad faces. Happy faces indicate number of candies won; sad faces indicate candies lost. One deck is disadvantageous; the other advantageous. Children are told to win as much as possible before the end of the "game" (i.e., after 50 card selections, unbeknownst to the child). The first 25 trials allowed children to sample from both decks; the last 25 trials are considered diagnostic of affective decision-making. The key dependent variable is the proportion of disadvantageous choices during trials 26–50. The task has been used with preschoolers but can be used with school-age children, too.

Day-Night Stroop. From Gerstadt, Hong, and Diamond (1994). Children are instructed to say the word "day" when shown a line drawing of the moon and stars, and "night" when shown a line drawing of the sun. The key dependent measure is the number of correct responses in the experimental condition. The Day-Night Stroop has been used in preschool and school-age children.

Delayed Response. Based on Hunter (e.g., 1917). In one version, an object is placed under one of two or more identical stimuli (e.g., cups). A delay is then imposed during which the stimuli are hidden by an opaque screen. After the delay, the screen is raised and the infant or child is allowed to obtain the stimulus. The primary dependent measure is the number of correct responses. Delayed response has been used with infants and children.

Dimensional Change Card Sort (DCCS). From Zelazo et al. (2003). Children are presented with cards depicting colored shapes that can be sorted differently, depending on whether one sorts them by color or by shape. Children are first told to sort by one dimension (e.g., color), and then told to sort by the other dimension (e.g., shape). The key dependent measure is number correct on the post-switch phase. The DCCS has been used with 3- to 5-year-old children, although versions have also been used with school-age children and adults.

Flexible Item Selection Task (FIST). From Jacques and Zelazo (2001), based on Feldman & Drasgow (1951). Children are shown a set of three cards and required first to select two cards that match each other on one dimension, and then to select a different pair of cards that match each other on another dimension. The primary dependent measure is number correct on the second selection. The FIST has been used with 3- to 5-year-old children, although more difficult versions could be used with older children.

Go-NoGo Task. Based on work by Luria (e.g., Luria, 1966). In a commonly used version of the Go-NoGo task, children are required to display a simple motor response to one cue, the Go stimulus, while refraining from responding to another stimulus, the No-Go stimulus. Scoring is based on reaction time, errors of commission (i.e., incorrectly responding to a No-Go stimulus), and errors of omission (not responding to a Go stimulus). The Go-NoGo task has been used mainly with school-age children.

Table 22.2 *Continued*

Handgame. Based on work by Luria (see Hughes, 1998b). Children first must imitate a pair of hand actions by the experimenter. Then, in the conflict condition, children must make the opposite responses (e.g., make a fist when the experimenter points a finger and point a finger when the experimenter makes a fist). The dependent measure is the number of errors in the conflict condition. The handgame has been used with preschoolers.

Object Reversal. Based on Overman et al. (1997). On each trial, children are presented with the same two objects and rewarded for reaching to one of them. After a certain number of trials, children are rewarded for reaching to the other object (i.e., the reward contingencies are reversed). The primary dependent variable is the number of trials needed to learn the reversal. The task has been used with young preschoolers, but could be used with infants and school-age children.

Self-Ordered Pointing. See Archibald & Kerns (1999). Children are presented with drawings of objects arranged in a matrix. The same objects are presented on each trial, but they appear in different locations. Participants are instructed to point to a different picture on each trial. The key dependent measure is the number of errors. Self-Ordered Pointing has been used with preschoolers and school-age children.

Stop-Signal Task. From Logan (1994). Children are presented via a computer with a series of stimuli and told to press one of two keys (e.g., X or O) depending on whether an X or an O appears on the screen, unless a tone (the stop signal) sounds (about 25% of all trials), in which case children should not press either key. Dependent measures are accuracy (correctly pressing a key), probability of stopping, and reaction time. The Stop-Signal Task is typically used with school-age children.

Stroop Test. From Stroop (1935). In the experimental condition, children are presented with color words (e.g., red) printed in non-matching colored ink (e.g., blue ink), and required to name the color of the ink. The key dependent measure is the number of correct responses. The Stroop Test has been used with literate school-age children.

Tower of Hanoi. Based on a popular nineteenth-century puzzle, the task consists of *n* disks of graduated size placed in a particular configuration across three pegs of the same size. Children must transfer the disks from a starting position to a specified goal state, observing a number of arbitrary rules. Problems differ in difficulty, which varies with the number of moves required for solution and the type of problem (e.g., tower-ending or flat-ending). The key dependent measure is the number of moves to solution. The task has been used with preschoolers and school-age children.

Tower of London. From Shallice (1982), based on the Tower of Hanoi. This tower task uses colored balls that must be moved on three pegs of graduated sizes. Children are presented with an initial arrangement of balls and with a target tower, and they are asked to describe how they would alter their initial arrangement so that it corresponds to the target tower. The task has been used with preschoolers and school-age children.

Wisconsin Card Sorting Test (WCST). Based on Grant and Berg (1948). Children are presented with stimulus cards that differ on various dimensions, and then children are shown individual cards that match different stimulus cards on different dimensions. Children must determine the rule according to which each card must be sorted, and the experimenter informs the child after each card whether the sorting is right or wrong. After a certain number of consecutive correct responses, the target dimension is shifted, and the child must discover this new sorting principle. The key dependent measures are perseverative errors and number of categories achieved. The WCST has been used with children older than about 6 years.

of EF. Accordingly, before reviewing behavioral evidence regarding typical and atypical development of EF, we describe briefly the results of recent research on PFC and its development. As a caveat, it should be noted that although EF has traditionally been linked to PFC, it clearly depends on the integrity of other brain regions as well (e.g., the limbic system). Indeed, although the terms are often used interchangeably, EF is *not* synonymous with PFC function: whereas some patients with PFC damage do not show impairments in EF (e.g., Shallice & Burgess, 1991), some patients with damage outside of PFC do (e.g., Anderson, Damasio, Jones, & Tranel, 1991). More generally, there are good reasons to reject a modular approach in the case of complex functions such as EF (Goldberg, 1995; Luria, 1966; Stuss & Benson, 1986).

Prefrontal cortex

PFC is the region of cerebral cortex anterior to pre-motor cortex and the supplementary motor area (and, according to some authors, excluding the anterior cingulate gyrus; Fuster, 1989; Stuss & Benson, 1986). In human beings, this region comprises between a quarter and a third of the cortex (Fuster, 1989). Although it is unclear whether this proportion is large relative to other species, recent evidence suggests that individual areas of PFC (e.g., Brodmann's area 10) may be larger in human beings than in other species, and that human PFC has unique patterns of interconnectivity (see Rilling, 2006; Semendeferi, Lu, Schenker, & Damasio, 2002). In general, the patterns of reciprocal connectivity between PFC and other, more subcortical and posterior, brain regions make PFC uniquely suited for the integration (or association) of information and the regulation of emotion, thought, and action.

Over the years, different authors have provided very different accounts of PFC function, perhaps emphasizing consequences of damage to different parts of PFC. PFC comprises several distinct areas that can be distinguished on the basis of neuroanatomical connections, the relative importance of different neurotransmitter systems, and behavioral correlations. These include orbitofrontal cortex (OFC), and dorsomedial (DM-PFC), ventrolateral (VL-PFC), dorsolateral (DL-PFC), and rostrolateral prefrontal cortices (RL-PFC). For the present purposes, however, we collapse across lateral regions, on the one hand, and ventral and medial regions, on the other, to highlight the difference between two broad areas, lateral PFC (L-PFC) and ventral and medial PFC (VM-PFC).

Lateral prefrontal cortex. L-PFC comprises the lateral portions of Brodmann's areas 9, 10, 11, and 12; areas 45 and 46; and the superior part of area 47 (cf. H. Damasio, 1996; Gazzaniga, Irvy, & Mangun, 1998) – regions that mainly receive their blood supply from the middle cerebral artery (H. Damasio, 1996; Stuss & Benson, 1986). In addition to its connections with VM-PFC, L-PFC is connected to a variety of brain areas that would allow it to play an important role in the integration of sensory and mnemonic information and the regulation of intellectual function and action. These include: the thalamus, parts of the basal ganglia (the dorsal caudate nucleus), the hippocampus, and primary and secondary association areas of neocortex, including posterior temporal, parietal, and occipital areas (e.g., Fuster, 1989). With respect to neurotransmitter systems, there is evidence that dopamine plays a particularly important role in L-PFC (see Robbins, 2000, for a review).

Ventral and medial prefrontal cortex. VM-PFC, as broadly defined here, consists of both ventral (orbital) and medial regions of PFC, including the medial portions of Brodmann's areas 9, 10, 11, and 12; areas 13 and 25; and the inferior portion of area 47. The medial regions receive their blood supply from the anterior cerebral artery (H. Damasio, 1996; Stuss & Benson, 1986). Unlike L-PFC, VM-PFC is part of a fronto-striatal circuit that has strong connections to the amygdala and other parts of the limbic system. Hence, VM-PFC is well suited for the integration of affective and non-affective information, and for the regulation of appetitive/motivated behavior.

Development of PFC. An early, influential idea held that PFC was not functional during childhood. The origin of this idea can perhaps be traced to Luria (1973, p. 87), who estimated that PFC did not "become finally prepared for action" until about 4–7 years of age. Golden (1981, p. 292) took this suggestion a step further, proposing that PFC was not functional at all until about 12–15 years of age, and noting that PFC development was often incomplete until age 24 years. The first part of this proposal has now been convincingly refuted: behavioral and comparative data (e.g., Diamond & Goldman-Rakic, 1989), imaging data (e.g., Chugani & Phelps, 1986), and case studies of children with brain lesions (Eslinger, Biddle, & Grattan, 1997) and closed head injuries (Scheibel & Levin, 1997) all indicate some PFC function as early as the end of infancy. For example, Diamond and Goldman-Rakic (1989) showed that in monkeys, performance on the A-not-B task (see table 22.2) depends on intact DL-PFC, which suggests that 12-month-old human infants who succeed on the task rely on DL-PFC. Further support for this suggestion comes from Bell and Fox (1992), who measured electroencephalographic (EEG) activity longitudinally in infants between 7 and 12 months of age, and found a correlation between performance on A-not-B (being able to tolerate longer delays), on the one hand, and frontal EEG power and frontal/parietal EEG coherence, on the other. As a final example, contrary to the notion that childhood lesions of PFC are symptomless ("silent"), several studies indicate that PFC damage does indeed produce symptoms in children, whether assessed retrospectively (e.g., Anderson, Bechara, Damasio, Tranel, & Damasio, 1999) or by direct testing during childhood (Jacobs, Harvey, & Anderson, 2007).

At the same time, however, there is some support for Golden's (1981) suggestion regarding silent lesions of PFC: Eslinger et al. (1997) reviewed several case studies of early PFC damage and found that the immediate consequences of PFC lesions in children are often less noticeable than the consequences of comparable lesions in adults. Moreover, behavioral impairments may appear later in development, when late-developing functions would normally emerge (cf. Goldman & Alexander, 1977), although it is unclear to what extent these impairments are secondary consequences of a disrupted epigenetic process. The fact that identical lesions can have different consequences at different ages (e.g., Jacobs et al., 2007; Kolb, Gibb, & Gorny, 2000; Moses & Stiles, 2002) underscores the need for a developmental approach to the problem of mapping function to neurological structure.

Indeed, it is clear that both PFC and PFC function follow an extremely protracted developmental course (Gogtay et al., 2004; Marsh, Gerber, & Peterson, 2008; Tsujimoto, 2008). Relevant measures include (but are not limited to) the following: (a) *head circumference* (e.g., Epstein, 1986), which shows peak growth rates at 7, 12, and 15 years; (b) *myelination* (e.g., Yakovlev & Lecours, 1967), which starts postnatally in PFC and continues into adulthood; (c) *interhemispheric connectivity*, which shows peak growth rates between 3 and 6 years, as indicated by structural imaging of anterior regions of the corpus callosum (Thompson et al., 2000); (d) *synaptic density* (in layer III of the middle frontal gyrus), which reaches a peak at about 1 year of age that is considerably higher than the adult level, remains high until about age 7 years, and then declines until about age 16, when the adult level is finally attained (e.g., Huttenlocher, 1990); (e) *cortical thickness* which shows the most complex (i.e., cubic) and protracted neurodevelopmental trajectory for PFC (particularly for DL-PFC; Shaw et al., 2008); and (f) *scalp electrical activity* (e.g., Barry et al., 2004), which shows increasing interhemispheric EEG coherences in the frontal regions (but only in the alpha bands) in late childhood.

A few general trends might be noted. First, age-related increases in white-matter volume appear to be monotonic. Second, grey-matter volume in PFC shows an inverted-U-shaped pattern of early increases followed by gradual decreases that start in late childhood and continue into adulthood (e.g., Gogtay et al., 2004; Huttenlocher, 1990; O'Donnell, Noseworthy, Levine, Brandt, & Dennis, 2005). Third, developmental increases in white-matter volume and decreases in gray-matter volume are more pronounced for boys than they are for girls (e.g., de Bellis et al., 2001). Fourth, OFC function seems to develop more rapidly in males (e.g., Overman, Bachevalier, Schuhmann, & Ryan, 1996), and seems to be under hormonal control (Clark & Goldman-Rakic, 1989). Fifth, several researchers have noted a shift from more diffuse to more focal activation of PFC during performance on measures of EF – age-related increases in activation in areas related to EF in adults, and age-related decreases in activation in areas unrelated to EF (e.g., Bunge, Dudukovic, Thomason, Vaidya, & Gabrieli, 2002; Durston et al., 2006; Luna et al., 2001).

Developmental theories of EF

Many early efforts to explain age-related changes in EF relied on the construct of inhibition (e.g., Luria, 1966), and this approach has remained popular (e.g., Kirkham, Cruess, & Diamond, 2003). Reconceptualizing EF as inhibitory control has some prima facie appeal because failures of EF are often manifested as perseverative errors. Perseveration implies that behavior is emitted that should have been inhibited, so perseveration seems to implicate inhibition by definition. However, to the extent that inhibition accounts make a substantive, empirical claim, the claim must be that individuals with EF deficits *try* to suppress interfering response tendencies but cannot do so because of an immature or inefficient inhibition mechanism.

An account of EF development that focuses solely on a weak or inefficient inhibition mechanism, however, is problematic for at least four reasons (see MacLeod, Dodd, Sheard, Wilson, & Bibi, 2003, for additional discussion). One limitation is that inhibition accounts have difficulty generating predictions regarding the specific situations that will pose problems for children at different ages. For example, 3-year-olds perseverate in certain card-sorting tasks, such as the Dimensional Change Card Sort (DCCS; see table 22.2; Frye, Zelazo, & Palfai, 1995), but not in the A-not-B task, where 9-month-old infants will search perseveratively despite seeing an object hidden at a new location. Although it is possible to claim that card sorting requires *more* inhibition than A-not-B, this claim would seem to be inevitably post hoc.

A second limitation is that inhibition is not a unitary construct. Several researchers distinguish, for example, between interference control, which refers to the suppression of interference due to stimulus competition, and behavioral inhibition, which refers to the suppression of a prepotent response (Friedman & Miyake, 2004; Nigg, 2000). Current inhibition theories often fail to specify which aspect of inhibition is crucial to the development of EF, which is important in light of evidence that different aspects of inhibition may be unrelated in behavior (Friedman & Myiake, 2004; Huizinga, Dolan, & Van der Molen, 2006; van der Sluis, de Jong, & van der Leij, 2007).

A third limitation of inhibition accounts is that they are probably too simple to capture the full range of phenomena that are covered by the term EF, including planning in tasks with minimal inhibitory demands (Tower of London vs. Tower of Hanoi; see table 22.2; Goel & Grafman, 1995), concept generation in fluency tasks, action monitoring, and source monitoring and other aspects of episodic retrieval. EF is often measured using an interference paradigm, but it need not be.

Fourth, the concept of inhibition may explain why an action is not executed or why interfering information is ignored, but it does not explain why the correct response is executed. For example, the construct of inhibition, by itself, fails to address how one decides what is to be inhibited. Hence, as a function, inhibition needs to interact with other functions, including problem representation and planning. As a consequence, inhibition may be necessary but not sufficient for a complete account of the development of EF and problem solving (Müller, Dick, Gela, Overton, & Zelazo, 2006). In fact, the concept of inhibition may not be necessary to explain children's performance on some EF tasks that would seem to demand it (Bub, Masson, & Lalonde, 2006).

In contrast to inhibition accounts, a number of researchers have attributed changes in EF to changes in actual or functional capacity of working memory (WM; e.g., Case, 1985; Diamond, 2002; Morton & Munakata, 2003; Roberts & Pennington, 1996). This approach probably has its origin in early work by Jacobson (1936), who demonstrated that PFC-lesioned monkeys showed impairments on a version of Hunter's (e.g., 1917) delayed-response task (see table 22.2). One well-articulated example comes from Morton and Munakata (2002), who distinguish between *active memory representations* and *latent memory traces*. Active memory representations correspond to WM and take the form of sustained, trial-specific activity in PFC, whereas latent memory traces are formed in more posterior cortex. Development of EF is hypothesized to occur as a result of increases in the strength of active memory representations, which, in turn, allow children to override prepotent tendencies mediated by latent memory traces.

Consistent with these WM approaches, developmental studies using delayed-response tasks (e.g., Hunter, 1917), span tasks (e.g., the counting span task; Case, 1985), and Self-Ordered Pointing (see table 22.2; Archibald & Kerns, 1999; Hongwanishkul,

Happaney, Lee, & Zelazo, 2005) have shown that there are regular age-related increases in WM throughout childhood (see Gathercole, Pickering, Ambridge, & Wearing, 2004). These increases could affect children's EF at any of the PS phases, but they would seem to be particularly important for planning and execution (especially, the intending phase of execution).

Another approach to the development of EF has been to suggest that EF involves both WM and inhibition (e.g., Diamond, 2002; Roberts & Pennington, 1996). Although this proposal is more complex than accounts that rely on either WM or inhibition alone, and it may provide a useful account of those aspects of EF associated with DL-PFC, it remains unclear whether it can account for the full range of EF phenomena (see Stuss, Eskes, & Foster, 1994).

In contrast to these approaches, the Cognitive Complexity and Control theory, revised (CCC-r; Zelazo, Müller, Frye, & Marcovitch, 2003), maintains that age-related changes in EF are the result of increases in the hierarchical complexity of the rules that children can formulate, maintain in WM, and use when solving problems. According to this model, children's plans are assumed to correspond literally to rules, formulated in potentially silent self-directed speech, as when we tell ourselves, "If I see a mailbox, then I need to mail this letter." Over the course of the preschool period, there are several age-related increases in the complexity of children's rule systems that can be observed in card sorting, social understanding, physical causality, morality, and other areas. Complexity is measured by the number of levels of embedding in these rule systems. For example, unlike 2.5-year-olds, 3-year-olds readily integrate two rules (e.g., "If red then here; if blue then there") into a single rule system (Zelazo & Reznick, 1991). However, 3-year-olds have difficulty representing a higher-order rule that allows them to switch flexibly between incompatible pairs of rules (e.g., "If sorting by color, then if red then here, if blue then there. If sorting by shape, then if car then here, if flower then there").

Different regions of lateral PFC are hypothesized to correspond to rule use at different levels of complexity (Bunge & Zelazo, 2006). According to the model, lateral PFC-mediated reprocessing allows one to reflect on relatively simple rules (i.e., at a higher level of consciousness; Zelazo, 2004) and formulate higher-order rules that control the application of these simpler rules. As individuals engage in reflective reprocessing, ascend through levels of consciousness, and formulate more complex rule systems, they recruit an increasingly complex hierarchical network of PFC regions (see Zelazo & Cunningham, 2007, for further discussion). This reprocessing fulfils the functions of WM (i.e., keeping rules in mind) and inhibitory control (i.e., more complex rules allow children to select relevant rules for guiding their behavior and avoid relying on outmoded rules, although of course this may be more or less difficult depending on the prepotency of the outmoded rules). Moreover, the ability to engage in several degrees of reflection, which typically emerges during the preschool years, is required to construe stimuli in terms of multiple dimensions.

The importance of complexity has been recognized in the developmental literature (e.g., see Halford and Andrews, chapter 27, this volume), and Halford et al. (Halford, Wilson, & Phillips, 1998; Andrews & Halford, 2002) also suggest that the systematic construction of increasingly complex relations between objects is a major dimension of cognitive development. Research in developmental cognitive neuroscience, however, has provided some support for all of these approaches to EF, and it now seems likely that EF involves the orchestration of a variety of processes, including inhibitory control, WM, and reflection and rule complexity.

EF in Typical Development

Although EF can be understood in fairly domain-general terms, a distinction may be made between the development of relatively "hot" affective aspects of EF more associated with VM-PFC and the development of relatively "cool" cognitive aspects more associated with L-PFC. Both types of EF may be understood in terms of the PS framework, but they differ in the extent to which they involve the regulation of affect and motivation (i.e., basic limbic-system functions, which Stuss & Alexander, 2000, refer to as the "four F's": feeding, fleeing, fighting, and sexual activity). Whereas cool EF is more likely to be elicited by relatively abstract, decontextualized problems, hot EF is required for problems that are characterized by high affective involvement or demand flexible appraisals of the affective significance of stimuli. This characterization of hot EF is consistent with recent proposals regarding the function of OFC, the ventral parts of what is here broadly referred to as VM-PFC. For example, on the basis of evidence that OFC is required for successful performance on simple tests of object reversal (see table 22.2) and extinction in OFC-lesioned monkeys and patients with OFC damage, Rolls (e.g., Rolls, Hornak, Wade, & McGrath, 1994) suggests that OFC is required for the flexible representation of the reinforcement value of stimuli.

Another example is A. Damasio's (e.g., 1994) *somatic marker theory*, according to which OFC (especially the ventromedial portion of OFC) is required for processing learned associations between affective reactions and specific scenarios. Support for this proposal comes from a number of studies by Bechara and colleagues (e.g. Bechara, Damasio, Damasio, & Anderson 1994; see also Bechara, Damasio, & Damasio, 2000), who developed a gambling task sensitive to OFC damage. Bechara et al. (1994) found that patients with OFC damage were more likely than healthy controls to make disadvantageous choices.

The distinction between two types of PS that put differential demands on affect and motivation makes considerable sense from a neuroanatomical point of view, and it is supported by task analyses. First, VM-PFC has close connections with the limbic system, whereas these connections are less direct in the case of L-PFC (they are partly mediated by OFC). Second, measures of OFC function, such as extinction, object reversal, and gambling, all require revising one's appraisal of the affective significance of stimuli. In all cases, one must learn to avoid or ignore something that previously elicited (appetitive) approach.

When thinking about the development of hot and cool EF, it will be important to consider that measures of these functions need to be arranged according to developmental level. An important determinant of developmental level seems to be task complexity, or more appropriately, the complexity of the cognitive processes that a task requires. This dimension may be orthogonal to the hot-cool dimension, although characterizing the relation between these dimensions remains an important question for research. In any case, from this perspective, a task such as object reversal is a relatively simple measure of hot EF, whereas gambling is relatively complex. Similarly, delayed response is a relatively simple measure of cool EF, whereas the WCST is relatively complex.

Finally, it should be kept in mind that both VM-PFC and L-PFC are parts of a single coordinated system, and in the normal case they work together – even in a single situation. Thus, as Damasio (e.g., 1994) suggests, decision-making is normally biased in an adaptive fashion by physiological reactions that predict rewards and punishments. Conversely, it seems likely that a successful approach to solving some affective problems is to reconceptualize the problem in relatively neutral, decontextualized terms, and try to solve it using cool EF. For these reasons, it is probably impossible to design a task that is a pure measure of hot or cool EF, although it is clearly possible to design tasks that emphasize one or the other.

Most developmental research on EF has focused on cool EF, often using global neuropsychological tests that are either taken directly from the adult literature or adapted from adult tasks. For example, several early studies used the WCST (Heaton, 1981), which provides an index of cool EF that spans all four phases of PS (for process decomposition, see Lie, Specht, Marshall, & Fink, 2006). Chelune and Baer (1986) documented a linear increase in performance on the WCST between the ages of 6 and 10 years, with 6-year-olds performing at the level of patients with PFC damage and 10-year-olds performing like healthy adults. This pattern was obtained for the three variables assessed: number of perseverative errors, number of categories achieved, and failures to maintain set. Several other studies (e.g., Levin et al., 1991; Somsen, 2007; Welsh, Pennington, & Groisser, 1991) also used the WCST with typically developing children (often in comparison with clinical samples), and these studies generally replicated Chelune and Baer's (1986) results, although some studies suggest a more protracted development that continues well into adolescence (Lin Chen, Yang, Hsiao, & Tien, 2000; Paniak, Miller, Murphy, Patterson, & Keizer, 1996).

Another widely used measure of EF is the Dimensional Change Card Sort (DCCS; see Zelazo, 2006), in which children are shown two target cards (e.g., a blue rabbit and a red boat) and asked to sort a series of bivalent test cards (e.g., red rabbits and blue boats) first according to one dimension (e.g., color), and then according to the other (e.g., shape). Most 3-year-olds perseverate during the post-switch phase, continuing to sort test cards by the first dimension (e.g., Zelazo et al., 2003). They do this despite being told the new rules on every trial, and despite correctly answering questions about the post-switch rules (e.g., "Where do the rabbits go in the shape game?"). In contrast, by 5 years of age, most children switch immediately on the DCCS when instructed to do so. Variants of this task have been used extensively to test hypotheses about EF and its development in early childhood (e.g., Bialystok, 1999; Bohlmann & Fenson, 2005; Diamond, Carlson, & Beck, 2005; Dick, Overton, & Kovacs, 2005; Kirkham et al., 2003; Kloo & Perner, 2005; Munakata & Yerys, 2001).

It is only relatively recently that researchers have become interested in the development of hot EF, and most of the measures employed are best considered global. For example, Overman and his colleagues (e.g., Overman, Bachevalier, Schuhmann, & McDonough-Ryan, 1997) studied object reversal in infants and young children between 15 and 54 months, and they found considerable development within this age range. As noted, object reversal is an example of hot EF because it requires one to revise one's assessment of whether an object should be approached or avoided.

To assess hot EF in somewhat older children, Kerr and Zelazo (2004) created a simplified Children's Gambling Task (see table 22.2) based on Bechara et al. (1994). The first 25 trials allowed children to sample from both decks; the last 25 trials were considered diagnostic of affective decision-making. Kerr and Zelazo (2004) found that during the last 25 trials, 3-year-olds made more disadvantageous choices (65.4%) than 4-year-olds (40.7%), and 3-year-olds made more such choices than would be expected by chance, whereas 4-year-olds made fewer. These results indicate that hot EF develops over the preschool period: 3-year-olds, but not 4-year-olds, perform like OFC patients insofar as they reliably make disadvantageous choices. Bunch, Andrews, and Halford (2007) replicated the findings that performance on the gambling task improves significantly between 3 and 5 years and demonstrated that the complexity of the gains-loss pattern affects performance. Further research (e.g., Crone & van der Molen, 2004; Hooper, Luciana, Conklin, & Yarger, 2004) has shown that performance on gambling tasks systematically improves between 6 years and adulthood, and that these changes cannot be explained by a WM demands or reward-oriented response style – the same developmental trend was also observed in a reversed gambling task in which losses were placed up front and rewards occurred infrequently.

EF according to the PS framework

We now turn to the PS framework, where EF is understood to proceed from problem representation to planning to execution to evaluation, and inflexibility can occur at each of these phases. For each PS phase, we first discuss relatively cool measures of EF and then consider hot measures. Although we made an effort to restrict this review to measures that are reasonably well focused on only one of the four phases (e.g., measures of planning that do not require plans to be executed), disagreement about how best to describe particular tasks is likely to remain.

Problem representation. In the Gestalt tradition, problem representation was often assessed using insight problems, which require flexible restructuring of the problem representation (e.g., Duncker, 1945). Unfortunately, very few studies have used this approach with children, and indeed, to date there have been very few developmental studies of cool problem representation. One exception is a study by Jacques and Zelazo (2001), who measured problem representation in preschoolers using the Flexible Item Selection Task (see table 22.2), a measure of EF adapted from Feldman and Drasgow's (1951) Visual-Verbal Test. On each trial of the Flexible Item Selection Task, children are shown a three-card set (e.g., a purple fish, a pink fish, and a pink telephone) and required to select two cards that match each other on one dimension (e.g., shape: the purple *fish* and the pink *fish*), and then select a different pair of cards that match each other on a different dimension (e.g., color: the *pink* fish and the *pink* telephone). Successful performance thus requires selecting one of the cards (referred to as the *pivot* item) on both selections, according to different dimensions. On the first selection, 3-year-olds were significantly worse than both 4- and 5-year-olds, who did not differ. On the second selection, 4-year-olds were worse than 5-year-olds, suggesting that although they understood the basic task instructions and could select the first pair correctly, they had trouble re-representing the test item in a different way (i.e., according to a different dimension).

Hot measures of problem representation include most tests of theory of mind, which require flexible problem representation insofar as children are required to represent something from multiple points of view (see Wellman, chapter 10, this volume). Moreover, theory of mind has been linked to VM-PFC through lesion studies and imaging studies with adults (e.g., Amodio & Frith, 2006; Frith & Frith, 2003). The exact role of affect and motivation in reasoning about self and other remains to be determined, but it is obvious that inter- and intrapersonal perspective-taking involves the flexible evaluation of the significance (or meaning) of a situation.

To date, the large majority of research on theory of mind has been conducted in 3- to 5-year-old children (see Wellman, chapter 10, this volume), although the development of theory of mind clearly continues beyond age 5 years. Among the most widely used preschool-age measures of theory of mind are those assessing strategic deception (e.g., Russell, Mauthner, Sharpe, & Tidswell, 1991) and understanding of false belief (e.g., Wimmer & Perner, 1983). Although most 4- and 5-year-olds perform well on these measures, 3-year-olds often respond incorrectly, suggesting a developmental advance in hot problem representation during the preschool years.

Planning. The best studies of planning, for our purpose, are those in which efforts have been made to develop tasks that are relatively pure measures of planning in order to minimize difficulties that may be attributed to other phases of PS such as execution (e.g., Kaller, Rahm, Spreer, Mader, & Unterrainer, 2008; Klahr & Robinson, 1981). For the most part, these studies employ well-defined problems such as the Tower of Hanoi and its variants, and require children to describe their plans without actually executing them.

Early work by Piaget (1976) using execution versions of the Tower of Hanoi revealed poor performance even among school-age children, and subsequent research focusing on planning has confirmed that performance on tower tasks follows a protracted developmental course. For example, Klahr and Robinson (1981) modified the original Tower of Hanoi by employing upside-down cans instead of disks, thereby inverting one of the arbitrary rules to "don't put a smaller can on top of a larger one," and embodying it as an inviolable task constraint. These authors also required children simply to *describe* their plans. Using their modified version, Klahr and Robinson (1981) found that 4-year-olds typically did well on 2- and 3-move problems, whereas 5-year-olds usually did well on 4-move problems, and 6-year-olds did well on 6-move problems. Thus, clear age differences emerged in the length of the problems that children could pass. Analysis of children's pass/fail patterns in different versions of the task indicates that there are corresponding changes in problem analysis and depth of search (i.e., the number of anticipated moves that must be remembered). More recent work employing the Tower of London has extended these results. For example, Luciana and Nelson (1998) found that on 4- and 5-move problems, even 8-year-old children (the oldest group of children included) performed significantly worse than adults.

Brooks, Frye, and Samuels (1996) examined planning in the hot EF context of strategic deception. These authors reasoned that 3-year-olds who perform poorly on measures of strategic deception (e.g. Russell et al., 1991) might have difficulty selecting an appropriate plan, or they might have difficulty executing a plan when it is appropriate to do so. To distinguish between these possibilities, the authors showed children demonstrations of two already formulated plans, one deceptive and one not, and asked children to select the one that would trick another person. Four-year-olds chose the deceptive plan, whereas 3-year-olds did not. These results suggest that there are changes in preschoolers' planning in the hot realm.

Execution. Following Luria's seminal work on children's rule use (see Zelazo & Jacques, 1996, for review), Zelazo and Reznick (1991) investigated rule use in 2.5- to 3-year-olds using a card sort in which children were presented with a pair of ad hoc rules (e.g, "If it's something found inside the house, then put it here. If it's something found outside the house, then put it there.") and then asked them to use these rules to separate 10 test cards. Two-and-a-half-year-olds failed to use the rules despite possessing knowledge about the cards, whereas 3-year-olds performed well. Subsequent research (Zelazo et al., 1995) found that 2.5-year-olds had difficulty even when they were provided with considerable aids and incentives. Analyses of children's errors revealed a tendency to repeat responses: when they erred, it usually involved putting a card into the box in which they had put a card on the previous trial. These results resemble those described by Luria for the one-light task in that 2.5-year-olds seemed to understand the task and the rules, and actually *started* to use the rules, but were susceptible to perseverative errors.

Three- to 5-year-olds' rule use has been assessed using the DCCS, described earlier. The DCCS puts two pairs of rules into opposition. Numerous studies have revealed that these age-related changes on the DCCS are robust and occur in a wide range of situations with a wide variety of task materials (see Garon et al., 2008). Zelazo et al. (2003) have interpreted these results as evidence that 3-year-olds have difficulty integrating incompatible pairs of rules into a single system of rules via a higher-order rule. Support for this interpretation comes from the finding that 3-year-olds demonstrate knowledge of the post-switch rules, even though they fail to use them (Zelazo et al., 1996, Exp. 4), and show predicted patterns of success and failure across different versions of the task (see Zelazo et al., 2003, for a review). By contrast, Kirkham et al. (2003) have attributed 3-year-olds' perseveration on the DCCS to deficits in inhibitory control (i.e., 3-year-olds fail to suppress attention to the pre-switch dimension in order to shift attention to the post-switch dimension). Following this interpretation, 3-year-olds should perform well when the values of the pre-switch dimension are removed from the target cards during the post-switch phase (e.g., if children were required to sort red rabbits and blue boats according to shape in the pre-switch phase, and then to sort red flowers and blue cars according to color in the post-switch phase). Results indicate, however, that 3-year-olds perform poorly under these circumstances, just as they do in the standard version of the DCCS (Müller et al., 2006; Zelazo et al., 2003).

The use of rules has also been studied using simple measures of selective attention (e.g., Davidson et al. 2006; Enns & Cameron, 1987). For example, Gerardi-Caulton (2000) used a spatial conflict (Simon) task with children aged 24, 30, and 36 months.

Children were presented with a shape (e.g. a star) on a screen, and instructed to press a response button that matched the picture. On some trials, the location of the response button and the location of the picture on the screen were congruent, and on other trials they were incongruent. All children performed more slowly and less accurately on incongruent trials, and this effect was more pronounced for younger children.

Rueda, Posner, Rothbart, and Davis-Stober (2004) studied the development of selective attention in children between the ages of 6 and 10 years using a flanker task (from the Attention Network Test). In this task, children were presented with a row of five fish, and told to press an arrow that corresponded to the left–right orientation of the middle fish. On congruent trials, the fish all faced the same way, and on incongruent trials the middle fish faced the opposite direction. Results showed improvement in reaction time and in accuracy on incongruent trials from ages 6 to 7 years.

Adding motivational significance to a rule-use task yields an assessment of execution in the context of hot EF. One classic paradigm is delay of gratification, which has been assessed using delay tasks and choice tasks (e.g., Mischel, Ebbesen, & Zeiss, 1972). Early studies generally failed to find age differences within the preschool range, but did find differences within the school-age years (see Mischel, Shoda, & Rodriguez, 1989, for review). Moreover, this research has identified a number of attentional and cognitive factors that contribute to the length of time that children elect to wait. For example, thinking about the abstract, non-arousing qualities of the preferred reward, instead of its concrete, arousing qualities positively influences children's ability to delay gratification. These findings suggest that one way to succeed on a hot EF task might be to convert it from a hot EF task into a cool EF task, underscoring the close relation between these two aspects of EF.

Two recent studies have examined delay of gratification in younger children using a modified choice task (Moore, in press; Moore, Barresi, & Thompson, 1998; Thompson et al., 1997). Thompson et al. (1997) found that two measures of future-oriented hot EF show similar developmental trajectories. Specifically, when given the option to choose between a small reward now or a larger reward later (prudence) and between a reward for self now or a reward for self and other later (altruism), 4- to 5-year-old children demonstrated significantly more prudence and altruism than 3-year-old children, and for the 3-year olds, there was a correlation between prudence and altruism when age was partialled out. In addition to replicating these results, Moore et al. (1998) found that prudence and altruism were related to performance on measures of theory of mind.

Prencipe and Zelazo (2005) used a version of this choice task to examine children's delay of gratification for self and other (the experimenter). Three-year-olds typically chose the immediate reward for themselves and the delayed reward for the experimenter, suggesting that they are capable of adaptive decision-making but have particular difficulty regulating approach behavior in motivationally significant situations. Self-regulation may be facilitated in part by the adoption of a third-person perspective on one's own behavior (Barresi & Moore, 1996).

Children may also use symbols to decontextualize concrete stimuli, creating *psychological distance* from the stimuli (Dewey, 1931/1985; Werner & Kaplan, 1963), which then might foster reflection and control. Carlson, Davis, and Leach (2005) assessed this possibility using the Less is More task, in which children are presented with two piles of candy, one large and one small, and must point to the small pile in order to obtain the large pile. Three-year-olds, compared to 4-year-olds, have difficulty inhibiting their tendency to point to the preferred, larger reward; they have difficulty reversing the simple stimulus–reward rules for the purposes of the task. Carlson et al. trained 3-year-olds on symbolic representations for the quantities of treats, in increasing degree of separation from reality before giving them the task (e.g., one-to-one correspondence with rocks vs. a mouse and elephant to stand for small and large amounts, respectively). Children in the symbol conditions performed better than children presented with real treats, and improved as a function of the degree of symbolic distancing from the real rewards.

Evaluation. Evaluation involves both error detection and error correction, and research with normal adults and patients (e.g., Konow & Pribram, 1970) underscores the importance of this distinction. In some situations, children's ability to detect errors seems to develop in advance of their ability to correct them (e.g., Gelman & Meck, 1983). For example, using a relatively cool measure of evaluation, Bullock and Lütkenhaus (1988) found that 18- and 24-month-old children could reliably distinguish between correctly and incorrectly built towers, even when they themselves failed to build the towers correctly. Moreover, even 17-month-olds gave evidence of monitoring their own performance qualitatively (e.g., by showing care about aligning blocks on a tower). However, it was not until 26 months that children consistently monitored their progress towards a goal (e.g., creating a tower identical to a model).

As opposed to the dissociation found in toddlers, Jacques, Zelazo, Kirkham, and Semcesen (1999) found that cool error detection and correction were more closely linked in preschool-age children. In this study, children were asked to evaluate the sorting of a puppet on the DCCS. Thus, the response execution requirement was removed from the task altogether. When 3-year-olds watched the puppet perseverate, they judged the puppet to be correct. When they saw the puppet sort correctly, they judged the puppet to be wrong. Moreover, children's judgments of the puppet were highly correlated with their own performance on the DCCS.

Finally, Gladstone (1969) examined both error detection and error correction in the context of extinction, which can be considered a measure of hot EF (see Rolls, Hornak, Wade, & McGrath, 1994). More specifically, he looked at rate of extinction on an operant task in which to-be-retrieved rewards were visible. After a certain amount of responding, it could be seen that the reward supply had been exhausted. Nonetheless, children below 3.5 years kept repeating their responses. Older children produced fewer responses during this extinction phase, with the oldest children (around 4.5 years) immediately ceasing to respond when it became apparent that the reward dispenser was empty. Gladstone argued that the younger children recognized the illogic of their extinction behavior, and were able to detect their errors, but had difficulty using this information to control their behavior. However, interpretation of children's performance remains unclear and future work might usefully investigate the relation between error detection and error correction in a variety of hot and cool contexts.

Summary. Evidence from diverse studies suggests that there are systematic changes during the preschool years and beyond in all phases of EF identified by the functional

PS model. Indeed, it seems likely that the various phases of PS develop together. For example, rule use in execution is likely facilitated by the evaluation of outcomes, which can then prompt reflection, leading to better problem representation and planning. In this way, intelligent activity can be reflected back into earlier phases of PS, where it can come to precede execution and contribute to the development of EF as a whole.

Consistent with the CCC-r (Zelazo et al., 2003), these changes in EF can be characterized in terms of the complexity of the problems that children can solve. For example, research on rule use has revealed that by 3 years of age, children can represent and employ a pair of arbitrary rules for sorting cards, but they are likely to perseverate if they are required to shift from one set of rules to an incompatible pair, or if they are required to use a pair of rules that conflicts with their a priori biases (i.e., their default rules). Nonetheless, it should be noted that there seem to be other influences on performance in addition to complexity, including, perhaps, degree of affective involvement (Morton, Trehub, & Zelazo, 2003). This would suggest that when complexity is controlled, hot EF tasks may be more difficult than cool EF tasks. For example, Gladstone (1976) failed to find a difference between 3- and 4-year-olds on his measure of extinction when blocks were used as a reward, whereas such differences were clearly evident when rewards consisted of candy, gum, and small toys. The use of highly appealing rewards may have increased the extent to which the task was a measure of hot EF, and consequently increased task difficulty.

One way in which the general issue of hot versus cool EF has been addressed is in the context of the relation between cool EF and theory of mind. As noted, changes in children's hot EF as measured by tests of theory of mind (see Wellman, chapter 10, this volume) co-occur with changes in cool EF as measured by various tasks, including the DCCS (e.g., Frye et al., 1995) and the windows task (Russell et al., 1991). Further, longitudinal studies (e.g., Carlson, Mandell, & Williams, 2004; Hughes, 1998a; see also Flynn, 2007) found that cool EF tasks at time 1 predicted performance on theory-of-mind tasks at time 2, even after age, verbal ability, and theory-of-mind scores at time 1 were taken into account.

The presence of a strong relation between cool EF and theory of mind is inconsistent with several theories of theory of mind (e.g., the "theory-theory," which predicts that individual children's development in one domain will be independent from their development in another), and it would not be predicted by the view that theory of mind is a domain-specific module (e.g., Baron-Cohen, 1997). Nonetheless, several theoretical possibilities remain (e.g., see Moses & Tahiroglu, in press; Perner & Lang, 1999, for discussion). From the present perspective, however, the question about how to interpret the relation between cool EF and theory of mind can be rephrased as one regarding the relation in development between hot and cool EF.

EF in Atypical Development

Difficulties with EF are prominent in a variety of disorders with childhood onset, including autism (e.g., O'Hearn, Asato, Ordaz, & Luna, 2008), conduct disorder (e.g. Séguin,

2004), obsessive–compulsive disorder (Pietrefesa & Evans, 2007), and attention deficit hyperactivity disorder (ADHD; e.g., Castellanos, Sonuga-Barke, Milham, & Tannock, 2006; Willcutt, Doyle, Nigg, Faraone, & Pennington, 2005), among others (see Zelazo & Müller, 2002, for further discussion). The exact role of EF in each of these different disorders remains unclear, but recent research has considered the possibility that different aspects of EF may be implicated in different forms of these disorders, perhaps for different reasons. For example, a multiple-deficit model of ADHD acknowledges that ADHD is a heterogeneous disorder, with different neuropsychological profiles, and that several pathways can lead to ADHD (Castellanos & Tannock, 2002; Nigg, Willcutt, Doyle, & Sonuga-Barke, 2005; Willcutt et al., 2005). In particular, Castellanos and colleagues (2006) have delineated hot and cool EF pathways such that "inattention symptoms may be associated with deficits in 'cool' EF, whereas hyperactivity/impulsivity symptoms will be found to reflect 'hot' EF deficits" (p. 119). Empirical studies suggest that hot EF (e.g., delay aversion) and cool EF (e.g., the Stop-Signal Task) are independent predictors of ADHD status (e.g., Solanto et al., 2001), and that even after controlling for WM, hot EF (Iowa Gambling Task) is associated with symptoms of hyperactivity/impulsivity, but not with symptoms of inattention (Toplak, Jain, & Tannock, 2005; but see Geurts, van der Oord, & Crone, 2006).

Conclusion

The construct of EF has long been recognized to be important but ill-defined. In this chapter, we present a PS framework for understanding EF that we believe provides a better account of EF than simpler constructs such as inhibition, and also avoids reifying homuncular constructs (e.g., a central executive [Baddeley, 1996], or a supervisory attentional system [Norman & Shallice, 1986]). Although EF can be understood in fairly domain-general terms, a distinction can be made between the development of relatively hot affective aspects of EF associated with VM-PFC and the development of more purely cognitive, cool aspects associated with L-PFC. Models of EF have traditionally been based on cool EF, and thus major questions for future research concern the development of hot EF, and its relation to cool EF, which echo old questions concerning the relation between cognition and affect (e.g., Damasio, 1994). Zelazo and Cunningham (2007), for example, proposed a neural model of EF, the iterative reprocessing model, that positions hot and cool EF on a continuum of reflective processing and emphasizes the way in which relatively hot and relatively cool aspects of EF interact when one is solving a problem.

Developmental research on both hot and cool EF has revealed that EF first emerges early in development, probably around the end of the first year of life, but also that it continues to develop across a wide range of ages, with adult-level performance on many standard tests of EF being reached at about 12 years of age, and performance on some measures continuing to change into adulthood. This developmental course runs parallel to the protracted growth of PFC. Moreover, failures of EF occur in different situations at different ages, and these situations can be ordered according to the complexity of the inferences required (Zelazo et al., 2003). Work on PFC is also beginning to take account of the role of hierarchical complexity (e.g., Koechlin & Summerfield, 2007; Stuss et al, 1999). Future work should also explore the role of conscious reflection as a process whereby more complex plans can be formulated (Zelazo, 2004) and the role of language in the formulation of these plans (Müller, Jacques, Brocki, & Zelazo, 2009).

From this perspective, age-related increases in complexity can be understood in terms of the hierarchical organization of the neurological concomitants of EF, and, given this organization, PFC lesions in development will have predictable consequences. Naturally, the challenge from a psychological point of view is to describe the hierarchical organization of the function of EF in terms of both underlying cognitive processes and corresponding brain systems.

Finally, EF difficulties may be a common consequence of many different perturbations of the epigenetic process (including many different types of developmental disorder), and different developmental disorders may involve impairments in different aspects of EF. Future work on EF from a developmental psychopathological perspective might explore the developmental relations between hot and cool EF in typical and atypical development and show more precisely how these types of EF are related to different regions of PFC and different neurotransmitter systems.

References

Amodio, D., & Frith, C. (2006). Meeting of minds: The medial frontal cortex and social cognition. *Nature Reviews Neuroscience*, *7*, 268–277.

Anderson, S. W., Bechara, A., Damasio H., Tranel, D., & Damasio A. R. (1999). Impairment of social and moral behavior related to early damage in human prefrontal cortex. *Nature Neuroscience*, *2*, 1032–1037.

Anderson, S. W., Damasio, H., Jones, R. D., & Tranel, D. (1991). Wisconsin card sorting performance as a measure of frontal lobe damage. *Journal of Clinical and Experimental Neuropsychology*, *13*, 909–922.

Andrews, G., & Halford, G. S. (2002). A cognitive complexity metric applied to cognitive development. *Cognitive Psychology*, *45*, 153–219.

Archibald, S. J., & Kerns, K. A. (1999). Identification and description of new tests of executive functioning in children. *Child Neuropsychology*, *5*, 115–129.

Baddeley, A. (1996). Exploring the central executive. *Quarterly Journal of Experimental Psychology: Human Experimental Psychology* [Special issue: Working memory], *49A*, 5–28.

Barkley, R. A. (1997). Behavioral inhibition, sustained attention, and executive functions: Constructing a unifying theory of ADHD. *Psychological Bulletin*, *121*, 65–94.

Baron-Cohen, S. (1997). Are children with autism superior at folk physics? In H. M. Wellman & K. Inagaki (Eds.), *The emergence of core domains of thought: Children's reasoning about physical, psychological, and biological phenomena* (pp. 45–54). San Francisco: Jossey-Bass.

Barresi, J., & Moore, C. (1996). Intentional relations and social understanding. *Behavioral and Brain Sciences*, *19*, 107–154.

Barry, R. J., Clarke, A. R., McCarthy, R., Selikowitz, M., Johnstone, S. J., & Rushby, J. A. (2004). Age and gender effects in EEG coherence: I. Developmental trends in normal children. *Clinical Neurophysiology*, *115*, 2252–2258.

Bechara, A., Damasio, A., Damasio, H., & Anderson, S. (1994). Insensitivity to future consequences following damage to human prefrontal cortex. *Cognition, 50*, 7–15.

Bechara, A., Damasio, H., & Damasio, A. R. (2000). Emotion, decision making and the orbitofrontal cortex. *Cerebral Cortex* [Special issue: The mysterious orbitofrontal cortex], *10*, 295–307.

Bell, J. A., & Fox, N. A. (1992). The relations between frontal brain electrical activity and cognitive development during infancy. *Child Development, 63*, 1142–1163.

Bialystok, E. (1999). Cognitive complexity and attentional control in the bilingual mind. *Child Development, 70*, 636–644.

Bohlmann, N. L., & Fenson, L. (2005). The effects of feedback on perseverative errors in preschool aged children. *Journal of Cognition and Development, 6*, 119–131.

Brooks, P. J., Frye, D., & Samuels, M. C. (1996). *The comprehension and production of deception for self and other.* Unpublished manuscript.

Bub, D. N., Masson, M. E. J., & Lalonde, C. E. (2006). Cognitive control in children: Stroop interference and suppression of word reading. *Psychological Science, 17*, 51–57.

Bullock, M., & Lütkenhaus, P. (1988). The development of volitional behavior in the toddler years. *Child Development, 59*, 664–674.

Bunch, K. M., Andrews, G., & Halford, G. S. (2007). Complexity effects on the children's gambling task. *Cognitive development, 22*, 376–383.

Bunge, S. A., Dudukovic, N. M., Thomason, M. E., Vaidya, C. J., & Gabrieli, J. D. E. (2002). *Development* of frontal lobe contributions to cognitive control in children: Evidence from fMRI. *Neuron, 33*, 301–311.

Bunge, S., & Zelazo, P. D. (2006). A brain-based account of the development of rule use in childhood. *Current Directions in Psychological Science, 15*, 118–121.

Carlson, S. M., Davis, A. C., & Leach, J. G. (2005). Less is more: executive function and symbolic representation in preschool children. *Psychological Science, 16*, 609–616.

Carlson, S., Mandell, D. J., & Williams, L. (2004). Executive function and theory of mind: Stability and prediction from ages 2 to 3. *Developmental Psychology, 40*, 1105–1122.

Case, R. (1985). *Intellectual development: Birth to adulthood.* Orlando, FL: Academic Press.

Castellanos, F. X., Sonuga-Barke, E. J. S., Milham, M. P., & Tannock, R. (2006). Characterizing cognition in ADHD: Beyond executive dysfunction. *Trends in Cognitive Sciences, 10*, 117–123.

Castellanos, F. X., & Tannock, R. (2002). *Neuroscience* of Attention-deficit/Hyperactivity disorder: The search for endophenotypes. *Nature Reviews Neuroscience, 3*, 617–628.

Chelune, G. J., & Baer, R. A. (1986). Developmental norms for the Wisconsin Card Sorting Test. *Journal of Clinical and Experimental Neuropsychology, 8*, 219–228.

Chugani, H., & Phelps, M. (1986, February 21). Maturational changes in cerebral function in infants determined by 18^{FDG} positron emission tomography. *Science, 231*, 840–843.

Clark, A. S., & Goldman-Rakic, P. S. (1989). Gonadal hormones influence the emergence of cortical function in nonhuman primates. *Behavioral Neuroscience, 103*, 1287–1295.

Crone, E. A., & van der Molen, M. W. (2004). Developmental changes in real life decision making: Performance on a gambling task previously shown to depend on the ventromedial prefrontal cortex. *Developmental Neuropsychology, 25*, 251–279.

Damasio, A. (1994). *Descartes' error: Emotion, reason, and the human brain.* New York: Grosset/Putnam.

Damasio, H. (1996). Human neuroanatomy relevant to decision-making. In A. R. Damasio, H. Damasio, & Y. Christen (Eds.), *Neurobiology of decision-making* (pp. 1–12). Berlin: Springer-Verlag.

Davidson, M. C., Amso, D., Cruess-Anderson, L., & Diamond, A. (2006). Development of cognitive control and executive functions from 4–13 years: Evidence from manipulations of memory, inhibition and task switching. *Neuropsychologia, 44*, 2037–2078.

De Bellis, M. D., Keshavan, M. S., Beers, S. R., Hall, J., Frustaci, K., Masalehdan, A., Noll, J., & Boring, A. M. (2001). Sex differences in brain maturation during childhood and adolescence. *Cerebral Cortex, 11*, 552–557.

Delis, D. C., Squire, L. R., Bihrle, A., & Massman, P. (1992). Componential analysis of problem-solving ability: Performance of patients with frontal lobe damage and amnesic patients on a new sorting test. *Neuropsychologia, 30*, 683–697.

Dempster, F. N. (1992). The rise and fall of the inhibitory mechanism: Toward a unified theory of cognitive development and aging. *Developmental Review, 12*, 45–75.

Denckla, M. B., & Reiss, A. L. (1997). Prefrontal-subcortical circuits in developmental disorders. In N. A. Krasnegor, G. R. Lyon, & P. S. Goldman-Rakic (Eds.), *Development of the prefrontal cortex: Evolution, neurobiology, and behavior* (pp. 283–293). Baltimore, MD: Paul Publishing Co., Inc.

Dewey, J. (1931/1985). Context and thought. In J. A. Boydston & A. Sharpe (Eds.), *John Dewey: The later works, 1925–1953* (Vol. 6, pp. 3–21). Carbondale, IL: Southern Illinois University Press.

Diamond, A. (2002). Normal development of prefrontal cortex from birth to young adulthood: Cognitive functions, anatomy, and biochemistry. In D. T. Stuss & R. T. Knight (Eds.), *Principles of frontal lobe function* (pp. 466–503). London: Oxford University Press.

Diamond, A., Carlson, S. M., & Beck, D. M. (2005). Preschool children's performance in task switching on the Dimensional Change Card Sort task: Separating dimensions aids the ability to switch. *Developmental Neuropsychology, 28*, 689–729.

Diamond, A., & Goldman-Rakic, P. S. (1989). Comparison of human infants and rhesus monkeys on Piaget's A-not-B task: Evidence for dependence on dorsolateral prefrontal cortex. *Experimental Brain Research, 74*, 24–40.

Dick, A. S., Overton, W. F., & Kovacs, S. L. (2005). The development of symbolic coordination: Representation of imagined objects, executive function, and theory of mind. *Journal of Cognitive Development, 6*, 133–161.

Duncker, K. (1945). On problem-solving. *Psychological Monographs, 58* (Whole No. 5).

Durston, S., Davidson, M. C., Tottenham, N., Galvan, A., Spicer, J., Fossella, J. A., & Casey, B. J. (2006). A shift from diffuse to focal cortical activity with development. *Developmental Science, 9*, 1–20.

Epstein, H. T. (1986). Stages in human brain development. *Developmental Brain Research, 30*, 114–119.

Eslinger, P. J., Biddle, K. R., & Grattan, L. M. (1997). Cognitive and social development in children with prefrontal cortex lesions. In G. R. Lyon & N. A. Krasnegor (Eds.), *Attention, memory, and executive function* (pp. 295–335). Baltimore, MD: Paul H. Brookes Publishing Co.

Feldman, M. J., & Drasgow, J. (1951). A visual-verbal test for schizophrenia. *Psychiatric Quarterly Supplement, 25*, 55–64.

Flynn, E. (2007). The role of inhibitory control in false belief understanding. *Infant and Child Development, 16*, 53–69.

Friedman, N. P., & Miyake, A. (2004). The relations between inhibition and interference control functions: A latent-variable analysis. *Journal of Experimental Psychology: General, 133*, 101–135.

Frith, C., & Frith, U. (2003). Development and neurophysiology of mentalizing. *Philosophical Transactions of the Royal Society B, Biological Sciences, 358*, 458–473.

Frye, D., Zelazo, P. D., & Palfai, T. (1995). Theory of mind and rule-based reasoning. *Cognitive Development, 10,* 483–527.

Fuster, J. (1989). *The prefrontal cortex: Anatomy, physiology and neuropsychology of the frontal lobe* (2nd ed.). New York: Raven.

Garon, N., Bryson, S. E., & Smith, I. M. (2008). Executive function in preschoolers: A review using an integrative framework. *Psychological Bulletin, 134,* 31–60.

Gathercole, S. E., Pickering, S., Ambridge, B., & Wearing, H. (2004). The structure of working memory from 4 to 15 years of age. *Developmental Psychology, 40,* 177–190.

Gazzaniga, M. S., Ivry, R. B., & Mangun, G. R. (1998). *Cognitive neuroscience: The biology of the mind.* New York: Norton.

Gelman, R., & Meck, D. (1983). Preschoolers' counting: Principles before skill. *Cognition, 13,* 494–505.

Gerardi-Caulton, G. (2000). Sensitivity to spatial conflict and the development of self-regulation in children 24–36 months of age. *Developmental Science, 3/4,* 397–404.

Gerstadt, C. L., Hong, Y. J., & Diamond, A. (1994). The relationship between cognition and action: Performance of children 3.5–7 years old on a Stroop-like dayight test. *Cognition, 53,* 129–153.

Geurts, H. M., van der Oord, S., & Crone, E. A. (2006). Hot and cool aspects of cognitive control in children with ADHD: Decision-making and inhibition. *Journal of Abnormal Child Psychology, 34,* 813–824.

Gladstone, R. (1969). Age, cognitive control and extinction. *Journal of Experimental Child Psychology, 7,* 31–35.

Gladstone, R. (1976). On the ability of young children to use significant cues intelligently. *The Journal of Genetic Psychology, 129,* 311–316.

Goel, V., & Grafman, J. (1995). Are the frontal lobes implicated in "planning" functions? Interpreting data from the Tower of Hanoi. *Neuropsychologia, 33,* 623–642.

Gogtay, N., Giedd, J. N., Lusk, L., Hayashi, K. M., Greenstein, D., Vaituzis, A. C., … Thompson, P. M. (2004). Dynamic mapping of human cortical development during childhood through early adulthood. *Proceedings of the National Academy of Sciences of the United States of America, 101,* 8174–8179.

Goldberg, E. (1995). Rise and fall of modular orthodoxy. *Journal of Clinical and Experimental Neuropsychology, 17,* 193–208.

Golden, C. J. (1981). The Luria-Nebraska children's battery: Theory and formulation. In G. W. Hynd & J. E. Obrzut (Eds.), *Neuropsychological assessment and the school-aged child* (pp. 277–302). New York: Grune & Stratton.

Goldman, P. S., & Alexander, G. E. (1977, June 16). Maturation of prefrontal cortex in the monkey revealed by local reversible cryogenic depression. *Nature, 267,* 613–615.

Grant, D. A., & Berg, E. A. (1948). A behavioral analysis of degree of reinforcement and ease of shifting to new responses in a Weigl-type card-sorting problem. *Journal of Experimental Psychology, 38,* 404–411.

Halford, G., Wilson, W. H., & Phillips, S. (1998). Processing capacity defined by relational complexity: Implications for comparative, developmental, and cognitive psychology. *Behavioral and Brain Sciences, 21,* 803–864.

Heaton, R. K. (1981). *A manual for the Wisconsin Card Sorting Test.* Odessa, FL: Psychological Assessment Resources.

Hill, E. (2004). Executive dysfunction in autism. *Trends in Cognitive Sciences, 8,* 26–32.

Hongwanishkul, D., Happaney, K. R., Lee, W., & Zelazo, P. D. (2005). Hot and cool executive function: Age-related changes and individual differences. *Developmental Neuropsychology, 28,* 617–644.

Hooper, C. J., Luciana, M., Conklin, H. M., & Yarger, R. S. (2004). Adolescents' performance on the Iowa gambling task: Implications for the development of decision making and ventromedial prefrontal cortex. *Developmental Psychology, 40,* 1148–1158.

Hughes, C. (1998a). Finding your marbles: Does preschoolers' strategic behavior predict later understanding of mind? *Developmental Psychology, 34,* 1326–1339.

Hughes, C. (1998b). Executive function in preschoolers: Links with theory of mind and verbal ability. *British Journal of Developmental Psychology, 16,* 233–253.

Huizinga, M., Dolan, C. V., & van der Molen, M. W. (2006). Age-related change in executive function: Developmental trends and a latent variable analysis *Neuropsychologia, 44,* 2017–2036.

Hunter, W. S. (1917). Delayed reaction in a child. *Psychological Review, 24,* 74–87.

Huttenlocher, P. R. (1990). Morphometric study of human cerebral cortex development. *Neuropsychologia, 28,* 517–527.

Jacobs, R., Harvey, A. S., & Anderson, V. (2007). Executive function following focal frontal lobe lesions: Impact of timing of lesion on outcome. *Cortex, 43,* 792–805.

Jacobson, C. F. (1936). Studies of cerebral functions in primates: I. The functions of the frontal association areas in monkeys. *Comparative Psychology Monographs, 13,* 1–30.

Jacques, S., & Zelazo, P. D. (2001). The Flexible Item Selection Task (FIST): A measure of executive function in preschoolers. *Developmental Neuropsychology, 20,* 573–591.

Jacques, S., Zelazo, P. D., Kirkham, N. Z., & Semcesen, T. K. (1999). Rule selection versus rule execution in preschoolers: An error-detection approach. *Developmental Psychology, 35,* 770–780.

Kaller, C. P., Rahm, B., Spreer, J., Mader, I., & Unterrainer, J. M. (2008). Thinking around the corner: The development of planning abilities. *Brain and Cognition, 67,* 360–370.

Kerr, A., & Zelazo, P. D. (2004). Development of "hot" executive function: The children's gambling task. *Brain and Cognition, 55,* 148–157.

Kirkham, N. Z., Cruess, L., & Diamond, A. (2003). Helping children apply their knowledge to their behavior on a dimension-switching task. *Developmental Science, 6,* 449–467.

Klahr, D., & Robinson, M. (1981). Formal assessment of problem solving and planning processes in preschool children. *Cognitive Psychology, 13,* 113–148.

Kloo, D., & Perner, J. (2005). Disentangling dimensions in the Dimensional Change Card Sorting task. *Developmental Science, 8,* 44–56.

Koechlin, E., & Summerfield, C. (2007). An information theoretical approach to prefrontal executive function. *Trends in Cognitive Sciences, 11,* 229–235.

Kolb, B., Gibb, R., & Gorny G. (2000). Cortical plasticity and the development of behavior after early frontal cortical injury. *Developmental Neuropsychology, 18,* 423–444.

Konow, A., & Pribram, K. H. (1970). Error recognition and utilization produced by injury to the frontal cortex in man. *Neuropsychologia, 8,* 489–491.

Lehto, J. E., Juujäarvi, P., Kooistra, L., & Pulkkinen, L. (2003). Dimensions of executive functioning: Evidence from children. *The British Journal of Developmental Psychology, 21,* 59–80.

Levin, H. S., Culhane, K. A., Hartmann, J., Evankovich, K., Mattson, A. J., Harward, H., Ringholz, G., Ewing-Cobbs, L., & Fletcher, J. M. (1991). Developmental changes in performance on tests of purported frontal lobe functioning. *Developmental Neuropsychology, 7,* 377–395.

Lie, C.-H., Specht, K., Marshall, J. C., & Fink, G. R. (2006). Using fMRI to decompose the neural processes underlying the Wisconsin Card Sorting Test. *NeuroImage, 30,* 1038–1049.

Lin, C. C. H., Chen, W. J., Yang, H., Hsiao, C. K., & Tien, A. Y. (2000). Performance on the Wisconsin Card Sorting Test among adolescents in Taiwan: Norms, factorial structure, and relation to schizotypy. *Journal of Clinical and Experimental Neuropsychology, 22,* 69–79.

Logan, G. D. (1994). On the ability to inhibit thought and action: A users' guide to the stop signal paradigm. In D. Dagenbach, & T. H. Carr (Eds.), *Inhibitory processes in attention, memory, and language* (pp. 189–239). San Diego: Academic Press.

Luciana, M., & Nelson, C. A. (1998). The functional emergence of prefrontally-guided working memory systems in four- to eight-year-old children. *Neuropsychologia, 36*, 273–293.

Luna, B., Thulborn, K. R., Munoz, D. P., Merriam, E. P., Garver, K. E., Minshew, N. J., … Sweeney, J. A. (2001). Maturation of widely distributed brain function subserves cognitive development. *NeuroImage, 13*, 786–793.

Luria, A. R. (1966). *Higher cortical functions in man* (2nd ed.). New York: Basic Books. (Original work published in 1962.)

Luria, A. R. (1973). *The working brain: An introduction to neuropsychology* (B. Haigh, Trans.). New York: Basic Books.

MacLeod, C. M., Dodd, M. D., Sheard, E. D., Wilson, D. E., & Bibi, U. (2003). In opposition to inhibition. In B. H. Ross (Ed.), *The psychology of learning and motivation* (Vol. 43, pp. 163–214). New York: Academic Press.

Marsh, R., Gerber, A. J., & Peterson, B. S. (2008). Neuroimaging studies of normal brain development and their relevance for understanding childhood neuropsychiatric disorders. *Journal of the American Academy of Child and Adolescent Psychiatry, 47*, 1233–1251.

Mischel, W., Ebbesen, E. B., & Zeiss, A. M. (1972). Cognitive and attentional mechanisms in delay of gratification. *Journal of Personality and Social Psychology, 21*, 204–218.

Mischel, W., Shoda, Y., & Rodriguez, M. L. (1989, May 26). Delay of gratification in children. *Science, 244*, 933–938.

Miyake, A., Friedman, N. P., Emerson, M. J., Witzki, A. H., Howerter, A., & Wager, T. (2000). The unity and diversity of executive functions and their contributions to complex "frontal lobe" tasks: A latent variable analysis. *Cognitive Psychology, 41*, 49–100.

Moore, C. (in press). The development of future oriented decision-making. In B. Sokol, U. Müller, J. I. M. Carpendale, A. Young, & G. Iarocci (Eds.), *Self- and social-regulation: Exploring the relations between social interaction, social cognition, and the development of executive functions.* New York: Oxford University Press.

Moore, C., Barresi, J., & Thompson, C. (1998). The cognitive basis of future-oriented prosocial behavior. *Social Development, 7*, 198–218.

Morton, J. B., & Munakata, Y. (2002). Active vs. latent representations: A neural network model of perseveration, dissociation, and décalage. *Developmental Psychobiology, 40*, 255–265.

Morton, J. B., Trehub, S. E., & Zelazo, P. D. (2003). Sources of inflexibility in 6-year-olds' understanding of emotion in speech. *Child Development, 74*, 1857–1868.

Moses, L. J., & Tahiroglu, D. (in press). Clarifying the relation between executive function and children's theories of mind. In B. Sokol, U. Müller, J. I. M. Carpendale, A. Young, & G. Iarocci (Eds.), *Self- and social-regulation: Exploring the relations between social interaction, social cognition, and the development of executive functions.* New York: Oxford University Press.

Moses, P., & Stiles, J. (2002). The lesion methodology: Contrasting views from adult and child studies, *Developmental Psychobiology, 40*, 266–277.

Müller, U., Dick, A. S., Gela, K., Overton, W. F., & Zelazo, P. D. (2006). The role of negative priming in preschoolers' flexible rule use on the Dimensional Change Card Sort task. *Child Development, 77*, 395–412.

Müller, U., Jacques, S., Brocki, K., & Zelazo, P. D. (2009). The executive functions of language in preschool children. In A. Winsler, C. Fernyhough, & N. Montero (Eds.), *Private speech, executive functioning, and the development of verbal self-regulation* (pp. 53–68). Cambridge: Cambridge University Press.

Munakata, Y., & Yerys, B. E. (2001). All together now: When dissociations between knowledge and action disappear. *Psychological Science, 12*, 335–337.

Nigg, J. T. (2000). On inhibition/disinhibition in developmental psychopathology: Views from cognitive and personality psychology and a working inhibition hypothesis. *Psychological Bulletin, 126*, 220–246.

Nigg, J. T., Willcutt, E. G., Doyle, A. E., & Sonuga-Barke, J. S. (2005). Causal heterogeneity in attention-deficit/hyperactivity disorder: Do we need neuropsychologically impaired subtypes? *Biological Psychiatry, 57*, 1224–1230.

Norman, D. A., & Shallice, T. (1986). Attention to action: Willed and automatic control of behavior. In R. J. Davidson, G. E. Schwartz, & D. Shapiro (Eds.), *Consciousness and self-regulation* (Vol. *4*, pp. 4–18). New York: Plenum.

O'Donnell, S., Noseworthy, M., Levine, B., Brandt, M., & Dennis, M. (2005). Cortical thickness of the frontopolar area in typically developing children and adolescents. *NeuroImage, 24*, 948–954.

O'Hearn, K., Asato, M., Ordaz, S., & Luna, B. (2008). Neurodevelopment and executive function in autism. *Development and Psychopathology, 20*, 1103–1132.

Overman, W. H., Bachevalier, J., Schuhmann, E., & McDonough-Ryan, P. (1997). Sexually dimorphic brain-behavior development: A comparative perspective. In N. A. Krasnegor & G. R. Lyon (Eds.), *Development of the prefrontal cortex: Evolution, neurobiology, and behavior* (pp. 337–357). Baltimore, MD: Paul H. Brookes Publishing Co.

Paniak, C., Miller, H. B., Murphy, D., Patterson, I., & Keizer, J. (1996). Canadian developmental norms for 9–14 year-olds on the Wisconsin Card Sorting Test. *Canadian Journal of Rehabilitation, 9*, 233–237.

Pennington, B. F. (1997). Dimensions of executive functions in normal and abnormal development. In N. A. Krasnegor, G. R. Lyon, & P. S. Goldman-Rakic (Eds.), *Development of the prefrontal cortex: Evolution, neurobiology, and behavior* (pp. 265–281). Baltimore: Paul H. Brookes Publishing Co.

Pennington, B. F., & Ozonoff, S. (1996). Executive functions and developmental psychopathology. *Journal of Child Psychology and Psychiatry, 37*, 51–87.

Perner, J., & Lang, B. (1999). Development of theory of mind and cognitive control. *Trends in Cognitive Science, 3*, 337–344.

Piaget, J. (1976). *The grasp of consciousness*. Cambridge, MA: Harvard University Press.

Pietrefesa, A. S., & Evans, D. W. (2007). Affective and neuropsychological correlates of children's rituals and compulsive-like behaviors: Continuities and discontinuities with obsessive–compulsive disorder. *Brain and Cognition, 65*, 36–46.

Prencipe, A., & Zelazo, P. D. (2005). Development of affective decision making for self and other: Evidence for the integration of first- and third-person perspectives. *Psychological Science, 16*, 501–505.

Rilling J. (2006). Human and nonhuman primate brains: are they allometrically scaled versions of the same design? *Evolutionary Anthropology, 15*, 66–77.

Robbins, T. W. (2000). Chemical neuromodulation of frontal-executive functions in humans and other animals. *Experimental Brain Research, 133*, 130–138.

Roberts, R. J., & Pennington, B. F. (1996). An interactive framework for examining prefrontal cognitive processes. *Developmental Neuropsychology, 12*, 105–126.

Rolls, E. T., Hornak, J., Wade, D., & McGrath, J. (1994). Emotion-related learning in patients with social and emotional changes associated with frontal lobe damage. *Journal of Neurology, Neurosurgery and Psychiatry, 57*, 1518–1524.

Rueda, M. R., Fan, J., Halparin, J., Gruber, D., Lercari, L. P., McCandliss, B. D., & Posner, M. I. (2004). Development of attention during childhood. *Neuropsychologia, 42*, 1029–1040.

Rueda, M. R., Posner, M. I., Rothbart, M. K., & Davis-Stober, C. P. (2004). Development of the time course for processing conflict: An event-related potentials study with 4 year olds and adults. *BMC Neuroscience, 5*, 1–13.

Russell, J., Mauthner, N., Sharpe, S., Tidswell, T. (1991). The "windows task" as a measure of strategic deception in preschoolers and autistic subjects. *British Journal of Developmental Psychology, 9*, 331–349.

Scheibel, R. S., & Levin, H. S. (1997). Frontal lobe dysfunction following closed head injury in children. In N. A. Krasnegor, G. R. Lyon, & P. S. Goldman-Rakic (Eds.), *Development of the prefrontal cortex: Evolution, neurobiology, and behavior* (pp. 241–263). Baltimore, MD: Paul Brookes Publishing Co.

Séguin, J. R. (2004). Neurocognitive elements of antisocial behavior: Relevance of an orbitofrontal cortex account. *Brain and Cognition, 55*, 185–197.

Semendeferi, K., Lu, A., Schenker, N., & Damasio, H. (2002). Humans and great apes share a large frontal cortex. *Nature Neuroscience, 5*, 272–276.

Shallice, T. (1982). Specific impairments of planning. In D. E. Broadbent & L. Weiskrantz (Eds.), *The neuropsychology of cognitive function* (pp. 199–209). London: The Royal Society.

Shallice, T., & Burgess, P. W. (1991). Deficits in strategy application following frontal lobe damage in man. *Brain, 111*, 727–741.

Shaw, P., Kabani, N. J., Lerch, J. P., Eckstrand, K., Lenroot, R., … Wise, S. P. (2008). Neurodevelopmental trajectories of the human cerebral cortex. *The Journal for Neuroscience, 28*, 3586–3594.

Solanto, M. V., Abikoff, H., Sonuga-Barke, E., Schachar, R., Logan, G., Wigal, T., … Turkel, E. (2001). The ecological validity of delay aversion and response inhibition as measures of impulsivity in AD/HD: A supplement to the NIMH Multi-Modal Treatment Study of AD/HD. *Journal of Abnormal Child Psychology, 29*, 215–228.

Somsen, R. J. M. (2007). The development of attention regulation in the Wisconsin Card Sorting task. *Developmental Science, 10*, 664–680.

Stroop, J. R. (1935). Studies of interference in serial verbal reactions. *Journal of Experimental Psychology, 18*, 643–662.

Stuss, D. T., & Alexander, M. P. (2000). Executive functions and the frontal lobes: A conceptual view. *Psychological Research, 63*, 289–298.

Stuss, D. T., & Benson, D. F. (1986). *The frontal lobes*. New York: Raven Press.

Stuss, D. T., Eskes, G. A., & Foster, J. K. (1994). Experimental neuropsychological studies of frontal lobe functions. In F. Boller, & J. Grafman (Eds.), *Handbook of neuropsychology* (Vol. 9, pp. 149–185). Amsterdam: Elsevier.

Stuss, D. T., Toth, J. P., Franchi, D., Alexander, M. P., Tipper, S., & Craik, F. I. M. (1999). Dissociation of attentional processes in patients with focal frontal and posterior lesions. *Neuropsychologia, 37*, 1005–1027.

Thompson, C., Barresi, J., & Moore, C. (1997). The development of future-oriented prudence and altruism in preschoolers. *Cognitive Development, 12*, 199–212.

Thompson, P. M., Giedd, J. N., Woods, R. P., MacDonald, D., Evans, A. C., & Toga, A. W. (2000, March). Growth patterns in the developing brain detected by using continuum mechanical tensor maps. *Nature, 404*, 190–193.

Toplak, M. E., Jain, U., & Tannock, R. (2005). Executive and motivational processes in adolescents with attention-deficit-hyperactivity disorder (ADHD). *Behavioral and Brain Functions*, 1:8. doi: 10.1186/1744-9081-1-8.

Tranel, D., Anderson, S. W., & Benton, A. (1994). Development of the concept of "executive function" and its relationship to the frontal lobes. In F. Boller & J. Grafman (Eds.), *Handbook of neuropsychology* (Vol. 9, pp. 125–148). Amsterdam: Elsevier.

Tsujimoto, S. (2008). The prefrontal cortex: Functional neural development during early childhood. *Neuroscientist, 14*, 345–358.

Van der Sluis, S., de Jong, P. F., & van der Leij, A. (2007). Executive functioning in children, and its relations with reasoning, reading, and arithmetic. *Intelligence, 35*, 427–449.

Welsh, M. C., Pennington, B. F., & Groisser, D. B. (1991). A normative-developmental study of executive function: A window on prefrontal function in children. *Developmental Neuropsychology, 7*, 131–149.

Werner, H., & Kaplan, H. (1963). *Symbol formation*. New York: Wiley.

Wiebe, S. A., Espy, K. A., & Charak, D. (2008). Using confirmatory factor analysis to understand executive control in preschool children: I. Latent structure. *Developmental Psychology, 44*, 575–587.

Willcutt, E. G., Doyle, A. E., Nigg, J. T., Faraone, S. V., & Pennington, B. F. (2005). Validity of the executive function theory of Attention-Deficit/Hyperactivity disorder: A meta-analytic review. *Biological Psychiatry, 57*, 1336–1346.

Wimmer, H., & Perner, J. (1983). Beliefs about beliefs: Representation and constraining function of wrong beliefs in young children's understanding of deception. *Cognition, 13*, 103–128.

Wise, S. P., Murray, E. A., & Gerfen, C. R. (1996). The frontal cortex-basal ganglia system in primates. *Critical Reviews in Neurobiology, 10*, 317–356.

Yakovlev, P. I., & Lecours, A. R. (1967). The myelogenetic cycles of regional maturation of the brain. In A. Minkowski (Ed.), *Regional development of the brain in early life* (pp. 3–70). Oxford: Blackwell.

Zelazo, P. D. (2004). The development of conscious control in childhood. *Trends in Cognitive Sciences, 8*, 12–17.

Zelazo, P. D. (2006). The Dimensional Change Card Sort (DCCS): A method of assessing executive function in children. *Nature Protocols, 1*, 297–301.

Zelazo, P. D., Carter, A., Reznick, J. S., & Frye, D. (1997). Early development of executive function: A problem-solving framework. *Review of General Psychology, 1*, 198–226.

Zelazo, P. D., & Cunningham, W. (2007). Executive function: Mechanisms underlying emotion regulation. In J. Gross (Ed.), *Handbook of emotion regulation*. New York: Guilford.

Zelazo, P. D., Frye, D., & Rapus, T. (1996). An age-related dissociation between knowing rules and using them. *Cognitive Development, 11*, 37–63.

Zelazo, P. D., & Jacques, S. (1996). Children's rule use: Representation, reflection and cognitive control. In R. Vasta (Ed.), *Annals of child development* (Vol. 12, pp. 119–176). London: Jessica Kingsley.

Zelazo, P. D., & Müller, U. (2002). Executive function in typical and atypical development. In U. Goswami, *Blackwell handbook of childhood cognitive development* (pp. 445–469). Oxford: Blackwell.

Zelazo, P. D., Müller, U., Frye, D., & Marcovitch, S. (2003). The development of executive function in early childhood. *Monographs of the Society for Research in Child Development, 68* (Serial No. 264).

Zelazo, P. D., & Reznick, J. S. (1991). Age-related asynchrony of knowledge and action. *Child Development, 62*, 719–735.

Zelazo, P. D., Reznick, J. S., & Piñon, D. E. (1995). Response control and the execution of verbal rules. *Developmental Psychology, 31*, 508–517.

CHAPTER TWENTY-THREE

Language and Cognition
Evidence from Disordered Language

Barbara Dodd and Sharon Crosbie

Introduction

This chapter explores the relationship between children's language development and cognitive ability from the perspective of communication disorder. Around 15% of children fail to acquire language milestones age appropriately. Their speech may be difficult to understand because they mispronounce many words. They may not understand others' speech, be able to construct complex sentences, or find the words they need to express ideas. Their use of language may be socially inappropriate. Phonological (speech sound system), syntactic (sentence structuring), semantic (meaning), and pragmatic (language use) functions may be impaired individually or in combination, and a deficit in one function often has implications for other functions. The causes of developmental communication disorders are various: environmental, physiological, or psychological, although most children have difficulties for which there is no known etiology.

Cognition involves the mental process of knowing: awareness, perception, memory, reasoning, and judgment. Definitions sometimes limit cognition to knowledge of a non-linguistic nature. For example, theories of normal adult abilities assume that innate properties of the human brain and typical experience will lead to similar perception and conception of objects irrespective of the language spoken (Jackendoff, 1996; Pinker, 1989). Recent findings, however, suggest that performance on cognitive experimental tasks involving preparation for language production is affected by the language spoken, influencing cognitive processes such as allocation of attention and non-linguistic similarity judgment (Gennari, Sloman, Malt, & Fitch, 2002; Papafragou, Hulbert, & Trueswell, 2008). Cognitive mechanisms that abstract patterns of spatially, causally, and temporally ordered information must analyze and integrate perceptual information to form inferences using both bottom-up and top-down mental processing (Kintsch, 2005).

Theories of both language and cognition (Chomsky, 1986; Piaget, 1952; Vygotsky, 1962) have primarily arisen from the study of normally developing children and adults. Interpretation of evidence from people with a communication disorder or a cognitive impairment is complicated. Mapping between linguistic and non-linguistic knowledge is not easily apparent when either one or both systems are impaired. One way of answering the general question "How does research on communication disorders in children inform the debate concerning the relationship between language and cognition?" is to identify more definite issues. Two specific questions seem crucial. The first is *Are children with an intellectual cognitive disability always language disordered?* In the first part of our chapter we present evidence showing that impaired cognition is associated with very different profiles of severity and type of language impairment. Next, we ask *Is language disorder in otherwise normal children associated with specific cognitive deficits?* The second part of this chapter reviews the evidence on language disorder in otherwise "normal" children. The data indicate that aspects of cognition are not always intact.

Language in Populations with Impaired Cognition

Up until the 1970s research suggested that cognitive impairment was inevitably associated with language delays and disorders. It was assumed that the severity of the cognitive impairment predicted language attainment across the board. For some congenital neurodevelopmental disorders, this relationship holds (Levy & Kave, 1999). Recent investigations, however, have led to three qualifications of that general assumption which have implications for the modularity of language and cognition as well as for the modularity of different aspects of language (phonology, syntax, and semantics):

- Specific causes of cognitive impairment are associated with different profiles of language disability.
- Specific aspects of language are differently affected within any one causal category of cognitive impairment (e.g. Down syndrome or Williams syndrome).
- Some individuals who are cognitively impaired have spared function of some aspects of language.

Etiology of cognitive impairment and language profile

The first qualification concerns the language profiles of individuals with cognitive impairment of different etiology. Two uncontroversial diagnostic categories of intellectual impairment are Down syndrome and Williams syndrome. Both are genetic conditions. Nearly all cases of Down syndrome (DS) result from the chromosomal disorder, trisomy 21. Williams syndrome (WS) is a congenital metabolic disorder of genetic origin (microdeletion of one elastin gene and its surrounding DNA on gene 7). The occurrence of DS is one infant in every thousand live births, compared to one infant born with WS in every 25,000 live births. Physiological factors associated with DS include: hearing loss; visual impairment; hypotonia (low muscle tone); cranio-facial abnormalities (e.g. wide pharynx); chronic upper respiratory tract infections; and cardiovascular defects. Individuals with WS are at risk for: hyperacusis (sensitive hearing, but no hearing loss); visual strabismus; motor difficulties (strength, balance, motor planning); hypercalcemia (high levels of calcium in the blood); gastrointestinal abnormalities; and renal and cardiovascular defects.

Both syndromes are characterized by intellectual impairment. People with DS constitute about 30% of the moderate to severe intellectually impaired population (25–55 IQ) (Vicari, 2006). While they do not differ from other cognitively impaired populations (matched for chronological age and IQ) on most behavioral measures, it is often claimed that their linguistic abilities are more impaired. In comparison with both typically developing and intellectually impaired mental-age matched peers, children with DS perform poorly on measures of comprehension of complex sentences (Kernan, 1990), mean length of utterance, sentence complexity, use of articles, verb inflections and pronouns (Rondal & Lambert, 1983), and articulation and phonology (Dodd & Thompson, 2001). Rondal and Edwards (1997) concluded "that some persistent speech and language differences may indeed exist between DS and non-DS mentally retarded persons" (p. 84).

Intellectual impairment in WS is predominantly in the moderate-to-mild range (40–70 IQ), and they are reported to have difficulties with number, problem solving, and spatial cognition (see Stevens & Karmiloff-Smith, 1997). Behavioral characteristics include hyperactivity and short attention span. In early childhood their linguistic skills are reported to lag behind cognition (Stojanovik & James, 2006). In contrast, by adolescence there have been some reports of *relatively* intact linguistic functioning. For example, Bellugi, Lai, and Wang (1997) found that the spontaneous language of the 30 adolescents in their study was "syntactically impeccable" and that grammatically complex sentences were produced. Rondal and Edwards (1997) concluded that phonological and morphosyntactic abilities are spared in relation to their level of cognitive impairment.

The differences identified in the linguistic abilities of children with DS and WS has generated numerous studies (Clahsen & Almazan, 1998; Grant, Karmiloff-Smith, Berthoud, & Cristophe, 1996; Jarrold, Baddeley, & Hewes, 1998; Karmiloff-Smith et al., 1997; Perovic, 2006; Stojanovik, Perkins, & Howard, 2004; Tyler et al., 1997). For example, Joffe and Varlokosta (2006) compared ten sets of three children with WS, DS (age range 5; 11–14) and typical development (TD; mean age 4.4 years) matched for mental age (from 3 years and 2 months to 6 years and 8 months). The results indicated that the children with WS and DS performed less well than TD controls on standardized and non-standardized measures of receptive and expressive grammar and semantics. Participants with WS tended to perform better than children with DS on standardized measures of receptive and expressive semantics and non-word repetition; and on non-standardized measures of morphosyntax. These differences however were not always statistically significant.

Despite the large number of studies, however, existing data are fragmentary. Research reports often have few subjects, focus on only one aspect of language, assume diagnostic groups are homogeneous, interpret data from a specific age level as being characteristic of all ages, and match different groups in different ways (e.g., mean length of utterance [MLU], performance IQ measures). Another fundamental issue concerns the assessment tasks used. Children are most often assessed on "static" standardized tests (e.g., the British

Picture Vocabulary Scale- 3; Dunn, Dunn, Whetton, & Burley, 1997) or similar non-standardized tasks designed to examine a particular sub-skill in depth (e.g., morphosyntax). Given cognitive impairment and educational experience, such tasks might not provide a fair reflection of language function. A static task (the PPVT-R) has been shown to underestimate the receptive language ability of children with DS, compared to dynamic assessment where mediation was used to focus children's attention on the task and inhibit impulsivity (Alony & Kozulin, 2007).

In their reviews, Mervis and Becerra (2007) and Karmiloff-Smith, Brown, Grice, and Paterson (2008) challenged the assumption that people with WS had any language ability that is "intact." Nevertheless, Karmiloff-Smith et al. (1997, p. 246) acknowledged that the grammatical ability of people with WS was "surprisingly good given WS level of mental retardation." For people with DS, the proposal that their linguistic impairment is greater than would be predicted by their cognitive abilities, is less controversial (Perovic 2006; Vicari, 2006). Different etiologies, then, are associated with different profiles of language strengths and weaknesses. The relationship between language and cognition is not necessarily linear.

Profile of communicative disability in one diagnostic category of cognitive impairment

The second factor that changed how the relationship between language and cognition is perceived arose from research indicating that different aspects of language could be impaired to different degrees within one individual. Research suggests that children with DS have difficulty acquiring the formal structure of language. Their ability to master the phonological and syntactic constraints of language would appear more impaired than expected given their cognitive ability. Ring and Clahsen (2005) and Perovic (2006) demonstrated that people with DS have a specific syntactic deficit in comprehending reflexive pronouns (e.g., myself, himself) and passive constructions. Perovic (2006, p. 1628) argued that these findings "are at odds with any proposal which states that the limited grammatical achievement in DS is related to a severe slowing down of linguistic development." Similarly, Fabretti, Pizzuto, Vicari, and Volterra (1997) compared the performance of DS and TD groups matched for MLU on a story description task. They found that although the two groups did not differ on a lexical measure, the participants with DS omitted more morphemes and used unusual syntactic and pragmatic forms. Other studies confirm that children with DS show specific problems in the knowledge and use of grammatical features (see Vicari, 2006).

In contrast, their *use* of language is considered less impaired. Children with DS are reported to use one-word utterances to request interesting objects in the same way as normally developing children matched for Piagetian stage (Greenwald & Leonard, 1979). Rondal and Edwards' (1997) review concluded that the variety of speech acts (questions, assertions, suggestions, commands) is appropriate for their cognitive level. They argued that the language profile of children with DS reflects relative strengths in thematic, semantic, and pragmatic measures and relative weaknesses in morphosyntactic and phonetic-phonological aspects.

The speech of both children and adults with DS not only clearly differentiates them from other etiological categories of cognitive impairment, but is also the aspect of their functional communication that is most impaired (Kumin, 1999; Bunn, Simon, Welsh, Watson, & Elliot, 2002). The speech of children with DS is often unintelligible. While the phonemes acquired are appropriate, the order of their emergence does not follow the typical order of acquisition. Research suggests that when compared with the speech of children matched for intellectual disability who do not have DS, a greater degree of disability is revealed. Phonological development is slow and difficult, and follows a different course to that of typically developing children. While delayed phonological acquisition typifies the speech of children who are intellectually disabled but do not have DS, children with DS have a specific difficulty and are prone to inconsistent pronunciation of the same words. For example, when 15 children with DS were asked to name the same pictures on a naming task on three separate occasions in one 45-minute session, more than 67% of the words were pronounced differently (e.g. umbrella produced as [ɤnbE, ɤnbEdɤ and ɤmbEjɤ]) (Dodd and Thompson, 2001).

The two important characteristics of the speech of people with DS that require explanation are that they make fewer errors in imitation than in spontaneous production of the same words (e.g., Lenneberg, 1967), and that their production is inconsistent (Borghi, 1990). Vicari's (2006) review concluded that hearing loss could not account for linguistic disorders associated with DS, indicating that impaired processing or output constraints are implicated (e.g., phonological short-term memory deficit; Hulme & Mackenzie, 1992). Bunn et al.'s (2002) study evaluated the hypothesis that a neuropsychological disconnection in information processing (speech perception tasks and speech production tasks occurring in different cerebral hemispheres) might account for the speech difficulties associated with DS. Their results indicated that although the participants with DS made more speech errors than cognitively matched controls when imitating four-word sequences, they also did so when labeling pictures. The participants with DS did not make more errors than controls, however, when they were reading the same words. These findings suggest that hemispheric disconnection cannot account for the speech disorder associated with DS.

Inconsistent speech errors (where the same lexical item is mispronounced in different ways) are reported for two other speech disordered populations. Kumin and Adams (2000) asserted that children with DS have childhood apraxia of speech (CAS) – a motor-speech disorder characterized by poor performance on diadochokinetic tasks, vowel errors, more errors in multisyllabic utterances, poor phonotactics, and inconsistency of word production (Ozanne, 2005). Another group of children with speech disorder make inconsistent speech errors (Dodd, Leahy, & Hambly, 1989) but can be primarily discriminated from children with CAS by their word-repetition behavior. Children with CAS perform less well when they imitate words than when they produce them spontaneously while children with an inconsistent speech disorder, like children with DS, are better in imitation than spontaneous production. These children's inconsistent speech difficulty is associated with a phonological planning deficit (Dodd, Holm, Crosbie, & McCormack, 2005) that can be successfully treated by a core vocabulary approach to intervention in both non-DS children with inconsistent speech disorder (Crosbie, Holm, & Dodd, 2005) and DS children (Dodd, McCormack, & Woodyatt, 1995). Another beneficial approach to intervention has been to teach children with DS to read (Buckley, 2003). Both intervention strategies provide children with information about how to plan phonological sequences for whole words, leading to consistent production with fewer segment errors and enhanced intelligibility.

In summary, one of the more frequent types of cognitive impairment (DS) is characterized by an uneven profile of linguistic ability. Research evidence suggests that while semantic and pragmatic functions are appropriate for cognitive level, phonology and aspects of syntax are specifically impaired. Not all individuals with DS, however, show the same profile of disability. In the next section, the remarkable linguistic abilities of two adults with cognitive impairment are described.

Savants: individuals with cognitive impairment but relatively spared language function

The term savant refers to exceptional people who despite cognitive impairment demonstrate remarkable ability in one particular domain (e.g., music, mathematics, art, or language). Rondal and Edwards (1997) summarize data on a dozen cases where language abilities were exceptional in comparison to IQ, Piagetian stage, and cause of cognitive impairment (e.g., Bellugi, Marks, Bihrle, & Ssabo, 1988; Cromer, 1991;Yamada, 1990). Two examples of exceptional language development despite cognitive impairment are now briefly reviewed.

Françoise. Rondal (1994a, 1994b) reported a detailed case study of a 32-year-old Frenchwoman with DS. Françoise had a verbal IQ of 70, and a non-verbal IQ of 64. She had difficulty with spatial subtests, arithmetic, and memory for numbers. On the Epreuves Differentielles d'Efficience Intellectuelle (Perron-Borelli & Misès, 1974), an intelligence test consisting of eight verbal and non-verbal subtests, Françoise achieved a verbal mental age of 9 years 10 months and a non-verbal mental age of 5 years 8 months. In terms of her non-verbal intellectual functioning, Françoise's performance is typical of adults with DS.

In contrast her spontaneous spoken language was fluent with appropriate intonation and her pronunciation was error free. Her mean length of utterance was 12.24 morphemes. Syntactically, Françoise produced complete sentences with correct word order. She made no errors in the construction of declarative, interrogative, imperative, emphatic, or exclamatory sentences either affirmatively or negatively. Complex constructions, like embedded clauses and passive voice, were used appropriately, articles were marked for number, gender, and for contrast between specific and non-specific reference. Extensive analyses of her spontaneous spoken language revealed Françoise's mastery of expressive syntax (see Rondal, 1994a, 1994b).

Psycholinguistic tasks assessing comprehension of complex grammatical constructions revealed Françoise's ability to be near normal. Her performance on standardized vocabulary tests was at the lower end of the normal range. Assessment of Françoise's language functioning revealed that she made occasional lexical errors in locutions (e.g., *y a* for *il y a*), adverbial derivations, and expressions. More importantly, Françoise's conversational speech showed difficulties with discourse organization. For example, although she used a range of conjunctive forms (e.g. *et, alors, mais, donc*) at the beginning of utterances, these forms did not establish relationships between utterances. Rondal and Edwards (1997, p. 94) interpreted this, and other phenomena, such as the repeated use of stereotyped expressions and the alternate introduction of two ideas, as an indication that "although discourse taken at the level of the speech turn ... is coherent, the larger text lacks cohesion."

While careful analyses and extensive testing revealed some limitations in Françoise's language functioning, they fail to detract from the major finding. Despite moderate cognitive impairments due to DS, which is typically associated with poor language skills, Françoise mastered her native language. The following case study is extraordinary because Christopher is multilingual.

Christopher. Christopher's remarkable linguistic skills were first described by O'Connor and Hermelin (1991), when he was 29 years old. Although he had a non-verbal IQ of 67, Christopher demonstrated the ability to translate into English from German, French, and Spanish. His morphosyntactic comprehension was adequate in all four languages and standardized vocabulary tests revealed above-average performance in English, German, French, and Spanish. Subsequently, Smith and Tsimpli's (1995) book presented detailed descriptions of Christopher's linguistic and cognitive abilities, exploring the extent to which he could use his formal linguistic knowledge to communicate effectively. The following summary is drawn from Smith and Tsimpli (1995).

> Christopher, born in 1962, cannot live independently. He has difficulty finding his way around and his gross and fine motor skills are poor. Perinatal brain damage was diagnosed at six weeks of age and Christopher's developmental milestones were delayed. He was considered to be cognitively impaired and attended special schools, eventually being transferred to a school for physically handicapped children. His main interests at home and at school were foreign languages. Christopher performed within normal limits on verbal assessments, and well below the normal range on most non-verbal tests.

After extensive testing of Christopher's linguistic abilities in English, Smith and Tsimpli (1995) concluded that "his knowledge of his first language is essentially perfect" (p. 43). Assessment included asking for judgments concerning sentence "goodness" and the correction of "bad" sentences (e.g., Stimulus: *Who did you say Mary met at John's party*? Correction *Whom did you say Mary met at John's party?*). Christopher demonstrated competence across a broad range of grammatical structures (e.g., declaratives, passives, negatives, interrogatives, involving variations in agreement and word-order). Similar tasks established that his lexical and semantic skills were exceptional given his cognitive deficit. Although he demonstrated adequate performance on tests of pragmatic skills (e.g., discourse) he was unable to understand jokes or handle irony and metaphor. This deficit reflected Christopher's difficulty with second-order representation (i.e., understanding a propositional form interpretatively rather than descriptively as in *No man is an island*). This finding indicated that despite intact grammar, Christopher's cognitive abilities limit his use of linguistic inference.

Christopher has varying degrees of knowledge (from elementary to fluent production and comprehension) of 16 languages: Danish, Dutch, Finnish, French, German, modern Greek, Hindi, Italian, Norwegian, Polish, Portuguese, Russian, Spanish, Swedish, Turkish, and Welsh. These languages represent a wide range of language families (Indo-European, Uralic, and Altaic) and include different word orders (subject–object–verb; subject–verb–object) and different scripts (Cyrillic, Greek, Devanagari). Smith and Tsimpli (1995) assessed Christopher's linguistic knowledge of modern Greek, French, Spanish, and Italian, those second languages in which he is most competent. His lexical and morphological skills were shown to be better than his syntactic ability. The grammar of his first language influenced judgments of the grammatical soundness of sentences in other languages and his use of syntax in other languages was limited. In contrast Christopher's acquisition of lexical and morphological information was exceptional. "He manifests an attention bordering on obsession with the orthographic form of words and their morphological make-up … identifying appropriate features of their number, case, gender and agreement system" (Smith & Tsimpli, 1995, p. 82).

Smith and Tsimpli (1995) concluded that Christopher's profile of abilities in his first and second languages provides evidence for the modularity of language. That is, that the mental processes that support language are distinct from other perceptual and mental functions. Bates (1997) disputed that Christopher's abilities, and those of other "language savants" can be explained by the notion of modularity. She argued that Christopher's linguistic strengths and weaknesses could be accounted for by a "special talent" in lexical learning and pattern recognition but impaired pragmatics ameliorated by an interest in foreign languages that were "his life's work and greatest achievement" (Bates, 1997, p. 10).

Bates's review argues that all aspects of the language of people with intellectual disability need to be intact for language and cognition to be considered as modular. Both Françoise and Christopher show a dichotomy between their formal language abilities and their higher language skills such as inferencing, non-literal language, humor, and discourse cohesion. For example, Françoise has excellent morphosyntax and phonology but difficulty using her formal linguistic skills in conversation. Similarly Christopher struggles with higher-level language skills (e.g., humor, discourse). Both cases demonstrate that language not only involves understanding of formal linguistic structure such as syntax and phonology, but also the ability to use knowledge of language to communicate. Both cases are exceptional in that they demonstrate that cognition does not always limit acquisition of the formal aspects of language ability. The next section examines this issue from another perspective.

Language Disorders in the Absence of Intellectual Impairment or Sensory Deficits

In this section the cognitive abilities of children with two different profiles of language function are examined. One group, children who have impaired morphosyntax and/or semantics, are usually classified as having a specific language impairment (SLI). SLI has an incidence of 7.6% among 5-year-olds, with 70% of these children continuing to have low language performance at age 18–20 (Ervin, 2001). The other group of children has a spoken phonological impairment that makes speech difficult or impossible to understand. Phonological impairment has an incidence of 6.4% with many children having consequent difficulties with literacy, academic achievement, and social relationships (Broomfield & Dodd, 2005; Dodd, 1995).

Specific language impairment

SLI is a diagnosis that describes children who fail to acquire normal language functions in the absence of any obvious cognitive or sensory deficits (Aram, Morris, & Hall, 1993; Bishop, 1997; Stark & Tallal, 1981). By definition these children appear to support the argument that language is modular (e.g. Smith & Tsimpli, 1995) and that intact cognition does not guarantee typical language development. However, investigation of children labeled as having SLI suggests that specific cognitive processes differ from those of their non-impaired peers.

Exploring the label: SLI. Diagnosis of SLI is based on exclusion criteria. Neurological, sensory, behavioral, and emotional causality must be ruled out before comparing the child's verbal and non-verbal functioning. A range of standardized assessments are used to compare language function to estimates of non-verbal performance (in terms of age-equivalent scores or standard deviation cut-off points, e.g., 2 standard deviations below the mean). If there is a mismatch between verbal and non-verbal performance, particularly when non-verbal performance falls within the normal range, a diagnosis of SLI is made.

Consequently children with SLI are not a homogenous group (e.g., Bishop, 1997). Recognition of this variation resulted in attempts to develop logical and clinically relevant classification systems. Traditional taxonomies of SLI (American Psychiatric Association, 1994) make a distinction between receptive (comprehension) and expressive subgroups. More detailed linguistically based classification systems (Aram & Nation, 1975; Bishop & Rosenbloom, 1987; Rapin, 1996) have greater relevance but were never validated.

Conti-Ramsden, Crutchley, and Botting (1997) studied the characteristics of a large national cohort of 7-year-old children attending language units in England. They used a battery of standardized tests and teacher opinion to examine the extent to which psychometric tests differentiated clusters of children with SLI. They compared their data with that of Rapin and Allen (1987) and identified similar, distinct subgroups. Conti-Ramsden and Botting (1999) reassessed the children in the cohort 1 year later addressing two important issues: the stability of the subgroups and stability of the children's classification. The same profiles of language difficulties described in the original study remained but individual children (45% of the sample) moved across subgroups primarily due to change in the children's vocabulary or phonology. Longitudinal studies are useful as they provide information about the stability of the disorder. However the results need to be interpreted in light of the fact that the children were receiving intensive speech and language therapy that might have altered their profile of abilities.

The use of standardized tests to collect data to establish subgroups is problematic because it limits the type of data available for analysis. Dunn, Flax, Sliwinski, and Aram (1996) suggest that standardized assessments are more restrictive and less sensitive to language disorder than clinical judgment. One cluster identified by Conti-Ramsden, Crutchley, and Botting (1997) illustrates this point. The children were attending a language unit and receiving intensive speech and language therapy input. They were judged to have a language disorder as their primary problem and had difficulty coping in mainstream schools even with support. Yet they performed well on all of the standardized assessments (>40th percentile, where 29–71 reflects the average range) except the British Ability Scales word-reading task. Conti-Ramsden and Botting (1999) concluded that this group of children should not be considered as language impaired because their profiles on standardized assessments appear normal. To address this issue, Dunn et al. (1996) suggested that information gathered from spontaneous language samples (utterance length and the number that contain grammatical errors, e.g., error in word order, tense markers) can reconcile the mismatch between the children who are clinically identified as having SLI and those identified by psychometric testing. They argued that a classification approach that relies solely on standardized tests fails to identify the underlying processes responsible for children's language profiles and how they use their language skills.

Despite the lack of empirically validated subgroups, it is nevertheless evident that SLI is not a unitary condition and that distinct profiles of difficulties exist (Bishop, 1997; Conti-Ramsden et al., 1997; Rapin & Allen, 1983). SLI has also been shown to be dynamic, with individuals' strengths and weaknesses changing over time. Bishop (1997) concluded that research assuming that children with SLI are a unitary group will lead to conflicting findings and different conclusions about what impaired mental processes underlie SLI.

Theories of underlying impairment. Theories of SLI fall into two main theoretically opposing positions: those that propose a specific-linguistic deficit, and those that attribute SLI to limitations in processing capacity (specific or general cognitive processing deficits).

To take theories of specific-linguistic deficit first, the hypothesis that SLI is the result of a specific-linguistic deficit stems from Chomsky's theory that language is innate. Children with SLI are thought to have impaired innate knowledge. There are a number of versions of the specific-linguistic theory, each detailing a specific deficit in linguistic knowledge (see Leonard, 1998). For example, the functional category deficit theory (Leonard, 1995) proposes that children with SLI have difficulty acquiring functional categories (e.g., determiners – *a*, *the*). In contrast, Rice, Wexler, and Cleave (1995) propose a particular difficulty with finite forms (e.g., *-ed*, *-s*, *be*, and *do*). They suggest that children with SLI have an extended period of time where finiteness markers are optional.

A relatively more general deficit in linguistic knowledge has been proposed by Gopnik (1990) who described the case of a bilingual dysphasic boy. Spontaneous language samples collected over an 18-month period indicated errors for a wide range of features (number, person, tense, aspect, and gender). Nevertheless, the boy demonstrated an understanding of the rules constraining thematic relations in simple sentences. Gopnik concluded that the profile of ability was consistent with a feature-deficit hypothesis (feature blindness) that was reflected by the child's impaired ability to formulate grammatical rules. An alternative account argues that children with SLI have a restricted range of contexts in which they can apply grammatical rules (see Leonard, 1998).

Other specific-linguistic accounts focus on deficits in acquisition of grammatical structure. For example, van der Lely (1998; van der Lely & Ullman, 2001) suggested that children with SLI have an impaired computational grammatical system where the application of structural linguistic rules is optional, in contrast to TD where they are obligatory. For example, children with SLI rely more on associative lexical memory for use of regular and irregular past tense forms in expressive grammar.

Leonard (1998) raises two problems for specific-linguistic accounts of SLI. The predictions made are only applicable to a limited number of languages, yet SLI exists in all languages so far studied. The second problem is that the language symptoms identified may be due to a non-linguistic impairment. For example, difficulty formulating grammatical rules may reflect a more general rule-abstraction deficit. It is also difficult for specific-linguistic theories to account for the dynamic nature of SLI. Further, accounts that fail to acknowledge the non-linguistic difficulties of children with SLI might be misleading.

Moving now to discuss processing-deficit theories, these suggest that deficits in cognitive mechanisms underlie the language impairments documented in children with SLI. Again, as seen in the linguistic theories of SLI, there are a number of versions of the processing-deficit theory, each detailing a specific processing deficit. These theories are briefly outlined.

The limited processing account stemmed from evidence that children with SLI process information more slowly than their peers (Johnston & Ellis-Weismer, 1983; Kail, 1994; Tallal & Piercy, 1973, 1975). For example, Lahey and Edwards (1996) compared the performance of 66 children with SLI to those without SLI on three tasks designed to stress different types of processing. The tasks were: naming pictures with the signal to respond presented at various delay intervals, primed naming, and vocal responding to non-linguistic stimuli. They divided the children with SLI into two groups: one with a receptive and expressive impairment and one with only expressive deficits. The children with receptive/expressive language disorder were slower on naming tasks and responding to non-linguistic stimuli than their peers. However, those children with expressive-only language deficits were not significantly slower than their peers, suggesting differences between children with different profiles of SLI. In contrast, Windsor and Hwang (1999) reported generally slow performance for all children with SLI across a range of language tasks, compared to their age-matched peers. Their "expressive" subgroup also had reading difficulties. These contradictory findings highlight the need for specific description of subject group characteristics in research.

A temporal processing deficit has been proposed as underlying SLI. One account suggests that SLI is the result of an impaired ability to respond to rapidly presented auditory information. Tallal and colleagues (e.g. Tallal, 1976; Tallal & Piercy, 1975) reported that children with SLI had a non-specific auditory temporal processing impairment. The children found it difficult to distinguish auditory stimuli if the critical identifying information was brief or if the stimuli were presented in rapid sequence, interfering with the perception of phonological structure (Tallal, 2000, 2004).

Some researchers question whether the deficit observed is one of temporal processing or poor discrimination of visual and auditory brief/rapid stimuli (Studdert-Kennedy & Mody, 1995). A careful longitudinal study by Bishop, Carlyon, Deeks, and Bishop (1999) assessed a range of auditory abilities including thresholds for detection of a brief backward masked tone, detection of frequency modulation, and pitch discrimination using temporal rapid cues.

In an alternative account of the temporal processing deficit, Corriveau, Pasquini, and Goswami's (2007) study reported that many children with SLI had auditory processing difficulties but these were not specific to brief, rapidly changing cues. The majority of children with SLI (70–80%) had difficulty detecting amplitude envelope rise time and the duration of simple tones (i.e., their difficulties were with the amplitude [speech] envelope suggesting a deficit in processing supra-segmental information). While Fernell, Norrelgen, Bozkurt, Hellberg, and Löwing (2002) found no problems with the children's temporal resolution in auditory perception in their study of 25 children with SLI, additional studies are needed to investigate supra-segmental auditory temporal processing as a causal factor in SLI.

An alternative hypothesis is that SLI is associated with *a phonological storage deficit*, which is measured by assessment of non-word repetition (Gathercole & Baddeley, 1990a). Phonological working memory refers to the system that temporarily stores information required for complex cognitive tasks, and has been linked to the setting up of phonological representations (Gathercole & Baddeley, 1990a) and vocabulary acquisition (Gathercole & Baddeley, 1989). Gathercole and Baddelely (1990b) compared six children with SLI and control groups, matched for verbal and non-verbal abilities, on a range of memory tasks. Children with SLI had significantly impaired phonological memory that could not be attributed to auditory perceptual processes, articulation rate, failure to encode material phonologically or failure to use sub-vocal rehearsal. It was concluded that the impairment arose from a deficit in phonological storage.

More recently, Gathercole (2006) proposed that children with SLI have a double deficit: impaired phonological storage and an unidentified skill specific to processing novel speech stimuli (non-words). Her summary of recent research indicated that there is "convergent evidence that phonological storage deficits may not be sufficient on their own to cause developmental impairments of language learning" (p. 535). Other candidate deficits that might combine with impaired phonological storage were identified as general working memory, inability to cope with excessive processing loads, and, perhaps, a temporal processing deficit.

In contrast, Joanisse and Seidenberg (1998) present evidence that the linguistic impairments in SLI could stem from basic *information-processing deficits* in phonology that also interfere with memory. They suggest that phonology is the link between perceptual deficits and impaired language abilities. In contrast, Chiat (2001) proposed that SLI arises from impaired phonological processing that disrupts the *mapping* process used to acquire language. Phonological processing plays a key role in the mapping process from segmentation of the auditory signal to the storage of lexical units, the identification of their semantics, and syntactic combination. The predicted effect of impaired phonological processing crosses levels of language and is not confined to any one area, e.g., semantic, syntactic, or phonological ability. As a result the phonological theory of SLI can account for a wide range of complex problems reported in SLI.

A genetic marker for SLI. Bishop's (2006) recent research has focused on genetically informative designs that use measures of underlying cognitive mechanisms rather than clinical diagnostic criteria. For example, Barry, Yasin, and Bishop (2007) compared the results of parents of children with and without SLI on a battery of psychometric tests and questionnaires. They found that non-word repetition gave the best discrimination between the parent groups and suggested that non-word repetition was a marker of family risk for language impairment. Bishop (2006) proposed a risk factor model for SLI where underlying deficits are considered to be probabilistic. As an example, an auditory deficit alone would be considered an environmental risk that may not give rise to SLI unless it was combined with a genetic risk factor. The risk factors are additive with a genetic risk having a stronger effect.

Non-word repetition has, then, emerged as an important tool because it is considered to be a marker for language impairment (for a meta-analysis, see Coady & Evans, 2007). For example, Botting and Conti-Ramsden (2003) examined three groups of children with communication disorders, autism, pragmatic impairment, and SLI, on a series of psycholinguistic markers. Recalling sentences, a subtest of the Clinical Evaluation of Language Fundamentals (Semel, Wiig, & Secord, 1995) was the most reliable universal marker for communication impairment, and non-word repetition was significantly lower for children with SLI than all other groups. Performance profiles on phonological working-memory tasks have differentiated children with SLI from TD peers, children with autism (Whitehouse, Barry, & Bishop, 2008), and children with developmental coordination disorder (Alloway & Archibald, 2008).

Non-word repetition, however taps many skills, from auditory perception to articulation ability. Poor performance on non-word repetition does not necessarily mean the child has a phonological storage deficit. Coady and Evans (2007) acknowledge that "while using the Non-word Repetition Test as an identifying tool says nothing about the nature of the underlying deficits, it does provide a way to group children so these deficits can be explored" (p. 33).

In summary, in the last decade there has been a shift away from the search for a single explanation for language impairment. As Bishop (2006) concludes "a 'single cause' approach is too simple to account for the clinical reality" of SLI (p. 1166). The heterogeneous nature of SLI reflects difficulties with assessment tools that constrain rather than illuminate the nature of SLI. In response there has been an increasing interest in psycholinguistic markers of language impairment. While establishing markers may lead to better identification and increased knowledge of specific cognitive processes involved in SLI, research has yet to examine whether the relationship between these processes and language ability are causative, correlative, or consequential. In contrast, research in phonological disorder implicates cognitive processing more explicitly.

Phonological disorder

Children with phonological disorders make errors of pronunciation that renders their speech difficult to understand. To produce a spoken word a child uses a stored representation, created from input information, to assemble a phonological plan that is constrained by their knowledge of the phonological system. This plan drives phonetic planning and articulatory execution (Chiat, 2000). Different deficits in this speech-processing chain can underlie speech difficulties. Consequently, children with phonological disorder are not a homogeneous group. They differ in severity, type of surface-error pattern, suspected causal and maintenance factors, and their response to different intervention approaches.

More than half the children with phonological difficulties have delayed development, i.e., they follow the normal course of acquisition but at a slower rate. There is some evidence (Dodd, Zhu, & Shatford, 2000; Renfrew & Geary, 1973) that spontaneous recovery can occur, and that a child with delayed developmental errors at one assessment may perform age-appropriately at a later assessment, despite having no intervention. In contrast, children with phonological disorder make errors in pronunciation that deviate from the normal developmental path (e.g., marking all initial consonants as [h]), rarely recover spontaneously (Dodd et al., 2000), and are at risk for later difficulties in the acquisition of literacy (Dodd et al., 1995). They are, by definition, within normal limits on non-verbal cognitive assessments at diagnosis and have intact comprehension. Expressive language may also be within normal limits. Alternatively, poor morphosyntactic performance may reflect deletion of word final consonants that precludes the marking of tense, plurality, and possession. Some children attempt to maximize their intelligibility by producing short utterances, leading to short MLU measures and low scores on sentence complexity.

Research has attempted to identify the types of deficits that might underlie phonological disorder using a psycholinguistic approach (Dodd, 1995; Hewlett, Gibbon, & Hardcastle, 1998; Stackhouse & Wells, 1997). Deficits identified include peripheral impairment of auditory or motor skills, and a cognitive-linguistic impairment (e.g., impaired ability to abstract phonological constraints).

Peripheral deficits. Impaired auditory processing skills have been hypothesized to underlie both speech and language disorders (Tallal, 1976). Dodd and McIntosh (2008) investigated the input, output, and cognitive-linguistic abilities of children with speech impairment (N = 78) and matched controls (N = 87). There was no difference between the groups when they judged consonant vowel syllables, presented auditorially, as the same or different, although some children with speech difficulty (around 7%) had impaired integration of heard and lip-read information in an auditory-visual speech perception task. Bishop (1997) pointed out, however, that it is difficult to determine whether poor performance on input processing tasks is causative, or reflects correlative or consequent symptoms.

Oro-motor skills have been the focus of considerable research. Some children's difficulties in producing intelligible speech can be accounted for in terms of precision of articulatory movement (Gibbon, Dent, & Hardcastle, 1993). A palatal prosthesis that records contact patterns of the tongue indicates that some children consistently mark differences between phonemes that listeners perceive as identical. For example a listener might perceive /r/ as /w/, despite oro-motor production patterns for /r/ and /w/ being distinct. Such covert distinctions cannot, however, explain error patterns like "all clusters are marked by /ɣ/", or "labiodental and alveolar sounds (f, v, l, s, z, t, d) become velars (k, g)." Dodd and McIntosh (2008) found that while no children in a TD control group performed below the normal range on the oro-motor diadochokinetic task (i.e., repetitions of *pat-a-cake*), three of the speech-impaired group had poor accuracy (substituting [t] for /k/) but age-appropriate intelligibility and fluency. No child in either group performed outside the normal range on the isolated movements task. On the sequenced movement task, two children with speech impairment performed below the normal range.

It does not seem plausible, then, that children presenting with markedly different speech profiles should always have either a specific peripheral auditory or oro-motor deficit, given the complexity of the phonological aspect of language. Rather, phonological errors may reflect children's attempts to solve the linguistic code of their native language.

Cognitive-linguistic impairment in rule abstraction. Many children's speech difficulty may lie in understanding the nature of the phonological system to be acquired. Pinker (1994, p. 480) defines phonology as "the component of grammar that determines the sound pattern of the language, including its inventory of phonemes, how they may be combined to form natural-sounding words, how the phonemes may be adjusted depending on their neighbours, and patterns of intonation, timing and stress." Each language's phonology is constrained in a specific way. For example, in English, words cannot begin with the velar nasal /ŋ/, although Cantonese words can. Phonological development involves acquisition of knowledge about these constraints and their implementation in word production. An impaired ability to derive and use the phonological constraints or rules to plan spoken output would result in atypical speech errors.

In Dodd and McIntosh's (2008) study, children with speech impairment performed more poorly than the controls on tasks assessing non-verbal rule abstraction and cognitive flexibility. In the first task, children were rewarded with a cartoon when touching a picture on a computer screen that was a particular color irrespective of shape (first rule "red," second rule "blue"), shape irrespective of color (third rule "circle"), or color and shape (fourth rule "blue triangle"). On this rule-abstraction task, 59% of the children with speech impairment derived no rules, compared to 25% of the control group, and whereas 25% of the control group derived all four rules, only one child with speech impairment performed that well.

The other task assessed cognitive flexibility using the *Favorite Item Selection Task* (FIST) (Jacques and Zelazo, 2001). Children were shown three pictures and asked to point to two that go together. When they have done that, they are asked to point to another two pictures that go together. The FIST has three preliminary trials and 15 test trials. The three pictures manipulate a combination of three dimensions: color, shape, and size. There were three cues within each dimension: color – red, blue, and yellow; shape – boat, shoe, and teapot; size – small, medium, and large. In each trial two dimensions are relevant for matching (e.g., color and size) and one is irrelevant (shape). For example, in one item the three pictures are of a small red teapot, small blue teapot, and medium blue teapot so that the important cues are small and blue. All children performed better than chance would predict on the first selection. On the second selection, however, 17% of children with speech difficulty performed at chance level, while only 3% of control participants did so.

The finding that many children with speech impairment have difficulties in non-verbal rule derivation and cognitive flexibility may mean that their pattern-recognition ability is impaired, affecting their ability to derive the rules of their native phonology. Given that their phonological systems give rise to consistent errors, it is obvious that the children can abstract phonological constraints. Their problem lies in identifying the right phonological features as salient (e.g., the need to contrast word final consonants) and in their persistence in the use of some inappropriate error patterns (e.g., marking clusters with a bilabial fricative), showing a lack of flexibility.

Previous research lends support to the hypothesis that a deficit in abstracting salient phonological features might underlie many speech difficulties of unknown origin. Studies have reported poor performance on phonological awareness (Dodd & Gillon, 1997; Gillon, 2004), and identification of illegal phonotactic speech sound combinations (Dodd et al., 1989). Further, many preschool children whose spoken phonological disorder is resolved through intervention later have difficulty acquiring literacy (Nathan, Stackhouse, Goulandris, & Snowling, 2004). Literacy is also a rule-governed system where rules must be learned to represent the spoken forms of words (Manis & Morrison, 1985). For example, when phonologically disordered children and reading-age matched controls were asked to spell orthographically transparent (e.g., *rent*), opaque (e.g., *yacht*), or rule-governed words (e.g. *bake*, *back*), they differed only on the rule-governed stimuli (Dodd & Cockerill, 1985).

In addition, intervention teaching the phonological rules of spoken phonology successfully resolves speech error patterns (Gierut, 1998; Crosbie et al., 2005). The question arising from these findings is why some children have difficulty learning phonological rules for speech and literacy. The research reviewed here suggests phonological disorder, in the absence of general cognitive impairment, can reflect peripheral deficits, but that most children have a specific cognitive deficit in abstracting appropriate rules and having the cognitive flexibility to change these rules.

Conclusion

The evidence reviewed in this chapter reveals the potential of research on language disorder to inform the debate on the relationship between language and cognition. However, that potential has not yet been realized. Standardized assessment tools provide limited (in accuracy, specificity, and scope) descriptive accounts of language function rather than explanation. Consequently most research focuses on identifying linguistic strengths and weaknesses rather than investigating the mental processes that underlie language performance. Further, the populations discussed in this chapter, particularly children with SLI, are heterogeneous populations. One important advance in the last decade has been a move away from the search for one underlying deficit that accounts for language impairment. Research that seeks to identify specific linguistic and cognitive skills has a greater potential to elucidate the relationship between cognition and language.

There is, however, one reservation about the use of evidence from impaired populations for understanding the "normal" development of language and cognition. Stevens and Karmiloff-Smith (1997, p. 758) caution that "equivalent behavioural outcomes (e.g. in vocabulary scores, syntactic performance, etc.) can stem from different brain structures and processes." Another important barrier to our understanding of the nature of the relationship between impaired cognition and language arises from the way both abilities are measured. There is a tendency for specific aspects of language (e.g. vocabulary *or* syntax *or* comprehension) to be thought generally representative of language ability. Similarly, cognition can be measured by assessments that include a range of abilities or a relatively specific ability. These two issues constrain the interpretation of evidence from the populations discussed.

Nevertheless, the research reviewed in this chapter on the relationship between language and cognition from the perspective of impaired language and impaired cognition allows some tentative conclusions. People with impaired cognition provide evidence that language is modular, at least to the extent that different aspects of language can be impaired differentially. SLI and phonological impairment are both associated with cognitive deficits, although the nature of the relationship between SLI and cognition – causal, consequent, or correlative – awaits clarification (Bishop, 1997). There is no one cause of either SLI or phonological impairment. Nor is there one linguistic profile associated with cognitive impairment. These findings allow researchers to refine their questions about the nature of the relationship between language and cognition.

References

Alloway, T., & Archibald, L. (2008). Working memory and learning in children with developmental coordination disorder and specific language impairment. *Journal of Learning Disabilities, 41*(3), 251–262.

Alony, S., & Kozulin, A. (2007). Dynamic assessment of receptive language in children with Down syndrome. *International Journal of Speech-Language Pathology, 9*(4), 323–331.

American Psychiatric Association (1994). *Diagnostic and statistical manual of mental disorders* (4th ed.) (DSM-IV). Washington DC: American Psychiatric Association.

Aram, D., Morris, R., & Hall, N. (1993). Clinical and research congruence in identifying children with specific language impairment. *Journal of Speech and Hearing Research, 36*(3), 580–591.

Aram, D. M., & Nation, J. E. (1975). Patterns of language behaviour in children with developmental language disorders. *Journal of Speech and Hearing Research, 18*, 229 – 241.

Barry, J., Yasin, I., & Bishop, D. (2007). Heritable risk factors associated with language impairments. *Genes, Brain and Behavior, 6*, 66–76.

Bates, E. (1997). On language savants and the structure of the mind: A review of Neil Smith & Ianthi-Maria Tsimpli, *The mind of a savant: Language learning and modularity. International Journal of Bilingualism, 1*(2), 163–179.

Bellugi, U., Lai, Z., & Wang, P. (1997). Language, communication and neural systems in Williams syndrome. *Mental Retardation and Developmental Disabilities Research Reviews, 3*, 333–342.

Bellugi, U., Marks, S., Bihrle, A., & Ssabo, H. (1988). Dissociation in language and cognitive functions in Williams Syndrome. In D. Bishop & K. Mogford (Eds.), *Language development in exceptional circumstances.* London: Churchill Livingstone.

Bishop, D. (1997). *Uncommon understanding: Development and disorders of language comprehension in children.* Hove, UK: Psychology Press.

Bishop, D. (2006). Developmental cognitive genetics: How psychology can inform genetics and vice versa. *Quarterly Journal of Experimental Psychology, 59*(7), 1153–1168.

Bishop, D., Carlyon, R., Deeks, J., & Bishop, S. (1999). Auditory temporal processing impairment: Neither necessary nor sufficient for causing language impairment in children. *Journal of Speech, Language and Hearing Research, 42*, 1295–1310.

Bishop, D., & Rosenbloom, L. (1987). Childhood language disorders classification and overview. In W. Yule & M. Rutter (Eds.), *Language development and disorders* (Vol. 101/102, pp. 16–41). Oxford: Mac Keith Press.

Borghi, R. (1990). Consonant phoneme and distinctive feature error patterns in speech. In D. Van Dyke, D. Lang, F. Heide, D. Van Duyne, M. Soucek (Eds.), *Clinical Perspectives in the Management of Down's Syndrome* (pp. 147–152). New York: Springer.

Botting, N., & Conti-Ramsden, G. (2003). Autism, primary pragmatic difficulties and specific language impairment: Can we distinguish them using psycholinguistic markers? *Developmental Medicine and Child Neurology, 45*, 515–545.

Broomfield, J., & Dodd, B. (2005). Clinical effectiveness. In Dodd, B. (Ed.), *Differential diagnosis and treatment of children with speech disorder* (2nd ed., pp. 211–230). London: Whurr.

Buckley, S. (2003). Literacy and language. In J. Rondal & S. Buckley (Eds.), *Speech and language intervention in Down syndrome* (pp. 132–153). London: Whurr.

Bunn, L., Simon, D., Welsh, T., Watson, C., and Elliot, D. (2002). Speech production errors in adults with and without Down syndrome following vernal, written and pictorial cues. *Developmental Neuropsychology, 21*(2), 157–172.

Chiat, S. (2000). *Understanding children with language problems.* Cambridge: Cambridge University Press.

Chiat, S. (2001). Mapping theories of developmental language impairment: Premises, predictions and evidence. *Language and Cognitive Processes, 16*(2–3), 113–142.

Chomsky, N. (1986). *Knowledge of language: Its nature, origin and use.* New York: Praeger.

Clauhsen, H., & Almazan, M. (1998). Syntax and morphology in Williams syndrome. *Cognition, 68*, 167–198.

Coady, J., & Evans, J. (2007). Uses and interpretation of non-word repetition tasks in children with and without specific language impairments (SLI). *International Journal of Language and Communication Disorders, 43*(1), 1–40.

Conti-Ramsden, G., & Botting, N. (1999). Classification of children with specific language impairment: Longitudinal considerations. *Journal of Speech, Language, and Hearing Research, 42*, 1195–1204.

Conti-Ramsden, G., Crutchley, A., & Botting, N. (1997). The extent to which psychometric tests differentiate subgroups of children with SLI. *Journal of Speech, Language, and Hearing Research, 40*, 765–777.

Corriveau, K., Pasquini, E., & Goswami, U. (2007). Basic auditory processing skills and specific language impairment: A new look at an old hypothesis. *Journal of Speech, Language, and Hearing Research, 50*(3), 647–667.

Cromer, R. (1991). *Language and thought in normal and handicapped children*. London: Blackwell.

Crosbie, S., Holm, A., & Dodd, B. (2005). Intervention for children with severe speech disorder: A comparison of two approaches. *International Journal of Language and Communication Disorders, 40*, 467–491.

Dodd, B. (1995). *Differential diagnosis and treatment of children with speech disorder*. London: Whurr.

Dodd, B., & Cockerill, H. (1985). Phonologically disordered children's spelling abilities. In J. E. Clark (Ed.), *The cultivated Australian. Beitrage zur Phonetik und Linguistik, 48* (pp. 404–415). Hamburg: Helmut Buske Verlag.

Dodd, B., & Gillon, G. (1997). The nature of the phonological deficit underlying disorders of spoken and written language. In Leong, C. K., & Joshi, R. M. (Eds.), *Cross-language studies of learning to read and spell* (pp. 53–70). Dordrecht: Kluwer Academic.

Dodd, B., Holm, A., Crosbie, S., & McCormack, P. (2005). Differential diagnosis of phonological disorders. In B. Dodd (Ed.), *Differential diagnosis and treatment of children with speech disorder* (2nd ed., pp. 44–70). London: Whurr.

Dodd, B., Leahy, J., & Hambly, G. (1989). Phonological disorders in children: underlying cognitive deficits. *British Journal of Developmental Psychology, 7*, 55–71.

Dodd, B., McCormack, P., & Woodyatt, G. (1995). An evaluation of an intervention program: The relationship between children's phonology and parents' communicative behavior. *American Journal on Mental Retardation, 98*, 632–645.

Dodd, B., & McIntosh, B. (2008). The input processing, cognitive linguistic and oro-motor skills of children with speech difficulty. *International Journal of Speech-Language Pathology, 10*(3), 169–178.

Dodd, B., & Thompson, L. (2001). Speech disorder in children with Down syndrome. *Journal of Intellectual Disability Research, 45*(4), 308–316.

Dodd, B., Zhu, H., & Shatford, C. (2000). Does speech disorder spontaneously resolve? In *Child language seminar 1999 proceedings*. London: City University Press.

Dunn, L., Dunn, L., Whetton, C., & Burley, J. (1997). *British picture vocabulary scale III*. Windsor: NFER-Nelson.

Dunn, M., Flax, J., Sliwinski, M., & Aram, D. (1996). The use of spontaneous language measures as criteria for identifying children with specific language impairment: An attempt to reconcile clinical and research incongruence. *Journal of Speech and Hearing Research, 39*(3), 643–654.

Ervin, M. (2001). *SLI: What we know and why it matters*. Retrieved July 29, 2007, from American Speech-Language-Hearing Association website: http://www.asha.org/about/publications/leader-online/archives/2001/sli.htm.

Fabretti, D., Pizzuto, E., Vicari, S., & Volterra, V. (1997). A story description task in children with Down syndrome: Lexical and morphosyntactic abilities. *Journal of Intellectual Disability Research, 41*, 165–179.

Fernell, E., Norrelgen, F., Bozkurt, I., Hellberg, G., & Löwing, K. (2002). Developmental profiles and auditory perception in 25 children attending special preschools for language-impaired children. *Acta Paediatrica, 91*(10), pp. 1108–1115.

Gathercole, S. (2006). Nonword repetition and word learning: The nature of the relationship. *Applied Psycholinguistics, 27*, 513–543.

Gathercole, S., & Baddeley, A. (1989). Evaluation of the role of phonological STM in the development of vocabulary in children: A longitudinal study. *Journal of Memory and Language, 28*, 200–213.

Gathercole, S., & Baddeley, A. (1990a). The role of phonological working memory in vocabulary acquisition: A study of young children learning new names. *British Journal of Psychology, 81*, 439–454.

Gathercole, S., & Baddeley, A. (1990b). Phonological memory deficits in language disordered children: Is there a causal connection? *Journal of memory and language, 29*(29), 336–360.

Gennari, S., Sloman, S., Malt, B., & Fitch, W. (2002). Motion events in language and cognition. *Cognition, 83*(1), 49–79.

Gibbon, F., Dent, H., & Hardcastle, W. (1993). Diagnosis and therapy of abnormal alveolar stops in a speech disordered child using EPG. *Clinical Linguistics and Phonetics, 7*(6), 247–267.

Gierut, J. (1998). Treatment efficacy: Functional phonological disorders in children. *Journal of Speech, Language and Hearing Research, 41*, S85–S100.

Gillon, G. (2004). *Phonological awareness: From research to practice.* New York: Guilford Press.

Gopnik, M. (1990). Feature blindness: A case study. *Language Acquisition, 1*(2), 139–164.

Grant, J., Karmiloff-Smith, A., Berthoud, I., & Cristophe, A. (1996). Is the language of people with Williams syndrome mere mimicry? Phonological short-term memory in a foreign language. *Cahiers de Psychologie Cognitive, 15*, 615–628.

Greenwald, C., & Leonard, L. (1979). Communicative and sensorimotor development of Down's syndrome children. *American Journal of Mental Retardation, 84*, 296–303.

Hewlett, N., Gibbon, F., & Hardcastle, W. (1998). When is a velar an alveolar? Evidence supporting a revised psycholinguistic model of speech production in children. *International Journal of Language and Communication Disorders, 33*, 161–176.

Hulme, C., & Mackenzie, S. (1992). *Working memory and severe learning difficulties.* Mahwah, NJ: Erlbaum.

Jackendoff, R. (1996). The architecture of the linguistic–spatial interface. In P. Bloom, M. Peterson, L. Nadel, & M. Garrett (Eds.), *Language and space* (pp. 1–30). Cambridge, MA: MIT Press.

Jacques, S., & Zelazo, P. (2001). The Flexible Item Selection Task (FIST): A measure of executive function in preschoolers. *Developmental Neuropsychology, 20*, 573–591.

Jarrold, C., Baddeley, A., & Hewes, A. (1998). Verbal and nonverbal abilities in the Williams syndrome phenotype: Evidence for diverging developmental trajectories. *Journal of Child Psychology and Psychiatry and Allied Disciplines, 39*, 511–523.

Joanisse, M., & Seidenberg, M. (1998). Specific language impairment: A deficit in grammar or processing? *Trends in Cognitive Sciences, 2*(7), 240–247.

Joffe, V., & Varlokosta, S. (2006). Language abilities in Williams syndrome: Exploring comprehension, production and repetition skills. *International Journal of Language and Communication Disorders, 9*(3), 213–225.

Johnston, J., & Ellis-Weismer, S. (1983). Mental rotation abilities in language-disordered children. *Journal of Speech and Hearing Research, 26*, 397–403.

Kail, R. (1994). A method for studying the generalized slowing hypothesis in children with specific language impairment. *Journal of Speech and Hearing Research, 37*, 418–421.

Karmiloff-Smith, A., Brown, J., Grice, S., & Paterson, S. (2008). Dethroning the myth: Cognitive dissociations and innate modularity in Williams syndrome. *Developmental Neuropsychology, 23*(1), 227–242.

Karmiloff-Smith, A., Grant, J., Berthoud, I., Davies, M., Howlin, P., & Udwin, O. (1997). Language and Williams syndrome: How intact is "intact"? *Child Development, 68*(2), 246–62.

Kernan, K. (1990). Comprehension of syntactically indicated sequence by Down's syndrome and other mentally retarded adults. *Journal of Mental Deficiency Research, 34*, 169–178.

Kintsch, W. (2005). An overview of top-down and bottom-up effects in comprehension: The CI perspective. *Discourse Processes, 39*(2), 125–128.

Kumin, L. (1999). Comprehensive speech and language treatment for infants, toddlers and children with Down syndrome. In T. Hassold & D. Patterson, *Down syndrome: A promising future, together.* New York: Wiley.

Kumin, L., & Adams, J. (2000). Developmental apraxia of speech and intelligibility in children with Down syndrome. *Down Syndrome Quarterly, 5*, 1–6.

Lahey, M., & Edwards, J. (1996). Why do children with specific language impairment name pictures more slowly than their peers? *Journal of Speech and Hearing Research, 39*, 1081–1098.

Lenneberg, E. (1967). *Biological foundations of language.* New York: Wiley.

Leonard, L. (1995). Functional categories in the grammars of children with specific language impairment. *Journal of Speech and Hearing Research, 38*(6), 1270–1283.

Leonard, L. (1998). *Children with specific language impairment.* Cambridge, MA: MIT Press.

Levy, Y., & Kave, G. (1999). Language breakdown and linguistic theory: A tutorial review. *Lingua, 107*, 95–113.

Manis, F., & Morrison, F. (1985). Reading disability: A deficit in rule learning? In L. Siegal & F. Morrison (Eds.), *Cognitive development in atypical children. Progress in cognitive development research.* New York: Springer-Verlag.

Mervis, C., & Becerra, A. (2007). Language and communicative development in Williams syndrome. *Mental Retardation and Developmental Disabilities Research Reviews, 13*, 3–15.

Nathan, L., Stackhouse, J., Goulandris, N., & Snowling, M. (2004). The development of early literacy skills among children with speech difficulties: A test of the "critical age hypothesis." *Journal of Speech, Language, and Hearing Research, 47*, 377–391.

O'Connor, N., & Hermelin, B. (1991). A specific linguistic ability. *American Journal of Mental Retardation, 95*, 673–680.

Ozanne, A. (2005). The search for developmental verbal dyspraxia. In B. Dodd (Ed.), *Differential diagnosis and treatment of children with speech disorder* (pp. 99–109). London: Whurr.

Papafragou, A., Hulbert, J., & Trueswell, J. (2008). Does language guide event perception: Evidence from eye-movements. *Cognition, 108*, 155–184.

Perovic, A. (2006). Syntactic deficit in Down syndrome: More evidence for the modular organisation of language. *Lingua, 116*, 1616–1630.

Perron-Borelli, M., & Misès, R. (1974). *Epreuves différentielles d'efficience intellectuelle.* Issy-les-Moulineaux, France: Editions Scientifiques et Psychologiques.

Piaget, J. (1952). *The origin of intelligence in the child.* London: Routledge & Kegan Paul.

Pinker, S. (1989). *Learnability and cognition: The acquisition of argument structure.* Cambridge, MA: MIT Press.

Pinker, S. (1994). *The language instinct.* London: Penguin.

Rapin, E. (1996). Practitioner review: Developmental language disorders: A clinical update. *Journal of Child Psychology and Psychiatry, 37*(6), 643–655.

Rapin I., & Allen, D. (1983). Developmental language disorders: Nosologic considerations. In U. Kirk (Ed.), *Neuropsychology of language, reading, and spelling* (pp. 155–184). New York: Academic Press.

Rapin, I., & Allen, D. (1987). Developmental dysphasia and autism in preschool children: Characteristics and subtypes. In J. Martin, P. Martin, P. Fletcher, P. Grunwell, & D. Hall (Eds.), *Proceedings of the first international symposium on specific speech and language disorders in children* (pp. 20–35). London: AFASIC.

Renfrew, C. E., & Geary, L. (1973). Prediction of persisting speech defect. *British Journal of Disorders of Communication, 8*, 37–47.

Rice, M., Wexler, K., & Cleave, P. (1995). Specific language impairment as a period of extended optimal infinitive. *Journal of Speech and Hearing Research, 38*, 850–863.

Ring, M., & Clahsen, H. (2005). Distinct patterns of language impairment in Down's syndrome and Williams syndrome: The case of syntactic chains. *Journal of Neurolinguistics, 18*, 479–501.

Rondal, J. A. (1994a). Exceptional cases of language development in mental retardation: The relative autonomy of language as a cognitive system. In H. Tager-Flushberg (Ed.), *Constraints on language acquisition: Studies of atypical children* (pp. 155–174). Hillsdale, NJ: Erlbaum.

Rondal, J. A. (1994b). Exceptional cases of language development in mental retardation: Natural experiments in language modularity. *Cahiers de Psychologie Cognitive, 13*, 427–467.

Rondal, J. A., & Edwards, S. (1997). *Language in mental retardation.* London: Whurr.

Rondal, J. A., & Lambert, J. L. (1983). The speech of mentally retarded adults in a dyadic communication situation: Some formal and informative aspects. *Psychologica Belgica, 23*, 49–56.

Semel, E., Wiig, E., & Secord, W. (1995). *Clinical evaluation of language fundamentals-3 UK*. London: Psychological Corporation.

Smith, N. V., & Tsimpli, I. M. (1995). *The mind of a savant: Language learning and modularity*. Oxford: Blackwell.

Stackhouse, J., & Wells, B. (1997). *Children's speech and literacy difficulties: A psycholinguistic framework*. London: Whurr.

Stark, R., & Tallal, P. (1981). Selection of children with specific language deficits. *Journal of Speech and Hearing Disorders, 46*, 114–122.

Stevens, T., & Karmiloff-Smith, A. (1997). Word learning in a special population: Do individuals with Williams syndrome obey lexical constraints. *Journal of Child Language, 24*, 737–765.

Stojanovik, V., and James, D. (2006). Short-term longitudinal study of a child with Williams syndrome. *International Journal of Language and Communication Disorder, 41*(2), 213–223.

Stojanovik, V., Perkins, M., & Howard, S. (2004). Williams syndrome and specific language impairment do not support claims for developmental double dissociations and innate modularity. *Journal of Neurolinguistics, 17*(6), 403–424.

Studdert-Kennedy, M., & Mody, M. (1995). Auditory temporal perception deficits in the reading-impaired: A critical review of the evidence. *Psychonomic Bulletin and Review, 2*(4), 508–514.

Tallal, P. (1976). Rapid auditory processing in normal and disordered language development. *Journal of Speech and Hearing Research, 19*, 561–571.

Tallal, P. (2000). Experimental studies of language learning impairments: From research to remediation. In D. V. M. Bishop & L. B. Leonard (Eds.), *Speech and language impairments in children: Causes, characteristics, intervention and outcome* (pp. 131–155). Hove, UK: Psychology Press.

Tallal, P. (2004). Improving language and literacy is a matter of time. *Nature Reviews Neuroscience, 5*, 721–728.

Tallal, P., & Piercy, M. (1973). Defects of non-verbal auditory perception in children with developmental aphasia. *Nature, 241*, 468–469.

Tallal, P., & Piercy, M. (1975). Developmental aphasia: The perception of brief vowels and extended stop consonants. *Neuropsychologia, 13*, 69–74.

Tyler, L., Karmiloff-Smith, A., Voice, K., Stevens, T., Grant, J., Udwin, O., Davies, M., & Howlin, P. (1997). Do individuals with Williams syndrome have bizarre semantics? Evidence for lexical organisation using an on-line task. *Cortex, 33*(3), 515–527.

Van der Lely, H. K. J. (1998). G-SLI in children: Movement, economy and deficits in the computational syntactic system. *Language Acquisition, 7*, 161–193.

Van der Lely, H. K. J., Rosen, S., & McClelland, A. (1998). Evidence for a grammar-specific deficit in children. *Current Biology, 8*, 1253–1258.

Van der Lely, H., & Ullman, M. (2001). Past tense morphology in specifically language impaired and normally developing children. *Language and Cognitive Processes, 16*, 177–217.

Vicari, S. (2006). Motor development and neuropsychological patterns in persons with Down syndrome. *Behaviour Genetics, 36*(3), 355–364.

Vygotsky, L. (1962). *Thought and Language*. Cambridge, MA: MIT Press.

Whitehouse, A., Barry, J., & Bishop, D. (2008). Further defining the language impairment of autism spectrum disorders: Is there a specific language impairment subtype? *Journal of Communication Disorders, 41*, 319–336.

Windsor, J., & Hwang, M. (1999). Testing the generalized slowing hypothesis in specific language impairment. *Journal of Speech, Language and Hearing Research, 42*, 1205–1218.

Yamada, J. (1990). *Laura: A case for the modularity of language*. Cambridge, MA: MIT Press.

CHAPTER TWENTY-FOUR

The Empathizing-Systemizing (E-S) Theory of Autism

A Cognitive Developmental Account

Simon Baron-Cohen

In the first edition of this Handbook, we put forward the Empathizing-Systemizing (E-S) theory of autism (Baron-Cohen, Wheelwright, Lawson, Griffin, & Hill, 2002). In this second edition, I take the opportunity to update that review. The E-S theory is proposed as an example of how the study of cognitive development can attempt to characterize atypical development.

Classic autism and Asperger syndrome share *three* core diagnostic features: (a) difficulties in social development, (b) and in the development of communication, alongside (c) unusually strong, narrow interests and repetitive behaviour (American Psychiatric Association, 1994). Since communication is always social, it might be more fruitful to think of autism and Asperger syndrome as sharing features in *two* broad areas: social-communication, and narrow interests/repetitive actions. As for distinguishing features, a diagnosis of Asperger syndrome requires that the child spoke on time and has average IQ or above.

Today the notion of an autistic spectrum is no longer defined by any sharp separation from "normality" (Wing, 1997). The clearest way of seeing this "normal" distribution of autistic traits is by looking at the results from the Autism Spectrum Quotient (or AQ) (Baron-Cohen, Hoekstra, Knickmeyer, & Wheelwright, 2006; Baron-Cohen, Wheelwright, Skinner, Martin, & Clubley, 2001). This is a screening instrument in the form of a questionnaire, either completed by a parent about his or her child, or by self-report (if the adult is "high-functioning"). There are 50 questions in the AQ in total,

Portions of this paper appeared in Baron-Cohen, S. (2008) Autism, hyper-systemizing, and truth, *Quarterly Journal of Experimental Psychology*, *61*, 64–75; and Baron-Cohen, S. (2008) Theories of the autistic mind, *The Psychologist*, *21*, 112–116. The author was supported by the MRC UK and the Nancy Lurie Marks Family Foundation during the period of this work.

and when administered to a large population the results resemble a "normal distribution." Most people without a diagnosis fall in the range 0–25; most with a diagnosis of an autism spectrum condition fall between 26 and 50. Eighty percent score above 32, and 99% score above 26. So the AQ neatly separates the groups, showing that 93% of the general population fall in the average range of the AQ, and 99% of the autistic population fall in the extreme (high-end) of the scale.

In the general population, males score slightly (but statistically significantly) higher than females. Since autism spectrum conditions are far more common in males than in females (classic autism occurs in four males for every one female, and Asperger syndrome occurs in nine males for every one female; Rutter, 1978), this may suggest that the number of autistic traits a person has is linked to a sex-linked biological factor – genetic or hormonal, or both (Baron-Cohen, Knickmeyer, & Belmonte, 2005; Baron-Cohen, Lutchmaya, & Knickmeyer, 2004). These two aspects – the autistic spectrum and the possibility of sex-linked explanations – have been at the core of my research and theorizing over recent years.

The Mindblindness Theory

In my early work I explored the theory that children with autism spectrum conditions are delayed in developing a *theory of mind* (ToM): the ability to put oneself into someone else's shoes, to imagine their thoughts and feelings (Baron-Cohen, 1995; Baron-Cohen, Leslie, & Frith, 1985). When we mindread or mentalize, we not only make sense of another person's behavior (why did their head swivel on their neck? Why did their eyes move left?), but we imagine a whole set of mental states (they have seen something of interest, they know something or want something) and we can predict what they might do next.

The mindblindness theory proposes that children with autism and Asperger syndrome are delayed in the development of their ToM, leaving them with degrees of *mindblindness*. As a consequence, they find other people's behavior confusing and unpredictable, even frightening. Evidence for this comes from difficulties they show at each point in the development of the capacity to mindread:

- Typical 14-month-olds show *joint attention* (such as pointing or following another person's gaze), during which they not only look at another person's face and eyes, but pay attention to what the other person is interested in (Scaife & Bruner, 1975). Children with autism and Asperger syndrome show reduced frequency of joint attention in toddlerhood (Swettenham et al., 1998).
- Typical 24-month-olds engage in *pretend play*, using their mindreading skills to be able to understand that in the other person's mind, they are just pretending (Leslie, 1987). Children with autism and Asperger syndrome show less pretend play, or their pretence is limited to more rule-based formats (Baron-Cohen, 1987).
- The typical 3-year-old child can pass the *seeing leads to knowing* test: understanding that merely touching a box is not enough to know what is inside (Pratt & Bryant,

1990). Children with autism and Asperger syndrome are delayed in this (Baron-Cohen & Goodhart, 1994).

- The typical 4-year-old child passes the "false belief" test, recognizing when someone else has a mistaken belief about the world (Wimmer & Perner, 1983). Most children with autism and Asperger syndrome are delayed in passing this test (Baron-Cohen et al., 1985).
- Deception is easily understood by the typical 4-year-old child (Sodian & Frith, 1992). Children with autism and Asperger syndrome tend to assume everyone is telling the truth, and may be shocked by the idea that other people may not say what they mean (Baron-Cohen, 1992; Baron-Cohen, 2007a). The typical 9-year-old can figure out what might hurt another's feelings and what might therefore be better left unspoken – *faux pas*. Children with Asperger syndrome are delayed by around 3 years in this skill, despite their normal IQ (Baron-Cohen, O'Riordan, Jones, Stone, & Plaisted, 1999).
- The typical 9-year-old can interpret another person's expressions from their eyes, to figure out what they might be thinking or feeling (see figure 24.1). Children with Asperger syndrome tend to find such tests far more difficult (Baron-Cohen, Wheelwright, Scahill, Lawson, & Spong, 2001), and the same is true when the adult test of *reading the mind in the eyes* is used (figure 24.2). Adults with autism and Asperger syndrome score below average on this test of *advanced* mindreading (Baron-Cohen, Wheelwright, Hill, Raste, & Plumb, 2001).

1. Feeling sorry 2. Bored

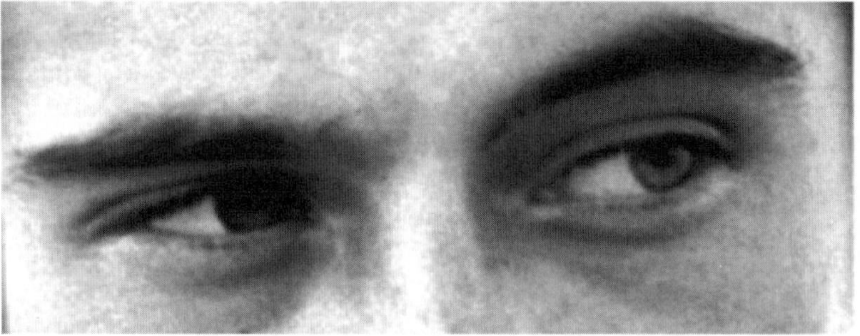

3. Interested 4. Joking

Figure 24.1 The child version of the *reading the mind in the eyes* test (Correct answer = interested.)

1. Sarcastic 2. Stern

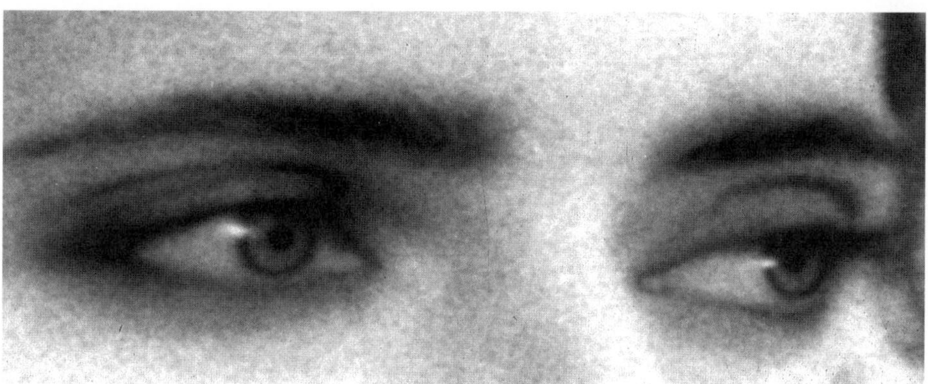

3. Suspicious 4. Dispirited

Figure 24.2 The adult version of the *reading the mind in the eyes* test (Correct answer = dispirited.)

A strength of the mindblindness theory is that it can make sense of the social and communication difficulties in autism and Asperger syndrome, and that it is universal in applying to all individuals on the autistic spectrum. Its shortcoming is that it cannot account for the non-social features. A second shortcoming of this theory is that whilst mind *reading* is one component of empathy, true empathy also requires an emotional response to another person's state of mind (Davis, 1994). Many people on the autistic spectrum also report that they are puzzled by how to *respond* to another person's emotions (Grandin, 1996). A final limitation of the mindblindness theory is that a range of clinical conditions show forms of mindblindness (such as patients with schizophrenia (Corcoran & Frith, 1997), or narcissistic and borderline personality disorders (Fonagy, 1989), and in some studies children with conduct disorder (Dodge, 1993), so this may not be specific to autism and Asperger syndrome.

Two key ways to revise this theory have been to explain the non-social areas of strength by reference to a second factor, and to broaden the concept of ToM to include an emotional reactivity dimension. Both of these revisions were behind the development of the next theory.

The Empathizing-Systemizing (E-S) Theory

This newer theory explains the social and communication difficulties in autism and Asperger syndrome by reference to delays and deficits in *empathy*, whilst explaining the areas of strength by reference to intact or even superior skill in *systemizing* (Baron-Cohen, 2002).

ToM is just the cognitive component of empathy. The second component of empathy is the response element: having an appropriate emotional reaction to another person's thoughts and feelings. This is referred to *affective empathy* (Davis, 1994). On the Empathy Quotient (EQ), a questionnaire either filled out by an adult about themselves, or by a parent about their child, both cognitive and affective empathy are assessed. On this scale, people with autism spectrum conditions score lower than comparison groups.

According to the E-S theory, autism and Asperger syndrome are best explained not just with reference to empathy (below average) but also with reference to a second psychological factor (systemizing), which is either average or even above average. So it is the discrepancy between E and S that determines if you are likely to develop an autism spectrum condition.

To understand this theory we need to turn to this second factor, the concept of *systemizing*. Systemizing is the drive to analyze or construct systems. These might be any kind of system. What defines a system is that it follows *rules*, and when we systemize we are trying to identify the rules that govern the system, in order to predict how that system will behave (Baron-Cohen, 2006). These are some of the major kinds of system:

- *Collectible* systems (e.g., distinguishing between types of stones or wood)
- *Mechanical* systems (e.g., a video-recorder or a window lock)
- *Numerical* systems (e.g., a train timetable or a calendar)
- *Abstract* systems (e.g., the syntax of a language, or musical notation)
- *Natural* systems (e.g., weather patterns, or tidal wave patterns)
- *Social* systems (e.g., a management hierarchy, or a dance routine with a dance partner)
- *Motoric* systems (e.g., throwing a Frisbee or bouncing on a trampoline)

In all these cases, you systemize by noting regularities (or structure) and rules. The rules tend to be derived by noting if A and B are *associated* in a systematic way. The evidence for intact or even unusually strong systemizing in autism and Asperger syndrome is that, in one study, such children performed above the level that one would expect on a physics test (Baron-Cohen, Wheelwright, Scahill, et al., 2001). Children with Asperger syndrome as young as 8–11 years old scored higher than a comparison group who were older (typical teenagers).

A second piece of evidence comes from studies using the Systemizing Quotient (SQ). The higher your score, the stronger your drive to systemize. People with high-functioning autism or Asperger syndrome score higher on the SQ compared to people in the general population (Baron-Cohen, Richler, Bisarya, Gurunathan, & Wheelwright, 2003). The above tests of systemizing are designed for children or adults with Asperger syndrome, not classic autism. However, children with classic autism perform better than controls on the *picture sequencing test* where the stories can be sequenced using physical-causal concepts (Baron-Cohen et al., 1986). They also score above average on a test of how to figure out how a Polaroid camera works, even though they have difficulties figuring out people's thoughts and feelings (Baron-Cohen et al., 1985; Perner et al., 1989). Both of these are signs of their intact or even strong systemizing.

The strength of the E-S theory is that it is a *two-factor theory* that can explain the cluster of both the social and non-social features in autism spectrum conditions. Below-average empathy is a simple way to explain the social-communication difficulties, whilst average or even above-average systemizing is a way of explaining the narrow interests, repetitive behavior, and resistance to change/need for sameness. This is because when you systemize, it is easiest to keep everything constant, and only vary one thing at a time. That way, you can see what might be causing what, rendering the world predictable.

When this theory first came out, one criticism of it was that it might only apply to the *high*-functioning individuals with autism or Asperger syndrome. Whilst their obsessions (with computers or math for example) could be seen in terms of strong systemizing (Baron-Cohen, Wheelwright, Stone, & Rutherford, 1999), surely this didn't apply to the *low*-functioning individuals? However, when we think of a child with autism, many of the classic behaviors can be seen as a reflection of their strong systemizing. Some examples are listed in table 24.1.

Like the Weak Central Coherence (WCC) theory (Frith, 1989), the E-S theory is about a different cognitive style (Happe, 1996). Like that theory, it also posits excellent attention to detail (in perception and memory), since when you systemize you have to pay attention to the tiny details. This is because each tiny detail in a system might have a functional role. Excellent attention to detail in autism has been repeatedly demonstrated (Jolliffe & Baron-Cohen, 2001; Mottron, Burack, Iarocci, Belleville, & Enns, 2003; O'Riordan, Plaisted, Driver, & Baron-Cohen, 2001; Shah & Frith, 1983, 1993). The difference between these two theories is that whilst the WCC theory sees people with autism spectrum conditions as drawn to detailed information (sometimes called local processing) for *negative* reasons (an alleged inability to integrate), the E-S theory sees this same quality (excellent attention to detail) as being highly purposeful: it exists in order to understand a system. Attention to detail is occurring for *positive* reasons: in the service of achieving an ultimate understanding of a system (however small and specific that system might be).

Whereas the WCC theory predicts that people with autism or Asperger syndrome will be forever lost in the detail and never achieve an understanding of the system as a whole (since this would require a global overview), the E-S theory predicts that over time the person may achieve an excellent understanding of a whole system, given the opportunity to observe and control all the variables in that system. The existence of talented mathematicians with Asperger syndrome like Richard Borcherds is proof that such individuals can

Table 24.1 Systemizing in classic autism and/or *Asperger syndrome (in italics)*

- **Sensory systemizing**
  - Tapping surfaces, or letting sand run through one's fingers
  - *Insisting on the same foods each day*
- **Motoric systemizing**
  - Spinning round and round, or rocking back and forth
  - *Learning knitting patterns or a tennis technique*
- **Collectible systemizing**
  - Collecting leaves or football stickers
  - *Making lists and catalogues*
- **Numerical systemizing**
  - Obsessions with calendars or train timetables
  - *Solving math problems*
- **Motion systemizing**
  - Watching washing machines spin round and round
  - *Analyzing exactly when a specific event occurs in a repeating cycle*
- **Spatial systemizing**
  - Obsessions with routes
  - *Developing drawing techniques*
- **Environmental systemizing**
  - Insisting on toy bricks being lined up in an invariant order
  - *Insisting that nothing is moved from its usual position in the room*
- **Social systemizing**
  - Saying the first half of a phrase or sentence and waiting for the other person to complete it
  - *Insisting on playing the same game whenever a child comes to play*
- **Natural systemizing**
  - Asking over and over again what the weather will be today
  - *Learning the Latin names of every plant and their optimal growing conditions*
- **Mechanical systemizing**
  - Learning to operate a video-recorder
  - *Fixing bicycles or taking apart gadgets and reassembling them*
- **Vocal/auditory/verbal systemizing**
  - Echoing sounds
  - *Collecting words and word meanings*
- **Systemizing action sequences**
  - Watching the same video over and over again
  - *Analyzing dance techniques*
- **Musical systemizing**
  - Playing a tune on an instrument over and over again
  - *Analyzing the musical structure of a song*

integrate the details into a true understanding of the system (Baron-Cohen, 2003). It is worth noting that the Executive Dysfunction (ED) theory (Ozonoff, Pennington, & Rogers, 1991; Rumsey & Hamberger, 1988; Russell, 1997) has even more difficulty in explaining instances of good understanding of a whole system, such as calendrical calculation, or indeed why the "obsessions" in autism and Asperger syndrome should center on systems at all.

So, when the low-functioning person with classic autism has shaken a piece of string thousands of times close to his eyes, whilst the ED theory sees this as perseveration arising from some neural dysfunction which would normally enable the individual to shift attention, the E-S theory sees the same behavior as a sign that the individual understands the physics of that string movement. He may be able to make it move in exactly the same way every time. When he makes a long, rapid sequence of sounds, he may know exactly that acoustic pattern, and get some pleasure from the confirmation that the sequence is the same every time. Much as a mathematician might feel an ultimate sense of pleasure that the "golden ratio" (that a + b/a = a/b) *always* comes out as 1.61803399, so the child – even with low-functioning autism – who produces the same outcome every time with his repetitive behavior appears to derive some emotional pleasure at the predictability of the world. This may be what is clinically described as "stimming" (Wing, 1997). Autism was originally described as involving "resistance to change" and "need for sameness" (Kanner, 1943), and here we see that this important clinical observation may be the hallmark of strong systemizing.

One further advantage of the E-S theory is that it can explain what is sometimes seen as an inability to "generalize" in autism spectrum conditions (Plaisted, O'Riordan, & Baron-Cohen, 1998; Rimland, 1964; Wing, 1997). According to the E-S theory, this is exactly what you would expect if the person is trying to understand each system as a *unique* system. A good systemizer is a splitter, not a lumper, since lumping things together can lead to missing key differences that enable you to predict how these two things behave differently. Finally, the E-S theory destigmatizes autism and Asperger syndrome, relating these to individual differences we see in the population (between the sexes, and within the sexes), rather than as categorically distinct or mysterious.

The Extreme Male Brain Theory

The E-S theory has been extended into the Extreme Male Brain (EMB) theory of autism (Baron-Cohen, 2002). This is because there are clear sex differences in empathizing (females performing better) and in systemizing (males performing better), such that autism and Asperger syndrome can be seen as an extreme of the typical male profile, a view first put forward by the pediatrician Hans Asperger (Asperger, 1944). To see how this theory is effectively just an extension of the E-S theory, one needs to understand that that theory posits two independent dimensions (E for empathy and S for systemizing) in which individual differences are observed in the population. When you plot these, five different "brain types" are seen:

- *Type E* (E > S): individuals whose empathy is stronger than their systemizing
- *Type S* (S > E): individuals whose systemizing is stronger than their empathy
- *Type B* (S = E): individuals whose empathy is as good (or as bad) as their systemizing (B stands for "balanced")
- *Extreme Type E* (E >> S): individuals whose empathy is above average, but who are challenged when it comes to systemizing
- *Extreme Type S* (S >> E): individuals whose systemizing is above average, but who are challenged when it comes to empathy

The E-S model predicts that more females have a brain of Type E, and more males have a brain of Type S. People with autism spectrum conditions, if they are an extreme of the male brain, are predicted to be more likely to have a brain of Extreme Type S. If one gives people in the general population measures of empathy and systemizing (the EQ and SQ), the results fit this model reasonably well. The majority of males (54%) *do* have a brain of Type S; many females (44%) have a brain of Type E; and the majority of people with autism and Asperger syndrome (65%) have an extreme of the male brain (Goldenfeld, Baron-Cohen, & Wheelwright, 2005).

Apart from the evidence from the SQ and EQ, there is other evidence that supports the EMB theory. Regarding tests of empathy, on the *faux pas test*, where a child has to recognize when someone has said something that could be hurtful, typically girls develop faster than boys, and children with autism spectrum conditions develop even slower than typical boys (Baron-Cohen, O'Riordan, et al., 1999). On the *reading the mind in the eyes test*, on average women score higher than men, and people with autism spectrum conditions score even lower than typical males (Baron-Cohen, Jolliffe, Mortimore, & Robertson, 1997). Regarding tests of attention to detail, on the *embedded figures test*, where one has to find a target shape as quickly as possible, on average males are faster than females, and people with autism are even faster than typical males (Jolliffe & Baron-Cohen, 1997).

Recently, the EMB theory has been extended to the level of neurology, with some interesting findings emerging (Baron-Cohen et al., 2005). Thus, in regions of the brain that on average are smaller in males than in females (e.g. the anterior cingulate, superior temporal gyrus, prefrontal cortex, and thalamus), people with autism have even smaller brain regions than typical males. In contrast, for measures of the brain that on average are bigger in males than in females (e.g., the size of the amygdala and cerebellum, overall brain size/weight, and head circumference), people with autism appear to exceed average male values. They have even bigger brain regions in the amygdala and cerebellum than typical males, and have been found to have even larger brains than typical males. Not all studies support this pattern but some do, and it will be important to study such patterns further. It will also be important to address the neurobiological mechanisms that may be causing this hyper-masculinization, one candidate being fetal testosterone (Auyeung et al., 2009).

In summary, the EMB theory is relatively new and may be important for understanding why more males develop autism and Asperger syndrome than do females. It remains in need of further examination. It extends the E-S theory which has the power to explain not just the social-communication deficits in autism spectrum conditions, but also the uneven cognitive profile, repetitive behavior, islets of ability, savant skills, and unusual narrow interests that are part of the atypical neurology of this subgroup in the population.

The Autistic Mind: In Search of "Truth"

The function of systemizing is to predict lawful events, including lawful change, or patterns in data. The hyper-systemizing theory of autism spectrum disorders can explain their preference for systems that change in highly lawful or predictable ways; why they become disabled when faced with systems characterized by less lawful change; and their "need for sameness" or "resistance to change." If "truth" is defined as lawful patterns in data then, according to the hyper-systemizing theory, one could view people with autism spectrum disorders as strongly driven to discover the "truth." I am defining the term "truth" as precise, reliable, consistent, or lawful patterns or structure in data. If a wheel is spinning round and round, there are consistent, lawful patterns to be detected. Sometimes the pattern will occur with 100% predictability (this particular person's birthday always falls on April 4), sometimes with relatively high predictability (daffodils typically bloom in the second week of March in England). Systemizing is the means by which we identify lawful patterns in data.

When we systemize, we make the *implicit* assumption that the pattern of data coming into our senses reveals the truth. My contention is that the autistic brain, being highly tuned to systemize, is the ultimate pattern-detector and truth-detector (Baron-Cohen, 2006). In a high-functioning individual on the autistic spectrum, such pattern-seeking can reveal scientific truths about the nature of reality, since their systemizing can help the individual understand how things work. What was previously dismissed as an "obsession" can be viewed more positively as a "strong, narrow interest" in a topic that, when harnessed, can lead the person with autism or Asperger syndrome to excel in a highly specific field.

Whilst systemizing can deliver truths in the form of laws, it can only do so in domains that are ultimately lawful. One reason why people with autism spectrum disorders (postulated to be hyper-systemizers) may struggle with empathy and be less interested in topics such as pure fiction, pretence, or deception is that these are not and never will be truth-oriented. Regarding the domain of emotions, human behavior is not 100% lawful. Different people can express the same emotion differently, or an emotion may even have no external expression. Regarding the domain of mental states, as Alan Leslie pointed out, the domain of mental states plays havoc with "truth relations." This is because of the opacity of mental states like "belief" or "pretence" (Leslie, 1987). The sentence "Mary believes that 'John is having an affair with his colleague'" is true if Mary believes it, irrespective of whether John really is having an affair. When we mindread, we have to keep track of what we believe to be true (John is not having an affair) whilst representing someone else's different (possibly false) belief – what they believe to be true (Mary believes he is). Empathy is therefore arguably impossible without such an ability to play with and even suspend the truth.

Hyper-Systemizing: Implications for Intervention

The E-S theory has implications for intervention, as is being tried by "systemizing empathy," presenting emotions in an autism-friendly format (Baron-Cohen, 2007b). In one example of a mindreading exercise, actors pose with facial expressions such that people with autism can teach themselves emotion-recognition via DVD or computer (www.jkp.com/mindreading). This involves taking the quite artificial approach of presenting mental states (such as emotional expressions) as if they are lawful and systemizable, even if they are not (Golan et al., 2006). The children's animation *The Transporters* (www.thetransporters.com) grafts human actors' facial expressions of emotion onto mechanical systems such as trains and trams that move in a highly predictable fashion, along tracks, so that even young children with autism are attracted to look at faces whilst they are drawn to watch the kind of material that is intrinsically rewarding for them (Golan et al., in press). Such approaches tailor the information to the learning style of the learner and these approaches have been evaluated and shown to lead to improvements in emotion recognition.

In conclusion, the E-S theory is an example of how the study of cognitive development in an atypical population (autism spectrum conditions) attempts to explain a wide range of otherwise disparate features. It is a theory that began at the psychological level (in the first edition of this Handbook) and is gradually being tested at deeper (neurobiological) levels. And it is a theory that has educational implications. As such it illustrates how psychology can contribute to both understanding etiology and clinical practice.

References

American Psychiatric Association (1994). *Diagnostic and statistical manual of mental disorders* (4th ed.) (DSM-IV). Washington DC: American Psychiatric Association.

Asperger, H. (1944). Die "Autistischen Psychopathen" im Kindesalter. *Archiv fur Psychiatrie und Nervenkrankheiten, 117*, 76–136.

Auyeung, B., Baron-Cohen, S., Chapman, E., Knickmeyer, R., Taylor, K., & Hackett, G., (2009). Foetal testosterone and autistic traits. *British Journal of Psychology, 100*, 1–22.

Baron-Cohen, S. (1987). Autism and symbolic play. *British Journal of Developmental Psychology, 5*, 139–148.

Baron-Cohen, S. (1992). Out of sight or out of mind: another look at deception in autism. *Journal of Child Psychology and Psychiatry, 33*, 1141–1155.

Baron-Cohen, S. (1995). *Mindblindness: An essay on autism and theory of mind.* Boston: MIT Press/Bradford Books.

Baron-Cohen, S. (2002). The extreme male brain theory of autism. *Trends in Cognitive Science, 6*, 248–254.

Baron-Cohen, S. (2003). *The essential difference: Men, women, and the extreme male brain*. London: Penguin.

Baron-Cohen, S. (2006). The hyper-systemizing, assortative mating theory of autism. *Progress in Neuropsychopharmacology and Biological Psychiatry, 30*, 865–872.

Baron-Cohen, S. (2007a). I cannot tell a lie. *In Character, 3*, 52–59.

Baron-Cohen, S. (2007b). Transported into a world of emotion. *The Psychologist, 20,* 76–77.

Baron-Cohen, S., & Goodhart, F. (1994). The "seeing leads to knowing" deficit in autism: The Pratt and Bryant probe. *British Journal of Developmental Psychology, 12,* 397–402.

Baron-Cohen, S., Hoekstra, R. A., Knickmeyer, R., & Wheelwright, S. (2006). The Autism-Spectrum Quotient (AQ) – Adolescent version. *Journal of Autism and Developmental Disorders, 36,* 343–350.

Baron-Cohen, S., Jolliffe, T., Mortimore, C., & Robertson, M. (1997). Another advanced test of theory of mind: Evidence from very high-functioning adults with autism or Asperger syndrome. *Journal of Child Psychology and Psychiatry, 38,* 813–822.

Baron-Cohen, S., Knickmeyer, R., & Belmonte, M. K. (2005). Sex differences in the brain: Implications for explaining autism. *Science, 310,* 819–823.

Baron-Cohen, S., Leslie, A. M., & Frith, U. (1985). Does the autistic child have a "theory of mind"? *Cognition, 21,* 37–46.

Baron-Cohen, S., Leslie, A. M., & Frith, U. (1986). Mechanical, behavioural and intentional understanding of picture stories in autistic children. *British Journal of Developmental Psychology, 4,* 113–125.

Baron-Cohen, S., Lutchmaya, S., & Knickmeyer, R. (2004). *Prenatal testosterone in mind: Amniotic fluid studies.* Cambridge, MA: MIT Press/Bradford Books.

Baron-Cohen, S., O'Riordan, M., Jones, R., Stone, V., & Plaisted, K. (1999). A new test of social sensitivity: Detection of faux pas in normal children and children with Asperger syndrome. *Journal of Autism and Developmental Disorders, 29,* 407–418.

Baron-Cohen, S., Richler, J., Bisarya, D., Gurunathan, N., & Wheelwright, S. (2003). The Systemising Quotient (SQ): An investigation of adults with Asperger syndrome or high-functioning autism and normal sex differences. *Philosophical Transactions of the Royal Society, 358,* 361–374.

Baron-Cohen, S., Wheelwright, S., Hill, J., Raste, Y., & Plumb, I. (2001). The "Reading the Mind in the Eyes" test revised version: A study with normal adults, and adults with Asperger syndrome or high-functioning autism. *Journal of Child Psychology and Psychiatry, 42,* 241–252.

Baron-Cohen, S., Wheelwright, S., Lawson, J., Griffin, R., & Hill, J. (2002). The exact mind: Empathizing and systemizing in autism spectrum conditions. In U. Goswami (Ed.), *Blackwell handbook of childhood cognitive development* (pp. 491–508). Oxford: Blackwell.

Baron-Cohen, S., Wheelwright, S., Scahill, V., Lawson, J., & Spong, A. (2001). Are intuitive physics and intuitive psychology independent? *Journal of Developmental and Learning Disorders, 5,* 47–78.

Baron-Cohen, S., Wheelwright, S., Skinner, R., Martin, J., & Clubley, E. (2001). The Autism Spectrum Quotient (AQ): Evidence from Asperger syndrome/high-functioning autism, males and females, scientists and mathematicians. *Journal of Autism and Developmental Disorders, 31,* 5–17.

Baron-Cohen, S., Wheelwright, S., Stone, V., & Rutherford, M. (1999). A mathematician, a physicist, and a computer scientist with Asperger syndrome: Performance on folk psychology and folk physics test. *Neurocase, 5,* 475–483.

Corcoran, R., & Frith, C. (1997). Conversational conduct and the symptoms of schizophrenia. *Cognitive Neuropsychiatry, 1,* 305–318.

Davis, M. H. (1994). *Empathy: A social psychological approach.* Colorado: Westview Press.

Dodge, K. A. (1993). Social-cognitive mechanisms in the development of conduct disorder and depression. *Annual Review of Psychology, 44,* 559–584.

Fonagy, P. (1989). On tolerating mental states: Theory of mind in borderline personality. *Bulletin of the Anna Freud Centre, 12,* 91–115.

Frith, U. (1989). *Autism: Explaining the enigma.* Oxford: Blackwell.

Golan, O., Baron-Cohen, S., Ashwin, E., Granader, Y., McClintock, S., Day, K., & Leggett, V. (in press). Enhancing emotion recognition in children with autism spectrum conditions: An intervention using animated vehicles with real emotional faces. *Journal of Autism and Developmental Disorders*.

Golan, O., Baron-Cohen, S., Wheelwright, S., & Hill, J. J. (2006). Systemising empathy: Teaching adults with Asperger syndrome to recognise complex emotions using interactive multi-media. *Development and Psychopathology*, *18*, 589–615.

Goldenfeld, N., Baron-Cohen, S., & Wheelwright, S. (2005). Empathizing and systemizing in males, females and autism. *Clinical Neuropsychiatry*, *2*, 338–345.

Grandin, T. (1996). *Thinking in pictures*. Vancouver, WA: Vintage Books.

Happe, F. (1996). *Autism*: UCL Press.

Jolliffe, T., & Baron-Cohen, S. (1997). Are people with autism or Asperger's syndrome faster than normal on the Embedded Figures Task? *Journal of Child Psychology and Psychiatry*, *38*, 527–534.

Jolliffe, T., & Baron-Cohen, S. (2001). A test of central coherence theory: Can adults with high-functioning autism or Asperger syndrome integrate fragments of an object? *Cognitive Neuropsychiatry*, *6*, 193–216.

Kanner, L. (1943). Autistic disturbance of affective contact. *Nervous Child*, *2*, 217–250.

Leslie, A. M. (1987). Pretence and representation: The origins of "theory of mind." *Psychological Review*, *94*, 412–426.

Mottron, L., Burack, J. A., Iarocci, G., Belleville, S., & Enns, J. T. (2003). Locally orientated perception with intact global processing among adolescents with high-functioning autism: evidence from multiple paradigms. *Journal of Child Psychology and Psychiatry*, *44*, 904–913.

O'Riordan, M., Plaisted, K., Driver, J., & Baron-Cohen, S. (2001). Superior visual search in autism. *Journal of Experimental Psychology: Human Perception and Performance*, *27*, 719–730.

Ozonoff, S., Pennington, B., & Rogers, S. (1991). Executive function deficits in high-functioning autistic children: Relationship to theory of mind. *Journal of Child Psychology and Psychiatry*, *32*, 1081–1106.

Perner, J., Frith, U., Leslie, A. M., & Leekam, S. (1989). Exploration of the autistic child's theory of mind: Knowledge, belief, and communication. *Child Development*, *60*, 689–700.

Plaisted, K., O'Riordan, M., & Baron-Cohen, S. (1998). Enhanced visual search for a conjunctive target in autism: A research note. *Journal of Child Psychology and Psychiatry*, *39*, 777–783.

Pratt, C., & Bryant, P. (1990). Young children understand that looking leads to knowing (so long as they are looking into a single barrel). *Child Development*, *61*, 973–983.

Rimland, B. (1964). *Infantile autism: The syndrome and its implications for a neural theory of behaviour*. New York: Appleton-Century-Crofts.

Rumsey, J., & Hamberger, S. (1988). Neuropsychological findings in high-functioning men with infantile autism, residual state. *Journal of Clinical and Experimental Neuropsychology*, *10*, 201–221.

Russell, J. (1997). How executive disorders can bring about an inadequate theory of mind. In J. Russell (Ed.), *Autism as an executive disorder*. Oxford: Oxford University Press.

Rutter, M. (1978). Diagnosis and definition. In M. Rutter & E. Schopler (Eds.), *Autism: A reappraisal of concepts and treatment* (pp. 1–26). New York: Plenum Press.

Scaife, M., & Bruner, J. (1975). The capacity for joint visual attention in the infant. *Nature*, *253*, 265–266.

Shah, A., & Frith, U. (1983). An islet of ability in autism: A research note. *Journal of Child Psychology and Psychiatry*, *24*, 613–620.

Shah, A., & Frith, U. (1993). Why do autistic individuals show superior performance on the block design test? *Journal of Child Psychology and Psychiatry*, *34*, 1351–1364.

Sodian, B., & Frith, U. (1992). Deception and sabotage in autistic, retarded, and normal children. *Journal of Child Psychology and Psychiatry, 33*, 591–606.

Swettenham, J., Baron-Cohen, S., Charman, T., Cox, A., Baird, G., Drew, A., Rees, L., & Wheelwright, S. (1998). The frequency and distribution of spontaneous attention shifts between social and non-social stimuli in autistic, typically developing, and non-autistic developmentally delayed infants. *Journal of Child Psychology and Psychiatry, 9*, 747–753.

Wimmer, H., & Perner, J. (1983). Beliefs about beliefs: Representation and constraining function of wrong beliefs in young children's understanding of deception. *Cognition, 13*, 103–128.

Wing, L. (1997). *The autistic spectrum*: Oxford: Pergamon.

PART IV

Theories of Cognitive Development

As in the first edition, the final section of this Handbook presents a selection of theoretical models for making sense of cognitive development. Cognitive developmental psychology is rich in data, but relatively sparse in theories. Productive explanatory frameworks can make sense of our data, and good theoretical frameworks can guide future research and inform educators and clinicians who work with young children. Most educators for example still rely on two extremely influential theoretical frameworks proposed in the last century, those of Piaget and Vygotsky. Both scientists created detailed theoretical models that guided – and continue to guide – much cognitive developmental research. Overviews of these two theories are presented in the chapters by Miller and Daniels. Newer theories of cognitive development as offered by information-processing theories and neuroconstructivism are discussed in the chapters by Halford and Andrews, and by Westermann, Thomas, and Karmiloff-Smith. The key topic of individual differences, which is important for both educational and clinical approaches to cognitive development, is covered in the final chapter in the Handbook, by Sternberg.

Miller's chapter on Piaget's theory (chapter 25) presents a very clear account of Piaget's claims and the empirical reactions to these claims that shaped the contemporary field of childhood cognitive development. She begins with a description of classic Piagetian theory, outlining the cognitive stages proposed by Piaget to reflect different kinds of mental logical structures. Piaget argued that children begin with an understanding of the world based on mental action schemes, followed by an understanding based on mental representations, and finally by an understanding based on internalized organized operations. Action schemes are organized patterns of behavior for interacting with the environment, such as sucking and grasping. Mental representations are detached from actions, whereas organized operations take the products of mental representations and combine and evaluate them. According to Piaget, cognition is an active, complex, and self-organizing system, similar to other biological systems. Empirical reactions to this theory were many and various, and so Miller concentrates on four key issues.

The first is whether a stage-based model is appropriate for describing cognitive development. The second is whether particular competencies may emerge earlier than Piaget supposed. The third is whether children's current cognitive structures really make it impossible for them to acquire new concepts that do not fit these structures, a research question of particular importance for education. The fourth is about the mechanisms underpinning cognitive development. Miller then demonstrates elegantly that all four of these issues still inform cognitive developmental research today. She shows that even apparently divergent approaches, such as the notion of naïve theories, fall out of Piaget's original account. In doing so, she touches on many of the themes that inform the chapters in this Handbook. Examples are the theme of informational enrichment versus conceptual change, the theme of innate biases that constrain learning, and the importance of general cognitive processes such as executive function. She also demonstrates that developmental cognitive neuroscience is supporting some of Piaget's insights, such as the intimate connections between action and cognition. Her conclusion is that we still need Piaget's theory today. Piaget asked the right questions about development.

In chapter 26, on Vygotsky's theory, Daniels notes the central importance accorded by Vygotsky to cultural and social experiences for psychological development, and charts the migration of Vygotsky's theory into "sociocultural theory" and "activity theory." One of Vygotsky's key claims was that cultural tools, such as forms of talk, ideas and beliefs, signs and symbols, shape children's cognitive development, and that the social, cultural, and historical influences on the formation of mind can be revealed by empirical study. In sociocultural theory, the mediation provided by speech is the main focus of inquiry, as "talk" both shapes children's possibilities for thought and action and is in turn shaped by these thoughts and actions. In activity theory, the child's activity is the focus of analysis, with one aim being to understand how the child actively shapes the forces that are shaping her. Daniels shows how Vygotsky's theory was itself shaped by his experiences in trying to develop a state system to educate "pedagogically neglected" children. The theory was intended to enable the development of new pedagogies for all learners, partly by identifying the psychological "tools" that could direct the mind and behavior of the child. The most important of these tools was language, but other symbolic systems such as maps and pretending also played a role in cognitive development, enabling the child to progress beyond the biological limits imposed by internal systems such as memory capacity. The child was seen as using these psychological tools for self-creation. A particularly important theoretical construct for development was the zone of proximal development (ZPD). The ZPD comprised the area of potential development that each individual could reach via the guidance of adults or in collaboration with more capable peers. The ZPD has been very influential in education, with respect to both assessment and instruction. The notion of a ZPD implies that teaching and assessment should be focused on the *potential* of the learner rather than on their demonstrated level of understanding. It also implies that teaching should create possibilities for development through active participation and collaboration. Rather than conceiving of instruction as simply face to face interaction or the simple transmission of prescribed knowledge and skills, the mutual influence of individual and supra-individual factors must be taken into account. Indeed, Daniels suggests that contemporary models of the ZPD should consider the potential afforded to the learner not just by adults and other individuals, but by institutions, social groups, and communities. Here there are obvious similarities to the theoretical views of Carpenter (chapter 4) and Tomasello (chapter 9). He finishes his chapter by considering the implications of biology for Vygotsky's theory. As he notes, a full account of human functioning in the social world requires an understanding of how the brain functions. In particular, the recognition by cognitive neuroscience of the intertwined nature of emotion and cognition may offer important future insights.

In chapter 27, on information-processing models of cognitive development, Halford and Andrews focus on some of the measures of cognitive complexity that have resulted from this theoretical approach. They argue that cognitive complexity is becoming a major organizing theme in cognitive development, and illustrate this in particular with respect to Halford's own theory of relational complexity. In information-processing theories, cognitive development is conceptualized via a computer metaphor. The child takes certain inputs, converts them into representations, and then uses these representations to compute certain outputs. Cognitive development is then explained by recourse to increasingly complex representations. As Halford and Andrews demonstrate, information-processing models of cognitive development provided the major theoretical alternative to Piaget's and Vygotsky's models prior to the advent of developmental cognitive neuroscience. Information-processing models also contributed to the development of the connectionist modeling approach, which comes into its own via neuroconstructivism. However, information-processing models began with "neo-Piagetian" theories. The goal of these theories was to explain the data collected by Piaget and by those working within a Piagetian framework in terms of the growth of information-processing abilities such as memory capacity and the ability to coordinate different inputs (such as the different dimensions of a stimulus). Halford and Andrews show that all the major information-processing theories (McLaughlin, Pascual-Leone, and Case) were based on these two fundamental components, the child's assumed available memory storage and the level of complexity at which the child was assumed to be capable of processing information (also discussed as the number of concepts that could be considered simultaneously). Clearly, it is difficult to distinguish these assumed components empirically, as cognitive development could either be due to the child making better use of available storage capacity with age (via increased processing efficiency or expertise), or to storage capacity itself increasing with age, or both. Halford and Andrews argue that a lot of "what develops" is accounted for by increased efficiency in the way that available capacity is utilized. One productive way of modeling this increased efficiency is by analyzing the complexity of the information that must be processed in a particular cognitive task, for example in terms of cognitive skills (Fischer), relational complexity (Halford), or rule complexity (Zelazo, see Zelazo & Müller, chapter 22). Halford and Andrews illustrate the difficulties inherent in attempting to arrive at objective analyses of conceptual complexity, and conclude that the optimal metric is to consider the number of relations that can be processed in parallel in the cognitive representation of a particular task. They then relate developmental increases in the ability to handle complexity with maturation of the prefrontal cortex in the brain. Halford and Andrews end by arguing that both cognitive and neuroscience approaches to understanding cognitive development have converged on the notion of complexity, suggesting that this is a critical principle for capturing cognitive development. However, as noted by Miller, Piaget also recognized the importance of complexity: in Piaget's stage theory, cognitive representations become increasingly more complex with development.

In chapter 28, Westermann, Thomas, and Karmiloff-Smith outline a new theoretical approach that has emerged since the first edition of this Handbook, neuroconstructivism. As they note, this approach also incorporates the idea of complexity. Experience-dependent learning by neural networks in the brain results in a progressive elaboration of the complexity of mental representations, with mental representations conceptualized as neural activation patterns in these networks. This is our neural networks metaphor. Importantly, the physical means by which these networks learn provides an important constraint on how complexity is understood. In other words, the "software" (the mental representations) and "hardware" (the neural structures) of the brain cannot be separated when studying development. At the same time, the social and cultural environment and the active acquisition of knowledge by the child provide additional constraints, hence neuroconstructivism is not reductionist. It does not claim that cognitive change can be explained solely on the basis of neural adaptation. Further, as there will be variations in the constraints at different stages of life (or in different developmental disorders, which are conceived as arising from altered constraints), a single theoretical framework can account for typical and atypical development, childhood, adult processing, and age-related cognitive decline. Westermann et al. also argue that attempts to capture the way that cognition is shaped by functional brain development have necessitated a new empirical methodology, focused on developmental trajectories. As Westermann et al. point out, much of the data in the field of children's cognitive development is actually static, demonstrating the abilities of infants and children at different ages. Neuroconstructivism aims to capture the causes and mechanisms of developmental change, characterizing development as a continuous trajectory shaped by multiple interacting biological and environmental constraints. Therefore, the development of computational models such as connectionist models has been very important. These models can explain the mechanisms that might underlie behavioral change in typical cognitive development. A good example earlier in this book comes from the connectionist models considered by Quinn (chapter 5) in his analysis of conceptual development. Connectionist models can also explain developmental mechanisms in atypical development, for example, whether one empirically observed feature of a disorder is the cause of other observed features via the developmental process.

A difficulty common to many theoretical models of cognitive development, including some of those discussed in this section, is how to conceptualize individual differences. In chapter 29, Sternberg concludes the Handbook by giving an overview of individual differences in cognitive development. Sternberg focuses on two paradigms for understanding individual differences, the psychometric paradigm and the systems paradigm. The psychometric paradigm has been an important one in psychology, leading to the development of standardized tests for the measurement of individual differences in cognitive development or in intelligence. The basic notions derived from psychometric theory (e.g., of verbal versus non-verbal intelligence) still govern test construction today. It is also still assumed that there is a general factor *g* underlying all individual differences in cognitive abilities, which may relate to processing speed. Sternberg reviews some of the recent biological evidence for conceiving processing speed in terms of the speed of conduction of neural impulses or action potentials. He concludes that the picture is mixed. However, as he notes, the production of "smart drugs" to enhance mental processing by affecting brain pharmacology has been rather successful, driven partly by a better understanding of the cognitive function of different neurotransmitters. He then considers systems paradigms of individual differences, which are based on the idea of multiple intelligences. For example, researchers such as Gardner have been influential in education, and discuss distinct kinds of intelligence such as "emotional" intelligence (the ability to understand and regulate one's emotions), "social" intelligence (the ability to interact effectively with other people), and "practical" intelligence (the ability to function effectively in everyday life). Sternberg's own theory of intelligence, the triarchic theory, is also a systems theory. However, rather than seeing intelligence as modular, Sternberg focuses on how different aspects of intelligence work together. In his theory, three types of intelligence (analytical, creative, and practical) function together to explain individual differences in performance and to explain individual variability with different kinds of problems. Sternberg also considers the role of heredity versus environment in individual differences in intelligence. He finishes by considering extremes in intelligence, via research on intellectual giftedness and intellectual disability.

Some emergent themes can be seen in these treatments of theories of cognitive development, themes which have also been reflected in many of the chapters in the preceding sections of this Handbook. Cognitive development is no longer conceptualized as happening in an encapsulated fashion in the brain of the individual child. It is seen as crucially dependent on interactions between the child, the social world, and the psychological (or cultural) tools available for mediating knowledge. This is captured powerfully by Vygotsky's theory, but is also critical to the developmental accounts offered for example in the chapters by Carpenter and Tomasello. The ways in which we talk to our children, the things that we talk to them about, the social contexts of the experiences that we provide for them, and the emotional contexts in which these experiences take place all play key roles in cognitive development. Parents and caretakers are acting, usually quite unconsciously, in ways that promote and influence cognitive change, and cognitive development is socially mediated in a surprising number of ways.

A second emergent theme is the centrality of experience-dependent learning. From the initial sensory learning of spatio-temporal structure by low-level perceptual mechanisms to the later shaping of neural networks by symbolic means such as language, cultural artifacts, and pretend play, simple biological learning mechanisms result in complex cognitive structures. Neural networks learn from every incremental experience, extract the patterns or regularities in environmental inputs, and then "fill in" when parts of previously experienced inputs are missing. The infant and child also select actively which experiences to prioritize, often guided by social cues (for example, "ostensive cueing," as discussed by Gergely in chapter 3) or by their emotional responses to environmental events. Importantly, this means that we can shape children's cognitive development by providing certain kinds of environmental events, as in the "teaching" experiments with infants discussed by Baillargeon, Li, Gertner, and Wu in chapter 1. As Daniels notes in this section, we also need to consider the impact on cognitive development of social groups and communities. The chapter on moral development by Nucci and Gingo (chapter 16) provides a nice example of the kind of cross-cultural analysis that can be informative.

Therefore, the crucial factors in explaining childhood cognitive development may be the augmentation of sensory-motor knowledge by information gained through active experience, by information transmitted through language and direct teaching (for example, via apprenticeship or scaffolding), by information experienced by pretend play and the imaginary games that occupy so much of children's unstructured time, and by social learning. Some of these developmental mechanisms were of course identified by Piaget and Vygotsky. As language is acquired, cognitive development is more likely to depend on the child's ability to reflect metacognitively on her own knowledge, and efficiently to inhibit competing knowledge that is interfering with the application of logic. In the early primary years, metacognition and executive function may take over as the drivers of cognitive development. Piaget's theory that logical development depends on qualitatively different kinds of reasoning becoming available at different ages appears to be wrong (e.g. Piaget, 1952). Nevertheless, Piaget's core idea that cognitive structures mirror mathematical systems appears to be correct. This is essentially the core assumption of modern connectionism (Abbott & Dayan, 1999), and again highlights the important role of research in neural networks and machine learning for understanding mechanisms of cognitive development (Meltzoff, Kuhl, Movellan, & Sejnowski, 2009). Cognitive neuroscience provides the scientific framework for exploring how perceptual spatio-temporal structure yields cognitive concepts at the level of neural networks, and how these networks are shaped further as language is acquired.

Indeed, one way of integrating the new theoretical frameworks offered by cognitive neuroscience with the more traditional frameworks offered by theorists like Piaget and Vygotsky is to combine both frameworks. New knowledge about the power of simple learning mechanisms to represent conceptual structure, coming from cognitive neuroscience, needs to be integrated with our knowledge about the importance of language, action and imaginative pretend play, knowledge construction, direct teaching, and being part of a community to cognitive development. One way of thinking about this is to propose that the new theoretical frameworks of neuroconstructivism and information processing help us to understand how the brain creates cognitive representations from perceptual input (Goswami, 2008). The older theoretical frameworks contributed by Piaget and Vygotsky help us to understand how the activities of the child along with the parent, sibling, peer, teacher, and larger community and culture enrich and develop these emergent conceptual representations into a rich and sophisticated cognitive system. Paradoxically, this analysis suggests that at the meta-level our new theoretical approaches to understanding cognitive development, such as neuroconstructivism, are neo-Piagetian and neo-Vygotskian in more ways than might immediately be apparent. In particular, neuroconstructivism offers us new ways forward in terms of characterizing the learning mechanisms that have been described as causally biased, explanation-based, self-organizing, and striving for equilibrium.

References

Abbott, L. F., & Dayan, P. (1999). The effect of correlated variability on the accuracy of a population code. *Neural Computation, 11*, 91–101.

Goswami, U. (2008). *Cognitive development: The learning brain.* Hove, UK: Psychology Press.

Meltzoff, A. N., Kuhl, P. K., Movellan, J., & Sejnowski, T. J. (2009). Foundations for a new science of learning. *Science, 325*, 284–288.

Piaget, J. (1952). *The child's conception of number.* London: Routledge & Kegan Paul.

CHAPTER TWENTY-FIVE

Piaget's Theory

Past, Present, and Future

Patricia H. Miller

Piaget (1952, p. 269) observed his 20-month-old son:

> Laurent is lying on his back but nevertheless resumes his experiments of the day before. He grasps in succession a celluloid swan, a box, etc., stretches out his arm and lets them fall. He distinctly varies the positions of the fall. Sometimes he stretches out his arm vertically, sometimes he holds it obliquely, in front of or behind his eyes, etc. When the object falls in a new position (for example on his pillow), he lets it fall two or three times more on the same place, as though to study the spatial relation; then he modifies the situation. At a certain moment the swan falls near his mouth: now, he does not suck it (even though this object habitually serves this purpose), but drops it three times more while merely making the gesture of opening his mouth.

Here we see some of the most provocative ideas from Piaget: by watching babies at play it is possible to access their minds, because they think in actions, which later will go underground and become abstract thinking. Children are like scientists in that they try out little action and thought experiments and thus actively construct knowledge about the world; in fact, the ideal endpoint of cognitive development is scientific thinking. In children's mundane behaviors, Piaget saw a remarkable underlying process of cognitive development at work. In his view, moment-to-moment specific encounters with objects or people lead to general ways of understanding the world. This understanding changes during development as thinking progresses through various stages from birth to maturity.

Piaget's theory was the first major theory of cognitive development and thus generated the first substantial body of research on children's thinking. His work and the reactions of researchers to it over the last few decades generated a set of key questions, or issues, about cognitive development that contemporary theories and research continue to address. These issues and their contemporary context are the focus of this chapter.

This chapter begins with the emergence of Piaget's theory, followed by key theoretical claims, and then reactions to the theory that clarified the main issues of cognitive development. Then the final sections show how researchers are addressing these issues today and how Piaget's theory still can make contributions to contemporary research on cognitive development.

The Emergence of Piaget's Theory

The Swiss psychologist, zoologist, and philosopher Jean Piaget (1896–1980) spent his life trying to answer fundamental philosophical questions about how humans acquire knowledge: How do we come to know something? Is objective knowledge, unbiased by the nature of the knower, even possible? By studying developmental changes in the process of knowing and in the organization of knowledge, Piaget felt that he could find answers to these questions. For example, he examined the traditional philosophical question of how humans acquire concepts of time, space, and causality by tracing the development of these concepts.

An amazingly productive scholar, Piaget published over 40 books and more than 100 articles or chapters on child psychology alone, not even counting his numerous publications in philosophy and education. Here is a sampling of his research topics: concepts of quantity, space, time, speed, physical causality, morality, and mind; logic and reasoning; relations between cognition and language, learning, perception, and emotions; and the roles of play, imitation, and social interaction. His theory energized the emerging field of cognitive developmental psychology in the mid-1960s.

The publication of Flavell's *Developmental Psychology of Jean Piaget* (1963), which brought Piaget's work to researchers in English-speaking countries, was followed by a dramatic surge in citations of Piaget's work (Siegler & Crowley, 1991) over the following three years. Piagetian-influenced research peaked in the late 1970s through the early 1980s when approximately a third of the articles in major developmental journals cited Piaget (Iaccino & Hogan, 1994). This was the "Piagetian stage" of developmental psychology. Today, Piaget's ideas so permeate research on cognitive development that his influence typically is not even noticed or acknowledged. As Flavell (1996, p. 202) noted, "I think we are in more danger of underappreciating Piaget than of overappreciating him, for much the same reason that fish are said to underappreciate the virtues of water."

Main Theoretical Claims

An adequate summary of Piaget's theory is beyond the scope of this chapter, and the reader is referred to other sources (e.g., Miller, 2002; Piaget, 1983; http://www.piaget.org). This description will emphasize classic Piagetian theory (through the 1960s) rather than the work towards the end of his career, because the former, and the reactions to it, are what shaped the contemporary field of cognitive development, and the later work, unfortunately, has received little attention.

Stages as structures of logic

Perhaps the boldest and most controversial of Piaget's claims is that cognitive development proceeds through a series of *stages*. Each stage is a period of time during which the child's thinking and behavior in a variety of situations tend to reflect a particular type of underlying mental logical structure, or general way of thinking. That is, each stage has a different structure, or set of mental actions, which allows a particular type of interaction between the child and the environment. Consequently, each stage provides a fundamentally different view of the world.

Piaget proposed that stages follow an invariant, universal sequence. Each stage derives from the previous stage, incorporates and transforms that stage, and prepares for the next stage. Piaget's stages are summarized in table 25.1. One of the most exciting ideas in Piaget's theory is that motor actions evolve over the years into abstract thought. Through millions of transactions with the environment and reflections on these transactions, children move from an understanding of the world based on action schemes, to one based on representations, to one based on internalized, organized operations. The beauty of this is that it is orderly.

During infancy, a cognitive structure is called a *scheme* – an organized pattern of behavior for interacting with the environment. A scheme is whatever is repeatable and generalizable in an action. The sucking scheme, then, describes the way infants put various objects into their mouths and suck them. As the scheme develops and becomes more differentiated, children classify objects into "suckables" and "non-suckables," with various subcategories such as hard suckables, soft suckables, and good-tasting suckables. These schemes become increasingly organized, as when sucking and grasping schemes eventually are organized into a higher-order structure that allows coordinated reaching for an object and bringing it to the mouth to suck.

Piaget constructed his model of infancy mainly by simply observing infants as they went about their daily business of playing and learning about the world. The task that attracted the most attention by far is the *object permanence* task – the understanding that objects exist even when you cannot see, feel, or hear them. For example, young infants who see an object placed in a box so that it is no longer visible act as though it no longer exists.

With preschoolers, Piaget had conversations about phenomena ranging from dreams to causes of the movement of clouds, which revealed their ability to mentally represent objects, events, and simple causes. The cognitive structures of school-age children consist of organized mental operations similar to systems of logic. For example, addition, subtraction, multiplication, and division are operations that are coordinated in the concept of number (e.g., the mental operation of reversing addition equals subtraction).

Piaget's most famous task was *conservation* (of number, weight, length, etc.). For example, he showed children two rows of eight objects, one right above the other. After they agreed that they had the same number he spread out one row and then asked whether

Table 25.1 Stages in Piaget's theory

Stage	Description
Sensorimotor period (roughly birth to 2 years)	Infants understand the world in terms of their overt, physical actions on the world. Simple reflexes gradually become more complex, intentional, and organized. Each action-based concept is a pattern of perceptual-motor interactions, for example, "things you can suck on." Piaget refers to a "logic of action."
Preoperational period (roughly 2–7 years)	Children use symbols (mental images, words, gestures) to represent objects and events. That is, they reconstruct the sensorimotor concepts of objects, relations, causality, space, and time in a new medium (mental representation) and a more highly organized structure. Despite the limitations of egocentrism, rigid thought, and limited role-taking and communication abilities, these symbols become increasingly organized and logical, so that children can think about causes.
Concrete operational period (roughly 7–11 years)	Logical structures permit children to perform various mental operations, which are internalized actions that can be reversed. Thinking now is more flexible and abstract. Actions are still the main source of knowledge, but the actions now are mental. Logic dominates over perceptions, such that children understand that quantities stay the same even though they change their appearance.
Formal operational period (roughly 11–15 years)	Mental operations now can be applied not only to concrete objects but also to purely verbal or logical statements, to the possible as well as the real, to the future as well as the present. Children take the results of concrete operations and generate hypotheses (propositions, statements) about their logical relations. Thus, they have operations on operations; thought has become truly logical, abstract, and hypothetical. The essence of formal operational thought is the *scientific method*. Children formulate a hypothesis and test it. They can imagine all possible outcomes and generate all possible combinations to test.

they still had the same number. An 8-year-old says they do, whereas a 4-year-old says that the longer row has more. According to Piaget, preoperational children fail this task because they lack reversible mental operations, which characterize concrete operations. Finally, formal operational children perform operations on operations, such as generating possible outcomes and evaluating them in light of evidence.

Processes of change: assimilation–accommodation cycles

Piaget's most general definition of intelligence is that it is adaptation to the environment. Just as humans adapt physically to the environment, so do they adapt mentally to the environment. The stages reflect different ways of adapting to the environment.

Adaptation involves two complementary processes: assimilation and accommodation. *Assimilation* is the process of applying what one knows, of fitting reality into one's current cognitive organization. When children think, they are constrained by their current cognitive structure. Some distorting of experience is inevitable as children attempt to incorporate, understand, or interpret this experience. A child's mind is not like a camera; experience is always filtered through the child's current ways of understanding.

Accommodation, the other side of the coin, refers to adjustments (advances) in cognitive organization that result from experience in the world. Objects have unique features that must be taken into account sooner or later. Accommodation occurs because the current structures have failed to interpret a particular object or event satisfactorily. The resulting reorganization of thought leads to a different and more satisfactory assimilation of the experience. Thus, assimilation and accommodation are closely intertwined in a series of cycles through development. For example, infants' attempts to apply their sucking and grasping schemes to a magnet are only partially successful because the magnet is new in certain ways (e.g., metallic, horseshoe shaped). As a result of this failure to "understand" (assimilate) the object or event, they must make minor cognitive adjustments or accommodations. This brings them to a slightly more advanced cognitive level. However, this new level makes them aware of other discrepancies, and so the assimilation–accommodation cycle continues. For Piaget, this is the main mechanism, or process, of development.

Knowledge through the active construction of concepts

Piaget saw cognition as an active, complex, self-organizing system. Children do not passively learn from experience. Instead, they actively construct knowledge through interacting with the world and reflecting on these experiences. A child knows or understands a ball or a rattle by acting on it – physically or mentally. Infants construct a world of objects to suck, grasp, throw, shake, and listen to. It seems impossible today that "the active child" was a revolutionary notion.

Reactions to Piaget's Theory: New Findings, New Issues

Once Piaget's theory became accessible to English-speaking developmentalists, a wave of research attempted to replicate, expand, or refute his theory. Such studies typically applied more rigorous experimental procedures, tested larger numbers of children, and performed fine-grained analyses of Piagetian tasks. The outcome was that Piaget's theory spawned many interesting new findings, paradigms, and tasks. Perhaps most importantly, this work took the developmental issues raised by Piaget in fruitful new directions and raised important new issues. The rest of this chapter outlines four main issues and shows how they shaped much of the contemporary field of cognitive development and continue to be the focus of this work today. The heading of each subsection identifies a major set of research findings from the mid-1960s until recently and the issue raised by this research.

Evidence against broad stages: is cognitive understanding domain-specific or general?

The attempts at replication showed that Piaget's findings, particularly the sequences in which concepts are acquired, generally were replicated. However, studies also began to identify some limits to the theory.

The strongest criticisms concerned Piaget's notion of stages. Research did not support the claim that children acquire concepts and broad conceptual structures that apply to all content areas. Instead, a child often performed at different cognitive levels on tasks that supposedly tapped the same stage. Moreover, a concept often was demonstrated earlier with simpler task demands than with more complex ones, and earlier in areas in which children had a great deal of experience and knowledge than in less familiar ones. For example, infants were more likely to demonstrate the concept of object permanence when the object was the mother than when it was a physical object (Bell, 1970). Given these inconsistencies, researchers asked whether the mind is less a coherent cognitive system than a "collection of different and unrelated mindlets" (Flavell, 1992) devoted to different contents. It seemed more accurate to depict cognition as concepts and related clusters of concepts that pertained to a particular domain, such as math, space, or quantity, rather than as a series of general stages.

It should be noted that Piaget himself acknowledged that a structure may apply only to a particular content area and may have to be constructed anew in various domains during a stage. He referred to *horizontal décalages* that occur when a general concept emerges earlier on some tasks than others. For example, the conservation of substance typically develops a year or two before conservation of weight. In Piaget's view, some stimuli "resist" the application of the cognitive structures. Still, researchers began to think of cognition as more domain-specific than domain-general.

Although the growing body of evidence of inconsistency in performance questioned Piaget's stage notion, it also stimulated several important theoretical accounts. Flavell (1982) offered more refined analyses of the possible nature of stages: the acquisition of each stage is an extended process, including an initial period of preparation during which the stage is somewhat unstable and a final period of maturity and stability that may come only after that stage has officially ended. Until this final point, the cognitive items may not become concordant, tightly organized, and interrelated into a true stage. Concepts or structures that characterize a stage are often only roughly synchronous in their development. For example, two concepts might begin their development at the same time but complete it at different times. Or they might begin and end their development at different times but have considerable temporal overlap. Finally, there may be more stage-like consistency in some cognitive domains than in others.

Theorists labeled as "neo-Piagetians" offered theoretical models of stages defined in terms of the complexity of their information-processing requirements rather than their logical structure. Case, Fischer, Pascual-Leone, Halford, Demetriou, and others (see Morra, Gobbo, Marini, & Sheese, 2008, for both historical and contemporary accounts of these models) often focused on changes in working memory – the capacity to hold several pieces of information in mind and perform mental operations on them. These theorists also included strategies, as well as contextual social or physical support for emerging skills, to develop broad, elegant theories that better articulate the processes underlying movement from one stage to another. For example, only after children have the working-memory capacity to hold two conflicting representations in mind simultaneously, such as "tall glasses have more" and "fat glasses have more" can they begin to try to integrate them to construct a new representation – taller is balanced by thinner.

Some researchers searched for alternative theoretical models more satisfactory than cognitive structures associated with stages; for example, specific rules used to solve problems in a particular domain. In the rule-assessment approach, Siegler (1978) drew on Piaget's method of examining children's errors for insight into their thinking to develop an elegant systematic account of the development of precise rules used to solve problems in particular domains. For example, on the balance-scale task, an early rule might be "The arm with the most weights always goes down" whereas a more advanced rule might be "When the two arms have the same number of weights the arm with the weights further from the fulcrum will go down." Instead of stage-like changes, cognitive development may consist of rule shifts on a particular task. Other models focused on the organization of children's knowledge base concerning a particular domain. Children shift from novice to expert status after experience in a particular domain such as chess, soccer, or dinosaurs (e.g., Chi, 1978), and thus show more organized and advanced thinking in that domain.

Evidence that children's level of performance could be moved around by a variety of task factors led to theories about how children actually apply their concepts in a particular setting. That is, theories about how cognitive *competence* is translated into *performance* (Flavell & Wohlwill, 1969). Researchers began to develop a theory of performance to supplement Piaget's theory of competence (i.e., cognitive structures). A child must not only understand that number is conserved when items are spread out but also be able to understand the task instructions, attend to number and ignore other attributes such as color and the salient length dimension, and have the working-memory capacity to remember the equivalence of the rows, the type of transformation, and the questions asked (e.g., Miller, 1978). Importantly, such work drew attention to the role of *quantitative* developmental changes in degree, amount, speed, or efficiency (e.g., of working memory) in *qualitative* stage-like changes in kind of thinking (e.g., non-conservers vs. conservers).

Thus, the reactions to Piaget's theory of stages raised an important issue: *Does cognitive development consist of concepts and cognitive structures applied to all content areas or of domain-specific concepts and limited conceptual systems?* What determines whether a structure will be applied to a particular content area? How can we decide what constitutes a "domain"? What information-processing skills are needed for competence to be expressed in performance in a particular task? How do qualitative (stage) and quantitative change (e.g., better working memory and attention) operate together during development? Researchers continue to address these issues today.

Demonstrations of early competencies: is there earlier development or different levels of a concept?

A second main challenge to Piaget's theory was research showing that his methods often underestimated children's understanding. The "miracle baby" (Gopnik, 1994, p. 133) experiments were particularly provocative. In these studies, experimenters eliminated or reduced Piaget's motor requirement, for example, that infants search for a hidden object in order to be credited with the concept of object permanence. Baillargeon (1987), for instance, found that 4-month-old infants, who should not yet possess the concept of object permanence, were surprised when a screen falling away from them seemed to pass through a now out-of-view box they had seen there shortly before. Other studies found infant precocious understanding in areas such as physical causality, time, number, and categorization (see Haith & Benson, 1998, and Spelke & Newport, 1998, for reviews). Together, these studies demonstrated that the "scientist in the crib" (Gopnik, Meltzoff, & Kuhl, 1999) shows impressive causal reasoning and seems to have key foundational concepts much earlier than Piaget thought.

Just as limitations in motor skills may mask young infants' knowledge, so may preschoolers' limited verbal skills underestimate their knowledge, because they may not understand the wording Piaget used during testing; for example, the meaning of "same number" and "amount." Or children may not have the verbal skills to provide a logical explanation for their answer (e.g., "You didn't add any water or take any away so it has to be the same"), which Piaget required in order to credit an understanding of conservation.

This concern with the considerable verbal requirements of tasks led to a number of clever attempts to devise less verbal, or non-verbal, assessments, such as expressions of surprise (Gelman, 1972), heart-rate changes (Bower, 1974), and choice of candy (Miller, 1976), to test for the presence or absence of certain concepts. For example, Gelman (1972) found that 3-year-olds noticed, and were surprised, when the number of toy mice changed (because the experimenter had surreptitiously removed one).

"Simplification studies" showed that complex materials and procedures also can underestimate the age at which children acquire various concepts. For example, young children demonstrate more knowledge about counting when there are only a few objects than when there are many (Gelman & Gallistel, 1978).

Thus, from these studies we learned that motor, verbal, and information-processing abilities may mask early competencies and that reducing these demands and simplifying materials and responses reveal greater knowledge. However, it was not clear what we should conclude from these studies. A "rich" interpretation of these findings is that Piaget underestimated young children's competencies. Some developmentalists argued for powerful biological constraints that permit the rapid acquisition of knowledge about language, mental states, and objects (Gelman & Williams, 1998; Spelke & Newport, 1998). However, given that Piaget's main claims concerned the sequence in which knowledge is acquired rather than the particular ages, showing that an ability emerged earlier than Piaget claimed is not necessarily damaging to his theory.

A more intriguing conclusion about these early competencies is the "lean" interpretation that they may reveal less advanced versions of, or perhaps precursors of, the later, more advanced concepts identified by Piaget. For example, young infants' apparent understanding of object permanence actually may reflect knowledge that, although related to object permanence, is more perceptual than conceptual (e.g., Meltzoff & Moore, 1998). These early perception-based understandings, or perceptual expectations, are important because they may support causal learning in various domains. Similarly, preschoolers' advanced competence on simplified concrete operational tasks actually may reflect only preoperational concepts, such as understanding the functional relations between two variables, rather than concrete operational concepts (Chapman, 1988; Lourenco & Machado, 1996). These simplified tasks provide so much perceptual support that they lack the conditions theoretically necessary for operational reasoning. Thus, these apparent concepts may actually be "precursors" to the concept in question.

In any case, it is clear that concepts have some sort of earlier development than Piaget thought. At first, a concept is fragile and thus demonstrated only in supportive contexts (i.e., perceptual supports, modest demands on the child's working memory and verbal ability). The fragile concept gradually strengthens and becomes less perceptual and more cognitive; or precursors emerge then bootstrap the development of the target, more abstract, concept.

Regardless of one's position on this issue, Piaget's claims made researchers think deeply about what it means to "have" a concept. This issue had important implications for assessment. If a variety of task manipulations affect the age at which children demonstrate understanding, how do you decide which task provides "accurate" assessment? The different methods of the Piagetians and subsequent researchers reflect different goals of assessment. Piaget was careful to avoid "false positive errors," that is, concluding that children have the concept when in fact they do not. Consequently, he used heavy verbal demands (e.g., explanations), complex materials, and a misleading visual array to ensure that only children who consider the concept logically necessary will persist. His challengers, in contrast, were more interested in avoiding "false negative errors" – concluding that children do not have the concept when in fact they do. Thus, whether a researcher is interested in the first manifestation or the final form of the concept influences the sort of assessment selected.

Research on early competencies was quite fruitful because it revealed positive acquisitions during the infancy and preschool years that complement Piaget's emphasis on the cognitive deficiencies of young children. For example, this work revealed that preoperational children know quite a bit about number. Gelman and Gallistel (1978) found that they understood a sequence of simple principles of counting; for example, the principle that numbers must always be used in the same order. That is, children who say "1, 2, 6, 9" follow this counting principle correctly if, when counting, they always use these numbers in this order. These early principles add to, rather than contradict, Piaget's work on more advanced concepts of number acquired several years later. In short, regardless of whether the various tests of Piaget's theory actually disproved some claims, the more important contribution of this burst of research energy was to contribute subtle theoretical ideas about levels of "having" a concept and a rich set of findings about related early concepts in infants and preschoolers.

Although demonstrations of surprisingly early competencies attracted the most attention, observations of surprising incompetence in adolescents and adults appeared as well. For example, adolescents and adults often, perhaps even typically, do not reason in formal operational ways (e.g., Byrnes, 1988). Also, showing apparent conservers fake evidence of non-conservation (e.g., Miller, 1973) sometimes suggested that the understanding of conservation was easily dislodged. Recent research suggests that even adults, who fully understand the concept of compensation of width and height and of conservation, still are influenced by the salience of the height of glasses. When students, or even experienced bartenders, were asked to pour 1.5 ounce shots from a bottle into a tall and slender or a short and wide glass, they poured more into the short, wide glasses – 30% more in the case of students (Wansink & van Ittersum, 2005).

In summary, finding that young children may possess greater competence and adolescents less competence than Piaget thought led to the issue: *Are there levels of understanding in many concepts and, if so, how do these levels differ?* Are these early competencies weaker more fragile versions of the full-blown concept or are they different (e.g., perception-based) but related skills that serve as precursors to, and even contribute to the development of, the full-blown concept? Does it even make sense to ask if a child "has" a concept?

Evidence that concepts can be trained: what are the cognitive constraints on the effects of experience on cognitive development?

Perhaps the largest body of research aimed at disproving Piaget's claims addressed whether children's current cognitive structures actually make it impossible for them to acquire particular new concepts, even with instruction. Some of the early studies were very straightforward – the experimenter simply explained the concept to the child. For example, in one study intended to train the conservation of length (Kingsley & Hall, 1967) this involved showing children the meaning of longer and shorter, showing them how to measure with a ruler, telling them that the ruler was more reliable than visual cues, and explaining that length is changed only by adding to or taking away and that moving an object does not change its length. Other studies taught the precursors, sometimes testing Piaget's claims about what mental operations lead to conservation. For example, does training children to use the mental operation of compensation (understanding that a change in width cancels any change in height during pouring) lead to conservation? Some training studies were unsuccessful, but many training studies successfully taught a new concept by teaching underlying operations, creating cognitive conflict, verbalizing the rule for the child, or redirecting attention to the relevant feature (Brainerd & Allen, 1971).

What did we learn from hundreds of conservation training studies? We learned that some young children sometimes, under some circumstances, can be taught concepts that they otherwise would not have acquired until months or even years later. Did training studies serve as a test of Piaget's theory? In a sense, no, because the sequence of acquiring concepts is more important than the age of acquisition.

Perhaps the most important lesson from training studies actually supported Piaget's theory: older children lacking the concept are more likely to learn from training than are younger ones, presumably because they are closer to acquiring the concept naturally. This is consistent with Piaget's arguments about cognitive readiness – that children can profit from instruction only if they have enough understanding to assimilate this new information into their present cognitive structures or accommodate their structures to the experience. However, more refined predictions are more difficult because it is not clear how to assess degree of readiness in children. The notion of cognitive readiness was applied to instruction in schools. Educators attempted to ensure that a child had the cognitive prerequisites for profiting from particular types of instruction and that they presented new concepts in the correct sequence.

The training studies also furthered our thinking about appropriate methods for assessing effects of cognitive training. One can determine the strength of any training effects only if there are generalization tests with other materials, delayed as well as immediate post-tests, and perhaps counter-suggestions that children must resist. Again, these studies identified levels of understanding.

In sum, training studies raised some very interesting issues: *What are the cognitive constraints on learning from experience?* How do learning and cognitive change differ? Is long-term change different from short-term change? How do you know which children are most ready to benefit from training? How do you know when a child has acquired a concept after instruction?

Evidence about mechanisms of development: what are the processes of developmental change?

Cognitive development is about both description of acquisitions at each age and explanations of how cognitive change comes about. Piaget proposed the following four-factor "formula" for development that points to processes of developmental change:

Development = Physical maturation + Experience with the physical environment
+ Social experience + Equilibration

In his view, development emerges from the continual complex interplay of innate and environmental factors. Innate factors include reflexes that provide the building blocks of cognition through a series of modifications during experience, a particular physical makeup unique to the human species, and inherited ways of interacting with the environment. Newborns know almost nothing about the world, but they are born with the tools that can lead them to know almost everything. Active experience with the world and interactions with other people provide information about the world that the child uses, through equilibration, to resolve cognitive conflict by constructing new concepts. Thus, *equilibration* is Piaget's main engine for change.

As an example of equilibration, in the liquid-conservation task children are in disequilibrium if they go back and forth between saying that the tall thin glass has more because it is tall and the short fat one has more because it is fat. However, researchers challenged this claim on both empirical and theoretical grounds. Young children are poor at detecting logical inconsistencies that might cause cognitive conflict and thus disequilibrium. For example, children do not see a problem with the claim that a man is both tall and very short until about age 6 (Ruffman, 1999). Moreover, Piaget's mechanisms of development were very imprecise, and thus researchers looked for other, more specific, mechanisms.

Examples of new mechanisms uncovered (Flavell, Miller, & Miller, 2002; Siegler & Alibali, 2005) include mental operations becoming increasingly automatic and less effortful as a result of practice, mental capacity for a variety of mental skills increasing as working memory increases, and cognitive conflict created by interactions with more advanced peers. Other examples are brain maturation, attending to and encoding new information, constructing strategies for problem solving, and improving skills at selecting strategies.

Cognitive developmental research today is increasingly focused on mechanisms of development. Issues include: *What are the processes underlying cognitive development? How do innate and environmental factors together cause development? What are the correlates, in brain activity, of cognitive change?*

In summary, post-Piagetian research questioned whether cognitive development is stage-like, revealed earlier competencies that challenged Piaget's proposed ages, and changed the focus to mechanisms of cognitive changes. The research led to new methods and identified the limits of the theory – what it could do and not do. The resulting issues have shaped contemporary research on cognitive development. As Flavell (1963, p. 412) concluded, "Piaget has staked out a lot of virgin territory in the area of cognitive growth. As is often the case with new explorations, the cartography was not always accurate. But at least there are stakes there now, and we cannot and should not ignore them." The developmental issues are stakes that guide contemporary researchers through the developing cognitive landscape.

Contemporary Piagetian-Influenced Work: Issues of Cognitive Development Revisited

Today, Piaget's theory has a pervasive, but often invisible, influence: it is simply assumed that children actively construct knowledge. Researchers search for an organized conceptual system underlying several different cognitive behaviors; for example, a child's intuitive theory of how genetics works or about the nature of minds. They try to identify how a new concept arises from a previous one, and consider both qualitative and quantitative change. They look at children's errors for clues to their belief systems.

Research also continues today on all four of the above issues, though again the ties to Piaget usually are implicit rather than explicit. In what content areas or theories are the four Piagetian-derived issues described above still debated today? What new directions have these issues taken recently?

Stages versus domain-specific cognition

In recent years, new statistical modeling techniques have permitted researchers to empirically map out patterns of development (e.g., Dawson-Tunik, Commons, Wilson, & Fischer, 2005), specifically, when during development there appear to be somewhat abrupt, stage-like improvements in cognition and when improvement is more gradual. For example, if items of corresponding levels of complexity of each task tend to cluster together, and there are gaps between these levels, this could be taken as evidence for stages – either within a domain or across domains.

Work continues on children's developing domain-specific understanding of various content areas examined by Piaget, particularly number (Bryant & Nunes, chapter 21, this volume), space (Liben & Christensen, chapter 17, this volume), biology (Gelman & Opfer, 2002; Opfer & Gelman, chapter 8, this volume), physics (Baillargeon, Li, Gertner & Wu, chapter 1, this volume; Wilkening & Cacchione, chapter 18, this volume), moral reasoning (Nucci & Gingo, chapter 16, this volume), and people (especially intentionality, Carpenter, chapter 4, this volume; and understanding minds, Wellman, chapter 10, this volume). Piaget's work on scientific reasoning, pretend play, symbolic development, causal reasoning, and inductive/deductive reasoning continues to inform current work in these domains (Kuhn; Lillard, Pinkham & Smith; DeLoache; Koslowski & Masnick; Goswami; all this volume).

Today, much of this work, especially with young children, falls within the *core-knowledge* approach, which examines children's organized "foundational" concepts about physics, psychology, and biology that are important to learn quickly early in life, in order to adapt and thrive. Knowing that dropped objects will fall, understanding others' intentions, and distinguishing between animate and inanimate entities are examples. Some of these researchers have a *theory-theory* approach (Gelman & Kalish, 2006; Wellman, chapter 10, this volume), which asserts that children develop informal, naïve theories about specific domains. Children's "theories" – organized, coherent systems of knowledge about a domain – clearly retain important elements from Piaget's theory of organized knowledge. Children test their causal-explanatory theories in their everyday interactions with objects and people, and change these theories as needed.

In "theory of mind," for example, children's understandings about the psychological causes of others' behavior change from one theory to another during development. The false-belief task is the most commonly used assessment. For example, children see a crayon box and, when asked what is in it say "crayons." The box is opened to reveal candles and children are asked what they thought was in the box before it was opened. Four-year-olds say "crayons" but 3-year-olds say "candles" – what they know to be the case rather than what they falsely believed. Four-year-olds are said to have a theory of mind based on understanding minds as representations that may be true or false; 3-year-olds' theory, in contrast, is based on understanding minds as corresponding to reality.

Early competencies

Several chapters (1–7) in this volume review recent work on stunning early competencies in infants' ability to imitate, detect other people's intentions, infer intentionality and causality when viewing animated shapes, understand physical qualities of objects such as permanence and containment, categorize objects, learn words, and remember. For example, infants understand the goal of another person's behavior (i.e., intentions) even if the goal was not achieved, as when the person reaches for an object unsuccessfully (Hamlin, Hallinan, & Woodward, 2008). Also, some researchers argue that, on some level, infants can add and subtract very small numbers and even differentiate between number ratios (McCrink & Wynn, 2004, 2007). Moreover, young children go beneath the surface changes of objects to infer unseen "essences" and underlying causal mechanisms that explain why an organism is a member of a particular category. Thus, a raccoon that is shaved, painted black and white, and implanted with an odor sac is still a raccoon rather than a skunk, and there is a "boyness" and "girlness" essence that causes gender-specific behaviors (Gelman, 2003).

The controversy mentioned in the earlier section on this issue – of whether these early competencies truly are the advanced, adult-like abilities that they seem or are qualitatively different from mature versions – recently was debated again by some of the key researchers in this area (Liben, 2008). As new methods, including neuroimaging, reveal more and more evidence of infants' conceptual understanding, the issue is perhaps more important than ever. How should we interpret changes in infant looking-time and patterns of cortical activity that seem to indicate sophisticated knowledge? For example, how should we interpret the following study (Quinn, Westerlund, & Nelson, 2006). Six-month-old infants were shown 36 different cat images (i.e., multiple instances from a common category, cats) then 20 novel cat images with 20 novel dog images interspersed. Both cat and dog novel images differed perceptually from the original cat images. Infants' brain activity was identical with cats 19–36 (the trials by which a "category" might be formed) and the 20 novel cats, but not the dogs. Thus, infants acted as though the novel cats, but not dogs, were members of that same category, cats. Looking behavior showed the same pattern (Mareschal & Quinn, 2001); thus there is converging evidence. The debate continues as to whether and how the adult concept of cat differs from that of infants. Are these infant competencies in fact categories or, instead, perceptual clusters? Does the adult concept reflect "informational enrichments" (Quinn, 2008) of the earlier knowledge or a more radical qualitative transformation?

Other new theoretical accounts of various early competencies (and incompetencies) have been offered. For example, young infants may possess representations of hidden objects that are strong enough to elicit looking but not strong enough to elicit the more effortful behavior of reaching for the objects (Munakata, McClelland, Johnson, & Siegler, 1997) – Piaget's litmus test for the assessment of object permanence. Innate learning biases to look for categories and causes may be operating as well.

Instruction/learning

Compared to the 1960s and 1970s, the number of recent conservation training studies is quite modest. However, these recent training studies have taken the field in some fascinating new directions. For example, conservation training is more effective when 5-year-old non-conservers have to explain the reasoning behind an adult's (correct) conservation answer than when they simply hear the adult's answer or hear the answer plus an explanation (Siegler, 1995), perhaps because it encourages children to notice and think about new aspects of the problem. Moreover, the children who benefited most were those who initially showed greater variability of reasoning. Another conservation example (Church & Goldin-Meadow, 1986) is that children sometimes show more advanced thinking with their hands (e.g., showing awareness of the increase in width of the container of liquid) than in their speech (i.e., saying that the taller container has more). Such children progressed more after training than did children with concordant behaviors. Moreover, children given conservation training with gestures (even with no objects present!) as well as verbal instruction improved more than children given only verbal instruction (Ping & Goldin-Meadow, 2008). These findings about variability and discordant representations offer a new perspective on the meaning of cognitive readiness to learn. Furthermore, this work on the role of gestures suggests the influence of an aspect of the environment not explored by Piagetians.

More generally, the blurring of learning and cognitive change in light of Piagetian work has led to interesting theoretical work on this issue. Learning now often is viewed as short-term cognitive change as a result of experience, and these microchanges often are studied with the microgenetic method (Miller & Coyle, 1999; Siegler, 1995). In this method, researchers examine changes in children's behavior from one trial to the next on similar tasks over several sessions separated by days or weeks. By looking up close at small moment-to-moment changes, researchers find clues to processes of change. The microgenetic method has revealed counterintuitive findings, such as children (a) dropping a good, more advanced strategy that produced a correct answer in favor of trying out another strategy and (b) keeping a strategy that produced an incorrect answer (Siegler,1996).

Still another theme concerning the role of environmental inputs is that the social transmission of information may play a greater role than Piaget thought. Parents or other people transmit knowledge, and children can thus benefit from the experience of others. Learning from conversations with parents may be especially important for unobservable phenomena such as religion (e.g., God's special powers and the afterlife) and certain scientific concepts such as the spherical shape of the earth or that thinking depends on the brain (Harris & Koenig, 2006). More generally, it is becoming clearer that social and cultural influences, such as schooling and the types of social support and conversations provided by parents in different cultures, significantly impact even Piagetian-like cognitive development (e.g., Gauvain & Perez, 2007).

Mechanisms of development

What drives development is arguably the main focus of cognitive developmental research today. One of the most active research areas on this topic is developmental cognitive neuroscience (see below), stimulated by advances in neuroimaging techniques. For example, neuroimaging reveals that maturation of the cortex correlates with cognitive milestones during development (Sowell et al., 2004). Of particular interest is frontal cortex development that facilitates the inhibition of dominant but less mature responses. It should be noted, however, that many brain changes reflect, rather than drive, development, as in the strengthening of some neural pathways and networks and pruning away of other neural connections as a result of experience. Other current research on mechanisms examines the role of working memory; "connectionist" models of associative learning simulate how children make connections between events that are reliably associated, and there is a rich literature on strategy development and selection (Siegler, 1989; Siegler & Alibali, 2005). One interesting finding related to Piaget's notion of equilibration as a force for change is that, as noted above, variability and contradictions in a child's behavior may be a source of conflict that sets in motion cognitive change (Goldin-Meadow, Alibali, & Church, 1993; Siegler, 1995).

Why We Still Need Piaget's Theory

What is still relevant today from Piagetian research? As this chapter has emphasized, issues about cognitive development from Piagetian theory and research challenging it have endured to guide current research. This last section will show how these issues are important in several main areas of contemporary research on cognitive development.

Some of the main topics dominating research on cognitive development today include: variability in performance (intra-person over time or inter-person), social cognition (especially theory of mind), cognitive self-regulation (especially executive functions), and brain processes underlying cognition and its development. The first two clearly derive from research stimulated by Piaget's theory, whereas the last two do not, but are included because they illustrate how drawing on Piaget's theory could benefit these research areas.

What might be useful from Piaget's theory for studying these four topics? The discussion below suggests that it would be fruitful to return to some of the core concepts and issues of cognitive development generated by Piagetian theory. In particular, for all four topics it would be useful to return to Flavell's classic papers on sequences (1972) and concurrences (1971) in the acquisition of concepts. Sequences, concurrences, organization, and the intertwining of qualitative and quantitative change can serve as guiding principles for analyzing change and identifying mechanisms of development.

Variability in cognitive performance

As described earlier, initial attempts to replicate Piaget's claims about consistency within each stage uncovered considerable variability in a child's performance across settings, tasks, or time. For example, in one study (Siegler, 1995) slightly over half of 5-year-olds classified as non-conservers generated a correct answer and satisfactory explanation on at least one conservation problem. Studies by Siegler and others documented, on a variety of tasks, variability between children, between similar tasks, and, most importantly, even within a given child on the same problem a few minutes apart (e.g., the same math problem). In fact, variability may be more common than consistency. Variability now is examined as a phenomenon of interest in its own right rather than as simply a problem for Piaget's theory.

The most developed theoretical account of variability is Siegler's (1996) overlapping waves theory, which depicts cognitive development as more like a series of overlapping waves than a series of discrete stages. For example, various strategies could be used to solve addition problems, such as solving 3 + 2 = 5 by counting 1-2-3-4-5, counting 3-4-5, or simply recalling the memorized answer. At any age, a child possesses several strategies that could be used, though they vary in their strength and frequency of use. This describes why there is variability – a child continues to use an old strategy after a new strategy begins to develop. Each strategy, like a wave, gathers strength over time, peaks, and then diminishes; immature strategies flow and ebb earlier than do more advanced strategies. Thus, a child is not in a particular stage regarding addition, but rather has a particular configuration of possible strategies from which he or she typically draws several different ones when solving a series of math problems.

This approach could be extended in interesting directions by drawing on several Piagetian notions. What is theoretically interesting in the sequences in which the strategies emerge? Drawing on Flavell's (1972) analysis, one might ask whether an earlier strategy scaffolds the development of a later strategy, is eventually replaced by the later strategy, or becomes a part of that strategy. Regarding concurrences, perhaps two co-existing strategies join together to construct a third more advanced strategy. These developmental sequences and concurrences provide important clues about processes of development. Also, concurrences in the emergence of two or more strategies would clarify the cognitive organization of children's strategies. Finally, it would be theoretically and empirically fruitful to study Siegler's wave model in terms of its nice integration of quantitative and qualitative development. Changes in strength and frequency of a strategy during development are quantitative changes, while changes in the configuration and organization of the set of potential strategies are qualitative changes. Quantitative changes may, for example, be the process by which qualitative change occurs, as when a new strategy becomes strong enough to force a reorganization of a child's hierarchy of strategies.

Theory of mind

The "theory-theory" approach to theory of mind (Wellman, chapter 10, this volume) has clear ties to Piaget's view that related concepts are closely interrelated and form a coherent cognitive system. Moreover, Piaget's work on egocentrism – preschoolers' tendency to perceive and interpret the world in terms of their own perspective, lacking the understanding that this perspective is just one of many – foreshadowed theory-of-mind research.

Theory-of-mind research has fruitfully examined concurrences in the emergence of understanding false belief, the appearance–reality distinction, and facial displays that hide inner emotions (e.g., Flavell, 1993) in order to address whether these abilities might reflect a more general concept (e.g., a distinction between mental representations and reality). However, researchers rarely have drawn on the analysis of sequences as a useful theoretical tool from Piagetian work. Based on such a sequential analysis of seven concepts by Wellman and Liu (2004) one could examine the developmental processes occurring between concept A (e.g., understanding that two people can have different beliefs about the same object), which develops before concept B (e.g., the development of the understanding of false belief). Specifically, A might scaffold B, be replaced by B (a different theory, such as desire–belief), or become a part of B. Or A and B might join together to construct a third, more advanced, theory of mind.

Executive functions

Executive functions (EF) include cognitive processes involved in goal-oriented behavior; for example, inhibition of prepotent responses, working memory, and shifting from one cognitive set (e.g., one attribute, color) to another (e.g., shape). Historically, EF research came from neuropsychology, not Piaget, because EF is associated with activity in the prefrontal cortex (Zelazo & Müller, chapter 22, this volume). Piagetian and EF approaches have only occasionally been brought together; for example, in theories by several neo-Piagetians, (e.g., Case, Pascual-Leone; see Morra et al., 2008, for descriptions) and others (Russell, 1999). One empirical link between EF and Piagetian work is that his object-permanence task was resurrected in recent years because of its potential to study toddlers' limited ability to inhibit. Of particular interest was Piaget's A-not-B task in which an object is hidden in location A for several trials and a toddler searches correctly under A. Then, as the toddler watches, the object is moved to location B, but the toddler persists in searching under A. It has been argued that these toddlers may not lack an understanding of object permanence but rather have difficulty with the memory demands and with inhibiting their prepotent response of searching the first hiding place (Diamond, 1985). Also, performance on formal operational tasks is related to EF (Emick & Welsh, 2005).

Several connecting points with Piaget can be identified. One is his notion of *centration* – young children's difficulty with cognitive shifting because of their tendency to attend to or think about one salient feature of an object or event (e.g., water height in a container) and ignore other features (fatness of container). They cannot mentally shift back and forth between height and width and see their compensatory relation. Relatedly, Piaget also found that preschoolers have trouble thinking about an object as first a boat and then blue in order to classify it along both dimensions simultaneously. Thus, both centration and double classification seem conceptually similar to the cognitive shifting component of EF. This rich body of Piagetian empirical and theoretical work could suggest new directions for this contemporary EF research.

The post-Piagetian work on concurrences would provide valuable guidance for one of the central debates in EF research today: Is EF a unitary construct or a set of somewhat independent components (inhibition, shifting, and working memory)? The research addressing this issue sometimes looks for concurrences (i.e., correlated development between two or more of these components). However, theoretical work on concurrences (e.g., Flavell, 1971,1982, 1992) goes well beyond these simplistic designs to suggest more ways to address some of the subtleties of concurrence: Do inhibition and shifting begin their development at the same time but complete it at different times? Do they begin and end their development at different times but have a considerable temporal overlap?

EF components do seem to emerge in a sequence (Anderson, 2002; Romine & Reynolds, 2005). Piagetian theory concerning sequences could enhance such work by asking, for example, whether one EF component, such as inhibition, might facilitate the development of a later-developing component such as shifting (Best & Miller, 2008). Or two EF components may be mutually facilitative, as each bootstraps the development of the other in a back-and-forth fashion. Another issue concerning sequences is the role of inhibition in cognitive sequences; any satisfactory theory of cognitive development must address the role of the inhibition of old behaviors as new ones develop (Houdé, 2000). When solving a Piaget-like numerical task, adults show a pattern of brain activity suggesting that they have to control a childlike non-conserver tendency to use the length-equals-number strategy that competes with the logic-based concept of conservation (Daurignac, Houdé, & Jouvent, 2006). Finally, theorizing about both sequences and qualitative–quantitative interactions could inform a topic of great current interest – the developmental relations between the development of EF and theory of mind (e.g., Carlson & Moses, 2001).

Developmental cognitive neuroscience

This booming area of research has produced considerable evidence concerning brain activity underlying various kinds of cognitions in infants and children (Nelson & Luciana, 2008) but rarely explicitly addresses Piagetian theory or the Piagetian-inspired issues described in this chapter (but see Segalowitz, 2007). One recent approach, *neuroconstructivism* (Westermann, Thomas, & Karmiloff-Smith, chapter 28, this volume), draws on the Piagetian emphasis on how humans construct increasingly complex conceptual systems as a result of active engagement with the world, within neural constraints. That is, concepts emerge from two-way interactions among genes, brain, cognition, behavior, and environment. Brain development and behavioral development are intertwined; each contributes to the development of the other in a back-and-forth fashion.

Beyond the obvious fact that the maturing brain makes possible more advanced thinking, cognitive neuroscience work has supported specific aspects of Piaget's theory. First, close connections exist between action and thinking, as when cognitive tasks activate both cognitive-control and motor areas of the brain (Diamond, 2000). The key role of action also is supported by the finding that adults' cortical activation is similar when they perform a particular action, think about performing it, or observe another person performing that same behavior (e.g., Rizzolatti & Craighero, 2004). Importantly, this link between actions and mental representations suggests a possible developmental mechanism for infants' apparent rudimentary understanding of others' intentions. Second, a few neuroscience studies showing parallel spurts in cognitive development and changes in brain activity (Fischer, 2008; Hudspeth & Pribram, 1992) suggest both a close developmental relation and qualitative change.

The Piagetian issues about cognitive organization, domain specificity, and sequences can provide new theoretical tools for developmental cognitive neuroscience work. Regarding the organization of knowledge, the typical developmental trend from diffuse to focal cortical activation (e.g., Durston & Casey, 2006) implies a change in brain organization. Moreover, by taking a "connectionist" approach to the object-permanence task it is possible to tie developmental changes on this task to changes in neural networks (correlations in activity across different areas of the brain) that, for example, integrate information about the object (Mareschal, Plunkett, & Harris, 1999). The same is true of rule use on the Piagetian balance-scale task (Quinlan, van der Mass, Jansen, Booij, & Rendell, 2007). Other questions about cognitive organization include: If the neural networks activated by two different tasks are overlapping, are the two cognitive skills involved more closely related conceptually than previously believed? How do different neural networks interact at various ages? What is the relation between these qualitative changes (in organization) and quantitative change (degree of activation)? The pruning of synapses during development is not only quantitative (i.e., a decrease) but also qualitative as the organization of neural networks changes.

Regarding the issue of domain specificity and core knowledge, which neural networks are activated by each task/concept? Do tasks believed to tap the same knowledge system in fact activate the same neural networks or different ones? Regarding sequences, it would be useful to ask, for example, whether there are consistent sequences in the development of neural networks that map on to known sequences in cognitive development.

In summary, this overview of four currently active research areas shows both what has been retained from Piaget's approach and how several Piagetian issues not addressed hold great promise for guiding future research in these four areas. These issues are important because they address the causes and mechanisms of development.

Conclusions

The extensions of, and challenges to, Piaget's theory stimulated clever new methods and provocative findings, and clarified enduring issues of development. Thus, Piagetian work has shaped contemporary research on cognitive development. Today, cognitive development still seems to be about systematic changes in somewhat coherent knowledge systems, at least in core domains. Early competencies in infancy and early childhood evolve over an extended period of time into more mature versions of these competencies. Change is both qualitative and quantitative, and processes of change are both innate and experiential. However, new parts of the developmental story include variability in performance, domain-specific core knowledge about minds and other domains, cognitive self-regulation, and changes in the brain that both constrain and enable development.

We still need Piagetian theory today to provide theoretical tools to analyze sequences, concurrences, and quantitative and qualitative change, thereby identifying potential mechanisms of change and clarifying cognitive organization. Piaget and his challengers asked the right questions about development and we try anew to answer them in new areas of research.

References

Anderson, P. (2002). Assessment and development of executive function (EF) during childhood. *Child Neuropsychology, 8*(2), 71–82.

Baillargeon, R. (1987). Object permanence in 3.5- and 4.5-month-old infants. *Developmental Psychology, 23*, 655–664.

Bell, S. M. (1970). The development of the concept of object as related to infant–mother attachment. *Child Development, 41*(2), 292–311.

Best, J. R., & Miller, P. H. (2008). *Developmental perspectives on executive function*. Manuscript under review.

Bower, T. G. R. (1974). *Development in infancy*. San Francisco: Freeman.

Brainerd, C. J., & Allen, T. W. (1971). Experimental inductions of the conservation of "first-order" quantitative invariants. *Psychological Bulletin, 75*, 128–144.

Byrnes, J. P. (1988). Formal operations: A systematic reformulation. *Developmental Review, 8*, 66–87.

Carlson, S. M., & Moses, L. J. (2001). Individual differences in inhibitory control and children's theory of mind. *Child Development, 72*(4), 1032–1053.

Chapman, M. (1988). *Constructive evolution: Origins and development of Piaget's thought.* Cambridge: Cambridge University Press.

Chi, M. T. H. (1978). Knowledge structures and memory development. In R. S. Siegler (Ed.), *Children's thinking. What develops?* Hillsdale, NJ: Erlbaum.

Church, R. B., & Goldin-Meadow, S. (1986). The mismatch between gesture and speech as an index of transitional knowledge. *Cognition, 23*, 43–71.

Daurignac, E., Houdé, O., & Jouvent, R. (2006). Negative priming in a numerical Piaget-like task as evidenced by ERP. *Journal of Cognitive Neuroscience, 18*(5), 730–736.

Dawson-Tunik, T. L., Commons, M., Wilson, M., & Fischer, K. W. (2005). The shape of development. *European Journal of Developmental Psychology, 2*(2), 163–195.

Diamond, A. (1985). The development of the ability to use recall to guide action, as indicated by infants' performance on AB. *Child Development, 56*, 868–883.

Diamond, A. (2000). Close interrelation of motor development and cognitive development and of the cerebellum and prefrontal cortex. *Child Development, 71*, 44–56.

Durston, S., & Casey, B. J. (2006). What have we learned about cognitive development from neuroimaging? *Neuropsychologia, 44*(11), 2149–2157.

Emick, J., & Welsh, M. (2005). Association between formal operational thought and executive function as measured by the Tower of Hanoi-Revised. *Learning and Individual Differences, 15*(3), 177–188.

Fischer, K. W. (2008). Dynamic cycles of cognitive and brain development: Measuring growth in mind, brain, and education. In A. M. Battro, K. W. Fischer, & P. J. Léna (Eds.), *The educated brain: Essays in neuroeducation* (pp. 127–150). Cambridge: Cambridge University Press.

Flavell, J. H. (1963). *The developmental psychology of Jean Piaget.* Princeton, NJ: Van Nostrand.

Flavell, J. H. (1971). Stage-related properties of cognitive development. *Cognitive Psychology, 2*, 421–453.

Flavell, J. H. (1972). An analysis of cognitive-developmental sequences. *Genetic Psychology Monographs, 86*, 279–350.

Flavell, J. H. (1982). On cognitive development. *Child Development, 53*, 1–10.

Flavell, J. H. (1992). Cognitive development: Past, present, and future. *Developmental Psychology, 28*(6), 998–1005.

Flavell, J. H. (1993). The development of children's understanding of false belief and the appearance–reality distinction. *International Journal of Psychology, 28*(5), 595–604.

Flavell, J. H. (1996). Piaget's legacy. *Psychological Science, 7*, 200–203.

Flavell, J. H., Miller, P. H., & Miller, S. A. (2002). *Cognitive development* (4th ed.). Upper Saddle River, NJ: Prentice-Hall.

Flavell, J. H., & Wohlwill, J. F. (1969). Formal and functional aspects of cognitive development. In D. Elkind & J. H. Flavell (Eds.), *Studies in cognitive growth: Essays in honor of Jean Piaget.* New York: Oxford University Press.

Gauvain, M., & Perez, S. M. (2007). The socialization of cognition. In J. C. Grusec & P. D. Hastings (Eds.), *Handbook of socialization: Theory and research* (pp. 588–613). New York: Guilford Press.

Gelman, R. (1972). Logical capacity of very young children: Number invariance rules. *Child Development, 43*, 75–90.

Gelman, R., & Gallistel, C. R. (1978). *The child's understanding of number.* Cambridge, MA: Harvard University Press.

Gelman, R., & Williams, E. M. (1998). Enabling constraints for cognitive development and learning: Domain specificity and epigenesis. In W. Damon (Series Ed.) & D. Kuhn & R. S. Siegler

(Vol. Eds.), *Handbook of child psychology: Vol. 2. Cognition, perception, and language* (5th ed., pp. 575–630). New York: Wiley.

Gelman, S. A. (2003). *The essential child: Origins of essentialism in everyday thought.* New York: Oxford University Press.

Gelman, S. A., & Kalish, C. W. (2006). Conceptual development. In W. Damon (Series Ed.) & D. Kuhn & R. Siegler (Vol. Eds.), *Handbook of child psychology: Vol. 2. Cognition, perception, and language* (6th ed., pp. 687–733). New York: Wiley.

Gelman, S. A., & Opfer, J. E. (2002). Development of the animate–inanimate distinction. In U. Goswami (Ed.), *Blackwell handbook of childhood cognitive development* (pp. 151–166). Malden, MA: Blackwell.

Goldin-Meadow, S., Alibali, M. W., & Church, R. B. (1993). Transitions in concept acquisition: Using the hand to read the mind. *Psychological Review, 100*, 279–297.

Gopnik, A. (1994). Apres le patron. *Cognitive Development, 9*, 131–138.

Gopnik, A., Meltzoff, A. N., & Kuhl, P. K. (1999). *The scientist in the crib; Minds, brains, and how children learn.* New York: Morrow.

Haith, M. M., & Benson, J. B. (1998). Infant cognition. In W. Damon (Series Ed.) & C. Kuhn & R. S. Siegler (Vol. Eds.), *Handbook of child psychology: Vol. 2. Cognition, perception, and language* (5th ed., pp. 199–254). New York: Wiley.

Hamlin, J. K., Hallinan, E. V., & Woodward, A. L. (2008). Do as I do: 7-month-old infants selectively reproduce others' goals. *Developmental Science, 11*(4), 487–494.

Harris, P., & Koenig, M. A. (2006). Trust in testimony: How children learn about science and religion. *Child Development, 77*(3), 505–524.

Houdé, O. (2000). Inhibition and cognitive development: Object, number, categorization, and reasoning. *Cognitive Development, 15*, 63–73.

Hudspeth, W. J., & Pribram, K. H. (1992). Psychophysiological indices of cerebral maturation. *International Journal of Psychophysiology, 12*, 19–29.

Iaccino, W. J., & Hogan, J. (1994, March). *Plotting the impact of Piaget.* Paper presented at the meeting of the Society for Research in Child Development, Boston.

Kingsley, R. C., & Hall, V. C. (1967). Training conservation through the use of learning sets. *Child Development, 38*(4), 1111–1126.

Liben, L. S. (Ed.) (2008). Continuities and discontinuities in children and scholarship [Special section]. *Child Development, 79*(6).

Lourenco, O., & Machado, A. (1996). In defense of Piaget's theory: A reply to 10 common criticisms. *Psychological Review, 103*, 143–164.

Mareschal, D., Plunkett, K., & Harris, P. (1999). A computational and neuropsychological account of object-oriented behaviors in infancy. *Developmental Science, 2*(3), 306–317.

Mareschal, D., & Quinn, P. C. (2001). Categorization in infancy. *Trends in Cognitive Sciences, 5*, 443–450.

McCrink, K., & Wynn, K. (2004). Large-number addition and subtraction by 9-month-old infants. *Psychological Science, 15*, 776–781.

McCrink, K., & Wynn, K. (2007). Ratio abstractions by 6-month-old infants. *Psychological Science, 18*(8), 740–745.

Meltzoff, A. N, & Moore, M. K. (1998). Object representation, identity, and the paradox of early permanence: Steps toward a new framework. *Infant Behavior and Development, 21*, 201–235.

Miller, P. H. (1978). Stimulus variables in conservation: An alternative approach to assessment. *Merrill-Palmer Quarterly, 24*, 141–160.

Miller, P. H. (2002). *Theories of developmental psychology* (4th ed.). New York: Worth.

Miller, P. H., & Coyle, T. R. (1999). Developmental change: Lessons from microgenesis. In E. K. Scholnick, K. Nelson, S. A. Gelman, & P. H. Miller (Eds.), *Conceptual development: Piaget's legacy*. Mahwah, NJ: Erlbaum.

Miller, S. A. (1973). Contradiction, surprise, and cognitive change: The effects of disconfirmation of belief on conservers and nonconservers. *Journal of Experimental Child Psychology, 15*, 47–62.

Miller, S. A. (1976). Nonverbal assessment of Piagetian concepts. *Psychological Bulletin, 83*, 405–430.

Morra, S., Gobbo, C., Marini, Z., & Sheese, R. (Eds.) (2008). *Cognitive development: Neo-Piagetian perspectives*. New York: Erlbaum.

Munakata, Y., McClelland, J. A., Johnson, M. H., & Siegler, R. S. (1997). Rethinking infant knowledge: Toward an adaptive process account of successes and failures in object permanence tasks. *Psychological Review, 104*, 686–713.

Nelson, C. A., & Luciana, M. (Eds.) (2008). *Handbook of developmental cognitive neuroscience* (2nd ed.). Cambridge, MA: MIT Press.

Piaget, J. (1952). *The origins of intelligence in children*. New York: International Universities Press.

Piaget, J. (1983). Piaget's theory. In P. H. Mussen (Series Ed.) & W. Kessen (Vol. Ed.), *Handbook of child psychology: Vol. 1. History, theory, and methods* (4th ed.). New York: Wiley.

Ping, R. M., & Goldin-Meadow, S. (2008). Hands in the air: Using ungrounded iconic gestures to teach children conservation of quantity. *Developmental Psychology, 44*, 1277–1287.

Quinlan, P. T., van der Maas, H. L. J., Jansen, B. R. J., Booij, O., & Rendell, M. (2007). Rethinking stages of cognitive development: An appraisal of connectionist models of the balance scale task. *Cognition 103*(3), 413–459.

Quinn, P. C. (2008). In defense of core competencies, quantitative change, and continuity. *Child Development, 79*(6), 1633–1638.

Quinn, P. C., Westerlund, A., & Nelson, C. A. (2006). Neural markers of categorization in 6-month-old infants. *Psychological Science, 17*, 59–66.

Rizzolatti, G., & Craighero, L. (2004). The mirror-neuron system. *Annual Review of Neuroscience, 27*, 169–192.

Romine, C. B., & Reynolds, C. R. (2005). A model of the development of frontal lobe function: Findings from a meta-analysis. *Applied Neuropsychology, 12*(4), 190–201.

Ruffman, T. (1999). Children's understanding of logical inconsistency. *Child Development, 70*, 872–886.

Russell, J. (1999). Cognitive development as an executive process – in part: A homeopathic dose of Piaget. *Developmental Science, 2*(30), 247–295.

Segalowitz, S. J. (2007). The role of neuroscience in historical and contemporary theories of human development. In D. Coch, G. Dawson, & K. W. Fischer (Eds.), *Human behavior, learning, and the developing brain: Typical development* (pp. 3–29). New York: Guilford Press.

Siegler, R. S. (1978). The origins of scientific reasoning. In R. S. Siegler (Ed.), *Children's thinking: What develops?* (pp. 109–149). Hillsdale, NJ: Erlbaum.

Siegler, R. S. (1989). Mechanisms of cognitive development. *Annual Review of Psychology, 40*, 353–379.

Siegler, R. S. (1995). How does change occur: A microgenetic study of number conservation. *Cognitive Psychology, 28*, 25–273.

Siegler, R. S. (1996). *Emerging minds: The process of change in children's thinking*. New York: Oxford University Press.

Siegler, R. S., & Alibali, M. W. (2005). *Children's thinking* (4th ed.). Upper Saddle River, NJ: Pearson/Prentice-Hall.

Siegler, R. S., & Crowley, K. (1991). The microgenetic method: A direct means for studying cognitive development. *American Psychologist, 46*, 606–620.

Sowell, E. R., Thompson, P. M., Leonard, C. M., Welcome, S. E., Kan, E., & Toga, A. W. (2004). Longitudinal mapping of cortical thickness and brain growth in normal children. *Journal of Neuroscience, 24*, 8223–8231.

Spelke, E. S., & Newport, E. L. (1998). Nativism, empiricism, and the development of knowledge. In W. Damon (Series Ed.) and R. M. Lerner (Vol. Ed.), *Handbook of child psychology: Vol. 1. Theoretical models of human development* (5th ed., pp. 275–340). New York: Wiley.

Wansink, B., & van Ittersum, K. (2005). Shape of glass and amount of alcohol poured: Comparative study of effect of practice and concentration. *British Medical Journal, 331*(7531), 1512–1514.

Wellman, H. M., & Liu, D. (2004). Scaling of theory-of-mind tasks. *Child Development, 75*(2), 523–541.

CHAPTER TWENTY-SIX

Vygotsky and Psychology

Harry Daniels

Introduction

In this chapter I will discuss some of the key elements of developments in psychology that have been attributed to the work of L. S. Vygotsky. In so doing I draw on Daniels (2008) where these arguments are rehearsed and developed. Vygotsky's (1978) non-dualist conception of mind claims that "intermental" (social) experience shapes "intramental" (psychological) development. This is understood as a mediated process in which culturally produced artifacts (such as forms of talk, representations in the form of ideas and beliefs, signs and symbols) shape and are shaped by human engagement with the world (Vygotsky, 1987, p. 78). This understanding of mediation was central to his analysis of the social, cultural, and historical influences on the formation of mind. I will provide a brief account of the key elements of this theory which carry with them radical implications for the work of applied psychologists working in education. I will then discuss recent developments in cognitive neuroscience in relation to this body of work.

There is a growing interest in what has become known as "sociocultural theory" and its near relative "activity theory." Both traditions are historically linked to the work of Vygotsky and both attempt to provide an account of learning and development as mediated processes. In sociocultural theory the emphasis is on semiotic mediation with a particular emphasis on speech. In this account cultural artifacts such as speech serve as tools which both shape possibilities for thought and action and in turn are shaped by those who use them. In activity theory it is activity itself which takes the centre stage in the analysis. Both approaches attempt to theorize and provide methodological tools for investigating the processes by which social, cultural, and historical factors shape human functioning. Neither account resorts to determinism in that they both acknowledge that in the course of their own development human beings also actively shape the very forces that are active in shaping them. This mediational model which entails the mutual influence of individual and supra-individual factors lies at the heart of many attempts to develop our understanding of the possibilities for interventions in processes of human learning and development. For many educators it provides important tools for the development of an understanding of pedagogy. Importantly, this body of theoretical work opens up, or rather insists upon, a pedagogic imagination that reflects on the processes of teaching and learning as much more than face-to-face interaction or the simple transmission of prescribed knowledge and skill.

The development of psychology as a discipline has passed through several stages. Each part of this history provides an important legacy for the next. One of the reasons that so many Western psychologists are reading the writings of a long-dead Russian may be that they are seeking to extend the insights of the so-called cognitive revolution and yet are painfully aware of the shortcomings of so many of its products (e.g., Hirst & Manier, 1995). The research practice of experimentation in artificial situations has provided valuable insights. In the past these have incurred the significant cost of underplaying the formative effects of the social situation of development. Tomasello is one of a group of researchers who are seeking to redress this problem. Certainly, in the past, context, however defined, remained under-theorized and its effects remained under-researched.

Vygotsky developed a theory within which social, cultural, and historical forces play a part in development. His attempts to theorize interpersonal and intrapersonal processes provide an important opening for discussions of determinism, reductionism, and agency within a framework of social formation. His free-ranging cross/multi-disciplinary contribution to twentieth-century intellectual life was supported by his own interpretation of both fellow Russian and European thinkers. He was developing a way of thinking that also found parallels with others beyond his place and time. This creative fusion and development of many perspectives and persuasions was cast adrift in the tragedy that befell the Soviet Union under Stalin. It was selectively molded, transformed, developed, and, in no small part, suppressed for many years.

At the outset I must draw attention to the culturally situated interpretations of Vygotsky's work which have been developed:

> The Vygotsky described in the books of J. Wertsch (1985) does not resemble the Vygotsky in the works of A. V. Brushlinskii (1994) or V. P. Zinchenko (1996). M. G. Iaroshevskii (1991) and Kozulin (1990) do not agree in their evaluations of Vygotskian theory with Van der Veer and Valsiner (1991), Veresov (1992), or Leontiev (1998). (Koshmanova, 2007, p. 62)

Although the texts themselves did achieve some small notoriety in unpublished form, both in the Soviet Union and in the West, they only really became known in the West in the 1970s. These ideas were originally forged at a time of rapid and intense social upheaval – the Russian Revolution. They were developed by someone who was charged with developing a state system for the education of "pedagogically neglected" children (Yaroshevsky, 1989, p. 96). This group included the homeless, of which there were a very large number, and those with special needs. In July 1924 the 28-year-old Lev Vygotsky was appointed to work in the People's Commissariat for Public Education. He argued that the culture of education as it had existed was itself in need of profound transformation and that this was possible in the new social circumstances that obtained in Russia. He embarked on the creation of psychological theories which he and others used as tools for the development of new pedagogies for all learners.

The original texts are themselves rich and complex. They afford a multiplicity of stimulating avenues for exploration and development. The nature and extent of this source of inspiration is captured in the following intriguing statement made by a modern-day Russian writer whose own imagination is inspired by his early twentieth-century countryman.

> Vygotsky's cultural-historical theory – resembles a city. A city with broad new avenues and ancient, narrow backstreets known only to longtime residents, with noisy, crowded plazas and quiet, deserted squares. … Sometimes dust storms and hurricanes rage, or the rain beats down long and hard and "the sky is overcast." (Puzyrei, 2007, pp. 85–86)

This image of a city with its popular as well as relatively unknown spaces, visible and invisible structures, which changes in time with a variety of tempos and rhythms captures the complexity and excitement of Vygotsky's legacy. It points to the political nature of the development of ideas (sometimes dust storms and hurricanes rage, or the rain beats down long and hard and "the sky is overcast") as well as the subtlety and complexity that underpins ostensible simplicity and the processes of its renewal.

One way of understanding Vygotsky is as a cultural psychologist. Michael Cole opens the first chapter of his recent book *Cultural Psychology* with a discussion of Wundt's conception of a psychology comprised of two parts. One part was the then (1880) new psychology of experimentation. The other, much less widely discussed, part of Wundt's contribution was concerned with "the task of understanding how culture enters into psychological processes" (Cole, 1996, p. 7). The work of the Russian school of Vygotsky, Luria, and Leontiev has influenced many of the twentieth-century social theorists who sought to address this agenda. A central theme for them was that of mediation.

Bakhtin's (1981, 1986) suggestion that language is "over populated with the intentions of others," reminds us that the processes of mediation are processes in which individuals operate with artifacts (e.g., words/texts) which are themselves shaped by, and have been shaped in, activities within which the values and meanings relayed in communication are contested and meaning negotiated. In this sense cultural residues reside in and constrain the possibilities for communication. Thus the mediational process is one which neither denies individual or collective agency nor denies social, cultural, historical constraint. Tensions are revealed in competing definitions of "culture" and the labeling of contemporary theoretical approaches as for example either sociocultural or cultural-historical. There are similar debates about the means of mediation. Some approaches have tended to focus on semiotic means of mediation (Wertsch, 1991) whereas others have tended to focus more on the system of activity itself (Engeström, 1993).

I wish to discuss the general concept of mediation within the Vygotskian thesis. Figure 26.1 represents the possibilities for subject–object relations. They are either unmediated, direct, and in some sense natural or they are mediated through culturally available artifacts. In much of the literature the term "tool" is used in place of artifact. I intend to discuss both the concept of tool as it appeared in the original writing and artifact as something that is imbued with meaning and value through its existence within a field of human activity.

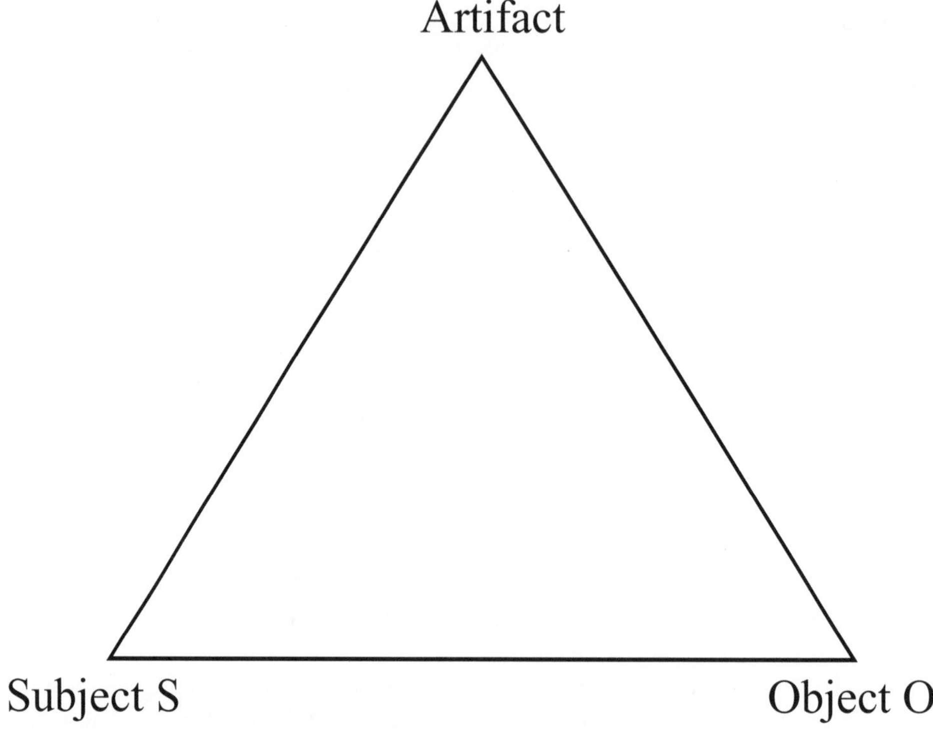

Figure 26.1 The basic triangular representation of mediation

Psychological Tools and Mediation

Vygotsky described psychological tools as devices for mastering mental processes. They were seen as artificial and of social rather than organic or individual origin. He gave the following examples of psychological tools: "language; various systems for counting; mnemonic techniques; algebraic symbol systems; works of art; writing; schemes, diagrams, maps and mechanical drawings; all sorts of conventional signs" (Vygotsky, 1960/1981, pp. 136–137).

In that the concept denies the possibility of total determinism through external forces it is associated with an intellectual baggage which is potentially highly charged, especially in the political context in which these ideas were originally promulgated. Vygotsky forged his ideas on mediation at a time when the emergent command-control version of the soviet state engineered by Stalin was keen to promote the unmediated effects of social organization on consciousness. In the extract reprinted below it is clear that Vygotsky was arguing that humans master themselves through external symbolic, cultural systems rather than being subjugated by and in them:

> this auxiliary stimulus possesses the specific function of reverse action, it transfers the psychological operation to higher and qualitatively new forms and permits the humans, by the aid of extrinsic stimuli, to control their behaviour from the outside. (Vygotsky, 1978, p. 40)

This emphasis on self-construction through and with those tools which are available brings two crucial issues to the foreground. Firstly, it speaks of the individual as an active agent in development. Secondly, it affirms the importance of contextual effects, in that development takes place through the use of those tools which are available at a particular time in a particular place. He distinguished between psychological and other tools and suggested that psychological tools can be used to direct the mind and behavior. In contrast, technical tools are used to bring about changes in other objects. Rather than changing objects in the environment, psychological tools are devices for influencing the mind and behavior of oneself or another. Vygotsky saw tools and symbols as two aspects of the same phenomena – a tool being technical and altering "the process of a natural adaptation by determining the form of labour operations," and a sign being psychological and altering "the entire flow and structure of mental functions" (Vygotsky, 1981, p. 137).

The symbolic function is thought of in the following way: "A symbol is something that someone intends to stand for or represent something other than itself" (DeLoache, 1995). This symbolic function evolves and as Waxman and Leddon point out "early acquisition is sufficiently constrained to permit infants to form fundamental categories of objects and to learn the words to express them, and sufficiently flexible to accommodate the systematic variations in the word-to-world mappings that occur across languages" (chapter 7, this volume). Vygotsky's point is that different symbolic forms may be put to different psychological purposes.

In the discussion of memory and thinking that constitutes chapter 3 of one of the more widely available collections of his writing, *Mind in Society*, Vygotsky stipulates that radical transformations take place in the relationships between psychological functions as a result of such mediated psychological activity. He suggests that "for the young child, to think means to recall; but for the adolescent, to recall means to think" (Vygotsky, 1978, p. 51). Human memory is seen as a function that is actively supported and transformed through the use of signs.

> Just as a mould gives shape to a substance, words can shape an activity into a structure. However, that structure may be changed or reshaped when children learn to use language in ways that allow them to go beyond previous experiences when planning future action. ... [O]nce children learn how to use the planning function of their language effectively, their psychological field changes radically. A view of the future is now an integral part of their approaches to their surroundings. (Vygotsky, 1978, p. 28)

Thus from Vygotsky's perspective the use of psychological tools:

1. Introduces several new functions connected with the use of the given tool and with its control. This is witnessed in the work of Hedegaard (1990) who showed how providing children with psychological tools in the form of theoretical models reveals the central relationships at play in a problem.

2. Abolishes and makes unnecessary several natural processes, whose work is accomplished by the tool, and alters the course and individual features (the intensity, duration, sequence, etc.) of all the mental processes that enter into the composition of the instrumental act, replacing some functions with others (i.e., it recreates and reorganizes the whole structure of behavior just as a technical tool recreates the whole structure of labor operations) (Vygotsky, 1981, pp., 139–140).

One of the many examples that Vygotsky gave of the latter was that of the creation of counting systems (notched sticks and knots) which enabled those using them to go beyond the limits of memory.

Psychological tools, just as material tools, are the products of human cultural-historical activity. The notion of artifact raises a central concern in the philosophy underpinning many sociocultural psychologies – the relation between the ideal and the material. An artifact is material in that it has been created through the modification of physical material in the process of goal-directed human actions. It is ideal in that the material form has been shaped to fulfill human intentions which underpin those earlier goals; these modified material forms exist in the present precisely because they successfully aided those human intentional goal-directed actions (Cole & Derry, 2005). Bakhurst (e.g., 1995) has done much to clarify the contribution of the Russian philosopher Ilyenkov to our understanding of the framework within which so much of the Russian perspective on mediation may be read. The idea is of meaning embodied or sedimented in objects as they are put into use in social worlds. For example, when someone has their house burgled they are usually much more upset about the loss of a family heirloom than, say, a CD player. The heirloom has meanings sedimented in it through the history of its use. The CD player rarely carries such intensity of meaning. This idea is central to the conceptual apparatus of theories of culturally mediated, historically developing, practical activity. This model of the process is part of the conceptual apparatus which is associated with Ilynekov's philosophy of "ideality" which engages with the way in which humans inscribe significance and value into the very physical objects of their environment (Bakhurst, 1995, p. 173). Deloache (chapter 12, this volume) provides a detailed account of a cognitive view of the use of symbolic artifacts.

The concept of mediation has developed far beyond the original notion of psychological tools. Contributions from disciplines as seemingly diverse as philosophy, cognitive psychology, and neurophysiology have given rise to the possibility of reconsidering the original Vygotskian position. This concept on which so much of the thesis depends has gained explicit and implicit support from a wide range of contributions. A model of dynamic interplay between socially formed and appropriated discourses and other artifacts, mental representations, and patterns of neurological activity in the formation of human thought has started to evolve. Discussions of the constraints and control over those discourses and other artifacts which are available socially in particular cultural contexts and which have specific historical origins and commitments gives rise to sociological considerations of production and distribution. Biological constraints and limitations are also to be understood in a robust model of the way in which social, cultural, and historical factors exercise a formative effect on human development. Crucially the emphasis on the human use of tools, signs/artifacts for self-creation, removes the

Vygotskian model from the domain of crude social determinism in which the social factors have a direct and unmediated effect on consciousness.

Development and Dialectics

Vygotsky (1978) formulated what he termed "general genetic law of cultural development" in which he asserts the primacy of the social in development in the context of his model of development as a mediated process:

> every function in the child's cultural development appears twice: first, on the social level, and later, on the individual level; first between people (interpsychological), and then inside the child (intrapsychological). (Vygotsky, 1978, p. 57)

The general genetic law of cultural development introduces the notion of some form of relationship between something which is defined as "social" and something which is defined as "individual." My use of the term "mediation" suggests that this is not necessarily a direct relationship from the social to the individual. However, there is an important conceptual move to be made between the dualism (in which entities such person and context are analytically distinct) I infer above and the dialectical relationship (which acknowledges methodological inseparability) which Cole implies below:

> The dual process of shaping and being shaped through culture implies that humans inhabit "intentional" (constituted) worlds within which the traditional dichotomies of subject and object, person and environment, and so on cannot be analytically separated and temporally ordered into independent and dependent variables. (Cole, 1996, p. 103)

Sameroff (1980) provided an important contribution to the debates on psychology and systems theory with the introduction of concept of "dialectics" within which development was seen as driven by internal contradictions. Earlier, Riegel (1976) and Wozniak (1975) had criticized traditional psychology with its emphasis on balance and equilibrium. It was Riegel who produced a manifesto for dialectical psychology which emphasized contradictions and their synchronizations in short- and long-term development both in the individual and in society (Riegel, 1976, p. 689). Surprisingly this work is rarely cited in discussions of Vygotsky's work. The details of their approach differ whilst the key emphasis on dialectical processes remains very similar. As Van der Veer and Valsiner (1991) remind us, Vygotsky most definitely adopted a dialectical worldview in that he seeks to develop and apply dialectical logic in his methodology. This was the case for his theories as well as his approach to method and criticism.

> A present day psychologist is most likely to adopt a non-dialectical "either–or" perspective when determining the "class membership" of one or other approach in psychology. Hence the frequent non-dialectical contrasts between "Piagetian" and "Vygotskian" approaches, or the widespread separation of psychologists into "social" versus "cognitive" categories which seem to occupy our minds in their meta-psychological activities … in direct contrast, for

> Vygotsky any two opposing directions of thought serve as opposites united with one another in the continuous whole – the discourse on ideas. This discourse is expected to lead us to a more adequate understanding of the human psyche, that is , to transcend the present state of theoretical knowledge, rather than force the existing variety of ideas into a strict classification of tendencies in the socially constructed scientific discipline of psychology. (Van der Veer & Valsiner, 1991, pp. 392–393)

Much of the Western writing which claims a Vygotskian root discusses his contribution in terms of accounts of internalization. Much effort has been expended attempting to clarify the movement from the social to the individual and yet relatively little attention has been paid to the reverse direction. Bruner's (1997) reminder about Vygotsky's liberationist version of Marxism serves to reinforce the view that his was a psychology which posited the active role of the person in their own cognitive and emotional creation rather than as being a crude social construction. The reference to a liberationist version of Marxism is prompted by Vygotsky's insistence on a model of development which seeks to theorize the progressive "liberation" of person from the direct control of environmental stimuli. Whether the emphasis was directly on creativity itself or through the use of expressions such as "mastering themselves from the outside" in his early work, Vygotsky discussed externalization at some length. It was in this discussion that he sought to articulate the way in which humans, as individuals or groups, are active in the creation of psychological tools and artifacts which may be used by others in processes of social and psychological transformation.

Concept Formation

Engeström has developed a model of transformation which he calls the expansive cycle in which internalization and externalization develop complementary roles. Engeström and Mietteinen (1999) provide a discussion of the internalization–externalization process at every level of activity. They relate internalization to the reproduction of culture and externalization to the creation of artifacts that may be used to transform culture. The rediscovered emphasis on externalization is important because it brings a perspective to concept formation which affirms the notion of active agency in learning and development. "Like Ilyenkov after him, Vygotsky recognises that as much as culture creates individuals, culture itself remains a human creation" (Bakhurst & Sypnowich, 1995, p. 11). Ways of thinking and feeling may be influenced and shaped by the availability of cultural artifacts which may themselves be the products of mediated activity.

As the now-accepted correct translation of Vygotsky's work *Thinking and Speech* implies, he was concerned to know how the social activity of speaking was connected with the active processes of thinking. 1927–1934 was the period when Vygotsky was particularly interested in concept formation. For Vygotsky scientific concepts are characterized by a high degree of generality and their relationship to objects in the real world is mediated through other concepts. By the use of "scientific concept," Vygotsky referred to concepts introduced by a teacher in school, and spontaneous concepts were those that were acquired by the child outside contexts in which explicit instruction was in place. Scientific concepts were described as those which form a coherent, logical hierarchical system. According to Vygotsky (1987) children can make deliberate use of scientific concepts; they are consciously aware of them and can reflect upon them.

The editors of the most recent translation of *Thinking and Speech* argue that when Vygotsky (1987) uses the terms "spontaneous thinking" or "spontaneous concepts" he is referring to the context of formation which is that of immediate, social, practical activity as against a context of instruction in a formal system of knowledge. Scientific concepts are through their very systematic nature open to the voluntary control of the child.

> [T]he dependence of scientific concepts on spontaneous concepts and their influence on them stems from the unique relationship that exists between the scientific concept and its object. … [T]his relationship is characterized by the fact that it is mediated through other concepts. Consequently, in its relationship to the object, the scientific concept includes a relationship to another concept, that is it includes the most basic element of a concept system. (Vygotsky,1987, p. 192)

Vygotsky argued that it was in communication that social understanding was made available for individual understanding. Within schooling word meanings themselves form the object of study. As Minick (1987) has argued, the differences between communication *with* words and communication *about* words marks the significant difference between communication within schooling and communication in everyday life. This is the difference that Kozulin (1998) refers to as repositioning. Communication about words within schooling leads to the development of scientific concepts by the individual. In this way communication performs a mediational function between the society of schooling and the individual. The need for instruction remains paramount within the original thesis. This is associated with the institution of the school and the teacher.

> [T]he fundamental difference between the problem which involves everyday concepts and that which involves scientific concepts is that the child solves the latter with the teacher's help. … [I]n a problem involving everyday concepts he must do with volition something that he does with ease spontaneously. (Vygotsky, 1987, p. 216)

The theoretical derivation of "scientific and everyday" in the original writing was somewhat provisional. For example, the association of the scientific with the school does not help to distinguish those aspects of schooling that act to add to everyday understanding without fostering the development of scientific concepts. The association also suggests that the development of scientific concepts must take place in the school and not outside it.

It may be as a consequence of the dualist perspective which remains so powerful, that the emphasis on the interdependence between the development of scientific and everyday concepts is also not always appreciated. Vygotsky argued that the systematic, organized, and hierarchical thinking that he associated with scientific concepts becomes gradually embedded in everyday referents and thus achieves a general sense in the contextual richness of everyday thought. Vygotsky thus presented an interconnected model of the relationship between scientific and everyday or spontaneous concepts. Similarly he argued that everyday thought is given structure and order in the context of systematic scientific thought. Vygotsky was keen to point out the relative strengths of both as they both contributed to each other.

Vygotsky argued that scientific concepts are not assimilated in ready-made or pre-packaged form. He insisted that the two forms of concept are brought into forms of relationship within which they both develop. An important corollary of this model of conceptual development is the denial of the possibility of direct pedagogic transmission of concepts.

> [P]edagogical experience demonstrates that direct instruction in concepts is impossible. It is pedagogically fruitless. The teacher who attempts to use this approach achieves nothing but a mindless learning of words, an empty verbalism that stimulates or imitates the presence of concepts in the child. Under these conditions, the child learns not the concept but the word, and this word is taken over by the child through memory rather than thought. Such knowledge turns out to be inadequate in any meaningful application. This mode of instruction is the basic defect of the purely scholastic verbal modes of teaching which have been universally condemned. It substitutes the learning of dead and empty verbal schemes for the mastery of living knowledge. (Vygotsky, 1987, p. 170)

If it is to be effective in the formation of scientific concepts, instruction must, according to Davydov (1988), be designed to foster conscious awareness of conceptual form and structure and thereby allow for individual access and control over acquired scientific concepts. It must also foster the interaction and development of everyday concepts with scientific concepts.

> [L]earning a foreign language raises the level of development of the child's native speech. His conscious awareness of linguistic forms, and the level of his abstraction of linguistic phenomena, increases. He develops a more conscious, voluntary capacity to use words as tools of thought and as a means of expressing ideas. … [B]y learning algebra, the child comes to understand arithmetic operations as particular instantiations of algebraic operations. This gives the child a freer, more abstract and generalized view of his operations with concrete quantities. Just as algebra frees the child's thought from the grasp of concrete numerical relations and raises it to the level of more abstract thought, learning a foreign language frees the child's verbal thought from the grasp of concrete linguistic forms of phenomena. (Vygotsky, 1987, p. 180)

Zone of Proximal Development

Wells (1999) distinguished between two definitions of the zone of proximal development (ZPD) within Vygotsky's original writing. One version in chapter 6 of *Mind in Society* places emphasis on dynamic assessment of children's intellectual abilities rather than more static measures such as IQ scores. Here Vygotsky defines the ZPD as:

> actual developmental level as determined by independent problem solving and the higher level of potential development as determined through problem solving under adult guidance or in collaboration with more capable peers. (Vygotsky, 1978, p. 86)

He elaborates on this definition in order to emphasize the difference between aided and unsupported performance.

> Suppose I investigate two children – both of whom are twelve years old chronologically and eight years old in terms of mental development. Can I say that they are the same age mentally? Of course. What does this mean? It means that they can independently deal with tasks up to the degree of difficulty that has been standardized for the eight-year-old level. Suppose I show … [these children] have various ways of dealing with a task … that the children solve the problem with my assistance. Under these circumstances it turns out that the first child can deal with problems up to a twelve-year-old's level. The second up to a nine-year-old's. Now are these children mentally the same? (Vygotsky, 1978, pp. 85–86)

His interest was in assessing the ways in which learners make progress. The focus on process as well as product in assessment has become embedded in the range of techniques now called "dynamic assessment" (e.g., Lidz & Elliot, 2000). The general practice of dynamic assessment is either explicitly or tacitly inspired by the work of Vygotsky. This contrasts sharply with practices which theorize a lag of learning behind development as in the case of Piaget or which theorize learning as development as in the case of Skinner.

There are stark differences in the ways in which many contemporary versions of the ZPD idea which have, at least, some root in Vygotskian theory become embedded in other psychological traditions. Wells (1999) pointed out that the second version of the ZPD is to be found in Vygotsky's last major work, *Thinking and Speech* (1978), and is embedded in chapter 6, in which he discussed "The Development of Scientific Concepts in Childhood." Instruction is foregrounded here rather than assessment.

> We have seen that instruction and development do not coincide. They are two different processes with very complex interrelationships. Instruction is only useful when it moves ahead of development. When it does, it impels or awakens a whole series of functions that are in a stage of maturation lying in the zone of proximal development. This is the major role of instruction in development. This is what distinguishes the instruction of the child from the training of animals. This is also what distinguishes instruction of the child which is directed toward his full development from instruction in specialised, technical skills such as typing or riding a bicycle. The formal aspect of each school subject is that in which the influence of instruction on development is realised. Instruction would be completely unnecessary if it merely utilised what had already matured in the developmental process, if it were not itself a source of development. (Vygotsky, 1987, p. 212)

Arguably, Vygotsky has not shifted his position on the nature of the ZPD in the time that lapsed between the writing of these two texts. Perhaps the differences of emphasis may be attributable to the changes in the social/political/professional circumstances in which he was working. In the earlier writing he was more concerned with assessment and indeed it was more acceptable to write about assessment. As his career developed the political pressure against assessment grew and his own interests, as Minick (1987) has shown, shifted away from relations between psychological functions and towards relations between psychological functioning and social circumstances.

In summary, Vygotsky discussed the ZPD in terms of assessment and instruction. Within both frames of reference he discussed the relationship between an individual learner and a supportive other or others even if that other was not physically present in the context in which learning was taking place.

Lave and Wenger (1991) argue that the operational definition of the ZPD has itself undergone many differing interpretations. Many different researchers have interpreted and developed the notion of the ZPD (e.g., Tharp & Gallimore, 1988; Wells, 1999), with the result that various models have emerged which apply, extend, and reconstruct Vygotsky's original conception. These differences may be seen to reveal the more general theoretical drift towards a broader more cultural and historical view of the "social" which is theorized as being progressively more intimately a part of the "individual." Thus Lave and Wenger (1991) distinguish between a "scaffolding," a "cultural," and a "collectivist" or "societal" interpretation of the original formulation of the ZPD. The "scaffolding" interpretation is one in which a distinction is made between support for the initial performance of tasks and subsequent performance without assistance: "the distance between problem-solving abilities exhibited by a learner working alone and that learner's problem-solving abilities when assisted by or collaborating with more-experienced people."

The term "scaffolding" could be taken to infer a "one-way" process within which the "scaffolder" constructs the scaffold and presents it for use to the novice. Newman, Griffin, and Cole (1989) argued that the ZPD is created through negotiation between the more advanced partner and the learner, rather than through the donation of a scaffold as some kind of prefabricated climbing frame. There is a similar emphasis on negotiation in Tharp and Gallimore (1988) who discussed "teaching as assisted performance," in those stages of the ZPD where assistance is required. The key question here seems to be with respect to where the "hints," "supports," or "scaffold" come from. Are they produced by "the more capable partner" or are they negotiated? Vygotsky is unclear on this matter.

The "cultural" interpretation of the ZPD is based on Vygotsky's distinction between scientific and everyday concepts. It is argued that a mature concept is achieved when the scientific and everyday versions have merged:

> the distance between the cultural knowledge provided by the socio-historical context – usually made accessible through instruction – and the everyday experience of individuals. Hedegaard calls this the distance between understood knowledge, as provided by instruction, and active knowledge, as owned by individuals. (Lave & Wenger, 1991, p. 76)

However as Lave and Wenger (1991) note, no account is taken of " the place of learning in the broader context of the structure in the social world." Vygotsky did not provide an extended social-psychological or sociological dimension of the pedagogy he discussed. Hedegaard (1998) discusses what she calls the "double move approach" in the process of concept formation within the ZPD. She suggests that "the teacher guides the learning activity both from the perspective of general concepts and from the perspective of engaging students in 'situated' problems that are meaningful in relation to their developmental stage and life situations" (Hedegaard, 1998, p. 120).

In the "collectivist," or "societal" perspective, Engeström defined ZPD as the "distance between the everyday actions of individuals and the historically new form of the societal activity that can be collectively generated" (Engeström, 1987, p. 174). Under such societal interpretations of the concept of the ZPD researchers tend to concentrate on processes of social transformation. This involves the study of learning beyond the context of pedagogical structuring, including the structure of the social world in the analysis, and taking into account in a central way the "conflictual nature of social practice" (Lave & Wenger, 1991, pp. 48–49). This would require an articulation of relations of power and control in the settings in which development is taking place.

These types of definition carry with them different implications for schooling and instruction. If the "social" in teaching and learning is constrained to a view of particular teaching technologies and procedures then the analysis of schooling is both truncated and partial. If the "social" in schooling is considered in socio-institutional terms then the gaze of the analysis of the impacts is altered and/or extended. This question of the scope of the definition is fundamental to one of my concerns about the ways in which pedagogy is theorized, described, and investigated. Pedagogy may be understood as face-to-face interaction between teacher and taught or it may be understood as a practice in which direct and indirect (or explicit and implicit) interpersonal and institutional factors exert a formative effect. Following Vygotsky's own insistence on the use of genetic (historical/developmental) analysis it is possible to discern a trajectory in his own writing towards a more socially connected account.

> Vygotsky seemed to be coming to recognise this issue near the end of his life. It is reflected in the difference between Chapters five and six of *Thinking and Speech* (1987). Both chapters deal with the ontogenetic transition from "complexes" to "genuine," or "scientific" concepts. However, the two chapters differ markedly in what they see as relevant developmental forces. In Chapter five (based on research with Shif and written during the early 1930s), concept development is treated primarily in terms of intramental processes, that is , children's conceptual development as they move from "unorganised heaps" to "complexes" to "concepts." In Chapter six (written in 1934), there is an essential shift in the way Vygotsky approaches these issues. He clearly continued to be interested in intramental functioning, but he shifted to approaching concept development from the perspective of how it emerges in institutionally situated activity. Specifically, he was concerned with how the forms of discourse encountered in the social institution of formal schooling provide a framework for the development of conceptual thinking. He did it by the teacher–child intermental functioning found in this setting. (Wertsch, Tulviste, & Hagstrom, 1993, p. 344)

It remains the case that most of Vygotsky's writing tends to focus on the more immediate interactional/interpersonal antecedents of independent or seemingly independent functioning. The first important implication of this is that teaching and assessment should be focused on the potential of the learner, rather than on a demonstrated level of achievement or understanding. The second is that teaching, or instruction, should create the possibilities for development, through the kind of active participation that characterizes collaboration, that it should be socially negotiated, and that it should entail transfer of control to the learner. It is in this way that the ZPD is created. Theories concerning the regulation of such practices within specific schools remained beyond the scope of Vygotsky's writing. The institutional regulation of the social practices of schooling is beyond the gaze of much of the empirical work that claims to be drawing on his work.

Vygotsky insisted that there is no necessary recourse to physical presence in accounts of support within the ZPD. With the following quotation he announced the possibility of virtual collaboration without the physical presence of the adult/teacher.

> [W]hen the school child solves a problem at home on the basis of a model that he has been shown in class, he continues to act in collaboration, though at the moment the teacher is not standing near him. From a psychological perspective, the solution of the second problem is similar to this solution of a problem at home. It is a solution accomplished with the teacher's help. This help – this aspect of collaboration – is invisibly present. It is contained in what looks from the outside like the child's independent solution of the problem. (Vygotsky, 1987, p. 216)

Vygotsky often seems to be concerned with a ZPD as a space where the learner is brought into the "knowing" of the other. The emphasis on multiple voices, engaged in the construction of a form of meaning which is not necessarily located within the individual, characterizes many current interpretations of Bakhtin's influence on a Vygotskian account. Valsiner cautioned against too much theoretical speculation of this nature and ponders on the social implications of an ordinary person announcing that they were either "seamlessly tied" to their living room or that their mind was filled with the "voices of others" (Valsiner, 1997, p. 237). On the other hand, Gergen (1995) developed a radical constructionist account of the learning processes. He was critical of both Vygotsky and Bruner suggesting "they remain deeply ambivalent concerning the significance of the social as opposed to the individual." These two positions serve to illustrate the ongoing tensions in the interpretation of the ZPD concept.

Valsiner provides another important cautionary note that must enter into this debate. He reminds us that much of the empirical work that has been undertaken runs the risk of confusing microgentic and ontogenetic processes.

> There exists an unwarranted (and implicit) assumption in received empirical practices in developmental psychology to consider the microgenetic and ontogenetic levels of development similar in their organisation. (Valsiner, 1997, p. 241)

If this slippage is permitted then the concept of appropriation can be used to render any form of social activity as formative in ontogenetic terms. Clearly this is not justified as not all social interaction or indeed teaching serves a developmental function.

Valsiner (1998) has recently reconstructed the notion of the ZPD, as part of a zone system, which extends beyond other notions of the ZPD. In a model which emphasizes canalization and co-construction he discussed organizational devices that provide the framework for constraint on development and possible directions of nearest future development. The constraints come within the zone of free movement (ZFM) and possibility is promoted within the zone of promoted action (ZPA). Valsiner (1997) argued that the zones are useful tools for explaining regulation of the developmental process, through the restructuring of the zones and the relationships between them.

The ZFM is a means he uses to describe the internal and external structuring of a child's access to different aspects of his or her environment (Valsiner, 1997, 1998). Valsiner (1997) argued that as the child develops, the ZFM becomes internalized, provid-

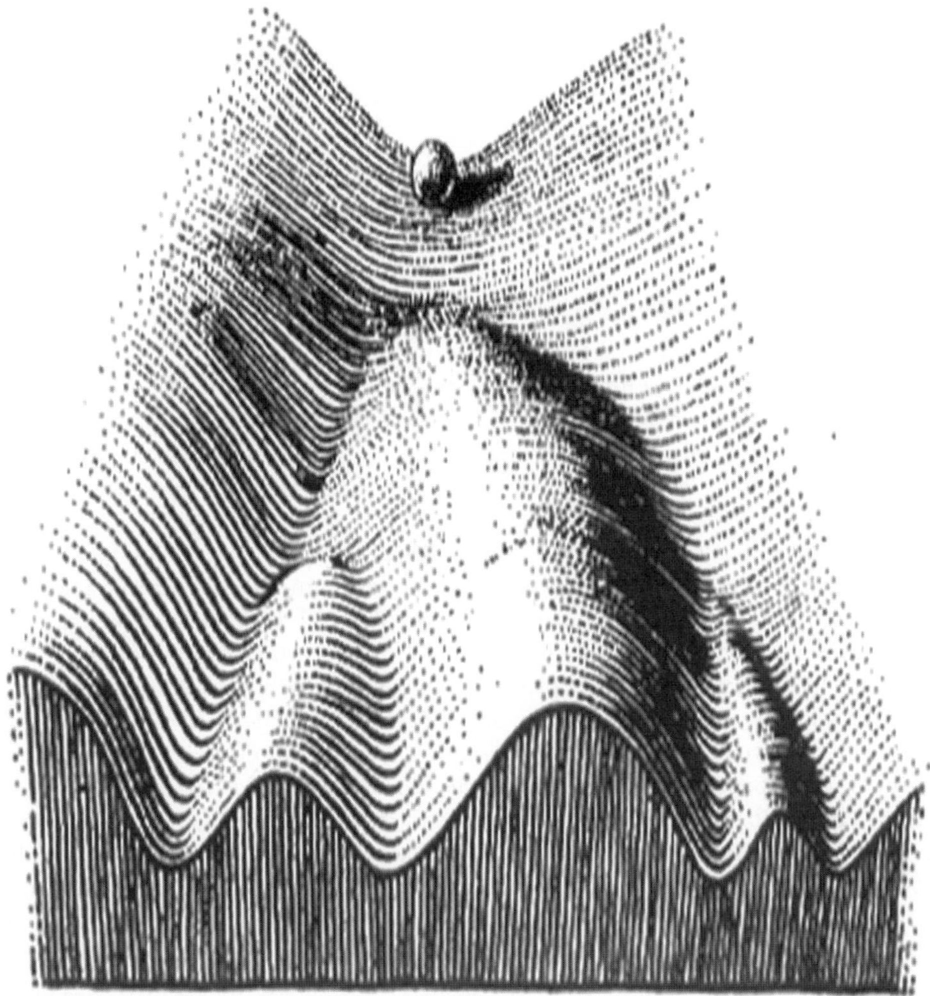

Figure 26.2 The ball represents cell fate. The valleys are the different fates the cell might roll into. (Waddington, 1956.)

ing a structure for personal thinking and feeling through semiotic regulation. The ZFM promotes canalization, through the constraints or restrictions created on and through possible child–environment interactions. This argument reminds me of Waddington's (1956) developmental chreods which were proposed as models of cell development within embryology. In figure 26.2 the ball represents cell fate. The valleys are the different fates the cell might roll into.

At the beginning of its journey, development is plastic, and a cell has many possible fates. However, as development proceeds, certain decisions cannot be reversed. The surface down which the ball rolls is itself subject to change.

Valsiner's ZFM could be linked with Gibson's (1979) idea of ecological affordance or Waddington's model of developmental chreods. All three speak of constraint yet not in an over-determined manner. However, it is important to remember that in Vygotsky's original writings he most certainly did not subscribe to the extreme relativism with which he has been popularly associated.

> We said that in collaboration the child can always do more than he can independently. We must add the stipulation that he cannot do infinitely more. What collaboration contributes to the child's performance is restricted to limits which are determined by the state of his development and his intellectual potential. (Vygotsky, 1987, p. 209)

Valsiner argued that the meanings and values of the caregiver will canalize and constrain the possibilities for interest and interaction. He recognized that this canalization process may lead to conflict. My own view is that this theory has not yet developed to the point where operational definitions of different forms of social practice may be generated, their consequences hypothesized and investigated.

In summary, the discussion of the ZPD has raised a number of questions for theories of cognitive development. For example: To what extent is the "social" other in the ZPD merely an individual with whom the learner interacts? This seems to reflect the tradition of experimental psychology rather than the tenets of an account of the social formation of mind. The reduction of the complexity of classroom life to a quasi-experimental dyad carries significant restrictions in terms of the generalizability and validity of findings. Crucially such studies do not allow for a critical examination of the effect of different forms of participant structure in learning situations. When considering different models of the ZPD it thus seems reasonable to ask: To what extent should we consider social groups, institutions, communities, and other cultural-historical dimensions within the ZPD? It also seems important to ask whether the changes that take place as a consequence of activity in a ZPD are best considered as acts of internalization or as incorporation of aspects of the social that may or may not remain present. Lastly and somewhat portentously: To what extent is the developing conscious mind an individual mind? This question echoes the work that is being developed on the formation of collective intentionality by Bleakley and Bligh (2008), Engeström (2006), Tomasello, and Carpenter (chapter 4, this volume) amongst others.

Biology in Development

Moll (1994) argues that an adequate account of Vygotsky's theory must ground the sociogenesis of cognition in a fundamental recognition of natural and biological possibility. He argues that natural constraints in cognitive development are not given enough attention in contemporary discussions of his work. Tudge and Winterhoff (1993) also explore this theme in the context of a critical review of Vygotsky's views on biological influences:

> the child's system of activity is determined at each specific stage both by the child's degree of organic development and by his or her degree of mastery in the use of tools. (Vygotsky, 1997, p. 21)

It is inescapable that Vygotsky did account for biological factors and individual differences. In his work on "defectology" he insists that individual differences in patterns of communication give rise to differences in patterns of social mediation and hence development.

> A bodily defect is, first of all, a social and not an organic abnormality of behaviour. A bodily defect in a person causes a certain attitude towards that person among the people around him. It is this attitude, and not the defect in itself, that affects the character of psychological relations to a child with impaired sense organs. (Yaroshevsky, 1989, p. 107)

However it is in the manner of social engagement that differences may arise and form their own dynamic.

> Whatever the anticipated outcome, always and in all circumstances, development, complicated by a defect, represents a creative (physical and psychological) process: the creation and re-creation of a child's personality based upon the restructuring of all the adaptive functions and upon the formation of new processes – overarching, substituting, equalising – generated by the handicap, and creating new, roundabout paths for development. (Knox & Stevens, 1993, p. 17)

Similarly Vygotsky was concerned that social responses to people with disabilities should not create problems of their own. Given that he argues that cultural tools and practices have a formative effect on development, then barriers to participation are a cause for concern. Barriers may be both social and biological. Specific forms of impairment may give rise to difficulty in participation in a society where most participants do not experience similar difficulties. The solution could be to seek alternate forms of participation either through transforming social practices in such a way as not to marginalize those with the impairment or through specific interventions such as supplementary forms of communication like Braille. In the past, and to a slightly lesser extent now, many people with disabilities remove themselves or are removed from certain aspects of society. Gallaudet University is an example of a setting where deaf people are educated with other deaf people. This setting is usually regarded as positive. There are many examples of social responses to people with disabilities where satisfactory communities are not the outcome. Vygotsky's suggestion is that transformations in patterns of participation carry with them implications for cognitive development. Exclusion carries cognitive consequences.

Ratner (1998) argues that higher psychological functions actually stimulate neuronal growth in particular directions and that they create their own biological mediations. And in so doing he provides an account of how experience impacts on biology. He draws on Donald (1991) in his assertion that they do not depend upon specialized biological mechanisms which predetermine them. The assertion is that higher forms of cognition co-opt brain systems that originally had similar but more limited functions. This accords with Vygotsky's position that:

> There is every reason to assume that the historical development of behaviour from primitive forms to the most complex and highest did not occur as a result of the appearance of new parts of the brain or the growth of parts already existing. (Vygotsky, 1998, p. 35)

Much has been written about the notion of plasticity of the brain (cf. Dennett, 1991) in which mutual transformation is posited rather than some form of unidirectional determination. Clark reconsiders the role of language as a tool which he argues acts as an adjunct of the brain in problem solving, "a tool that alters the nature of the computational tasks involved in various kinds of problem solving" (Clark, 1996, p. 193). This accords with the assertion that modern developmental cognitive neuroscientific approaches emphasize that "there is no single cause of anything" and "nothing is determined" (Morton, 2004). The emphasis shifts to models of learning that emphasize the complexity of interaction between biology and educational environments, and that mitigation is always possible (Morton, 2004).

Similarly, Dennett (1991) argues that advanced cognitive skills should be viewed not so much as the manifestation of the innate hardware of the brain but more as the ways in which the biological material is programmed and reprogrammed through the input that arises from specific cultures and use of language. He discusses the "myriad microsettings in the plasticity of the brain" (Dennett, 1991, p. 219). This accords with the criticism of approaches to artificial intelligence which "bundle into the machine a set of operational capacities which in real life emerge only from the interactions between machine (brain) and world" (Clark, 1996, p. 64).

Moves to develop a dynamic account of plasticity at the level of neurological function echo the assertion that Tomasello (1999) makes with respect to the role of genetic material in human cognitive evolution. His argument is that dichotomies, such as "nature–nurture," which have linguistically structured so much of the debate, are outmoded. They are not sufficiently powerful tools for the consideration of the issues. There are also brain-imaging experiment studies which are suggestive of the Vygotskian account of mediation arguing that in cognition and action, material symbols may be the link between internal representations and objects and words in the world (Roepstorff, 2008).

> [T]he material world … may come to a productive interplay with previous experiences, as they are represented as particular configurations in brains. … It appears to allow for "the world" to be a major driving force in providing objects … material and symbolic, just as the representations in the brain are. (Roepstorff, 2008, p. 2053)

Tomasello, Dennett, Clark, and Damasio in their differing ways suggest a forthcoming development of the place of biology in the development of thinking. The early stages of this development suggest a high degree of compatibility with a sociogenetic account of development whilst it must be recognized that it is only more recently that the importance of social behavior has made forays into the neurosciences (e.g., Adolphs, 2003).

Waddington's model of canalization in epigenesis provides a way of thinking about development that is not over-determined by biology. It provides less clarity on the mechanisms of plasticity. There are clear warnings about overly narrow-minded approaches to this quest (cf. Stetsenko, 2008) yet it is interesting to note that almost 20 years after his death, two neuropsychological books of Vygotsky's close colleague Luria remained among the top 10 essential readings in neuropsychology as identified by practicing North American neuropsychologists (Ryan, Prifitera, & Cummins, 1982).

Affect and Cognition

This challenge to refine models of development and functioning is heightened when the implications of Vygotsky's opposition to a dualistic account of affective and cognitive functions is brought into the conceptual framework. He was clear in his views on the matter:

> [Thought] is not born of other thoughts. Thought has its origins in the motivating sphere of consciousness, a sphere that includes our inclinations and needs, our interests and impulses, and our affect and emotions. The affective and volitional tendency stands behind thought. Only here do we find the answer to the final "why" in the analysis of thinking. (Vygotsky, 1987, p. 282)
>
> When we approach the problem of the interrelation between thought and language and other aspects of mind, the first question that arises is that of intellect and affect. Their separation as subjects of study is a major weakness of traditional psychology, since it makes the thought process appear as an autonomous flow of "thoughts thinking themselves" segregated from the fullness of life, from personal needs and interests, the inclinations and impulses of the thinker. [E]very idea contains a transmuted affective attitude toward the bit of reality to which it refers. (Vygotsky, 1986, p. 10)

In the last year of his life, Vygotsky turned his attention to a new unit of analysis, namely, *perezhivanie*. This concept may be equated with lived or emotional experience.

> The emotional experience [*perezhivanie*] arising from any situation or from any aspect of his environment, determines what kind of influence this situation or this environment will have on the child. Therefore, it is not any of the factors themselves (if taken without the reference of the child) which determines how they will influence the future course of his development, but the same factors refracted through the prism of the child's emotional experience. (Vygotsky, 1994, p. 339)
>
> Vygotsky understood perezhivanie as the integration of cognitive and affective elements, which always presupposes the presence of emotions. Vygotsky used this concept in order to emphasize the wholeness of the psychological development of children, integrating external and internal elements at each stage of development. … According to Bozhovich, for a short period of time Vygotsky considered perezhivanie as the "unity" of psychological development in the study of the social situation of development. (Gonzalez-Rey, 2002, p. 136)

This idea has been largely ignored in the development of post Vygotskian theory. It was refined in the writing of Vasilyuk (1991) when he introduced the notion of experiencing defined as a particular form of activity directed towards the restoration of meaning in life. He contrasted his activity-theory-based understanding with that of a reflection of a state in the subject's consciousness and with forms of contemplation. Notions of experiencing and identity formation may become part of an understanding of learning that includes a systematic and coherent analysis of the wider social structuring of society as an inseparable part of the analysis.

Recent advances in neuroscience (Damasio, 1999) and cognitive psychology (Clark, 1996, 1998) open the way for rethinking mind/biology/social setting transactions. Damasio is concerned with the role of feelings in the ways that humans make sense of the information that the social world provides to the sense organs. He presents a dynamic view of the construction of the "autobiographical self" which is the product of continual revision and change.

Damasio argues that social interaction influences the brain, giving rise to brain states that in turn generate "feelings" or "emotions." These then feed back into social interaction, shaping its course and direction.

> The neurological systems that support decision making generally are the same systems that support social and moral behavior. Without adequate access to emotional, social, and moral feedback, in effect the important elements of culture, learning cannot inform real-world functioning as effectively. (Immordino-Yang & Damasio, 2007, p. 6)

Cromby discusses the empirical evidence for some of Damasio's arguments:

> evidence that feelings are the default mode of our engagement with the world comes from Zajonc's studies … from Sperry and Gazzaniga's work with split-brain patients … from … investigation of basic affect systems. … [I]f the brain is entirely deprived of feedback from the body then consciousness also disappears. (Cromby, 2007, p. 112)

There are an increasing number of studies across a range of fields of focus (interactional/educational [Johnson, 2006], social [Cacioppo, 2002], cognitive [Gazzaniga, 2000], affective [Panksepp, 1998], etc.) which are seeking to relate social, cognitive, and affective processes to the functioning and development of the brain. There is much to be done to drag some of the theorizing away from the intellectual silos of the past if a new vision of dialectical development is to be created.

Vygotsky and his followers provide some evidence and much speculation on the sociogenetic nature of human development and functioning. This body of work is rapidly expanding and exerting influence over a wide range of studies in the social sciences. A full and robust account of human functioning in the social world cannot be developed in the absence of an understanding of how the brain functions in the overall system of human development. It seems that we have evidence that there is a complex and mutually shaping system in play. As yet we know little of the detail of the forms of exchange that are enacted.

References

Adolphs, R. (2003). Cognitive neuroscience of human social behavior. *Nature Reviews Neuroscience*, *4*, 165–78.

Bakhtin, M. M. (1981). *The dialogic imagination: Four essays* (ed. M. Holquist, trans. C. Emerson & M. Holquist). Austin: University of Texas Press.

Bakhtin, M. M. (1986). *Speech genres and other late essays* (ed. C. Emerson & M. Holquist). Austin: University of Texas Press.

Bakhurst D. (1995). Lessons from Ilyenkov. *The Communication Review 1*(2), 155–178.

Bakhurst, D., & Sypnowich, C. (1995). Introduction. In *The social self: Inquiries in social construction*. London: Sage.

Bleakley A., and Bligh J. (2008). Students learning from patients: Let's get real in medical education. *Advances in Health Sciences Education 13*, 89–107.

Bruner, J. (1997). Celebrating divergence: Piaget and Vygotsky. *Human Development, 40*, 63–73.

Brushlinskii, A. V. (1994). Diskussii. *Psikhologicheskii Zhurnal, 22*(4), 115–126.

Cacioppo, J. T. (2002). *Foundations in social neuroscience. Social neuroscience series*. Cambridge, MA: MIT Press.

Clark, A. (1996). *Being there: Putting brain, body and world together again*. Cambridge: MA: MIT Press.

Clark, A. (1998). Magic words: How language augments human computation. In P. Carruthers & J. Boucher (Eds.), *Language and thought: Interdisciplinary themes*. Cambridge University Press: Cambridge. Reprinted in J. Toribio & A. Clark (Eds.), *Artificial Intelligence and Cognitive Science: Vol. 4. Language and meaning*. New York: Garland Press.

Cole, M. (1996). *Cultural psychology: A once and future discipline*. Cambridge MA: Harvard University Press.

Cole, M., & Derry, J. (2005). We have met technology and it is us. In R. J. Sternberg & D. Preiss (Eds.), *Intelligence and technology: The impact of tools on the nature and development of human abilities*. Mahwah, NJ: Erlbaum.

Cromby, J. (2007). Toward a psychology of feeling. *International Journal of Critical Psychology, 21*, 94–118.

Damasio, A. (1999). *The feeling of what happens: Body and emotion in the making of consciousness*. New York: Harcourt Brace & Co.

Daniels, H. (2008). *Vygotsky and Research* London: Routledge.

Davydov, V. V. (1988). Problems of developmental teaching: The experience of theoretical and experimental psychological research. Parts 1–3. *Soviet Education, 30*(8), 3–87; *30*(9), 3–56; *30*(10), 2–42.

DeLoache, J. S. (1995). Early understanding and use of symbols: The model model. *Current Directions in Psychological Science, 4*, 109–113.

Dennett, D. (1991). *Consciousness explained*. New York: Little Brown and Co.

Donald, M. (1991). *Origins of the modern mind: Three stages in the evolution of culture and cognition*. Cambridge, MA: Harvard University Press.

Engeström Y. (1987). *Learning by expanding*. Helsinki: Orienta-Konsultit Oy.

Engeström, Y. (1993). Developmental studies on work as a test bench of activity theory. In S. Chaikin & J. Lave (Eds.), *Understanding practice: Perspectives on activity and context*. Cambridge: Cambridge University Press.

Engeström, Y. (2006). Collaborative intentionality capital: Object-oriented interagency in multi-organizational fields. Retrieved from http://www.edu.helsinki.fi/activity/people/engestro/.

Engeström, Y., & Mietteinen, R. (1999). Introduction. In Y. Engeström, R. Miettinen, & R. L. Punamaki (Eds.), *Perspectives on activity theory*. Cambridge: Cambridge University Press.

Gazzaniga, M. S. (1998). Principles of human brain organisation derived from split-brain studies. *Neuron, 14*, 217–228.

Gazzaniga, M. S. (2000). *The new cognitive neurosciences*. Cambridge, MA: MIT Press.

Gergen, K. J. (1995). Social construction and the educational process. In P. Steffe & J. Gale (Eds.), *Constructivism in education* (pp. 17–39). Hillsdale, NJ: Erlbaum.

Gibson, J. J. (1979). *The ecological approach to visual perception.* Boston: Houghton Mifflin.

Gonzalez-Rey, F. (2002). L. S. Vygotsky and the question of personality in the cultural-historical approach. In D. Robbins & A. Stetsenko (Eds.), *Voices within Vygotsky's non-classical psychology: Past, present, future.* New York: Nova Science.

Hedegaard, M. (1998). Situated learning and cognition: Theoretical learning of cognition. *Mind Culture and Activity, 5*(2), 114–126.

Hedegaard, M. (1990). The zone of proximal development as basis for instruction. In L. C. Moll (Ed.), *Vygotsky and education: Instructional implications and applications of sociohistorical psychology* (pp. 349–371). Cambridge: Cambridge University Press.

Hirst, W., & Manier, D. (1995). Opening vistas for cognitive psychology. In L. M. W. Martin, K. Nelson, & E. Tobach (Eds.), *Sociocultural psychology: Theory and practice of doing and knowing.* Cambridge: Cambridge University Press.

Iaroshevskii, M. G. (Ed.) (1991). *Repressirovannaia nauka.* Leningrad: Nauka (vol. 1); St Petersburg: Nauka (vol. 2).

Immordino-Yang, M. H., & Damasio, A. R. (2007). We feel, therefore we learn: The relevance of affective and social neuroscience to education. *Mind, Brain and Education, 1,* 3–10.

Johnson, S. (2006). The neuroscience of the mentor–learner relationship. *New Directions for Adult and Continuing Education, 110,* 63–69.

Knox, J. E., & Stevens, C. (1993). Vygotsky and soviet Russian defectology: An introduction to Vygotsky. In *The collected works of L. S. Vygotsky: Vol. 2. Problems of abnormal psychology and learning disabilities.* New York: Plenum Press.

Koshmanova, T. S. (2007). Vygotskian scholars: Visions and implementation of cultural-historical theory. *Journal of Russian and East European Psychology, 45*(2), 61–95.

Kozulin, A., (1998). *Psychological tools. A sociocultural approach to education.* London: Harvard University Press.

Lave, J., & Wenger, E. (1991). *Situated learning: Legitimate peripheral participation.* Cambridge: Cambridge University Press.

Leont'ev [Leontiev], A. N. (1998). Uchenie o srede v pedologicheskih rabotakh Vygotskogo. *Voprosy Psikhologii, 1,* 108–24.

Lidz, C. S., & Elliott, J. G. (Eds.) (2000). *Dynamic assessment: Prevailing models and applications.* New York: Elsevier.

Minick, N. (1987). The Development of Vygotsky's thought: An introduction. In R. W. Rieber & A. S. Carton (Eds.), *The collected works of L. S. Vygotsky* (*Vol. 1*). New York: Plenum Press.

Moll, I. (1994). Reclaiming the natural line in Vygotsky's theory of cognitive development. *Human Development, 37*(6), 333–342.

Morton, J. (2004). *Understanding developmental disorders: A causal modelling approach.* Oxford: Blackwell.

Newman, D., Griffin, P., & Cole, M. (1989). *The construction zone: Working for cognitive change in school.* Cambridge: Cambridge University Press.

Panksepp, J. (1998). *Affective neuroscience: The foundations of human and animal emotions.* New York: Oxford University Press.

Puzyrei A. A. (2007). Contemporary psychology and Vygotsky's cultural-historical theory. *Journal of Russian and East European Psychology, 45*(1), 8–93.

Ratner, C. (1998). Prologue. In R. Rieber (Ed.), & M. J. Hall (Trans.), *The Collected Works of L. S. Vygotsky: Vol. 5. Child Psychology.* London: Plenum Press.

Riegel, K. F. (1976). The dialectics of human development. *American Psychologist,* October, 689–700.

Roepstorff, A. (2008). Things to think with: Words and objects as material symbols. *Philosophical Transactions of the Royal Society B*, *363*, 2049–2054.

Ryan, J. J., Prifitera, A., & Cummins, S. J. (1982). Essential books in clinical neuropsychology. *Professional Psychology*, *13*, 674–676.

Sameroff, A. J. (1980). Development and the dialectic: The need for a systems approach. In W. A. Collins (Ed.), *The Concept of Development: Minnesota Symposia on Child Psychology*, *15*, 83–103.

Stetsenko, A. (2008). From relational ontology to transformative activist stance on development and learning: Expanding Vygotsky's (CHAT) project. *Cultural Studies of Science Education*, *3*, 471–491.

Tharp, R. G., & Gallimore, R. (1988). *Rousing minds to life: Teaching, learning, and schooling in social context*. Cambridge: Cambridge University Press.

Tomasello, M. (1999). *The cultural origins of human cognition*. Cambridge, MA: Harvard University Press.

Tudge, J. R. H., & Winterhoff, P. A. (1993). Vygotsky, Piaget, and Bandura: Perspectives on the relations between the social world and cognitive development. *Human Development*, *36*, 61–81.

Valsiner, J. (1997). *Culture and the development of children's action: A theory of human development* (2nd ed.). New York: Wiley.

Valsiner, J. (1998). *The guided mind: A sociogenetic approach to personality*. Cambridge, MA: Harvard University Press.

Van der Veer, R. & Valsiner, J. (1991). *Understanding Vygotsky: A quest for synthesis*. Oxford: Blackwell.

Vasilyuk, F. (1991). *The psychology of experiencing: The resolution of life's critical situations*. Hemel Hempstead: Harvester.

Veresov, N. N. (1992). Kul'tura i tvorchestvo kak psikhologicheskie idei. *Voprosy Psikhologii*, *1–2*, 124–28.

Vygotsky, L. S. (1960/1981). The instrumental method in psychology. In *The concept of activity in Soviet psychology*, ed. and trans. J. V. Wertsch (pp. 134–143). Armonk, NY: Sharpe.

Vygotsky, L. S. (1978). *Mind in society: The development of higher psychological processes*, ed. and trans. M. Cole, V. John-Steiner, S. Scribner, & E. Souberman. Cambridge, MA: Harvard University Press.

Vygotsky, L. S. (1981). The development of higher forms of attention. In *The concept of activity in Soviet psychology*, ed. and trans. J. V. Wertsch (pp. 189–240). Armonk, NY: Sharpe.

Vygotsky, L. S. (1986). *Thought and language*, ed. and trans. A. Kozulin. Cambridge, MA: MIT Press.

Vygotsky, L. S. (1987). *The collected works of L. S. Vygotsky. Vol.1: Problems of general psychology [Including the volume Thinking and speech]*, ed. R. W. Rieber & A. S. Carton, trans. N. Minick. New York: Plenum Press. Originally published in 1934.

Vygotsky, L. S (1994). The socialist alteration of man. In *The Vygotsky reader* (pp. 175–184). Oxford: Blackwell. Originally published 1930.

Vygotsky, L. S. (1997). *Educational psychology*. Boca Raton, FL.: St. Lucie Press. Originally written 1921–1923.

Vygotsky, L. S. (1998). *The collected works of L. S. Vygotsky: Vol. 5. Child psychology*, ed. R. Rieber, trans. M. J. Hall. London: Plenum Press.

Waddington, C. H. (1956). *The strategy of genes*. London: George Allen and Unwin.

Wells, G. (1999). *Dialogic inquiry: Toward a sociocultural practice and theory of education*. Cambridge: Cambridge University Press.

Wertsch, J. V. (1985). *Vygotsky and the social formation of mind*. Cambridge, MA: Harvard University Press.

Wertsch, J. V. (1991). *Voices of the mind: A sociocultural approach to mediated action*. Cambridge, MA: Harvard University Press.

Wertsch, J. V., Tulviste, P., & Hagstrom, F. (1993). A sociocultural approach to agency. In E. A. Forman, N. Minick, & C. A. Stone (Eds.), *Contexts for learning: Sociocultural dynamics in children's development*. Oxford: Oxford University Press.

Wozniak, R. H. (1975). A dialectic paradigm for psychological research: Implications drawn from the history of psychology in the Soviet Union. *Human Development, 18*, 18–34.

Yaroshevsky, M. (1989). *Lev Vygotsky*. Moscow: Progress Publishers.

Zajonc, R. B. (1980). Feeling and thinking: Preferences need no inferences. *American Psychologist, 35*(2), 151–175.

Zajonc, R. B. (1984). On the primacy of affect. *American Psychologist, 39*(2), 117–123.

Zinchenko, V. P. (1996). Ot klassicheskoi k organicheskoi psikhologii. *Voprosy Psikhologii, 5*, 7–20.

CHAPTER TWENTY-SEVEN

Information-Processing Models of Cognitive Development

Graeme S. Halford and Glenda Andrews

Information-processing models help us to understand the data of cognitive development, to gain new insights, and to frame new and useful questions. They also bring new concepts into the field from the related areas, including cognitive psychology, cognitive science, and neuroscience. These concepts tend to provide new ways of analyzing and understanding the processes of cognitive development. Specifically, information-processing theories have yielded measures of cognitive complexity, which can be a major organizing theme in cognitive development, if it is found that children tend to master more complex concepts later.

A dominant early approach has been the neo-Piagetian models, which sought to explain the course of cognitive development, as observed by Piaget and his collaborators, in terms of the growth of information processing.

Neo-Piagetian Models

Several models developed in parallel in this field, often with considerable interaction between the theorists.

McLaughlin

The model of McLaughlin (1963), although not the first information-processing theory in the field, can probably be regarded as beginning the modern era of models in this category. McLaughlin proposed that Piagetian stage was determined by the number of concepts that could be considered simultaneously. Piaget's sensorimotor, preoperational, concrete operational and formal operational stages required $2^0 = 1$, $2^1 = 2$, $2^2 = 4$ and

$2^3 = 8$ concepts to be considered simultaneously. To illustrate, consider a set of objects with two attributes – shape (triangle, non-triangle) and color (red, non-red). This defines four possible categories: red triangle, red non-triangle, non-red triangle, and non-red non-triangle. Thus two binary valued attributes yield four categories, or $2^2 = 4$. Now consider a set of objects with three attributes – shape (triangle, non-triangle), color (red, non-red), and size (large, non-large). Now there are 8 possible categories of objects: large red triangle, large red non-triangle, ... non-large non-red non-triangle. Thus three binary valued attributes yield $2^3 = 8$ categories.

McLaughlin proposed that the number of categories that a child could consider simultaneously was determined by memory span. A child with a span of 2 could consider $2^1 = 2$ concepts, and this would put the child at the preoperational stage. A child with a span of 3 or 4 could consider, $2^2 = 4$ concepts, and would be in the concrete operational stage. A child with a span or 5 to 8 could consider $2^3 = 8$ concepts, and would be in the formal operational stage. McLaughlin pointed to a correspondence between the development of span and the progression through Piaget's stages of cognitive development.

However McLaughlin did not apply the theory to analyze or predict performance on any specific cognitive tasks. Nevertheless, McLaughlin's suggestion inspired a lot of thought by subsequent cognitive developmentalists, including our own work. Interestingly, Feldman (2000) has shown that complexity of concept learning can be defined by the length of the shortest Boolean expression that is equivalent to the concept, an idea that is broadly consistent with McLaughlin's. Feldman's formulation applies to experimental concept learning (Shepard, Hovland, & Jenkins, 1961) whereas McLaughlin's theory applies to cognitive development, but there is enough common ground here to suggest that this approach to analysis of complexity might not yet have run its full course. McLaughlin's formulation was the first serious attempt to quantify complexity of concepts that are important in cognitive development.

Pascual-Leone

The model of Pascual-Leone (1970) was first theory of complexity in cognitive development to be empirically tested. He proposed that children's cognitive functioning was governed by central-computing space, or *M*-space, that corresponded to the number of separate schemes that they could coordinate. The value of M was $a + 1$ at age 3 and increased by 1 every 2 years, reaching a value of $a + 7$ at age 15, where a is a parameter that represents the processing space required for instructions and for the general task situation, and which is constant over age. To illustrate, Pascual-Leone proposed that a child for whom $M = a + 2$ would be in the last substage of Piaget's preoperational stage, and would on average be 5–6 years old.

Pascual-Leone developed the compound stimulus visual information (CSVI) task to assess *M*-space. The stimuli varied over eight dimensions, such as shape, color, size, whether the figure was closed or open, whether there was a circle in the centre, and so on. Children were trained to produce a specific response for the positive attribute on each dimension (e.g., raise a hand if the shape was square, clap hands if the color was red, etc.). Testing consisted of presenting stimuli varying in from five attributes (for 5-year-olds) to eight attributes (for 11-year-olds) and determining the number of responses given out of the total for the stimulus (e.g., given a stimulus with five positive attributes, a child might give four of the five responses they had been trained to give for that set of attributes). The number of active schemes was then estimated using the Bose-Einstein occupancy model. A good fit to the expected age norms was obtained.

Pascual-Leone then demonstrated that the *M*-space demands of some well-known cognitive developmental tasks predicted the ages at which these were attained. For example, Pascual-Leone and Smith (1969) analyzed class inclusion as requiring an M-space of three, because it is a union of two classes, A and A′ that are included in B (e.g., apples and bananas are included in fruit). It therefore requires coordination of a scheme for each of these classes, in addition to the schemes representing instructions and the task situation. The requirement to coordinate three schemes is consistent with attainment of class inclusion at approximately age 7, when *M*-space reaches three schemes.

The conception which Pascual-Leone introduced in 1970 has resulted in a repertoire of techniques for assessing children's processing capacity, and research related to the paradigm continues at the present time. A number of detailed comparisons have been made between Baddeley's (1990) working-memory model and Pascual-Leone's *M*-space (Baddeley & Hitch, 2000; de Ribaupierre & Bailleux, 1994, 2000; Kemps, De Rammelaere, & Desmet, 2000). See also a reply by Pascual-Leone (2000). The links between *M* capacity, inhibitory control, executive processes (e.g., shifting, updating), and processing speed have also been examined (Im-Bolter, Johnson, & Pascual-Leone, 2006; Johnson, Im-Bolter, & Pascual-Leone, 2003).

Case

Case (1985) proposed that children's cognitive processes develop because they make better use of the available capacity. Specifically, Case proposed that total processing space (TPS) could be flexibly allocated to operating space (OS) or short-term storage space (STSS), i.e.:

$$\text{TPS} = \text{OS} + \text{STSS}$$

Total processing space was held to be constant over age, after infancy. Demands for operating space declined with age because of increased processing efficiency, thereby making more of the TPS available as short-term storage space. The increase in short-term memory span with age was attributed to more efficient processing, which also became the main factor responsible for cognitive development, according to the model. Their empirical methods are well illustrated by Case, Kurland, and Goldberg (1982) who assumed that participants who processed faster were more efficient, and required less operating space, leaving more short-term storage space. Therefore their recall would be superior. Consistent with the theory, short-term memory span for words was found to be well predicted by speed of rehearsal. A striking finding was that when adults' rehearsal rate was reduced to that of 6-year-olds their spans were reduced correspondingly.

These findings appeared to offer a straightforward and elegant solution to the problem of whether processing capacity increased with age. They were consistent with the claim by Chi (1978) that memory performance reflected familiarity or expertise rather than capacity. Chi measured recall of 10-year-olds' and adults' memories for digit strings and for chess positions. With digits, the usual finding that adults' recall was superior was obtained. However the children in the sample had much greater knowledge of chess than the adults, and their recall of chess pieces on a board was superior to that of the adults. This finding, like that of Case et al. (1982) was taken to indicate that memory capacity was not responsible for increases in span with age. Note however that, while both studies demonstrate an effect of variables other than capacity, processing speed in the Case et al. study, and domain knowledge in Chi's study, they do not assess capacity. Neither Case et al.'s nor Chi's (1978) findings rule out an increase in capacity with age, which is what more recent evidence indicates (Andrews, Halford, Bunch, Bowden, & Jones, 2003; Cowan, 2001; Halford, Cowan, & Andrews, 2007; Quartz & Sejnowski, 1997).

The theory that processing space is a single resource that can be flexibly allocated to processing or storage is hard to reconcile with findings from working-memory research. Halford, Maybery, O'Hare, and Grant (1994) gave children a memory preload, comprised of a string of digits, then a cognitive task to perform, then they were asked to recall the preload. This procedure separates the processing and storage demands that are combined in many working-memory measures, and the difficulty of the cognitive task was manipulated independently of the concurrent memory-storage task. They found that a concurrent short-term memory load does not interfere with reasoning as would be expected according to Case's position.

Another aspect of Case's early work has withstood the test of time. This is the insight that cognitive development depends heavily on learning to use the available capacity more efficiently. Processing capacity is limited in both children and adults (Cowan, 2001; Halford, Cowan, & Andrews, 2007; Luck & Vogel, 1997) and therefore cognitive processes require strategies that utilize the limited capacity effectively. The postulate that total processing capacity remains constant over age is no longer tenable, but it is true that

increased efficiency in the way capacity is utilized accounts for a lot of what develops. The historic contribution from this phase of Case's work may be that he was the first to realize the importance of processing efficiency in cognitive development, and to build this principle into a systematic theory.

He also anticipated more recent neuroscience evidence on growth of processing capacity. Case (1992b) reviewed evidence that the frontal cortex continues to develop for at least two decades after birth, and electroencephalographic (EEG) coherence between frontal and posterior lobes also increases. He then drew attention to correspondence between growth of EEG coherence and development of working memory over ages 4–10 years. This work arguably marks the beginning of attempts to base systematic cognitive development theory on neuroscience data.

In his later work Case (1992a, 1992b; Case et al., 1996) developed the concept of central conceptual structures, defined as "an internal network of concepts and conceptual relations that plays a central role in permitting children to think about a wide range of situations at a new epistemic level, and to develop a new set of control structures for dealing with them" (Case, 1992a, p. 130). Development of central conceptual structures passes through the sequence of four major neo-Piagetian stages:

The *sensorimotor* stage is concerned with coordination between actions and reactions, or between actions and effects, for example when pushing a lever on a piece of apparatus sets it vibrating, producing an interesting sight or sound.

The *interrelational* stage is concerned with relations, such as one end of a beam moving down while the other moves up. At more advanced levels, coordination between relations occurs, so placing a heavier weight on one end of a beam and a lighter weight on the other is linked to one end of the beam going down while the other end goes up.

The *dimensional* stage is concerned with dimensional units, such as numbers, weights, or distances. Thus the child has progressed from relations between objects or events to thinking about relations between dimensional units such as number of weights, or between distances.

The *vectorial* (or abstract dimensional) stage is one in which dimensional structures are coordinated to produce abstract systems of dimensions, for example when ratios of weights and distances are converted to new ratios having a common term.

Each major stage is divided into substages that represent increasing structural complexity within the major stage. Complexity is defined by the number of nested goals required to perform the task. In order to predict which side of a balance beam would go down, at the simplest, *preliminary* substage there is a single goal, to determine which side of the balance would go down. The strategy is to simply look at the balance beam to determine which side looks heavier. At the next, *unifocal* substage, there is a hierarchy of two nested goals, to predict which side of the beam will go down, and a subgoal to determine which side has the larger number of weights. At the *bifocal* substage there are three nested goals, and at the *elaborated coordination* substage there are four nested goals.

The number of goals children can maintain, and hence the complexity of the problems they can solve, is determined by the size of STSS, which increases from 1 to 4, due to both maturation and experience. This progression occurs within each of the major stages. This means that the short-term storage load is reset to 1 when the child progresses to the next major stage, so a task that imposed a load of 4 at the elaborated coordination substage of interrelational stage would impose a load of 1 at substage 1 of the dimensional stage. The transition from one stage to another is achieved by coordinating two existing structures into a higher-order structure.

Case (1992a; Case et al., 1996) applied the theory to a wide range of domains, including scientific and mathematical knowledge, spatial and musical reasoning, understanding narrative and social roles, and motor development. However the metric is not general to all tasks, but is specific to performance within one of the major stages.

Fischer

The theory of Fischer (1980; Fischer & Rose, 1996) was based on cognitive skill theory, where skill refers to control over sources of variation in a person's own behavior. There are four major stages or tiers: the reflex, sensorimotor, representational, and abstract. Within each tier there is a recurring cycle of four levels: the set, mapping (of sets), system (composition of mappings), and system of systems. As with Case's theory, the highest level of one tier is shared with the lowest level of the next, and represents a transition between tiers.

A set is a source of variation over which some cognitive process exercises control.

> In an action, the person can control the relevant variations in the behaviors on things. An infant who can consistently grasp a rattle has a set for grasping that rattle. (Fischer, 1980, p. 481)

In more conventional terms, a set is really a variable, but it implies correspondences between events or objects and actions: "The thing is always included with the behavior in the definition of a set" (Fischer, 1980, p. 481).

A set is the lowest level of structure within a tier. A single sensorimotor set would typically develop around 15–17 weeks of age. The next level is a mapping between sets. A sensorimotor mapping would typically develop at 7–8 months. An example would be coordination of looking at an object in order to grasp it. The next level is a system, which is really a coordination of two mappings. An example would be when the child drops a piece of bread and watches it fall, then breaks off a crumb and watches it fall. There is a mapping between dropping and watching the piece of bread and another between dropping and watching the crumb. By varying one set, the dropping, and observing the result, seeing the bread fall, the child develops a concept of means–end links. The next level is a system of sensorimotor systems, and is a mapping between two systems from the previous level. However it is also the first level of the representational tier, and is a single representational set.

Fischer (1980) illustrates the levels of the representational tier with a spring-and-cord gadget, in which a weight hangs from a cord that passes around a pulley to a coil spring that is attached to a vertical surface. As extra weight is added the spring stretches and the string moves around the pulley so that the horizontal part of the cord becomes shorter and the vertical part becomes longer, though the overall length of the cord is of course constant, which is a form of conservation of length (Piaget, 1950). A 4- to 5-year-old child who had experience with the gadget could use size of the weight to control the length of the spring. This is mapping one set, (variable) weight, into the other, spring length. The child might also make mappings between horizontal to vertical length of cord, or between any two of the four sets: weight, vertical and horizontal cord length, and spring length. However, understanding is disjointed because each of these mappings exists independently, and there is no integration such as recognizing that the horizontal and vertical lengths of cord are segments of one cord of constant length. A representational system is formed by relating two representational mappings. An example would be a mapping between the horizontal and vertical lengths of cord with one weight, and another mapping between the horizontal and vertical lengths with a different weight. Relating these mappings shows how the horizontal length decreases as the vertical length increases, and vice versa, which in turn leads to recognition that changes in the lengths compensate each other, leading to the idea that the total length of the string is conserved. Thus the subtle and important concept of conservation emerges from the coordination of lower-level structures. The next level is a system of representational systems, which is a single abstract set. Development then proceeds through the remaining three levels of the abstract tier: the abstract mapping, abstract system, and the system of abstract systems, which is identified with principles.

Complexity increases within a tier in a manner that bears a striking correspondence to McLaughlin's (1963) complexity scale. The four levels within a tier comprise a set, then a mapping between two sets, then a system which is a mapping between two mappings of sets and is equivalent to four sets, then a mapping between two systems, which comprises eight sets (see, for example, Fischer, 1980, figure 2, p. 490). This corresponds to McLaughlin's (1963) four levels defined as $2^0 = 1$, $2^1 = 2$, $2^2 = 4$ and $2^3 = 8$ concepts considered simultaneously. This again illustrates the underlying common ground between different information-processing theories of cognitive development.

Fischer also has an extensive consideration of transformation rules for creating the transition from one level to another. The first rule is intercoordination, which is a process of combining skills at one level to produce a skill at the next level. An example would be the two mappings between horizontal and vertical lengths of cord under different weights, as mentioned earlier. The mappings are intercoordinated to create a system, and recognition of the compensating changes between horizontal and vertical lengths emerges from the intercoordination. The other rules are compounding, focusing, substitution, and differentiation.

Fischer's (1980) formulation has been retained in essence in his later work, but there have been two major developments of the model. One has been to link the model to dynamic growth functions (Van der Maas & Molenaar, 1992; van Geert, 1993) while the other has been to link it to spurts in brain growth (Fischer & Bidell, 1998; Fischer & Rose, 1996; Thatcher, 1994). Dynamic systems models of cognitive development are considered by Thelen and Smith (2006) but we will try to indicate briefly how Fischer's theory has developed along these lines. Firstly, it is proposed that the major reorganizations between levels, as outlined above, correspond to growth spurts or other discontinuities in brain growth. Furthermore, these dynamic changes can occur concurrently in many independent systems, which might be localized in different regions of the brain. It is also proposed that each new level is marked by a new behavioral control system, which is supported by a new kind of neural network (Fischer & Rose, 1996). Fischer, Stewart, and Stein (2008) propose that knowledge is built from repeated reconstructions that move towards higher complexity and abstraction, though with many reversals and recoveries. Fischer also proposes that the recurring cycles of development that occur in each tier are supported by observations of brain growth. A more comprehensive summary is given by Fischer and Bidell (2006).

The implications of the recent developments of Fischer's theory are profound and sophisticated. They offer a resolution of the anomaly, crucial to understanding development, that there is both variability and consistency in cognitive development. Dynamic systems produce variability from a relatively small set of common processes. The application of dynamic systems theory to the database provided by cognitive developmental stage theory is one of the greatest achievements of Fischer and his colleagues.

Attempts at Synthesis

Attempts have been made to synthesize the neo-Piagetian theories (Chapman, 1987, 1990; Chapman & Lindenberger, 1989; Demetriou, Doise, & van Lieshout, 1998; Demetriou, Efklides, & Platsidou, 1993). Chapman's approach was arguably more directly based on information-processing concepts. He postulated that:

> the total capacity requirement of a given form of reasoning is equal to the number of operatory variables that are assigned values simultaneously in employing that form of reasoning in a particular task. (Chapman & Lindenberger, 1989, p. 238)

We will consider his analysis of class inclusion. A concrete example might comprise a set of beads, some red (A) and some blue (A′), all of which are wooden (B). Therefore A and A′ are included in B ($A \cup A' = B$). The child is asked to decide whether there are more red than wooden beads. Solving the problem entails assigning values to the class variables, A, A′, and B, that is recognizing that A = red beads, A′ = blue beads, and B = wooden beads, which is a form of variable binding. Chapman and Lindenberger refer to this as the coordination of intension (the defining properties of the class) and extension (objects belonging to the class).

Chapman (1987) analyzed tasks in terms of the number of schemes required for solution:

> One of the main hypotheses generated by the proposed model is that the notion of attentional capacity can be explicated in terms of the number of representational schemes coordinated by an inferential scheme. (Chapman, 1987, p. 310)

However he interpreted schemes in a way that was very like variables:

> A further property of representational schemes is that they can be generalized beyond their immediate context and embedded in more abstract schemes without losing their identity. (Chapman, 1987, p. 309)

Chapman was very much aware of the inherent difficulties in objective analyses of complexity. After a penetrating review of the neo-Piagetian theories of Case, Pascual-Leone, and Halford, Chapman (1990) commented:

> In summary, neo-Piagetian theorists have not yet developed a method of task analysis (a) that is sufficiently rigorous to result in unambiguous predictions and (b) that can be applied with equal facility to both cognitive tasks and measurement tasks. (Chapman, 1990, p. 273)

In his later work, Chapman was more explicit in analyzing complexity in terms of variables. Perhaps therefore one of the most important achievements of Chapman and his collaborators was to have realized that the best way to analyze complexity of cognitive tasks is to determine the number of variables that have to be instantiated in parallel.

Variables can be analyzed more objectively than schemes. The concept of scheme is so flexible that it may be difficult for independent observers to agree on the number of schemes required for a task.

Processing Speed

Evidence for a global processing-speed factor that increases with development was provided by Kail (1986, 1988a, 1991; Kail & Park, 1992). The methodology was based on measuring changes in processing speed with age across a number of rather different tasks, and is well illustrated by Kail (1988a). Children were tested on a memory search task in which they studied a set of one, three, or five digits, then a single-digit probe was presented and children had to decide whether it had been in the study set. Visual search was similar except that the study set was a single digit, and children had to determine whether this digit appeared in a probe set of one to five digits. Processing speed can be measured in both tasks by the slope of the function relating probe set size to response time. Other tasks used included mental rotation, in which children had to judge whether a pair of letters presented in different orientations were identical or were mirror images, and a mental addition task in which children had to determine the correctness of sums such as 3 + 8 = 10. There was also an analogical reasoning task with two 3 × 3 matrices. Children had to determine whether the geometric figures in the cells changed according to the same rule in both matrices. It was found that the change in processing speed over the age range 8–22 years was very similar across all task domains, and was best fitted by an exponential function that was common to the tasks. This led Kail to propose that changes in processing speed over age reflected processing capacity rather than learning.

While these findings offer some of the strongest evidence for growth of processing capacity with age, they have not been without controversy. One issue has been whether the findings are compatible with some kind of learning model (e.g. Stigler, Nusbaum, & Chalip, 1988; but see also Kail, 1988b, 1990, 1991). The global nature of the processing-speed factor has also been challenged by Ridderinkhof and van der Molen (1997) who argued that process-specific factors may be involved. There is also a cause-and-effect question: Does increased speed cause an increase in processing capacity, or the reverse? A possible answer comes from neural net models. Increased capacity reduces processing time in some neural nets because it reduces the number of cycles required for the net to settle into the solution that best fits the parallel-acting constraints. Alternatively it is possible that higher processing speed permits more information to be processed before activation decays. This issue seems likely to remain active for some time (see, for example, Cowan, 1998; Halford, Wilson, & Phillips, 1998a). These controversies notwithstanding, the discovery of a global processing-speed factor must be considered one of the major achievements in the field. Processing speed has emerged as a major factor in cognitive development across the lifespan (Cerella & Hale, 1994; Kail & Salthouse, 1994; Salthouse, 1996) and it has found application in a number of other contexts (Kail, 1997, 1998, 2000; Kail & Hall, 1999).

Further issues have been raised by Anderson (1992), who proposes that individual differences reflect processing efficiency, whereas cognitive development depends on knowledge elaboration and maturation of modules. He reviews evidence that individual differences in intelligence are stable over the course of development, and are related to measures of processing speed such as inspection time, which is the exposure duration required to detect which of two vertical lines is longer. This has been found to correlate with intelligence (Nettelbeck, 1987).

Cognitive development, on the other hand, is considered to be heavily dependent on maturation of specialized modules that are functionally independent, complex processes of evolutionary importance, independent of general intelligence. Anderson proposes that there are modules for perception of 3-dimensional space, phonological encoding, syntactic parsing, and theory of mind. The mechanisms that enable us to see in 3-dimensional space are specialized for processing visual information, and are complex, but do not correlate with intelligence. Although it is likely that some functions, especially in perception, are modular, it is a much greater leap to propose that cognitive development and individual differences in intelligence exist in separate, watertight compartments. It seems more likely that cognitive development also depends on acquisition of domain-general processes, such as memory storage and retrieval functions, and analogical reasoning (Halford & Andrews, 2004, 2007).

Cognitive Complexity

The orderly interpretation of findings in cognitive development depends on having a metric for cognitive complexity. It is only by comparing complexities that we can determine whether young children's performance on a given task is precocious.

Relational Complexity theory

One such approach, which has its origins partly in the neo-Piagetian approach, is Relational Complexity (RC) theory (Halford et al., 1998b; Halford, Cowan, & Andrews, 2007). Complexity is defined in terms of relations that can be processed in parallel. The essential idea is that each argument of a relation represents a source of variation, or a dimension, and an *n*-ary relation is a set of points in *n*-dimensional space. Thus relations of higher *arity* are more complex, so a unary relation is less complex than a binary relation, which is less complex than a ternary relation, and so on. Processing load increases with relational complexity, and empirical evidence indicates that quaternary relations are the most complex that adults can process in parallel (Halford, Baker, McCredden, & Bain, 2005). This is consistent with limitations in short-term memory capacity (Cowan, 2001). Normative data suggests that unary relations are processed at a median age of

1 year, binary relations at 2 years, ternary relations at 5 years, and quaternary relations at 11 years.

Concepts too complex to be processed in parallel are handled by *segmentation* (decomposition into smaller segments that can be processed serially) and *conceptual chunking* (recoding into less complex relations, but at the cost of making some relations inaccessible). For example, $v = st^{-1}$ (velocity = distance/time) is a ternary relation, but can be recoded to a unary relation, a binding between a variable and a constant. However this makes relations between velocity, distance, and time inaccessible (e.g., if velocity is represented as a single variable, we cannot answer questions such as "How is speed affected if the distance is doubled and time held constant?").

Complex tasks are normally segmented into steps, each of which is of sufficiently low relational complexity to be processed in parallel. The steps are processed serially. Expertise is important for devising strategies that reduce the complexity of relations that have to be processed in parallel, though a lower limit is usually imposed by the structure of the task. The effective relational complexity of a task is the most complex relation that has to be performed in parallel, using the most efficient strategy available. Complexity analyses are based on principles that are common across domains and methodologies.

We can illustrate relational complexity with the class inclusion task, discussed earlier, comprised of wooden beads, most of which are red, while the remainder are blue. Children are asked "Are there more wooden beads or more red ones?" Young children tend to say there are more red ones. The possible causes of error have been the subject of much controversy (Breslow, 1981; Bryant & Trabasso, 1971; Halford, 1993; Hodkin, 1987; Markovits, Dumas, & Malfait, 1995; McGarrigle, Grieve, & Hughes, 1978; Pears & Bryant, 1990; Siegel, McCabe, Brand, & Matthews, 1978; Thayer & Collyer, 1978) but when allowance is made for these, we still have a complexity factor that influences performance. The problem is that in order to determine which class is the superordinate and which are the subclasses, children must consider the relations among the superordinate class and the two subclasses. A class such as wooden beads is not inherently a superordinate, and its status is defined by its relations to the subordinates. That is, wooden is a superordinate because it includes red and blue beads. All three sets and the relations between them are necessary to understand that the subclasses are included in the superordinate class. This entails a ternary relation. If the task is represented as a series of separate binary relations that are not integrated, then the full implications of the entire relational structure among the classes (e.g., that the superordinate class is necessarily more numerous than the major subclass) will be missed.

Andrews and Halford (2002) investigated the emergence of ternary-relational processing in the class inclusion task as well as five other content domains (transitive inference, hierarchical classification, sentence comprehension, cardinality, and hypothesis testing). The percentages of children who processed ternary relations were 16% at age 3–4 years, 48% at age 5, 70% at age 6, and 78% at age 7–8. The majority of children at each age succeeded on comparable binary-relational items. In this and other research (e.g., Andrews & Halford, 1998; Bunch, Andrews, & Halford, 2007; Halford, Andrews, & Jensen, 2002; Halford, Bunch, & McCredden, 2007) relational complexity was manipulated independently of other factors, and substantial complexity effects were observed. An important point about capacity to process complex concepts is that it develops in parallel with the acquisition and organization of knowledge, and there is considerable interaction between the two sets of processes. Knowledge and complexity aspects of cognitive development have been considered in detail by Halford, Cowan, and Andrews (2007), who also provide objective principles for analysis of cognitive complexity.

A number of unequivocal developmental predictions have been made in advance using RC theory (Halford, 1993). For example, 2-year-olds should be able to discriminate either weight or distance, but not both, on the balance scale, which has been confirmed by Halford, Andrews, Dalton, Boag, and Zielinski (2002). It was also predicted that structural complexity would be a factor in concept of mind (Halford, 1993), which was confirmed by Davis and Pratt (1995), Frye, Zelazo, and Palfai (1995), Gordon and Olson (1998), Andrews et al. (2003), and Keenan, Olson, and Marini (1998).

Cognitive Complexity and Control theory

Another complexity approach to cognitive development is Cognitive Complexity and Control (CCC) theory (Zelazo, Müller, Frye, & Marcovitch, 2003). This theory, which developed independently of RC theory, focuses on the complexity of the rules children are able to use. There are four types of rules that vary in complexity. The simplest are single stimulus–reward associations, which can be represented either implicitly or explicitly (e.g., when reversal of the association is required). Condition–action (if–then) rules are more complex than associations. In univalent rule pairs each stimulus is associated with a separate response (e.g., red light – stop; green light – go). Bivalent rule pairs are more complex because each stimulus is associated with two different responses, the correct response being determined by the context. For example, in the Dimensional Change Card Sorting (DCCS; Zelazo, 2006) task, a red boat is sorted with a red flower in the color game, but when the context changes to the shape game, the red boat is sorted with the blue boat. Higher-order rules integrate pairs of bivalent rules into rule hierarchies which facilitate selection among task sets (Zelazo et al., 2003). Older children construct more complex rules than younger children. Reversal of stimulus–reward associations has been demonstrated in non-human animals and children as young as 30 months (Overman, Bachevalier, Schuhmann, & Ryan, 1996). From 3 years, children can use a pair of arbitrary univalent rules, but they experience difficulty with bivalent rule pairs. Around 5 years, children can integrate two incompatible pairs of bivalent rules into a single rule system via a higher-order rule (Zelazo, Jacques, Burack, & Frye, 2002). Predictions derived from CCC theory have been supported by empirical research in that success on tasks that involve higher-order rules is not usually observed before 4.5 to 5 years of age (e.g., Frye et al., 1995; Kerr & Zelazo, 2004).

CCC-R (i.e., Cognitive Complexity and Control theory, revised; see Zelazo & Müller, chapter 22, this volume) and RC theories developed independently, but they share common ground. Analyses based on rule complexity and relational complexity are translatable in many situations. For example, according to CCC theory, correct responding on the DCCS (Zelazo et al., 2003), false-belief and appearance–reality tasks (Frye et al., 1995), and the Children's Gambling Task (Kerr & Zelazo, 2004) requires higher-order rules. In RC theory, these tasks are ternary-relational (Andrews, et al., 2003; Bunch et al., 2007; Halford, Bunch, & McCredden, 2007). However, whereas CCC theory applies to tasks with a hierarchical structure, RC theory can also be applied to tasks with non-hierarchical structures.

Both complexity approaches propose that maturation of the frontal lobes underpins age-related increases in children's ability to deal with increasing complexity. There is abundant evidence for the protracted maturation of prefrontal regions. Measures of synaptic density and elimination (Huttenlocher & Dabholkar, 1997), and of myelination (Paterson, Heim, Friedman, Choudhury, & Benasich, 2006) show that prefrontal regions are the last to reach maturation. Dramatic changes in myelination continue in the dorsal, medial, and lateral regions of the frontal cortex during adolescence (Nelson, Thomas, & De Haan, 2006). Glucose metabolism in the frontal and association cortices increases between 8 and 12 months (Chugani & Phelps, 1986). Within the frontal lobes grey matter maturation occurs earliest in the orbitofrontal cortex (OFC), Brodmann area (BA) 11, later in the ventrolateral prefrontal cortex (VL-PFC; BA44, BA45, BA47), and later still in dorsolateral prefrontal cortex (BA9 and BA46), coinciding with its later myelination (Gogtay et al., 2004).

Studies of brain function in adults show that relational processing involves the prefrontal cortex. Waltz et al. (1999) studied patients with brain lesions due to dementia. Patients with damage to the dorsolateral prefrontal cortex (DL-PFC) could use single binary-relational premises but they could not integrate two premises in a transitive inference task. Premise integration is ternary-relational (Andrews & Halford, 1998; Halford et al., 1998b). Similar results were obtained for a matrix reasoning task that required relational integration. Brain-imaging studies have implicated the DL-PFC and rostrolateral prefrontal cortex (RL-PFC) in relational integration, and as relational complexity increases more anterior regions appear to be recruited (Christoff & Owen, 2006; Christoff et al., 2001; Kroger et al., 2002). Smith, Keramatian, and Christoff (2007) demonstrated that a relational match-to-sample task reliably activates RL-PFC in adults. Ramnani & Owen (2004) proposed that the functions of the anterior prefrontal cortex (APFC) are distinguished more by the coordination and integration of information processing than by cognitive domain. This is consistent with Christoff and Owen's (2006) proposal that the functions of the RL-PFC are related more to cognitive complexity than to a cognitive domain.

Brain-imaging studies of the developing brain are still quite scarce. However performance on the Piagetian A-not-B task appears to be associated with maturity of brain systems involving the prefrontal cortex. Bell and Fox (1992) found that toleration of longer delays in 12-month-olds was associated with more mature patterns of EEG brain activity. Bell (2001) recorded EEG activity while 8-month-olds performed a looking version of the A-not-B task. High-performing infants showed task-related increases in EEG power in four scalp regions (frontal pole, medial frontal, parietal, occipital), suggesting the involvement of both frontal and non-frontal brain regions. They also showed increased EEG coherence between medial frontal and parietal sites, suggesting that these regions were working together in the task, and lower coherence between two frontal pairs of electrodes in the right than left hemisphere, consistent with more advanced differentiation. Low-performing infants showed more hemispheric symmetry. Lesion research with non-human primates implicates the DL-PFC (BA8, BA9, BA10), but not the hippocampus in A-not-B task performance (Diamond, 1990; Diamond, Zola-Morgan, & Squire, 1989).

Bunge and Zelazo (2006) proposed a brain-based account of the development of rule use in childhood which links the four rule types to different prefrontal cortex sub-regions. Simple stimulus–reward associations involve the OFC (BA11). Univalent and bivalent conditional rules involve the VL-PFC (BA44, BA45, BA47) and the DL-PFC (BA9, BA46). Higher-order rules recruit the RL-PFC (the lateral portion of BA10).

Imaging studies involving children aged from 8 to 12 years (Crone et al., 2009) are consistent with these complexity accounts. Extending brain-imaging research to examine acquisition of complex rules and relations in younger 3- to 8-year-old children is an important area for future research, although the difficulties associated with using these techniques with young children are far from trivial.

Levels of Cognitive Functioning

Levels of cognitive function have been defined by a number of writers, including Campbell and Bickhard (1986) and Karmiloff-Smith and her collaborators (Clark & Karmiloff-Smith, 1993; Karmiloff-Smith, 1992, 1994). The most influential at present is probably that of Karmiloff-Smith, based on the implicit–explicit distinction. It is considered by Westermann, Thomas, and Karmiloff-Smith (chapter 28, this volume), but has links to the other information-processing approaches. Level-I, or implicit knowledge, is an effective basis for performance, but is not accessible to other cognitive processes, and cannot be modified strategically. It is *knowledge in the system* but not *knowledge to the system.* There are three levels of explicit knowledge that become progressively more accessible, modifiable, and available to consciousness and verbal report. Unlike neo-Piagetian models, representational redescription occurs independently in each domain, and is not age- or stage-linked. Nevertheless representational redescription attempts to integrate Piagetian constructivism and Fodor's (1983) concept of innate knowledge.

The nature of representational redescription has been only partly specified. Phillips, Halford, and Wilson (1995) proposed that the implicit–explicit distinction can be captured by the distinction between associative and relational knowledge. Karmiloff-Smith (1994) has speculated about neural net models that might make the transition from one level to another. However much remains to be done to address this fundamental issue.

Process Models of Cognitive Development

A number of information-processing models of concept acquisition have been developed. The Q-SOAR model of Simon and Klahr (1995) applied Newell's (1990) SOAR architecture to Gelman's (1982) study of number conservation acquisition. Children are shown two equal rows of objects, asked to count each row in turn and say how many each contains, then to say whether they are the same or different. Then one row is transformed (e.g. by spacing objects more widely, increasing the length of the row, without adding any items) then the child is asked whether each row still contains the same number, and whether they are the same or different.

The preconserving child cannot answer this question. This is represented in Q-SOAR as an impasse. The model then searches for a solution to the problem, using a procedure based on the work of Klahr and Wallace (1976). This entails quantifying the sets before and after the transformation, noting that they were the same before the transformation, that they are the same after the transformation, and finally that the transformation did not change the relation between the sets. This process uses knowledge already available, including quantifying the sets, comparing them, recalling results of quantification and comparison, and noticing the effect of transformations (both conserving and non-conserving). With repeated experience, the model gradually learns to classify the action of spacing out the items as a conserving transformation.

Following work on rule assessment (Briars & Siegler, 1984; Siegler, 1981), Siegler and his collaborators conducted an extensive study of strategy development (Siegler, 1999; Siegler & Chen, 1998; Siegler & Jenkins, 1989; Siegler & Shipley, 1995; Siegler & Shrager, 1984). Two of the models were concerned with development of addition strategies in young children. When asked to add two single-digit numbers, they choose between a set of strategies including retrieving the answer from memory, decomposing the numbers (e.g., 3 + 5 = 4 + 4 = 8), counting both sets (counting right through a set of 3 and a set of 5, perhaps using fingers), and the *min strategy* of counting on from the larger set (e.g., 4, 5, 6, 7, 8, so 3 + 5 = 8).

Their early strategy-choice model was based on distribution of associations (Siegler & Shrager, 1984). The idea is that each addition sum is associated with answers of varying strengths so for a given sample of children 2 + 1 might yield the answer "3" 80% of the time, "1" or "2" 4%, "4" 3%, and so on. The chance of an answer being chosen is a function of its associative strength relative to competing answers. The more peaked the distribution the more likely it will be that a single answer will occur. However it will be adopted only if it is above the confidence criterion. If not, alternative strategies, such as counting, are sought.

In their later work Siegler and his collaborators developed the Adaptive Strategy Choice Model (ASCM, pronounced "Ask-em"). This model makes more active strategy choices. At the beginning ASCM knows only the small set of strategies typically used by 4-year-olds, but it has general cognitive skills for choosing and evaluating strategies. The model is trained on a set of elementary addition facts, then the min strategy is added to the model's repertoire. The model chooses a strategy for each problem on the basis of the past speed and accuracy of the strategy and on similarity between the current problem and past problems where a strategy has been used. Each time a strategy is used the record of its success is updated and the projected strength of the strategy for that problem is calculated. The strength of association between a problem and a specific answer is increased or decreased depending on the success of the answer. One of the strengths of the model is that it can account for variability, both between children and between different strategies used by the same child for a particular class of problems. Most importantly it provides a reasonably accurate account of strategy development in children over age.

Relational Knowledge and Analogy

One of the most fundamental problems in cognitive development is children's acquisition of relational and dimensional knowledge, yet there has been little systematic study of it. One of the most interesting research projects in this area is that by Smith, Gasser, and Sandhofer (1997). Examining evidence from children's word acquisition, Smith noted that dimensional adjectives (e.g. "wet," "soft," "big," "red") are learned relatively slowly as compared with, say, nouns. Smith postulated that to learn dimension words, children must learn three kinds of mappings; between words and objects ("red" for red objects), word–word maps ("red," "blue," etc., are associated with color), and property–property maps ("They are the same color"). Smith argues that early use of relational terms is holistic, but relational terms gradually become organized into dimensions (by about 5 years of age). This enables recognition that "more than" is the opposite of "less than" and recognition of transitivity of relations (e.g. $a > b$ and $b > c \rightarrow a > c$).

Recognition of the role of analogy in cognition and cognitive development increased rapidly in the 1980s. Gentner (1983) provided a workable conceptualization of human analogical reasoning with her theory that analogy is a mapping from a familiar structure, the base, to an unfamiliar structure, the target. The mapping is validated by correspondence between the structures in base and target. One difficulty is that analogical reasoning has sometimes been difficult to produce in the laboratory (Gick & Holyoak, 1983) but it occurs readily in real life (Dunbar, 2001) so this difficulty might be overcome by using more naturalistic procedures. Computational models of analogical mapping (e.g., Falkenhainer, Forbus, & Gentner, 1989; Holyoak & Thagard, 1989; Hummel & Holyoak, 1997) helped to clarify the nature of the process, and its role as a mechanism of cognitive development has been explored (e.g. Halford, 1993). The DORA (Discovery Of Relations by Analogy) model (Doumas, Hummel, & Sandhofer, 2008) has also provided an existence proof for acquisition of structured knowledge by self-supervised learning from examples.

Much of the developmental interest in analogy has centered around the age of attainment (Gentner & Ratterman, 1991; Gentner, Rattermann, Markman, & Kotovsky, 1995; Goswami, 1996; Goswami & Brown, 1989). There is no reason to doubt that simple proportional analogies of the form A is to B as C is to D can be performed by children under 5 years. Indeed, according to complexity analyses by Halford and his collaborators (Halford, 1993; Halford et al., 1998b) they should be possible at around 1.5–2 years. Analogies that require parallel processing of more complex relations are predicted to be consistent with the age norms for that level of relational complexity.

Symbolic Neural Net Models

Neural net models, considered by Westermann, Thomas, and Karmiloff-Smith (chapter 28, this volume), have become one of the most important types of computational models of cognitive development. However questions about the ability of some early models to account for symbolic processes (Fodor & Pylyshyn, 1988; Marcus, 1998a, 1998b; Smolensky, 1988) have given rise to symbolic neural net models (Halford, Wilson, et al., 1994; Hummel & Holyoak, 1997; Shastri & Ajjanagadde, 1993). We will briefly consider two attempts to build symbolic neural net models of cognitive development.

The first is a neural net implementation of the processing complexity theory of Halford et al. (1998b) discussed earlier. It is based on the Structured Tensor Analogical Reasoning (STAR) model of Halford, Wilson, et al. (1994). The essential idea is that the structural properties of higher cognition can be captured by the representation and processing of relations. Representation of a relation entails a symbol for the relation, plus a representation of the related entities. These must be bound together in a way that preserves the truth of the relation. Consider a simple binary relation, such as larger-than. An instance of larger-than, in predicate calculus notation, is larger-than(elephant,mouse). In our model we represent this by having a set of units representing each component, larger-than, elephant, and mouse. Each set of units corresponds to a set of activation values, or vector. The binding is represented by computing the tensor (outer) product of the vectors, producing a 3-dimensional matrix. More complex relations correspond to binding more entities, and therefore to tensor products of higher rank. Thus a binary relation entails binding three entities, the symbol and two arguments, a ternary relation to binding four entities, the symbol and three arguments, and so on. Tensor product nets are shown schematically in figure 27.1, together with the approximate Piagetian stage with which each level of relational complexity is identified in the theory of Halford et al. (1998b).

This model is designed to represent structure with a neural net architecture. Thus the components retain their identity in the compound representation. In the Rank 3 tensor product representing larger(elephant,mouse) the vectors representing larger, elephant, and mouse are retained. Also, any component can be retrieved, given the remaining components, a property that Halford et al. (1998b) call omni-directional access. The relations in a net can be modified online, by changing the relation symbol. This is one of the properties of explicit knowledge defined by Clark and Karmiloff-Smith (1993). The model can handle higher cognitive processes such as analogical reasoning, and mathematical operations. Because the number of neural units, and therefore the computational cost, increases exponentially with complexity of relations, the model provides a natural explanation for the link between processing loads and relational complexity observed by Halford et al. (1998b). On the other hand this model does not have the learning functions that are a major benefit of multilayered net models, such as the balance-scale model of McClelland (1995), and consequently does not handle the emergent properties of these models. Therefore at the present time it appears that symbolic and multilayered net models should be seen as complementary, and the next step forward might depend on hybrids, or on models that capture the properties of both classes of nets.

The model of Smith, Gasser and Sandhofer (1997) simulates children's acquisition of dimensional terms. It employs the three-layered net architecture, but can probably be categorized as a symbolic model because it specifically addresses acquisition of symbolic knowledge. An object with four perceptible attributes is coded in the input layer. There is a separate input that codes the relevant dimension, such as color. There is a further input indicating whether two successive objects are the same or different on the specified dimension. The representations in the hidden layer are copied to a perceptual buffer

Piagetian stage	No. of rank	dimensions	Cognitive processes	Typical tasks	PDP implementation
Preconceptual	1	2	**Unary relations**	**match-to-sample, identity position, integration, category label distinct from category**	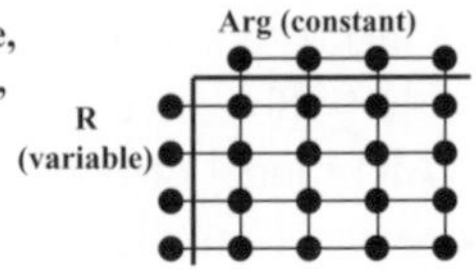 Arg (constant); R (variable)
Intuitive	2	3	**Binary relations, Univariate functions**	**relational match-to sample, A-not-B, complementary categories**	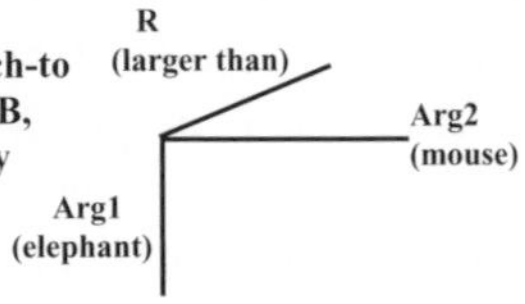 R (larger than); Arg2 (mouse); Arg1 (elephant)
Concrete operational	3	4	**Ternary relations, Binary operations, Bivariate functions**	**transitive inference, hierarchical categories, concept of mind**	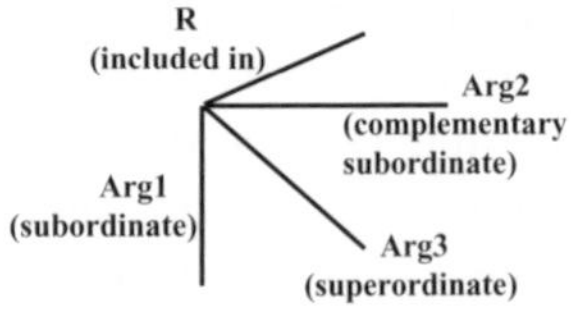 R (included in); Arg2 (complementary subordinate); Arg1 (subordinate); Arg3 (superordinate)
Formal	4	5	**Quaternary relations Compositions of Binary operations**	**proportion, balance-scale**	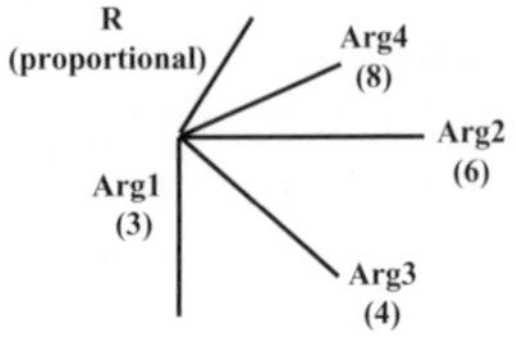 R (proportional); Arg4 (8); Arg2 (6); Arg1 (3); Arg3 (4)

Figure 27.1 Representational ranks

(analogous to the context units in the simple recurrent net; Elman et al., 1996). The net is trained to produce the appropriate dimensional attribute (e.g., red). The training is constrained by property–property maps. If two successive objects are the same on the specified dimension, the output must be the same for both of them. The success of the model tends to support the authors' claim that culturally transmitted information about the sameness of objects on specified dimensions (e.g., "these flowers are the same color") is important for children's acquisition of dimensional terms.

Conclusion

One of the most striking things about research on information-processing approaches to cognitive development is the richness of both empirical and theoretical work in the field.

Another is that information-processing approaches to cognitive development have told us a lot about the nature of the underlying processes in cognitive development. This means that we now have a lot more information about what is happening when a child is performing a task. This yields a lot of insights and offers genuinely new ways of understanding many issues. A third observation is the success with which information-processing conceptions have been linked to neuroscience and to neural net models. While no one would pretend that all problems have been solved in these areas, they certainly offer exciting possibilities for the future. A fourth observation is that we now have genuine process models of the way structured knowledge, that is so vital to cognitive development, is acquired. Fifth, a good deal of common ground has emerged from neo-Piagetian models about what constitutes conceptual complexity in cognition. This yielded a complexity metric, based on the number of related variables in a cognitive representation, that enables tasks to be compared for complexity, and tasks of equivalent complexity to be recognized, independent of domain or methodology. Furthermore it can be applied, not only to cognitive development, but to cognition generally. This is an illustration of the way cognitive development research can contribute to general cognition and cognitive science.

It is always nice to finish with a single principle that captures the essence of what has been learned from an extended body of research. One such principle emerges jointly from cognitive and neuroscience research. This is that with maturation and development, there is an increase in the ability to process complex information. Research that we have reviewed indicates that the anterior prefrontal cortex is specialized for coordination and integration of information, and for processing complex relationships. The anterior prefrontal cortex is also late developing, so we would expect that these functions will improve due to maturation. Basic cognitive functions, including associative learning and many perceptual functions, will be as efficient in infants and young children as in older children and adults. But complex processing, such as occurs in reasoning, as well as in language production and comprehension, is a factor that will become more efficient with age. This improvement will be influenced by both maturation and experience, because experience also contributes to neurocognitive development. However it means that simple conceptions that cognitive development depends on maturation or on learning, are imprecise and misleading. Some functions mature early, whereas complex cognitive functions mature later, and this needs to be taken into account in educational and child-rearing contexts.

References

Anderson, M. (1992). *Intelligence and development: A cognitive theory*. Oxford: Blackwell.

Andrews, G., & Halford, G. S. (1998). Children's ability to make transitive inferences: The importance of premise integration and structural complexity. *Cognitive Development, 13*, 479–513.

Andrews, G., & Halford, G. S. (2002). A cognitive complexity metric applied to cognitive development. *Cognitive Psychology, 45*, 153–219.

Andrews, G., Halford, G. S., Bunch, K. M., Bowden, D., & Jones, T. J. (2003). Theory of mind and relational complexity. *Child Development, 74*, 1435–1458.

Baddeley, A. D. (1990). *Human memory: Theory and practice.* Needham Heights, MA: Allyn & Bacon.

Baddeley, A. D., & Hitch, G. J. (2000). Development of working memory: Should the Pascual-Leone and the Baddeley and Hitch models be merged? *Journal of Experimental Child Psychology, 77*, 128–137.

Bell, M. A. (2001). Brain electrical activity associated with cognitive processing during a looking version of the A-not-B task. *Infancy, 2*, 311–330.

Bell, M. A., & Fox, N. A. (1992). The relations between frontal brain electrical activity and cognitive development during infancy. *Child Development, 63*, 1142–1163.

Bunch, K., Andrews G., & Halford, G. S. (2007). Complexity effects on the children's gambling task. *Cognitive Development, 22*, 376–383.

Bunge, S. A., & Zelazo, P. D. (2006). A brain-based account of the development of rule use in childhood. *Current Directions in Psychological Science, 15*, 118–121.

Breslow, L. (1981). Reevaluation of the literature on the development of transitive inferences. *Psychological Bulletin, 89*, 325–351.

Briars, D., & Siegler, R. S. (1984). A featural analysis of preschoolers' counting knowledge. *Developmental Psychology, 20*, 607–618.

Bryant, P. E., & Trabasso, T. (1971). Transitive inferences and memory in young children. *Nature, 232*, 456–458.

Campbell, R. L., & Bickhard, M. H. (1986). *Knowing levels and developmental stages.* Basel: Karger.

Case, R. (1985). *Intellectual development: Birth to adulthood.* New York: Academic Press.

Case, R. (1992a). *The mind's staircase: Exploring the conceptual underpinnings of children's thought and knowledge.* Hillsdale, NJ: Erlbaum.

Case, R. (1992b). The role of the frontal lobes in the regulation of cognitive development. *Brain and Cognition, 20*, 51–73.

Case, R., Kurland, M., & Goldberg, J. (1982). Operational efficiency and the growth of short-term memory span. *Journal of Experimental Child Psychology, 33*, 386–404.

Case, R., Okamoto, Y., Griffin, S., McKeough, A., Bleiker, C., Henderson, B., & Stephenson, K. M. (1996). The role of central conceptual structures in the development of children's thought. *Monographs of the Society for Research in Child Development, 61* (1–2, Serial No. 246).

Cerella, J., & Hale, S. (1994). The rise and fall in information-processing rates over the life span. *Acta Psychologica, 86*, 109–197.

Chapman, M. (1987). Piaget, attentional capacity, and the functional limitations of formal structure. *Advances in Child Development and Behaviour, 20*, 289–334.

Chapman, M. (1990). Cognitive development and the growth of capacity: Issues in NeoPiagetian theory. In J. T. Enns (Ed.), *The development of attention: Research and theory* (pp. 263–287). Amsterdam: Elsevier.

Chapman, M., & Lindenberger, U. (1989). Concrete operations and attentional capacity. *Journal of Experimental Child Psychology, 47*, 236–258.

Chi, M. T. H. (1978). Knowledge structures and memory development. In R. S. Siegler (Ed.), *Children's thinking: What develops?* (pp. 73–96). Hillsdale, NJ: Erlbaum.

Christoff, K., & Owen, A. M. (2006). Improving reverse neuroimaging inference: Cognitive domain versus cognitive complexity. *Trends in Cognitive Sciences, 10*, 352–353.

Christoff, K., Prabhakaran, V., Dorfman, J., Zhao, Z., Kroger, J., Holyoak, K. J., & Gabrieli, J. D. E. (2001). Rostrolateral prefrontal cortex involvement in relational integration during reasoning. *NeuroImage, 14*, 1136–1149.

Chugani, H. T., & Phelps, M. E. (1986). Maturational changes in cerebral function in infants determined by FDG positron emission tomography. *Science, 231*, 840–843.

Clark, A., & Karmiloff-Smith, A. (1993). The cognizer's innards: A psychological and philosophical perspective on the development of thought. *Mind and Language, 8*, 487–519.

Cowan, N. (1998). What is more explanatory, processing capacity or processing speed? *Behavioral and Brain Sciences, 21*, 835–836.

Cowan, N. (2001). The magical number 4 in short-term memory: A reconsideration of mental storage capacity. *Behavioral and Brain Sciences, 24*(1), 87–114.

Crone, E. A., Wendelken, C., van Leijenhorst, L., Honomichl, R. D., Christoff, K., & Bunge, S. A. (2009). Neurocognitive development of relational reasoning. *Developmental Science, 12*, 55–66.

Davis, H. L., & Pratt, C. (1995). The development of children's theory of mind: The working memory explanation. *Australian Journal of Psychology, 47*, 25–31.

Demetriou, A., Doise, W., & van Lieshout, C. (Eds.) (1998). *Life-span developmental psychology*. Chichester: Wiley.

Demetriou, A., Efklides, A., & Platsidou, M. (1993). The architecture and dynamics of developing mind: Experiential structuralism as a frame for unifying cognitive developmental theories. *Monographs of the Society for Research in Child Development, 58* (5, Serial No. 234).

De Ribaupierre, A., & Bailleux, C. (1994). Developmental change in a spatial task of attentional capacity: An essay toward an integration of two working memory models. *International Journal of Behavioral Development, 17*, 5–35.

De Ribaupierre, A., & Bailleux, C. (2000). The development of working memory: Further note on the comparability of two models of working memory. *Journal of Experimental Child Psychology, 77*, 110–127.

Diamond, A. (1990). The development of neural bases of memory function as indexed by the AB and delayed response tasks in human infants and rhesus monkeys. In A. Diamond (Ed.), *The development of neural bases of higher cortical function* (pp. 267–317). New York: New York Academy of Science Press.

Diamond, A., Zola-Morgan, S., & Squire, L. R. (1989). Successful performance by monkeys with lesions of the hippocampal formation on AB and object retrieval, two tasks that mark developmental changes in human infants. *Behavioral Neuroscience, 103*, 526–537.

Doumas, L. A., Hummel, J. E., & Sandhofer, C. A. (2008). A theory of the discovery and predication of relational concepts. *Psychological Review, 115*, 1–43.

Dunbar, K. (2001). The analogical paradox: Why analogy is so easy in naturalistic settings, yet so difficult in the psychological laboratory. In D. Gentner, K. J. Holyoak, & B. K. Kokinov (Eds.), *The analogical mind: Perspectives from cognitive science*. Cambridge, MA: MIT Press.

Elman, J. L., Bates, E. A., Johnson, M. H., Karmiloff-Smith, A., Parisi, D., & Plunkett, K. (1996). *Rethinking innateness: A connectionist perspective on development*. London: MIT Press.

Falkenhainer, B., Forbus, K. D., & Gentner, D. (1989). The structure-mapping engine: Algorithm and examples. *Artificial Intelligence, 41*, 1–63.

Feldman, J. (2000). Minimization of Boolean complexity in human concept learning. *Nature, 407*(6804), 630–632.

Fischer, K. W. (1980). A theory of cognitive development: The control and construction of hierarchies of skills. *Psychological Review, 87*, 477–531.

Fischer, K. W., & Bidell, T. R. (1998). Dynamic development of psychological structures in action and thought. In W. Damon & R. M. Lerner (Eds.), *Handbook of child psychology: Vol. 1. Theoretical models of human development* (5th ed., pp. 467–561). New York: Wiley.

Fischer, K. W., & Bidell, T. R. (2006). Dynamic development of action and thought. In W. Damon & R. M. Lerner (Eds.), *Handbook of child psychology: Vol. 1. Theoretical models of human development* (6th ed., pp. 313–399). New York: Wiley.

Fischer, K. W., & Rose, S. P. (1996). Dynamic growth cycles of brain and cognitive development. In R. W. Thatcher, G. R. Lyon, J. Rumsey, & N. Kresnegor (Eds.), *Developmental neuroimaging: Mapping the development of brain and behavior* (pp. 263–283). San Diego: Academic Press.

Fischer, K. W., Stewart, J., & Stein, Z. (2008). Process and skill: Analysing dynamic structure of growth. In F. Riffert & H-J. Sander (Eds.), *Researching with Whitehead: System and adventure* (pp. 327–367). Munich: Verlag Karl Alber.

Fodor, J. A. (1983). *Modularity of mind: An essay on faculty psychology*. Cambridge, MA: MIT Press.

Fodor, J. A., & Pylyshyn, Z. W. (1988). Connectionism and cognitive architecture: A critical analysis. *Cognition, 28*, 3–71.

Frye, D., Zelazo, P. D., & Palfai, T. (1995). Theory of mind and rule-based reasoning. *Cognitive Development, 10*, 483–527.

Gelman, R. (1982). Accessing one-to-one correspondence: Still another paper about conservation. *British Journal of Psychology, 73*, 209–220.

Gentner, D. (1983). Structure-mapping: A theoretical framework for analogy. *Cognitive Science, 7*, 155–170.

Gentner, D., & Ratterman, M. J. (1991). Language and the career of similarity. In S. A. Gelman & J. P. Byrnes (Eds.), *Perspectives on language and thought: Interrelations in development.* Cambridge: Cambridge University Press.

Gentner, D., Rattermann, M. J., Markman, A., & Kotovsky, L. (1995). Two forces in the development of relational similarity. In T. Simon & G. S. Halford (Eds.), *Developing cognitive competence: New approaches to process modeling* (pp. 263–313). Hillsdale, NJ: Erlbaum.

Gick, M. L., & Holyoak, K. J. (1983). Schema induction and analogical transfer. *Cognitive Psychology, 15*, 1–38.

Gogtay, N., Giedd, J. N., Lusk, L., Hayashi, K. M., Greenstein, P., Vaituzis, A. C., … Thompson, P. M. (2004). Dynamic mapping of human cortical development during childhood through early adulthood. *Proceedings of the National Academy of Sciences of the United States of America, 101*, 8174–8179.

Gordon, A. C. L., & Olson, D. R. (1998). The relation between acquisition of a theory of mind and the capacity to hold in mind. *Journal of Experimental Child Psychology, 68*, 70–83.

Goswami, U. (1996). Analogical reasoning and cognitive development. In H. Reese (Ed.), *Advances in child development and behavior* (Vol. 26, pp. 91–138). San Diego: Academic Press.

Goswami, U., & Brown, A. L. (1989). Melting chocolate and melting snowmen: Analogical reasoning and causal relations. *Cognition, 35*, 69–95.

Halford, G. S. (1993). *Children's understanding: The development of mental models.* Hillsdale, NJ: Erlbaum.

Halford, G. S., & Andrews, G. (2004). The development of deductive reasoning: How important is complexity? *Thinking and Reasoning, 10*, 123–145.

Halford, G. S., & Andrews, G. (2007). Domain general processes in higher cognition: Analogical reasoning, schema induction and capacity limitations. In M. J. Roberts (Ed.), *Integrating the mind.* (pp. 302–331). Hove, UK: Psychology Press.

Halford, G. S., Andrews, G., Dalton, C., Boag, C., & Zielinski, T. (2002). Young children's performance on the balance scale: The influence of relational complexity. *Journal of Experimental Child Psychology, 81*, 417–445.

Halford, G. S., Andrews, G., & Jensen, I. (2002). Integration of category induction and hierarchical classification: One paradigm at two levels of complexity. *Journal of Cognition and Development, 3*(2), 143–177.

Halford, G. S., Baker R., McCredden, J. E., & Bain, J. D. (2005). How many variables can humans process? *Psychological Science, 16*(1), 70–76.

Halford, G. S., Bunch, K., & McCredden, J. E. (2007). Problem decomposability as a factor in complexity of the Dimensional Change Card Sort Task. *Cognitive Development, 22*, 384–391.

Halford, G. S., Cowan, N., & Andrews, G. (2007). Separating cognitive capacity from knowledge: A new hypothesis. *Trends in Cognitive Sciences, 11*, 237–242.

Halford, G. S., Maybery, M. T., O'Hare, A. W., & Grant, P. (1994). The development of memory and processing capacity. *Child Development, 65*, 1338–1356.

Halford, G. S., Wilson, W. H., Guo, J., Gayler, R. W., Wiles, J., & Stewart, J. E. M. (1994). Connectionist implications for processing capacity limitations in analogies. In K. J. Holyoak & J. Barnden (Eds.), *Advances in connectionist and neural computation theory: Vol. 2. Analogical connections* (pp. 363–415). Norwood, NJ: Ablex.

Halford, G. S., Wilson, W. H., & Phillips, S. (1998a). Authors' response: Relational complexity metric is effective when assessments are based on actual cognitive processes. *Behavioral and Brain Sciences, 21*, 848–864.

Halford, G. S., Wilson, W. H., & Phillips, S. (1998b). Processing capacity defined by relational complexity: Implications for comparative, developmental, and cognitive psychology. *Behavioral and Brain Sciences, 21*, 803–831.

Hodkin, B. (1987). Performance model analysis in class inclusion: An illustration with two language conditions. *Developmental Psychology, 23*, 683–689.

Holyoak, K. J., & Thagard, P. (1989). Analogical mapping by constraint satisfaction. *Cognitive Science, 13*, 295–355.

Hummel, J. E., & Holyoak, K. J. (1997). Distributed representations of structure: A theory of analogical access and mapping. *Psychological Review, 104*, 427–466.

Huttenlocher, P. R., & Dabholkar, A. S. (1997). Regional differences in synaptogenesis in human cerebral cortex. *The Journal of Comparative Neurology, 387*, 167–178.

Im-Bolter, N., Johnson, J., & Pascual-Leone, J. (2006). Processing limitations in children with specific language impairment: The role of executive function. *Child Development, 77*, 1822–1841.

Johnson, J., Im-Bolter, N., & Pascual-Leone, J. (2003). Development of mental attention in gifted and mainstream children: The role of mental capacity, inhibition, and speed of processing. *Child Development, 74*, 1594–1614.

Kail, R. (1986). Sources of age differences in speed of processing. *Child Development, 57*, 969–987.

Kail, R. (1988a). Developmental functions for speeds of cognitive processes. *Journal of Experimental Child Psychology, 45*, 339–364.

Kail, R. (1988b). Reply to Sigler, Nusbaum, and Chalip. *Child Development, 59*, 1154–1157.

Kail, R. (1990). *More evidence for a common, central constraint on speed of processing*. Amsterdam: North Holland.

Kail, R. (1991). Controlled and automatic processing during mental rotation. *Journal of Experimental Child Psychology, 51*, 337–347.

Kail, R. (1997). Phonological skill and articulation time independently contribute to the development of memory span. *Journal of Experimental Child Psychology, 67*, 57–68.

Kail, R. (1998). Speed of information processing in patients with multiple sclerosis. *Journal of Clinical and Experimental Neuropsychology, 20*, 98–106.

Kail, R. (2000). Speed of information processing: Developmental change and links to intelligence. *Journal of School Psychology, 38*, 51–61.

Kail, R., & Hall, L. K. (1999). Sources of developmental change in children's word-problem performance. *Journal of Educational Psychology, 91*, 660–668.

Kail, R., & Park, Y. (1992). Global developmental change in processing time. *Merrill-Palmer Quarterly, 38*, 525–541.

Kail, R., & Salthouse, T. A. (1994). Processing speed as a mental capacity. *Acta Psychologica, 86*, 199–225.

Karmiloff-Smith, A. (1992). *Beyond modularity: A developmental perspective on cognitive science*. Cambridge, MA: MIT Press.

Karmiloff-Smith, A. (1994). Précis of "Beyond modularity: A developmental perspective on cognitive science." *Behavioral and Brain Sciences, 17*, 693–745.

Keenan, T., Olson, D. R., & Marini, Z. (1998). Working memory and children's developing understanding of mind. *Australian Journal of Psychology, 50*, 76–82.

Kemps, E., De Rammelaere, S., & Desmet, T. (2000). The development of working memory: Exploring the complementarity of two models. *Journal of Experimental Child Psychology, 77*, 89–109.

Kerr, A., & Zelazo, P. D. (2004). Development of "hot" executive function: The children's gambling task. *Brain and Cognition, 55*, 148–157.

Klahr, D., & Wallace, J. G. (1976). *Cognitive development: An information processing view*. Hillsdale, NJ: Erlbaum.

Kroger, J. K., Sabb, F. W., Fales, C. L., Bookheimer, S. Y., Cohen, M. S., & Holyoak, K. J. (2002). Recruitment of anterior dorsolateral prefrontal cortex in human reasoning: A parametric study of relational complexity. *Cerebral Cortex, 12*, 477–485.

Luck, S. J., & Vogel, E. K. (1997). The capacity of visual working memory for features and conjunctions. *Nature, 390*(6657), 279–281.

Marcus, G. F. (1998a). Can connectionism save constructivism? *Cognition, 66*, 153–182.

Marcus, G. F. (1998b). Rethinking eliminative connectionism. *Cognitive Psychology, 37*, 243–282.

Markovits, H., Dumas, C., & Malfait, N. (1995). Understanding transitivity of a spatial relationship: A developmental analysis. *Journal of Experimental Child Psychology, 59*, 124–141.

McClelland, J. L. (1995). A connectionist perspective on knowledge and development. In T. Simon & G. S. Halford (Eds.), *Developing cognitive competence: New approaches to cognitive modeling* (pp. 157–204). Hillsdale, NJ: Erlbaum.

McGarrigle, J., Grieve, R., & Hughes, M. (1978). Interpreting inclusion: A contribution to the study of the child's cognitive and linguistic development. *Journal of Experimental Child Psychology, 26*, 528–550.

McLaughlin, G. H. (1963). Psycho-logic: A possible alternative to Piaget's formulation. *British Journal of Educational Psychology, 33*, 61–67.

Nelson, C. A., III, Thomas, K. M., & de Haan, M. (2006). Neural bases of cognitive development. In D. Kuhn & R. Siegler (Eds.), *Handbook of child psychology: Vol. 2. Cognition, perception, and language* (6th ed., pp. 3–57). Hoboken, NJ: Wiley.

Nettelbeck, T. (1987). *Inspection time and intelligence*. Norwood, NJ: Ablex.

Newell, A. (1990). *Unified theories of cognition*. Cambridge, MA: Harvard University Press.

Overman, W. H., Bachevalier, J., Schuhmann, E., & Ryan, P. (1996). Cognitive gender differences in very young children parallel biologically based cognitive gender differences in monkeys. *Behavioural Neuroscience, 110*, 673–684.

Pascual-Leone, J. A. (1970). A mathematical model for the transition rule in Piaget's developmental stages. *Acta Psychologica, 32*, 301–345.

Pascual-Leone, J. A. (2000). Reflections on working memory: Are the two models complementary? *Journal of Experimental Child Psychology, 77*, 138–154.

Pascual-Leone, J. A., & Smith, J. (1969). The encoding and decoding of symbols by children: A new experimental paradigm and a neo-Piagetian model. *Journal of Experimental Child Psychology, 8*, 328–355.

Paterson, S. J., Heim, S., Friedman, J. T., Choudhury, N., & Benasich, A. A. (2006). Development of structure and function in the infant brain: Implications for cognition, language and social behaviour. *Neuroscience and Biobehavioral Reviews, 30*, 1087–1105.

Pears, R., & Bryant, P. (1990). Transitive inferences by young children about spatial position. *British Journal of Psychology, 81*, 497–510.

Phillips, S., Halford, G. S., & Wilson, W. H. (1995). *The processing of associations versus the processing of relations and symbols: A systematic comparison.* Paper presented at the Proceedings of the Seventeenth Annual Conference of the Cognitive Science Society, Pittsburgh, PA.

Piaget, J. (1950). *The psychology of intelligence*, trans. M. Piercy & D. E. Berlyne. London: Routledge & Kegan Paul. Originally published 1947.

Quartz, S. R., & Sejnowski, T. J. (1997). The neural basis of cognitive development: A constructivist manifesto. *Behavioral and Brain Sciences, 20*, 537–596.

Ramnani, N., & Owen, A. M. (2004). Anterior prefrontal cortex: Insights into function from anatomy and neuroimaging. *Nature Reviews Neuroscience, 5*, 184–194.

Ridderinkhof, K. R., & van der Molen, M. W. (1997). Mental resources, processing speed, and inhibitory control: A developmental perspective. *Biological Psychology, 45*, 241–261.

Salthouse, T. A. (1996). The processing-speed theory of adult age differences in cognition. *Psychological Review, 103*, 403–428.

Shastri, L., & Ajjanagadde, V. (1993). From simple associations to systematic reasoning: A connectionist representation of rules, variables, and dynamic bindings using temporal synchrony. *Behavioral and Brain Sciences, 16*, 417–494.

Shepard, R. N., Hovland, C. I., & Jenkins, H. M. (1961). Learning and memorization of classifications. *Psychological Monographs, 75*(13) (Whole No. 517), 42.

Siegel, L. S., McCabe, A. E., Brand, J., & Matthews, J. (1978). Evidence for the understanding of class inclusion in preschool children: Linguistic factors and training effects. *Child Development, 49*, 688–693.

Siegler, R. S. (1981). Developmental sequences within and between concepts. *Monographs of the Society for Research in Child Development, 46*, 1–84.

Siegler, R. S. (1999). Strategic development. *Trends in Cognitive Science, 3*(11), 430–435.

Siegler, R. S., & Chen, Z. (1998). Developmental differences in rule learning: A microgenetic analysis. *Cognitive Psychology, 36*(3), 273–310.

Siegler, R. S., & Jenkins, E. A. (1989). *How children discover new strategies.* Hillsdale, NJ: Erlbaum.

Siegler, R. S., & Shipley, C. (1995). Variation, selection, and cognitive change. In T. Simon & G. S. Halford (Eds.), *Developing cognitive competence: New approaches to process modeling* (pp. 31–76). Hillsdale, NJ: Erlbaum.

Siegler, R. S., & Shrager, J. (1984). *Strategy choices in addition and subtraction: How do children know what to do?* Hillsdale, NJ: Erlbaum.

Simon, T., & Klahr, D. (1995). A computational theory of children's learning about number conservation. In T. Simon & G. S. Halford (Eds.), *Developing cognitive competence: New approaches to process modeling* (pp. 315–353). Hillsdale, NJ: Erlbaum.

Smith, L. B., Gasser, M., & Sandhofer, C. M. (1997) Learning to talk about the properties of objects: A network model of the development of dimensions. In R. L. Goldstone, P. G. Schyns, & D. L. Medin (Eds.), *Perceptual learning: The psychology of learning and motivation* (Vol. 36, pp. 219–255). San Diego: Academic Press.

Smith, R., Keramatian, K., & Christoff, K. (2007). Localising the rostrolateral prefrontal cortex at the individual level. *NeuroImage, 36*, 1387–1396.

Smolensky, P. (1988). On the proper treatment of connectionism. *Behavioral and Brain Sciences, 11*, 1–74.

Stigler, J. W., Nusbaum, H. C., & Chalip, L. (1988). Developmental changes in speed of processing: Central limiting mechanism of skill transfer? *Child Development, 59*, 1144–1153.

Thatcher, R. W. (1994). Cyclic cortical reorganization: Origins of human cognitive development. In G. Dawson & K. W. Fischer (Eds.), *Human Behavior and the Developing Brain* (pp. 232–266). New York: Guilford Press.

Thayer, E. S., & Collyer, C. E. (1978). The development of transitive inference: A review of recent approaches. *Psychological Bulletin, 85*, 1327–1343.

Thelen, E., & Smith, L. B. (2006). Dynamic systems theories. In W. Damon & R. M. Lerner (Ed.), *Handbook of child psychology: Vol. 1. Theoretical models of human development* (6th ed.). Hoboken, NJ: Wiley.

Van der Maas, H. L. J., & Molenaar, P. C. M. (1992). Stagewise cognitive development: An application of catastrophe theory. *Psychological Review, 99*, 395–417.

Van Geert, P. (1993). A dynamic systems model of cognitive growth: Competition and support under limited resource conditions. In L. Smith & E. Thelen (Eds.), *A dynamic systems approach to development: Applications* (pp. 265–331). Cambridge, MA: MIT Press.

Waltz, J. A., Knowlton, B. J., Holyoak, K. J., Boone, K. B., Mishkin, F. S., de Menezes Santos, M., Thomas, C. R., & Miller, B. L. (1999). A system for relational reasoning in human prefrontal cortex. *Psychological Science, 10*, 119–125.

Zelazo, P. D. (2006). The Dimensional Change Card Sort (DCCS): A method of assessing executive function in children. *Nature Protocols, 1*, 297–301.

Zelazo, P. D., Jacques, S., Burack, J. A., & Frye, D. (2002). The relation between theory of mind and rule use: Evidence from persons with autism-spectrum disorders. *Infant and Child Development, 11*, 171–195.

Zelazo, P. D., Müller, U., Frye, D., & Marcovitch, S. (2003). The development of executive function. *Monographs of the Society for Research in Child Development, 68*(3), 1–155.

CHAPTER TWENTY-EIGHT

Neuroconstructivism

Gert Westermann, Michael S. C. Thomas, and Annette Karmiloff-Smith

Introduction

In this chapter, we outline the neuroconstructivist framework for studying cognitive development. Neuroconstructivism builds on the Piagetian view that development constitutes a progressive elaboration in the complexity of mental representations via experience-dependent processes. However, neuroconstructivism is also informed by recent theories of functional brain development, under the view that the character of cognition will be shaped by the physical system that implements it. First, we begin by outlining the main premises of the neuroconstructivist framework. Second, we describe one of the emerging methodologies on which neuroconstructivism relies – the modeling of development in complex neurocomputational systems. Third, we turn to consider atypical development, and the way it can shed light on the constraints shaping the typical developmental process. Fourth, we describe a new empirical methodology that has been designed to analyze the primary data on which neuroconstructivism relies: developmental trajectories. Finally, we review recent findings on genetic influences on brain development, and indicate how these may shape our conceptions of cognition.

The Neuroconstructivist Framework

Perhaps surprisingly the bulk of existing research in developmental psychology is not strictly developmental at all. Instead it is concerned with static snapshots of the abilities of infants and children at different ages. For example, we know that in language develop-

This work was funded by ESRC grant RES-000-22-3394, EC grant 0209088 (NEST) and UK MRC grant G0300188. Thanks to Frank Baughman for his help in the preparation of Figure 28.2.

ment, 6-month-old infants can discriminate between all speech sounds, but by 12 months of age they have lost the ability to discriminate between non-native sounds (Werker & Tees, 1984). In object categorization we know that 3- to 4-month-old infants are capable of forming perceptual categories on the basis of animal pictures, but only by 10 months are they able to encode the correlations between object features to constrain categories (Younger & Cohen, 1986). And Piaget showed that children younger than around 7 years, but not at 10 years, lack the concept of conservation; that is, they do not understand that the physical characteristics of an object or substance remain the same even when its appearance changes (Piaget, 1955). However, the perhaps biggest challenge facing developmental psychologists is to link these individual observations into a developmental trajectory and to explain the causes of developmental change that allow the child to progress from one set of abilities to another, more complex, one. A recent attempt to provide such a developmental framework is neuroconstructivism (Mareschal, Johnson, et al., 2007; Westermann et al., 2007).

The neuroconstructivist approach characterizes development as a trajectory that is shaped by multiple interacting biological and environmental constraints. The central aspect of understanding cognitive development in this framework is the explanation of how these constraints affect the development of the neural networks of the brain that give rise to progressively more complex mental representations. Brain and cognitive development are linked by characterizing mental representations as neural activation patterns that are realized in the developing neural network of the brain. By considering constraints at all levels from the gene to the social environment, neuroconstructivism draws on, and integrates, different views of brain and cognitive development such as (a) probabilistic epigenesis which emphasizes the interactions between experience and gene expression (Gottlieb, 2007), (b) neural constructivism which focuses on the experience-dependent elaboration of neural networks in the brain (Purves, 1994; Quartz & Sejnowski, 1997), (c) the "interactive specialization" view of brain development which focuses on the mutually constraining interactions of different brain regions in shaping the developing brain (Johnson, 2001), (d) embodiment views that emphasize the importance of the body in cognitive development and processing (Clark, 1999; Smith, 2005), (e) Piaget's constructivist approach to development that stresses the proactive acquisition of knowledge by the child, and (f) approaches highlighting the role of the evolving social environment for the developing child.

The neuroconstructivist approach has in part been motivated by advances in infancy research that allow for the investigation of brain and cognitive development in parallel (Johnson, 1997; Nelson & Luciana, 2001). First, in the past 15 years our ability to investigate the developing brain has progressed dramatically through the application of sophisticated imaging methods such as functional MRI, event-related potential (ERP), magnetoencephalography, and near infra-red spectroscopy to infancy research. Second, new experimental methods such as preferential looking, head-turn paradigms and eye tracking have been developed and refined to study the abilities of even very young infants in a range of behavioral domains. Third, computational modeling has enabled the development and testing of brain-inspired models of cognitive behavior in which the effect of changed constraints on cognitive outcomes can be investigated. And finally, great progress has been made in characterizing gene–environment interactions in development.

Acknowledging the close link between brain and cognitive development has important implications pertaining to the study of cognitive development. Perhaps most importantly, neuroconstructivism rejects the widely accepted separation of levels of description proposed by Marr (Marr, 1982). Marr argued that a process can be described and analyzed independently on three different levels: the computational, algorithmic, and implementational levels. This widely accepted approach was inspired by the computer metaphor of the mind which separates between the "software" of mental processes and the underlying "hardware" of the brain, and it argued that the nature of mental processes could be studied without regard to the nature of its implementation. However, the neuroconstructivist approach is incompatible with this assumption. This is because the changing brain constrains the possible mental representations (neural activation patterns), but at the same time through the mechanisms of experience-dependent brain development, neural activity itself changes the underlying brain structures. In the language of the computer metaphor, the hardware constrains the software, but the software changes the underlying hardware. This interdependency between levels makes it clear that hardware and software cannot be studied independently from one another. It also means that, despite highlighting the importance of brain development for cognitive development, neuroconstructivism does not advocate a reductionist viewpoint in which cognitive change should be explained solely on the basis of neural adaptation. Instead, neuroconstructivism argues for consistency between levels of description and an acknowledgement that processes described best at one level can change those at a different level and vice versa.

A second implication of the neuroconstructivist viewpoint is that development, adult processing, and age-related decline can in principle be accounted for within a single framework by characterizing the variations in constraints that operate at different stages of life. Likewise, in the neuroconstructivist framework atypical development can be explained as arising from a set of altered constraints that push development off its normal track (Karmiloff-Smith, 1998). We will return to this point below.

Sources of Constraints in Neuroconstructivist Development

In this section we describe the different levels of constraints that shape development and we define a common set of developmental mechanisms and principles that operate across all levels.

Genes

In the past decade the view of a genetic blueprint for development has been radically changed. This traditional view postulated a one-directional chain from gene (DNA) to RNA transcription to protein structures. Development was seen as the progressive unfolding of the information in the genome. In contrast, more recent work has found many instances of gene–environment interactions, recognizing that the expression of genes is often subject to environmental and behavioral influences (Lickliter & Honeycutt, 2003; Rutter, 2007). This probabilistic epigenetic view of development (Gottlieb, 2007) emphasizes that gene expression is not strictly preprogrammed but is regulated by signals from the internal and external environment, and that development is therefore subject to bidirectional interactions between genes, neural activity, and the physical and social environments of the developing child. For example, a longitudinal study of the effect of life stress on depression (Caspi et al., 2003) revealed that although genetic factors affected the susceptibility to depressive symptoms, this effect was modulated by stressful life experiences earlier in life. Another recent study (Wiebe et al., 2009) reported interactions between genotype and prenatal exposure to smoking in preschoolers on tasks requiring executive control: those children with a particular genotype performed poorly in these tests only if they also had been exposed prenatally to tobacco. With reference to the nature–nurture debate these results therefore suggest that development proceeds through interactions between genes and the environment that are so closely linked that an attempt to quantify either contribution makes no sense (Karmiloff-Smith, 2006). We return to epigenetic approaches to explaining atypical development below.

Encellment (neural constructivism)

The development of a neuron is constrained by its cellular environment throughout development. Even at early stages of fetal development the way in which an individual cell develops is influenced by molecular interactions with its neighboring cells. At later stages in development, neural activity, generated spontaneously or through sensory stimulation, can affect the functional and structural development of neural networks in various ways (Butz, Wörgötter, & van Ooyen, 2009; Quartz, 1999). Neural activity can guide the outgrowth and retraction of neural axons and dendrites, leading to addition or loss of synaptic connections between neurons and to synaptic rewiring, modifying the connection patterns between neurons. These mechanisms can act rapidly with parallel progressive and regressive events (Hua & Smith, 2004). Together they lead to the experience-dependent elaboration and stabilization of functional neural networks (Quartz & Sejnowski, 1997). Evidence for the role of experience on neural development has come, among others, from studies in which rats were reared in environments of different complexities (Rosenzweig & Bennett, 1996), and this work has led to a wider research effort to identify the neural consequences of environmental enrichment (Sale, Berardi, & Maffei, 2009; van Praag, Kempermann, & Gage, 2000). In these studies it was reliably shown that the brains of rats growing up in stimulating environments with other rats, toys, and opportunities for physical exercise, had markedly increased cortical weight and thickness, more dendritic arborization, and a higher number and size of synapses. Furthermore, these animals showed increased hippocampal synaptogenesis and less age-related cell death. These structural changes went hand in hand with increased cognitive function, improved learning and memory, and reduced age-related cognitive decline. Some of the observed changes were associated with altered gene expression, pointing further towards a role of gene–environment interactions in experience-dependent brain development.

From a neuroconstructivist perspective these mechanisms are important because they indicate that experiences can alter the neural networks that are in place to support the processing of these experiences. The nature of mental representations, realized through neural activation patterns, is constrained by the structure of the neural networks supporting them. The fact that these activation patterns can in turn themselves modulate the structure of these networks provides a mechanism by which progressively more complex representations can be built onto simpler ones by the gradual adaptation of the constraints (neural structures) to the experiences (neural activation patterns).

Embrainment (interactive specialization)

As individual neurons are linked to other neurons affecting their development, so entire functional brain regions develop in a network with other regions through a process of interactive specialization (Johnson, 2001). This view of brain development is different from the more traditional modular view which focuses on the development of encapsulated functional brain regions in isolation. It is supported by functional neuroimaging research showing that the functional specialization of brain regions is highly context sensitive and depends on interactions with other brain regions through feedback processes and top-down modulation (Friston & Price, 2001). This process becomes most evident in brain organization in people who lack one sensory modality. For example, in individuals who have been blind from an early age, the brain area that is the primary visual cortex in seeing people is recruited for the tactile modality instead, i.e., Braille reading (Sadato et al., 1996). Interfering with normal processing in this area through transcranial magnetic stimulation (TMS) affects tactile identification of Braille letters in blind but not in seeing people who instead display impaired visual processing when stimulated in this area (Cohen et al., 1997). It therefore appears that the functional development of cortical regions is strongly constrained by available sensory inputs and that the final organization of the cortex is an outcome of interactive processes such as competition for space.

Embodiment

The fact that the brain is embedded in a body has a profound impact on the constraints on cognitive development. On the one hand the body develops in parallel with cognitive abilities and serves to change the information available to the child. In this way the developing body can serve as an information filter to the brain. For example, during the first months of life visual acuity is low, leading to less detailed visual input than in the mature visual system. Likewise, the infant's ability to manipulate her environment develops progressively as she moves from lying to sitting, reaching and grasping, crawling and walking, allowing her to actively generate new inputs to her sensory systems with increased sophistication. It has been speculated that the gradual increase in complexity of sensory inputs might be beneficial to the developing child (Newport, 1990; Turkewitz & Kenny, 1985). According to this "less is more" hypothesis, initially only the coarser aspects of the environment are processed and more detail is added gradually, supporting the development of progressively more complex mental representations while protecting the immature mind from being overloaded with irrelevant detail too early.

On the other hand, the body also serves to constrain the mental computations necessary to solve a problem. For example, the structure of the skeleton, muscles, tendons, and ligaments, together with continuous proprioceptive feedback, affords only certain movement trajectories in reaching for an object, thus greatly simplifying the computations that are necessary to execute that movement.

The embodiment view highlights that proactive exploration and manipulation of the environment are an essential part of cognitive development. The child does not passively absorb information but actively generates and selects the information from which to learn. This view also suggests that the classic view of cognition – the mind receiving rich representations of the external world, operating offline on these representations, and generating outputs – neglects real-time interactions and dynamical loops between body, brain, and environment (Kleim, Vij, Ballard, & Greenough, 1997).

Ensocialment

The final constraint in the neuroconstructivist framework is the social environment in which a child develops. For example, it has long been acknowledged that the contingent timing of interactions between a mother and child can have a profound effect on the development of secure attachment, the expression of emotions, as well as social and cognitive development (reviewed in Harrist & Waugh, 2002). By contrast, an atypical social environment – for example early traumatic experiences such as death of a parent, maternal depression, child abuse, or neglect – can have severe adverse effects on the neural and behavioral development of the infant (Cirulli, Berry, & Alleva, 2003; Kaufman, Plotsky, Nemeroff, & Charney, 2000; Murray, 1992).

Common principles

The neuroconstructivist framework identifies a number of common principles and mechanisms that operate across all levels of analysis and shape the development of neural structures and, thus, mental representations. The main principle is *context dependence*. On all levels, the constraints that shape the developing neural system establish a context that affects the specific outcome of development. This is true for the cellular environment of the developing neuron, for interacting brain regions, and for the specific details of the biological and social environment of the child. A specific context is realized through the processes of *competition, cooperation*, *chronotopy*, and *proactivity*. Competition leads to the specialization of components in a system, allowing for the development of more complex representations. Likewise, cooperation leads to the integration between subcomponents and for existing knowledge to be re-used at higher levels. Chronotopy refers to the temporal aspect of development: events occur at a point in time that is defined by a temporal context, such as sequences of gene expression, or adaptive plasticity occurring at different times in different parts of the developing system. Development relies on proactivity in selecting information from the environment.

Together, these mechanisms lead to the *progressive specialization* of the learning system. Some neural circuits, once wired, may be hard to alter. Likewise, cognitive function becomes more entrenched and committed to a specific function, possibly becoming less sensitive to inputs outside its range (Scott, Pascalis, & Nelson, 2007).

These constraints and mechanisms result in a learning trajectory that at each point in time is determined by the immediate demands of the environment instead of converging towards an adult goal state. This local adaptation can often be achieved by small adaptations of the existing mental representations, resulting in *partial representations*, e.g., for objects, that are fragmented and distributed across a range of brain regions. Such distributed, modality-specific representations have recently become the focus of investigation in adults (Barsalou, Simmons, Barbey, & Wilson, 2003; Pulvermüller, 2001).

Neuroconstructivism and Computational Modeling

Characterizing development as the outcome of local changes in response to multiple interacting constraints, and linking neural and cognitive development, lends itself to specification through computational modeling, particularly the connectionist approach to modeling cognitive development (Elman et al., 1996; Mareschal, Sirois, Westermann, & Johnson, 2007; Quinlan, 2003; Spencer, Thomas, & McClelland, 2009). Connectionist models are computational systems loosely based on the principles of neural information processing. As such they are placed on a level of description above biological neural networks but aim to explain behavior on the basis of the same style of computations as the brain. Moreover, connectionist models have the ability to learn from data and are therefore relevant for explaining the mechanisms underlying behavioral change in cognitive development.

A connectionist model consists of a large number of interconnected units that are idealized simplifications of biological neurons (although it should be noted that modelers do not assume that an artificial neuron in any sense stands for a biological neuron). Typically, each unit receives excitatory or inhibitory inputs from other neurons through weighted connections, sums up this activation, and, if this activation exceeds a threshold, becomes active itself. Often these units are arranged in layers (see figure 28.1). In many models activation thus flows from an input layer that receives input from the environment, to internal layers of the network and on to an output layer that generates a response that is visible to the environment. There are different manners in which connectionist models learn, but learning nearly always proceeds by adjusting the strengths of the connections between the units. One of the most common learning principles is *backpropagation of error* (Rumelhart, Hinton, & Williams, 1986). In this *supervised* learning paradigm, activation flows through a layered network in response to an input, resulting in a pattern of activation over the units of the output layer. In supervised learning there is a teaching signal corresponding to the desired output for a specific input. This teaching signal can be construed as explicit feedback from a parent, or as the child comparing a prediction with an actual subsequent experience. The difference between the output that is generated by the network and the desired output is computed as the network error. This error is then used to strengthen or weaken the connection weights in order to change the flow of activation in such a way that on presentation of the same input, the network output will match the desired output more closely. Since a network is usually trained on a large number of data and each weight change is very small, there is pressure on the model to

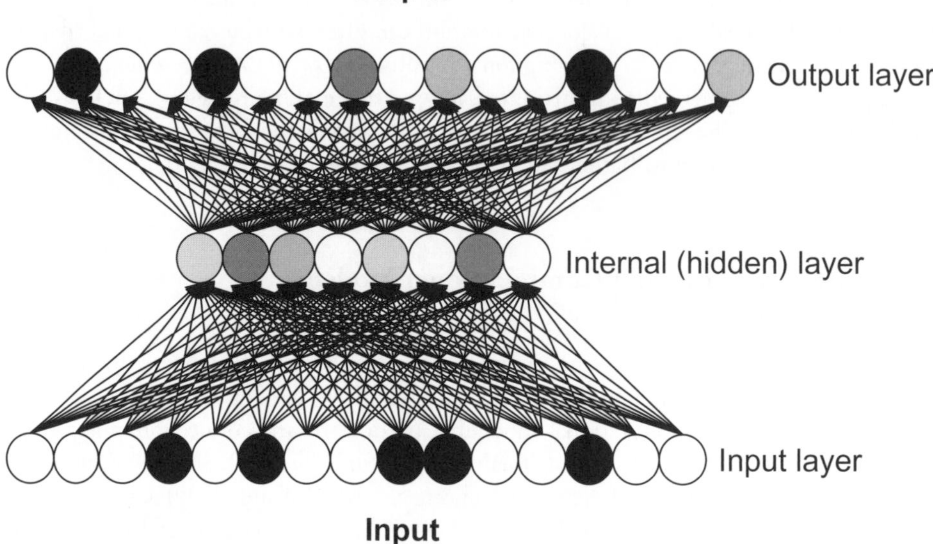

Figure 28.1 A typical connectionist model with three layers. The input layer receives stimulation from the environment. The resulting activation of the input units is propagated to hidden and output units through weighted interconnections. The output layer produces a response visible in the environment. Different grey scales indicate the activation levels of the units

develop a weight pattern that produces the correct output for all inputs. This pressure leads the model to extract generalizations from the data, which often allows it to produce meaningful outputs for previously unseen stimuli.

Another commonly used type of connectionist model is based on *unsupervised* learning. In this paradigm, output units are often arranged in the form of a map (such as in the *Kohonen feature map*) (Kohonen, 1982), and the model learns to cluster input stimuli on this map on the basis of their similarities. In these models there is no teaching signal because the model's task is to make sense of the input data merely based on the structure of these data. Unsupervised models are attractive because they tend to form topographic maps like those found in many parts of the cortex. In self-organizing topographic feature maps, the similarity relationships from a high-dimensional environment (such as the visual world) are preserved on the 2-dimensional mapping in that similar items occupy nearby positions on the map. Their closeness to cortical maps has led some researchers to claim a higher biological plausibility for unsupervised than for supervised models (e.g., Li, 2003). However, as clearly not all learning is unsupervised, both supervised and unsupervised models have their place in the modeling of cognitive development.

The validity of a computational model of development, that is, its ability to explain the mechanisms underlying cognitive change, can be assessed in different ways. Where developmental change is assessed in laboratory studies, the model can likewise be exposed to experimental situations in which stimuli are presented in a controlled fashion. An example of this approach has been the modeling of the development of infant categorization between 4 and 10 months of age. In experimental studies using the preferential-looking paradigm, Younger and Cohen (1986) found that 4-month-old infants were able to form categories on the basis of the perceptual features of cartoon animals. When 10-month-olds were shown the same animal pictures they categorized them in different ways, indicating that they, but not the 4-month-olds, were sensitive to the correlational structure between object features. This transition from feature-based to correlation-based category formation was modeled in a connectionist system that was exposed to encodings of the same stimuli that the infants had seen (Westermann & Mareschal, 2004). By gradually changing the function by which network units integrate their incoming activations, the model displayed a developmental trajectory that at one point mimicked the 4-month-olds' behavior, and, at a later point, the 10-month-olds' behavior. The change in the network function leading to this behavioral change was interpreted as infants developing the progressive ability to form more precise internal representations of objects in their environment on the basis of experience-dependent neural tuning during their first year of life (see Thomas, 2004, for discussion).

In cases where development is assessed outside the laboratory, such as in language development, a model can be exposed to data that reflect a child's experience in the real world. For example, several connectionist models have been used to investigate the mechanisms underlying children's learning of the English past tense (e.g., Plunkett & Juola, 1999; Rumelhart & McClelland, 1986; Westermann, 1998). These models are usually trained on a set of verbs that reflects the frequency of occurrence in spoken (and sometimes written) language. In this case, the characteristic error patterns observed in children of different ages are compared with the performance of the model at different stages of learning.

Finally, the validity of a model can be assessed by generating predictions that can then be tested against children's performance. As noted above, connectionist models often generalize to previously unseen stimuli in meaningful ways (for example, to new objects in categorization studies or nonsense words in past-tense learning), and these generalizations can be assessed against the behavior of children tested on the same stimuli.

Connectionist models are an ideal tool to study development within the neuroconstructivist framework, because the learning trajectory in a model is likewise the outcome of local adaptations to interacting constraints. In contrast to child development, however, in a model these constraints are precisely known and can be manipulated by the modeler to observe changes to the developmental trajectory and the learning outcome. A model has intrinsic constraints such as the number of units, the pattern of connections between units, and the way in which environmental inputs are encoded for processing; plasticity constraints such as the function and parameters of the weight update rule; and environmental constraints such as the type, frequency, and order of the stimuli presented to the model. More recently, insights from developmental cognitive neuroscience have been incorporated into connectionist modeling by allowing for experience-dependent structural development and the gradual integration of network subcomponents (Mareschal, Sirois, et al., 2007; Westermann, Sirois, Shultz, & Mareschal, 2006), adding further constraints to the developmental model.

As we will discuss below, manipulating these constraints is particularly well suited to exploring the causes and consequences of atypical development.

Neuroconstructivism and Developmental Disorders

Developmental disorders can shed light on the way in which constraints at the genetic, neural, physical, and social levels of description operate to shape cognitive development. Several questions come to the fore in considering what happens when a child's development does not proceed as expected. It is important to establish the role that the developmental process itself plays in producing the behavioral impairments that are observed in, for example, the older child with autism or language impairment. It is also important to consider the extent to which emerging impairments are influenced by the interactivity of brain systems or by disruption to the timing and order in which developmental events usually unfold. Finally, we must consider how the child's social context can serve to attenuate or exaggerate deficits.

Variability is a pervasive feature of cognitive development, both in terms of intelligence in typically developing children and in the possibilities of development impairments. Disorders can have several causes. They can stem from genetic abnormalities, such as in Down syndrome (DS), Williams syndrome (WS), and fragile X syndrome (FXS). They can be identified on the basis of behavioral impairments, such as in autism, specific language impairment (SLI), attention deficit hyperactivity disorder (ADHD), or dyslexia. In the case of behaviorally defined disorders, genetic influence is frequently suspected as these conditions can run in families, but the genetic basis is not fully understood. Finally, disorders can be caused by atypical environments, either biochemical, such as mothers taking drugs during pregnancy, or psychological, such as cases of deprivation or abuse.

Notably, some developmental disorders can exhibit uneven cognitive profiles. For example, there may be particular problems in language but less so in non-verbal areas (e.g., SLI). Some abilities can appear relatively stronger against a background of low IQ (e.g., face recognition in WS). To understand disorders, we must explain both how development can be generally poor, perhaps occurring more slowly than usually, perhaps terminating at low levels of ability, and also how abilities can be impaired to different extents (Thomas, Purser, & Richardson, in press).

Within the neuroconstructivist framework, developmental disorders can be understood through altered constraints that push the developmental trajectory off its normal track. Atypical development can, like typical development, be characterized as an adaptation to multiple interacting constraints, only that in this case the constraints are different. These atypical constraints then lead to different (suboptimal) outcomes possibly through a deflection in the process of representation construction. This explanation of atypical development stands in contrast to theories that assume that disorders arise from isolated failures of particular functional modules to develop (see Karmiloff-Smith, 1998, 2009, and Thomas et al., in press, for discussion). Modular explanations were characteristic of early investigations of several disorders: autism was initially viewed in terms of the failure of an innate, dedicated theory-of-mind module to develop (Frith, Morton, & Leslie, 1991); and SLI in terms of selective damage to a genetically pre-specified syntactic module (van der Lely, 2005).

Empirical evidence supports the role of development in producing atypical cognitive profiles, because these profiles do not necessarily retain a consistent shape across development. For example, when Paterson, Brown, Gsödl, Johnson, and Karmiloff-Smith (1999) explored the language and number abilities of toddlers with DS and WS, they found a different relative pattern to that observed in adults with these disorders. The profile in early childhood was not a miniature version of the adult profile.

The neuroconstructivist approach places the developmental process at the heart of explanations of developmental deficits (Karmiloff-Smith, 1998). Empirically, the framework encourages researchers to focus on trajectories of development, rather than static snapshots of behavior at different ages in comparison to typically developing children matched for chronological or mental age. The theoretical emphasis is that the disordered system is still developing but it does not possess the information or neurocomputational constraints that enable it to acquire a domain. Notably, in some circumstances, atypical underlying cognitive processes may be sufficient to generate normal levels of behavior on particular tasks: for example, as demonstrated by research on face recognition in children with autism and WS (Annaz, Karmiloff-Smith, Johnson, & Thomas, 2009; Karmiloff-Smith et al., 2004). In other cases, the atypical constraints may even produce better than typical performance for a given behavioral task, such as in some aspects of perception in autism (Mottron, Belleville, & Menard, 1999; Shah & Frith, 1983). Such possibilities make it clear how a neuroconstructivist developmental framework differs from viewing disorders as if they were normal systems with broken parts. Nevertheless, a modular view of developmental disorders still persists amongst some researchers. Thus Temple and Clahsen (2002, p. 770) argue that "there remains no empirical evidence in any developmental disorder that the ultimate functional architecture has fundamentally different organization from normal, rather than merely lacking or having reduced development of components of normal functional architecture."

Several of the core ideas of neuroconstructivism are emphasized by the study of atypical development. For example, in some cases localization and specialization of cortical areas appear atypical (Karmiloff-Smith, 2009). Adults with WS exhibit face-recognition skills in the normal range but examination of ERPs reveals different neural activity compared to typical controls (e.g., Grice et al., 2001). Neuroimaging data have suggested differences in the constraints of *chronotopy*, in terms of the changes in connectivity (and associated plasticity) over time in disorders such as autism and DS (e.g., Becker, Armstrong, & Chan, 1986; Chugani et al., 1999). Differences in *input encoding* have been proposed to have cascading effects on the context in which other cognitive abilities are acquired (e.g., in autism, SLI, and dyslexia). Alterations in the level of abstraction achieved in forming internal representations, or in the dimensions of similarity that those representations encode, can play a material role in the ability of other brain systems to employ this information to drive other processes. It is possible that in autism, SLI, and dyslexia, for example, the consequence of atypical similarity structure in the input representations results in a processing deficit much higher up in a hierarchy of representational systems.

Differences in *embodiment* may also impact on the trajectory of development. For example, Sieratzki and Woll (1998) proposed that in children with spinal muscular atrophy – a disorder that reduces early mobility – language development might be accelerated as a compensatory way for the young child to control his/her environment. Lastly, an atypical child co-specifies an *atypical social environment* – for example, in the expectations and reactions of parents and peers – which has also been observed to influence these children's development (e.g., Cardoso-Martins, Mervis, & Mervis, 1985).

Of course, when we place an emphasis on development as a trajectory, and atypical development as an atypically constrained trajectory, it becomes increasingly important to specify what is different about the constraints and mechanisms of change in a given disorder. Here again, computational modeling offers a very useful tool.

Modeling Atypical Development

Constructing a computational model of development involves making a range of decisions. These include the nature of the input and output representations corresponding to the target cognitive domain, the regime of training experiences, the specific architecture and learning algorithm, and a set of free parameters. These are concrete realizations of the constraints that act on or shape the normal developmental trajectory (Mareschal & Thomas, 2007; Spencer, Thomas, & McClelland, 2009). Because the constraints can be systematically varied and the effects of such variation on performance investigated in detail, models provide a mechanistic means to explore candidate ways in which developmental impairments can arise.

From a formal learning perspective, alterations to the model's constraints can produce a number of effects. They may change the nature of the *hypothesis space* that can be reached (i.e., the knowledge that can be stored); they can change the nature of the *search* of an existing hypothesis space (i.e., how information from the environment can be used to acquire this knowledge); they can change the *inductive bias* which the system uses to generalize its knowledge to novel situations; or they can change the set of *training examples*, either in the system's autonomous, self-guided sampling of the environment or when the environment is itself impoverished.

One of the virtues of implemented models is that they allow us to simulate the consequences of changes to a complex system in which behavior is generated by the ongoing interaction of many components. These outcomes are not always predictable using analytical means (and are therefore called "emergent properties"). One issue to which models have been applied is the consequence of multiple ongoing interactions across development between the components that make up a whole cognitive system. Baughman and Thomas (2008) used *dynamical systems modeling* to simulate development in different types of cognitive architecture that were constructed from multiple interacting components. These architectures included distributed, modular, hemispheric, central processor, and hierarchical designs. Baughman and Thomas examined how early damage to a single component led to consequent impairments over development. In some cases, the initial damage was followed by compensation from surrounding components. In other cases, causal interactions between components across development caused the impairment to spread through the system. Several factors determined the exact pattern, including the architecture, the location of the early damage within that architecture with respect to connectivity, and the nature of the initial impairment. The model highlighted the importance of understanding causal connectivity in explaining the origin of uneven cognitive profiles.

One ongoing debate in the field of development disorders is their relation to acquired disorders following brain damage. Is a child with SLI similar in any way to the adult with acquired aphasia? Modeling generated insights into this question by investigating the consequences of damaging a learning system in its initial state (analogous to a developmental disorder) compared to damaging a system in its trained state (analogous to an adult acquired deficit). Using a backpropagation connectionist model of development, Thomas and Karmiloff-Smith (2002) demonstrated that some types of damage hurt the system more in the "adult" state (e.g., severing network connections) while others hurt the system more in the "infant" state (e.g., adding noise to processing). The adult system tolerates noise because it already possesses an accurate representation of the knowledge, but loss of network structure leads to a decrement in performance since connections contain established knowledge. By contrast, the infant system tolerates loss of connections because it can reorganize remaining resources to acquire the knowledge, but is impaired by noisy processing since this blurs the knowledge that the system has to learn. Empirical evidence supports the importance of a good representation of the input during language acquisition. When McDonald (1997) analyzed the conditions for successful and unsuccessful language acquisition across a range of populations (including early and late first-language learners, early and late second-language learners, and individuals with DS, WS, and SLI), the results indicated that good representations of speech sounds (or components of signs for sign language) were key in predicting the successful acquisition of a language. This included acquisition of higher-level aspects such as syntax.

Models can also be used to establish whether one empirically observed feature of a disorder can serve as a causal explanation for other observed features via the development process. Triesch, Teuscher, Deák, and Carlson (2006) proposed a computational model of the emergence of gaze-following skills in infant–caregiver interactions. They constructed their model to test the idea that the emergence of gaze following may be explained in terms of the infant's gradual discovery that monitoring the caregiver's direction of gaze is predictive of where rewarding objects will be located in the environment. They based their model of gaze following on a biologically plausible reward-driven mechanism called temporal difference learning, which is a type of *reinforcement learning*. Reinforcement learning is a way of training computational models where certain outcomes are associated with rewards. In the current context, the model learned a sequence of actions that lead to a reward. The infant was construed as an agent situated in an environment. The agent generated actions based on what it perceived from the environment, and then potentially received a reward for its action, along with updated information of the new state of the environment. In the Triesch et al. model, the environment depicted a range of locations containing either the caregiver, an interesting object, or nothing. If the infant looked at the caregiver, information would also be available on the direction of the caregiver's gaze (i.e., whether the caregiver was looking at the infant or at some location in the environment). Rewards were available to the infant for fixating an object or the caregiver, but rewards reduced over time as the infant became bored. A schematic of the model is shown in figure 28.2.

The model demonstrated three results. First, through rewards gained during exploration of the simulated environment, the model successfully acquired gaze-following behavior. Second, when the intrinsic reward value of observing faces was lowered to simulate

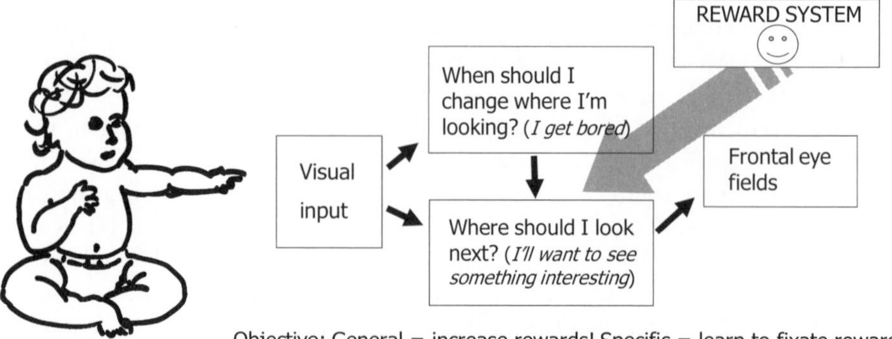

Figure 28.2 Schematic of Triesch, Teuscher, Deák, and Carlson's (2006) computational model of the development of gaze-following behavior, based on reinforcement learning

autism (e.g., Annaz et al., 2009; Dawson, Meltzoff, Osterling, Rinaldi, & Brown, 1998) or raised to simulate WS (e.g., Bellugi, Lichtenberger, Jones, Lai, & St George, 2000; Jones et al., 2000), the result in both cases was an atypical developmental trajectory, with the emergence of gaze following absent or substantially delayed. Empirically, deficits in shared attention (mutual gaze to a common object) are observed in both developmental disorders (Laing et al., 2002; Osterling & Dawson, 1994). Third, the implemented model could be used to predict possible deficits in other disorders. For example, it has been proposed that ADHD may in part stem from deficits in the reward-learning system (Williams & Dayan, 2005; Williams & Taylor, 2004). Richardson and Thomas (2006) demonstrated that appropriate parameter changes applied to the Triesch et al. model to simulate ADHD also produced impairments in the development of early gaze behavior. If the genetic influence on ADHD (e.g., Banaschewski et al., 2005) means that precursors to the childhood behavioral symptoms can also be observed in infancy, then the Richardson and Thomas simulation predicts that atypical gaze following may be such a precursor.

The gaze-following model underscores a key theoretical point at the heart of neuroconstructivism. Disorders that appear very different in their adult states may in fact be traced back to infant systems that share much in common, but differ in certain low-level neurocomputational properties (see Mareschal, Johnson, et al., 2007). It is development itself – together with the characteristics of the system that is undergoing development – that produces divergent behavioral profiles.

Recent Developments in Methodology: The Use of Trajectory Analysis

The neuroconstructivist focus on change over time generates a need for methods that allow us to describe, analyze, and compare the trajectories followed by different cognitive systems. This is especially the case when we wish to study variations in the trajectories found in typically or atypically developing children. New methods have been designed for just this purpose (see, e.g., Thomas et al., 2009).

The use of trajectories to study cognitive variation contrasts with a static "snapshot" approach to measuring differences. For example, when researchers investigate behavioral deficits in individuals with developmental disorders, a common methodology is to use a *matching* approach. The research asks, does the disorder group show behavior appropriate for its mean age? To answer this question, the disorder group is matched with two separate typically developing control groups, one match based on chronological age (CA) and a second match based on mental age (MA) derived from a relevant standardized test. If the disorder group shows an impairment compared with the CA-matched group but not with the MA-matched group, individuals with the disorder are considered to exhibit developmental delay on this ability. If, by contrast, the disorder group shows an impairment compared with both control groups, then the disorder group is considered to exhibit developmental deviance or atypicality (see, e.g., Hodapp, Burack, & Zigler, 1990; Leonard, 1998). The matching approach dispenses with age as an explicit factor by virtue of its design, but necessarily this restricts its ability to describe change over developmental time.

An alternative analytical methodology is based on the idea of trajectories or growth models (Annaz et al., 2009; Annaz, Karmiloff-Smith, & Thomas, 2008; Jarrold & Brock, 2004; Karmiloff-Smith, 1998; Karmiloff-Smith et al., 2004; Rice, 2004; Rice, Warren, & Betz, 2005; Singer Harris, Bellugi, Bates, Jones, & Rossen, 1997; Thomas et al., 2001, 2006, 2009). In this alternative approach, the aim is to construct a function linking performance with age on a specific experimental task and then to assess whether this function differs between the typically developing group and the disorder group. The use of trajectories in the study of development has its origin in growth curve modeling (see, e.g., Chapman, Hesketh, & Kistler, 2002; Rice, 2004; Rice et al., 2005; Singer Harris et al., 1997; Thelen & Smith, 1994; van Geert, 1991) and in the wider consideration of the shape of change in development (Elman et al., 1996; Karmiloff-Smith, 1998). In the context of disorder research, the impetus to move from matching to trajectory-based studies was a motivation to place development at the heart of explanations of developmental deficits, since as we have argued, the phenotype associated with any neurodevelopmental disorder does not emerge full-blown at birth but, rather, develops gradually and sometimes in transformative ways with age. This can only be studied by following atypical profiles over time.

Focusing on the example of disorder research, the aim of the trajectory methodology approach is twofold. First, it seeks to construct a function linking performance with age for a specific experimental task. Separate functions are constructed for the typically developing group and for the disorder group, and the functions are then compared. Second, it aims to shed light on the causal interactions between cognitive components across development. To do so, it establishes the *developmental relations* between different experimental tasks, assessing the extent to which performance on one task predicts performance on another task over time. Once more, the developmental relations found in the disorder group can be compared against those observed in a typically developing group. Trajectories may be constructed in three ways: (a) they may be constructed on the basis of data collected at a single point in time, in a cross-sectional sample of individuals varying in age and/or ability; (b) they may be constructed on the basis of data collected at multiple points in time, tracing longitudinally changes in individuals usually of the same age; or (c) they may combine both methods, with individuals who vary in age followed over two or more measurement points. In most cases, analyses employ linear or non-linear regression methods, for example comparing the gradients and intercepts of best-fit regression lines between groups (Thomas et al., 2009).

The trajectory methodology makes several demands of behavioral measures. It relies on the use of experimental tasks that yield *sensitivity* across the age and ability range of the children under study, that avoid *floor and ceiling effects* where possible, and that have *conceptual coherence* with the domain under investigation. Conceptual coherence means that the behavior must tap the same underlying cognitive processes at different age and ability levels. It is worth noting that the first of these criteria, task sensitivity across a wide age range, may be one of the hardest to fulfill. This is particularly the case in domains that are characterized by early development, where measures may exhibit ceiling effects at a point when other domains are still showing marked behavioral change over time. In the domain of language, for example, speech development reaches ceiling levels of accuracy much earlier than vocabulary or syntax. This can compromise our ability to assess developmental relations between abilities that plateau at different ages. Currently, one of the biggest challenges facing the study of cognitive development is to calibrate measurement systems to afford age-level sensitivity while at the same time retaining conceptual coherence over large spans of time.

There are currently few theoretically interesting behavioral measures that tap development over a very wide age range. Sometimes researchers are tempted to rely on subtests from standardized test batteries (IQ tests), since these are often constructed with a wide age range in mind. However, despite being psychometrically sound measures, standardized tests are frequently very blunt measures of the development of individual cognitive processes. One alternative is to appeal to more sensitive dependent measures such as reaction time. Although reaction times can be noisy, they continue to exhibit developmental change when accuracy levels are at ceiling. A second alternative is to use implicit rather than explicit measures of performance to assess underlying cognitive processes. Implicit measures are online, time-sensitive assessments of behavior in which the participants are usually unaware of the experimental variables under manipulation, such as the frequency or imageability of words in a speeded recognition task (Karmiloff-Smith et al., 1998).

Lastly, it is important to stress that irrespective of the correct theoretical explanation of a given disorder, trajectories are descriptively powerful because they distinguish between multiple ways that development can differ. For example, trajectories may differ in their onset, in their rate, in their shape, in their monotonicity (whether they consistently increase over time or go up and down), and the point and level at which performance asymptotes. An accurate and detailed characterization of empirical patterns of change is a necessary precursor to formulating causal accounts of developmental impairments.

Recent Developments in the Genetic Bases of Atypical Development

Much work has been done to uncover the genes contributing to various developmental disorders. For some, e.g., autism, SLI, and dyslexia, behavioral genetics has identified multiple genes of small effect as contributing to the phenotypic outcome (Plomin, DeFries, Craig, & McGuffin, 2002). In others, such as WS, DS, and FXS, for which molecular genetics has already identified the gene or set of genes playing a role in the phenotypic outcome, efforts are placed on uncovering the function(s) of individual genes. These functions are rarely if ever at the cognitive level, although animal models are sometimes interpreted to suggest this. An example of this approach is spatial cognition in WS. Here, members of a family who had a tiny deletion (ELN and LIMK1) within the WS-critical region (WSCR) displayed spatial deficits similar to those found in WS. This was taken to indicate that the LIMK1 gene was a major contributor to spatial cognition (Frangiskakis et al., 1996).

LIMK1 knockout mice likewise revealed spatial deficits in the Morris maze (Meng et al., 2002), providing further apparent evidence for an important role of LIMK1 in spatial processing. Although subsequent research on other LIMK1 patients revealed no spatial deficits, thereby challenging this view (Gray, Karmiloff-Smith, Funnell, & Tassabehji, 2006; Karmiloff-Smith et al., 2003; Tassabehji et al., 1999), this misses the neuroconstructivist point. It is not only the final effects of a gene's downstream pathway on cognitive-level outcomes that matters, but also LIMK1 expression over developmental time, thus to examine its basic-level functions during embryogenesis and postnatal development. Indeed, LIMK1 is involved in dendritic spine growth and synaptic regulation across the brain, and not expressed solely in parietal cortex to form a spatial cognition module.

While animal models are useful for testing hypotheses about human disorders, obviously we must compare like with like at the cognitive level. The LIMK1 knockout mice were tested in the Morris water maze (Meng et al., 2002), a task that necessitated the mouse updating the representation of its position in space each time it moved. By contrast, the human spatial tasks had participants seated stationary at a table representing relations between objects. Therefore, while one problem involves egocentric space, the other involves allocentric space. This discrepancy has recently been remedied by designing human tasks that resemble the water maze (a pool filled with balls for children to search for a tin full of surprises) or using mouse designs which resemble the human tasks, with the aim of bringing the cognitive demands of tasks in line across species comparisons. Obviously, it will be crucial to study both species across developmental time.

Although rare, partial deletion patients are useful in narrowing down the contributions of certain genes to phenotypic outcomes. Several patients with differing sized deletions within the WSCR have been identified. This allows us not only to examine basic functions, but also to analyze downstream and longer-term effects on aspects of cognition (Karmiloff-Smith et al, 2003; Tassabehji, Hammond, Karmiloff-Smith et al., 2005). For example, one patient, HR, has only three of the 28 WS genes not deleted, yet she displays subtle differences with the WS full-blown phenotype (less of an overly friendly personality profile, somewhat less impaired intellectually, neither the gait nor the monotonous tone of those with classic WS). Cases like these enable us to hone in on the contributions of specific genes and their interactions with other genes to the phenotypic outcome. Here again, development plays a crucial role. HR examined at 28 months had scores matching CA controls on general cognitive abilities. By 42 months, however, her performance was close to age-matched children with WS, and by 60 months her cognitive profile was identical to that of WS, although she remains different in personality and facial morphology. So, when making genotype/phenotype correlations, it is critical to take developmental time into account (Karmiloff-Smith, Scerif, & Thomas, 2002).

Would it be simpler to study a disorder caused by a single gene mutation (FXS) rather than the 28 genes deleted in Williams syndrome? This question would only make sense if genes coded directly for cognitive-level outcomes. In reality, genotype/phenotype correlations in FXS are just as complex as in other syndromes. FXS is caused by an expansion of the CGG repeat at the beginning of the FMR1 gene on the X chromosome. Healthy individuals have between 7 and any number up to 60 repeats with 30 repeats at the FMR1 gene site. In most affected individuals, significant expansion of repeats (>200) results in hypermethylation and silencing of the FMR1 gene, a lack of messenger RNA, and a diminution of the FMR1 gene's protein product (Verkerk et al., 1991).

Realizing that the FMR1 gene is involved in brain-wide processes such as synaptic regulation, the complexities of the cognitive outcome from a single gene make sense: problems with attention, language, number, and spatial cognition (Cornish, Scerif, & Karmiloff-Smith, 2007).

Note that different genetic mutations may result in similar phenotypic outcomes. For example, although autism spectrum disorder (ASD) is considered by some to present with the opposite profile from WS, in fact they display numerous phenotypic similarities, such as atypical pointing, triadic attention, sustained and selective attention, deficits in identifying complex emotional expressions, problems with pragmatics of language, auditory memory and theory-of-mind deficits, and a focus on features at the expense of global configuration. This suggests that multiple genes contribute to outcomes in both ASD and WS. Clearly the likelihood of one gene/one outcome is exceedingly small.

The importance of tracing gene expression over time became particularly clear with respect to the FOXP2 gene, originally claimed to be directly involved in speech and language deficits (Gopnik & Crago, 1991; Pinker, 2001). A British family (KE) had yielded several generations of children with speech and language impairments. When affected family members were discovered to have a FOXP2 mutation on chromosome 7 (Lai, Gerrelli, Monaco, Fisher, & Copp, 2003), some hailed this as the gene contributing to human language evolution (Pinker, 2001; Whiten, 2007). But in-depth molecular analyses in humans (Groszer et al., 2008), chimpanzees (Enard et al., 2002), and birds showed that the function of this gene was widespread and contributed to the rapid coordination of sequential processing and its timing. FOXP2 is expressed more during learning than during other periods of development (Haesler et al., 2004), and its expression becomes increasingly confined to motor regions (Lai et al, 2003). Why, in the human case, the mutation affects speech/language more than other domains is because speech/language is the domain in which the rapid coordination of sequential processing and its timing is critical. But FOXP2 is not specific to that domain. It also affects other domains, albeit more subtly. Indeed, it was shown that the KE family also had problems with imitating non-linguistic oral articulation, with fine-motor control, and with the perception/production of rhythm (Alcock, Passingham, Watkins, & Vargha-Khadem, 2000), suggesting a domain-general effect of differing impact.

Note that neuroconstructivism does not rule out domain-specificity; it argues that it cannot be taken for granted when one domain is more impaired than another (Karmiloff-Smith, 1998). Rather, developmental trajectories and cross-domain interactions must always be explored. Unlike the nativist perspective, neuroconstructivism offers a truly developmental approach that focuses on change and emergent outcomes. Genes do not act in isolation in a predetermined way. The profiles of downstream genes to which FOXP2 binds suggest roles in a wide range of general, not domain-specific, functions including morphogenesis, neuronal development, axon guidance, synaptic plasticity, and neurotransmission (Teramisu & White, 2007). This differs from theorizing at the level of cognitive modules and points to the multilevel complexities of genotype/phenotype relations in understanding human development in any domain.

In general, researchers must always recall that development really counts. For example, were one to discover, as is the case with WS adult brains, that parietal cortex is proportionally small, it cannot be automatically assumed that this causes their problems with spatial cognition and number. A question that must always be raised is whether parietal cortex started out smaller in proportion to other cortical areas or whether parietal cortex *became* small over time because of atypical processing in that region. Only a truly developmental approach can address such questions.

In our view, developmental disorders are explicable at a very different level from high-level cognitive modules; rather phenotypic outcomes are probably due to perturbations in far more basic processes early in development, such as a lack of pruning or over-exuberant pruning, of differences in synaptogenesis, of differences in the density/type of neurons, in differing firing thresholds, in poor signal-to-noise ratios, or generally in terms of atypical timing across developing systems. Rather than invoking a start state of innately-specified modules handed down by evolution, the neuroconstructivist approach argues for increased plasticity for learning (Finlay, 2007), i.e., for a limited number of domain-relevant biases, which *become* domain-specific over developmental time via their competitive interaction with each other when attempting to process environmental inputs (Johnson, 2001; Karmiloff-Smith, 1998). In other words, neuroconstructivism maintains that if the adult brain contains modules, then these *emerge developmentally* during the ontogenetic process of gradual localization/ specialization of function, i.e., progressive modularization (Elman et al., 1996; Johnson, 2001; Karmiloff-Smith, 1992, 1998). In this sense, it is probable that domain-specific outcomes enabled by gene–environment interactions may not even be possible without the gradual process of development over time.

Conclusion

In this chapter we have described neuroconstructivism as a new framework for understanding and explaining cognitive development, with cognition defined as based on patterns of neural activity that constitute mental representations. The main tenet of this approach is that development is a trajectory that is shaped by constraints at different levels of the organism, from genes to the social environment. Importantly there are also tight interactive loops between these levels: for example, neural activity affects the structural development of the brain's neural networks, partially mediated through the activity-dependent expression of genes. The structure of the network in turn constrains the possible patterns of activity. Neural activity leads to behavior by which the physical and social environment can be manipulated, leading to new experiences and thus new patterns of neural activity.

It is not necessary for an explanation of development to be useful that all changes and interactions are fully characterized: for example, in many cases it will not be necessary to specify the genetic mechanisms by which neural activation is translated into experience-dependent neural plasticity. What is important, however, is to consider the implications of the dynamic nature of these constraints and their interactions. Ignoring them (or not knowing about them) has led researchers to develop theories of development in which a genetic blueprint leads to a preprogrammed maturation of encapsulated modules with innate functionality. On the opposite extreme, radical empiricist views would have argued for an "anything goes" view of development under total plasticity. Neuroconstructivism rejects both views and instead it follows the Piagetian constructivist notion of proactive interactions between the individual and the environment in which a strongly constrained developing system comes to optimally adapt to these constraints, be they "typical" constraints in typical development or altered constraints in atypical development. Investigating the nature of these constraints and their role in shaping the developmental trajectory is at the heart of the neuroconstructivist endeavor.

Note

1 An introduction to these methods can be found at http://www.psyc.bbk.ac.uk/research/DNL/stats/Thomas_trajectories.html.

References

Alcock, K. J., Passingham, R. E., Watkins, K., Vargha-Khadem, F. (2000). Pitch and timing abilities in inherited speech and language impairment. *Brain and Language*, *75*(1), 34–46.

Annaz, D., Karmiloff-Smith, A., Johnson, M. H., & Thomas, M. S. C. (2009). A cross-syndrome study of the development of holistic face recognition in children with autism, Down syndrome and Williams syndrome. *Journal of Experimental Child Psychology*, *102*, 456–486.

Annaz, D., Karmiloff-Smith, A., & Thomas, M. S. C. (2008). The importance of tracing developmental trajectories for clinical child neuropsychology. In J. Reed & J. Warner Rogers (Eds.), *Child neuropsychology: Concepts, theory and practice* (pp. 7–18). Oxford: Wiley-Blackwell.

Banaschewski, T., Hollis, C., Oosterlaan, J., Roeyers, H., Rubia, K., Willcutt, E., & Taylor, E. (2005). Towards an understanding of unique and shared pathways in the psychopathophysiology of ADHD. *Developmental Science*, *8*, 132–140.

Barsalou, L. W., Simmons, W. K., Barbey, A. K., & Wilson, C. D. (2003). Grounding conceptual knowledge in modality-specific systems. *Trends in Cognitive Sciences*, *7*, 84–91.

Baughman, F. D., & Thomas, M. S. C. (2008). Specific impairments in cognitive development: A dynamical systems approach. In B. C. Love, K. McRae, & V. M. Sloutsky (Eds.), *Proceedings of the 30th Annual Conference of the Cognitive Science Society* (pp. 1819–1824). Austin, TX: Cognitive Science Society.

Becker, L. E., Armstrong, D. L., & Chan, F. (1986). Dendritic atrophy in children with Down's syndrome. *Annals of Neurology, 20,* 520–526.

Bellugi, U., Lichtenberger, L., Jones, W., Lai, Z., & St George, M. (2000). The neurocognitive profile of Williams syndrome: A complex pattern of strengths and weaknesses. *Journal of Cognitive Neuroscience, 12,* 1–29.

Butz, M., Wörgötter, F., & van Ooyen, A. (2009). Activity-dependent structural plasticity. *Brain Research Reviews, 60,* 287–305.

Cardoso-Martins, C., Mervis, C. B., & Mervis, C. A. (1985). Early vocabulary acquisition by children with Down syndrome. *American Journal of Mental Deficiency, 90*(2), 177–184.

Caspi, A., Sugden, K., Moffitt, T. E., Taylor, A., Craig, I. W., Harrington, H., ... Poulton, R. (2003). Influence of life stress on depression: Moderation by a polymorphism in the 5-HTT gene. *Science, 301,* 386–389.

Chapman, R. S., Hesketh, L. J., & Kistler, D. J. (2002). Predicting longitudinal change in language production and comprehension in individuals with Down syndrome: Hierarchical linear modeling. *Journal of Speech, Language, and Hearing Research, 45,* 902–915.

Chugani, D. C., Muzik, O., Behen, M., Rothermel, R., Janisse, J. J., Lee, J., Chugani, H. T. (1999). Developmental changes in serotonin synthesis capacity in autistic and non-autistic children. *Annals of Neurology, 45,* 287–295.

Cirulli, F., Berry, A., & Alleva, E. (2003). Early disruption of the mother–infant relationship: Effects on brain plasticity and implications for psychopathology. *Neuroscience and Biobehavioral Reviews, 27,* 73–82.

Clark, A. (1999). An embodied cognitive science? *Trends in Cognitive Sciences, 3,* 345–351.

Cohen, L. G., Celnik, P., Pascual-Leone, A., Corwell, B., Falz, L., Dambrosia, J., ... Hallett, M. (1997). Functional relevance of cross-modal plasticity in blind humans. *Nature, 389,* 180–183.

Cornish, K., Scerif, G., & Karmiloff-Smith, A. (2007). Tracing syndrome-specific trajectories of attention across the lifespan. *Cortex, 43*(6), 672–685.

Dawson, G., Meltzoff, A. N., Osterling, J., Rinaldi, J., & Brown, E. (1998). Children with autism fail to orient to naturally occurring social stimuli. *Journal of Autism and Developmental Disorders, 28,* 479–485.

Elman, J. L., Bates, E. A., Johnson, M. H., Karmiloff-Smith, A., Parisi, D., & Plunkett, K. (1996). *Rethinking innateness: A connectionist perspective on development.* Cambridge, MA: MIT Press.

Enard, W., Przeworski, M., Fisher, S. E., Lai, C. S., Wiebe, V., Kitano, T., Monaco, A. P., & Pääbo, S. (2002). Molecular evolution of FOXP2, a gene involved in speech and language. *Nature, 418,* 869–872.

Finlay, B. L. (2007). E pluribus unum: Too many unique human capacities and too many theories. In S. Gangestad & J. Simpson (Eds.), *The evolution of mind: Fundamental questions and controversies.* (pp. 294–304). New York: Guilford Press.

Frangiskakis, J. M., Ewart, A. K., Morris, A. C., Mervis, C. B., Bertrand, J., Robinson, B. F., ... Keating, M. T. (1996). LIM-kinase1 hemizygosity implicated in impaired visuospatial constructive cognition. *Cell, 86,* 59–69.

Friston, K. J., & Price, C. J. (2001). Dynamic representations and generative models of brain function. *Brain Research Bulletin, 54,* 275–285.

Frith, U., Morton, J., & Leslie, A. M. (1991). The cognitive basis of a biological disorder: Autism. *Trends in Neurosciences, 14*(10), 433–438.

Gopnik, M., & Crago, M. B. (1991). Familial aggregation of a developmental language disorder. *Cognition, 39,* 1–30.

Gottlieb, G. (2007). Probabilistic epigenesis. *Developmental Science, 10,* 1–11.

Gray, V., Karmiloff-Smith, A., Funnell, E., & Tassabehji, M. (2006). In-depth analysis of spatial cognition in Williams syndrome: A critical assessment of the role of the LIMK1 gene. *Neuropsychologia, 44*(5), 679–685.

Grice, S., Spratling, M. W., Karmiloff-Smith, A., Halit, H., Csibra, G., de Haan, M., & Johnson, M. H. (2001). Disordered visual processing and oscillatory brain activity in autism and Williams syndrome. *NeuroReport, 12,* 2697–2700.

Groszer, M., Jeats, D. A., Deacon, R. M. J., de Bono, J. P., Orasad-Mulcare, S., Gaub, S., … Fisher, S. E. (2008). Impaired synaptic plasticity and motor learning in mice with a point mutation implicated in human speech deficits. *Current Biology, 18,* 354–362.

Haesler, S., Wada, K., Nshdejan, A., Morrisey, E. E., Lints, T., Jarvis, E. D., & Scharff, C. (2004). FOXP2 expression in avian vocal learners and non-learners. *Journal of Neuroscience, 24,* 3164–3175.

Harrist, A. W., & Waugh, R. M. (2002). Dyadic synchrony: Its structure and function in children's development. *Developmental Review, 22,* 555–592.

Hodapp, R. M., Burack, J. A., & Zigler, E. (Eds.) (1990). *Issues in the developmental approach to mental retardation.* New York: Cambridge University Press.

Hua, J. Y., & Smith, S. J. (2004). Neural activity and the dynamics of central nervous system development. *Nature Neuroscience, 7,* 327–332.

Jarrold, C., & Brock, J. (2004). To match or not to match? Methodological issues in autism-related research. *Journal of Autism and Developmental Disorders, 34,* 81–86.

Johnson, M. H. (1997). *Developmental cognitive neuroscience.* Oxford: Blackwell.

Johnson, M. H. (2001). Functional brain development in humans. *Nature Reviews Neuroscience, 2,* 475–483.

Jones, W., Bellugi, U., Lai, Z., Chiles, M., Reilly, J., Lincoln, A., & Adolphs, R. (2000). Hypersociability in Williams syndrome. *Journal of Cognitive Neuroscience, 12,* 30–46.

Karmiloff-Smith, A. (1992). *Beyond modularity: A developmental perspective on cognitive science.* Cambridge, MA: MIT Press/Bradford Books.

Karmiloff-Smith, A. (1998). Development itself is the key to understanding developmental disorders. *Trends in Cognitive Sciences, 2,* 389–398.

Karmiloff-Smith, A. (2006). The tortuous route from genes to behaviour: A neuroconstructivist approach. *Cognitive, Affective and Behavioural Neuroscience, 6*(1), 9–17.

Karmiloff-Smith, A. (2009). Nativism vs. neuroconstructivism: Rethinking developmental disorders [Special issue on the interplay of biology and environment]. *Developmental Psychology, 45*(1), 56–63.

Karmiloff-Smith, A., Grant, J., Ewing, S., Carette, M. J., Metcalfe, K., Donnai, D., Read, A. P., Tassabehji, M. (2003). Using case study comparisons to explore genotype–phenotype correlations in Williams-Beuren syndrome. *Journal of Medical Genetics, 40*(2), 136–140.

Karmiloff-Smith, A., Scerif, G., & Thomas, M. S. C. (2002). Different approaches to relating genotype to phenotype in developmental disorders. *Developmental Psychobiology, 40,* 311–322.

Karmiloff-Smith, A., Thomas, M. S. C., Annaz, D., Humphreys, K., Ewing, S., Grice, S., Brace, N., Van Duuren, M., Pike, G., & Campbell, R. (2004). Exploring the Williams syndrome face-processing debate: The importance of building developmental trajectories. *Journal of Child Psychology and Psychiatry and Allied Disciplines, 45,* 1258–1274.

Karmiloff-Smith, A., Tyler, L. K., Voice, K., Sims, K., Udwin, O., Howlin, P., & Davies, M. (1998). Linguistic dissociations in Williams syndrome: Evaluating receptive syntax in on-line and off-line tasks. *Neuropsychologia, 36*, 343–351.

Kaufman, J., Plotsky, P. M., Nemeroff, C. B., & Charney, D. S. (2000). Effects of early adverse experiences on brain structure and function: Clinical implications. *Biological Psychiatry, 48*, 778–790.

Kleim, J. A., Vij, K., Ballard, D. H., & Greenough, W. T. (1997). Learning-dependent synaptic modifications in the cerebellar cortex of the adult rat persist for at least four weeks. *Journal of Neuroscience, 17*, 717–721.

Kohonen, T. (1982). Self-organized formation of topologically correct feature maps. *Biological Cybernetics, 43*, 59–69.

Lai, C. S., Gerrelli, D., Monaco, A. P., Fisher, S. E., & Copp, A. J. (2003). FOXP2 expression during brain development coincides with adult sites of pathology in a severe speech and language disorder. *Brain, 126*, 2455–2462.

Laing, E., Butterworth, G., Ansari, D., Gsödl, M., Laing, E., Barnham, Z., ... Karmiloff-Smith, A. (2002). Atypical linguistic and socio-communicative development in toddlers with Williams syndrome. *Developmental Science, 5*(2), 233–246.

Leonard, L. B. (1998). *Children with specific language impairment.* Cambridge, MA: MIT Press.

Li, P. (2003). Language acquisition in a self-organizing neural network model. In P. Quinlan (Ed.), *Connectionist models of development: Developmental processes in real and artificial neural networks* (pp. 115–149). New York: Psychology Press.

Lickliter, R., & Honeycutt, H. (2003). Developmental dynamics: Toward a biologically plausible evolutionary psychology. *Psychological Bulletin, 129*, 819–835.

Mareschal, D., Johnson, M. H., Sirois, S., Spratling, M. W., Thomas, M. D. C., & Westermann, G. (2007). *Neuroconstructivism: How the brain constructs cognition.* Oxford: Oxford University Press.

Mareschal, D., Sirois, S., Westermann, G., & Johnson, M. (Eds.) (2007). *Neuroconstructivism: Vol. 2. Perspectives and prospects.* Oxford: Oxford University Press.

Mareschal, D., & Thomas M. S. C. (2007). Computational modeling in developmental psychology. *IEEE Transactions on Evolutionary Computation [Special issue on autonomous mental development], 11*(2), 137–150.

Marr, D. (1982). *Vision.* San Francisco: H. Freeman and Co.

McDonald, J. L. (1997). Language acquisition: The acquisition of linguistic structure in normal and special populations. *Annual Review of Psychology, 48*, 215–241.

Meng, Y., Zhang, Y., Tregoubov, V., Janus, C., Cruz, L., Jackson, M., ... Falls, D. (2002). Abnormal spine morphology and enhanced LTP in LIMK-1 knockout mice. *Neuron, 35*, 121–133.

Mottron, L., Belleville, S., & Menard, E., (1999). Local bias in autistic subjects as evidenced by graphic tasks: Perceptual hierarchization or working memory deficit? *Journal of Child Psychology and Psychiatry, 40*(5), 743–55.

Murray, L. (1992). The impact of postnatal depression on infant development. *Journal of Child Psychology and Psychiatry, 33*, 543–561.

Nelson, C. A., & Luciana, M. (Eds.) (2001). *Handbook of developmental cognitive neuroscience.* Cambridge, MA: MIT Press.

Newport, E. L. (1990). Maturational constraints on language learning. *Cognitive Science, 14*, 11–28.

Osterling, J., & Dawson, G. (1994). Early recognition of children with autism: A study of first birthday home video tapes. *Journal of Autism and Developmental Disorders, 24*, 247–257.

Paterson, S. J., Brown, J. H., Gsödl, M. K., Johnson, M. H., & Karmiloff-Smith, A. (1999). Cognitive modularity and genetic disorders. *Science, 286*(5448), 2355–2358.

Piaget, J. (1955). *The child's construction of reality.* Routledge & Kegan Paul.

Pinker, S. (2001). Talk of genetics and vice versa. *Nature, 413*, 465–466.

Plomin, R., DeFries, J. C., Craig, I. W., & McGuffin, P. (Eds) (2002). *Behavioral genetics in the postgenomic era.* Washington DC: APA Books.

Plunkett, K., & Juola, P. (1999). A connectionist model of English past tense and plural morphology. *Cognitive Science, 23*, 463–490.

Pulvermüller, F. (2001). Brain reflections of words and their meaning. *Trends in Cognitive Sciences, 5*, 517–524.

Purves, D. (1994). *Neural activity and the growth of the brain.* Cambridge: Cambridge University Press.

Quartz, S. R. (1999). The constructivist brain. *Trends in Cognitive Sciences, 3*, 48–57.

Quartz, S. R., & Sejnowski, T. J. (1997). The neural basis of cognitive development: A constructivist manifesto. *Behavioral and Brain Sciences, 20*, 537–596.

Quinlan, P. T. (Ed.) (2003). *Connectionist models of development.* Hove, UK: Psychology Press.

Rice, M. L. (2004). Growth models of developmental language disorders. In M. L. Rice & S. F. Warren (Eds.), *Developmental language disorders: From phenotypes to etiologies* (pp. 207–240). Mahwah, NJ: Erlbaum.

Rice, M. L., Warren, S. F., & Betz, S. (2005). Language symptoms of developmental language disorders: An overview of autism, Down syndrome, fragile X, specific language impairment, and Williams syndrome. *Applied Psycholinguistics, 26*, 7–27.

Richardson, F., & Thomas, M. S. C. (2006). The benefits of computational modeling for the study of developmental disorders: Extending the Triesch et al. model to ADHD. *Developmental Science, 9*, 151–155.

Rosenzweig, M. R., & Bennett, E. L. (1996). Psychobiology of plasticity: Effects of training and experience on brain and behavior. *Behavioural Brain Research, 78*, 57–65.

Rumelhart, D. E., Hinton, G. E., & Williams, R. J. (1986). Learning representations by back-propagating errors. *Nature, 323*, 533–536.

Rumelhart, D. E., & McClelland, J. L. (1986). On learning the past tense of English verbs: Implicit rules or parallel distributed processing? In J. L. McClelland, D. Rumelhart, & the PDP Research Group (Eds.), *Parallel distributed processing: explorations in the microstructure of cognition: Vol. 1. Foundations* (pp. 318–362). Cambridge, MA: MIT Press.

Rutter, M. (2007). Gene–environment interdependence. *Developmental Science, 10*, 12–18.

Sadato, N., Pascual-Leone, A., Grafman, J., Ibañez, V., Deiber, M.-P., Dold, G., & Hallett, M. (1996). Activation of the primary visual cortex by Braille reading in blind subjects. *Nature, 380*, 526–528.

Sale, A., Berardi, N., & Maffei, L. (2009). Enrich the environment to empower the brain. *Trends in Neurosciences, 32*, 233–239.

Scott, L. S., Pascalis, O., & Nelson, C. A. (2007). A domain-general theory of the development of perceptual discrimination. *Current Directions in Psychological Science, 16*, 197–201.

Shah, A., & Frith, U. (1993). Why do autistic individuals show superior performance on the block design task? *Journal of Child Psychology and Psychiatry, 8*, 1351–1364.

Sieratzki, J. S., & Woll, B. (1998). Toddling into language: Precocious language development in motor-impaired children with spinal muscular atrophy. In A. Greenhill, M. Hughes, H. Littlefield, & H. Walsh (Eds.), *Proceedings of the 22nd Annual Boston University Conference on Language Development* (Vol. 2, pp. 684–694). Somerville, MA: Cascadilla Press.

Singer Harris, N. G., Bellugi, U., Bates, E., Jones, W., & Rossen, M. (1997). Contrasting profiles of language development in children with Williams and Down syndromes. *Developmental Neuropsychology, 13*, 345–370.

Smith, L. B. (2005). Cognition as a dynamic system: Principles from embodiment. *Developmental Review, 25*, 278–298.

Spencer, J., Thomas, M. S. C., & McClelland, J. L. (2009). *Toward a new unified theory of development: Connectionism and dynamical systems theory reconsidered.* Oxford: Oxford University Press.

Tassabehji, M., Hammond, P., Karmiloff-Smith, A., Thompson, P., Thorgeirsson, S. S., Durkin, M. E., ... Donnai, D. (2005). GTF2IRD1 in craniofacial development of humans and mice. *Science, 310*(5751), 1184–1187.

Tassabehji, M., Metcalfe, K., Karmiloff-Smith, A., Carette, M. J., Grant, J., Dennis, N., ... Donnai, D. (1999). Williams syndrome: Use of chromosomal microdeletions as a tool to dissect cognitive and physical phenotypes. *American Journal of Human Genetics, 64*, 118–125.

Temple, C., & Clahsen, H. (2002). How connectionist simulations fail to account for developmental disorders in children. *Behavioral and Brain Sciences, 25*, 769–770.

Teramisu, I., & White, S. A. (2006). FOXP2 regulation during undirected singing in adult songbirds. *Journal of Neuroscience, 26*, 7390–7394.

Thelen, E., & Smith, L. B. (1994). *A dynamic systems approach to the development of cognition and action*. Cambridge, MA: MIT Press.

Thomas, M. S. C. (2004). How do simple connectionist networks achieve a shift from "featural" to "correlational" processing in categorisation? *Infancy, 5*(2), 199–207.

Thomas, M. S. C., Annaz, D., Ansari, D., Scerif, G., Jarrold, C., & Karmiloff-Smith, A. (2009). Using developmental trajectories to understand developmental disorders. *Journal of Speech, Language, and Hearing Research, 52*, 336–358.

Thomas, M. S. C., Dockrell, J. E., Messer, D., Parmigiani, C., Ansari, D., & Karmiloff-Smith, A. (2006). Speeded naming, frequency, and the development of the lexicon in Williams syndrome. *Language and Cognitive Processes, 21*, 721–759.

Thomas, M. S. C., Grant, J., Barham, Z., Gsödl, M., Laing, E., Lakusta, L., ... Karmiloff-Smith, A. (2001). Past tense formation in Williams syndrome. *Language and Cognitive Processes, 16*, 143–176.

Thomas, M. S. C., & Karmiloff-Smith, A. (2002). Are developmental disorders like cases of adult brain damage? Implications from connectionist modeling. *Behavioral and Brain Sciences, 25*(6), 727–788.

Thomas, M. S. C., Purser, H. R. M., & Richardson, F. M. (in press). Modularity and developmental disorders. In P. D. Zelazo (Ed.), *Oxford handbook of developmental psychology*. Oxford: Oxford University Press.

Triesch, J., Teuscher, C., Deák, G., &. Carlson, E. (2006). Gaze following: Why (not) learn it? *Developmental Science, 9*, 125–147.

Turkewitz, G., & Kenny, P. A. (1985). The role of developmental limitations of sensory input on sensory/perceptual organization. *Journal of Developmental and Behavioral Pediatrics, 6*, 302–306.

Van der Lely, H. K. J. (2005). Domain-specific cognitive systems: Insight from grammatical-SLI. *Trends in Cognitive Sciences, 9*(2), 53–59.

Van Geert, P. (1991). A dynamic systems model of cognitive and language growth. *Psychological Review, 98*, 3–53.

Van Praag, H., Kempermann, G., & Gage, F. H. (2000). Neural consequences of environmental enrichment. *Nature Reviews Neuroscience, 1*, 191–198.

Verkerk, A. M., Pieretti, M., Sutcliffe, J. S., Fu, Y.-H., Kuhl, D. P., Pizzuti, A., ... Warren, S. T. (1991). Identification of a gene (FMR-1) containing a CGG repeat coincident with a breakpoint cluster region exhibiting length variation in fragile X syndrome. *Cell, 65*, 905–914.

Werker, J. F., & Tees, R. C. (1984). Cross-language speech-perception: Evidence for perceptual reorganization during the 1st year of life. *Infant Behavior and Development, 7*, 49–63.

Westermann, G. (1998). Emergent modularity and U-shaped learning in a constructivist neural network learning the English past tense. In M. A. Gernsbacher & S. J. Derry (Eds.), *Proceedings of the Twentieth Annual Conference of the Cognitive Science Society* (pp. 1130–1135). Hillsdale, NJ: Erlbaum.

Westermann, G., & Mareschal, D. (2004). From parts to wholes: Mechanisms of development in infant visual object processing. *Infancy, 5*, 131–151.

Westermann, G., Mareschal, D., Johnson, M. H., Sirois, S., Spratling, M., & Thomas, M. S. C. (2007). Neuroconstructivism. *Developmental Science, 10*, 75–83.

Westermann, G., Sirois, S., Shultz, T. R., & Mareschal, D. (2006). Modeling developmental cognitive neuroscience. *Trends in Cognitive Sciences, 10*, 227–233.

Whiten, A. (2007). *Imaginative minds.* Talk given at The British Academy, London.

Wiebe, S. A., Espy, K. A., Stopp, C., Respass, J., Stewart, P., Jameson, T. R., Gilbert, D. G., & Huggenvik, J. I. (2009). Gene–environment interactions across development: Exploring DRD2 genotype and prenatal smoking effects on self-regulation. *Developmental Psychology, 45*, 31–44.

Williams, J. O. H., & Dayan, P. (2005). Dopamine, learning, and impulsivity: A biological account of ADHD. *Journal of Child and Adolescent Psychopharmacology, 15*(2), 160–179.

Williams, J. O. H., & Taylor, E. (2004). Dopamine appetite and cognitive impairment in attention deficit/hyperactivity disorder. *Neural Plasticity, 11*(1), 115–132.

Younger, B. A., & Cohen, L. B. (1986). Developmental change in infants' perception of correlations among attributes. *Child Development, 57*, 803–815.

CHAPTER TWENTY-NINE

Individual Differences in Cognitive Development

Robert J. Sternberg

What is it that leads children to be similar in some ways but different in others, whether they are identical twins, fraternal twins, ordinary siblings, or simply two children of the same age? This chapter will deal with this question. The focus of the chapter will be on cognitive skills, although, of course, children can be similar and different with respect to many other kinds of skills as well.

The chapter is divided into five parts. In the first part of the chapter, I will briefly describe seven main paradigms that have been used for understanding individual differences in cognitive development. In the second part of the chapter, I will discuss at some length three of these paradigms for understanding individual differences in cognition. In the third part of the chapter, I will discuss origins and stability of individual differences, in particular, issues of heritability and modifiability of cognitive skills. In the fourth part of the chapter, I will discuss extremes in individual differences: giftedness and retardation in cognitive skills. In the fifth part of the chapter, I will discuss group differences and their relationship to individual differences in cognitive skills.

Paradigms for Understanding Individual Differences in Cognition and Cognitive Development

Several different paradigms have been proposed for understanding individual differences. Some of the main paradigms are the psychometric paradigm, the learning paradigm, the Piagetian paradigm (see Miller, chapter 25, this volume), the Vygotskian paradigm (see Daniels, chapter 26, this volume), the information-processing paradigm, the biological paradigm, and the systems paradigm (Sternberg, 1990; see also Sternberg, 2000; Sternberg & S. Kaufman, in press; Sternberg & Powell, 1983).

The psychometric paradigm seeks understanding of development through the use of psychometric theory and tests. Cognitive development might be understood partly in terms of differentiation of cognitive factors, with the sources of individual differences underlying task performance becoming more specific over age. Individual differences might derive, in part, from more differentiation at a given age, or from higher scores on factors, representing greater degrees of facility in an ability. For example, one child might have a higher verbal-comprehension factor score than another, signifying greater ability to understand verbal materials.

The learning paradigm (see Bjorklund, 2004; Sternberg & Powell, 1983) provides understanding of cognitive development in terms of mechanisms of classical and instrumental conditioning, and possibly social learning as well. Individual differences derive from rates of reinforcement and from the discriminative value of the reinforcements. For example, a child who is reinforced frequently and only (or largely) for using English correctly might develop better verbal skills than would a child who receives less reinforcement or who is reinforced for using poor English.

The information-processing paradigm (Bjorklund, 2004; Chen & Siegler, 2000; Klahr, 1992; Sternberg, 1984; see also Deary, 2000; Lohman, 2000; Siegler & Alibali, 2004) provides an understanding of cognitive development through specification of how knowledge, mental representations, mental processes, and strategies develop with age. Individual differences are understood in terms of differences in the effectiveness of these elements. For example, one child might be able to execute a set of mental processes more quickly than does another child, or might be able to choose a strategy for solving a problem that is a better strategy than that chosen by another child.

The biological paradigm (Grigorenko, 2000; Sternberg & J. Kaufman, 2001; Travis, 2007; P. A. Vernon, Wickett, Bazana, & Stelmack, 2000) seeks an understanding of cognitive development through an understanding of mechanisms of genetic transmission of characteristics, synaptogenesis, neural conduction, brain evolution, and so forth. Individual differences might be understood, for example, in terms of different genes inherited by two different children. Most biological researchers conceptualize biological effects as occurring in interaction with the environment. In other words, biological mechanisms affect the child's adaptation to the environment, but the environment also affects how biological mechanisms unfold.

The systems paradigm (e.g., Gardner, 1999, 2006; Sternberg, 1997, 2005; Thelen, 1992; Thelen & Smith, 1998) seeks an understanding of cognitive development in terms of the interactions of a dynamic system with many interacting elements. Individual differences arise when certain elements of the system are more effective than others, resulting in better performance of the system as a whole. For example, someone who is better at recognizing when he or she has a problem will be more likely to develop mechanisms for solving that problem than will be someone who does not recognize that the problem exists.

In sum, there are a variety of paradigms for understanding cognitive development and individual differences in such development. Consider in more detail three of these paradigms.

Three Paradigms for Studying Individual Differences in Cognition: A Detailed Analysis

Three of the most widely used paradigms for studying individual differences in cognitive development are the psychometric, biological, and systems paradigms.

The psychometric paradigm

Psychometric theories are unique among the paradigms mentioned above in relying primarily upon individual differences both in their formulation and in their verification (or falsification). Psychometric researchers use techniques of data analysis to discover common patterns of individual differences across cognitive tests. These patterns are then hypothesized to emanate from latent sources of individual differences, namely, cognitive abilities. One approach, stemming from Galton (1883) and J. M. Cattell (1890), was to use a series of psychophysical tests to measure individual differences in cognitive abilities.

Others have followed up on this approach of studying individual differences in speed and efficiency of information processing (Anderson, 1992; Deary, 2000; Jensen, 1998).

The Binetian Paradigm. Alfred Binet and Theodore Simon, commissioned in 1904 by the Minister of Public Instruction in Paris to create a test that would insure that children with developmental disability would receive an adequate education, took a different tack from that of Galton and Cattell. Binet and Simon (1916) proposed a theory consisting of three distinct elements: direction, adaptation, and criticism. These elements, under other names (such as *metacognition*), are still viewed today as important to individual differences in cognition. Direction consists in knowing what has to be done and how it is to be accomplished. When children are required to add two numbers, for example, they give themselves a series of instructions on how to proceed and these instructions form the direction of thought. Adaptation refers to children's selection and monitoring of their strategy during the course of task performance. For example, in solving a mathematics problem, there may be several alternative strategies children can use (see, e.g., McNeil, Uttal, Jarvin, & Sternberg, 2009; Siegler, 1996; Siegler & Jenkins, 1989), and adaptation would be involved in deciding which strategy to select. Criticism or control is the ability to criticize one's own thoughts and actions. For example, after solving a mathematical word problem, a child might wish to evaluate the solution to make sure it is sensible.

The ideas of Binet and Simon were brought to the United States by a professor of psychology at Stanford University, L. M. Terman, who was involved in the construction of early versions of what has come to be called the Stanford-Binet Intelligence Test. Examples of tests would include verbal absurdities, which requires recognition of why each of a set of statements is foolish; similarities and differences, which requires children to say how each of two objects is the same as, and different from, the other;

comprehension, which requires children to solve practical problems of the sort encountered in everyday life; and naming the days of the week. The most recent version of this test is still widely used (Roid, 2006).

The ideas of Binet are strongly linked to current notions about metacognition, that is, children's knowledge and control of their cognitive processing (e.g., Demetriou, Efklides, & Platsidou, 1993; Dunloski & Metcalfe, 2008; Flavell, 1992; Gopnik & Meltzoff, 1997; Goswami, 1996). In a sense, Binet was the first or certainly one of the first metacognitive theorists, recognizing the importance of children's understanding of their own behavior for their cognitive development. Indeed, children with developmental disability, who have low IQs, are distinguished largely for their lack of adequate metacognitive functioning (Borkowski & Cavanaugh, 1979; Butterfield & Belmont, 1977; Campione, Brown, & Ferrara, 1982).

Because intelligence tests have been central to the measurement of individual differences in the development of cognitive skills, it is worth saying something about how they are interpreted.

Intelligence testing as a means of assessing individual differences in cognition. Intelligence tests contain a wide variety of contents, as the examples above indicate. Originally, these tests were designed to yield a mental age, which refers to a child's level of intelligence in comparison to the "average" child of a given age. If, for example, a child performs at a level comparable to that of an average 12-year-old, the child's mental age will be 12, regardless of the child's chronological (physical) age. The tests were designed to yield an intelligence quotient, or IQ, which is the ratio between mental age and chronological age multiplied by 100. A score of 100 signifies that mental age is equivalent to chronological age. The IQ of 100 is thus the average IQ. A score above 100 indicates above-average intelligence and a score below 100 indicates below-average intelligence.

For a variety of reasons, the concept of mental age proved to be problematical. For example, it implied a kind of continuous mental development that was found not to exist and it implied that mental age would keep increasing indefinitely, which it did not. As a result, IQs in recent years have been computed on the basis of relative performance within a given age group. The IQs derived from this procedure are commonly referred to as *deviation IQs*, to distinguish them from the *ratio IQs* obtained by the older method. Deviation IQ scores are set to have a mean of 100 and a standard deviation of 15 or 16. The most widely used test for children is the Wechsler Intelligence Scale for Children, fourth edition (WISC-IV; Wechsler, 2003). (There is also a Wechsler test for preschool children, the Wechsler Preschool and Primary Scale of Intelligence – WPPSI-III). The WISC-IV measures individual differences in cognitive abilities through two main scales – a verbal scale and a performance scale. The verbal scale includes tests such as similarities, which requires an indication of a way in which two different objects are alike; arithmetic, which requires solution of arithmetic word problems; vocabulary, which requires definition of common English words; and comprehension, which requires understanding of common societal customs. The performance scale includes tests such as picture completion, which requires identification of a missing part in a picture of an object, and picture arrangement, which requires rearrangement of a scrambled set of cartoon-like pictures into an order that tells a coherent story.

Factor theories. Psychologists such as Binet and Wechsler grounded their work in tests of intelligence. Other researchers used tests, but grounded their work in theories of intelligence. The researchers tested children with tests based on their theories and then analyzed their data. One technique of data analysis they used is factor analysis, which analyzes correlations or covariances among cognitive tests in order to produce a set of hypothetical underlying factors (abilities). Psychometric theories generally have been grounded in the factor as the basic unit of individual differences in cognitive abilities.

The earliest such theory was that of Spearman (1904, 1927), a theory that is still widely accepted today (see, e.g., Brand, 1996; Herrnstein & Murray, 1994; Jensen, 1998; see essays in Sternberg & Grigorenko, 2002). According to Spearman, underlying all individual differences in cognitive abilities is a general factor, or *g* factor, which Spearman believed to be due to differences in mental energy. This factor was alleged to permeate performance of all cognitive tests. Spearman also posited specific factors, or *s* factors, which were each specific to single tests.

Not all theorists have accepted the idea of a single factor as responsible for most individual differences in cognition. Thurstone (1938) suggested that seven primary mental abilities underlie individual differences in cognition. The seven factors in Thurstone's theory are verbal comprehension, measured by vocabulary tests; number, measured by tests of computation and simple mathematical problem solving; memory, measured by tests of picture and word recall; perceptual speed, measured by tests that require the test-taker to recognize small differences in pictures or to cross out the *a*'s in strings of letters; space, measured by tests requiring mental rotation of pictures or other objects; verbal fluency, measured by speed with which one can think of words beginning with a certain letter; and inductive reasoning, measured by tests such as analogies and number-series completions.

In recent times, many psychometric theorists have settled on hierarchical models as useful characterizations of individual differences in cognitive abilities. These models combine the general factor of Spearman with the primary kinds of mental abilities of Thurstone by suggesting that the abilities are related hierarchically. One such model, developed by R. B. Cattell (1971), proposes that general intelligence – at the top of the hierarchy – comprises two major subfactors: fluid ability and crystallized. Fluid ability represents the acquisition of new information, or the grasping of new relations and abstractions regarding known information, as required in inductive-reasoning tests such as analogies and series completions. Crystallized ability represents the accumulation of knowledge over the lifespan of the child and is measured, for example, in tests of vocabulary, of general information, and of achievement. Subsumed within these two major subfactors are other, more specific, factors.

A more detailed hierarchical model, based on a reanalysis of many data sets from hundreds of studies, has been proposed by Carroll (1993). At the top of the hierarchy is general ability; in the middle of the hierarchy are various broad abilities, such as learning and memory processes and the effortless production of many ideas. At the bottom of the hierarchy are many narrow, specific abilities such as spelling ability and reasoning speed. Other similar hierarchical models have been proposed as well (e.g., Gustafsson, 1988; Horn, 1994; P. E. Vernon, 1971).

According to psychometric theorists, children differ from each other intellectually primarily by virtue of differences in their abilities as revealed by scores on the underlying factors of intelligence. Herrnstein and Murray (1994), among others (e.g., Jensen, 1998), have argued that children with low levels of *g*, or general intelligence, are handicapped both in school and in life, and are less capable of succeeding in a wide variety of life activities, including school performance, getting along with others, and, later in life, performance on the job. Many, although certainly not all, psychometric theorists tend to emphasize the role that genes play in the development of intelligence, and tend to view levels of intelligence as relatively fixed rather than as modifiable (e.g., Bouchard, 1998).

The biological paradigm

Several studies suggest that the speed of conduction of neural impulses may correlate with intelligence as measured by IQ tests (e.g., McGarry-Roberts, Stelmack, & Campbell, 1992; P. A. Vernon & Mori, 1992), although the evidence is mixed. Some investigators (e.g., P. A. Vernon & Mori, 1992) have suggested that this research supports a view that intelligence is based on neural efficiency.

P. A. Vernon and Mori (1992) measured nerve-conduction velocity in the median nerve of the arm using electrodes. They found significant correlations between conduction velocity and IQ (around .4). A meta-analysis of nine studies that have investigated the relation between peripheral nerve-conduction velocity and psychometrically measured intelligence yields mixed results (P. A. Vernon et al., 2000). Some of the studies have yielded positive correlations (e.g., P. A. Vernon & Mori); others have yielded trivial correlations (e.g., Reed & Jensen, 1991). Clearly, the jury is still out on the relation of peripheral nerve-conduction velocity – rate of conduction over the length of the axons – to IQ.

Electrophysiological and metabolic evidence. Electrophysiological research has suggested that complex patterns of electrical activity in the brain, which are prompted by specific stimuli, sometimes correlate with scores on IQ tests. Many of the early studies used simple sensory processing as the basis for eliciting the waveforms (Barrett & Eysenck, 1992; Caryl, 1994). Typical correlations in these early studies were at about the .3 level between the latency of event-related potential waves elicited by visual stimuli and scores on tests of intelligence.

In a typical study, Reed and Jensen (1992) used performance during a pattern-reversal task (e.g., using a checkerboard where the black squares changed to white and the white squares to black) to measure two medium-latency event-related potentials, N70 and P100. The correlations between the latency measures and IQ were small (in the range of −.1 to −.2) but significant in some cases. (Correlations were negative because longer latencies corresponded to lower IQs.)

One of the most interesting areas of biological research on intelligence involves examining the rate of cortical glucose metabolism. Richard Haier and his colleagues have studied cortical glucose metabolic rates using PET scan analysis while subjects solved Raven Matrix problems or played the computer game Tetris (Haier, Siegel, Tang, Abel, & Buchsbaum, 1992). In both studies they found that more intelligent subjects showed lower metabolic rates, suggesting that more intelligent individuals expend less effort when working on these tasks. The direction of this relationship, however, remains to be shown. It is not clear whether smarter people expend less glucose, or lower glucose metabolism contributes to higher intelligence. More intelligent people appear to use their brains more efficiently. Using functional magnetic resonance imaging (fMRI), John Duncan and his colleagues (2000) have found that intelligence, or at least the general component of it, seems to be localized in the lateral frontal cortex.

Another biological approach to intelligence involves the search for drugs that enhance intellectual abilities. Drugs like Adderall (a stimulant) and Provigil (which induces wakefulness) are being used to increase intellectual performance, including by students taking tests (Carey, 2008). There is a feeling among some that use of these drugs is somehow not ethical. Yet, caffeine is used by millions of people to enhance cognitive performance. It has been known for some time that caffeine increases cognitive performance (Revelle, Humphreys, Simon, & Gilliland, 1980). Thus, if ethical issues are to be raised, they will have to be raised for all performance-enhancing drugs, including caffeine.

Genes. There are now a number of genes that have been associated with intelligence and its development. Grigorenko (2009) has reviewed some of these findings. According to Grigorenko (2009),

> there have been numerous studies of a variety of candidate genes [for reviews, see (Deary, Spinath, & Bates, 2006; Posthuma & de Geus, 2006; Shaw, 2007)]. Among these genes are (a) neurotransmitters and genes related to their metabolism (e.g., catechol-O-methyl transferase, *COMT* located at 22q11; monoamine oxidase A gene, *MAOA* at Xp11; cholinergic muscarinic 2 receptor, *CHRM2* at 7q33; dopamine D2 receptor, *DRD2* at 11q23; serotonin receptor 2A, *HTR2A* at 13q13, metabotrophic glutamate receptor, *GRM3* at 7q21, and the adrenergic alpha 2A receptor gene, *ADRA2A* at 10q25); (b) genes related to developmental processes, broadly defined (e.g., cathepsin D, *CTSD* at 11p15; succinic semialdehyde dehydrogenase, *ALDH5A1* at 6p22; type-I membrane protein related to beta-glucosidases, *klotho* at 13q13; brain-derived neurotrophic factor, *BDNF*, at 11p14; muscle segment homeobox 1, *MSX1* at 4p16; synaptosomal-associated protein 25, *SNAP25*, at 20p12); and (c) genes of variable functions (e.g., heat shock 70kDa protein 8, *HSPA8* at 11q24; insulin-like growth factor 2 receptor, *IGF2R* at 6q25; prion protein, *PRNP* at 20p13; dystrobrevin binding protein 1, *DTNBP1* at 6p22; apolipoprotein E, *APOE* at 19q13; cystathionine-beta-synthase, *CBS* at 21q22; major histocompatibility complex, class II, DR, *HLA-DRB1* at 6p21).

The systems paradigm

Systems theories attempt to go beyond psychometric methods and static factors in explaining the development of individual differences in cognitive abilities. Two such theories are the theory of multiple intelligences and the triarchic theory of intelligence.

The theory of multiple intelligences. Gardner (1983, 1993, 1999, 2006) does not view individual differences in cognition, or even intelligence, as singular. Nor does he even speak of multiple cognitive abilities. Rather, he speaks of multiple intelligences. According to his theory, there are eight (or possibly 10) distinct multiple intelligences. These intelligences are (a) linguistic intelligence, which is used when a child reads a book, writes a paper, or even speaks to a friend; (b) logical-mathematical intelligence, which is used when a child solves a school mathematics problem, or counts change, or tries to make a logical argument in speaking to an authority figure; (c) spatial intelligence, which is used when a child needs to get from one place to another, reads a map, or needs to fit his or her clothes in a trunk when preparing for a camping trip; (d) musical intelligence, which is used when a child sings a song, plays the trumpet, or reads music; (e) bodily-kinesthetic intelligence, which is used when a child dances, plays basketball, runs a race, or throws a ball; (f) interpersonal intelligence, which is used when a child relates to other people, such as when he or she tries to understand a sibling's behavior, motives, or emotions; (g) intrapersonal intelligence, which is used when a child tries to understand himself or herself; and (h) naturalist intelligence, which is used when a child tries to understand patterns in the natural world, such as the kinds of places where trees can and cannot grow. Gardner has also speculated that there may be an additional intelligence, existential intelligence, relating to understanding of matters of existence and one's place in the universe.

Gardner has used converging operations to gather evidence to support his theory of the multiple sources of individual differences in cognition. The base of evidence used by Gardner includes (but is not limited to) the distinctive effects of localized brain damage on specific kinds of intelligences, distinctive patterns of development in each kind of intelligence across the lifespan, evidence from exceptional individuals (from both ends of the spectrum), and evolutionary theory. More recent work suggest that abilities are diffused rather than being isolated in the brain (e.g., Duncan et al., 2000).

Gardner's view of the mind is modular. Modularity theorists believe that different abilities – such as Gardner's intelligences – can be isolated as emanating from distinct portions or modules of the brain. Thus, a major task of existing and future research on intelligence would be to isolate the portions of the brain responsible for each of the intelligences. Gardner has speculated as to at least some of these relevant portions, but hard evidence for the existence of the separate intelligences has yet to be produced: the theory is in need of predictive empirical verification.

There may be multiple kinds of intelligence beyond those suggested by Gardner. For example, Salovey and Mayer (1990; see also Mayer, Salovey, & Caruso, 2000) have suggested the existence of *emotional intelligence*, which involves the child's ability to understand and regulate one's emotions (see also Goleman, 1995), and which appears to be relatively distinct from intelligence as it is conventionally conceived. For example, a child who, upon feeling frustrated, inappropriately gets angry and throws temper tantrums might be viewed as having a lower level of emotional intelligence than another child who reacts to frustration in a more prosocial way. Other investigators have discussed a concept of *social intelligence*, which is a form of intelligence used in interacting effectively with other people (Cantor & Kihlstrom, 1987; Kihlstrom & Cantor, 2000; Ford, 1994). For example, a child who effectively relates to other children on the playground might be viewed as effective in social intelligence. Still other investigators have suggested a concept of *practical intelligence*, or the ability to function effectively in everyday life (Sternberg et al., 2000; Wagner, 2000). A child high in practical intelligence, for example, would know how to allocate time in order to get his or her homework done on time. Clearly, psychological concepts of intelligence are becoming much broader than they were just a few years ago. At the same time, not all psychologists accept these broader conceptions.

The triarchic theory. Whereas Gardner emphasizes the separateness of the various aspects of intelligence, I have tended to emphasize the extent to which these aspects work together in the triarchic theory of successful intelligence (Sternberg, 1985, 1988, 1997, 1999a, 1999b, 2005). According to the triarchic theory, intelligence comprises three aspects, which deal with the relation of intelligence (a) to the internal world, (b) to experience, and (c) to the external world. Intelligence draws on three kinds of information-processing components: (a) metacomponents – executive processes used to plan, monitor, and evaluate problem solving; (b) performance components – lower-order processes used for implementing the commands of the metacomponents; and (c) knowledge-acquisition components – the processes used for learning how to solve the problems in the first place. Individual differences in cognition derive largely from individual differences in the execution of these three kinds of components. The components are highly interdependent.

Suppose a child was asked by his parents to justify their buying him a toy he wants. To succeed the child would need to draw on all three types of components. The child would use metacomponents to decide on a line of argument (e.g., that the toy is highly educational), plan the line or argument, monitor the argument to see whether it is winning over his parents, and evaluate how well the finished product succeeds in accomplishing his goals (i.e., do his parents buy the toy for him?). He would draw on past uses of knowledge-acquisition components to know what kinds of arguments do and do not work with his parents. He would also use performance components for the actual argumentation. In practice, the three kinds of components do not function in isolation. For example, if monitoring the argument reveals that it is not working, the child may then use performance components to initiate another line of argument. He also stores the knowledge learned about kinds of arguments that do not work with his parents.

These three kinds of components all contribute to three relatively distinct aspects of intelligence. In this "triarchy" of intelligence, analytical abilities are used to analyze, evaluate, critique, or judge, as when a child decides whether to hand over a toy to his sister that the sister argues she has a right to play with. A metacomponent, such as that of planning, might be used by the sister analytically to devise a strategy to convince her brother to let her play with the toy. Creative abilities are used to create, invent, discover, and imagine, as when a child invents novel arguments why he really needs a toy (e.g., that he may see a way to improve on it and thereby start his own line of toys to be sold on the internet). Practical abilities are used to apply, utilize, and implement ideas in the real world, as when the child realizes that despite his wonderful arguments, his parents just are not going to buy him the toy and it is time to quit arguing and wait for another day. Research suggests that the three types of abilities – analytical, creative, and practical – are statistically relatively independent (Sternberg, 1985; Sternberg et al., 2000; Sternberg, Grigorenko, Ferrari, & Clinkenbeard, 1999; Sternberg & Lubart, 1995; Sternberg & the Rainbow Project Collaborators, 2005, 2006). Moreover, it is possible to increase prediction of school success and reduce ethnic-group differences by measuring not only the analytical abilities assessed by conventional tests, but also creative and practical ones (Sternberg and the Rainbow Project Collaborators, 2006). Including creative and practical assessments also decreases ethnic-group differences in tests of achievement, relative to just including memory and analytical items (Stemler, Grigorenko, Jarvin, & Sternberg, 2006).

According to the triarchic theory, children may apply their intelligence to many different kinds of problems. For example, some people may be more intelligent in the face of abstract, academic problems, whereas others may be more intelligent in the face of concrete, practical problems. The theory does not define an intelligent child as someone who necessarily excels in all aspects of intelligence. Rather, intelligent children know their own strengths and weaknesses and find ways to capitalize on their strengths and either to compensate for or to correct their weaknesses. For example, a child strong in verbal skills but not in quantitative skills might choose to become a writer rather than an accountant. The point is to make the most of one's strengths and to find ways to improve upon, or at least to live comfortably with, one's weaknesses. Some children are extreme in their strengths and weaknesses, and we consider such children next.

Heredity, Environment, and Modifiability

Since ancient times, people have speculated on the extent to which individual differences among people are due to nature – or heredity – and the extent to which they are due to nurture – or environment. The ancient nature–nurture controversy continues in regard to cognitive skills (Birney, Citron-Pousty, Lutz, & Sternberg, 2005; Grigorenko & Sternberg, 2003; Sternberg & Grigorenko, 1997). However, today, the large majority of psychologists believe that differences in cognitive skills result from a combination of hereditary and environmental factors.

The degree to which heredity contributes to individual differences in cognitive skills is often expressed in terms of a heritability coefficient, a number on a scale from 0 to 1, such that a coefficient of 0 means that heredity has no influence on variation among children, whereas a coefficient of 1 means that heredity is the only influence on such variation. This coefficient can be applied to cognitive skills or to any other attributes, such as height, weight, or running skills. The heritability coefficient is limited in the information it conveys because it does not adequately account for gene–environment interaction – for example, the extent to which genes can affect the environments people choose and the environments people live in can affect their ultimate choices of mates and hence the genes carried over to their children. Also important are epigenetic effects, or changes in gene expression induced by mechanisms other than changes in DNA.

It is important to remember that the heritability coefficient indicates variation in measured attributes. The heritability coefficient can tell us only about genetic effects that result in individual differences among children. It tells us nothing about genetic effects where there are no, or only trivial, differences. For example, both how tall you are and how many fingers you have at birth are in large part genetically preprogrammed. But we can use the coefficient of heritability only to assess genetic effects on height, where there are large individual differences. We cannot use the coefficient to understand number of fingers at birth because there is so little variation across children.

It is also important to realize that heritability tells us nothing about the *modifiability* of cognitive skills. A trait can be heritable and yet modifiable. For example, height is highly heritable, with a heritability coefficient greater than .9 in most populations. Yet heights of Europeans and North Americans increased by over 5 cm between 1920 and 1970 (Van Wieringen, 1978). Consider, as another example, attributes of corn. Many attributes of corn, including height, are highly heritable. But if one batch of corn seeds were planted in the rich fertile fields of Iowa, and another similar batch were planted in the Mojave Desert, the batch planted in Iowa undoubtedly would grow taller and thrive better, regardless of the heritability of the attributes of the corn. In this case, environment would largely determine how well the corn grew (Lewontin, 1974).

These issues apply not just to corn, but also to children. Ramey and his colleagues have shown that it is possible to take children with relatively low IQs, place them in an educational environment that enriches their cognitive functioning, and thereby substantially increase their cognitive skills as measured by tests of IQ and other kinds of cognitive tests (Ramey & Ramey, 1998, 2000). Similar children, lacking such interventions, show no comparable gains. In other words, two children with similar genetic predispositions can show very different cognitive performances depending on the environments in which they find themselves.

Current estimates of the heritability coefficient of various cognitive skills are based almost exclusively on performance on conventional tests of intelligence. The estimates can be no better than the tests and we have already seen that the tests define intelligence somewhat narrowly. Among Gardner's intelligences, for example, they measure primarily linguistic, logical-mathematical, and perhaps spatial intelligences. In Sternberg's terms, they measure only analytical abilities.

How can we estimate the heritability of cognitive skills (at least that portion of them measured by the conventional tests)? Several methods have been used. The main ones are studies of separated identical twins, studies of identical versus fraternal twins, and studies of adopted children (Mackintosh, 1998; Plomin, DeFries, McClearn, & McGuffin, 2008; Sternberg & Grigorenko, 1997).

Separated identical twins

Identical twins have identical genes. No one knows exactly why identical twinning occurs, but we do know that identical twins result when a sperm fertilizes an egg, and then the newly formed embryo splits in two, resulting in two embryos with identical genes. Suppose that a set of identical twins is born, and then one of the twins is immediately whisked away to a new environment, chosen at random, so that no relationship exists between the environments in which the two twins are raised. The two twins would have identical genes, but any similarity between their environments would be due only to chance. If we then created a number of such twin pairs, we would be able to estimate the contribution of heredity to individual differences in intelligence by correlating the measured intelligence of each child with that of his or her identical twin. The twins would have in common all their heredity but none of their environment (except any aspects that might be similar due to chance). In studies of twins reared apart, the various estimates tend to fall within roughly the same heritability-coefficient range of .6 to .8 (e.g., Bouchard & McGue, 1981; Juel-Nielsen, 1965; Newman, Freeman, & Holzinger, 1937; Shields, 1962; see Plomin et al., 2008).These relatively high figures must be interpreted with some caution, however, as the supposedly random assortment of environments was not truly random. Placement authorities tend to place twins in environments relatively similar to those the twins had left. Therefore variation that is actually environmental is included in the correlation that is supposed to represent only the effect of heredity.

Identical versus fraternal twins

Another way to estimate heritability is to compare the correlation of IQs for identical versus fraternal twins. The idea is that whereas identical twins share identical genes, fraternal twins share only the same genes as would any brother or sister. On average, fraternal twins share only 50% of their genes. To the extent that the identical and fraternal twin pairs share similar environments due to age, we should not get environmental differences due merely to variations in age among sibling pairs. If environments are nearly the same for both twins, differences in the correlation of intelligence scores between fraternal and identical twins should be attributable to heredity. According to a review by Bouchard and McGue (1981), these data lead to a heritability estimate of about .75, again suggesting a high level of heritability. More recent estimates are similar, although quite variable (Mackintosh, 1998). Social class moderates heritability. In particular, heritability is substantially lower in children of lower socioeconomic class (Turkheimer, Haley, D'Onofrio, Waldron, & Gottesman, 2003). Thus, environments matter more for children of lower socioeconomic class.

These data may be affected by the fact that fraternal twins often do not share environments to the same extent that identical ones do, particularly if the fraternal twins are not same-sexed twins. Parents tend to treat identical twins more nearly alike than they do fraternal twins, even to the extent of having them dress the same way. Moreover, the twins themselves are likely to respond differently if they are identical, perhaps seeking out more apparent identity with their twin. Thus, once again, the contribution of environment may be underestimated to some extent.

Adoption

Yet another way to examine hereditary versus environmental contributions to intelligence is by comparing the correlation between the IQs of adopted children with those of their biological parents, on the one hand, and their adoptive parents, on the other. Biological parents provide adopted children with their genes, and adoptive parents provide the children their environments. So, to the extent that heredity matters, the higher correlation should be with the intelligence of the biological rather than the adoptive parents; to the extent that environment matters, the higher correlation should be that with the intelligence of the adoptive rather than the biological parents. In some families, it is also possible to compare the IQs of the adopted children to the IQs of either biological or adoptive siblings.

Many psychologists who have studied intelligence as measured by IQ believe the heritability of intelligence to be about .5 in children, and somewhat higher in adults (Mackintosh, 1998; Plomin et al. 2008), for whom the early effects of the child-rearing environment have receded. However, there probably is no one coefficient of heritability that applies to all populations under all circumstances. Indeed, changes in distributions of genes or in environments can change the estimates. One way of changing the environment is through concerted efforts to modify cognitive skills.

Modifying cognitive skills

At one time, it was believed that cognitive abilities are fixed, and that we are stuck forever with whatever level of cognitive abilities we have at birth. Today, many researchers believe that cognitive abilities are malleable – that the skills deriving from these abilities can be shaped and even increased through various kinds of interventions (Bransford & Stein, 1993; Detterman & Sternberg, 1982; Grotzer & Perkins, 2000; Halpern, 1996; Mayer, 2000; Perkins & Grotzer, 1997; Sternberg & Grigorenko, 2007; Sternberg, Kaufman, & Grigorenko, 2008; Sternberg & Spear-Swerling, 1996). For example, the Head Start program was initiated in the 1960s as a way of providing preschoolers with an edge on cognitive skills and accomplishments when they started school. Long-term follow-ups have indicated that by mid-adolescence, children who participated in the program were more than a grade ahead of matched controls who were not in the program (Lazar & Darlington, 1982; Zigler & Berman, 1983). Children in the program also scored higher on a variety of tests of scholastic achievement, were less likely to need remedial attention, and were less likely to show behavioral problems. Although such measures are not truly measures of intelligence, they show strong positive correlations with intelligence tests. A number of other programs have also shown some success in environments outside of the family home (e.g., Adams, 1986).

Support for the importance of home environment was found by Bradley and Caldwell (1984) in regard to the development of cognitive skills in young children. These researchers found that several factors in the early home environment, before children start school, may be linked to high IQ scores: emotional and verbal responsivity of the primary caregiver and the caregiver's involvement with the child, avoidance of restriction and punishment, organization of the physical environment and activity schedule, provision of appropriate play materials, and opportunities for variety in daily stimulation. Further, Bradley and Caldwell found that these factors more effectively predicted IQ scores than did socioeconomic status or family-structure variables. Note, however, that the Bradley-Caldwell study pertained to preschool children, and children's IQ scores do not begin to predict adult IQ scores well until about age 4. Moreover, before age 7, the scores are not very stable (Bloom, 1964).

Perhaps the best evidence for the modifiability of cognitive skills comes from research by Flynn (1987, 1998, 2007; see also Neisser, 1998). This research suggests that ever since recordkeeping began early in the twentieth century, IQ scores have been increasing roughly nine points per generation (every 30 years). This result is sometimes referred to as the *Flynn effect*. From any point of view, this increase is large. No one knows exactly why such large increases have occurred, although the explanation must be environmental, because the period of time involved is too brief for genetic mutations to have had an effect. If psychologists were able to understand the cause of the increase, they might be able to apply what they learned to increasing the intellectual skills of children within a given generation.

Altogether, evidence now indicates that environment, motivation, and training can profoundly affect cognitive skills. Heredity may set some kind of upper limit on how cognitively skillful a child can become. However, we now know that for any attribute that is partly genetic, there is a reaction range – the broad limits within which a particular attribute can be expressed in various possible ways, given the inherited potential for expression of the attribute in a particular child. Thus, each child's cognitive skills can be developed further within this broad range of potential skills. We have no reason to believe that children now reach the upper limits in the development of their cognitive skills. To the contrary, the evidence suggests that, although we cannot work miracles, we can do quite a bit to help children become more cognitively adept.

Extremes in Cognitive Skills

Intellectual giftedness

Psychologists differ in terms of how they define the intellectually gifted (Callahan, 2000; Chart, Grigorenko, & Sternberg, 2008; Sternberg & Davidson, 2005; Winner, 1997). Some use an exclusively IQ-based criterion. For example, many programs for the gifted screen largely on the basis of scores on conventional intelligence tests, taking children in perhaps the top 1% (IQ roughly equal to 135 or above) or 2% (IQ roughly equal to 132 or above) for their programs. Others also supplement the assessment of IQ as a basis of giftedness with other criteria, such as school or career achievements or other measures of gifted performance.

Probably the most well-known studies of gifted children were conducted by Terman. Terman conducted a *longitudinal study*, research which followed particular individuals over the course of their lifespans (Terman, 1925; Terman & Oden, 1959). The study has continued even after Terman's death. In his sample of the gifted, Terman included children from California under age 11 with IQs over 140, as well as children in the 11- to 14-year age bracket with slightly lower IQs. The mean IQ of the 643 research participants selected was 151; only 22 of these participants had IQs lower than 140. The accomplishments in later life of the selected group were extraordinary by any criterion. For example, 31 men from the study were listed in *Who's Who in America*. There were numerous highly successful businessmen, as well as individuals who were successful in all of the professions. As with all correlational data, it would be difficult to assign a causal role to IQ in accounting for the accomplishments of the successful individuals in the study, as other factors such as familial socioeconomic status and the final educational level achieved by these individuals could also be important.

Today, many, if not most, psychologists look to more than IQ for the identification of the intellectually gifted. (See Sternberg & Davidson, 1986, 2005, and Winner, 1996, for descriptions of a variety of theories of giftedness.) For example, Renzulli (1986; Renzulli & Reis, 2004) has suggested that high motivation, or commitment to tasks, and high creativity are important to giftedness, in addition to above-average (although not necessarily outstanding) cognitive abilities. Perhaps gifted children are children who are good at something – sometimes just one thing – but who find a way of capitalizing on that something to make the most of their capabilities (Sternberg, 1985, 2007). All of these theorists are in agreement that there is more to giftedness than a high IQ. Indeed, children can be creatively or practically gifted, and not even show up as particularly distinguished at all on an IQ test (Sternberg, 1997, 2005).

In one set of studies, high-school students from all around the United States and some other countries were identified in terms of analytical, creative, and practical giftedness (Sternberg & Clinkenbeard, 1995; Sternberg, Ferrari, Clinkenbeard, & Grigorenko, 1996). In many cases, students who were gifted in one of these kinds of abilities were not gifted in others. The identified students were then taught a college-level course that emphasized analytical, creative, or practical forms of instruction. Some students were in an instructional condition that matched their pattern of cognitive skills. Other students were taught in a way that mismatched their pattern of cognitive skills. Students' achievement was also evaluated in all three ways. It was found that students achieved at higher levels when they were taught in a way that matched their pattern of cognitive skills. In general, the best teaching is teaching that enables students both to capitalize on their strengths *and* to correct or compensate for their weaknesses (Sternberg, Torff, & Grigorenko, 1998).

These findings raise a potentially important issue. Research suggests that intelligence tests are not *biased* in a narrow statistical sense: they do not tend, on average, falsely to predict criterion performance for particular groups (Mackintosh, 1998). For example, lower intelligence-test scores tend to be associated with lower school achievement for children from a variety of groups. But if intelligence tests measure a somewhat narrow set of skills and schools also tend to value this narrow set of skills, then there is a possibility that both the predictor (such as an intelligence test) and the criterion (such as school grades) share the same bias. Statistical analyses would fail to detect bias because both the predictor and the criterion that is predicted share the same bias. The bias is not in the predictor (the test), per se, but in the entire system of prediction (the test, the measure of achievement, and their interrelation). Perhaps if intelligence tests and schools both valued creative and practical abilities as well as analytical abilities, children now identified as relatively lacking in intelligence would be viewed as more intelligent.

Developmental disability (intellectual disability)

Developmental disability refers to low levels of intelligence, including low adaptive competence (Detterman, Gabriel, & Ruthsatz, 2000; Detterman & Thompson, 1997). But how should we determine a precise definition of developmental disability and whom we should label as having developmental disability? Different viewpoints lead to different conclusions.

The American Association on Intellectual and Developmental Disabilities no longer uses the term "mental retardation." It instead uses the term "intellectual disability." It defines intellectual disability as "a disability characterized by significant limitations both in intellectual functioning and in adaptive behavior as expressed in conceptual, social, and practical adaptive skills. This disability originates before the age of 18" (American Association on Intellectual and Developmental Disabilities, 2008). Someone with developmental disability, or intellectual disability, shows both low IQ and low adaptive competence, the latter of which refers to how a child (or an adult) gets along in the world. In other words, to be labeled as having a developmental disability, a child not only would have to perform poorly on an intelligence test but also would have to show problems adapting to the environment, both conceptually and socially. A child whose performance was normal in every way except for low IQ would not, by this definition, be classified as having a developmental disability. Adaptive life skills are judged in a variety of domains, such as communication (as in talking to someone or writing them a letter), self-care (as in dressing oneself or using the toilet), home living (as in preparing meals), and social interaction (as in meeting the expectations of others).

It is not always easy to assess adaptive competence, however, as the following example (Edgerton, 1967) shows. A man with developmental disability (who had scored low on tests of intelligence) was unable to tell time – an indication of some kind of cognitive deficit. However, the man employed a clever compensatory strategy. He wore a nonfunctional watch, so that whenever he wanted to know the time, he could stop, look at his watch, pretend to notice that his watch did not work, and then ask a nearby stranger (who would have observed his behavior) to tell him the correct time. How should we assess this man's adaptive competence – in terms of his strategy for determining the time or in terms of his inability to tell time by looking at a watch? Did the man have intellectual disability, and if so, why?

Zigler (1982; see also Hodapp & Dykens, 1994) believes that some children with intellectual disability simply develop mentally at a slower rate than do children with normal intelligence. Most investigators, however, seek not only to look at quantitative differences in rates of development but also at qualitative differences in performance. A key qualitative difference centers on metacognitive skill. There is fairly widespread agreement that children with intellectual disabilities have difficulties with the executive processes of cognition, such as planning, monitoring, and evaluating their strategies for task performance (Campione, Brown, & Ferrara, 1982). An example would be their planning to rehearse lists of words they are asked to memorize (Brown, Campione, Bray, & Wilcox, 1973). To what extent might such difficulties be based on hereditary factors and to what extent on environmental factors?

Both environmental and hereditary factors may contribute to developmental disability (Grigorenko, 2000; Sternberg & Grigorenko, 1997). Environmental influences before birth may cause permanent disability – for example, developmental disability resulting from a mother's inadequate nutrition or ingestion of toxins such as alcohol during the child's prenatal development (Olson, 1994). A child exposed to an impoverished environment or denied opportunities for even basic instruction in the home might display developmental disability. Even a brief trauma, such as from a car accident or a fall, can injure the brain, causing developmental disability.

Although we do not understand the subtle influences of heredity on intelligence very well at present, we do know of several genetic syndromes that clearly cause developmental disability. For example, one of the more common genetic causes of developmental disability is Down syndrome, once called "mongolism." This syndrome results from the presence of extra chromosomal material on one of the chromosomes. The extra material disrupts the normal biochemical messages and results in developmental disability and other features of this syndrome.

Group Differences in Cognitive Abilities

Cultural and societal analyses of cognitive skills render it particularly important to consider carefully the meaning of group differences in measured IQ (Fischer, Jankowski, & Lucas, 1996; Loehlin, 2000). For example, on average, African Americans score somewhat lower than Caucasians on conventional standardized tests of intelligence (Herrnstein & Murray, 1994); but it is important to remember that Italian American scores used to be considerably lower than they are now. Scores of groups can fluctuate. Scores of African Americans have been showing an increasing pattern over time, just as have scores for other groups.

Available evidence to date suggests an environmental explanation for these group differences (Nisbett, 1998; Sternberg, Grigorenko, & Kidd, 2005). For example, in one study, offspring of American servicemen born to German women during the Allied occupation of Germany after the Second World War revealed no significant difference between IQs of children of African American versus white servicemen (Eyferth, 1961). This result suggests that given similar environments, the children of the two groups (African American and white) of servicemen performed equally on tests of intelligence. Another study found that children adopted by white families obtained higher IQ scores than did children adopted by African American families, again suggesting environmental factors contributing to the difference between the two groups (Moore, 1986). Another way of studying group differences has been through trans-racial adoption studies, where white parents have adopted African American children (Scarr & Weinberg, 1976; Scarr, Weinberg, & Waldman, 1993; Weinberg, Scarr, & Waldman, 1992). The results of these studies have been somewhat difficult to interpret, in that both white and African American children who were adopted in the study showed decreases in IQ after a 10-year follow-up on their performance.

Group differences may thus originate from a number of factors, many of which change over time. The result is that group differences are not immutable: a group that scores, on average, lower than another group at one given time may score, on average, lower, the same, or even higher at another time.

For example, environmental factors such as poverty, under-nutrition, and illness might affect intelligence (Sternberg et al., 2000). One mechanism is through resources. Children who are poor often do not have the resources in the home and school that children from more affluent environments have. Another mechanism is through attention to and concentration on the skills being taught in school. Children who are undernourished or ill may find it hard to concentrate in school, and therefore may profit less from the instruction they receive. A third mechanism is the system of rewards in the environment. Children who grow up in economically deprived environments may note that the children who are most rewarded are not those who do well in school, but rather those who find ways of earning the money they need to survive, whatever these ways may be. It is unlikely that there is any one mechanism that fully explains the effects of these various variables. It is also important to realize that whatever these mechanisms are, they can start in utero, not just after birth. For example fetal alcohol syndrome results in reduced IQ, and has its effects prenatally, before the child even enters the world outside the mother's womb.

The preceding arguments with respect to culture and group differences may make it clear why it is so difficult to come up with what everyone would consider a culture-fair test – a test that is equally appropriate for members of all cultures and that comprises items that are equally fair to members of all cultures. If members of different cultures have different ideas of what it means to be intelligent, then the very behaviors that may be considered intelligent in one culture may be viewed as unintelligent in another. Indeed, there is abundant evidence that members of different cultures in fact do have different conceptions of intelligence (Berry, 1974; Greenfield, 1997; Grigorenko et al., 2001; Sternberg & Kaufman, 1998).

Almost everyone would like to construct only culture-fair tests. Unfortunately, at present and for the foreseeable future, there exist no perfectly culture-fair tests of intelligence. Even among the tests devised to date, performance on those tests that have been labeled as "culture-fair" seems to be influenced in some degree by cultural factors, such as years of schooling and academic achievements (e.g., Ceci, 1996). In sum, one must be careful about drawing conclusions regarding group differences in intelligence (Greenfield, 1997; Loehlin, 2000) that may appear to be justified on the surface but that represent only a superficial analysis of group differences.

The development of culture-fair tests based on each culture's own definition of intelligence may be an unrealistic goal, but it is possible to provide culture-relevant tests. Culture-relevant tests employ skills and knowledge that relate to the cultural experiences of the test-takers. Content and procedures are used in testing that are appropriate to the cultural context of the test-takers. For example, 14-year-old boys performed poorly on a task when it was couched as a cupcake-baking task but performed well when it was framed as a battery-charging task (Ceci & Bronfenbrenner, 1985). Brazilian maids had no difficulty with proportional reasoning when hypothetically purchasing food but had great difficulty with it when hypothetically purchasing medicinal herbs (Schliemann & Magalhües, 1990). Brazilian children whose poverty had forced them to become street vendors showed no difficulty in performing complex arithmetic computations when selling things but had great difficulty performing similar calculations in a classroom (Carraher, Carraher, & Schliemann, 1985; Ceci & Roazzi, 1994; Nuñes, 1994). Young Kenyan children who knew more of the natural herbal medicines they needed to treat parasitic illnesses actually did worse on IQ tests than did children who had less of this practical knowledge (Sternberg et al., 2001). Eskimo children who had superb knowledge of hunting, fishing, indigenous foods and medicines, and geographic navigation using natural landmarks were, for the most part, considered not very bright by their teachers in school (Grigorenko et al., 2004). These children learned better when taught in practical ways that made use of objects in their environments (e.g., fish racks) than when taught in abstract ways linked to conventional textbooks (Sternberg, Lipka, Newman, Wildfeuer, & Grigorenko, 2007).

To summarize, the causes as well as the manifestations of individual and group differences in cognitive skills are complex. At times, superficial comparisons are made between individuals or groups with little attempt to gain serious insight into either the causes or the modifiability of these differences. The study of individual differences in cognitive development needs to concentrate not just on cataloguing such differences, but, rather, on understanding their causes. Intervention efforts need to focus on modification with the view that cognitive skills almost always can be increased, at least to some degree.

Conclusion

This chapter has described some major paradigms for understanding individual differences in cognitive development, three of which were described in detail. Some of the paradigms have waned in recent years, such as the Piagetian one, whereas others have waxed, such as the biological one. Eventually, one would hope that the paradigms would be more integrated. For example, Piaget looked at himself as taking what he called a genetic-epistemological approach, and he had training in biology. If there is one major lesson of the research, it is that there are no glib explanations. For example, attempts such as that by Herrnstein and Murray (1994) to explain many societal differences in terms of general intelligence are today seen by many as more "explaining away" than "explaining" developmental and differential effects. It is tempting to seek the easy explanations. The problem is that they do not adequately account for the complexity that underlies human cognitive development and individual differences in it.

References

Adams, J. L. (1986). *The care and feeding of ideas: A guide to encouraging creativity*. Reading, MA: Addison-Wesley Publishing Company.

Anderson, M. (1992). *Intelligence and development: A cognitive theory*. Oxford: Blackwell.

Barrett, P. T., & Eysenck, H. J. (1992). Brain evoked potentials and intelligence: The Hendrickson paradigm. *Intelligence, 16*(3–4), 361–381.

Berry, J. W. (1974). Radical cultural relativism and the concept of intelligence. In J. W. Berry & P. R. Dasen (Eds.), *Culture and cognition: Readings in cross-cultural psychology* (pp. 225–229). London: Methuen.

Binet, A., & Simon, T. (1916). *The development of intelligence in children*. Baltimore: Williams & Wilkins. (Originally published in 1905).

Birney, D. P., Citron-Pousty, J. H., Lutz, D. J., & Sternberg, R. J. (2005). The development of cognitive and intellectual abilities. In M. H. Bornstein & M. E. Lamb (Eds.), *Developmental science: An advanced textbook* (5th ed., pp. 327–358). Mahwah, NJ: Erlbaum.

Bjorklund, D. F. (2004). *Children's thinking: Cognitive development and individual differences.* Belmont, CA: Wadsworth.

Bloom, B. S. (1964). *Stability and change in human characteristics.* New York: Wiley.

Borkowski, J. G., & Cavanaugh, J. C. (1979). Maintenance and generalization of skills and strategies by the retarded. In N. R. Ellis (Ed.), *Handbook of mental deficiency, psychological theory, and research* (2nd ed., pp. 569–617). Hillsdale, NJ: Erlbaum.

Bouchard, T. J. (1998). Genetic and environmental influences on adult intelligence and special mental abilities. *Human Biology, 70*, 257–279.

Bouchard, T. J., Jr., & McGue, M. (1981). Familial studies of intelligence: A review. *Science, 212*, 1055–1059.

Bradley, R. H., & Caldwell, B. M. (1984). 174 Children: A study of the relationship between home environment and cognitive development during the first 5 years. In A. W. Gottfried (Ed.), *Home environment and early cognitive development: Longitudinal research.* San Diego: Academic Press.

Brand, C. (1996). *The g factor: General intelligence and its implications.* Chichester, UK: Wiley.

Bransford, J. D., & Stein, B. S. (1993). *The ideal problem solver: A guide for improving thinking, learning, and creativity* (2nd ed.). New York: W. H. Freeman and Company.

Brown, A. L., Campione, J. C., Bray, N. W., & Wilcox, B. L. (1973). Keeping track of changing variables: Effects of rehearsal training and rehearsal prevention in normal and retarded adolescents. *Journal of Experimental Psychology, 101*, 123–131.

Butterfield, E. C., & Belmont, J. M. (1977). Assessing and improving the cognitive functions of mentally retarded people. In I. Bialer & M. Sternlicht (Eds.), *The psychology of developmental disability: Issues and approaches.* New York: Psychological Dimensions.

Callahan, C. M. (2000). Intelligence and giftedness. In R. J. Sternberg (Ed.), *Handbook of intelligence* (pp.159–175). New York: Cambridge University Press.

Campione, J. C., Brown, A. L., & Ferrara, R. (1982). Developmental disability and intelligence. In R. J. Sternberg (Ed.), *Handbook of human intelligence* (pp. 392–490). New York: Cambridge University Press.

Cantor, N., & Kihlstrom, J. F. (1987). *Personality and social intelligence.* Englewood Cliffs, NJ: Prentice-Hall.

Carey, B. (2008, March 9). Brain enhancement is wrong, right? *The New York Times.* Retrieved October 26, 2008, from http://www.nytimes.com/2008/03/09/weekinreview/09carey.html.

Carraher, T. N., Carraher, D., & Schliemann, A. D. (1985). Mathematics in the streets and in schools. *British Journal of Developmental Psychology, 3*, 21–29.

Carroll, J. B. (1993). *Human cognitive abilities: A survey of factor-analytic studies.* New York: Cambridge University Press.

Caryl, P. G. (1994). Early event-related potentials correlate with inspection time and intelligence. *Intelligence, 18*, 15–46.

Cattell, J. M. (1890). Mental tests and measurements. *Mind, 15*, 373–380.

Cattell, R. B. (1971). *Abilities: Their structure, growth, and action.* Boston: Houghton Mifflin.

Ceci, S. J. (1996). *On intelligence … more or less* (expanded ed.). Cambridge, MA: Harvard University Press.

Ceci, S. J., & Bronfenbrenner, U. (1985). Don't forget to take the cupcakes out of the oven: Strategic time-monitoring, prospective memory and context. *Child Development, 56*, 175–190.

Ceci, S. J., & Roazzi, A. (1994). The effects of context on cognition: Postcards from Brazil. In R. J. Sternberg & R. K. Wagner (Eds.), *Mind in context: Interactionist perspectives on human intelligence* (pp. 74–101). New York: Cambridge University Press.

Chart, H., Grigorenko, E. L., & Sternberg, R. J. (2008). Identification: The Aurora Battery. In J. A. Plucker & C. M. Callahan (Eds.), *Critical issues and practices in gifted education* (pp. 281–301). Waco, TX: Prufrock.

Chen, Z., & Siegler, R. S. (2000). Intellectual development in childhood. In R. J. Sternberg (Ed.), *Handbook of intelligence* (pp. 92–116). New York: Cambridge University Press.

Deary, I. J. (2000). Simple information processing and intelligence. In R. J. Sternberg (Ed.), *Handbook of intelligence* (pp. 267–284). New York: Cambridge University Press.

Deary, I. J., Spinath, F. M., & Bates, T. C. (2006). Genetics of intelligence. *European Journal of Human Genetics, 14*, 690–700.

Demetriou, A., Efklides, A., & Platsidou, M. (1993). The architecture and dynamics of developing mind. *Monographs of the Society for Research in Child Development* (Serial No. 234).

Detterman, D. K., Gabriel, L. T., & Ruthsatz, J. M. (2000). Intelligence and developmental disability. In R. J. Sternberg (Ed.), *Handbook of intelligence* (pp. 141–158). New York: Cambridge University Press.

Detterman, D. K., & Sternberg, R. J. (Eds.). (1982). *How and how much can intelligence be increased?* Norwood, NJ: Erlbaum.

Detterman, D. K., & Thompson, L. A. (1997). IQ, schooling, and developmental disabilities: What's so special about special education? *American Psychologist, 52*, 1082–1091.

Duncan, J., Seitz, R. J., Kolodny, J., Bor, D., Herzog, H., Ahmed, A., Newell, F. N., & Emslie, H. (2000). A neural basis for general intelligence. *Science, 289*, 457–460.

Dunloski, J., & Metcalfe, J. (2008). *Metacognition: A textbook for cognitive, educational, life span and applied psychology*. Thousand Oaks, CA: Sage.

Edgerton, R. (1967). *The cloak of competence*. Berkeley: University of California Press.

Eyferth, K. (1961). Leistungen verschiedener Gruppen von Besatzungskindern im Hamburg-Wechsler Intelligenztest für Kinder (HAWIK). *Archiv für die gesamte Psychologie, 113*, 222–241.

Fischer, C. S., Jankowski, M. S., & Lucas, S. R. (1996). *Inequality by design: Cracking the Bell Curve myth*. New Jersey: Princeton University Press.

Flavell, J. H. (1992). Cognitive development: Past, present, and future. *Developmental Psychology, 28*, 998–1005.

Flynn, J. R. (1987). Massive IQ gains in 14 nations. *Psychological Bulletin, 101*, 171–191.

Flynn, J. R. (1998). WAIS-III and WISC-III gains in the United States from 1972 to 1995: How to compensate for obsolete norms. *Perceptual and Motor Skills, 86*, 1231–1239.

Flynn, J. R. (2007). *What is intelligence?: Beyond the Flynn effect*. New York: Cambridge University Press.

Ford, M. E. (1994). A living systems approach to the integration of personality and intelligence. In R. J. Sternberg, & P. Ruzgis (Eds), *Personality and intelligence* (pp. 188–217). New York: Cambridge University Press.

American Association on Intellectual and Developmental Disabilities (2008). Frequently asked questions on intellectual disability and the AAIDD definition. Retrieved June 7, 2008, from http://www.aaidd.org/Policies/faq_mental_retardation.shtml.

Galton, F. (1883). *Inquiry into human faculty and its development*. London: Macmillan.

Gardner, H. (1983). *Frames of mind: The theory of multiple intelligences*. New York: Basic Books.

Gardner, H. (1993). *Multiple intelligences: The theory in practice*. New York: Basic Books.

Gardner, H. (1999). *Intelligence reframed: Multiple intelligences for the 21st century*. New York: Basic Books.

Gardner, H. (2006). *Multiple intelligences: New horizons in theory and practice*. New York: Basic Books.

Goleman, D. (1995). *Emotional intelligence.* New York: Bantam Books.

Gopnik, A., & Meltzoff, A. (1997). *Words, thoughts, and theories.* Cambridge: MA: MIT Press.

Goswami, U. (1996). Analogical reasoning and cognitive development. In H. Reese (Ed.), *Advances in child development and behavior* (Vol. 26). San Diego: Academic Press.

Greenfield, P. M. (1997). You can't take it with you: Why abilities assessments don't cross cultures. *American Psychologist, 52*(10), 1115–1124.

Grigorenko, E. L. (2000). Heritability and intelligence. In R. J. Sternberg (Ed.), *Handbook of intelligence* (pp. 53–92). New York: Cambridge University Press.

Grigorenko, E. L. (2009). What is so stylish about styles? Comments on the genetic etiology of intellectual styles. In L.-F. Zhang & R. J. Sternberg (Eds.), *Perspectives on intellectual styles* (pp. 233–252). New York: Springer.

Grigorenko, E. L., Geissler, P. W., Prince, R., Okatcha, F., Nokes, C., Kenny, D. A., Bundy, D. A., & Sternberg, R. J. (2001). The organization of Luo conceptions of intelligence: A study of implicit theories in a Kenyan village. *International Journal of Behavioral Development, 25*(4), 367–378.

Grigorenko, E. L., Meier, E., Lipka, J., Mohatt, G., Yanez, E., & Sternberg, R. J. (2004). Academic and practical intelligence: A case study of the Yup'ik in Alaska. *Learning and Individual Differences, 14*, 183–207.

Grigorenko, E. L., & Sternberg, R. J. (2003). The nature–nurture issue. In A. Slater & J. Gavin Bremner (Eds.), *An introduction to developmental psychology* (pp. 64–91). Oxford: Blackwell.

Grotzer, T. A., & Perkins, D. A. (2000). Teaching of intelligence: A performance conception. In R. J. Sternberg (Ed.), *Handbook of intelligence* (pp. 492–515). New York: Cambridge University Press.

Gustafsson, J. E. (1988). Hierarchical models of the structure of cognitive abilities. In R. J. Sternberg (Ed.), *Advances in the psychology of human intelligence* (Vol. 4, pp. 35–71). Hillsdale, NJ: Erlbaum.

Haier, R. J., Siegel, B., Tang, C., Abel, L., & Buchsbaum, M. S. (1992). Intelligence and changes in regional cerebral glucose metabolic rate following learning. *Intelligence, 16*(3–4), 415–426.

Halpern, D. F. (1996). *Thought and knowledge: An introduction to critical thinking* (2nd ed.). Mahwah, NJ: Erlbaum.

Herrnstein, R. J., & Murray, C. (1994). *The bell curve.* New York: Free Press.

Hodapp, R. M., Dykens, E. M. (1994). Developmental disability's two cultures of behavioral research. *American Journal on Developmental disability, 98*, 675–687.

Horn, J. L. (1994). Theory of fluid and crystallized intelligence. In R. J. Sternberg (Ed.), *The encyclopedia of human intelligence* (Vol. 1, pp. 443–451). New York: Macmillan.

Jensen, A. R. (1998). *The g factor: The science of mental ability.* Westport, CT: Praeger/Greenwood.

Juel-Nielsen, N. (1965). *Individual and environment: A psychiatric-psychological investigation of monozygotic twins reared apart.* New York: Humanities Press.

Kihlstrom, J., & Cantor, N. (2000). Social intelligence. In R. J. Sternberg (Ed.), *Handbook of intelligence* (pp. 359–379). New York: Cambridge University Press.

Klahr, D. (1992). Information processing approaches to cognitive development. In M. H. Bornstein & M. E. Lamb (Eds.), *Developmental psychology: An advanced textbook* (3rd ed.). Hillsdale, NJ: Erlbaum.

Lazar, I., & Darlington, R. (1982). Lasting effects of early education: A report from the consortium for longitudinal studies. *Monographs of the Society for Research in Child Development, 47* (2–3, Serial No. 195).

Lewontin, R. (1974). The analysis of variance and the analysis of cause. *American Journal of Human Genetics, 26*, 400–411.

Loehlin, J. C. (2000). Group differences in intelligence. In R. J. Sternberg (Ed.), *Handbook of intelligence* (pp. 176–193). New York: Cambridge University Press.

Lohman, D. F. (2000). Complex information processing and intelligence. In R. J. Sternberg (Ed.), *Handbook of intelligence* (pp. 285–340). New York: Cambridge University Press.

Mackintosh, N. J. (1998). *IQ and human intelligence.* Oxford: Oxford University Press.

Mayer, J. D., Salovey, P., & Caruso, D. (2000). *Models of emotional intelligence.* In R. J. Sternberg (Ed.), *Handbook of intelligence* (pp. 396–420). New York: Cambridge University Press.

McGarry-Roberts, P. A., Stelmack, R. M., & Campbell, K. B. (1992). Intelligence, reaction time, and event-related potentials. *Intelligence, 16*(3–4), 289–313.

McNeil, N. M., Uttal, D. H., Jarvin, L., & Sternberg, R. J. (2009). Should you show me the money? Concrete objects both hurt and help performance on mathematics problems. *Learning and Instruction, 19*, 171–184.

Moore, E. G. J. (1986). Family socialization and the IQ test performance of traditionally and transracially adopted black children. *Developmental Psychology, 22*, 317–326.

Neisser, U. (Ed.) (1998). *The rising curve.* Washington DC: American Psychological Association.

Newman, H. H., Freeman, F. N., & Holzinger, K. J. (1937). *Twins: A study of heredity and environment.* Chicago: University of Chicago Press.

Nisbett, R. E. (1998). Race, genetics, and IQ. In C. Jencks, & M. Phillips (Eds.), *The Black–White test score gap* (pp. 86–102). Washington DC: Brookings Institution.

Nuñes, T. (1994). Street intelligence. In R. J. Sternberg (Ed.), *Encyclopedia of human intelligence* (Vol. 2, pp. 1045–1049). New York: Macmillan.

Olson, H. C. (1994). Fetal alcohol syndrome. In R. J. Sternberg (Ed.), *Encyclopedia of human intelligence* (Vol. 1, pp. 439–443). New York: Macmillan.

Perkins, D. N., & Grotzer, T. A. (1997). Teaching intelligence. *American Psychologist, 52*, 1125–1133.

Plomin, R., DeFries, J. C., McClearn, J. E., & McGuffin, P. (2008). *Behavioral genetics* (5th ed.). New York: Worth.

Posthuma, D., & de Geus, E. J. C. (2006). Progress in the molecular-genetic study of intelligence. *Current Directions in Psychological Science, 15*, 151–155.

Ramey, C. T., & Ramey, S. L. (1998). Early intervention and early experience. *American Psychologist, 53*, 109–120.

Ramey, C. T., & Ramey, S. L. (2000). Intelligence and public policy. In R. J. Sternberg (Ed.), *Handbook of intelligence* (pp. 534–548). New York: Cambridge University Press.

Reed, T. E., & Jensen, A. R. (1992). Conduction velocity in a brain nerve pathway of normal adults correlates with intelligence level. *Intelligence, 16*(3–4), 259–272.

Renzulli, J. S. (1986). The three-ring conception of giftedness: A developmental model for creative productivity. In R. J. Sternberg & J. E. Davidson (Eds.), *Conceptions of giftedness* (pp. 53–92). New York: Cambridge University Press.

Renzulli, J. S., & Reis S. (2004). *Identification of students for gifted and talented programs.* Thousand Oaks, CA: Corwin.

Revelle, W., Humphreys, M. S., Simon, L., & Gilliland, K. (1980). The interactive effect of personality, time of day, and caffeine: a test of the arousal model. *Journal of Experimental Psychology: General, 109*, 1–31.

Roid, G. H. (2006). *Stanford-Binet intelligence scales* (5th ed.). Rolling Meadows, IL: Riverside.

Salovey, P., & Mayer, J. D. (1990). Emotional intelligence. *Imagination, Cognition, and Personality, 9*, 185–211.

Scarr, S., & Weinberg, R. A. (1976). IQ test performance of black children adopted by white families. *American Psychologist, 31*, 726–739.

Scarr, S., Weinberg, R. A., Waldman, L. D. (1993). IQ correlations in transracial adoptive families. *Intelligence, 17*, 541–545.

Schliemann, A. D., & Magalhües, V. P. (1990). Proportional reasoning: From shops, to kitchens, laboratories, and, hopefully, schools. *Proceedings of the Fourteenth International Conference for the Psychology of Mathematics Education*, Oaxtepec, Mexico.

Shaw, P. (2007). Intelligence and the developing human brain. *Bioessays, 29*, 962–973.

Shields, J. (1962). *Monozygotic twins brought up apart and brought up together*. London: Oxford University Press.

Siegler, R. S. (1996). *Emerging minds: The process of change in children's thinking*. New York: Oxford University Press.

Siegler, R. S., & Alibali, M. W. (2004). *Children's thinking* (4th ed.). Englewood Cliffs, NJ: Prentice-Hall.

Siegler, R., & Jenkins, E. A. (1989). *How children discover new strategies*. Hillsdale, NJ: Erlbaum.

Spearman, C. (1904). "General intelligence," objectively determined and measured. *American Journal of Psychology, 15*(2), 201–293.

Spearman, C. (1927). *The abilities of man*. London: Macmillan.

Steele, C. M. (1997). A threat in the air: How stereotypes shape intellectual identity and performance. *American Psychologist, 52*(6), 613–629.

Stemler, S. E., Grigorenko, E. L., Jarvin, L., & Sternberg, R. J. (2006). Using the theory of successful intelligence as a basis for augmenting AP exams in psychology and statistics. *Contemporary Educational Psychology, 31*(2), 344–376.

Sternberg, R. J. (Ed.) (1984). *Mechanisms of cognitive development*. New York: Freeman.

Sternberg, R. J. (1985). *Beyond IQ: A triarchic theory of human intelligence*. New York: Cambridge University Press.

Sternberg, R. J. (1988). *The triarchic mind: A theory of human intelligence*. New York: Viking.

Sternberg, R. J. (1990). *Metaphors of mind*. New York: Cambridge University Press.

Sternberg, R. J. (1997). *Successful intelligence*. New York: Plume.

Sternberg, R. J. (1999a). Successful intelligence: Finding a balance. *Trends in Cognitive Sciences, 3*, 436–442.

Sternberg, R. J. (1999b). The theory of successful intelligence. *Review of General Psychology, 3*, 292–316.

Sternberg, R. J. (Ed.) (2000). *Handbook of intelligence*. New York: Cambridge University Press.

Sternberg, R. J. (2005). The theory of successful intelligence. *Interamerican Journal of Psychology, 39*(2), 189–202.

Sternberg, R. J. (2007). Culture, instruction, and assessment. *Comparative Education, 43*(1), 5–22.

Sternberg, R. J., Clinkenbeard, P. R. (1995). A triarchic model of identifying, teaching, and assessing gifted children. *Roeper Review, 17*(4), 255–260.

Sternberg, R. J., & Davidson, J. E. (Eds.) (1986). *Conceptions of giftedness*. New York: Cambridge University Press.

Sternberg, R. J., & Davidson, J. E. (Eds.) (2005). *Conceptions of giftedness* (2nd ed.). New York: Cambridge University Press.

Sternberg, R. J., Ferrari, M., Clinkenbeard, P. R., & Grigorenko, E. L. (1996). Identification, instruction, and assessment of gifted children: A construct validation of a triarchic model. *Gifted Child Quarterly, 40*(3), 129–137.

Sternberg, R. J., Forsythe, G. B., Hedlund, J., Horvath, J., Snook, S., Williams, W. M., Wagner, R. K., Grigorenko, E. L. (2000). *Practical intelligence in everyday life*. New York: Cambridge University Press.

Sternberg, R. J., & Grigorenko, E. L. (Eds.) (1997). *Intelligence, heredity, and environment.* New York: Cambridge University Press.
Sternberg, R. J., & Grigorenko E. L. (Eds.). (2002). *The general factor of intelligence: How general is it?* Mahwah, NJ: Erlbaum.
Sternberg, R. J., & Grigorenko, E. L. (2007). *Teaching for successful intelligence* (2nd ed.). Thousand Oaks, CA: Corwin Press.
Sternberg, R. J., Grigorenko, E. L., Ferrari, M., & Clinkenbeard, P. (1999). A triarchic analysis of an aptitude-treatment interaction. *European Journal of Psychological Assessment, 15*, 1–11.
Sternberg, R. J., Grigorenko, E. L., & Kidd, K. K. (2005). Intelligence, race, and genetics. *American Psychologist, 60*(1), 46–59.
Sternberg, R. J., & Kaufman, J. C. (1998). Human abilities. *Annual Review of Psychology, 49*, 479–502.
Sternberg, R. J., & Kaufman, J. C. (Eds.) (2001). *The evolution of intelligence.* Mahwah, NJ: Erlbaum.
Sternberg, R. J., & Kaufman, S. (in press). *Cambridge handbook of intelligence.* New York: Cambridge University Press.
Sternberg, R. J., Kaufman, J. C., & Grigorenko, E. L. (2008). *Applied intelligence.* New York: Cambridge University Press.
Sternberg, R. J., Lipka, J., Newman, T., Wildfeuer, S., & Grigorenko, E. L. (2007). Triarchically-based instruction and assessment of sixth-grade mathematics in a Yup'ik cultural setting in Alaska. *International Journal of Giftedness and Creativity, 21*(2), 6–19.
Sternberg, R. J., & Lubart, T. I. (1995). *Defying the crowd: Cultivating creativity in a culture of conformity.* New York: Free Press.
Sternberg, R. J., Nokes, K., Geissler, P. W., Prince, R., Okatcha, F., Bundy, D. A., & Grigorenko, E. L. (2001). The relationship between academic and practical intelligence: A case study in Kenya. *Intelligence, 29*, 401–418.
Sternberg, R. J., & Powell, J. S. (1983). The development of intelligence. In P. H. Mussen (Series Ed.) & J. Flavell & E. M. Markman (Vol. Eds.), *Handbook of child psychology* (3rd ed., pp. 341–419). New York: Wiley.
Sternberg, R. J., & The Rainbow Project Collaborators (2005). Augmenting the SAT through assessments of analytical, practical, and creative skills. In W. Camara & E. Kimmel (Eds.), *Choosing students: Higher education admission tools for the 21st century* (pp. 159–176). Mahwah, NJ: Erlbaum.
Sternberg, R. J., & The Rainbow Project Collaborators (2006). The Rainbow Project: Enhancing the SAT through assessments of analytical, practical and creative skills. *Intelligence, 34*(4), 321–350.
Sternberg, R. J., & Spear-Swerling, L. (1996). *Teaching for thinking.* Washington DC: American Psychological Association.
Sternberg, R. J., Torff, B., & Grigorenko, E. L. (1998). Teaching triarchically improves school achievement. *Journal of Educational Psychology, 90*(3), 1–11.
Terman, L. M. (1925). *Genetic studies of genius: Mental and physical traits of a thousand gifted children* (Vol. 1). Stanford, CA: Stanford University Press.
Terman, L. M., & Oden, M. H. (1959). *Genetic studies of genius: The gifted group at midlife* (Vol. 4). Stanford, CA: Stanford University Press.
Thelen, E. (1992). Development as a dynamic system. *Current Directions in Psychological Science, 1*, 189–193.
Thelen, E., & Smith, L. B. (1998). Dynamic systems theories. In W. Damon (Series Ed.) & R. M. Lerner (Vol. Ed.), *Handbook of child psychology: Vol. 1. Theoretical models of human development* (5th ed.). New York: Wiley.

Thurstone, L. L. (1938). *Primary mental abilities*. Chicago: University of Chicago Press.
Travis, A. (2007). *Cognitive evolution: The biological imprint of applied intelligence*. Boca Raton, FL: Universal.
Turkheimer, E., Haley, A., D'Onofrio, B., Waldron, M., & Gottesman, I. I. (2003). Socioeconomic status modifies heritability of IQ in young children. *Psychological Science, 14*, 623–628.
Van Wieringen, J. C. (1978). Secular growth changes. In F. Falker & J. M. Tanner (Eds.), *Human growth* (Vol. 2). New York: Plenum.
Vernon, P. A., & Mori, M. (1992). Intelligence, reaction times, and peripheral nerve conduction velocity. *Intelligence, 16*(3–4), 273–288.
Vernon, P. A., Wickett, J. C., Bazana, P. G., & Stelmack, R. M. (2000). The neuropsychology and psychophysiology of human intelligence. In R. J. Sternberg (Ed.), *Handbook of intelligence* (pp. 245–264). New York: Cambridge University Press.
Vernon, P. E. (1971). *The structure of human abilities*. London: Methuen.
Vygotsky, L. (1978). *Mind in society*. Cambridge, MA: Harvard University Press.
Wagner, R. K. (2000). Practical intelligence. In R. J. Sternberg (Ed.), *Handbook of human intelligence* (pp. 380–395). New York: Cambridge University Press.
Wechsler, D. (2003). *Manual for the Wechsler Intelligence Scales for Children* (4th ed.) (WISC-IV). San Antonio, TX: Harcourt Assessment.
Weinberg, R. A., Scarr, S., & Waldman, I. D. (1992). The Minnesota Transracial Adoption Study: A follow-up of IQ test performance at adolescence. *Intelligence, 16*(1), 117–135.
Winner, E. (1996). *Gifted children: Myths and realities*. New York: Basic Books.
Winner, E. (1997). Exceptionally high intelligence and schooling. *American Psychologist, 52*, 1070–1081.
Wissler, C. (1901). The correlation of mental and physical tests. *Psychological Review, Monograph Supplement, 3*(6).
Zigler, E. (1982). Development versus difference theories of developmental disability and the problem of motivation. In E. Zigler & D. Balla (Eds.), *Developmental disability: The developmental–difference controversy*. Hillsdale, NJ: Erlbaum.
Zigler, E., & Berman, W. (1983). Discerning the future of early childhood intervention. *American Psychologist, 38*, 894–906.

Index

Note: Page numbers in *italics* refer to tables; page numbers in **bold** refer to figures.